Real Estate Finance and Investments

THE McGRAW-HILL/IRWIN SERIES IN FINANCE, INSURANCE AND REAL ESTATE

Stephen A. Ross
Franco Modigliani Professor of Finance and Economics
Sloan School of Management
Massachusetts Institute of Technology
Consulting Editor

FINANCIAL MANAGEMENT

Benninga and Sarig
Corporate Finance: *A Valuation Approach*

Block and Hirt
Foundations of Financial Management
Tenth Edition

Brealey and Myers
Principles of Corporate Finance
Sixth Edition

Brealey, Myers and Marcus
Fundamentals of Corporate Finance
Third Edition

Brooks
FinGame Online 3.0

Bruner
Case Studies in Finance: *Managing for Corporate Value Creation*
Third Edition

Chew
The New Corporate Finance: *Where Theory Meets Practice*
Third Edition

Grinblatt and Titman
Financial Markets and Corporate Strategy
Second Edition

Helfert
Techniques of Financial Analysis: *A Guide to Value Creation*
Tenth Edition

Higgins
Analysis for Financial Management
Sixth Edition

Kester, Fruhan, Piper and Ruback
Case Problems in Finance
Eleventh Edition

Nunnally and Plath
Cases in Finance
Second Edition

Ross, Westerfield and Jaffe
Corporate Finance
Sixth Edition

Ross, Westerfield and Jordan
Essentials of Corporate Finance
Third Edition

Ross, Westerfield and Jordan
Fundamentals of Corporate Finance
Fifth Edition

Smith
The Modern Theory of Corporate Finance
Second Edition

White
Financial Analysis with an Electronic Calculator
Fourth Edition

INVESTMENTS

Bodie, Kane and Marcus
Essentials of Investments
Fourth Edition

Bodie, Kane and Marcus
Investments
Fifth Edition

Cohen, Zinbarg and Zeikel
Investment Analysis and Portfolio Management
Fifth Edition

Corrado and Jordan
Fundamentals of Investments: *Valuation and Management*
Second Edition

Farrell
Portfolio Management: *Theory and Applications*
Second Edition

Hirt and Block
Fundamentals of Investment Management
Sixth Edition

FINANCIAL INSTITUTIONS AND MARKETS

Cornett and Saunders
Fundamentals of Financial Institutions Management

Rose
Commercial Bank Management
Fifth Edition

Rose
Money and Capital Markets: *Financial Institutions and Instruments in a Global Marketplace*
Seventh Edition

Santomero and Babbel
Financial Markets, Instruments, and Institutions
Second Edition

Saunders
Financial Institutions Management: *A Modern Perspective*
Third Edition

Saunders and Cornett
Financial Markets and Institutions: *A Modern Perspective*

INTERNATIONAL FINANCE

Beim and Calomiris
Emerging Financial Markets

Eun and Resnick
International Financial Management
Second Edition

Levich
International Financial Markets: *Prices and Policies*
Second Edition

REAL ESTATE

Brueggeman and Fisher
Real Estate Finance and Investments
Eleventh Edition

Corgel, Ling and Smith
Real Estate Perspectives: *An Introduction to Real Estate*
Fourth Edition

FINANCIAL PLANNING AND INSURANCE

Allen, Melone, Rosenbloom and VanDerhei
Pension Planning: *Pension, Profit-Sharing, and Other Deferred Compensation Plans*
Eighth Edition

Crawford
Life and Health Insurance Law
Eighth Edition (LOMA)

Harrington and Niehaus
Risk Management and Insurance

Hirsch
Casualty Claim Practice
Sixth Edition

Kapoor, Dlabay and Hughes
Personal Finance
Sixth Edition

Skipper
International Risk and Insurance: *An Environmental-Managerial Approach*

Williams, Smith and Young
Risk Management and Insurance
Eighth Edition

ELEVENTH EDITION

Real Estate Finance and Investments

William B. Brueggeman, Ph.D.
Corrigan Chair in Real Estate
Edwin L. Cox School of Business
Southern Methodist University

Jeffrey D. Fisher, Ph.D.
Charles H. and Barbara F. Dunn Professor of Real Estate
Kelley School of Business
Indiana University

McGraw-Hill Irwin

Boston Burr Ridge, IL Dubuque, IA Madison, WI New York San Francisco St. Louis
Bangkok Bogotá Caracas Kuala Lumpur Lisbon London Madrid Mexico City
Milan Montreal New Delhi Santiago Seoul Singapore Sydney Taipei Toronto

The McGraw-Hill Companies

McGraw-Hill Irwin

Real Estate Finance Investment

Published by McGraw-Hill/Irwin, an imprint of The McGraw-Hill Companies, Inc. 1221 Avenue of the Americas, New York, NY, 10020.

Some ancillaries, including electronic and print components, may not be available to customers outside the United States.

This book is printed on acid-free paper.

5 6 7 8 9 0 CCW/CCW 0 9 8 7 6 5 4 3

ISBN 007365809X

Publisher: *John E. Biernat*
Executive editor: *Stephen M. Patterson*
Editorial assistant: *Jennifer Rizzi*
Executive marketing manager: *Rhonda Seelinger*
Project manager: *Laura Ward Majersky*
Production supervisor: *Debra R. Sylvester*
Supplement producer: *Nate Perry*
Media technology producer: *Mark Molsky*
Cover and interior design: *Mary E. Kazak*
Cover photograph: *Photography by David Heald © Solomon R. Guggenheim Foundation, New York.*
Compositor: *GAC Indianapolis*
Typeface: *10/12 Times Roman*
Printer: *Courier Westford*

Library of Congress Cataloging-in-Publication Data

Brueggeman, William B.
Real estate finance and investments / William B. Brueggeman, Jeffrey D. Fisher.
p. cm. — (The McGraw-Hill/Irwin series in finance, insurance, and real estate)
Includes index.
ISBN 0-07-365809-X (alk. paper)
1. Mortgage loans—United States. 2. Real property—United States—Finance. I. Fisher, Jeffrey D. II. Title. III. Series.
HG2040.5.U5 B78 2002
332.7'2—dc21

2001040328

www.mhhe.com

PREFACE

The world of real estate finance and investments continues to evolve as real estate equity investments and mortgages play an expanding role as investments in both private and public markets. Similarly, this book continues to evolve to provide students with the tools that they need to understand and analyze real estate markets and the investment alternatives available to both debt and equity investors. The revisions we have made in this edition of the book reflect the need for students to expand their understanding of these topics when preparing for a career in the field of real estate.

Public market vehicles for financing and investing in commercial real estate such as commercial mortgage-backed securities (CMBS) and real estate investment trusts (REITs) have matured since the last edition of this book. We have completely revised the chapter on REITs and expanded the coverage of CMBS accordingly.

We have also expanded the discussion of the importance of the underlying economic factors that ultimately affect the value of properties. Factors that affect the supply and demand for different property types are very dynamic and ultimately affect the risk and value of residential and commercial properties.

We continue the tradition of having a book that is very "user friendly" for students. Calculator solutions are shown for many of the problems. Traditional table solutions are also shown in the early chapters to aid in the understanding of the time-value-of-money concepts being illustrated. We are also making computer spreadsheets available that can be used to solve many of the end-of-chapter problems.

This book can be used by professionals as well as by academics and students. We have always strived to include material that is used in everyday practice. Our goal continues to be to help everyone advance their ability to analyze and better understand the institutions and instruments common in real estate markets.

We would like to thank several people who contributed to the eleventh edition revision. Eric Clausen updated the information on FHA, VA, and conventional loans in Chapter 6. Ron Donohue with the Hoyt Group made substantial revisions to the chapter on REITs. Jacey Leonard assisted with the revision of the Instructor's Manual and with the creation of Excel spreadsheet templates that are available for use with the book.

We also continue to be indebted to people who have contributed to previous editions, especially the late Henry E. Hoagland, who wrote the first edition of this book and Leo D. Stone, who participated in several editions. Finally, we thank all of the adopters of the previous editions of the book who with their feedback have made us feel that we have helped them prepare students for successful careers in real estate.

William B. Brueggeman
Jeffrey D. Fisher

BRIEF CONTENTS

CONTENTS

PART I

INTRODUCTION

PART IV

Financing Proposed Projects

15 Financing Project Development 433

16 Financing Land Development Projects 467

PART V

Real Estate Capital Markets and Securities

17 The Secondary Mortgage Market: Pass-Through Securities 495

CHAPTER

1

Overview of Real Estate Finance and Investments

Real estate finance and investments is a field of study that requires an understanding of many important subjects: property law, mortgage underwriting practices, mortgage insurance programs, financial analysis, valuation principles, federal income tax laws, investment analysis, real estate development, and capital markets. This book is intended to provide the reader with a foundation in each of these areas. It is oriented toward the student who has had some exposure to basic finance—and perhaps real estate principles—and desires a more advanced treatment of the subject. The emphasis of the book is real estate financial and investment analysis. However, at various points in the text we give descriptions of important institutional characteristics, which complement our analysis with insights into business practice.

This chapter provides an overview of the contents of the book. The subjects addressed throughout form the basis for much of what is needed for professionals who are in or about to enter the field of real estate finance. Although the breadth of coverage may seem to include very diverse topics, these topics contain analytic approaches and methodologies that can be transferred to many different problem areas. Students may find that they have a much better understanding of basic finance after they have learned to apply it to real estate.

Exhibit 1–1 is a flowchart of the organization of the book, its major parts, and the chapters within those parts. The student will obtain the necessary background for each chapter by reading the chapters in numerical order. However, there are other ways to progress through the material, particularly for the more advanced student. For example, a course of study emphasizing real estate finance could proceed from Part II, "Financing Residential Properties," to Part V, "Real Estate Capital Markets and Securities" with emphasis on mortgage-backed securities. Similarly, a course of study focusing on income property financing and investment could proceed from Part I directly to Part III.

Part IV is important for courses of study that illustrate the differences between the analysis of existing and proposed (construction and land development) projects. Techniques used to evaluate and finance these projects differ significantly. The student who wants to proceed from Part II or Part III directly to Part V can do so without any loss of continuity.

EXHIBIT 1–1 Chapter Flowchart—Real Estate Finance and Investments

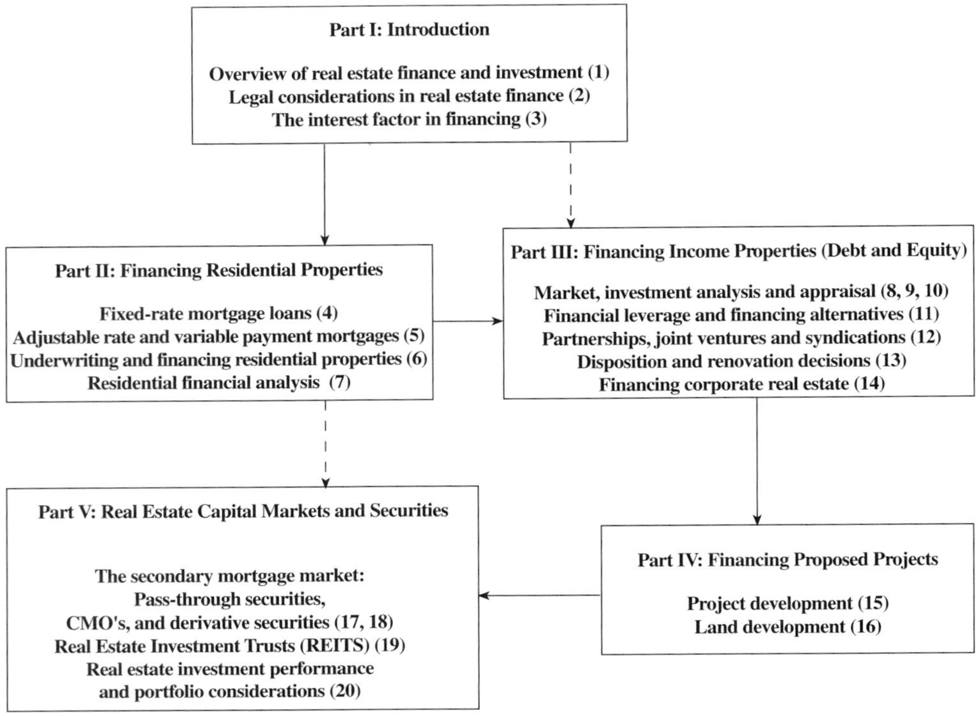

Part I: Introduction
Overview of real estate finance and investment (1)
Legal considerations in real estate finance (2)
The interest factor in financing (3)
Part II: Financing Residential Properties
Fixed-rate mortgage loans (4)
Adjustable rate and variable payment mortgages (5)
Underwriting and financing residential properties (6)
Residential financial analysis (7)
Part III: Financing Income Properties (Debt and Equity)
Market, investment analysis and appraisal (8, 9, 10)
Financial leverage and financing alternatives (11)
Partnerships, joint ventures and syndications (12)
Disposition and renovation decisions (13)
Financing corporate real estate (14)
Part V: Real Estate Capital Markets and Securities
The secondary mortgage market:
Pass-through securities,
CMO's, and derivative securities (17, 18)
Real Estate Investment Trusts (REITS) (19)
Real estate investment performance
and portfolio considerations (20)
Part IV: Financing Proposed Projects
Project development (15)
Land development (16)

Introduction

Part I provides the background information necessary for an in-depth study of real estate finance and investment. Many readers may already be familiar with this material. Chapter 2 contains a summary of important legal considerations in real estate finance while Chapter 3 reviews compound interest calculations that form the basis for mortgage calculations and much of the financial analysis throughout the remainder of the text.

When transactions involving a specific good or service occur repetitively in a free market economy, a number of institutional and legal arrangements evolve to standardize and facilitate this activity. Financing real estate is no exception. When the acquisition or development of residential or commercial properties is financed, the nature of the borrower's interest in the property, which is generally used as security for a loan, must be identified and acceptable to the lender who advances the funds. Real estate transactions are significant in economic magnitude and societal importance. Many interests in real estate can be either conveyed or used as security for lending. Our legal system has evolved to accommodate commercial activities related to the vast number of transactions that occur in our economy. For example, to be legally valid, real estate transactions must meet the following requirements: They have to be documented, put in writing, and take the form of a contract. Commitments made to finance these transactions are also documented, usually in the form of a mortgage and a note. Mortgages identify the property that is used to secure a loan and contain promises made by the borrower to fulfill certain other obligations to the lender. Notes identify the amount of indebtedness between lender and borrower and the terms of repayment.

Chapter 2 contains a summary of the rights and interests in real estate that may be conveyed or used as security for mortgage loans. Covered in more detail are the legal nature of mortgages and the contents normally included in most mortgages. Because changes in property law are most important at the state and local levels, the nature of interests acquired by lenders and the remedies available to them should borrowers default will vary from state to state and among localities. While the scope of this book makes it impossible to compare the differences between states, we can distinguish the major differences in mortgage contracts. Further, various covenants (promises) commonly included in mortgage agreements are described in some detail. Much of the necessary documentation in residential financing has been standardized to facilitate the eventual sale of many mortgages in the secondary mortgage market. Finally, foreclosure and alternatives to foreclosure by the lender are explored and discussed in some detail.

The review of compound interest (time value of money) calculations in Chapter 3 includes understanding compounding (future value) and present value (discounting) calculations. The basic mathematics of compound interest and discounting are reviewed for annual as well as other, particularly monthly, compounding periods needed for mortgage calculations.

Financing Residential Properties

We often take home ownership and mortgage financing of residential properties for granted. However, not until after the Great Depression of the 1930s did Congress take the responsibility for improving housing standards and providing the framework for the vast system of housing finance that we know today. The mortgage insurance programs of the Federal Housing Administration (FHA) followed by the mortgage and guarantee programs of the Veterans Administration (VA) put into place mechanisms for vastly reducing default losses on loans made to households seeking mortgage financing. These programs provided lenders with sufficient protection to encourage them to make mortgage loans in substantial volume.

Part II covers many important topics in residential financing. Exhibit 1–2 outlines the many considerations that borrowers and lenders must make when borrowers seek residential financing. The process involves deciding on the type of mortgage with respect to the pattern of repayment (i.e., fixed or adjustable interest rates) and whether a conventional mortgage loan or a mortgage with FHA insurance or a VA guarantee should be chosen. These decisions are sometimes complex, particularly when one chooses between fixed and adjustable interest rates and compares closing cost requirements. Chapters 4 through 6 contain a detailed analysis of these topics for all types of mortgages with emphasis on loan selection and underwriting.

Deciding how a property should be financed at the time of acquisition is important, but other considerations at that time and subsequently are also important to most borrowers. Chapter 7 deals with these issues:

1. Computing the effective cost of financing, including loan fees and charges. This methodology allows for a comparison of loans with different terms such as the interest rate, fees, and maturity.

EXHIBIT 1–2 Residential Mortgage Financing (borrower and lender considerations)

Stage I: Loan Selection	*Stage II: Loan Underwriting*	*Stage III: Loan Closing*
A. Type of mortgage 1. Fixed interest rate 2. Adjustable interest rate 3. Other	A. Verification of income/assets 1. Determination of payment-to-income ratios 2. Credit history 3. Other savings and assets	A. Documentation 1. RESPA 2. Federal Truth in Lending
B. Type of mortgage insurance/guaranty 1. None—conventional loan 2. Private insurance 3. FHA 4. VA	B. Appraisal of property value 1. Relationship to loan amount 2. Determination of maximum loan-to-value amount	B. Transfer of title 1. Deed to buyer 2. Funds to seller from buyer and lender

2. Computing the marginal or incremental cost of acquiring additional loan amounts (i.e., 75 percent, 80 percent, 90 percent, 95 percent of value). This analysis will help the buyer decide whether to make a large or small down payment when acquiring a property.
3. Calculating the benefits and costs of refinancing. This decision must be made when interest rates decline after a loan has been made. The borrower must usually decide whether benefits from savings due to lower payments will exceed the costs that must be paid to undertake refinancing.
4. Comparing financing options provided by a lender or the option of assuming a mortgage previously made by the seller. These alternatives, coupled with the possibility of acquiring second mortgage financing, are also of concern to borrowers.
5. Identifying the many different tax treatments that apply to interest deductions for each type of mortgage. This task is necessary because a borrower has many mortgage payment alternatives to consider.

Financing Income-Producing Properties

Part III (Chapters 8 to 14) provides an in-depth look at some of the more important aspects of financing and pricing income-producing properties. Exhibit 1–3 provides an outline of the topics and techniques used to analyze income properties. The outline is a logical progression of steps that an investor would take when (1) acquiring a property, (2) considering the tax consequences of the transaction, (3) deciding what type and how much, if any, financing to use in making the acquisition, and (4) attempting to gauge the amount of risk taken for a specific type of property and how that risk could change with the application of financial leverage.

The above four areas are usually undertaken when the investor purchases a property at a specific price; that is, the investor is usually asking, "If I pay a specific price for the property and I use a certain amount of debt, what will be my rate of return on

EXHIBIT 1–3 Important Considerations in Analyzing Income-Producing Properties

A. Economic influences on property values.
   1. Regional economic drivers.
   2. Economic base analysis.
   3. Supply and demand analysis.
   4. Location decisions.

B. Estimating cash flows from a real estate investment.
   1. Examining lease provisions; base rents, escalations, expense stops.
   2. Developing pro forma operating statements.
   3. Estimating operating cash flows.
   4. Estimating cash flows when properties are sold.
   5. Performing a "pretax" profitability analysis.
   6. Identifying sources of risk in real estate investment.
   7. Determining the sensitivity of investment performance to each cash flow projection.
   8. Evaluating the expected return and risk of an investment.

C. Considering federal income taxes.
   1. Classifying income according to the current tax law.
   2. Methods of depreciation allowable for residential and commercial income-producing real estate.
   3. Provisions applying to amortization of financing and other fees.
   4. Rehabilitation and historic building tax credits.
   5. Developing pro forma statements of after-tax income from operation and the sale of real estate.
   6. Combining pretax cash flows with after-tax income to arrive at after-tax cash flow.
   7. Performing an "after-tax" profitability analysis.

D. Evaluating the role of financing and leverage in real estate investment analysis.
   1. Identifying alternative types of debt financing.
   2. Evaluating the impact of financial leverage on the return on equity—positive and negative leverages.
   3. Computing the break-even or maximum interest rate that can be paid while retaining positive leverage.
   4. Evaluating the impact of tax deductibility of mortgage interest in the analysis.
   5. Evaluating how financing affects the riskiness of an investment.

E. Valuation of income properties.
   1. Three approaches to estimating value: cost, sales comparison, and income capitalization.
   2. The relationship between appraisal and investment analysis.

F. The decision to hold or sell, refinance, or renovate.
   1. Marginal rates of return for holding versus selling.
   2. Refinancing in lieu of selling.
   3. Comparing the costs versus the benefits of renovating.

G. Corporate real estate.
   1. The decision to own or lease.
   2. The decision to sell and lease back real estate.
   3. The relationship of real estate to the value of the firm.

H. Real estate partnerships, joint ventures, and syndication.
   1. The nature of limited partnership structuring.
   2. The framework for distributing cash flow and taxable income and losses.
   3. The importance of the equity interest in the partnership.
   4. Tax rules, substantial economic effect, capital gains, and cash distributions upon dissolution of the partnership.
   5. Tax treatment of fees and expenses of the partnership.

equity before and after taxes?" Based on that price the investor may also ask, "What is the risk associated with the investment?"

Part D of the outline (see Exhibit 1–3) changes the point of view somewhat and asks, "How much *should be paid* for the investment if a specific rate of return on equity invested is desired?" Chapter 9 focuses on the question, "How much should a typical investor be willing to pay?" These questions are important because an investor normally does not want to pay more for a given property than other investors are willing to pay. This topic is of equal importance to the lender, because the lender must consider the value of the property used as security for financing. To accomplish this analysis, we explain in detail the three approaches (cost, sales comparison, and income capitalization) used to estimate value.

Each item listed in parts A–D of the outline usually has more relevance for individuals and institutional investors *at the time* they are considering the purchase of property. Part E shows considerations that are vital to decision making *after* the asset has been purchased. The fundamental approach to the sell-or-hold decision is to first ascertain the market value of the investor's equity. Then the investor must decide whether the cash realized if the asset were sold can be reinvested in an alternative investment of equal risk. The new investment would have to earn a rate of return at least equivalent to the future cash flow that would be given up if the project were sold. This framework, which is discussed in Chapter 13, provides the proper guide to formulating the decision by the investor to continue to own or to sell. Chapter 13 also evaluates the decision to refinance. Refinancing may be viewed as a method of removing equity from a project free of taxes, as opposed to selling an asset to raise capital. The decision to refinance may also be a part of the decision to renovate a property.

Part F considers real estate from the perspective of the user; including leasing versus owning and the control of facilities, which are important to all businesses. These topics are explained in considerable detail in Chapter 14.

The last item on the outline (see Exhibit 1–3), real estate partnerships, joint ventures, and syndication, considers how a group of investors can pool funds to acquire full or partial ownership of real estate assets. Investors should evaluate this kind of investment on both a pretax and aftertax basis in accordance with the techniques outlined in parts A–D. Although the type of syndication that was prominent in the early 1980s is unlikely to occur in the future (because it was motivated by the favorable tax environment of that period), it is still important to understand the nature of limited partnerships. Indeed, many of the real estate investment trusts (REITs) formed in recent years were structured so that the REIT was a general partner in a limited partnership.

Financing Real Estate Development

Real estate development and financing is frequently not well understood by many individuals working on the periphery of this activity because most real estate activities involve the resale, financing, and leasing of *existing* properties. Real estate development deals with either (1) the preparation of land with an intent to resell sites to project developers (e.g., a business park), (2) the development of a single, large-scale project on one specific site, or (3) the development of mixed use projects (e.g., a shopping mall or office-hotel complex). These activities usually require interim financing during the construction and development phase and permanent financing after improvements have been made and the property is leased to tenants.

The goals of Chapters 15 and 16 are to provide (1) a brief introduction to the nature of the real estate development process, (2) a basic understanding of development financing, (3) some insight into how lenders underwrite such projects, and (4) a framework to ascertain whether development projects are economically feasible. We provide a detailed analysis on lending arrangements and requirements, and detailed schedules relating to the way that funds are "drawn down" as needed to complete construction. A very useful approach to estimating construction period interest is presented in the appendix to Chapter 15. Construction interest, which may account for up to 15 to 20 percent of total development costs, must be estimated carefully. Loans made during construction are based on interest rates tied to the prime rate. Consequently, they can change significantly, particularly when interest rates are high and volatile. Individuals who aspire to work in real estate development or to work for lenders to development companies should have a general understanding of these concepts.

Real Estate Capital Markets and Securities

Chapters 17 and 18 deal exclusively with the secondary mortgage market, a market in which institutions originating mortgage loans either sell such loans or issue mortgage-backed securities against pools of loans, which are then sold to other intermediaries and institutions. The secondary mortgage market has grown tremendously in recent years. Two government-related agencies, the Federal National Mortgage Association (Fannie Mae) and the Federal Home Loan Mortgage Company (Freddie Mac), have been the dominant institutions providing capital to facilitate transactions in the secondary mortgage market. The Government National Mortgage Association (Ginnie Mae) has provided guarantees needed to facilitate much of the mortgage securitization that has occurred. These entities are largely involved with residential mortgage loans that are pooled and then secured. A parallel development in commercial mortgage-backed securities has been occurring more slowly. Eventually, it should provide an opportunity for lenders and investors to make a significant new secondary market in those mortgages.

In addition, Chapters 17 and 18 analyze in-depth the various types of securities used in the secondary mortgage market. They describe in detail the securities currently issued against mortgage pools and give examples that show how mortgage pools are formed. Cash flow patterns in and out of these pools are described for each security type, and the methodology used to value such securities is carefully considered. The various securities considered include (1) mortgage-backed bonds, (2) mortgage pass-through securities, (3) mortgage pay-through securities, and (4) collateralized mortgage obligations.

The tremendous growth of real estate investment trusts (REITs) has brought about one of the most significant changes in the financing of real estate. Although the REIT is not a new investment vehicle, it was not a significant source of capital for real estate until recent tax law changes and other events made public markets a viable way of raising equity capital for real estate. Chapter 19 discusses this important form of real estate ownership and how techniques learned in earlier chapters can be applied to the analysis of REITs.

Real estate is an important component of a multiasset portfolio that may also include stocks, bonds, and other investments. Chapter 20 discusses the role that real estate plays in portfolios held by investors, especially institutions such as pension funds.

Many of these institutions have amassed real estate investment portfolios worth billions of dollars and must know how to measure investment return and risk on their portfolios. They must also understand the trade-offs between risk and return that usually occur as portfolios are diversified. In Chapter 20, we use statistical concepts to develop risk measures for individual investments as well as investment portfolios. Different portfolio weights are used to examine how risk and return vary in relation to the addition and deletion of various investments. We explain many important sources of investment return data and use historic data on common stocks, corporate and government bonds, mortgage-backed securities, and so on to develop important concepts. Readers interested in institutional investment activity in real estate should find this chapter extremely important and timely.

Conclusion

It is clear that numerous concepts and techniques are important in real estate finance and investment analysis. This book covers these topics by starting with the basics and progressing in complexity in a number of ways—for example, from analysis of individual mortgages to analysis of mortgage-backed securities, and from analysis of residential mortgages to analysis of more complex mortgages used to finance income properties. Also, the book progresses from the analysis of individual properties used as collateral for mortgages to more complex forms of ownership such as partnerships and real estate investment trusts. Although the rigor of the material appears to increase as you read the book from beginning to end, all of the concepts and techniques presented are used in practice and will prepare you for a career in real estate finance and investments. Good luck.

CHAPTER 2

LEGAL CONSIDERATIONS IN REAL ESTATE FINANCE

Ownership of most physical assets is claimed by virtue of possession (e.g., furniture, jewelry, and other items). However, this is not the case for real estate investments because as we will see in this chapter, ownership can be quite different from possession and a variety of legal factors affect the ownership rights associated with real estate. The economic benefits expected by lenders, investors, and other parties in a real estate transaction are affected by these legal factors. We first consider the legal rights associated with ownership of real estate and the various ways of defining and protecting these rights. We then consider the legal rights of lenders and how those rights are defined and protected by various clauses in the mortgage agreement. When reading this chapter, try to see how these legal considerations ultimately affect the expected benefits and risk associated with investing in or financing a real estate investment.

Property Rights and Estates

The term **real estate** is often used to refer to things that are not movable such as **land** and improvements permanently attached to the land. The **ownership rights** associated with the real estate are referred to as **real property.** Real property is contrasted with **personal property.** The latter refers to things that are movable such as automobiles, shares of stock, etc. and does not include land or things permanently attached to the land.[1]

It is important to distinguish between physical real estate assets and ownership rights in real property because many parties can have different ownership rights in a given parcel of real estate. Our legal system offers ways for the person financing or investing in real estate to be creative and to apportion these various interests among parties. For example, a person may have ownership rights to a property for his or her lifetime (a life estate), after which the ownership rights will be transferred to a different person (as a reversion or remainder). A company may have rights to the minerals under the land, and another person may have ownership rights to space above

[1]Certain items known as *fixtures* are items that were personal property but have become real property because they have either been attached to the land or building in a somewhat permanent manner or are intended to be used with the land and building on a permanent basis. Examples include built-in dishwashers, furnaces, and garage door openers.

the land (e.g., ownership of a condominium unit on the upper floor of a building or even airspace above the building).

We generally refer to **property rights** as the right of a person to the possession, use, enjoyment, and disposal of his or her property. With respect to its application to real estate, *interest* is a broad legal term used to denote a property right. The holder of an interest in real estate enjoys some right, or degree of control or use and, in turn, may receive payment for the sale of such an interest. This interest, to the extent that its value can be determined, may also be bought, sold, or used as collateral for a loan.

The value of a particular parcel of real estate can be viewed as the total price individuals are willing to pay for the flow of benefits associated with all of these rights. An individual does not have to be an owner per se to have rights to some of the benefits of real estate. For example, a person who leases the land, a **lessee,** has the right to exclusive use of the property for a period of time. This right of use has value to the lessee, even though the term of the lease is fixed. In exchange for the right to use the property, the lessee is willing to pay a rent for the term of the lease. A holder of a mortgage also has some rights as a nonowner in real estate pledged as security for a loan. These rights vary with state law and the terms of the mortgage, but, in general, the lender (or mortgagee) has a right to repossess or bring about the sale of a property if the borrower defaults on the mortgage loan. The mortgage provides the lender with what is referred to as a **secured interest.** Obviously this right has value to the lender in the event of default and reduces the quantity of rights possessed by the owner.

It should be clear that some understanding of the legal characteristics of real estate is essential to analyzing the relative benefits that accrue to the various parties who have some rights in a particular property. In most real estate financing and investment transactions, we generally think in terms of investing, selling, or borrowing based on one owner possessing all property rights in the real estate. However, as we have discussed, all or a portion of these rights may be restricted or transferred to others. Remarkably, the various holders of these separate rights generally enjoy their respective rights in relative harmony. However, conflicts arise occasionally concerning the relative rights and priorities to be accorded to the holders of these interests. The potential for such conflicts may also affect the value or price individuals may be willing to pay for an interest in real estate and, ultimately, the value of property.

Definition of an Estate

The term **estate** is used to denote a **possessory** or **potentially possessory interest** in real estate, that is, an estate which is either presently possessory or may ripen into a **possessory estate** in the future (e.g., at the end of a lease). A possessory interest involves the general right to occupy and *use* the property during the periods of possession. The modern notion of an "estate" continues to retain the English common law connotation of any interest in real estate that carries the right of exclusive possession, which includes the right to sell, use, lease, or even exclude others from the property.

Not all interests in real property are estates. An **easement** is a **nonpossessory interest** in land. It is the right to use the land owned or leased by someone else for some special purpose (e.g., as a right of way to and from one's property). An easement entails only a limited user privilege and not privileges associated with ownership. Another important example of an interest in real estate that is not deemed to be an estate is the interest of a lender (**mortgagee**) in the property of the borrower (**mortgagor**). Mortgages are generally regarded in contemporary American law to be mere liens on the estates of others.

Classification of Estates

Estates in Possession versus Estates Not in Possession. Two broad categories of estates can be distinguished on the basis of the nature of rights accompanying the ownership of such estates. An estate in possession (a present estate in land) entitles its owner to immediate enjoyment of the rights to that estate. An estate not in possession (a future estate in land), on the other hand, does not convey the rights of the estate until some time in the future, if at all. An estate not in possession, in other words, represents a *future* possessory interest in property. Generally, it does not convert to an estate in possession until the occurrence of a particular event. Estates in possession are by far the more common. When most people think of estates, they ordinarily have in mind estates in possession. Obviously, lenders and investors are very interested in the nature of the estate possessed by the owner when considering the purchase or financing of a particular estate in property.

Freehold versus Leasehold Estates. Estates in possession are of two general types: freehold estates and leasehold estates. These types of estates are technically distinguished on the basis of the definiteness or certainty of their duration. A **freehold estate** lasts for an indefinite period of time; that is, there is no definitely ascertainable date on which the estate ends. A **leasehold estate,** on the other hand, expires on a definite date. Aside from this technical distinction, a freehold estate connotes ownership of the property by the estate holder, whereas a leasehold estate implies only the right to *possess* and *use* the property owned by another for a period of time.

Examples of Freehold Estates

It is beyond the scope of this chapter to review all the possible types of freehold estates. We will discuss two of the most common examples, however, to convey the importance of knowing the type of estate that is associated with a particular transaction.

Fee Simple Estate. A **fee simple estate,** also known as a fee simple absolute estate, is the freehold estate that represents the most complete form of ownership of real estate. A holder of a fee simple estate is free to divide up the fee into lesser estates and sell, lease, or borrow against them as he or she wishes, subject to the laws of the state in which the property is located. In addition to controls imposed by government, the use of property may also be controlled by **deed restrictions,** which are essentially private contractual agreements imposed by former owners (usually developers and subdividers of real estate) to use or not to use property in certain ways. Deed restrictions are usually used to control use of the land so that a future owner does not act in a manner that would reduce the value of the surrounding property. Apart from controls that may be imposed by government or deed restrictions, no special conditions, limitations, or restrictions are placed on the right of a holder of a fee simple estate to enjoy the property, lease it to others, sell it, or even give it away. It is this estate in property which investors and lenders encounter in most investment and lending transactions.

Life Estates. It is possible to have a freehold estate that has less ownership rights than a fee simple estate. One example is a **life estate,** which is a freehold estate that lasts only as long as the life of the owner of the estate or the life of some other person. Upon the death of that person, the property reverts back to the original grantor (transferor of property), his or her heirs, or any other designated person. Most life estates result from the terms of the conveyance of the property. For example, a grantor may wish to make a gift of his or her property prior to death, yet wish to retain the use and enjoyment of the property until that time. This can be accomplished by making a conveyance of the property subject to a reserved life estate. A life estate can be leased, mortgaged, or sold. However, parties concerned with this estate should be aware that the estate will end with the death of the holder of the life estate (or that of the person whose life determines the duration of the estate). Because of the uncertainty surrounding the duration of the life estate, its marketability and value as collateral are severely limited.

Estates Not Yet in Possession (Future Estates)

The preceding discussion concerned estates in possession, which entitled the owner to immediate enjoyment of the estate. Here we discuss estates not in possession, or **future estates,** which do not convey the right to enjoy the property until some time in the future. The two most important types of future estates are the reversion and the remainder.

Reversion. A **reversion** exists when the holder of an estate in land (the grantor) conveys to another person (a grantee) a present estate in the property that has less ownership rights than the grantor's own estate and retains for the grantor or the grantor's heirs the right to take back, at some time in the future, the full estate that the grantor enjoyed before the conveyance. In this case, the grantor is said to have a reversionary fee interest in the property held by the grantee. A reversionary interest can be sold or mortgaged because it is an actual interest in the property.

Remainder. A **remainder** exists when the grantor of a present estate with less ownership rights than the grantor's own estate conveys to a third person the reversionary interest the grantor or the grantor's heirs would otherwise have in the property upon termination of the grantee's estate. A remainder is the future estate for the third person. Like a reversion, a remainder is a mortgageable interest in property.

Leasehold Estates

There are two major types of leasehold estates: estates for years and estates from year to year. There are two other types, but they are not common.[2] Leasehold estates are classified on the basis of the manner in which they are created and terminated.

Estate for Years. An **estate for years** is the type of leasehold estate investors and lenders are most likely to encounter. It is created by a lease that specifies an exact duration for the tenancy. The period of tenancy may be less than one year and still be an estate for years as long as the lease agreement specifies the termination date. The lease, as well as all contracts involving transactions in real estate, is usually written. Indeed, a lease is generally required by the statute of frauds to be in writing when it covers a term longer than one year. The rights and duties of the landlord and tenant and other provisions related to the tenancy are normally stated in the lease agreement.

An estate for years can be as long as 99 years (by custom, leases seldom exceed 99 years in duration), giving the lessee the right to use and control the property for that time in exchange for rental payments. To the extent that the specified rental payments fall below the market rental rate of the property during the life of the lease, the lease has value (leasehold value) to the lessee. The value of this interest in the property can be borrowed against or even sold. For example, if the lessee has the

---

[2] *Estate at Will:* An estate at will is created when a landlord consents to the possession of the property by another person but without any agreement as to the payment of rent or the term of the tenancy. Such estates are of indefinite duration. *Estate at Sufferance:* An estate at sufferance occurs when the tenant holds possession of the property without consent or knowledge of the landlord after the termination of one of the other three estates.

right to occupy the property for $1,000 per year when its fair market value is $2,000 per year, the $1,000 excess represents value to the lessee, which may be borrowed against or sold (assuming no lease covenants prevent it).

While a property is leased, the original fee owner is considered to have a *leased fee* estate. This means that he or she has given up some property rights to the lessee (the leasehold estate). The value of the leased fee estate will now depend on the amount of the lease payments expected during the term of the lease plus the value of the property when the lease terminates and the original owner receives the reversionary interest. Hence, a leased fee estate may be used as security for a loan or may be sold.

Estate from Year to Year. An **estate from year to year** (also known as an estate from period to period, or simply as a periodic tenancy) continues for successive periods until either party gives proper notice of its intent to terminate at the end of one or more subsequent periods. A "period" usually corresponds to the rent-paying period. Thus, such a tenancy commonly runs from month to month, although it can run for any period up to one year. Such estates can be created by explicit agreement between the parties, although a definite termination date is not specified. Since these estates are generally short term (a year or less), the agreement can be, and frequently is, oral. This type of estate can also be created without the express consent of the landlord. A common example is seen when the tenant "holds over" or continues to occupy an estate for years beyond the expiration date, and the landlord accepts payment of rent or gives some other evidence of tacit consent.

If present tenants are to remain in possession after the transfer or sale of property, the grantee should agree to take title subject to existing leases. The agreement should provide for prorating of rents and the transfer of deposits to the grantee. Buyers of property encumbered by leases should always reserve the right to examine and approve leases to ensure that they are in force, are not in default, and are free from undesirable provisions.

Assurance of Title

When considering the purchase of real estate, buyers must be in a position to assess the quantity and quality of ownership rights that they are acquiring. **Title assurance** refers to the means by which buyers of real estate "(1) learn in advance whether their sellers have and can convey the quality of title they claim to possess, and (2) receive compensation if the title, after transfer, turns out not to be as represented."[3] Lenders are also concerned about title assurance because the quality of title affects the collateral value of the property in which they may have a secured interest. Before we examine the mechanisms used for title assurance, we must briefly review the concepts of title and deed.

The Meaning of Title

Title is an abstract term frequently used to refer to documents, records, and acts that prove ownership. Title establishes the quantity of rights in real estate being conveyed from seller to buyer. The previous section briefly examined some of the various types of ownership rights and possessory interests that can be involved in a parcel of real estate. We saw, for example, that one person may hold title in fee simple ownership,

[3]Grant S. Nelson and Dale A. Whitman, *Real Estate Transfer, Finance and Development,* 2nd ed. (St. Paul, MN: West Publishing, 1981), p. 167.

convey title to a life estate to someone else, and convey the right to reversion upon termination of the life estate to yet another person. Hence, there are many possible combinations of rights and interests.

An **abstract of title** is a historical summary of the publicly recorded documents that affect a title. The quality of the title conveyed from seller to buyer depends upon the effect these documents have upon the seller's rightful possession of his or her property.

Essentially, title exists only for freehold estates. A leasehold estate, on the other hand, is typically created by a contract (called a lease) between a person who holds title (the **lessor**) and another person (the lessee), whereby possession of the property is granted by the owner to the other person for a period of time. The existence of leases on a property will, however, affect the nature of the rights that can be conveyed to a new buyer because lease terms are binding on the new owner unless waived by the lessee. Because investors and lenders are concerned about the nature and extent of the rights they are acquiring or financing, leases encumbering the property can have a profound impact on a property's value.

Deeds

Usually title is conveyed from one person (the grantor) to another (the grantee) by means of a written instrument called a **deed.**[4] [We use the term *grantor* instead of *seller* because title may also be transferred by the owner (grantor) to an heir (grantee) by means of a will; hence the terms *grantor* and *grantee.*] To be a valid conveyance of ownership interests in real property, all deeds must be in writing and meet certain other legal requirements of the state in which the property is located.

Generally, a purchaser wants the deed to convey a good *and* marketable title to the property. A good title is one that is valid in fact; that is, the grantor does lawfully have the title he or she claims to have to the property. However, a good title, because of the lack of sufficient documentation (as in the case of title by adverse possession) or encumbrances on the property, may be unmarketable. A marketable title is one that is not merely valid in fact but is also "free from reasonable doubt," one that is "reasonably free from litigation," and "one which readily can be sold or mortgaged to a reasonably prudent purchaser or mortgagee (mortgage lender)."[5]

An encumbrance on a title does not automatically make it unmarketable. A purchaser may be willing to take title to the property subject to the encumbrance. But the deed should note all encumbrances on the title so that a potential purchaser can rationally decide whether to purchase the property and to arrive at the appropriate price given any risks, costs, or restrictions posed by the encumbrances.

Methods of Title Assurance

There are three general ways in which a buyer has assurance that a title is good and marketable. First, the seller may provide a warranty as part of the deed. Second, there may be a search of relevant recorded documents to determine whether there is reason to question the quality of the title. This is usually done by an attorney and is accompanied by a legal opinion. Third, title insurance may be purchased to cover unexpected problems with the title.

[4] A deed is not the only way by which ownership rights in real property are conveyed. Titles are also transferred by wills, court decrees, and grants of land from the government to private persons. In addition, lawful title to property can also be acquired by means of adverse possession.

[5] *Black's Law Dictionary,* 5th ed. (St. Paul, MN: West Publishing, 1979).

Title Covenants in Deeds

The major types of deeds can be distinguished on the basis of the types of guarantees that the grantor makes with respect to the quality of the title. Guarantees, or warranties as they are more commonly called, pertain to the quality of the title. They are contained within the deed instrument as **deed covenants,** which are clauses whereby the grantor makes a promise that something is either done, shall be done, or shall not be done, or stipulates the truth of certain facts. It is important to understand that any deed, no matter how complete the warranties contained therein, can only convey the quality of title that the grantor actually has to the property. This is why most buyers of real estate usually obtain independent assurance of the validity and marketability of the title from a third party. Nonetheless, deed covenants do represent a significant form of protection for the buyer because the law provides for recourse in the form of a suit for damages against the grantor should they be breached. Depending on the type of deed used in conveyance, the grantee may have extensive claims or no claim at all against the grantor for defects of title. There is, of course, the possibility that the grantor's ability to pay damages to the grantee may be insufficient to cover the grantee's losses and costs.

General Warranty Deed. A **general warranty deed** is the most commonly used deed in real estate transactions and the most desirable type of deed from the buyer's perspective. It offers the most comprehensive warranties about the quality of the title. Essentially, the grantor warrants that the title he or she conveys to the property is free and clear of all encumbrances other than those specifically listed in the deed. Probably the most significant covenants generally contained in such a deed are the following: (1) a covenant that the grantor has good (legally valid) title to the property, (2) a covenant that the grantor has the right to convey the property, (3) a covenant to compensate the grantee for loss of property or eviction suffered by the grantee as a result of someone else having a superior claim to the property, and (4) a covenant against encumbrances on the property other than those specifically stated in the deed. In a general warranty deed, these covenants cover all conveyances of the property from the time of the original source of title to the present.

Special Warranty Deed. A **special warranty deed** makes the same warranties as a general warranty deed except that it limits their application to defects and encumbrances that occurred only while the grantor held title to the property. Unlike the warranties in a general warranty deed, those in a special warranty deed do not apply to title problems caused or created by predecessors in title.

Quitclaim Deed. A **quitclaim deed** offers the grantee the least protection. Such a deed simply conveys to the grantee whatever rights, interests, and title that the grantor may have in the property. No warranties are made about the nature of these rights and interests or of the quality of the grantor's title to the property. The quitclaim deed simply says that the grantor "quits" whatever "claim" he or she has in the property (which may well be none) in favor of the grantee.[6]

Very few buyers of real estate rely solely on the guarantees of title provided in deeds of conveyance by the seller. The two methods that buyers employ most often

---

[6]Quitclaim deeds are appropriately and frequently used to clear up technical defects or "clouds" on the title to a property. Where the record indicates a person may have any potential claim to the property, obtaining a quitclaim deed from him will eliminate the risk that such a claim will be made in the future.

to obtain assurance of title independent of the guarantees provided by the seller are an attorney's opinion of title and title insurance.[7]

Abstract and Opinion Method

Obtaining a lawyer's opinion of title used to be the most common method of title assurance before the widespread availability of title insurance. Although its use has been reduced by title insurance, this older method of title assurance is still widely used today, especially in the South and East.

Essentially, the abstract and opinion method is a two-step process. First, there is a search of the title record, which involves locating and examining all of the instruments in the public records that have affected the title of the property in question.[8] Second, when the title search is completed, a lawyer studies the relevant public records and other facts and proceedings affecting title for the purpose of arriving at an expert opinion of the character of the title. Based upon this study of the abstract or the record, the lawyer will give his or her judgment whether the title is good and marketable. If the title is found to be "clouded," the opinion should state what defects or encumbrances were uncovered by an examination of the records, and it should also state what the lawyer thinks can and should be done to "cure" the defects uncovered.

Because a lawyer's responsibility is limited to what appears in the records, the lawyer cannot be held liable for any defect in the title not disclosed therein. For example, a forged deed or one signed by a person judged to be incompetent would show good record title and a purchaser would have no recourse against the attorney or title company because abstracts and opinions are expressly limited to matters of public record. Any liability borne by the lawyer is based upon proof of his or her negligence or lack of professional skill in the examination of the records. Either would be difficult to prove. Rather than rely on the lawyer's opinion, most lenders and investors today prefer to purchase title insurance, which eliminates this risk.

The Title Insurance Method

Title insurance was developed to cure the inadequacies of title validation accomplished through an abstract and legal opinion. Title insurance does all that a carefully drawn abstract and a well-considered opinion by a competent lawyer are expected to do. In addition, it adds the principle of insurance to the above services and undertakes to spread the risk of *unseen hazards* among all who benefit from it.

Elimination of risk arising from unseen hazards in the public record has caused many investors and lenders to prefer this method of title assurance. In fact, title insurance is required for any mortgage that is traded in the secondary mortgage market. The title insurance process starts with a careful analysis of the records. The information available to the commercial title insurance company may be even more complete than that found in the public records. Skilled technicians at title insurance companies examine all available evidence of the title to determine its character. If their conclusions warrant, the title company will insure the title to a property and assume risks that are not even disclosed in the public records or in its own files. In short, title insurance ensures that the title is good and marketable.

---

[7]There are other types of deeds, such as the bargain and sale deed, and deeds that are given by third-party fiduciaries, such as a sheriff's deed or a trustee's deed.

[8]Most of the instruments that affect title to real estate are recorded, in accordance with the recording acts of the various states, at what is typically called the county recorder's office. But some instruments that affect title may be recorded in other places. The nature of these other places where records are filed vary from state to state.

What title insurance is supposed to add to the abstract system and the opinion of skilled lawyers may be summarized as follows: (1) definite contract liability to the premium payer, (2) reserves sufficient to meet insured losses, (3) supervision by an agency of the state in which the title insurance company operates, and (4) protection to the policyholder against financial losses that may show up at any future time because of any kind of title defect, disclosed or hidden. Despite these advantages, the abstract and opinion method may still be used because of its lower cost. In general, one method, but not both, is used when purchasing property, to avoid the duplication of effort and cost.

Kinds of Title Insurance Policies. There are two kinds of title insurance policies. The owner's policy insures the interests of a new property owner. The lender's (or mortgagee) policy insures the interests of the mortgagee. The owner's policy is payable to the owner (or to the heirs of the owner); the lender's policy is payable to the mortgagee.

Both policies are paid for with a one-time premium. The one-time premium for the owner's policy may be paid by either the seller or the buyer, depending on the terms of the purchase contract, which are influenced by local custom and market conditions. It is almost universal practice for the borrower to pay the cost of the mortgagee's policy.

Recording Acts

All states have enacted statutes known as **recording acts.** Although the recording acts are not uniform among the states, these acts in general provide a publicly accessible system for assessing and establishing claims or interests in real estate as against all other parties. These statutes also provide a set of authoritative rules for resolving priority disputes among competing claimants to interests in real estate. As part of this system, procedures have been established for placing documents affecting claims to real estate interests on the public record and for maintaining these records to make information available concerning almost all interests in real estate. Once an instrument creating a claim on an interest in real estate has been duly recorded, the recording is deemed to give constructive notice of this interest "to the world." Constructive notice means that the recording acts deem a person to have whatever information is contained in the public records—information that could be obtained by a reasonably diligent investigation of the records whether or not the investigator actually has knowledge of the information recorded. Instruments affecting virtually all interests in real estate, including deeds, mortgages, assignments of mortgages, liens on real estate, land contracts, long-term leases, easements, restrictive covenants, and options to buy, are covered by recording acts.

Most recording acts say that in order to establish and preserve a claim to an interest in real estate that will take precedence in law against future claimants, the instrument creating that claim must be recorded in accordance with state law. These acts were designed in part to protect an innocent person who purchased an interest in real estate in good faith unaware that the interest had already been acquired by another. For example, if A conveyed to B, who did not record the instrument establishing his claim, and later A conveyed the same interest to C, who did record, C's claim would be superior to B's if he was unaware of the prior conveyance and paid

Box 2.1

Fire Station Bought for $2,272, Thanks to Blunder!

According to the *Star State Reporter* in Gary, Indiana, "The city of Gary was certainly surprised to learn that Munster resident Joseph F. Belovich had bought its Fire Station 7 for $2,272." Especially since the fire station was not for sale! But a court ruled that Belovich owned the property, because he bought it at a tax-delinquent sale and properly filed the deed with the Lake County recorder's office. The city had never recorded the deed when it bought the land on which it constructed the fire station. According to the article, Belovich asked the city to pay him $1 million to buy the property from him or he wants the fire department evicted.

Because the city's deed was not recorded, the former owner of the land was billed for the property taxes and the taxes were not paid. The delinquent taxes accumulated and the property was auctioned by the county in 1984 for delinquent taxes. Belovich bought the property at the sale and filed the deed on December 10, 1984.

Belovich is also seeking back rent, attorney fees, and other related damages, plus 12 percent interest. The outcome of this case was not yet determined at the time of this writing.

valuable consideration to A for the conveyance. B's only claim would be to file a suit against A for fraud.

Mechanics' Liens. One cloud on the title which may not be disclosed by the public records is a **mechanics' lien.** In general, mechanics' liens give unpaid contractors, workers, and material suppliers the right to attach a lien on the real estate to which they added their labor or materials. To obtain the payment owed them, they may foreclose such liens by forcing a judicial sale of the encumbered property. They are then paid from the proceeds of the sale. Use of mechanics' liens exists in every state, although the nature of the statutes varies.

Mechanics' liens are permitted to be recorded "after the fact." In other words, state laws generally give contractors, laborers, or suppliers of materials a certain period of time following the completion of work or delivery of materials during which to file their lien. When the lien is filed it "relates back" and takes priority over all liens filed after the time when materials were first delivered or work first performed on the real estate. As a result, until the end of the time allowed for filing (generally 60 days), a purchaser of an interest in newly constructed or improved real estate cannot be sure that the interest will be unencumbered or that the interest will have the priority bargained for. As a precaution, lenders and purchasers of such real estate should require the seller to provide an affidavit stating that at closing, all moneys due to contractors and subcontractors have been fully paid. In the event liens are filed after the closing, a breach of the vendor's covenants in the affidavit can easily be proven, and the vendor can be held liable for the discharge of those liens.

The Mortgage Instrument

In the following discussion of mortgages, we will concentrate on loans used for the purchase of owner-occupied residential property. Although much of the information covered here also applies to other types of loans (e.g., construction and land development loans), additional material relating specifically to these loans will be discussed in later chapters.

Utilization of mortgage financing has been the most common method of financing the purchase of real estate. Under this method, the buyer usually borrows funds from an institutional lender (e.g., a savings and loan association, a savings bank, a commercial bank, or life insurance company) and uses these and other funds to purchase a property. When funds are borrowed with the express intent of using the proceeds to acquire real estate that will serve as a security for a loan, the mortgage serving as evidence of the loan security is commonly called a **purchase-money mortgage.** Real estate is generally regarded by lenders as excellent security for a loan, and lenders acquire a secured interest in the real estate with a mortgage.

Definition of a Mortgage

In its most general sense, a **mortgage** is created in a transaction whereby one party pledges real property to another party as security for an obligation owed to that party. A **promissory note** is normally executed contemporaneously with the mortgage. This note creates the obligation to repay the loan in accordance with its terms and is secured by the mortgage. The elements essential to the existence of a mortgage are an *obligation* to pay or perform and a *pledge* of property as security for that obligation. The obligation secured by a mortgage need not be monetary. It may be, for example, an agreement to perform some service or to perform some other specified actions.[9]

Note versus Mortgage

Normally, the underlying obligation secured by a mortgage is evidenced by a separate promissory note. The note admits the debt and generally makes the borrower personally liable for the obligation. The mortgage is usually a separate document that pledges the designated property as security for the debt. If the lender is completely confident that the borrower has sufficient assets now, would continue to have those assets over the term of the loan, and would meet the underlying obligation, no mortgage would be necessary. In case of default, the mortgagee may elect to disregard the mortgage and sue on the note. The judgment awarded the mortgagee as a result of a suit on the note may be attached to other property of the mortgagor which, when sold to satisfy the judgment lien, may enable the mortgagee to recover the amount of the claim more readily than if he or she foreclosed on the mortgage. In practice, the mortgagee will normally elect to sue on the note and foreclose on the mortgage simultaneously.

Mortgages typically include clauses containing important covenants for both the mortgagor and mortgagee. These clauses are frequently repeated in the promissory note, or the note may incorporate these covenants by reference to the mortgage. Promissory notes typically contain clauses specifying the interest rate, repayment terms, maturity dates and other clauses dealing with notices of default, the rights of mortgagors and mortgagees upon default, late payment fees, prepayment fees, and

---

[9]To be an obligation secured by a mortgage, an obligation which is not itself an explicitly monetary one must be reducible to monetary terms. In other words, a dollar value must be placed on it.

other clauses. The note also generally empowers the mortgagee to require immediate and full payment of the entire amount of debt secured by the mortgage (referred to as acceleration) in case of the mortgagor's default. Without an acceleration clause the mortgagee could only sue for the amount of the payments currently in default. Another clause, which may be included in the note, requires full payment of the entire debt upon the transfer of the mortgagor's interest in the property without the mortgagor's consent. This is referred to as a due-on-sale clause.

Interests That Can Be Mortgaged

Most people are accustomed to thinking of a mortgage in relation to full, or fee simple, ownership. But any interest in real estate that is subject to sale, grant, or assignment—that is, any interest that can be transferred—can be mortgaged. Thus, such diverse interests as fee simple estates, life estates, estates for years, remainders, reversions, leasehold interests, and options to purchase real estate, among others, are all mortgageable interests as far as legal theory is concerned. Whether, as a matter of sound business judgment, mortgagees would be willing to lend money against some of the lesser interests in land is quite another question.

Minimum Mortgage Requirements

A mortgage involves a transfer of an interest in real estate. Accordingly, the statute of frauds requires that it must be in writing. The vast volume of mortgage lending today is institutional lending, and institutional mortgages are formal documents. There is, however, no specific form required for a valid mortgage. Indeed, although most mortgages are formal documents, a valid mortgage could be handwritten. The requirements of a valid mortgage document are (1) wording that appropriately expresses the intent of the parties to create a security interest in real property for the benefit of the mortgage and (2) other items required by state law.

In the United States, mortgage law has traditionally been within the jurisdiction of state law; by and large, mortgages continue to be governed primarily by state law. Thus, to be enforceable, a mortgage must meet requirements imposed by the law of the state in which the property offered as security is located.

Whether a printed form of mortgage instrument is used or an attorney draws up a special form, the following subjects should always be included:

1. Appropriate identification of mortgagor and mortgagee.
2. Proper description of the property that has a lien.
3. Covenants of seisin and warranty.[10]
4. Provision for release of dower rights.[11]
5. Any other desired covenants and contractual agreements.

All of the terms and contractual agreements recited in the note can be included in the mortgage as well by making reference to the note in the mortgage document.

Although the bulk of mortgage law remains within the jurisdiction of state law, a wide range of federal regulations also are operative in the area of mortgage law. Moreover, in recent years the federal government has acted to directly preempt state

[10]A *covenant* is a promise or binding assurance. *Seisin* is the state of owning the quantum of title being conveyed.

[11]*Dower* is the interest in a husband's real estate transferred by law to the widow after his death. The common law counterpart running in favor of the husband as a widower is called *curtesy.* Many states now have a statutory allowance from the decedent's estate in lieu of dower and curtesy.

law in a number of areas (e.g., overturning state usury laws,[12] overturning state restrictions on the operation of due-on-sale clauses, and establishing conditions for allowing prepayment of the mortgage debt and for setting prepayment penalties).

In addition, the federal government has exerted a strong but indirect influence on mortgage transactions by means of its sponsorship of the agencies and quasi-private institutions that support and, for all practical purposes, constitute the secondary market for residential mortgages. The Federal National Mortgage Association (FNMA) and the Federal Home Loan Mortgage Corporation (FHLMC) have adopted joint standardized mortgage forms for the purpose of facilitating secondary market transactions on a nationwide basis. The joint FNMA-FHLMC uniform mortgage form has been so widely adopted by residential mortgage lenders that it has largely replaced the use of mortgage forms used by individual institutions. One reason for the popularity of this form with residential lenders is that it is readily acceptable by the major secondary market institutions, should the lender desire to sell the mortgage after it has been originated.

Important Mortgage Clauses

It is beyond the scope of this chapter to discuss all the clauses that might be found in a mortgage document. We will mention some of the more important clauses, however, so that the reader gains an appreciation of the effect these clauses may have on the position of the borrower and lender.

Funds for Taxes and Insurance. This clause requires the mortgagor to pay amounts needed to cover property taxes and property fire and casualty insurance, plus mortgage insurance premiums, if required by the lender, in monthly installments in advance of when they are due unless such payments are prohibited by state law. The purpose of this clause is to enable the mortgagee to pay these charges out of money provided by the mortgagor when they become due instead of relying on the mortgagor to make timely payments on his own. The mortgagee is thereby better able to protect his or her security interest against liens for taxes, which normally have priority over the first mortgage, and against lapses in insurance coverage. Such funds are generally held in an escrow or trust account for the mortgagor.

Charges and Liens. This clause requires the mortgagor to pay all taxes, assessments, charges, and claims assessed against the property that have priority over the mortgage and to pay all leasehold payments, if applicable. The reason for this clause is that the mortgagee's security interest can be wiped out if these claims, or liens, are not paid or discharged, since they generally can attain priority over the interests of the mortgagee. For example, if taxes and assessments are not paid, a first mortgage on the property can be wiped out at a sale to satisfy the tax lien, unless the mortgagee is either the successful bidder at the tax sale or pays the tax due to keep the property from being sold at the tax sale.

Hazard Insurance. This clause requires the mortgagor to obtain and maintain insurance against loss or damage to the property caused by fire and other hazards, such as windstorms, hail, explosion, and smoke. In effect, this clause acknowledges that the mortgagee as well as the mortgagor has an insurable interest in the mortgaged property. The mortgagee's insurable interest is the amount of the mortgage debt.

[12]Usury laws prohibit charging unconscionable and exorbitant rates or amounts of interest for the use of money. A usurious loan is one whose interest rate exceeds that permitted by usury laws.

Preservation and Maintenance of the Property. This clause obligates the mortgagor to maintain the property in good condition and to not engage in or permit acts of waste.[13] This clause recognizes that the mortgagee has a valid interest in preventing the mortgaged property from deteriorating to the extent that the collateral value of the property is impaired.

Transfer of Property or a Beneficial Interest in Borrower. This clause, known as the **due-on-sale clause,** allows the mortgagee to accelerate the debt (i.e., to take action to make the outstanding loan balance plus accrued interest immediately due and payable) when the property, or some interest in the property, is transferred without the written consent of the mortgagee. The purpose of the due-on-sale clause is to enable the mortgagee to protect his or her security interest by approving any new owner. The clause also permits the mortgagee to increase the interest rate on the loan to current market rates. This, of course, reduces the possibility of the new owner assuming a loan with an attractive interest rate.

Borrower's Rights to Reinstate. This clause deals with the mortgagor's right to reinstate the original repayment terms in the note after the mortgagee has caused an acceleration of the debt. It gives the mortgagor the right to have foreclosure proceedings discontinued at any time before a judgment is entered enforcing the mortgage (i.e., before a decree for the sale of the property is given) if the mortgagor does the following:

1. Pays to the mortgagee all sums which would then be due had no acceleration occurred.
2. Cures any default of any other covenants or agreements.
3. Pays all expenses incurred by the lender in enforcing its mortgage.
4. Takes such action as the mortgagee may reasonably require to ensure that the mortgagee's rights in the property and the mortgagor's obligations to pay are unchanged.

Acceleration; Remedies. This clause provides that notice must be given to the mortgagor, which specifies (1) the default, (2) the action required to cure the default, (3) the time by which the default must be cured, and (4) that failure to cure the default may result in acceleration of the debt secured by the mortgage. Absent this clause, a mortgagee can only sue a delinquent mortgagor for payments then in default.

Lender in Possession. This clause provides that upon acceleration or abandonment of the property, the mortgagee (or a judicially appointed receiver) may enter the property and collect rents until the mortgage is foreclosed. Rents collected must be applied first to the costs of managing and operating the property, and then to the mortgage debt, real estate taxes, insurances, and other obligations of the mortgagor as specified in the mortgage.

Release. The **release clause** obligates the mortgagee to discharge the mortgage and deliver written evidence to the mortgagor thereof when all amounts of indebtedness secured by the mortgage have been paid off. The certificate of release should

[13] *Waste* is the abuse or destructive use of property by one in rightful possession.

be recorded in the proper official records to clear the title of the estate to which the mortgage had been attached. The mortgagor does not have to pay the mortgagee for the release but does have to pay the costs of recording the release.

Prepayment. The lender is not required to accept advance payments unless there is a provision to this effect, known as a **prepayment clause.** The clause may permit prepayment in full or in part, and the lender, at his or her option, may choose to charge the penalty provided. Lenders will typically choose not to enforce the penalty provision when current interest rates exceed the rate on the mortgage note being prepaid. This clause can be viewed as giving the lender an option of accepting payment when it is advantageous.

Future Advances. While it is expected that a mortgage will always state the total amount of the debt it is expected to secure, this amount may be in nature of a forecast of the total debt to be incurred in installments. In other words, a mortgage may cover **future advances** as well as current advances. For example, a mortgage may be so written that it will protect several successive loans under a general line of credit extended by the mortgagee to the mortgagor. In case the total amount cannot be forecasted with accuracy, at least the general nature of the advances or loans must be apparent from the wording of the mortgage.

An illustration of a mortgage for future advances, sometimes called an **open-end mortgage,** takes the form of construction loans. Here the borrower arranges in advance with a mortgagee for a total amount, usually definitely stated in the mortgage, that will be advanced, in stages, under the mortgage to meet the part of the costs of construction as it progresses. As the structure progresses, the mortgagor has the right to call upon the mortgagee for successive advances on the loan. All improvements become security under the terms of the mortgage as they are constructed.

Subordination Clause. By means of this clause, a first mortgage holder agrees to make its mortgage junior in priority to the mortgage of another lender. A **subordination clause** might be used in situations where the seller provides financing by taking back a mortgage from the buyer, and the buyer also intends to obtain a mortgage from a bank or other financial institution, usually to develop or construct an improvement. Financial institutions will generally require that their loans have first mortgage priority. Consequently, the seller must agree to include a subordination clause in the mortgage whereby the seller agrees to subordinate the priority of the mortgage to the bank loan. This ensures that even if the seller's mortgage is recorded before the bank loan, it will be subordinate to the bank loan.

Assumption of Mortgage

When the mortgagor transfers his or her rights to another, the question arises, "Does the grantee agree to become liable for payment of the mortgage debt and relieve the mortgagor of his or her personal obligation?" If this is the intention of both parties, the **assumption of the mortgage** by the grantee may accomplish the purpose. The deed, after specifying the nature of the mortgage which encumbers the property, will contain a clause to the effect that the grantee assumes and agrees to pay the amount of the obligations owed to the mortgagee as part consideration for the conveyance of title. Where an assumption is undertaken by the grantee, it should be couched in language that leaves no doubt about the intent.

An assumption agreement takes the form of a contract of indemnity. It shifts the responsibility for the payment of the debt from the grantor to the grantee. Thereafter, the grantor stands in the position of a surety (guarantee) for the payment of the debt. However, such an arrangement binds only the parties to it: the grantor and the grantee. Since the mortgagee is not ordinarily a party to such an agreement, he or she is not bound by it. As a consequence, the mortgagee may still hold the original mortgagor liable. Thus, if a property is sold with a loan assumption and the new owner defaults on the loan, the lender can hold the previous owner liable unless the previous owner was released from the debt.

Release of Grantor from Assumed Debt. When a mortgagor owning property grants that property to another and the grantee assumes the grantor's mortgage, the lender may or may not release the grantor from personal liability for the mortgage debt. The decision of release will depend on the value of the property as security, the grantee's financial capabilities, and other factors affecting the lender's attitudes toward the transaction. A mortgagee cannot be expected to release an antecedent mortgagor if the result will be to increase the credit risk, unless the mortgagee is compensated in some way (e.g., a higher interest rate).

Acquiring Title "Subject to" a Mortgage

In contrast to the assumption of the personal obligation to pay the debt, grantees may not be willing to accept this responsibility. In this case, they may ask grantors to allow them to take title **"subject to" the mortgage.** So long as the grantees are financially able and think it will be to their advantage, they will keep up payments on the mortgage and observe its other covenants. Under normal conditions, if they purchased the property at a fair price, it will be to their advantage to avoid default on the mortgage to protect their own equity.

But should the grantees reach the conclusion that there is no longer any advantage to making further payments, or should they become financially unable to do so, they may default on their payments. By so doing, they run the risk of losing whatever equity they have in the property. However, grantees cannot be held personally liable for the amount of the debt that they assumed. Grantors are still personally liable and may be held liable for any deficiency judgment resulting from the foreclosure sale.

It is obviously riskier for grantors to sell property subject to the mortgage. Given a choice, they would generally prefer that responsible grantees assume the mortgage unless they are compensated for the additional risk they undertake as a surety (e.g., by receiving a higher price for the property).

Property Covered by a Mortgage

The property that is covered by the mortgage as security for the loan includes not only the land and any existing buildings on the land, but also easements and fixtures. In addition, the mortgage agreement may provide that property covered by the mortgage also includes rights to natural resources (e.g., mineral, timber, oil and gas, and water rights) and even rights to rents and profits from the real estate. An easement that runs with the property is generally regarded by the law as being covered by the mortgage, regardless of whether the easement is created before or after the mortgage is executed. Such an easement, if in existence at the time the property is mortgaged, is covered by the mortgage even if it is not mentioned in the mortgage. Foreclosure of the mortgage will not extinguish this easement. An easement created subsequent to the recording of a mortgage, however, will be extinguished by the foreclosure.

Issues involving fixtures have generated a considerable amount of legal controversy. In general, a **fixture** is an item of tangible personal property (also referred to as chattel) that has become affixed to or is intended to be used with the real estate so as to be considered part of the property. The law is in general agreement that fixtures are covered by the mortgage, with the exception of "trade fixtures"[14] installed by a tenant.

A mortgage will usually contain what is called an **after-acquired property clause** as part of its description of the type of property to be covered by the mortgage. This provision states in effect that property acquired subsequent to the execution of the mortgage that becomes part of the real estate is included in the security covered by the mortgage. After-acquired property includes additional improvements erected on the property or fixtures that become part of the property at any time in the future for as long as the debt remains outstanding. The courts have generally affirmed the validity of after-acquired property clauses, and the Uniform Land Transactions Act (ULTA) expressly accepts their validity.[15]

Junior Mortgages

In simple real estate financing transactions, such as those involving single residences, the character of the mortgage structure is easily defined. The senior or prior mortgage is usually called a first mortgage. All others are given the class name of **junior mortgages.** In any particular situation, there may be one or more junior mortgages or none at all. One junior lien, usually called a second mortgage, is sometimes used to bridge the gap between the price of the property and the sum of the first mortgage and the amount of money available to the purchaser to use as a down payment. Traditionally second mortgages are short term and carry a higher rate of interest than first mortgages because of the additional risk associated with their junior status.

Recording of Mortgages

Unless the statutes of the state require it, recording is not essential to the validity of a mortgage because it is an agreement between the mortgagor and the mortgagee. The act of recording creates no rights that did not exist before, but it does give others notice of the existence and effect of the mortgage. A recorded mortgage protects its holder by giving him or her priority over the subsequent acts of the mortgagor. For example, if a mortgagee failed to record the mortgage, the mortgagor could mortgage the property to a second lender. If this second lender had no notice of the prior unrecorded mortgage, the second lender would have a lien prior to that of the original mortgagee. In general, the priority of successive liens is determined by the time they are accepted for record.

---

[14]Trade fixtures are personal property used by tenants in businesses. Such fixtures retain the character of personal property (e.g., shelves used to display merchandise).

[15]For a discussion and case law materials related to after-acquired property clauses, see Grant S. Nelson and Dale A. Whitman, *Real Estate Transfer, Finance, and Development,* 2nd ed. (St. Paul, MN: West Publishing, 1981), pp. 633–39; see also Kratovil and Werner, *Modern Mortgage Law and Practice,* 2nd ed., pp.114–17.

As we have discussed, the recording acts provide opportunities for the protection of holders of interests in property, but at the same time they place responsibilities upon them to make use of these opportunities. Failure to inspect the records for prior liens or to record the mortgage may result in loss to the mortgagee. In most states, *junior lienors* of record without notice of the existence of a senior mortgage will have priority over an unrecorded senior mortgage. Even subsequent recording of a senior mortgage lien will generally not elevate it to a higher priority.

Other Financing Sources

Seller Financing

A source of credit for a real property buyer is often the seller. If the seller is willing to take back a mortgage as part or full payment of the purchase price, it is referred to as **seller financing.** This type of financing is used when:

1. Third-party mortgage financing is too expensive or unavailable.
2. The buyer does not qualify for long-term mortgage credit because of a low down payment or difficulty meeting monthly payments.
3. The seller desires to take advantage of the installment method of reporting the gain from the sale.
4. The seller desires to artificially raise the price of the property by offering a lower-than-market interest rate on the mortgage, thereby creating more capital gains and less interest or ordinary income.[16]

Any mortgage given by a buyer to secure payment of all or part of the purchase price of a property is called a purchase-money mortgage. It can be a first mortgage, which might be the case if the seller is providing all of the financing necessary to consummate the transaction. It is more likely to take the form of a second mortgage that is used to bridge the gap between an available first mortgage and the buyer's down payment. As such, it must be differentiated from mortgages given to secure a loan from a third party for the purchase of the property. The third-party lender (e.g., a financial institution), will normally want its mortgage to be a first mortgage. Thus the purchase-money mortgage must either be recorded after the third-party loan or contain a subordination clause as defined earlier.

Land Contracts

One form of financing real estate that has been widely used over the years is commonly referred to as a land contract. The term **land contract** has a variety of aliases, including real estate contract, installment sales contract, agreement to convey, and contract for deed. As the last term implies, the land contract seller promises to convey title at such time as the purchaser completes the performance of the obligation called for in the contract. Such performance usually means payment of the purchase price in stipulated installments, much the same way as under a note and mortgage.

It should be emphasized that a land contract is not a mortgage. Under the land contract, the sellers retain the title in their name. The deed record shows that the sellers are still the owners of the property, but the land contract is supposed to tie

[16]The use of this technique has been limited by the "unstated interest rule."

their hands to make sure that the sellers or their assigns ultimately transfer title to the vendees or their heirs or assigns.

The land contract may be used as a substitute for either a vendor's lien (a lien implied by courts of equity arising from the purchaser having received property for which he or she has not yet fully paid) or a purchase-money mortgage. Like the former, it is often a fragile type of evidence of the vendee's equity and would normally not be preferred over the purchase-money mortgage if the latter were available. However, in cases where there is no down payment or a small down payment, or in states that have long redemption periods during which the vendee has the right to possession and to collection of rents even though in default, sellers of land may refuse to give a deed and take back a mortgage until a very substantial part of the purchase price has been paid.

Several points of comparison exist between purchase-money mortgages and land contracts. A land contract buyer does not have title to the property and therefore cannot control whether the property will be mortgaged subsequent to the execution of the land contract or be made subject to covenants, easements, or mechanics' liens in the future by the contract seller. Most land contracts contain a clause allowing the seller to mortgage property up to an amount equal to the buyer's indebtedness to the seller. The buyer would have this protection if mortgage financing were used because limits would be made explicit and the buyer would have title. Furthermore, the possibility of forfeiture of the land contract interest may exist without any of the procedural protections afforded mortgages. It is suggested that all such points of comparison should be considered in making the decision whether to buy or sell on land contract or to obtain mortgage financing. In general, land contracts are used in many of the same situations as purchase-money mortgages (e.g., where the buyer has difficulty obtaining third-party financing).

Recording of Land Contracts. State laws provide for the recording of conveyances of land and instruments affecting title. Land contracts generally are considered instruments affecting title and are consequently admissible to record. Recording land contracts is not essential to their validity; it merely gives notice of their existence to third parties.

Mortgage Default

We have discussed the various property rights associated with real estate. Next consider some of the problems that result when one of the parties does not fulfill a contractual obligation associated with its property right. The legal ramifications of these problems affect the financial security of other parties' rights and are thus an important aspect of real estate finance.

One of the most important risks in making a mortgage loan is that the borrower will default on his or her obligation in some way, so that the lender may not receive the expected mortgage payments. The risk associated with mortgage loans depends in part on the rights of the lender if and when such default occurs. Thus, it is important to understand the legal ramifications of mortgage default.

What Constitutes Default?

Default is a failure to fulfill a contract, agreement, or duty, especially a financial obligation. It follows that a **mortgage default** can result from any breach of the mortgage contract. The most common default is the failure to meet an installment payment of the interest and principal. Failure to pay taxes or insurance premiums when due may also result in a default, which may precipitate an acceleration of the debt and a foreclosure action. Indeed, some mortgages have clauses that make specific stipulations to this effect. Even a failure to keep the security in repair may constitute a *technical default,* but a technical default seldom results in an actual foreclosure sale. It might be difficult for the mortgagee to prove that the repair clause in the mortgage had been broken unless the property showed definite evidence of the effects of waste.

From another point of view, default is defined first in the breach of the letter of the contract and then in the attitude of the mortgagee. This means that even though there is a breach of contract, the mortgagee may see fit to ignore it or to postpone doing something about it. In case of default accompanied by abandonment, the probabilities are that the mortgagee will act quickly to protect his or her interests against vandalism, neglect, and waste. If, on the other hand, the mortgagor is of good character, has generally met obligations promptly in the past, wishes to retain an interest in the property, and is only temporarily unable to meet obligations, a default is not likely to be immediately declared by the mortgagee.

Alternatives to Foreclosure: Workouts

Foreclosure involves the sale of property by the courts to satisfy the unpaid debt. The details of this process are discussed later. Because of the time involved and the various costs associated with foreclosure (and possibly repair of any damage to the property), lenders often prefer to seek an alternative to actual foreclosure.

Although mortgage contracts normally indicate definite penalties to follow any breach therein, experience has shown that in spite of provisions for prompt action in case of a default in mortgage payments, many commitments are not met in strict accordance with the letter of the contract. Instead, whenever mortgagors get into financial trouble and are unable to meet their obligations, adjustments of the payments or other terms are likely to follow if both the borrower and lender believe that the conditions are temporary and will be remedied.

The term **workout** is often used to describe the various activities undertaken to deal with a mortgagor who is in financial trouble. Many times the parties make a workout agreement that sets forth the rules by which, during a specified period of time, they will conduct themselves and their discussions. The lender agrees to refrain from exercising legal remedies. In exchange the borrower acknowledges his or her financial difficulty and agrees to certain conditions such as supplying specified information to the lender and establishing a cash account in which receipts from the property are deposited.

Five alternatives can be considered in a workout:

1. Restructuring the mortgage loan.
2. Transfer of the mortgage to a new owner.
3. Voluntary conveyancy of the title to the mortgagee.
4. A "friendly foreclosure."
5. A prepackaged bankruptcy.

Restructuring the Mortgage Loan

Loans can be restructured in many ways. Such restructuring will usually involve lower interest rates, accruals of interest, or extended maturity dates. If the original loan is nonrecourse to the borrower, the lender may want to obtain personal recourse against the borrower as part of the loan restructuring agreement. This makes the borrower subject to significantly more downside risk if the restructuring fails. The lender also may want a participation in the performance of the property to enhance the lender's upside potential as compensation for being willing to restructure the loan. For example, the lender could ask for a percentage of any increase in the income of the property over its current level.

Recasting of Mortgages. Once a mortgage is executed and placed on record, its form may change substantially before it is redeemed. It may be recast for any one of several reasons. A mortgage can be renegotiated at any time, but most frequently it is recast by changing the terms of the mortgage (either temporarily or permanently) to avoid or cure a default.

Where mortgage terms such as the interest rate, amortization period, or payment amounts are changed, mortgagees must exercise care to avoid losing their priority over intervening lienors. The mere extension of time of payment will not generally impair the priority of the extended mortgage. Courts, however, are watchful to protect intervening lienors against prejudice, and mortgages may lose priority to the extent that changes in the interest rate, payment amounts, or the amount of indebtedness place additional burdens on the mortgagor.[17]

Extension Agreements. Occasionally, a mortgagor in financial difficulty may seek permission from the mortgagee to extend the mortgage terms for a period of time. This is known as a mortgage **extension agreement.** A mortgagor may request a longer amortization period for the remaining principal balance or temporary grace period for the payment of principal or interest payments or both. In responding to such a request, the mortgagee needs to consider the following issues:

1. What is the condition of the security? Has it been reasonably well maintained or does it show the effects of waste and neglect?
2. Have there been any intervening liens? These are liens recorded or attached after the recordation of the mortgage but before any modifications to it. If so, what is their effect upon an extension agreement? If such liens exist, it is possible that the extension of an existing mortgage may amount to a cancellation of the mortgage and the making of a new one. If so, this could advance the priority of intervening liens.
3. What is the surety status of any grantees who have assumed the mortgage? Will an extension of time for the payment of the debt secured by the mortgage terminate the liability of such sureties? The best way for mortgagees to protect themselves against the possibilities implied in these questions is to secure the consent of the extension agreement from all sureties to the extension. As parties to it, they can have no grounds for opposing it. But if they are not made parties to the extension—particularly if changes in the terms of the mortgage through the extension agreement tend to increase the obligations for which the sureties are liable—then care should be exercised to ensure that those sureties who refuse to sign the agreement

[17]Recasting of mortgages to admit interests not present at the time the mortgages were executed is sometimes necessary. For example, the mortgage may make no provision for an easement of a public utility company that requires access to the rear of the site covered by the mortgage. Since the installation of the services of the utility will normally add to rather than subtract from the value of the security, the mortgagee will usually be glad to approve the change. Nevertheless, it will require a recasting of the mortgage to the extent indicated.

are not released by the extension agreement. The possibility of foreclosure and a deficiency judgment against them may be a sufficient inducement to obtain their agreement to be parties to the extension.

The exact nature of an extension agreement depends upon the bargaining position of mortgagor and mortgagee. If mortgagors can refinance the loan on more favorable terms, they will probably not apply for an extension agreement. Alternatively, they may have to make changes that favor the mortgagee, such as an increase in the interest rate.

Alternative to Extension Agreement. An alternative to an extension agreement has the mortgagee agree informally to a temporary extension without making any changes in the formal recorded agreement between the parties. If the mortgagor is unable to meet all monthly mortgage payments, these too may be waived temporarily or forgiven in whole or in part. For example, simply raising the question of such an agreement suggests that the mortgagor cannot pay the matured principal of the loan. Therefore, some informal arrangement may be made to permit the mortgagor to retain possession of the property in return for meeting monthly payments, which may or may not include principal installments. The use of this kind of informal agreement can be troublesome, but, in general, if it is reached, the amounts demanded will be adjusted to the present payment capacities of the borrower. Should the borrower's financial condition improve, the lender may again insist that the originally scheduled payments resume.

The use of such an alternative to a definite extension agreement may serve the temporary needs of both mortgagors and mortgagees. If the latter feel that the security amply protects their lien, the mortgagees can afford to be lenient in helping mortgagors adjust their financial arrangements during a difficult period. If the mortgagors also feel that any real equity exists in the property, they will wish to protect it if at all possible.

Transfer of Mortgage to a New Owner

Mortgagors who are unable or unwilling to meet their mortgage obligations may be able to find someone who is willing to purchase the property and either assume the mortgage liability or take the property "subject to" the existing mortgage. (Recall the discussion in the previous chapter of the legal distinction between these two alternatives.) The new purchaser may be willing to accept the **transfer of mortgage** if he or she thinks the value of the property exceeds the balance due on the mortgage. In either case, the seller retains personal liability for the debt. However, if the seller is about to default and expects to lose the property anyway, he or she may be willing to take a chance on a new purchaser fulfilling the mortgage obligation. The risk is that the new buyer will default, and the seller will again have responsibility for the debt and get the property back.

Recall that if purchasers acquire the property "subject to" the existing debt, they do not acquire any personal liability for the debt. Thus, they can only lose any equity personally invested to acquire the property. This equity investment may be quite small where the sellers are financially distressed and face foreclosure. Thus, the buyers may have little to lose by taking a chance on acquiring the property subject to the mortgage. If it turns out to be a good investment, they will continue to make payments on the debt, but if they find that the value of the property is unlikely to exceed the mortgage debt within a reasonable time frame, they can simply stop making payments and let the sellers reacquire the property. Thus, we see that in this situation buyers of the property "subject to" a mortgage have in effect purchased an option. The equity buyers invest is payment for this option, which allows them to take a chance on the property value increasing after it is acquired. We can therefore see why purchasers might even give the sellers money to acquire a property subject to a mortgage even if the *current* value of the property is less than the mortgage balance.

For example, suppose a property has a mortgage balance of $100,000. Property values in the area are currently depressed, and the owner believes that only $99,000 could be obtained on an outright sale. However, a buyer is willing to acquire the property at a price of $101,000 "subject to" the existing mortgage. Thus, $2,000 is paid for the option of tying up the property in hopes that property values rise above their current level.[18] If the property does not rise in value to more than $100,000 (less any additional principal payments that have been made), the purchaser could simply walk away, and the original owner again becomes responsible for the mortgage. If the property rises in value to more than $101,000, the purchaser stands to make a profit and would continue to make payments on the mortgage.

It should be clear that knowledge of various legal alternatives (e.g., being able to purchase a property "subject to" versus assuming a mortgage) can allow a buyer and seller to arrive at an agreement that best meets their financial objectives. Thus, legal alternatives can often be evaluated in a financial context.

Voluntary Conveyance

Borrowers (mortgagors) who can no longer meet the mortgage obligation may attempt to "sell" their equity to the mortgagees. For example, suppose that the mortgagors are unable to meet their obligations and face foreclosure of their equity. To save time, trouble, and expense associated with foreclosure, the mortgagees may make or accept a proposal to take title from the mortgagors. If they both agree that the property value exceeds the mortgage balance, a sum may be paid to the mortgagors for their equity. If the value is less than the mortgage balance, the lenders may still be willing to accept title and release the mortgagors from the mortgage debt. This **voluntary conveyance** might be done because the cost of foreclosure may exceed the expected benefit of pursuing that course of action.

When voluntary conveyances are used, title is usually transferred with a warranty or quitclaim deed from mortgagors to mortgagees. The mortgagors should insist upon a release to make sure that they are no longer bound under their note and mortgage, especially in situations where the mortgage balance is near or in excess of the property value. Otherwise, the mortgagors may find that they still have a personal obligation to pay the mortgage note. The conveyance to the mortgagees in exchange for a release from the mortgage debt is frequently referred to as giving *deed in lieu of foreclosure* of the mortgage. A deed in lieu of foreclosure has the advantage of speed and minimizes the expense of transferring the property and the uncertainty of litigation. It also avoids the negative publicity of foreclosure or bankruptcy. A deed in lieu of foreclosure does not cut off subordinate interests in the property. The lender must make arrangements with all other creditors. There are also potential bankruptcy problems. The transfer may be voidable as a preferential transfer. In addition to the legal questions involved in voluntary conveyances, the mortgagee frequently faces very practical financial issues as well. If there are junior liens outstanding, they are not

[18]The seller would receive $1,000 in cash, but since the seller had −$1,000 in equity he or she receives the economic benefit of $2,000, which is also the difference between the price paid and the market value of the property.

eliminated by a voluntary conveyance. Indeed, their holders may be in a better position than before if the title to the property passes to a more financially sound owner. Unless in some manner these junior liens are released from the property in question—possibly by agreement with their holders to transfer them to other property owned by the mortgagor or even on occasion to cancel them—the mortgagee may find it necessary to foreclose instead of taking a voluntary conveyance because the title conveyed is subject to junior liens. Foreclosure provides the mortgagee with a lawful method of becoming free from the liens of the junior claimants.

Friendly Foreclosure

Foreclosure can be time-consuming and expensive, and there can be damage to the property during this time period. A **"friendly foreclosure"** is a foreclosure action in which the borrower submits to the jurisdiction of the court, waives any right to assert defenses and claims and to appeal or collaterally attack any judgment, and otherwise agrees to cooperate with the lender in the litigation. This can shorten the time required to effect a foreclosure. This also cuts off subordinate liens and provides better protection in case of the borrower's subsequent bankruptcy. A friendly foreclosure normally takes more time than a voluntary conveyance but is less time-consuming than an unfriendly foreclosure. This is discussed in more detail in the next section.

Prepackaged Bankruptcy

The mortgagee must consider the risk that the mortgagor will use the threat of filing for bankruptcy as a way of reducing some of his or her obligation under the original mortgage agreement. Bankruptcy can have significant consequences for secured lenders. To the extent that the collateral securing the debt is worth less than the principal amount of the debt, the deficiency will be treated as an unsecured debt. In a **prepackaged bankruptcy,** before filing the bankruptcy petition, borrowers agree with all their creditors to the terms on which they will turn their assets over to its creditors in exchange for a discharge of liabilities. This can save a considerable amount of time and expense compared with the case where the terms are not agreed upon in advance. The consequences of bankruptcy are discussed further in the last section of this chapter.

Foreclosure

In practice, most mortgagees are not anxious to take property from mortgagors, particularly where the mortgagors have candidly communicated with the mortgagees concerning the default and have made realistic proposals to cure the default over a reasonable period of time. Because the management and disposal of property requires skills that are usually outside of the range of expertise of most lenders and therefore costly to acquire, mortgagees prefer to collect the amounts owed them and are likely to be lenient and patient when circumstances warrant it. Seldom do mortgagees insist upon the exact letter of their contract. Nor do they rush into court to insist upon **foreclosure** at the first evidence of default, but after patience and leniency have been extended to delinquent mortgagors, eventually a settlement becomes necessary and foreclosure proceedings are started.

Judicial Foreclosure

In general, the mortgagee possesses two types of remedies to protect his or her interests in case of default by the mortgagor. First, the lender may obtain **judicial foreclosure;** that is to sue on the debt, obtain judgment, and execute the judgment against property of the mortgagor. In a judicial foreclosure, property subject to attachment and execution[19] is not limited to the mortgaged property. This judgment may be levied against any of the mortgagor's property not otherwise legally exempt[20] from execution.

Second, the lender may bring a foreclosure suit and obtain a decree of foreclosure and sale. If the sale of the mortgaged property realizes a price high enough to meet the expenses of the sale and the claims of the mortgagee and still leave a balance, this balance goes to the mortgagor. While foreclosure and sale of the property may be undertaken in two separate actions, they are usually pursued simultaneously in practice.

Redemption

Redemption is the process of canceling or annulling a title conveyed by a foreclosure sale by paying the debt or fulfilling the other conditions in the mortgage. It can be accomplished by paying the full amount of the debt, interest, and costs due to the mortgagee. The *equity of redemption*[21] must be asserted prior to foreclosure. Once the foreclosure sale has been confirmed, the mortgagor can no longer redeem the property, except in states that provide for a statutory period for redemption after foreclosure. The right to redeem after foreclosure is called the right of *statutory redemption,* which exists in about half of the states. Generally, the period for statutory redemption runs about six months to one year after the foreclosure sale. In a number of states, instead of granting the mortgagor a right to redeem after the foreclosure sale, state laws postpone the sale to provide a longer period of time to pay a debt that is in default.

Sales of Property

The advertising of the sale, the place where it takes place, and the method of sale are governed by state law. While details differ, the results are approximately the same in all states.

Fixing a Price. A mortgage foreclosure sale emanates from the assumption that a public auction is a satisfactory way to realize the best possible price in selling property. Hence, in some jurisdictions the highest bidder gets the property irrespective of its cost, the amount of liens against it, or any other consideration. Despite this requirement of a public sale, in most cases only the mortgagee or the mortgagee and a small number of bidders appear at the foreclosure sale and, as a result, the mortgagee is usually the successful bidder. The mortgagee can use his or her claims as a medium of exchange in the purchase, except for costs, which must be paid in cash. Others must pay cash for their purchases (which may be in the form of a loan obtained from another lender with an agreement granting to it the new mortgage),

---

[19] *Attachment* is the act or process of seizing property of a debtor by court order in order to secure the debt of a creditor in the event judgment is rendered. *Execution* is the process of authorizing the sheriff or other competent officer to seize and sell property of the debtor in satisfaction of a judgment previously rendered in favor of a creditor.

[20] Most states provide by statute that a certain amount of a borrower's property shall be free from all liability from levy and sale as a result of the enforcement (execution) of a money judgment. These statutes typically provide that some amount of personal property and equity in a borrower's home not secured by a purchase-money lien shall be set off and free from seizure and sale in order to provide the borrower with a minimum amount of property to maintain his or her family on their road to financial recovery.

[21] The *equity of redemption* is the right of a mortgagor to redeem his or her property from default, the period from the time of default until foreclosure proceedings are begun.

unless the successful bidder can arrange with the mortgagee to keep his or her lien alive by renegotiating or assuming the existing indebtedness. As a consequence, frequently only the mortgagee makes any serious bid for the property. Because lenders generally prefer to avoid owning and liquidating foreclosed properties, they will normally bid the full amount of their claim only where it is less than or equal to the market value of the security less foreclosure, resale, and holding costs. Rarely will lenders bid in excess of their claim in an attempt to outbid other buyers at the sale.

In a few states an "upset" price is fixed in advance of the sale. This means that an appraisal by agents of the court fixes a minimum value for the property that must be reached in the bidding or the court will refuse to confirm the sale. This is not a common practice because it is quite difficult for the court to fix the price that the property must bring at the foreclosure sale. On the one hand, the court is interested in doing justice to the mortgagor. Since a deficiency judgment may be decreed in case the mortgagee is not completely satisfied from the proceeds of the sale, the lower the price, the larger the deficiency judgment. On the other hand, the mortgagee's rights also must be protected. If the court insists on too high a price, no sale would be effected, and hence the mortgagee would receive no satisfaction of his or her claims.

Deed of Trust. The historical development of the law has commonly led, in some jurisdictions, to the finance of real estate by a **deed of trust** instead of a regular mortgage. There are three parties to a loan secured by a deed of trust. The *borrower* (creator of the trust) conveys the title to the property to be used as security to a *trustee,* who holds it as security for the benefit of the *holder of the note* executed by the borrower when the loan was made. The conveyance to the trustee is by deed, but the transfer is accompanied by a trust agreement, either as a part of the deed or in addition to it, setting forth the terms of the security arrangement and giving the trustee the power of sale in event of default.

The deed of trust is commonly used in Alabama, Arkansas, California, Colorado, the District of Columbia, Delaware, Illinois, Mississippi, Missouri, Nevada, New Mexico, Tennessee, Texas, Utah, Virginia, and West Virginia. Deeds of trust are not used extensively in other states because courts there have held that any conveyance of real estate given to secure a debt is a mortgage, irrespective of the form of the instrument used. This interpretation greatly restricts the trustee's power of sale, often requiring the expense and delay of a court process up to and including foreclosure. States imposing this restriction have sought to ensure that a reasonable sale price and all other appropriate benefits are obtained for both borrower and noteholder before the property is sold.

Where the deed of trust is used according to its terms, the trustee is authorized in case of default to foreclose the borrower's equity by a sale of the property at public auction. After a proper time period for advertisement, the trustee must account to both parties for the proceeds of the sale. The parties are entitled to their share as their interest may appear, after expenses of the sale, including compensation to the trustee, have been met. The deed of trust has the advantage of normally being more expeditious than a mortgage foreclosure.

Deed of Trust and Mortgage Compared. The deed of trust is such a mixture of trust and mortgage law that anyone using it should act under the counsel of a local real estate lawyer. In general, however, the legal rules surrounding the creation and evidence of the debt in the form of a note, rights of the borrower left in possession, legal description of the property, creation of a valid lien on after-acquired property, and recording are the same for mortgages and deeds of trust. Similarly, a property subject to a deed of trust may be sold subject to the deed of trust either with or without an assumption of the debt by the purchaser. Borrowers may sell their interest or borrow money using the interest as security. Technically, borrowers have a reversionary interest in the property, and title to the property reverts to them upon payment of the debt. In the event of failure or refusal of a trustee to execute a reconveyance when the borrowers repay their debt, the trustee may be forced to act by legal process, whereby the borrowers would obtain a court order forcing the trustee to act.

In California, where deeds of trust and mortgages are used side by side, several distinctions are made between the two instruments. Whereas a mortgage may be discharged by a simple acknowledgment of satisfaction on the record, a reconveyance of title is considered necessary to extinguish a deed of trust.[22] Recording requirements for mortgages and deeds of trust also differ. Under the recording laws of most states, mortgage assignments may be, and in some states must be, recorded. Assignments of a deed of trust, however, need not be recorded and in some states are not eligible for recordation. The recording of the original deed of trust gives notice of the lien against the property, and only the trustee has the power to clear the record through a reconveyance of the property.

Nature of Title at Foreclosure Sale. The purchaser of property at a foreclosure sale is, in effect, the purchaser of the rights of the mortgagor whose interests are cut off by the sale. Even though the sale is conducted under court supervision, the court makes no representation concerning the nature of the title that a buyer will receive. Any title defects that existed prior to the foreclosure sale will continue with the title as it passes to the purchaser. If a junior lienor has been omitted in the suit for foreclosure, his or her claims will not be cut off by such suit. As long as lienor claims are not cut off, the purchaser acquires the property subject to those liens instead of a fee simple unencumbered.

Parties to Foreclosure Suit. When the holders of a senior mortgage bring suit to foreclose their mortgage, they must join in the suit all who share the mortgagor's interest. These include not only junior mortgage holders but judgment creditors, purchasers at an execution sale, and trustees in bankruptcy, if any. Failure to include all of these might improve their position with the foreclosure of the senior lien. For example, should the senior mortgagee become the successful bidder at the foreclosure sale, and should a junior lienor of record not be joined in the suit, it is possible that when the senior mortgagee takes title to the land, the junior mortgagee may acquire the position of a senior lienor. To avoid this possibility, every foreclosure action should be preceded by a careful search of the record to discover all junior lien claimants who should be joined in the foreclosure suit.

Should any junior lienors think that they have an equity to protect, they have the right to purchase the property at a foreclosure sale, paying off or otherwise providing for the interests of the claimants whose liens are superior to theirs. It might

[22]Some states do not require reconveyance to extinguish a deed of trust. Instead, the secured beneficiary of the trust (noteholder) signs a request for release of the deed of trust, which is presented by the borrower to the trustee together with the canceled note and the deed of trust. The trustee issues a release of trust, which is then recorded at the appropriate office of public records for the county.

be, for example, that a senior mortgagee has a $50,000 lien on a property that a junior mortgagee with a $10,000 lien considers to be worth more than $50,000. If the junior lienor does not bid for the property, the senior mortgagee may bid it in for $50,000 (in the absence of other bidders) and cut off the junior lienor's equity, causing a loss to the junior lienor. By taking over responsibility for the senior mortgage, the junior lienor could bid up to $60,000 for the property without providing additional funds. In this event, it is not uncommon for a senior claimant to agree in advance upon the method of settlement of his or her claims. This may include an agreement to renew the senior mortgagee's claim, either with or without a reduction in the amount.

The purchaser at the foreclosure sale takes over the property free of the lien of the mortgage being foreclosed, but also free of all holders of junior liens who have been joined in the foreclosure action. If the senior mortgage holder or a third party purchases the property at a foreclosure sale, all such junior liens are of no further force or effect.

If junior lienholders bring suit for foreclosure, they should not join the senior lienholders in the suit. Instead, they should sue subject to the senior lien, but this means they are not obligated to pay off the senior lienholders. Junior lienholders may prefer to keep the senior mortgage alive. Holders of the senior lien may join the action voluntarily and sometimes do so to make sure that their interests are fully protected. They may wish to have the court determine the amount to be assumed by the purchaser which is due them. Or should there be any questions about the order of priority of this lien, senior lienholders may join the foreclosure action to have this question answered. Again they may have a side agreement with the junior lienors to continue their mortgage unchanged in amount. In case the junior mortgage holders plan to buy the property at the foreclosure sale, they may prefer to pay off the senior lien as well. This must be done with the consent of the lienholders if they are not a party to the suit. This practice represents a redemption of the senior mortgage and follows the English maxim of "redeem up, but foreclose down." This concept is fairly obvious. It simply means that junior mortgagees must honor the prior position of senior mortgagees, but junior mortgagees may wipe out liens junior to theirs. For example, say a property now worth $100,000 is encumbered as follows:

First mortgage, A	$ 90,000
Second mortgage, B	20,000
Third mortgage, C	10,000
Total mortgage liens	$120,000

In a foreclosure action, mortgagee B has a buying power of $110,000 without raising additional funds if he is able to keep the first mortgage undisturbed, or if he refinances it. If he buys the property at the foreclosure sale for no more than $110,000, the third mortgage lien will be completely cut off by foreclosure.

Holders of junior liens destroyed in a foreclosure action are entitled to have the surplus of sale price over senior mortgage claims applied to their claims. If there is no surplus, they are entitled to a judgment for the full amount of their claims. From that time on, they are merely general, unsecured creditors of the mortgagor, unless the latter should own other real estate to which such judgments would attach.

Effect of Foreclosure on Junior Lienors

If a senior mortgage holder brings foreclosure suit and joins junior claimants in the suit, the question arises, "What happens to the claims of those cut off by the foreclosure sale?" Any surplus remaining after satisfying the costs of foreclosure and the claims of the senior lienor is distributed according to the priority rights of junior claims. Sometimes the distribution of this surplus is not as simple as it sounds. Frequent disputes concerning the order of priority require action by the court to establish the order of settlement.

Where a senior mortgage is properly foreclosed, it extinguishes the *lien* of the junior mortgage, but the *debt* secured by the mortgage is unaffected. Where there is no surplus from the foreclosure sale or where it is insufficient to meet all claims, the holders of such claims still maintain their rights to pursue the mortgagors on whatever personal obligation they have incurred by obtaining the mortgage. This legal right may or may not result in satisfaction of the claims of lienholders. Such obligations are not extinguished and may be enforced at some future time should the mortgagors ever recover their economic status sufficiently to make pursuit of claims against them worthwhile.

Deficiency Judgment

While a sale of the mortgaged property may result in a surplus to which the mortgagor is entitled, it may on the contrary be sold at a price that fails to satisfy the claims of the mortgagee. Any deficit is a continuing claim by the mortgagee against the mortgagor. The mortgagor is personally obligated to pay the debt evidenced by the promissory note. Since mortgages may involve one or more specific properties, the mortgagee will normally look to such property to provide primary security for his or her claim, but any deficiency remains the obligation of the mortgagor. Any deficit remaining after a foreclosure and sale of the property is known as a **deficiency judgment.**

Deficiency judgments are unsecured claims—unless the mortgagor owns other real estate—and take their place alongside other debts of the mortgagor. Unlike the mortgage from which such judgment springs, the latter gives the holder no right of preference against any of the non-real estate assets of the debtor.[23] Hence, the value of deficiency judgments is always open to serious question. This is true in part because of the ways by which they can be avoided or defeated.

Debtors seeking to avoid the deficiency judgment may plan accordingly. Since such judgments attach only to real estate or other property that the debtors hold or may acquire in the future, the debtors may see that they do not acquire any future property interests or, if they do, they will be careful to have titles recorded in names other than their own.

Considerable sentiment exists in some quarters in favor of legislation to abolish deficiency judgments altogether, leaving mortgagees with only the property to protect their claims. Several states strictly limit the applicability of deficiency judgments. Of course, this increases the possibility that a borrower will walk away from a property if its market value falls below the loan balance.

Taxes in Default

Payment of property taxes is an obligation of the mortgagor. As such, taxes constitute a prior lien against the security. Transfers of title always take into account accrued but

[23]Deficiency judgments become a lien on all real estate owned by the judgment debtor in the county or counties where the judgment is entered. To the extent that there is equity in the real estate that is not exempt from execution, the judgment can be considered secured and the creditor can enforce his lien through foreclosure and sale of the property to which the lien attaches.

unpaid taxes. Mortgages commonly contain tax clauses giving the mortgagee the right to pay taxes not paid regularly by the mortgagor. The amounts so paid are then added to the claims of the mortgagee. While the lien of taxes gives tax-collecting authorities the right to foreclose in case of default, this right is seldom exercised on first or even second default. Instead, the taxing authority from time to time may pursue an alternative policy of selling tax liens with deeds to follow. Since tax liens constitute superior liens prior to the claims of mortgagees if the taxing authorities have observed statutory procedure, and since they customarily carry high effective rates of interest, mortgagees may prefer to maintain the priority claim of tax liens by paying delinquent taxes and adding them to their claims.

If foreclosure becomes necessary, mortgagees include all taxes they have paid. At the time of a foreclosure sale, the purchaser usually is expected to pay all delinquent taxes, thus making the tax status of the property current.

Tax Sales. Where mortgagees do not act to protect their interests against tax liens, sooner or later taxing authorities will bring pressure to collect delinquent taxes. In effect, if not in form, the **tax sale** procedure is intended to parallel that followed in the foreclosure of mortgages. At the time of the tax sale, the purchaser receives a tax certificate, which is then subject to redemption in nearly all states. The period of redemption is usually two or three years. If the property is not redeemed by the delinquent taxpayer within this period, the purchaser at the tax sale is then entitled to receive a deed to the property.

Tax titles are usually looked upon as weak evidence of ownership. The interest of the tax collector is to find someone willing and able to pay taxes for someone else in return for a claim against the property. The collector is not greatly concerned about passing good title. There is no suggestion of warranty. In addition to any defects in title regardless of delinquent taxes, the unconcern of the tax collector may in turn result in added clouds on the title. Among the latter, the following may occur:

1. Because of inaccurate description of the property or incorrect records of ownership, the notice of sale may be defective.
2. The property owner may have been denied due process or his or her day in court.
3. The line of authority for the sale may not be clear.
4. Irregularities and carelessness, even in minor procedural matters, may cause the tax sale to be invalidated.

All of these depend in part upon the recuperative powers of the delinquent taxpayers. If they have lost interest in the property or lack the financial resources to protect their interests, delinquent taxpayers may interpose no objections to the plans of the purchaser at the tax sale. Nevertheless, the risk is great enough to suggest caution and due attention even to minor details before purchasing tax liens.

In the absence of bidders at a tax sale—which might occur in periods of depression or in the sale of inexpensive vacant land—the property usually reverts to the state, the county, or some other local governmental unit. State and local units can be careless and neglect to take steps to realize a fair price when they dispose of property so acquired. A sale by the governmental unit, given full compliance with statutory requirements, normally offers a very short period of redemption after which the mortgagor and the mortgagee lose to the purchaser all rights to the property. Mortgagees should diligently monitor tax sale notices to ensure that their lien rights on property sold at tax sales are not affected.

Bankruptcy

Bankruptcy may be defined as a proceeding in which the court takes over the property of a debtor to satisfy the claims of creditors. The goal is to relieve the debtor of all liabilities, so that he or she may become financially solvent. The potential for bankruptcy under Chapters 7, 11, and 13 of the Bankruptcy Code affects the value of real estate as collateral. Lenders must be aware of the possibility that a borrower may file bankruptcy and must know how such a filing will change their positions. Both real estate investors and lenders must have a basic understanding of their rights in a bankruptcy proceeding to effectively negotiate with one another and resolve their differences short of a bankruptcy proceeding. Although a comprehensive examination of the Bankruptcy Code is beyond the scope of this text, several areas of bankruptcy law of particular importance to real estate investors and lenders are discussed below.

Chapter 7 Liquidation

The purpose of Chapter 7, or "straight bankruptcy," is to give debtors a fresh start by discharging all of their debts and liquidating their nonexempt assets. Chapter 7 is available to any person regardless of the extent of his or her assets or liabilities. A Chapter 7 petition can be filed voluntarily by a debtor or involuntarily by petitioning creditors, except that a farmer may not be forced into an involuntary proceeding.

Upon the filing of a Chapter 7 petition, the court appoints an interim trustee who is charged with evaluating the financial condition of the debtor and reporting at the first meeting of creditors whether there will be assets available for liquidation and distribution to unsecured creditors. The trustee's job is to oversee the liquidation of nonexempt assets and to evaluate claims filed by creditors. The ultimate objective of a Chapter 7 bankruptcy is the orderly liquidation of the debtor's assets and the distribution of the proceeds according to the legal rights and priorities of the various creditor claimants.

A lender whose loan to the debtor is secured by a mortgage on real estate will normally be paid in full if the value of the security exceeds the balance due under the mortgage. To foreclose on the mortgage and sell the debtor's property, the lender must first petition the bankruptcy court. If the debtor is not behind in the mortgage payments and desires to retain the property, he or she may do so by reaffirming the mortgage debt. This means that although the debtor's obligation to repay the debt has been discharged in bankruptcy, the debtor makes a new agreement after the discharge to repay the debt.

Chapter 11

An alternative to Chapter 7 is a Chapter 11 bankruptcy, which is available to owners of a business. Whereas a Chapter 7 bankruptcy normally results in the liquidation of the debtor's assets, a Chapter 11 proceeding looks to the preservation of the debtor's assets while a plan of reorganization to rehabilitate the debtor is formulated. Within 120 days after filing a Chapter 11 bankruptcy petition, this plan of reorganization must be filed by the debtor with the court. The plan must classify the various claims against the debtor's assets and specify the treatment of the debts of each class. In a typical reorganization plan, the rights and duties of the parties are redefined in one of two ways. The plan may restructure the debt to provide for reduced payments over an extended period, or the plan may scale down the debt, reducing the debtor's obligation to an amount less than the full claim.

Once a plan is filed, the proponent of the plan, usually the debtor, must solicit creditor acceptance. Once holders of two-thirds of the total amount of the claims and a majority of the total number of claim holders assent to the plan, the court will analyze the plan and determine whether it meets the technical prerequisites for judicial confirmation. Even if one or more creditor classes dissent, the court can still confirm the plan if it meets certain statutory requirements. This alternative method of confirmation is known as *cramdown.*

The cramdown provisions under Chapter 11 provide borrowers with the ability to restructure their secured (e.g., mortgage) and unsecured indebtedness by executing a plan of reorganization that outlines the mechanics for getting borrowers back on their feet and states how different classes of claims and interests will be treated. The cramdown provisions are essential to keeping the borrowers whole during a reorganization. Without a cramdown provision, secured lenders could always block the proposed reorganization by refusing to approve the plan and foreclose on the major assets of the borrower.

Under the Bankruptcy Code, a plan of reorganization may seriously impact secured lenders by impairing their claim. Despite this impairment, the plan may be confirmed by the court over the objections of the secured lenders. The law, however, makes some provision for secured lenders who do not approve the plan. One provision allows the borrower to keep the secured property but requires that the lender must receive present or deferred payments having a present value equal to the value of the collateral. A second provision calls for a sale of the collateral with the lender's lien attaching to the proceeds of the sale. A final catch-all provision requires the secured lender's realization of the "indubitable equivalent" of his or her claims.

Chapter 11 bankruptcy proceedings are of great concern to lenders who may find that their security is tied up for years during the reorganization of the debtor's financial affairs. Even lenders holding mortgages on a Chapter 11 debtor's personal residence may find that they are unable to foreclose on their liens where such a foreclosure would interfere with the debtor's plan of reorganization. In sum, the basic object of a Chapter 11 bankruptcy is to provide for a court-supervised reorganization, instead of a liquidation, of a financially troubled business.

Chapter 13

A Chapter 13 petition in bankruptcy, also known as a *wage earner proceeding,* represents an attractive alternative to the liquidation applied in Chapter 7. Like Chapter 11, a Chapter 13 proceeding envisions the formulation of a plan designed for the rehabilitation of the debtor. Such plans provide that funding of the plan will come from future wages and earnings of the debtor. Any debtor with regular income who has unsecured debts of less than $100,000 and secured debts of less than $350,000 qualifies for Chapter 13 relief. Thus a Chapter 13 bankruptcy is the one most likely to be used by an individual.

The heart of Chapter 13 is the repayment plan, which is proposed by the debtor and, assuming it meets certain tests and conditions, is subject to confirmation by the court over objections of creditors. In a Chapter 13 plan, debtors propose to pay off their obligations and reorganize their affairs. The plan may call for payments over a three- to five-year period. Unlike a Chapter 7 or Chapter 11 bankruptcy that can be filed by debtors only every six years, a Chapter 13 plan can be filed immediately after completion of a prior bankruptcy liquidation or payment plan as long as it is filed in good faith.

During the period covered by the plan, creditors must accept payment as provided in the plan and may not otherwise seek to collect their debts. Assuming successful completion of the plan, debtors receive a discharge of all debts provided for in the plan other than long-term obligations for payments that continue beyond the period of the plan's duration. However, the plan may not modify the rights of mortgagees whose liens are secured only by property used by the debtors as their personal residence. This "preferred treatment" for such mortgagees under Chapter 13 is justified because the success of a reorganization plan could be jeopardized if foreclosure of this mortgage disrupts the affairs of the debtors by forcing them to seek other shelter. Although the plan may not "modify" the rights of secured lenders, lenders desiring to accelerate the balance of any indebtedness upon default to raise the interest rate should be aware of the borrower's right to cure a default in bankruptcy (by making arrangements to pay amounts currently in default over the period of the plan) and reinstate the mortgage. Thus, although a plan may not "modify" the rights of lenders whose debt is secured by liens on the debtor's personal residence, the filing of a Chapter 13 will likely prevent an imminent foreclosure and allow for repayment of arrearages existing on the date of the filing to be carried over a reasonable period of time. Where the plan calls for curing the arrearages and no modification of the schedule of current payments, courts will normally approve the plan because it does not materially affect the rights of such lenders.

Conclusion

This chapter discussed legal considerations important in creating and defining various rights to real property. This is important in the study of real estate finance since it is these rights that are purchased, sold, and mortgaged. Thus, an understanding of the various rights associated with real estate is necessary to properly evaluate a real estate financial decision. Legal considerations affect the risk of receiving the economic benefit associated with one's property rights. For example, we have discussed the importance of having a marketable title. Any defects in the title may result in a loss of benefits to the owner and jeopardize the collateral value of the real estate for the mortgage lender. To some extent, this risk is controlled and minimized by the use of title assurance methods, including title insurance and the use of general warranty deeds.

Knowing the various ways of petitioning property rights may also result in maximizing the value of a particular property, since it allows parties with different needs (e.g., users, equity investors, lenders) to have a claim on the property rights that best meet those needs. Thus, the total value of all the rights associated with a property may exceed that of a property where there could be no mortgage, no leases, or other ways to separate rights.

This chapter also discussed many of the legal ramifications associated with default, foreclosure, and bankruptcy. The probability of one or more of these events occurring and the rights of the parties if it occurs ultimately affects the value of the various property rights. These legal considerations should be kept in mind as we discuss the risks associated with mortgage lending in later chapters. Clearly, the legal rights of borrowers and lenders affect the degree of risk assumed by each party and, thus, the value of entering into various transactions.

The availability of various legal alternatives can be viewed as a way of controlling and shifting risk between the various parties to a transaction. The probability of default or bankruptcy by a borrower and the legal alternatives available to each party affect the expected return to the lender from the loan. In later chapters we will discuss how the amount of the loan relative to the value of the property is used by the lender to control risk. The reader should keep in mind the fact that loan covenants as discussed in this chapter also control the risk.

Key Terms

abstract of title 14
after-acquired property clause 25
assumption of the mortgage 23
bankruptcy 39
deed 14
deed covenants 15
deed of trust 34
deed restrictions 11
deficiency judgment 37
due-on-sale clause 22
easement 10
estate 10
estate for years 12
estate from year to year 13
extension agreement 29
fee simple estate 11
fixture 25
foreclosure 32
freehold estate 11
"friendly foreclosure" 32
future advances 23
future estates 12
general warranty deed 15
judicial foreclosure 32
junior mortgages 25
land contract 26
leasehold estate 11
lessee 10
lessor 14
life estate 11
mechanics' lien 18
mortgage 19
mortgage default 27
mortgagee 10
mortgagor 10
nonpossessory interest 10
open-end mortgage 23
ownership rights 9
personal property 9
possessory estate 10
possessory interest 10
potentially possessory interest 10
prepackaged bankruptcy 32
prepayment clause 23
promissory note 19
property rights 10
purchase-money mortgage 19
quitclaim deed 15
real estate 9
real property 9
recasting a mortgage 29
recording acts 17
redemption 33
release clause 22
remainder 12
reversion 12
secured interest 10
seller financing 26
special warranty deed 15
"subject to" the mortgage 24
subordination clause 23
tax sale 38
title 13
title assurance 13
transfer of mortgage 30
voluntary conveyance 31
workout 28

Questions

1. What is the difference between real estate, real property, and personal property?
2. What is meant by an estate? Why are estates important in real estate finance?
3. How can a leased fee estate have a value that could be transferred to another party?
4. What is an abstract of title?
5. Name the three general methods of title assurance and briefly describe each. Which would you recommend to a friend purchasing a home? Why?
6. What purpose is served when a mortgage lender records his or her mortgage?
7. Would it be legal for you to give a quitclaim deed for the Statue of Liberty to your friend?
8. How is a promissory note different from a mortgage?
9. What is the purpose and effect of each of the following clauses:
   a. Acceleration clause?
   b. Prepayment clause?
   c. Due-on-sale clause?

10. How does a purchase-money mortgage differ from a land contract?
11. How can mechanics' liens achieve priority over first mortgages that were recorded prior to the mechanics' lien?
12. Name several mortgageable interests in real estate and comment on their risk as collateral to lenders.
13. What is meant by mortgage foreclosure, and what alternatives are there to such action?
14. Explain the difference between a buyer assuming the mortgage and taking title "subject to" the mortgage.
15. What dangers are encountered by mortgagees and unreleased mortgagors when property is sold "subject to" a mortgage?
16. What is the difference between the equity of redemption and statutory redemption?
17. What special advantages does a mortgagee have in bidding at the foreclosure sale where the mortgagee is the foreclosing party? How much will the mortgagee normally bid at the sale?
18. Is a foreclosure sale sometimes desirable or even necessary when the mortgagor is willing to give a voluntary deed?
19. What is a deficiency judgment and how is its value to a lender affected by the Bankruptcy Code?
20. What are the risks to the lender if a borrower declares bankruptcy?

Problems

1. Five years ago Smith purchased a home from Jones. Smith's attorney, Able, examined the abstract of title and rendered his opinion that no defects or encumbrances existed against the home. Smith has now contracted to sell the home to Tims. Tims's attorney now determines that Able had overlooked a judgment lien against the home, which was recorded before Smith purchased the home from Jones. What is Smith's recourse? What is Tims's recourse against Smith?
2. Henry Wallace owns the building at 123 City Avenue, which has been vacant for many years. He leases the building to Doug Griffin on a long-term fixed-rate lease for $1,000 per month. Doug Griffin does not record his lease or any memorandum thereof. Before Mr. Griffin moves in, General Motors announces it is building a large manufacturing plant next door. Mr. Wallace then signs a lease with Charles Gregory, who is willing to pay $10,000 per month to lease the same building. Mr. Gregory has no notice of Mr. Wallace's prior lease with Mr. Griffin. Who is entitled to occupancy? What can Mr. Griffin do?
3 *a.* Sedgewick arranged for an open-end mortgage loan from the Second National Bank in amounts up to $50,000. The loan was closed and Sedgewick drew $30,000 initially. Three months later he drew the remaining $20,000. What is the bank's position concerning the possibility of intervening liens?
   b. Assume there was no definite agreement for future advances between Sedgewick and the bank at the time the initial $30,000 loan was closed. Would your answer be different?
4. Last year Jones obtained a mortgage loan for $100,000. He just inherited a large sum of money and is contemplating prepaying the entire loan balance to save interest. What are his rights to prepay the loan?
5. First Bank Company holds a note from Jason Black and a first mortgage on real estate owned by Jason Black to secure it. Mr. Black sold his property to Robert Frasca, and Robert Frasca assumed the mortgage. The bank did not give Mr. Black a release from his debt. Subsequently Mr. Frasca defaulted in payment on the note. After some negotiating, the bank extended the term of the note and increased the interest rate. What is Mr. Black's position at this stage of the transaction?
6. Mort owns a property. Jessica Rosen holds a first mortgage against it, and Alex Nelligan holds a second mortgage. Mort defaults on his mortgage payments. Ms. Rosen forecloses without joining Mr. Nelligan in the foreclosure suit. The property is sold to Shelia McBride at the foreclosure sale. What are Mr. Nelligan's rights?
7. What would your answer be in problem 6 if Mr. Nelligan's mortgage was not recorded?
8. In problem 6, what if Mr. Nelligan was joined in the foreclosure suit but forgot to attend the sale and bid? Does Mr. Nelligan have any other way of getting Ms. Rosen to pay?
9. Bob entered into a land contract to purchase real estate from Sam. The purchase price was to be paid over a 10-year period by monthly amortization. At the end of five years, Bob defaulted, having failed to

make his required payments. The contract provided that in event of default, the seller could declare a forfeiture after a period of 30 days and repossess the property. If the court should consider the land contract an equitable mortgage, what might be the rights of Bob and Sam?

10. A debtor has filed a plan to reorganize his affairs under Chapter 13 of the Bankruptcy Code. The plan calls for payment of 10 cents on the dollar to all unsecured creditors over the next three years. The only secured creditor is Last Bank and Trust, whose lien is secured by the debtor's personal residence. The plan calls for curing the present payments in arrears over one year and reducing the scheduled payments by 50 percent for three years. Will the court approve the debtor's plan? Why or why not?

CHAPTER 3

The Interest Factor in Financing

Financing the purchase of real estate usually involves borrowing on a long- or short-term basis. Because large amounts are usually borrowed in relation to the prices paid for real estate, financing costs are usually significant in amount and weigh heavily in the decision to buy property. Individuals involved in real estate finance must understand how these costs are computed and how various provisions in loan agreements affect financing costs and mortgage payments. Familiarity with the mathematics of compound interest is essential in understanding mortgage payment calculations, how loan provisions affect financing costs, and how borrowing decisions affect investment returns. It is also important for investment analysis calculations that we examine later in this text. This chapter provides an introduction to the mathematics of compound interest. It forms a basis for concepts discussed in financing single family properties, income-producing properties, and in funding construction and development projects.

Compound Interest

Understanding the process of compounding in finance requires the knowledge of only a few basic formulas. At the root of these formulas is the most elementary relationship, **compound interest.** For example, if an individual makes a bank deposit of $10,000 that is compounded at an annual interest rate of 6 percent, what will be the value of the deposit at the end of one year? In examining this problem, one should be aware that any compounding problem has four basic components:

1. An initial deposit, or present value of an investment of money.
2. An interest rate.
3. Time.
4. Value at some specified future period.

In our problem, the deposit is $10,000, interest is to be earned at an annual rate of 6 percent, time is one year, and value at the end of the year is what we would like to know. We have four components, three of which are known and one that is unknown.

Compound or Future Value

In the preceding problem, we would like to determine what value will exist at the end of one year if a single deposit or payment of $10,000 is made at the beginning of the year and the deposit balance earns a 6 percent rate of interest. To find the solution, we must introduce some terminology:

PV = **present value,** or principal at the beginning of the year
i = the interest rate
I = dollar amount of interest earned during the year
FV = principal at the end of n years, or **future value**
n = number of years

In this problem, then, $PV = \$10{,}000$, $i = 6$ percent, $n =$ one year, and FV, or the value after one year, is what we would like to know.

The value after one year can be determined by examining the following relationship:

$$FV = PV + I_1$$

or the future value, FV, at the end of one year equals the deposit made at the beginning of the year, PV, plus the dollar amount of interest I_1 earned in the first period. Because $PV = \$10{,}000$, we can find FV by determining I_1. Since we are compounding annually, FV is easily determined to be $10,600, which is shown in Exhibit 3–1.

Multiple Periods. To find the value at the end of two years, we continue the compounding process by taking the value at the end of one year, $10,600, making it the deposit at the beginning of the second year, and compounding again. This is shown in Exhibit 3–2.

Exhibit 3–2 shows that a total future value of $11,236 has been accumulated at the end of the second year. Note that in the second year, interest is earned not only

EXHIBIT 3–1 Compound Interest Calculation for One Year

$$\begin{aligned} I_1 &= PV \times i \\ &= \$10{,}000(.06) \\ &= \$600 \end{aligned}$$

Future value at the end of one year ($n = 1$ year) is determined as

$$\begin{aligned} FV &= PV + I_1 \\ &= \$10{,}000 + \$600 \\ &= \$10{,}600 \end{aligned}$$

or

$$\begin{aligned} FV &= PV(1 + i) \\ &= \$10{,}000(1 + .06) \\ &= \$10{,}600 \end{aligned}$$

on the original deposit of \$10,000, but also on the interest (\$600) that was earned during the first year. *The concept of earning interest on interest is the essential idea that must be understood in the compounding process and is the cornerstone of all financial tables and concepts in the mathematics of finance.*

From the computation in Exhibit 3–2, it should be pointed out that the value at the end of year 2 could have been determined directly from *PV* as follows:

$$FV = PV(1 + i)(1 + i)$$
$$= PV(1+i)^2$$

In our problem, then, when $n = 2$ years

$$FV = PV(1 + i)^2$$
$$= \$10{,}000(1 + .06)^2$$
$$= \$10{,}000(1.123600)$$
$$= \$11{,}236$$

From this computation, the \$11,236 value at the end of two years is identical to the result that we obtained in Exhibit 3–2. Being able to compute *FV directly* from *PV* is a very important relationship because it means that the future value, or value of any deposit or payment left to compound for any number of periods, can be determined from *PV* by simple multiplication. Therefore, if we want to determine the future value of a deposit made today that is left to compound for any number of years, we can find the solution with the general formula for compound interest, which is

$$FV = PV(1 + i)^n$$

By substituting the appropriate values for *PV*, *i*, and *n*, we can determine *FV* for any desired number of years.[1]

Other Compounding Intervals. In the preceding section, the discussion of compounding applies to cases where funds were compounded only once per year. Many savings accounts, bonds, mortgages, and other investments provide for monthly, quarterly, or semiannual compounding. Because we will be covering mortgage

EXHIBIT 3–2 Compound Interest Calculation for Two Years

$$\$10{,}600(.06) = I_2$$
$$\$636 = I_2$$

and value at the end of two years, or $n = 2$ years, is now

$$\$10{,}600 + I_2 = FV$$
$$\$10{,}600 + \$636 = \$11{,}236$$

[1]At this point, the reader may realize that these problems can be solved with a financial calculator. We will illustrate the use of a financial calculator to solve many of the problems in this and other chapters in this book.

loans extensively in a later chapter, which involves monthly compounding almost exclusively, it is very important that we consider the other compounding intervals.

When compounding periods other than annual are considered, a simple modification can be made to the general formula for compound interest. To change the general formula:

$$FV = PV(1 + i)^n$$

where

$$n = \text{years}$$
$$i = \text{annual interest rate}$$
$$PV = \text{deposit}$$

to any compounding period, we divide the annual interest rate (i) by the desired number of compounding intervals *within* one year. We then increase the number of time periods (n) by multiplying by the desired number of compounding intervals *within* one year. For example, let m be the number of intervals *within* one year in which compounding is to occur, and let n be the number of years in the general formula. Then we have

$$FV = PV\left[1 + \frac{i}{m}\right]^{n \cdot m}$$

Therefore, if interest is to be earned on the \$10,000 deposit at an annual rate of 6 percent, compounded monthly, to determine the future value at the end of one year, where $m = 12$, we have

$$\begin{aligned} FV &= \$10{,}000\left[1 + \frac{.06}{12}\right]^{1 \cdot 12} \\ &= \$10{,}000(1.061678) \\ &= \$10{,}616.78 \end{aligned}$$

If we compare the results of monthly compounding with those from compounding annually, we can immediately see the benefits of monthly compounding. If our initial deposit is compounded monthly, we would have \$10,616.78 at the end of the year, compared with \$10,600.00 when annual compounding is used.

Another way of looking at this result is to compute an **effective annual yield** (*EAY*) on both investments. This is done by assuming that \$10,000 is deposited at the beginning of the year and that all proceeds are withdrawn at the end of the year. For the deposit that is compounded monthly, we obtain

$$\begin{aligned} EAY &= \frac{FV - PV}{PV} \\ &= \frac{\$10{,}616.78 - \$10{,}000.00}{\$10{,}000} \\ &= 6.1678\% \end{aligned}$$

The result can be compared with the effective annual yield obtained when annual compounding is used, or

$$EAY = \frac{\$10{,}600 - \$10{,}000}{\$10{,}000}$$
$$= 6\%$$

From this comparison, we can conclude that the effective annual yield is higher when monthly compounding is used. This comparison should immediately illustrate the difference between computing interest at a *nominal* annual rate of interest and computing interest at the same nominal annual rate of interest, *compounded monthly.* Both deposits are compounded at the same nominal annual rate of interest (6 percent); however, one is compounded 12 times at a monthly rate of (.06 × 12), or .005, on the ending monthly balance, while the other is compounded only once, at the end of the year at the rate of .06. It is customary in the United States to use a nominal rate of interest in contracts, savings accounts, mortgage notes, and other transactions. How payments will be made or interest accumulated (i.e., annually, monthly, daily) is then specified. It is up to the parties involved in the transaction to ascertain the effective annual yield.

From the above analysis, one result should be very clear. Whenever the nominal annual interest rates offered on two investments are equal, the investment with the more frequent compounding interval within the year will always result in a higher effective annual yield. In our example, we could say that a 6 percent annual rate of interest compounded monthly provides an effective annual yield of 6.168 percent.[2]

Other investments offer semiannual, quarterly, and daily compounding. In these cases, the basic formula for compound interest is modified as follows:

Compounding Interval		*Modified Formula*
Semiannually,	$m = 2$	$FV = PV\left[1 + \frac{i}{2}\right]^{n \cdot 2}$
Quarterly,	$m = 4$	$FV = PV\left[1 + \frac{i}{4}\right]^{n \cdot 4}$
Daily,	$m = 365$	$FV = PV\left[1 + \frac{i}{365}\right]^{n \cdot 365}$

For example, if a deposit of $10,000 is made and an annual rate of 6 percent compounded daily is to be earned, we have

$$FV = \$10{,}000\left[1 + \frac{.06}{365}\right]^{1 \cdot 365}$$
$$= \$10{,}000(1.061831)$$
$$= \$10{,}618.31$$

[2]Many savings institutions that compound savings monthly or daily usually quote a nominal annual rate of interest but point out that if funds are left on deposit for one year, a higher effective annual yield will be earned.

and the effective annual yield would be 6.1831 percent. If the money was left on deposit for two years, the exponent would change to 2 × 365, and *FV* at the end of two years would be $11,274.86.

Throughout this book, we will also follow the convention of using nominal rates of interest in all problems, examples, and so on. Hence, the term *interest rate* means a *nominal,* annual rate of interest. This means that when comparing two alternatives with *different* compounding intervals, the nominal interest rate should not be used as the basis for comparisons. In these cases, the concept of effective annual yield should be used when developing solutions.

Use of Compound Interest Tables

Finding a solution to a compounding problem involving many periods is very awkward because of the amount of multiplication required. Calculators that are programmed with compound interest functions eliminate much of the detail of financial calculations. Another shortcut for finding solutions to compound interest problems can be used by consulting interest factors that have been developed in tables in Appendixes A and B. Appendix A contains interest factors for selected nominal interest rates and years based on the assumption of *annual* compounding intervals. Appendix B contains interest factors for selected nominal interest rates and years based on the assumption of *monthly* compounding intervals. These two compounding periods were chosen because they represent the compounding intervals most frequently used throughout this book.

In both appendixes, the interest factors used for compounding single deposits are contained in column 1, Amount of $1 at Compound Interest. Essentially, these interest factors have been computed from the general formula for compound interest for annual compounding and from the formula, as modified, for monthly compounding for various combinations of *i* and years.

To become familiar with the use of these tables, interest factors for annual compounding (now referred to as *IF*) for the future value (*FV*) of $1 for various interest rates are shown in Exhibit 3–3. (These factors have been taken directly from column 1 in each table for respective interest rates contained in Appendix A.)

In the problem discussed earlier, we wanted to determine the future value of a $10,000 deposit compounded at an annual rate of 6 percent after one year. Looking at the 6 percent column in Exhibit 3–3 corresponding to the row for one year, we find the interest factor 1.060000. When multiplied by $10,000, this interest factor gives us the solution to our problem.

EXHIBIT 3–3 Amount of $1 at Compound Interest (column 1, Appendix A), annual compounding factors

	Rate			
Year	*6%*	*10%*	*15%*	*20%*
1	1.060000	1.100000	1.150000	1.200000
2	1.123600	1.210000	1.322500	1.440000
3	1.191016	1.331000	1.520875	1.728000
4	1.262477	1.464100	1.749006	2.073600
5	1.338226	1.610510	2.011357	2.488320

$$FV = \$10{,}000(FVIF, 6\%, 1 \text{ yr.})$$
$$= \$10{,}000(1.060000)$$

The interest factor for the future value of \$1, at 6 percent for one year (abbreviated as *FVIF,* 6%, 1 yr.) is 1.060000—the same result had we computed $(1 + .06)^1$ or 1.06 from the general formula for compound interest. In other words,

$$(FVIF, 6\%, 1 \text{ yr.}) = (1 + .06)^1 = 1.06$$

The interest factors in the tables in Appendix A allow us to find a solution to any compounding problem as long as we know the deposit (*PV*), the interest rate (*i*), and the number of periods (*n*) over which annual compounding is to occur. You may also find this solution by using a financial calculator.

Question: What is the future value of \$5,000 deposited for four years compounded at an annual rate of 10 percent?

Solution:

$$FV = \$5{,}000(FVIF, 10\%, 4 \text{ yrs.})$$
$$= \$5{,}000(1.464100)$$
$$= \$7.320.50$$

As was the case with the interest factors for annual compounding, interest factors for monthly compounding for selected interest rates and years have been computed from the modified formula $PV(1 + i/12)^{n \cdot 12}$ and are compiled in tables contained in Appendix B. To familiarize the student with these tables, interest factors for selected interest rates and periods have been taken from column 1, *Amount of \$1 at Compound Interest,* from tables in Appendix B and are shown in Exhibit 3–4.

EXHIBIT 3–4 Amount of \$1 at Compound Interest (column 1, Appendix B, monthly compounding factors)

	Rate		
Month	*6%*	*8%*	
1	1.005000	1.006670	
2	1.010025	1.013378	
3	1.015075	1.020134	
4	1.020151	1.026935	
5	1.025251	1.033781	
6	1.030378	1.040673	
7	1.035529	1.047610	
8	1.040707	1.054595	
9	1.045911	1.061625	
10	1.051140	1.068703	
11	1.056396	1.075827	
12	1.061678	1.083000	
Year			*Month*
1	1.061678	1.083000	12
2	1.127160	1.172888	24
3	1.196681	1.270237	36
4	1.270489	1.375666	48

In our earlier problem, we wanted to determine the future value of a \$10,000 deposit that earned interest at an annual rate of 6 percent, compounded *monthly.* This can be easily determined by selecting the appropriate interest factor from the 6 percent column for 12 months, or 1 year, in Exhibit 3–4. That factor is 1.061678. Hence, to determine the value of the deposit at the end of 12 months, or 1 year, we have

$$\begin{aligned} FV &= \$10{,}000(MFVIF, 6\%, 12 \text{ mos.}) \\ &= \$10{,}000(1.061678) \\ &= \$10{,}616.78 \end{aligned}$$

In other words, the interest factor for a 6 percent rate of interest compounded *monthly* for one year (*MFVIF,* 6%, 12 mos.) is 1.061678, which is the same result that we would obtain if we expanded $(1 + .06/12)^{1 \cdot 12}$ by multiplying, or

$$(MFVIF, 6\%, 12 \text{ mos.}) = \left[1 + \frac{.06}{12}\right]^{1 \cdot 12} = 1.061678$$

Note the letter *M* in our abbreviation for the *monthly compound interest equation.* Instead of writing $(1 + .06/12)^{1 \cdot 12}$ and expanding the equation to obtain the monthly interest factor, we simply indicate that a monthly interest factor was either calculated or obtained from Appendix B when we use the abbreviation (*MFVIF,* 6%, 12 mos.). When *M* is not included in the abbreviation, *annual* compounding is assumed, and those annual interest factors should be calculated or obtained from Appendix A. Hence, calculating or using the interest factors shown in column 1 in the tables contained in Appendix B allows us to find the solution to any monthly compounding problem as long as we know the deposit (*PV*), the interest rate (*i*), and the number (*n*) of months or years over which compounding is to occur.

Question: What is the future value of a single \$5,000 deposit earning 8 percent interest, compounded monthly, at the end of two years?

Solution:

$$\begin{aligned} FV &= \$5{,}000\left[1 + \frac{.08}{12}\right]^{2 \cdot 12} \\ &= \$5{,}000(MFVIF, 8\%, 24 \text{ mos.}) \\ &= \$5{,}000(1.172888) \\ &= \$5{,}864.44 \end{aligned}$$

Use of Financial Calculators

Finding a solution to a compounding problem involving many periods is greatly simplified with the use of a calculator. Calculators programmed with compound interest functions eliminate the need for financial tables and much of the detail involved in financial calculations. We will present alternative solutions to most of the time value of money problems in the remainder of this text using the general format of a financial calculator. Refer to your specific calculator manual to confirm whether all operations are similar. Unless specified otherwise, the solutions assume that payments are made at the *end* of each period, and that money spent is (−) and money received is (+). The problems use the following format:

n = number of years, unless stated otherwise
i = interest rate per year, unless stated otherwise
PV = present value
PMT = payments
FV = future value

Solutions will follow the format above, with the variable being solved listed last.

For example, in the problem discussed earlier, we wanted to determine the future value of a \$10,000 deposit compounded at an annual rate of 6 percent after one year.

Solution: n = 1 year
i = 6%
PMT = 0
PV = \$10,000
FV = \$10,600

The same problem compounded monthly would follow the format listed below. Note: Several calculators have a function for a number of periods. In such cases, the number of periods and interest are typically stated on an annual basis, and the number of periods is entered separately.

Solution: n = 12 (1 year × 12 periods per year)
i = .5% (6%/12 periods per year)
PMT = 0
PV = −\$10,000
FV = \$10,616.78

The same problem compounded daily would look like this.

Solution: n = 365 (1 year × 365 periods per year)
i = .0164 (6%/365 periods per year)
PMT = 0
PV = −\$10,000
Solve for FV:
FV = \$10,618.31

Question: What is the future value of \$5,000 deposited for four years compounded at an annual rate of 10 percent?

Solution: n = 4 years
i = 10%
PMT = 0
PV = −\$5,000
FV = \$7,320.50

Question: What is the future value of a single \$5,000 deposit earning 8 percent interest, compounded monthly, at the end of two years?

Solution: $n = 24$ (2 years × 12 periods)
$i = .666\%$ (8%/12 periods)
$PMT = 0$
$PV = -\$5{,}000$
$FV = \$5{,}864.44$

Present Value

In the preceding section, we were concerned with determining value at some time in the *future*; that is, we considered the case where a deposit had been made and compounded into the future to yield some unknown future value.

In this section, we are interested in the problem of knowing the future cash receipts for an investment and of determining how much should be paid for the investment at *present.* The concept of present value is based on the idea that money has time value. Time value simply means that if an investor is offered the choice between receiving $1 today or receiving $1 in the future, the proper choice will always be to receive the $1 today because this $1 can be invested in some opportunity that will earn interest, which is always preferable to receiving only $1 in the future. In this sense, money is said to have *time value.*

When determining how much should be paid *today* for an investment that is expected to produce income in the *future,* we must apply an adjustment called **discounting** to income received in the future to reflect the time value of money. The concept of present value lays the cornerstone for calculating mortgage payments, determining the true cost of mortgage loans, and finding the value of an income property, all of which are very important concepts in real estate finance.

A Graphic Illustration of Present Value

An example of how discounting becomes an important concept in financing can be seen from the following problem. Suppose an individual is considering an investment that promises a cash return of $10,600 at the end of one year. The investor believes this investment should yield an annual rate of 6 percent. The question is how much should the investor pay *today* if $10,600 is to be received at the *end* of the year and the investor requires a 6 percent return compounded annually on the amount invested?

The problem can be seen more clearly by comparing it with the problem of finding the compound value of $1 discussed in the first part of this chapter. In that discussion, we were concerned with finding the future value of a $10,000 deposit compounded monthly at 6 percent for one year. This comparison is depicted in Exhibit 3–5.

In Exhibit 3–5 note that with compounding, we are concerned with determining the *future value* of an investment. With discounting, we are concerned with just the opposite concept; that is, what *present value* or *price* should be paid *today* for a particular investment, assuming a desired rate of interest is to be earned?

Because we know from the preceding section that $10,000 compounded annually at a rate of 6 percent results in a future value of $10,600 at the end of one year, $10,000 is the present value of this investment. However, had we not done the compounding problem in the preceding section, how would we know that $10,000 equals the present value of the investment? Let us again examine the compounding

EXHIBIT 3–5 Comparison of Future Value and Present Value

		Month					
		2	4	6	8	10	12
Compounding at 6%	$10,000	⟶					Future value(?)
Discounting at 6%	Present value(?)	⟵					$10,600

problem considered in the previous section. To determine future value, recall the general equation for compound interest:

$$FV = PV(1 + i)^n$$

In our present value problem, *PV* becomes the *unknown* because *FV*, or the future value to be received at the end of one year, $n = 1$ year, is *known* to be \$10,600. Because the interest rate (i) is also known to be 6 percent, *PV* is the only value that is not known. *PV*, the present value or amount we should pay for the investment today, can be easily determined by rearranging terms in the above compounding formula as follows:

$$FV = PV(1 + i)^n$$

$$PV = FV \frac{1}{(1 + i)^n}$$

In our problem, then, we can determine *PV* directly by substituting the known values into the above expression as follows:

$$\begin{aligned} PV &= FV \frac{1}{(1 + i)^n} \\ &= \$10{,}600 \frac{1}{(1 + .06)^1} \\ &= \$10{,}600 \frac{1}{1.06} \\ &= \$10{,}600 \times (.943396) \\ &= \$10{,}000 \end{aligned}$$

Note that the procedure used in solving for the present value is simply to multiply the future value, *FV*, by 1 divided by $(1 + i)^n$. We know from the section on compounding that in our problem $(1 + i)^n$ is $(1 + .06)^1$ or (*FVIF*, 6%, 1 yr.), which equals 1.06. Dividing 1 by 1.06 yields .943396. This result is important in present value analysis because it shows the relationship between future value and present value.

Because we see from Exhibit 3–5 that the discounting process is the opposite of compounding, to find the present value of any investment is simply to compound in a "reverse sense." This is done in our problem by taking the reciprocal of the interest factor for the compound value of \$1 at 6 percent, $1 \div 1.06$ or .943396,

Box 3.1

Use of a Financial Calculator:

Solving for the present value of payments or income streams is very similar to the proceeding format when we were solving for future values:

Calculator Solution

$n = 1$ year
$i = 6\%$
$PMT = \$0$
$FV = 10{,}600$

Solve for present value:
$PV = -\$10{,}000$

Note: the negative *PV* indicates that this is a cash outflow.

which we abbreviate as (*PVIF,* 6%, 1 yr.), multiplying it by the future value of the investment to find its present value. We can now say that $10,600 received at the end of one year, when discounted by 6 percent, has a present value of $10,000. Alternatively, if we are offered an investment that promises to yield $10,600 after one year and we want to earn a 6 percent annual return, we should not pay more than $10,000 for the investment (it is on the $10,000 present value that we earn the 6 percent interest).

Use of Present Value Tables. Because the discounting process is the reverse of compounding, and the interest factor for discounting $1 \div (1 + i)^n$ is simply the reciprocal of the interest factor for compounding, a series of interest factors have been developed that enable us to solve directly for present value (*PV*). Instead of having to multiply out the term $(1 + i)^n$ and to divide the result into 1 each time we want to discount, all of that work has been done for us and compiled in column 4 in the tables in Appendix A, Present Value Reversion of $1, for annual compounding (monthly factors are contained in Appendix B). Exhibit 3–6 contains a sample of factors to be used when discounting that are taken directly from column 4 in the tables for selected interest rates in Appendix A.

In our problem, we want to know how much should be paid for an investment with a future value of $10,600 to be received at the end of one year if the investor demands an annual return of 6 percent. The solution can be found by calculating or selecting the (*PVIF,* 6%, 1 yr.) or from the 6 percent column in Exhibit 3–6, or .943396. The $10,600 future value can now be multiplied by .943396, resulting in a present value (*PV*) of $10,000.

Question: How much should an investor pay today for a real estate investment that will return $20,000 at the end of three years, assuming the investor desires an annual return of 15 percent interest on the amount invested?

EXHIBIT 3–6 Present Value Reversion of $1 (column 4, Appendix A, annual discounting factors)

	Rate		
Year	*6%*	*10%*	*15%*
1	.943396	.909091	.869565
2	.889996	.826446	.756144
3	.839619	.751315	.657516
4	.792094	.683013	.571753
5	.747258	.620921	.497177
6	.704961	.564474	.432328

Solution:

$$PV = \$20{,}000 \times \frac{1}{(1 + .15)^3}$$

$$= \$20{,}000(PVIF,\ 15\%,\ 3\text{ yrs.})$$

$$= \$20{,}000(.657516)$$

$$= \$13{,}150.32$$

The investor should pay no more than $13,150.32 today for the investment promising a return of $20,000 after three years if a 15 percent return on investment is desired.[3]

Calculator Solution

$n = 3$ years
$i = 15\%$
$PMT = 0$
$FV = \$20{,}000$

Solve for present value:
$PV = -\$13{,}150.32$

Because we can use the discounting process to find the present value of a future value when *annual* compounding is assumed, we can also apply the same methodology assuming *monthly* discounting. For example, in our illustration involving monthly compounding, the future value of $10,000 at an annual rate of interest of 6 percent compounded monthly was $10,616.80. An important question an investor should consider is how much should be paid today for the future value of $10,616.80 received at the end of one year, assuming that a 6 percent return compounded *monthly* is required?

[3]An accepted convention in finance is that when one refers to a percentage return on investment, a nominal annual interest rate is assumed. If solutions are computed based on different compounding intervals within a year, such as monthly, the solution should be designated as an *annual rate of interest compounded monthly.* The latter solution may then be converted, if desired, to an effective annual yield, as shown previously.

EXHIBIT 3–7 Present Value Reversion of $1 (column 4, Appendix B, monthly discounting factors)

	Rate			
Month	*6%*	*8%*	*9%*	
1	.995025	.993377	.992556	
2	.990075	.986799	.985167	
3	.985149	.980264	.977833	
4	.980248	.973772	.970554	
5	.975371	.967323	.963329	
6	.970518	.960917	.956158	
7	.965690	.954553	.949040	
8	.960885	.948232	.941975	
9	.956105	.941952	.934963	
10	.951348	.935714	.928003	
11	.946615	.929517	.921095	
12	.941905	.923361	.914238	
Year				*Month*
1	.941905	.932583	.923361	12
2	.887186	.869712	.852596	24
3	.835645	.811079	.787255	36
4	.787098	.756399	.726921	48

We could answer this question by finding the reciprocal of the formula used to compound monthly, $1 \div (1 + i/12)^{1 \cdot 12}$, and multiply that result by the future value of $10,616.78 to find the present value (*PV*). We may calculate this factor or, following the procedure used in annual discounting, we could use the series of factors that have been calculated and included in table form. These factors, assuming a monthly discounting process, are contained in column 4 in the tables in Appendix B. A sample of factors for selected interest rates and years is shown in Exhibit 3–7.

In our problem, we want to determine the present value of $10,616.80 received at the end of one year, assuming a desired rate of return of 6 percent, compounded monthly. By going to the 6 percent column and the row corresponding to one year (12 months) and selecting the interest factor .941905, we can now multiply $10,616.80 × (.941905) = $10,000 and see that $10,000 is the maximum amount one should pay today for the investment.

Calculator Solution

$n = 1$ year × 12 periods = 12
$i = 6\% \div 12$ periods = .5%
$PMT = 0$
$FV = 10{,}616.80$

Solve for present value:
$PV = -\$10{,}000$

Question: How much should an investor pay to receive \$12,000 three years (36 months) from now, assuming that the investor desires an annual return of 9 percent compounded *monthly?*

Solution:

$$\begin{aligned} PV &= \$12{,}000(MPVIF,\ 9\%,\ 36 \text{ mos.}) \\ &= \$12{,}000(.764149) \\ &= \$9{,}169.79 \end{aligned}$$

Calculator Solution

$n = 3 \times 12 = 36$
$i = 9\% \div 12 = .75\%$
$PMT = 0$
$FV = 12{,}000$

Solve for present value:
$PV = -\$9{,}169.79$

The investor should pay no more than \$9,169.79 for the investment, or the present value (*PV*) of the investment is \$9,169.79. (Again note the use of *M* in our abbreviation designating monthly discounting.)

Compound or Future Value of an Annuity

The first section of this chapter dealt with finding the compound or future value of a *single deposit* or payment made only once, at the beginning of a period. An equally relevant consideration involves a series of equal deposits or payments made at equal intervals. For example, assume deposits of \$1,000 are made at the *end* of each year for a period of five years and interest is compounded at an annual rate of 5 percent. What is the future value at the end of the period for a series of deposits plus all compound interest? In this case, the problem involves equal payments (*P*), or deposits, made at equal time intervals. This series of deposits or payments is defined as an **annuity.** Because we know how to find the answer to a problem where only one deposit is made, it is logical and correct to assume that the same basic compounding process applies when dealing with annuities. However, that process is only a partial solution to the problem because we are dealing with a series of deposits that occur annually.

To compute the sum of all deposits made in each succeeding year and include compound interest on deposits only when it is earned, the general formula for compounded interest must be expanded as follows:

$$FVA = P(1 + i)^{n-1} + P(1 + i)^{n-2} + \cdots + P$$

This may also be written as

$$FVA = P \times \sum_{t=1}^{n-1} (1 + i)^t + P$$

which simply means that we may take the constant payment or annuity *P* and multiply it by the "sum of" the series $1 + i$ expanded from time $t = 1$ to the period $n - 1$,

EXHIBIT 3–8 Future Value of an Annuity of $1,000 per Year Compounded at 5 Percent Annually (column 1, Appendix A)

Year	Deposit	IF	Future Value
1	$1,000 × (*FVIF*, 5%, 4 yrs.)	= $1,000 × 1.215506	= $1,215.51*
2	1,000 × (*FVIF*, 5%, 3 yrs.)	= 1,000 × 1.157625	= 1,157.63*
3	1,000 × (*FVIF*, 5%, 2 yrs.)	= 1,000 × 1.102500	= 1,102.50
4	1,000 × (*FVIF*, 5%, 1 yr.)	= 1,000 × 1.050000	= 1,050.00
5	1,000 × 1.000000	= 1,000 × 1.000000	= 1,000.00
	Also	= 1,000 × 5.525631	= $5,525.63*

*Rounded.

plus *P*.[4] Hence, the symbol Σ represents the "sum of" that series and is simply a shortcut notation to be used in place of writing $1 + i$ repetitively.

In this expression, *FVA* is the **future value of an annuity** or the sum of all deposits, *P*, compounded at an annual rate, *i*, for *n* years. The important thing to note in the expression, however, is that each deposit is assumed to be at the *end* of each year and is compounded through year *n*. The final deposit does not earn interest because it occurs at the end of the final year. Since we are dealing in our example with a series of $1,000 deposits made over a five-year period, the first $1,000 deposit is compounded for four periods ($n - 1$), the $1,000 deposit made at the beginning of the second year is compounded for three periods ($n - 2$), and so on, until the last deposit, *P*, is reached. The last deposit is not compounded because it is deposited at the end of the fifth year.[5]

To compute the value of these deposits, we could construct a solution like that shown in Exhibit 3–8. Note that each $1,000 deposit is compounded from the end of the year in which the deposit was made to the end of the next year. In other words, as shown in our expanded formula above, the deposit at the end of year 1 is compounded for four years, the deposit made at the beginning of the second year is compounded for three years, and so on. By carrying this process out one year at a time, we determined the solution, or $5,525.63, when the compounded amounts in the extreme right-hand column are added.

Although the future value of $1,000 per period, *FVA*, can be determined in the manner shown in Exhibit 3–8, careful examination of the compounding process reveals another, easier way to find the solution. Note that the $1,000 deposit occurs annually and never changes; it is constant. When the deposits are constant, it is possible to sum all of the individual *IF*s as 5.525631. By multiplying $1,000 by 5.525631, a solution of $5,525.63 is obtained, as shown at the bottom of the right-hand column in Exhibit 3–8.

[4] The formula shown here is the formula for an *ordinary annuity* which assumes all deposits are made at the *end* of each year. The final *P* in the expression means that the last payment is not compounded. The letter *A* in *FVA* signifies that an annuity is being evaluated.

[5] The reader should be aware that this formulation is used for *ordinary annuities* or when payments or receipts occur at the end of a period. This is different from the formula for an *annuity due*, which assumes deposits are made at the *beginning* of the year.

EXHIBIT 3–9 Accumulation of $1 per Period (column 2, Appendix A, annual compounding factors)

	Rate		
Year	*5%*	*6%*	*10%*
1	1.000000	1.000000	1.000000
2	2.050000	2.060000	2.100000
3	3.152500	3.183600	3.310000
4	4.310125	4.374616	4.641000
5	5.525631	5.637093	6.105100
6	6.801913	6.975319	7.715610
7	8.142008	8.393838	9.487171
8	9.549109	9.897468	11.435888

Use of Compound Interest Tables for Annuities

Because the *IF*s in Exhibit 3–8 can be added when annuities are being considered, a series of new interest factors have been calculated for various interest rates in column 2 of Appendix A, *Accumulation of $1 per Period.* A sample of these factors, now referred to as *FVIFA, i%*, yrs., has been taken directly from column 2 in Appendix A and compiled in Exhibit 3–9 (note the use of the letter *A* after *FVIF,* which designates that the series of deposits being considered is an annuity and not the deposit of a single amount).

In the problem at hand, to determine the future value of $1,000 deposited annually at 5 percent for five years, note that if we go to the 5 percent column in Exhibit 3–9 and obtain the *IF* that corresponds to five years, we can find the solution to our problem as follows:

$$\begin{aligned} FVA &= P(FVIFA,\ 5\%,\ 5 \text{ yrs.}) \\ &= \$1{,}000(FVIFA,\ 5\%,\ 5 \text{ yrs.}) \\ &= \$1{,}000(5.525631) \\ &= \$5{,}525.63 \end{aligned}$$

This amount corresponds to the solution obtained from the long series of multiplications carried out in Exhibit 3–8.

Calculator Solution

$n = 5$
$i = 5\%$
$PV = 0$
$PMT = -\$1{,}000$

Solve for future value:
$FV = \$5{,}525.63$

Question: What is the future value of \$800 deposited each year for six years, compounded annually at 10 percent interest after six years?

Solution:

$$\begin{aligned} FV &= \$800(FVIFA,\ 10\%,\ 6\text{ yrs.}) \\ &= \$800(7.715610) \\ &= \$6{,}172.49 \end{aligned}$$

Calculator Solution

$n = 6$
$i = 10\%$
$PV = 0$
$PMT = -\$800$

Solve for future value:
$FV = \$6{,}172.49$

The same procedure used for compounding annuities for amounts deposited or paid annually can also be applied to monthly annuities. A very simple modification can be made to the formulation used for annual annuities by substituting $i/12$ in place of i and adding the number of compounding periods per year (m) in the annual formulation, as follows:

$$FVA = P\left[1 + \frac{i}{12}\right]^{n \cdot m - 1} + P\left[1 + \frac{i}{12}\right]^{n \cdot m - 2} + \cdots + P$$

or

$$FVA = P \cdot \sum_{t=1}^{n \cdot m - 1} \left[1 + \frac{i}{12}\right]^{t} + P$$

However, in this formulation, $n \cdot m$ represents months. Deposits or payments P are made monthly and are constant in amount. Hence, the interest factors used to compound each monthly deposit may be added (as they were for annual deposits in Exhibit 3–8), and a new series for compounding monthly annuities can be computed. This has been done for selected interest rates and years. The factors for compounding monthly annuities are contained in column 2 in Appendix B tables.[6]

Question: An investor pays \$200 per month into a real estate investment that promises to pay an annual rate of interest of 8 percent compounded *monthly.* If the investor makes consecutive monthly payments for five years, what is the future value at the end of five years?

Solution:

$$\begin{aligned} FVA &= \$200(MFVIFA,\ 8\%,\ 60\text{ mos.}) \\ &= \$200(73.476856) \\ &= \$14{,}695.37 \end{aligned}$$

[6]Like annual compounding, this formulation assumes that deposits are made at the *end* of each month, or that an ordinary annuity is being compounded.

Calculator Solution

$n = 5 \times 12 = 60$ months
$i = 8\%/12 = .666\%$
$PV = 0$
$PMT = -\$200$

Solve for future value:
$FV = \$14{,}695.34$

In this case, the value of payments earning interest at an annual rate of 8 percent compounded monthly can be found by multiplying the $200 monthly annuity by the interest factor for the accumulation of $1 per period in column 2 in Appendix B tables, or $200(73.476856) = $14,695.37.

Present Value of an Annuity

In the preceding section, our primary concern was to determine the future value of an annuity, or constant payments received at equal time intervals. In this section, we consider the **present value of an annuity (*PVA*),** or the series of annual income receipts the investment produces over time. Because an investor may have to consider a series of income payments when deciding whether to invest, this is an important problem. Recall that when dealing with the present value of a single receipt, or ending value, *PV*, we took the basic formula for compounding interest and rearranged it to determine the present value of an investment as follows:

$$FV = PV(1 + i)^n$$

$$PV = FV \div (1 + i)^n$$

$$PV = FV \cdot \frac{1}{(1 + i)^n}$$

To consider the present value of an annuity, or *PVA,* we need only consider the sum of individual present value for all receipts. This can be done by modifying the basic present value formula as follows:

$$PVA = R\,\frac{1}{(1 + i)^1} + R\,\frac{1}{(1 + i)^2} + R\,\frac{1}{(1 + i)^3} + \cdots + R\,\frac{1}{(1 + i)^n}$$

or this can be written as

$$PVA = R \sum_{t=1}^{n} \frac{1}{(1 + i)^t}$$

Note in this expression that each receipt, *R,* is discounted for the number of years corresponding to the time when the funds were actually received. In other words, the first receipt would occur at the end of the first period and would be discounted only one period, or $R \cdot [1 \div (1 + i)^1]$. The second receipt would be discounted for two periods, or $R \cdot [1 \div (1 + i)^2]$, and so on.

Calculator Solution

$n = 6$
$i = 6\%$
$PMT = -\$500$
$FV = 0$

Solve for present value:
$PV = \$2{,}458.66$

Assuming an individual is considering an investment that will provide a series of annual cash receipts of $500 for a period of six years, and the investor desires a 6 percent return, how much should the investor pay for the investment today? We can begin by considering the present value of the $500 receipt in year 1, as shown in Exhibit 3–10. Note that the present value of the $500 receipt is discounted for one year at 6 percent. This is done because the income of $500 for the first year is not received until the end of the first period, and our investor only wants to pay an amount today (present value) that will assure a 6 percent return on the amount paid today. Therefore, by discounting this $500 receipt by the interest factor in column 5 for one year in the 6 percent tables in Appendix A, or .943396, the present value is $471.70. Note that the second $500 income payment is received at the end of the second year. Therefore, it should be discounted for *two* years at 6 percent. Its present value is found by multiplying $500 by the interest factor in column 5 in the 6 percent tables for two years, or .889996, giving a present value of $445. This process can be continued for each receipt for the remaining three years (see Exhibit 3–10). The present value of the entire series of $500 income payments can be found by adding the series of receipts discounted each month in the far right-hand column, which totals $2,458.66.

However, because the $500 series of payments is constant, we may simply sum all interest factors to obtain one interest factor that can be multiplied by $500 to obtain the same present value (see Exhibit 3–10). The sum of all interest factors for 6 percent is 4.917324. When 4.917324 is multiplied by $500, the present value, $2,458.66, found in the lengthy series of multiplications carried in Exhibit 3–10, is again determined.

EXHIBIT 3–10 Present Value of $500 per Year (discounted at 6 percent annually)

Year	*Receipt*	*IF**	*Present Value*
1	$500 × (*PVIF*, 6%, 1 yr.)	= $500 × .943396	= $ 471.70
2	500 × (*PVIF*, 6%, 2 yrs.)	= 500 × .889996	= 445.00
3	500 × (*PVIF*, 6%, 3 yrs.)	= 500 × .839619	= 419.81
4	500 × (*PVIF*, 6%, 4 yrs.)	= 500 × .792094	= 396.05
5	500 × (*PVIF*, 6%, 5 yrs.)	= 500 × .747258	= 373.63
6	500 × (*PVIF*, 6%, 6 yrs.)	= 500 × .704961	= 352.48
	Also	$500 × 4.917324	= $2,458.66†

*Column 4, Appendix A.
†Rounded.

Use of the Present Value of an Annuity Table

Because the interest factors in Exhibit 3–10 may be summed, as long as the income payments are equal in amount and received at equal intervals, this combination obviously takes a lot of work out of problem solving. The sums of *IF*s for various interest rates, now referred to as (*PVIFA, i%, n* yrs.), have been compiled in table form and are listed in column 5, Present Value of Ordinary Annuity $1 per Period, in the tables in Appendix A. To familiarize you with discounting annuities, we have developed Exhibit 3–11 to show the *IF*s for the present value of $1 per period (annuity). These *IF*s were taken directly from column 5 in the tables contained in Appendix A for a sample of interest rates. In our problem, we want to determine the present value of $500 received annually for six years, assuming a desired annual rate of return of 6 percent. How much should an investor pay for this total investment today and be assured of earning the desired return? We can solve this problem by computing the solution with a calculator or by looking at Exhibit 3–11, finding the 6 percent column, and looking down the column until we locate the *IF* in the row corresponding to six years. The *IF* is 4.917324. Thus

$$\begin{aligned} PVA &= \$500(PVIFA,\ 6\%,\ 6\text{ yrs.}) \\ &= \$500(4.917324) \\ &= \$2{,}458.66 \end{aligned}$$

This solution corresponds to that obtained in Exhibit 3–10.

Question: An investor has an opportunity to invest in a rental property that will provide net cash returns of $400 per year for three years. The investor believes that an annual return of 10 percent should be earned on this investment. How much should the investor pay for the rental property?

Solution:

$$\begin{aligned} PVA &= \$400(PVIFA,\ 10\%,\ 3\text{ yrs.}) \\ &= \$400(2.486852) \\ &= \$994.74 \end{aligned}$$

The investor should pay no more than $994.74 for the investment property. With that amount a 10 percent return will be earned. (Again, note the use of the letter *A* after *PVIF,* indicating an annuity is being evaluated.)

EXHIBIT 3–11 Present Value of Ordinary Annuity $1 per Period (column 5, Appendix A, annual discounting factors)

	Rate			
Year	*5%*	*6%*	*10%*	*15%*
1	.952381	.943396	.909091	.869565
2	1.859410	1.833393	1.735537	1.625709
3	2.723248	2.673012	2.486852	2.283225
4	3.545951	3.465106	3.169865	2.854978
5	4.329477	4.212364	3.790787	3.352155
6	5.075692	4.917324	4.355261	3.784483
7	5.786373	5.582381	4.868419	4.160420
8	6.463213	6.209794	5.334926	4.487322

Calculator Solution

$n = 3$
$i = 10\%$
$PMT = -\$400$
$FV = 0$

Solve for present value:
$PV = \$994.74$

Based on the logic used in discounting annuities paid or received annually, the same procedure can be applied to cash receipts paid or received *monthly.* In this case, the formula used to discount annual annuities is simply modified to reflect monthly receipts or payments, and the discounting interval is changed to reflect monthly compounding:

$$PVA = P\left[\frac{1}{1+\frac{i}{12}}\right]^1 + P\left[\frac{1}{1+\frac{i}{12}}\right]^2 + \cdots + P\left[\frac{1}{1+\frac{i}{12}}\right]^{12\cdot n}$$

where payments (P) occur monthly, the exponents represent months running from 1 through $n \cdot m$, and *PVA* represents the present value of an annuity received over $n \cdot m$ months.

Like annual discounting, computation of the present value of an annuity can be very cumbersome if one has to expand the above formula for each problem, particularly if the problem involves cash receipts or payments over many months. Hence, a series of interest factors have been computed by expanding the above formula for each monthly interval and adding the resulting interest factors (this was performed with discounting annual annuities in Exhibit 3–10). These factors are contained in column 5 in tables in Appendix B. Like the annual tables, the column is labeled *Present Value of Ordinary Annuity of $1 per Period;* however, the period in this case is one month. A sample of these factors for given interest rates and years has been taken directly from column 5, Appendix B, and included in Exhibit 3–12. Hence, if an investor wants to know how much he or she should pay today for an investment that would pay $500 at the end of each month for the next 12 months and earn an annual rate of 6 percent compounded monthly on the investment, the investor can easily compute the solution with a calculator or determine it by consulting Exhibit 3–12. Looking to the 6 percent column and dropping down to the row corresponding to 12 months, the factor 11.618932 is found. Multiplying $500 by 11.618932 results in $5,809.47, or the amount that the investor should pay today if a 6 percent rate of return compounded monthly is desired.

Question: A real estate partnership predicts that it will pay $300 at the end of each month to its partners over the next six months. Assuming the partners desire an 8 percent return compounded monthly on their investment, how much should they pay?

Solution:

$$\begin{aligned} PVA &= \$300(MPVIFA, 8\%, 6 \text{ mos.}) \\ &= \$300(5.862452) \\ &= \$1,758.74 \end{aligned}$$

EXHIBIT 3–12 Present Value of Ordinary Annuity of $1 per Period (column 5, Appendix B, monthly discounting factors)

	Rate		
Month	*6%*	*8%*	
1	.995025	.993377	
2	1.985099	1.980176	
3	2.970248	2.960440	
4	3.950496	3.934212	
5	4.925866	4.901535	
6	5.896384	5.862452	
7	6.862074	6.817005	
8	7.882959	7.765237	
9	8.779064	8.707189	
10	9.730412	9.642903	
11	10.677027	10.572420	
12	11.618932	11.495782	
Year			*Month*
1	11.618932	11.495782	12
2	22.562866	22.110544	24
3	32.871016	31.911806	36
4	42.580318	40.961913	48

Calculator Solution

$n = 6$ months

$i = 8\% \div 12 = .6666\%$

$PMT = -\$300$

$FV = 0$

Solve for present value:

$PV = \$1{,}758.74$

Accumulation of a Future Sum

The previous two sections have dealt with compounding and discounting single payments on annuities. In some instances, however, it is necessary to determine a series of payments necessary to *accumulate a future sum,* taking into account the fact that such payments will be accumulating interest as they are deposited. For example, assume we have a debt of $20,000 that must be repaid in one lump sum at the end of five years. We would like to make a series of equal annual payments (an annuity) at the end of each of the five years, so that we will have $20,000 at the end of the fifth year from the accumulated deposits plus interest. Assuming that we can earn 10 percent interest per year on those deposits, how much should each annual deposit be?

In this case, we are dealing with accumulating a future sum. Exhibit 3–5 indicates that we will be compounding a series of deposits (P), or an annuity, to achieve that future value. Hence, we can work with the procedure for determining future values by compounding as follows:

$$P(FVIFA, 10\%, 5 \text{ yrs.}) = \$20{,}000$$
$$P(6.105100) = \$20{,}000$$
$$P = \$20{,}000 \div 6.105100$$
$$= \$3{,}275.95$$

Calculator Solution

$n = 5$
$i = 10\%$
$PV = 0$
$FV = \$20{,}000$

Solve for annual payments:
$PMT = -\$3{,}275.95$

This computation merely indicates that when compounded at an annual interest rate of 10 percent, the unknown series of equal deposits (*P*) will result in the accumulation of \$20,000 at the end of five years. Given the interest factor for compounding an annual annuity (*FVIFA*) from column 2 in the tables in Appendix A, or 6.105100, we know that the unknown deposit, *P,* when multiplied by that factor will result in \$20,000. Hence, by dividing \$20,000 by the interest factor for compounding an annual annuity, we can obtain the necessary annual payment of \$3,275.95. The result tells us that if we make deposits of \$3,275.95 at the end of each year for five years, and each of those deposits earns interest at an annual rate of 10 percent, a total of \$20,000 will be accumulated at the end of five years.

We can see from the above computation, that dividing \$20,000 by 6.105100 is equivalent to multiplying \$20,000 by (1 ÷ 6.105100), or .163797, and the same \$3,275.95 solution results. The factor .163797 is referred to in real estate finance as a **sinking-fund factor (SFF),** which is also used in other applications in real estate. These sinking-fund factors (or reciprocals of interest factors for compounding annuities) are contained in column 3 in Appendix A for annual deposits (the reader should either locate or compute the factor .163797) and Appendix B for monthly deposits. In the latter case, if we want to know what monthly payments would be necessary to pay off the \$20,000 debt at the end of five years, taking into account that each deposit will earn an annual rate of 10 percent compounded monthly, we can easily multiply \$20,000 times .012914 (the sinking-fund factor, column 3, Appendix B tables) to obtain \$258.28 per month as the required series of deposits.

Determining Yields or Internal Rates of Return on Investments

Up to now, this chapter has demonstrated how to determine future values in the case of compounding and present values in the case of discounting. Each topic is important in its own right, but each has also provided tools for determining an equally important component used extensively in real estate financing, that is, calculating rates of return or **investment yields.** In other words, the concepts illustrated in the compounding and discounting processes can also be used to determine rates of return, or yields, on investments, mortgage loans, and so on. These concepts must be mastered because procedures used here will form the basis for much of what follows in succeeding chapters.

We have concentrated previously on determining the future value of an investment made today when compounded at some given rate of interest, or the present investment value of a stream of cash returns received in the future when discounted at a given rate of interest. In this section, we are concerned with problems where we know what an investment will cost today and what the future stream of cash returns will be, but we do not know what **yield** or **rate of return** will be earned if the investment is made.

Investments with Single Receipts

In many cases, investors and lenders are concerned with the problem of what rate of compound interest, or investment yield, will be earned if an investment is undertaken. To illustrate the investment yield concept, assume an investor has an opportunity today to buy an unimproved one-acre lot for \$5,639. The lot is expected to appreciate in value and to be worth \$15,000 after seven years. What rate of interest (or investment yield) would be earned on the \$5,639 investment in the property if it were made today, held for seven years, and sold for \$15,000?

To solve for the unknown rate, we can formulate the problem as follows:

$$PV = R \cdot \frac{1}{(1+i)^n}$$

$$\$5{,}639 = \$15{,}000 \cdot \frac{1}{(1+i)^7}$$

We want to know the annual rate of compound interest, i, that, when substituted into the above equation, will make the \$15,000 receipt equal to the \$5,639 investment outlay, or present value, today.

Unfortunately, there is no "easy way" of finding a solution to the unknown, or i, directly. What follows are a number of approaches to finding it. (For readers using electronic calculators or who have access to computers, the material that follows may be lightly reviewed.)

The trial-and-error approach is one way to solve for i. A value for i is estimated; then the equation is solved to ascertain whether the future value, or \$15,000, when discounted to present value, PV, will equal \$5,639. When the correct value for i is found, the solution for present value should yield \$5,639.

How do we begin the search for i? One way is to simply guess a solution. Let's try 10 percent. Mathematically we ask, if

$$PV = \$15{,}000 \frac{1}{(1+.10)^7}$$

is $PV = \$5{,}639$?

Solving for PV, we have

$$PV = (\$15{,}000)(.513158)$$
$$= \$7{,}697$$

We note that \$7,697 or PV is much greater than the desired PV, or \$5,639. This means that the yield, or rate of compound interest earned on the investment, is *greater* than 10 percent. Hence, we must continue the discounting process by increasing i.

Our next "trial" will be 15 percent. Substituting, we have

$$\begin{aligned} PV &= \$15{,}000\,\frac{1}{(1+.15)^7} \\ &= \$15{,}000(.375937) \\ &= \$5{,}639 \end{aligned}$$

This time *PV* equals \$5,639. This "guess" was correct. From this result, we have determined that the yield or internal rate of return, *i*, earned on the investment is equal to 15 percent. We have, in essence, "removed" interest compounded at the rate of 15 percent for seven years from the \$15,000 receipt of cash, leaving the initial deposit, or present value, of \$5,639.

When trying to find the yield in which only one future value is involved, we can use an alternative approach where the interest factor, *PVIF,* in the financial tables is first determined as follows:

$$\begin{aligned} \$5{,}639 &= \$15{,}000(PVIF,\ ?\%,\ 7\text{ yrs.}) \\ \$5{,}639 \div \$15{,}000 &= (PVIF,\ ?\%,\ 7\text{ yrs.}) \\ .375933 &= (PVIF,\ ?\%,\ 7\text{ yrs.}) \end{aligned}$$

The above calculations show that the interest factor is .375933, but we still do not know the interest rate. However, we do know that the time period over which the investment is to appreciate in value is seven years. Because *PVIF* is .375933 and the term of investment is seven years, the interest tables in Appendix A allow us to easily find the correct interest rate. Since the cash return of \$15,000 is a single receipt, we need only locate an *IF* for the present value reversion of \$1 equal to .375933 in column 4 in the row corresponding to seven years for some interest rate. We begin the search for the interest rate by choosing an arbitrary interest rate, say 5 percent. The 5 percent table in Appendix A shows that the *IF* in column 4 for seven years is .710681, which is larger than .375933. Moving to the 10 percent table, the *IF* for seven years is .513158, which is lower than the *IF* at 5 percent but comes closer to the *IF* we are looking for. Continuing this trial-and-error process, the 15 percent table indicates that the *IF* in column 4 for seven years is .375937; therefore the interest rate we desire is 15 percent. We know this is the correct interest factor because \$15,000 (.375937) = \$5,639.

Calculator Solution

$n = 7$
$PV = -\$5{,}639$
$PMT = 0$
$FV = \$15{,}000$

Solve for investment yield:
$i = 15\%$

What does this interest rate, or yield, mean? It means that the \$5,639 investment made today, held for seven years, and sold for \$15,000, is equivalent to investing

$5,639 today and letting it compound annually at an interest rate of 15 percent (note the correspondence between the terms *interest rate* and *yield*).[7] This fact can be determined with the following computation:

$$FV = \$5{,}639(FVIF, 15\%, 7 \text{ yrs.})$$
$$= \$5{,}639(2.660020)$$
$$= \$15{,}000$$

This calculation simply shows that $5,639 compounded annually at an interest rate of 15 percent for seven years is $15,000. Hence, making this investment is equivalent to earning a rate of return of 15 percent. This rate of return is usually referred to as the *investment yield* or the **internal rate of return.**

Calculator Solution

$n = 7$
$i = 15\%$
$PV = -\$5{,}639$
$PMT = 0$

Solve for future value:
$FV = \$15{,}000$

The internal rate of return integrates the concepts of compounding and present value. It represents a way of measuring a return on investment, expressed as a compound rate of interest, over the entire investment period. For example, if an investor is faced with making an investment in an income-producing venture, regardless of how the cash returns are patterned, the internal rate of return provides a guide or comparison for the investor. It tells the investor what the equivalent compound interest rate will be on the investment being considered. In the example of the unimproved one-acre lot, the 15 percent yield or internal rate of return is equivalent to making a deposit of $5,639 and allowing it to compound monthly at an annual interest rate of 15 percent for seven years. After seven years, the investor would receive $15,000, which includes the original investment of $5,639 plus all compound interest. With the internal rate of return known, the investor can make an easier judgment about what investment to make. If the 15 percent return is adequate, it will be made; if not, the investor should reject it.[8]

The concepts of the internal rate of return or yield, present value, and compounding are indispensable tools that are continually used in real estate finance and investment. The reader should not venture beyond this section without firmly grasping the concepts that have been explained. These concepts form the basis for the remainder of this chapter and the chapters which follow.

[7]We are now using the terms *yield* and *internal rate of return* for *i*, instead of the interest rate. It is generally accepted practice to use these terms when evaluating most investments. The term *interest rate* is generally used when a loan is being evaluated. The two concepts are very similar, but the reader should become accustomed to these differences in usage.

[8]When comparing different investments, the investor must also consider any differences in risk. This topic is discussed in later chapters.

Yields on Investment Annuities

The concepts illustrated for a single receipt of cash (when the unimproved lot was sold) also apply to situations where a *series* of cash receipts is involved. Consequently, a yield or internal rate of return also can be computed on these types of investments.

Suppose an investor has the opportunity to make an investment in real estate costing \$3,170 that would provide him with cash income of \$1,000 at the end of *each year* for four years. What investment yield, or internal rate of return, would the investor earn on the \$3,170? In this case, we have a series of receipts that we wish to discount by an unknown rate to make the present value of the \$1,000 annuity equal the original investment of \$3,170. We need to find a solution for i in this problem, or the rate of interest that will make the present value of the \$1,000 four-year annuity equal to \$3,170. Using our shorthand notation, we have

$$\$3{,}170 = \$1{,}000(PVIFA,\ ?\%,\ 4\text{ yrs.})$$

Recalling the notation for the present value of an annuity PVA, we have

$$PVA = R \cdot \sum_{t=1}^{n} \frac{1}{(1+i)^t}$$

Substituting gives

$$\$3{,}170 = 1{,}000 \cdot \sum_{t=1}^{n} \frac{1}{(1+i)^t}$$

Using our shorthand notation, we can express our problem as follows:

$$\begin{aligned} PVA &= R(PVIFA,\ ?\%,\ 4\text{ yrs.}) \\ \$3{,}170 &= \$1{,}000(PVIFA,\ ?\%,\ 4\text{ yrs.}) \\ \$3{,}170 \div \$1{,}000 &= (PVIFA,\ ?\%,\ 4\text{ yrs.}) \\ 3.170000 &= (PVIFA,\ ?\%,\ 4\text{ yrs.}) \end{aligned}$$

Calculator Solution

$n = 4$
$PV = -\$3{,}170$
$PMT = \$1{,}000$
$FV = 0$

Solve for investment yield:
$i = 10\%$

This procedure is similar to solving for the yield or internal rate of return on single receipts discussed in the preceding section, except that we are now dealing with an annuity (note the use of the letter *A* after *PVIF* in our abbreviated formula). Using the same procedure as before we solve for the interest factor for a four-year period that will correspond to some interest rate. To determine what the interest rate is, search the tables in Appendix A (column 5) in the four-year row until you find a factor very close to 3.1700. A careful search reveals that the factor will be found in the 10 percent tables (the reader should verify this). Hence, based on this procedure,

EXHIBIT 3–13 Illustration of the Internal Rate of Return (*IRR*) and Components of Cash Receipts

	Year			
	1	*2*	*3*	*4*
Investment (balance)	$3,170	$2,487	$1,736	$ 910
IRR at 10%	317	249*	174*	91*
Cash received	$1,000	$1,000	$1,000	$1,000
Less: Cash yield at 10%	317	249	174	90*
Recovery of investment	$ 683	$ 751	$ 826	$ 910
Investment (beginning of year)	$3,170	$2,487	$1,736	$ 910
Less: Recovery of investment	683	751	826	910
Investment (end of year)	$2,487	$1,736	$ 910	$ 0

*Rounded.

we have determined that the investment yield or internal rate of return (*IRR*) on the $3,170 invested is 10 percent. A more in-depth analysis of what the internal rate of return means is presented in Exhibit 3–13.

When the internal rate of return is computed, two characteristics are present (see Exhibit 3–13). One is the *recovery of capital* in each period, and the other is *interest earned* in each period. In other words, when the *IRR* is computed based on the $3,170 investment and the $1,000 received each year, *implicit* in the *IRR* computation is the *full recovery* of the $3,170 investment *plus* interest compounded annually at 10 percent. Hence, the 10 percent investment yield is really a rate of compound interest earned on an outstanding investment balance from year to year. Of the total $4,000 received during the four-year period, total interest earned is $830 and capital recovery is $3,170.

Monthly Annuities: Investment Yields. A similar application for investment yields can be made in cases where monthly cash annuities will be received as a return on investment. For example, assume that an investor makes an investment of $51,593 to receive $400 at the end of each month for the next 20 years (240 months). What annual rate of return, compounded monthly, would be earned on the $51,593? The solution can be easily determined with the following procedure:

$$R(MPVIFA, ?\%, 20 \text{ yrs.}) = PVA$$

$$\$400(MPVIFA, ?\%, 20 \text{ yrs.}) = \$51{,}593$$

$$(MPVIFA, ?\%, 20 \text{ yrs.}) = \$51{,}593 \div \$400$$

$$= 128.9825$$

Calculator Solution

$$n = 20 \times 12 = 240$$
$$PV = -\$51{,}593$$
$$PMT = \$400$$
$$FV = 0$$

Solve for investment yield:

i (monthly) = 0.5833%

i (annualized) = .005833 × 12 or 7%

As was the case with finding the *IRR* for investments with annual receipts, we find the interest factor for the present value of an ordinary annuity of $1 per month for 20 years for an interest rate compounded monthly (note the *M* in our shorthand notation), which is 128.9825. In Appendix B, column 5 in the 20-year row of various interest rates, we find the interest rate that corresponds to that factor is 7 percent. Hence, the *IRR* is 7 percent compounded monthly on the $51,593 investment. Both the recovery of $51,593 plus $44,407 in interest was embedded in the stream of $400 monthly cash receipts over the 20-year period.

Effective Annual Yields: Extensions

Earlier in this chapter, we dealt with the problem of determining equivalent annual yields in cases where there were more than one compounding interval within a year. In our example, we showed the effective annual yield for a $10,000 investment compounded annually, monthly, and daily to be 6, 6.1678, and 6.1831 percent, respectively. In many situations, we may already know the *effective annual yield (EAY)* and would like to know what the *nominal annual rate* of interest compounded monthly (or for any period less than one year) must be to earn the desired effective annual yield. For example, we considered a problem in which compounding occurred monthly based on a nominal annual rate of interest of 6 percent. Because compounding occurred in monthly intervals, an effective annual interest rate larger than the nominal rate resulted. Assuming that we wanted to know what the nominal annual rate of interest, compounded *monthly,* would have to be to provide a desired *EAY* of 6 percent, we can employ the following formula, where *ENAR* is the **equivalent nominal annual rate,** compounded monthly:

$$ENAR = [(1 + EAY)^{1/m} - 1] \cdot m$$

In our problem, we would have

$$\begin{aligned} ENAR &= [(1 + .06)^{1/m} - 1] \cdot 12 \\ &= [(1 + .06)^{.083333} - 1] \cdot 12 \\ &= [1.004868 - 1] \cdot 12 \\ &= .0584106 \text{ or } 5.84106\% \text{ (rounded)} \end{aligned}$$

To illustrate this concept, if we have investment A, which will provide an effective annual yield of 6 percent, and we are considering investment B, which will provide interest compounded monthly, we would want to know what the equivalent nominal annual rate (*ENAR*) of interest, compounded monthly, would have to be on investment B to provide the *same* effective annual yield of 6 percent. That rate would be an annual rate of 5.84106 percent compounded monthly.

$$\begin{aligned} FV &= \$1(MFVIF, 5.84106\%, 12 \text{ mos.}) \\ &= \$1\left[1 + \frac{.0584106}{12}\right]^{12} \\ &= \$1.06 \text{ (rounded)} \end{aligned}$$

From our example, we know that the *EAY* is (\$1.06 − \$1.00) ÷ \$1.00, or 6 percent. Hence, we now know that an investment of equal risk, with returns compounded *monthly,* must have an annual nominal rate of interest of at least 5.84106 percent to provide us with an equivalent, effective annual yield of 6 percent. Obviously, this application can be modified for any investment with different compounding periods by altering m in the above formula.

Calculator Solution

$n = 12$ months
$i = 5.84106 \div 12 = .486755\%$
$PV = -\$1$
$PMT = 0$

Solve for future value:
$FV = \$1.06$

Solving for Annual Yields with Partial Periods: An Extension

Many investments produce monthly cash flows but call for investment returns to be calculated as an annual return (with annual compounding periods). Furthermore, the investment may be sold within a year (say after 5 months into a calendar year). How can monthly cash flows that may also include periods within a calendar year be expressed as an annual rate of interest? Consider the following example.

An investment is made in the amount of \$8,000 and the contract calls for investment returns to be reported as compounded annually. Monthly cash flows of \$500 are received for 17 months. What is the *annual* return on the investment? This can be determined as follows:

Step 1:

Calculator Solution

$n = 17$ months
$i = ?$
$PMT = 500$
$PV = -\$8,000$
$FV = 0$

Solve for i:
$i = .682083$

Step 2: The monthly interest rate of .682083 can now be used to determine the annual rate as follows:

Calculator Solution

$PV = -\$1$
$i = .682083$
$PMT = 0$
$n = 12$
$FV = ?$
Solve for FV:
$FV = 1.084991$

Step 3: The annual rate of interest would be:

$$FV - PV = 1.084991 - 1.000 = .084991 \text{ or } 8.5\%$$

Therefore, this investment over a 17-month period has produced an *effective annual yield* (EAY) of 8.5 percent. Note that this yield is much higher than an annual rate, compounded monthly, which would be $.682083 \times 12 = 8.19$ percent.

Conclusion

This chapter introduced and illustrated the mathematics of compound interest in financial analysis. Although this may be a review for many readers, a thorough understanding of this topic is essential in real estate finance. The concepts and techniques introduced in this chapter are used throughout the remainder of this text to solve a variety of problems encountered in real estate finance. In the following two chapters, we apply the mathematics of finance to the calculation of mortgage payments and the effective cost of various alternative mortgage instruments. Later we apply the mathematics of finance to the analysis of income property investments. Although this chapter illustrated the use of financial tables, these tables are not necessary to solve any of the problems in the remainder of the book. In fact, an alternative calculator solution is also provided for many of the problems. The table solutions are only shown so that the readers can see the mathematics behind the calculator solutions. As we move toward more advanced material, it is assumed that readers can obtain the solutions using a financial calculator or by using a spreadsheet program on a personal computer.

Key Terms

Questions

1. What is the essential concept in understanding compound interest?
2. How are the interest factors in column 1, in the Appendix B tables, developed?
3. What general rule can be developed concerning maximum values and compounding intervals within a year? What is an equivalent annual yield?
4. What does the time value of money mean? How is it related to present value? What process is used to find present value?
5. How does discounting, as used in determining present value, relate to compounding, as used in determining future value? How would present value ever be used?
6. What are the interest factors in column 4 in the Appendix A tables? How are they developed?
7. What is an annuity? How is it defined? What is the difference between an ordinary annuity and an annuity due?
8. Why can't interest factors for annuities be used when evaluating the present value of an uneven series of receipts? What factors must be used to discount a series of uneven receipts?
9. What is the sinking-fund factor? How and why is it used?
10. What is an internal rate of return? How is it used? How does it relate to the concept of compound interest?

Problems

1. Jim makes a deposit of $12,000 in a bank account. The deposit is to earn interest annually at the rate of 9 percent for seven years.
   a. How much will Jim have on deposit at the end of seven years?
   b. Assuming the deposit earned a 9 percent rate of interest compounded quarterly, how much would he have at the end of seven years?
   c. In comparing (*a*) and (*b*), what are the respective effective annual yields? (*Hint:* Consider the value of each deposit after one year only.) Which alternative is better?
2. Would you prefer making a $25,000 investment that will earn interest at the rate of 7 percent compounded monthly or making the same $25,000 investment at 8 percent compounded annually. (*Hint:* Consider one year only.)
3. John is considering the purchase of a lot. He can buy the lot today and expects the price to rise to $15,000 at the end of 10 years. He believes that he should earn an investment yield of 10 percent annually on his investment. The asking price for the lot is $7,000. Should he buy it? What is the effective annual yield of the investment if John purchases the property for $7,000 and is able to sell it 10 years later for $15,000?
4. An investor can make an investment in a real estate development and receive an expected cash return of $45,000 after six years. Based on a careful study of other investment alternatives, she believes that an 18 percent annual return compounded quarterly is a reasonable return to earn on this investment. How much should she pay for it today?
5. Jones can deposit $5,000 at the end of each six-month period for the next 12 years and earn interest at an annual rate of 8.5 percent, compounded semiannually. What will the value of the investment be after 12 years? If the deposits were made at the beginning of each period, what would the value of the investment be after 12 years?
6. Suppose you deposit $1,250 at the end of each quarter in an account that will earn interest at an annual rate of 15 percent compounded quarterly. How much will you have at the end of four years?
7. Suppose you deposit $2,500 at the end of year 1, nothing at the end of year 2, $750 at the end of year 3, and $1,300 at the end of year 4. Assuming that these amounts will be compounded at an annual rate of 9 percent, how much will you have on deposit at the end of five years?

8. An investor is considering an investment that will pay $2,150 at the end of each year for the next 10 years. He expects to earn an annual return of 18 percent on his investment. How much should he pay today for the investment? How much should he pay if the investment returns are paid at the beginning of each year?
9. Suppose you have the opportunity to make an investment in a real estate venture that expects to pay investors $750 at the end of each month for the next eight years. You believe that a reasonable return on your investment should be 17 percent compounded monthly.
   a. How much should you pay for the investment?
   b. What will be the total sum of cash you will receive over the next eight years?
   c. Why is there such a large difference between (*a*) and (*b*)?
10. Walt is evaluating an investment that will provide the following returns at the end of each of the following years: year l, $12,500; year 2, $10,000; year 3, $7,500; year 4, $5,000; year 5, $2,500; year 6, $0; and year 7, $12,500. Walt believes that he should earn an annual rate of 9 percent on this investment, compounded monthly. How much should he pay for this investment?
11. A loan of $50,000 is due 10 years from today. The borrower wants to make annual payments at the end of each year into a sinking fund that will earn interest at an annual rate of 10 percent. What will the annual payments have to be? Suppose that the monthly payments earn 10 percent interest, compounded monthly. What would the annual payments have to be?
12. The Dallas Development Corporation is considering the purchase of an apartment project for $100,000. They estimate that they will receive $15,000 at the end of each year for the next 10 years. At the end of the 10th year, the apartment project will be worth nothing. If Dallas purchases the project, what will be its internal rate of return? If the company insists on a 9 percent return compounded annually on its investment, is this a good investment?
13. A corporation is considering the purchase of an interest in a real estate syndication at a price of $75,000. In return, the syndication promises to pay $1,020 at the end of each month for the next 25 years (300 months). If purchased, what is the expected internal rate of return, compounded monthly? How much total cash would be received on the investment? How much is profit and how much is return of capital?
14. An investment in a real estate venture will provide returns at the end of the next four years as follows: year 1, $5,500; year 2, $7,500; year 3, $9,500; and year 4, $12,500. An investor wants to earn a 13 percent *annual* return on her investment. How much should she pay for the investment? Assuming that the investor wanted to earn an annual rate of 13 percent compounded *monthly*, how much would she pay for this investment? Why are these two amounts different?
15. A pension fund is making an investment of $100,000 today and expects to receive $1,500 at the end of each month for the next five years. At the end of the fifth year, the capital investment of $100,000 will be returned. What is the internal rate of return on this investment?
16. An investor has the opportunity to make an investment that will provide an effective annual yield of 10 percent. She is considering two other investments of equal risk that will provide compound interest monthly and quarterly, respectively. What must the equivalent nominal annual rate (*ENAR*) be for each of these two investments to ensure that an equivalent annual yield of 10 percent is earned?
17. An investment producing cash flows in the amount of $1,000 per month is undertaken for a period of 28 months. The investor pays $24,000 for the investment and the contract stipulates that investment returns must be calculated as annual returns (annual compounding). What would be the annual interest rate reported to the investor? What would be the annual rate compounded monthly for this investment?

CHAPTER 4

Fixed Rate Mortgage Loans

This chapter deals with various approaches to pricing and structuring fixed interest rate mortgage loans. By *pricing* a loan, we refer to the rate of interest, fees, and other terms that lenders offer and that borrowers are willing to accept when mortgage loans are made. As a part of the pricing process, we also stress the supply and demand for loanable funds, the role of inflation, and how both affect the rate of interest. As to loan structuring, we review the many innovations in mortgage payment patterns that have evolved from changes in the economic environment.

Another major objective of this chapter is to illustrate techniques for determining the yield to the lender and actual cost to the borrower when various provisions exist in loan agreements. Lenders on real estate commonly include various charges and fees in addition to the interest rate as a condition of making a loan. These charges may include loan discounts, origination fees, prepayment penalties, or prepaid interest. In addition, various amortization or loan repayment schedules can be agreed upon by the borrower and lender to facilitate financing a particular real estate transaction. Because these provisions often affect the cost of borrowing, the methodology used to compute the yield to the lender (cost to the borrower) is stressed in this chapter.

Determinants of Mortgage Interest Rates: A Brief Overview

Changing economic conditions have forced the real estate finance industry to go through an important evolution. These changing conditions now require lenders and borrowers to have a better understanding of the sources of funds used for lending and the nature of how risk, economic growth, and inflation affect the availability and cost of mortgage funds.

When considering the determinants of interest rates on mortgage loans used to finance single family residences, we must also consider the demand and supply of mortgage funds. Most mortgage lenders are intermediaries or institutions that serve as conduits linking flows of funds from savers to borrowers. Borrowers use the savings in the form of mortgage credit. The market rate of **interest** on mortgage loans is established by what borrowers are willing to pay for the use of funds over a specified period of time and what lenders are willing to accept in the way of compensation for the use of such funds. On the demand side of the market, it can be safely said that the demand for mortgage loans is a **derived demand,** or determined by the demand for housing.

The demand for housing is generally determined by the number of households desiring housing, household income, size, age, tastes, preferences for other goods, and the interest rate that must be paid to acquire mortgage credit. Hence, the demand for housing establishes, in large part, the demand for mortgage credit at various rates of interest.

The supply side of the mortgage market is established by what interest rates lenders are willing to accept when providing funds to borrowers. The amount of credit that they are willing to supply is a function of their cost of attracting funds from savers, the cost of managing and originating loans, losses from loan defaults and foreclosures, and, in the case of fixed interest rate loans, potential losses due to unexpected changes in interest rates after a loan is made.

When supplying funds to the mortgage market, lenders also consider returns and the associated risk of loss on alternative investments in relation to returns available on mortgages. Hence, the mortgage market should also be thought of as part of a larger capital market, where lenders and investors evaluate returns available on mortgages and all competing forms of investment and the relative risks associated with each. Should lenders believe that a greater return can be earned by making more mortgage loans (after taking into account the costs and the risk of loss) than would be the case if they invested in corporate bonds or business loans, more funds would be allocated to mortgage loans, and vice versa. Hence, lender decisions to allocate funds to mortgages are also made relative to returns and risk on alternative loans and investment opportunities.

The Real Rate of Interest: Underlying Considerations

When discussing market interest rates on mortgages, we should keep in mind that these interest rates are based on a number of considerations. We pointed out earlier that the supply of funds allocated to mortgage lending in the economy is, in part, determined by the returns and risks on all possible forms of debt and investment opportunities.

One fundamental relationship that is common to investments requiring use of funds in the economy is that they earn at least the **real rate of interest.**[1] This is the minimum rate of interest that must be earned by savers to induce them to divert the use of resources (funds) from present consumption to future consumption. To convince individuals to make this diversion, income in future periods must be expected to increase sufficiently from interest earnings to divert current income from consumption to savings. If expected returns earned on those savings are high enough to provide enough future consumption, adequate amounts of current savings will occur.

Interest Rates and Inflation Expectations

In addition to the real rate of interest, a concern that all investors have when making investment decisions is how *inflation* will affect investment returns. The rate of inflation is of particular importance to investors and lenders making or purchasing loans made at fixed rates of interest over long periods of time. Hence, when deciding

[1]If the reader can visualize an investment portfolio containing investments in all productive activities in the economy based on the weight that any particular activity has to the total value of all productive activity in the economy, the rate of current earnings on such a portfolio would be equivalent to the real rate of interest. Such a rate would also be the rate required by economic units to save rather than consume from current income.

whether to make such commitments, lenders and investors must be convinced that interest rate commitments are sufficiently high to compensate for any expected loss in purchasing power during the period that the investment or loan is outstanding; otherwise, an inadequate real return will be earned. Therefore, a consensus of what lenders and investors expect inflation to be during the time that their loans and investments are outstanding is also incorporated into interest rates at the time investments and loans are made.

To illustrate the relationship between the **nominal interest rate,** or the contract interest rate agreed on by borrowers and lenders, and real rates of interest, suppose a $10,000 loan is made at a nominal or contract rate of 10 percent with all principal and interest due at the end of one year. At the end of the year, the lender would receive $11,000, or $10,000 plus $10,000 times (.10). If the rate of inflation during that year was 6 percent, then the $11,000 received at the end of the year would be worth about $10,377 ($11,000 ÷ 1.06). Thus, although the nominal rate of interest is 10 percent, the *real* rate on the mortgage is just under 4 percent ($377 ÷ $10,000 = 3.77%). Therefore, we conclude that if the lender wanted a 4 percent real rate of interest, the lender would have to charge a nominal rate of approximately 10 percent to compensate for the expected change in price levels due to inflation.[2]

We can summarize by saying that the nominal interest rate on any investment is partially determined by the real interest rate *plus a premium* for the expected rate of inflation. In our example, the real rate of 4 percent plus an inflation premium of 6 percent equals 10 percent. Note that this premium is based on the rate of inflation *expected* at the time that the loan is made. The possibility that inflation will be more or less than expected is one of many risks that lenders and investors must also consider.

Interest Rates and Risk

In addition to expected inflation, lenders and investors are also concerned about various *risks* undertaken when making loans and investments. Lenders and investors are concerned about whether interest rates and returns available on various loans and investments compensate adequately for risk. Alternatively, will a particular loan or investment provide an adequate risk-adjusted return?

Many types of risk could be discussed for various investments, but they are beyond the scope of this book. Consequently, we will focus on risks affecting mortgage loans. Many of these risks are, however, present to greater and lesser degrees in other loans and investments.

Default Risk. When making mortgage loans, one major concern of lenders is the risk that borrowers will default on obligations to repay interest and principal. This is referred to as **default risk,** and it varies with the nature of the loan and the creditworthiness of individual borrowers. The possibility that default may occur means that lenders must charge a premium, or higher rate of interest, to offset possible loan losses. Default risk relates to the likelihood that a borrower's income may fall after a loan is made, thereby jeopardizing the receipt of future mortgage payments.

---

[2]Actually the nominal rate of interest should be (1.06 × 1.04) − 1, or 10.24 percent, if a real rate of 4 percent is desired. For convenience throughout this text, we will *add* the real rate and premium for expected inflation as an approximation to the nominal interest rate. We should point out that the relationship of expected inflation and interest rates has long been a subject of much research. While we show a very simple, additive relationship in our discussion, there may be interaction between real interest rates and inflation. The specific relationship between the two is not known exactly. Hence, the student should treat this discussion at a conceptual or general level of interpretation.

Similarly, a property's value could fall below the loan balance at some future time, which could result in a borrower defaulting on payments and a loss to the lender.

Interest Rate Risk. An additional complication in lending and investing arises from the uncertainty in today's world about the future supply of savings, demand for housing, and future levels of inflation. Thus interest rates at a given point of time can only reflect the market consensus of what these factors are expected to be. Investors and lenders also incur the risk that the interest rate charged on a particular loan may be insufficient should economic conditions change drastically *after* a loan is made. The magnitude of these changes may have warranted a higher interest rate when the loan was made. The uncertainty about what interest rate to charge when a loan is made can be referred to as **interest rate risk.**

For example, **anticipated inflation** may have been 6 percent at the time our $10,000 loan was made. But if *actual* inflation turns out to be 8 percent, this means the interest rate that should have been charged is 12 percent. In this case, we say that the anticipated rate of inflation at the time the loan was made was 6 percent. However, because **unanticipated inflation** of 2 percent occurred, the lender will lose $200 in purchasing power (2 percent of $10,000) because the rate of interest was too low. This does not mean that lenders did not charge the "correct" interest rate *at the time the loan was made*. At that time, the inflation was expected to be 6 percent. Therefore, to be competitive, a 10 percent interest rate had to be charged. However, the additional 2 percent was unanticipated by all lenders in the market. It is unanticipated inflation that constitutes a major component of interest rate risk to all lenders.

The possibility that too low an interest rate was charged at the time the loan was made is a major source of risk to the lender. Hence, a premium for this risk must also be charged or reflected in the market rate of interest. Interest rate risk affects all loans, particularly those that are made with fixed interest rates, that is, where the interest rate is set for a lengthy period of time when the loan is made. Being averse to risk, lenders must charge a premium to incur this risk.

Prepayment Risk. Residential mortgage loans typically allow borrowers to prepay loans without penalty. This gives borrowers the option to prepay the loan. If loans are prepaid when interest rates fall, lenders must forgo the opportunity to earn interest income that would have been earned at the original contract rate. As funds from the prepaid loans are reinvested by lenders, a lower rate of interest will be earned. When interest rates increase, however, the loan is not as likely to be prepaid. The risk that the loan will be prepaid when interest rates fall below the loan contract rate is referred to as **prepayment risk.**

Other Risks. There are additional risks that lenders and investors consider that may vary by type of loan or investment. For example, the *liquidity* or *marketability* of loans and investments will also affect the size of the premium that must be earned. Securities that can be easily sold and resold in well-established markets will require lower premiums than those that are more difficult to sell. This is called **liquidity risk.**

Legislative risk is another risk associated with mortgage lending that also may result in a premium. It can refer to changes in the regulatory environment in which markets operate; for example, regulations affecting the tax status of mortgages, rent controls, state and federal laws affecting interest rates, and so on, are all possibilities that lenders face after making loans for specified periods of time. Lenders must assess the likelihood that such events may occur and be certain that they are compensated for undertaking these risks when loans are made.

A Summary of Factors Important in Mortgage Pricing

We can now see that the interest rate charged on a particular mortgage loan will depend on the real interest rate, anticipated inflation, interest rate risk, default risk, prepayment risk, and other risks. These relationships can be summarized in general as follows:

$$i = r + p + f$$

In other words, when pricing or setting the rate of interest i on a mortgage loan, the lender must charge a premium p sufficiently high to compensate for default and other risks and a premium f that reflects anticipated inflation to earn a real rate of interest r, which is competitive with real returns available on other investment opportunities in the economy. If lenders systematically *underestimate* any of the components in the above equation, they will suffer real economic losses.

Pricing decisions by lenders are rendered complex because mortgage loans are made at fixed interest rates for long periods of time. For example, if we assume that a mortgage loan is to be made with a one-year maturity, the interest rate charged at origination should be based on what the lender expects each of the components discussed above to be during the coming year. More specifically,

$$i_t = r_1 + p_1 + f_1$$

or the mortgage interest rate i at origination (time t) would be based on the lender's expectations of what the real rate of interest, the rate of inflation, and risk premiums (for risks taken in conjunction with making the mortgage loan over and above the level of risk reflected in the real rate of interest) should be for the term of the loan.

Development of Mortgage Payment Patterns

Given the many types of financial instruments that have evolved in recent years, there is no longer a "common" or "standard" mortgage pattern available in residential financing. Prior to the 1970s, changes in mortgage instruments generally occurred gradually. When changes did occur, they were considered major. This pattern of gradual change existed for many years because of a relatively stable economic environment characterized by *very low rates of inflation.* Because of volatility in interest rates and inflation during the 1970s, changes in the design of mortgage loan instruments have now become very common. To gain insight into the structural changes in mortgage loan payment patterns and why they have evolved into the various forms available today, we briefly review the history of this evolutionary process and the economic influences that have forced the many changes that we observe today.

Early Mortgage Lending Patterns

Prior to the 1930s and 1940s, a very common practice in mortgage lending was the requirement of a substantial down payment from borrowers trying to purchase housing. Lenders would limit maximum loan amounts to 50 percent of property value, and the term of the loan would vary. Five years was commonly the maximum term available. Payments were generally "interest only," with the full loan balance due after five years. At that time, it would be expected that another loan would be made, usually for a lesser amount as the borrower saved on his or her own account and applied those savings to reduce the amount of the loan.

Based on the above description, a few relationships should be obvious to the reader. First, mortgage loans were considered very risky and only relatively wealthy individuals could qualify for a mortgage loan because of the large down payment required by the lender. Second, lenders considered the borrower's ability to repay the loan far more important than the collateral value represented by the real estate; consequently, the borrower's ability to earn income and retire the debt "on his own" was critical in the lending decision. Finally, the loan could be called, or not renewed, after five years, which presented the possibility that if economic conditions were unfavorable the borrower could be required to repay the full loan balance at that time.

The Constant Amortization Mortgage Loan (CAM)

After the depression, the U. S. economy experienced a relatively long period of economic prosperity characterized by relatively high real growth and low rates of inflation. As employment and real income increased, lenders began to recognize the possibility that longer-term loans could be made because households were earning greater real incomes. This influence resulted in lower risks to lenders, since households were more likely to repay their debt and housing values were not likely to decline. Hence, lenders were willing to make a longer-run assessment of both the borrower and the collateral when making lending decisions.

Given the economic environment just described, lenders devised the **self-amortizing loan,** a longer-term loan with monthly payments consisting of partial repayment of principal (**amortization** means the process of loan repayment over time). Indeed, a first effort to accomplish this was referred to as the **constant amortization mortgage (CAM)** loan. Payments on CAMs were determined first by computing a constant amount of each monthly payment to be applied to principal. Interest was then computed on the monthly loan balance and added to the monthly amount of amortization. The total monthly payment was determined by adding the constant amount of monthly amortization to interest on the outstanding loan balance. An example of a CAM is as follows: a loan was made for $60,000 for a 30-year term at 12 percent (annual rate compounded monthly); payments were to be made monthly and were to consist of *both* interest and amortization (or reduction of principal), so that the loan would be repaid at the end of 30 years.[3]

Amortization was determined by dividing the number of months or term of the loan (360) into the loan amount ($60,000) resulting in a reduction of principal of $166.67 per month. Interest would be computed on the outstanding loan balance and then be added to amortization to determine the monthly payment. An illustration of the payment pattern and loan balance is shown in Exhibit 4–1.

The computations in Exhibit 4–1 show that the initial monthly payment of $766.67 included amortization of $166.67, plus interest computed on the outstanding loan balance. The total monthly payment would decline each month by a constant amount or $1.67 (.01 × $166.67). The loan payment and balance patterns are shown in Exhibit 4–2.

By instituting the constant amortization mortgage, lenders recognized that in a growing economy, borrowers could partially repay the loan over time, through the

[3]Actually, mortgage interest rates were much lower than 12 percent in the postdepression period, and the term of the loan would have been closer to 20 years. We are using 12 percent interest and a 30-year term so that our later examples will be comparable with this one.

EXHIBIT 4–1 Monthly Payments and Loan Balance (constant amortization loan)

(1) Month	(2) Opening Balance ×	(3) Interest (.12 ÷ 12)	(4) Amortization	(3) + (4) Monthly Payment*	(2) − (4) Ending Balance
1	$60,000.00	$600.00	$166.67	$766.67	$59,833.33
2	59,833.33	598.33	166.67	765.00	59,666.66
3	59,666.66	596.67	166.67	763.34	59,499.99
4	59,499.99	595.00	166.67	761.67	59,333.32
5	59,333.32	593.33	166.67	760.00	59,166.65
6	59,166.65	591.67	166.67	758.34	58,999.98
.	.	.	.	.	.
.	.	.	.	.	.
.	.	.	.	.	.
360	166.67	1.67	166.67	168.34	–0–

*Monthly payments decline by $1.67, or the amount of monthly amortization ($60,000 ÷ 360) times the monthly interest rate (.12 ÷ 12). In this case we have ($60,000 ÷ 360)(12 ÷ 12), or $1.67.

EXHIBIT 4–2 Loan Payment and Balance Patterns (constant amortization loan)

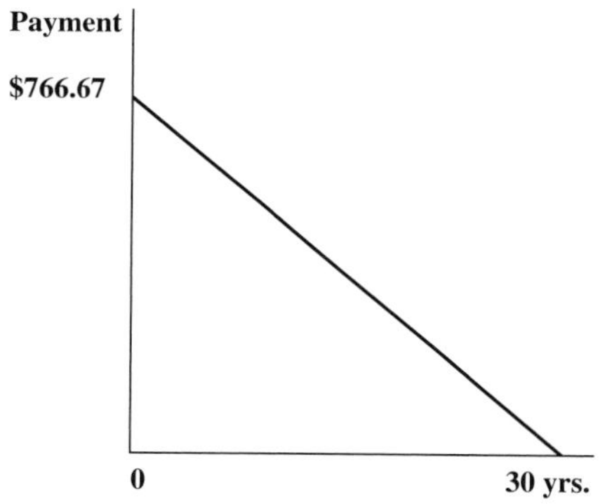

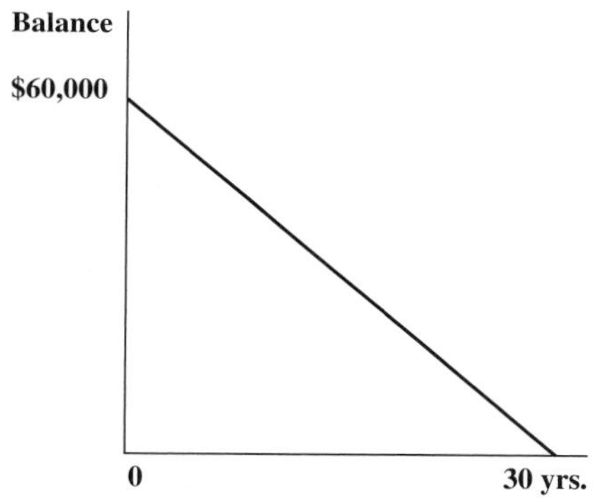

amortization process, as opposed to being left to their own devices to reduce the loan balance when the term of the loan ended, which was the case with the shorter-term, "interest only," loan pattern previously discussed.

While the constant amortization payment pattern was considered an improvement, it was still very conservative because it placed primary emphasis on the amortization of the loan and gave much less recognition to the fact that in an economy with long periods of sustained real growth, a borrower's income was more likely to increase, not decline. Therefore, the prospect that a borrower's ability to repay debt more slowly from an income stream that was expected to grow seemed to be reasonable enough to warrant further modification in mortgage lending instruments. Indeed, the CAM was a relatively short-lived phenomenon and quickly gave rise to the more familiar fully amortizing, constant payment mortgage loan, to which we now turn.

Fully Amortizing, Constant Payment Mortgage Loan (CPM)

The most common loan payment pattern used in real estate finance from the postdepression era to the present, and one which is still very prevalent today, is the fully amortizing, **constant payment mortgage (CPM).** This loan payment pattern is used extensively in financing single family residences and in long-term mortgage lending on income-producing properties such as multifamily apartment complexes and shopping centers. This payment pattern means simply that a level, or constant, monthly payment is calculated on an original loan amount at a fixed rate of interest for a given term. Like the CAM, payment includes interest and *some* (though not a constant) repayment of principal. At the end of the term of the CPM loan, the original loan amount, or **principal,** is completely repaid, or fully amortized, and the lender has earned a fixed rate of interest on the monthly loan balance. However, the amount of amortization varies each month with the CPM loan.

To illustrate how the monthly loan payment calculation is made, we turn to our previous example of a \$60,000 loan made at 12 percent interest for 30 years. What are the constant monthly mortgage payments on this loan, assuming it is to be fully amortized at the end of 30 years? Based on our knowledge of discounting annuities from the preceding chapter, the problem is really no more than finding the present value of an annuity and can be formulated as follows:

$$PV = R \cdot \sum_{t=1}^{n} \left[\frac{1}{1 + \frac{i}{12}} \right]^t$$

where

PV = present value
R = annuity
i = fixed interest rate on mortgage
n = number of months loan will remain outstanding

Calculator Solution

$n = 30 \times 12 = 360$
$i = 12 / 12 = 1$
$PV = -\$60{,}000$
$FV = 0$

Solve for payment:
$PMT = \$617.17$

In this case, we are interested in solving for R, or the constant monthly payment (annuity) that will fully repay the loan amount (PV) and earn the lender 12 percent interest compounded monthly. Using the shorthand notation developed in the previous chapter, we can also determine the monthly payment on the \$60,000 loan as shown in Exhibit 4–3.

Looking again at the calculation of the monthly mortgage payment in Exhibit 4–3, we should give particular attention to the following step in the solution:

$$(MP)\ \text{Monthly payment} = \$60{,}000 \div 97.218331$$

which is also equivalent to

EXHIBIT 4–3 Determining Constant Monthly Payments—Fully Amortized Mortgage

$$\begin{aligned}\text{Monthly payments} \times (\textit{MPVIFA}, 12\%, 360 \text{ mos.}) &= \$60{,}000\\ \text{Monthly payments} \times 97.218331 &= \$60{,}000\\ \text{Monthly payments} &= \$60{,}000 \div 97.218331\\ &= \$617.17\end{aligned}$$

$$\begin{aligned}&= \$60{,}000(1 \div 97.218331)\\ &= \$60{,}000(.010286126)\\ &= \$617.17\end{aligned}$$

Note that dividing \$60,000 by the *IF* 97.218331 is identical to multiplying \$60,000 by (1 ÷ 97.218331), or .010286126. This simple fact enables us to simplify calculations of this kind considerably.

Mortgage Loan Constants. Prior to the widespread use of financial calculators, manually performing multiplication was easier and more convenient than long division, particularly when decimals were involved. Consequently, a series of new interest factors, called **loan constants,** were developed for various interest rates and loan maturities. These loan constants enable a simple multiplication to be made (\$60,000 × .010286126) to determine monthly mortgage payments instead of the more awkward division (\$60,000 ÷ 97.218331). The factor used for multiplication in our example, .010286126, is the loan constant for 360 months at 12 percent interest. In Appendixes A and B, column 6 is titled "Installment to Amortize \$1." This means that a factor multiplied by the original principal gives the payments necessary to amortize (or pay off) principal and earn interest on the unamortized loan balance at a given interest rate over a prescribed number of years. It is customary to refer to this factor as the loan constant in mortgage lending. Factors are provided for loans requiring annual payments (Appendix A) and for monthly payments (Appendix B) in those tables. Given an interest rate and term of a loan, one can find the appropriate loan constant by looking down column 6 and finding the factor in the row corresponding to the number of years for which the loan is to be made. The loan constant can then be multiplied by any beginning loan amount to obtain the monthly mortgage payments necessary to amortize the loan fully by the maturity date.[4]

Exhibit 4–4 provides a sample of monthly loan constants for various interest rates and loan maturities. Returning to our problem of finding the monthly mortgage payment for a \$60,000 loan made at 12 percent for 30 years, we locate the 12 percent column and look down until we find the row corresponding to 30 years where the loan constant is .010286 (rounded).[5]

---

[4]With a financial calculator, the loan constant can be calculated as $n = 360$, $i = .12 \div 12$, $PV = -1$, solve for *PMT*: $PMT = .010286126$.

[5]Because of rounding (to six decimal places), the loan constant is .010286. When we multiply \$60,000 by the rounded constant, we get a monthly payment of \$617.16. The more exact solution is \$617.17. In many problems in future chapters we use the mortgage constants in column 6 in tables in Appendixes A and B. Hence, readers should be aware that small discrepancies between their solutions and ours may occur when financial calculators are used, because calculator solutions may be rounded off to eight or more decimal places. We have attempted to carry out solutions to at least six decimal places.

EXHIBIT 4–4 Monthly Mortgage Loan Constants (column 6, Appendix B)

		Interest Rate			
Years	*Months*	*9%*	*10%*	*11%*	*12%*
5	60	.020758	.021247	.021742	.022244
10	120	.012668	.013215	.013775	.014347
15	180	.010143	.010746	.011366	.012002
20	240	.008997	.009650	.010322	.011011
25	300	.008392	.009087	.009801	.010532
30	360	.008046	.008776	.009523	.010286

Analysis of Principal and Interest. It should be obvious that the sum of all mortgage payments made over the 30-year (360 months) period is $617.17 × 360, or $222,181.20. This amount is far greater than the original loan of $60,000. Why are the total payments so much higher than the amount of the loan? The reason is that interest must be paid monthly over the entire term of the loan on the outstanding loan balance. This relationship is shown in Exhibit 4–5.

The pattern developed in Exhibit 4–5 shows in month 1 a beginning mortgage balance, or loan principal, of $60,000. The monthly payment, which was calculated to be $617.17, includes interest of $600.00 in the first month. Interest is determined by multiplying the beginning loan amount of $60,000 by the annual rate of 12 percent divided by 12 months (.12 ÷ 12) to obtain monthly interest of $600. The difference between $617.17 (column 2) and $600.00 (column 3) gives the amount of loan amortization or principal reduction (column 4) of $17.17 during the first month. The beginning loan balance of $60,000 less the principal reduction in the first month of $17.17 gives the balance at the end of the first month of $59,982.83, which provides the beginning balance for the interest calculation in the second month. This process continues through the 360th month, or to the end of the 30th year, when the loan balance diminishes to zero.

The initial, relatively low principal reduction shown in column 6 in Exhibit 4–5 results in a high portion of interest charges in the early monthly payments. Note that the ending loan balance after the first six months (column 6) is $59,894.36; thus only $105.64 has been amortized from the original balance of $60,000 after six months. Interest paid during the same six-month period totals $3,597.38. The explanation for the high interest component in each monthly payment is that the lender earns an annual 12 percent return (1 percent monthly) on the outstanding monthly loan balance. Because the loan is being repaid over a 30-year period, obviously the loan balance is reduced only very slightly at first and monthly interest charges are correspondingly high. Exhibit 4–5 also shows that the pattern of high interest charges in the early years of the loan reverses as the loan begins to mature. Note that during the last months of the loan, interest charges fall off sharply and principal reduction increases.

Interest, Principal, and Loan Balance Illustrated. Exhibit 4–6 (panel A) illustrates the loan payment pattern over time, by indicating the relative proportions of interest and principal in each monthly payment over the 30-year term of the loan. Exhibit 4–6 (panel B) shows the rate of decline in the loan balance over the same 30-year period. It is clear that the relative share of interest as a percentage of the

EXHIBIT 4–5 Loan Amortization Pattern, $60,000 Loan at 12 Percent Interest for 30 Years

Month	Beginning Loan Balance	Monthly Payment	Interest (.12 ÷ 12)	Amortization*	Ending Loan Balance
1	$60,000.00	$617.17	$600.00	$ 17.17	$59,982.83
2	59,982.83	617.17	599.83	17.34	59,965.49
3	59,965.49	617.17	599.65	17.52	59,947.97
4	59,947.97	617.17	599.48	17.69	59,930.28
5	59,930.28	617.17	599.30	17.87	59,912.41
6	59,912.41	617.17	599.12	18.05	59,894.36
.	.	.	.	.	.
.	.	.	.	.	.
.	.	.	.	.	.
358	1,815.08	617.17	18.15	599.02	1,216.06
359	1,216.06	617.17	12.16	605.01	611.06
360	611.06	617.17	6.11	611.06	-0-

*Amortization increases each month by the factor 1 + i/12; that is, 17.17(1.01) = 17.34, etc.

total monthly mortgage payment declines very slowly at first. Note in panel A that halfway into the term of the mortgage, or after 15 years, interest still makes up $514.24 of the $617.17 monthly payment and principal the difference ($617.17 − $514.24 = $102.93). Further, the loan balance (panel B) is approximately $51,424. Total mortgage payments of $111,090.60 ($617.17 × 180 months) have been made through the 15th year, with approximately $8,576 (or $60,000 − $51,424) of the loan repaid at that point. This pattern reverses with time. Note in panel A that after 25 years, interest makes up only $277.45 of the monthly payment, and the loan balance (panel B) has declined sharply to $27,745.

Constant Payment and Constant Amortization Loans: A Comparison

At this point, it is instructive to compare the payment and loan balance patterns of the constant payment and constant amortization loans. Although the constant amortization mortgage (CAM) was not used for an extensive period of time, the change to the constant payment mortgage (CPM) was a dramatic modification in mortgage lending instruments and the forces that brought this change about, and its impact on borrowers and lenders should be understood.

Exhibit 4–7 compares loan payment patterns (panel A) and mortgage loan balance patterns (panel B) for types of mortgages with the same loan terms. To make this comparison, we consider the same $60,000 loan made at 12 percent for 30 years. A very important pattern shown in panel A is the significant reduction in the initial monthly payment for the CPM compared with the CAM. Recall that if the CAM were made, the initial monthly payment would have been $766.67. If a CPM were made, however, the initial monthly payment would be $617.17. The reason for such a large difference in initial payments ($149.50) is that while the $766.67 CAM payment *declines* through time, the $617.27 CPM remains *level* throughout the life of the loan. It should be stressed, however, that the present value of both payment

EXHIBIT 4–6 Monthly Payment, Principal, Interest, and Loan Balances for a Constant Payment Mortgage

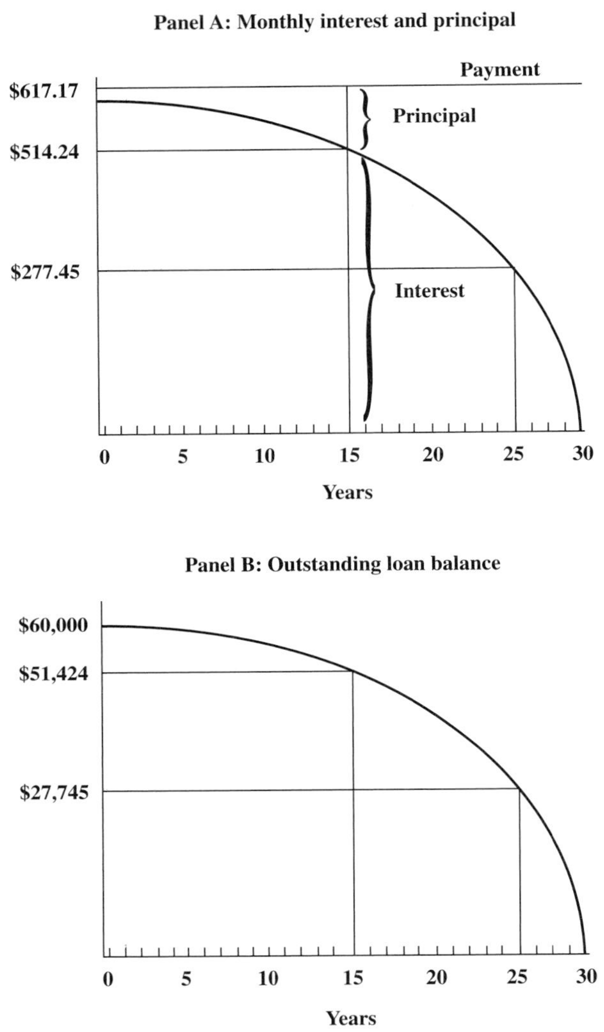

streams is equal to $60,000. This equivalency results from the fact that although the CPM is below that of the CAM for approximately 10 years (dashed line, panel A), beyond the 10th year the CPM payment exceeds the CAM payment. Hence, the present value of the difference between all monthly payments prior to the 10th year (where CAM > CPM) is eventually offset by the present value of monthly payments beyond year 10 (where CPM > CAM for the next 20 years).

Another important pattern emerges in panel B of Exhibit 4–7. The CPM loan balance always exceeds that of the CAM prior to the 360th month, because the rate of amortization for the CPM is far less than that of the CAM. In other words, with a CAM, more of each monthly payment represents amortization of principal compared with the monthly payment of the CPM. Hence, the CPM loan balance is

EXHIBIT 4–7 Comparison of Monthly Payments and Loan Balances (constant payment versus constant amortization loans)

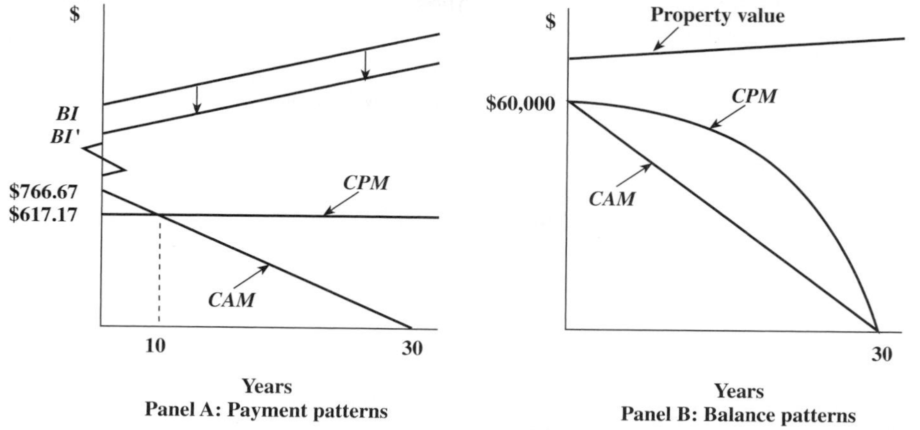

reduced more slowly. This can be seen easily, as the initial monthly interest charge for both loans would be 12 percent times 12 [.01 × ($60,000) = $600]. For the CAM, amortization would be $766.67 − $600 = $166.67, leaving a balance of $59,833.33. In the case of the CPM, we would have $617.17 − $600.00 = $17.17, leaving a balance of $59,982.83. Hence the CPM, with its lower payment, reduces the loan balance more slowly. More total interest will be earned by the CPM lender over the 30-year loan period, although the lender's return will be 12 percent, compounded monthly, in each case.

While the mechanics of the payment and balance patterns are interesting, an *economic interpretation* of the difference in the two mortgage payments and its impact in the marketplace is equally important. Looking back to panel A of Exhibit 4–7, we have already pointed out that the initial monthly payment for a CPM was considerably less compared with that of a CAM. This significant reduction in payment also meant that more households could *qualify* for a constant payment mortgage than for a constant amortization mortgage. This point is illustrated in panel A, which shows that if borrowers were required to have a minimum beginning income of (*BI*) to qualify for a CAM, lenders could require a lower income (*BI*′) if a CPM were made and still have the same cushion or protection against default (or *BI* − *CAM* = *BI*′ − CPM). In this case, borrower income could be lower by $149.50 or an amount equal to the difference in the initial CAM payment of $766.67 and the CAM payment of $617.17. This shift to the CPM pattern, however, was based on the fact that lenders were convinced that borrower incomes would increase and that property values (*PV*, panel B) would either remain steady or increase over time. In an economy experiencing real economic growth with relatively stable prices, increases in income and property values would reduce borrower default risk associated with a CPM loan. Hence, this fundamental change to the CPM pattern occurred after lenders realized the ability of households to meet mortgage payments from *future income*, as well as *current income*, was not as risky as first believed. Further, as real incomes increased, property values were likely to remain higher than the outstanding loan balance over the term of the loan; hence the collateral value of the real estate relative to the more slowly declining mortgage loan balance was considered by lenders to be adequate.

Determining Loan Balances

Because most mortgage loans are repaid before they mature, mortgage lenders must be able to determine the balance on a fully amortized CPM loan at any time. As previously indicated, even though most loans are made for terms of 25 or 30 years, nationwide statistics indicate that households move because of job changes, purchases of different houses, and so on. Hence, mortgages are usually repaid from 8 to 12 years after they are made. Therefore, it is very important to know what the loan balance will be at any time when financing real estate with this type of mortgage.

Calculator Solution

$n = 20 \times 12 = 240$
$i = 12\% \div 12 = 1\%$
$PMT = -\$617.17$
$FV = 0$

Solve for mortgage balance:
$PV = \$56{,}051.02$

To illustrate, let us return to the previous example of the \$60,000 CPM loan made at 12 percent interest for a term of 30 years. After 10 years, the borrower decides to sell the property and to buy another one. To do so, the existing loan must be paid off. How much will have to be repaid to the lender after 10 years? We could construct a loan balance schedule as in Exhibit 4–5; however, this is time-consuming and unnecessary. Finding loan balances for CPMs can be accomplished in two easier ways. First, one can simply find the present value of the \$617.17 payments at the 12 percent contract rate of interest *for the 20 years remaining until maturity*. For example:

$$\begin{aligned} \text{Mortgage balance } (MB) &= \$617.17(MPVIFA, 12\%, 20 \text{ yrs.}) \\ &= \$617.17(90.819416) \\ &= \$56{,}051.02 \end{aligned}$$

The unpaid balance after 10 years is \$56,051.02. This exercise also points out another interesting fact. Because the payments include interest and a reduction of principal each month, by "removing" all interest from all remaining payments, it follows that only the principal can remain. Discounting the \$617.17 monthly payments at an annual rate of 12 percent compounded monthly is a process that really amounts to "removing interest" from the payments. Hence, after "removing interest" by discounting, we ascertain that the unamortized or unpaid balance must be \$56,051.02.

An alternative method for finding mortgage balances at any time in the life of the mortgage is to divide the interest factor for the accumulation of \$1 per period (*FVA*), from column 2 in Appendix B for the year in which the balance is desired, by the accumulation of \$1 per period factor for the original term of the mortgage, and then to subtract that result from 1. The result of this computation is the loan balance expressed as a percentage of the original amount. This is referred to as the **monthly loan balance factor (MLBF).** To illustrate:

$$1 - \frac{(MFVIFA,\ 12\%,\ 10\ \text{yrs.})}{(MFVIFA,\ 12\%,\ 30\ \text{yrs.})} = \%\ \text{loan balance}$$

$$1 - (230.03869 \div 3494.9641) = 93.42\%$$

Calculator Solution

% of loan balance:

$$1 - \frac{FV \text{ at } n = 10 \text{ years}}{FV \text{ at } n = 30 \text{ years}}$$

FV at 10 years:
$n = 120$, $i = 1\%$, $PMT = -1$, $PV = 0$

Solve for FV: \$230.03869

FV at 30 years:
$n = 360$, $i = 1\%$, $PMT = -1$, $PV = 0$

Solve for FV: \$3,494.9641
$1 - (\$230.03869 \div \$3{,}494.9641) = 93.42\%$

This is a more general formula that can be used regardless of the original dollar amount of the loan or payments because it gives a solution in percentage form. In this case, we determine that approximately 93.42 percent, or \$56,052, of the original loan balance (\$60,000) is still outstanding. This solution is nearly the same result that we obtained by discounting. The difference is due to rounding.

Calculator Solution

$PV = -\$60{,}000$
$n = 10 \times 12 = 120$
$i = 12\% \div 12 = 1\%$
$PMT = \$617.17$
Solve for future value:
$FV = \$56{,}050.24$ (difference due to rounding of payment)

Another way of finding a loan balance is to use a financial calculator, most of which have a built-in amortization function. Alternatively, the balance of a loan can be found by calculating the future value (FV) of the payments (PMT) if the initial loan amount is also entered as a present value (PV). The number of periods (n) entered in the calculator is the number of periods (e.g., months) that the loan has already been amortized and the interest rate (i) is the contract rate on the loan.

Loan Closing Costs and Effective Borrowing Costs: Fully Amortized Loans

Loan closing costs are incurred in many types of real estate financing, including residential property, income property, construction, and land development loans. Closing costs can generally be placed in one of three categories: statutory costs, third-party charges, and additional finance charges.

Statutory Costs. At the same time that a mortgage loan is closed between borrower and lender, certain charges for legal requirements pertaining to title transfer, recording of the deed, and other fees required by state and local law are usually charged to the buyer of the property, who is usually the borrower. These **statutory costs** are usually collected at the title closing, which may occur at the same time as the loan closing. In some states the lender may conduct both the loan and title closing. These statutory charges are made for services performed by governmental agencies for the borrower; consequently, they do not provide income to the lender. As such, statutory costs should not be included as additional finance charges because they do not affect the cost of borrowing. These charges would generally have to be paid even if a property was bought for cash and no financing was involved.

Third-Party Charges. Charges for services such as legal fees, appraisals, surveys, past inspection, and title insurance are called **third-party charges.** Like statutory charges, these charges may occur even if the buyer paid cash to buy a property. If a loan is made, charges for these services may be collected by the lender or title company at a title closing, but they are in turn paid out to third parties; hence, they usually do not constitute additional income to the lender and are usually not associated with financing the real estate being purchased.

Additional Finance Charges. Closing costs that do affect the cost of borrowing are additional finance charges levied by the lender. These charges constitute additional income to the lender and must be included as a part of the cost of borrowing. Generally, lenders refer to these additional charges as *loan fees*. Loan fees are intended to cover expenses incurred by the lender for processing loan applications, preparation of loan documentation and amortization schedules, obtaining credit reports, and any other expenses that the lender believes should be recovered from the borrower. Sometimes these charges are itemized separately in the loan closing statement, and sometimes they are grouped under the general category of *loan origination fees*. These fees are generally the "fixed cost" element of originating mortgage loans.

Lenders usually charge these costs to borrowers when the loan is made, or "closed," rather than charging higher interest rates. They do this because if the loan is repaid soon after closing, the additional interest earned by the lender as of the repayment date may not be enough to offset the fixed costs of loan origination. For example, assume that the prevailing interest rate on a $60,000 mortgage is 12 percent and that it will cost the lender $1,000 to close the loan. If the lender chose to increase the interest rate to 12.25 percent to recover these origination costs, an additional $150 (approximately) would be collected during the first year ($60,000 × .0025). If the loan was repaid after the first year, the lender would not recover the full $1,000 in origination costs. This is why lenders attempt to "price" these origination costs separately.

Another charge, which may be itemized separately or included in the overall category of loan origination fees, is **loan discount fees,** or **points.**[6] This charge also represents an additional finance charge, but its primary purpose is to *raise the yield* on a mortgage loan. In the context of real estate lending, loan discounting amounts to a borrower and lender negotiating the terms of a loan based on a certain loan amount. The lender then discounts the loan by charging a fee, which will be deducted from the contract loan to the borrower. Payments made by the borrower, however, are based on the contract amount of the loan. For example, assume a

[6]Lenders in some areas of the country refer to loan discounts as "discount points" or simply "points." In conventional mortgage lending, the borrower usually pays this charge, which adds to financing costs. In this chapter, we are concerned with conventional lending situations where the borrower pays the loan discount as a part of origination fees.

borrower and lender agree on a $60,000 loan at 12 percent interest for 30 years. The lender actually disburses $58,200 to the borrower by including a loan discount charge of 3 percent (points), or $1,800. The borrower is required to repay $60,000 at 12 percent interest for 30 years. However, because the borrower actually receives $58,200 but must repay $60,000 plus interest, it is clear that the actual borrowing cost to the buyer is greater than 12 percent.

Why do pricing practices such as discounting to increase yields exist? Many reasons have been advanced. One reason given by lenders is that mortgage rates tend to be somewhat "sticky" in upward and downward moves. For example, suppose that the prevailing rate is 12 percent and market pressures push rates upward. However, instead of one lender moving the rate to perhaps 12.25 or 12.50 percent, the lender may still quote 12 percent as the loan rate but charge loan discount points.

Many mortgage loans are originated by lenders and then sold to investors. These loans may be sold to yield the investor the same rate of interest that the lender expects to charge borrowers. However, if interest rates rise before the date that the loan is originated but after the date on which the lender and investor agree on the yield on mortgages to be sold, the lender will add discount points to profit from the increase in interest rates. In this case, the loan will be originated at an interest rate equal to the yield promised to the investor, and the lender will earn the discount points.

Another reason for loan discount fees is that lenders believe that, in this way, they can better price the loan to the *risk* they take. For example, in the beginning of this chapter we referred to the risk premium component (p) of the interest rate. However, the risk for some individual borrowers is slightly higher than it is for others. Further, these loans may require more time and expense to process and control. Hence, discount points may be charged by the lender (in addition to origination fees) to compensate for the slightly higher risk.

The practice of using loan origination and discount fees has historically prevailed throughout the lending industry. It is important to understand (1) that these charges increase borrowing costs and (2) how to include them in computing effective borrowing costs on loan alternatives when financing any real estate transaction.

Loan Fees and Borrowing Costs. To illustrate loan fees and their effects on borrowing costs in more detail, consider the following problem: A borrower would like to finance a property for 30 years at 12 percent interest. The lender indicates that an origination fee of 3 percent of the loan amount will be charged to obtain the loan. What is the actual interest cost of the loan?

We structure the problem by determining the amount of the origination fee [.03 × ($60,000) = $1,800]. Second, we know that the monthly mortgage payments based on $60,000 for 30 years at 12 percent will be $617.17. Now we can determine the effect of the origination fee on the interest rate being charged as follows:

Contractual loan amount	$60,000
Less: Origination fee	1,800
Net cash disbursed by lender	$58,200
Amount to be repaid:	
Based on $60,000 contractual loan amount, $617.17 for 30 years.	

In other words, the amount actually disbursed by the lender will be $58,200, but the repayment will be made on the basis of $60,000 plus interest at 12 percent compounded monthly, in the amount of $617.17 each month. Consequently, the lender will earn a yield on the $58,200 actually disbursed, which must be greater than 12 percent. To solve for the effective interest cost on the loan, we proceed as follows:

$$\text{Monthly payment} \times (MPVIFA, ?\%, 30 \text{ yrs.}) = \text{Amount disbursed}$$
$$\$617.17 \times (MPVIFA, ?\%, 30 \text{ yrs.}) = \$58{,}200$$
$$(MPVIFA, ?\%, 30 \text{ yrs.}) = \$58{,}200 \div \$617.17$$
$$(MPVIFA, ?\%, 30 \text{ yrs.}) = 94.301408$$

Using the procedure for solving yields on investment annuities, we see that this calculation results in an interest factor of 94.301408. We know that the loan will be outstanding for a period of 30 years. Therefore, to find the actual interest cost of this loan we want to locate an interest factor in column 5 for 30 years in Appendix B that equals 94.301408. A close inspection of Appendix B reveals that the interest factor that we are looking for falls between factors in the 12 percent and 13 percent tables.

Using a financial calculator, we can calculate the **effective interest cost** of the loan, assuming it is outstanding until maturity, as 12.41. This yield is obviously higher than the 12 percent contract, or nominal, rate of interest specified in the note or mortgage.

Calculator Solution

$$n = 30 \times 12 = 360$$
$$PMT = -\$617.17$$
$$PV = \$58{,}200$$
$$FV = 0$$

Solve for yield:

$$i\ (\text{monthly}) = 1.034324\%$$
$$i\ (\text{annualized}) = 12.41\%$$

This computation forms the basis for a widely used rule of thumb in real estate finance; that is, for every 2 percentage points in the origination fee charged the borrower, the effective cost to the borrower, or investment yield earned by the lender, increases by approximately one-fourth of a percent above the contract rate. Note that in our solution, we obtained an effective rate of 12.41 percent, versus 12.375 percent using the approximation. While this estimate is close to the yield calculated in one example, we have assumed that the loan remains outstanding until maturity. However, most loans on the average are "prepaid" or paid off long before maturity. Hence, this rule of thumb, while helpful, generally provides only an estimate of the effective cost (yield) of most mortgage loans.[7]

Truth-in-Lending Requirements and the Annual Percentage Rate

Because of problems involving loan fees and the potential abuse by some lenders of charging high fees to unwary borrowers, Congress passed a federal Truth-in-Lending Act.[8] As a result of this legislation, the lender must disclose to the borrower the **annual percentage rate (*APR*)** being charged on the loan. Calculation of the *APR* is generally made in the manner shown in the preceding example. The *APR* in this

[7]This rule of thumb will become very inaccurate if the payoff period is very short relative to the maturity and when the level of interest rates increases.

[8]See Regulation Z of the Federal Reserve Board, 12 C.F.R., sec. 226, as amended.

case would be disclosed at closing to the borrower by rounding the effective interest rate up or down to the nearest one-eighth of a percent. In this case, the 12.41 percent effective rate would be rounded to the nearest one-eighth of a percent and disclosed to be 12.375 percent. The *APR*, then, does reflect origination fees and discount points and treats them as additional income or yield to the lender regardless of what costs, if any, the fees are intended to cover.[9]

Loan Fees and Early Repayment: Fully Amortized Loans

An important effect of loan fees and early loan repayment must now be examined in terms of the effect on interest cost. We will show in this section that when loan fees are charged and the loan is paid off before maturity, the effective interest cost of the loan increases even further than when the loan is repaid at maturity.

To demonstrate this point, we again assume our borrower obtained the $60,000 loan at 12 percent for 30 years and was charged an $1,800 (3 percent) loan origination fee. At the end of *five years*, the borrower decides to sell the property. The mortgage contains a due-on-sale clause; hence, the loan balance must be repaid at the time the property is sold. What will be the effective interest cost on the loan as a result of both the origination fee and early loan repayment?

To determine the effective interest cost on the loan, we first find the outstanding loan balance after five years to be $58,598.16. To solve for the yield to the lender (cost to the borrower), we proceed by finding the rate at which to discount the monthly payments of $617.17 *and* the lump-sum payment of $58,598.16 after five years so that the present value of both equals $58,200, or the amount actually disbursed by the lender.

This presents a new type of discounting problem. We are dealing with an annuity in the form of monthly payments for five years *and* a loan balance, or single lump-sum receipt of cash, at the end of five years. To find the yield on this loan, we proceed as follows:

$$\$58{,}200 = \$617.17(MPVIFA, ?\%, 5 \text{ yrs.}) + \$58{,}598.16(MPVIF, ?\%, 5 \text{ yrs.})$$

This formulation simply says that we want to find the interest rate (?%) that will make the present value of both the $617.17 monthly annuity and the $58,598.16 received at the end of five years equal to the amount disbursed. Take special note that the two interest factors used in the above formulation are different. One factor, *MPVIF*, is used to discount the single receipt or loan balance. The other factor, *MPVIFA*, will be used to discount the payments, or monthly annuity. Hence, we cannot use the method of dividing the disbursement by the monthly annuity to find an interest factor, as we did above, because we also have the loan balance of $58,598.16 to take into account. How do we solve this problem? We find the answer by trial and error; that is, we must begin choosing interest rates and then select the interest factors for five years corresponding to (*MPVIFA*) in column 5 and (*MPVIF*) in column 4. We then multiply these factors by the cash payments and determine whether the calculated present value is equal to $58,200. When we have found the interest rate that gives us a present value of $58,200, we have the solution we want.

[9]Generally the *APR* disclosed to the borrower is the effective interest rate computed under the assumption that the loan will be outstanding until maturity rounded to the *nearest* one-eighth percent. If the reader desires greater accuracy in these computations, consult *Computational Procedures Manual for Supplement 1 to Regulation Z of the Federal Reserve Board: Calculator Instructions* (Office of the Comptroller of the Currency, February 1978).

From the above analysis, we can conclude that the actual yield (or actual interest cost) that we have computed to be approximately 12.82 percent is higher than both the contract interest rate of 12 percent and the 12.41 percent yield computed assuming that the loan was outstanding until maturity. This is true because the $1,800 origination fee is earned over only 5 years instead of 30 years, which is equivalent to earning a higher rate of compound interest on the $58,200 disbursed. Hence, when this additional amount earned is coupled with the 12 percent interest being earned on the monthly loan balance, this increases yield to 12.82 percent.[10]

Calculator Solution

1. Solve for remaining balance:

$$n = 25 \times 12 = 300$$
$$i = 12\% \div 12 = 1\%$$
$$PMT = -\$617.17$$
$$FV = 0$$

Solve for remaining balance:

$$PV = \$58,598.16$$

2. Next, solve for the interest payment, holding a 30-year loan, for 5 years, and discounted by the loan origination fee:

$$n = 5 \times 12 = 60$$
$$PMT = -\$617.17$$
$$PV = \$58,200$$
$$FV = \$58,598.16$$

Solve for yield:

$$i \text{ (monthly)} = 1.069\%$$
$$\text{Annual interest} = 1.069\% \times 12 = 12.82\%$$

Another point is that the 12.82 percent yield is not reported to the borrower as the "annual percentage rate" required under the Truth-in-Lending Act. The reason is that neither the borrower nor lender knows for certain that the loan will be repaid ahead of schedule. Therefore, 12.375 percent will still be reported as the *APR* and 12 percent will be the contract rate, although the actual yield to the lender in this case will be 12.82 percent. It should be remembered that the annual percentage rate under truth-in-lending requirements never takes into account early repayment of loans. The *APR* calculation takes into account origination fees, but always assumes the loan is paid off at maturity.

Relationship between Yield and Time. Based on the preceding discussion, we can make some general observations about the relationship of mortgage yields and the time during which mortgages are outstanding. The first observation is that the effective interest cost on a mortgage will always be equal to the contract rate of interest when no finance charges are made at the time of loan origination or repayment. This follows because, as we saw in Exhibit 4–6, the level payment pattern

[10]If the loan is repaid in less than one year, the yield becomes larger and approaches infinity should the loan be repaid immediately after closing.

assures the lender of earning only a given annual rate of interest, compounded monthly, on the monthly outstanding loan balance. Hence the outstanding mortgage balance can be repaid at any time, and the lender's yield (borrower's cost) will not be affected. It will be equal to the contract rate of interest.

The second observation is that if origination or financing fees are charged to the borrower, the following occurs: (1) the effective yield will be higher than the contract rate of interest, and (2) the yield will increase as repayment occurs sooner in the life of the mortgage. These relationships can be explained by referring to Exhibit 4–8, where the two curves, *A* and *B* represent the mortgage yield pattern under two assumptions. Curve *A* represents the effective yield, or cost, when no financing fees are charged to the borrower. In our previous example, the yield would remain at 12 percent, equal to the contract rate of interest regardless of when the loan is repaid; hence, the horizontal line is over the range of 0 to 30 years. Curve *B* represents a series of loan yields computed under the assumptions that a 3 percent origination fee is charged to the borrower and that the loan is prepaid in various years prior to maturity. In our example, we note that the yield earned by the borrower is 15.26 percent if the loan is repaid one year after closing and that it diminishes and eventually equals 12.41 percent after 30 years. Hence, we can again conclude that if financing fees are charged to the buyer, the effective yield to the lender (cost to the borrower) can range from one that is extremely high if prepaid, say, after one year (the yield in that case would be approximately 15.26 percent) to a yield that would be considerably lower if repaid at maturity, or 12.41 percent. If a borrower knows when he or she expects to repay a loan, this method of computing the effective borrowing cost

EXHIBIT 4–8 Relationship between Mortgage Yield and Financing Fees at Various Repayment Dates

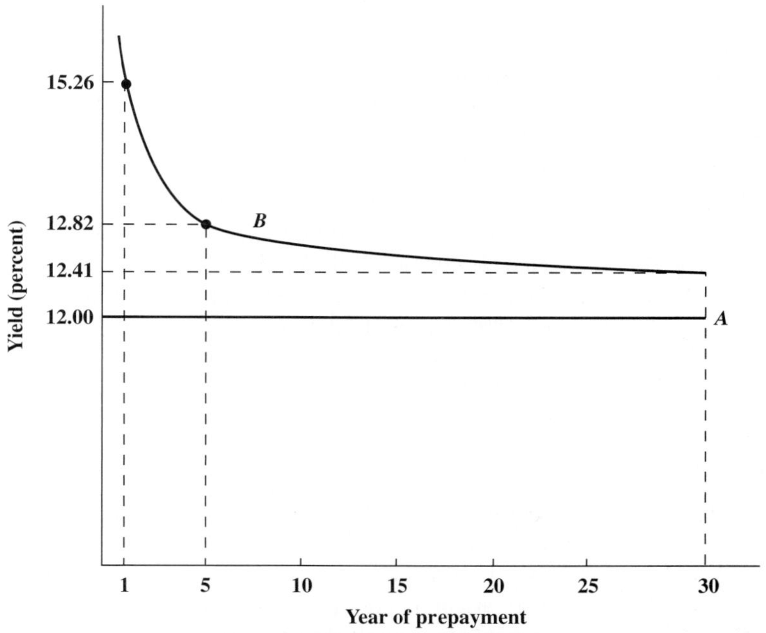

should be used. This is particularly important if the borrower is comparing alternative loans with different terms.

Prepayment Penalties. Many borrowers mistakenly take for granted that a loan can be prepaid in part or in full anytime before the maturity date. This is not the case; if the mortgage note is silent on this matter, the borrower may have to negotiate the privilege of early repayment with the lender. However, many mortgages provide explicitly that the borrower can pay a **prepayment penalty** should the borrower desire to prepay the loan.

One rationale for a prepayment penalty is that the lender may be trying to recover a portion of loan origination costs not charged to the borrower at closing. This may have been done by the lender to compete for the loan by making initial closing costs lower for the borrower. Another reason for prepayment penalties is that the lender has agreed to extend funds for a specified time, 30 years in our present example. Early payment from the lender's view may represent an unanticipated inflow of funds that may or may not be readily reinvested in periods when mortgage rates are stable or are expected to decline. However, if interest rates undergo a sustained increase over long periods of time, lenders usually welcome early repayments since they may be able to loan out funds again at higher rates of interest.

Another reason for prepayment penalties is that they are not included in the computation of the *APR*; hence, they are not included in the *APR* disclosure to the borrower. Borrowers may not be able to determine the effect of these penalties on borrowing costs and therefore the penalties represent a technique lenders use to increase yields. Some states have begun prohibiting the enforceability of prepayment penalties to individuals financing residences if the loan has been outstanding more than some specified minimum number of years. Also, in areas where penalties are allowed, lenders will waive them if the buyer of a property agrees to originate a new loan with the same lender.

Because of the use of prepayment penalties, we want to know the effective mortgage loan yield (interest cost) when both a loan discount fee and a prepayment penalty are charged on the loan. To illustrate, we consider both the effects of the 3 percent loan discount and a 3 percent prepayment penalty on the outstanding loan balance for the $60,000, 30-year loan with a contract interest rate of 12 percent used in the preceding section. We assume the loan is the effective interest cost to the borrower (yield to the lender). To solve for the yield, mortgage funds actually disbursed in this case will be $60,000 minus the origination fee of $1,800, or $58,200. Taking the loan discount fee into account, we want to find the discount rate which, when used to discount the series of monthly payments of $617.17 plus the outstanding loan balance of $58,598.16 and the prepayment penalty of $1,758 (3 percent of $58,598.16), or a total of $60,356, will result in a present value equal to the amount of funds actually disbursed, $58,200.

This is done as follows:

$$\$58{,}200 = \$617.17(MPVIFA, ?\%, 5 \text{ yrs.}) + \$60{,}356(MPVIF, ?\%, 5 \text{ yrs.})$$

Following the same thinking used in the previous section, we note that a 3 percent origination fee and a 3 percent prepayment penalty are unlikely to increase the yield of this loan beyond 14 percent. Using a financial calculator, we find the answer to be 13.25 percent. With a 3 percent origination fee, early payment in the fifth year, and a 3 percent prepayment penalty, we see that the effective yield on the loan will increase to about 13.25 percent.

Calculator Solution

$$n = 5 \times 12 = 60$$
$$PMT = -\$617.17$$
$$PV = \$58{,}200$$
$$FV = -\$60{,}356$$

Solve for effective yield:
i (monthly) = 1.10425%
Annual interest = 13.25%

In this case, the *APR* will still be disclosed at 12.375 percent, which reflects the loan discount only, not the prepayment penalty, and assumes the loan is repaid at the end of 30 years. The actual yield computed here of 13.25 percent is a marked difference from both the loan contract rate of 12 percent and the disclosed *APR* of 12.375 percent.

Charging Fees to Achieve Yield, or Pricing CPMs

In the preceding examples, we have developed the notion of the effective borrowing costs and yield from a given set of loan terms. However, we should consider how these are determined by lenders when "pricing" a loan. As we discussed earlier in the chapter, lenders generally have alternatives in which they can invest funds. Hence, they will determine available yields on those alternatives for given maturities and weigh those yields and risks against yields and risks on mortgage loans. Similarly, competitive lending terms established by other lenders establish yields that managers must consider when establishing loan terms. By continually monitoring alternatives and competitive conditions, management establishes loan offer terms for various categories of loans, given established underwriting and credit standards for borrowers. Hence a set of terms designed to achieve a competitive yield on categories of loans representing various ratios of loan-to-property value (70 percent loans, 80 percent loans, etc.) are established for borrowers who are acceptable risks. These terms are then revised as competitive conditions change.

If, based on competitive yields available on alternative investments of equal risk, managers of a lending institution believe that a 13 percent yield is competitive on 80 percent mortgages with terms of 30 years and expected repayment periods of 10 years, how can they set terms on all loans made in the 80 percent category to ensure a 13 percent yield? Obviously, one way is to price all loans being originated at a contract rate of 13 percent. However, management may also consider pricing loans at 12 percent interest and charging either loan fees or prepayment penalties or both to achieve the required yield. Why would lenders do this? Because (1) they have fixed origination costs to recover, and (2) competitors may still be originating loans at a contract rate of 12 percent.

To illustrate how fees for all loans in a specific category can be set, we consider the following formula:

$$ND = MLC(MPVIFA, 13\%, 10 \text{ yrs.}) + MLBF(MPVIF, 13\%, 10 \text{ yrs.})$$

where

MLC = Monthly loan constant factor at 12 percent contract rate for 30 years
$MLBF$ = Loan balance factor for a 30-year loan, after 10 years, at 12 percent
ND = Net disbursement (unknown) as percent of total loan

Substituting values for a 13 percent, 30-year loan in the preceding expression, we have

$$\begin{aligned} ND &= .010286(66.974419) + .9342(.27444) \\ &= .9453 \end{aligned}$$

The result $ND = .9453$ means that the net disbursement at loan closing should be 94.53 percent, or 94.5 percent (rounded), of the loan amount. Therefore if the loan is priced by offering terms of 12 percent interest and a 5.5 percent origination fee (100% − 94.5%) and the loan is repaid in 10 years, management will have its 13 percent yield.

The above formula can be used for any loan category for which a solution is desired. The application was used here for the 80 percent loan category. Note that the numerical value of 80 percent does not appear in the formula. Hence, the formula can be used for all 13 percent, 30-year loans.

Inflation and Mortgage Pricing Problems

The fully amortizing, constant payment mortgage has been the most widely used mortgage instrument in the United States for some time. In more recent times, particularly during the 1970s and early 1980s, inflation and its effect on this "standard" mortgage instrument have caused problems for both lenders and borrowers. Because of these problems, a number of different mortgage instruments have been proposed as alternatives to the standard mortgage instrument. In this section, we outline the problems that inflation has brought for both borrowers and lenders who have relied on the standard mortgage instrument. Also included is a detailed description of the graduated payment mortgage. This mortgage is also a fixed interest rate mortgage and has been used in place of the constant payment mortgage, particularly during periods of rising interest rates.

Effects on Lenders and Borrowers

How does inflation relate to mortgage lending and cause difficulty for lenders and borrowers desiring to make constant payment loans with fixed interest rates? The answer to this question can be easily illustrated. Let's assume initially that a \$60,000 loan is made at a time when no inflation is expected. The loan is expected to be outstanding for a 30-year period. Because there is no inflation, an inflation premium (f) is not required; hence, the lender will earn a return equivalent to the riskless interest rate (r), plus a premium for risk (p) over the period of the loan.[11] We assume that the interest rate charged under such assumptions would be 4 percent, representing a 3 percent real rate of interest and a risk premium of 1 percent over the period of the loan. Assuming a constant payment, fixed interest rate loan made in an inflationless environment, the lender would collect constant payments of approximately \$286 per month, based on the loan constant for 4 percent and 30 years. This amount is shown in Exhibit 4–9 as a straight line (RP) over the life of the loan and represents the series of *constant real payments* necessary to earn the lender a 3 percent fixed real return plus a 1 percent risk premium each year that the loan is outstanding.

[11] Actually the interest rate charged will be related to the expected repayment period that may occur before maturity. However, this will not alter the concept being illustrated. The figures chosen here are arbitrary. Some studies indicate that the real rate of interest has historically been in the 1 to 3 percent range and risk premium on mortgages in the 2 to 3 percent range.

EXHIBIT 4–9 Real and Nominal Values of Mortgage Payments

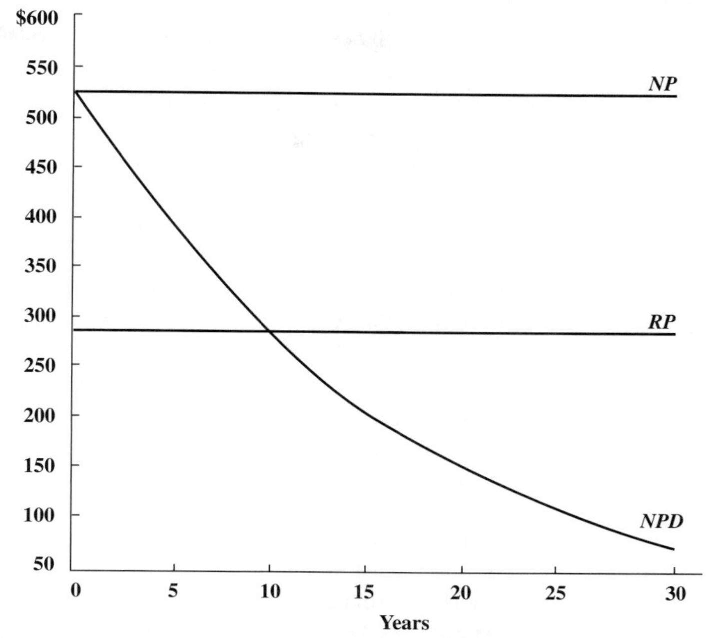

NP = Nominal payments.
RP = Real payments.
NPD = Nominal payments deflated.

Now assume that the same loan is made in an inflationary environment where a 6 percent rate of inflation is expected to prevail during each year that the loan is outstanding. The interest rate on the mortgage loan would now have to increase to approximately 10 percent for the lender to earn the same real return. This includes the base rate of 4 percent earned when no inflation was expected, plus an inflation premium of 6 percent.[12] Given that the standard mortgage instrument is to be used, the lender must now collect approximately $527 a month (rounded). This new payment pattern is shown in Exhibit 4–9 as the horizontal line labeled *NP*, representing a constant series of nominal payments received over the term of the loan. Hence, included in the series of nominal payments are amounts that will provide the lender with a 4 percent basic rate of interest representing a real return and risk premium, plus a 6 percent inflation premium over the 30-year loan term.

In our example, an expected inflation rate of 6 percent caused an 84 percent rise in the monthly mortgage payments from $286 to $527, or $241 per month. Why is there such a significant increase in these monthly payments? The reason can be easily seen by again examining curve *NPD* in Exhibit 4–9. This curve represents the real value of the monthly payments that the lender will receive over the 30-year loan period. It is determined by "deflating" the $527 nominal monthly payments by the

[12]The nominal interest rate would actually be (1 + .04)(1 + .06) − 1 or 10.24 percent. However, as indicated earlier, we use 10 percent to simplify calculations.

rate of inflation.[13] The *NPD* curve is important because the lender, realizing that inflation is going to occur, expects that the constant stream of $527 payments to be received over time will be worth less and less because of lost purchasing power. Hence, to receive the full 10 percent interest necessary to leave enough for a 4 percent real return and risk premium over the life of the loan, more "real dollars" must be collected in the *early* years of the loan (payments collected toward the *end* of the life of the mortgage will be worth much less in purchasing power).

To illustrate, let's examine the deflated or real value of the $527 payments collected each month, as represented by the curve *NPD*. Note that for about the first 10 years of the loan life, the real value of these payments is greater than those for the 4 percent loan. However, after 10 years, the real value of these payments falls below the payments required on the 4 percent loan. However, even though the two payment streams differ, the real value of the nominal payment stream is equal to the required real payments at 4 percent, or $NPD = RP$. This means that from the stream of nominal $527 monthly receipts, the lender will ultimately earn the same real value as a stream of $286 payments or 4 percent on investment after deflating the nominal payments by the inflation rate. However, in order to earn the same real interest rate, the real value of the payment stream (*NPD*) must be greater than *RP* in the early years, since it will fall below *RP* in the later years. This relationship is referred to as *tilting* the real payment stream in the early years to make up for the loss in purchasing power in later years.

This **tilt effect** also has a considerable impact on the borrower. Recall that with no inflation the borrower faced a $286 payment; however, with inflation a $527 monthly payment is necessary. When the loan is first originated, the difference in the two payments is about $241 per month and represents an additional amount of real or current dollars that the borrower must allocate from current real *income* to meet mortgage payments.

Over time, this burden moderates. For example, by the end of the first year, the real value of the $527 payments deflated by the 6 percent rate of inflation would be about $497 per month and the borrower's real income will have increased by 3 percent, or by the real rate of growth in the economy. At that time, the borrower will have more real income to pay declining real mortgage payments. The important point is that even though the borrower's income is increasing both in real and nominal terms each year, it is not enough to offset the tilt effect in the early years of a loan. From this analysis, it becomes apparent from Exhibit 4–9 why it is so difficult for first-time home buyers to qualify for constant payment, fixed interest rate loans during periods of rising inflation. With the general rate of inflation and growth in the economy, borrower incomes will grow gradually or on a year-by-year basis. However, as expected inflation increases, lenders must build estimates of the full increase into current interest rates "up front," or *when the loan is made*. This causes a dramatic increase in required real monthly payments relative to the borrower's current real income.

One final observation about the tilt effect is that, as the rate of inflation increases, the tilt effect increases. In Exhibit 4–10, we show the effect of an increase in inflation from 6 percent in our previous example to 8 percent per year. Note that nominal monthly payments increase from $527 to $617 per month, the latter figure based on an increase in the mortgage interest rate to 12 percent. The impact of the tilt effect on

[13] Deflating an income stream is done by computing the monthly inflation factor $.06 \div 12$, or .005, and multiplying $\$527(1 \div 1.005)^1$ in the first month, $\$527(1 \div 1.005)^2$ in the second month, and so on, until the end of year 30.

EXHIBIT 4–10 Relationship between Real and Nominal Payments at Various Rates of Inflation

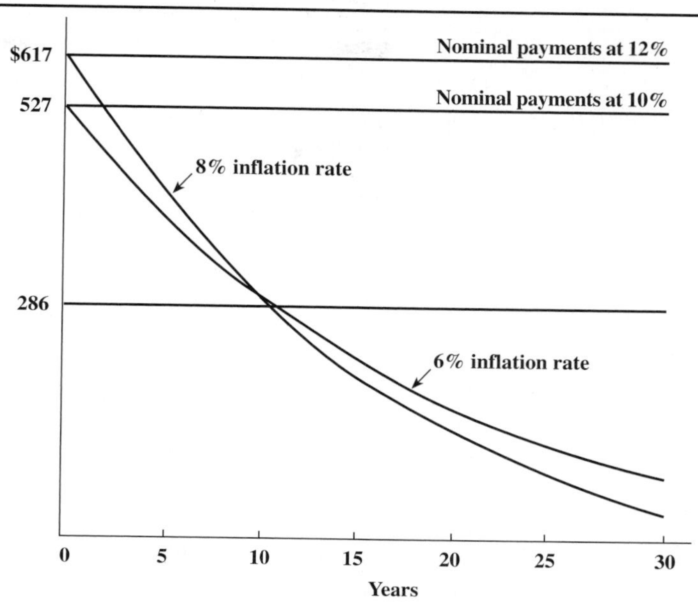

a constant payment loan when inflation is expected to be 8 percent can be seen relative to the effect when inflation was expected to be 6 percent. Note that when the $617 monthly payments are deflated at 8 percent (*NPD @ 8%*) for inflation, the burden of the real payments to be made by the borrower increases relative to the real payments required when inflation was 6 percent in the early years of the loan. The curve corresponding to monthly payments deflated at 8 percent indicates that the real value of monthly payments on the 12 percent mortgage exceeds the real value of payments on the 10 percent mortgage for about the first 10 years of the loan term. This is true even though the lender will earn a 4 percent real return on both mortgages after inflation. Further, if we again assume that the "average" borrower's real income will increase by 3 percent, regardless of the rate of inflation, as inflation increases from 6 percent to 8 percent it is clear that the borrower will have to allocate even more current real income to mortgage payments. This indicates that in the early years of the mortgage, the burden of the tilt effect on borrowers increases as the rate of inflation increases. This increased burden is due solely to (1) the nature of the mortgage instrument, that is, a constant payment, fixed interest rate mortgage, and (2) the rate of inflation. Further, the tilt effect makes it even more difficult for borrowers to qualify for loans based on their current income and make payments from current income.

The Graduated Payment Mortgage (GPM)

In an attempt to deal with the problem of inflation and its impact on mortgage interest rates and monthly payments, lenders have instituted new mortgage instruments. One such instrument is the **graduated payment mortgage (GPM).** The objective of a GPM is to provide for a series of mortgage payments that are *lower* in the initial years of the loan than they would be with a standard mortgage loan. GPM payments then gradually increase at a predetermined rate as borrower incomes are expected to rise over time. The payment pattern thus offsets the tilt effect

EXHIBIT 4–11 Comparison of GPM Payments and Standard Constant Payments ($60,000, 30-year maturity, various interest rates)

	Interest Rate				
	10%	*11%*	*12%*	*13%*	*14%*
Constant Payments	$526.54	$571.39	$617.17	$663.72	$710.94
GPM payments graduated (7.5% annually)					
1	$400.22	$436.96	$474.83	$513.71	$553.51
2	430.24	469.73	510.44	552.24	595.03
3	462.51	504.96	548.72	593.66	639.65
4	497.19	542.83	589.87	638.18	687.63
5	534.48	583.55	634.11	686.04	739.20
6–30	574.57	627.31	681.67	737.50	794.64

to some extent, reducing the burden faced by households when meeting mortgage payments from current income in an inflationary environment.[14]

An example of the payment pattern for the graduated payment mortgage is illustrated in Exhibit 4–11. The exhibit contains information on how payments should be structured for the 30-year, $60,000 loan used in our previous examples. GPMs can have a number of plans allowing for differences in initial payment levels, rates of graduation, and graduation periods.[15] Exhibit 4–11 contains information on one of the more popular payment plans in use today. This plan allows for a 7.5 percent rate of graduation in monthly payments over 5 years, after which time the payments level off for the remaining 25 years. Computing initial payments on a mortgage of this kind is complex.

Looking at the information contained in Exhibit 4–11, we see that for a standard constant payment mortgage (CPM) loan of $60,000 originated at 12 percent for 30 years, the required constant monthly payments would be $617.17. A GPM loan made for the same amount and interest rate, where the monthly payments are increased (graduated) at the end of each year at a predetermined rate of 7.5 percent, begins with an initial payment of approximately $474.83. This initial payment will then increase by 7.5 percent per year to an amount equal to $681.67 at the beginning of year 6 and will remain constant from that point until the end of year 30. Compared with $617.17 in the constant payment mortgage, GPM payments are initially lower by $142.34 in the first year. The difference becomes smaller over time. The graduated payment level reaches approximately the same payment under the standard mortgage between the fourth and fifth years after origination. GPM payments exceed constant payments by $64.50 ($681.67 − $617.17) beginning in year 6. GPM payments then remain at the $681.67 level for the remaining 25 years of the loan term.

Exhibit 4–12 provides a comparison of payment patterns for a graduated payment mortgage (GPM), a constant payment mortgage (CPM), and a constant amortization mortgage (CAM). GPM payments are based on the 7.5 percent

[14]The Federal Housing Administration initiated the first widely accepted graduated payment plan under its Section 245 program. For more detail, see the *HUD Handbook 4240.2* rev., Graduated Payment Mortgage Program, Sect. 245. These handbooks are available from HUD regional insuring offices.

[15]For a current update on plans available, contact a regional insuring office of the FHA, which is a division of the Department of Housing and Urban Development.

EXHIBIT 4–12 Comparison of Mortgage Payment Patterns (Loan amount = $60,000, Maturity = 30 years, Interest 12% *GPM* add: 7.5% graduation rate, 5 years)

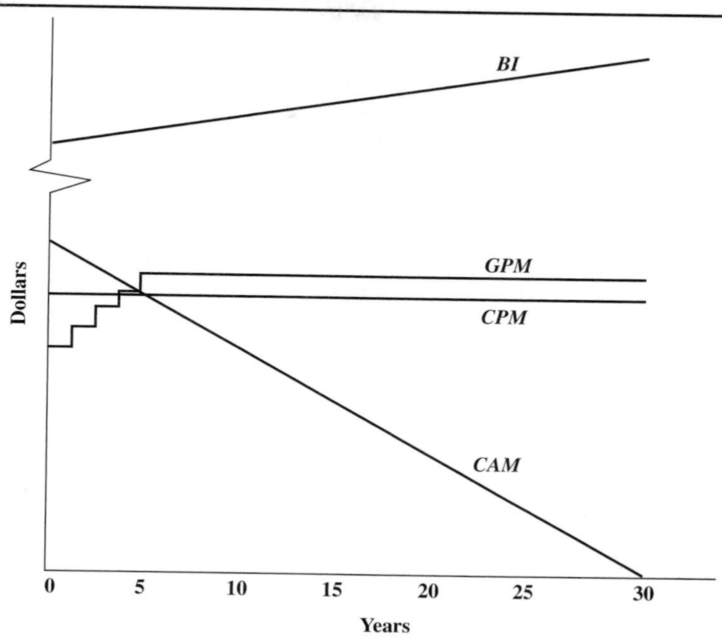

graduation plan. All three loans are assumed to be originated for $60,000 at 12 percent interest for 30 years. Note that the GPM is below that of the CPM for approximately five years, at which point the GPM payments begin to exceed CPM payments. The reason for this pattern should be obvious. Under either payment plan, the yield to the lender must be an annual rate of 12 percent compounded monthly, assuming no origination fees, penalties, and so on. Therefore, because the GPM payments are below those of the CPM in the early years, GPM payments must eventually exceed the level payment on the CPM loan to "make up" for the lower payments on the GPM in the early years. Hence, if the borrower chooses the GPM in our example, the payments will exceed those of a standard CPM mortgage from years 6 to 30.

The advantages of the GPM program are obvious from the borrower's standpoint. The initial payment level under the GPM plan shown in Exhibit 4–12 is significantly lower than under the CPM plan. Further, in the early years, GPM payments correspond more closely to increases in borrower's income *BI*. Hence, the burden of the tilt effect requiring borrowers to allocate more current real dollars for mortgage payments from current real income in an inflationary environment is reduced somewhat with the GPM. Based on this analysis, it is easy to conclude that the GPM significantly reduces monthly payments for borrowers in the early years of the mortgage loan, corresponds more closely to increases in borrower income, and therefore may increase the demand for mortgage credit by borrowers.

When judged relative to the CAM, the CPM and GPM clearly provide for initial payments that are far below payments required for the CAM with the same terms. It is important to stress that higher rates of inflation have caused a modification in mortgage instruments over time. Even though all three mortgage instruments provide the same yield (12 percent), changes in mortgage payments have clearly been structured to reduce initial payments. This has been done with the expectation that growth in real incomes and expected inflation will extend into the future, resulting in sufficiently high borrower incomes to repay the debt while reducing initial payments sufficiently to reduce the payment burden at the time of loan origination.

Outstanding Loan Balances: GPMs. Because the initial loan payments under GPM plans are usually lower than payments necessary to cover the monthly interest, the outstanding loan balance under the GPM will *increase* during the initial years of the loan. It will remain higher than that of the standard CPM mortgage until full repayment occurs at maturity. A comparison of loan balances for a GPM and a standard mortgage, based on the 12 percent, $60,000, 30-year terms used in our previous example, are shown in Exhibit 4–14.

Exhibit 4–13 indicates that the mortgage balance with the GPM *increases* until approximately year 5, when it begins to decline until it reaches zero in year 30. Hence, if a borrower sold this property during the first four years after making a GPM loan, more would be owed than originally borrowed. The loan balance increases during the first four years after origination because the initial GPM payments are lower than the monthly interest requirements at 12 percent. Therefore, no amortization of principal occurs until payments increase in later periods. To illustrate, in our previous example, the interest requirements under a GPM after the first month of origination would be $60,000 $\times$ (.12 $\div$ 12), or $600.00. The GPM payments during the first year of the loan are only $474.83, which are less than the monthly interest requirement of $600.00. The difference, or $125.17, must be added to the initial loan balance of $60,000, as if that difference represented an additional amount *borrowed* each month. This $125.17 monthly difference is referred to as **negative amortization.** Further, this shortfall in interest must also accumulate interest at the rate of 12 percent compounded monthly. Hence, during the first year, $125.17 per month plus monthly compound interest must be added to the $60,000 loan balance. This process amounts to compounding a monthly annuity of $125.17

EXHIBIT 4–13 Determining Loan Balance on a GPM ($60,000 loan, 12%, 30 years, 7.5 % rate of graduation)

Year	*Beginning Balance*	*Required Monthly Interest Payment*	*GPM Payment*	*First Month Loan Amortization*	*Change in Balance*	*Ending Balance*
1	$60,000.00	$600.00	$474.83	$125.17	$1,587.47	$61,587.47
2	61,587.47	615.87	510.44	105.43	1,337.12	62,924.59
3	62,924.59	629.25	548.72	80.53	1,021.32	63,945.91
4	63,945.91	639.46	589.87	49.59	628.93	64,574.84
5	64,574.84	645.75	634.11	11.64	147.62	64,722.46*
6	64,722.46	647.22	681.67	(34.45)	(436.91)	64,285.55

*Maximum balance. During the sixth year, the payments ($681.67) will exceed required interest ($647.22), and loan amortization will begin.

at 12 percent per month and adding that result to the initial loan balance to determine the balance at year-end. The amount added to the loan balance at the end of the year will be \$125.17 (*MFVIFA*, 12%, 12 mos.) or \$125.17(12.682503) = \$1,587.47.

Calculator Solution

$n = 12$
$i = 12\% \div 12 = 1\%$
$PMT = \$474.83$
$PV = -\$60{,}000$

Solve for future value:
$FV = \$61{,}587.47$

Calculator Solution

$n = 12$
$i = 12\% \div 12 = 1\%$
$PMT = \$125.17$
$PV = 0$

Solve for additional loan balance:
$FV = -\$1{,}587.47$

The importance of the increasing GPM loan balance and negative amortization can be seen in relationship to the property value also (see Exhibit 4–14). It is important to note the "margin of safety," or difference between property value and loan balance. This margin is much *lower* when a GPM loan balance is compared with that of a CPM. This makes a GPM loan riskier to the lender than a CPM, because more consideration must be given to *future* market values of real estate and *future* borrower income. For example, let's assume that the GPM borrower decides to sell a property after five years. When compared with the CPM, the lender will have received relatively lower monthly payments up to that point. Further, because of negative amortization the proceeds from sale of the property must be great enough to repay the loan balance that has increased relative to the original amount borrowed. In short, with a GPM, the lender must now be more concerned about trends in real estate values because resale value will constitute a more important source of funds for loan repayment.

GPM Mortgages and Effective Borrowing Costs. A closing note in this chapter considers the question of the effective interest cost and GPMs. In the absence of origination fees and prepayment penalties, the yield on GPMs, like yields on CAMs and CPMs, is equal to the contract rate of interest as specified in the note because the GPM, like the CPM, is a fixed interest rate mortgage. This is true whether or not the GPM loan, like CAM and CPM loans, is repaid before maturity. However, to the extent points or origination fees are charged, the effective yield on a GPM will be *greater* than the contract rate of interest, and it will increase the earlier the loan is repaid. When computing yields on GPMs originated with points, the same procedure should be followed as described with the standard CPM; that is, the interest

EXHIBIT 4–14 Loan Balances for Constant Payment, Graduated Payment, and Constant Payment Mortgages as Compared with Expected House Value

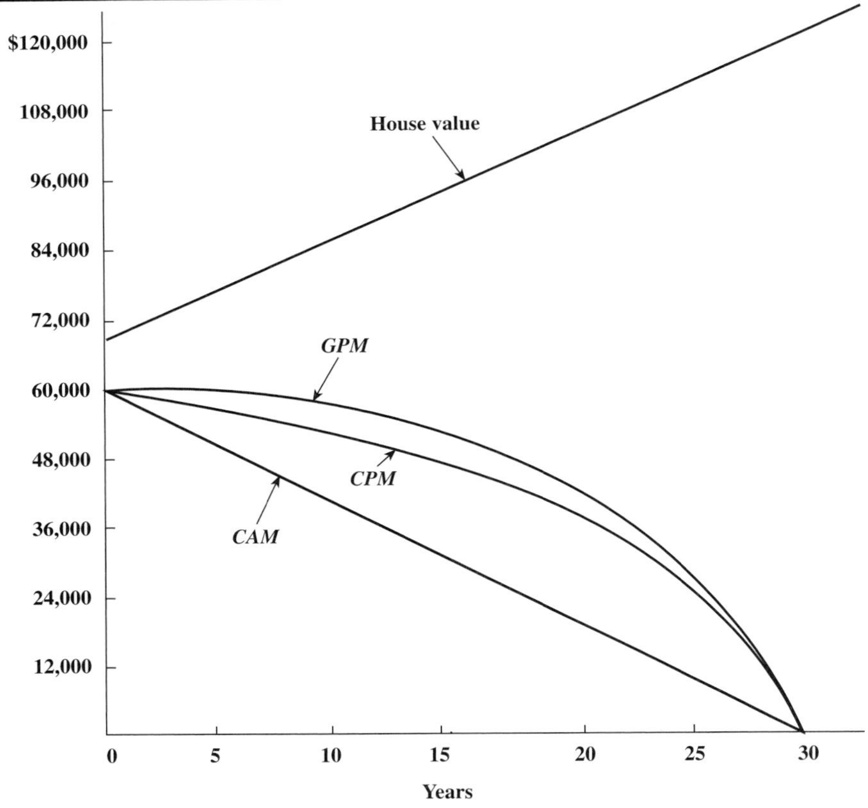

rate making the stream of GPM payments equal to the funds disbursed after deducting financing fees is the effective cost of the loan. Where origination fees are charged on GPMs, the authors have computed results that are very close to those computed for standard mortgage loans with the same terms and origination fees. This is true regardless of the loan amount or rate of graduation on the GPM. In the GPM discussed above, for example, if 3 points are charged and the loan is repaid after 5 years, the effective cost would be about 12.78 percent, compared with 12.82 on a CPM with the same terms.[16] Is a borrower better off or worse off with a GPM or a CPM loan? Generally, if a standard loan and a GPM are originated at the same

[16]Computations for the effective interest cost on GPMs are much more difficult than those for the CPM because the amount disbursed must be set equal to a series of seven annuities, representing different payments for 12 periods in each of the six years, with the final annuity payment covering years 6 to 30. Similarly, when finding loan balances, we may use for GPMs the same procedure demonstrated for CPMs; that is, the remaining payment streams would be discounted at the contract rate of interest and the present value would be determined. However, determining loan balances on GPMs may involve discounting a series of one or more annuities spanning many different 12-month intervals if any remaining CPM payments differ.

rate of interest and have the same fees, there will be little, if any, difference in their effective costs. However, because the graduated payment pattern reduces the tilt effect, the borrower is definitely better off with a GPM *if it can be obtained at the same interest rate* as the standard mortgage.

Would a GPM generally be available at the same interest rate as a standard CPM mortgage? It would appear that because of the additional risk taken by the lender—in the form of an increasing loan balance due to negative amortization in the early years of the loan and lower initial monthly cash flows received from reduced payments—the GPM lender would require a *higher risk premium* than the CPM lender. Hence, all things being equal, a slightly higher interest rate may be required on a GPM than on a CPM. This would tend to neutralize some of the positive features of the GPM compared with the CPM.

Reverse Annuity Mortgages (RAMs)

In recent years **reverse annuity mortgages** have become important, particularly as a greater percentage of the home-owning population is approaching retirement and seeking ways to supplement their retirement income. For example, assume that a household owns a residential property worth $500,000 today. They would like to use the value of the property to supplement their retirement income with a RAM. A lender agrees to make a loan in an amount not to exceed $250,000 for a period of 10 years. However, instead of giving the borrower cash in the amount of $250,000, the lender agrees to let the borrower take down the loan in monthly installments over the life of the mortgage. The lender will charge an interest rate of 10 percent on the loan. What will be the maximum monthly payments to the borrower under these terms? We can solve for this as follows:

$$FV = PMT * MPVIFA, \text{ 120 months, (10\% interest)}$$
$$\$250{,}000 = PMT * MPVIFA, \text{ 120 months, (10\% interest)}$$

Calculator Solution

$FV = -\$250{,}000$
$i = 10\% \div 12$
$PMT = ?$
$n = 120$
$PV = 0$

Solve for $PMT = \$1{,}220.44$

Looking at this example, note that the borrower can supplement his income by drawing $1,220.44 from the lender each month for 120 months, at the end of which time the lender will be owed a total of $250,000. At that time, the lender can collect the balance assuming that the property is sold; or if members of the retired households are still surviving and the property value has increased, then a new RAM loan can be negotiated based on the appraised value of the property and current market interest rates.

Conclusion

In this chapter, we discussed various approaches to pricing and structuring fixed interest rate mortgage loans. We saw that the price or interest rate on the loan depends on a number of factors including various types of risk that affect mortgage lenders. It is important that we keep these risk factors in mind in future chapters because alternative mortgage instruments are often designed in some way that alter the risk characteristics. Although the focus of this chapter has been on residential mortgages, the concepts and calculations are equally important for commercial mortgages, which are discussed in later chapters. We will find that the riskiness of the mortgage is also a factor in the risk and expected rate of return for investors in real estate income properties.

Key Terms

Questions

1. What are the major differences between CAM, CPM, and GPM loans? What are the advantages to borrowers and risks to lenders for each? What elements do each of the loans have in common?
2. Define *amortization*.
3. Why do the monthly payments in the beginning months of a CPM loan contain a higher proportion of interest than principal repayment?
4. What are loan closing costs? How can they be categorized? Which of the categories influence borrowing costs and why?
5. Does repaying a loan early ever affect the actual or true interest cost to the borrower?
6. Why do lenders charge origination fees, especially loan discount fees?
7. What is the connection between the Truth-in-Lending Act and the annual percentage rate (*APR*)?
8. Does the annual percentage rate always equal the effective borrowing cost?
9. What is meant by a real rate of interest?
10. What is a risk premium in the context of mortgage lending?
11. When mortgage lenders establish interest rates through competition, an expected inflation premium is said to be part of the interest rate. What does this mean?
12. Why do monthly mortgage payments increase so sharply during periods of inflation? What does the tilt effect have to do with this?
13. As inflation increases, the impact of the tilt effect is said to become even more burdensome on borrowers. Why is this so?
14. A mortgage loan is made to Mr. Jones for $30,000 at 10 percent interest for 20 years. If Mr. Jones has a choice between a CPM and a CAM, which one would result in his paying a greater amount of total interest over the life of the mortgage? Would one of these mortgages be likely to have a higher interest rate than the other? Explain your answer.
15. A borrower makes a GPM mortgage loan. It is originated for $50,000 and carries a 10 percent rate of interest for 30 years. If the borrower decides to prepay the loan after 10 years, would he be paying a higher yield, lower yield, or the same yield as the contract rate originally agreed on? How would this

yield compare with that on a CPM or CAM made on the same terms?

16. Would a lender be likely to originate a GPM at the same rate of interest as a standard CPM loan?

17. What is *negative amortization*? Why does it occur with a GPM? What happens to the mortgage balance of a GPM over time?

Problems

1. A borrower obtains a fully amortizing CPM mortgage loan for $125,000 at 11 percent interest for 20 years. What will be the monthly payment on the loan? What would the initial six payments be with a CAM?
2. A fully amortizing mortgage loan is made for $80,000 at 9 percent interest for 25 years. Payments are to be made monthly. Calculate:
   a. Monthly payments.
   b. Interest and principal payments during month 1.
   c. Total principal and total interest paid over 25 years.
   d. The outstanding loan balance if the loan is repaid at the end of year 10.
   e. Total monthly interest and principal payments through year 10.
   f. What would the breakdown of interest and principal be during month 50?
3. A constant payment, fully amortizing, mortgage loan is made for $100,000 at 8 percent interest for 30 years. What would payments be if they are calculated:
   a. Monthly.
   b. Quarterly.
   c. Annually.
   d. Weekly.
4. Regarding problem (3), how much total interest and principal would be paid over the entire 30-year life of the mortgage in each case? Which payment pattern would have the greatest amount of interest payable over the 30-year term of the loan? Why?
5. A mortgage loan is made for $100,000 at 8 percent interest for 20 years.
   a. Calculate the monthly payment for a CPM mortgage.
   b. What will the *total* of payments be for the entire 20-year period? Of this total how much will be interest?
   c. Assume the loan is repaid at the end of 8 years. What will be the outstanding balance? How much total interest will have been collected by then?
   d. The borrower now chooses to reduce the loan balance by $5,000 at the end of year 5.
      (1) What will be the new loan maturity assuming that loan payments are not reduced?
      (2) Assume the loan maturity will not be reduced. What will the new payments be?
6. A 30-year mortgage loan was made 10 years ago for $75,000 at 10 percent interest. The borrower would like to prepay the mortgage balance by $10,000.
   a. Assuming he can reduce his monthly mortgage payments, what is the new mortgage payment?
   b. Assuming the loan maturity is shortened and using the original monthly payments, what is the new loan maturity?
7. A mortgage is made for $100,000 at 7.5 percent interest. If the monthly payments were $1,000 per month, when will the loan be repaid?
8. A mortgage is made for $80,000 for 25 years. Total monthly payments will be $900 per month. What is the interest rate on the loan?
9. A mortgage is made for $60,000 for a term of 10 years. The borrower and lender agree that a balance of $20,000 will remain and be repaid as a lump sum at that time.
   a. If the interest rate is 9 percent, what must monthly payments be over the 10-year period?
   b. If the borrower chooses to repay the loan after 5 years instead of at the end of year 10, what must the loan balance be?
10. A mortgage is made for $80,000 at 12 percent interest for 10 years. The lender and borrower agree that monthly payments will be "interest only" and will require *no* loan amortization.
    a. What will the monthly payments be?
    b. What will be the loan balance after 5 years?
    c. If the loan is repaid after 5 years, what will be the yield to the lender?
    d. Instead of being repaid after 5 years, what will be the yield if the loan is repaid after 10 years?
11. A lender makes a loan for $90,000 for 10 years at 8 percent interest. The lender and borrower agree that payments will be monthly and that a balance of $20,000 will remain and be repaid at the end of year 10. Assuming 2 points are charged by the

lender, what will be the yield if the loan is repaid at the end of year 10? What must the loan balance be if it is repaid after year 4? What would be the yield to the lender if the loan is repaid at the end of year 4?

12. A loan for $50,000 is made for 10 years at 8 percent interest and *no monthly payments* are scheduled.
    a. How much will be due at the end of 10 years?
    b. What will be the yield to the lender if it is repaid after 8 years? (Assume monthly compounding.)
    c. If 1 point is charged in (*b*) what will be the yield to the lender?

13. John wants to buy a property for $105,000 and wants an 80 percent loan for $84,000. A lender indicates that a fully amortizing loan can be obtained for 30 years (360 months) at 12 percent interest; however, a loan origination fee of $3,500 will also be necessary for John to obtain the loan.
    a. How much will the lender actually disburse?
    b. What is the effective interest cost to the borrower, assuming that the mortgage is paid off after 30 years (full term)?
    c. What is the annual percentage rate (*APR*) that the lender must disclose to the borrower? (Recall that APRs are rounded up or down to the nearest 1/8 percent).
    d. If John pays off the loan after five years, what is the effective interest charge? Why is it different from the *APR* in (*c*)?
    e. Assume the lender also imposes a prepayment penalty of 2 percent of the outstanding loan balance if the loan is repaid within eight years of closing. If John repays the loan after five years with the prepayment penalty, what is the effective interest cost? Why is it different from the *APR* in (*c*)?

14. A lender is considering what terms to allow on a loan. Current market terms are 9 percent interest for 25 years, and the borrower, Rich, has requested a loan of $100,000. The lender believes that extra credit analysis and careful loan control will have to be exercised because Rich has never borrowed such a large sum before. In addition, the lender expects that market rates will move upward very soon, perhaps even before the loan is closed. To be on the safe side, the lender decides to extend to Rich a CPM loan commitment for $95,000 at 9 percent interest for 25 years; however, the lender wants to charge a loan origination fee to make the mortgage loan yield 10 percent. What origination fee should the lender charge? What fee should be charged if it is expected that the loan that will be repaid after 10 years?

15. A homeowner purchases a property for $70,000. He finances the purchase with a GPM carrying a 12 percent interest rate. A 7.5 percent rate of graduation will be applied to monthly payments beginning each year after the loan is originated for a period of five years. The initial payment will be $498.57 per month. The initial loan amount is $63,000 for a term of 30 years. The homeowner expects to sell the property after seven years.
    a. If he can sell the property for $80,000, what will the net proceeds be from the sale?
    b. What would the payment be if a CPM loan was available?
    c. Assume the loan is originated with two discount points. What is the effective yield on the GPM?

16. A borrower is faced with choosing between two loans. Loan A is available for $75,000 at 10 percent interest for 30 years, with 6 points to be included in closing costs. Loan B would be made for the same amount, but for 11 percent interest for 30 years, with 2 points to be included in the closing costs.
    a. If the loan is repaid after 15 years, which loan would be the better choice?
    b. If the loan is repaid after five years, which loan is the better choice?

17. A reverse annuity mortgage is made with a balance not to exceed $300,000 on a property now valued at $700,000. The loan calls for monthly payments to be made to the borrower for 120 months at an interest rate of 11 percent.
    a. What will the monthly payments be?
    b. Assume that the borrower must have monthly payments of $2,000 for the first 50 months of the loan. Remaining payments from months 51 to 120 must be determined so that the $300,000 maximum is not exceeded in month 120. What must payments to the borrower be during months 51 to 120?

CHAPTER

5

Adjustable Rate and Variable Payment Mortgages

In the preceding chapter, we discussed the evolution of fixed interest rate mortgage instruments, giving particular attention to payment patterns. We saw how payment structures have evolved in response to changes in the economic environment, particularly when the impact of inflation on interest rates and mortgage payments was considered. While many of those changes alleviated problems faced by *borrowers*, depending on the degree of uncertainty in expectations of inflation and interest rates, those remedies may be inadequate from the viewpoint of *lenders*. These inadequacies stem from the fact that although payment patterns can be altered to suit borrowers as expectations change, the constant amortization mortgage (CAM), constant payment mortgage (CPM), and graduated payment mortgage (GPM) are all originated in *fixed interest rates* and all have *predetermined payment patterns*. Consequently, neither the interest rate nor payment pattern will change, regardless of economic conditions. Loans made at fixed interest rates (FRMs) may cause serious problems for lenders who must pay market interest rates on savings because market interest rates may change suddenly, and lenders who have made an overabundance of fixed interest rate mortgages may encounter serious difficulty as interest costs on savings rise relative to interest revenues from mortgage loans.

This chapter deals with a variety of mortgages that are made with either *adjustable* interest rates (called **adjustable rate mortgages—ARMs**) or with variable payment provisions that change with economic conditions. These instruments differ from fixed interest rate mortgages (FRMs) in that they are designed to adjust in one or more ways to changes in economic conditions. Rather than making mortgages with fixed rates of interest over long periods of time, these mortgages provide an alternative method of financing through which lenders and borrowers *share* the risk of interest rate changes, or **interest rate risk.** This enables lenders to match changes in interest costs with changes in interest revenue more effectively and thus provide borrowers with potentially lower financing costs.

In this chapter, we begin by discussing the price level adjusted mortgage (PLAM), which is one type of variable payment mortgage. Although not used widely, the PLAM illustrates many of the problems that must be considered by lenders and borrowers in financial decision making. We then consider ARMs and issues relative to how they are "priced." As a part of the analysis of ARMs, we investigate the effects of limitations on (1) interest rate changes, (2) payment increases, and (3) negative amortization and the resultant effects on ARM loan yields. We also consider how these mortgages should be priced relative to FRMs and other ARMs made on different loan terms. At the conclusion of the chapter, we consider the shared appreciation mortgage (SAM), whose repayment terms are partially based on appreciation in property values.

ARMs and Lender Considerations

To this point, we have considered *borrower* concerns regarding mortgage loans. More specifically, we have concerned ourselves with how payment patterns have been modified to offset problems caused by the "tilt effect," thereby making more households eligible for loans. To complete the discussion of mortgage lending, we must briefly consider problems faced by *lenders* and their cost of funds.

Recall from the previous chapter that we approached the tilt effect and GPMs with fixed interest rates from the perspective of borrowers. We indicated that because of the tilt problem, borrowers had an increasingly difficult time qualifying for loans in inflationary times, even though their incomes may have been rising. From the perspective of *lenders*, fixed interest rate mortgages are a potential problem regardless of what the payment pattern may be (i.e., a CAM, CPM, or GPM). One major problem with FRMs is that the interest rate is fixed on the date of origination and remains fixed until the loan is repaid. Hence, from the day of origination, lenders are underwriting the risk of any significant changes in the implicit components of mortgage interest rates, that is, the real rate of interest r, the risk premium p, and the premium for expected inflation f. To the extent that lenders underestimate any or all of these components at the time of mortgage origination, they will incur a financial loss. For example, assume that a mortgage loan for $60,000 is made for 30 years at 10 percent interest with an expected repayment period of 10 years. This mortgage would require monthly payments of about $527 (rounded). Should such a loan be made, it must follow that the consensus of lenders at the time the loan is made is that a 10 percent rate of interest is sufficiently high to compensate them for all forms of risk bearing expected to occur over the time that the loan is expected to be outstanding. If over that time, one or more of the components of the mortgage interest rate i are significantly higher than was anticipated at the time of origination, lenders will suffer a loss.[1] If, for example, lenders make an inaccurate prediction of inflation and unanticipated inflation occurs, warranting a 12 percent interest rate instead of 10 percent, the magnitude of the loss to the lender is determined as follows:

$$\begin{aligned} PV &= \$527(MPVIFA, 12\%, 120 \text{ mos.}) + MB(MPVIF, 12\%, 120 \text{ mos.}) \\ &= \$527(69.700522) + \$54{,}563(.302995) \\ &= \$53{,}264 \end{aligned}$$

The loss would be equal to $60,000 − $53,264 = $6,736. Hence, in this case, a 2 percent rate of **unanticipated inflation** would result in a financial loss of $6,736 or 11.2 percent of the loan amount. Based on this example, it should be easy to see the relationship between *interest rate risk* and potential losses to lenders. That there

[1]There are many reasons why lenders may inaccurately predict the components of i over the expected repayment period. Monetary growth may expand or contract, causing changes in the rate of inflation (f). General economic activity may expand (contract), resulting in a change in the general level of investment and employment, thereby affecting real interest rates and default risk (r and p).

is always some additional risk because of the *uncertainty* about expected levels of each of the components of i is one of the reasons why a risk premium p is demanded by lenders. To the extent that this uncertainty about future levels of r and f increases, p will also increase, and vice versa.[2]

Calculator Solution

1st step: Determine mortgage balance

$n = 20 \times 12 = 240$ (# of remaining payments)
$i = 10\% \div 12 = .8333\%$ (stated interest rate)
$PMT = \$527.00$
$FV = 0$
Solve for PV of payments:
$PV = -\$54{,}610$

2nd step: Discount payments and mortgage balance at 12%

$n = 10 \times 12 = 120$
$i = 12\% \div 12 = 1\%$
$PMT = \$527$
$FV = \$54{,}610$
Solve for PV of mortgage balance:
$PV = -\$53{,}279$
Loss = \$60,000 − 53,279 = \$6,721

Note: Calculator answer differs due to rounding.

It should be noted that losses incurred by lenders result in gains to borrowers. Of course, one could argue that if interest rates declined then lenders would gain. However, when this occurs, borrowers usually try to refinance their loans. This pattern implies that with fixed interest rate lending, risk bearing is not "symmetric," or evenly balanced; that is, lenders bear the risk of loss when interest rates increase, which is not equally offset by gains if interest rates decline because borrowers can usually prepay loans and will do so when interest rates decline. This was referred to as prepayment risk in Chapter 4. This problem has also motivated lenders to turn to ARMs and other loan instruments.

Another serious problem faced by lenders during periods of rising interest rates is illustrated in Exhibit 5–1. In the exhibit, we present two components of a hypothetical, abbreviated balance sheet for a savings institution. On the asset side of the balance sheet, we assume that the institution has made only FRM loans. We also provide estimates of loan maturities and yields that will be earned on those loans. On the liability side, we detail the deposit accounts by maturity and also show the interest cost paid to savers for each maturity category. From this hypothetical, partial balance sheet, we compute a weighted average yield for FRM mortgages on the asset side that is 12 percent, with an average expected maturity of four to five years. On the deposit, or liability, side of the balance sheet, we compute a weighted average

[2]The reader should realize that there will always be some likelihood that expected levels of r and f will not always be accurate because of *unanticipated* changes. During some time periods, when economic conditions are stable, the uncertainty in these estimates is likely to be less, whereas in other periods, uncertainty may be greater. Hence, the *uncertainty* of these estimates is what causes interest rate risk and, in turn, larger or smaller risk premiums.

EXHIBIT 5–1 Hypothetical Breakdown of Mortgages and Savings Accounts by Expected Maturity

Mortgages			Deposits		
Percent of Total	*Expected Yield (percent)*	*Expected Maturity (years)*	*Percent of Total*	*Interest Rate (percent)*	*Maturity (years)*
33.3	11	2–3	33.3	9	0*
33.3	12	4–5	33.3	10	1
33.3	13	6–7	33.3	11	2
Weighted average	12	4.5		10	1

*Withdrawable without notice.

EXHIBIT 5–2 Hypothetical Breakdown of Mortgages and Savings Accounts by Expected Maturity (after interest rate changes)

Mortgages			Deposits		
Percent of Total	*Expected Yield (percent)*	*Expected Maturity (years)*	*Percent of Total*	*Interest Rate (percent)*	*Maturity (years)*
33.3	11	2–3	33.3	11	0*
33.3	12	4–5	33.3	10	1
33.3	13	6–7	33.3	11	2
Weighted average	12	4.5		10.7	1

*Withdrawable without notice.

cost of funds, which is equal to 10 percent with an average maturity of one year. An estimate of the lender's net revenue before operating costs, or "spread," would be approximately equal to 12 percent minus 10 percent, or 2 percent of assets. From this net revenue, the institution would have to meet its operating costs, cover loan default losses, and earn a profit.

Difficulties that a savings institution may encounter during a period of unexpected changes in interest rates can be seen if we consider a 2 percent increase in interest cost associated with the deposit category with a zero maturity, or where savings deposits can be withdrawn at any time. Should that sudden, unanticipated increase in interest rates occur, we note in Exhibit 5–2 that the new weighted average cost of funds increases to 10.7 percent. On the asset side of the balance sheet, however, the weighted average yield on FRM loans does not change. Net revenue would decline from 2.0 to 1.3 percent of assets (12 percent minus 10.7 percent). This savings institution would now have a smaller amount of income, or **spread,** from which to pay operating costs and earn a profit. Clearly, this organization will find it more difficult to earn a profit after the sudden increase in interest rates than it did previously. Further, as time passes, if interest rates on deposits continued to rise, this would cause even more difficulty. Even if rates did not continue to rise, the spread will continue to narrow as deposits mature before mortgages are repaid. For example after one year the rate on new deposits, which was 10 percent, will also rise as deposits mature and are replaced with new one-year deposits. Of course, some new mortgages might be made during the year to partially offset this reduction.

It should be obvious to the reader that this lender's profitability problem was brought about by an *imbalance* in the maturity structure of assets and liabilities. The weighted average maturity of assets is much greater than the weighted average maturity of liabilities. Over time this imbalance, or "gap," can become even more acute if interest costs rise and deposit maturities become shorter relative to asset maturities. This imbalance is sometimes referred to as the classic problem of a savings institution—"borrowing short and lending long." This means that the savings institution has accepted deposits, certificates of deposit, and so on, with relatively short maturities and has used most of the funds to finance fixed rate mortgage loans with longer maturities.[3] To the extent that this imbalance, sometimes called the **maturity gap,** exists between assets and liabilities for savings institutions, the firms are exposed to a considerable risk that the cost of deposits may change relative to the yield on assets. Clearly, if deposit costs for lenders increase relative to yields on their assets, lenders are worse off.[4]

To accomplish the shifting of interest rate risk, mortgage lenders have devised adjustable interest rate mortgage instruments with many different features. When developing these instruments, lenders have generally attempted to accomplish two goals: (1) to make these more complex mortgage instruments acceptable to borrowers and (2) to make mortgage instruments flexible enough, in terms of interest rate and payment features, so that problems concerning deposit instability and cost of funds are alleviated. In the sections that follow, we will discuss many types of mortgage instruments, some of which pass interest rate risk fully to the borrower and some of which pass interest rate risk partially to the borrower. We will also discuss how these various mortgages are "priced," that is, how the initial interest rate and other fees vary in accordance with risks shared by the borrower and lender. Rather than attempt to describe specific details on the many varieties of ARMs, we provide a generic framework that focuses on how changes in payments, interest rates, loan balances, and maturity occur in relation to market conditions. In this way, the student should be able to deal with mortgages containing many combinations of features that change in response to market conditions over time.

The Price Level Adjusted Mortgage (PLAM)

One concept that has been discussed as a remedy to the imbalance problem for savings institutions is the **price level adjusted mortgage (PLAM)**. Recall from the discussion in the previous chapter on the determinants of mortgage interest rates, i—an expected real rate of interest (r), a risk premium (p), and an expected inflation (f)—we displayed the following equation:

$$i = r + p + f$$

[3]Obviously lenders could protect themselves by investing in shorter-term assets, such as Treasury bills, to "match" zero maturity deposit accounts. Indeed, most lenders attempt to do this and still maintain a significant proportion of mortgages in their loan portfolio. Nonetheless, it is still very difficult to make an "exact" match. To reduce this risk, lenders have turned to designing lending instruments, including ARMs, with interest rates that change with market conditions and deposits costs.

[4]Of course, to the extent interest rates fall, they are better off. However, the risk is in not knowing what the outcome will be.

We also indicated that perhaps the most difficult variable in the equation to predict was a premium for expected inflation (*f*). To help reduce interest rate risk, or the uncertainty of inflation and its effect on interest rates, it has been suggested that lenders should *originate* mortgages at interest rates that reflect expectations of the real interest rate plus a risk premium for the likelihood of loss due to default on a given mortgage loan, or $r + p$.

After estimating initial values for *r* and *p*, the PLAM loan balance would be adjusted up or down by a price index. Payments would then be based on a new loan balance, adjusted for inflation. This would shift the risk of changes in market interest rates brought about by inflation (*f*) to borrowers and relieve lenders of the difficult task of forecasting future interest movements when originating loans. The lender would still bear the risk of any unanticipated change in *r* or *p*.[5]

PLAM: Payment Mechanics

An example of a PLAM loan would have payments based on a rate of interest consisting only of expectations for *r* and *p* for an expected maturity period. Payments would be adjusted periodically, based on the indexed value of the *mortgage balance* for the remaining loan term. To illustrate, assume that a mortgage is made for \$60,000 for 30 years at an interest rate of 4 percent, or a lender's estimate of $r + p$. The lender and borrower may agree that the loan balance will be indexed to the Consumer Price Index (CPI) and adjusted annually. Initial monthly payments would be based on \$60,000 at 4 percent for 30 years, or approximately \$286. After one year, the loan balance, based on a 30-year amortization schedule for the 4 percent interest rate would be about \$58,943. If it is assumed that the CPI increased by 6 percent during the first year of the loan, the *loan balance* at the end of year 1 would become \$58,943 (1.06), or \$62,480. This balance would be repaid over 29 remaining years. Monthly payments, beginning in the second year, would be based on the higher-indexed loan balance of \$62,480 at the same 4 percent interest rate for 29 years, or \$304 per month. This process would continue each year thereafter: (1) computing the loan balance using an amortization schedule based on a 4 percent interest rate for the remaining term, (2) increasing the balance by the change in the CPI during the next year, and (3) computing the new payment over the remaining loan term.

Assuming inflation continued at an annual rate of 6 percent for the remaining loan term, Exhibit 5–3 shows the nominal payment and loan balance pattern every year for the PLAM loan. There are many patterns that should be pointed out in Exhibit 5–3. Note that the PLAM payments shown in panel A increase at approximately the same rate as the change in the price level, or 6 percent over the life of the loan. This increase in payments continues over the life of the loan even though loan amortization begins to occur as the number of remaining years to maturity declines (see panel B). This pattern of rising payments occurs because (1) the effect of the

[5]Although we are treating each of these variables making up *i* as independent and additive, they may not be independent and may well interact with one another. For example, the risk premium (*p*) is partially dependent on the likelihood that a borrower's income and wealth will rise or fall, which may depend on changes in the economy and, hence, the underlying real rate of interest (*r*). Changes in income would affect the likelihood of default on a loan because of payments rising relative to income (which may rise or fall) or the loan balance exceeding the market value of the house. Similarly, we do not fully understand the relationship between inflation (*f*) and real growth (*r*) and possible interaction between them. Hence, the reader should be aware that we are dealing with these influences in a conceptual way to illustrate the importance of each component, but we do not mean to imply that the specification of *i* is this simplistic.

EXHIBIT 5–3 Payments and Loan Balance Patterns, $60,000 PLAM, 4%, Inflation = 6% per Year, versus $60,000 CPM, 10% Interest, 30 Years

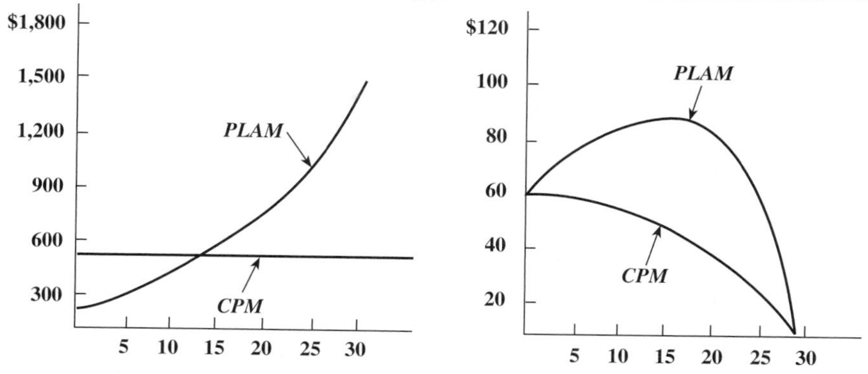

Panel A: Monthly payments

Panel B: Outstanding loan balances ($000s)

increasing price index on the loan balance and (2) each succeeding year's payment is computed over a shorter remaining loan term.[6] It is also interesting to compare the payments on this PLAM to a $60,000, constant payment FRM made at 10 percent for 30 years. Payments on the FRM would be approximately $527, as compared to the initial PLAM payment of $286. Thus, it would appear that many more households could qualify to purchase housing with PLAMs when compared to CPMs. Further, PLAMs would appear to help remedy problems of savings imbalance and interest rate risk faced by savings institutions. This is because mortgage yields would correspond more closely with changes in interest rates on deposits.

The PLAM is not without problems, however. Panel B in Exhibit 5–3 shows that the loan balance on the PLAM increases to about 155 percent of the original loan amount, or from $60,000 to approximately $93,000, after 15 years. Although housing prices have appreciated considerably during the 1960s and 1970s, housing is only one of many components making up the CPI. Hence, should prices of other goods represented in the CPI increase faster than housing prices, indexing loan balances to the CPI could result in loan balances increasing faster than property values. If this occurred, borrowers would have an incentive to default. This possibility would place a considerable burden on lenders because now, instead of dealing with inflation and fixed interest rate loans, they would have to establish adequate down payment levels for all borrowers, forecast future housing prices, and be assured that the value of the property that serves as collateral for the mortgage would always be greater than the outstanding loan balance. Hence, it is questionable whether the CPI is the proper index to use when adjusting PLAM balances.

[6]The reader should realize that the process of adjustments occurring at the end of each year can be viewed as an annual series of new mortgage loan originations. As such, payments may be modified based on different rates of interest or maturities, with the outstanding loan balance always representing the new amount being borrowed. Hence, it is possible for changes in interest rates or maturities to be renegotiated or varied by the lender and borrower at any time to moderate or increase monthly payments.

A second problem with PLAMs has to do with the relationship between mortgage payments and borrower incomes. It would appear that the tilt problem would be greatly reduced, because payments would be matched more closely with borrower incomes. However, this assumes that both the CPI, which is used to index the PLAM, and borrower incomes change in the same way. A desired ratio between mortgage payments and borrower incomes may be easy to maintain as long as incomes keep pace with increases in the CPI. Over the long run this relationship may be possible as increases in income and mortgage payments "balance out." However, if inflation increases sharply, it is not likely that borrower incomes would increase at the same rate in the short run. During such periods, the payment burden may increase and households may find it more difficult to make mortgage payments. Because of this possibility and the need to develop a desired relationship to mortgage payments, lenders would have to estimate future income for households in different occupational categories and the relationship of that income to inflation. The problems of rising loan balances and payments just discussed make estimating the risk premium (p) that lenders must charge extremely difficult.

A third problem with PLAMs is that the price level chosen for indexation is usually measured on a historical, or ex post facto basis. In other words, the index is based on data collected in the *previous period* but published currently. Inasmuch as mortgage payments are to be made in the future, historic prices may not be an accurate indication of future prices. To illustrate, the change in the CPI may have been 10 percent during the past year (published currently). This figure would be used to index the outstanding mortgage balance, which will determine payments during the *next* year. If the rate of increase in the CPI subsequently slowed to 2 percent during the next year, it is easy to see that mortgage payments would be rising at a faster rate (10 percent) than current prices (2 percent) and, perhaps, faster than borrower incomes. Although borrower incomes may have increased by 10 percent in the previous year, the lag between realization of income in one period and higher payments in the next still presents a problem. This lag problem could become even more distorted in our example if the CPI were to decline and then increase. For this reason, many observers believe that if the PLAM programs were adopted extensively, the time intervals between payment adjustment periods would have to be shortened considerably. This time is called an adjustment interval.

A final problem lenders see with PLAMs involves a modification in the types of deposits offered. If PLAMs were used to a large extent, lenders would probably have to develop new types of deposit accounts, which would also be made available at some basic rate of interest and indexed to the price level. This would have to occur so that when prices and interest rates increase, yields on both PLAM loans and savings deposits would rise together. Otherwise, revenue from mortgages could fluctuate more than deposit costs, and a profit squeeze could develop.

While PLAMs offer the potential for a better match between the costs of deposits and returns on assets than fixed interest rate mortgages, PLAMs have not been tried to any significant extent because of the problems listed above. Further, savers can achieve their desired objectives through a variety of available savings instruments that are not indexed to price levels. They can invest their savings in short-term securities and reinvest them very frequently, thereby reducing their interest rate risk exposure. Such investments could include Treasury bills, certificates of deposit, or unit shares in money market funds. By having a choice among short-term investment vehicles with yields that are very sensitive to changes in inflation, savers may believe that they can hedge adequately against the risk of unanticipated inflation without requiring price-indexed deposits. Lenders, on the other hand, are probably willing to bear some of the interest rate risk associated with inflation; therefore they have not seen the need to shift this risk completely to borrowers by implementing PLAMs. Many PLAM features are, however, very attractive and these features form the framework for understanding the ARMs now being offered in the marketplace.

ARMs: An Overview

Rather than using changes in the price level as a mechanism to adjust mortgage interest rates and payments, lenders are choosing a variety of mortgages with *interest rates* that are *indexed to other market interest rates*. By choosing indexes based on interest rates rather than on a price index, lenders partially avoid having to estimate real interest rates and risk premiums for the entire period that loans are expected to be outstanding. With ARMs, lenders are, in effect, making a loan, with terms that are updated to current interest rate levels at the end of each adjustment period. By using an interest rate index instead of an ex post measure of inflation based on the CPI or any other price index, lenders earn expected yields based on *expected future values* for r, p, and f over a future period of time. Because interest rates are a reflection of lender and borrower expectations of r, p, and f over specific future periods of time, revisions of ARMs are always based on future expectations. The terms of a mortgage are tied to an index of such rates and are continuously updated in the market. Hence, an ARM provides for adjustments that are more timely for lenders than a PLAM because values for r, p, and f are revised at *specific* time intervals to reflect market expectations of future values for *each* component of i *between adjustment dates*. For example, the value for f, or expected inflation, is based on an estimate of *future* prices rather than a past measure as exemplified in the CPI or other price indexes. Similarly, values for r and p are based on the market's current assessment of borrower incomes, housing values, and other risks in the prospective economic environment between adjustment dates.

ARMs Illustrated

We can begin to illustrate ARM mechanics with a simple example. An ARM for \$60,000 with an *initial* interest rate of 10 percent is originated with a term of 30 years, but its payments are to be adjusted at the end of each year based on an interest rate determined by a specified index at that time. Based on these initial loan terms, monthly payments would be approximately \$527 per month for the first year. If the market index were to rise at the end of one year and change the interest rate on the ARM to 12 percent, payments would be determined based on the outstanding loan balance for 29 years as follows:

$$\begin{aligned} MP &= \$59{,}666(MLC,\ 12\%,\ 348 \text{ mos.}) \\ &= \$59{,}666(.010324) \\ &= \$616 \text{ (rounded)} \end{aligned}$$

Hence, the new 12 percent interest rate on the ARM at the end of the first year is an updated estimate or consensus of all lenders and borrowers as to what the components of i will be for the *coming year*.

Calculator Solution

Discount mortgage balance at 12%

$n = 29 \times 12 = 348$

$i = 12\% \div 12 = 1\%$

$PV = \$59{,}666$

$FV = 0$

Solve for payments:

$PMT = \$616$

At least three observations should be made concerning our simple example.

1. The use of ARMs does not completely eliminate the possibility of lenders realizing losses because of *interest rate risk*. In our example, the yield to the lender on the ARM during the first year was 10 percent. If market rates move to 12 percent *the day after* the ARM is originated, the lender would sustain a 2 percent loss for the 12-month period. Obviously, this loss would be eliminated if the adjustment period was reduced to one day, or the loss could be reduced to the extent the adjustment period was less than one year.
2. The longer the adjustment interval, the greater the interest rate risk to the lender. Hence, the expected yield on such a mortgage should be greater. This idea will be elaborated on later in the chapter.
3. Finally, as the lender assumes *less* interest rate risk, the borrower incurs *more* interest rate risk, depending on the nature of the index chosen and the frequency of payment adjustments. This point can be appreciated if one thinks of a FRM where the lender assumes the full risk of future interest rate changes and compares it to an ARM with payments adjusting freely with market conditions. Clearly, in the latter case the borrower would be assuming more interest rate risk and the lender less. Because the borrower assumes more risk, the *initial interest rate* on an ARM should generally be *less* than that on a FRM. Further, because the lender is shifting interest rate risk to the borrower, the lender should also expect, at the time of loan amortization, to earn a lower yield on an ARM over the term of the loan.

Anytime the process of risk bearing is analyzed, individual borrowers and lenders differ in the degree to which they are willing to assume risk. Consequently, the market for ARMs contains a large set of mortgage instruments that differ with respect to how risk is to be shared between borrowers and lenders.

ARM Indexes. One differentiating feature among ARMs is the range of *indexes* used to establish future mortgage terms. Some commonly used indexes are:

- Interest rates on six-month Treasury bills.
- Interest rates on one-year Treasury securities.
- Interest rates on three-year Treasury securities.
- Interest rates on five-year Treasury securities.
- The weighted average national cost of funds (deposits) index.
- The national average of fixed interest rates on mortgage loans made on previously existing homes.

There are many other components of ARMs in addition to indexing and interest rate adjustments that must be discussed if ARMs are to be adequately understood. These characteristics also determine how much interest rate risk is being passed from lenders to borrowers and, therefore, how much risk the borrower accepts.

Other ARM Characteristics. The following list contains a description of some of the general characteristics frequently found in adjustable rate mortgages:

- *Initial interest rate.* The initial rate on an ARM will usually be determined based on market conditions at the time that the loan is made. However, it will almost always be *lower* than the prevailing rates on fixed interest rate mortgages. An ARM lender should also expect to earn a lower yield because the lender in an ARM loan is assuming less interest rate risk. Hence, at the time of origination, the initial interest rate on the ARM will usually be lower than that on a FRM.[7]
- *Index.* The **index** is the interest rate series (such as one from the above list) agreed on by both the borrower and the lender and over which the lender has no control. This index may be very short term or long term in nature.
- *Adjustment interval.* The period of time between mortgage payment adjustments is called the **adjustment interval.** This time period is usually six months or one year. However, it could be as long as every three to five years, or it could be as short as one month or less.
- *Margin.* A constant spread, or premium in addition to the index chosen for an ARM, is known as the **margin.**
- *Composite rate.* The sum of the index plus the margin used to establish the new rate of interest for ARMs after each adjustment interval is the **composite rate.** It can differ from the initial interest rate on the date of origination.
- *Limitations or caps.* Maximum *increases* allowed in payments, interest rates, maturity extensions, and negative amortization (or loan balances) between adjustment intervals or over the life of the loan, as provided for in an ARM agreement, are called **caps.**
- *Negative amortization.* To the extent the interest in a given year is not covered by the payment due to a payment cap, the difference in interest may be compounded at current rates and added to the outstanding loan balance. When additions to the outstanding loan balance are allowed, such amounts are referred to as **negative amortization** (see discussion of GPMs in the previous chapter).
- *Floors.* Maximum *reductions* in payments or interest rates between adjustment intervals or over the life of the loan are called **floors.**
- *Assumability.* The ability of the borrower to allow a subsequent purchaser of a property to assume a loan under the existing terms.
- *Discount points.* As with FRMs, these points or fees are also used with ARMs to change the lender's yield in relation to risk.
- *Prepayment privilege.* As with FRMs, the borrower usually has the right to prepay the loan. This prepayment privilege is usually allowed *without penalty.*

A brief illustration of how these features might be used in quoting ARM terms follows: A loan is made for $60,000 for a period of 30 years at an *initial interest rate*

[7]One exception to this rule would occur if the yield curve, discussed in the previous chapter, is inverted or "humped." This would mean that short-term interest rates are higher than long-term interest rates and hence the initial interest rate on an ARM tied to an index with a shorter maturity would be greater than that on a FRM with a longer maturity.

of 10 percent. Payments will be *adjusted annually* based on the *index* of yields on one year U.S. Treasury obligations on the payment adjustment date, plus a *margin* of 2 percent. Payment increases will be *capped*, based on a maximum increase of a 2 percent increase in the interest rate in any one year, or a total increase of 5 percent over the life of the mortgage (this is sometimes referred to as a 2/5 rate cap). Should the *composite rate* exceed the interest rate cap at the time of payment adjustment, *negative amortization* will be computed and added to the outstanding loan balance. There will be a 2 percent *floor*, or limit on the extent to which the interest rate may fall each year, regardless of the decline in the market index. The loan will *not be assumable*; that is, the outstanding loan balance must be repaid in the event the property is sold. Later in the chapter, we will show how future payments and loan balances are calculated on a loan like the one described above.

Clearly, many other combinations of the above provisions could be used to allocate interest rate risk between the lender and borrower, depending on borrower qualifications and willingness to assume risk. Space does not allow for an in-depth analysis of all of these combinations. What we will provide, however, is a framework which should provide the necessary tools that can be used to analyze any given set of ARM provisions.

Problems Lenders and Borrowers Face with ARMs

Many problems regarding adjustable rate mortgages concern lenders and borrowers. With respect to borrowers, these features are more complex and difficult to understand than provisions usually present in a constant payment mortgage. This complexity is compounded by the fact that many ARMs contain more than one feature that may change in response to conditions in the mortgage market. It is more difficult for borrowers to determine the effect of each feature, both individually or combined, on borrowing costs. Some of these features will be more important than others, and the relative importance of each feature may change over an interest rate cycle.

Lenders also face significant uncertainty when making ARMs. They must find the proper combination of options to include in the mortgage instrument to satisfy borrower requirements, including how much risk borrowers are willing to bear. Lenders must also estimate the yields they expect to earn on these loans and how the pattern of yields corresponds to expected changes in their cost of funds. While lenders may pass much of the interest rate risk to borrowers with ARMs—to the extent that they improperly price or establish too low an initial interest rate on these loans—they still may earn an inadequate yield and have difficulty paying market interest rates to savers. In this sense, while they may be better off because of their ability to add ARMs to their asset portfolios, lenders have to a degree replaced the problems that they faced with standard, fixed interest rate CPM loans with a different set of problems. In other words, ARMs may not completely relieve lenders from the possibility of making loans with *expected yields* that may be inadequate in relation to future deposit costs. To the extent that lenders select inappropriate indexes, margins, adjustment periods, and so on, they may still be underwriting a considerable amount of interest rate risk that may adversely affect profitability.

Lacking market experience, borrowers also face the decision regarding ARMs. On the positive side, these loans will generally be priced at an *initial* interest rate *below* that of a FRM. Hence, in periods of very high long-term interest rates, the tilt effect is reduced and more households should be able to qualify for loans with ARMs than they would with FRMs. As a result, a more continuous flow of funds should be available to borrowers than would be the case if only FRMs were available. On the other hand, households must also budget a more uncertain monthly payment flow from their incomes from year to year with ARMs.

Finally, because of the fact that ARMs may shift all or part of the interest rate risk to the borrower, the *risk of default* will generally increase to the lender, thereby reducing some of the benefits gained from shifting interest rate risk to borrowers. For example, if a lender were to shift all interest rate risk to a borrower by requiring payments in accordance with any changes in interest rates without limit, it is clear that the risk of default would increase considerably. Similarly, the way in which ARM payment patterns are structured may also affect default risk. As a result, in practice, lenders must assess the likelihood that a borrower will default under a number of different ARM plans that shift all or a part of the interest rate risk to borrowers. In the remainder of this chapter, we focus on interest rate risk and default risk change in relation to the types of ARMs negotiated by lenders and borrowers. The aspect of default risk concerned with the underwriting of such mortgage loans in relation to borrower income, type of employment, and the value of the house being purchased is considered in detail in the next two chapters.

Risk Premiums, Interest Rate Risk, and Default Risk on ARMs

It is very difficult to determine how expected yields will vary among ARMs containing different repayment characteristics. However, for any given class of borrowers, the expected yield (cost) of borrowing with an ARM generally depends on the ARM provisions described in detail earlier: (1) the initial interest rate, (2) the index to which the interest rate is tied, (3) the margin, or spread, over the index chosen for a given ARM, (4) discount points charged at origination, (5) the frequency of payment adjustments, and (6) the inclusion of caps or floors on the interest rate, payments, or loan balances. The loan amount and each of the six characteristics listed will determine the cash outflow or amount loaned, expected monthly payments, and the expected loan balance for an expected time period from which an expected yield (internal rate of return) can be computed. In addition to understanding how each of the above relationships is likely to affect the expected yield (or cost of borrowing), further complications include understanding how combinations of these terms may *interact* over time and possibly amplify or reduce *default risk* to the lender.

While much has been said about benefits to lenders from shifting interest rate risk to borrowers, there are added risks that lenders must assume with ARMs. The combination of the six characteristics also affects default risk either (1) by the ability of the borrower to make mortgage payments or (2) by increasing the loan balance too high in relation to the value of the house, assuming negative amortization is allowed. While we discuss lender underwriting standards used to gauge default risk in more detail in the next chapter, we also want to stress the importance of default risk in our present discussion.

A useful way to approach the relationships between interest rate risk and default risk for an individual and lender is to examine panel A of Exhibit 5–4. The exhibit shows the risk premium (p) demanded by the lender on the vertical axis and interest rate risk assumed by the lender on the horizontal axis. Looking at line A–B in the exhibit, we see that as more interest rate risk is assumed by the lender (less by the borrower), the lender will demand a higher risk premium. Hence, the interest rate risk curve is positively sloped. In the extreme, if the lender assumes all interest rate risk (point B) this would be equivalent to the amount of interest rate risk assumed with a FRM. Note that when the lender assumes no interest rate risk, the borrower is assuming all interest rate risk. This is represented by the intersection of the interest rate risk line at the origin of the diagram (point A).

EXHIBIT 5–4 The Relationship between Interest Rate Risk, Default Risk, and Risk Premiums

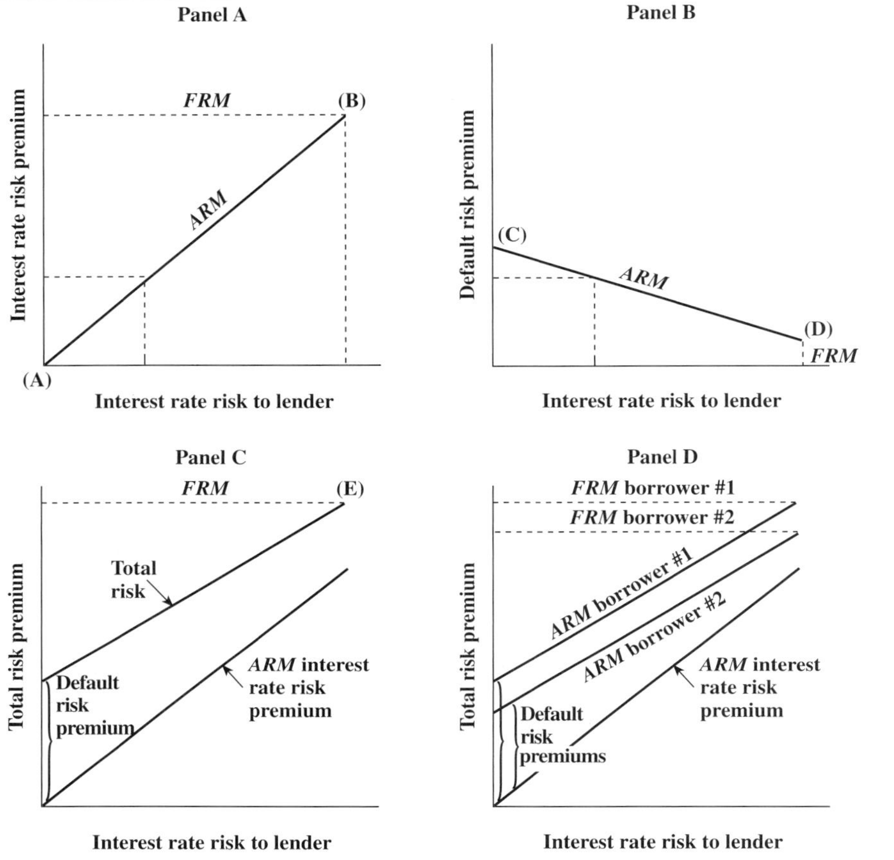

When interest rate risk assumed by the borrower increases (as would be the case with an ARM with *no cap* on payments or the interest rate), *default risk* assumed by the lender increases (see panel B). Default risk is greatest at point C, where there are no restrictions on ARM interest rates or payments, because the borrower faces a greater likelihood that unanticipated changes in interest rates may cause significant increases in payments ("payment shock") relative to income. Hence, the likelihood of default is greater when the borrower assumes all interest rate risk. However, as more interest rate risk is assumed by the lender, we should note in panel B that risk of borrower default declines because payment shock to the borrower is restricted when caps on payments or interest rates are used. In essence, by assuming more interest rate risk, the *lender* absorbs more shock, thereby reducing *borrower* default risk. This pattern is exhibited in panel B where the default risk curve is shown as negatively related to the risk premium demanded by the lender as interest rate risk to the lender increases. However, the level of default risk never declines below the risk assumed by the lender on a fixed rate mortgage (point D), which is also coincident with the lender's assumption of all interest rate risk (point B in panel A).

The total risk curve (see panel C of Exhibit 5–4), establishes the risk premium demanded by the lender for both risks (interest rate risk and default risk) assumed under various ARM terms. The total amount of risk assumed by the lender corresponds to various combinations of ARM terms ranging from the assumption of all interest rate risk by the borrower (panel A, point A) to the assumption of all interest rate risk by the lender (panel A, point B) coupled with the amount of default risk incurred by the lender given different levels of interest rate risk (panel B). Hence, panel C shows the total risk premium the lender should earn, given levels of interest rate risk and default risk that correspond to various levels of interest rate risk. However, the total risk premium should not exceed the total premium that would be earned on a FRM (panel C, point E).

Panel D in Exhibit 5–4 shows the relationship between total risk and the risk premium demanded by the lender for *different borrowers*. Note that the amount of *interest rate risk* remains the same for each borrower; however, *default risk* differs. Hence, the premium charged by the lender on ARMs will vary, depending on the amount of default risk being assumed for each borrower, (1) or (2), and how that default risk interacts with expected changes in interest rate risk. We should point out that many other non-interest rate factors can cause default such as loss of employment, divorce, and so on. We focus here only on how default risk changes with fluctuations in interest rates.

Exhibit 5–4 is appropriate only for specific borrowers, however. To date, the exact relationship between default risk and interest rate risk for many different classes of borrowers has not been studied extensively. Hence, you cannot generalize the example shown to all borrowers and lenders in the mortgage market. However, it is safe to say that ARM loans will only be made to an individual borrower as long as the expected benefits to the lender from shifting interest rate risk exceed potential default losses. Similarly, as long as a given borrower is willing to undertake interest rate risk in exchange for paying a lower risk premium to a lender, the ARM will be acceptable to the borrower.

While Exhibit 5–4 graphically portrays the risk/return trade-off faced by lenders and borrowers, ARM terms may be structured in many ways to provide a trade-off between interest rate and default risk that is satisfactory to both. These terms could include many possible combinations of initial interest rates, margin, points, the index chosen, frequency of payment adjustments, caps on payments, and so on. We will explore various combinations of ARM terms later in this chapter.

From the above discussion, then, mortgage lending (borrowing) can be viewed as a process of *pricing risk*, with the expected yield being the return received (paid) by lenders (borrowers) for making loans with terms under which lenders and borrowers bear various amounts of risk. The terms utilized in construction of an ARM (e.g., initial rate, index, adjustment period, caps) are simply the "tools" at the disposal of borrowers and lenders to negotiate and allocate the amounts of interest rate and default risk being shared.[8]

---

[8]If risk could be quantified, or reduced to some unit quantity such as dollars, an agreement could be devised that would specify exactly how much risk was being shared. However, because risk is an abstract concept, this is not possible. This is the reason why borrowers and lenders include various provisions in contracts to share risk under any set of unknown future economic conditions.

Expected Yield Relationships and Interest Rate Risk

While the contracting process used by lenders and borrowers to allocate risk is a complicated one, there are some general relationships regarding interest rate risk and yields that can be employed in this process. The following general relationships regarding interest rate risk may be useful when comparing ARMs with FRMs and comparing ARMs containing different loan provisions with one another. The relationships focus on the effects of interest rate risk on ARM yields, given the conclusion that an ARM will never be made unless the expected benefit to a lender from shifting interest rate risk to a borrower exceeds expected losses from default risk. Proceeding with this assumption when evaluating ARM terms, interest rate risk, and expected yields to lenders, we should consider the following relationships:

1. At the time of origination, the *expected* yield on an ARM should be less than the *expected* yield on a FRM, to the extent that benefits to lenders from shifting interest rate risk exceed increases in default risk to borrowers. Otherwise, the borrower and lender will always prefer a FRM. Coincident with the lower expected ARM yield, the *initial interest rate* on an ARM will *usually* be less than that of a FRM.[9]

2. Adjustable rate mortgages tied to short-term indexes are generally riskier to borrowers than ARMs tied to long-term indexes because the latter are generally more variable than long-term interest rates. Therefore, the more risk-averse ARM borrowers will generally prefer ARMs tied to a longer-term index and they should be willing to pay more (a higher risk premium and expected yield to the lender). Less risk-averse borrowers will prefer a shorter term index and will expect to pay less for taking additional interest rate risk. Borrowers who prefer no interest rate risk will choose a fixed rate mortgage and will pay the highest total risk premium to the lender.

3. Coincidentally with (2), ARMs with shorter time intervals between adjustments in payments are generally riskier to borrowers than those with longer time periods because, although an ARM may be tied to a short-term index, the adjustment period may not coincide with the index. For example, an ARM may be adjusted every *three* years based on the value of the *one-year* index at the time of adjustment. Hence, the more frequent the adjustment interval, the lower the interest rate risk to lenders because ARM payments will reflect current market conditions irrespective of the index chosen. Borrowers preferring no adjustment in payments will choose FRMs.

4. To the extent ARMs contain maximum caps on interest rate adjustments, the interest rate risk incurred by borrowers will be lower. Hence, the expected yield realized by lenders should be higher than if no restrictions were present. The expected yield will vary with the size of the limitations. When floors are used, the risk to the borrower is greater because of the limit placed on the decline in the interest rate used to compute ARM payments in any given year. Borrowers who prefer certainty in payments and interest rates will choose a FRM, which will always provide the highest *expected* yield to the lender.

5. If an ARM has negative amortization due to a payment cap, then the effect of changes in interest rates will not materially reduce interest rate risk to borrowers or the expected yield to lenders because any interest foregone because of limitations or caps will be deferred and become a part of the loan balance. Any amounts of negative amortization will also accrue compound interest and must be eventually paid by borrowers.

---

[9] Although the initial interest rate on an ARM should generally be less than that of a FRM, in cases where short-term interest rates are greater than long-term rates and an ARM is tied to a short-term rate, it is possible that the initial rate on an ARM may be greater than an initial interest rate on a FRM. However, the *expected yield* on an ARM should be lower because yields are computed to maturity, which includes expected future interest rate patterns.

Initial ARM Terms. In the preceding section, we described some general relationships regarding ARM loan terms, risk bearing, and what lenders (borrowers) should expect to yield (pay) over the life of the ARM contract, or repayment period. We must point out, however, that lenders and borrowers also negotiate certain *initial* loan provisions that (1) will be known at the point of origination and (2) will affect expected yields. Once the index frequency of payment adjustments, rates of payments, and negative amortization have been negotiated, the magnitude of the effect on lenders and borrowers will be determined solely by future market conditions. However, the initial terms on ARMs, or the loan amount, maturity, initial interest rate, margin, and discount points, are quantifiable and can be negotiated with complete certainty at the time the loan is made. These initial loan terms will reflect the net effect of (1) the amount of interest rate risk assumed by the lender as determined by the index chosen, adjustment period, any caps or negative amortization, and (2) the amount of default risk assumed by the lender as determined by the amount of interest rate risk shifted to a specific borrower. Exhibit 5–5 contains a summary of hypothetical loan terms being quoted on three ARMs and one FRM.

A careful review of these loans reveals considerable differences in terms. We note that the initial interest rate for ARM I is 8 percent, for ARM II it is 9 percent, and for ARM III it is 11 percent, while the fixed interest rate mortgage is quoted at 14 percent. Why is this?

A quick review of the terms for ARM I shows that it has the same terms (*b*)–(*f*) as ARMs II and III, however, characteristics (*g*)–(*i*) reveal that future payments and interest rates are *unrestricted* since there are no caps on payments or interest rates. These terms may now be compared with ARM II, which has a cap of 7.5 percent between any adjustment period plus a provision for negative amortization. ARM III has an interest rate cap of 2 percent between adjustment periods and 5 percent over the life of the loan. When all three ARMs are compared, it is clear that the borrower is assuming more interest rate risk with ARM I than with any of the other ARMs. Hence, the expected yield on ARM I to the lender should be *less*, when compared with other ARMs, for an otherwise qualified borrower (i.e., a borrower with an acceptable level of default risk under all three ARM choices).

Because the *expected yield* should be *less* for ARM I, the *initial interest rate* will also generally be *lower* than each of the initial rates shown for the other ARM alternatives. Given that all ARMs are tied to the same index and have the same margin and discount points, the only way to "price" ARM I to achieve a lower expected yield is to *reduce* the initial interest rate relative to the other ARMs. ARM I should also have the largest discount, or spread, relative to the interest rate on the FRM. This would be expected because the borrower is bearing all interest rate risk; hence, the lender should expect to earn a lower risk premium and therefore a lower *yield* on ARM I when compared with the FRM (again, default risk is assumed to be acceptable for this borrower if ARM I is made).

Using a lower initial rate as an inducement for borrowers to accept more interest rate risk and unrestricted payments in the future is obviously only one of many combinations of terms that may be used to differentiate ARM I from ARMs II and III and from the FRM. For example, the lender could keep the initial rate on ARM I the same as that offered on ARM II, but reduce the margin on ARM I or charge fewer discount points, or both. Other terms, such as the choice of index, payment adjustment intervals, and so on, could also be varied with these three terms to accomplish the same objectives.

Exhibit 5–5 Comparison of Hypothetical Loan Terms

Contents	*ARM I*	*ARM II*	*ARM III*	*FRM*
(*a*) Initial interest rate	8%	9%	11%	14%
(*b*) Loan maturity	30	30	30	30
(*c*) Maturity of instruments making up index	1 year	1 year	1 year	—
(*d*) Percent margin above index	2%	2%	2%	—
(*e*) Adjustment interval	1 year	1 year	1 year	—
(*f*) Points	2%	2%	2%	2%
(*g*) Payment cap	None	7.5%	—	—
(*h*) Interest rate cap	None	None	2%, 5%*	—
(*i*) Negative amortization	—	Yes	—	—

*2 percent maximum annual increase, 5 percent total increase over the loan term.

Moving to ARMs II and III in Exhibit 5–5, we note that both have initial interest rates that are greater than the initial rate on ARM I. The interest rate on ARM II is greater than that of ARM I because ARM II has a cap on payments that reduces payment uncertainty for the borrower.

When ARM III is compared to ARMs I and II, the interest rate risk assumed by the lender is clearly greater because payments are limited by interest rate caps. In this case, should market interest rates rise, the interest rate cap would restrict interest payments and not allow the lender to recover any lost interest. When compared with ARMs I and II, ARM III provides that more interest rate risk will be borne by the lender. Hence, it should be originated at a higher initial rate of interest.

Important note should be taken of other possibilities in Exhibit 5–5. If other terms, such as the index and adjustment interval, were to be changed, we would also expect changes in the initial loan terms. Suppose that in ARM I an index based on securities with longer maturities were to be chosen or payment intervals were longer than those shown. We would then expect either or all of the initial rate, index, or points to *increase* because of lower interest rate risk to the borrower; the risk is less because indexes tied to securities based on longer maturities are not as volatile as those based on shorter maturities. Obviously the same would hold true for the other ARMs if a longer-term index and payment interval were used. Indeed, if such changes were made to the other ARMs, they would become more like a FRM. If longer-term indexes and lower caps were used on ARMs II and III, interest rate risk bearing would become greater for the lender; hence, the expected yield earned by the lender should approach that of a FRM as of the date of origination.

ARM Payment Mechanics

To illustrate how payment adjustments and loan balances are determined over the term for the ARMs in Exhibit 5–5, consider the example of a loan amount of $60,000 with a term of 30 years. We assume that the ARM interest rate will be adjusted annually. Hence, the first adjustment will occur at the beginning of the second year. At that time, the composite rate on the loan will be determined by the index of one-year U.S. Treasury securities, plus a 2 percent margin. If we assume (1) that the index of one-year Treasury securities takes on a pattern of 10, 13, 15, and 10 percent for the *next* four years, based on forward rates in existence at the time each ARM is originated, and (2) that monthly payment and interest rate adjustments are made annually, what would payment adjustments, loan balances, and expected yields be for an ARM with these assumed characteristics?

No Caps or Limitations on Payments or Interest Rates. The first case to consider is ARM I, where payments are unrestricted or allowed to move up or down with the index without limit. What would be the payment pattern on such an ARM given that the expected distribution of future interest rates actually occurred? This unrestricted case, where no limitations apply to payments or interest, is straightforward to deal with.

The first four columns of Exhibit 5–6 contain the data needed for our computations. Note that we assume that the initial interest rate is 8 percent for the first year, but after the first year the index *plus* the 2 percent margin establish what the payment will be. From the beginning of year 2 through the beginning of year 5 the interest rates used to determine payments are 12, 15, 17, and 12, respectively, based on our assumptions. As previously pointed out, ARMs tied to the same index may vary with respect to the initial rate of interest, the margin, and, perhaps, discount points offered by lenders. These components are usually set by competitive conditions in the lending area and are the primary variables (along with caps or other restrictions) with which lenders compete when pricing loans. Lenders have no control over the index and, therefore, must rely on other components with which to compete when pricing the loan.

The payments column of Exhibit 5–6 is based on a series of relatively simple computations. They are carried out as though a new loan is originated at the end of each year based on a new rate of interest, as determined by the index plus the margin, applied to the outstanding loan balance. For example, the initial mortgage payment (*MP*) is determined as

$$\begin{aligned} MP &= \$60{,}000(MLC, 8\%, 360 \text{ mos.}) \\ &= \$60{,}000(.007338) \\ &= \$440.28 \end{aligned}$$

The mortgage balance (*MB*) at the end of the first year will be

$$\begin{aligned} MB_1 &= \$440.28(MPVIFA, 8\%, 348 \text{ mos.}) \\ &= \$440.28\ (135.145031)\ (\text{rounded}) \\ &= \$59{,}502 \end{aligned}$$

At the beginning of year 2, payments would be computed based on a new interest rate of 12 percent for the remaining loan term of 348 months. Hence, the new payment would be

$$\begin{aligned} MP_2 &= \$59{,}502(MLC, 12\%, 348 \text{ mos.}) \\ &= \$614.30 \end{aligned}$$

The mortgage loan balance at the end of the second year would be

$$\begin{aligned} MB_2 &= \$614.30(MPVIFA, 12\%, 336 \text{ mos.}) \\ &= \$614.30(96.468019) \\ &= \$59.260 \end{aligned}$$

The process of (1) computing the loan balance, based on the interest rate applicable during the year for which the balance is desired, and (2) computing the new payment, based on any change in the index at the end of the appropriate adjustment interval, would continue after each adjustment interval over the remaining life of the loan.

EXHIBIT 5–6 Summary Data and Results: ARM I (unrestricted case)

(1) Year	(2) Index	+	(3) Margin	=	(4) Interest Rate	(5) Payments	(6) Percent Change in Payments	(7) Balance†
1					8%*	$440.28		$59,502
2	10%		2%		12	614.30	+39.5	59,260
3	13		2		15	752.27	+22.5	59,106
4	15		2		17	846.21	+12.5	58,990
5	10		2		12	617.60	−27.0	58,639

*Initial rate.
†Rounded.

Calculator Solution
1st step: Determine 1st year payment
n = 30 × 12 = 360
i = 8% ÷ 12 = .66666%
PV = $60,000
FV = 0
Solve for payment:
PMT = −$440.26
2nd step: Determine 1st year MB
n = 29 × 12 = 348
i = 8% ÷ 12 = .66666%
PMT = −$440.26
FV = 0
Solve for *MB:*
PV = $59,499
3rd step: Determine 2nd year payment
n = 29 × 12 = 348
i = 12% ÷ 12 = 1%
PV = $59,499
FV = 0
Solve for payment:
PMT = −$614.25
4th step: Determine 2nd year MB
n = 28 × 12 = 336
i = 12% ÷ 12 = 1%
PMT = −$614.25
FV = 0
Solve for *MB*:
PV = $59,255

Looking again at Exhibit 5–6, we carry out the computations using the hypothetical interest rate pattern. Assuming no restrictions or caps on interest rates or payments, we see considerable variation in the payment pattern. Payments increase by as much as 39.5 percent and decline by as much as 27 percent during the first five years. For borrowers who have a strong aversion to interest rate risk and the coincident variability in payments, the unrestricted ARM, tied to a short-term instrument, may not be desirable. One final pattern should be noted in Exhibit 5–6: regardless of the interest rate pattern chosen, the loan is amortizing. The rate of amortization will differ, however, depending on the rate of interest in effect at each adjustment interval.

The default risk associated with ARM I should also be clear from Exhibit 5–6. Note that although the initial payment level is low, the variation in payments over the five-year period is great. Clearly, for a borrower to take this risk, the lender must view the borrower's future income or present and future wealth as sufficient to cover significant changes in monthly payments.

Payment Caps and Negative Amortization. We now consider ARM II where the lender and borrower have agreed that to moderate possible interest rate fluctuations in the future, there will be a cap, or maximum rate, of 7.5 percent at which *payments* can increase between adjustment intervals. In this case, however, any difference between payments and interest that should be earned, based on unrestricted changes in interest rates, will be added to the loan balance. As previously discussed, this type of ARM contains a payment cap and *negative amortization*.[10]

Because this ARM allows for a payment cap and negative amortization, the receipt of more cash flow is pushed further into the future than in the unrestricted case. Therefore, interest rate risk to the lender is somewhat greater than with ARM I, so we assume that the initial rate on the mortgage is quoted to be 9 percent while the margin will remain at 2 percent. Exhibit 5–7 contains computations of the payment and loan balance patterns for the ARM just described. As shown in the exhibit, based on an unrestricted change in our hypothetical pattern of interest rates, monthly payments in the second year would be $615.18, or 27.4 percent higher than the $482.77 payment required during the first year. A payment of $615.18 would obviously be greater than the 7.5 percent maximum allowable increase; hence the payment would be capped at $518.98, or 7.5 percent more than $482.77. However, because this ARM requires negative amortization, the difference between interest charged during year 2, or 12 percent, and the amount actually paid will be added to the outstanding loan balance plus compound interest.

Negative amortization is computed by using the method shown for the GPM in Chapter 4. Exhibit 5–7 contains a breakdown of interest and amortization for ARM II. Note that during the first year when loan payments are computed at 9 percent interest, monthly amortization occurs and the loan balance is reduced. After the first year, monthly payments must be computed *first* based on the unrestricted interest rate (column 3) to determine whether payments will increase at a rate greater than 7.5 percent. If uncapped payments would exceed 7.5 percent, then the payment cap (column 4) becomes operative and actual payments will be restricted to a 7.5 percent increase. The monthly interest that is accruing on the loan balance at the unrestricted rate is (.12 ÷ 12)$59,590 = $595.90 (column 6). However, the payment that will actually be made is $518.98. The difference, $76.92 (column 7), must be added to the loan balance with compound interest. Hence, the difference in year 2,

[10]Most ARM programs no longer allow negative amortization. However, we include this example to illustrate how mortgage payment mechanics can be modified to include negative amortization when necessary.

EXHIBIT 5–7 Determination of Payment Limits (negative amortization: ARM II, with payment cap = 7.5 percent annually)

(1) Beginning of Year	*(2)* Balance (rounded)	*(3)* Uncapped Payment	Percent Change in Payments	*(4)* Payment Capped at 7.5 Percent
1	$60,000	$482.77		$482.77
2	59,590	615.18	+27.4	518.98
3	60,566	768.91	+48.2	557.90
4	63,128	903.79	+62.0	599.74
5	66,952	700.96	+16.8	644.72

(5) Monthly Interest Rate	*(6)* Monthly Interest (5) × (2)	*(7)* Monthly Amortization (4) − (6)	*(8)* Annual Amortization (7) × MFVIFA in (5)
.09 ÷ 12	$450.00	$ 32.77	$ 409.87
.12 ÷ 12	595.90	(76.92)	(975.54)
.15 ÷ 12	757.08	(199.18)	(2,561.53)
.17 ÷ 12	894.31	(294.57)	(3,823.69)
.12 ÷ 12	669.52	(24.80)	(314.53)

$76.92 per month, is compounded at 1 percent per month (column 8) resulting in an increase of $975.54 in the loan balance.[11]

Payments in the third year of the ARM are determined by again establishing whether uncapped payments would increase by more than 7.5 percent. To determine this, we find that the loan balance, which includes the previous year's negative amortization, is $59,590 + $975.54 = $60,566 (rounded). The *unrestricted* interest rate of 15 percent for the remaining 336 months is used to compute the uncapped payment. Uncapped payments based on the unrestricted rate of 15 percent would be $768.91. This is a 48 percent increase from $518.98; hence the payment will again be capped at a 7.5 percent increase, and negative amortization will be computed on the interest shortfall, compounded at 15 percent monthly, and added to the loan balance. This process is repeated for each adjustment interval over the life of the loan.[12] Actual loan balances with payments capped at 7.5 percent are shown in Exhibit 5–8.

Another observation regarding ARM II (see Exhibit 5–7) has to do with the increase in both the payment and loan balance during year 5 even though there is a significant decline in the interest index from 17 to 12 percent. This occurs because

[11]It would be possible to moderate fluctuations in monthly payments to some degree by extending the loan maturity. This could be done by simply substituting the desired maturity at any adjustment interval and computing payments based on the prevailing index and the new maturity desired. If the maturity was extended, it would reduce monthly payments somewhat, thereby moderating fluctuations in monthly payments.

[12]ARMs with negative amortization provisions usually limit increases in the loan balance during the life of the loan because it is possible for the loan balance to increase to a level that exceeds the value of the property serving as security for the loan. Consequently, lenders and borrowers must agree that if a pre-specified maximum is reached, the lender must either forgo further accumulation of interest in the loan balance or require that monthly payments be increased at that time.

EXHIBIT 5–8 ARM II: Loan Balances When Payments Are Capped at 7.5 Percent Annually (negative amortization allowed)

Year	*Index*	*Margin*	*Interest Rate*	*Payments*	*Percent Change in Payments*	*Loan Balances*	*Percent Change In Balance*†
1			9%*	$482.77			
2	10%	2%	12	518.98	+7.5	$60,566	+.6
3	13	2	15	557.90	+7.5	63,128	+4.2
4	15	2	17	599.74	+7.5	66,952	+6.1
5	10	2	12	644.72	+7.5	67,267	+.5

*Origination rate.
†Rounded.

the loan balance has increased, due to past negative amortization, to $66,952 at the end of year 4. Even though the interest rate declines to 12 percent, monthly interest will be $669.52, which is in excess of the maximum 7.5 percent increase from the $599.74 payment in the preceding year. Hence, payments would increase by 7.5 percent, even though interest rates have declined.

Interest Rate Caps. The final case that we consider with ARMs is a common pattern in which interest rates are capped or limited (see Exhibit 5–9). In ARM III, the increase in interest rates is limited to 2 percent during any one adjustment interval (year in our example) and to a *total* of 5 percent over the life of the loan. If interest rates ever exceed these caps, payments are limited. Hence, the interest rate cap also acts as a payment cap because the maximum increase in interest rate determines the maximum increase in mortgage payments. This means that if the index plus the margin exceeds these caps, the lender will lose any amount of interest above the capped rates.[13] Exhibit 5–9 illustrates the payment mechanics of ARM III, where the interest rate quoted at origination, 11 percent, is higher than it is with ARMs I and II because the latter two have unrestricted interest rates while ARM III has interest rate caps. Therefore the lender is taking more interest rate risk with ARM III because of the possibility that the cap will be exceeded and interest will be lost. To compensate for this possibility, the lender will charge a higher initial interest rate and should expect to earn a higher expected yield.

The payment patterns shown in Exhibit 5–9 are determined from the loan balance established at the end of each adjustment interval. Payments are then computed based on the indicated rate of interest for the remaining term. Results of computations show that, compared with ARM I (the unrestricted case), payments on ARM III are higher initially, then remain generally lower than payments on ARM I for the remaining term. Hence, borrowers would have to have more income to qualify for ARM III and default risk to the lender should be lower. The loan balances for both

[13]In many cases, ARMs may contain floors as well as a cap. In our example, this would mean that a maximum reduction of 2 percent in the mortgage rate would be allowed, regardless of the decline in the index. These floors have limited effectiveness, however, because if a significant decline in the index occurs and the loan agreement allows for prepayment, borrowers may *refinance* with a new mortgage loan at a rate that is lower than the floor would allow.

EXHIBIT 5–9 Summary Data and Results: ARM III Interest Rates Capped at 2 Percent, 5 Percent (no negative amortization allowed)

Year	Index + Margin	Capped Interest Rate	Payments	Percent Change in Payments	Balance
1		11%	$571.39		$59,730
2	12%	12	616.63	+7.9	59,485
3	15	14	708.37	+14.9	59,301
4	17	16	801.65	+13.2	59,159
5	12	12	619.37	−22.7	58,807

ARMs are about the same in year 5. ARM III payments begin at a higher level than those of ARM II, because of the higher initial rate of interest and remain higher over the term of the loan. However, because of negative amortization, loan balances over time for ARM II are significantly higher than for ARM III.

Expected Yields on ARMs: A Comparison

In the preceding sections, we examined three kinds of ARMs with provisions commonly used in real estate lending. Other considerations are also important to lenders and borrowers. One important issue is the *yield* to lenders, or *cost* to borrowers, for each category of loan. Given the changes in interest rates, payments, and loan balances, it is not obvious what these yields (costs) will be.

Computing Yields on ARMs. To compare yields on ARMs, the yield (cost) to the lender (borrower) must be computed for each alternative by solving for the internal rate of return, or the rate of discount. This rate makes the present value of all expected mortgage payments and the loan balance in the year of repayment equal to the initial loan amount less discount points (or $58,800) for each alternative. To illustrate, consider the case of the *unrestricted* ARM I which is paid off in year 5. Using data from Exhibit 5–6, we compute the internal rate of return (or yield) as shown in Exhibit 5–10.

From the computations shown in Exhibit 5–10, we see that the solution is approximately 13.0 percent.[14] This means that even though the *initial* rate of interest was 8 percent and the forward rates of interest are expected to range from 8 to 17 percent over the five-year period, the *expected* yield (cost) is 13.0 percent. Hence by computing the internal rate of return we have a result that can be compared among alternative ARMs.

Before comparing results for each ARM considered, we examine the computational procedure used in Exhibit 5–10. Essentially, we are discounting a series of grouped cash flows. In the present case, we are dealing with five groups of monthly cash flows and a single receipt (the loan balance). Note that we discount each group of monthly cash flows by using the present value of a monthly annuity factor of 13 percent (column 3). However, this procedure gives us a present value for a *one-year group* of 12 monthly payments and does not take into account that the cash flows occurring from years 2 through 5 are not received during year 1. Hence, each of the

[14]Using a financial calculator yields a solution of 13.0 percent. We will rely on this result in our discussion.

EXHIBIT 5–10 Computing the IRR for an Unrestricted ARM, Payoff at End of Year 5

(1) Year	(2) Monthly Payments		(3) MPVIFA, 13%, 12 Months		(4) MPVIF, 13%, Years 1–5		(5) PV
1	$ 440.28	×	11.196042	×	—	=	$ 4,929.39
2	614.30	×	11.196042	×	.878710	=	6,043.53
3	752.27	×	11.196042	×	.772130	=	6,503.22
4	846.21	×	11.196042	×	.678478	=	6,428.04
5	617.60	×	11.196042	×	.596185	=	4,122.43
5	$58,639.00	×	—	×	.523874	=	30,719.45
							$58,746.06*

*Desired *PV* = $58,800: *IRR* approximately 13 percent.

grouped cash flows must be discounted again by the present value of $1 factor to recognize that the present value of each group of cash flows is not received at the same time. This is carried out in column 4. The loan balance, or $58,639, is then discounted as a lump sum.

Concluding Observations: ARMs, Borrower, Lender, and Market Behavior. Recalling the graphic analysis of the risk premium and the relationship between interest rate and default risk in Exhibit 5–4, we now show how risk premiums demanded for ARMs I–III would fall on the total risk curve in Exhibit 5–11. This diagram basically indicates that moving from ARM I to ARM III, interest rate risk to the lender increases. However, based on panel B in Exhibit 5–4, we recall that as interest rate risk increases to the lender, default risk for a specific borrower declines due to interest rate changes. Following the market rule that benefits to the lender (from shifting interest rate risk to the borrower) *must exceed* expected default risk for the ARM to be originated, we see in Exhibit 5–11 that the total risk premium, and hence the expected yield to the lender, increases as we move from ARM I to ARM III. All expected ARM yields remain below that of the FRM, as they should.

We also know that, in general, the initial interest rate and expected yield for all ARMs should be lower than that of a FRM on the day of origination. The extent to which the initial rate and expected yield on an ARM will be lower than that on a FRM or another ARM, depends on the terms relative to payments, caps, and so on. Terms that are more unrestricted and shift more interest rate risk to the borrower will generally have initial interest rates that are discounted furthest from FRMs. They will also be discounted from ARMs containing caps on payment and interest rate increases. Hence, when a borrower is faced with selecting from a given set of ARMs with different terms and expectations of forward interest rates, an expected yield must be calculated before a comparison among adjustable rate mortgages and a fixed rate mortgage can be accomplished. While there is no guarantee that the *expected* yield calculated at origination will be the actual yield or cost of funds over the term of the ARM, the expected yield represents the *best estimate* of the cost of an ARM based on information available at the time of origination.

EXHIBIT 5–11 Ranking ARMs Based on Total Risk

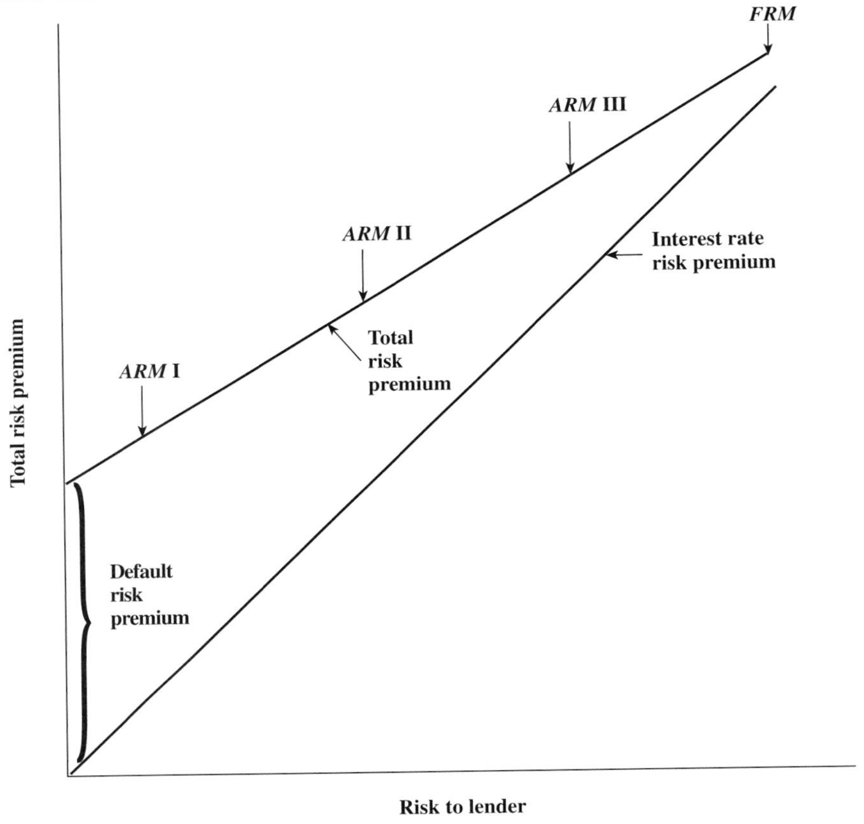

Shared Appreciation Mortgages

The final type of mortgage that we will consider is one referred to as the **shared appreciation mortgage (SAM).** This mortgage design is also intended to deal with the problem of uncertain future inflation. It is similar in some ways to the price level adjusted mortgage (PLAM) considered earlier because it has a lower contract interest rate that is then adjusted for inflation. However, the nature of the adjustment is quite different. Recall that the PLAM had the loan balance adjusted periodically based on the change in a price level index. With the SAM, the lender receives an agreed upon percentage of the appreciation in the value of the home used as collateral for the loan.

To illustrate this loan, we return to our example of the $60,000 loan. When we considered this loan as a constant payment mortgage (CPM), we assumed it had a 12 percent interest rate with a 30-year loan term. Let us assume the same lender is willing to make a SAM at a 9 percent contract rate with the lender receiving one-half of any appreciation in the value of the home. (The lender will not share in any depreciation, however.) The loan will be amortized over 30 years, but the payment to the lender for price appreciation is due either at the end of 10 years or whenever the home is sold, if it is sold before the 10 years are up. If the home is not sold by the end of the 10 years, an appraisal is made to determine what amount is due the lender.

Payments on the loan based on the 9 percent contract rate will be $482.77 per month. Recall that the payment based on the 12 percent market rate was $617.17. We will assume that the home is currently worth $90,000 and that it is expected to increase at the inflation rate of 6 percent per year. After 10 years, the home will be worth $\$90{,}000(1.06)^{10} = \$161{,}176$. Thus the appreciation is $\$161{,}176 - \$90{,}000 = \$71{,}176$, and the lender will receive one-half of this, or $35,588. In addition, the lender will receive the loan balance based on the initial 9 percent, 30-year term of $53,657.

One of the first things to consider when analyzing this loan is what the effective yield will be, based on the payments and price appreciation assumed above. This is a relatively simple calculation. The payment stream will consist of annual payments and the sum of the loan balance plus the amount of appreciation paid to the lender at the end of the 10 years. We want to find the discount rate that equates these payments with the $60,000 loan amount. We have

$$\$60{,}000 = \$482.77(MPVIFA, ?\%, 10 \text{ yrs.}) + \$89{,}245(MPVIF, ?\%, 10 \text{ yrs.})$$

Using a financial calculator, we find the yield to be 12.17 percent, which is slightly higher than the fixed rate CPM. The actual yield will depend on what the actual appreciation in the home is over the 10-year period. It could be greater or less than 12.17 percent. One would expect the yield on the SAM to be greater than that of a CPM because a greater amount of the yield is determined by the appreciation, which in turn is uncertain and comprises a greater amount of cash flow received in year 10.

Like the PLAM, the SAM begins with payments based on a lower interest rate. However, the payments on the PLAM are adjusted after the first year based on inflation for the previous year. With the SAM, payments remain the same. The adjustment for inflation is made all at once at a previously agreed upon future time, 10 years in our example. The inflation premium is usually paid by the borrower from the sale of the home or from funds obtained by refinancing. Thus the borrower is not faced with continually increasing mortgage payments as is the case with the PLAM. The adjustment is also based on the inflation rate for the home instead of a more general inflation index, which may not correlate with the increase in the value of the home.

From the foregoing discussion, it is clear that the SAM provides an alternative way for the lender to be compensated for increases in inflation and thus transfers much of the risk of price level increases to the borrower. The SAM has not been used extensively by borrowers and lenders for several possible reasons.

1. Lenders may prefer not to wait years before receiving compensation for price level increases.

2. While borrowers may like the idea of the inflation adjustment depending only on the increase in the value of the home and not on the more general price index, lenders may be concerned with how well a particular house will keep up with inflation. Clearly, there are many factors besides inflation that affect the future value of a house.

3. The amount of appreciation in the value of the home depends on actions by borrowers after the loan is closed, such as how well the property is maintained. Borrowers may have less incentive to maintain their homes because the lender shares in any increase in home value resulting from good maintenance.

4. Until recently, it was not clear whether the appreciation paid to a lender would be considered "contingent" interest or a reduction in the capital gain from the

sale of the home. This is important for tax purposes. It has recently been ruled that appreciation is contingent interest and is therefore deductible against ordinary income. This is more attractive than if appreciation reduced only capital gains, which are taxed at a lower effective rate.

Conclusion

In this chapter, we have shown how mortgage loan terms can be modified to incorporate variable interest rates. Loans with adjustable interest rates become necessary from time to time, depending on the rate of economic expansion and expected rates of inflation. In many situations, when the expected rate of inflation accelerates and becomes more uncertain, questions arise as to whether borrowers or lenders will bear the risk of future interest rate changes. During these times, fixed interest rate lending becomes very costly to borrowers because fixed interest rates and mortgage payments increase at a greater rate than borrower incomes. This imbalance between loan payments and borrower incomes motivates both borrowers and lenders to seek ways to modify loan agreements so that real estate purchases can be financed at loan payment levels that are commensurate with current borrower incomes. ARM loans provide one solution to the imbalance problem. Through a variety of options, including the benchmark index chosen for ARM interest rates; the volatility of the index; frequency of payment adjustment; annual and over-the-loan life interest rate caps; and negative amortization and other features, lenders and borrowers can negotiate loans and payment structures that result in interest rate risk-sharing agreements that are satisfactory to all parties.

Key Terms

adjustable rate mortgage (ARM) 115
adjustment interval 125
caps 125
composite rate 125
floors 125
index 125
interest rate risk 115
margin 125
maturity gap 119
negative amortization 125
price level adjusted mortgage (PLAM) 119
shared appreciation mortgage (SAM) 140
spread 118
unanticipated inflation 116

Questions

1. In the previous chapter, significant problems about the ability of borrowers to meet mortgage payments and the evolution of fixed interest rate mortgages with various payment patterns were discussed. Why didn't this evolution address problems faced by lenders? What have lenders done in recent years to overcome these problems?
2. What is meant by the "spread" and "maturity gap" problems faced by savings institutions that supply much of the funds made available for mortgage loans?
3. How do inflationary expectations influence interest rates on mortgage loans?
4. How does the price level adjusted mortgage (PLAM) address the problem of uncertainty in inflationary expectations? What are some of the practical limitations in implementing a PLAM program?
5. Why do adjustable rate mortgages (ARMs) seem to be a more suitable alternative for mortgage lending than PLAMs?
6. List each of the main terms likely to be negotiated in an ARM. What does pricing an ARM using these terms mean?
7. What is the difference between interest rate risk and default risk? How do combinations of terms in ARMs affect the allocation of risk between borrowers and lenders?
8. Which of the following two ARMs is likely to be priced higher; that is, offered with a higher initial interest rate? ARM A has a margin of 3 percent and is tied to a three-year index with payments adjustable every two years; payments cannot increase by more than 10 percent from the preceding period; the term

is 30 years and no assumption or points will be allowed. ARM B has a margin of 3 percent and is tied to a one-year index with payments to be adjusted each year; payments cannot increase by more than 10 percent from the preceding period; the term is 30 years and no assumption or points are allowed.

9. What are forward rates of interest? How are they determined? What do they have to do with indexes used to adjust ARM payments?
10. How do ARMs help lenders with their gap management problems? What strategy would lenders like to use in structuring ARM terms with deposit liabilities?
11. Distinguish between the initial rate of interest and expected yield on an ARM. What is the general relationship between the two? How do they generally reflect ARM terms?
12. If an ARM is priced with an initial interest rate of 8 percent and a margin of 2 percent (when the ARM index is also 8 percent at origination) and a fixed rate mortgage (FRM) with constant payment is available at 11 percent, what does this imply about inflation and the forward rates in the yield curve at the time of origination? What is implied if a FRM were available at 10 percent? 12 percent?
13. What is a SAM? Contrast it with a PLAM and an ARM.

Problems

1. A price level adjusted mortgage (PLAM) is made with the following terms:

   Amount = $95,000
   Initial interest rate = 4 percent
   Term = 30 years
   Points = 6 percent

   Payments to be adjusted at the beginning of each year.

   Assuming inflation is expected to increase at the rate of 6 percent per year for the next five years:

   a. Compute the payments at the beginning of each year.
   b. What is the loan balance at the end of the fifth year?
   c. What is the yield to the lender on such a mortgage?

2. A borrower has been analyzing different adjustable rate mortgage (ARM) alternatives for the purchase of his new home. The borrower anticipates owning the home for five years. The lender first offers a $75,000, 15-year ARM with the following terms:

   Initial interest rate = 9 percent
   Index = 1-year Treasuries
   Payments adjusted each year
   Margin = 2 percent
   Interest rate cap = None
   Payment cap = None
   Negative amortization = Not allowed
   Discount points = 2 percent

   Based on estimated forward rates, the index to which the ARM is tied is forecasted as follows: End of year (*EOY*)1 = 10 percent; *EOY* 2 = 8 percent; *EOY* 3 = 12 percent; *EOY* 4 = 14 percent.

   Compute the payments, loan balances, and yield for the unrestricted ARM for the five-year period.

3. Refer to problem 2. As a second ARM alternative, assume the borrower can borrow $75,000 for 30 years with the following terms:

   Initial interest rate = 10 percent
   Index = 1-year Treasuries
   Payments adjusted each year
   Margin = 2 percent
   Interest rate cap = 2/5
   Payment cap = N/A
   Negative amortization = yes
   Discount points = 2 percent

   Based on estimated forward rates, the index to which the ARM is tied is forecasted as follows: End of year (*EOY*)1 = 10 percent; *EOY* 2 = 8 percent; *EOY* 3 = 12 percent; *EOY* 4 = 14 percent.

   Compute the payments, loan balances, and yield for the ARM for the five-year period.

4. Refer to problem 2. Assume that a lender offers a 30-year, $75,000 adjustable rate mortgage with the following terms:

   Initial interest rate = 10.5 percent
   Index = 1-year Treasuries
   Payments adjusted each year
   Margin = 2 percent
   Interest rate cap = 2 percent annually;
   5 percent lifetime
   Discount points = 2 percent

   Based on estimated forward rates, the index to which the ARM is tied is forecasted as follows: End of year (*EOY*)1 = 10 percent; *EOY* 2 = 8 percent; *EOY* 3 = 12 percent; *EOY* 4 = 14 percent.

Compute the payments, loan balances, and yield for the ARM for the five-year period.

5. MakeNu Mortgage Company is offering home buyers a new mortgage instrument called the Stable Home Mortgage. This mortgage is composed of both a fixed rate and an adjustable rate component. Mrs. Maria Perez is interested in financing the purchase of a new home. The home, which costs $100,000, is to be financed by Stable Home Mortgages (SHM) on the following terms:

   a. The SHM requires a 5 percent down payment, costs the borrower 2 discount points, and allows 75 percent of the mortgage to be fixed and 25 percent to be adjustable. The fixed portion of the loan is for 30 years at an annual interest rate of 10.5 percent. Having neither an interest rate nor payment cap, the adjustable portion is also for 30 years with the following terms:

      Initial interest rate = 9 percent

      Index = 1-year Treasuries

      Payments adjusted each year

      Margin = 2 percent

      Interest rate cap = none

      Payment cap = none

   The projected one year U.S. Treasury-bill index, to which the ARM is tied, is as follows: End of year (*EOY*)1 = 10 percent; *EOY* 2 = 11 percent; *EOY* 3 = 8 percent; *EOY* 4 = 12 percent.

   Calculate Mrs. Perez's total monthly payments and end-of-year loan balances for the first five years. Calculate the lender's yield, assuming Mrs. Perez repays the loan after five years.

   b. Repeat part (*a*) under the assumption that the initial interest rate is 9.5 percent and there is an annual interest rate cap of 1 percent.

6. A SAM is made for $95,000 at an initial rate of 8 percent for 30 years. The lender will have a 30 percent share in any increase in the value of the property over the next five years. The property is expected to increase a total of 25 percent over its initial value of $110,000.

   a. What would be the lender's yield, assuming that the property is sold after five years?

   b. Assuming that the lender desires a 12 percent annual yield over the next five years, at what rate would the property have to appreciate to provide this yield?

   c. How would your answer to parts (*a*) and (*b*) change if 2 discount points are charged on the loan?

7. A mortgage loan is made for $100,000 for a 30-year period at 12 percent interest. The borrower and lender have negotiated a monthly payment of $800.

   a. What will be the loan balance at the end of year 5? year 30?

   b. How much interest will be paid and accrued as negative amortization in year 1? year 5?

CHAPTER

6

Underwriting and Financing Residential Properties

This chapter deals with the process of seeking long-term mortgage financing for owner-occupied residential properties. Here we focus on two aspects of this process: loan *underwriting* and *closing*. When discussing the underwriting process, we consider borrower and property characteristics and how loan terms are established. We also consider the size of the loan relative to property value, loan payments relative to borrower income, and default risk undertaken by lenders. We discuss the use of mortgage insurance or guarantees that may be necessary to grant a given loan request in cases where the total risk of lending to a specific borrower is too great for a given lender to undertake. Insurance may be provided by private insurers, or, depending on the property and borrower characteristics, insurance or guarantees may be available from various government agencies.

We look at the loan closing process in terms of the necessary accounting between the borrower, lender, seller, and other parties to a transaction in which transfer of title and a loan closing occur simultaneously, and we consider federal regulations that require certain practices from the lender regarding uniform disclosure of interest charges, closing statements, and collection of credit and other information about the borrower.

Underwriting Default Risk

The process of evaluating a borrower's loan request in terms of potential profitability and risk is referred to as **underwriting.** This function is usually performed by a loan officer at a financial institution, such as a savings and loan association, commercial bank, mutual savings bank, or mortgage banking company. The loan officer performs this analysis based on information contained in (1) the loan application submitted by the borrower and (2) an appraisal of the property. This analysis is made in the context of a lending policy, or guidelines, that a particular institution specifies. In some cases, lenders will require that borrowers obtain **default insurance.** The borrower purchases this insurance policy to protect the lender from potential losses should the borrower default on the loan. In such cases, the lender is not willing to bear the total risk of borrower default, or the loan may be sold to a third-party investor (recall the process of assignment of the note and mortgage discussed in Chapter 2). In the latter case, the lender must consider underwriting standards required by such investors; otherwise the lender may lose the option of selling mortgages later. In deciding whether a loan application should be accepted or rejected, the loan officer follows some fundamental concepts in loan risk analysis.

Before beginning a detailed discussion of specific underwriting standards and policies, we first consider some basic relationships and terms used in mortgage underwriting. Two fundamental relationships that must be assessed by any lender when considering the risk of making a mortgage loan are the expected **payment-to-income ratio** and the **loan-to-value ratio.** The payment-to-income ratio is simply the monthly payment on the loan amount being applied for plus other housing expenses divided by the borrower's income. The loan-to-value ratio is the loan amount requested divided by the estimated property value.

The first ratio is important because the borrower will generally be personally liable on the note, and must be able to make payments either as scheduled (in the case of a *fixed rate mortgage*) or as market conditions change interest rates (in the case of *adjustable rate mortgages*). Clearly, the greater the ratio of mortgage payment to income for a given borrower, the greater is default risk. Hence, a higher risk premium must be earned by the lender. Similarly, because the property being acquired by the borrower also serves as security for the note, as the loan-to-value ratio increases, the likelihood of loss increases. This is because the property may not bring a sufficient price at a foreclosure sale to cover the outstanding loan balance, any past due payments, and foreclosure costs. Therefore, the major problems facing a lender when reviewing a loan request made by a borrower are (1) assessing the many variables that affect default risk, (2) determining whether a fixed interest rate or adjustable rate mortgage can be made, and (3) if the total risk on a particular loan request is too great, deciding whether the loan should be refused or made with default insurance or guarantees from third parties.

Classification of Mortgage Loans

In previous chapters, we discussed and classified mortgage loans mainly in terms of interest rate risk, that is, whether a loan was a fixed rate mortgage (FRM) or an adjustable rate mortgage (ARM). While those chapters also included basic discussion of default risk, specific methods and procedures for assessing borrower default risk are primary topics in this chapter.

Recall from the previous chapter that default risk was defined as a potential loss that could occur if the borrower failed to make payment on a loan. This failure could be caused by a borrower having insufficient income, or because the market value of the property fell below the outstanding mortgage balance, or both. There are several ways that default risk can be shared. Default risk may be fully assumed by the lender, shared by the lender and a third-party insurer, or fully assumed by a third-party insurer or guarantor. To facilitate discussion, we use the following classifications:

1. Conventional mortgages.
2. Insured conventional mortgages.
3. FHA insured mortgages.
4. VA guaranteed mortgage loans.

Conventional Mortgage Loans

Conventional mortgage loans are negotiated between a borrower and lender. From these negotiations, the loan-to-value ratio, interest rate (or ARM terms), and the payment-to-income ratio are established. The loan-to-value ratio establishes the borrower's down payment, or equity. Should the borrower default on the loan, both the lender and borrower may incur losses. Losses usually include any past due interest, costs of selling the property, and the extent to which the sale price is less than the mortgage balance. In the event of loss, the borrower absorbs such losses first to the extent of any equity. If losses exceed the amount of borrower equity, the lender will then incur a loss, which then becomes a claim against the borrower and (depending on state law) may be used to attach other assets owned by the borrower (recall the discussion of deficiency judgments in Chapter 2).

Typically, if the borrower desires a conventional loan, the maximum loan amount will be 80 percent of the value of the real estate being purchased. Recently, many lenders have been lending up to 90 percent of the value without mortgage insurance. Location of the property—for example, in a platted subdivision with city utilities—is a key factor. Because the lender must look to the sale of the property for repayment of the mortgage loan should the borrower default, regulations governing the operation of most savings institutions generally require that for conventional loans, equity of at least 20 percent of value must be provided by the borrower.[1] Therefore, such losses must exceed 20 percent of the original property value before the lender would suffer a loss.

Insured Conventional Mortgage Loans

In many instances, borrowers do not have the necessary wealth to make a down payment of 20 percent of value when purchasing a property. However, if the income-earning ability of the borrower and the location of the property being acquired are satisfactory, lenders may be willing to grant a loan request in excess of 80 percent of value with a condition that the borrower purchase **mortgage insurance** against default risk. Many firms provide this insurance for a premium, which is paid by the borrower and is based on the amount of risk assumed by the mortgage insurer. A useful way of thinking about mortgage insurance is to view the borrower as negotiating for a larger loan from the lender, then paying an insurer to assume the increase in default risk above that taken by the lender on a conventional loan. In other words, only the amount of the loan in *excess* of 80 percent of the property value at the time of loan origination is usually covered under the mortgage insurance policy. Therefore, if a mortgage is made for 95 percent of value and private mortgage insurance is purchased, the borrower would make an equity down payment of 5 percent of the property value and the mortgage lender would make a 95 percent loan. However, the lender would have 80 percent of the loan amount at risk and the mortgage insurer would insure any losses to the lender in an amount equal to 15 percent of the property value. The interest rate charged on this type of loan might be higher than the rate on an uninsured conventional loan because the amount of the loan is greater (95 percent versus 80 percent).

Mortgage insurers are private companies that operate by collecting premiums from borrowers based on the incremental risk being assumed as loan amounts rise above 80 percent. These premiums are pooled and the insurers maintain reserves that are used to pay claims to lenders should mortgage defaults occur. These companies

---

[1]Federal regulations require that residential mortgages cannot be made in excess of 90 percent of value without mortgage insurance. For further information see the *Code of Federal Regulations,* 12 CFR Section 545.32(d)(2).

can usually take this additional risk at a premium that would be lower than individual lenders would have to charge because they insure many different borrowers making mortgage loans nationally whereas individual lenders make loans to fewer individuals in fewer geographic regions. Consequently, mortgage insurers are able to diversify the additional default risk more effectively than a single lender can. A single lender could be more adversely affected should an economic decline occur in a particular region.

When an insured conventional mortgage is made, the maximum loan that a borrower is likely to obtain will be 95 percent of value although some lenders will go even higher. Because a greater potential for loss exists and much of the risk of loss is being assumed by the mortgage insurer, underwriting requirements that the lender uses to evaluate the borrower are likely to be heavily influenced by the insurer. Lenders must rigidly adhere to these standards when this type of loan is considered. Premiums will be based on the extent to which the loan-to-value ratio exceeds 80 percent for any given borrower.

FHA Insured Mortgage Loans

A mortgage loan can also be insured by the **Federal Housing Administration (FHA).** Unlike conventional insurance, which protects the lender against some portion of the potential loan loss, FHA mortgage insurance insures the lender *completely* against any default losses. It should be stressed that FHA does not make loans but provides insurance. Because FHA accepts the entire risk of borrower default, it maintains strict qualification procedures before the borrower and property will be accepted under its insurance program.

The FHA was created in 1934 with the passage of the Federal Housing Act.[2] The original intent of the FHA was to stabilize the housing industry after the Depression of the early 1930s. It also has had a long-standing policy objective to make housing affordable to lower- and middle-income families. This has been accomplished by allowing such families to purchase homes with lower down payments than would be required under conventional lending standards. The FHA operates as an insurance program, collecting premiums and maintaining reserves for payment of lender claims. Because FHA mortgage loans are made with higher loan-to-value ratios than conventional uninsured loans and because the FHA assumes the entire risk of default, mortgage insurance premiums charged by FHA are usually higher than conventional premiums, reflecting the additional risk taken by FHA.

Why is there a need for both FHA and private mortgage insurance? Regulations place loan maximums on FHA insured mortgage loans which may not be sufficient for many borrowers who purchase higher-priced properties.[3] Hence, qualified borrowers will normally choose a conventional, privately insured loan when a larger loan is necessary to purchase higher-priced property with a low down payment. In general, borrowers with higher incomes, who desire to purchase higher-valued properties with low down payments, opt for private mortgage insurance because the loan amount can be greater than the maximum available under FHA at a lower insurance cost. FHA borrowers are likely to have lower incomes and purchase properties in lower price ranges, within the maximum loan limits set by FHA. Because

[2]The National Housing Act of 1934, as amended.

[3]For a discussion of FHA maximum insurable loan amounts, see *HUD Handbook 4000.2* and subsequent revisions. FHA maximum insurable loan amounts depend on the geographic region in which the loan is made. These amounts also change from time to time.

Box 6.1

Redesigned FHA Seen Adding New Supply To Market

Some significant changes may be in store for the secondary market if the Federal Housing Administration is converted into a government-owned corporation. One of the first changes that may take place, according to housing experts, is that as many as 1 million new mortgages will hit the markets over the next 10 years. "The financial markets will respond well once they know what the mortgages are," said William Apgar, executive director of the Joint Center for Housing Studies at Harvard University. "In terms of new mortgages, yes, they'll be riskier, and for a while they might sell at a discount," he said. "But once the markets have time to adjust to the risk, and the risk becomes known, they will be priced accordingly," Apgar told MBSL in a recent interview. He was speaking in Washington last week after the release of a Harvard study which supports conversion of the existing FHA into a federally owned corporation.

Apgar estimated that the Clinton administration's plan to convert the current FHA structure into a government-owned mortgage insurance entity—now being called the Federal Housing Corp.—will bring as many as 1 million additional mortgages over the next 10 years to the markets, or about 100,000 mortgages a year. The most obvious example of new mortgage products, according to industry experts, would be those that take into account nontraditional underwriting standards. Administration plans also call for the FHA to target its insurance programs primarily to first-time homebuyers, currently underserved minorities, immigrants and people living in central cities, all segments which have a homeownership rate well below the national average of 63 percent. "The key will be to expand to new markets," Apgar said. David Crowe, staff vice president for housing policy at the National Association of Home Builders, agrees that expanding the market could be the major benefit of converting the FHA into a government corporation. "The most likely situation is that the corporate-like structure will give the FHA the flexibility and the adaptability to serve people who can't now get into the market. My reading is that their intent is to fix what's broken and in the process make access available to more people," Crowe said.

But aside from added product, Apgar said that he believes the market will see new kinds of mortgages being developed. New mortgages, he said, could soon be tailored to the markets now being cultivated by the FHA, the Federal Home Loan Mortgage Corp., the Federal National Mortgage Association and others. Apgar compared the debut of new mortgage products to that of the initial 30-year mortgage in the 1930s. Prior to 1934, home mortgages were generally five-year balloons with a hefty down payment requirement. "If you go back to 1934 (when the FHA was created) the thought was that the 30-year mortgage was not bankable," Apgar said. But once the market and FHA established a track record of how 30-year mortgages performed, they became a part of everyday life that supports housing today. Apgar said that he expects a similar pattern to develop with new mortgage products that, for example, carry underwriting standards that are not typically seen in the secondary market.

Freddie Mac officials seem to have a different view. They expect very little difference with a new FHA-type structure, even in volume terms. "The basic mortgage product won't change," said Robert Van Order, Freddie Mac chief economist. "The direction of interest rates and inflation is the overwhelmingly important factor in determining mortgage volume," he said. But Van Order also noted that the only issue that could directly affect Wall Street is what happens to prepayments as a result of new

(continued)

mortgage products and their performance or default rate. Even with new mortgage products coming into the secondary market, Van Order said that defaults have very little impact on prepayments. "If you have to put an average to prepayments, defaults would make a 20-basis point difference versus 10 percent on the average prepayment rate on Freddie Mac mortgage securities," Van Order said. "From a standpoint of the investors, the numbers are small and won't affect them a great deal," he added.

Source: "Mortgage-Backed Securities Letter," June 5, 1995 v10 i23, Investment Dealers' Digest, Inc.

of the borrowers' lower incomes, lenders may insist that the entire mortgage loan be insured; consequently, these borrowers will pay higher insurance premiums to FHA.

FHA extends insurance to buyers under a number of programs. The most common is Section 203b, which insures loans on one- to four-family detached residences. This program requires fixed interest rate financing with a term of between 15 and 30 years. Other FHA loan programs include Section 251, an ARM program; Section 234c, a condominium insurance program; and Section 245, a graduated payment mortgage insurance program.[4]

VA Guaranteed Mortgage Loans

Qualified veterans who desire to purchase a residential property and who meet certain length-of-service tests, may obtain a mortgage loan guarantee from the **Department of Veterans Affairs (VA).** The VA provides **guarantees** that compensate lenders for losses on loans made to veterans (borrowers). The amount of the guarantee varies with the home loan amount and the veteran's remaining entitlement. The guarantee generally equals or exceeds 25 percent of the loan amount. This amount, in effect, represents what would otherwise be a down payment in conventional financing under the VA's GI loan program. As is the case with the FHA program, VA does not make mortgage loans. It does, however, make direct loans to the public in connection with the sale of repossessions. Unlike the FHA program, the VA provides a loan guarantee, not default insurance. The certificate of guarantee is provided at no charge to the lender. All losses incurred by VA under this program are paid by the U.S. Government through its budget allocation to the Department of Veterans Affairs. In recent years, however, the program has not incurred any net losses due to the funding fees paid by veterans on each loan.

The amount of the loan that may be guaranteed is generally limited to the amount shown on the **Certificate of Reasonable Value (CRV),** with the following exceptions:

1. For regular refinancing loans (cash-out), the loan is limited to 90 percent of the amount on the CRV.
2. Loans to refinance construction loans, installment land sale contracts, and loans assumed by veterans at interest rates higher than the proposed refinance rate are not subject to the 90 percent limit. However, these types of refinancing loans may not exceed the lesser of the VA reasonable value or the sum of the outstanding balance of the loan plus allowable closing

[4]For a detailed listing of FHA mortgage insurance programs, see *HUD Handbook 4000.2*.

costs and discounts. In construction loan cases, "balance of the loan" includes the balances of construction financing and lot lien(s), if any.

3. For graduated payment mortgage loans, a cash down payment is required.
4. For Energy Efficient Mortgages, the loan amount may be increased by the cost of the energy conservation improvements up to $6,000. When energy efficiency improvements are made in conjunction with a refinancing loan that is subject to the 90 percent of value limit, the maximum loan is 90 percent of the CRV, plus the cost of the energy efficiency improvements.
5. Any loan amount may be increased by the amount of the VA funding fee, and the loan may exceed the reasonable value of the property by this amount.

The maximum loan entitlement available to any veteran is $36,000; however, a guarantee of up to $50,750 is available on loans of more than $144,000. The maximum guarantee on a loan is the lesser of the veteran's available entitlement or:

1. For loans up to $45,000, 50 percent of the loan.
2. For loans between $45,000 and $144,000 the minimum guaranteed amount is $22,500 with a maximum guarantee of up to 40 percent of the loan not to exceed $36,000.
3. For loans of more than $144,000 made for the purchase or construction of a home or to purchase a residential unit in a condominium or to refinance an existing VA guaranteed loan for interest rate reduction, 25 percent of the loan up to $50,750.
4. For joint loans involving the use of two or more veterans' entitlements, not to exceed the dollar or percentage limits established above. For joint loans involving a veteran and a nonveteran who is not the veteran's spouse, the VA guarantee will be limited to that portion of the loan allocable to the veteran's interest in the property.

For loans to refinance existing VA loans in which entitlement used on existing loans will be restored for reuse on refinancing loans secured by the same properties, the provisions above are applicable regardless of the amount of the guarantee on the existing loan. However, a minimum of 25 percent of the loan amount will be guaranteed for interest rate reduction refinancing loans (IRRRLs). Unlike IRRRLs, the maximum guarantee for "cash-out" refinancing of an existing VA loan, which was originally guaranteed in excess of $36,000, is limited by law to $36,000.

Energy Efficient Mortgages are processed by considering the portion of the loan attributable to the energy efficiency improvements to be guaranteed, without charge to the veteran's guarantee entitlement, to the same extent as would apply to a loan that did not include energy-related improvements.

Contrary to the FHA and conventional mortgages discussed earlier, VA loan guarantees are extended to fixed interest and adjustable rate mortgages only. Fixed payment, adjustable rate (ARM), graduated payment, growing equity and buydown mortgages are permissible loan repayment patterns permitted under VA guidelines. VA guaranteed mortgages must also allow for prepayment at any time without penalty and the loan must be assumable (with lender approval). VA loans may also be used to construct new homes, repair and improve existing homes, refinance an existing property, acquire a home and make energy efficient improvements, and acquire mobile homes and farms as long as the latter will be used as the borrowers' primary residence.

Veterans may use their VA home loan entitlement more than once. Essentially, qualified veterans receive an entitlement that never expires. The amount of entitlement available to a borrower at any given time depends on the current guarantee maximum, amounts of previously used entitlement, plus any amounts restored from previously used entitlement. For example, the current maximum entitlement is $36,000. If a borrower purchased a property for $80,000, the VA would issue a certificate of guarantee for 40 percent or $32,000, leaving $4,000 of entitlement for future use by the borrower. If after a time the borrower meets the legal requirements for restoration, the $32,000 of previously used entitlement would be added back to the remaining entitlement, making the full entitlement $36,000 once more.

There is an exception to the maximum entitlement for loans of more than $144,000. If a borrower purchases a property in excess of $144,000, the VA would issue a certificate of guarantee for 25 percent of the loan amount not to exceed $50,750. In this case, no residual entitlement remains even if the full amount of $50,750 has not been used. For example, the borrower purchases a property for $180,000 and the VA issues a 25 percent guarantee, or $45,000. There is no residual entitlement of $5,750 since this exception to the $36,000 maximum entitlement is designed to help offset the cost of housing in high-cost areas and not to extend benefits in general.

If the borrower sells the property on assumption to another qualified veteran borrower with entitlement who agrees to substitute his entitlement for the entitlement used by the original borrower on the loan, the original borrower's entitlement would be restored.

Many other influences affect the amount of entitlement for which a borrower may qualify, for example, when both husband and wife are qualified veterans.[5]

The Underwriting Process

Regardless of the type of mortgage (conventional, conventional insured, FHA, or VA), much of the underwriting process is common to all types of mortgage loans. The underwriter begins by collecting the data for deciding whether credit should be extended. The goal of this process is to determine whether the loan-to-value ratio, the payment-to-income ratio, assets of the borrower, and borrower credit history are acceptable to the lender or the lender and insurer. Next we discuss (1) how borrower income is estimated and the relationship of that income to the proposed mortgage payments and other obligations of the borrower, and (2) how the value of the property is established through an appraisal.

Borrower Income

The underwriting process usually begins with the underwriter obtaining the data needed to decide about extending credit. An item of primary importance will be borrower income. To gather the necessary data regarding income, the borrower is requested to allow the lender to (1) verify place of employment, (2) verify wages, and (3) inquire as to whether employment is likely to continue into the future. Typically, where a borrower is employed on a full-time basis and obtains regular income from this employment, there is little problem in verifying income. In cases where a

[5]For a discussion of VA loan guarantee eligibility requirements, see Title 38, U.S. Code, Section 3701.

borrower's income is derived from more than a single source, the process of verifying the amount and the likelihood of that income continuing is more difficult.

Other possible income sources include these:

- Part-time employment.
- Working spouse.
- Rentals.
- Alimony or child support.
- Commissions.
- Self-employment.
- Bonuses.
- Dividends or interest.
- Retirement annuity.
- Social Security.
- Public assistance.

Generally, two tests must be met before any of these sources will be included in establishing borrower income in the underwriting process. First, the underwriter must judge that the income is likely to continue. This usually means that a source of income must have already occurred continuously for a sufficient time for the underwriter to judge whether that income will continue. Second, the income must be verifiable, usually by reviewing the borrower's federal income tax returns for at least two years. When the income is nontaxable, such as distributions from retirement annuities, canceled checks or verification of deposits may be used to verify the existence of the income.

In addition to deciding what sources of income should be included, difficulties also arise when determining how much income should be used in the underwriting process. For example, the amount of income from a particular source may vary from period to period. When income is variable in nature, such as the earnings from commission sales positions, rentals, or self-employment, a borrower's income will generally be averaged over a period of at least two years from amounts shown on tax returns. Any expenses incurred in earning that income will be deducted from the amount of income earned.

When two individuals are employed, the question arises of what constitutes income. The general rule applied by the lender takes a long-run viewpoint, that is, it asks whether both individuals will remain employed indefinitely, or at least until the income of one is sufficient to meet the monthly mortgage payments. This question often presents difficulty when the value of the property and the loan amount being requested are high in relation to the income of only one of the earners. Obviously, the lender will have to exercise judgment about the future stability of the joint incomes. Generally, if both parties have been employed for several consecutive years, future income stability is more likely. If the intent of one of the parties is to end employment after a given number of years and this individual is presently employed in a professional activity with employment stability, both incomes may be included for the time both expect to remain employed. An estimate may be made as to what the primary worker's total income will be at the time the other party ceases employment.

Although income forms much of the basis for risk analysis by the lender, recent federal regulations have limited the extent to which lenders may obtain information or make inferences concerning a loan applicant's background. Regulation B of the

Board of Governors of the Federal Reserve System provides guidelines that lenders must comply with when gathering information about potential borrowers.[6]

Verification of Borrower Assets

Another step in the data collection process is the verification of borrower assets. Assets of the borrower must at least be sufficient to close the transaction. This means that borrower assets must be sufficient to pay closing costs and make a down payment. Moreover, lenders usually do not allow borrowed funds to be used as the borrower's down payment. Thus, how long a borrower's assets have been on deposit will be used as an important indicator of whether the borrower is planning to use borrowed funds to make a down payment. Gifts, on the other hand, are usually allowed for all funds necessary to close. A gift letter stating that no repayment is required, signed by both the borrower and gift donor, is usually required. The lender will usually document the transfer of funds from the donor's account to the borrower's account. Any assets that are not required to close the lending transaction will reflect favorably upon the creditworthiness of the borrower.

Other assets of the applicant also play an important role in rating the loan quality by the lender. The rating is improved if the applicant has demonstrated a consistent ability to save as evidenced by savings accounts or investments in other property, ownership of life insurance (cash value), purchase of securities, and the like, as well as the ability to carry the obligations associated with the acquisition of these assets. For example, an older applicant whose remaining life expectancy is less than the term of the mortgage being sought may be granted a loan with the desired maturity, even though it exceeds the years of life expectancy remaining, if adequate life insurance exists to pay off the mortgage loan in the event death occurs before the loan is repaid. In most cases, the lender will request that the applicant sign a request allowing other financial institutions, investment companies, and credit agencies to disclose to the lender the nature and amount of the applicant's assets. These could include stocks, bonds, savings accounts, and any recent activity in the accounts.

Assessment of Credit History

Typically, the underwriter will also make a judgment about the acceptability of the borrower's past payment history on other obligations. Credit reports from a central credit bureau, located in most cities, will give a history on a borrower's payment habits for up to 10 years. Such things as slow payment of past borrower obligations

[6](a) The use of sex, marital status, race, religion, age, or national origin in a credit underwriting procedure is prohibited. (b) Creditors may not inquire into birth control practices or into childbearing capabilities or intentions, or assume, from her age, that an applicant or an applicant's spouse may drop out of the labor force due to childbearing and thus have an interruption of income. (c) A creditor may not discount part-time income but may examine the probable continuity of the applicant's job. (d) A creditor may ask and consider whether and to what extent an applicant's income is affected by obligations to make alimony or child support or maintenance payments. (e) A creditor may ask to what extent an applicant is relying on alimony or child support or maintenance payments to repay the debt being requested, but the applicant must first be informed that no such disclosure is necessary if the applicant does not rely on such income to obtain the credit. Where the applicant chooses to rely on alimony, a creditor shall consider such payments as income to the extent the payments are likely to be made consistently. (f) Applicants receiving public assistance payments cannot be denied access to credit. If these payments and security provided for the loan meet normal underwriting standards, credit must be extended. (g) An individual may apply for credit without obligating a spouse to repay the obligation, as long as underwriting standards of the lender are met. (h) A creditor shall not take into account the existence of a telephone listing in the name of an applicant when evaluating applications. A creditor may take into account the existence of a telephone in the applicant's home. (i) Upon the request of an applicant, creditor will be required to provide reasons for terminating or denying credit.

may reflect unfavorably upon the loan applicant. Many examples of adverse credit experience will surely cause the loan application to be rejected. However, a brief interruption in an otherwise acceptable credit history caused by explainable events such as divorce or interruption in income will sometimes be overlooked by the underwriter if an explanation is provided—assuming that the borrower has recovered financially from the adverse circumstances that caused this problem. Even bankruptcy may not automatically cause a loan application to be rejected if there were extenuating circumstances and the borrower has had several years of acceptable history since the problem occurred.

Estimated Housing Expense

Determining the housing expense used to establish the payment-to-income ratio that a borrower is proposing to undertake is relatively straightforward. The following is a list of items that are likely to be included in the estimate of monthly housing expense:

- Principal and interest on the mortgage being applied for.
- Mortgage insurance (if any).
- Property taxes.
- Hazard insurance.
- Condominium or cooperative homeowners association dues (if applicable).

The underwriter will have to estimate many of these items because their exact amounts will not be known at the time of underwriting. Very often the lender may require that the borrower pay monthly, prorated installments toward mortgage insurance, hazard insurance, and property taxes, in addition to the mortgage payment. Judgment concerning the risk associated with making the mortgage loan will depend upon the total cost of home ownership relative to borrower income. If this total cost of home ownership is too high, then an applicant's loan application may be rejected. Specific examples of how these expenses are estimated and related to income will be discussed later in the chapter.

Other Obligations

In most cases, borrowers will have other obligations in addition to the mortgage loan being applied for. Obvious examples include auto loans, credit card accounts, other mortgage debts, or alimony and child support payments. The underwriter will request that the borrower disclose all debts at the time of application, then verify these commitments by obtaining a credit report with the approval of the borrower. Courthouse records in the borrower's county of residence also may be checked to determine whether there are any judgments outstanding against the borrower for unpaid debts. Another item on the credit report of importance to the underwriter will be whether the borrower has ever filed for bankruptcy.

Compensating Factors

It is possible that the underwriter will find other favorable factors about the borrower that can offset certain unfavorable factors during the underwriting process. Typically, it is considered favorable for a borrower to have liquid assets that could be used to make her monthly mortgage payment should the borrower's income be interrupted. Another favorable factor is if the borrower is employed in a field where his skills are in high demand and the likelihood is that his income will increase over time. These factors may prove sufficient to allow a borrower to devote more income to housing expenses, even if the borrower's proposed housing expense ratio is higher than for other borrowers with similar incomes. Of course, making a substantial equity down payment as part of the purchase price is considered favorable as well. When any or all of the conditions exist, it is possible that underwriting policies may be relaxed to some degree.

After all of the factual data described above have been determined, the loan underwriter will consider whether or not the loan in question should be granted. The process of making this evaluation varies, depending upon the kind of loan the borrower is seeking. The following examples of the underwriting process in conventional, insured conventional, FHA, and VA loan transactions should help to illustrate this point.

The Underwriting Process Illustrated

This chapter section illustrates how each of the four types of mortgage loans described above is generally underwritten by lenders. As indicated earlier, one goal of underwriting is to establish whether the risk of borrower default is acceptable and whether the loan should be granted. We will consider each type of mortgage (conventional, insured conventional, FHA, and VA) separately. In this section, we look at how the maximum mortgage amount is established, how it is related to property value, and how that relationship varies with each type of mortgage. We also discuss (1) proposed housing expenses and other obligations relative to borrower income, (2) the criteria used to establish acceptable relationships between expenses and income, which will serve as the basis for the lending decision, and (3) the role of appraisals in establishing the loan-to-value ratio.

To facilitate the discussion, we use the sample borrower information in Exhibit 6–1 to illustrate the underwriting process for each category of mortgage loans. Details about the underwriting criteria will be sufficient to allow generalizations beyond the cases used in our discussion.

Underwriting Standards—Conventional and Insured Conventional Mortgages

Looking at the data shown in Exhibit 6–1, we see that in addition to the verification of income and outstanding debts, the lender has estimated both property taxes and hazard insurance (fire, storm, etc.), which are also used in estimating housing expenses. These expenses establish the monthly payment-to-income ratio for the borrower-applicants. Looking at Exhibit 6–2, we see some of the general underwriting standards that lenders will apply in making the decision to grant or deny the loan request. In other words, after assembling the facts necessary to establish monthly housing expenses and other obligations, the lender will compute the necessary ratios and compare them to the general standards used by the lenders and mortgage insurers. This will help determine whether the default risk is acceptable, given the prevailing rate of interest. Lenders and insurers establish these underwriting standards, or maximum allowable ratios based on loss experience from previously underwritten loans. Interpret these ratios as a general guide, however, because there may be other assets or compensating factors to be considered as a part of the underwriting process.

Also note in Exhibit 6–2 that, in the case of ARMs, more stringent underwriting standards may have to be met in certain cases. This is because an increase in interest rates could result in either an increase in payments or an increase in the loan balance due to a payment cap and negative amortization. Lenders refer to cases where negative amortization is *expected* as *scheduled amortization* and usually take it into account when underwriting the ARM by requiring a *lower* loan-to-value ratio. If payments are likely to be adjusted because the composite rate (current ARM

EXHIBIT 6–1 Sample Underwriting Illustration: Borrower and Property Characteristics

Name of borrower:	John and Jane J. Jones
Income:	$3,542 monthly from salaried employment of both spouses, $42,500 annually
Debts:	Installment obligation of $181 per month with 35 months remaining
	Credit card obligations, $50 per month with more than 12 months remaining
Sale price:	$76,700
Appraised value:	$77,000
Estimated property taxes:	$797 annually
Hazard insurance:	$552 annually
Desired mortgage:	FRM with a 30-year term, constant payment

EXHIBIT 6–2 General Industry Standards for Underwriting Conventional and Insured Conventional Loans

	Conventional (percent)		Insured Conventional (percent)	
	FRMs	*ARMs*	*FRMs*	*ARMs*
Maximum ratios allowed:				
Loan-to-value	80	80	95	90*–95
Payment-to-income	28	25†–28	28	25†–28
Total obligations to income	36	33†–36	36	33†–36

*Conventional ARMs with loan-to-value ratios in excess of 90 percent are generally not available, although some lenders will loan in excess of 90 percent at a higher interest rate. Graduated payment mortgages (GPMs) are usually limited to 90 percent loan-to-value ratios because of scheduled negative amortization.

†Generally, the higher ratios are allowed; however, if the conventional ARM or GPM allows for the possibility of maximum increases in monthly payments beyond prescribed limits. The lower ratios must be met for the loan to be insured.

index plus margin) at the time of origination is higher than the initial interest rate, the underwriter will probably consider the scheduled payment increase when reviewing the payment-to-income ratio.[7] Note that conventional GPMs are usually underwritten on the basis of scheduled amortization, which is known at the time of origination, and the loan-to-value ratio is usually restricted to 90 percent. Also, in the case of ARMs, initial maximum payment-to-income ratios may be lowered if the mortgage agreement provides for the possibility of monthly payments exceeding prescribed maximums. For example, if an ARM is made with a payment cap greater than 15 percent annually, or the interest rate cap exceeds 2 percent annually

[7]When the composite rate is higher than the initial rate at the time of origination, the latter rate is referred to as the *teaser rate*, because lenders may be using it as an incentive for borrowers to make ARMs. When the first payment adjustment occurs, payments will increase substantially if the composite rate is still considerably higher than the initial rate. This increase in ARM payments is referred to as *payment shock* in the lending industry.

or 5 percent over the life of the mortgage, lower ratios will usually be required. This latter restriction also applies to GPMs.

When computing these ratios for the conventional and insured conventional cases, we take relevant information from Exhibit 6–1 and compute the necessary ratios shown in Exhibit 6–3. Note that in the two cases being considered, the insured conventional loan is larger (95 percent versus 80 percent) and is made at a higher interest rate. Also, the insured loan requires a monthly mortgage insurance premium, and the conventional loan does not. The ratios calculated and shown at the bottom of the exhibit indicate that the borrower would probably qualify for either a conventional loan or an insured conventional loan, given that those ratios fall well below the maximum ratios allowed under the general underwriting standards shown in Exhibit 6–2. Whether the borrower will prefer the conventional or insured conventional loan depends on the amount available for a down payment (20 percent or 5 percent of appraised value) and whether the borrower wants to pay additional interest and insurance charges. The latter choice also depends on whether the borrower has sufficient funds to make either down payment requirement. If the borrower could afford to make either down payment, the borrower must decide whether the difference (15 percent) can be reinvested at a rate of interest in excess of the added interest and insurance charges. (A procedure that may be used to choose between loans that differ in amount and interest rates will be presented in detail in Chapter 7.)

Underwriting Standards—FHA Insured Mortgages

If the borrower in our example is considering an FHA insured mortgage, a similar approach is used to underwriting, with some notable exceptions. To begin our general discussion of FHA underwriting, we point out that unlike the conventional underwriting process, which provides for loan amounts as a percentage of appraised value (80 percent, 95 percent, etc.), FHA has a specific procedure that is used to establish the *maximum insurable loan amount* for which they are willing to issue an insurance binder. This process is generally described in Exhibit 6–4.

Exhibit 6–4 shows that FHA provides for a closing cost allowance (to be discussed) in its definition of total acquisition cost, which is used as a basis for establishing the maximum loan amount.[8] To the extent the borrower pays closing costs that are equal to or greater than the FHA allowance, the acquisition cost increases. Note that FHA also gives the borrower the option to finance the up-front mortgage insurance premium. This additional amount financed is added to the maximum mortgage amount to arrive at the total amount financed, $76,326. Monthly payments are calculated on this latter amount. Also note that the maximum loan amount is computed on a graduated basis when the total acquisition is greater than $50,000. That is, calculate 97 percent of the first $25,000, which is equal to $24,250, then 95 percent of the remainder, subject to a maximum loan-to-value ratio established under the Omnibus Budget Reconciliation Act of 1990, and an absolute maximum loan amount that FHA is willing to insure.[9] If the total acquisition cost is less than or equal to $50,000, then the maximum mortgage amount is 97 percent. These graduated rates and maximums are subject to change by FHA at any time, based on prevailing economic conditions.

---

[8]Examples of various closing costs to be discussed later in the chapter include origination fees, appraisal fees, credit report fees, and transfer taxes.

[9]The maximum loan-to-value limits under the Omnibus Budget Reconciliation Act of 1990 are 98.75 percent if the appraised value is $50,000 or less or 97.75 percent if that value is in excess of $50,000. These limits are subject to change at any time.

EXHIBIT 6–3 Computation of Borrower Qualification (conventional and insured conventional loan examples)

	Conventional	*Insured Conventional*
Loan amount requested	$61,360	$72,865
Terms	*FRM* 30 yr., 9.25%	*FRM* 30 yr., 9.5%
Loan-to-value ratio	80%	95%
Borrower income (A)	$ 3,542	$ 3,542
Housing expenses		
Principal and interest	$ 505	$ 613
Property taxes	66	66
Hazard insurance	46	46
Mortgage insurance	—	21*
Housing expense (B)	617	746
Add:		
Installment debt†	181	181
Credit cards	50	50
Total obligations (C)	$ 848	$ 977
Housing expense ratio (B ÷ A)	17%	21%
Total obligation ratio (C ÷ A)	24%	28%

*Based on the second year's premium, or .35 percent of the loan balance outstanding at the end of the first year, divided by 12 months. The first year's premium is likely to be higher (0.8 percent) and is usually collected in advance as a part of closing cost (to be discussed). Monthly mortgage insurance premiums that lower the amount of money needed at closing are now available. The lender using them is invoiced monthly instead of annually.

†Usually defined as an obligation with at least 11 remaining monthly payments. However, any obligation that in the judgment of the underwriter, requires a large monthly outlay relative to income may be included, even if the number of remaining payments is less than 11.

It should be stressed that FHA has established its own standards for both of these qualifying ratios (see bottom of the exhibit), which it uses uniformly for FRM, GPM, and ARM loans. This practice of computing ratios based on current income at the time of loan originations is followed even though monthly payments with a GPM or ARM may change in future periods. However, for FHA to insure ARMs, they must conform to very rigid specifications. For example, ARMs cannot have negative amortization and are currently subject to interest rate caps of 1 percent annually and 5 percent over the term of the loan. GPMs are also subject to specific limits on allowable payment increases. The current allowable scheduled increases in payments are

Plan 1 2.5 percent payment increases annually for 5 years.
Plan 2 5 percent payment increases for 5 years.
Plan 3 7.5 percent payment increases for 5 years.
Plan 4 2 percent payment increases for 10 years.
Plan 5 3 percent payment increases for 10 years.

Further, the original mortgage balance for a GPM at the time of origination plus all interest that is scheduled to be accrued over the life of the loan may not exceed 97 percent of the original appraised value.

Because of the very limited variations in payments allowed by FHA in its ARM and GPM programs, a single set of underwriting ratios (bottom of Exhibit 6–4) is generally used on both types of mortgages, as well as on FRMs. This stands in contrast to the range in ratios used by underwriters when reviewing conventional ARMs (see Exhibit 6–2).

EXHIBIT 6–4 Determination of Maximum Loan Amount and Borrower Qualification Ratios (FHA example)

SECTION I. Maximum Loan Amount Calculation

First Calculation		
Lower of price or appraised value	$76,700	
Plus: Closing cost allowance*	1,350	
Acquisition cost	$78,050	
97 percent of the first $25,000		$24,250
95 percent of the remainder		50,397
Maximum loan amount under first calculation		$74,647
Second Calculation		
Lower of price or appraised value		$76,700
Times: Maximum loan-to-value ratio—Value > $50,000		97.75%
Maximum loan amount under second calculation		$74,974
Maximum loan amount†—lesser of the first or second calculation		$74,647
Plus: Financed mortgage insurance premium† of 2.25%‡		1,679
Amount financed		$76,326

SECTION II. Computation of Qualifying Ratios

Gross income (monthly) (A)	$ 3,542
Housing Expense	
Principal, interest, and up-front mortgage insurance premium ($76,326, 9.5%, 30 years)	$ 642
Property taxes	66
Hazard insurance	46
Annual mortgage insurance premium‡	31
Total housing expense (B)	$ 785
Other Obligations	
Installment debt§	$ 181
Credit cards	50
Total obligations (C)	$ 1,016

Qualifying Ratios (percent)	*Applicant Ratios (percent)*	*FHA Maximum Ratios (percent)*
Housing expense ratio B / A	22	29
Total obligations ratio C / A	29	41

*The FHA provides for a closing cost allowance in determining the loan amount. Limits on this amount vary by region.

†The maximum loan amount may not exceed limits set by FHA regulations. These limits vary by city and change over time.

‡The mortgage insurance premium is composed of two components, an up-front insurance premium, which may be financed or paid in cash, and an annual fee, which varies in terms of amount and term according to the loan-to-value ratio. See U.S. Department of Housing and Urban Development *Mortgagee Letter 94–14* and revisions for a complete discussion on mortgage insurance premiums.

§Usually debt with 10 installments remaining. However, the underwriter can increase or decrease the number of installments depending on the total number of obligations outstanding and the relationship to borrower income.

As in the case of conventional lending, the underwriter is likely to take into account other assets, the credit history, and offsetting factors when deciding to accept or reject a loan application. Because FHA requires tax adjustments in its underwriting process, the qualifying ratios used as standards in determining the adequacy of borrower income are higher than those used in the conventional cases. These ratios are also based on FHA's loss experience in the operation of its insurance fund. Our hypothetical borrower-applicants, then, would likely qualify for an FHA insured loan. FHA uses one additional underwriting test, however, which is discussed in the next section.

Underwriting Standards—VA Guaranteed Mortgages

The underwriting process followed by the Veterans Administration differs considerably in its approach to establishing the adequacy of borrower income in relation to the loan request. The VA procedure stresses the notion of **residual income,** which is a process whereby gross income is reduced by all monthly outlays for housing, expenses, taxes, all debt obligations, and recurring job-related expenses (see Exhibit 6–5). The difference, or residual income, is then examined to establish whether VA deems it adequate for supporting the borrower's family.

A few items are of particular importance. The mortgage loan amount is equal to the sale price, $76,700, plus a funding fee ranging from 0.5–3.0 percent of the loan request to help the borrower fund closing costs (to be discussed).[10] Because the loan request is equal to or less than the maximum loan amount, it would qualify for a guarantee.[11] In addition, because the VA is providing a guarantee, no monthly mortgage insurance premium is required of the borrower. Based on the borrower-applicant information in Exhibit 6–1, with a family size of two and no minor dependents, our hypothetical borrowers should qualify for a VA guaranteed loan. They would also meet the supplemental test as used as a secondary underwriting tool by the FHA.

---

[10]VA typically allows the funding fee (which is paid to VA) to be included in the veteran's loan amount. The funding fee charged depends on the amount of down payment paid by the borrower. If the down payment is 10 percent or greater, the funding fee is 1.25 percent. If the down payment is from 5 percent to 10 percent, the fee is 1.5 percent; anything less than 5 percent requires a fee of 2.0 percent. If the veteran has a service-related disability, the veteran is not required to pay any funding fee on the VA loan. If the funding fee was 2.0 percent, .02 times 76,700, or $1,534, is included in the loan amount of $76,700 + $1,534, or $78,234. Any closing costs in excess of $1,534 would be required of the borrower at closing. However, the VA also monitors what it considers to be excessive closing costs when considering whether to extend its guarantee.

[11]The down payment plus VA guarantee must always equal 25 percent of the lesser of purchase price or appraised value. Because the current maximum guarantee is $36,000, a loan of up to $144,000 can be made with no down payment.

H.R. 995, signed on Oct. 13, 1994, increased the maximum entitlement for purchase loans or interest rate reduction refinance loans (IRRRL) above $144,000 to $50,750.

VA loans are also fully assumable. There are two types of assumptions: (1) nonqualifying assumptions, where the buyer may or may not be a veteran or qualify with VA before assuming the loan; (2) qualifying assumptions, where the buyer assumes the loan with VA approval. In the former case, if the loan closed prior to March 1, 1988, the loan may be assumed without qualification and the veteran who originated the loan remains personally liable on the note. In the latter case, loans closed after March 1, 1988, require the buyer to qualify for the assumption. The veteran has no liability because the buyer qualified with VA prior to assuming the loan.

When a VA mortgage loan is assumed, the buyer is not required to be a veteran and is not charged for the mortgage guarantee. If, however, the buyer is a veteran and the seller can induce him to substitute his guarantee for the guarantee used by the seller, then the seller's VA entitlement can be restored and used again. Also, in many instances, increases in VA guarantees provided for by Congress are retroactive. As a result, a veteran who used his maximum VA guarantee in one period may have an additional VA guarantee in a subsequent period.

In the case of an FHA assumption, if the seller paid the up-front FHA insurance premium, the buyer will pay the seller for a prorated share of the insurance in relation to the number of months remaining until maturity. However, if the up-front insurance premium was financed, the buyer must continue to pay the insurance premium as a part of the monthly payment.

EXHIBIT 6–5 Determination of Borrower Qualification (VA guaranteed loan example)

Residual income technique		
Gross income		$3,542
Less federal income taxes		602
State income taxes		106
Social Security taxes		266
All debts*		231
Maintenance		58
Utilities		134
Principal and interest payment†		657
Property taxes		66
Hazard insurance		46
Job-related, or child care expense		50
Residual income		$1,326
Minimum residual income for family of:‡	1	424
	2	710
	3	855
	4	964
	5	999
	6	1,079
	7	1,159

*Usually includes obligations with six monthly installments remaining; however, the underwriter may include any obligations considered material relative to the borrower's income.

†Based on a loan amount of $78,138 at 9.5 percent for 30 years (rounded).

‡Residual income figures are determined by region of the country and loan amount. The figures used in this exhibit are based on the Midwest region for loan amounts of $70,000 and above.

Underwriting and Loan Amounts—A Summary

It is useful at this point to summarize some pertinent data before moving on to the next topic, closing costs. Exhibit 6–6 provides a summary breakdown of some of the more important characteristics considered thus far. The first item to be noted is that although we begin with the same appraised value in all cases, the loan amount will vary by mortgage category. This variation is based on the fact that we have assumed that a loan-to-value ratio of 80 percent is to be used in the case of the conventional loan and a 95 percent loan is to be made in the insured conventional loan case with any additional closing costs to be paid by the borrower in both cases. In the FHA case, the loan amount is higher because of the higher loan-to-value ratio allowed by FHA (97 percent and 95 percent of portions of the loan request) *and* because a closing cost allowance may be financed under this program. In the case of the VA, the loan amount is 100 percent of the lower of price or appraised value, plus an allowance for closing costs. Also note that an additional term, *amount financed*, is used in the exhibit. This is the amount upon which the monthly interest and principal will be calculated. In three of the cases it is equal to the loan amount. In the FHA case, the amount financed includes the total insurance premium or 2.25 percent of the loan balance (or an additional $1,679) that the lender is also financing and that must be repaid as a part of monthly principal and interest on the total loan amount.

Other items of importance in Exhibit 6–6 are the interest rates and notes regarding insurance costs. In our example, we have assumed that the interest rate on the conventional loan will be 9.25 percent, or lower than the rate charged in all other cases. This is because the amount of funds being loaned is lower than in all other

EXHIBIT 6–6 Summary of Underwriting Results

	Conventional	*Insured Conventional*	*FHA Insured*	*VA Guaranteed*
(a) Lower of price/ appraised value	$76,700	$76,700	$76,700	$76,700
(b) Loan amount	$61,360	$72,865	$74,647	$76,700
(c) Amount financed	$61,360	$72,865	$76,326	$78,138
(d) Interest rate	9.25%	9.5%	9.5%	9.5%
(e) Term	30 years	30 years	30 years	30 years
(f) Insurance fee	N.A.	*	†	N.A.

*0.8 percent of loan at closing, .35 percent per year, payable monthly.

†Two components: an up-front mortgage insurance premium that may either be financed or paid at closing and a monthly insurance premium that varies according to the loan term, loan-to-value ratio, and date of loan closing.

cases. Another important item about interest rates in the exhibit is that all of these rates are competitively determined through negotiation between borrower and lender and will change over time. Do not infer from our example that there is a fixed spread between interest rates on conventional and other loan types. These illustrations are used as *examples only*. Similarly, we assume the terms of the mortgages to be 30 years. While FHA and VA loans are available in 15- to 30-year terms, 30-year loans are used most frequently under these programs. Conventional mortgages, however, are frequently made for 15, 20, and 25 years. Finally, keep in mind that in developing the estimates of housing expenses, total obligations, and other expenses used in underwriting, we have assumed the same estimates in many of our examples for similar expense categories (utilities, maintenance, debts, etc.). In reality these estimates may differ, depending on the specific regulations, policies, cost manuals, and guidelines that the various insurers and lenders involved in the underwriting process use.[12] While there are many other peculiarities associated with underwriting each type of loan, we have attempted to limit the technical detail and to focus on the major differences between underwriting approaches and regulations in order to help you understand the more important attributes of the process.

Property Appraisal

At some point in the application and underwriting process, the lender must estimate whether the market value of the property serving as security for repayment of the debt is sufficiently high to pay the loan balance in the event of default. This estimate of value is usually made by an appraiser on the staff of the lender or by an independent fee appraiser. The latter is someone who specializes in performing appraisals for lenders and investors for a fee. Such an individual must be unrelated to the parties to the transaction and must have no vested or financial interest in the property being appraised. Lenders use independent appraisers when the volume of appraisals required by loan applications is not sufficiently high to warrant employing one permanently on staff or when staff appraisers face a temporary overload of appraisal requests. Such appraisals are then reviewed by the lending institution.

[12]FHA and VA closing cost estimates may vary regionally, or even locally, and are updated continuously. In some instances, an appraiser may even make specific estimates of utilities and maintenance items for a given property.

The objective of the appraisal is to establish a **market value,** usually meaning the most probable price that would be paid for a property under competitive market conditions. The reader should understand that this notion of *value* may be different from the *price* that an individual buyer (such as the loan applicant) may be willing to pay for the property. For example, the borrower-applicant's *individual preference* for attributes of the property being acquired may be such that she may be willing to pay a significantly higher price for a property than the *majority* of potential buyers in the market. Because the lender is more concerned about what the market price would be in the event of default, the appraiser must make an independent estimate of the most probable price that a property would bring if it were sold under competitive market conditions, where individuals other than the borrower would be bidding. In a sense, the appraiser's estimate of value will help the lender determine whether the price being offered by the borrower-applicant is an "outlier," or a price that is significantly different from what would be paid by most buyers in the market for similar properties. Although there are some differences in appraisal requirements used in conventional, FHA, and VA mortgage underwriting, the general approaches to estimating value are similar.

To produce an estimate of value, the appraiser generally begins with an assessment of national, regional, and local economic conditions, stressing income, population, employment, and interest rate trends, which form the determinants of demand for the property in question. Supply is examined by assessing the relative cost of land and the factors of production (wages, capital). Current market equilibrium conditions in the housing market are then considered by examining the current availability (inventory) of housing units, absorption rates, rental vacancies, and trends in rents to gauge the likelihood of any short-run price movements that may affect the estimate of value. Finally, the appraiser examines the submarket, usually encompassing the neighborhood, including nearby retail, educational, and religious facilities, to establish any premiums that might be paid for the property because of its proximity to those facilities.

In estimating the value for the specific property (usually referred to as the "subject" property), the appraiser will rely on three approaches: the market, cost, and income capitalization approaches, although in residential appraisals only two approaches, cost and market, are usually reliable. The **sales comparison approach** involves selecting properties that have sold most recently and that are *most comparable* to the subject. Adjustments are made for dissimilarities (such as size of dwelling, lot, amenities), which the appraiser attempts to keep at a minimum, in accordance with the concept of comparability. This approach is based on the principle that buyers should be willing to pay the same price for otherwise identical properties. By adjusting the sale price of comparable properties for dissimilarities, the appraiser is trying to make properties that have recently sold as identical as possible to the subject. The adjusted price of the comparables can then be used to price the subject.

The **cost approach** involves estimating the cost to reproduce the structure (less depreciation), then adding the value of the land (site) to it in arriving at a value. The rationale for this approach is that no knowledgeable buyer would pay more for a property than it can be reproduced for. Finally, the **income approach** is a process whereby comparable residences that are currently *renting* for income are used to estimate the value of the subject. This process usually involves establishing a ratio between the selling price and income of such recently sold comparables. The rent is then adjusted for dissimilarities with the subject. A comparable rent for the subject is then established and the ratio of price to rent for comparables is used to convert the adjusted rent into a value for the subject. This latter approach is not frequently used because it is generally the least reliable method—the number of comparable residences that are rented are few and not sold as often as owner-occupied residences.

Based on these approaches, the appraiser makes a final estimate of value and reports it to the lender. The lender will review the report and, if he is in agreement with the approach used by the appraiser, use the *lower* of appraised value or the market price in establishing the maximum loan amount. The loan amount is also subject to the adequacy of the borrower's income to carry the monthly payments based on prevailing loan terms. For a more detailed examination of each of these approaches, we now consider a problem example. In the example, we use the uniform appraisal form (see Exhibit 6–7, Panels A and B) required by the Federal National Mortgage Association and Federal Home Loan Mortgage Corporation. Most residential mortgages made today utilize this form, since it is a part of the required documentation should any lender desire to sell a loan to either of these entities after origination.[13]

The Sales Comparison Approach. As previously indicated, when using this method the appraiser estimates the value of a property by comparing the selling prices of properties similar to, and near, the property being appraised. Because no two properties are exactly alike, the appraiser adjusts the values of similar properties (called **comparable properties**) for dissimilarities. These differences are isolated, and adjustments are made by the appraiser, who, using her judgment and knowledge of current market conditions, establishes what the market value is for each major attribute of a comparable that is different from the subject property. Because the value of the subject property is unknown, the price of the *comparables* will be adjusted until all differences have been taken into account. If this process is carried out correctly, the adjusted value of the comparable properties should then be approximately equal to the price of the subject property. In selecting the comparables, the appraiser must be careful to establish that the sales of the comparable properties were arm's-length transactions between the buyer and seller. For instance, if the seller were under duress, as in a foreclosure situation, or if a sale were between relatives, such sales would not be desirable for use as comparables because buyers may not have paid a fair market price for the properties. Once the appraiser has determined that the comparable sales were arm's-length transactions, the appraiser's process of adjusting the comparable sales can begin.

To illustrate how the appraiser will adjust the comparable sales for any differences between the subject property and the comparable properties, Exhibit 6–7 contains a property description in Panel A and an example of the three approaches to value used in the appraisal process in Panel B. Note that Panel A contains the identification of the property and a general description of the property. Section II of

---

[13]For more detailed information see *Underwriting Guidelines, Home Mortgages,* Federal Home Loan Mortgage Corporation, July 1985. The sale of mortgages to institutions in the secondary mortgage market will be covered in a later chapter. While all residential appraisals are made using the three approaches to value discussed above, additional specifications concerning condition and construction quality of the dwelling being appraised are sometimes included in FHA and VA appraisals. While such specifications are too numerous to be considered here, the following sources provide additional information: (1) for an overview of FHA appraisal policies, see *HUD Handbook 4150.1,* "Valuation Analysis for Home Mortgage Insurance," April 1983; (2) for VA appraisal standards, see *VA Bulletin CNU-2-86*, "Procedures for Making VA Appraisals," March 21, 1986, and Department of Veterans Benefits Circular 26–86–9, "Appraisal Review Guidelines," March 10, 1986.

Exhibit 6–7 (Panel A) Property Descriptions

Property Description & Analysis **UNIFORM RESIDENTIAL APPRAISAL REPORT** **File No.**

SUBJECT

Property Address 482 Liberty Street — Census Tract 1005.00
City Anytown, USA. — County — State — Zip Code
Legal Description Lot 78, 1st Section Happy Acres Farm
Owner/Occupant John and Jane J. Jones — Map Reference 33-84
Sale Price $ 76,700 — Date of Sale 3-01-96
Loan charges/concessions to be paid by seller $ None
R.E. Taxes $ 797.00 — Tax Year — HOA $/Mo. None
Lender/Client XYZ Federal Savings and Loan Assoc.

PROPERTY RIGHTS APPRAISED: [x] Fee Simple; [ ] Leasehold; [ ] Condominium (HUD/VA); [ ] De Minimis PUD

LENDER DISCRETIONARY USE: Sale Price $; Date ; Mortgage Amount $; Mortgage Type ; Discount Points and Other Concessions ; Paid by Seller $; Source

NEIGHBORHOOD

LOCATION	[ ] Urban	[x] Suburban	[ ] Rural
BUILT UP	[x] Over 75%	[ ] 25-75%	[ ] Under 25%
GROWTH RATE	[ ] Rapid	[x] Stable	[ ] Slow
PROPERTY VALUES	[ ] Increasing	[x] Stable	[ ] Declining
DEMAND/SUPPLY	[ ] Shortage	[x] In Balance	[ ] Over Supply
MARKETING TIME	[ ] Under 3 Mos.	[x] 3-6 Mos.	[ ] Over 6 Mos.

PRESENT LAND USE	%
Single Family	80
2-4 Family	10
Multi-family	10
Commercial	
Industrial	
Vacant	

LAND USE CHANGE: Not Likely [x]; Likely [ ]; In process [ ]; To:

PREDOMINANT OCCUPANCY: Owner [x]; Tenant [ ]; Vacant (0-5%) [ ]; Vacant (over 5%) [ ]

SINGLE FAMILY HOUSING	PRICE $ (000)	AGE (yrs)
Low	55	10
High	80	20
Predominant	65	15

NEIGHBORHOOD ANALYSIS	Good	Avg.	Fair	Poor
Employment Stability		x		
Convenience to Employment		x		
Convenience to Shopping			x	
Convenience to Schools	x			
Adequacy of Public Transportation		x		
Recreation Facilities			x	
Adequacy of Utilities		x		
Property Compatibility		x		
Protection from Detrimental Cond.		x		
Police & Fire Protection			x	
General Appearance of Properties		x		
Appeal to Market		x		

Note: Race or the racial composition of the neighborhood are not considered reliable appraisal factors.
COMMENTS: shopping is approximately two miles away at I-75 and Colerain, City Park one mile north. Other recreational facilities of a private nature. Fire protection is voluntary unit. Other aspects average or better.

SITE

Dimensions 60x125x72x140
Site Area 8,745 Sq.Ft. — Corner Lot Yes
Zoning Classification R-2 (Min.Size 7500 Sq.Ft.) — Zoning Compliance Yes
HIGHEST & BEST USE: Present Use Single family res. — Other Use

UTILITIES	Public	Other
Electricity	x	
Gas	x	
Water	x	
Sanitary Sewer	x	
Storm Sewer		

SITE IMPROVEMENTS	Type	Public	Private
Street	Macadem	x	
Curb/Gutter	Concrete	x	
Sidewalk	Concrete	x	
Street Lights			
Alley			

Topography Level
Size Typical in neighborhood
Shape Typical in neighborhood
Drainage Good
View Average
Landscaping Typical in neighborhood
Driveway
Apparent Easements
FEMA Flood Hazard Yes* — No x
FEMA* Map/Zone

COMMENTS (Apparent adverse easements, encroachments, special assessments, slide areas, etc.): None

IMPROVEMENTS

GENERAL DESCRIPTION: Units 1; Stories 1; Type (Det./Att.) Det.; Design (Style) Rambler; Existing Yes; Proposed ; Under Construction ; Age (Yrs.) 10; Effective Age (Yrs.) 10-12

EXTERIOR DESCRIPTION: Foundation Concrete; Exterior Walls Brick; Roof Surface Cedar Shingle; Gutters & Dwnspts. Galv. Iron; Window Type Dbl. Hung Wood; Storm Sash Yes; Screens Yes; Manufactured House No

FOUNDATION: Slab Concrete; Crawl Space None; Basement Yes; Sump Pump No; Dampness None; Settlement None; Infestation None

BASEMENT: Area Sq. Ft. 1316; % Finished 0; Ceiling ; Walls ; Floor Concrete; Outside Entry Yes

INSULATION: Roof [x]; Ceiling [x]; Walls [x]; Floor [x]; None [ ]; Adequacy [x]; Energy Efficient Items: R-38 Ceiling, R-19 Walls

ROOM LIST

ROOMS	Foyer	Living	Dining	Kitchen	Den	Family Rm	Rec. Rm.	Bedrooms	# Baths	Laundry	Other	Area Sq. Ft.
Basement												
Level 1	x	x	x	x		x		3	2			
Level 2												

Finished area above grade contains: 7 Rooms; 3 Bedroom(s); 2 Bath(s); 1645 Square Feet of Gross Living Area

INTERIOR

SURFACES (Materials/Condition): Floors Hardwood/Good; Walls Plaster; Trim/Finish Wood; Bath Floor Ceramic Tile; Bath Wainscot Ceramic; Doors ; Fireplace(s) #

HEATING: Type FWA; Fuel Gas; Condition Good; Adequacy x
COOLING: Central x; Other ; Condition ; Adequacy x

KITCHEN EQUIP.: Refrigerator [x]; Range/Oven [x]; Disposal [x]; Dishwasher [x]; Fan/Hood [x]; Compactor [ ]; Washer/Dryer [ ]; Microwave [x]; Intercom [ ]

ATTIC: None [ ]; Stairs [ ]; Drop Stair [x]; Scuttle [ ]; Floor [ ]; Heated [ ]; Finished [ ]

IMPROVEMENT ANALYSIS	Good	Avg.	Fair	Poor
Quality of Construction	x			
Condition of Improvements	x			
Room Sizes/Layout		x		
Closets and Storage		x		
Energy Efficiency	x			
Plumbing-Adequacy & Condition		x		
Electrical-Adequacy & Condition		x		
Kitchen Cabinets-Adequacy & Cond.		x		
Compatibility to Neighborhood		x		
Appeal & Marketability		x		

Estimated Remaining Economic Life 45 Yrs.
Estimated Remaining Physical Life 60 Yrs.

AUTOS

CAR STORAGE: Garage [ ]; No. Cars 1; Carport [x]; Condition ; None [ ]; Attached [ ]; Detached [ ]; Built-In [ ]; Adequate [x]; Inadequate [ ]; Electric Door [ ]; House Entry [ ]; Outside Entry [ ]; Basement Entry [ ]

COMMENTS

Additional features: Fireplace in living room; rear concrete covered patio (22x12); 4 ft. high chain link fence around rear yard.

Depreciation (Physical, functional and external inadequacies, repairs needed, modernization, etc.): Additional insulation (floor and ceiling) and automatic thermostat were added in 1979

General market conditions and prevalence and impact in subject/market area regarding loan discounts, interest buydowns and concessions:

Freddie Mac Form 70 10/86 12Ch. AO Forms and Worms Inc.,® 315 Whitney Ave., New Haven, CT 06511 1(800) 243-4545 Item #111710 Fannie Mae Form 1004 10/86

EXHIBIT 6–7 (Panel B) Property Valuation

Valuation Section **UNIFORM RESIDENTIAL APPRAISAL REPORT** **File No.**

Purpose of Appraisal is to estimate Market Value as defined in the Certification & Statement of Limiting Conditions.

COST APPROACH

BUILDING SKETCH (SHOW GROSS LIVING AREA ABOVE GRADE)
If for Freddie Mac or Fannie Mae, show only square foot calculations and cost approach comments in this space

Measurements		No. Stories	=	Sq.Ft.
42x37	x	1		1,554
24x3.8	x	1		91
Total gross living area				1,645sq.ft

ESTIMATED REPRODUCTION COST-NEW-OF IMPROVEMENTS:

Dwelling 1,645 Sq. Ft. @ $ 38.09	=	$62,658
1,316 Sq. Ft. @ $ 7.89	=	10,383
Extras soft wtr.sys.;d/w. disp.	=	
range/oven;f/h; fireplace	=	3,240
Special Energy Efficient Items R-30 Insultn.	=	500
Porches, Patios, etc. and fence	=	1,800
Garage/Carport 200 Sq. Ft. @ $ 6.50	=	1,300
Total Estimated Cost New	=	$79,881
Less Depreciation: Physical 13,500; Functional —; External 7,500	=	$21,000
Depreciated Value of Improvements	=	$58,881
Site Imp. "as is" (driveway, landscaping, etc.)	=	$ 3,050
ESTIMATED SITE VALUE	=	$15,500
(If leasehold, show only leasehold value.)		
INDICATED VALUE BY COST APPROACH	=	$77,431

(Not Required by Freddie Mac and Fannie Mae)
Does property conform to applicable HUD/VA property standards? ☒ Yes ☐ No
If No, explain:

Construction Warranty ☐ Yes ☒ No
Name of Warranty Program
Warranty Coverage Expires

SALES COMPARISON ANALYSIS

The undersigned has recited three recent sales of properties most similar and proximate to subject and has considered these in the market analysis. The description includes a dollar adjustment, reflecting market reaction to those items of significant variation between the subject and comparable properties. If a significant item in the comparable property is superior to, or more favorable than, the subject property, a minus (−) adjustment is made, thus reducing the indicated value of subject; if a significant item in the comparable is inferior to, or less favorable than, the subject property, a plus (+) adjustment is made, thus increasing the indicated value of the subject.

ITEM	SUBJECT	COMPARABLE NO. 1		COMPARABLE NO. 2		COMPARABLE NO. 3	
Address	482 Liberty	478 Liberty St.		225 West 17th Street		110 East 16th Street	
Proximity to Subject		Adjacent		2 blocks West		3 blocks SE	
Sales Price	$ 76,700		$ 65,000		$ 73,500		$ 67,500
Price/Gross Liv. Area	$ 46.63 ☑	$ 46.43 ☑		$ 44.54 ☑		$ 42.19 ☑	
Data Source	Sales con-tract	Present Owner		Appraiser's Files		Selling Broker	
VALUE ADJUSTMENTS	DESCRIPTION	DESCRIPTION	+(−)$ Adjustment	DESCRIPTION	+(−)$ Adjustment	DESCRIPTION	+(−)$ Adjustment
Sales or Financing Concessions		None	–	None	–	None	–
Date of Sale/Time	3-1-96	1-29-96	–	2-14-96	–	12-17-95	–
Location	Avg.Suburb	Similar		Similar		Similar	–
Site/View	Corner Lot	Inside Lot	1,950	Inside Lot	1,950	Corner Lot	–
Design and Appeal	Rambler-Avg.	Similar		Similar		Similar	–
Quality of Construction	Good	Good		Good		Good	–
Age	20 years	19 years		20 years		13 years	(3,250)
Condition	Good	Good		Good		Int.Paint Fair	950
Above Grade Room Count (Total / Bdrms / Baths)	7 / 3 / 2	6 / 1 / 1.5	7,500	7 / 3 / 2	–	7 / 3 / 1	
Gross Living Area	1,645 Sq. Ft.	1,400 Sq. Ft.		1,650 Sq. Ft.		1,600 Sq. Ft.	2,800
Basement & Finished Rooms Below Grade	80% Bsmt Area Unfinished	Full Bsmt Rec. Room	(1,950)	Full Bsmt, Rec Rm, ½ Bath	(2,800)	50% Bsmt Unfinished	3,200
Functional Utility	Good	Good	–	Good	–	Fair	2,800
Heating/Cooling	Central	Central	–	None	2,500	Central	–
Garage/Carport	1Car att.C/P	Similar	–	2 Car att.Gar.	(4,000)	2 Car att.Gar.	(4,000)
Porches, Patio, Pools, etc.	Fence, Rear Patio	Fence, Rear Screen Porch	(1,200)	Fence, Rear Patio	–	No Fence, Rear Screen Porch	(500)
Special Energy Efficient Items	R-38 Ceiling Ins. Solar HW Heater	No solar HW Heater	3,900	No solar HW Heater	3,900	Inf. Insulatn. No solar HW Heater	4,600
Fireplace(s)	Living Room	Similar	–	No Fireplace	1,800	No Fireplace	1,800
Other (e.g. kitchen equip., remodeling)	Range/Oven Disp., Dish Washer	Similar	–	Similar	–	No Built-in Appliance	500
Net Adj. (total)		☒ + ☐ −	$ 10,200	☒ + ☐ −	$ 3,350	☒ + ☐ −	$ 8,900
Indicated Value of Subject			$ 75,200		$ 76,850		$ 76,400

Comments on Sales Comparison: Sale No. 1 is recent sale of smaller house next door to subject and indicated value reflects considerable net adjustments as does sale No. 3. Sale No. 2 is most comparable to subject and required only a few moderate size adjustments consequently most weight is assigned to its indicated value.

INDICATED VALUE BY SALES COMPARISON APPROACH .... $ 76,850

INDICATED VALUE BY INCOME APPROACH (If Applicable) Estimated Market Rent $ 650 /Mo. x Gross Rent Multiplier ______ = $ 75,400

This appraisal is made ☒ "as is" ☐ subject to the repairs, alterations, inspections or conditions listed below ☐ completion per plans and specifications.

Comments and Conditions of Appraisal: Property is at the top of the neighborhood value, but at estimated value it is readily saleable.

RECONCILIATION

Final Reconciliation: Most weight is given to market approach as the comps are recent sales and are fairly similar and in close proximity to subject. Less weight is assigned to cost approach due to the difficulty in reliably establishing depreciation. Least weight given to income approach.

This appraisal is based upon the above requirements, the certification, contingent and limiting conditions, and Market Value definition that are stated in

☐ FmHA, HUD &/or VA instructions.

☐ Freddie Mac Form 439 (Rev. 7/86)/Fannie Mae Form 1004B (Rev. 7/86) filed with client December 1, 19 95 ☐ attached.

I (WE) ESTIMATE THE MARKET VALUE, AS DEFINED, OF THE SUBJECT PROPERTY AS OF March 7, **19** 96 **to be $** 77,000

I (We) certify: that to the best of my (our) knowledge and belief the facts and data used herein are true and correct; that I (we) personally inspected the subject property, both inside and out, and have made an exterior inspection of all comparable sales cited in this report; and that I (we) have no undisclosed interest, present or prospective therein.

Appraiser(s) SIGNATURE ______ NAME ______

Review Appraiser (if applicable) SIGNATURE ______ NAME ______ ☒ Did ☐ Did Not Inspect Property

Freddie Mac Form 70 10/86 12Ch Forms and Worms Inc.,® 315 Whitney Ave., New Haven, CT 06511 1(800) 243-4545 Fannie Mae Form 1004 10/86

Panel B provides an example of the sales comparison approach to value. Some of the items that the appraiser will have to adjust the comparable properties for are (1) time since the comparable has been sold, (2) location, (3) view, (4) design appeal, (5) quality of construction, (6) age of the property, (7) condition, (8) size of rooms, (9) quality of interior finish, (10) functional utility, (11) type and condition of major systems such as central heat and air, and (12) sale or financing concessions.

When making these adjustments, the appraiser adds or subtracts from the value of the *comparable properties* to reflect the differences in market value between comparable and subject property that are caused by different attributes. If the subject property is superior to the comparable property with regard to a particular attribute, then the appraiser will *add* to the value of the *comparable property*. If the subject property has attributes that are inferior to the comparable property, then the appraiser will *subtract* from the value of the *comparable property*. Recall that the value of the subject is unknown; hence, *adjustments must be made to the comparable properties*. After all adjustments have been made to the comparables, the adjusted values of the comparables should be approximately equal to the value of the subject.

The amount that the appraiser adds to or subtracts from the price of a comparable property is an estimate of the *market value* of attributes that are different when comparing the subject with comparable property. For example, in dealing with differences in the *site*, in Panel B (middle) we see that comparables 1 and 2 are both "inferior" to the subject in the sense that the subject is a corner location and the comparables are not. The appraiser judges that such a difference is worth $1,950 in additional market value for the subject, and hence *increases* or adjusts up the prices of the *comparables* by $1,950. On the other hand, we note that comparable 2 has a two-car garage whereas the subject has only a one-car garage. In this case, the price of the *comparable* is adjusted *down* by the difference in the value of a two-car versus a one-car garage ($4,000). Again, the idea is to adjust the *comparables* until all positive and negative characteristics are priced and added to or subtracted from the comparables, leaving a residual value (after adjustments) that should be equal in price to the bundle of characteristics contained in the subject property. The residual values of all comparables, after adjustments, should approach the value of the subject, which is unknown.

How does the appraiser estimate the value of these characteristics? Estimating is done on the basis of experience, judgment, and knowledge of how individual buyers and sellers tend to *price* these attributes in various neighborhoods, given the site and other property characteristics. In other words, the appraiser must be able to *identify* and *defend* the estimated increase or decrease in the total price of a property, given the addition or removal of one or more characteristics (garage, bedroom, bath, etc.). This may seem to be a difficult task: however, in many housing markets hundreds of properties are sold each week and the appraiser generally has access to this data. A process of comparison and continuous updating of information makes the estimation possible. It should be stressed that under the sales comparison approach to value, adjustments are *not* based on the *cost* of constructing improvements. This is because the *market* may not value the addition the same way that an individual may. For example, the cost of adding a swimming pool to a property in an area of small, older, lower-priced homes may not be recovered in the market price when the property is sold, even though the current owner may believe that the value of this addition is at least equal to its cost. In this case, the addition to *market value may not be equal to the cost of constructing the pool* because the appraiser may judge that buyers composing the market for the property are not willing to pay as much for such an improvement as the current owner. Hence the swimming pool may be referred to as an *overimprovement* to the property, and its full cost may not be reflected in the sale price.[14]

To obtain the final estimate of value under the sales comparison approach, the appraiser gives a *qualitative* weight to the residual price for each comparable. The weight assigned to each price depends on how many adjustments were made to each comparable. If many adjustments were made to a comparable, it would be given less weight, and vice versa. The appraiser then assesses the final estimates for each comparable in relation to the qualitative weights (see the comments at the bottom of Panel B, Exhibit 6–7) given to each, and arrives at a final estimate of value.

A common concern of appraisers when using the sales comparison approach to value is the possibility that a comparable sale price may contain financing benefits paid for by the seller of a property. This situation occurs when the seller of a comparable is attempting to help the buyer qualify for a loan and has paid points or discount fees for the buyer, or has taken back a second mortgage at a below-market rate of interest, which usually reduces the borrower's-buyer's monthly payments and cost of financing the property.[15] Sellers often recover such financing costs by charging a higher price for the property. If this property is used later by an appraiser as a comparable to estimate the value of another property, its price may be overstated. This is a difficult situation for appraisers because unless they know the conditions of a property's sale, it will not always be clear whether the seller of a property has paid some of the buyer's financing costs. During times when interest rates are rising and buyers find it difficult to qualify, seller-paid financing is common. During these times, appraisers usually verify that a comparable transaction does not include seller financing by speaking directly with one of the parties to the transaction or the settlement agent before using the comparable in the appraisal process. If seller financing has been used in the transaction, the appraiser must reflect this in his estimate of value by estimating the cost of the seller financing and subtracting this amount from the comparable value.[16] In the example shown in our exhibit, we see that no seller financing was present in any of the comparable sales. Based on the various adjustments to comparables and the appraiser's weighting of these estimates, a value of $76,850 is assigned to the property being appraised under the sales comparison approach.

The sales comparison approach gives the most reliable indication of value when there are a number of current sales of highly comparable properties and information about the circumstances surrounding the transaction is easy to obtain. When these conditions are in effect, appraisers prefer the sales comparison approach.

---

[14]Overimprovements occur when individuals make improvements that they may prefer and/or believe will add value to the property. However, the market may not agree and, hence, will not pay for the cost of the improvement. Similarly, a homeowner can also make an underimprovement, for example, if too small a house is built on a large site. In this case, individuals may not be willing to pay as much for the property as they would have if the relationship between the site and the improvement had been in conformity with other properties in the market area. Many textbooks are available on appraising if you want to pursue the topic.

[15]This is sometimes referred to as "creative" financing in residential transactions. This problem is more prevalent in periods of high interest rates, when buyers have a difficult time qualifying for a loan. In these situations, sellers may finance all or part of the purchase at below market rates of interest or contribute in some way to the buyer's cost of financing.

[16]This will be analyzed in detail in the next chapter.

The Cost Approach. When using the cost approach, the appraiser establishes a value for the site on which the improvement is located, then determines the cost of reproducing the improvement and adds the two. After adding the cost of the improvement and land value, the appraiser deducts an amount for any depreciation (if appropriate) that improvements have suffered since they were constructed. If the improvement has just been completed, the latter adjustment is usually unnecessary unless it was poorly designed or located. This procedure is illustrated at the top of Exhibit 6–7, Panel B.

In arriving at the estimate of land value, a procedure similar to that followed in the sales comparison approach just described is used. Comparable sites that have been recently sold are selected, and adjustments are made for differences in location, size, shape, and topography. In estimating the improvement cost, the appraiser will usually consult cost manuals for material, labor, and profit (overhead) as well as verifying with local construction companies the costs associated with constructing improvements with specific physical and qualitative dimensions. Based on these sources, estimates of construction costs per square foot are made for living space, basements, garages, and second floors. Individual estimates are then made for fixtures (kitchen, bath, etc.), landscaping, and additional improvements (pool, porches, etc.).

In the event the improvement is not newly constructed, there are three types of depreciation that the appraiser will deduct from the cost estimate just described. The first is depreciation in the property's value resulting from normal wear and is referred to as physical depreciation. Examples of physical depreciation would include curable items, such as worn carpeting or walls needing paint, or incurable items, such as foundation settling, which may detract from a property's appearance but do not affect the usefulness of the structure. The second is depreciation resulting from internal property characteristics that make the property less livable or marketable than it was when first constructed. This is referred to as functional obsolescence. Examples of incurable functional obsolescence may include excessive amounts of hallway space. Curable obsolescence would include replacement of lighting fixtures. The third type of depreciation the appraiser will consider is called external obsolescence. It is caused by characteristics external to the property, such as changing land uses in a neighborhood that will cause a structure to become obsolete before the actual building would wear out. Examples of external factors that would cause economic depreciation to occur include pollution, shifting land uses, or changing legal restrictions on land use.

The older a property becomes the more difficult it is for the appraiser to estimate the amount of depreciation that should be used in the appraisal process. In the example shown in Exhibit 6–7, Panel B, we see that the appraiser has estimated that for the subject property (which is 10 years old), physical depreciation amounts to $13,500, economic depreciation is $7,500, and no functional obsolescence was apparent. Based on the cost approach to value, we see that the appraiser assigns a value of $77,400 to the subject property.

The cost approach to value usually provides the most reliable estimate of value when comparable properties are newly constructed and require very few adjustments for depreciation. Appraisers also consider the cost approach when determining value if only a few transactions involving comparable properties exist and the sales comparison approach to value is difficult to use.

The Income Approach. A third appraisal method establishes market value of property by determining how much an investor is willing to pay for the income stream that a property produces. Using this method, the appraiser attempts to establish the relationship between a property's sale price and the monthly income stream it would produce, if rented. The appraiser typically uses sales of a rental property similar to the subject property and determines the ratio of sale price to monthly rental income. This ratio is referred to as the **gross rent multiplier.** The value of the subject property would then be estimated by judging what the subject property should rent for (again by looking at comparable rental units and adjusting for dissimilarities), then multiplying this estimate by the ratio established from comparable sales.

In our example we see in the lower portion of Panel B in Exhibit 6–7 that the appraiser has estimated that, if rented, the subject would bring $650 per month. Given that comparable properties have recently sold for 116 times their monthly rents, it is reasonable that the same relationship would hold for the subject also. Hence a value of $75,400, or $650 × 116, is arrived at by using the income approach.

Typically the income approach is difficult to use because sales of single-family rental properties are rare in an area. When this is the case, appraisers tend to rely on the sales comparison and *cost* approaches when establishing value. However, it should be stressed that for some properties, such as condominiums, where many units are frequently rented, the income approach may provide a reliable estimate of value.

Final Estimate of Value. The appraiser must reconcile the different estimates of value provided by the sales comparison, income, and cost approaches to value when making a final estimate of value. This is accomplished by using a qualitative weighting method, in much the same way as in the sales comparison approach. The appraiser assigns subjective weights to each of the three values based on the reliability of the data and the number of adjustments that had to be made in each technique. More weight would be given to the method requiring fewer adjustments where data is verifiable, current, and complete. In our example, we see that the final estimate of value is $77,000, which, as the appraiser points out, is closest to the sales comparison and cost approaches.

Property Appraisal and Actual Sale Price. In our example the sale price of a property agreed on between a buyer and seller does not exactly correspond to the lender's appraised value. For example, a buyer and a seller agreed on a price of $76,700 for the property and the appraised value obtained by the lender was $77,000. The lender will generally use $76,700, or the lower of sale price or appraised value, as the value on which the loan will be based, unless there is convincing evidence to change it.

Property Values over Time. A cardinal rule followed by lenders is that the value of a mortgaged property should never fall below the outstanding loan balance at any time during the life of the mortgage. In other words, the lender wants to be assured that the market value of the property will always be higher than the loan balance in the event of default by the borrower.

An additional consideration for the lender when considering the relationship of the mortgage balance and property value over time will be the potential effect of any *increases* in the mortgage balance relative to property value. This may present problems in the case of mortgage programs in which loan balance may, or will, increase after the time of loan origination. Recall the discussion in Chapter 4 of the effects of negative amortization in graduated payment mortgage programs and of adjustable rate mortgage programs in Chapter 5.

While the lender may consider the outlined factors in the appraisal process, the lender may not make a lending decision based upon the racial or national origin of individuals living in a neighborhood. This discrimination in making mortgage loans in a neighborhood is known as **redlining** and is prohibited under the **Equal Credit Opportunity Act (ECOA).** Under this act, the lender may not discourage loan applications from borrowers or use discriminatory appraisal practices relative to the neighborhood where the borrower resides. Enforcement of ECOA appraisal guidelines may represent a problem for lenders when (1) neighborhoods have had declining value patterns over time and the risk that this pattern will continue is high, and (2) a large protected minority resides in the neighborhood. ECOA requirements do not prevent lenders from refusing to make loans in such areas, but they do prohibit racial or ethnic considerations from being determining factors in the lending decision.[17]

Loan Commitments The initial loan application, completed by the borrower and submitted for evaluation by the lender, does not represent a binding contract. Normally it represents a mechanism to gather information concerning the loan, the borrower, and the property. After completion of the underwriting process and after negotiation between the borrower and lender, if the loan application is approved, the lender will issue a loan commitment. The loan commitment is binding and details the loan amount and the terms on which the lender is willing to lend. The commitment usually carries an expiration date, setting the time by which the borrower must accept the terms of the loan offer or lose the commitment.

Conclusion

Readers should now have a general understanding of underwriting procedures for residential mortgages as well as the different types of loans available for residential financing. This chapter also introduced fundamental relationships used when assessing default risk involved in making a mortgage loan. We presented four different types of mortgage loans along with examples of each. The borrowers' circumstances will dictate what type of loan is best for their particular situation. This chapter is not intended to be inclusive of all possible variations and rules for underwriting. Rather it is a concise guide to general underwriting procedures and techniques. References to FHA and VA publications have been included for readers who want additional detail on underwriting criteria.

The three approaches used by appraisers to estimate the market value of residential properties have been presented. Lenders and investors should be familiar with these techniques and with the assumptions made by each to estimate value. Chapter 9 has additional discussion of appraisal with emphasis on commercial real estate.

Key Terms

Certificate of Reasonable Value (CRV) 150
comparable properties 165
conventional mortgage loans 147
cost approach 164
default insurance 145
Department of Veterans Affairs (VA) 150
Equal Credit Opportunity Act (ECOA) 172
Federal Housing Administration (FHA) 148
FHA insured mortgages 148
gross rent multiplier 171
guarantees 150
income approach 164
loan-to-value ratio 146
market value 164

[17]For an expanded discussion of the ECOA, see 12 CFR 202.1.

Questions

1. What does underwriting mean in real estate lending?
2. Describe the residual income, net effective income, and gross income approaches to underwriting. What kinds of mortgage loans are usually associated with each?
3. Why would a lender be concerned about payment shock, negative amortization, and the existence of a teaser rate when underwriting an adjustable rate mortgage?
4. Compare the differences between private and FHA mortgage insurance from the lender's perspective. What similarities exist?
5. How do private or public mortgage insurance, hazard insurance, and mortgage cancellation insurance each serve to reduce default risk from the lender's perspective?
6. Under Regulation B of the Board of Governors of the Federal Reserve Board, what guidelines must a lender follow when underwriting a loan?
7. Why is the income approach to value often difficult to use on a single family residential appraisal?
8. What are the differences between the cost and sales comparison approaches to appraising property?

Problems

1. Ms. Sally Strutter is considering the purchase of a residence for $60,000. She desires a fixed-rate, constant-payment 30-year mortgage. Ms. Strutter requests some information from you concerning what types of loans are available on her proposed purchase. After questioning, you determine that she is single, a veteran, and eligible for a VA guaranteed mortgage. The amount of guarantee available to her would be the current VA maximum because Ms. Strutter has never used any of her loan guarantee benefits. Her current occupation is stockbroker, and she has earned $36,000 annually over the last several years. Typically, Ms. Strutter has incurred expenses of $5,000 annually in earning that income. Her credit record is exceptional, and her only current obligation is an auto loan with a payment of $100 monthly for the next 36 months. Ms. Strutter has $7,000 in savings at the current time.

   After some research you are able to compile the following information about the borrower and the property in the proposed transaction:

Borrower Data

Monthly federal income taxes	$439
Monthly state income taxes	$ 78
Monthly FICA withholding	$194

Property Characteristics

Current owner's hazard insurance premium	$ 36 monthly
Property taxes	$ 33 monthly
Maintenance expenses	$ 45 monthly average
Utilities	$105 monthly average

   In addition, you decide that should the borrower want an FHA 203b mortgage, the closing cost allowance authorized by FHA in this region for determining the mortgage balance would be about $1,000. The property has been appraised for $60,000.

   a. Calculate the *maximum* mortgage amount for conventional insured, FHA, and VA mortgages for the borrower. Do not include any costs of mortgage insurance in these mortgage amounts.

   b. You determine that the appropriate FHA up-front mortgage insurance premium on the loan requested is 3.8 percent of the mortgage amount and the annual mortgage insurance premium will be .5 percent of the beginning loan balance. Furthermore, you determine that the renewal premium on conventional mortgage insurance will be .35 percent of the mortgage balance outstanding annually. You believe that the available interest rate on each of the three loan types being considered will be 9.5 percent. Also, Ms. Strutter indicates she would like to finance the FHA insurance premium or the VA funding fee in the loan amount rather than pay them in cash at closing. What effect does this have on the mortgage amounts? What would Ms. Strutter's monthly payment for principal, interest, and mortgage insurance or guarantee be on each of the loans being considered?

c. Would Ms. Strutter qualify for each of the loans being considered?

d. Which loan appears to be best for Ms. Strutter? Give specific reasons.

2. As a new appraiser with the firm of Smith, Turner, and Brown, you have been given your first appraisal assignment. The subject property is located at 322 Rock Creek Road in a new suburb of a large metropolitan area. The property is like many others in the area, with three bedrooms, two baths, a living room, a den, a large kitchen, and a two-car garage. The residence has about 1,800 square feet of air-conditioned space and is of traditional design. The property is located on an interior lot with no potential flooding problems. The quality of construction appears to be about average for the market area.

From the office file you have obtained the locations of and driven by comparable properties to use in the appraisal process that have the following characteristics:

	Comparable I	*Comparable II*	*Comparable III*
Address	123 Clay St.	301 Cherry Lane	119 Avenue X
Sale price	$85,000	$79,000	$75,000
Time of sale	6 months ago	7 months ago	13 months ago
Design	Modern	Traditional	Traditional
Parking	2-car garage	2-car carport	1-car garage
Location	Corner lot	Interior lot	Interior lot
Drainage	Good	Below average	Good
Bedrooms	Four	Three	Two
Baths	Two	Two	Two
Construction	Average	Average	Below average

After discussing the matter with your boss, you have come to some conclusions concerning what you believe the different attributes of the comparable properties are likely to be worth in the market area. Appreciation in house values in the area has been very low over the past eight months, and you think that any properties that have sold within that period would probably not require any adjustments for the time of sale. However, one of the comparable properties sold over a year ago, and you think it will require a $1,500 upward adjustment. Your boss has also indicated that properties in the area that are located near the creek sell for about $1,200 less than other properties in the area because of a slower rate of runoff after heavy rains. Properties on corner lots generally sell for a premium of about $1,000. Houses with the fashionable modern design usually bring about $1,000 more than those that have traditional design characteristics. Because three-bedroom homes are considered desirable by buyers in the area, an additional fourth bedroom will generally only add about $1,200 in value to a property. However, properties that contain only two bedrooms are rather difficult to sell, and often bring $2,000 less than their three-bedroom counterparts when they are sold. Most homes in the area have a two-car garage, but when properties have a one-car garage, they usually sell for about $800 less. A two-car open carport generally reduces the value of the property by a similar amount, or $800. The inferior construction quality exhibited by comparable III should reduce its value by about $1,500.

a. Complete the sales comparison approach to value and assign an estimate of value to the subject property. Give specific reasons for your choice of value.

b. Assume that the value of the lot the subject property is constructed on is $13,000. Air-conditioned space in the dwelling would cost about $36.00 per square foot to reproduce, and the garage would cost approximately $3,700 to reproduce. Complete the *cost* approach to value, assuming that, because the property is new, no depreciation of the structure is required.

3. Joe is considering the purchase of a primary residence, but there are several properties he likes in

different price ranges. He wants the most for his money and is not sure how to best use his VA entitlement. He feels he will be moving again in a few years and wants to be sure he still has VA entitlement available if he is unable to sell his residence before he has to relocate and purchase a new primary residence.

a. What is the minimum purchase price for a home that would use all of Joe's VA entitlement?

b. Joe decides that the purchase price found in *(a)* will not buy him a large enough home, and since his entire VA entitlement will be completely used at that price anyway, what is the maximum purchase price Joe can select for the same entitlement?

c. If Joe decides that the home that can be bought with the purchase price in *(b)* will also be too small, what is the maximum purchase price Joe can select and still expect the VA to provide a loan guaranty?

CHAPTER

7

Residential Financial Analysis

In previous chapters, we have considered the analytics of various types of mortgages used in real estate finance. This chapter extends those concepts to various questions related to the financing of owner-occupied residential properties. Questions raised include how to compare two loans with different loan terms (e.g., amount of loan, interest rate), how to decide whether to refinance or prepay a loan, and whether a loan assumption is desirable. We will also evaluate the effect of below-market financing on the sale price of a house. This is important because one must often pay a higher price for a home that appears to have favorable financing.

Incremental Borrowing Cost

We begin by considering how to evaluate two loan alternatives where one alternative involves borrowing additional funds relative to the other. For example, assume a borrower is purchasing a property for $100,000 and faces two possible loan alternatives. A lender is willing to make an 80 percent first mortgage loan, or $80,000, for 25 years at 12 percent interest. The same lender is also willing to lend 90 percent, or $90,000, for 25 years at 13 percent. Both loans will have fixed interest rates and constant payment mortgages. How should the borrower compare these alternatives?

To analyze this problem, emphasis should be placed on a basic concept called the **marginal** or **incremental cost of borrowing.** Based on the material presented in earlier chapters, we know how to compute the effective cost of borrowing for one specific loan. However, it is equally important in real estate finance to be able to compare financing alternatives whereby the borrower can finance the purchase of real estate in more than one way or under different lending terms.

In the problem at hand, we are considering differences in the amount of the loan and the interest rate. A loan can be made for $80,000 for 25 years at 12 percent, or $90,000 can be borrowed for 25 years at 13 percent interest. Because there are no origination fees, we know from Chapter 4 that the effective interest cost for the two loans will be 12 percent and 13 percent, respectively. However, an important cost that the borrower should compute is the cost to acquire the incremental or additional $10,000, should he choose to take the $90,000 loan over the $80,000 loan. At first glance, you may think that because the interest rate on the $90,000 loan is 13 percent, the cost of acquiring the additional $10,000 is also 13 percent. This is *not* so. Careful analysis of the two loans reveals that if the borrower wants to borrow the additional \$10,000 available with the \$90,000 loan at 13 percent, he or she also must pay an *additional* 1 percent interest on the first \$80,000 borrowed. This increases the cost of obtaining the additional \$10,000 considerably. The \$90,000 loan has a larger payment due not only to the additional \$10,000 being borrowed but also to the higher interest rate being charged on the entire amount. To determine the cost of the additional \$10,000, we must consider how much the additional payment will be on the \$90,000 loan compared with the \$80,000 loan.[1] This difference should then be compared with the additional \$10,000 borrowed. This can be done as follows:[2]

	Loan Amount		*Loan Constant*		*Monthly Payments*
Alt. II at 13%	\$90,000	×	.0112784	=	\$1,015.05
Alt. I at 12%	80,000	×	.0105322	=	842.58
Difference	\$10,000		Difference		\$ 172.47

We want to find the annual rate of interest, compounded monthly, that makes the present value of the difference in mortgage payments, or \$172.47, equal to \$10,000, or the incremental amount of loan proceeds received. As previously discussed, one approach is to solve directly for the interest factor. We have

$$\$172.47(MPVIFA,\ ?\%,\ 25\text{ yrs.}) = \$10{,}000$$
$$(MPVIFA,\ ?\%,\ 25\text{ yrs.}) = \$10{,}000 \div \$172.47 = 57.977737$$

We have computed the monthly *interest factor* for the \$172.47 annuity to be 57.977737. Looking at column 5 in Appendix B, we see that this factor is close to the 25-year factors in the 20 percent interest rate table. A financial calculator indicates that the answer is 20.57 percent. Hence, if our borrower desires to borrow the additional \$10,000 with the \$90,000 loan, the cost of doing so will be more than 20 percent, a rate considerably higher than 13 percent. This cost is referred to as the marginal or incremental cost of borrowing. The 13 percent rate on the \$90,000 loan can be thought of as a weighted average of the 12 percent rate on the \$80,000 loan and the 20.57 percent rate on the additional \$10,000. That is,

$$\left[\frac{80{,}000}{90{,}000} \times 12\%\right] + \left[\frac{10{,}000}{90{,}000} \times 20.57\%\right] = 12.95\% \text{ or } 13\% \text{ (rounded)}$$

The borrower must consider this cost when evaluating whether the additional \$10,000 should be borrowed. If the borrower has sufficient funds so that the \$10,000 would not have to be borrowed, it tells the borrower what rate of interest must be earned on funds *not* invested in a property because of the larger amount borrowed. In other words, by obtaining a larger loan (\$90,000 versus \$80,000), the borrower's down payment will be \$10,000 less than it would have been on the \$80,000 loan. Hence, unless the borrower can earn 20.57 percent interest or more on a \$10,000 investment of equal risk on funds not invested in the property, he or she would be better off with the smaller loan of \$80,000.

[1]Although we use an \$80,000 and a \$90,000 loan in our example, the calculation can be generalized to other loans that are the same percentage of the property value.

[2]Loan constants from the tables in the appendixes may give slightly different answers than financial calculators because of rounding errors. Carrying the loan constant out additional decimal places alleviates the problem.

Calculator Solution

$n = 25 \times 12 = 300$
$PV = -\$10{,}000$
$PMT = \$172.47$
$FV = 0$

Solve for incremental cost of borrowing:
$i = 20.57\%$ (annual)

If the borrower does not have enough funds for a down payment on the $80,000 loan and needs to borrow $90,000, the incremental borrowing cost indicates the cost of obtaining the extra $10,000 by obtaining a larger first mortgage. There may be alternative ways of obtaining the extra $10,000. For example, if the borrower could obtain a second mortgage for $10,000 at a rate *less* than 20.57 percent, this may be a better alternative than a 90 percent loan.[3] Therefore, the marginal cost concept is also an *opportunity cost* concept in that it tells the borrower the minimum rate of interest that must be earned, or the maximum amount that should be paid, on any additional amounts borrowed.

It should be noted that the 20.57 percent figure we calculated also represents the *return* that the lender earns on the additional $10,000 loaned to the borrower; that is, the *cost* of a loan to the borrower will reflect the *return* on the loan to the lender. Of course, keep in mind that the figures we are calculating do not take federal income tax considerations into account, which are also important in determining returns and costs (see the appendix to this chapter). For example, if the borrower is in a higher tax bracket than the lender, the after-tax cost to the borrower will be less than the after-tax return to the lender.

Early Repayment

We should also note that in this example, the incremental cost of borrowing will depend on when the loan is repaid. For example, if the loan is repaid after five years instead of being held for the entire loan term, the incremental borrowing cost increases from 20.57 to 20.83 percent. To see this, we modify the above analysis to consider that if the loan is repaid after five years, the amount that would be repaid on the $80,000 loan will differ from the amount that would be repaid on the $90,000 loan. Thus, in addition to considering the difference in payments between the two loans, we must also consider the difference in the loan balances at the time the loan is repaid. We can find the incremental borrowing cost as follows:

	Loan Amount		*Loan Constant*		*Monthly Payments*	*Loan Balance after Five Years*
Alt. II at 13%	$90,000	×	.0112784	=	$1,015.05	$86,639.88
Alt. I at 12%	80,000	×	.0105322	=	842.58	76,522.56
Difference	$10,000		Difference		$ 172.47	$10,117.32

[3]A lower effective cost for a second mortgage means that the borrower pays less interest each month. However, if the second mortgage has a term less than 25 years, the total monthly payments will be higher with the $80,000 first mortgage and a $10,000 second mortgage than with a $90,000 first mortgage. Thus, some borrowers may prefer to choose a higher effective borrowing cost to have lower monthly payments.

Computing the marginal cost, we have

$$\$172.47(MPVIFA, ?\%, 5 \text{ yrs.}) + \$10{,}117.32(MPVIF, ?\%, 5 \text{ yrs.}) = \$10{,}000$$

In this case, we cannot simply solve for an interest factor and use the tables to find the interest rate because two present value factors are in the above equation. To find the answer, we must find the interest rate that makes the present value of the monthly annuity and lump sum equal to $10,000. The method for doing this was presented in Chapter 3. We can verify that the incremental borrowing cost is now 20.83 percent, the result of early repayment. As we will see in the next section, the impact of early payment may be greater when points are also involved on one or both of the loans.

Calculator Solution

$n = 5 \times 12 = 60$
$PV = -\$10{,}000$
$PMT = \$172.47$
$FV = 10{,}117.32$

Solve for marginal cost:
$i = 1.7360$ (monthly)
$i = 1.7360 \times 12 = 20.83\%$ (annual)

Origination Fees

It should be apparent that the concept of incremental borrowing cost is extremely important when deciding how much should be borrowed to finance a given transaction. In the preceding section, the two alternatives considered were fairly straightforward; the only differences between them were the interest rate and the amount borrowed. In most cases, financing alternatives under consideration will have *different* interest rates as the amount borrowed increases and, possibly, *different* loan maturities. Also, loan origination fees will usually be charged on the loan alternatives. This section considers differences in loan fees on two loan alternatives. We will consider differences in loan maturities later.

The first case is the incremental cost of borrowing when loan origination fees are charged on two 25-year loan alternatives. For example, if a $1,600 origination fee (2 points) is charged on the $80,000 loan and a $2,700 fee (3 points) is charged on the $90,000 loan, how does this affect the incremental cost of borrowing? These differences can be easily included in the cost computation as follows.

Differences in amounts borrowed and payments:

	Loan	–	*Fees*	=	*Net Amount Disbursed*	*Loan*		*Loan Constant*	=	*Monthly Payments*
Alt. II at 13%	$90,000	–	$2,700	=	$87,300	$90,000	×	.0112784	=	$1,015.05
Alt. I at 12%	80,000	–	1,600	=	78,400	80,000	×	.0105322	=	842.58
			Difference	=	$ 8,900			Difference	=	$ 172.47

We want to find an annual rate of interest, compounded monthly, that makes the present value of the difference in mortgage payments, or $172.47, equal to $8,900, or the incremental amount of loan proceeds received. Using a financial calculator, we find that the exact answer is 23.18 percent. Hence, the marginal cost increases to about 23.2 percent when the effects of an additional $1,100 in origination fees charged on the $90,000 loan are included in the analysis. Thus, the borrower only benefits from an additional $8,900 instead of $10,000.

Calculator Solution

$n = 25 \times 12 = 300$
$PV = -\$8{,}900$
$PMT = \$172.47$
$FV = 0$
$i = 1.9316 \times 12 = 23.18\%$

As before, the marginal or incremental cost of borrowing increases if the loan is repaid before maturity. For example, if the loan in the above problem were repaid after five years, the incremental cost would increase to about 24.67 percent.

Incremental Borrowing Cost versus a Second Mortgage

The incremental borrowing cost obviously depends on how much the interest rate increases with the loan-to-value ratio. In the examples considered previously, the interest rate increased from 12 percent to 13 percent (a differential of 1 percent) when the loan-to-value ratio increased from 80 percent to 90 percent. When no points were charged and the loan was held until maturity, the incremental borrowing cost was 20.57 percent. The incremental borrowing cost would increase if the differential between the rate on the 80 percent loan and the 90 percent loan were greater than 1 percent. Conversely, the incremental borrowing cost would decrease if the differential were less than 1 percent.

Because borrowers have a choice between obtaining a 90 percent loan or an 80 percent loan plus a second mortgage for the remaining 10 percent, we would expect the incremental borrowing cost to be competitive with the rate on a second mortgage with the same maturity. In the example, if a second mortgage with a maturity of 25 years can be obtained with an effective borrowing cost that is much less than 20.57 percent, then the 90 percent loan is not competitive; it implies that the 1 percent yield differential between the 90 percent loan and the 80 percent loan is too great. Lenders would have to adjust the differential (or the second mortgage rate) so that the incremental borrowing cost is about the same as the effective cost of a second mortgage.

In Exhibit 7–1, we calculate the incremental borrowing cost for the alternatives discussed earlier, which assume that the loan is prepaid after five years. The exhibit shows how the incremental borrowing cost is affected by the interest rate differential on the 90 percent loan and the 80 percent loan. A 0 percent interest rate differential means that the contract interest rate, which is 12 percent, is the same for both loans. A 1 percent differential means the contract rate is 1 percent higher (e.g., 13 percent for the 90 percent loan).

When the interest rate differential is zero, the incremental cost is the same as the effective cost of the loan. For example, with no points the incremental cost is exactly 12 percent, the same as the interest rate for the 80 percent loan. As the interest rate differential increases, the incremental borrowing cost increases. The incremental cost increases by about the same rate for each loan.

Suppose that a second mortgage for 10 percent of the purchase price (on top of an 80 percent first mortgage) can be obtained with an effective cost of 20 percent with a 25-year maturity. This is added to Exhibit 7–1.[4] This implies that, to be

[4]To compare this rate with the incremental borrowing cost, this must be the effective cost of the loan, considering any points and the effect of prepayment.

EXHIBIT 7–1 Incremental Borrowing Cost versus Interest Rate Differential

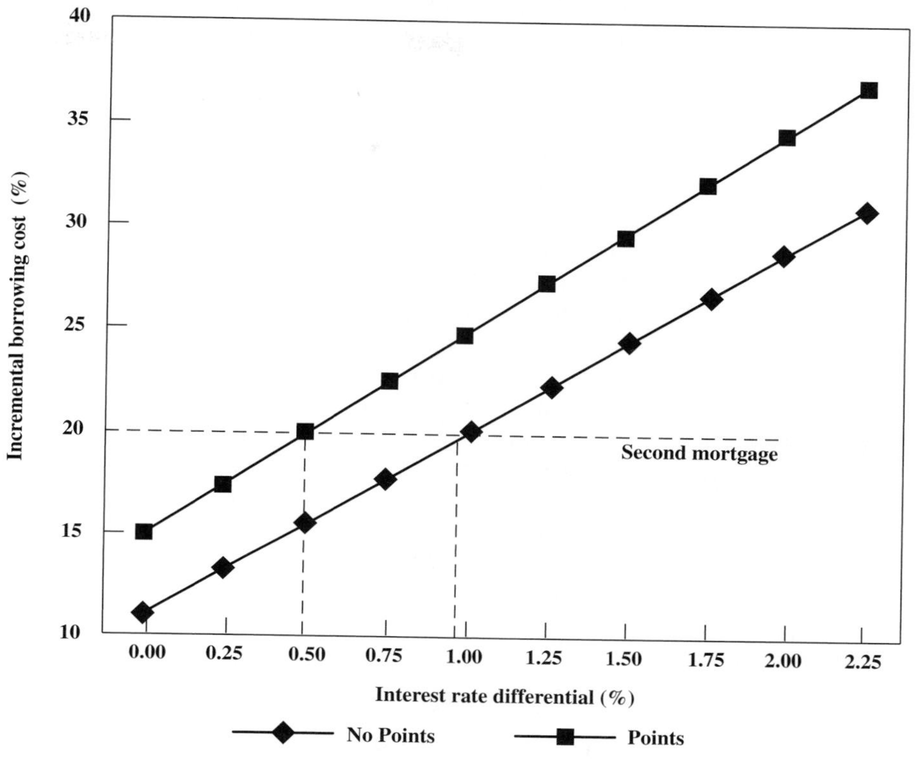

competitive, the 90 percent loan should be priced so that its incremental cost over an 80 percent loan is 20 percent. Suppose lenders expect the loan to be prepaid on average after five years and that they want to charge 2 points on an 80 percent loan and 3 points on a 90 percent loan as we have assumed in the previous examples. This implies that the interest rate differential should be about .50 percent or 50 basis points (see Exhibit 7–1). Alternatively, if lenders do not want to charge any points on either loan, the interest rate differential would have to be about 90 basis points.

Relationship between the Incremental Cost and the Loan-to-Value Ratio

In the previous section, we illustrated the calculation of the incremental borrowing cost for a 90 percent loan ($90,000) with a 13 percent interest rate versus an 80 percent loan ($80,000) with a 12 percent interest rate. Where there were no points and the loan was held until maturity, the incremental cost was 20.57 percent. The incremental borrowing cost is the amount that lenders require on the amount added to the loan that increases the loan-to-value ratio from 80 percent to 90 percent. As discussed previously, this incremental return should be competitive with the return required for a second mortgage for 10 percent of value. The incremental borrowing cost represents the return that lenders require at the margin for lending additional funds; that is, increasing the loan-to-value ratio, whether this is done with a larger first mortgage or a second mortgage.

In the previous examples, we used the difference in interest rates for the entire loan amount (e.g., the rate on an 80 percent loan versus the rate on a 90 percent loan) to calculate the implied cost of the incremental 10 percent loan. In theory, however, it is the incremental cost of the extra amount loaned that must reflect the equilibrium required rate of return for the level of default risk associated with the additional amount loaned. As the loan-to-value ratio increases, the level of default risk also increases. Thus, we would expect the incremental borrowing cost to rise with the loan-to-value ratio. This, in turn, pulls up the average cost of the entire loan. Exhibit 7–2 shows the relationship between the rate for the incremental amount borrowed (incremental borrowing cost) and the average rate for the entire loan (effective rate for a loan with a particular loan-to-value ratio). To compare the results with the previous examples, the calculations in the exhibit are based on a loan term of 25 years, the assumption that the loan is held until maturity, and no points. Loans are assumed to be made in increments of 10 percent of value. The average and incremental rates are the same for a loan-to-value ratio of 10 percent because this is the first incremental loan amount. The incremental rate then increases as the loan-to-value ratio increases. The incremental rate rises faster than the average rate for the entire loan because the average rate for the entire loan is a weighted average of the incremental cost of each of the previous incremental costs. This is the familiar relationship between marginal and average costs; that is, the marginal cost pulls up the average cost as long as the marginal cost is greater than the average cost.

The exhibit indicates, for example, that the average cost for an 80 percent loan is 12 percent. The marginal cost of a 90 percent loan is about 21 percent. This implies that the average cost of a 90 percent loan can be approximated as a weighted average as follows:

$$\text{Average cost of 90\% loan} = (80/90 \times 12\%) + (10/90 \times 21\%)$$
$$\text{Average cost of 90\% loan} = 13\%$$

Note that these are the same numbers (rounded) as calculated in the previous section for the same loan when the loan had no points and was held until maturity.[5]

Because the incremental borrowing cost must be competitive with the rate for a second mortgage, the rate for the incremental amount borrowed shown in Exhibit 7–2 should also approximate the market rate for a second mortgage. Because it is inefficient for lenders to make loans with low loan-to-value ratios,[6] however, we may not actually observe quotes for loans at the lower end of the loan-to-value range; that is, a borrower may have to pay the same rate for any loan that is less than 60 percent of value. This means that the incremental cost and average cost might not actually begin to rise until the loan-to-value ratio exceeds 60 percent.

Differences in Maturities

In the previous examples, the loan alternatives considered had the same maturities (25 years). How does one determine the incremental cost of alternatives that have different maturities as well as different interest rates? Do differences in maturities materially change results? We examine these questions by changing our previous example and assuming that the $90,000 alternative has a 30-year maturity and a higher interest rate. How would the analysis be changed? We first must compute the following information:

[5]This formula is an approximation because the relative weight of each loan actually changes slightly over time as the loans are amortized. Because each loan is amortized over 25 years, the loan-to-value ratio of the 80 percent loan must drop much faster than that of the 10 percent loan because both loan-to-value ratios must be zero at loan maturity.

[6]The transactions cost would be the same as loans with a higher loan-to-value ratio.

Exhibit 7–2 Effect of Loan-to-Value Ratio on Loan Cost

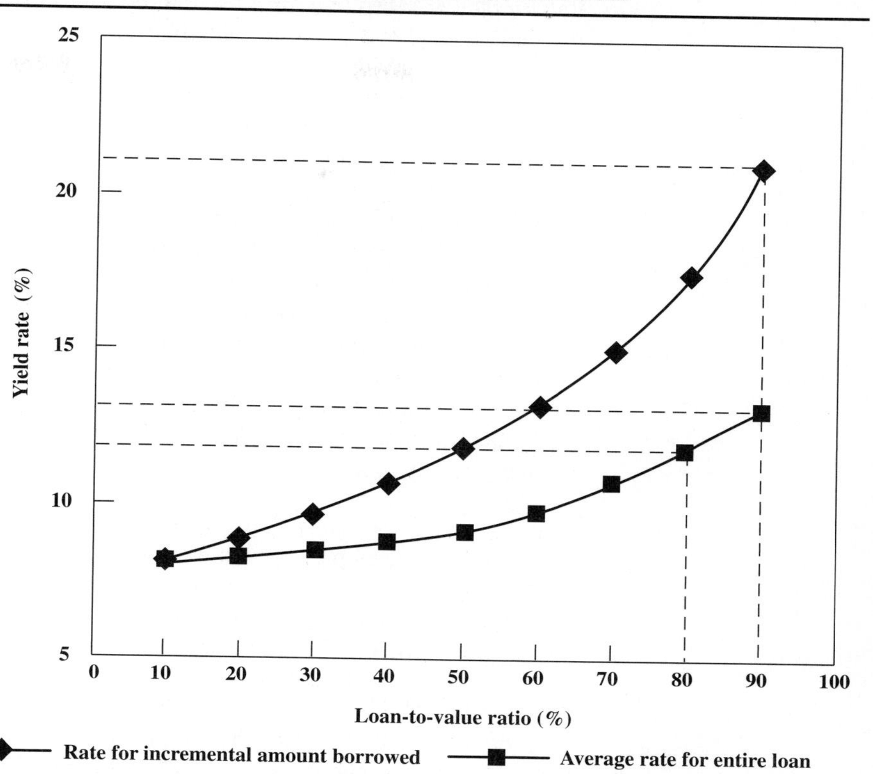

	Loan	Payments Years 1–25	Payments Years 26–30
Alt. III at 13%, 30 yrs.	$90,000	$995.58	$995.58
Alt. I at 12%, 25 yrs.	80,000	842.58	–0–
Difference	$10,000	$153.00	$995.58

In this case, we compute the monthly payment for a $90,000, 30-year loan at 13 percent interest, which is $995.58. However, there are two differences in the series of monthly payments relevant to our example. For the first 25 years, the borrower will pay an additional $153.00 per month for alternative III. For the final five-year period, years 26 through 30, the difference between payments will be the full $995.58 payment on alternative III because the $80,000 loan would be repaid after 25 years. Hence, the incremental cost must be computed by considering the payment differences as two annuities or grouped cash flows as follows:

$$\$153.00(MPVIFA,\ ?\%,\ 25\text{ yrs.}) + \$995.58(MPVIFA,\ ?\%,\ 5\text{ yrs.})\,(MPVIF,\ ?\%,\ 25\text{ yrs.}) = \$10{,}000$$

In the above formulation, the second annuity of $995.58 runs for 5 years, but it is not received until the end of year 25 and therefore must also be discounted for 25 years.[7] We cannot solve directly for the interest factor because there are two unknown factors. Thus, we must use the procedures outlined in Chapter 4 to calculate the yield (cost). Using an estimate of 19 percent and discounting, we get

$$PV = \$153.01(62.590755) + \$995.58(38.549682)(.008980)$$
$$= \$9{,}921.65$$

Calculator Solution
Requires cash flow analysis:
Initial flow = −$10,000
Flow 1 = $153.00
# of times = 300 (years 1–25)
Flow 2 = $995.58
# of times = 60 (years 26–30)
Solve for *IRR*
IRR (monthly) = 1.5719%
IRR (annualized) = 18.86%

Because the desired present value is $10,000, the answer must be slightly less than 19 percent. Using a calculator that can solve for an *IRR* with uneven, or grouped, cash flows, we find the solution is 18.86 percent. Hence, the marginal or incremental cost of borrowing the additional $10,000 given that (1) the interest rate increases from 12 percent to 13 percent, and (2) the loan term increases from 25 years to 30 years will be about 18.86 percent. Compare this with the incremental cost of 20.57 percent in the first example where no fees were charged but both maturities were 25 years. The reason the marginal cost is lower in this case is that although a higher rate must be paid on the $90,000 loan, it will be repaid over a longer maturity period, 30 years. Even though the borrower pays a higher rate for the $90,000 loan, there is a benefit to having a longer amortization period (and thus lower monthly payments) on the $90,000 loan.

Note that if the borrower expects to repay the loan before maturity, both the differences in monthly payments and loan balances in the year of repayment must be taken into account when computing the marginal borrowing cost. Also, should any origination fees be charged, the incremental funds disbursed by the lender should be reduced accordingly.

Loan Refinancing

On occasion, an opportunity may arise for an individual to refinance a mortgage loan at a reduced rate of interest. For example, during 1986 and 1992, interest rates fell sufficiently to cause many borrowers to refinance their home mortgages.

The fundamental relationships to know in any **loan refinancing** decision include at least three ingredients: (1) terms on the present outstanding loan, (2) new loan terms being considered, and (3) any charges associated with paying off the existing loan or acquiring the new loan (e.g., prepayment penalties on the existing loan

[7]Alternatively, we could compute the present value of the second annuity as follows: $995.58 (*MPVIFA*, ?%, 30 yrs. − 25 yrs.).

or origination and closing fees on the new loan). To illustrate, assume a borrower made a mortgage loan 5 years ago for $80,000 at 15 percent interest for 30 years (monthly payment). After 5 years, interest rates fall, and a new mortgage loan is available at 14 percent for 25 years. The loan balance on the existing loan is $78,976.50. Suppose that the prepayment penalty of 2 percent must be paid on the existing loan, and the lender who is making the new loan available also requires an origination fee of $2,500 plus $25 for incidental closing costs if the new loan is made. Should the borrower refinance?

In answering this question, we must analyze the costs associated with refinancing and the benefits or savings that accrue because of the reduction in interest charges should the borrower choose to refinance. The costs associated with refinancing are as follows:

Cost to refinance:		
Prepayment penalty:	(2% × $78,976.50)	$1,580
Origination fee, new loan		2,500
Recording, etc., new loan		25
		$4,105

Benefits from refinancing are obviously the interest savings that result from a lower interest rate. Hence, if refinancing occurs, the monthly mortgage payment under the new loan terms will be lower than payments under the existing mortgage. Monthly benefits would be $60.88 as shown:

Monthly savings due to refinancing:	
Monthly payments, existing loan, $80,000, 15%, 30 years	$1,011.56
Monthly payments, new loan, $78,976.50, 14%, 25 years	950.69
Difference in monthly payments	$ 60.87

One way to approach this problem is to ask whether it is worth "investing," or paying out, $4,105 (charges for refinancing) to save $60.87 per month over the term of the loan. Perhaps the $4,105 could be invested in a more profitable alternative? To analyze this question, we should determine what rate of return is earned on the investment of $4,105 for 25 years, given that $60.87 per month represents a savings. Using a financial calculator, we find that the yield on our $4,105 investment, with savings of $60.87 per month over 25 years, is equivalent to earning 17.57 percent per year. If another alternative equal in risk, which provides a 17.57 percent annual return, cannot be found, the refinancing should be undertaken. This return appears to be attractive because it is higher than the market rate of 14 percent that must be paid on the new loan. Thus, refinancing is probably desirable.

Early Repayment: Loan Refinancing

If the property is not held for the full 25 years the monthly savings of $60.87 do not occur for the entire 25-year term, and therefore the refinancing is not as attractive. If we assume the borrower plans to hold the property for only 10 more years after refinancing, is refinancing still worthwhile? To analyze this alternative, note that the $4,105 cost will not change should the refinancing be undertaken; however, the benefits (savings) will change. The $60.87 monthly benefits will be realized for only 10 years. In addition, since the borrower expects to repay the refinanced loan after 10 years, there will be a difference between loan balances on the existing loan and the new loan due to different amortization rates. We assume that there will be no prepayment penalty on either loan if they are prepaid ten years from now.

Loan balance, 15th year—existing loan*	$72,275
Loan balance, 10th year—new loan†	71,386
Difference	$ 889

*Based on $80,000, 15 percent, 30 years prepaid after 15 years.
†Based on $78,976, 14 percent, 25 years, prepaid after 10 years.

The new calculation comparing loan balances under the existing loan and the new loan terms, should the new loan be made, shows that if refinancing occurs the amount saved with the lower loan balance is $889. Hence, total savings with refinancing would be $60.87 per month for 10 years, plus $889 at the end of 10 years. Do these savings justify an outlay of $4,105 in refinancing costs? To answer this question, we compute the return on the \$4,105 outlay as follows:

$$\$60.87(MPVIFA, ?\%, 10 \text{ yrs.}) + \$889(MPVIF, ?\%, 10 \text{ yrs.}) = \$4{,}105$$

Because the loan is repaid early and the monthly savings of $60.87 will not be received over the full 25-year period, the yield must be below the 17.57 percent yield computed in the previous example. The yield earned due to refinancing will be 14.21 percent per year for the 10-year period.

Calculator Solution

$n = 10 \times 12 = 120$
$PV = -\$4{,}105$
$PMT = \$60.87$
$FV = \$889$

Solve for yield:
$i = 14.21\%$

Obviously, this return is lower than the 17.57 percent computed under the assumption the loan will be repaid after 25 years. This is true because the refinancing cost of $4,105 remained the same, while the savings stream of $60.87 was shortened from 25 years to 10 years. Although an additional $889 was saved because of differences in loan balances, it did not offset the reduction in monthly savings that would have occurred from year 10 through year 25. The relationship between the *IRR* and the number of years the loan is held after refinancing is illustrated in Exhibit 7–3. Note that the returns from refinancing are negative if the loan is held for only five years after prepayment. The return rises sharply for each additional year the loan is held after prepayment until it is held for about 15 additional years. In analyzing refinancing decisions, then, not only must we compare costs and benefits (savings), but also the time period one expects to hold a property.[8]

[8]Obviously, the shorter the time period that the borrower expects to be in the home after refinancing, the lower the return on "investing" in refinancing. In fact if the period of time is relatively short, the return could be negative. Hence, if a borrower expects to sell a property within a short time after refinancing, it will be difficult to justify refinancing.

EXHIBIT 7–3 ***IRR*** **from Savings When Refinancing**

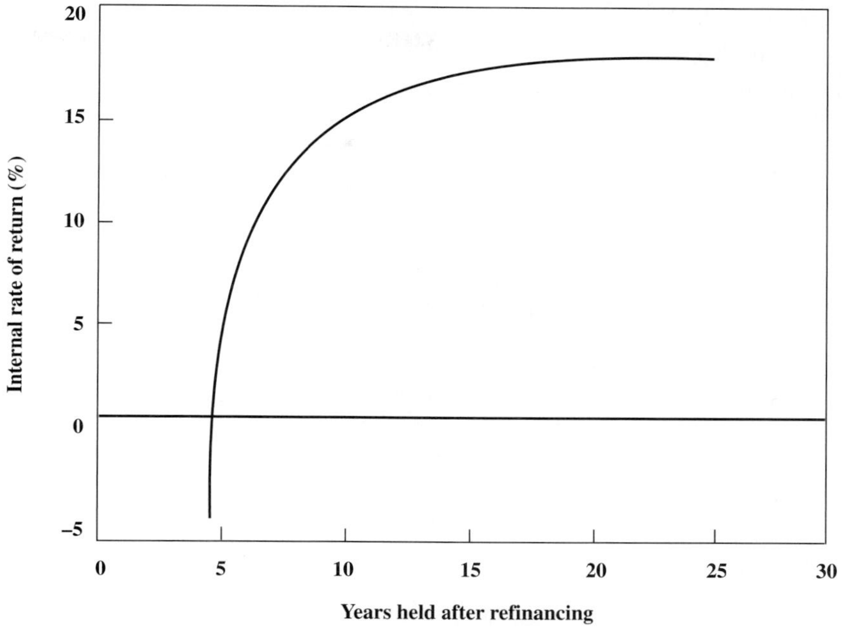

Effective Cost of Refinancing

The refinancing problem can also be analyzed by using an extension of the effective cost concept discussed earlier. We know that points increase the effective cost of a loan. In our problem, the borrower would be making a new loan for \$78,976.50 but must pay \$4,105 in "fees" to do so. Although these fees include the prepayment penalty on the old loan, this can be thought of as a cost of making a new loan by refinancing, or the **effective cost of refinancing.** Thus, the borrower in effect receives \$78,976.50 less \$4,105 or \$74,871.50. Payments on the new loan when made at 14 percent for 25 years would be \$950.69. To find the effective cost where the loan is held to maturity, or 25 years, we proceed as follows:

$$\$950.69(MPVIFA,\ ?\%,\ 25\text{ yrs.}) = \$74{,}871.50$$

Calculator Solution

$n = 25 \times 12 = 300$
$PV = -\$74{,}871.50$
$PMT = \$950.69$
$FV = 0$

Solve for yield:
$i = 14.86\%$

Using the tables or a financial calculator, we obtain an interest rate of 14.86 percent. This can be interpreted as the effective cost of obtaining the new loan by refinancing. Since this cost is *less* than the rate on the old loan (15 percent), refinancing would seem to be desirable.[9] Thus, we arrive at the same conclusion we got when calculating the return on investing in refinancing.

Borrowing the Refinancing Costs

In the above analysis, we assumed that the borrower had to pay (as a cash outlay) the refinancing costs of $4,105. However, it is likely that if the borrower is going to the trouble of refinancing, he or she may also be able to borrow the refinancing costs.[10] How does this affect our analysis?

The borrower now gets a loan for the loan balance of $78,976.50 plus the fees of $4,105.00 for a total of $83,081.50. Payments at the 14 percent rate (assuming the interest rate is still the same) would be $1,000.10.[11] What do we compare this to now that the borrower has no cash outlay when refinancing? The answer is simple. These payments are still less than those on the old loan ($1,011.56). Given that the borrower has lower payments ($11.46) for 300 months without any cash outlay, it is desirable to refinance.[12]

We could, of course, also compute the effective cost of refinancing as we did in the previous section. In this case, the total amount of the loan is $83,081.50; however, the borrower, in effect, only benefits from $78,976.50 (the loan amount less the refinancing costs). Using the payment of $1,000.10 and assuming the new loan is held for the full loan term, we can calculate the effective cost as follows:

$$\$1{,}000.10(\mathit{MPVIFA},\ ?\%,\ 25\ \text{yrs.}) = \$78{,}976.50$$

Solving for the effective interest rate, we obtain an answer of 14.81 percent, which is virtually the same as we obtained in the previous section. The only reason the answer is slightly lower is that the origination fee on the new loan was assumed to remain at $2,500 even though the amount of the loan was increased to cover the refinancing costs.

Calculator Solution

$n = 25 \times 12 = 300$
$PV = -\$78{,}976.50$
$PMT = \$1{,}000.10$
$FV = 0$

Solve for effective interest rate:
$i = 14.81\%$

Note that whether we calculate a return on investing in refinancing, or we calculate the effective cost of refinancing, we arrive at the same conclusion. Often there are many ways of considering a problem that lead to similar conclusions. It is infor-

[9]Any points that had been paid on the old loan would not be relevant since they are a "sunk cost"; that is, they have already been paid and are not affected by refinancing. Thus, only the current interest rate on the old loan should be compared with the effective cost of the new loan.

[10]The borrower will probably have sufficient equity in the home to do so since, if the old loan was held for several years, the borrower has reduced the balance on the old loan and the home may have increased in value.

[11]If this approach were used to analyze the case where the loan was to be repaid early, the additional loan balance on the refinanced loan would have to be considered. This would reduce the benefit of the lower payments.

[12]If the interest rate was higher, then we would also want to consider the incremental cost of the additional $4,105, as considered earlier in the chapter.

mative to look at a problem several ways to gain skill in handling the wide variety of financial alternatives one may encounter. Knowing alternative ways of analyzing a problem also reduces the chance of applying an incorrect technique to solve it.

Early Loan Repayment: Lender Inducements

After a period of rising interest rates, borrowers may have a loan that has an interest rate below the market rate. Earlier we considered the situation where interest rates had fallen and the borrower may find it beneficial to refinance at a lower interest rate even if additional fees and penalties have to be paid to the lender. Where interest rates have risen considerably, the situation may be the opposite. Banks may be willing to "pay" the borrower to induce him or her to repay the loan early. That is, the lender may offer the borrower a discount to pay off the balance of a below market interest rate loan.[13] How much of a discount should be offered?

Suppose a borrower has a loan that was made 10 years ago. The original loan amount was $75,000 to be amortized over 15 years at 8 percent interest. The balance of the loan is now $35,348, and the payments are $716.74 per month. If the current market interest is 12 percent, then the lender would like to have the loan paid off early so that funds could be loaned to someone else at the market rate. The borrower has no incentive to prepay the loan even if he or she has $35,348 available to do so. However, the bank may be willing to offer the borrower a discount to prepay the loan. Suppose the lender discounts the loan by $2,000, so that only $33,348 must be paid to the lender. Is this attractive to the borrower?

Calculator Solution

$n =$ $5 \times 12 = 60$
$PV =$ $-\$33,348$
$PMT =$ $\$716.74$
$FV =$ 0

Solve for return:
$i =$ 10.50%

By accepting the discount, the borrower, in effect, earns a return on the funds used to repay the loan; that is, by making a payment of $33,348 to the lender the borrower saves $716.74 per month. To calculate the return earned by prepaying the loan, we have

$$\$716.74(MPVIFA,\ ?\%,\ 5\text{ yrs.}) = \$33,348$$

Scanning the tables for the *MPVIFA,* or using a financial calculator, we find the return to be about 10.5 percent. Thus, the interest savings represent a 10.5 percent return on the "investment" made to repay the loan.[14] Whether this represents an attractive proposition for the borrower depends on what alternatives he or she has for investing the $33,348.

---

[13]This is particularly true if the loan is assumable.

[14]The above analysis does not consider the impact of federal income taxes. The IRS has ruled that when a lender discounts a loan such that the borrower does not have to repay the contract loan balance, the discount represents "loan forgiveness" and as such is considered taxable income. Thus, the borrower would have to pay taxes on the $2,000 discount. For an investor in the 40 percent tax bracket, the taxes would be $800. Thus, the net result is as if the borrower only received a discount of $2,000 − $800 = $1,200. This clearly reduces the benefit to the borrower to repay the loan.

In the preceding example, we assumed that the borrower had the funds ($33,348) to prepay the below market rate loan. Several other possibilities could be considered. One is that the borrower would refinance some or all of the loan at the market rate. Another is that the borrower wants to increase the loan balance by refinancing. In either case, the lender may still be willing to provide an inducement for the borrower to refinance since the existing loan is at a below market rate. However, the approach taken to analyze the problem depends on whether, on balance, the borrower gives funds to the lender to reduce the loan balance in exchange for the lower payments or the borrower receives additional funds in exchange for an additional loan payment.

Market Value of a Loan

We have considered several problems in which the balance of a loan was determined after payments had been made for a number of years. The balance of the loan represents the amount that the borrower must repay the lender to satisfy the loan contract. (Any prepayment penalties must be added to the loan balance.) The loan balance may be interpreted as the "contract" or "book value" of the loan. However, if interest rates have changed since the origination of the loan, the loan balance will probably not represent the "market" value of the loan.

The **market value of a loan** is the amount that a new lender or investor would pay to receive the remaining payments on the loan. It can be thought of as the amount that could be loaned so that the remaining payments on the loan would give the lender a return equal to the current market rate of interest.

To find the market value of a loan, you simply calculate the present value of the remaining payments at the market rate of interest. For example, suppose a loan was made five years ago for $80,000 with an interest rate of 10 percent and monthly payments over a 20-year loan term. Payments on the loan are $772.02 per month. As we know, one way of finding the current balance of the loan is to compute the present value of the remaining loan payments at the *contract* interest rate of 10 percent. We have

$$\begin{aligned} \text{Loan balance} &= \$772.02(MPVIFA,\ 10\%,\ 15\text{ yrs.}) \\ &= \$772.02(93.057439) \\ &= \$71{,}842 \end{aligned}$$

To find the market value of the loan, we compute the present value of the remaining payments at the market interest rate. Suppose that rate is currently 15 percent. We have

$$\begin{aligned} \text{Market value} &= \$772.02(MPVIFA,\ 15\%,\ 15\text{ yrs.}) \\ &= \$772.02(71.449643) \\ &= \$55{,}161 \end{aligned}$$

Thus the market value of the loan is $55,161 compared to a loan balance of $71,842. The $55,161 is the amount that the lender would receive if the loan were sold to another lender, investor, or the secondary market.[15] We could say that the

[15]It is informative to look at an alternative approach that yields the same answer. Suppose we were to make a loan for $71,842 at the market rate of 15 percent for the remaining loan term of 15 years. The payment would be $1,005.49. This is $233.47 higher than the contract payment. If we discount this *difference* in payments for the 15-year period at the market rate we get a present value of $16,681. Subtracting this difference from the loan balance results in the market value of the loan.

above loan is selling at a "discount." The amount of the difference in this case would be $71,842 − $55,161 = $16,681. We could also say that the mortgage is selling at a discount of 23 percent of its "face" value.

Calculator Solution
Loan balance:
$n = 15 \times 12 = 180$
$i = 10\% \div 12 = 0.8333\%$
$PMT = \$772.02$
$FV = 0$

Solve for loan balance:
$PV = \$71,842$

Market value:
(change i to 15%)
$i = 15\% \div 12 = 1.25\%$

Solve for market value:
$PV = \$55,161$

The market value of the loan is lower than the contract loan balance in this example because interest rates have risen relative to the interest rate (10 percent) at which the loan was originated 10 years ago. However, the borrower is required to make payments based on 10 percent even though market rates have risen to 15 percent. This is one reason why adjustable rate mortgages have become more attractive to lenders (see Chapter 5). With an adjustable rate mortgage, the market value of the outstanding loan will not differ as much as a new loan originated at market rates of interest. Indeed, if the interest rate on the outstanding loan could be adjusted at each payment interval and there were no limitations (caps) on the amount of the adjustment, the contract rate on the loan would always equal the market rate. In this event, the loan balance and market value for such a loan would always be equal because future payments would be based on current rates of interest.

Effective Cost of Two or More Loans

Many situations exist where the buyer of a home may be considering a combination of two or more loans (e.g., a first and a second mortgage to finance the home). One situation is the assumption of a loan that has a favorable rate of interest.[16] However, the amount of cash necessary for the buyer to assume a mortgage may be prohibitive. This can occur when the seller has already paid down the balance of the loan and when the home has appreciated in value since it was originally financed by the seller. Thus, the buyer must use a second mortgage to bridge the gap between the amount available from the loan assumption and the desired total loan amount.

[16]In many areas of the United States, properties are sold on assumption. However, in many other areas, the right to sell on assumption is precluded explicitly in the mortgage or by the lender not approving the new buyer. Lending practices vary widely, depending on tradition and economic conditions in a given area.

Suppose an individual bought a $100,000 property and made a mortgage loan 5 years ago for $80,000 at 10 percent interest for a term of 25 years. Due to price appreciation the market value of the property has risen in value over the past five years to $115,000. The amount of cash equity required by the buyer to assume the seller's loan would be $39,669, determined as follows:

Purchase price	$115,000
Seller's mortgage balance	
($80,000, 10%, 25 yrs., after 5 yrs.)	75,331
Cash equity required to assume	$ 39,669

If the buyer does not have $39,669 in cash, even though he or she desires an assumption, the transaction may not be completed. One alternative open to the buyer who could not make the large cash outlay may be to obtain a second mortgage. However, using a second mortgage will be justified in this case only if the terms of the second mortgage, when combined with the terms on the assumed mortgage, will make the borrower as well or better off than if the entire purchase had been financed with a new mortgage. If the entire purchase can be financed with a new $92,000 loan (80 percent of value) at 12 percent for 20 years, we must know how to combine a second mortgage with the assumed mortgage to determine whether the assumption would be as attractive as the new mortgage loan. Suppose a second mortgage for $16,669 ($92,000 − $75,331) could be obtained at a 14 percent rate for a 20-year term. To analyze this problem, we compute the combined mortgage payments on the assumed loan and a second mortgage loan made for 20 years at 14 percent.

Monthly payment, assumed loan*	$726.96
Monthly payment, second mortgage loan†	207.28
	$934.24

*Based on original $80,000 loan, at 10 percent, for 25 years.
†Based on second mortgage loan of $16,669 at 14 percent, for 20 years.

The combined monthly payments equal $934.24. We now want to compute the effective cost of the combined payments that are made on the combined loan of $92,000. We have

$$\$934.24(MPVIFA,\ ?\%,\ 20\text{ yrs.}) = \$92{,}000$$
$$MPVIFA = 98.475766$$

Using a financial calculator, we find an answer of 10.75 percent. This is the cost of obtaining $92,000 with the loan assumption and second mortgage. Since this is less than the cost of obtaining $92,000 with a new first mortgage at a rate of 12 percent, the borrower is still better off with the loan assumption and a second mortgage.[17] It

[17]It should be apparent that such a high interest rate can be paid on the second mortgage because $75,331, the amount assumed, carries a 10 percent rate and represents about 82 percent of the $92,000 to be financed, while the second mortgage of $16,669 represents only 18 percent. When weighted together by the respective interest rates, the total rate paid on the combined amounts is influenced more by the amount assumed at 10 percent. As an approximation of the average of "blended" rate for the two loans, we have (.82 times 10%) + (.18 times 14%) = 10.72%, which is approximately the same as the answer we found using the present value factors above.

is important to note, however, that the preceding analysis does not consider the fact that the seller of the home may have *raised the price of the home* to capture the benefit of the assumable below market rate loan. Later in the chapter, we will consider this in our analysis.

Calculator Solution

$n = 20 \times 12 = 240$
$PV = -\$92{,}000$
$PMT = \$934.24$
$FV = 0$

Effective yield:
$i = 10.75\%$

Second Mortgages and Shorter Maturities

In most cases, second mortgages may not be available for a 20-year period. If a five-year term were available on a second mortgage loan at 14 percent interest, would the borrower still be better off by assuming the existing mortgage and taking a second mortgage? To answer this question, we must determine the combined interest cost on the assumed mortgage, which carries a rate of 10 percent for 20 remaining years, and the second mortgage, which would carry a rate of 14 percent for 5 years. This combined rate can then be compared with the current 12 percent rate for 20 years presently available, should the property be financed with an entirely new mortgage loan.

To combine terms on the assumable mortgage and second mortgage, we add monthly payments together as follows:

	Monthly Payments
Assumed loan*	$ 726.96
Second mortgage†	387.86
Total	$1,114.82

*Based on original terms: $80,000, 10 percent, 25 years.
†Based on $16,669, 14 percent, 5 years.

The sum of the two monthly payments is equal to $1,114.82. However, the combined $1,114.82 monthly payments will be made for only five years. After five years, the second mortgage will be completely repaid, and only the $726.96 payments on the assumed loan will be made through the 20th year.

Whether the combined mortgages should be used by the borrower can now be determined by again solving for the combined cost of borrowing. This cost is based on the monthly payments under both the assumed loan and second mortgage, for the respective number of months payments must be made, in relation to the $92,000 amount being financed. These costs are easily seen as the monthly payments of $387.86 on the second mortgage for *5 years* and the monthly payments of $726.96 on the assumed mortgage for *20 years*, both discounted by an interest rate that results in the present value of $92,000.

$$\$387.86(MPVIFA,\ ?\%,\ 5\text{ yrs.}) + \$726.96(MPVIFA,\ ?\%,\ 20\text{ yrs.}) = \$92{,}000$$

We must find the interest rate that makes the present value of the combined monthly mortgage payments (grouped cash flows) equal to $92,000. Using a financial calculator, we find that the combined interest cost on the existing mortgage assumed for 20 years and the second mortgage for 5 years is 10.29 percent. This combined package of financing must again be compared to the 12 percent interest rate currently available on an $80,000 mortgage for 20 years. Because the effective cost of the two combined loans is less than the market rate, this is the best alternative. It should be noted, however, that for the first 5 years the combined monthly payments of $1,114.82, should the assumption and second mortgage combination be made, would be higher than the payments with a new mortgage for $92,000 at 12 percent for 20 years, which would be $1,013.00 per month. Although this is offset by the lower $726.96 payments after five years, the borrower must decide which pattern of monthly loan payments fits his or her income pattern, in addition to simply choosing the loan alternative with the lower effective borrowing cost. A borrower may be willing to pay a higher effective cost for a loan (or combination of loans) that has lower monthly payments.

Calculator Solution
Requires cash flow analysis:
Initial flow = −$92,000
Flow 1 = $1,114.82
Number of times = 60 (years 1–5)
Flow 2 = $726.96
Number of times = 180 (years 6–20)

Solve for *IRR*:
IRR (monthly) = 0.8573%
IRR (annualized) = 10.29%

Effect of Below Market Financing on House Prices

In many situations, a home buyer may have an opportunity to purchase a home and obtain financing at a below market interest rate. We have previously discussed one case where the seller of the house had a below market rate loan that could be assumed by the buyer. Below market financing might also be provided by the seller of the home with a *purchase money mortgage*. In this case, the seller provides some or all of the financing to the buyer at an interest rate lower than the current market rate. Indeed, this type of financing is common during periods of tight credit and high interest rates.

Obviously, below market rate loans have value to the buyer. However, because the informed seller of the home also recognizes the value of this type of financing, we would expect the seller to increase the price of the house to reflect it. That is, the "price" of the house would be higher with below market financing than market rate financing.

We now consider how a buyer would analyze whether to purchase a house with below market financing if the house price is higher than that of an otherwise comparable home that does not have below market financing. Suppose a home could be purchased for $105,000 subject to an assumable loan at a 9 percent interest rate with a 15-year remaining term, a balance of $70,000, and payments of $709.99 per month. A comparable home without any special financing costs $100,000, and a loan for $70,000 could be obtained at a market rate of 11 percent with a 15-year term. Which alternative is best for the buyer? Note that we are assuming that the two loan amounts are the same. In analyzing this problem, we must consider whether it is desirable for the buyer to pay an additional $5,000 in cash for the home (additional equity invested) to receive the benefit of lower payments on the below market loan. The calculations are as follows:

	Down Payment	*Payment*
Market rate loan	$30,000	$795.62
Loan assumption	35,000	709.99
Difference	$ 5,000	$ 85.63
$85.63 times (*MPVIFA*, ?%, 180 mos.) =		$ 5,000

Using a financial calculator, we find that making the additional $5,000 down payment would result in earning the equivalent of 19.41 percent because of the lower monthly loan payments. Alternatively, should the buyer decide not to pay the additional $5,000, he or she would have to find a return of 19.41 percent on the $5,000 in an investment with comparable risk. Because the 19.41 percent rate is higher than the 11 percent market rate, buying the house with below market financing appears to be desirable.

Calculator Solution

$n = 15 \times 12 = 180$
$PV = -\$5{,}000$
$PMT = \$85.63$
$FV = 0$

Solve for yield:

$i = 1.6177\%$ per month

or

$i = 19.41\%$ per year

Assuming a Lower Loan Balance

For simplicity, it was assumed in the above example that the balance of the assumable (below market) loan was the same as the amount available for a new loan at the market rate. As discussed previously, an assumable loan may have a lower balance than a new market rate loan because the seller has paid down the loan and the home may have increased in value. Suppose the balance on the assumable loan in our example is only $50,000 and monthly payments are $507.13. The buyer, however, needs financing of $70,000, the amount that can normally be borrowed at market rates. The borrower may also obtain a second mortgage of $20,000 for 15 years at a 14 percent rate, with payments of $266.35 per month. Is it still desirable to assume the loan, take a second mortgage, and pay $5,000 more for the house? We can make the following calculations:

	Down Payment	Payment
Market rate loan	$30,000	$795.62
Loan assumption + Second mortgage	35,000	773.48*
	$ 5,000	$ 22.14

*$507.13 on the $50,000 loan assumption plus $266.35 on the second mortgage.

The return is now −2.90 percent. The buyer is clearly better off by not paying $5,000 more for the house to assume the loan. How much more would the buyer be willing to pay? This is the subject of the next section.

Cash Equivalency

In the previous section, we considered how a buyer could analyze whether a premium should be paid for a home with a below market rate loan. We now extend that discussion to consider how much the buyer *could* pay to be indifferent to purchasing the home with a below market rate loan or one that must be financed at the market rate.

We will use the example from the last section, where a $70,000 loan could be assumed at a 9 percent rate with a remaining term of 15 years and payments of $709.99 per month. Recall that a comparable home with no special financing available would sell for $100,000 and could be financed at a market rate of 11 percent. How much more than $100,000 could the buyer pay if he or she chose to assume the 9 percent loan and still be as well off as if the property were purchased for $100,000 and financed with an 11 percent loan? We first find the present value of the payments that can be assumed using the *market* rate.

$$
\begin{aligned}
PV &= \$709.99(MPVIFA,\ 11\%,\ 180\text{ mos.}) \\
&= \$709.99(87.981937) \\
&= \$62,466.30
\end{aligned}
$$

This is the market value or **cash equivalent value** of the assumable loan. It represents the price at which the old loan could be sold to a new lender/investor.

Calculator Solution

$n = 15 \times 12 = 180$
$i = 11\% \div 12 = 0.91666\%$
$PMT = \$709.99$
$FV = 0$

Market value:
$PV = \$62,446.30$

By assuming the existing loan balance, the buyer of the house would obtain financing equal to $70,000.00 instead of $62,466.30 for the same $709.99 payment. Thus, the buyer receives a net benefit of $70,000.00 − $62,466.30 = $7,533.70. Therefore, the buyer could pay $7,533.70 more for the home, or $107,534 (rounded).

In the previous section, we calculated that the return to the buyer would be 19.41 percent if an additional \$5,000 more, or \$105,000, were paid for the home. It is possible to verify that by paying \$107,534 for the home, the buyer's return would be exactly 11 percent, the same as the market interest rate on the loan.

Based on the above analysis, the home with the assumable loan could probably sell for as high as \$107,534. The buyer would be paying a cash equivalent value of \$100,000 for the house plus an additional **financing premium** of \$7,534 to obtain the benefit of the below market rate loan. The value of the house is still \$100,000. This is referred to as the cash equivalent value of the house. This differs from the *price* paid for the house, which includes the \$7,534 financing premium. The recognition of this premium is important because if we knew that the property had actually sold for \$107,534 but did not consider that it had an assumable below market rate loan, we would have an inflated opinion about the real worth of the house. Alternatively, the buyer would never want to agree to pay \$107,534 for the property unless the 9 percent below market financing could be obtained. During the early 1980s, when below market rate loans were common, appraisers were criticized for not taking financing premiums into consideration when using sales of homes with below market rate loans as comparables in determining the value of houses that had no special financing.

Note that the amount of cash (equity) invested in the home is \$107,534, \$70,000 or \$37,534. When this is added to the cash equivalent value of the loan of \$62,466, we obtain the cash equivalent value of the property of \$100,000.

Cash Equivalency: Smaller Loan Balance

In the previous section, we determined the indifference price for a property that had an assumable below market rate loan. The loan balance was the same as the buyer could obtain with a market rate loan. However, when loan assumptions occur, it is likely that the loan balance is significantly less than would normally be desired. We now modify the example in the last section by considering that the balance of the assumable 9 percent loan is only \$50,000 and the buyer would have to borrow an additional \$20,000 through a second mortgage to obtain the \$70,000 needed. We assume that the second mortgage could be obtained at a 14 percent rate for a 15-year term. We continue to assume that a \$70,000 new first mortgage (70 percent of the house value) could be obtained at an 11 percent rate with a 15-year term.[18] Now how much could the buyer pay for the house and be indifferent to the two methods of financing?

We now find the present value of the *sum* of the payments on the assumable loan (\$507.13) plus payments on the second mortgage (\$266.35), using the 11 percent market rate.

$$\begin{aligned} PV &= \$773.48(MPVIFA,\ 11\%,\ 180\text{ mos.}) \\ &= \$773.48(87.981937) \\ &= \$68{,}052.27 \end{aligned}$$

[18]Even if the buyer didn't need a second mortgage, we can only evaluate the benefit of the loan assumption by comparing it with what is currently available in the market. Since market rates are usually based on a loan-to-value ratio of 70 percent or more, a second mortgage must be considered in the analysis.

The difference between the present value ($68,052.27) and the $70,000 available at the market rate is $1,947.73. Thus, the buyer would now pay only an additional $1,947.73 for the home to get the below market rate loan. Thus, the home would probably sell for no more than $101,950 (rounded). This is considerably less than the $107,500 obtained where the assumable loan had a balance of $70,000 instead of $50,000. There are two reasons that the premium is less: First, because the balance of the assumable loan is less, the saving (from lower payments) is less. Second, because this balance is less than the amount of the loan that could be obtained at the market rate, the benefit from lower payments on the assumable loan is reduced by the necessity of obtaining a second mortgage at a higher interest rate than the rate on a new first mortgage. It is important to realize that when carrying out this analysis, the need for a second mortgage must be considered; otherwise the benefit of the loan assumption is overstated.

Calculator Solution

$n = 15 \times 12 = 180$

$i = 11\% \div 12 = 0.91666\%$

$PMT = \$773.48$

$FV = 0$

Market rate:

$PV = \$68,052.27$

Cash Equivalency: Concluding Comments

In the previous two sections, we showed how to analyze the impact of below market financing on the sale price of a property. It is important to recognize the relationship between the price at which a property sells and any special (e.g., below market) financing that might be available. Although we have considered several examples of cash equivalency calculations, we have only introduced a few of the possible situations that could arise in practice. At least three additional situations could arise that would affect the analysis.

1. If the below market financing is not transferable to a subsequent buyer, this means that a previous buyer may not benefit from the below market rate loan for its remaining term. This obviously affects any financing premiums that would be paid for properties.
2. Even if below market loans were always assumable by subsequent buyers, the value of this type of financing over the remaining term of the loan to a subsequent buyer depends on the market rate of interest at the time of subsequent sales. These rates may be higher or lower than rates prevailing at the time that the present owner purchased the property. If market rates at the time the property is sold are no longer greater than the contract rate on the assumable loan, then the subsequent buyer would not pay a premium. Hence, the likelihood of subsequent sales and interest rates at such points in time adds an element of uncertainty to the benefit of assuming any loan and should tend to reduce the amount buyers are willing to pay for such loans.
3. Even if the buyer plans to own the property for a time period exceeding the loan term, interest rates could drop after the loan is assumed. Because

borrowers can usually refinance when interest rates drop, a below market rate loan has less value if interest rates are expected to fall. In effect, the value of the below market financing is reduced by the "option" to refinance if interest rates fall.

All of the situations discussed above tend to reduce the premium a buyer would pay for a below market interest rate loan. Thus, our analysis is likely to indicate the *upper limit* on the premium associated with below market rate loans. The best way to verify the value of such premiums is by observing how much more buyers pay for below market financing in contrast to houses without special financing.

Wraparound Loans

Wraparound loans are used to obtain additional financing on a property while keeping an existing loan in place. The wraparound lender makes a loan for a face amount equal to the existing loan balance plus the amount of additional financing. The wraparound lender agrees to make the payments on the existing loan as long as the borrower makes payments on the wraparound loan. Instead of making payments on the original loan in addition to payments on a second mortgage, the borrower makes a payment only on the wraparound loan.

Suppose a homeowner named Smith has an existing loan with a balance of $90,000 and monthly payments of $860.09. The interest rate on the loan is 8 percent and the remaining loan term is 15 years. From the time Smith originally obtained this loan, the home has risen in value to $150,000. Smith's current loan balance is 60 percent of the current value of the property. He would like to borrow an additional $30,000, which would increase his debt to $120,000 or 80 percent of the property value.

Assume that the current effective interest rate on a first mortgage with an 80 percent loan-to-value ratio is 11.5 percent with a term of 15 years, and the current effective interest rate on a second mortgage for an *additional* 20 percent of value ($30,000) would be 15.5 percent for a term of 15 years.

A lender different than the holder of Smith's existing loan is willing to make a wraparound loan for $120,000 at a 10 percent rate for a 15-year term. Payments on this loan would be $1,289.53 per month. If Smith makes this loan, the wraparound lender will take over the payments on Smith's current loan; that is, Smith will pay $1,289.53 to the wraparound lender, and the wraparound lender will make the $860.09 payment on the original loan. Thus, Smith's payment would increase by $429.44 ($1,289.53 − $860.09) per month. Because the wraparound lender is taking over the payments on the old loan, Smith will actually receive only $30,000 in cash (the $120,000 amount for the wraparound loan less the $90,000 balance of Smith's current loan).

Is the wraparound loan a desirable alternative for Smith to obtain an additional $30,000? The rate on the $120,000 wraparound loan (10 percent) is less than the market rate (11.5 percent) on a new first mortgage for the entire $120,000. Thus, the wraparound loan would be more desirable than refinancing with a new first mortgage.[19] Why would the wraparound lender make a loan that has a lower rate than a

[19] It is assumed that there are no points on the wraparound loan so that the effective cost of the wraparound loan is 10 percent. The cost of a wraparound loan can be compared with the cost of a new first mortgage because both rates reflect the cost of a loan for $120,000.

new first mortgage? The answer is that the wraparound lender is primarily concerned with earning a competitive rate of return on the *incremental* funds loaned (i.e., the additional \$30,000). It is the effective cost of the incremental funds loaned that the borrower also should be concerned about.

What is the cost of the incremental \$30,000? This is analogous to determining the incremental borrowing cost of a loan that we discussed at the beginning of the chapter. That is, we want to know the incremental cost of the 80 percent wraparound loan versus the 60 percent existing loan. To get the additional \$30,000 on the wraparound loan, the borrower must pay a 10 percent interest rate on the entire \$120,000, not solely the additional \$30,000. Because the rate on the existing \$90,000 is only 8 percent, the incremental cost of the additional \$30,000 is greater than 10 percent. The question is whether the incremental cost is more or less than the 15.5 percent rate for a second mortgage of \$30,000.

The incremental borrowing cost of the wraparound loan can be determined by finding the interest rate that equates the present value of the additional payment with the additional funds received. We have:

$$\$429.44(MPVIFA,\ ?\%,\ 180\text{ mos.}) = \$30{,}000$$
$$MPVIFA = 69.8584$$

Using the tables and interpolating or using a financial calculator, we find that the interest rate is 15.46 percent or about 15.5 percent. This is the same rate as that for a second mortgage, which is what we would expect. The wraparound lender can charge a lower rate on the wraparound loan and still earn a competitive rate on the incremental funds loaned because the existing loan is at a below market rate. The wraparound rate of 10 percent is, in effect, a weighted average of the rate on the existing loan (8 percent) and the rate on a second mortgage (15.5 percent).[20] If the existing loan were at the market rate for a 60 percent loan, then the wraparound rate would have to be equal to the rate on an 80 percent loan, so that the wraparound lender would earn a rate of return on the incremental funds equal to a second mortgage rate.

Calculator Solution

$n = 15 \times 12 = 180$
$PV = -\$30{,}000$
$PMT = \$429.44$
$FV = 0$

Effective yield:
$i = 15.46\%$

Is there any reason why the wraparound lender should be willing to make the loan at a rate that is more attractive than a second mortgage? The wraparound loan is, in effect, a second mortgage because the original loan is still intact. Furthermore, the loan-to-value ratio is increased by the same amount with the wraparound loan as it would be with a second mortgage. However, the wraparound loan has one advantage: The wraparound lender makes the payments on the first mortgage loan. Hence,

[20]The weighted average is $(90{,}000 \div 120{,}000 \times 8\%) + (30{,}000 \div 120{,}000 \times 15.5\%) = 9.875$ percent or about 10 percent, which is the rate on the wraparound loan. Note that the weighted average is less than the 11.5 percent rate on a new \$120,000 first mortgage, which indicates that the existing loan is at a below market rate.

control is retained over default in its payment, whereas if a second mortgage was made, the second mortgage lender would not necessarily be aware of a default on the first mortgage loan and might not be included in foreclosure action resulting from it. In a typical wraparound mortgage agreement, the wraparound lender is obligated to make payments on the original mortgage only to the extent that payments are received from the borrower, and the borrower agrees to comply with all of the covenants in the original mortgage except payment. Any default by the borrower will be realized by the wraparound lender who may not want to see the property go into foreclosure. The wraparound lender may make advances on the first mortgage and add them to the balance on the wraparound loan, foreclose on its mortgage, or negotiate for the title to the property in lieu of foreclosure, while still making payments on the first lien. Thus, the wraparound lender may be willing to earn an incremental return that is slightly lower than a second mortgage rate.

It should be noted that the original mortgage may contain a prohibition against further encumbrances or a due-on-sale clause that may preclude use of a wraparound loan to access equity in, or finance the sale of, property. In the absence of these restrictions, the original lender may also be willing to work out a deal with Smith that would be attractive to both of them. For example, this lender might offer Smith a new first mortgage at the same 10 percent rate as the wraparound loan (rather than the 11.5 percent market rate on a first mortgage) if Smith agrees to borrow the additional $30,000 from the bank. Again, because the 10 percent rate applies to the entire $90,000 (not only the additional $30,000) the original lender can earn an incremental return of 15.5 percent on the incremental funds advanced. Thus, the existing lender can earn a competitive rate of return on the new funds and keep the existing borrower as a customer. The lender still earns only 8 percent on the existing loan, but this would also be true if the borrower gets a second mortgage or a wraparound loan from a different lender. Thus, the original lender may be willing to, in effect, offer the same deal as a wraparound lender by charging a rate on a new first mortgage that is equal to the wraparound rate of 10 percent.[21]

Buydown Loans

The final type of loan situation we consider is the **buydown loan.** With a buydown loan, the seller of the home (frequently a builder) pays an amount to a lender to buy down or lower the interest rate on the loan for the borrower for a specific period of time. This may be done in periods of high interest rates to help borrowers qualify for financing. For example, suppose interest rates are currently 15 percent and a purchaser of a builder's home has only enough income to qualify for a loan at a 13 percent fixed rate. Let's assume that the loan will be for $75,000 with monthly amortization based on a 30-year term. Payments based on the market rate of 15 percent would be $948.33 per month. Payments at a 13 percent rate would only be $829.65 per month. Based on the buyer's income, the buyer would qualify to make payments of $829.65 but not $948.33. Suppose the builder wanted to buy down the interest rate from 15 to 13 percent, thereby enabling the bank to make the loan, so that payments are only $829.65 per month for the first five years of the loan term but will increase to $948.33 for the remaining loan term. To accomplish this, the

[21]This is often referred to as a "blended rate" because the 10 percent rate is a weighted average of the rate on the existing loan and the rate on the incremental funds loaned.

builder would have to make up the difference in payments ($118.68 per month for the five-year period). If this difference were paid by the builder to the lender at the time the loan closed, the amount paid would have to be the present value of the difference in payments, discounted at the market rate of 15 percent. Thus we have

$$\begin{aligned}\text{Buydown} &= \$118.68(MPVIFA,\ 15\%,\ 60\ \text{mos.})\\ &= \$118.68(42.034592)\\ &= \$4{,}988.67\end{aligned}$$

The builder would therefore pay $4,988.67 to the lender to buy down the loan. When coupled with the payments received from the buyer, the lender would earn a market rate of 15 percent and be willing to qualify the buyer.

Calculator Solution

$n = 5 \times 12 = 60$

$i = 15\% \div 12 = 1.25\%$

$PMT = \$118.68$

$FV = 0$

Solve for buydown loan:

$PV = \$4{,}988.67$

The buydown has the advantage of allowing borrowers to qualify for the loan when their current income might not otherwise meet the lender's payment-to-income criteria. Based on our discussion of cash equivalent value, however, you should realize that the builder will probably have added the buydown amount to the price of the home. Thus, the borrower might be better off bargaining for a lower price on the home and obtaining his or her own loan at the market rate. Probably the same home or a similar one could be obtained for $4,988.67 less without a buydown. The borrower is, in effect, paying $4,988.67 in "points" to lower the interest rate to 13 percent from 15 percent.

It should also be noted that many buydowns are executed with graduated payments for three or five years; that is, they may be initiated with monthly payments of $829.65 and step up each year by a specified amount until $948.33 is reached in the fifth year.

Some buydown programs are also used in conjunction with adjustable rate mortgages, where the initial rate of interest will be bought down. Because initial rates on ARMs are typically lower than those on fixed rate mortgages, this results in even lower initial payments, thereby allowing more buyers to qualify. However, this type of buydown practice has been discouraged because payments may increase considerably, particularly if there is an increase in the market rate of interest. In these cases, payments would rise because of higher market rates and because future payments have not been bought down.

Conclusion

This chapter has illustrated a number of problems concerning residential financing situations that borrowers and lenders might face. In today's era of creative financing, many other examples could be discussed. However, we have chosen examples that illustrate the main concepts and approaches to solving important problems. These can be applied to other situations that you might want to analyze. Thus, this chapter should be viewed as introducing various tools that can be used to handle other types of residential financing problems.

To keep our analysis as straightforward as possible and focus on the key new concepts we wanted to introduce, we have used fixed rate mortgages in all our examples in this chapter. However, the analyses also apply to other types of mortgages.

Although we have analyzed only residential financing problems in this chapter, all of the concepts apply equally to the analysis of income-producing or investment real estate. Thus, in later chapters that deal with income property, we will again refer to many of the concepts introduced here.

Key Terms

buydown loan 201
cash equivalent value 196
effective cost of refinancing 187
financing premium 197
incremental cost of borrowing 176
loan refinancing 184
marginal cost of borrowing 176
market value of a loan 190
origination fees 179
wraparound loan 199

Questions

1. Why do points increase the effective interest rate for a mortgage loan more if the loan is held for a shorter time period than a longer time period?
2. What factors must be considered when deciding whether to refinance a loan after interest rates have declined?
3. Why might the market value of a loan differ from its outstanding balance?
4. Why might a borrower be willing to pay a higher price for a home with an assumable loan?
5. What is a buydown loan? What parties are usually involved in this kind of loan?
6. Why might a wraparound lender provide a wraparound loan at a lower rate than a new first mortgage?
7. Assuming the borrower is in no danger of default, under what conditions might a lender be willing to accept a lesser amount from a borrower than the outstanding balance of a loan and still consider the loan paid in full?
8. Under what conditions might a home with an assumable loan sell for more than comparable homes with no assumable loans available?
9. What is meant by the incremental cost of borrowing additional funds?
10. Is the incremental cost of borrowing additional funds affected significantly by early repayment of the loan?

Problems

1. A borrower can obtain an 80 percent loan at an 8 percent interest rate with monthly payments amortized over 25 years. Alternatively, he could obtain a 90 percent loan at an 8.5 percent rate with the same loan term. The borrower plans to stay in the home for the entire loan term.
   a. What is the incremental cost of borrowing the additional funds? (Hint: The dollar amount of the loan doesn't affect the answer.)
   b. How would your answer change if two points were charged on the 90 percent loan?
   c. Would your answer to part (*b*) change if the borrower planned to be in the home only five years?
2. A potential homeowner has $60,000 to invest in a $280,000 home. He can obtain either a $220,000 loan at 9.5 percent for 20 years or a $180,000 loan at 9 percent for 20 years and a second mortgage of $40,000 at 13 percent for 20 years.
   a. Which alternative should the borrower choose, assuming he will be in the house for the full loan term?
   b. Would your answer change if the borrower plans to be in the home only five years?
   c. Would your answers to (*a*) and (*b*) change if the second mortgage had a 10-year term?

3. A homeowner obtained a mortgage 5 years ago for $95,000 at 11 percent amortized over 30 years. Mortgage rates have dropped, so that a 25-year loan can be obtained at 10 percent. There is no prepayment penalty on the mortgage balance of the original loan, but three points will be charged on the new loan and other closing costs will be $2,000.
   a. Should the borrower refinance if he plans to be in the home for the remaining loan term? Assume the homeowner borrows only an amount equal to the outstanding balance of the loan.
   b. Would your answer change if he planned to be in the home only 5 more years?
4. Secondary Mortgage Purchasing Company (SMPC) wants to buy your mortgage from the local savings and loan. The original balance of your mortgage was $140,000 and was obtained 5 years ago at 10 percent interest for 30 years.
   a. What should SMPC pay if they want an 11 percent return?
   b. How would your answer to part (*a*) change if Secondary Mortgage expected the loan to be repaid after five years?
5. You have a choice between the following two identical homes: Home A is priced at $150,000 with 80 percent financing at a 10.5 percent interest rate for 20 years. Home B is priced at $160,000 with an assumable mortgage of $100,000 at 9 percent interest with 20 years remaining. Monthly payments are $899.73. A second mortgage for $20,000 can be obtained at 13 percent interest for 20 years.
   a. With no preference other than financing, which house would you choose?
   b. How would your answer change if the *seller* of home B provided a second mortgage for $20,000 at the same 9 percent rate as the assumable loan?
   c. How would your answer change if the seller of home B provided a second mortgage for $30,000 at the same 9 percent rate as the assumable loan so that no additional down payment would be required by the buyer if the loan were assumed?
6. A homeowner has lived for 15 years in a home, the value of which has risen to $200,000. The balance on the original mortgage is $100,000 and the monthly payments are $1,100 with 15 years remaining. The homeowner would like to obtain $50,000 in additional financing. A new first mortgage for $150,000 can be obtained at a 12.5 percent rate and a second mortgage for $50,000 at a 14 percent rate with a 15-year term. Alternatively, a wraparound loan for $150,000 can be obtained at a 12 percent rate and a 15-year term. Which alternative should the homeowner choose?
7. A home builder is offering $100,000 loans for his homes at 9 percent for 25 years. Current market rates are 9.5 percent for 25-year loans. The home would normally sell for $110,000 without any special financing.
   a. At what price should the builder sell the homes to earn, in effect, the market rate of interest on the loan? Assume that the buyer would have the loan for the entire term of 25 years.
   b. How would your answer to part (*a*) change if the home is resold after 10 years and the loan repaid?
8. A home is available for sale that could normally be financed with an $80,000 loan at a 10 percent rate with monthly payments over a 25-year term. Payments would be $726.96 per month. The builder is offering buyers a mortgage that reduces the payments by 50 percent for the first year and 25 percent for the second year. After the second year, regular payments of $726.96 would be made.
   a. How much would you expect the builder to have to give the bank to buy down the payments as indicated?
   b. Would you recommend the home be purchased if it was selling for $5,000 more than similar homes that do not have the buydown available?
9. An appraiser is looking for comparable sales and finds a house that recently sold for $200,000. She finds that the buyer was able to assume the seller's mortgage which had a 7 percent interest rate. The balance of the loan at the time of sale was $140,000 with a remaining term of 15 years (monthly payments). The appraiser determines that if a $140,000 loan was obtained on the same property, the market rate for a 15-year loan would have been 8 percent with no points.
   a. Assume that the buyer expected to benefit from the interest savings on the assumable loan for the entire loan term. What is the cash equivalent value of the house?
   b. How would your answer to part (*a*) change if you assumed that the buyer only expected to benefit from interest savings for five years because he would probably sell or refinance after five years?

APPENDIX
AFTER-TAX EFFECTIVE INTEREST RATE

The preceding chapters have dealt with numerous situations where financing alternatives were evaluated. In all cases, the analysis was made without considering that mortgage interest is tax-deductible. An obvious question is whether consideration of federal income taxes affects the conclusions in our analyses. To gain insight into this question, we first consider the after-tax effective cost of a standard fixed-rate mortgage loan.

Example

Suppose a borrower makes a $100,000 loan with annual payments at a 10 percent rate and a 10-year term. Payments are made on an annual basis to simplify the initial illustration. The annual loan payment is calculated as follows:

$$\begin{aligned}\text{Annual payment} &= \$100{,}000 \div (\textit{PVIFA}, 10\%, 10 \text{ yrs.})\\ &= \$100{,}000 \div 6.14439\\ &= \$16{,}275\end{aligned}$$

A loan schedule is calculated in Exhibit 7A–1 for the 10-year loan term. The pretax cost of this loan is simply 10 percent because there are no points or prepayment penalties. We now want to see the effect of interest being tax-deductible. The tax benefit of the interest tax deduction is calculated by multiplying the loan interest each year by the borrower's tax rate. For example, the first year interest is $10,000. At a 28 percent tax rate, this means that the borrower can reduce taxes by $2,800 by deducting the interest.

The after-tax cost of the loan can now be found by subtracting the tax savings from the loan payment. The after-tax cost is calculated in Exhibit 7A–2.

EXHIBIT 7A–1 Loan Schedule

End of Year	*Payment*	*Interest*	*Principal*	*Balance*
1	$16,275	$10,000	$ 6,275	$93,725
2	16,275	9,373	6,902	86,823
3	16,275	8,682	7,592	79,231
4	16,275	7,923	8,351	70,880
5	16,275	7,088	9,187	61,693
6	16,275	6,169	10,105	51,588
7	16,275	5,159	11,116	40,472
8	16,275	4,047	12,227	28,245
9	16,275	2,825	13,450	14,795
10	16,275	1,480	14,795	0

EXHIBIT 7A–2 After-Tax Cost of Loan Payment

Year	*Payment*	*After-Tax Value of Deduction**	*After-Tax Payment*
1	$16,275	$2,800	$13,475
2	16,275	2,624	13,650
3	16,275	2,431	13,843
4	16,275	2,218	14,056
5	16,275	1,985	14,290
6	16,275	1,727	14,547
7	16,275	1,444	14,830
8	16,275	1,133	15,141
9	16,275	791	15,484
10	16,275	414	15,860

*Interest times tax rate

EXHIBIT 7A–3 Net Present Value of After-Tax Payments

Year	*ATCF*	*PVIF*	*Present Value*
0	−$100,000	$1.00000	−$100,000
1	13,475	0.93284	12,570
2	13,650	0.87018	11,878
3	13,843	0.81174	11,237
4	14,056	0.75722	10,644
5	14,290	0.70636	10,094
6	14,547	0.65892	9,585
7	14,830	0.61466	9,115
8	15,141	0.57338	8,682
9	15,484	0.53487	8,282
10	15,860	0.49894	7,913
Total present value			0

To calculate the after-tax effective cost of borrowing, we need to find the annual compound interest rate that equates the after-tax payments to the initial amount of the loan ($100,000). Calculating this rate indicates an after-tax cost of borrowing of exactly 7.2 percent. This is verified in Exhibit 7A–3.

Adding the present value column in Exhibit 7A–3 results in a net present value of zero, which verifies that the after-tax cost is 7.2 percent.

Now that we have performed the calculations the "long way," you may wonder if the pretax and after-tax costs are in some way related to the borrower's tax rate. There is a very simple relationship in this situation:

$$\begin{aligned}\text{After-tax effective cost} &= (\text{Pretax effective cost}) \times \\ &\quad (1 - \text{tax rate}) \\ &= 10\% \, (1 - .28) \\ &= 7.2\%\end{aligned}$$

We see that the after-tax borrowing cost is inversely proportional to the complement of the borrower's tax rate; that is, if the tax rate is 28 percent, the complement of the tax rate is 72 percent and the after-tax cost is 72 percent of the pretax cost. (In effect, the entire interest cost is tax-deductible.) This relationship will hold even if the loan is repaid early. The relationship also applies to loans with points if the points are deductible when they are paid. If the points cannot be deducted in the same year they are paid, the relationship will not hold exactly. Even where it doesn't hold exactly, it is usually a good approximation of the effective cost.[22] It should also be clear that the higher the borrower's tax rate, the more the benefit of the interest tax deduction.

Monthly Payments

The above example assumed that the payments on the loan were made annually; for example, at the end of the year, which coincided with the time the borrower received the tax deduction. If the loan payments were monthly, would the answer differ significantly? If we assumed that the buyer realized tax benefits from the interest deductions monthly, then the answer would not change at all. It could be argued that taxes are paid only once each year (on April 15 of the following year!) and thus the tax deduction is not received at the exact same time as the loan payment. However, knowing that the tax benefit from the interest deduction will affect tax forms at the end of the year may also mean that borrowers pay less estimated taxes during the year.[23] Furthermore, borrowers may have less taxes withheld from their monthly pay because they know that the interest will reduce their taxable income at the end of the year. Because of these possibilities, it may be more realistic to assume, when calculating the after-tax cost of financing, that interest deductions occur at different points in time than the mortgage payment. However, even if the tax deduction was not assumed to occur until the end of the year, it would not affect the calculated effective interest rate significantly. Thus, for practical purposes, we can conclude that the after-tax effective monthly interest cost is equal to the pretax effective monthly cost multiplied by the complement of the investor's tax rate (1 − Tax rate).

Effect of After-Tax Interest Cost on Loan Decisions

We have seen that the after-tax effective interest rate is directly proportional to the borrower's tax rate. This will be true as long as the interest is tax-deductible in the year it is paid.[24] When this is true, tax considerations will not affect any of the conclusions regarding selection from alternative mortgages because taxes affect each loan in a similar manner. Thus, we can still compare pretax effective interest costs when choosing a loan and be confident that tax considerations will not affect financing decisions. Similarly, we can compute the incremental borrowing cost, the effective cost of refinancing, and other decision criteria discussed in the preceding chapter on a pretax basis. We do not mean to imply that interest deductions for tax purposes are an unimportant consideration when deciding to borrow money. Clearly, a borrower should consider the tax deductibility of the interest payments as part of the cost of making borrowing decisions. The *higher* a borrower's tax rate, the lower the after-tax cost of borrowing. This affects one's willingness to borrow on investment real estate, as you will see later in the book when we evaluate financial leverage.

Negative Amortization Loans

We have seen that the after-tax effective cost of a loan is equal to the pretax effective cost multiplied by the complement of the investor's tax rate. This is true as long as all interest "charged" on the loan is tax deductible in the year that the interest is paid. By interest charged we mean the portion of each monthly payment which is *not* principal.

In the case of loans with negative amortization, interest charged will exceed the payment during some or all of the loan term. One example we have discussed is the graduated payment mortgage (GPM). We will now see how the after-tax effective cost is calculated for a loan with negative amortization. Consider a loan for $100,000 at a 10 percent interest rate with *annual* payments of $8,000 per year for the first five years, followed by payments of $12,000 per year until the entire balance is repaid.

Because interest charged is $10,000 (.10 × $100,000) the first year and the payment is only $8,000, negative amortization will be $2,000. This increases the balance of the loan to $102,000 after one year. Interest the second year is, therefore, $10,200 (.10 × $102,000). Proceeding in this manner, we can construct the loan schedule in Exhibit 7A–4.

---

[22]For example, if points are charged on loans for *income* property, the relationship may not hold exactly. This is because the timing of the tax deduction for the points may not correspond with the actual payment of the points. Whereas the points are paid at the time the loan is closed, they must be amortized over the loan term for tax purposes. Points paid when purchasing an owner-occupied residence are generally deductible, although points paid when refinancing a residence must be amortized over the loan term.

[23]The IRS requires taxpayers to estimate their tax liability and in many cases quarterly payments must be made to the IRS.

[24]Some alternative mortgages such as the graduated payment mortgage have interest charged (due to negative amortization) which is not deductible in the year it is paid. This is discussed later in this appendix.

From the exhibit, we see that negative amortization for the first five years increases the balance. In year 6, when the payments increase to more than the interest charged, the loan balance begins to decline. However, it takes until year 15 before the balance decreases below the initial $100,000.

The question now is how much interest can the borrower deduct for tax purposes each year? Most borrowers, at least with owner-occupied homes, compute taxes on a "cash basis"; that is, their income and expenses for tax purposes are based on actual cash income and expenditures.[25] For these borrowers, *current tax regulations require that interest deductions may not exceed the amount of payment*. Thus, in our example, only $8,000 could be deducted each year during the first five years. Starting with year 6, we see that the payment exceeds the interest. What happens to the interest that could *not* be deducted during the first five years (due to the negative amortization)? The answer is that the borrower can continue to deduct the entire loan payment *until the loan balance is reduced to its initial balance*, in this case, $100,000. Thus, the borrower can deduct the $12,000 payment until year 14. In year 15, the borrower can deduct the $10,161 interest, plus the remaining negative amortization that will reduce the balance to $100,000, or $1,630. After year 15, interest is deducted at the applicable rate in the same manner used on any constant payment mortgage. Exhibit 7A–5 illustrates the relationship among the mortgage payment, interest charges, and loan balance in this example.

Exhibit 7A–4 Loan Schedule

Year	*Beginning Balance*	*Payment*	*Interest*	*Amortization*
1	$100,000	$ 8,000	$10,000	$(2,000)
2	102,000	8,000	10,200	(2,200)
3	104,200	8,000	10,420	(2,420)
4	106,620	8,000	10,662	(2,662)
5	109,282	8,000	10,928	(2,928)
6	112,210	12,000	11,221	779
7	111,431	12,000	11,143	857
8	110,574	12,000	11,057	943
9	109,631	12,000	10,963	1,037
10	108,594	12,000	10,859	1,141
11	107,453	12,000	10,745	1,255
12	106,198	12,000	10,620	1,380
13	104,818	12,000	10,482	1,518
14	103,300	12,000	10,330	1,670
15	101,630	12,000	10,161	1,837
16	99,793	12,000	9,979	2,021
.	.	.	.	.
.	.	.	.	.
.	.	.	.	.

After-Tax Effective Cost. We now have the information we need to calculate the tax deductions and after-tax effective cost of the loan. We can create the schedule in Exhibit 7A–6.

We could compute the effective cost for the entire loan term or for repayment of the loan at any time prior to the end of the loan term. For purpose of illustration, we will compute the after-tax effective cost for repayment of the loan at the *end* of year 15 when the balance is $99,793. We have the following cash flows:

Year	*After-Tax Cash Flow*
0	−$100,000
1–5	5,760
6–14	8,640
15	108,492

The *IRR* for the above cash flows is 7.32 percent. Recall that the pretax effective cost was 10 percent; thus, we see that the after-tax effective cost is slightly higher than it would be for a fully amortizing loan, which would have an after-tax effective cost of exactly 7.2 percent. The higher after-tax effective cost for the negative amortization loan occurs because of the *deferral* of interest deductions. During the period of time that the loan balance was increased, less interest is deducted than is charged. The portion of interest that is not tax-deductible during those years becomes deductible from the time the loan balance begins to fall until it reaches the original balance.

Conclusion

The tax deductibility of interest payments reduces the after-tax cost of debt. As long as the entire amount of interest charged in a given year is tax deductible that year, there is a very simple relationship between the pretax cost of a loan and the after-tax cost. The after-tax cost is equal to the pretax cost multiplied by the complement of the borrower's tax rate. That is

$$\text{After-tax cost} = (\text{Pretax cost})(1 - \text{Tax rate})$$

If the entire amount of interest charged is *not* deductible, as was illustrated for negative amortization loans, the effective after-tax cost will be higher than it would be for the fully amortized loan. This results from the delay in receiving the tax deduction. However, even in this situation, multiplying the pretax cost times the complement of the borrower's tax rate provides a close approximation of the after-tax borrowing cost.

If all loans evaluated for tax purposes are treated about the same, taxes do not have to be considered in the analysis

[25]The alternative is an "accrual basis," where an accrual-based accounting system is used to determine income and expenses.

EXHIBIT 7A–5 Tax Deductions—Negative Amortization Loan

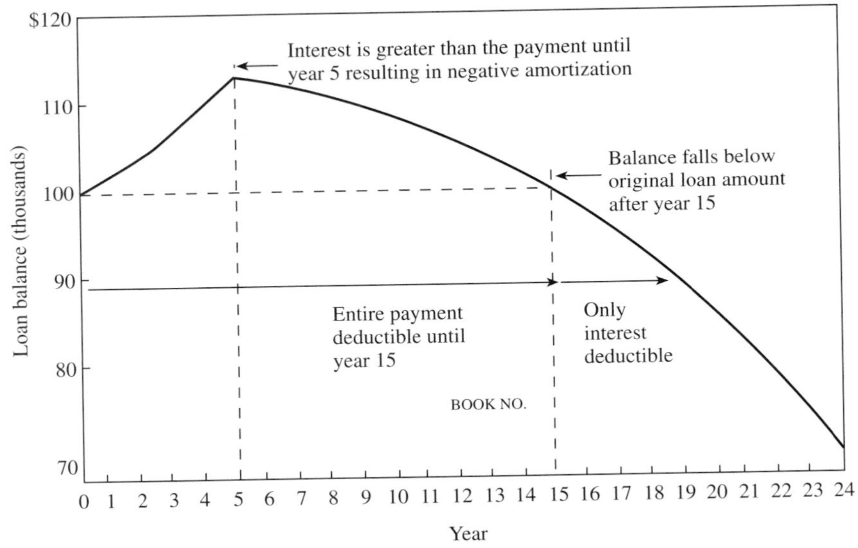

EXHIBIT 7A–6 After-Tax Payments

Year	*Payment*	*Interest Deductions*	*Tax* Savings*	*After-Tax Payment*
1	$ 8,000	$ 8,000	$2,240	$5,760
2	8,000	8,000	2,240	5,760
3	8,000	8,000	2,240	5,760
4	8,000	8,000	2,240	5,760
5	8,000	8,000	2,240	5,760
6	12,000	12,000	3,360	8,640
7	12,000	12,000	3,360	8,640
8	12,000	12,000	3,360	8,640
9	12,000	12,000	3,360	8,640
10	12,000	12,000	3,360	8,640
11	12,000	12,000	3,360	8,640
12	12,000	12,000	3,360	8,640
13	12,000	12,000	3,360	8,640
14	12,000	12,000	3,360	8,640
15	12,000	11,791	3,302	8,699

*28 percent tax rate.

since they affect all loans in the same manner and thus "wash out" in the final analysis. Thus, the types of analyses discussed in previous chapters can still be made without explicitly considering taxes. However, tax deductibility of interest is still important when deciding whether to borrow in the first place since it reduces the cost of using debt to finance the purchase of real estate. This is particularly important when determining whether to borrow money for investment property since the after-tax cost of the funds borrowed must be compared with the after-tax return on the property (before considering borrowing money) to see whether it is favorable to use debt to finance the purchase.

Problems

1. A $100,000 loan can be obtained at a 10 percent rate with monthly payments over a 15-year term.
   a. What is the after-tax effective interest rate on the loan, assuming the borrower is in a 30 percent tax bracket and the loan is held only three years? Assume that the benefit of interest deductions for tax purposes occurs at the same time payments are made.
   b. Calculate the after-tax effective cost for the above loan, assuming 5 points are charged and that the points are tax-deductible at the time they are paid.
   c. How does the after-tax cost in part (*b*) compare with the pretax effective cost of the loan?
2. A mortgage for $100,000 is made with *initial* payments of $500 per month for the first year. The interest rate is 9 percent. After the first year, payments will increase to an amount that makes the loan fully amortizable over the remaining 24 years with constant monthly payments.
   a. Calculate the interest deductions for the loan for the first year.
   b. How much, if any, interest must be deferred until the second year?
   c. How much interest will be deducted in the second year?

CHAPTER

8

Introduction to Income-Producing Properties and Valuation Fundamentals

In this chapter our focus is on income-producing properties. We begin by identifying the major property types and the economic forces that affect their value. We will consider supply and demand relationships, location analysis, and the competitive nature of the real estate business. We will then turn to principles used in real estate valuation. In that discussion, we will consider the three major approaches used in valuation, that is, the **sales comparison, income capitalization,** and **cost approaches** to value. In discussing these approaches, our goal is to explain and illustrate techniques used in the industry to collect and analyze market data to estimate current property values. These estimates are important because they may be used by investors, sellers, lenders, insurers, taxation officials, courts of law, and others, in cases where a property value may serve as the basis for making a decision. While many investors may also rely on these estimates, the primary objective of the approaches explained in this chapter is to provide evidence of value based on the price a property would bring if it were offered for sale in a competitive market. The reader should also understand that when an estimate of value is made, no assurance is being given that if such a property is acquired it would be a good investment for a particular investor. That is the focus of the next chapter. Finally, in this chapter we will also consider how to interpret the *influences* of macroeconomic changes on property values.

Property Types

We begin with Exhibit 8–1 which outlines major classifications used to identify and group different types of real estate. The two major categories used to classify property are residential and nonresidential. Residential properties include *single family houses* and *multifamily properties* such as apartments. Condominiums and co-ops are also included as residential properties.

EXHIBIT 8–1 Classification of Real Estate Uses

- I. Residential
  - Single family
    - Detached
    - Cluster developments
    - Zero lot line developments
  - Multifamily
    - High rise (usually *CBD*)
    - Low rise
    - Garden apartments (usually suburban)
- II. Nonresidential
  - Office
    - Major multitenant—*CBD*
    - Single or multitenant—suburban
    - Single tenant—built to suit
    - Combination office/showroom
  - Retail
    - Regional shopping centers/malls
    - Neighborhood centers
    - Community centers
    - Strip centers
    - Specialty centers
    - Discount centers
  - Industrial
    - Heavy industrial
    - Light industrial warehouse
    - Office/warehouse
    - Warehouse:
      - Distribution
      - Research and development (R&D)
      - Flex space
      - Office-showroom
  - Hotel/Motel
    - Business/convention
    - Full service
    - Tourist/resort
      - Limited service
      - Extended stay
      - All suites
  - Recreational
    - Country clubs
    - Marinas/resorts
    - Sports complexes
  - Institutional (special purpose)
    - Hospital/convalescent
    - Universities
    - Government
    - Other
- III. Mixed use developments
  - Combinations of one or more of the above uses

In general, residential properties are properties that provide residences for individuals or families. Although hotels and motels can also be thought of as providing residences for people, they are considered to be transient or temporary residences and thus are not categorized as residential property. In the discussion that follows, we use the same categories, which are logical from an economic perspective because factors that affect the supply and demand for hotels and motels are quite different from those that affect residential properties used as a residence.

Single family dwellings are usually thought of as individual, detached units developed in subdivision tracts. Other variants include cluster home developments where owners share "green space" in outdoor areas and "zero lot line" developments that contain single family and detached units.

The second major category of residential housing is income producing and referred to as multifamily housing. It is usually differentiated by location (urban or suburban) and size of structure (high rise, low rise, or garden apartments). High-rise apartments are usually found near or close to the central business district (*CBD*) of cities because land costs are greater than in suburban areas.

Nonresidential properties are typically broken down into five major subcategories: commercial, industrial, hotel/motel, recreational, and institutional. **Commercial real estate** includes both office buildings and retail space. As is the case for many of the categories, the same *building* can contain both commercial and retail space. In fact, the same building could contain residential as well as nonresidential uses of space. A combination of end uses in one property is usually referred to as a *mixed use development.* Thus, the categories being discussed should be viewed more as a convenient way of categorizing the use of space for the purpose of analyzing supply, demand, and thus investment potential for that space.

Office buildings range from major multitenant buildings found in the central business districts of most large cities to single tenant buildings, often built with the needs of a specific tenant or tenants in mind. An example of the latter would be a medical office building near a hospital.

Retail properties vary from large regional shopping centers containing over a million square feet of space to small stores occupied by individual tenants found in almost every town. As indicated earlier, it is also common to find retail space combined with office space, particularly on the first floor of office buildings in major cities.

Industrial real estate includes property used for light or heavy manufacturing as well as associated warehouse space. This category includes special-purpose buildings designed specifically for industrial use that would be difficult to convert to another use, buildings used by wholesale distributors, and combinations of warehouse/showroom and office facilities. Older buildings that were initially used as office space often "filter down" to become warehouse or light industrial space.

Hotels and motels vary considerably in size and facilities available. Motels and smaller hotels are used primarily as a place for business travelers and families to spend a night. These properties may have limited amenities and will often be located very close to a major highway. Hotels designed for tourists who plan to stay longer will usually provide dining facilities, a swimming pool, and other amenities. They will also typically be located near other attractions that tourists visit. Hotels at "destination resorts" provide the greatest amount of amenities. These are resorts that are away from major cities where the guests usually stay for several days or even several weeks. Facilities at these resort hotels can be quite luxurious, with several dining rooms, swimming pools, nearby golf courses, and so forth. Hotels that cater to convention business may be either a popular destination resort or located near the center of a major city. People who go to conventions usually want a variety of choices for dining and want to be able to "combine business with pleasure."

Recreational real estate includes uses such as country clubs, marinas, sports complexes, and so on. These are very specialized uses, usually associated with retail space that complements the recreational activity (e.g., golf shops). Dining facilities and possibly hotel facilities may also be present.

Institutional real estate is a general category for property that is used by a special institution such as a government agency, a hospital, or a university. The physical structure could be similar to other properties; government office space, for example, would be similar to other offices, and could in fact be in the same building. However, space used by institutions such as universities and hospitals is usually designed for a specific purpose and not easily adaptable for other uses.

Regional Economic Influences on Property Values

An important concept in real estate analysis is the fact that the profitability of income-producing properties is highly *dependent* on the regional or geographic area in which they are located. Profitability for such properties is highly influenced by the nature of the industries, businesses, and so on that are attracted to a region. Business activity and growth determine employment and income in a region, which influences the demand for all property types. In short, when undertaking a real estate analysis, the analyst must identify the *regional economic drivers* and make a judgment about whether these drivers will provide a source of growth or decline in a region. To determine the latter, trends must be established for the future global outlook for growth in those industries (i.e., computer technology, communication technology, medical-pharmaceutical, and tourism/recreation).

Why do certain kinds of economic activity tend to "cluster" more in some regions and urban areas than others? We do not intend to provide an extensive discussion of the phenomena here as there have been volumes written on this subject by many regional economists. However, we do believe that an understanding of the underpinnings of this economic behavior is critical when thinking about the relative attractiveness of real estate investments. As we will stress in this chapter and in others, making an investment in a specific real estate asset cannot be separated completely from *making an investment in an economic region* because the real estate is permanently located in that region. Therefore, the need to know the forces that drive economic growth in an area is essential to the success of an investment.

Analogy with the Law of Comparative Advantage

This concept, stated very simply, says that some geographic regions have a comparative advantage over other regions in that certain goods/services can be produced more efficiently and profitably in that region than in other regions. This advantage may exist because of: (1) natural advantages (e.g., seaport, minerals, low cost energy, and beaches), (2) employee characteristics such as a highly trained, educated workforce (e.g., location of universities, workforce training in technical industries), (3) proximity to many major consumer markets (e.g., transportation hub). Regional examples would include high-tech research and development (California, Seattle, Boston), oil and gas exploration (Houston), communication and computer assembly (Austin, Houston, San Diego), medical technology/clinics (Minnesota, Boston), and production of entertainment (Los Angeles). These industries tend to locate in certain geographic areas because land, labor, and capital can be combined cost-effectively or revenues can be enhanced by businesses in those regions. This simple concept is very useful in real estate investing because when researching markets for real estate investment opportunities, those markets having industries with the highest likelihood of future growth should rank high on the priority list.

Identifying Regional Economic "Drivers" or Base Industries. One obvious way to identify the drivers of economic growth in an area is to identify those businesses producing the greatest *profits*. Unfortunately, data pertaining to profits is difficult to collect on a regional basis because (1) much of it is private information and (2) for publicly owned firms, multiple operating divisions may make profits by region very difficult to break down. Therefore, trying to ascertain how much profit is produced by firms in a specific region is difficult. As a result, many analysts rely on *employment data* that are collected by the U. S. Department of Labor and by various agencies in all 50 states. The underlying logic for using employment data for real estate investment research is that expanding businesses will have expanding needs for labor. Identifying the number of employees in an industry classification in a region will help to identify those industries with a comparative advantage in that region and those employers must have workspace in office buildings, warehouses, and other kinds of real estate. While employment data are generally thought to be the best tool available for analysis, this method is not ideal because labor may not always be added in direct proportion to increases in revenues or the output of goods and services produced by a company. Furthermore, the method may tend to underestimate the importance of less labor-intensive businesses in a region that may be very profitable and pay high wages to a few employees.

Economic Base Analysis—Location Quotients

One widely accepted approach in regional economic analysis is to calculate what are referred to as **location quotients** for a region. This is done very simply by using the following relationship:

$$\frac{\left(\dfrac{RE_j}{RE_{TOT}}\right)}{\left(\dfrac{USE_j}{USE_{TOT}}\right)} \gtreqless 1.0?$$

Terms in this relationship are as follows:

RE	=	Regional employment
USE	=	U.S. Employment
j	=	Industry classification
TOT	=	Total

For example, if we let *j* represent the computer assembly industrial classification, then this ratio will tell us if the proportion of regional employment (*RE*) in the computer assembly business (*j*) as a percentage of total employment in that region (RE_{TOT}) is greater or less than those employed in industry *j* throughout the United States as a percentage of the total employment throughout the country. If this ratio is *greater* that 1.0, then industry (*j*) would be identified as a *base* or *driver industry* for a region because it employs a greater than proportionate amount of workers in that industry than is the case for the United States as a whole. Obviously, if the ratio is *less* than 1.0, then that industry would not be a base industry. Industry classifications with ratios less than 1.0 are usually referred to as *supporting industries.* Examples of the latter could be accounting firms, advertising firms, and so on. These supporting businesses are also important for real estate investment particularly for retail establishments, personnel services, and similar firms, all of whom must also lease operating space in properties.

Data classifications for various industries (designated above as *j*) have been developed and published by the U.S. Office of Management and Budget and are used by the U.S. Department of Labor. This department collects and categorizes data on all employees in the United States. Depending on the level of detail desired, all employment data are broken into several industry classifications. These classifications are referred to as Standard Industrial Classification, or SIC codes.[1] The data are collected in 315 metropolitan areas.

Employment Multipliers. This aspect of economic base analysis is conducted to determine how *total employment* in a region is affected by changes in *base employment.* After a complete analysis is conducted for every employment classification (*j*) in a region and all base employment has been identified with location quotients and totaled, employment in the remaining category is totaled and a ratio of *total* to *basic* employment is calculated. If for example, total employment in a metropolitan area equals 1,000,000 and base employment or employment in classifications with a location quotient >1.0 totals 400,000, supporting employment would be 600,000. In this case, the total employment to basic employment ratio would be 1,000,000 ÷ 400,000 or 2.5. Therefore, if a forecast called for a 40,000 jobs increase in *all basic employment* categories, it may be the case that *total employment* would increase by 40,000 × 2.5 or 100,000, of which 60,000 would be supporting employment.[2] Obviously, a real estate investor would like to know how many of the 100,000 expected new jobs would be likely to occur in warehouses, offices, or retail properties and how many new houses and apartments should be developed to provide shelter for these workers. A detailed breakdown by SIC code would shed light on the former while the expected age distribution, sizes of households, and wages likely to be earned would help in the latter case.[3] It should be stressed that there can also be instances where employment in base industries in a metropolitan area may be expected to decline. In these instances, total employment rates would also be expected to decline by an amount greater than declines in base industry employment.

In Exhibits 8–2 and 8–3, we provide examples from a recent economic base study of the expected effects of growth in high-tech industries using the location quotient approach. High-tech *SIC codes* are identified in Exhibit 8–2. High-tech job classifications were chosen by the authors of the study because employment in these industries were deemed likely to grow at rates in excess of the U.S. total employment ratio.[4] Employment data from companies in those SIC codes in each metropolitan area were then obtained and location quotients were calculated. Those Metropolitan Statistical Areas (MSAs) likely to benefit from expansion in such industries are identified in Exhibit 8–3. The exhibit also includes the number of SIC codes within the high-tech definition with location quotients greater than 1.0.

---

[1] See *Standard Industrial Classification Manual,* Office of Management and Budget, Executive Office of the President, U.S. Government Printing Office, Washington, DC, various editions.

[2] This example assumes that a proportional, or linear relationship between base and total employment exists. Over time this may, or may not, be the case.

[3] The U.S. Bureau of the Census provides periodic estimates of population characteristics by region in various population, housing, and related reports.

[4] See *America's High-Tech Economy,* by Ross C. Devol, Milken Institute, Santa Monica, CA. Employment data used in the study were provided by Regional Financial Associates.

EXHIBIT 8–2 High-Tech Industries (SIC codes)

SIC Code	*Manufacturing Sectors*
283	Drugs
357	Computer and office equipment
366	Communications equipment
367	Electronic components and accessories
372	Aircraft and parts
376	Guided missiles, space vehicles, and parts
381	Search, detection, navigation, guidance, aeronautical, and nautical systems instruments and equipment
382	Laboratory apparatus and analytical, optical, measuring and controlling instruments
384	Surgical, medical, and dental instruments and supplies
SIC Code	*Service Sectors*
481	Telephone communications services
737	Computer programming, data processing, and other computer-related services
781	Motion picture production, and allied services
871	Engineering, architectural and surveying services
873	Research development and testing services

Source: Milken Institute, Santa Monica, CA.

Supply and Demand Analysis

We have discussed the importance of the economic base in determining the success of investments in income-producing property. Market rents for properties also depend on the supply and demand for space by tenants. In this section, we look more closely at market forces that affect both the supply and demand for space and how this affects real estate investments.

Equilibrium Market Rental Rate. At any point in time, a fixed stock of space exists in the market in previously constructed buildings. Some of this space will be leased. The remaining space constitutes vacancies, or supply of space available for lease. The price at which an owner can lease the space depends on the market rental rate on comparable properties. The amount of existing space that building owners are willing to lease at different rental rates is expressed by a supply curve as illustrated in Exhibit 8–4. As the market rental rate rises, more space is supplied by building owners. The maximum amount of space that can be leased at any given point in time is limited, however, to the existing stock of space.

At lower market rental rates, some of the existing space may not be made available for lease. This space may be deliberately held vacant by owners in anticipation of higher market rents in the future. Alternatively, they may prefer to convert the space to a different use rather than rent it under the existing use at the current market rate for that use. A certain amount of space will also always be vacant because of tenants moving and the time it takes for newly constructed space to be offered for lease. This stock of space will change over time due to construction of new buildings and demolition of existing buildings.

EXHIBIT 8–3 Top 50 Milken Institute High-Tech Locations, 1998

Rank in Total High-Tech Employment	*Number of LQs greater than 1**	*Rank in Total High-Tech Employment*	*Number of LQs greater than 1**
1. San Jose, CA	10	26. Portland–Vancouver, OR–WA	2
2. Dallas, TX	7	27. Boulder–Longmont, CO	9
3. Los Angeles–Long Beach, CA	5	28. Kalamazoo–Battle Creek, MI	2
4. Boston, MA	11	29. Indianapolis, IN	4
5. Seattle–Bellevue–Everett, WA	6	30. Nassau–Suffolk, NY	7
6. Washington, DC–MD–VA–WV	5	31. Kansas City, MO–KS	2
7. Albuquerque, NM	3	32. Minneapolis–St. Paul, MN–WI	4
8. Chicago, IL	4	33. Lubbock, TX	2
9. New York, NY	2	34. St. Louis, MO–IL	4
10. Atlanta, GA	4	35. Cedar Rapids, IA	5
11. Middlesex–Somerset–Hunterdon, NJ	7	36. Orlando, FL	4
12. Phoenix–Mesa, AZ	1	37. Sacramento, CA	6
13. Orange County, CA	10	38. Detroit, MI	2
14. Oakland, CA	8	39. Wichita, KS	3
15. Philadelphia, PA	4	40. Tucson, AZ	5
16. Rochester, MN	1	41. Ft. Worth–Arlington, TX	4
17. San Diego, CA	9	42. Colorado Springs, CO	9
18. Raleigh–Durham–Chapel Hill, NC	7	43. Monmouth–Ocean City, NJ	4
19. Denver, CO	3	44. Bergen–Passaic, NJ	6
20. Newark, NJ	5	45. Melbourne–Titusville–Palm Bay, FL	7
21. Austin–San Marcos, TX	4	46. San Antonio, TX	3
22. San Francisco, CA	5	47. Pittsburgh, PA	2
23. Houston, TX	2	48. Atlantic City–Cape May, NJ	1
24. Boise, ID	2	49. West Palm Beach–Boca Raton, FL	3
25. New Haven–Bridgeport, CT	10	50. Huntsville, AL	7

* The location quotient (LQ) equals percent of employment in an industry in metro areas divided by percent of employment in the same industry in the United States. If LQ > 1.0, the industry is more concentrated in the metro area than in the United States on average.

Sources: Milken Institute; Regional Financial Associates.

Exhibit 8–4 also shows the *demand* for space from users. As the rental rate falls, firms are more willing to use additional space in their operations rather than other factor inputs such as labor and capital. As shown in the exhibit, the intersection of the supply and demand curves determines the equilibrium market rental rate as well as the amount of space that is leased. The total space that is leased at a given point in time includes space that was leased in previous periods. The difference between the existing stock of space and the total amount leased at the market rate represents vacant space. This is a normal or equilibrium market vacancy rate.

The supply curve illustrated in Exhibit 8–4 depicts a short-run equilibrium for a period of time during which the total supply of existing space is fixed and does not increase due to new construction or decrease due to demolition. That is, the supply of space includes existing space that was constructed in the past based on an analysis of the rental market at that point in time. Changes in the market for space after an ad-

EXHIBIT 8–4 Rental Market Equilibrium

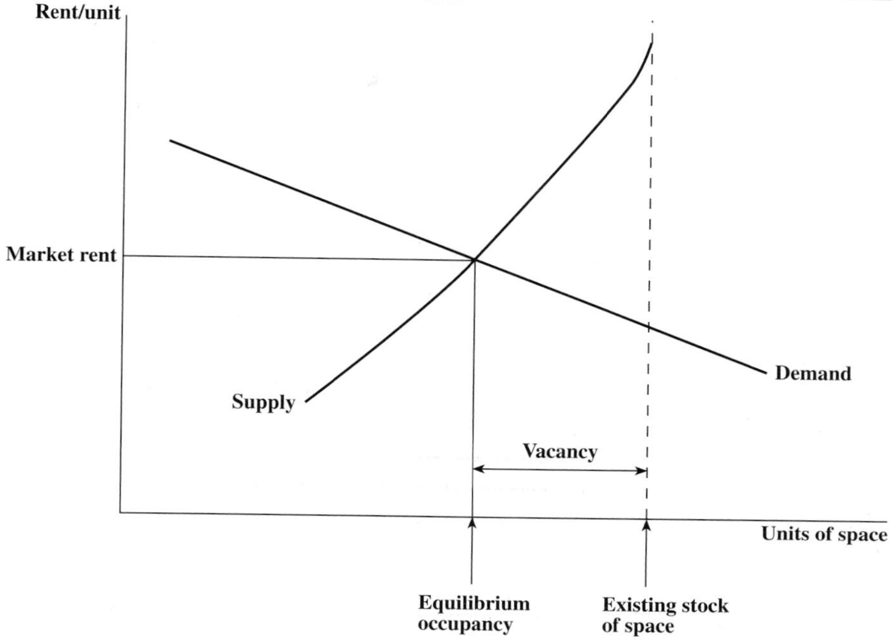

ditional building is constructed can result in a change in the market rental rate. For example, suppose the demand for office space increases because new firms are locating in the area and office employment is increasing. This is indicated by a shift in the demand curve from D to D' in Exhibit 8–5. Based on the supply curve for existing space offered for lease, the market rent would rise from R to R'. The increase in demand is likely to result in an increase in the construction of new space, however, because the profitability of developing new space increases at the higher market rents and lower market vacancy rate. The amount of new space that is actually developed depends on the profitability of developing new space as well as the supply of land for development. As new space is developed and the stock of space increases, the maximum amount of space that can be offered for lease increases from S_{max} to S'_{max} and shifts the entire supply curve from S to S' as shown in Exhibit 8–5. Based on the new supply curve (after new space is constructed) equilibrium rents decrease from R' to R''. In other words, the rental rate does not rise as much as it would have in the absence of new construction. Depending on the quantity of space added by the new construction, it is possible that rental rates could fall below the level they were at before demand increased if more space is developed than was needed to meet the increase in demand.

This analysis considered an increase in the demand for space, which was followed by an increase in the supply of space. A *decrease* in the demand for space causes an opposite movement in the demand curve and a reduction in the equilibrium market rental rate. This results in an increase in the vacancy rate. Because the stock of space already exists, the higher vacancy rate may persist until the demand for space increases. Some decrease in the existing stock may occur due to depreciation and demolition of older buildings, but this occurs over a long period of time.

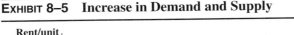

EXHIBIT 8–5 Increase in Demand and Supply

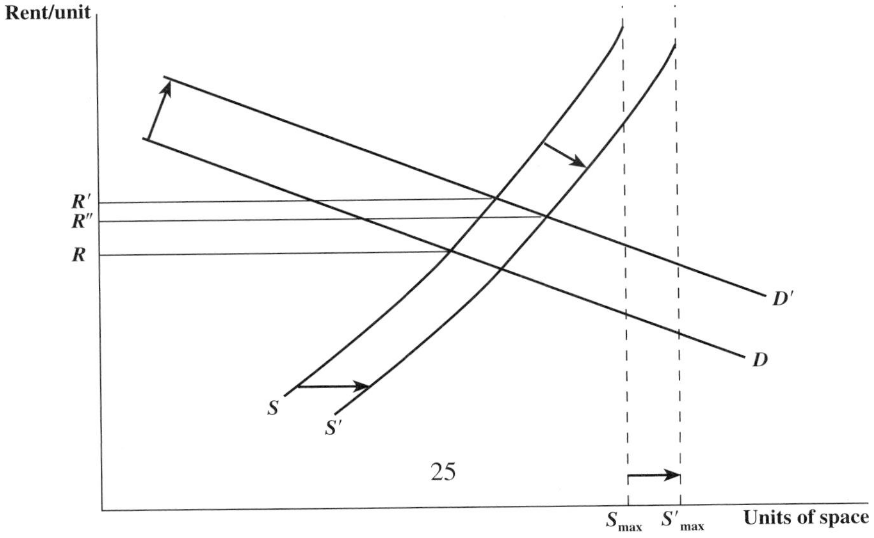

Implications for Risk In general, market rent depends on changes in the demand for space as well as expected changes in the supply of space as we discussed. Expected and unexpected changes in market rental rates over the entire economic life of a property affect the return and risk associated with investing in that property. Changes in the demand for space can result from a number of factors that affect the economic base of the area where the property is located. Changes in the supply of space can result from developers reacting to anticipated increases in the demand for space or a belief that they can attract a sufficient number of tenants from existing buildings to make their building profitable. The investor must evaluate how changes in the market rental rate due to changes in supply and demand can affect the income potential of a possible investment as well as the volatility in income. Even if the investment is an existing building that has already been leased, the income can be affected when the existing leases expire and are renewed at the market rent at that time. As we will see later in this chapter, *leases* can be structured to shift some of the risk from the owner/lessor to the user/lessee.

Local Market Studies of Supply and Demand

While it is useful to think of supply and demand relationships in the abstract, when making real estate investments a market analysis must usually be undertaken to determine the level of vacancies, rents, the amount of new construction underway, and when the property will be ready for occupancy. This is important because, as we will see later in this chapter, a forecast of rents, vacancies, and expenses must be made when a property is under consideration for investment. Exhibit 8–6 contains a summary of many of the variables that must be considered when undertaking a market study. All of these relationships are generally dependent, or derived from, the types of employment generated by the economic base of the area and the levels of supporting employment discussed in the previous section. However, in order to consider the demand for space by type of property, more detail is necessary. When considering investments in apartment and retail properties, in addition to forecasting the number of new employees, information is needed on the quality of job creation

EXHIBIT 8–6 Determinants of Supply and Demand—Major Property Types

Demand Influences:

Apartments:
Number of households, age of persons in households, size of household incomes, interest rates, affordability, apartment rents, housing prices.

Office Space:
Categories of employment with very high proportions of office use include: service and professional employment including attorneys, accountants, engineers, insurance, real estate brokerages and related activity, banking, financial services, consultants, medical–dental, pharmaceutical, etc.

Warehouse Space:
Categories of employment with high concentrations in warehouse use: wholesaling, trucking, distribution, assembly, manufacturing, sales/service, etc.

Retail Space:
Demand indications include: household incomes, age, gender, population, size and tastes/preferences.

Supply Influences:

Vacancy rates, interest rates and financing availability, age and combination of existing supply stock, construction costs, land costs

Property Type		*Typical Construction Periods*
Apartments	Suburban garden walkup	6–18 months
	Urban mid, high-rise	18–24 months
Office Buildings	Suburban low-rise	18–24 months
	CBD mid, high-rise	24–48 months
Retail	Strip/stand-alone	6–12 months
	Neighborhood/community	12–24 months
	Enclosed malls	36–48 months
Warehouse	Suburban, single level	9–12+ months

indicated by the salaries and wages that will be earned by individuals in the area, as well as their ages, sizes of households, and other related information. This information will provide a better understanding regarding the *type* of apartments and retail merchandise desired, which will, in turn, indicate which submarkets are likely to benefit from economic growth.

Similarly, when considering investments in warehouses and office properties, a deeper understanding of the nature and kinds of employment produced by growth in the economic base will help in investment analysis. For example, when one considers employment growth in New York City, it is likely that much of the employment will be occurring in offices. On the other hand, if considering Detroit, a higher percentage of employment growth is likely to occur in industrial and warehouse properties. Exhibit 8–6 provides the reader with some idea of the variables that influence the demand for various property types.

For the supply side of each market, developers of each property type also carefully consider each of the same variables in Exhibit 8–6. However, they must also weigh the costs of financing and the economic benefits of acquiring land and undertaking development in other locations. The exhibit provides some idea as to the time required to develop various property types. Based on this information, it should be fairly clear that the supply of space available in any market tends to be fixed in the short run and unlike many other goods and services, requires lead time to adjust to increases in demand. Furthermore, trying to establish the quantity of space that can be produced effectively relative to the size of a submarket is also important when completing an investment study.

Location and User-Tenants

After briefly examining a method for identifying the economic drivers affecting cities and regions, we now turn to a conceptual framework for determining how locations *within* a city are evaluated by businesses. It goes without saying that location is an important attribute in real estate. Successful real estate investors and developers must also realize that location as viewed by *user-tenants* is also important to recognize. We mean that successful real estate investors and developers should understand the *business operations* of potential *tenant-users and how certain locations will appeal to those users.* Recall that many users of real estate are business firms that operate to make a profit. Consequently, most real estate decisions made by these users are considered in terms of how leasing space in alternative locations will generate more profit by: (1) increasing sales revenue or (2) reducing the cost of operations, or (3) some combination of both. A very basic illustration of the relationship between user profits and locations is shown in Exhibit 8–7.

Looking at Exhibit 8–7, when evaluating three locations in Big City, it is clear that User A will realize more profit in location (1) because revenues are greater and its operating expenses are invariant to location. User A can afford to pay more rent per square foot in location (1) and potentially earn a greater profit than it would in locations (2) and (3). User B, on the other hand, will be best off in location (3) because its *revenues* are invariant to location, and its expenses will be lowest in that location. Location (2) appears to be suboptimal for both Users A and B and may also be appealing to businesses that are different from Users A and B.

Because profitability will vary by location, the above analysis also implies that (1) User A and other users who are either in competition with User A or who operate businesses in which location significantly affects *sales revenue* (examples could be retailers, restaurants, or certain service providers) will tend to cluster near location (1) as they anticipate earning higher profits there. These firms will compete with one another by bidding for space in that location. The location will take on the characteristics of a *submarket* containing those tenant-users selling goods and services to consumers who are sensitive to the location.

On the other hand, User B, whose *expenses* are very sensitive to location, will choose location (3) because it will tend to lower costs and thus produce higher profits. Competitors of User B and firms that are not necessarily in the same business as User B but that have *similar operating cost structures* will compete for space in and around location (3). Examples of user-tenants in this location might include wholesale distributors occupying large warehouses. Such distributors may charge the same price for products to all customers in a region; however, its delivery expenses will vary by location. Therefore, it will tend to choose a location in an area that will minimize delivery expenses.

This process of profit analysis and competition by many different firms for space in locations that tend to maximize profits produces certain general land-use results in real estate markets. These are:

EXHIBIT 8–7 Relationship between User Revenue, Expenses, and Profits per Square Foot by Location

	Locations in Big City, USA		
	(1)	*(2)*	*(3)*
User A:			
Revenue	$120	$100	$ 90
Less: Expenses	80	80	80
Profit	$ 40	$ 20	$ 10
User B:			
Revenue	$100	$100	$100
Less: Expenses	90	80	70
Profit	$ 10	$ 20	$ 30

1. The process of firms competing for space will result in the highest rents possible for the most profitable locations and, ultimately, the highest land value and best development for a site (e.g., office, retail, warehouse, apartment or hotel).
2. Locations will tend to be dominated by clusters of users with revenue or operating expense structures that relate in similar ways to a given location.
3. Locations with the greatest appeal to users will tend to produce higher rents and also to exhibit highest spatial *densities.* Developers will attempt to build multistory projects or cluster buildings on very desirable sites so that they may earn the highest rents per square foot. This process will tend to attract tenants whose operations can be conducted in relatively small amounts of space or in multistory structures while still enabling them to earn higher revenues and profits.
4. Some locations are competed for by firms that are most cost-sensitive. These firms tend to require large amounts of land and large facilities on which to conduct larger scales of operations at lower rents per square foot.

When viewing location in this way, the reader can begin to understand how and why land-use patterns and submarkets develop within urban areas. It should also help the reader understand why retail and high-rise office developments occur in some areas while warehouses requiring large quantities of land on single levels occur in others. Of course, these patterns of land use are also affected by zoning and historic land-use patterns in urban markets. However, even the latter influences are subject to periodic changes.

In summary, a key concept to understand is that for most business users, real estate is considered to be an *operating input* that is used with labor to produce output. In other words, business firms in their operations combine labor and materials *with* real estate at a location to produce goods and services. For example, law, accounting, and advertising firms produce services for clients and employees and real estate are major *inputs* in the *production* of their client services that are sold from a specific location. Retailers may combine large quantities of merchandise and salespersons on land and in buildings to produce a merchandise/service mix that appeals to customers. Further, the distribution of their goods and merchandise may require a large quantity of land and warehouse buildings with relatively few employees to break down, re-sort, and deliver merchandise to customers. The point of these examples is that because business users view real estate as an input that affects operating expenses and/or revenues, the relationships between land and building space requirements, rent, the number of employees, and revenues should be viewed in the context of various locations. These resources tend to be combined by businesses so that they maximize profit. Land-use patterns follow this pattern of business location decision making.

The Business of Real Estate

One additional decision that must be made by tenant-users is whether it is more cost-effective to *lease* or *purchase* their real estate requirements. This question is important because in addition to location, it also lies at the heart of understanding the real estate business.

Contrary to popular belief, the vast majority of real estate used by business firms is *leased* and not owned. This is true in spite of the vast number of buildings with signs that carry a name of a major corporation on the exterior.[5] Why is this the case? There are many important reasons:

1. Most tenants find *leasing to be more cost-effective than owning.* This is particularly true when their space requirements are less than the quantity of space they would have to purchase in order to satisfy their needs in a desired location. For example, assume that a user needs 20,000 square feet of space to operate profitably, and it must have such space in a specific location. However, only buildings with a minimum size of 100,000 square feet are available for purchase in that location. In this case, the user will usually opt to *lease* the 20,000 square feet of space as opposed to purchasing a 100,000 square foot building. Leasing will usually be preferred because purchasing would include the responsibility for leasing the remaining 80,000 square feet of excess space to other users. Purchasing would generally not be optimal because:
   a. Owning would require a large commitment of capital to purchase the 100,000 square foot facility. Such capital could be used in other business activities.
   b. A purchase would "put the user in the real estate business." That is, the user would have to take the risk of owning and also have the real estate business "know how" to lease, collect rents, maintain, and insure, the additional 80,000 square feet of space that it does not use.
2. Even if a tenant could occupy the entire 100,000 square feet in a building, it might still choose to lease because:
   a. Owning would *reduce* operating flexibility. For example, if the firm would decide to leave a metropolitan area and/or consolidate or expand, in a different location in the same metro area, it might have to sell the entire property. This could take a considerable amount of time and tie up personnel and capital. If it had leased the property, it could move upon the lease expiration date or even negotiate a release from the owner/lessor.

[5] These signs usually identify the major corporate tenant in a building, who is granted the right to construct a sign by the property owner in its lease agreement.

b. If it owns the property, the firm must operate, maintain, and repair the facility. These activities may result in the loss of focus on its core business activities. For example, a technology consulting firm may be better off focusing all of its effort on consulting with clients and not have the worry of owning, operating, leasing, and managing the building that it occupies. Operating and managing properties is usually done more cost-effectively by firms who specialize in real estate operations.

c. If the firm decided to *size down* from using 100,000 square feet, as the owner of the building it would have to engage a broker to find an additional user or buyer for the excess space. Furthermore, it might have to renovate the space to suit the requirements of the new tenant. Again, this would mean undertaking unrelated real estate business activities.

In summary, the primary point is that history is replete with evidence of corporations who ventured away from their core businesses and engaged in real estate investment and development. Results have been mixed at best. The real estate industry includes economic functions that are *specialized in nature* and are separate and distinct from the operations of the many different business activities conducted by tenant-users. These noncore real estate business activities include the risks of (1) selecting the "right tract" of land and developing the "right amount" of space, (2) leasing that space to many different tenants, (3) hiring personnel, collecting rents, and maintaining the facility, (4) finding financing for the investment or development, (5) doing continuous research about real estate markets in order to decide when to sell, raise or lower rents, renovate, and so on. These are a few examples of many of the functions requiring special skills that can be performed most cost-effectively by real estate firms who specialize in these activities. Business firm–users are best left to focus on their primary activities (e.g., lawyers, accountants and advertising companies serving clients, and retailers serving their customers). These users will generally not be as effective in real estate development, investment, leasing, and so on, as those firms who specialize in these activities.

One general exception to the above observations may occur if a single tenant-user requires its own facilities for its corporate headquarters or must have unique features such as high-tech labs, specialized computer installations, security or other features that are unique. In these very special cases, ownership may be preferred to leasing. It has been estimated that over 80 percent of all office buildings and retail properties is *leased* to tenants. This number is slightly lower for industrial/warehouse properties, of which 37 percent is estimated to be occupied by owners and 63 percent is leased to user-tenants. In summary, the reader should be aware that the real estate business is an activity that involves many firms who specialize in providing services to users. It is generally more cost-effective for users to lease their space requirements rather than attempting to provide them themselves.

The "Market" for Income-Producing Real Estate

Given the preceding discussion about (1) the general relationships between users seeking a location to maximize profits, (2) the general desirability of users to lease rather than own the space they need in their operations, and (3) the real estate business/industry performing the functions and risks associated with developing, owning, leasing, and maintaining land and buildings more cost-effectively than tenant-users, it is clear that an enormous market for real estate services has emerged.

When approaching the subject of making real estate investments, it is necessary to understand how this competitive market operates and the nature of the negotiations between owners of real estate and tenant-users. It is also important to understand how owner/investors in real estate must differentiate between expenses associated with operating buildings from expenses that are related to the business operations of a tenant. Such expenses should be allocated by owners to users. In this way, property owners will not pay a disproportionate share of expenses and/or bear risks associated with the operations of a tenant-user.

It can be best summarized to say that in this market for real estate services, tenants are searching for locations that provide the highest profit (either through greater revenues or lower costs) and real estate investor-owners stand ready to take the risks of developing and/or leasing and operating real estate for tenant-users. Real estate owners engage in providing these services in exchange for rent. However, as will be seen below, the term *rent* is a very general term and, though important, is not adequate to explain how expenses are allocated between owners and renters. In order to estimate total occupancy costs for tenants and profits for owners, there are many other areas of negotiation between real estate owners and business-users of real estate or tenants in addition to rent. These may include additional rights and responsibilities of both parties that are usually contained in *leases*. Lease contents are important because they affect how much income may be produced from an investment property, the legal responsibilities, and any future options negotiated between owners and tenants that may ultimately affect the value of an investment.

Valuation Fundamentals

The last section introduced property markets and discussed markets, supply and demand, then introduced how concepts affecting users of real estate and locations interact to impact the value of income-producing property. In this section, we will focus on various methods that can be used to estimate the market value of a property. Market value is a key consideration when financing or investing in income-producing properties. It is defined in the *Uniform Standards of Professional Appraisal Practice* as follows:[6]

> The most probable price which a property should bring in a competitive and open market under all conditions requisite to a fair sale, the buyer and seller each acting prudently and knowledgeably, and assuming the price is not affected by undue stimulus. Implicit in this definition is the consummation of a sale as of a specified date and the passing of title from seller to buyer under conditions whereby:
>
> 1. Buyer and seller are typically motivated;
> 2. Both parties are well-informed or well-advised, and acting in what they consider their best interests;
> 3. A reasonable time is allowed for exposure in the open market;
> 4. Payment is made in terms of cash in United States dollars or in terms of financial arrangements comparable thereto; and
> 5. The price represents the normal consideration for the property sold unaffected by special or creative financing or sales concessions granted by anyone associated with the sale.

[6] *Uniform Standards of Professional Appraisal Practice,* Appraisal Standards Board of The Appraisal Foundation, Washington, DC, 1995.

A property's market value is the basis for the lending decision because the property will be either the full or partial security for the loan. When making investment decisions, the investor will not normally want to pay more than the market value of the property. Similarly, the lender will not want to lend more than a proportion of the market value of the property because if the property must eventually be sold due to foreclosure of the loan, it would probably not sell for more than its market value. In the context of real estate finance, appraisal reports on properties are a part of the documentation required by lenders when considering whether to make mortgage loans. Because lenders and borrowers or investors use appraisals in decision making, they should be familiar with the generally accepted approaches to appraisal or valuation. There are many other instances when estimates of property values must be made after a property is acquired. These include valuations for insurance purposes, property tax assessments, investment performance reports for investors, and so on. These estimates may have to be made annually or even more frequently regardless of whether or not a property is sold. The purpose of this chapter is to explain the appraisal process and the three approaches ordinarily used in valuation.

Appraisal Process and Approaches to Valuation

An appraisal is an *estimate* of value. In making this estimate, appraisers use a systematic approach referred to as the **appraisal process.** First, they ascertain the physical and legal identification of the property involved. Second, they identify the property rights to be appraised or valued. For example, the property rights being valued may involve fee simple ownership of the property or something other than fee simple such as a leased fee estate. Third, appraisers specify the purpose of the appraisal. Besides an estimate of market value for lending and investment decisions, appraisals are also made in situations involving condemnation of property, insurance losses, and property tax assessments. Fourth, appraisers specify the effective date of the estimate of value. Since market conditions change over time, the estimate must be related to a specific date. Fifth, appraisers must gather and analyze market data, then sixth, apply appropriate techniques to derive the estimate of value. This process is the main concern of this chapter.

Appraisal Process

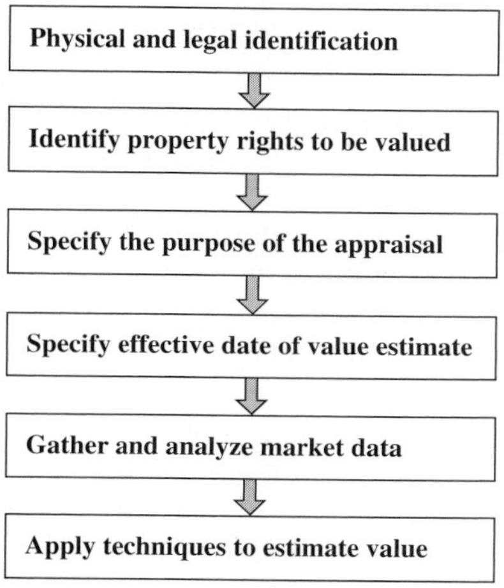

In the appraisal process, a considerable amount of market data must be collected and analyzed. Market data on rents, costs, vacancies, supply and demand factors, expenses, and any other data considered to be an important influence on property values must be collected, summarized, and interpreted by the analyst when making an estimate of value. It is not the intent of this book to cover how to conduct market studies and collect data for making appraisals. In real estate finance, it is more commonly the case that lenders, borrowers, and investors will use the appraisal report to make lending and investment decisions. However, the user must understand the approach used by the appraiser in estimating value. By understanding these approaches, the user will be in a better position to decide whether the appropriate market data have been used and whether appropriate techniques have been used to estimate the value.

The role of appraisals cannot be overemphasized because appraised values are used as a basis for lending and investing. Methods and procedures used in establishing values are thoroughly reviewed and evaluated by lenders to prevent overborrowing on properties and by investors to avoid overpaying for properties. Lenders want to be assured that both the initial property value and the pattern of property value over time exceed the outstanding loan balance for any given property over the term of the loan.

In income property appraisals, at least two of three approaches are normally used: the *sales comparison approach,* the *income capitalization approach,* and/or the *cost approach.* We review the essentials of each approach here to provide insight into the process followed by appraisers in establishing the market value of income property.

Sales Comparison Approach

The **sales comparison approach** to value is based on data provided from recent sales of properties *highly comparable* to the property being appraised. This approach is sometimes referred to as the *market approach.* These sales must be "arm's-length" transactions, or sales between unrelated individuals. They should represent normal market transactions with no unusual circumstances, such as foreclosure, sales involving public entities, and so on. In short, when trying to establish market value for a property, current transaction prices are important benchmarks to use because they indicate what investors have paid to acquire properties.

To the extent that there are differences in size, scale, location, age, and quality of construction between the project being valued and recent sales of comparable properties, adjustments must be made to compensate for such differences. Obviously, when this approach is used, the more differences that must be adjusted for, the more dissimilar are the properties being compared, and the less reliable the sales comparison approach. The *rationale for the sales comparison approach* lies in the principle that an informed investor would never pay more for a property than what other investors have recently paid for comparable properties. Selection of data on properties that are truly comparable along all important dimensions, and that require relatively minor adjustments because of differences in building characteristics or locational characteristics, is critical to the successful use of this approach.

In developing the sales comparison approach to valuation, the appraiser summarizes and uses sales transaction data on comparable properties from the market area analysis in the development of expected rents and value estimates for the property being appraised. Exhibit 8–8 illustrates an example of some of the data that

EXHIBIT 8–8 Market Area Analysis and Sales Data (sales comparison approach, hypothetical office building)

		Comparable Properties		
Item	*Subject Property*	*1*	*2*	*3*
Sale date	—	Recent	1 year ago	2 years ago
Price	—	$355,000	$375,000	$413,300
Gross annual rent	—	$ 58,000	$ 61,000	$ 69,000
Gross square feet	13,300	14,500	13,750	15,390
Price per square foot*	—	$ 24.48	$ 22.27	$ 26.86
Rent per square foot*	—	$ 4.00	$ 4.44	$ 4.48
Proximity to subject†	—	2 mi.	2.5 mi.	3.5 mi.
Frontage lineal feet	300	240	310	350
Number floors	2	2	2	2
Number elevators	1	1	1	1
Age	New	3 yrs.	4 yrs.	6 yrs.
Exterior	Brick	Brick	Stucco	Brick
Construction‡	Average	Average	Average	Average
Landscaping‡	Average	Average	Average	Average

*Gross square footage (rounded).

†In this example the subject property is considered to be at the best location, and locations further away are less desirable.

‡Quality.

could be used in the development of a sales comparison approach for a hypothetical small office building and three comparable properties.

Based on the data developed from the market area analysis shown in Exhibit 8–8, we see that the subject property being appraised is very comparable to three small office buildings that have recently sold. A careful analysis of the data reveals relatively minor deviations in gross square footage, location, front footage on major streets, construction type and quality, parking space, and age of structures. The procedure that may be used to estimate value via the sales comparison approach is to attempt to adjust for the deviations between the property being appraised and the comparables. This adjustment can usually be accomplished in one of two ways. The price per square foot paid for each comparable can be adjusted to determine the market value for the subject, or the relationship between gross rental income and sale prices on the comparable can be applied to the subject with appropriate adjustment. Exhibit 8–9 shows how the price per square foot adjustment could be carried out.

Such adjustments on a square footage basis require adjustments for any major physical or locational deviations between the property being valued and the comparables recently sold. Adjustments on the square footage cost should be made *relative to* the property being valued; that is, the comparable data must be adjusted as though one wants to make the comparables identical to the subject property. Positive features that comparables possess relative to the subject property require negative adjustments, and negative features require positive adjustments. The appraiser makes all percentage adjustments based on knowledge of current market values and how various favorable and unfavorable attributes of comparable properties would affect the value of the subject. When adjusting for age differentials, front footage, or differences in the percentage of leasable square footage, the appraiser must be

EXHIBIT 8–9 Adjustments from Comparables to Subject Property

	Comparable 1	Comparable 2	Comparable 3
Sale price	$355,000	$375,000	$413,300
Square footage	14,500	13,750	15,390
Sale price per square foot	$ 24.48	$ 27.27	$ 26.86
Adjustments			
Sale date	—	+4%	+7%
Square footage	−5%	−4%	−12%
Location	+7%	+12%	+15%
Frontage	+10%	−14%	−15%
Age of structure	+8%	+10%	+15%
Net difference	+20%	+8%	+10%
Adjusted price	$426,000	$405,000	$454,630
Adjusted price per square foot	$ 29.38	$ 29.45	$ 29.54
Estimated price per square foot for subject	= $ 29.50		
Indicated market value			
$29.50 × 13,300 square feet	= $392,350		

able to estimate the value of such attributes and how the addition or deletion of those attributes affects the value of properties. It should be stressed that the *cost* of these attributes should not always be added or subtracted to ascertain value. This is because buyers of properties establish what the value of each attribute of a property is and how each attribute interacts with others. Hence, the appraiser should be concerned with the effect that the addition or deletion of an attribute will have on total property value, holding all other attributes constant. In other words, the appraiser is concerned with the marginal change in value. This marginal change in value may not correspond to the cost of adding or deleting an attribute. *This is a subjective process and such adjustments should be justified with evidence based on recent experience with highly comparable properties; otherwise, serious errors can result.*

In the above example the price of each of the comparable properties was divided by the number of square feet of the building to adjust for differences in the size of the property. This adjustment was made under the assumption that the price for an office building is directly related to its size in square feet. In this case the price per square foot is considered a **unit of comparison.**

Income Capitalization Approach

This approach to property valuation is based on the principle that the value of a property is related to its ability to produce cash flow. When attempting to estimate value using this approach, the analyst must take into account the many market influences that affect cash flows as well as extracting data from the sale of competitive properties deemed comparable to the property being evaluated. In this section, three techniques commonly are discussed. Two of the techniques, the gross income multiplier and direct capitalization methods, rely heavily on current market transactions involving the sale of comparable properties. These techniques resemble the sales comparison method discussed in the previous section in many ways. The focus of these techniques is to determine a market value that is consistent with prices being paid for comparable properties trading in the marketplace. However, rather that giving priority to adjusting for differences in value by adding and subtracting directly from the prices of comparable properties for physical and locational attributes, these two methods tend to focus first on the income-producing aspect of comparable properties relative to the prices at which they were sold. Adjustments are then made for physical and locational dissimilarities.

The third income capitalization technique discussed in this section is the discounted present value method. This method differs considerably from the gross income multiplier and direct capitalization techniques in that a forecast of future income production and expected investment return is used. The point of view utilized is more like that of an investor trying to value properties by using a technique that incorporates many of the same steps and information that he would use to make an investment decision. The following is a discussion of these three techniques.

Gross Income Multipliers. One technique used in conjunction with the income capitalization approach to valuation is to develop what are referred to as **gross income multipliers.** These are relationships between gross income and sale prices for all comparable properties that are applied to the subject property. This technique also requires that an estimate of the gross income be made for the subject property. The gross income multiplier (*GIM*) is defined as

$$GIM = \frac{\text{Sales price}}{\text{Gross income}}$$

or simply the ratio of sale price to gross income. Such multipliers are developed for the properties comparable to the office building being valued. In this case, gross income can be considered a unit of comparison. From the data developed in Exhibit 8–10, we can see that the *GIM*s range from 5.99 to 6.15, which means that the comparable properties sold for 5.99 to 6.15 *times* current gross income. If the subject property is comparable, it too should sell for roughly a price that bears the same relationship to its gross income.

In arriving at a value for the subject property, then, the appraiser must develop an estimate of gross income based on the market data on comparables shown in Exhibit 8–10. For the comparable properties the gross income should be annual income at the time the property is sold (i.e., what it will be during the first year for the purchaser). Similarly, gross income for the subject will be for the first year of operation after the date for which the property is being appraised.

Some appraisers use **potential gross income** (which assumes all the space is occupied) when developing *GIM*s. Others use **effective gross income,** which is based on occupied space (potential gross income less vacancies). The results should be similar if the appraiser is consistent for the comparable and subject properties. If there are significant differences in the vacancy rates among the comparable properties, then using effective gross income may be more appropriate. Of course, this may indicate that the properties are not really very comparable and may be in *different market segments.*

This approach is very similar to the direct capitalization approach, however instead of using *NOI* as the focal point of the method, it relies on gross rent. Therefore, an additional assumption critical to the use of this method is that the operating expenses are the same for all properties. If for some reason this assumption is not valid, then this technique should not be used.

Care should be taken here to ensure that significant changes in *lease agreements* are not expected to occur. For example, if a major increase in rent is expected

EXHIBIT 8–10 Development of *GIM* (comparable properties)

		Comparable Properties		
	Subject Property	*1*	*2*	*3*
Sale price	?	\$355,000	\$375,000	\$413,300
Current gross income	\$36,600	58,000	61,000	69,000
GIM	?	6.12×	6.15×	5.99×

on a comparable due to a lease expiration in the near future, this must be taken into account and adjusted for. In addition to comparability in physical attributes, location, and leases, it is also assumed that no material differences in operating expenses exist between comparables. If material differences do exist, this technique should not be relied on.

From the range of *GIM*s shown in Exhibit 8–10, the appraiser also must select an appropriate *GIM* for the subject property. This is done by observing the range in *GIM*s for the comparable properties as shown in Exhibit 8–10. Rather than simply averaging the *GIM*s in the table, the appraiser would normally give more or less weight to a particular comparable when choosing a rate to apply to the subject property. For example, the appraiser may believe that of the three comparable properties, the third one should be given the most weight because it was the most recent sale. Thus, the appraiser might believe the *GIM* should be closer to that for the second and third comparable properties. The experience and judgment of the appraiser are important parts of this process. Assuming that the appraiser chooses a *GIM* of 6 times as "appropriate" for the subject property, its indicated value would be \$59,185 times 6 or \$355,110.

Direct Capitalization

In cases where it is suspected that differences in operating expenses exist between comparables, the focus of the analysis should be shifted from gross income multipliers to *net operating income* (*NOI*) and the **direct capitalization** technique. Additional financial information that may be used in this analysis is summarized in Exhibit 8–11. This information centers on aspects of the net operating income-producing capability of the subject property and the three properties selected as comparables from market transactions data.

As shown in Exhibit 8–11, the price, rent and operating expense ratios have been obtained from brokers who were involved in the sale of the comparable properties. (Data were obtained with the permission of the buyer and seller of the comparable properties.) In each case, the **net operating income (*NOI*)** was obtained by subtracting operating expenses from rents reported on the comparables at the time of sale. The reader should note the definitions used to identify all items of rent, income, and expenses in Exhibit 8–11. After determining the *NOI*, it is then divided by the transaction price to obtain what is defined in the industry as the **capitalization rate** (sometimes referred to as the "cap rate" and *designated as R*) for the three comparable properties. Note that the cap rates, or *R*s, for the three comparables range from .084 to .099.

Given that the *NOI* for the subject property is \$36,600, we would like to determine its value using the following relationship:

$$\text{Value} = NOI \div R$$

EXHIBIT 8–11 Income, Expense and Price Relationships

	Subject Property	Comparable Properties *(1)*	*(2)*	*(3)*
Price	?	$355,000	$375,000	$413,300
Effective Gross Income	$60,000	58,000	61,000	69,000
% operating expense	39%	48%	42%	41%
NOI	36,600	30,160	35,380	40,710
NOI ÷ Price = (*R*)	?	.084	.094	.099

Definitions of Common Income and Expense Items

Rental Income at Full Occupancy. An estimate of revenues expected to be received from existing tenants based on lease terms plus any vacant space priced at market rents.

\+ **Other Income.** Examples may include: revenues from parking, laundry and cable TV fees, application fees, net deposits, etc.

= **Potential Gross Income (PGI).** Total cash flow possible from all sources and activities relative to the property ownership.

− **Vacancy and Collection Losses.** Estimated rent losses from unoccupied space or due to unpaid rents and losses from other sources.

= **Effective Gross Income (EGI).** All sources of potential income less vacancy and collection losses.

− **Real Estate Taxes.** Based on assessed value by the county and/or other tax assessing entities.

− **Insurance.** Property owners usually provide for insurance on the premises (building, parking lots, etc.) for property damage and for personal injury.

− **Utilities.** Cost of electric, water, etc. that may be paid in full or part by property owners, depending on lease terms.

− **Repair and Maintenance.** Estimates of cash outlays for recurring items expected to be replaced within three years or less of economic use.

− **Administrative and General.** Allocations of costs for personnel and expenses from an off-site activity. That is, a real estate company with many properties under its ownership may allocate a percentage of certain costs (e.g., human resources, payroll, accounting) to the operating expenses of its individual properties.

− **Management and Leasing Expenses.** Supervisory on-site–management employees who lease, collect rents, pay expenses, etc. These may be the employees of the property owner or include payment by the property owner for services outsourced to other companies who specialize in property management and leasing and earn fees and commissions.

− **Salaries.** On-site employees who maintain "make ready" and repair, etc. the property.

− **Reserve for Replacements.** An annualized estimate of costs of certain items that must be replaced but have a useful life in excess of three years (parking garages, elevators, roof, air conditioning systems).

= **(*NOI*) Net Operating Income.** An annual estimate of the net operating income resulting from the compilation of all of the above items.

By substituting $36,600 for *NOI* for our subject property and dividing by an *estimate* of *R* which we obtain from the comparable sales data, we hope to estimate the value for the office building that we are analyzing. The question is which *R* should be selected from which comparable sale? Should we select an average of three *R*s, or what?

The best procedure to follow at this point is to choose an R based on a careful reexamination of the data in Exhibits 8–8 through 8–11 to determine the comparables that are *most* like the subject property. To complete this example, if the subject is more closely related to comparables (2) and (3), then an R ranging between .094 and .099 is probably warranted. Assuming that comparable (2) is most similar and .095 is chosen, then the value for our subject may be estimated as follows:

$$\begin{aligned}\text{Subject property value} &= \$36{,}600 \div .095\\ &= \$385{,}263\end{aligned}$$

Further Interpretation—Application and Limitations. Essentially, this method uses income and expense data from current sales comparisons as market *benchmarks.* This only assures that if a price of $385,263 is paid for the subject property, this price appears to be reasonable, or "in-line" with prices currently being paid for comparable properties. In this case, buyers of properties should not expect to pay less or sellers expect to receive more than this estimated market price. It should be stressed, however, that this approach to valuation *does not assure that this property will be a good investment if purchased.* It only assures the buyer that it is a competitive market price and that if the method is applied correctly, the buyer is probably not overpaying or underpaying for the property relative to what other investors have paid for similar properties. The question of *whether or not it is a good investment will depend on the future growth in rents, income and property values.* These aspects are not specifically considered as a part of this or the gross income multiplier technique and, therefore, no conclusions can be drawn as to the *investment potential* of this property. That must be determined by estimating the future course of the economic base in the market in which the property is located—the leases, rents, expenses, major repairs, and so on. We will consider these factors when we address *investment analysis* in the next chapter.

Direct Capitalization—A Note of Caution

The above discussion of direct capitalization that concerns the relationship between value, and *NOI* and cap rates derived from comparable sales is an important one. However, it must be stressed that when using direct capitalization, properties chosen as comparables must be *truly comparable* to, and/or competitive with, the property under consideration for investment. The term *comparability* means very similar in quality, of construction, size, age, functionality, location, and operating efficiency. It also means comparability in terms of lease maturities, lease options, rent escalators, and any other major lease attributes such as easements, title restrictions, and so on. While these attributes may be similar for many property investments, they may not be for many other investments. An example of the importance of the latter might be two office properties that have sold at the same time and that are locationally and functionally comparable. However, one office property may be leased by *four* tenants on a long-term lease basis with many lease options, and the other property may be leased to 30 small tenants with shorter-term average lease maturities and with many other different lease characteristics. It may be possible that the *NOI*s for the two properties were similar when they were sold. However, because of the differences in the *leases* and *attendant risk,* the prices for both, and therefore the cap rates, should be different. This also means that if an investor chooses to develop a cap rate (R) based on these two sales to use in pricing a property being considered for purchase, many adjustments will have to be made to reflect differences in the leases, in addition to any additional differences in physical, locational, and other attributes among the comparables. Making such adjustments is not always easy. As a result, assigning the "correct" cap rate is difficult and an incorrect one could result in a serious pricing error.

Another area of caution has to do with the treatment of capital outlays for any necessary replacement of building components that are nonrecurring or nonoperating in nature. Other items such as tenant improvements and commissions should also be accounted for. When making estimates of value based on the *NOI* obtained from the sales of comparable properties, the reader *must* determine whether or not, or how, outlays for tenant improvements and capital requirements were included in the data. *Industry practice varies on this issue.* Many appraisers estimate an *annual average outlay* for such items and adjust *NOI* downward by deducting such outlays much like an annual expense. In cases where properties are *highly comparable,* this practice may not materially affect the estimate of value as long as its treatment is consistent for all properties being used in the analysis. However, when properties used in this approach are somewhat dissimilar in that material differences in outlays of a nonrecurring nature are expected, then the reader must make adjustments for such items. If such adjustments are believed to be material and difficult to make, then this generally implies that the properties in question may really not be that comparable. Therefore, the results of this approach should be interpreted with caution.

When is it appropriate to use direct capitalization? Cap rates are important market benchmarks that are widely used in the real estate industry. However, it should be stressed again that estimating a property's value on a forecast of *NOI* for one year and applying a cap rate generated from data collected on the sales of comparable properties can prove to be problematic.

Discounted Present Value Techniques

This final income capitalization technique is based on the principle that investors will pay no more for a property than the present value of all *future NOIs.* Finding the value for a property that is expected to produce income over a very long economic life requires many assumptions and in-depth knowledge of discounted cash flow techniques and *approximations* that make finding present values over long economic lives manageable. It is also necessary to understand the assumptions underlying present value mechanics when such approximations are used. For these reasons, most professionals who value properties prefer to use direct capitalization or one of the sales comparison approaches when possible. However, this method is used by professionals when necessary. To illustrate this method we use an apartment example. Recall that we have already considered many income and expense relationships in the previous chapter. Our forecast of *NOI* is made for a time period during which we can foresee any material change in market supply or demand conditions that could affect rents. In short, we want to forecast and analyze cash flow over a period for which we have knowledge regarding existing tenants, lease terms, and supply and demand market conditions.

Forecasting *NOI*. *Based on our knowledge of market supply and demand,* lease terms, as well as income and expenses, we have made a forecast for the Hypothetical Hills apartment complex. We believe that a forecast for a 10-year period is appropriate and this forecast is shown in Exhibit 8–12. We believe that because Hypothetical Hills is relatively new and unique both in terms of location and design, there are very few comparable properties that have been sold recently with which to compare it. Therefore, the sales comparison method described in the preceding section may not produce a reliable estimate of value. In our forecast, we believe that

EXHIBIT 8–12 Ten Year *NOI* Forecast, Hypothetical Hills Apartments

Year	*NOI*	*% Growth*	*Year*	*NOI*	*% Growth*
1	$338,800	—	6	416,127	3
2	355,740	5	7	428,611	3
3	373,527	5	8	441,469	3
4	388,468	4	9	450,299	2
5	404,007	4	10	459,304	2

vacancy rates for Hypothetical Hills will remain below average relative to other apartment properties. Furthermore, the sales comparison method would probably not be useful because our estimate that cash flows are expected to grow at an *above average* rate ranging from 5 percent to 3 percent for the first seven years is not characteristic of growth expected for other apartment investment opportunities. *NOI* will then stabilize at a long-term rate of about 2 percent in year 9 and thereafter. We also believe that this 2 percent growth rate will eventually become consistent with long-run supply and demand conditions and those for competing apartment projects. Based on our forecast of cash flows and knowledge of market conditions, we conclude that other apartment properties are not as comparable as would be desired in order to use the sales comparison method.

Selection of a Discount Rate (*r*)

After estimating *NOI* over an expected period of analysis in the preceding section, step 3 in the present value approach to income capitalization requires the selection of a **discount rate** or **required internal rate of return** (r) over the investment period. Conceptually, this discount rate should be thought of as a required return for a real estate investment based on its risk when compared with returns earned on competing investments and other capital market benchmarks. For example, if the period of analysis is 10 years for our prospective real estate investment, the discount rate selected should be greater than: (1) the interest rate on a 10-year U.S. Treasury bond, (2) the interest rate on a 10-year commercial mortgage loan, and (3) the weighted average of corporate bond rates, or the borrowing rates for tenants in the property being evaluated.[7] A risk premium for real estate ownership and its attendant risks related to operation and disposition should also be included to arrive at a reasonable discount rate. Exhibit 8–13 depicts the above discussion conceptually in terms of expected returns relative to the risk that may be expected on different asset classes. In the case of income-producing real estate, the diagram indicates that expected returns should be above expected returns for Treasury bonds, commercial mortgages, and corporate bonds, but below those of expected returns on riskier common stocks. It should be stressed however, that this conceptualization depicts the average returns for all income-producing real estate as a sector. Risk on individual properties may be higher or lower than risk relative to the "average" property

[7] This is because when properties are leased, tenants are, in a sense, substituting lease obligations created by renting, for loans that would be used if tenants chose to build and finance properties using banks with debt. Therefore, in addition to credit risks, because real estate investors take the added risk associated with operating real estate, they should earn a return greater than the interest rate that tenants would otherwise pay on mortgage debt. If real estate investors could not earn more than this rate, each investor would be better off being a lender and making loans to tenants.

EXHIBIT 8–13 Risk and Return Trade-off by Type of Investment

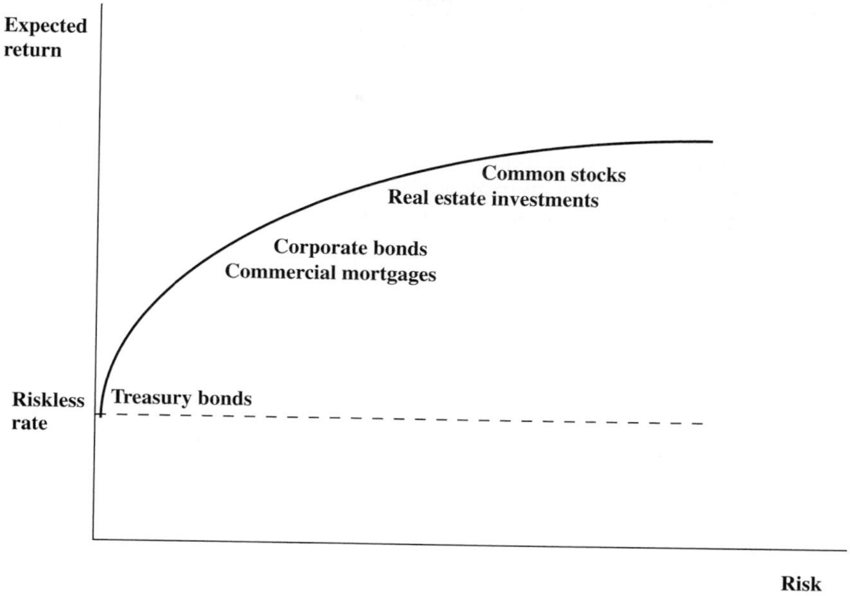

and therefore, expected returns on individual properties may be greater or less than this average. In our example, after considering the risk on other competing properties, we have selected 12 percent as the internal rate of return that we should expect to earn if we invest in the Hypothetical Hills Apartments.

Thus far, we have completed three of the *four* steps that we need to estimate present value, that is:

1. A forecast of *NOI*.
2. Selection of a relevant period of analysis or the **holding period** for the investment.
3. Selection of a discount rate or required rate of return (r) for the period selected in (2).

In the fourth step, we must deal with the present value of expected *NOI beyond the 10-year period* of analysis. We will represent these cash flows with a **reversion value** (*REV*) or *resale price.* Returning to our estimate of cash flow in Exhibit 8–12, note that we have estimated that *NOI* will *stabilize* from year 8 and beyond at a rate of 2 percent per year. In our example, we assume that the property value or *REV* will be established at the end of year 9. As you will see, this will require a cash flow forecast beginning in year 10 and a long-term growth assumption from that point until the end of the economic life of the property. In making this estimate for *REV,* the following major assumptions are being made:

1. The demand for apartments in this market region will tend to grow in a stable, long-term relationship with growth in the U.S. economy.

2. There will be no *major* or *structural* changes in the determinants of supply and/or demand for apartments from year 10 and thereafter.
3. If these assumptions cannot be made, a year-by-year forecast of *NOI* beyond year 10 must be made until a period of stability is expected to be reached.

Using Approximations to Estimate Reversion Values

At this point, the reader is probably wondering how the value for *REV* will be estimated at the end of year 9, particularly for an asset such as Hypothetical Hills, a new apartment community that is expected to have a long economic life, perhaps 50 years or more. The following are three techniques that are used frequently to do this.

(A) Developing Terminal Cap Rates Based on Expected Long-Term Cash Flows. Clearly, forecasting cash flows each year from year 10 through 50 would not be practical. One approach that could be used is to *approximate* the present value of cash flow for the remaining economic life of the asset by using a **terminal cap rate (R_T)**. This approach may be used only under very restrictive assumptions regarding the pattern of cash flow that is expected from the end of the holding period through the end of the useful life of the asset and its relationship to the required rate of return (r) that investors expect to earn on investment.

These are:

Case 1: $R_T = (r - g)$ when average long-run growth (g) in *NOI* is expected to be *positive.*

Case 2: $R_T = (r)$ when long-run growth (g) in *NOI* is expected to be level or zero.

Case 3: $R_T = (r + g)$ when average long-run growth (g) in *NOI* is expected to be negative or decline.

Depending on the long-run scenario chosen for the remaining economic life *after* the holding period, an estimate for (g) must be selected in order to estimate *REV.* In our case, we have estimated that from year 10 until the end of the economic life, *NOI* will tend toward an average growth rate (g) of 2 percent per year. Based on this set of assumptions, the reversion value (*REV*) for Hypothetical Hills Apartments at the end of year 9, based on a 10-year projection period, can be approximated as follows:

$$REV_9 = (NOI_{10}) \div (r - g)$$

This means that the estimated resale price or reversion value REV_9 is equal to *NOI* in year 10 which is shown in Exhibit 8–12 as $459,304 divided by r, which is the 12 percent discount rate or required rate of return that we have selected, minus the stabilized or long-term expected growth rate in cash flow, designated as (g), or 2 percent. The relationship $(r - g)$ in period 9 is also referred to by industry practitioners as a *terminal* capitalization rate, designated as R_T.

$$\begin{aligned} REV_9 &= NOI_{10} \div (R_T) \\ REV_9 &= \$459{,}304 \div (.12 - .02) \\ REV_9 &= \$459{,}304 \div .10, \text{ or} \\ REV_9 &= \$4{,}593{,}040 \end{aligned}$$

Note: $R_T = (r - g)$
$R_T = .10$

Now that we have estimated the reversion value in year 9, or REV_9, which is the present value of expected cash flows from year 10 through the end of the expected

EXHIBIT 8–14 Final Calculation of Present Value for Hypothetical Hills Apartments

End of Year	(a) NOI	(b) PVNOI @ 12%	(c) REV	(d) PVREV @ 12%	(e) (b + d) Total PV
1	$338,800	$302,500			$ 302,500
2	355,740	283,594			283,594
3	373,527	265,869			265,869
4	388,468	246,878			246,878
5	404,007	229,244			229,244
6	416,127	210,823			210,823
7	428,611	193,882			193,882
8	441,469	178,302			178,302
9	450,299	162,382	$4,593,040*	$1,656,296	1,818,676
					$3,729,771

* Calculated as: *NOI* in year 9 = $450,299 × 1.02 = $459,304 and $459,304 ÷ .10 = $4,593,040.

economic life of the property, we can now estimate the present value for the property over its *entire economic life* beginning in year 1, as shown in Exhibit 8–14.

To summarize, the present value, (*PV*), of estimated cash flows for this property can be illustrated as:

$$PV = PVNOI + PVREV$$
$$PV = \$3{,}729{,}771$$

This exercise completes our analysis, which, based on our assumptions, yields a present value or property value *today* of $3,729,771 for Hypothetical Hills. If an investor were to pay this price for the property and own it for 9 years and then sell it for $4,593,040, she would earn an *IRR* of 12 percent on the initial investment of $3,729,771. We should again point out that using the *terminal cap rate* of R_T, or .10, produces a REV_9 of $4,593,040. This result is heavily dependent on the *NOI* continuing to grow at 2 percent per year from years 10 through 50 discounted at 12 percent.

(B) Estimating the Terminal Cap Rate Directly from Sales Transactions Data. Note that the above example produced a relationship between the cap rate at time period zero, $338,800 ÷ $3,729,771 or .09, and the terminal cap rate of .10. This pattern is very commonly assumed in real estate valuation, when markets are believed to be, or will eventually reach, equilibrium or a "steady state." In our example, we show a terminal cap rate (R_T) that is greater than the **"going in" cap rate (*R*).** This assumption is frequently made because over time, as properties age and depreciate, the production of income declines, therefore the expected growth in *NOI* for an older property should be less than that of a new property. This also means that holding all else constant when compared to newly developed properties, a property that is 10-years old should sell for a lower price relative to its *NOI* (higher cap rate) than a new one. *An analyst may be able to verify today that this is the case by comparing cap rates from the sale of older properties with cap rates on newer properties.* Holding all else constant, the difference between cap rates on older properties and newer properties should reflect economic depreciation.

Referring again to our example, recall that when we made our estimates of cash flows in Exhibit 8–12, we recognized that because of its somewhat unique attributes, the expected growth for Hypothetical Hills would be significantly higher than that of other properties for the first 7 years. After that period, *NOI* would be expected to take on a long-run growth rate of about two percent. In other words, when making these estimates of *NOI,* we recognize that Hypothetical Hills will not be able to sustain above-normal growth relative to its competition forever. This is because (1) More competing properties will be developed thereby increasing supply and reducing the ability of Hypothetical Hills to earn rent premiums, (2) Hypothetical Hills will be older and its functions and style likely to become obsolescent. As a result, its uniqueness relative to the competition will diminish. Recognizing this likelihood, a practitioner may choose to estimate the terminal cap rate for Hypothetical Hills directly by collecting sales data for properties that are *now 10-years old, that are likely to be representative of how Hypothetical Hills will compete* in the apartment market 10 years from now. This approach, while widely used, is obviously problematical and requires considerable judgment by the analyst. Assuming that (1) Data from the current sale of 10-year old properties can be obtained, (2) The cap rate determined from such sales data is .10, and (3) The analyst believes that the trend in value for Hypothetical Hills will eventually converge with those of the comparables, the analyst may choose to use .10 as the terminal cap rate. Clearly, these assumptions should be looked at carefully by an investor relying on this approach to value.

While the above discussion may be helpful to you in understanding terminal cap rates, this approach will only hold when other major influences affecting the value of properties, such as investor expectations regarding interest rates, economic growth, and so on, are not expected to change. If, at the time a property is being valued, investors expect interest rates, economic growth, rents, risk, and so on, to change for all properties, then these changes also must be included in the analysis. Therefore, it may be possible that when combined with such economic changes, terminal cap rates may be *greater or less* than those indicated by older properties that have recently sold. We will address the combined effects and such influences later in this chapter.

(C) Estimating the Resale Price Based on an Expected Change in Property Values. An alternative that is sometimes used in lieu of using a terminal cap rate (R_T) to estimate the resale price of a property is to assume that *property values* will change at a specified compound rate each year. If, for example, we estimate that the value of a property and its *net operating income* are expected to increase by 3 percent per year, we can estimate the value of the property (V) based on this assumption using the information below:

Year	*Estimated NOI*	*Estimated Resale Price*
1	$500,000	
2	515,000	
3	530,450	
4	546,364	
5	562,754	$(1.03)^5 \times PV$

Note that in year 5 we have expressed the resale price as a function of the unknown present value (*PV*). This is because although we do not know the resale price, we believe it will be $(1.03)^5$ greater than the present value (*PV*). We may use algebra to solve for the present value. Our valuation premise is that the value of the property (*PV*) is equal to the present value of the above *NOI*. Thus, assuming a discount rate of 13 percent over a 5-year holding period, we can write the following algebraic expression:

$$PV = \frac{500{,}000}{(1.13)^1} + \frac{515{,}000}{(1.13)^2} + \frac{530{,}450}{(1.13)^3} + \frac{546{,}364}{(1.13)^4} + \frac{562{,}754}{(1.13)^5} + \frac{1.03^5 \times PV}{(1.13)^5}$$

Solving the above expression for *PV* we have:

$$\begin{aligned} PV &= 442{,}478 + 403{,}321 + 367{,}628 + 335{,}095 + 305{,}440 + (0.629208 \times V) \\ PV &= 1{,}853{,}962 + (0.629208 \times PV) \\ .370792V &= 1{,}853{,}962 \\ PV &= 5{,}000{,}000 \end{aligned}$$

Thus, the present value[8] would be \$5,000,000. In cases where we assume that growth in *NOI* and property value will be the same, this also implies that the capitalization rate will be constant over time. That is, at any point in time the ratio of income to value will be the same, 10 percent. In these examples, *NOI* during year 1 was \$500,000 and the value was estimated to be \$5 million which results in a 10 percent current, or what real estate investors may refer to as the "going in" capitalization rate.

Using the same analysis, it should follow that if we know that the value of the property is \$5 million, then holding all else constant, the assumptions in this problem imply a resale price at the end of a five-year holding period of \$5,796,370, or \$5,000,000 $(1 + .03)^5$. As we have seen, this figure can be obtained either by discounting the *NOI* over the remaining economic life (year 6 forward) at a 13 percent rate or by compounding the initial value at a 3 percent rate over the five-year holding period.

Finally, the reader may have realized that in the example above we could have obtained the going in capitalization rate of 10 percent by the same $r - g$ relationship discussed previously for the terminal capitalization rate. That is, $R = r - g$ or $R = 13\% - 3\% = 10\%$. The value would then be found by dividing the year 1 *NOI* by *R* or \$500,000/.10 = \$5,000,000. This works in this example because it was assumed that *NOI* and value changed at the same compound rate (3 percent) each year.

Extending the Present Value Approach: A Note on Land Values

In this section, we raise the question "What determines land values?" What causes land prices to move up and down? We have all heard of cases of parcels of land trading at prices that fluctuate up or down and wondered why this pattern occurs. There is a framework underlying the process that should help us to better understand land markets and their valuation process. To illustrate, we consider an example of a new office building on a site that is expected to produce *NOI* of \$500,000 for the coming operating year. The improvements are expected to last 75 years and

[8] Note that .629208 (*PV*) results from 1.03^5 (*PV*) *PVIF*, 13%, 5 yrs., or 1.159274 (*PV*).542760.

NOI is expected to *grow* each year by 3 percent and investors expect an *IRR* of 13 percent. We would value the property as:

$$PV = \frac{NOI_1}{r - g} \text{ or } \frac{NOI_1}{R}$$

$$PV = \frac{\$500{,}000}{.13 - .03} \text{ or } \frac{\$500{,}000}{.10}$$

$$PV = \$5{,}000{,}000$$

In our example, an office building on the site would produce \$500,000 in year 1 and grow at 3 percent (g) per year thereafter. Investors in similar office buildings are expecting 13 percent (r) on their investment and/or comparable office buildings are trading based on cap rates (R) of 10 percent, thereby producing a present value of \$5,000,000. Now assuming that a new building would cost \$4,000,000 to construct, the implied, or residual, land value would be \$5,000,000 − \$4,000,000 or \$1,000,000. The idea here is that **residual land value** is the residual value, or difference between total property value and the cost of constructing an improvement on a given site.

A Note on Volatility in Land Prices

It may be useful to introduce at this point the causes of land price volatility. Many readers can probably relate to times when land prices in certain areas increase suddenly, then subside and perhaps increase again. One observation may be that it is simply investor speculation causing such price fluctuations. While this may be the case from time to time, it is more likely that a fundamental change in a location has occurred, or is expected to occur, thereby changing one of the variables in our present value equation. To illustrate, we return to our office property example discussed earlier and two alternative scenarios for expected *NOI.*

Recall that expected *NOI* for our office property was \$500,000 and the land value was \$1,000,000. If we assume that because of unanticipated demand, our initial estimate of *NOI* increases by 10 percent to \$550,000, holding all else constant, total property value would rise to \$5,500,000. However building construction costs would be unaffected in the short run and remain at \$4,000,000, thereby producing a land value of \$1,500,000. The latter value, represents a 50 percent increase in land value given only a 10 percent increase in expected *NOI.* Conversely, if *NOI* was initially overestimated and was only \$450,000, then the value would fall to \$4,500,000 and cause land value to drop 50 percent. Similarly, if in addition to the difference in initial *NOI* other changes in our present value equation (such as higher or lower growth rates (g)) were to occur, the resultant effect on land value could be more pronounced. These changes in expected *NOI* and/or expected values for (r) and/or (g) are the basic causes of volatility in land prices.

"Highest and Best Use" Analysis

One additional use of the land residual method of valuation is to establish the type of property improvement that should be developed on the land. In our example, we used an office project; however, would the land be better used for a retail, warehouse or apartment project? The answer lies in determining what use will provide the *highest total property value.* This analysis is also called the **highest and best use** of the land. For example, in Exhibit 8–15, we provide estimates of *NOI* for each property type that *could* be developed on the Albert tract currently for sale at a price of \$1,000,000. We assume that a market study has been conducted, that rents and expenses have been estimated, and that investors must have a rate of return consistent with the risk associated with the possible uses shown in Exhibit 8–15.

Results in Exhibit 8–15 indicate that a retail project would be the highest and best use of the Albert tract. Such a property would be expected to produce a total property value of $7,500,000 and an implied land value of $3,500,000. If the asking price for the land is $1,000,000 then a developer can immediately realize value by developing a retail project (or by building the retail site for $1,000,000 and selling for $3,500,000). Adjacent land values will then begin to increase as developers compete and develop more retail sites and as the supply of retail development increases, land values will decline to a normal range. In summary, it is the *expected use* of the land and its future income that determines its value. As developers and investors envision what will bring the highest property value, competition for sites and prices paid based on expected site developments will ultimately determine land values.

Mortgage-Equity Capitalization: An Extension of Approaches to Valuation

In our recent discussion, value was found by discounting the *NOI* and resale proceeds for the property. The discount rate chosen was called a "free and clear" discount rate; that is, it did not consider whether the property was to be financed, for example, or how much debt versus equity was used. In effect, we discounted the entire income available from the property as though the investor were paying cash for the entire purchase price. We did not consider the possibility of financing and how that income may be split among holders of debt (mortgage lenders) and equity investors. When considering financing, the discount rate used to value a property subject to debt must be consistent with this assumption; that is, the discount rate must reflect rates of return expected on equity invested. As we will see in Chapter 11, it must reflect the *risk* associated with financial leverage. We now discuss how the value of a property can be estimated by explicitly taking into consideration the requirements of the mortgage lender and equity investor—hence the term **mortgage-equity capitalization.**

This method for estimating value is based on the concept that total value (V) must be equal to the present value of expected mortgage financing (M) and the present value of equity investment (E) made by investors. That is,

EXHIBIT 8–15 Highest and Best Use Analysis—Albert Tract

Use	*(a) Year 1 NOI*	*(b) (r − g)*	*(c) R*	*(a ÷ c = d) Implied Property Value (PV)*	*(e) Bldg. Cost*	*(d) − (e) Implied Land Value (residual)*
Office	$500,000	.13 − .03	.10	$5,000,000	$4,000,000	$1,000,000
Retail	600,000	.12 − .04	.08	7,500,000	4,000,000	3,500,000
Apartment	400,000	.12 − .03	.09	4,444,444	4,000,000	444,000
Warehouse	400,000	.10 − .02	.08	5,000,000	4,000,000	1,000,000

$$V = M + E$$

To illustrate, suppose the *NOI* for a small income property is expected to be $50,000 for the first year. Financing will be based on a 1.2 *DCR* applied to the first year *NOI,* will have an 11 percent interest rate, and will be amortized over 20 years with monthly payments. We will see in Chapter 11 that financing for real estate income property is frequently based on a target first-year debt coverage ratio. The *NOI* will increase 3 percent per year after the first year. The investor expects to hold the property for five years. The resale price is estimated by applying an 11 percent terminal capitalization rate to the sixth year *NOI.* Investors require a 12 percent rate of return on equity (yield rate) for this type of property. Note that the discount rate of 13 percent and terminal capitalization rate of 11 percent imply an average annual compound growth in income after year 5 (for the remaining economic life of the property) of 2 percent per year. This is less than the 3 percent growth assumed for the first five years. As we have discussed, growth rates and capitalization rates can change over time.

We first determine the annual debt service (*DS*) as follows:

$$DS = NOI_1 \div DCR$$
$$DS = \$50{,}000 \div 1.20 = \$41{,}667$$

This equation results in a monthly mortgage payment of $41,667 ÷ 12 = $3,472.22. The amount of the mortgage can be found by discounting the monthly payments at the mortgage rate of 11 percent over the 20-year term. The amount of the mortgage can be thought of as the value of the mortgage (*M*) assuming that 11 percent is the current market rate for the mortgage.

We can now project the cash flows over a five-year holding period as follows:

	Operating Years Year					
	1	2	3	4	5	6
NOI	$50,000	$51,500	$53,045	$54,636	$ 56,275	$57,964
DS	41,667	41,667	41,667	41,667	41,667	N/A*
Cash flow	$ 8,333	$ 9,833	$11,378	$12,969	$ 14,608	
Resale:						
Resale in year 5					$526,945	
Less mortgage balance					305,495	
Cash flow					$221,450	
Total cash flow	$ 8,333	$ 9,833	$11,378	$12,969	$236,058	

*Shown only to estimate the resale price at the end of the five-year holding period.

The present value of the cash flows in this example at a 12 percent discount rate is $165,566. This represents the value of the equity investors' interest in the property (*E*). The total property value (*PV*) can now be found by summing the value of the mortgage (*M*) and the value of the equity (*E*). We have

$$PV = M + E$$
$$PV = \$336{,}394 + \$165{,}566$$
$$PV = \$501{,}960$$

The above value implies a going-in capitalization rate of about 10 percent ($50,000 ÷ $501,960). Note that this is less than the 11 percent rate used to estimate the resale price. As emphasized previously, the capitalization rate can change over time depending on assumptions about how income will change after the property is sold.

We can also calculate the first-year equity dividend rate based on the above equity value. (Recall that the equity dividend rate is equal to the first-year cash flow to the equity investor divided by initial equity investment.) The equity dividend rate is equal to \$8,333 ÷ \$165,566 or about 5 percent. Also, the loan-to-value ratio implied by the estimated value is \$336,394 ÷ \$501,960 or 67 percent.

We must emphasize that in the above formulation, proceeds to be realized by the equity investor are discounted at an investment yield rate (k), which is not the same "free and clear" rate (r) that was used for discounting *NOI,* because the equity that an investor is willing to invest in a project is equal to the discounted value of all cash returns to be realized on *equity* investment and not *total* investment. When attempting to estimate E, an estimate must be obtained for k, or the before-tax internal rate of return (*BTIRR*) investors expect to realize on their equity over the entire period of investment. In the previous cases, no leverage was assumed. Hence, the discount rate, r, reflects the required return on a total investment, or "all cash" basis, because the investor did not use any debt financing. For this reason we would also expect k to be greater than r because of the increased risk to the equity investor when financing is used.

As indicated previously, determining the mortgage interest rate and other mortgage terms and what percentage of value lenders would be willing to lend on a particular property is relatively straightforward. However, estimating the internal rate of return on equity (k) that investors expect to earn over an expected period of ownership is more complex. We do not normally know what cash flows were being estimated by an investor when a comparable property was purchased. Furthermore, k based on *historical data* may not be indicative of *future* trends. A few general guidelines, however, can be followed when estimating k.

1. We know that the risk premium should be *greater* for an equity investor than it would be for the mortgage lender. This equity position is riskier because the equity investor takes more risk than the mortgage lender since all debt-service (*DS*) requirements must be paid from *NOI* before the equity investor realizes any *BTCF.* Also, because the property serves as security for the loan, the lender has first claim against proceeds from the sale of a property; that is, the mortgage balance must be paid from the proceeds from sales before any cash is received by the equity investor. Hence, the equity investor is in a residual position, or one in which the claims of the lender must be met before the equity investor receives any return.

2. We know that the rate of return required by an equity investor (k) should be higher than that for the entire property (r) because of the risk associated with financial leverage.

3. When estimating the required investment yield on equity for a particular project, yields on other investments such as corporate bonds and stock can serve as a point of reference for estimation. Of course, adjustments must be made for differences in risk between the property being valued and any benchmark or average yields developed from other markets.

Cost Approach

The rationale for using the **cost approach** to valuing (appraising) properties is that any informed buyer of real estate would not pay more for a property than what it would cost to buy the land and build the structure. For a new property, the cost approach ordinarily involves determining the construction cost of building a given improvement, then adding the market value of the land. In the case of existing buildings, the appraiser first estimates the cost of replacing the building. This estimate is reduced by estimating any **physical deterioration, functional obsolescence,** or **external obsolescence** (discussed below) in arriving at the estimated value of the building. This approach is procedurally identical to the cost approach detailed in Chapter 6 for residential financing. In the case of income-producing property, however, structural design and equipment variations and locational influences make the cost estimation process much more complex. Consequently, the cost approach may at times be difficult to apply, particularly if the property is not new.

Many techniques can be used in conjunction with the cost approach to value. The technique chosen to estimate value will generally depend on (1) the age of the structure being valued, (2) whether the structure is highly specialized in design or function, and (3) the availability of data to be used for cost estimating. Generally if a project is in the proposal stage, cost data will be developed from plans and drawings by an appraiser or estimator. Cost estimation services are available for appraisers from the Marshall and Swift Company and the Boeckh Division of the American Appraisal Company.

EXHIBIT 8–16 Cost Breakdown—Hypothetical Office-Warehouse Complex (73,500 square feet: 8,000 office; 65,500 warehouse; 3 land acres; projected economic life, 50 years)

Component	*Cost*	*PSF*
	Hard Costs	
Excavation—back fill	$ 31,500	
Foundation	47,250	
Framing (steel)	160,500	
Corrugated steel exterior walls	267,750	
Brick facade (front)—glass	51,000	
Floor finishing, concrete	61,000	
Floor covering, offices	17,500	
Roof trusses, covering	115,040	
Interior finish, offices	57,400	
Lighting fixtures, electrical work	83,400	
Plumbing	114,500	
Heating-A/C	157,500	
Interior cranes, scales	139,060	
Loading docks, rail extension	96,000	
On-site parking, streets, gutters	176,000	
Subtotal	$1,575,000	$21.43
	Soft Costs	
Architect, attorney, accounting	$ 200,000	
Construction interest	125,000	
Builder profit	250,000	
Subtotal	575,000	
Land cost (by comparison)	350,000	
Value per cost approach	$2,500,000	$34.00

Box 8.1

Market value is not necessarily the same as construction cost. This can be seen from the following comparison of the job cost versus the value added by the following remodeling projects.

Project	Job Cost	Value Added	Cost Recouped
Two-story addition	$50,415	$43,004	85%
Minor kitchen work	8,014	7,874	98
Major kitchen work	23,243	19,797	85
Add bathroom	11,639	10,378	89
Remodel bathroom	8,365	6,747	81
Add master suite	35,560	29,252	82
Add family room	32,024	26,451	83
Convert home office	7,709	4,501	58
Finish attic bedroom	21,795	17,932	82
Replace siding	5,211	3,559	68
Replace windows	5,488	3,771	69
Add deck	6,528	4,606	71

Source: *Remodeling,* Scripps Howard News Service, reproduced courtesy of the *Indianapolis Star.*

If a project is in the proposal stage, specifications for material and equipment will have been set out in detail, usually making it possible to arrive at a relatively accurate cost estimate. Exhibit 8–16 contains a breakdown of hard and soft costs for a hypothetical office-warehouse complex in the proposal state of development. The cost breakdown shown in Exhibit 8–16 is based on categories that generally correspond to how various subcontractors would make bid estimates on improvements. This procedure is quite common for new, nontechnical construction.

In addition to the hard-cost categories shown in Exhibit 8–16 for our hypothetical office-warehouse complex, we see two additional categories. One represents a soft-cost category, which includes estimated outlays for services and intangible costs necessary when designing and developing a project. The other category represents land cost. Estimates of land value are made from comparisons with other recent land sales. The sales chosen to estimate value should be **comparable properties** to the land underlying the improvement being valued.

In cases where the project to be appraised includes an *existing* improvement, the detailed cost breakdown shown in Exhibit 8–16 is more difficult to use because the appraiser must estimate physical and economic depreciation on the component parts. Generally, when the cost approach to value is used for an existing improvement, the cost to replace the improvement is estimated and adjusted downward for depreciation caused by (1) physical deterioration, (2) functional or structural obsolescence due to the availability of more efficient layout designs and technological changes that reduce operating costs, and (3) external obsolescence that may result from changes outside of the property such as excessive traffic, noise, or pollution. These three categories of depreciation are very difficult to determine and, in many cases, require the judgment of appraisers who specialize in such problems. Adjusting downward for depreciation is especially difficult for industrial properties,

Exhibit 8–17 Estimates of Depreciation and Obsolescence on Improved Property

Replacement cost estimate	$1,750,000
1. Physical deterioration	
a. Repairable (curable)	
Interior finish	25,500
Floor covering	5,200
Lighting fixtures	17,000
Total	$ 47,700
b. Nonrepairable (incurable)	
15 years divided by 50 years (age to economic life)	30%
2. Functional obsolescence	
Layout design (inefficiency)	
Increasing operating cost (annually)	$ 15,600
3. External obsolescence	
Loss in rent per year*	4,000
Site value by comparison	$ 200,000

*Portion attributable to the building.

special-use facilities such as public buildings, and properties that are bought and sold infrequently.

To illustrate how adjustments must be made to reflect physical, functional, and economic depreciation, we consider a different property, a 15-year-old office-warehouse complex. The improvement, if constructed today and "costed out" at *current prices* using a procedure similar to that shown in Exhibit 8–16, would be $1,750,000. However, because the structure is 15 years old, certain adjustments must be made for necessary repairs, changes in design technology, and depreciation, as shown in Exhibit 8–17.

The essence of the cost approach for existing properties is first to price the improvement at its current **replacement cost.** Then that amount is reduced by any costs (1) that can be expended to upgrade the improvement or to cure obvious deterioration due mainly to needed maintenance or (2) that correspond to the economic loss associated with nonrepairable (or incurable) factors due to changes in design or layout efficiency that may make newer buildings less expensive to operate.

Hence, in our example, the appraiser estimates that a purchaser of the property would have to incur a cost of $47,700 simply to replace worn-out items, the result of deferred maintenance and replacement (curable physical deterioration). However, because the structure is 15 years old and the economic life was 50 years when the building was constructed, the appraiser estimates that structural nonrepairable or incurable depreciation due to wear and tear (incurable physical deterioration) would represent about 30 percent of current reproduction cost. This percentage was developed in the example by the ratio of age to economic life, or 15 divided by 50. This estimate assumes that the building will wear out evenly (at a rate of 2 percent per year—100 percent divided by 50 years) over its 50-year life. Because 15 years have passed, based on these assumptions, the building would be 30 percent depreciated. Estimates of physical depreciation are not always based on these simple assumptions. Many structures may wear out faster or slower over time. In such cases the appraiser should consider the **effective age** of the property rather than its actual age.

As for functional obsolescence in our example, the appraiser estimates that operating costs will be $15,600 higher on the existing structure when compared with a completely new building. The higher costs could be caused, for example, by the lack of suspended ceilings in an older structure, by posts and columns that might affect traffic and storage patterns, or by an older conveyor system designed into the initial structure. This $15,600 additional annual expense could represent added costs in manpower, machinery, and so on, due to functional inadequacies. This additional expense is treated as a discounted annuity because the increase in operating costs is expected to be $15,600 per year for the next 35 years. Assuming the buyer could earn 10 percent annually on other investments, the adjustment for functional obsolescence would reduce the total operating costs to a present value of $150,449. It is assumed that the owner could invest in a similar real estate venture or an investment of equal risk and earn 10 percent on total investment. This was discussed in more detail in our consideration of the income capitalization approach earlier in the chapter.

Finally, the appraiser estimates $4,000 per year for external obsolescence. This cost accounts for environmental changes, such as pollution, noise, neighborhood changes, and other *external* influences that result in lower rents (or higher expenses) when present. Estimates for these characteristics must be obtained from comparable sites where none of these external influences are present. Because the land value is being estimated separately from the building value, the effect of economic obsolescence on the land value will already be accounted for in the estimated land value. Thus, during the adjustment for the effect of locational obsolescence on the *building* value, the estimated rent loss should represent only that portion of the total rent loss (land and building) that applies to the building. For example, the appraiser might estimate that the rent for the entire property will be $5,000 per year less due to the locational obsolescence. However, if there were separate leases on the building and the land, the appraiser might expect that the building would rent for $4,000 less, whereas the land would rent for $1,000 less. This loss in building rent is capitalized and used to reduce the building value. In our example, we assume this rent loss to be $4,000 per year. As was the case with functional obsolescence, this loss in income will also be discounted at 10 percent. The discounted value of this loss is $38,577. In practice, this estimate is extremely difficult to make. The appraiser must often use considerable judgment as to what the total rent loss would be and how much would be allocated to the building.

Adjustments to the replacement cost estimate for the existing improvement in our example are shown in Exhibit 8–18. Note that any repairable or curable depreciation or obsolescence should be subtracted from the replacement cost estimate before any reduction is made for nonrepairable or incurable costs (30 percent in our example). In other words, even after adjusting for the curable items, productivity loss due to functional obsolescence and structural depreciation would still exist. The estimate for those incurable items must be made based on the assumption that all curable items are repaired.

In summary, the cost approach is most reliable where the structure is relatively new and depreciation does not present serious complications. However, when adjustments have to be made for depreciation and obsolescence, and when it is difficult to find comparable land sales, the cost approach is less desirable. This usually occurs where older, improved properties are being valued. However, where there are very few sales and market data are scarce, the cost approach to valuing older properties may be the only method available.

EXHIBIT 8–18 Adjustment of Replacement Cost Estimate

Replacement costs at current prices	$1,750,000
Less: Repairable physical depreciation	47,700
Subtotal	$1,702,300
Nonrepairable (incurable) physical depreciation, 30%	510,690
Functional obsolescence (incurable):	
$15,600(*PVIFA*, 10%, 35 yrs.)	
$15,600(9.644159)	150,449
Economic-locational obsolescence:	
$4,000(*PVIFA*, 10%, 35 yrs.)	
$4,000(9.644159)	38,577
Add: Site value (by comparison)	200,000
Value per cost approach	$1,202,584
or (rounded)	$1,200,000

Conclusion

We have demonstrated three approaches to valuation along with many of the techniques used in conjunction with each. Many combinations of approaches and techniques to valuation could be used; approaches and techniques should be chosen that best complement the data available for estimation. Stated another way, *the availability and quality of data should always dictate the methods and approaches chosen for valuation.* If perfect information were available, then theoretically the same value would result regardless of the method chosen, be it cost, market, or income capitalization. Even with imperfect information, the three approaches to value should correspond to some extent, which is the reason appraisal reports will typically contain estimates of value based on at least two approaches to determining value. While this procedure helps to corroborate the opinion of value, in the final analysis, it is up to the user of the report to interpret, understand, and critically analyze the assumptions, techniques, and methods used to estimate value. Appraisals are only estimates of market value based on market conditions and information available at the time of the appraisal. Economic conditions are subject to much uncertainty, and appraisals should be interpreted and used in light of that uncertainty. Lenders and investors should be familiar with the techniques used by appraisers and with the assumptions made in developing the estimate of value. The appraisal should be viewed as a complement, not a substitute, for sound underwriting or investment analysis by the particular lender or investor.

Key Terms

appraisal process 225
capitalization rate 230
commercial real estate 211
comparable properties 245
cost approach 209, 243
direct capitalization 230
discount rate 234
economic base 213
economic drivers 213
effective age 246
effective gross income 229
external obsolescence 244
functional obsolescence 244
"going in" cap rate (*R*) 237
gross income multiplier 229
highest and best use 240
holding period 235
hotels and motels 211
income capitalization approach 209
industrial real estate 211
institutional real estate 212
location quotient 213
mortgage-equity capitalization 241
net operating income (*NOI*) 230
nonresidential properties 211
physical deterioration 244
potential gross income 229
recreational real estate 211

Questions

1. What is the economic rationale for the cost approach? Under what conditions would the cost approach tend to give the best value estimate?
2. What is the economic rationale for the market approach? What information is necessary to use this approach? What does it mean for a property to be comparable?
3. What is a capitalization rate? What are the different ways of arriving at this rate to use for an appraisal?
4. If investors buy properties based on expected future benefits, what is the rationale for appraising a property without making any income or resale price projections?
5. What is the relationship between a discount rate and a capitalization rate?
6. What is meant by a unit of comparison? Why is it important?
7. Why do you think appraisers usually use three different approaches when estimating value?
8. Under what conditions should financing be explicitly considered when estimating the value of a property?
9. What is meant by depreciation for the cost approach?
10. When may a "terminal" cap rate be lower than a "going in" cap rate? When may it be higher?
11. In general, what effect would a reduction in risk have on "going in" cap rates? What would this effect be if it occurred at the same time as an unexpected increase in demand? What would the effect on property values be?
12. What are some of the potential problems with using a "going in" capitalization rate that is obtained from previous property sales transactions to value a property being offered for sale today?

Problems

1. Zenith Investment Company is considering the purchase of an office property. It has done an extensive market analysis and has estimated that based on current market supply/demand relationships, rents, and its estimate of operating expenses, annual *NOI* will be as follows:

Year	*NOI*
1	$1,000,000
2	1,000,000
3	1,000,000
4	1,200,000
5	1,250,000
6	1,300,000
7	1,339,000
8	1,379,170

A market that is currently oversupplied is expected to result in cash flows remaining *flat* for the next three years at $1,000,000. During years 4, 5, and 6, market rents are expected to be higher. It is further expected that beginning in year 7 and every year thereafter, *NOI* will tend to reflect a stable, balanced market and should grow at 3 percent per year indefinitely. Zenith believes that investors should earn a 12 percent return (r) on an investment of this kind.

a. Assuming that the investment is expected to be owned for seven years, what would be the value for this property at the end of year 7?

b. What would the terminal capitalization rate (R_T) be at the end of year 7? (Assume no material economic depreciation.)

c. What would the value be today?

d. What would the capitalization rate (R) be based on year 1 *NOI*?

2. Ace Investment Company is considering the purchase of the Apartment Arms project. Next year's *NOI* and cash flow is expected to be $2,000,000 and based on Ace's economic forecast, market supply and demand and vacancy levels appear to be in balance and as a result, NOI should increase at 4 percent each year for the foreseeable future. Ace believes that it should earn at least a 13 percent return on its investment.

a. Assuming the above facts, what would the estimated value for the property be today?

b. What cap rates should be indicated from recently sold properties that are comparable to Apartment Arms?

c. Assume that in part (*a*), that the required return is 14 percent, what would the value be today?

d. Assume results in part (*c*). What must the investor consider relative to "comparable" sales in (*b*) that may account for the differences in value?

3. Acme Investors is considering the purchase of the undeveloped Baker Tract of land. It is currently zoned for agricultural use. If purchased, however, Acme must decide how to have the property rezoned for commercial use and then how to develop the site. Based on its market study, Acme has made estimates for the two uses that it deems possible, that is, office or retail. Based on its estimates, the land could be developed as follows:

	Office	*Retail*
Rentable square feet	100,000	80,000
Rents per square foot	\$24.00	\$30.00
Operating expense ratio	40%	50%
Avg. growth in *NOI* per annum	3%	3%
Required return (r)	13%	14%
Total construction cost per square foot	\$100	\$100

Which would be the highest and best use of this site?

4. Ajax Investment Company is considering the purchase of land that could be developed into a class A office project. At the present time, Ajax believes that the site could support a 300,000 rentable square foot project with average rents of \$20 per square foot and operating expenses equal to 40 percent of that amount. It also expects rents to grow at 3 percent indefinitely and believes that Ajax should earn a 12 percent return (r) on investment. The building would cost \$100 per square foot to build:

a. What would the estimated property value *and* land value be under the above assumptions?

b. If rents are suddenly expected to *grow* at 4 percent indefinitely, what would the property value and land value be now? What percentage change in land value would this be relative to the land value in (*a*)?

c. If instead of (*b*), suppose growth in rents are expected to *fall* by 2 percent and rents will grow only by 1 percent because of excessive supply, what would land value be now? What percentage change would this be relative to the land value in (*a*)?

d. Suppose the land owner is asking \$7,000,000 for the land. *Under assumptions in part (a)* would this project be feasible?

e. If the land *must* be acquired for \$7,000,000, returning to the assumptions in (*a*), how much of a change in the following would have to occur to make the project feasible? (Consider each item one at a time and hold all other variables constant.)

1. Expected return on investment (r)
2. Expected (g) or growth in cash flows
3. Building cost
4. Rents

5. Armor Investment Company is considering the acquisition of a heavily depreciated building on 10 acres of land. At some time in the future it will demolish the building and build something more desirable. In the interim it expects to rent the building as a storage facility and expects to collect cash flows equal to \$100,000 next year. However because depreciation is expected to increase, Armor expects cash flows to decline at a rate of 4 percent per year indefinitely. Armor expects to earn an *IRR* on investment return (r) at 13 percent:

What is the value of this property?

6. Athena Investment Company is considering the purchase of an office property. After a careful review of the market and the leases that are in place, Athena believes that next year's cash flow will be \$100,000. It also believes that the cash flow will rise in the amount of \$5,000 each year for the foreseeable future. It plans to own the property for at least 10 years. Based on a review of property sales of properties that are *now* 10 years older than the subject property, Athena has determined that cap rates are in a range of .10. Athena believes that it should earn an *IRR* (required return) of at least 11 percent.

a. What is the estimated value of this office property (assume a .10 terminal cap rate)?

b. What is the current, or going in, cap rate for this property?

c. What accounts for the difference between the cap rate in (*b*) and .10 terminal cap rate?

d. What assumptions are being made regarding future economic conditions when using current comparable sales to estimate terminal cap rates?

7. An investor is considering the purchase of an existing suburban office building approximately five years old. The building, when constructed, was estimated to have an economic life of 50 years, and the building-to-value ratio was 80 percent. Based on current cost estimates, the structure would cost \$5 million to reproduce today. The building is expected to continue to wear out evenly over the 50-year period of its economic life. Estimates of other economic costs associated with the improvement are as follows:

Repairable physical depreciation	$300,000 to repair
Functional obsolescence (repairable)	$200,000 to repair
Functional obsolescence (nonrepairable)	$25,000 per year rent loss

The land value has been established at $1 million by comparable sales in the area. The investor believes that an appropriate opportunity cost for any deferred outlays or costs should be 12 percent per year. What would be the estimated value for this property?

8. ABC Residential Investors, LLP, is considering the purchase of a 120-unit apartment complex in Steel City, Pennsylvania. A market study of the area reveals that an average rental of $600 per month per unit could be realized in the appropriate market area. During the last six months, two very comparable apartment complexes have sold in the same market area.

   The Oaks, a 140-unit project, sold for $9 million. Its rental schedule indicates that the average rent per unit is $550 per month. Palms, a 90-unit complex, is presently renting units at $650 per month, and its selling price was $6.6 million. The mix of number of bedrooms and sizes of units for both complexes is very similar to that of the subject property, and both appear to have normal vacancy rates of about 10 percent annually. All rents are net as tenants pay all utilities and expenses.

   a. Based on the data provided here, how would an appraiser establish an estimate of value?

   b. What other information would be desirable in reaching a conclusion about the probable value for the property?

9. The *NOI* for a small income property is expected to be $150,000 for the first year. Financing will be based on a 1.2 *DCR* applied to the first year *NOI,* will have a 10 percent interest rate, and will be amortized over 20 years with monthly payments. The *NOI* will increase 3 percent per year after the first year. The investor expects to hold the property for five years. The resale price is estimated by applying a 9 percent terminal capitalization rate to the sixth-year *NOI.* Investors require a 12 percent rate of return on *equity* (equity yield rate) for this type of property.

   a. What is the present value of the equity interest in the property?

   b. What is the total present value of the property (mortgage and equity interests)?

   c. Based on your answer to part (*b*), what is the implied overall capitalization rate?

10. Sammie's Club wants to buy a 320,000-square-foot distribution facility on the northern edge of a large midwestern city. The subject facility is presently renting for $4 per square foot. Based on recent market activity, two properties have sold within a two-mile distance from the subject facility and are very comparable in size, design, and age. One facility is 350,000 square feet and is presently being leased for $3.90 per square foot annually. The second facility contains 300,000 square feet and is being leased for $4.10 per square foot. Market data indicate that current vacancies and operating expenses should run approximately 50 percent of gross income for these facilities. The first facility sold for $9.4 million, and the second sold for $7.9 million.

    a. With a direct capitalization rate approach to value, how would you estimate value for the subject distribution facility?

    b. What additional information would be desirable before the final direct rate (*R*) is selected?

APPENDIX: RECONCILIATION OF THE SALES COMPARISON AND INCOME CAPITALIZATION APPROACHES

Reconciliation: Sales Comparison and Income Capitalization Approaches

Based on the preceding discussion, it is obvious that both the sales comparison and income capitalization approaches to valuation have positive and negative aspects in their respective applications. Therefore, it is probably a good policy to use both approaches to valuing properties when possible. This is because comparable market data are *always beneficial* in a valuation analysis. When the sales comparison method is used, cap rates reflect what investors are *currently paying* for comparable properties. Any property currently for sale should tend to sell for a price that is *similar* to prices paid for highly comparable properties that have recently sold. This will be true no matter what the present value method produces based on forecasts of cash flows, holding periods, discount rates, and reversion values. On the other hand, much of the time, properties that have sold recently are not always *truly comparable* to properties available for purchase. Consequently, the exclusive use of direct capitalization, even when adjusted for different property attributes, is not always well advised. For these reasons, a careful analysis using both the present value approach and sales comparisons can be helpful.

Exploring the Relationships between Changing Market Conditions, Cap Rates, and Property Values

Thus far, we have illustrated the *mechanics* or approaches to valuation by using case examples. Investors who are active in real estate valuation and investing must always try to interpret changing market conditions and the effect that these changes are having on cap rates and property values. In other words, as analysts track the sales of properties they may observe that cap rates ($NOI \div V$) from these transactions may be increasing or decreasing. What does this mean? What causes cap rates to rise and fall? In this section, we introduce certain changes in market conditions and try to interpret the effects of those changes on property values and cap rates.

Scenario 1. Effects of Changes in "Going In" Cap Rates in Response to Supply and Demand. To illustrate what effects short-run conditions of excess *supply and demand,* or real market forces, may have on cap rates both in the current time period as well as in future time periods, we consider scenarios relative to a base case. Exhibit 8A–1 summarizes these cases. In the base case, we assume that market supply and demand *are currently in balance,* and that long term growth in rents and *NOI* is expected to be 3 percent and that investors expect returns of $r = 12$ percent. The reader should recall our earlier discussion pointing out that when using present value techniques in practice, *NOI* and cash flow may be different because of items such as capital expenditures and nonrecurring outlays. *To simplify the discussion and for purposes of illustration, we are assuming that NOI and cash flows in all examples that follow are equal.* Returning to our discussion, we show *NOI* to be \$100,000 in year 1 which is expected to grow at 3 percent per year. At the end of year 5, we show *REV,* which is based on year 6 *NOI,* divided by $(r - g)$, or $\$115{,}927 \div (.12 - .03) = \$1{,}288{,}082$. Because of the short period of analysis in our example, we do not consider the possible influence of economic depreciation on the terminal cap rate. However if the period of analysis were longer, or the analyst believed that economic depreciation would occur, then it should be considered. Note that in Panel B, these base case assumptions produce a *present value* of \$1,111,111, and a going in cap rate (R) of .09. This is a result consistent with a condition of a market equilibrium, or when supply and demand are thought to be in balance. Furthermore, investors have no reason to believe that market imbalances are likely for the foreseeable future. They believe that future growth is expected to produce real increases in *NOI* at the rate of 3 percent per year and investors in properties such as the one illustrated, expect to continue to earn a return of 12 percent. We now consider change in cap rates brought on by *unexpected changes* that bring on market conditions of excess supply and demand.

In case A, we show the effects of an unexpected change in short-run conditions relative to the base case. This is a condition of *oversupply* which we now expect to last three years and during which time rents are expected to be flat. Note that *NOI* remains at \$100,000 for three years. Then demand increases and *NOI* resumes a long-run growth pattern of 3 percent per year beginning in year 4. This assumption, in turn, produces results shown in Panel B and case A. Note that under conditions of three years of excess supply (holding all else constant), *present value declines* to \$1,054,776 and *cap rates (R) rise* to .095. Obviously R is now greater than .09 shown in the base case. *In short, conditions of excess supply produce rising cap rates.* Therefore, market conditions should show comparable property values falling because of higher market cap rates.

In case B, we show the effects of an unexpected short-run condition of *excess demand* that lasts for a period of four years, after which, supply adjusts and a long-term growth pattern at 3 percent per year is restored. Such a condition could be brought about by a sudden increase in employment in a market, thereby increasing demand relative to supply. Note in Panel B, case B, that present value increases to \$1,166,989 and *cap rates fall* to .086 relative to results in the base case. Therefore, when demand exceeds supply of available rental space, this tends to reduce cap rates, and to increase property values.

EXHIBIT 8A–1 Scenario 1: Short-Run Relationships between Supply and Demand, Investor Returns and "Going In" Cap Rates

Panel A:
Market Scenario:

		Year (1)	(2)	(3)	(4)	(5)	(6)
Base Case: Market in balance $g = 3\%$	*NOI*	$100,000	$103,000	$106,090	$109,273	$ 112,551	$115,927
	REV					1,288,082	
Case A: Excess supply	*NOI*	100,000	100,000	100,000	103,000	106,090	109,273
	REV					1,214,141	
Case B: Excess demand	*NOI*	100,000	105,000	110,250	115,762	119,235	122,812
	REV					1,364,578	

Panel B:
Expected Result:

			Commentary
Base Case:	*NOI* *PV* @ 12% Cap rate (*R*)	$ 100,000 $ 1,111,111 .090	*Market supply/demand in balance.* Long-term growth in *NOI* = 3% and investor expected return, *r* = 12%.
Case A:	*NOI* *PV* @ 12% Cap rate (*R*)	$ 100,000 $1,054,776 .095	Excess supply expected for 3 years. Rents remain flat, then increase at long-term growth 3% in year 4 and thereafter. Therefore, property values would be expected to *fall* and cap rates would be expected to *rise* relative to the base case.
Case B:	*NOI* *PV* @ 12% Cap rate (*R*)	$ 100,000 $1,166,989 .086	Excess demand causes *NOI* to rise at above normal growth (5%) for four years. Rents then revert to long growth (3%) beginning in year 5 and thereafter. Therefore, property values would be expected to *rise* and cap rates *fall* relative to the base case.

In summary, the goal of this exercise is to demonstrate the effects of changes in market conditions on property values and cap rates. In essence, *excess supply tends to drive PV down and cap rates up.* Investors are discounting lower rents and, therefore, future case flows brought on by excess supply and are only willing to purchase properties at lower prices and higher cap rates. Conversely, *excess demand tends to drive PV higher and cap rates lower* as investors discount higher than normal cash flows thereby producing higher property value and lower cap rates.

Scenario 2: Effects of Changes in Financial Market Conditions on "Going In" Cap Rates. In the previous section, we illustrated the effects of how *real* market influences, that is, the *supply* of new space available for occupancy and the *demand* for such space affect both property values and capitalization rates. In this section, we illustrate the effects of changes in *financial markets,* primarily through changes in interest rates, on property values and capitalization rates relative to the same base case contained in Exhibit 8A–2. In case C, we show the effect of an unanticipated, *increase* in long-term interest rates that also causes expected returns (*r*) to increase from 12 percent to 13 percent. Note that this increase is assumed to occur *holding all else constant.* This means that future rents, *NOI,* and so on, remain unaffected. The results of this increase in

EXHIBIT 8A–2 Scenario 2: Relationship between Changes in Interest Rates, Investor Returns, and "Going In" Cap Rates

Panel A: **Market Scenario:**		Year (*1*)	(*2*)	(*3*)	(*4*)	(*5*)	(*6*)
Base Case:	*NOI*	$100,000	$103,000	$106,090	$109,273	$ 112,551	$115,927
	REV					1,288,082	
Case C: Interest Rates Rise, $r = 13\%$	*NOI*	100,000	103,000	106,090	109,273	112,551	115,927
	REV					1,159,274	
Case D: Interest Rates Fall, $r = 11\%$	*NOI*	100,000	103,000	106,090	109,273	112,551	115,927
	REV					1,449,093	

Panel B: **Expected Result:**			Commentary
Base Case:	*NOI* *PV* @ 12% Cap rate (*R*)	$ 100,000 1,111,111 .09	Base case: Market supply/Demand in balance. Long-term growth in *NOI* = 3% and investor expected return, $r = 12\%$.
Case C:	*NOI* *PV* @ 13% Cap rate (*R*)	$ 100,000 1,000,000 .10	Relative to the base case, property values *decline* because of a higher discount rate (13%) and cap rates *rise*.
Case D:	*NOI* *PV* @ 11% Cap rate (*R*)	$ 100,000 1,250,000 .08	Relative to the base case, property values *rise* because of lower discount rates (11%) and cap rates *fall*.

interest rates is shown in Panel B where present value declines to $1,000,000 relative to the base case of $1,111,111 and cap rates rise to .10 from .09 in the base case.[9]

In case D, we consider a decrease in interest rates and therefore required returns of 11 percent relative to the 12 percent used in the base case. Again, holding all else constant, property values *rise* ($1,250,000) relative to the base case ($1,111,111) because *NOI* remains the same while investors' expected returns fall to 11 percent. Also, cap rates fall from .09 in the base case to .08.

The conclusions to be drawn here are that, holding all else constant, *rising* interest rates generally result in higher required returns (r) and higher cap rates. This, in turn, results in lower property values than would otherwise be the case if interest rates had not changed. Conversely, when interest rates *decline,* required returns also decline and property values rise. This tends to produce *lower cap rates.*

Scenario 3: Effects of Combined Changes in Financial Market Conditions and Real Market Influences on "Going In" Cap Rates. In Exhibit 8A–3 we consider the effects of an unanticipated increase in *interest rates,* coupled with market conditions consisting of real market changes including short-run excess supply and short-run excess demand. The base case shows that both real and financial market force affecting supply and demand are currently producing a balanced market. However in case E, because of an increase of 1 percent in long-term interest rates, investors how expect to earn 13 percent. When coupled

[9] Of course, in reality, the *exact* effect on present value may be different than what we have depicted. The reader should view this exercise more in terms of *direction of impact,* not in terms of exact dollar magnitudes.

EXHIBIT 8A–3 Scenario 3: Relationship between Excess Supply/Demand Conditions, Interest Rates, Investor Returns and "Going In" Cap Rates

Panel A:

Market Scenario:		Year (1)	(2)	(3)	(4)	(5)	(6)
Base Case:	*NOI*	$100,000	$103,000	$106,090	$109,273	$ 112,551	$115,927
	REV					1,288,082	
Case E: Oversupply and 13% return	*NOI*	100,000	100,000	100,000	103,000	106,090	109,273
	REV					1,092,727	
Case F: Excess demand and 13% return	*NOI*	100,000	105,000	110,250	115,762	119,235	122,812
	REV					1,228,120	
Case G: Oversupply and 11% return	*NOI*	100,000	100,000	100,000	103,000	106,090	109,273
	REV					1,365,909	
Case H: Excess demand and 11% return	*NOI*	100,000	105,000	110,250	115,762	119,235	122,812
	REV					1,535,150	

Panel B:

Expected Result:			Commentary
Base Case:	*NOI*	$ 100,000	Base case $g=3\%$, Expected return=13%. Causes cap rate (R) to increase relative to Scenario A in Exhibit 8–15 and property values *decline.*
	PV	1,111,111	
	Cap rate	.09	
Case E:	*NOI*	100,000	Oversupply *and* rising interest rates cause property values to *decline* and cap rates (R) to *increase* relative to the base case.
	PV	949,957	
	Cap rate	.105	
Case F:	*NOI*	100,000	Although excess demand exists, when combined with rising interest rates, property values *rise* although by not as much as in the base case.
	PV	1,049,424	
	Cap rate	.095	
Case G:	*NOI*	100,000	Falling interest rates exert a *positive* effect on property values, however, this effect is offset to some extent by an oversupplied market. The result is *slightly higher* property values and *slightly lower* cap rates relative to the base case.
	PV	1,185,780	
	Cap rate	.084	
Case H:	*NOI*	100,000	Both falling interest rates and excess demand combine to produce the most *positive* effect on property values and dramatically *lower* cap rates relative to the base case.
	PV	1,313,977	
	Cap rate	.076	

with a market condition of excess supply, the combined results produce a major *decline in property values* and a significant *increase in cap rates.* Note that this combination of excess supply and rising interest rates produces the lowest present values when compared to all other scenarios. This is because investors demand greater returns on real estate investments in a market that is being oversupplied by developers. This produces flat rents and *NOI* that are discounted by a larger discount rate. Case F, which depicts a combination of rising demand and rising interest rates, tends to produce a slightly lower *PV* and higher cap rate than would be the case under case E because the condition of excess demand is producing both higher rents and *NOI*; however, these higher cash flows are being discounted at a higher discount rate because of rising interest rates.

Cases G and H shown in Exhibit 8A–3 show the effects of falling interest rates under conditions of excess supply and demand respectively. In these cases, the combination of excess demand and falling interest rates (case H) produces the greatest effect, in which there are dramatically lower cap rates relative to the base case and all other cases. Case G also produces a favorable result in terms of lower cap rates, however, the excess supply condition produces a present value that is somewhat lower than that shown in Case H because of lower rents.

A Closing Note on Cap Rates and Market Conditions

In the above scenarios we may summarize as follows: Lower market cap rates (higher property values) tend to be brought about by:

1. Unanticipated increases in the demand for real estate relative to supply.
2. Unanticipated decreases in interest rates.
3. Both (1) and (2).

Higher market cap rates (lower property values) tend to be brought about by:

1. Unanticipated increases in the supply for real estate relative to demand.
2. Unanticipated increases in interest rates.
3. Both (1) and (2).

There are obviously *many other factors* that contribute to increases and decreases in cap rates. These could include changes in the risk associated with a given property or could be due to changes in neighborhood characteristics and/or many other factors.

A Word of Caution—Simultaneous Effects of Real Market Forces and Interest Rates on Property Values

It should be stressed that the above illustrations were developed under strict assumptions regarding the timing and duration of conditions of excess supply and demand as well as the extent and duration of interest rate changes. These examples were developed to demonstrate to the reader the effects of changes in market conditions on property values and cap rates by using the benefit of numerical examples. In practice, projections of these relationships are difficult to make as are the forecasts of the dollar magnitude of such changes on property values. There are many combinations of real market forces and interest rates that may be considered. Furthermore, we have not considered the possible *interaction* between changes in any one of these market forces on other market influences. For example, the effects of changes in interest rates may persist for a long period of time and affect the *long-term* growth in supply and demand and the pattern in *NOI* far beyond three years. Nonetheless, we believe that understanding these relationships is useful.

In practice, investors must know how to incorporate these relationships into forecasts. When valuing specific properties investors must consider:

1. Current market supply and demand conditions and how long such conditions will last.
2. The effects of such conditions on rents and *NOI*.
3. The future course of interest rates that may be affected by more global, non-real estate specific influences such as global economic growth and inflationary pressures.
4. The contents of leases that have been executed on the property being evaluated and whether conditions in (1), (2), and (3) will materially affect rents, expenses and tenant default rates.

CHAPTER

9

Introduction to Leases, Projecting Cash Flows, and Investment Value

In the previous chapter, we considered many *general relationships* affecting property values. The goal of that chapter was to provide the reader with an understanding of approaches used to estimate value for many different users—buyers, sellers, lenders, insurers, tax administrators, and so on. All of these parties are concerned that the value for a given property is current. Therefore, market information based on recent sales is very important. In this chapter we *extend* the analysis to a more detailed level with a focus on the investment value of properties. We consider more detailed information that is usually made available to potential buyers of properties. This would include information on leases, tenants, operating expenses, and other property-specific data that can be used to establish an investment value. We emphasize the differences between property types and the lease characteristics common to each type. We also consider (1) necessary outlays for needed repairs or improvements that would have to be made if a property was acquired, (2) risk, and (3) offering prices that can be made that will achieve a desired return on investment.

We begin with an explanation of leases and the determination of rental income. We follow with basic examples of an investment analysis for each of the major property types.

Leases

Income properties are typically leased to tenants for a specified period of time. The **lease** assigns rights, duties, and responsibilities between the **lessor** (owner) and the **lessee** (tenant) that affect each party for the duration of the lease. The terms of the lease include legal considerations that are designed to protect the interests of both the lessor and the lessee and specify how payments are to be made over the term of the lease. The lessor is usually the owner of the property. Thus, we tend to use these terms interchangeably. Similarly, the lessee is typically the tenant who occupies and uses the space, and the terms *lessee* and *user-tenant* are used interchangeably. The lease agreement usually includes the following items:

- The date of the lease agreement.
- The occupancy date, the rent due date, and the length of the lease term.

- The parties to the lease, namely, the lessor and lessee.
- A description and measurement of the leased premises.
- The allowed uses for the property.
- Any restrictions on alteration or improvements to the property.
- The responsibility for maintenance and repair of the tenant's space.
- Any restrictions on the operation of the tenant's business.
- Any restrictions on assignment or subletting of the space to a third party.
- The use of common areas and facilities, such as lobbies, rest rooms, and parking lots.
- Requirements for a tenant to obtain personal injury and personal property insurance.
- The method of handling delinquent payments and conditions for surrender of premises.
- The amount of base or minimum rent and the method used to calculate any additional rent.
- The responsibility for payment of specific expenses by the lessee and/or the lessor.
- Any tenant improvement allowances—improvements to the tenant's space that are paid for by the owner.
- Any concessions, for example, a free rent period.
- Any lease renewal options.

General Lease Terms for Specific Property Types

The following discussion will outline some of the general ways in which leases differ among different types of properties.

Hotel and motel rooms are typically rented on a day-to-day basis for obvious reasons. Rental housing and apartments are usually leased on an annual basis, although shorter or longer leases may occur. Lease terms are usually renegotiated after the end of each lease term.

Office space tends to be leased for three- to five-year terms with the tenant often having the option to lease for one additional three- to five-year term. Depending on market conditions, the lease may include provisions for rent increases each year by either a specified dollar amount (set-up provisions) or an amount based on inflation adjustment (e.g., CPI). Tenants are often responsible for paying their share of certain expenses such as property taxes, insurance, and maintenance. This is done by using either a net lease or expense pass-throughs.

Lease terms in retail space vary considerably. Smaller retail establishments may lease space only for one or two years, whereas larger establishments may be willing to commit to much longer lease terms. Leases for larger shopping centers, especially malls, usually have percentage leases with minimum rents.

Leases for industrial property are often highly individualized due to the special-purpose nature of the building. Although three- to five-year leases are common, many tenants will prefer longer-term leases, especially when equipment is to be installed that is expensive and inconvenient to move over relatively short periods of time. This is particularly true for manufacturing firms where operating expenses can be quite uncertain. Thus, the leases are typically net leases, with the tenant paying taxes, insurance, and maintenance as well as utilities.

Financial Contents of Leases

Rent. Because real property has a long economic life and transaction costs (i.e., moving, re-leasing, etc.) are high for both parties, owners and users usually prefer to contract for the use of the property for various periods of time.[1] The initial rent that must be paid under the lease contract is usually a specified dollar amount, which we refer to as the **base rent.** This base amount may change for a number of reasons depending on the method used to calculate rent over the term of the lease. Some leases include **step-up provisions** that specify that the rent will increase periodically by predetermined amounts over the term of the lease. This is analogous to a graduated payment mortgage. There is no uncertainty as to the amount and date of each increase in rental payments.

Another way of providing for increases in rents is to adjust the rent according to a specified index. The consumer price index (CPI) is commonly used for this purpose. That is, the rental rate is adjusted periodically according to the change in the CPI. Other indexes can be used. For example, in New York City it is common to use the Porter's Wage Index. Use of price indexes like the CPI to adjust rents differs from step-up leases because the actual change in rents is not known in advance. **CPI adjustment** shifts the risk of unexpected increases in the level of inflation to the tenant and tends to preserve the real value of the lease payments. In return for receiving a CPI adjustment in the lease, we would expect the lessor to accept a lower base rent than would be the case if there were no CPI adjustment. The use of the CPI is illustrated in an office building lease example later in this chapter.

Leases for shopping centers often include provisions for rents to be partially based on the tenant's sales volume. This is referred to as **percentage rent.** In this case a *minimum rent* usually must be paid regardless of the tenant's sales level. Then, if the tenant's sales volume exceeds a specified minimum amount, rent is calculated as a percentage of sales. The amount that the total rent exceeds the minimum rent is referred to as *overage rent.*

Responsibility for Expenses. The leases should identify which party has the responsibility for paying for building operating expenses such as property taxes, insurance, utilities, and maintenance. Two extreme lease types place all or none of this responsibility with the tenant. If all operating expenses are paid by the lessor, the lease is referred to as a **gross or full-service, lease.** In this case the owner bears the risk of all unexpected changes in operating expenses. Alternatively, if all operating expenses (perhaps with the exception of management fees) are paid by the tenant, the lease is usually referred to as a **net lease.** Historically, the term *net-net-net lease* or *triple net lease* was used to refer to a lease that required the tenant to pay for property taxes, insurance, and maintenance in addition to rent. In this case, the tenant bears the entire risk of unexpected changes in operating expenses.

As in many contracts, responsibilities can be shared between parties. One alternative would require the lessor to pay operating expenses up to a specified amount, referred to as an **expense stop.** The expense stop is usually based on the level of expenses associated with the operation of the building at the time the lease is signed. If expenses increase above the stop during the term of the lease, all or a portion of the increase is "passed through" to the tenant and added to the base rent. The amount above which expenses are passed through to tenants may be limited to only certain

[1] Another element of the rent calculation is the quantity of space, or rentable square footage, leased by the tenant. This will be discussed later in more detail.

expense categories or to all expense categories. In cases where the tenant leases only a portion of a building, the amount of the **expense pass-through** is usually based on the total of such expenses incurred in the operation of the building, pro rated based on the amount of space leased by the tenant. This type of lease is similar to the use of a net lease, with the exception that only increases in operating expenses are passed through to the tenant. The lessor retains the benefit of any decrease in operating expenses. Leases with expense pass-through provisions may also have a cap on the amount of expenses that can be passed through. For example, the lease may allow expenses to be passed through if they exceed $5 per square foot up to a maximum of $9 per square foot. In this case, the most the tenant would have to pay is $4 per square foot. The use of expense pass-through provisions are illustrated for an office building lease later in this chapter. One general rule that usually applies to expenses is that the property owner should not bear the risk of expenses associated with the operation of a user/tenant. Leases are usually designed with this in mind. That is, owners should bear the expenses associated with the operation of the buildings and tenants should bear expenses associated with operating their businesses.

Concessions. Lease contracts may also include concessions that effectively lower the rental rate. For example, there may be a **free rent** period during which no rent is paid. These concessions or discounts tend to be used during periods when markets are oversupplied with rentable space. For example, a tenant may not be required to pay rent during the first year of a five-year lease. This may be done in lieu of an average rent reduction over the entire lease term. In this way, in the later years of the lease, higher rents would be paid. Another form of concession is for the lessor to pay for the cost of tenant improvements.

Other Important Contents in Leases. All rents are a function of location, age, quality and condition of the premises. However given these attributes, there are generally rent premiums and discounts for certain locations within a property.

Rent Premiums

- *Apartments:* near pool, amenities, parking, better views, higher floors—with elevators.
- *Office:* ground floor, top floors with unobstructed views, building corners, proximity to an elevator lobby or transfer point, first floor of an elevator bank.
- *Retail:* frontage in lineal feet along mallway, nearness to anchor or major tenants or near main mall entrance.
- *Warehouse:* near entrance to industrial parks, good proximity to freeways, ample turning radius for transport vehicles.

Rent Discounts

- *Apartments:* on periphery of site, inferior views, higher floors—no elevators.
- *Office:* middle floors and areas not adjacent to the elevator bank, or with obstructed and/or undesirable views.
- *Retail:* nonmajor walkways in malls, second or third levels in multi-level malls.
- *Warehouse:* poor ingress/egress and poor traffic circulation on the site.
- Larger users pay lower average rent per square foot than smaller users.

Other issues that must be negotiated in leases include:

Fixed versus Variable Base Rents: Leases with fixed lease payments generally carry higher initial base rents than leases with indexed or adjustable rent clauses, particularly when rents are likely to be adjusted upward at specific times during the term of the lease.

Tenant Improvements: An agreement between owner and tenant concerning the amount that the owner will pay for tenant improvements (called TIs). This could include bookcases, doors, lighting, carpets, wall coverings, etc. This allowance is usually expressed as dollars per square foot of usable space that the owner will budget for a tenant to finish or refinish space. Any cost in excess of the agreed amount is to be paid by the tenant.

Lease Concessions: Any free rent, move-in allowance, buyout of an existing lease, designated parking, or any separate or exclusive property entrances and exits that will be provided for by the owner.

Signage: Purpose to grant one or more tenants the right to display a name inside and/or outside of the building for an additional fee. In the case of anchor tenants, signage may be offered at no charge as an inducement to lease space.

- The size and design of the sign are to be carefully controlled by the landlord, particularly in retail leases, and, when given exclusively to one tenant, may warrant a premium in the base rental rate.
- Other potential tenants may shy away from a retail or an office building featuring a competitor's name. There may be "prestige" issues involved, depending on the tenant mix in the building.

Non-compete Clause: Limits the ability of a property owner to lease space in the building to competitors of existing tenants.

- Some exclusive retail shops generally insist upon an exclusive use provision prohibiting any similar shop from leasing space anywhere or in proximity in the building in order to protect sales (e.g., jewelry stores, leather goods).
- *Business Image Trade Secrets:* A tenant may insist upon an exclusive use provision prohibiting a competitor from leasing space on the same floor or anywhere in the building in order to protect its image and/or trade secrets that may be overheard in shared common areas such as lobbies, elevators, etc.
- *Lease Approval by Other Large Anchor Tenants*[2]: Included in many retail leases so as to protect the image or limit competition. An anchor tenant may want the right to approve any major lease agreements so as to protect the general quality of retailing in the building.

Nondilution or Radius Clause: When property owners contract with a large user tenant to lease space in a shopping center, the property owner may require the tenant to agree not to lease any additional space in the same market/trade area specifically defined (e.g., within a radius of 5 miles).

Lender Approval of Major Leases: Lender/mortgagees usually have the right to approve all major leases (e.g., 5,000 sq. ft. or more) being negotiated between property owners and tenants.

---

[2]The term **anchor tenants** usually refers to the largest user-lessees occupying space in a property. In many cases because they lease a very large amount of space, they receive large rent discounts from property owners and demand many of the clauses listed above.

Tenant Right of First Refusal. Tenants may have the right to rent contiguous space when it becomes available, or to purchase the property should the owner decide to sell.

Tenant right to "put back" space. Tenant may have the right to decrease space rented in the event that tenant desires to reduce space needs.

Other Issues: Other options in lease agreements are usually focused on "events", that is, unanticipated economic or other types of occurrences that may cause the termination of the lease or cause the landlord or tenant to incur additional cost or bear additional risk. The list below illustrates some general areas of concern that should be anticipated and dealt with in a lease:

- Should the merger of a tenant or a landlord with another party terminate the lease?
- Should there be a termination of lease upon the sale of property by the current property owner?
- Will there be an expansion or additional construction on or near the site by the landlord in the future? What are the duties/responsibilities of the landlord to the tenant?
- What if a material modification in access/egress to the site by the owner is undertaken, what are the duties/responsibilities to tenant?
- *Eminent domain.* What adjustments will be made by the owner for the tenant if the state condemns part of the property for a right of way?

Determining Lease Revenue. In order to determine revenue, the base rent per square foot of *rentable area* must be multiplied by the quantity leased to tenants. While this may seem to be a straightforward calculation, it is not always as easy as it seems. This is particularly true in buildings where multiple tenants use and share common space. We will provide a hypothetical example using an office building to give the reader some idea of how rentable space is determined. However, depending on the city in which a building is located, local practices may affect how these calculations will be done. It is useful to begin with some terminology.

Rentable Area in a Building. It is useful to think about the rentable area in a building as the total area that could be rented to a *single tenant-user*. This would usually equal the total area on all floors and the lobby, less the nonrentable area which usually includes the thickness of exterior walls, any columns or protrusions through the floors such as elevator shafts or structural supports, mechanical equipment closets, basements, and so on, needed by the owner to maintain or operate the building. It would *include* areas such as elevator landings, lobbies, or reception areas, bathrooms, or any areas that could be used by a tenant and their visitors/clients (these latter areas are also referred to as common areas). To illustrate, if we assume that a building contains 250,000 square feet of gross building area and of that area, 200,000 square feet *could be rented and occupied by one tenant*, and base rents are $20 per square foot, then total rent would equal $20 times the rentable area of 200,000 feet or $4,000,000 per year. Tenants would make payments based on this amount prorated monthly by dividing by 12.

Multiple Tenants–Rental Area per Floor. In cases where many tenants share a building, each tenant will occupy its **usable area** on a floor. For example, if four tenants share one floor equally and that floor has a total of 20,000 square feet that is partitioned off into equal interior office spaces of 4,500 square feet each, then the total usable space on the floor is 18,000 square feet. However, there would be 20,000 square feet of usable *area* if only one tenant leased the entire floor. Therefore, when multiple tenants share a floor, the difference in the total possible usable area on a floor, (or space that would be used if only one tenant occupied that floor) and usable area occupied by multiple tenants, is a common area of 2,000 square feet to be used by all four tenants and their clients/visitors. In this instance, the owner will prorate the 2,000 square feet of common area among the four tenant users to determine the *rentable area* for each tenant by using a **load factor** which is calculated as follows:

$$\text{Load factor per floor} = \frac{\text{Rentable area per floor}}{\text{Usable area per floor}}$$

$$1.111 = \frac{20{,}000}{18{,}000}$$

Therefore, for a tenant with usable area of 4,500 square feet, rentable area for the tenant would be calculated as $4{,}500 \times 1.111 = 5{,}000$ square feet. The tenant would pay rent based on its rentable area of 5,000 square feet.

In many cases, the load factor per floor may be further adjusted for additional areas in the building. For example, a large office building may contain an "oversized" and elaborate lobby and may have other common areas (rooftop observations, etc.). In our example, if we assume that the 200,000 rentable square feet is distributed evenly over 10 floors (square building), and the first floor is a lobby and common area containing 20,000 square feet, then an owner *may attempt* to prorate this lobby common area among all tenants in the building. One way that this might be done is to take the ratio of the other common area (lobby) of 20,000 square feet ÷ 200,000 square feet total rentable area which is 10 percent. The load factor for a floor (1.111) may then be increased by another 10 percent or $1.111 \times 1.10 = 1.222$ (total load factor). Our tenant's rentable area would then be calculated as: (Usable area) (Total load factor) or $4{,}500 \times 1.222$ or 5,500 square feet. Assuming \$20 per square foot base rents, total rental revenue to the owner from this tenant would be:

$$\$20 \times (4.500 \times 1.222) = \text{Rent per year}$$
$$20 \times 5{,}500 = \$110{,}000$$

Therefore, when tenants shop for office space in a multitenanted office building, they will not only be interested in the base rent per square foot. They will also be interested in how the **rentable area** is determined, including the *load factors* that will be applied to the usable area they occupy to determine total rentable area. Rentable area is the quantity against which the base rent will be multiplied to determine rent payments. In many cases, when tenants compare buildings for possible occupancy, they compare load factors as "efficiency measures". High load factors generally indicate a large number of common areas and therefore *lower* "building efficiency". However, if an image-conscious tenant desires a spacious area in which to receive its clients and large common areas, this qualitative consideration may offset low efficiency.

Effective Rent

From the above discussion we know that a number of provisions affect rents and expenses as well as options that may be included in a lease. These provisions, in combination, determine the expected series of rental payments and the degree of risk that is borne by the owner/lessor versus the tenant/lessee over the term of the lease.

Because of the large number of possible combinations of lease terms, cash flows may vary considerably from lease to lease, making it difficult to establish what the lease cost is, as well as making comparisons between leases difficult. Therefore, it is useful to calculate a single measure or **effective rent** that can be used for comparison of leasing alternatives. To calculate the effective rent we will use the following procedure:

1. Calculate the present value of the expected net rental stream. The net rental stream is the amount received after considering expenses that the owner must pay. Note that the focus here is on income to the *owner* of the building.
2. Calculate an equivalent level annuity over the term of the lease. An equivalent level annuity has the same present value as the original cash flow stream.

To illustrate, we will calculate the effective rent that would be collected by the lessor for different lease structures. Because the responsibility for payment of operating expenses can vary considerably for different lease structures, the effective rent will be calculated *net* of any operating expenses that must be paid by the lessor. That is, any operating expenses that must be paid by the lessor will be subtracted from the rental income. A similar procedure would be used to calculate the effective rent paid by the lessee. In this case the amount of operating expenses that the lessee is responsible for paying would be *added* to the rent each year.

The effective rent will be calculated for the following six alternatives for a five-year lease on 1,000-square feet of rentable space:

1. *Net lease with steps.* Rent will be $10 per square foot the first year and will increase by $1 per square foot each year until the end of the lease. All operating expenses will be paid by the tenant.
2. *Net lease with one year of free rent.* No rental payment will be required during the first year. Rent the second year will be $14.50 per square foot and increase by $1 per square foot each year. All operating expenses will be paid by the tenant.
3. *Net lease with CPI adjustments.* The rent will be $11 per square foot the first year. After the first year, the rent will be increased by the amount of any increase in the CPI; in other words, a 100 percent CPI adjustment. The CPI is expected to be 2 percent during the second year, 3 percent the third year, 4 percent the fourth year, and 5 percent the fifth year.
4. *Gross lease.* Rent will be $17.50 per square foot each year with the lessor responsible for payment of all operating expenses. Expenses are estimated to be $4 during the first year and increase by 50 cents per year thereafter.
5. *Gross lease with expense stop.* Rent will be $15.50 per square foot the first year with the lessor responsible for payment of expenses up to an expense stop of $4 per square foot. Expenses are estimated to be $4 during the first year and increase by 50 cents per year thereafter.
6. *Gross lease with expense stop and CPI adjustment.* Rent will be $14.50 per square foot the first year and increase by the full amount of any change in the CPI after the first year with an expense stop at $4 per square foot. The CPI and operating expenses are assumed to change by the same amount as outlined above.

Based on the above assumptions, the effective rent can be calculated using the information in Exhibit 9–1. For each lease alternative, the average rent, present value of the rental stream, and the effective rent is shown in the exhibit. A 10 percent discount rate is used to calculate the present value and convert the present value into an effective rent. This rate should reflect the riskiness of the rental stream as discussed below. The effective rent varies for each alternative. This is expected because the risk differs for each alternative.

To illustrate calculation of the effective rent, the following calculations can be made for the first lease alternative:

1. Find the present value of the net rental income assuming a discount rate of 10 percent is appropriate.

$$PV = \frac{\$10.00}{1.10} + \frac{\$11.00}{(1.10)^2} + \frac{\$12.00}{(1.10)^3} + \frac{\$13.00}{(1.10)^4} + \frac{\$14.00}{(1.10)^5}$$
$$= \$44.77$$

2. Calculate the equivalent level annuity with the same present value.

$$\text{Effective rent} = \frac{PV}{PVIFA,\ 10\%,\ 5\ \text{years}}$$
$$= \frac{\$44.77}{3.79079}$$
$$= \$11.81$$

Note that with this type of lease, the tenant bears the risk of any unexpected change in operating expenses. Although the lease includes a step-up, higher-than-anticipated inflation could erode the real value of the rental income.

The same procedure can be used to calculate the effective rent for the remaining five alternatives. The second lease alternative is similar to the first but has a free rent period. The rent must obviously be higher in years 2 through 4 to result in an effective rent similar to the first alternative. Because the calculation of effective rent considers the effect of the free rent period on the present value of the rental stream, we might expect the effective rent to be the same as the first alternative. Default risk might be considered slightly higher, however, because if the tenant defaults after the first year, the lessor will have received no income from the lease. Thus, a slightly higher effective rent is reasonable.

Some tenants take advantage of free rent periods by defaulting on the lease at the end of the free rent period and moving to another building that also offers free rent. One way of avoiding this problem is to have the free rent period be at the end of the lease. Building owners prefer to have the rent highest at the end of the lease term, however, when they are more likely to sell the property.

The third alternative includes a CPI adjustment rather than fixed step-ups. Because the risk of unexpected inflation is shifted to the lessee, we might expect the effective rent (based on the expected change in the CPI) to be lower than the first two alternatives because the lessee bears more risk of unanticipated inflation. In this case the effective rent is \$11.61 per square foot.

The fourth alternative is a gross lease. This is much riskier for the lessor (less risky for the lessee) than any of the net leases. The lessor bears the risk if operating expenses differ from what was expected. Thus, we would expect the effective rent to be higher. In this case the effective rent is \$12.59.

The fifth alternative also is a gross lease but includes an expense stop (but no CPI adjustment). This shifts the risk of increases in expenses to the tenant while allowing the lessor to retain the benefit of any decrease in expenses. Thus, it is less risky for the lessor than the net lease and has a lower effective rent of \$11.50 per square foot.

EXHIBIT 9–1 Comparison of Effective Rents

1. Net Lease with Steps

Year	*1*	*2*	*3*	*4*	*5*
Net rent	$10.00	$11.00	$12.00	$13.00	$14.00
Average rent		12.00			
Present value		44.77			
Effective rent		11.81			

2. Net Lease with Free Rent

Year	*1*	*2*	*3*	*4*	*5*
Net rent		$14.50	$15.50	$16.50	$17.50
Average rent		12.80			
Present value		45.76			
Effective rent		12.07			

3. Net Lease with 100% CPI Adjustment

Year	*1*	*2*	*3*	*4*	*5*
Expected CPI	NA	2.00%	3.00%	4.00%	5.00%
Net rent	$11.00	$11.22	$11.56	$12.02	$12.62
Average rent		$11.68			
Present value		44.00			
Effective rent		11.61			

4. Gross Lease

Year	*1*	*2*	*3*	*4*	*5*
Gross rent	$17.50	$17.50	$17.50	$17.50	$17.50
Less expenses	4.00	4.50	5.00	5.50	6.00
Net rent	13.50	13.00	12.50	12.00	11.50
Average rent		$12.50			
Present value		47.74			
Effective rent		12.59			

5. Gross Lease with Expense Stop at $4.00

Year	*1*	*2*	*3*	*4*	*5*
Gross rent	$15.50	$15.50	$15.50	$15.50	$15.50
Less expenses	4.00	4.50	5.00	5.50	6.00
Plus reimbursement	0.00	0.50	1.00	1.50	2.00
Net rent	11.50	11.50	11.50	11.50	11.50
Average rent		$11.50			
Present value		43.59			
Effective rent		11.50			

6. Gross Lease with Expense Stop at $4.00 and CPI Adjustment

Year	*1*	*2*	*3*	*4*	*5*
Expected CPI	NA	2.00%	3.00%	4.00%	5.00%
Gross rent	$14.50	$14.79	$15.23	$15.84	$16.64
Less expenses	4.00	4.50	5.00	5.50	6.00
Plus reimbursement	0.00	0.50	1.00	1.50	2.00
Net rent	10.50	10.79	11.23	11.84	12.64
Average rent		$11.40			
Present value		42.84			
Effective rent		11.30			

The final alternative is a gross lease that combines a CPI adjustment with an expense stop. This shifts the risk of any increase in expenses to the tenant while retaining the benefit of any decrease in expenses and shifts the risk of any unexpected increase in expenses to the tenant. Thus, we would expect the effective rent to be the lowest for this alternative.

From the preceding examples, it should be clear that the effective rent is only a measure of the expected return to the lessor (cost to the lessee). Effective rents cannot be compared without considering differences in risk. The effective rent is useful, however, when it is desirable to compare the expected returns from different lease alternatives in a single measure.

Income Potential—Real Estate Assets

In this section we consider four major property types, that is, apartment, office, and retail buildings and industrial/warehouses. Our goal is to familiarize the reader with the operating and lease characteristics for each and how forecasts of cash flow may be developed.

The term **market rent** refers to the price that must be paid by a potential tenant to use a particular type of space under then current market conditions. The rent depends on many factors, including (1) the outlook for the national economy, (2) the economic base of the area in which the property is located, (3) the demand for the type of space provided by the property in the location being analyzed, and (4) the supply of similar competitive space.

For example, the market rent on office buildings depends on the number of firms doing business in the area as well as the likelihood of new firms locating in the area, the number of employees these firms currently employ and are expected to employ in the near future, and the amount of space that the firm needs for its employees to do their job. These factors can be very difficult to estimate as they depend upon many uncertain and complex factors. The number of employees and amount of space per employee that is needed by a particular type of firm may be quite different in the future than it was in the past, due to changes in the way the firm does business, especially with advances in technology.

Similarly, the market rent on apartments depends on the demographic makeup of the population and median income of families in the area in which the property is located, the cost and availability of homes or condominiums to purchase as an alternative to renting an apartment, and other factors. Market rents for retail space also depend on the demographic makeup of the population and the median income of families as well as the percentage of income they typically spend on various goods and services from retail establishments in a particular area. Real estate investors must also be very concerned with the *credit quality* of tenants. As a part of the leasing process, credit reports, bank references, and references from suppliers and customers are also important.

Real estate is a durable asset that has a relatively long economic life. The market rent at a given point in time is the price that users must pay for the use of a particular unit of space, for example, the rent per square foot of leasable area in a building. Market rents can change many times over the economic life of the building because of changes in the demand for space from potential users and/or changes in the supply of space as additions or deletions are made to the stock of available space. These changes are one source of volatility that will affect the rental income from properties over time. The value of a particular property at any point in time depends on the present value of the rental income expected from the building over its remaining economic life. Thus, real estate investors must consider how changes in the supply and demand for space might affect market rental rates over the economic life of the property.

Vacancy

As indicated previously, all space available in a building may not be leased at a particular time. This is because tenants leave after their lease has expired (or walk away from their lease before it expires!), or it could be that the space has never been rented, especially if it is in a newly constructed building. To project income for a property, it is therefore necessary to project how much of the space will be occupied by tenants during the anticipated holding period for the project. There should always be some allowance for vacant space, even in markets where leasing activity is strong, because as tenant turnover occurs it takes time to make space ready and to re-lease space to new tenants. Hence, there will always be some loss in rents, even in buildings occupied by a few larger tenants.

It is more difficult to project vacancy for newly constructed properties. While some leases may be signed before a project is completed, it is possible that less than full occupancy will be achieved immediately after construction is completed. In these cases, projections must be made as to how long it will take for remaining space to be "absorbed" by the market. That is, how long will it take for occupancy to reach a normal level? Obviously the longer it takes for space to be rented, the less income the investor will receive during the initial years of the project. Because this affects cash flows in the early years of the holding period, it will also have a significant impact on the investment value of a property.

At this point it is useful to make a few additional observations. First, when dealing with an acquisition of a property and developing a pro forma statement that will be used in an investment analysis, it is important to stress that such a forecast should contain a summary of *cash flow only.* The focus on cash flow is stressed and should be differentiated from statements that stress accounting income determined in accordance with generally accepted accounting principles (GAAP). While the latter may be important when producing annual reports, taxes, and so on, it should not be used in making an analysis for acquisitions of properties. Second, the term *net operating income* (*NOI*) was discussed in the previous chapter and is used extensively in the real estate investment business. In this chapter, we also focus on *cash flow*, that is, a summary of all cash inflows and outflows. We make this distinction because when undertaking an investment analysis, we will usually have access to detailed rent and expense information from the seller of the property or his agent. We will usually make an inspection of the property and estimate the extent of needed outlays for tenant improvements that may be necessary as leases mature and the property is made ready for new tenants, or outlays for major repairs after the property is inspected. As a result, we will be in a better position to make annual estimates of cash outflows for such items than to make average estimates for these expenses. In Exhibit 9–2 we list data sources that may be used to help compile appropriate benchmarks for operating expenses and other data that may be relevant when developing financial projections for various properties. In summary, when analyzing financial statements the reader should pay particular attention to how the treatment of outlays for tenant improvements, repairs, and replacements are included in statements of cash flows. In this chapter, rather than using an average outlay for such items, we will make an estimate of cash outflows for the year in which the outlay is expected to occur.

EXHIBIT 9–2 Useful Data Sources for Income Property Research

Type of Property	*Source*
Apartment, condominium, cooperative	*Income and Expense Analysis: Apartments, Condominiums and Cooperatives* (Chicago: Institute of Real Estate Management, annually)
Office buildings	*Office Building Experience Exchange Report* (Washington, DC: Building Owners and Managers Association International, annually)
Shopping centers	*The Dollars and Cents of Shopping Centers* (Washington, DC: Urban Land Institute)
Industrial parks	*Site Selection Handbook* (Atlanta: Conway Publications, Inc.)

Valuation of a Lease Fee Estate

In the preceding chapter, it was assumed that all properties being valued did not have a material number of existing leases. In these cases, it can be said that properties are acquired as *fee simple estates*. However, in many situations when properties are being considered for purchase, there are often existing leases in place. Such properties are said to be purchased as *lease fee estates*. Similarly, when valuing properties and selecting comparable properties from recent sales, many of these properties will also have existing leases. When using such comparables, it is very important to investigate whether or not existing leases are present and the contents of such leases. Failure to investigate these cases can result in serious errors when estimating value.

For example, let us assume Property A has an existing net lease with payments for the next five years at $400,000 per year. At the end of the five-year period, the lease is scheduled to expire and rents could then be negotiated on a year-to-year basis at market rates. Alternatively, Property B which is exactly comparable to A, can be expected to produce net rent of $500,000 per year with an escalation of 3 percent per year because it has no existing leases and market rents can be earned each year. Assuming this to be the case, we have:

	Cash Flow—Year 5					
PV	*(1)*	*(2)*	*(3)*	*(4)*	*(5)*	REV_5
Property A = $4,461,296	$400,000	$400,000	$400,000	$400,000	$400,000	$5,627,540
Property B = $4,908,366	500,000	515,000	530,450	546,364	562,754	5,627,540

We should also note that the reversion value at the end of year 5 (REV_5) is assumed to be the same in both cases because the lease on Property A will have expired and the rents can be adjusted up to market rates at the end of that year and every year thereafter, thereby making the reversion value the same as in Case B from year 6 into the future. Therefore, from year 5 on, cash flows are assumed to be the same in both cases and will produce the same *REV* at that time. We assume that the same required return of 13 percent is to be earned on both properties. However, note that both the present value and "going in" cap rates for both sales are very different. After discounting, we show a value of $4.46 million for A versus $4.91 million for B or a difference of about $450,000. Furthermore, the cap rates are .09 for Property A and .102 for Property B, respectively. One point to be made then is, if a property is under consideration for purchase (say Property C) and it is highly comparable to both Properties A and B, but very little information is available on the existing leases for A and B, then using cap rates from either sale could produce very different estimates of value. Indeed, if the *NOI* for Property C was $450,00, then depending on which cap rate was chosen, the estimated value could range from ($450,000 ÷ .09), or $5,000,000, to ($450,000 ÷ .102), or $4,411,765. This would be a difference of $588,235. Therefore, it is *important* when selecting comparable properties for valuation purposes, to be certain that *in addition* to the physical and locational characteristics of the properties, the contents of *existing leases* on such comparables are also very similar to the lease contents of the property under consideration for purchase.

Basic Investment Analysis—Apartment Properties

We begin our discussion of the necessary components for basic investment analysis by considering Waterfall Court Apartments, a luxury apartment complex being offered for sale by M&M Realty on behalf of the seller, Georgia Limited Partnership. M&M has provided us with offering material which requires that we sign a **confidentiality agreement** in which we agree not to divulge any information provided to us regarding Waterfall Court to other parties. M&M Realty will serve as the exclusive agent for Georgia L.P. and will provide any additional information regarding the offering to all potential buyers.

Exhibit 9–3 provides information on the location, number, and mix of units contained in the property.[3] Our goal is to provide the reader with the type of information that should be included in the preliminary competitive financial analysis of this property.

Exhibit 9–4 provides the broker's Statement of Cash Flow. When undertaking an investment analysis, we begin with expected rent per unit as indicated on the broker's statement that must be validated: (1) by using the rent roll that will be supplied by the present owner, (2) with a competitive analysis of other apartment communities in the relevant market area, and (3) by reviewing economic base studies dealing with the market economy. In addition to rent, other cash flows may be realized from covered parking and long-term net leases signed with CCC Corporation, which is using seven units as extended-stay facilities for their executives in training. Also, the mix of units (1,2, and 3) should be reviewed to determine whether this is consistent with what potential renters in the area currently want. A competitive analysis indicates that Waterfall is very similar to comparables 1 and 2 in terms of unit mix, parking, condition, and amenities. Comparable 3 is more densely developed with 1 bedroom apartments and its parking ratios are lower than all others. It appears that the average rent for Waterfall is reasonable relative to the competition.

Other property attributes and calculations that should be considered are whether the number of units per acre (usually set by zoning) are currently the maximum allowable. This may be important if zoning laws have changed and now allow development of 20 or more units per acre. Similarly, the average number of parking spaces (2.0) per unit or 400 spaces, should also be considered relative to the competition. The amenity package should also be considered in relation to expected

[3]Some investors refer to this initial evaluation as part of a "phase one" due diligence process, or a very preliminary financial analysis. A full due diligence investigation will be carried out if this preliminary evaluation appears to be satisfactory to the investor.

EXHIBIT 9–3 Investment Information—Waterfall Court Apartments Projections Made by Power Brokers, Inc.

Name of Property:
Waterfall Court Apartments

Location:
Suburbia, USA

Improvement Description:
A 196-unit luxury garden apartment community located on a major north-south arterial. The property is newly constructed and has a high level of amenities, including 100% direct access garages. All buildings are of two-story construction with 90% brick exteriors.

Seller:
Georgia Ltd. Partnership

Rent and Income Escalation = 4%
Expense, Vacancy and Reserve Escalation = 3%

Principal Amenities:
Direct access garages with automatic garage door openers. Washer/dryer connections (full-size) in all units, swimming pool and heated spa, fitness center, business center, jogging trail, limited access gates, parking spaces: 400/some covered.

Land Area/Density:
10.1561 acres

Unit Mix

1 Bedroom–1 Bath	104 units
2 Bedroom–2 Bath	84 units
3 Bedroom–2 Bath	8 units

Age:
3 years old

Average Monthly Rent:
$1,010/unit ($.95 sq. ft)

Asking Price:
$15,000,000

Waterfall Court Apartment: Preliminary Competitive Market Analysis

		Comparables/Competitors		
	Waterfall	*(1)*	*(2)*	*(3)*
Units per acre:	19.3	20.0	21.0	25.0
Unit mix:				
1BR/1Bath	53%	44%	50%	60%
2BR/2Bath	43%	50%	48%	40%
3BR/3Bath	4%	6%	2%	-0-
Parking spaces/unit:	2.01	2.00	1.95	1.50
Age:	3yrs.	3yrs	3yrs	5yrs
Condition/amenities:	Good	Excellent	Good	Good
Avg. monthly rent per unit:	$1,010	$1,020	$1,000	$950
Price per unit:	$77,577	$76,000	$75,000	$71,000

rents (.95 per square foot monthly) and to what the competition is currently offering in the way of exercise and recreation facilities, TV cable/satellite services, washer/dryer hookups, and so on.

As for expenses, the broker's statement anticipates that on-site expenses will include: salaries for on-site personnel who maintain and "make units ready" for tenants in the community. An operating risk that must be considered by apartment investors is the relative short nature of lease maturities, the potential tenant turnover, and downtime due to vacancies. Experience in large metropolitan areas indicates that as many as 60 percent of apartments in a given property may turn over each year. Turnover-related losses in revenue because of vacancies must be considered in

EXHIBIT 9–4 Waterfall Court Apartments—Cash Flow Projections Provided by Power Brokers, Inc.

	(Yr. 1)	*(Yr. 2)*	*(Yr. 3)*	*(Yr. 4)*	*(Yr. 5)*	*(Yr. 6)*
Income:						
Rental income	$2,201,281	$2,289,332	$2,380,906	$2,476,142	$2,575,187	$2,678,195
Covered garage rents	5,184	5,391	5,607	5,831	6,065	6,307
Net corporate income	32,400	33,696	35,044	36,446	37,903	39,420
Other income	55,172	57,379	59,674	62,061	64,543	67,125
Potential Gross Income (PGI)	$2,294,037	$2,385,798	$2,481,230	$2,580,480	$2,683,699	$2,791,047
Less: Vacancy & collection loss	103,232	106,329	109,518	112,804	116,188	119,674
Effective Gross Income (EGI)	$2,190,805	$2,256,529	$2,371,712	$2,467,676	$2,567,511	$2,671,373
Expenses:						
Salaries	$ 162,970	$ 167,859	$ 172,895	$ 178,082	$ 183,424	$ 188,927
Repair & maintenance cost	154,660	159,300	164,079	169,001	174,071	179,293
Management fee	75,726	77,998	80,338	82,748	85,230	87,787
Administration & general	19,600	20,188	20,794	21,417	22,060	22,722
Utilities	105,000	108,150	111,395	114,736	118,178	121,724
Real estate taxes	248,000	255,440	263,103	270,996	279,126	287,500
Insurance	21,756	22,409	23,081	23,773	24,487	25,221
Advertising	37,400	38,522	39,678	40,868	42,094	43,357
Total Expenses	$ 825,112	$ 849,865	$ 875,361	$ 901,622	$ 928,671	$ 956,531
Less: Reserve for replacements	135,280	139,338	143,519	147,824	152,259	156,827
Net Operating Income (*NOI*)	$1,230,413	$1,267,326	$1,352,832	$1,418,229	$1,486,581	$1,558,015

Broker's indicated "going in" cap rate: $1,230,413 ÷ $15,000,000 = 0.082
Broker's indicated reversion value (*REV* year 5): Year 6 *NOI* ÷ .090 = $17,311,278
Broker's indicated *IRR* on $15,000,000 asking price for 5 years: 11.35% (rounded)

conjunction with recurring repairs and maintenance expenses involved in making units ready for new tenants in making cash flow projections. In our example, they are included in repair and maintenance expense. A management fee for oversight of all leasing, rent collection, tenant relations, and so on, and an off-site administrative fee for payroll, insurance, tax property, and other bookkeeping services necessary for operations have also been estimated. These items should be validated from payment records and/or the appropriate agency or vendors. The broker's estimate for capital outlays has been made at $135,280 in year 1. This amount has been isolated and estimated separately from repairs and maintenance in the cash flow statement because it may not be cyclical in nature like many operating expenses. Contrary to most other property types, tenants occupying apartment properties usually sign leases with maturities of either 6 or 12 months. Furthermore, tenants usually pay for their own utilities, insurance, and so on, which usually relieves the investor of making payments for these items and recovering expenses from tenants. However, there are utility costs for common areas in the apartment community that must be paid by the owner.

Based on projections supplied in Exhibit 9–4, we see that the broker's analysis produces an *IRR* of 11.35 percent based on assumptions that include rent increases of 4 percent per year and an asking price of $15,000,000. Other important information includes a "going in" cap rate of .082 and reversion value of $17,311,278 based on a terminal cap rate of .090 applied to projected *NOI* in year 6.

EXHIBIT 9–5 Waterfall Court—Adjusted Statement of Cash Flow Produced by Adventure Investment Co.

	(Yr. 1)	(Yr. 2)	(Yr. 3)	(Yr. 4)	(Yr. 5)	(Yr. 6)
Income:						
Rental income	$2,201,281	$2,256,313	$2,324,002	$2,405,343	$2,489,529	$2,576,663
Covered garage rents	5,184	5,314	5,473	5,665	5,863	6,068
Net corporate income	32,400	33,210	34,206	35,404	36,643	37,925
Other income	55,172	56,551	58,248	60,287	62,397	64,580
Potential Gross Income (PGI)	$2,294,037	$2,351,388	$2,421,930	$2,506,697	$2,594,431	$2,685,237
Less: Vacancy and collection loss	103,232	106,329	109,518	112,804	116,188	119,674
Effective Gross Income (EGI)	$2,190,805	$2,245,059	$2,312,411	$2,393,893	$2,478,243	$2,565,563
Expenses:						
Salaries	$ 162,970	$ 167,859	$ 172,895	$ 178,082	$ 183,424	$ 188,927
Repair & maintenance cost	154,660	159,300	164,079	169,001	174,071	179,293
Management fee	75,726	77,998	80,338	82,748	85,230	87,787
Administration & general	19,600	20,188	20,794	21,417	22,060	22,722
Utilities	105,000	108,150	111,395	114,736	118,178	121,724
Real estate taxes	248,000	255,440	263,103	270,996	279,126	287,500
Insurance	21,756	22,409	23,081	23,773	24,487	25,221
Advertising	37,400	38,522	39,678	40,868	42,094	43,357
Total Expenses	$ 825,112	$ 849,865	$ 875,361	$ 901,622	$ 928,671	$ 956,531
Less: Reserve for replacements	135,280	139,338	143,519	147,824	152,259	156,827
Net Operating Income (*NOI*)	$1,230,413	$1,255,856	$1,293,531	$1,344,447	$1,397,314	$1,452,205

Indicated reversion value = $1,452,205 ÷ 0.09 = $16,135,611
Indicated price (PV) @ 11.35% required return = $14,171,789
Indicated "going in" cap rate = $1,230,413 ÷ $14,171,789 = 0.087

Data supplied in Exhibit 9–4 provides a starting point for you to make an analysis of Waterfall Court. As Exhibit 9–5 shows, you believe that Waterfall will underperform in the early years of ownership because rent and income escalation will be lower, beginning in year 2 at 2.5 percent, not 4 percent as projected by Power Brokers. You forecast that rent and income growth will increase 3 percent in year 3 and will grow at 3.5 percent thereafter. You agree with Power Brokers as to the rate that expenses are expected to increase for all years. The rental adjustment means that the *NOI* projected in Exhibit 9–4 will be lower each year and the reversion value is also likely to be lower. Note that although the going in cap rate is higher, however, the terminal cap rate appears to be reasonable, as does the expected *IRR* that is indicated by Power Brokers 11.35 percent. Applying these assumptions to rents produces the modified statement shown in Exhibit 9–5. Your modified projections should produce a price of $14,171,789, or 5 percent (rounded) lower than the $15,000,000 price being asked by Power Brokers.

Obviously, you should realize that this analysis is an *initial exercise* in financial and investment analysis. As such, changes in expected rates of appreciation, in estimates for *NOI* each year, in the asking price, and in the number of years used in the analysis will be undertaken as a part of a *more complete analysis*. We will consider changes in many of these relationships in the problems at the end of the chapter. Furthermore, an investor may choose to use mortgage financing to acquire the project in which case the amount of debt and equity required for investment will also become important in the analysis. This, as well as interest and depreciation deductions and taxes are also relevant. These subjects will be discussed in more depth in the chapters that follow.

Basic Investment Analysis—Office Properties

We begin this section by considering a very basic property summary being evaluated by Adventure Properties.

Rock Falls Office Park is located in Southwestern City and is described in Exhibit 9–6. The asking price for the investment is $23,500,000. All information has been compiled in an offering made available from Zebar Realty Associates, a brokerage firm in Southwestern City representing the seller. As the agent/broker for the seller, Zebar Realty has provided us with a diskette containing confidential and detailed lease summaries for all tenants. Zebar also stands ready to answer questions or to obtain additional information from the seller regarding any aspect of the property. Essentially, this office property consists of five buildings situated on 18 acres, containing 262,580 square feet of *rentable* space, currently leased and occupied by eight tenants. ABC Capital is the largest, occupying 161,641 square feet. A summary of pertinent lease information in Exhibit 9–6 shows the number of years remaining on each lease and the general credit quality of each tenant. It is important to note that about 60 percent of rentable space occupied by ABC Capital is scheduled for lease renewal four years from now, and ABC is a tenant with a very high credit rating.

- ABC Capital—handles processing and billing for a full range of branded credit cards offered by third party companies. (AA credit) Net lease, with passthrough of pro rata share of property taxes.
- Entity Mortgage—provides single-family residential mortgage financing in the niche market of reverse mortgages and home equity loans. (A credit)
- U.S. Meetings—founded in 1962, designs and implements corporate meeting and incentive programs for clients ranging from privately owned business to large multinational corporations. (bank reference—positive)
- Brink Systems—founded in 1991. A national provider of electronic payment, cash dispensing and e-commerce services. Processes transactions for more than 50,000 merchants and at over 6,000 ATM locations nationwide. (bank reference—positive)
- Feerless—service company for automated/electronic scales. In business for 15 years. (good credit)
- Café Royal—headquarters location for popular restaurant chains concentrated in the Southwest. (credit check pending)
- Cyber Image—computer consulting firm providing web page construction and related services. In business for 3 years. (bank reference—positive)
- Information Resources—provides electronic library systems to public and corporate users. In business one year. (credit check pending)

Exhibit 9–7 provides financial data relative to leases signed by tenants occupying space in Rock Falls Office Park. Note that the lease for the anchor tenant, ABC

EXHIBIT 9–6 Rock Falls Office Park—Property Summary—Offering Broker: Zebar Realty

Location: Suburban Office Submarket 20 miles north of Southwestern City, USA.
Size: 262,580 rentable square feet. Year built: 10 years ago.
Configuration: 5 buildings on 18 acres, 1,050 surface parking spaces.
Current Occupancy: 98%.
Quality of Construction: B grade, precise concrete panel, exposed aggregate finish, reflective glass panels.
Other: Good freeway access.
Asking Price: $23,500,000.

Tenant Lease Data	*Rentable Square Feet*	*Percent of Total Space*	*Years to Expiration*
Vacant	5,500	2.1%	-
Feerless, Inc.	4,600	1.8	2
Cafè Royal, Inc.	3,025	1.2	2
Entity Mortgage	31,100	11.8	3
Brink Systems, Inc.	14,226	5.4	4
ABC Capital	161,641	61.6	4
Information Resources	4,162	1.6	5
Cyber Image	9,671	3.7	6
U.S. Meetings	28,655	10.9	9
Total rentable square feet	262,580	100.0%	-

Capital, calls for a *net* payment of $12.50 per square foot with an escalator of 3 percent per year. In addition, ABC must reimburse the property owner for its pro rata share of property taxes. The remaining tenants have signed *gross* leases for $17.00 per square foot, which is much higher than ABC's rent. However, for gross leases, an expense stop is included whereby the property owner pays up to $9.00 per square foot in operating expenses each year. Tenants must pay all expenses in excess of $9.00 per square foot.

The pro forma statement of cash flow for the base year as developed by Zebar Realty is shown in Exhibit 9–8. Some of the more important relationships in the exhibit include total revenue which is comprised of base rents for all 5 buildings, less vacancies, which produces effective gross income (EGI). EGI is expected to increase at 3 percent per year. Regarding expenses, the net lease agreement with ABC Capital calls for a "pass-through" for property taxes based on the percentage of square footage that it occupies in the project. This will result in a recovery of $153,897 of the entire $250,000 tax bill.

Operating expenses total $954,390 and recoveries from gross lease tenants total $95,439 during year 1. Given that total operating expenses per square foot for buildings occupied by tenants with gross leases are expected to be $10.00 ($954,390 ÷ 95,439 sq. ft.) and the expense stop is $9.00, it means that $1.00 × 95,439 sq. ft. or $95,439 will be recovered by the owner from those tenants during year 1. ABC Capital will pay all operating expenses attributable to its space *directly.* Based on Zebar's projections, if $23,500,000 is paid for the property, the investor will earn a 13.8 percent *IRR*.

EXHIBIT 9–7 Rock Falls Office Park—Financial Data—Projections by Zebar Realty

Analysis Period: 5 years

Net Rentable Area Occupied:

Building 1 (single story)	63,987 square feet
Building 2 (single story)	53,593
Building 3 (single story)	44,061
Building 4 (single story)	34,612
Building 5 (single story)	60,827
Total occupied	257,080
Vacant (buildings 4 and 5)	5,500
Total rentable space	262,580 square feet

Leases/Rents:

Buildings 4,5	$17.00 gross with 3% step-ups (95,439)
Buildings 1,2, and 3	$12.50 net with 3% step-ups (161,641)

Real Estate Taxes:
$250,000, growing at 3% per annum.

Operating Expenses:
Currently $10.00 per square foot on 95,439 square feet occupied by gross lease tenants, growing at 3% per annum.

Expense Recoveries:
Expense stop, $9.00 per year (fixed) on gross leases only.

Expected Property Value Escalation:
4% per year, $REV_5 = \$28{,}591{,}343$.

Reserve for Replacements:
$50,000 year 1, increasing by $10,000 annually.

You have been asked to make an analysis of this investment. You have investigated exhibit 9–8 carefully and have begun to adjust the statement provided by Zebar. Your property management team that has just returned from a visit to the property has advised you that more extensive repairs and improvements will be required than the amounts projected by Zebar as reserve for replacements in Exhibit 9–8. For example, $100,000 will have to be expended immediately if the property is acquired. Amounts shown in Exhibit 9–9 will have to be expended *in addition* to the amounts projected by Zebar. Further, your accounting/financial staff advises you that amounts projected for nonreimbursable management fees are probably too low and should be increased by an additional $40,000 in year 1 and will escalate at 3 percent thereafter.

Both of these adjustments are made and shown in Exhibit 9-9. Furthermore, you believe that the 4 percent appreciation rate used by Zebar for the property value is too aggressive and should be lowered to 3 percent which is more consistent with rent growth. You also believe that because of the number of existing leases involved, the use of cap rates from comparable sales is not reliable. Therefore, you have chosen to estimate a property appreciation rate in lieu of a terminal cap rate to determine the reversion value (*REV*). Also, the reversion value based on the property appreciation rate should be based on the final transaction price paid for the property and not the asking price of $23,500,000. The procedure for finding the present value of Rock Falls is indicated in Exhibit 9–9.

EXHIBIT 9–8 Rock Falls Office Park–Cash Flow Projections Provided by Zebar Realty

	(Yr. 1)	*(Yr. 2)*	*(Yr. 3)*	*(Yr. 4)*	*(Yr. 5)*
Revenue:					
Bldg. 1, 2, 3 (161,641 sf)	$2,020,512	$2,081,127	$2,143,561	$2,207,868	$2,274,104
Bldg. 4, 5 (100,939 sf)	1,715,963	1,767,442	1,820,465	1,875,079	1,931,331
Potential Gross Income (PGI)	$3,736,475	$3,848,569	$3,964,026	$4,082,947	$4,205,435
Less: Vacancy (5,500 sf)	93,500	96,305	99,194	102,170	105,235
Effective Gross Income (EGI)	$3,642,975	$3,752,264	$3,864,832	$3,980,777	$4,100,201
Expenses:					
Operating expenses*	$ 954,390	$ 983,022	$1,012,512	$1,042,888	$1,074,174
Property taxes	250,000	257,500	265,225	273,182	281,377
Leasing, advertising & other†	209,289	215,568	222,035	228,696	235,465
Administration‡	110,000	113,300	116,699	120,200	123,806
Income before recoveries	$2,119,296	$2,182,875	$2,248,361	$2,315,812	$2,385,378
Add: Recoveries					
Operating expenses	95,439	124,071	153,561	189,936	215,223
Property taxes	154,000	158,620	163,379	168,280	173,328
Less: Reserve for replacements	50,000	60,000	70,000	80,000	90,000
Net Operating Income (*NOI*):	$2,318,735	$2,405,566	$2,495,301	$2,594,028	$2,683,929

Broker asking price: $23,500,000
Broker indicated "going in" cap rate: $2,318,735 ÷ $23,500,000 = .0987
Broker indicated *IRR:* 13.8%

*Includes utilities, security, management, repairs and maintenance and other on-site costs.
†Includes leasing, commissions and promotion (not recoverable).
‡Includes off-site expenses for legal, accounting, asset management overhead and other costs (not recoverable).

You show that the results of the adjustments made in Exhibit 9–9 indicate that if Adventure is to earn a target 14 percent required return, the offer should be $19,843,668. This offer is based on a present value of $19,943,668 less $100,000 in repairs that we would make immediately after closing.

Summary

The goal of the above analysis has been to provide a *very basic* example of how an office property being offered for sale may be analyzed by an investor. In general, projections made by the broker are based on information provided by the seller. A prospective buyer must analyze these projections, question the broker, and review lease agreements. This will help to establish rents and expenses based on the operation of the property. Expenses must be categorized as (1) those that are the obligation of the owner, (2) those that will be paid directly by tenants, and (3) those that will be recovered from tenants. When making the analysis, you should identify additional expenses that are not recoverable as they will be the responsibility of the owner-investor. You should also identify any major outlays that may be required because of deferred maintenance or because items have worn out. Estimates of property and rent escalation rates must be reviewed and evaluated based on market research and economic base analysis. Finally, you must establish a required rate of return. Adjustments to the projected operating statements can then be incorporated and an estimate of investment value can be made.

EXHIBIT 9–9 Rock Falls Office Park—Adjusted Statement of Cash Flow Produced by Adventure Investment Co.

Explanation:

a. Reserve for replacements estimates by the Brokers are too low. *Additional* capital outlays expected by Adventure are:

at Acquisition	\$100,000	year 4	\$322,000
year 2	\$110,000	year 5	\$93,000
year 3	\$141,000		

b. Escalation in property value should be 3%, not 4%. Also, escalation should be projected based on the final offering price, not \$23,500,000.

c. Off-site administration costs (not reimbursable) are too low. Initial level should be increased by \$40,000 with 3% annual increases.

d. Adventure's required rate of return = 14%, which is close to 13.8%, or Zebar's estimated *IRR*.

Adjustments:

	(Yr. 1)	*(Yr. 2)*	*(Yr. 3)*	*(Yr. 4)*	*(Yr. 5)*
Zebar Projected *NOI*	\$2,318,735	\$2,405,566	\$2,495,301	\$2,594,301	\$2,683,929
Less:					
Administrative costs	40,000	41,200	42,436	43,709	45,020
Additional capital outlays		110,000	141,000	322,000	93,000
Net cash flow	\$2,278,735	\$2,254,366	\$2,311,865	\$2,228,592	\$2,545,909

Discount rate = 14%

Present value of property: $PV = PVNCF + PVREV$

$$PV = \$7{,}935{,}765 + PVREV$$
$$= \$7{,}935{,}765 + [(1.03)^5\,(PV)(IFPV\$1, 14\%, 5\ yrs)]$$
$$= \$7{,}935{,}765 + 1.159274\,(PV)(.519369)$$
$$= \$7{,}935{,}765 + .602091\,(PV)$$
$$0.397909\,PV = \$7{,}935{,}765$$
$$PV = \$19{,}943{,}668$$

Adventure offer price: *PV* of \$19,943,668 − \$100,000, or \$19,843,668

Adventure "going in" cap rate = \$2,278,735 ÷ \$19,843,668 = .1143

Adventure indicated *IRR* after repairs and acquisition expenses of \$300,000: 13.72%

Adventure reversion value = $REV = \$19{,}943{,}668(1.03)^5 = \$23{,}120{,}177$

Basic Investment Analysis—Retail Properties

The following is an introductory analysis of retail property investment. You have been asked to perform a preliminary analysis for Adventure Investment Company. Exhibit 9–10 provides a summary of information for the Power Community Retail Center, a partially enclosed shopping mall with 270,000 of rentable square feet in Anytown, USA. The data have been provided by Producer Brokerage Associates on behalf of the owner who wants to sell the property as soon as possible.

Essentially, the property is occupied by 50 in-line retail tenants, 25 retail/ service tenants (insurance agent, travel service, etc.) and one major anchor grocer tenant. As Exhibit 9–10 shows, the grocer-anchor tenant pays only \$8.00 per square foot in rent.

EXHIBIT 9–10 Power Community Retail Center—Provided by Producer Brokerage Co.

Location: Anytown, USA
Description: 270,000 sq. ft. rentable area, grocery anchored, 16 acres. A partially enclosed, community shopping center anchored by a Coger grocery store whose lease is up for renewal this year. Some retail/service tenants occupy space on the second level toward the rear of the property. Various retail pads are available for lease or purchase and are located on the periphery of the property. Kiosks are located in enclosed area of mallway and are leased to vendors of convenience/impulse merchandise.

Property Information	*Anchor Tenant*	*In-Line Tenants*	*Outparcels, Kiosks*	*Retail/Service/ Other Tenants*
Square feet (rentable)	80,000	120,000	10,000	60,000
Number of tenants	1	50	10	25
Avg. base rent (net)	$8.00	$15.00	$20.00	$14.00
Rent escalator (expected)	0	3%	3%	3%
CAM charges	$1.50	Calculated	Net leases	Calculated
Operating expenses (escalator)	-	3%	N/A	-
Other recoveries (taxes, etc)	0	Prorated	N/A	Prorated
Remaining average lease terms	1 year	3 years	2 years	3 years

Broker's property value escalator = 4%
Broker's overage rents escalator = 3%

The owner of the mall indicates that average *sales per square foot* for all retail activity in the mall is now $425 which he believes justifies the average $15.00 per square foot rents for **in-line tenants.** Other retail/service tenants pay an average base rent of $14.00 per square foot. Some tenants have negotiated leases with the owner that call for **overage rents,** which are negotiated when a tenant believes the base rent to be too high. This may be true in spite of the location of the space in the center, its drawing power, and average sales per square foot cited by the owner. In essence these tenants desire the property owner to take part of the business risk and, in exchange, are willing to pay the owner a base rent plus a percentage of their sales revenue. The overage rent calculation is *negotiated* between the landlord and the tenant and is based on an agreed-on **breakpoint sales volume,** above which the property owner will receive a percentage of sales revenue as additional rent. Of course, the mall owner has the right to receive periodic certified statements of sales revenue from the tenant and to audit accounting records should any disputes occur.

In addition to rents, retail leases also call for the anchor tenant and all other tenants to contribute to **common area maintenance** (CAM) expenses. Because retail properties contain very large public walkways, parking, and other facilities (common areas), expenses will be incurred by the owner to maintain, heat, and cool such areas, as well as to provide for the security and maintenance of parking lots and other areas in the mallways. It should be noted that in addition to a lower base rent, the anchor tenant has also negotiated a CAM charge of $1.50 per square foot per year. In-line and retail/service tenants are required to pay the remaining CAM charges. It should be apparent that in order for an investor in a retail property to earn a competitive return on investment, the rent and CAM "discount" enjoyed by the anchor tenant must be offset by rent and CAM "premiums" paid by in-line tenants. These latter tenants must judge whether or not such premiums are warranted by customer traffic, sales per square foot, and other benefits. If the anchor tenant is given too high a discount on rent and CAM charges, amounts that in-line tenants may be asked to pay could be too high relative to the margins they earn on their merchandise, thereby making the mall relatively unattractive as a place of business. These tenants may choose to rent space in a competing retail location.

Exhibit 9–11 contains a pro forma statement of cash flows estimated by the broker as a part of the investment analysis package being marketed for Power Community Center. The estimated gross potential income is the sum of base rents, plus overage from selected retail tenants, plus lease income from the retail/service tenants. The latter group pay rents based on a net lease agreement. However, there is also recovery paid to the owner for their share of CAM and property taxes. In addition to base rents, and overage paid to the mall owner, some miscellaneous income is also received during Christmas and other holidays from vendors who temporarily operate during those periods.

Total expense outlays paid by the property owner are expected to be $2,600,000, some of which is not reimbursable. These outlays are expected to increase at 3 percent per year. Amounts includable as CAM charges for heating/cooling, security, property taxes, insurance, and so on, associated with operations including the common areas of the mall should total $1,440,000. The anchor's share of $120,000 leaves $1,320,000, or $7.33 per square foot of CAM charges for all nonanchor tenants. Note that CAM charges usually include operating expenses and repair and

EXHIBIT 9–11 Power Retail Center—Cash Flow Projections Provided by Producer Brokerage

	(Yr. 1)	*(Yr. 2)*	*(Yr. 3)*	*(Yr. 4)*	*(Yr. 5)*
Rents					
Anchor	$ 640,000	$ 640,000	$ 640,000	$ 640,000	$ 640,000
In-line tenants	1,800,000	1,854,000	1,909,620	1,966,909	2,025,916
Office tenants	840,000	865,200	891,156	917,891	945,427
Kiosks	200,000	206,000	212,180	218,545	225,102
Overage	125,000	128,750	132,613	136,591	140,689
Miscellaneous	20,000	20,600	21,218	21,855	22,510
Potential Gross Income (PGI)	$3,625,000	$3,714,550	$3,806,787	$3,901,790	$3,999,644
Vacancy	50,000	51,500	53,045	54,636	56,275
Effective Gross Income (EGI)	3,575,000	3,663,050	3,753,742	3,847,154	3,943,368
Less: Operating expenses	2,600,000	2,678,000	2,758,340	2,841,090	2,926,323
Add: Reimbursables	1,440,000	1,483,200	1,527,696	1,573,527	1,620,733
Net Operating Income (*NOI*)	$2,415,000	$2,468,250	$2,523,098	$2,579,590	$2,637,778
Breakdown of CAM Charges					
Total expenses subject to reimbursement:	1,440,000	1,483,200	1,527,696	1,573,527	1,620,733
Less: Anchors share 80,000 × $1.50	120,000	120,000	120,000	120,000	120,000
In-line/other tenants' share of CAM	$1,320,000	$1,363,200	$1,407,696	$1,453,527	$1,500,733

Broker's indicated property value escalation = $25,000,000 $(1.04)^5$ = $30,416,323 in year 5
Broker's indicated *IRR:* 13.4%
Broker's indicated cap rate (going in) $2,415,000 ÷ $25,000,000 = 0.097

maintenance only and should not include outlays for major capital repairs such as roofs, replacement for HVAC equipment and so on.

After carefully analyzing the broker's statement you believe that certain adjustments must be made. For example, your property management staff has provided you with a statement that shows additional outlays for major capital items and improvements that are not included as a part of the broker's statement for Power Center (see Exhibit 9–11). These costs are considerably more than the average reserve for replacements estimated by Producer Brokerage, particularly during years 2 and 3. These costs could be related to reconstruction and repair of items such as parking lots and garages, HVAC, roofs, and tenant improvements; outlays are estimated for the year in which they are expected to occur.

As indicated in Exhibit 9–11, the average lease term for in-line tenants is relatively short, therefore an investor should be particularly aware of the high likelihood of tenant turnover, particularly in years 2 and 3. Estimates shown in Exhibit 9–12 reflect this likelihood with higher provisions for tenant improvements and leasing commissions included as other outlays in those years. In spite of the turnover however, overage and operating expenses are expected to be in the ranges indicated in Exhibit 9–12 for the forecast period. Additional investigation leads you to believe

EXHIBIT 9–12 Power Retail Center Revised Cash Flow Projections—Adventure Investment Company

	(Yr. 1)	*(Yr. 2)*	*(Yr. 3)*	*(Yr. 4)*	*(Yr. 5)*
Rents					
Anchor	$ 560,000	$ 560,000	$ 560,000	$ 560,000	$ 560,000
In-line tenants	1,800,000	1,854,000	1,909,620	1,966,909	2,025,916
Office tenants	840,000	865,200	891,156	917,891	945,427
Kiosks	200,000	206,000	212,180	218,545	225,102
Overage	125,000	128,750	132,613	136,591	140,689
Miscellaneous	20,000	20,600	21,218	21,855	22,510
Potential Gross Income (PGI)	$3,545,000	$3,634,550	3,726,787	$3,821,790	$3,919,644
Vacancy	50,000	51,500	53,045	54,636	56,275
Effective Gross Income (EGI)	$3,495,000	$3,583,050	$3,673,742	$3,767,154	$3,863,368
Less: Operating expenses	2,600,000	2,678,000	2,758,340	2,841,090	2,926,323
Add: Reimbursables	1,400,000	1,483,200	1,527,696	1,573,527	1,620,733
Net Operating Income (*NOI*):	$2,335,000	$2,388,250	$2,443,098	$2,499,590	$2,557,778
Capital outlays and other	155,000	367,270	668,350	70,000	71,900
Net cash flow	$2,180,000	$2,020,980	$1,774,748	$2,429,590	$2,485,878

Adventure Investment Company Analysis:

Indicated price @ 13% required return:

$$
\begin{aligned}
PV &= PVNCF + PVREV \\
&= \$7{,}581{,}265 + PV(1.03)^5(IFPV\$1{,}13\%,\ 5\text{yrs.}) \\
&= \$7{,}581{,}266 + PV(1.159274)(.542760) \\
&= \$7{,}581{,}267 + (.629208)PV \\
(.370792)\ PV &= \$7{,}581{,}267 \\
PV &= \$20{,}446{,}145 \text{ (indicated price)}
\end{aligned}
$$

that the anchor tenant will demand that its base rent be reduced to $7.00 per square foot and its CAM reduced to $1.00 per square foot effective immediately, or it will move out. A market survey indicates that this pattern of rent is competitive with that of other large, anchor grocer-tenants are paying in comparable locations. You also believe that the expected sale price after a 5-year period of ownership is too aggressive and should be lowered to 3 percent. These adjustments are made and the cash flow is adjusted as shown in Exhibit 9–12. Your supervisor has indicated that if Adventure purchases Power Center, it must offer a price that will result in a 13 percent required return. Based on the adjustments made to the broker's statement, you estimate that the offering price should be $20,446,145. Note that this price is considerably lower than the asking price of $25,000,000.

Basic Investment Analysis—Warehouse Properties

The final illustration of an investment analysis of a property type in this chapter deals with industrial warehouse properties. This property type is different from office and retail properties in many ways. Exhibit 9–13 provides a summary of important data for Northern Distribution Center, a large distribution/warehouse facility located in Mid City, USA, being marketed by Industrial Brokers, Inc.

The primary focus of this analysis will be on a *single tenant* as opposed to a **multitenanted property** such as was the case in our previous examples. Although our example will focus on a single tenant, the reader should be able to modify a warehouse investment to reflect multiple tenants occupying the site. In our example, Anything.Dot.Com is the sole tenant of the property and much of the focus will be on the tenant; the real estate will tend to be secondary in the evaluation. Why is this so? A careful analysis of the lease contents reveals that it is a *triple net* or *absolute net lease*. This means that Anything.Dot.Com is responsible for all expenses associated with operating its own business and all expenses associated with operating, maintaining, and making material repairs for the building and property. The rents paid by Anything are the sole source of cash flow to the owner of this property. Because of the nature of the lease agreement, net operating income and cash flow are equivalent in this example. The lease has a term of 15 years with two rent renewal periods of 5 years each. Obviously, the value of these renewals depends on what market rents will be at the end of years 10 and 15.

Triple net leases represent a relatively stable cash flow to property owners. In a sense, cash flow from such a lease can be thought of as being similar to that from a less-than-investment-grade corporate bond. Cash flows would consist of a base level of income and an escalator, or call option, against future income or appreciation in property values. However, the fixed term of the lease also prohibits the owner from realizing any *interim* market rent increases in excess of base rents, should such market opportunities occur because rents may only be adjusted at designated times. Also, because leases are estates that must be honored by all subsequent property owners, any future sale of this property is made *subject to* the lease terms made with Anything.Dot.Com. This could represent a source of risk to a warehouse investor because the credit rating for Anything could change materially during the term of the lease. For example, an improvement in Anything.Dot.Com's credit would tend to *enhance* the project value. However, should there be a default on the lease or a bankruptcy, this would affect the marketability of the property as delays might occur in removing the tenant from the property and could cause a reduction in property value. Additionally, the real estate would again become the

EXHIBIT 9–13 Northern Distribution Center—Data Provided by Industrial Brokers, Inc.

Location: Mid City, USA
Key Factors:

- A single-story, single-tenant distribution facility located in Mid City. The property was completed 5 years ago. The building contains 164,300 rentable square feet of space.
- The Center is 100% leased to Anything.Dot.Com for fifteen (15) years on an *absolute net lease.* Lease allows for two, five-year rent reviews at market rates.
- The long-term, net leased nature of the property should generate a very stable cash flow stream. Cash flows will significantly increase over the remaining lease term, given the 6.7% step rent increases.
- The building is cross docked and offers 26′–30′ clear heights, 50 × 40 column spacing, 120′ truck courts, asphalt parking for 408 cars, and approximately 5% office finished.
- Asking price: $20,915,000
- Cap rate: .089
- Lease: Absolute triple net. Tenant pays all taxes, repairs, maintenance, utilities, and insurance. All major repairs must be approved by owner.
- Rental and Step-ups: Base: $3.31 per square foot, expected 6.7% escalator in option years 5 and 10 during remaining lease term.
- Expected property value escalation: 2% per year

Net Cash Flow Summary—Northern Distribution Center—Projected by Industrial Brokers, Inc.

Year	*Cash Flow*	*Reversion*
0	–0–	
1	$1,867,853	
2	1,867,853	
3	1,867,853	
4	1,867,853	
5	1,867,853	
6	1,992,977	
7	1,992,977	
8	1,992,977	
9	1,992,977	
10	1,992,977	
11	2,126,530	
12	2,126,530	
13	2,126,530	
14	2,126,530	
15	2,126,530	$25,210,911
16	2,268,982	

Broker indicated *IRR:* 10.0%

Broker indicated terminal cap rate: .09

focal point of attention as brokers attempted to re-lease the space and the maintenance expended by Anything during the lease term would affect its marketability.

Based on a preliminary examination of broker-produced cash flows for the Northern Distribution Center, if: (1) the asking price of $20,915,000 was paid, and (2) the cash flows shown in Exhibit 9–13 and appreciation rate were accurately

EXHIBIT 9–14 Revised Statement of Cash Flow—Northern Distribution Center—Adventure Investment Company

- Revised escalators downward from 6.7% to 5%.
- Increase required return from 10.0% to 11.0%.
- Reversion value in year 15 based on *NOI* in year 16, capitalized at terminal cap rate of .095, higher than "terminal cap rate" indicated on broker statement.

Revised Cash Flows:

Year	*CF*	*Reversion*
0	0	
1	$1,867,833	
2	1,867,833	
3	1,867,833	
4	1,867,833	
5	1,867,833	
6	1,961,225	
7	1,961,225	
8	1,961,225	
9	1,961,225	
10	1,961,225	
11	2,059,286	
12	2,059,286	
13	2,059,286	
14	2,059,286	
15	2,059,286	$22,760,526
16	2,162,250	

Adventure's estimated price (*PV*) = $18,642,433
*NOI year 16 ÷ Terminal cap rate or : $2,162,250 ÷ .095 = REV_{15}

estimated, then an expected *IRR* of 10.00 percent would result. However, based on the modifications shown in Exhibit 9–14, the analyst at Adventure Investments has revised many of the assumptions made by Industrial Property Brokers. The analyst believes that the rent growth is too aggressive, and because of the credit risk posed by Anything.Dot.Com, the required rate of return should be increased to 11 percent. Furthermore, she believes the terminal cap rate should be increased because of the onset of material economic depreciation after 15 years, which will affect the ability of the future operating income potential of the property. When the assumptions are incorporated into the analysis, the price that Adventure will offer for the Northern Distribution Center is $18,642,433. This price reflects Adventure's expectations regarding future income and property growth and meets the target rate of return (11 percent) that it believes is necessary to undertake the investment.

Conclusion

The purpose of this chapter has been to familiarize the reader with lease provisions and operating characteristics generally representative of major property types. The illustrations have shown that regional economic conditions, market supply and demand, lease terms, tenant credit, investment risk, and the ability of property owners to pass through operating costs are all important considerations in income property analysis. Furthermore, the ability to modify and develop pro forma cash flow statements and to undertake a competitive market analysis serve as the foundations for analysis and for estimating an investment value for properties being sought for acquisition. These latter topics are the topic for chapters that follow.

Key Terms

anchor tenant 261
base rent 259
breakpoint sales volume 279
common area maintenance 279
concessions 260
confidentiality agreement 270
CPI adjustment 259
effective rent 264
expense pass-through 260
expense stop 259
free rent 260
gross (full service) lease 259
in-line tenants 279
investment value 278
lease 257
lease concessions 261
lessee 257
lessor 257
load factor 263
market rent 267
multitenanted property 282
net lease 259
noncompete clause 261
overage rents 279
percentage rent 259
radius clause 261
rentable area 263
right of first refusal 262
step-up provisions 259
tenant improvements 261
usable area 262

Questions

1. How does the use of leases shift risk from the lessor to the lessee?
2. What is the difference between an expected rate of return and an actual rate of return?
3. What is the difference between base or face rents and effective rents?

Problems

1. A building owner is evaluating the following alternatives for leasing space in an office building for the next five years:

   Net lease with steps. Rent will be $15 per square foot the first year and will increase by $1.50 per square foot each year until the end of the lease. All operating expenses will be paid by the tenant.

   Net lease with CPI adjustments. The rent will be $16 per square foot the first year. After the first year, the rent will be increased by the amount of any increase in the CPI. The CPI is expected to increase 3 percent per year.

   Gross lease. Rent will be $30 per square foot each year with the lessor responsible for payment of all operating expenses. Expenses are estimated to be $9 during the first year and increase by $1 per year thereafter.

   Gross lease with expense stop and CPI adjustment. Rent will be $22 the first year and increase by the full amount of any change in the CPI after the first year with an expense stop at $9.00 per square foot. The CPI and operating expenses are assumed to change by the same amount as outlined above.

   a. Calculate the effective rent to the owner (after expenses) for each lease alternative using a 10 percent discount rate.

   b. How would you rank the alternatives in terms of risk to the property owner?

   c. Considering your answers to parts (*a*) and (*b*), how would you compare the four alternatives?

2. As CFO for Everything.Com, you are shopping for 5,000 square feet of *usable* office space for 25 of your employees in Center City, USA. A leasing broker shows you space in Apex Atrium, a 10-story multitenanted office building. This building contains 300,000 square feet of gross building area. A total of 45,000 square feet is interior space and is nonrentable. The nonrentable space consists of areas contained in the basement, elevator core, and other mechanical and structural components. An additional 30,000 square feet of common area is the lobby area usable by all tenants. The 5,000 square feet of usable area that you are looking for is on the seventh floor, contains 28,000 square feet of rentable area, and is leased by other tenants who occupy a combined total of 20,000 square feet of usable space. The leasing broker indicated that base rents will be $30 per square foot of *rentable area*.
   a. Calculate total rentable area in the building (excluding lobby).
   b. Calculate the load factor and common area on the seventh floor only.
   c. Calculate the rentable area, including the load factor for common areas on the seventh and the total rent per square foot that will be paid by Everything.Com for the coming year if it chooses to lease the space.
   d. Adjust (*b*) assuming that the owner attempts to increase the load factor for other common areas in the building.
   e. Calculate total rent per square foot, assuming that adjusted load factors are applied to usable area for both the common areas on the seventh floor.
3. Exercise: Refer to Exhibits 9–3, 9-4, and 9–5 regarding Waterfall Court Apartments. Your boss has conducted a second, more careful examination of the property, and believes that your assumptions shown in Exhibit 9–5 are very realistic. However he believes that future capital outlays are still *underestimated* by $10,000 each year and the vacancy and collection losses should be 5.5 percent of potential gross income each year, beginning at $126,172 in year 1.
   a. What will these changes have on expected *NOI* in Exhibit 9–5?
   b. Assuming all changes in (*a*), how much should be offered now for Waterfall Courts if you would earn the same expected *IRR* of 11.37%?
   c. If you believe that after the changes in (*a*) are made, you would earn an *IRR* of 12 percent, what should your offer be?
4. Exercise: Refer to Exhibits 9–6, 9–7, and 9–8 for Rock Falls Office Park. After reviewing your financials in Exhibit 9–9, your boss thinks that operating expenses should begin at $11.00 per square foot and are likely to increase 4 percent per year with no changes in the expense stop. Furthermore, he believes that tenant improvement costs are still underestimated in years 2 and 5 by $50,000 in each year.
   a. What effect will these changes have on the expected cash flow in Exhibits 9–8 and 9–9?
   b. Assuming all changes in (*a*) how much should be offered for Rock Falls Office Park if the same expected *IRR* of 14 percent is to be earned?
   c. What if after all changes in (*a*) are made, you believe that an expected *IRR* of 15 percent should be earned. What would your offer be now?
5. Exercise: Refer to Exhibits 9–10, 9–11, and 9–12 for Power Community Retail Center. Your boss has reviewed your work in Exhibit 9–12 and believes that when its lease is up for renewal, the anchor tenant will demand that its base rent be *reduced* to $6.75 per square foot and its CAM charges be *reduced* to $0.75 per square foot, or it will move out. These rates appear to be consistent with what other anchor tenants are currently paying in comparable shopping centers.
   a. What effect will this have on the *NOI* and net cash flow each year in Exhibit 9-12?
   b. Assuming all changes in (*a*) how much should be offered for Power Retail Center if the same expected *IRR* of 13 percent is to be earned? If you now require an *IRR* of 14 percent, what would you offer?
   c. Assuming that you *must make up this loss in cash flow,* approximately how much would you have to charge all other *in-line* tenants in base rents and CAM charges to offset the loss? (Ignore any effects on outparcels, kiosks, office tenants, etc.)
6. Exercise: Refer to Exhibits 9–13 and 9–14 for the Northern Distribution Center. Your boss has told you to assume that the expected escalator in option years 5 and 10 will only be 4 percent.
   a. What will the new *NOI* be over the term of the lease in Exhibit 9–14?
   b. Assuming all changes in (*a*) and assuming the same reversion value in year 15, how much should be offered for Northern Distribution Center if your required *IRR* is changed to 11 percent?

CHAPTER

10 Investment and Risk Analysis

The investor must consider many variables when acquiring income properties, among them market factors, occupancy rates, tax influences, the level of risk, the amount of debt financing, and the proper procedures to use when measuring return on investment. Lenders are concerned with many of the same questions because these factors affect the value and marketability of the properties being used as collateral for loans. In addition, lenders are concerned with whether properties they finance will generate enough cash flow to cover the loan payments. This chapter provides the framework for analyzing additional issues addressed in many of the remaining chapters in this text.

Motivations for Investing

We have seen that there are many different categories of income property. We now consider why investors and lenders choose investments in one or more of these properties. We first consider the equity investor. The term **equity** refers to funds invested by an "owner" or the person acquiring the property. The particular form of ownership could be any of the freehold estates discussed in Chapter 2. That is, equity funds could be invested in a fee simple estate, a leased fee estate, a leasehold estate, and so forth. We contrast equity funds with debt, which is provided by a lender with the real estate used as collateral for the loan as discussed in Chapter 2.

What motivates the investor to make an equity investment in income properties? First, investors anticipate that market demand for space in the property will be sufficient to produce net income after collecting rents and paying operating expenses. This income constitutes part of an investor's return (before considering taxes and financing costs).

Second, the investor anticipates selling properties after holding them for some period of time. (A discussion regarding how long a property will be held is discussed in Chapter 13.) Investors often expect prices to rise over the holding period, particularly in an inflationary environment. Thus any price increase also contributes to an investor's return.

A third reason for investing in real estate is to achieve diversification. By this we mean that most investors want to hold a variety of different types of investments such as stocks, bonds, money market funds, and real estate.

A final reason for investing in real estate, which may be more important to some investors than others, is the preferential tax benefits that may result. Because of favorable tax treatment of real estate, investors paid little or no taxes on returns from real estate investments for many years. Although many of these favorable tax benefits have been eliminated over the years, understanding real estate tax law is still important. Investors must be able to understand changes in such laws and interpret their interaction on rents and real estate values. As tax laws change, investor decisions regarding purchase prices, how much financing should be used, and when to sell the property are also affected.

Motivations for Investing in Income Properties

1. Rate of return.
2. Price appreciation.
3. Diversification.
4. Tax benefits.

Real Estate Market Characteristics and Investment Strategies

Based on our discussion of economic base analysis and local supply and demand analysis in previous chapters, it should be evident that expected market conditions are important when making estimates of future cash flows. For example, if supply and demand for a given property type are considered to be out of balance and these conditions are expected to persist, the effects on vacancies and rents should be taken into account in forecasts of cash flows. If done properly, estimates of value and investment returns will reflect these expectations. What follows is a description of: (1) the cyclical nature of the real estate market and (2) a description of various *investment styles* that are widely used in all segments of the investment community (stocks, bonds, real estate, and so on). As the reader will come to realize, descriptions used to identify these "styles of investing" usually correspond to some underlying expectations regarding market conditions. We *do not advocate* any one, or combination of such investment styles. Nonetheless, these terms and descriptions are widely used by investment professionals to help classify and describe conditions in investment markets, and the reader should be aware of what they are.

"The Real Estate Cycle"

It may be useful at this point to discuss the cyclical nature of the real estate industry as background material for the more specific investment styles and strategies we will discuss. Some underlying facts regarding the real estate industry are (1) It is a very large market, both in terms of the number of properties and square footage, (2) It is highly competitive, and (3) Ownership is highly fragmented, that is, no one owner or developer controls a significant share of the real estate market in major cities in the United States.

It is also a fact that when local real estate owners and investors sense that vacancy rates are declining and rents are rising, it generally implies that the amount of leaseable space is also declining. As a result, more development may be feasible. As a result, developers begin to conduct highest and best use studies for specific sites and also analyze markets to determine if additional space, if developed, can be leased profitably. Because many competing developers may sense this opportunity simultaneously, they may all begin to obtain financing and develop at once in order to satisfy the demand. Even though there may be a definite need for additional space, the potential for overdevelopment will exist as each developer rushes to deliver additional space to the market before competitors. There is no way to determine exactly how much space should be developed because the depth and extent of demand is difficult to predict. As a result, the real estate industry is sometimes said to be prone to periodic *cycles* of "overdevelopment." Because of the highly competitive nature of the industry and its difficulty in forecasting demand, there are certain times when excess supply is unintentionally produced thereby increasing vacancy rates, reducing rents, and causing volatility in property values.

The cyclical nature of this market pattern is shown in Exhibit 10–1, which shows a *hypothetical cycle* for all property types relative to a "normal" level of occupancy for each property type. All points above the normal occupancy range for each property type indicate a condition of high occupancy and rising rents. This is a condition when further development is likely. All areas below the normal range indicate a condition of low occupancy and the potential for declining rents, a condition not suitable for development.[1] To illustrate, based on the pattern shown in Exhibit 10–1, apartment properties are in a recovery phase of the cycle after experiencing a condition either of excess supply or lack of demand. As implied in the exhibit, this property class is expected to continue to "recover" as the occupancy rate improves and demand increases relative to supply.

On the other hand, office properties are shown to be in a condition of high occupancy due to either excess demand or a shortage of rentable space. This market imbalance is expected to result in rising occupancy and higher rents. Therefore, this market segment may be expected to undergo future development. Warehouse properties appear to be in a well-balanced condition. No material change in occupancy or rents is expected and, as a result, no unexpected amount of development is likely. Retail properties, however, are in a declining occupancy phase of the cycle due to either an excessive amount of space for lease or lack of demand. The graph also indicates that retail occupancy is expected to decline further.

In summary, Exhibit 10–1 is intended to provide a framework of the supply/demand balance for each property type at one point in time. Based on the current stage in this cycle, investors considering investing in apartments should anticipate a period of vacancies and soft rents in cash flow projections even though this market is in recovery. Office property investors should expect to enjoy a period of low vacancies and higher than normal rents. However, these investors should also expect more office development and, therefore competition that will eventually result in rents, occupancies, and cash flows trending back to normal levels. Warehouse investors should not expect material changes in vacancies or rents. Retail property investors, on the other hand, should expect deteriorating conditions to continue and should forecast a continuing decline and an eventual turning point in cash flow forecasts. The time period associated with the cycle in Exhibit 10–1 is very difficult to forecast. It may be expected to exist only for a short period and must be continuously reevaluated as (1) new construction is being completed, or (2) the market experiences an unanticipated surge in demand for space. While the illustration in Exhibit 10–1 is very simplistic, it does serve as a starting point for investors in

[1]It should not be inferred from this exhibit that the normal level of occupancy shown in the graph is exactly the same for each property. This is a conceptual exhibit and is intended to depict general market conditions.

EXHIBIT 10–1 "The Real Estate Cycle"

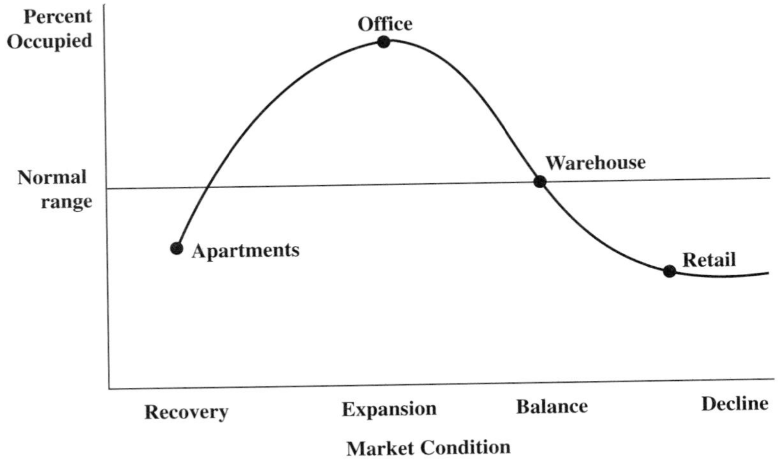

understanding the nature of the supply/demand balance by property type and should help the reader understand the general strategies that follow.

Investment Strategies

Thus far, we have approached the subject of pricing and investing in properties by stressing that investors should carefully make forecasts of future cash flows given the expected market supply, demand, and capital market conditions. This section contains a summary of some strategies or styles that are followed by real estate investors and portfolio managers. These styles are chosen with the intent of realizing superior investment performance. Think about these styles in conjunction with the discussion of the real estate cycle and formulate a critique of each approach. Exhibit 10–2 provides you with a general perspective on real estate market cycles and investment strategies. It should be obvious that many of these strategies overlap and may include combinations of one or more strategies. For example, an investor may combine a sector strategy with a timing strategy in that sector. Nevertheless, these strategies may be helpful in understanding much of the industry terminology that is used when describing the current state of a real estate market and the motivations of those seeking real estate investments.

Making Investments: Projecting Cash Flows

We will now look more closely at how investors and lenders project expected cash flows when they consider investing in income-producing properties. This will be followed by a discussion of various performance measures used to determine the attractiveness of a particular property.

Office Building Example

To illustrate how to make a projection of income, we consider the possible purchase of a 100,000-square-foot office building by an investor for $8.5 million. Construction

EXHIBIT 10–2 Investment Styles Used by Real Estate Investors—Sector Investing

A. Property Sector Investing

This style is based on the belief that over the long term, based on economic and demographic research, one *property type* will outperform other property sectors. For example, if research shows that prospects for the office sector are excellent and that this sector will outperform the retail, apartment, and warehouse property sectors over the long term, then an investor would specialize in office properties as a preferred sector investment. After the sector is chosen, then specific properties in specific cities and locations would be acquired. (This style is analogous to mutual funds that are created to invest only in stocks in specific industry sectors such as the computer industry, energy, and Internet companies.)

B. Contrarian Investing

This strategy is based on the premise that some major economic, technological, or other event will make the investment outlook for a given property type poor and "out of favor" among investors. Contrarians believe that investors tend to overreact to negative news and tend to oversell out-of-favor properties. For example, many investors now believe that because of direct marketing, the growth in e-commerce may have a very negative effect on retail properties. If the majority of investors believe that retail investments will perform poorly and sell them, a contrarian may wait until these retail properties become available at very low prices, then *purchase* them with the expectation that after other investors realize that this property sector has been oversold, a price recovery will occur.

C. Market Timing

This strategy is based on the belief that with an understanding of the stage of each property type in the real estate cycle and future economic conditions, some investors have the ability to predict when to buy or sell properties. For example in Exhibit 10–1, if investors believe that occupancy and rents will definitely improve and that the apartment market has definitely passed the bottom of its cycle and is in a recovery phase, then apartments would become a target investment for a "market timer." Similarly, if further decline is expected in the retail property sector in a given market *because of excess supply,* a market timer may attempt to "time or wait" to enter this market when it appears the excess supply of space is about to be eliminated, and then acquire properties in the hope of realizing a profit as market prices cycle upward. (Note that this strategy may be different from contrarians who tend to respond to external events such as e-commerce, while timers tend to emphasize current supply/demand or cyclical conditions in their evaluation of property markets.) Many market timers also believe that they should sell when a specific property type and market reaches a peak and buy a different property type in a *different* market. This variant of timing is sometimes referred to as a property sector *rotation strategy.*

D. Growth Investing

This strategy is based on "discovering," through research, those properties in markets that are likely to experience significant or above average *appreciation in value.* Investors in these properties believe that economic conditions favor demand for specific property types in specific growth markets. This investment style is heavily dependent on the value of market research and the ability to understand changes in the economic environment/technology, and its effects on all real estate sectors. For example, growth in e-commerce and technology may be expected to *favor* warehouse properties in specific strategic geographic locations (such as those discussed in Chapter 8). A growth investor would search those strategic locations to invest in warehouse properties. These properties would be purchased with the expectation that as more investors discover these markets and properties, they will make investments and drive prices up, thereby producing superior appreciation in property values. Investors using the strategy should expect to bear more risk than average as these markets are apt to expand and contract in concert with the industries that are driving the demand for space.

E. Value Investing

This strategy is based more on a "tried and true" performance approach where research is directed toward finding those properties that have been "overlooked" by investors. Based on careful research efforts, value investors try to identify properties with the ability to produce greater than expected income, and appreciation. For example, investors may prefer to invest in office properties that are located in central business districts and leased on a long-term basis to many large corporate tenants. In this case, rental income is more assured as tenants are large tenants with good credit histories. Because many leases may be about ready to expire, the ability of landlords to increase rents may be good. In trying to execute this strategy, investors attempt to focus on properties that have been overlooked by other investors and, therefore, appear to be undervalued.

F. Strategy as to Size of Property

This strategy is based on a preference for a subsector within a property type because investor/owners believe that they can better understand the operation of tenant-users and, therefore, better understand the demand for space in that subsector. As a result, such property owners tend to specialize in one property sector believing that it may be more cost-effective to lease and manage that property type. For example, an investor/owner may choose to invest *only* in neighborhood or community size retail shopping centers and not invest in larger regional malls. Or, an investor may prefer to invest in small, low-rise suburban office buildings rather than high-rise buildings located in central cities. They believe that a better understanding of these property subsectors and the tenants in these market sectors will be more profitable than would be the case if they invested in larger, more complicated, properties.

G. Strategy as to Tenants

This strategy is based on a preference for properties leased to multiple tenants or leased to a single or very few tenants. In the former case, owners may prefer to take the risk of higher tenant turnover because the ability to adjust rents to market levels more frequently is also greater. On the other hand, many investors may prefer properties that are leased to single tenants. These properties may be less risky because of low tenant turnover and the creditworthiness of tenants. These properties may be preferred even though they do not usually offer the opportunity for frequent adjustment in rents.

H. Arbitrage Investing

This strategy is based on the ability of investors to recognize differences in prices that buyers are willing to pay for the same real estate investments in different markets. For example, this strategy has been used by investors who buy properties directly in *private* market transactions then earn a profit by creating an publicly traded entity, such as a REIT, and issuing stock to the public. In this case, positive arbitrage profits are realized when the total market value of the REIT stock sold to the public exceeds the acquisition cost of the individual properties plus the cost of issuing stock.

I. Turnaround/Special Situation/Value-Added Opportunistic Investing

These strategies are generally based on the belief that successful investments that can be made by investors who see opportunities by changing or modifying the use of existing properties. For example investors may:

1. Acquire a large portfolio of underperforming or undermanaged properties. After a period of more intensive leasing, renovation, and property management, these properties can be sold one at the time, such that the total amount received when all properties are sold exceeds the initial total cost.
2. Acquire "real estate rich" firms that own an extensive amount of real estate in their business. These firms may not realize that the market value of their real estate is not fully reflected in the value of their business operation. In this event an investor might realize that the value of the business and the value of the real estate are separable. Consequently, a gain may be earned by acquiring the firm then selling its real estate. The necessary space to run the business could then be leased. If successful, the value of the real estate and the value of the business after separation would be greater than the previously combined entity.
3. Acquire properties needing renovation, upgrading, or repositioning. The success of this investment plan is usually dependent on:
   a. The ability to purchase properties at a discount.

b. Management understanding the opportunity and how to upgrade, modify, or perhaps reposition the property (e.g., from office use to retail use). The success of such an investment may also be dependent on an exit strategy such as:
(1.) Market acceptance of the repositioned assets.
(2.) The ability of buyers to obtain financing to purchase such assets.

J. Investing in "Trophy or "Blue Chip" Properties
This strategy is based on a "blue chip" approach to investing, that is, only very visible, well-located properties should be the targets for acquisition. While similar to value investing discussed above, investors in trophy assets believe that properties with some unique historical, architectural, or locational attribute (e.g., Empire State Building, Rockefeller Center, Transamerica Tower, Mall of America, Watergate Apartments) will stand the test of time and prove to be excellent investments for the long term.

of the Monument Tower office building was completed two years ago. The first tenants signed five-year leases at that time (two years ago). The remaining space was leased at various times during the past two years. Additional assumptions are as follows:

Current market rent (per square foot) $15.00
Gross square feet: 100,000 Leaseable: 96,000
Projected increase in market rent per year 4.00%
Management costs (percent of effective gross income) 5.00%
Estimated annual increase in the consumer price index 4.00%

The importance of these assumptions should become clear as we discuss the example. A summary of the leases that would be honored by the investor if the building is purchased is shown below.

Summary Lease Information—Monument Tower Office Building

Tenant	*Square Foot*	*Current Rent (per square foot)*	*Current Rental*	*Remaining Lease Term (years)*	*CPI Adjustment (percent)*
Tenant 1	30,000	$14.00	$ 420,000	3	50.00
Tenant 2	25,000	14.00	350,000	3	50.00
Tenant 3	15,000	14.00	210,000	3	50.00
Tenant 4	10,000	14.50	145,000	4	50.00
Tenant 5	10,000	15.00	150,000	5	50.00
Tenant 6	6,000	15.00	90,000	5	50.00
Total	96,000		$1,365,000		

Note: Additional assumptions about the tenant's responsibility for increases in operating expenses (expense stops) will be discussed later.

Base Rent

From this summary we see that there are six tenants, occupying a total of 96,000 square feet of rentable space. The remaining 4,000 square feet of space is used for heating, air conditioning, stairs, elevators, and so on, and is not rentable. The first three tenants to occupy the building leased most of the space. The market rate at the time they signed the lease (two years ago) was lower and they are *currently* paying \$14.00 per square foot.[2] These leases were made for five years, and thus three years remain on each lease. A fourth tenant signed a lease last year and is currently paying \$14.50 per square foot on the lease. The last two tenants just signed their leases at a rate of \$15.00 per square foot, the current rental rate for comparable space.

CPI Adjustment

In this example, we illustrate how rental adjustments are made based on expected increases in the consumer price index (CPI). As shown in an earlier chapter, there are a number of other ways that rent collections can be negotiated. In this example, we assume the rental rate is adjusted each year based on any increase in the CPI that occurred that year. One possibility is that rents are increased by the same percentage amount that the CPI increases. For example, if the CPI rises 4 percent as projected in our example, then the base rent would be increased 4 percent. However, lease payments are not always increased by the full amount of the increase in the CPI. Inclusion of inflationary adjustments in lease terms depends on market conditions and the willingness of tenants to bear the risk of unanticipated inflation. Inflation adjustments may be limited by caps or by specific step-ups in base rents. Further, as we have discussed, many building operating expenses incurred by owners are passed through to tenants. Because tenants will be paying a portion of these expenses (which will increase with inflation), it is not always necessary for a building owner to charge rents that are fully adjusted to the rate of inflation. On the other hand, if the market has an oversupply of space, no adjustment in base rent for inflation may be possible. Another reason rents may not be adjusted by the full amount of the CPI is that the lease can have a separate provision to reimburse the owner for any increase in expenses. This is discussed in the following section.

In our example, we assume that rents will increase by 50 percent of any increase in the CPI. Our assumption that the CPI will increase at a rate of 4 percent per year means that the base rental payment will increase by 2 percent per year (50 percent of 4 percent).

Based on our assumptions, the base rental income can be projected as shown in the projected rental income summary for Monument Tower below: You can verify some of the numbers in the exhibit by recalling that, as discussed above, base rents depend on (1) the initial base rent at the time the lease is signed, (2) CPI adjustments to the base rent, and (3) the market rent prevailing at the time of lease renewals.

Projected Rental Income—Monument Tower

Year	*1*	*2*	*3*	*4*	*5*	*6*
Tenant 1	\$ 420,000	\$ 428,400	\$ 436,968	\$ 506,189	\$ 516,313	\$ 526,639
Tenant 2	350,000	357,000	364,140	421,824	430,260	438,866
Tenant 3	210,000	214,200	218,484	253,094	258,156	263,319
Tenant 4	145,000	147,900	150,858	153,875	175,479	178,988
Tenant 5	150,000	153,000	156,060	159,181	162,365	182,498
Tenant 6	90,000	91,800	93,636	95,509	97,419	109,499
Total	\$1,365,000	\$1,392,300	\$1,420,146	\$1,589,672	\$1,639,992	\$1,699,809

[2]The initial rent on the lease when it was signed two years ago may have been lower than \$14.00 but it has increased due to consumer price index (CPI) adjustments.

Market rent for our example is \$15 per square foot during the first year. This is also the base rent for leases signed that year. Base rent on the leases is projected to increase at 2 percent per year because of the CPI adjustment (half of 4 percent). However, we use a 4 percent annual rate of increase for projecting market rents that will be in effect when leases are renewed. This is because space will be re-leased at market rates at the expiration of each of the leases, and we assume that market rates will increase at the same rate as the CPI.

It appears that a tenant will face much higher rents when the lease is renewed because the new lease is based on a market rate that is projected to rise by the full amount of the CPI, whereas the tenant's rent has increased by only half the CPI over the term of the lease. However, we will see in the next section that the amount of expenses for which the tenant must reimburse the owner when the lease is renewed may also be reduced.

In the case of the first tenant, the initial base rent is \$420,000, which is projected to increase 2 percent per year due to the CPI adjustment until the lease expires in the third year. The base rent in year 4 is projected to be \$506,189,[3] which assumes the market rent (which applies to new leases) of \$15 per square foot will have increased 4 percent per year by that time.

Expense Stops

We have discussed the use of a CPI adjustment to increase rents for unanticipated inflation. Office leases also commonly include a provision that protects the owner from increases in operating expenses beyond what they were during the year the lease was signed because of extraordinary expenses that may be related to the operation of one or more tenants. In our example, each lease for the office building has an **expense stop.** As briefly discussed in Chapter 8, these stops place an upper limit on the amount of operating expenses that will have to be paid by the owner. Any operating expenses in excess of the stop must be paid by the tenant. The amount of the stop is usually based on (1) the tenant's pro rata share (percent of total rentable area), (2) categories of expenses that the lessor and lessee agree will be included in the stop, and (3) the actual amount of operating expenses at the time the lease is signed.

For a newer property the tenant and property owner usually negotiate the amount of the stop. For older properties the owner generally provides the prospective tenant with operating expense statements, and the stop will be based on the tenant's pro rata share of the actual expenses on such statements plus an estimate of any expected increase during the first year of the lease.

In this case the lessor and lessee agreed that the stop will include all operating expenses. However, the owner of the property will incur property management expenses that will not be chargeable to the tenants. All amounts in excess of the expense stop must be paid by the tenant in addition to the base rent specified in the lease. For example, if the expense stop in the lease is \$4.00 per square foot and current expenses are \$4.45 per square foot, then the tenant must pay the owner 45 cents per square foot as an expense reimbursement. The reason for an expense stop is obviously to assure the owner that net income in subsequent years will be at least equal to the initial net income. Using expense stops is particularly important in leases containing fixed base rents (those without CPI adjustments). If expense stops are not used, operating expenses may rise during the term of the lease and net income will decline. The particular expenses passed through to the tenants are negotiable and vary with market conditions. In our

[3] $\$15(1.04)^3 \times 30{,}000$ square feet = \$506,189.

example, we have assumed that all expenses except expenses relating to leasing and a reserve for replacements will be passed through. Tenants are usually reluctant to allow these expenses to be passed through because they are the responsibility of the building owner, and any attempt to pass these through to tenants may be viewed as excessive.

Expense stops in the existing lease are assumed to be as follows:

Lease	*Stop*
Tenant 1	$4.00
Tenant 2	4.00
Tenant 3	4.00
Tenant 4	4.25
Tenant 5	4.45
Tenant 6	4.45

Panel A of Exhibit 10–3 shows the current expenses for the office building and the estimated annual increase in the expenses.

We can see from Panel A of Exhibit 10–3 that the projection of total operating expenses subject to expense stops is $427,200 or $4.45 per rentable square foot. Panel B shows projections for the increase in each expense category. Future rates of increase depend on estimates of how each cost is expected to change. In our example, utilities (heat and air conditioning) are expected to increase at a higher rate than the other items. We assume that property taxes will be level for two years, but then will increase when property values are reassessed. We expect property taxes to be level again for at least four years after the reassessment.

Panel C of Exhibit 10–3 uses the information on expense projections and expense stops to project expense reimbursements. Note that in year 1 the first four tenants will be making expense reimbursements to the owner because actual expenses are $4.45 per square foot, which exceeds the $4.00 expense stops in their leases. Also note that no expense reimbursement is projected for the year that leases are renewed because the stops included in lease renewals will be based on actual expenses at that time.

Net Operating Income

Based on the rental information and expense information in Exhibit 10–3, we can project **net operating income *(NOI)*** for the office building. Exhibit 10–4 projects net operating income for the next six years. Recall that we assumed management expenses to be 5 percent of **effective gross income *(EGI)*.** *EGI* is the actual rent expected to be collected after allowing for any vacancy. Our example projects vacancy at 5 percent of the base rent, beginning in the fourth year when the original leases are renewed. The management expense may be incurred by the owner or paid to a property management company. In either case it is not passed on to the tenant, so the owner has an incentive to control management expenses.

Note that net expenses (before management) are level ($393,700) after gross expenses are netted against the expense reimbursement (before management expenses) for the first three years. Expenses rise in years 4 and 5, since some of the leases are being renewed at new (higher) expense stops that reflect the estimated expenses per square foot at the time of the lease renewal. Note also that the analyst believes that, if acquired, Monument Tower will not require any major capital outlays

EXHIBIT 10–3 Summary of Operating Expenses—Monument Tower

Panel A: First-Year Expenses and Projected Increases

	Dollars	*Dollars per Square Foot*	*Projected Increases*
Property tax	$148,800	$1.55	Level 2 yrs. 10% increase, then level
Insurance	14,400	0.15	Increase 4.00% per yr.
Utilities	120,000	1.25	Increase 5.00 per yr.
Janitorial	76,800	0.80	Increase 3.00 per yr.
Maintenance	67,200	0.70	Increase 3.00 per yr.
Total	$427,200	$4.45	

Panel B: Projection of Expenses per Year

	1	*2*	*3*	*4*	*5*	*6*
Property tax	$148,800	$148,800	$163,680	$163,680	$163,680	$163,680
Insurance	14,400	14,976	15,575	16,198	16,846	17,520
Utilities	120,000	126,000	132,300	138,915	145,861	153,154
Janitorial	76,800	79,104	81,477	83,921	86,439	89,032
Maintenance	67,200	69,216	71,292	73,431	75,634	77,903
Total operating expenses	$427,200	$438,096	$464,325	$476,146	$488,460	$501,289
Per square foot	$4.4500	$4.5635	$4.8367	$4.9599	$5.0881	$ 5.2218

Panel C: Projected Expense Reimbursement per Year*

	1	*2*	*3*	*4*	*5*	*6*
Tenant 1	$13,500	$16,905	$25,101	$ 0	$ 3,848	$ 7,857
Tenant 2	11,250	14,088	20,918	0	3,207	6,548
Tenant 3	6,750	8,453	12,551	0	1,924	3,929
Tenant 4	2,000	3,135	5,867	7,099	0	1,336
Tenant 5	0	1,135	3,867	5,099	6,381	0
Tenant 6	0	681	2,320	3,059	3,829	0
Total	$33,500	$44,396	$70,625	$15,256	$19,189	$19,670

*We have made an estimate for a potential vacancy in Exhibit 10–4 that may occur when any of Tenants 1, 2, or 3 is scheduled to renew their lease. It is possible that any or all of these tenants may vacate and a new tenant, or tenants, would have to occupy that space at market rents. However, there may be some revenue loss during this time required for re-leasing.

during the projections period. If such outlays were deemed to be necessary, they should be included in the forecasted cash flows.

Although expense stops provide for some reimbursement and protect owners against increases in expenses, they do not provide for any increase in *NOI* to offset inflation. An expense stop simply guarantees that *NOI* will not decline. Thus, we see why it may be desirable to have a CPI adjustment as in our example. *A CPI adjustment allows the NOI to increase each year even if no leases are renewed.* We can now also see why the CPI adjustment does not have to be for the full amount of the increase in CPI. As we have seen, the expense stop has already adjusted for the effect of any increase in expenses due to inflation or any other factors. In general, expense stops and inflationary adjustments should be considered along with the initial base rent as part of the "price" of using space.

EXHIBIT 10–4 Projected Net Operating Income

	Year					
	1	*2*	*3*	*4*	*5*	*6*
Base rent	$1,365,000	$1,392,300	$1,420,146	$1,589,672	$1,639,992	$1,699,809
Vacancy	0	0	0	79,484	82,000	84,990
EGI	1,365,000	1,392,300	1,420,146	1,510,189	1,557,992	1,614,819
Operating expenses	427,200	438,096	464,325	476,146	488,460	501,289
Less: reimbursements	33,500	44,396	70,625	15,256	19,189	19,670
Subtotal	393,700	393,700	393,700	460,890	469,271	481,619
Add: management expenses	68,250	69,615	71,007	75,509	77,900	80,741
Total expenses	$ 461,950	$ 463,315	$ 464,707	$ 536, 399	$ 547,170	$ 562,360
NOI	$ 903,050	$ 928,985	$ 955,439	$ 973,790	$1,010,822	$1,052,459

Expected Outlays for Replacements and Capital Improvements

As discussed in Chapter 8, the analyst should also consider outlays of a recurring nature for replacement of items that wear out in the normal operating cycle of a property. These items may be included in operating expenses. In the case of capital outlays for major, nonrecurring items such as roof replacement, parking garage construction, and so on, these should be shown as an additional deduction from *NOI* in the year that the outlay will occur. In our example, Monument Tower is not expected to require any major capital outlays during the six-year projection made in Exhibit 10–4.

Introduction to Debt Financing

Usually an investor will pay for a property by combining his own money (equity) with a loan (debt): Purchase price equals debt plus equity. In Chapter 11 we will discuss reasons why both equity investors and lenders often find a combination of equity and debt desirable for real estate ownership. For now we will focus on how the use of debt affects the cash flows a real estate investor expects to receive.

To illustrate, we again return to our previous example of the Monument office building. Let us assume that an investor can obtain a loan at a 10 percent interest rate to be amortized over 20 years with monthly payments. The amount of the loan is 70 percent of the proposed purchase price (.70 × $8,500,000), or $5,950,000. Monthly payments would be $57,418.79, or $689,025 per year. Traditional investment analysis computes loan payments based on monthly payments (assuming that is the way the payments will be made), but all cash flows are summarized on an annual basis for financial projections.

Exhibit 10–5 shows a summary loan schedule for the property for the first five years. From this point on projections will be made for five years under the assumption that the property will be sold after five years. The reason for projecting *NOI* for an *additional* year will become apparent when we discuss estimating the sale price of the property at the end of the five-year holding period.

Exhibit 10–6 shows the results of including the financing costs in the calculation of cash flows to the equity investor.

EXHIBIT 10–5 Summary Loan Information

	End of Year				
	1	*2*	*3*	*4*	*5*
Payment	$ 689,025	$ 689,025	$ 689,025	$ 689,025	$ 689,025
Mortgage balance	5,851,543	5,742,776	5,622,620	5,489,883	5,343,245
Interest	590,569	580,259	568,869	556,288	542,388
Principal	98,457	108,767	120,156	132,738	146,637

EXHIBIT 10–6 Estimates of Before-Tax Cash Flow

	Year				
	1	*2*	*3*	*4*	*5*
Net operating income *(NOI)*	$903,050	$928,985	$955,439	$973,790	$1,010,822
Less: debt service *(DS)*	689,025	689,025	689,025	689,025	689,025
Before-tax cash flow	$214,025	$239,960	$266,414	$284,765	$ 321,797

Subtracting debt service from *NOI* results in before-tax cash flow from operations ($BTCF_o$). $BTCF_o$ is also referred to as the **equity dividend** because it represents the cash flow that will actually be received by the investor each year, analogous to a dividend on common stocks.

Introduction to Investment Analysis

In general, when we refer to **investment analysis** in real estate we are referring to analyzing a particular property to evaluate its investment potential. This analysis should also help answer other important questions: Should the property be purchased? How long should it be held? How should it be financed? What are the tax implications of owning the investment? How risky is the investment?

We will provide the analytic tools to answer these questions in the next several chapters. However, we can now begin to answer the first question: Should the property be purchased at a price of $8.5 million? To illustrate how we might approach this question, we continue with the pro forma statements from the office building example introduced above.

Measures of Investment Performance Using Ratios

We first consider several common measures of investment performance that might be referred to as ratio measures. These are relatively simple measures, yet they provide a starting point for our analysis. They are also often used to screen an investment. That is, if one of the ratios indicates a poor investment, then the analyst may not take the time to do a more comprehensive analysis.

Price per Square Foot. A preliminary measure of the reasonableness of the proposed purchase price for the property is the price per square foot. For our property, we have an asking price of $8.5 million and gross building area of 100,000 square feet. This results in a price per gross square foot of $85. Similarly, the *rentable* square footage is 96,000, resulting in a price per rentable square foot of $88.54. These prices may also be compared with comparable properties to determine if they are in line with what other investors have paid for similar space. Of course, we assume that the similar space is in fact comparable and will command the same income and resale potential. We are looking for significant departures from the norm. Another way of determining whether the asking price is reasonable would be to consider what a new office building on a comparable lot would cost per square foot. If it could be built for $70.00 per square foot (including land), we would have to question whether the asking price of the building is reasonable. If the cost of a new building was $85.00 per square foot of rentable area, however, we might feel that a premium of $3.54 per square foot ($88.54 − $85.00) is justified, considering that our building is fully leased and may therefore be less risky than building and leasing a new one.

Capitalization Rate. Another preliminary test of reasonableness of the purchase price for the property is the ratio of first-year *NOI* to the asking price. This is referred to as the **capitalization rate** or cap rate as introduced in Chapters 8 and 9. In this case we have $903,050 ÷ $8,500,000, or 10.62 percent, which is just under 11 percent. What does this mean? It certainly is *not* a rate of return on investment (like an *IRR*) because it doesn't consider future income from operations and resale of the property at the end of the holding period. However, this ratio or cap rate can be compared with rates for comparable office buildings that have recently sold. For example, a nearby office building may have recently sold for $10 million. An analysis of its leases at the time it sold indicates that it would produce an *NOI* of about $1.1 million for the upcoming year. Its ratio of *NOI* to sale price reflects a capitalization rate of 11 percent and provides a rough indication that the price for our property may be competitive. Of course, we have to be careful when using this approach for a number of reasons. First, the nature of the leases for the two properties may be quite different (e.g., different expiration dates, renewal options, escalations). Operating expenses over time may also be different for various reasons (the building may be older or less functionally efficient; it may have a different type of mechanical system, etc.). Further, because the location of the two properties may be slightly different, and because future income and expenses may not be the same for the two properties, the potential for price increases may be quite different. Thus the capitalization rate is only a starting point in our analysis. It does, however, represent a benchmark or a norm from which we are looking for significant deviations. For example, if the capitalization rates were in the range of 15 percent for most similar properties as compared to 10 percent for our property, it would probably indicate that the asking price for the property we are considering may be too high relative to what other investors have recently paid for comparable properties.

Equity Dividend Rate. The capitalization rate discussed above relates the entire *NOI* to the value of the property. An analogous measure from the equity investor's point of view is the equity dividend rate. This rate is calculated by dividing the *BTCF* (also referred to as the equity dividend) in the first year by the initial *equity investment.* The investor's initial *equity* in the project *is equal to the purchase price less* the amount borrowed. Thus the equity is $8,500,000 − $5,950,000 = $2,550,000. The equity dividend rate is therefore $214,025 ÷ $2,550,000 = 8.39

percent. This is a rough measure of current return on equity. Note, however, that it is not an investment yield because it does not take into account future cash flows from operation or sale of the property. The difference between the equity dividend rate and an investment yield or *IRR* for the equity investor is an important one, which we will discuss later in the chapter.

Debt Coverage Ratios. To obtain financing on the property, the lender must be satisfied that it is a good investment. One consideration obviously is the rate of return the lender will receive over the term of the loan, which depends on factors such as the interest rate charged, points, and so forth, as discussed earlier in this text. But the lender's rate of return is only one consideration. The lender will also evaluate the riskiness of the loan. One widely used indication of the riskiness of the loan is the degree to which the *NOI* from the property is expected to exceed the mortgage payments. The lender would like a sufficient cushion so that if the *NOI* is less than anticipated (e.g., from unexpected vacancy) the borrower will still be able to make the mortgage payments without using personal funds.

A common measure of this risk is the **debt coverage ratio (DCR).** The *DCR* is the ratio of *NOI* to the mortgage payment. When *NOI* is projected to change over time, the investor typically uses first-year *NOI*. For the office building example, the projected *NOI* in year 1 is $903,050. The mortgage payment (debt service) is $689,025. These figures result in a debt coverage ratio of 1.31. Lenders typically want the debt coverage ratio to be at least 1.2. The *DCR*s for each of the five years the property will be held are summarized as follows:

	Year				
	1	*2*	*3*	*4*	*5*
DCR	1.31	1.35	1.39	1.41	1.47

We see that this project has a debt coverage of about 1.3 for the first year, and the projected ratio increases each year thereafter. Thus it meets the minimum debt coverage ratio typically required by lenders.

Estimated Sale Price

To calculate measures of investment performance over an investment holding period, we must also estimate what our property might sell for. We first need to choose a holding period over which to analyze the investment. For now we will choose five years. When estimating a sale price, investors commonly use two general procedures. The first procedure is to estimate a rate at which property values in general are expected to increase in the area. This is sometimes related to expected inflation rates, although office buildings in some areas may do better or worse than the overall inflation rate for the economy depending on employment. For our office building, we assumed that the market rental rate would increase 4 percent per year. However, the rate at which *NOI* increases depends on the nature of the expense stops and the degree to which the lease payments are adjusted with the CPI. In our example the increase in *NOI* for the five-year lease term is about 3 percent per year. It seems reasonable, therefore, that the price for our property would also increase about 3 percent per year. Using the asking price as a starting point, a 3 percent annual increase would result in a sale price after five years of about $9,850,000.[4] Two problems are associated with using this approach to estimate the resale price. First, it is based on the assumed purchase price, which we may decide is not what the property is really worth once we complete our analysis. Second, it assumes that the resale price depends on how the historical value (purchase price) changed over time rather than looking forward to what will happen in the future. The approach to estimating a resale price discussed below addresses these issues.

A second way of estimating a resale price is to use the capitalization rate concept discussed in an earlier chapter. Recall that the capitalization rate (cap rate for short) is defined as the ratio of the first-year *NOI* to the purchase price. For our office building example the cap rate is 10.62 percent.[5] This ratio expresses the relationship between the purchase price of the property and the *NOI* that the purchaser expects to receive during the first year of ownership. As discussed earlier, the investor may find that, in general, office buildings that have recently been purchased by other investors have capitalization rates around 11 percent.

To estimate the resale price at the end of a five-year holding period, we could assume that investors at that time would also purchase properties at prices that result in a capitalization rate of around 11 percent.[6] Because we assume the property will be sold at the end of the fifth year, the *NOI* in year 6 is the first-year *NOI* to the new owner. Using *NOI* of $1,052,459 in year 6 and a capitalization rate of 11 percent results in an estimated resale price of $9,567,809.[7]

We now have two separate estimates of the resale price. Using a growth rate we arrived at an estimate of $9,850,000. Using a capitalization rate we arrived at an estimate of about $9,550,000. Considering both estimated prices, we might conclude that for purposes of analysis an estimated resale price about midpoint between these two estimates or about $9.7 million would be reasonable. Clearly, the analyst must use some judgment at this point regarding what is a reasonable estimate for the resale price. We are simply pointing out some of the considerations that might go into the investor's thought process. No single precise methodology can be rigidly followed. It is also common to round off the numerical estimate to convey the subjective nature of the estimate.

Before-Tax Cash Flow from Sale

When the property is sold, the mortgage balance must be repaid from the sale proceeds. Repayment results in before-tax cash flow from sale ($BTCF_s$). After the fifth year, the mortgage balance is $5,343,245. Subtracting this from the sale price of $9,700,000 results in before-tax cash flow ($BTCF_s$) of $4,356,755. We can summarize the process as follows:

---

[4]$8,500,000 times $(1.03)^5$.

[5]This is sometimes referred to as the "going in" cap rate because it applies to the rate at the time of purchase.

[6]This assumes that no significant changes will occur in the market for office space during the six-year period that would change the relationship between *NOI* and value. The capitalization rate could change if a change in the supply and demand for office space that affects market rental rates or if the rate of return required by investors in office space changes.

[7]When a capitalization rate is used to estimate the resale price it is often referred to as a *terminal capitalization rate.*

Estimates of Cash Flows from Sale in Year 5	
Sales price	\$9,700,000
Mortgage balance	− 5,343,245
Before-tax cash flow ($BTCF_s$)	\$4,356,755

Measures of Investment Performance Based on Cash Flow Projections

We now consider measures of investment performance that make use of the cash flow projections we have developed. These measures are more comprehensive than the ratio measures considered earlier because they explicitly consider cash flows over the entire investment holding period.

Net Present Value *(NPV)*. We now have the necessary information to calculate different measures of investment performance for the property that consider the entire holding period. To simplify calculations, it is common practice to assume that all cash flows will be received at the end of the year (the sum of all monthly cash flows received during the year). We begin with a calculation of the net present value *(NPV)*. Because our analysis will not consider federal income taxes (this is considered in the next chapter), it is a before-tax analysis. We will refer to the net present value being calculated as the *BTNPV.*

A summary of the cash flows for our office building (assuming it is purchased at the asking price) is as follows:

Year	*Cash Flow*
0 (equity)	(\$2,550,000)
1	214,025
2	239,960
3	266,414
4	284,765
5	4,678,551

The cash flow in year 5 includes *both* the cash flow from operating the property in year 5 (\$321,797) plus the estimated sales proceeds (\$4,356,755).

To find the *NPV* first calculate the present value *(PV)* of all the estimated future cash flows. Then subtract (net against) the initial cash outlay (equity) invested to acquire the investment from this present value to obtain the net present value. Thus, *NPV* measures the extent, if any, that the present value of cash flows to be received from the investment exceeds the equity invested in the office building. A positive *NPV* indicates that the value of the investment, in present value terms, exceeds the equity investment. The *NPV* obviously depends on the discount rate used to calculate the present value of the cash inflows. This discount rate should reflect the minimum rate of return the investor requires to make the investment, considering the riskiness of the investment. *NPV* is an opportunity cost concept in that the return required for the investment being analyzed should be at least as good as the return available on comparable investments. By investing in the property being analyzed, the investor must forgo the return that could have been earned on alternative investment opportunities.

Let's assume that the appropriate discount rate for the office building being analyzed is 18 percent. What is the *BTNPV?* Using the cash flows calculated on the previous page, the *BTNPV* is as follows:

Year	Cash Flow	Present Value (18%)
1	$ 214,025	$ 181,377
2	239,960	172,335
3	266,414	162,148
4	284,765	146,878
5	4,678,551	2,045,038
Total present value		2,707,776
Less initial equity investment		2,550,000
Net present value *(NPV)*		$ 157,776

We see that the *BTNPV* is $157,776. What does this mean? First, it indicates that the expected return for the investment is greater than the 18 percent discount rate. Second, we can say that the investor could invest $157,776 more equity capital and still earn the required 18 percent rate of return.

Internal Rate of Return. Based on material covered in earlier chapters, we have already seen that we can find an investment yield or *IRR* by finding the discount rate that equates the present value of the future cash inflows with the initial cash outflow. Recall that the initial equity investment is $2,550,000, found by subtracting the $5,950,000 loan amount from the $8,500,000 purchase price. Exhibit 10–7 presents the cash flows.

You should confirm that this process results in an *IRR* of 19.64 percent, which we will refer to as the *BTIRR* since it is a before-tax *IRR*. This is the before-tax yield that the investor may expect to earn on equity over the investment period.

Is the return adequate? The answer to this question depends on what the investor can earn on comparable investments, such as similar office buildings or even other real estate investments with similar risk characteristics. We have discussed comparing capitalization rates and price per square foot with comparable properties. Similarly, we could also ask what rate of return we would expect to earn had we bought another property at the price paid by another investor. This may give us some idea of what returns other investors are expecting. Of course, we would have to make our own projections of *NOI* and resale price unless the other investor told us exactly what he was thinking. We would also make similar projections and *IRR* calculations for other properties that are for sale, using their asking price. That is, we should earn a return that is at least as good as the return we could earn on other properties that are for sale that have similar risk characteristics.

Another test of the reasonableness of the *BTIRR* is to compare it with the effective interest cost of any mortgage financing that could be obtained to purchase the property. Normally, we would expect the return on the property to be greater than the effective cost of financing on the property, because the investor accepts more risk than the lender. The lender assumes less risk because a lender would have first claim on income and proceeds from sale of the property should there be a default. For example, we should expect that the *IRR* for the office building (*BTIRR* of 19.64

EXHIBIT 10–7 Cash-Flow Summary—Monument Tower

	End of Year					
	0	*1*	*2*	*3*	*4*	*5*
Before-tax cash flow		$214,025	$239,960	$266,414	$284,765	$4,678,551
Equity	$−2,550,000					
Total	$−2,550,000	$214,025	$239,960	$266,414	$284,765	$4,678,551

percent) would be more than the 10 percent mortgage interest rate. Otherwise, the investor would be better off lending on real estate rather than investing in it. Later in this chapter we will discuss approaches to measuring and evaluating risk to investors. Then in Chapter 12 we will show how debt affects that risk and return for equity investors.

Abuses in Pro Forma Cash Flow Projections

When making pro forma cash flow projections for real estate income properties, the analysts must be realistic about the assumptions being made. The following nine abuses common in pro forma cash flow projections were identified by Vernon Martin III in an article by that title in *Real Estate Review:*

1. Mismatched growth rates between rental income and expenses.
2. Failure to consider rental concessions and effective rents.
3. Absence of lease-by-lease analysis in properties encumbered by long-term leases.
4. Figures that project that expense recovery income will increase at the same growth rate as other expenses in a property encumbered by gross leases with expense stops.
5. Projections for vacancy and collection losses that are not synchronized with market conditions.
6. Use of operating expense categories that do not include all cost items. Common omissions are tenant improvements and leasing commissions.
7. Use of ending capitalization rates that are lower than starting capitalization rates. Reversion capitalization rates should be related to the property's age and remaining economic life.
8. Underestimation of sales and other reversion costs.
9. Use of an inappropriate internal rate of return (discount rate).

Summary of Investment Analysis Calculations

Exhibit 10–8 shows a summary of the calculations for the office building. The performance measures in Exhibit 10–8 should all be compared with other investment alternatives. The comparison will give a good indication of whether acquisition of the office building is a good investment. However, these measures may still not be sufficient to allow us to decide whether we should purchase the investment because we have not yet considered how *federal income taxes* might affect the results. We also need to know more about the *riskiness* of the investment so that we can be reasonably sure that we are comparing the performance measures outlined in Exhibit 10–8 with alternatives of comparable risk, as we discuss in the next section. We will also want to know whether we should borrow more or less money, and whether there are other, better ways of financing the property. Chapter 12 covers financing.

EXHIBIT 10–8 Summary of Monument Tower Office Building Investment Analysis Measures

Price/gross square footage	$ 85.00
Price/net square footage	$ 88.54
Capitalization rate	10.62%
IRR (BTIRR)	19.64%
NPV (18% discount rate)	$157,776

Being able to obtain a loan on the property also depends on the appraised value an independent appraiser presents. This value may be more or less than the investor is willing to pay. If the appraised value is too low, it will be difficult to finance the property with the amount of debt that we have assumed in our projections.

It should be obvious that we have only begun to do the in-depth analysis the potential acquisition of our office building requires. Whether investors consider all of these issues in practice depends on their level of sophistication. Our objective will be to cover all the issues that *should* be considered to be certain of making an intelligent investment decision.

Risk Analysis

We have discussed how to calculate the *IRR, NPV,* and other measures of investment performance. Because of risk differences, comparing *IRR*s or *NPV*s when making choices among alternative investments is usually not possible. Indeed, such a comparison may only be made if we assume that the risk associated with the different investments being analyzed is the same. Because risk usually is not the same, we provide some techniques for evaluating risk that enable us to make a more complete comparison of alternatives. We will provide a brief discussion of sources of risk and how they may differ among investment alternatives.

Comparing Investment Returns

To begin our discussion, we will briefly explore considerations that investors should take into account when comparing measures of return on investment on a specific real estate investment with other real estate investments and other investments generally.

After the investor has gone through a reasonably detailed analysis of an income-producing property, and after having developed measures of return on the investment, the investor must decide whether or not the investment will provide an adequate or competitive return. The answer to this question will depend on (1) the nature of alternative real estate investments, (2) other investments that are available to the investor, (3) the respective returns that those alternatives are expected to yield, and (4) differences in *risk* between the investment being considered relative to those alternative investments available to the investor.

In Exhibit 10–9, we have constructed a hypothetical relationship between rates of return and risk for various classes of alternative investments. The vertical axis represents the expected return,[8] and the horizontal axis represents the degree of risk

[8]To be most comparable, returns should be calculated on an after-tax basis as discussed later in this chapter.

inherent in each category of investment. Note that we are dealing with the average risk for an entire class of assets. There are obviously significant differences in risk within each class. For example, some bonds will be riskier than other bonds within the general bond category. Also, less variance occurs within some asset classes than others (e.g., Treasury bills are considered to be riskless). Assets within one category may have more risk than some of the assets in a higher risk category. For example, some bonds are riskier than some stocks, even though as a *class,* stocks are riskier than bonds.

Risk, as presented in Exhibit 10–9, is considered only by class of investments in relative terms; that is, as one moves to the right on the axis, an investment is considered riskier and to the left less risky. Hence, investments with higher risks should yield investors higher returns and vice versa.

Note that, based on the risk-return "ranking" indicated in Exhibit 10–9, the security with the lowest return, U.S. Treasury bills, also has the lowest risk.[9] As we move out on the risk-return line in the exhibit, we see that expected before-tax returns on investments in real estate offer a considerably higher expected return but are also much riskier than investing in U.S. Treasury bills.

Types of Risk

What are the investment characteristics peculiar to real estate that make it riskier than investing in government securities? Similarly, what risk characteristics differentiate real estate investment from the other alternatives such as common stock, corporate bonds, and municipal bonds also shown in Exhibit 10–9? To answer this question we must consider the source of risk differences among various categories of investments. What follows is a brief summary of major investment risk characteristics that must be considered by investors when deciding among alternative investments.

Business Risk. Real estate investors are in the business of renting space. They incur the risk of loss due to fluctuations in economic activity that affect the variability of income produced by the property. Changes in economic conditions often affect some properties more than others depending on the type of property, its location, and any existing leases. Many regions of the country and locations within cities experience differences in the rate of growth due to changes in demand, population changes, and so on. Those properties that are affected to a greater degree than others would be riskier. A property with a well-diversified tenant mix is likely to be less subject to business risk. Similarly, properties with leases that provide the owner with protection against unexpected changes in expenses (e.g., with expense stops in the lease) would have less business risk.

Financial Risk. The use of debt financing (referred to as financial leverage) magnifies the business risk. Financial risk increases as the amount of debt on a real estate investment is increased. The degree of financial risk also depends on the cost and structure of the debt. For example, a loan that gives the lender a participation in any appreciation in the value of the property in exchange for lower monthly payments may have less financial risk. Chapter 11 provides a further discussion of financial leverage and the use of different types of loans such as participation loans.

[9] Treasury bills are usually considered riskless, although they are subject to some interest rate risk and inflation risk.

EXHIBIT 10–9 Risk and Return (alternative investments)

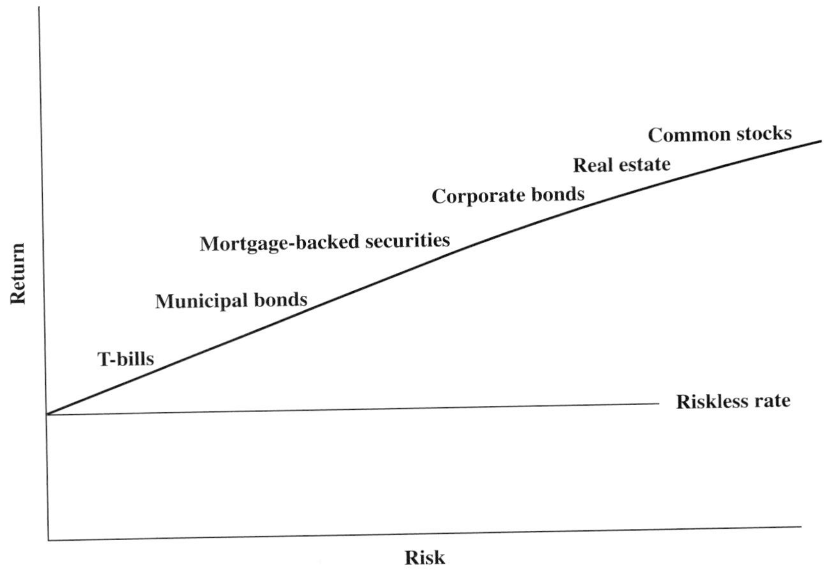

Liquidity Risk. This risk occurs when a continuous market with many buyers and sellers and frequent transactions is not available. The more difficult an investment is to liquidate, the greater the risk that a price concession may have to be given to a buyer should the seller have to dispose of the investment quickly. Real estate has a relatively high degree of liquidity risk. It can take from six months to a year or more to sell real estate income properties, especially during periods of weak demand for investment real estate such as occurred during the early 1990s. Special purpose properties would tend to have much more liquidity risk than properties that can easily be adapted to alternative uses.

Inflation Risk. Unexpected inflation can reduce an investor's rate of return if the income from the investment does not increase sufficiently to offset the impact of inflation, thereby reducing the real value of the investment. Some investments are more favorably or adversely affected by inflation than others. Real estate has historically done well during periods of inflation. This might be attributed to the use of leases that allow the *NOI* to adjust with unexpected changes in inflation. Furthermore, the replacement cost of real estate tends to increase with inflation. During periods of high vacancy rates, however, when the demand for space is weak and new construction is not feasible, the income from real estate does not tend to increase with unexpected inflation.

Management Risk. Most real estate investments require management to keep the space leased and maintained to preserve the value of the investment. The rate of return that the investor earns can depend on the competency of the management. This risk is based on the capability of management and its ability to innovate, respond to competitive conditions, and operate the business activity efficiently. Some properties require a higher level of management expertise than others. For example, regional malls require continuous marketing of the mall and leasing of space to keep a viable mix of tenants that draws customers to the mall.

Interest Rate Risk. Changes in interest rates will affect the price of all securities and investments. Depending on the relative maturity (short-term versus long-term investments), however, some investment prices will respond more than others, thereby increasing the potential for loss or gain. Real estate tends to be highly levered, and thus the rate of return earned by equity investors can be affected by changes in interest rates. Even if an existing investor has a fixed-rate mortgage or no mortgage, an increase in the level of interest rates may lower the price that a subsequent buyer is willing to pay. Furthermore, yield rates that investors require for real estate tend to move with the overall level of interest rates in the economy.

Legislative Risk. Real estate is subject to numerous regulations such as tax laws, rent control, zoning, and other restrictions imposed by government. Legislative risk results from the fact that changes in regulations can adversely affect the profitability of the investment. Some state and local governments have more restrictive legislation than others—especially for new development.

Environmental Risk. The value of real estate is often affected by changes in its environment or sudden awareness that the existing environment is potentially hazardous. For example, while it used to be common to use asbestos to insulate buildings, asbestos in buildings is now perceived as a potential health hazard. A property may also have become contaminated by toxic waste that is spilled or was once buried on the site or an adjacent site. Environmental risk can cause more of a loss than the other risks mentioned because the investor can be subject to cleanup costs that far exceed the value of the property.

In the final analysis, a prospective investor in a specific real estate project must estimate and compute an expected return on the project and compare that return with expected returns on other *specific* real estate investments as well as all other investments. Any risk differentials must then be carefully considered relative to any risk premium, or difference in expected returns, in all such comparisons. Investors must then make the final judgment as to whether an investment is justified.

Due Diligence in Real Estate Investment Risk Analysis

The term **due diligence** is used in the real estate investment community to describe the investigation that an investor should undertake when considering the acquisition of a property.[10] Although this process should be followed by any investor, it is particularly important when a firm is making investments on behalf of other investors. Essentially, due diligence is a process of discovering information needed to assess whether or not investment risk is suitable given a set of investment objectives. Exhibit 10–10 provides a general checklist of the areas that should be investigated along with some commentary regarding the importance of each. In most cases, a prospective investor will insist that any risks discovered in the due diligence process must be remedied by the current property owner as a condition of sale.

[10]The term is also used to describe investigations that should be undertaken in corporate mergers, formation of partnerships, and so on.

Exhibit 10–10 Sample Due Diligence Checklist

Areas of Review	Commentary
1. Rent roll analysis	Review to determine whether rent information and the payment history of tenants provided by the property owner is accurate and to discover whether there are any disagreements between tenants and landlord (e.g., withholding of rent) that may result in a future confrontation with tenants. Tenant creditworthiness and rent arrearages as well as bankruptcies are also important.
2. Lease agreement review Renewal option rights Expansion option rights First refusal rights Permitted uses Restrictive uses Tenant improvements Commissions Parking Signage	Review to determine the contents of leases as well as options that tenants possess and the responsibility and calculation of expenses. This may affect future expansion commitments relative to rents, expenses, expansions, etc. Also, commitments made to tenants by the current owner regarding parking, future improvements, payment of commissions, rights to sublet, erect signs, etc. Discover and review any amendments to existing leases.
3. Review of service and maintenance agreements Landscape, janitorial, trash removal elevator, security, building systems certificates of occupancy, mechanical, fire inspection, etc.	Review made to establish the frequency and extent of any problems with building equipment and the steps taken to remedy/repair/replace by the owner. Chronic problems in this area could indicate future major expenses, problems obtaining insurance coverage, etc. All equipment warranties should also be reviewed.
4. Pending or threatened matters review	Review to determine if there are any condemnation proceedings, tax suits, regulatory suits, governmental litigation, or private lawsuits that may affect the property.
5. Review of title/deed documents to determine: Nature and extent of easements Deed restrictions Quality of title Existence of liens • Financing liens • Mechanics liens • Tax liens • Judgment liens	Examination to reveal any easements granted to other parties that could benefit or detract from the value of the property. It should also reveal any liens that may exist because of unpaid taxes, disputes over payments due to suppliers and contractors, and the existence of civil judgements against the current property owner.
6. Property survey Boundary lines Location of buildings, structures, and other improvements.	Important review to determine whether or not the physical improvements are properly located on the site, or if they are in violation of any legal boundaries or site restrictions including rights of way, setback requirements, etc. It should also address issues regarding the location of all rights of way, driveways, walkways, curbcuts, utility lines, streams, rivers, and ditches and the location of any setback lines and of all roads, streets, and highways bordering the property, showing access to and from these.
7. Government compliance Compliance with current zoning ordinances, permitted uses/ grandfather provisions including: • Parking ratios • Setback lines • Height limitations • Density limitations (*a*) Number of units (*b*) Floor area ratios • Environmental regulations: toxic waste/air quality	Review to determine whether the current and intended use of the property is allowed under zoning. Also to determine whether any grandfather provisions currently apply. Environmental concerns may include a number of issues including the existence of toxic wastes, destruction of wetlands, trees, endangered species, etc., and whether a property lies in a designated special flood hazard area or the 100-year flood plain. This review is usually performed by an environmental engineering firm and requires an opinion letter.

8. Physical inspection Management files on repairs, maintenance and warranties	Survey taken to determine the physical condition of the structure and if defects exist, whether needed repairs are covered by warranties. A report should be prepared assessing the existence of "as-built" plans and specifications, the condition of building systems, structures, utilities, foundation, walls, adequacy, and availability of utilities. The presence of communication devices, such as satellite dishes, any variances from "as built" plans and specifications, and the existence of defects should be noted. Should also indicate compliance with ADA (Americans with Disabilities Act) regulations.
9. Tax matters Property taxes • Assessed value • Special assessments • Payment history	Review to determine whether payment of all taxes and assessments are current. Also to discover any abatements or existence of special local tax districts, etc.
10. Insurance policies **11. Engineering studies** **12. Market studies** **13. List of personal property**	These reviews would include the insurance claims history and any denial of insurance to the current property owner. The investor has a right to ask for any reports commissioned by the current property owner such as market studies, engineering studies, etc., that may be relevant to the transaction. The investor may request a list of personal property that may be conveyed with the real property in order to avoid disputes.

Sensitivity Analysis

We have discussed various types of risk that must be considered when evaluating different investment alternatives. Unfortunately, it is not easy to *measure* the riskiness of an investment. We will learn that there are different ways of measuring risk, depending on the degree and manner in which the analyst attempts to quantify the risk.

The performance of some properties will be more sensitive to unexpected changes in market conditions than that of other properties. For example, the effect of unexpected inflation on the net operating income for a property is affected by lease provisions such as expense stops and CPI adjustments. A property that is located in an area that has limited land available for new development is likely to be less sensitive to the risk that vacancy rates will increase as a result of overbuilding.

One of the most straightforward ways of analyzing risk is to do sensitivity analysis or a what-if analysis of the property. This involves changing one or more of the key assumptions for which there is uncertainty to see how sensitive the investment performance of the property is to changes in that assumption. Assumptions that are typically examined in a sensitivity analysis include the expected market rental rate, vacancy rates, operating expenses, and the expected resale price.

A sensitivity analysis starts with a *base case,* that is, a set of assumptions to be analyzed that will provide a frame of reference for the sensitivity analysis. This set of assumptions usually represents the analyst's best estimate of the most likely situation.[11]

Once the base case set of assumptions is identified, the analyst first computes the *IRR, NPV,* and other measures of investment performance using this base set of assumptions. Then the analyst varies the assumptions one or more at a time to see how each change affects the results. Usually the approach to changing assumptions is to (1) Change a single assumption at a time, or (2) Identify several scenarios in which more than one variable changes within a particular scenario.

[11]In a statistical sense the "most likely" case would be the one with the highest probability of occurrence. We will consider probabilities in more detail in a later section.

Exhibit 10–11

Resale Price	*Annual Change**	BTIRR
$ 7,300,000	−3.00%	6.17%
7,900,000	−1.45	10.25
8,500,000	0.00	13.76
9,100,000	1.37	16.86
9,700,000	2.68	19.64
10,300,000	3.92	22.16
10,900,000	5.10	24.48
11,500,000	6.23	26.63
12,100,000	7.32	28.64

*Compound annual rate of change from the purchase price of $8.5 million.

Change a Single Assumption at a Time. The advantage of this approach is that it allows the analyst to isolate the impact of a specific input assumption. For example, in the office building analyzed earlier in this chapter, we estimated the *IRR* to be 19.64 percent under a specific set of assumptions that might be considered a base case. Included in these assumptions was an estimate that the property would sell for $9.7 million after five years. What if the property sells for more or less than this? How would a change in sale price affect the *IRR?* Exhibit 10–11 shows the *IRR* for a range of possible resale prices. This chart shows how sensitive the *IRR* is to a change in the resale price. Exhibit 10–12 graphs the results.

Scenarios. An alternative to changing a single variable at a time is to identify different scenarios. The base case assumptions might be viewed as a most likely scenario. Similarly, one could conceive of a pessimistic scenario in which the assumptions reflect a situation where things don't go as well as the most likely scenario. For example, vacancy might be higher, which in turn might mean future market rents are lower, and the resale price is lower. Scenario analysis allows the analyst to see how much investment performance is affected by a combination of negative or worst case assumptions. Likewise, a set of optimistic assumptions would be identified that indicates how well the investment would perform if everything goes well. We will illustrate the use of scenarios later in this chapter.

Partitioning the IRR

We have given a considerable amount of attention to the development of the internal rate of return on equity invested in real estate projects. While this measure of return is useful in helping the investor to decide whether or not to invest in a project, it is helpful to "partition" that rate of return to obtain some idea as to the relative weights of components of the return and some idea as to the timing of the receipt of the largest portion of that return.

To illustrate what we mean by **partitioning the IRR,** recall that the internal rate of return on equity investment in real estate comprises two sources of cash flow: (1) cash flow from operations and (2) cash flow from the sale of the investment.

In Exhibit 10–12, we present the cash flow from operating the property ($BTCF_o$) and the cash flow from sale of the property ($BTCF_s$) for the office building example. Recall that the internal rate of return on equity for a five-year holding

EXHIBIT 10–12 Monument Tower Example
Sensitivity of *IRR* to Resale Price

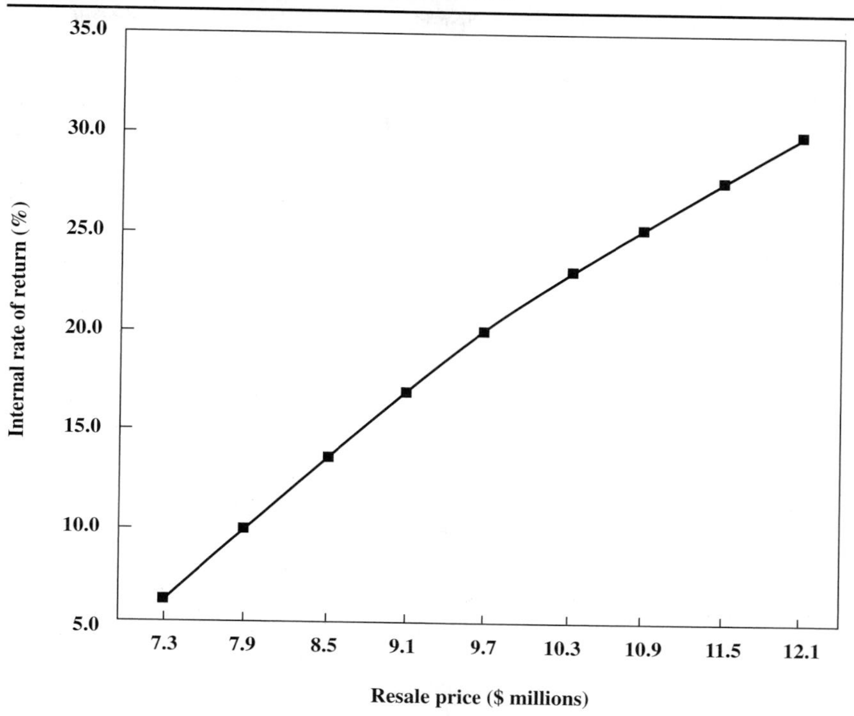

period was 19.64 percent. However, because both of the above-mentioned sources of cash flow make up the 19.64 percent internal rate of return, we have no way of knowing what proportion *each component bears to the total return.* A breakdown of each component would be useful to an investor concerned with how much of the return is made up of cash flow from *operations* realized from the project and how much is due to proceeds from *sale* in value of the property.

To consider these problems, it is a simple matter to reconsider the present value of the $BTCF_o$ and $BTCF_s$ in a slightly different manner as shown in Exhibit 10–13. We should note that all cash flow components the investor expects to receive from the project are discounted to find the internal rate of return of 19.64 percent. Then the *PV* of $BTCF_o$ and $BTCF_s$, are summed to get the total *PV* of $2,550,000. The ratio of the *PV* of $BTCF_o$ and *PV* of $BTCF_s$ can now be taken to the total present value. These ratios now represent the respective proportion of the internal rate of return made up by cash flow (30 percent) and cash flow from appreciation and sale after five years (70 percent).

Why is partitioning an internal rate of return important? Because it helps the investor to determine how much of the return depends on annual operating cash flow and how much depends on the projected cash flow from resale. Generally more certainty is associated with projecting cash flows that will occur during the operating years of the investment—especially when they are partially determined by existing leases. The resale price depends on expected cash flows that will occur beyond the current holding period. Thus, it would seem that the greater a proportion of the

EXHIBIT 10–13 Partitioning the *IRR*—Monument Tower Office Building

***PV* of *BTCF*$_o$:** Year	*Cash Flow*	IFPV	*Present Value*
1	$214,025	0.835859	$178,895
2	239,960	0.698661	167,650
3	266,414	0.583982	155,581
4	284,765	0.488127	139,001
5	321,797	0.408005	131,295
Total			$772,422
***PV* of *BTCF*$_s$:**			
5	$4,356,755	0.408005	$1,777,578
PV of *BTCF*$_o$′		$772,422	
PV of *BTCFs*′		1,777,578	
Total *PV*		$2,550,000	

Ratio of:
PV, BTCF$_o$ to Total *PV* = 30%
PV, BTCF$_s$ to Total *PV* = 70%

internal rate of return is made up of *expected appreciation in the future,* the greater the risk facing the investor. For example, the investment returns for the office building, with its 19.64 percent *IRR,* is made up of 30 percent annual *BTCF*$_o$′ and 70 percent *BTCF*$_s$. A second project might also require an investment of $2,550,000 and also provide the investor with the same *IRR* of 19.64 percent. When the *IRR* is partitioned, however, we may find that the proportions of the return are much different—suppose 3 percent from annual *BTCF*$_o$ and 97 percent from *BTCF*$_s$. Hence, even though both investments have a 19.64 percent *IRR,* a much higher proportion of the return in the second case depends on future appreciation in property value.[12] Given this outcome, the investor may want to compare any differences in risk between projects more carefully because even though the two projects are estimated to yield the same *IRR,* the likelihood of significant risk differences between the two is strong.

Variation in Returns and Risk

Many of the sources of risk discussed in the chapter, such as business risk, financial risk, and so on, affect returns on real estate investment by making such returns more *variable.* Generally speaking, the higher the variability in returns, the greater the risk in a project. For example, consider the office building that we have been analyzing. Assume that we are considering two additional properties for investment, a hotel and an apartment building.

To illustrate, Exhibit 10–14 contains an estimate of the internal rate of return over a five-year investment period for the three properties under three different economic scenarios. Essentially, Exhibit 10–14 shows estimates of the *IRR* for all three investments under three general economic scenarios that could occur over the investment period.[13] That is, the investor would estimate rents and expenses for both

[12]Be aware that it is possible to have negative *BTCF* and still have a *positive IRR.* Hence it is important to take the operating cash flows into account in addition to the *IRR.*

[13]The information in Exhibit 10–11 was used to select the rates of return for the office building. The pessimistic scenario assumes that the building is sold for $7.3 million and the optimistic scenario assumes that it is sold for $12.1 million.

Exhibit 10–14

Office Building

	Return (R)	*Probability (P)*	*R × P*	*R − Expected Return*	*P × (R − Expected Return)²*
Pessimistic	6.17%	25.00%	1.54%	−12.35%	0.3812%
Most likely	19.64	50.00	9.82	1.12	0.0062
Optimistic	28.64	25.00	7.16	10.12	0.2559
Σ Expected return			18.52%	Variance	0.6434%
				Std. Dev.	8.02%

Apartment Building

	Return (R)	*Probability (P)*	*R × P*	*R − Expected Return*	*P × (R − Expected Return)²*
Pessimistic	10.00%	25.00%	2.50%	−5.00%	0.0625%
Most likely	15.00	50.00	7.50	0.00	0.0000
Optimistic	20.00	25.00	5.00	5.00	0.0625
Σ Expected return			15.00%	Variance	0.1250%
				Std. Dev.	3.54%

Hotel

	Return (R)	*Probability (P)*	*R × P*	*R − Expected Return*	*P × (R − Expected Return)²*
Pessimistic	5.00%	25.00%	1.25%	−15.00%	0.5625%
Most likely	20.00	50.00	10.00	0.00	0.0000
Optimistic	35.00	25.00	8.75	15.00	0.5625
Σ Expected return			20.00%	Variance	1.1250%
				Std. Dev.	10.61%

Summary

Property	*Expected Return*	*Risk*
Office	18.52%	8.02%
Apartment	15.00	3.54
Hotel	20.00	10.61

investment alternatives under three assumptions regarding economic conditions. Then, given the debt-service effects (and perhaps the tax effects) appropriate for each investment, the cash flow would be projected as well as an estimate of the property value at the end of the investment period.

After computing the *IRR* under each case, the investor could then estimate the probability that each of the economic scenarios that affect the income-producing potential for each alternative will occur. The estimated *IRR,* when multiplied by the probability that a given economic scenario will occur, produces the expected return for each investment.

Based on the results in Exhibit 10–14, we see that the hotel property produces the highest expected return, 20 percent, compared to the 18.52 percent expected return for the office building and 15 percent for the apartment building. Does this mean that the hotel property should be selected over the office building and the apartment building? Not necessarily. At this point the reader should recall our discussion of risk characteristics in the chapter and how each investment may be affected by those considerations. A property that provides a high expected return may also be riskier relative to investments with somewhat lower returns.

In dealing with the problem of comparing risk and return among investments, some techniques can be used to complement the qualitative considerations discussed at the end of the chapter. We now turn to a more quantitative discussion of the treatment of projected risk.

In trying to deal with all risk characteristics particular to an investment, some researchers and market analysts argue that in combination these risks (e.g., business risk, financial risk, and the other risks discussed in the chapter) serve to induce *variability in a project's rate of return.* In our above example, the hotel project is riskier than the commercial property or apartment, and, in fact, if you closely examine the estimates of *IRR* under each economic scenario, you encounter a much *wider range* in possible *IRR*s with the hotel property compared to the other properties. In fact, if we diagramed the relationship between the probability of the possible economic states of nature and the expected *IRR* for each economic state of nature, we would have a pattern such as that shown in Exhibit 10–15. In that exhibit, we have plotted the probability of the state of the economy and expected *IRR* on each investment given the state of the economy. We have "smoothed" the curves in the diagram between each probability point to show what the *IRR* would most likely be at points between those specifically estimated. The key concept to grasp from the exhibit is that even though the expected return for the hotel property is higher than that computed for the office building, the range of expected returns for the hotel property is far greater than that for the office building. The narrowness in the range of outcomes for the office building relative to the outcomes for the hotel property indicates that there is *lower variability* in expected returns for the office building than for the recreation property. Many analysts consider *lower variability* in returns to be associated with *lower risk,* and vice versa. Therefore, by using a statistical measure of *variance,* the investor has an indication of the extent of the risk in an investment.

Measures of Variance and Risk. Computing the statistical variance in returns is a very simple procedure as Exhibit 10–14 shows for the three properties. The *standard deviation about the mean return* for the hotel property is 10.61 percent, which is *greater* than that for the office building, which is only 8.02 percent, or for the apartment, which is 3.54 percent. This measure of *dispersion* tells us that the actual return for the apartment building is *more likely* to be *closer* to its expected return of 15.0 percent when compared to the hotel property or the office building. Because the standard deviation for the hotel property is 10.61 percent, the actual return for the hotel property is *less likely* to be closer to its expected return of 20 percent, when compared to the office building or apartment property. Hence, if variation in returns is a good indicator of risk, then the hotel is clearly the riskiest of the three investments.

If the probability distribution of *IRR*s for the two investments being considered is normal, the standard deviation of returns for each investment also gives us valuable information. The standard deviation gives us a specific range within which we can expect the actual return for each investment to fall in relation to its expected return. For example, for the hotel property, we can expect its *actual* return to fall within + or − one standard deviation of its expected return of 20 percent, 68 percent of the time. This means that 68 percent of the time we can expect the return on the hotel property to fall between 9.39 and 30.61 percent. We can expect its actual

EXHIBIT 10–15 Probability Distribution of *IRRs* (office, apartment and hotel properties)

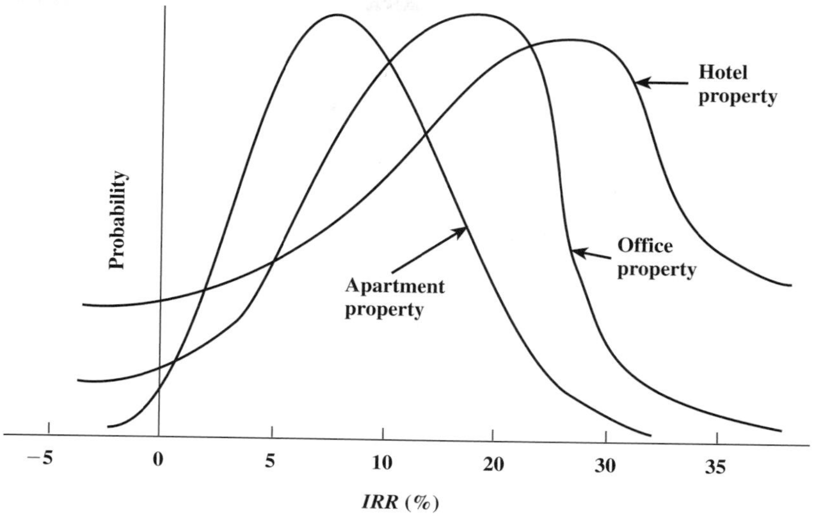

return to fall within + or − two standard deviations from its expected return approximately 95.5 percent of the time and + or − three standard deviations from its expected return approximately 99.7 percent of the time. In contrast, the actual return on the apartment building will fall in a much more narrow range of + or − one standard deviation from its expected return, or 15 percent + 3.54 percent = 18.54 percent and 15 percent − 3.54 percent = 11.46 percent, about 68 percent of the time, and so on.

Risk and Return. The relevance of these statistical measures, in addition to giving the investor a more quantitative perspective on dispersion and variance as proxies for risk, can also be related to the *IRR* in developing a measure of *risk per unit of expected return.* To do so for the investments, divide the standard deviation of the *IRR*s by the expected mean *IRR*. For the office building this computation would be 8.02 ÷ 18.52, or 0.433; for the hotel property it would be 10.61 ÷ 20.0, or 0.5305; and for the apartment it would be 3.54 ÷ 15, or 0.236. This statistic, called the *coefficient of variation,* is a measure of relative variation; that is, it measures *risk per unit of expected return.* In the case of the hotel property, the coefficient of variation is higher than that of the office building. The apartment has the lowest coefficient of variation. This suggests that return per unit of risk for the apartment building is not as high as it is for the office building and hotel. This comparison does not necessarily mean that the investor will decide not to accept the additional risk in exchange for the additional return; it depends on the investor's attitude toward risk. All investors are assumed to be *risk averse,* which means that they require a higher expected return as compensation for incurring additional risk. We cannot say, however, how much that return should be for a particular investor. If the returns for each of the three properties we have analyzed are based on market prices for each property, then the trade-off between risk and return reflects the price of risk in the

EXHIBIT 10–16 Risk versus Return

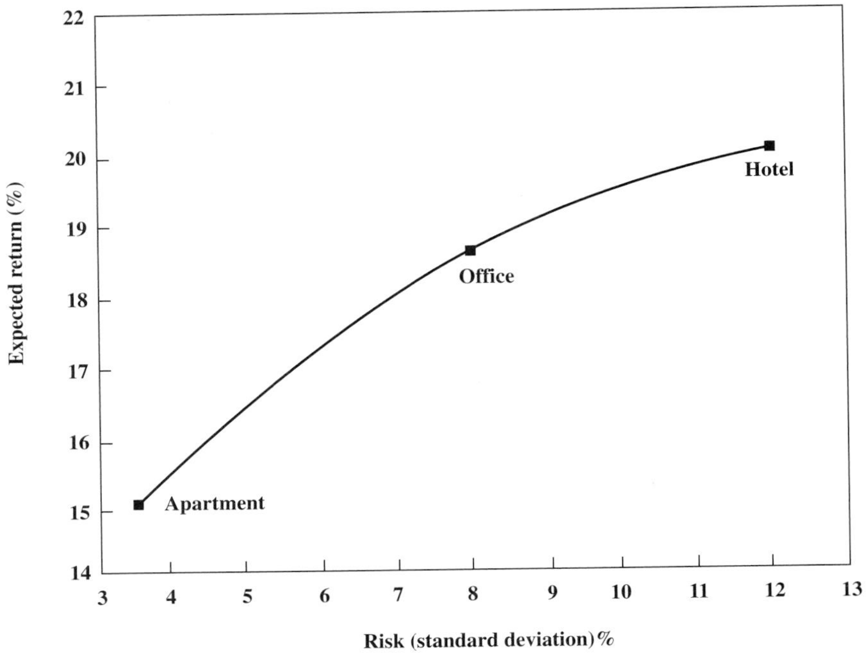

market, which implies that investors would purchase each of the above properties based on their risk and return characteristics.

In Exhibit 10–16 we plot the expected return versus the risk (standard deviation) for each of the three properties. This exhibit is similar to Exhibit 10–9, which showed the risk and return trade-off for all assets. In fact, the part of the curve represented by Exhibit 10–16 can be thought of as a small slice from the portion of Exhibit 10–9 that passes through real estate as an asset class.

Extensions. We have not considered the possibility of reducing risk (variance) by combining investments into a *portfolio.* By developing a portfolio of *different* investment properties, and also including stocks and bonds, the investor can significantly reduce risk through *diversification.* For example, economic events that result in the pessimistic scenario for the hotel property do not necessarily affect the apartment or office properties, and vice versa. Hence the returns for the three properties may not be perfectly correlated. Diversifying among the three investment types rather than choosing only one can reduce the overall risk of the portfolio. Diversification lowers the variance of total returns from all investments in a portfolio because high and low returns tend to offset one another when combined, resulting in less variation about an expected mean return for the entire investment portfolio. In the context of Exhibit 10–16, then, the portfolio would have an expected return and variance that is to the left of the curve in the exhibit, in other words, less risk for the same expected rate of return.

Taxation of Income-Producing Real Estate

Earlier in this chapter we introduced investment analysis of income-producing property. We calculated measures of investment performance such as the *IRR* and *NPV.* However, these calculations did not consider the effect of federal income taxes on the investment and financing decision; consequently, we referred to the analysis thus far as a before-tax analysis. We now extend investment analysis to include the effect of federal income taxes, which is referred to as an after-tax analysis.

Our discussion of taxes is intended only as a general overview of how taxes affect after-tax rates of return for real estate income property. Tax laws change frequently, and many complexities in the tax law are beyond the scope of this chapter. It is important, however, to have a sense of how tax laws influence investment decisions and how possible tax law changes may affect the desirability of real estate relative to other investments.

This chapter does *not* deal with real estate held as a *personal residence* by individuals. Special rules apply to the taxation of personal residences. For example, personal residences cannot be depreciated for tax purposes. We also assume that the property is not held for resale to others. Individuals holding property for resale to others in the ordinary course of business are referred to as **dealers,** *not investors.* Examples of individuals or firms with *dealer* status would be developers who develop lots for resale, builders of houses for resale, or others who do not intend to hold real estate as an investment, but rather for immediate resale. Real property held for resale by a dealer is *not depreciable* for tax purposes. (Depreciation rules are discussed later in the chapter.)

In this chapter we only consider property "held for use in a trade or business." *Most income-producing real estate investments are included in this category.* An owner acquires real estate with the intent to operate, modify, or do whatever necessary to produce income in a trade or business. Individuals in other occupations who own and operate rental properties are also in this category, although they must be actively engaged in the management of the property. Investors in a partnership, corporation, or trust may also hold property for use in a trade or business.[14] Real estate used in trade or businesses includes land and improvements such as income-producing rental properties and commercial properties, which are subject to depreciation. This category of real estate is the primary focus of the chapter.

Owners of real estate used in the production of income in a trade or business report income from rents and may deduct expenses incurred in operating the property, such as maintenance, repair, and utilities. They may also deduct property taxes, interest on mortgage loans made to acquire property, and interest on loans made in the operation of the business. In addition, they are allowed deductions for depreciation, and when properties are sold, certain capital gain and loss provisions (discussed in a later section) also apply.

Taxable Income from Operation of Real Estate

We have discussed at length how to calculate net operating income *(NOI)* for income-producing property. Recall that the calculation of *NOI* involves deducting

[14]Real estate used for the production of income in a trade or business is categorized as Section 1231 assets. Capital equipment (such as machinery) purchased by businesses that use such assets in the production of income are also designated as Section 1231 assets.

expenses associated with *operating* a property, such as property taxes, insurance, maintenance, management, and utilities. Then, subtracting the mortgage payment from the *NOI* results in before-tax cash flow from operating the property $(BTCF_o)$. We will now see that **taxable income** from operating real estate income property differs from $BTCF_o$ for two main reasons.[15] First, only the *interest* portion of a loan payment, not the total payment, is deductible from *NOI* for tax purposes. Second, the tax code allows owners to deduct a **depreciation allowance** from *NOI*. Thus, taxable income from operating a real estate income property can be stated as follows:

$$\text{Taxable Income} = NOI - \text{Interest} - \text{Depreciation Allowance}$$

The amount of interest deductible in a given taxable year equals the total interest paid to the lender during that year. We have discussed the separation of loan payments into principal and interest in considerable detail in earlier chapters.[16] We have not covered calculating depreciation allowances for tax purposes yet, and we will discuss this subject in the following section.

Depreciation Allowances

Physical assets like buildings suffer from physical depreciation over time that, *ceteris paribus,* reduces their economic value. Because buildings must ultimately be replaced, and because tax law allows investment in improvements to be recovered before income produced from the improvement is taxed, the investor may take a deduction for capital recovery (depreciation) from net operating income prior to the determination of taxable income. Otherwise, net operating income and taxable income would be overstated by an amount equal to the annual decrease in value due to economic depreciation. Thus, in theory, investors should only be taxed on the income net of this economic allowance for depreciation. This is the theoretical basis for tax depreciation.

However, because of inflation, changes in supply and demand, and other economic factors that also affect the value of real estate, it is difficult to know what portion of any net change in value is caused by physical depreciation. Further, our tax system has historically provided for depreciation allowances that are greater than any actual decline in the economic value of the property. As we will see, to the extent that tax depreciation *allowances* exceed *actual* economic depreciation, investors realize tax benefits. Exhibit 10–17 summarizes the methods for computing depreciation allowances that various tax laws in effect in recent years have allowed.

It should be obvious from the exhibit that tax policy on depreciation allowances has varied considerably. As indicated, this is because, historically, Congress has provided for allowances in excess of economic depreciation to stimulate investment in real estate in the belief that this policy would increase construction and, hence, the supply of rentable space in the economy. Unfortunately, it may also have contributed to much of the overbuilding that occurred during the early 1980s. As shown in the exhibit, the Tax Reform Act (TRA), which passed in 1986, lengthened depreciable life from its length during the period from 1981 to 1986. Increasing the depreciable life of real estate is one of several features in the 1986 law that reduced the favorable tax treatment that real estate had enjoyed previously. Later in this chapter we will see that depreciation is one source of tax benefits to investors in real estate.

[15] Additional differences will be shown in later chapters.

[16] You may want to review the appendix to Chapter 7 at this time.

EXHIBIT 10–17 Depreciation Rules for Real Estate*

Years	*Depreciable Life*	*Methods Allowed*
1969–1980	Useful life, approximately 30–40 years	Accelerated or straight line†
1981–1983	15 years	ACRS based on 175% of straight-line depreciation‡
1984–1985	18 years	ACRS based on 175% of straight-line depreciation‡
1986	19 years	ACRS based on 175% of straight-line depreciation‡
1987–1992	27.5 years for residential	Straight line
	31.5 years for nonresidential	Straight line
1993–?	27.5 years for residential	Straight line
	39 years for nonresidential	Straight line

*Some real estate investments also include personal property such as furniture and fixtures. Personal property can be depreciated over a much shorter time period than the real property (e.g., 8 years under the current tax law).

†Investors generally selected accelerated depreciation methods that ranged from 125 to 200 percent of straight-line depreciation, depending on whether the property was residential or nonresidential, new or existing.

‡Because of severe "recapture" rules that affected investors who used accelerated depreciation on nonresidential real estate, most investors used straight-line depreciation in nonresidential real estate during this period.

Depreciable Basis. The amount that can be depreciated for real estate improvements depends on the **depreciable basis** of the asset. The basis for a real estate investment is generally equal to the *cost* of the improvements (unless inherited or acquired by gift). *Cost* is generally defined to include the acquisition price of the improvements plus any installation costs associated with placing them into service. The cost of any capital improvements to the property made during the ownership period is also included in the basis when such outlays are made. Only improvements can be depreciated, not the cost of land. In this chapter, we focus on the tax treatment for existing properties. (Differences for properties that will be *developed and constructed* are discussed in a later chapter.)

Loan Points

Points paid in connection with obtaining a loan to purchase, refinance, or operate a real estate income property investment must be deducted ratably over the term of the loan. For example, suppose an investor secures a loan for $800,000 to purchase an office building. The loan is to be amortized over a 25-year term but has a term of 10 years with a balloon payment due at the end of the 10th year. Suppose two points, or $16,000, are paid on the loan. For tax purposes, the $16,000 would have to be amortized over 10 years, or $1,600 per year. If the investor sells the property before the points are fully amortized (year 10 in this example) the balance can be expensed in the year of sale. Thus in the above example, if the property is sold and the loan is repaid after five years, $8,000 could be expensed.

Tax Liability and After-Tax Cash Flow

Once we have calculated taxable income, we can calculate the tax liability that results from operating the property. The tax liability is calculated by multiplying the taxable income by the investor's marginal tax rate. The **marginal tax rate** is the rate that the *additional* income from the investment under consideration will be taxed. In general, we can think of it as the investor's tax bracket. The tax rate that corresponds to a particular tax bracket is the rate that applies to an *additional* or *marginal* dollar

EXHIBIT 10–18 2000 Marginal Ordinary Income Tax Rates for a Married Taxpayer Filing Jointly

Taxable Income	*Marginal Tax Rate*
$0–$43,850	15%
43,851–105,950	28
105,951–161,450	31
161,451–288,350	36
Over 288,350	39.6

of income that falls in a particular bracket. For investment decisions, we want to know how the additional income from adding the particular investment under consideration will affect the investor's taxes. Thus, we are interested in knowing what marginal tax rate (or rates) applies to the investment. For example, suppose the individual to whom the rates in Exhibit 10–18 apply already has taxable income of $100,000. Furthermore, suppose a real estate investment would produce taxable income of $10,000. According to the exhibit, the additional $10,000 of income would be taxed at a 31 percent rate, resulting in $3,100 in taxes.

Taxable Income from Disposal of Depreciable Real Property

In establishing whether a taxable **capital gain** or loss has occurred when a property is sold, we must determine the gross sales price. The gross sales price is equal to any cash or other property received in payment for the property sold, plus any liabilities against the property assumed by the buyer. Any selling expenses (e.g., legal fees, recording fees, and brokerage fees) may then be deducted to establish *net sales proceeds.* To determine gain or loss, subtract the *adjusted basis* of the property from net sales proceeds. The adjusted basis of a property is its *original basis* (cost of land and improvements, acquisition and installation fees) plus the cost of any capital improvement, alterations, or additions made during the period of ownership, less accumulated depreciation taken to date. Any excess of the net sales proceeds over the adjusted basis results in a taxable gain, and any deficit results in a taxable loss.

In the case of depreciable real estate held for use in trade or business, *net* gains on the sale are treated as long-term capital gains. The tax rate on long-term capital gains is often less than the rate on ordinary income. For example, the 1993 Tax Act set the maximum capital gain tax rate at 28 percent even if the investor is in a higher tax bracket for ordinary income. In 1997 the capital gain tax rate was lowered to 20 percent for that portion of the gain due to any increase in the value of the property and 25 percent for that portion of the gain due to depreciation taken during the seller's holding period.

After-Tax Investment Analysis

We now consider the effect of federal income taxes on the office building investment analysis example introduced earlier in this chapter. As a starting point for our discussion, Exhibit 10–19 summarizes the calculation of before-tax cash flow from the office building example introduced earlier in the chapter.

EXHIBIT 10–19 Estimates of Before-Tax Cash Flow from Operations and Sale

	Year				
	1	*2*	*3*	*4*	*5*
Cash flow from operations:					
Net operating income *(NOI)*	$903,050	$928,985	$955,439	$973,790	$1,010,822
Less debt service *(DS)*	689,025	689,025	689,025	689,025	689,025
Before-tax cash flow	$214,025	$239,960	$266,414	$284,765	$ 321,797
Estimates of cash flows from sale in year 5:					
Sales price					$9,700,000
Less mortgage balance					5,343,245
Before-tax cash flow $(BTCF_s)$					$4,356,755

After-Tax Cash Flow from Operations

We have estimated *before-tax* cash flows from the investment and now must determine the increase or decrease in the investor's taxable income as a result of undertaking it. Because taxes will either increase or decrease as a result of the investment, the increase or decrease must be added to or subtracted from before-tax cash flows to determine cash flow on an *after-tax* basis. To do this we must consider how much taxable income is produced each year from operations and then consider taxes in the year that the property is sold. Exhibit 10–20 shows the calculation of taxable income and after-tax cash flow from operating the property. In Exhibit 10–20 we see that we can find taxable income by subtracting interest and depreciation from the *NOI.* Note that only the interest, not the total loan payment, is tax deductible. In our example, interest was based on having a $5,950,000 loan amortized over a 20-year term with monthly payments based on a 10 percent interest rate. Exhibit 10–21 reproduces the summary loan schedule from earlier in this chapter.

Depreciation. Taxable income is also affected by an allowance for *depreciation.* As discussed earlier in the chapter, residential properties may be depreciated over 27.5 years, and nonresidential real property must be depreciated over 39 years. Both must be depreciated on a straight-line basis.[17] Also recall that only the improvements, not land, can be depreciated. Thus, we need to know what portion of the $8.5 million purchase price of the office building represents building improvements as opposed to land. For our case example, we assume that land cost requirements are 15 percent of the purchase price or $1,275,000, leaving improvements of $7,225,000. Dividing improvement cost by 39 results in an annual depreciation deduction of $185,256.[18]

[17]In the case of mixed use properties (those with both residential and nonresidential uses), if *one* of the uses produces 80 percent of revenues, the total improvement may be depreciated over the tax life corresponding to that use.

[18]The IRS publishes tables that taxpayers must use to calculate depreciation deductions. The tables assume that the investor purchases the property in the middle of the month, and they prorate the first-year depreciation according to the actual month of the year the property is purchased. We are simply dividing by 39 years.

EXHIBIT 10–20 Taxable Income and After-Tax Cash Flow from Operations

Taxable income:					
Net operating income *(NOI)*	$903,050	$928,985	$955,439	$973,790	$1,010,822
Less: interest	590,569	580,259	568,869	556,288	542,388
depreciation	185,256	185,256	185,256	185,256	185,256
Taxable income (loss)	127,225	163,470	201,313	232,246	283,177
Tax (at 36%)	$ 45,801	$ 58,849	$ 72,473	$ 83,609	$ 101,944
After-tax cash flow:					
Before-tax cash flow *(BTCF)*	$214,025	$239,960	$266,414	$284,765	$ 321,797
Less: tax	45,801	58,849	72,473	83,609	101,944
After-tax cash flow *(ATCF)*	$168,224	$181,110	$193,941	$201,156	$ 219,853

Recall that depreciation allowances represent recovery of capital and do not represent an actual cash outflow for the investor (that occurs when the property is acquired). The deduction only affects taxable income and not operating cash flows. In our example, taxable income is $127,225 in year 1. Assuming the investor is in a 36 percent tax bracket, the increase in tax liability as a result of owning the property will be $45,801 (.36 × $127,225). Subtracting this from before-tax cash flow results in after-tax cash flow of $168,224 in year 1.

Note that taxable income is *positive* during each year in this example. If the taxable income were negative (i.e., a tax loss), additional assumptions would have to be made regarding the investor's ability to use the losses to offset other taxable income. We discuss negative taxable income later in this chapter.

After-Tax Cash Flow from Sale

Exhibit 10–22 illustrates how sale of the property affects the investor's taxable income. When determining the investor's capital gain from sale of the property, we should keep in mind that the investor will have depreciated the property for five years. Hence, the investor's *cost basis* in the property will be reduced. In our example, depreciation was $185,256 per year for five years, resulting in total depreciation (accumulated depreciation) of $926,282. Subtracting the accumulated depreciation from the original cost basis of the property (cost of the land and improvements) results in an adjusted basis of $7,573,718. (Adjusted basis is also sometimes referred to as the *book value* of the property.) The difference between the adjusted basis ($7,573,718) and the sale price ($9,700,000) is the capital gain, $2,126,282. As discussed earlier, the portion of this gain due to price appreciation (sale price less original cost basis) has a maximum capital gain tax rate of 20 percent. The portion of the gain due to depreciation taken over the holding period (accumulated depreciation) has a maximum tax rate of 25 percent. Thus, the capital gain tax in this example can be calculated as shown at the top of the next page.

Subtracting tax from the before-tax cash flow results in **after-tax cash flow** from sale of $3,885,184.

Price appreciation ($9,700,000 − $8,500,000)		$1,200,000
Accumulated depreciation		926,282
Total gain		$2,126,282
Tax on price appreciation	$1,200,000 × .20 =	$ 240,000
Tax on accumulated depreciation	926,282 × .25 =	231,571
Total capital gain tax		$ 471,571

After-Tax IRR

Using the information from Exhibits 10–20 and 10–22, we may now calculate the after-tax *IRR*. Exhibit 10–23 summarizes the cash flows along with the before-tax cash flows for comparison. As we might expect, the after-tax *IRR* of 15.17 percent is lower than the before-tax *IRR,* which is 19.64 percent. However, although the investor's tax rate was 36 percent, the after-tax *IRR* is not 36 percent lower than the before-tax *IRR*. Rather, it is about 23 percent lower (1 − 15.17 ÷ 19.64 = 22.76%).

Effective Tax Rate

In the previous section, we indicated that the after-tax *IRR* is 23 percent lower than the before-tax *IRR,* even though the investor had a 36 percent marginal tax rate. In this case we would say that the **effective tax rate** on income from this investment would be 23 percent. Why is the effective tax rate on this investment lower than the marginal tax rate? The reason is that investors can reduce taxable income each year by the amount of depreciation deductions even though the property is not really

EXHIBIT 10–21 Summary Loan Information

	End of Year				
	1	*2*	*3*	*4*	*5*
Payment	$ 689,025	$ 689,025	$ 689,025	$ 689,025	$ 689,025
Mortgage balance	5,851,543	5,742,776	5,622,620	5,489,883	5,343,245
Interest	590,569	580,259	568,869	556,288	542,388
Principal	98,457	108,767	120,156	132,738	146,637

EXHIBIT 10–22 After-Tax Cash Flow from Sale in Year 5

Sale price			$9,700,000
Less mortgage balance			5,343,245
Before-tax cash flow *($BTCF_s$)*			4,356,755
Taxes in year of sale			
Sale price		$9,700,000	
Original cost basis	$8,500,000		
Accumulated depreciation	926,282		
Adjusted basis		7,573,718	
Capital gain		$2,126,282	
Tax on gain*			471,571
After-tax cash flow from sale *($ATCF_s$)*			$3,885,184

*[($9,700,000 − 8,500,000) × .20] + [$926,282 × .25].

EXHIBIT 10–23 Cash Flow Summary

	End of Year					
	0	*1*	*2*	*3*	*4*	*5*
Before-tax cash flow	$−2,550,000	$214,025	$239,960	$266,314	$284,765	$4,678,551
After-tax cash flow	−2,550,000	168,224	181,110	193,941	201,156	4,105,037

Before-tax *IRR(BTIRR)* = 19.64%
After-tax *IRR (ATIRR)* = 15.17%

EXHIBIT 10–24 After-Tax Net Present Value (13% discount rate)

Present value of *ATCF* from operations (Exhibit 10–19)	$ 667,817
Present value of *ATCF* from reversion (Exhibit 10–22)	2,108,722
Total present value	2,776,539
Less: original equity investment	−2,550,000
After-tax net present value	$ 226,539

decreasing in value. In fact, in this example it is increasing in value. Although depreciation allowances also reduce the adjusted basis of the property each year and will eventually result in an increase in taxes paid on the capital gain in the year of sale, the "time value of money" makes lower taxes paid on income each year a benefit to the investor. Furthermore, recall that the portion of capital gain due to depreciation recapture was taxed at 25 percent. Thus, the investor is able to defer taxes until the property is sold and convert (through depreciation deductions) some of the ordinary income to capital gains, which are taxed at a lower rate for investors who are in tax brackets above 25 percent.

After-Tax NPV

Earlier in the chapter, we calculated a net present value for the office building example using before-tax cash flows. Similarly, we can calculate the *NPV* using after-tax cash flows. Exhibit 10–24 summarizes the calculations using a 13 percent discount rate. Note that a lower, *after*-tax discount rate was applied to the after-tax cash flows to obtain the **after-tax net present value.** The after-tax discount rate depends on the after-tax return that can be earned on alternative investments of comparable risk.

A Note about Passive Losses

Starting with the Tax Reform Act of 1986, income and loss from all sources including real estate, had to be divided into three categories as follows:

1. ***Passive income*** *(or loss):* Income or loss from a trade or business where the investor does not materially participate in the management or operation of the property. Material participation is defined as "involvement in the

operations of the activity on a regular, continuous, and substantial basis." Investment in rental real estate is considered to be a passive activity. Hence, even if an investor materially participates in the operation of the property, income and losses earned from such activity is categorized as passive income or loss. Income (or loss) received by a limited partner in a partnership is considered passive by definition.

2. ***Active income*** *(or loss):* Salaries, wages, fees for services, and income from a trade or business in which the investor materially participates. However, even if a taxpayer materially participates, income or loss from rental activity is not considered active income. Thus, income from rental housing, office buildings, shopping centers, and other real estate activities in which a taxpayer is a landlord is not classified as active income (or loss). This income or loss is classified as *passive income.* However, the operation of a hotel, other transient lodging, or a nursing home is *not* a rental activity, and therefore its owners will have active income if they materially participate.
3. ***Portfolio income*** *(or loss):* Interest and dividend income from stocks, bonds, and some categories of real estate that are classified as *capital assets.* As stated earlier in the chapter, most real estate investments are classified as being held for a trade or business and not as capital assets. Examples of portfolio income from real estate activity include dividends received on shares in a real estate investment trust (REIT) or income received on long-term land leases or net leases on real estate where the owner does not materially participate in its operation.

These income classifications are very important because, in general, passive losses cannot be used to offset income from another category (special exceptions are discussed in the next section). This stipulation is referred to as the *passive activity loss limitation* (PAL). Prior to the 1986 Tax Reform Act, many investors purchased real estate that was held as a trade or business by a limited partnership in which the individual investor (limited partner) did not materially participate. These investments often produced (and may still be producing) tax losses that the investor used to offset other taxable income. The passive activity loss limitation prevents investors from offsetting taxable income with passive losses. Passive losses produced from real estate investments and other passive activities now must be used to offset passive income earned during the tax year. Any remaining or unused passive losses must be "suspended" and carried forward to offset any passive income earned in future years.

When an investment producing passive income is *sold* and a capital gain occurs, any unused or suspended losses from that activity (1) must first be used to offset any capital gain from the sale of that activity, (2) must then be used to offset any other passive income produced from other passive activities during that year, and (3) can then be used to offset *any income,* including active and portfolio income earned during that year. To the extent that unused losses remain, they may be carried forward into succeeding years as capital losses, not subject to passive loss rules. For Section 1231 property, any remaining losses would be deductible as ordinary losses.

In cases where the sale of a passive activity, such as real estate, produces a capital loss, *and* unused suspended losses from previous years also remain, the unused passive losses may be used to offset any other sources of income (active, passive, or portfolio). Of the capital loss portion, $3,000 of the loss may be used to offset any other source of income that year. Any excess must be carried forward to the next taxable year as a capital loss. It would no longer be subject to passive loss rules, and the excess as well as any unused passive losses may be deducted from ordinary income as a Section 1231 loss.[19]

Special Exceptions to PAL Rules

One special exception to the PAL rules that was included in the 1986 Tax Reform Act applies to individual rental property owners (other than limited partners). These investors are allowed to offset active income with up to $25,000 of passive activity losses (to the extent such losses exceed income from passive activities) from rental real estate activities in which the individual *actively* participates. Active participation is less restrictive than the material participation standard referred to earlier and requires less personal involvement. In general, the individual must own a 10 percent or greater interest in the activity and be involved in management decisions, such as selection of tenants and determination of rents, or must arrange for others to provide services (e.g., a property manager to manage the property on a day-to-day basis).

The TRA phases out this special rule for individuals with adjusted gross incomes between $100,000 and $150,000. It reduces the $25,000 loss allowance by 50 percent of the amount of the individual's adjusted gross income when such income for the taxable year exceeds $100,000. Thus, individuals with an adjusted gross income of $120,000 would only be allowed to use up to $15,000 of any passive losses to reduce active income. An individual with adjusted gross income in excess of $150,000 would receive no loss allowance.

The Tax Act of 1993 introduced a second exception to the PAL rules that provides relief for real estate brokers, sales associates, and other real estate professionals who can demonstrate "material involvement in the real estate business."[20] These individuals are eligible to deduct unlimited real estate losses if (1) more than half of all personal services they perform during the year are for real property trades or businesses in which they materially participate, and (2) they perform more than 750 hours of service per year in those real estate activities.

Conclusion

This chapter has introduced concepts and techniques important in the analysis of real estate income property. We discussed ways of projecting cash flows for an investor and ways of evaluating those cash flows with various measures of investment performance. The performance measures discussed in this chapter (*IRR, NPV, DCR,* etc.) will be used throughout the remainder of the text.

This chapter also pointed out the importance of considering risk when analyzing investments. Rates of return for alternative investments cannot be compared if the investments have different degrees of risk. We introduced several ways the investor can attempt to evaluate the riskiness of a real estate investment, including sensitivity analysis, partitioning the return, and the use of probability distributions to compute the expected return and standard deviation of the return.

Although the techniques in this chapter provide a good initial analysis of a project, as demonstrated by the office building example, many questions remain to explore in more depth. For example, How will taxes affect the performance of the property? Are there alternative ways of financing the property that would be better? The remaining chapters in this part of the text will cover these and other questions.

Another area this chapter covered was the key tax considerations that affect real estate investment decisions.

[19]For further explanation see P. Fass, R. Haft, L. Loffman, and S. Presant, *Tax Reform Act of 1986* (New York: Clark Boardman, 1986).

[20]Material involvement generally means that the taxpayer is involved in real estate operations on a regular, continuous, and substantial basis. Limited partners (discussed in Chapter 12) do not materially participate because active involvement could cause them to lose their limited liability status.

These considerations include determining the appropriate marginal tax rate, rules for depreciating real property, calculation of taxable income from operation of the property, and calculation of capital gain. These tax considerations will enter into different types of analyses that we will address in many of the remaining chapters of the text. In several cases we will be applying the tax rules introduced in this chapter to see how they affect investment. We will consider issues such as these: What is the optimal time to dispose of a property? Is it profitable to renovate a building? Additional tax considerations, such as the taxation of limited partnerships and development projects, will also be introduced in future chapters. Remember, however, that tax laws are subject to revisions that can have a substantial impact on the calculation of taxable income and taxes for real estate income property. Thus, this chapter is not intended to be a substitute for a comprehensive analysis of how current and future tax laws may affect a specific investor. It does, however, point out the general issues that investors should take into consideration regardless of the specifics of the tax law in effect at a particular point in time.

Key Terms

Questions

1. What are the primary benefits from investing in real estate income property?
2. What factors affect a property's projected *NOI?*
3. What factors would result in a property increasing in value over a holding period?
4. How do you think expense stops and CPI adjustments in leases affect the riskiness of the lease from the lessor's point of view?
5. Why should investors be concerned about market rents if they are purchasing a property subject to leases?
6. Discuss the pros and cons of using growth rates versus terminal cap rates to project a resale price.
7. What is the rationale for applying a terminal cap rate to the income one year after the end of the investment holding period?
8. Why is an overall rate not an *IRR?* In general, what factors could cause an *IRR* to be higher than an overall rate?
9. When might it be incorrect to apply a growth rate to the initial value to estimate the reversion?

10. What is meant by *equity?*
11. What are the similarities and differences between an overall rate and an equity dividend rate?
12. What is the significance of a debt coverage ratio?
13. What is meant by partitioning the internal rate of return? Why is this procedure meaningful?
14. What is a risk premium? Why does such a premium exist between interest rates on mortgages and rates of return earned on equity invested in real estate?
15. What are some of the types of risk that should be considered when analyzing real estate and other categories of investment?
16. What is the difference between business risk and financial risk?
17. Why is the variance (or standard deviation) used as a measure of risk? What are the advantages and disadvantages of this risk measure?
18. What is meant by a *tax shelter?*
19. How is the gain from the sale of real estate taxed?
20. What is meant by an *effective tax rate?* What does it measure?
21. Do you think taxes affect the value of real estate versus other investments?
22. What is the significance of the passive activity loss limitation (PAL) rules for real estate investors?

Problems

1. An office building has three floors of rentable space with a single tenant on each floor. The first floor has 20,000 square feet of rentable space and is currently renting for $15 per square foot. Three years remain on the lease. The lease has an expense stop at $4 per square foot. The second floor has 15,000 square feet of rentable space and is leasing for $15.50 per square foot and has four years remaining on the lease. This lease has an expense stop at $4.50 per square foot. The third floor has 15,000 square feet of leasable space and a lease just signed for the next five years at a rental rate of $17 per square foot, which is the current market rate. The expense stop is at $5 per square foot, which is what expenses per square foot are estimated to be during the next year (excluding management). Management expenses are expected to be 5 percent of effective gross income and are not included in the expense stop. Each lease also has a CPI adjustment that provides for the base rent to increase at half the increase in the CPI. The CPI is projected to increase 3 percent per year. Estimated operating expenses for the next year include the following:

Property taxes	$100,000
Insurance	10,000
Utilities	75,000
Janitorial	25,000
Maintenance	40,000
Total	$250,000

All expenses are projected to increase 3 percent per year. The market rental rate at which leases are expected to be renewed is also projected to increase 3 percent per year. When a lease is renewed, it would have an expense stop equal to operating expenses per square foot during the first year of the lease.

To account for any time that may be necessary to find new tenants after the first leases expire, vacancy is estimated to be 10 percent of *EGI* for the last two years (years 4 and 5).

a. Project the effective gross income *(EGI)* for the next five years.

b. Project the expense reimbursements for the next five years.

c. Project the net operating income *(NOI)* for next five years.

d. How much does the *NOI* increase (average compound rate) over the five years?

e. Assuming the property is purchased for $5 million what is the overall capitalization rate (going-in rate)?

2. You are an employee of University Consultants, Ltd., and have been given the following assignment. You are to present an investment analysis of a new small residential income-producing property for sale to a potential investor. The asking price for the property is $1,250,000; rents are estimated at $200,000 during the first year and are expected to grow at 3 percent per year thereafter. Vacancies and collection losses are expected to be 10 percent of rents. Operating expenses will be 35 percent of effective gross income. A 70 percent loan can be obtained at 11 percent interest for 30 years. The property is expected to appreciate in value at 3 percent per year and is expected to be owned for five years and then sold.

a. What is the investor's expected before-tax internal rate of return on equity invested *(BTIRR)?*

b. What is the first-year debt coverage ratio?

c. What is the terminal capitalization rate?

d. What is the *NPV* using a 14 percent discount rate? What does this mean?

e. What is the profitability index using a 14 percent discount rate? What does this mean?

3. Two investments have the following pattern of expected returns:

Investment A					
Year	*1*	*2*	*3*	*4*	*4 (sale)*
BTCF	\$5,000	\$10,000	\$12,000	\$15,000	\$120,000

Investment B					
Year	*1*	*2*	*3*	*4*	*4 (sale)*
BTCF	\$2,000	\$4,000	\$1,000	\$5,000	\$180,000

Investment A requires an outlay of \$110,000 and Investment B requires an outlay of \$120,000.

a. What is the *BTIRR* on each investment?

b. If the *BTIRR* were partitioned based on $BTCF_o$ and $BTCF_s$, what proportions of the *BTIRR* would be represented by each?

c. What do these proportions mean?

4. Mike Riskless is considering two projects. He has estimated the *IRR* for each under three possible scenarios and assigned probabilities of occurrence to each scenario.

State of Economy	*Probability*	*Estimated* BTIRR *Investment I*	*Estimated* BTIRR *Investment II*
Optimistic	0.20	0.15	0.20
Most likely	0.60	0.10	0.15
Pessimistic	0.20	0.05	0.05
	1.00		

Riskless is aware that the pattern of returns for Investment II looks very attractive relative to Investment I; however, he believes that Investment II could be more risky than Investment I. He would like to know how he can compare the two investments considering both the risk and return on each. What do you suggest?

5. An investor has projected three possible scenarios for a project as follows:

Pessimistic—NOI will be \$200,000 the first year, then decrease 2 percent per year over a five-year holding period. The property will sell for \$1.8 million after five years.

Most likely—NOI will be level at \$200,000 per year for the next five years (level *NOI*) and the property will sell for \$2 million.

Optimistic—NOI will be \$200,000 the first year and increase 3 percent per year over a five-year holding period. The property will then sell for \$2.2 million.

The asking price for the property is \$2 million. The investor thinks there is about a 30 percent probability for the pessimistic scenario, a 40 percent probability for the most likely scenario, and a 30 percent probability for the optimistic scenario.

a. Compute the *IRR* for each scenario.

b. Compute the expected *IRR*.

c. Compute the variance and standard deviation of the *IRR*s.

d. Would this project be better than one with a 12 percent expected return and a standard deviation of 4 percent?

6. (Extension of problem 2) You are still an employee of University Consultants, Ltd.

The investor tells you she would also like to know how tax considerations affect your investment analysis. You determine that the building represents 90 percent of value and would be depreciated over 39 years (use 1/39 per year). The potential investor indicates that she is in the 36 percent tax bracket and has enough passive income from other activities so that any passive losses from this activity would not be subject to any passive activity loss limitations. Capital gains from price appreciation will be taxed at 20 percent and depreciation recapture will be taxed at 25 percent.

a. What is the investor's expected after-tax internal rate of return on equity invested *(ATIRR)?* How does this compare with the before-tax *IRR (BTIRR)* calculated earlier?

b. What is the effective tax rate and before-tax equivalent yield?

c. How would you evaluate the tax benefits of this investment?

d. Recalculate the *ATIRR* in part (*b*) under the assumption that the investor *cannot* deduct any of the passive losses (they all become suspended) until the property is sold after five years.

CHAPTER

11

Financial Leverage and Financing Alternatives

In Chapter 7 we introduced a number of issues related to analyzing financing alternatives. Important concepts from that chapter include the effective cost of borrowing (before and after tax), and the incremental cost of borrowing additional funds. We also discussed how to evaluate whether a loan should be refinanced when interest rates decline. Although this discussion focused on *residential* property, all of the above concepts also apply to the analysis of income property.

The three preceding chapters have dealt with analyzing investment returns and risk on income property. In that analysis, we introduced financing and alluded to its effect on the before- and after-tax cash flow to the equity investor.

The purpose of this chapter will be to extend the discussion of debt from the earlier chapters in three additional ways. First, we consider how the level of financing affects the investor's before- and after-tax *IRR*. Second, we consider important underwriting procedures used by lenders when financing is sought by investors. Third, we consider several different financing alternatives that are used with real estate income property. Since it is impossible to discuss all the varieties of loans that are used in practice, we will concentrate on the primary alternatives and focus our discussion on concepts and techniques that you can apply to any type of financing alternative that you might consider.

Introduction to Financial Leverage

Why should an investor use debt? One obvious reason is simply that the investor may not have enough equity capital to buy the property. On the other hand, the investor may have enough equity capital but may choose to borrow anyway and use the excess equity to buy other properties. Because equity funds could be spread over several properties, the investor could reduce the overall risk of the portfolio. A second reason to borrow is to take advantage of the tax deductibility of mortgage interest, which amplifies tax benefits to the equity investor. The third reason usually given for using debt is to realize the potential benefit associated with financial leverage. **Financial leverage** is defined as benefits that may result for an investor who borrows money at a rate of interest lower than the expected rate of return on total funds invested in a property. If the return on the total investment invested in a property is greater than the rate of interest on the debt, the return on equity is magnified.

To examine the way financial leverage affects the investor's rate of return, we consider investment in a small commercial property with the following assumptions:

Purchase price	
Building value	$ 85,000
Land value	15,000
Total value	$100,000
Loan assumptions	
Loan amount	$ 80,000
Interest rate	10.00%
Term	Interest only
Income assumptions	
NOI	$12,000 per year (level)
Income tax rate*	28.00%
Depreciation	31.5 years (straight line)†
Resale price	$100,000
Holding period	5 years

*Used to illustrate this example only. Tax rates are subject to change.

†Recall from Chapter 10 that the Tax Act of 1993 allows residential property to be depreciated over 27.5 years and nonresidential property to be depreciated over 39 years. These rates are subject to change, however, and we use 31.5 years in this example for illustration only.

Using those assumptions, we obtain the cash flow estimates shown in Exhibit 11–1.

Exhibit 11–2 shows the cash flow summary and *IRR* calculations for the cash flows in Exhibit 11–1. From Exhibit 11–2 we see that the before-tax *IRR* (*BTIRR*) is 20 percent and the after-tax *IRR* (*ATIRR*) is 15.40 percent with an 80 percent loan. We now consider how these returns would be affected by a change in the amount of debt. Exhibits 11–3 and 11–4 show the cash flow and return calculations for the example assuming *no loan* is used.

From Exhibit 11–4 we see that both the *BTIRR* and *ATIRR* have fallen. That is, both returns are higher with debt than without debt. When this occurs, we say that the investment has **positive** or **favorable financial leverage.** We now examine the conditions that result in positive financial leverage more carefully. To do so, we first look at the conditions for positive leverage on a *before-tax* basis (the effect of leverage on *BTIRR*). Later, we examine the relationship on an *after-tax* basis (on *ATIRR*).

Conditions for Positive Leverage—Before Tax

In the example when no debt was used, the *BTIRR* was 12 percent. We will refer to this as the *unlevered BTIRR,* since it equals the return when no debt is used. In the case where 80 percent debt was used, the *BTIRR* increased to 20 percent. Why does this increase occur? It occurs because the *unlevered BTIRR is greater than the interest rate paid on the debt.*[1] The interest rate on the debt was 10 percent, which is less than the 12 percent unlevered *BTIRR*. We could say that the return on investment (before debt) is greater than the rate that has to be paid on the debt. This differential (12 percent versus 10 percent) means that positive leverage exists that will magnify the *BTIRR* on equity.

This relationship is formalized in a formula that estimates the return on equity, given the return on the property and the mortgage interest rate:[2]

[1]More precisely, the unlevered *IRR* is greater than the effective cost of the loan. Recall that the effective cost of a loan reflects points, prepayments, and other factors that affect the borrower.

[2]This is an approximation when the ratio of debt to equity changes over time.

EXHIBIT 11–1 Cash Flow for Commercial Building

	Estimates of Cash Flow from Operations Year				
	1	2	3	4	5
A. Before-tax cash flow:					
Net operating income (*NOI*)	$12,000	$12,000	$12,000	$12,000	$12,000
Less debt service (*DS*)	8,000	8,000	8,000	8,000	8,000
Before-tax cash flow	$ 4,000	$ 4,000	$ 4,000	$ 4,000	$ 4,000
B. Taxable income or loss:					
Net operating income (*NOI*)	$12,000	$12,000	$12,000	$12,000	$12,000
Less interest	8,000	8,000	8,000	8,000	8,000
Depreciation	2,698	2,698	2,698	2,698	2,698
Taxable income (loss)	1,302	1,302	1,302	1,302	1,302
Tax	$ 364	$ 364	$ 364	$ 364	$ 364
C. After-tax cash flow:					
Before-tax cash flow (*BTCF*)	$ 4,000	$ 4,000	$ 4,000	$ 4,000	$ 4,000
Less tax	364	364	364	364	364
After-tax cash flow (*ATCF*)	$ 3,636	$ 3,636	$ 3,636	$ 3,636	$ 3,636

Estimates of Cash Flows from Sale in Year 5

Sale price			$100,000
Less mortgage balance			80,000
Before-tax cash flow ($BTCF_s$)			$ 20,000
Taxes in year of sale			
Sale price		$100,000	
Original cost basis	$100,000		
Less accumulated depreciation	13,492		
Adjusted basis		86,508	
Capital gain		$ 13,492	
Tax from sale			3,778
After-tax cash flow from sale ($ATCF_s$)			$ 16,222

$$BTIRR_E = BTIRR_P + (BTIRR_P - BTIRR_D)\,(D/E)$$

where

$BTIRR_E$ = before-tax *IRR* on equity invested
$BTIRR_P$ = before-tax *IRR* on total investment in the property (debt and equity)
$BTIRR_D$ = before-tax *IRR* on debt (effective cost of the loan considering points)
D/E = ratio of debt to equity

Using the numbers for our example we have

$$BTIRR_E = 12.00\% + (12.00\% - 10.00\%) \times (80\% \div 20\%)$$
$$= 20.00\%$$

This formula indicates that as long as $BTIRR_P$ is greater than $BTIRR_D$, then $BTIRR_E$ will be greater than $BTIRR_P$. This situation is referred to as favorable or positive leverage. Whenever leverage is positive, the greater the amount of debt, the higher

EXHIBIT 11–2 Cash Flow Summary and *IRR*

	End of Year					
	0	1	2	3	4	5
BTCF	\$−20,000	\$4,000	\$4,000	\$4,000	\$4,000	24,000
ATCF	−20,000	3,636	3,636	3,636	3,636	19,858

Before-tax *IRR* (*BTIRR*) = 20.00%
After-tax *IRR* (*ATIRR*) = 15.40%

EXHIBIT 11–3 Cash Flow Estimates (no loan)

	Estimates of Cash Flow from Operations Year				
	1	2	3	4	5
A. Before-tax cash flow:					
Net operating income (*NOI*)	\$12,000	\$12,000	\$12,000	\$12,000	\$12,000
Less debt service (*DS*)	0	0	0	0	0
Before-tax cash flow	\$12,000	\$12,000	\$12,000	\$12,000	\$12,000
B. Taxable income or loss:					
Net operating income (*NOI*)	\$12,000	\$12,000	\$12,000	\$12,000	\$12,000
Less interest	0	0	0	0	0
Depreciation	2,698	2,698	2,698	2,698	2,698
Taxable income (loss)	9,302	9,302	9,302	9,302	9,302
Tax	\$ 2,604	\$ 2,604	\$ 2,604	\$ 2,604	\$ 2,604
C. After-tax cash flow:					
Before-tax cash flow (*BTCF*)	\$12,000	\$12,000	\$12,000	\$12,000	\$12,000
Less tax	2,604	2,604	2,604	2,604	2,604
After-tax cash flow (*ATCF*)	\$ 9,396	\$ 9,396	\$ 9,396	\$ 9,396	\$ 9,396

Estimates of Cash Flows from Sale in Year 5

Sale price			\$100,000
Less mortgage balance			0
Before-tax cash flow ($BTCF_s$)			\$100,000
Taxes in year of sale			
Sale price		\$100,000	
Original cost basis	\$100,000		
Less accumulated depreciation	13,492		
Adjusted basis		86,508	
Capital gain		\$ 13,492	
Tax from sale			3,778
After-tax cash flow from sale ($ATCF_s$)			\$ 96,222

EXHIBIT 11–4 Cash Flow Summary and Rates of Return (no loan)

	Cash Flow Summary End of Year					
	0	*1*	*2*	*3*	*4*	*5*
Before-tax cash flow	$–100,000	$12,000	$12,000	$12,000	$12,000	$112,000
After-tax cash flow	–100,000	9,396	9,396	9,396	9,396	105,618

Before-tax *IRR* (*BTIRR*) = 12.00%
After-tax *IRR* (*ATIRR*) = 8.76%

EXHIBIT 11–5 Before- and After-Tax Leverage

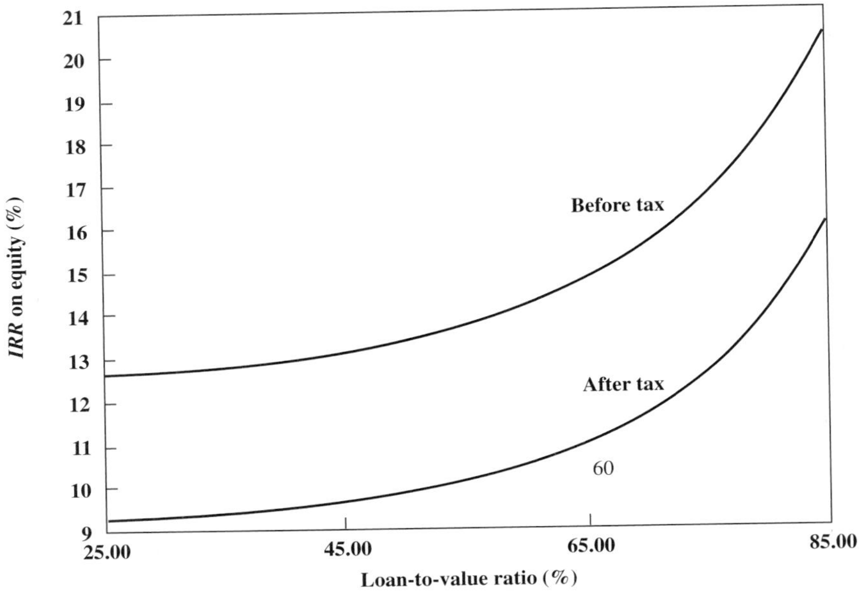

the return to the equity investor. From this result many investors conclude that they should borrow as much as possible. (We will see later that this conclusion is not necessarily valid when risk is considered.) The graph in Exhibit 11–5 illustrates the effect of different loan-to-value ratios on the *IRR* for our example.

While the relationships in Exhibit 11–5 are relatively straightforward, the amount of debt that may be used is limited. What are the limits? First, for various amounts of debt the debt coverage ratio may exceed the lender's limits, as discussed in Chapter 10. Because the *NOI* does not change when more debt is used, increasing the amount of debt increases the debt service relative to the *NOI*. Second, at higher loan-to-value ratios and declining debt coverage ratios, risk to the lender increases. As a result, the interest rate on additional debt will also increase. Indeed, at some point $BTIRR_p$ may no longer exceed $BTIRR_D$ (leverage will no longer be positive). Third, additional borrowing has additional risks for the equity investor. We will deal with the effect of leverage on risk more formally later in this chapter. However, we can point out now that leverage works both ways in the sense that it can magnify either returns or losses. That is, if the loan offers **negative (unfavorable) financial leverage,** or $ATIRR_D > BTIRR_P$, the use of more debt will magnify losses on equity invested in the property. We saw earlier that $BTIRR_P$ must exceed $BTIRR_D$ for the leverage to be favorable. Suppose that the interest rate is 14 percent instead of 10 percent. This results in negative leverage because the unlevered $BTIRR_E$ (12 percent) is now less than the 14 percent cost of debt. Exhibit 11–6 illustrates the effect that different loan-to-value ratios will have on the before- and after-tax *IRR*s. Note that when $BTIRR_P$ is less than $BTIRR_D$, then $BTIRR_E$ is also less than $BTIRR_D$ and declines even further as the amount borrowed (debt-to-equity ratio) increases. The next section develops this relationship more formally.

Conditions for Positive Leverage—After Tax

Looking at the after-tax IRR (ATIRR) in Exhibits 11–2 and 11–4, we see that ATIRRP (on total investment) is 8.76 percent and ATIRR on equity invested is 15.4 percent. Thus, the investor has favorable or positive leverage on an after-tax basis. That is, the expected after-tax IRR is higher if we can borrow money at a 10 percent rate as assumed in the example. How can leverage be favorable if the unlevered ATIRR (8.76 percent) is less than the cost of debt (10 percent)? The reason is because interest is tax deductible; hence we must consider the after-tax cost of debt. Because there are no points involved in this example, the after-tax cost of debt is equal to the before-tax cost times $(1 - t)$, where t is the tax rate. Thus the after-tax cost of debt is

$$.10(1 - .28) = 7.2\%$$

In the previous section we showed a formula to estimate the return on equity, given the return on the property and the mortgage interest rate. That formula can be modified to consider taxes as follows:

$$ATIRR_E = ATIRR_P + (ATIRR_P - ATIRR_D)\,(D/E)$$

where

$ATIRR_E$ = After-tax *IRR* on equity invested
$ATIRR_P$ = After-tax *IRR* on total funds invested in the property
$ATIRR_D$ = After-tax *IRR* on debt (effective after-tax cost of the loan)
D/E = Ratio of debt to equity

Using the above equation we have

$$\begin{aligned} ATIRR_E &= 8.76\% + (8.76\% - 7.2\%)\,(80\% \div 20\%) \\ &= 15.00\% \end{aligned}$$

Hence the approximation is 15 percent versus the actual *ATIRR* of 15.40 percent, as shown in Exhibit 11–2. The formula is an approximation because the debt-to-equity ratio increases over the holding period. That is, although the initial debt-to-equity ratio is 4.0 (\$80,000 ÷ \$20,000), when the property is sold, the debt is still \$80,000, but the equity is \$16,222 ($ATCF_S$ of \$96,222 less the loan of \$80,000), resulting in a debt-to-equity ratio of 4.93. Thus, the average *D/E* for the holding period is greater than the initial *D/E* of 4 that we used in the formula. However, using the initial *D/E* is still a good approximation. And the pivotal point for leverage is still the after-tax cost of debt. That is, for leverage to be favorable on an *after-tax* basis, the after-tax return on total funds invested must exceed the after-tax cost of the debt. For example, in our illustration, if the $ATIRR_P$ was less than 7.2 percent, leverage would be unfavorable.

EXHIBIT 11–6 Before- and After-Tax Leverage

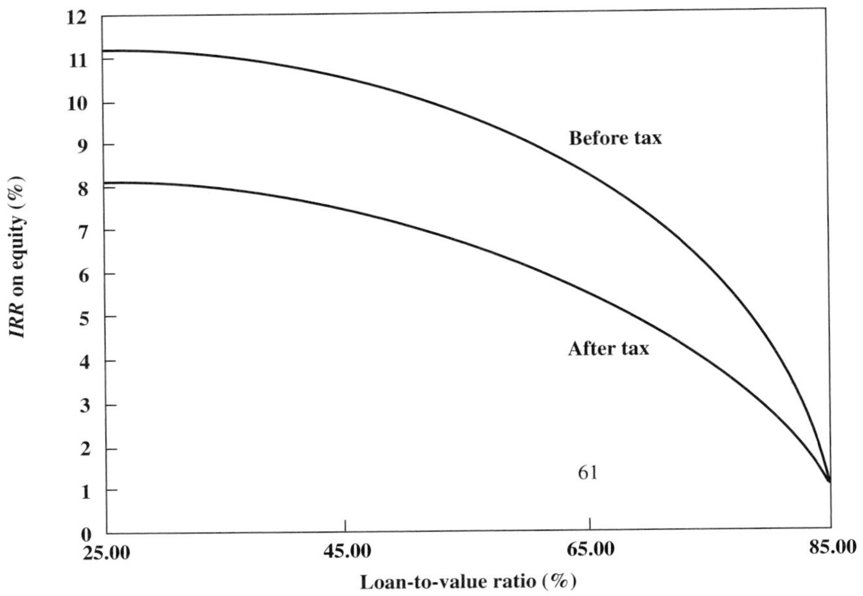

It is useful to summarize the various *IRR* calculations we have made for the office example. Exhibit 11–7 shows the before- and after-tax *IRR* with and without a loan. It is important to understand the difference between each of these returns. When using the term *return* (or *IRR*), it is obviously very important to specify whether that return is before tax or after tax, and whether it is based on having a loan (a *levered* return) or not having a loan (an *unlevered* return).

Break-Even Interest Rate

In the previous discussion we saw that the relationship between the after-tax *IRR* on the property (before debt) and the after-tax cost of debt determines whether leverage is favorable or unfavorable. It is sometimes useful to determine the maximum interest rate that could be paid on the debt before the leverage becomes unfavorable. This is referred to as the **break-even interest rate** and represents the interest rate at which the leverage is neutral (neither favorable or unfavorable). By examining the after-tax leverage equation in the previous section, we see that the point of neutral leverage can be expressed as follows:

$$ATIRR_D = ATIRR_P$$

Based on this relationship, we want to know the interest rate that will result in an after-tax cost of debt that is equal to the after-tax *IRR* on total funds invested in the property. In general, recall from Chapter 7 that the after-tax cost of debt, $ATIRR_D$, can be estimated as follows:

$$ATIRR_D = BTIRR_D(1 - t)$$

Exhibit 11–7 Summary *IRR* Measures

	$BTIRR_E$	$ATIRR_E$
No loan*	12.00%	8.76%
80% loan	20.00%	15.40%

*Note that $IRR_E = IRR_P$ when there is no loan.

Exhibit 11–8 Effect of Interest Rates on the After-Tax *IRR* on Equity

	$ATIRR_E$ (%) Loan to Value		
Interest Rate (%)	*60%*	*70%*	*80%*
10.00	10.83	11.86	13.73
10.50	10.36	11.16	12.61
11.00	9.89	10.45	11.48
11.50	9.41	9.73	10.32
12.00	8.92	9.01	9.16
12.50	8.44	8.27	7.98
13.00	7.95	7.53	6.78
13.50	7.45	6.79	5.57
14.00	6.95	6.03	4.34
14.50	6.45	5.27	3.10
15.00	5.95	4.50	1.85
15.50	5.44	3.73	0.58
16.00	4.92	2.94	−0.70

Solving this for the before-tax cost of debt, we have

$$BTIRR_D = \frac{ATIRR_D}{1 - t}$$

Because the break-even point for leverage occurs when $ATIRR_D = ATIRR_P$, we can substitute $ATIRR_P$ for $ATIRR_D$ in the above equation and obtain a break-even interest rate:

$$BTIRR_D = \frac{ATIRR_p}{1 - t}$$

For our example, the break-even interest rate (*BEIR*) would be

$$\frac{8.76\%}{1 - .28} = 12.17\%$$

This means that regardless of the amount borrowed, or degree of leverage desired, the maximum rate of interest that may be paid on debt and not reduce the return on equity is 12.17 percent. To demonstrate this concept further, Exhibit 11–8 shows the after-tax *IRR* for interest rates ranging from 10 to 16 percent for three different loan-to-value ratios. Note that for interest rates above the break-even interest rate of

EXHIBIT 11–9 After-Tax *IRR* versus Interest Rates

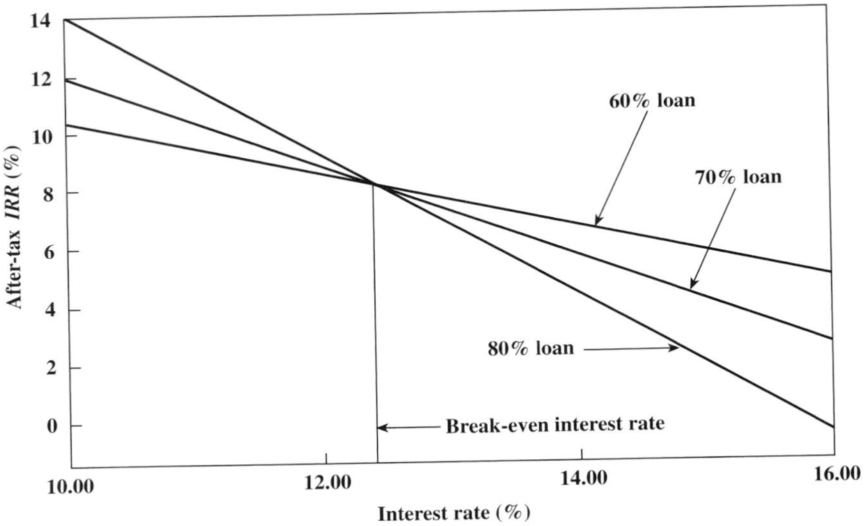

12.17 percent, the after-tax *IRR* for equity investor ($ATIRR_E$) is less than the after-tax *IRR* on total investment ($ATIRR_P$), which is 8.76 percent. Conversely, for interest rates below the break-even interest rate, the after-tax *IRR* for the equity investor is greater than the after-tax *IRR* on the property.

Exhibit 11–9 graphs the information in Exhibit 11–8 and shows the break-even interest rate. Again note that the break-even interest rate remains 12.17 percent regardless of the amount borrowed (that is, 60, 70, or 80 percent of the property value).

If an investor borrowed funds at an effective interest rate that was just equal to the break-even interest rate, leverage would be neutral; that is, it would not be unfavorable or favorable. However, at the break-even interest rate $ATIRR_P$ is exactly equal to $ATIRR_D$ (by definition), which means that $ATIRR_E$ will exactly equal $ATIRR_D$. That is, the investor earns the same after-tax rate of return as a lender in the same project. But borrowing at the break-even interest rate will not provide a risk premium for the equity investor. Equity investors normally require a risk premium because they bear the risk of variations in the performance of the property. We will show this situation more formally in the section following the next one.

Leverage and the Incremental Cost of Debt

As mentioned earlier in this chapter, at high amounts of debt a higher interest rate may have to be paid to obtain additional financing. We know that favorable leverage occurs as long as the effective cost of debt is less than the break-even interest rate. Thus we might conclude that it is advantageous to borrow additional funds as long as the cost of those funds is less than the break-even interest rate. We now show that this conclusion is not necessarily true. Recall that in Chapter 7 we discussed the concept of the **incremental cost of debt** as it related to loans on residential property. We showed that the decision to borrow additional funds should be made by considering the incremental or marginal cost of the additional funds obtained. Knowing the incremental cost of funds is equally important in analyzing the amount to borrow on income property.

In the example we have been using, an 80 percent loan was available at a 10 percent interest rate. This rate was less than the break-even interest rate of 12.17 percent; thus we concluded that leverage was favorable. Now suppose that the investor can obtain an 85 percent loan, but at a 10.25 percent interest rate instead of 10 percent (we assume the loan would be an interest-only loan for simplicity). We might conclude that borrowing the additional funds is desirable because the rate on the 85 percent loan (10.25 percent) is less than the break-even interest rate of 12.17 percent. However, the *incremental* cost of the additional $5,000 received on the 85 percent loan is 14.25 percent.[3] This cost is greater than the break-even interest rate of 12.17 percent. Thus, obtaining the additional loan is not desirable. Looking only at the 10.25 percent rate on the entire loan would not lead to the correct decision because it does not focus on the cost of the additional funds received. Recall from Chapter 7 that whenever the investor has a choice of obtaining a higher loan amount at a higher interest rate, an incremental cost is associated with obtaining the additional funds. Thus, we should compare this incremental cost with the break-even interest rate when deciding to borrow additional funds.

Risk and Leverage

We have seen how favorable financial leverage can increase $BTIRR_E$ and $ATIRR_E$. We also saw that increasing the amount of debt magnifies the effect of leverage. It is no wonder that many people conclude that they should borrow as much as possible (look at the number of "no money down" seminars and advocates of using "OPM," or other people's money). The point of the following discussion is to emphasize that *there is an implicit cost associated with the use of financial leverage.* This cost comes in the form of *higher risk.* Recall that we referred to risk as **financial risk** in Chapter 10. To illustrate, consider the following investment opportunity:

Total project costs (land, improvements, etc.) will be $1 million. In our initial example, the investor does not use debt to finance the project. Three possible scenarios for a project are as follows:

Pessimistic—*NOI* will be $100,000 the first year and decrease 2 percent per year over a five-year holding period. The property will sell for $900,000 after five years.

Most likely—*NOI* will be level at $110,000 per year for the next five years, and the property will sell for $1.1 million.

Optimistic—*NOI* will be $120,000 the first year and increase 5 percent per year for five years. The property will then sell for $1.3 million.

The investor thinks probability for the pessimistic scenario is about 20 percent, for the most likely scenario, 50 percent, and for the optimistic scenario, 30 percent.

[3]Interest on the 85 percent loan is (.1025)($85,000) = $8,712. Subtracting the $8,000 interest on the 80 percent loan (.10) ($80,000), we obtain a difference of $712.50 per year. Dividing this by the $5,000 additional funds received results in an incremental cost of 14.25 percent. Note that because it is an interest only loan, the total payments are the same as the interest payments. And because the balance of the loan does not change, the *IRR* can be found by simply dividing the payment by the loan amount, rather than using present value factors.

Using the preceding information, we have computed (calculations not shown) $BTIRR_P$ for each scenario, the expected $BTIRR_P$, the variance of the $BTIRR_P$s, and the standard deviation of the $BTIRR_P$s. The results are as follows:

Unlevered

	(1) Estimated $BTIRR_P$	*(2) Expected* $BTIRR_P$*	*(3) Deviation (1) − (2)*	*(4) Squared Deviation*	*(5) Probability*	*(6) Product (4)(5)*
Pessimistic	7.93	13.06	−5.13	26.31	0.20	5.26
Most likely	12.56	13.06	−0.50	0.25	0.50	0.12
Optimistic	17.31	13.06	4.25	18.07	0.30	5.42
					Variance	10.81

Standard deviation $= \sqrt{10.81} = 3.29$

*7.93(.2) + 12.56(.5) + 17.31(.3) = 13.06%.

We now assume the same investment is financed with a loan for $900,000, which is obtained at a 10 percent interest rate for a 15-year term. What will be the expected $BTIRR_E$ and the standard deviation of the $BTIRR_E$? The results are as follows:

Levered

	(1) Estimated $BTIRR_E$	*(2) Expected* $BTIRR_E$*	*(3) Deviation (1) − (2)*	*(4) Squared Deviation*	*(5) Probability*	*(6) Product (4)(5)*
Pessimistic	−5.09	26.49	−31.58	997.36	0.20	199.47
Most likely	25.99	26.49	−0.50	0.25	0.50	0.13
Optimistic	48.38	26.49	21.89	479.13	0.30	143.74
					Variance	343.34

Standard deviation $= \sqrt{343.34} = 18.53$

*15.09(.2) + 25.99(.5) + 48.38(.3) = 26.49.

Note that under the most likely and optimistic scenarios, estimated *IRR*s are higher with the loan (levered) than with no loan (unlevered), indicating that these cases offer favorable leverage. In the pessimistic case, however, the estimated return is lower, indicating that if that scenario occurs, leverage will be very unfavorable. Looking at the range in expected $BTIRR_E$, however, which is higher with the loan, one might think that it is still a good idea to borrow. Note, however, that the standard deviation is considerably higher in the levered case, 18.53 percent versus 3.29 percent. Thus, the investment is clearly riskier when leverage is used. (This would also be true regardless of whether the leverage is favorable or unfavorable.) The point is that the decision to use leverage cannot be made by only looking at $BTIRR_P$ and $BTIRR_E$. The investor must ask whether the higher expected return with leverage is commensurate with the higher risk. Alternatively, the investor should ask if there is a way to realize the higher return with less risk, such as another investment in a different property or in the same property but with a different way of financing.

Underwriting Loans on Income Properties

Chapter 7 dealt with residential underwriting and lending. However, there are many additional issues that must be addressed by lenders when loan applications from investors in *commercial* and *multifamily* properties are evaluated. We focus only on the areas of major concern in the explanation that follows.

Market Study and Appraisal

When applying for debt financing, lenders usually require that the application be accompanied by a *market study* that includes an analysis of the economic base (see Chapter 8), and prospective employment growth for the city or region in which the property is located. Also included should be an analysis of the submarket showing vacancy rates and rents on competing properties, as well as any new construction and the expected demand by renters. In short, the lender must be assured that occupancy and rent will be adequate to support mortgage loan payments.

In addition to a market analysis for higher value properties, the loan application must be accompanied by an *appraisal* of the property being financed. This appraisal will usually be done by a third party (i.e., not the lender or the borrower), who will use one or more of the sales comparison, income capitalization, or cost approaches to value discussed in detail in Chapter 8. Each approach used to estimate value will be carefully reviewed by the lender, who may change any assumptions that are viewed to be too aggressive or otherwise inconsistent with the lender's assessment of the market, and a property value for lending purposes will be established. The loan will be secured by a mortgage on the property; therefore the lender must be certain that the value of the property is sufficient to repay the loan in the event that the investor defaults and the property must be sold.

Borrower Financials

In addition to the mortgage security provided by the property, unless stated otherwise the borrower/investor will provide additional loan security in the form of personal liability on the note. Therefore, the lender will require a set of personal financial statements, or in the case of a corporate borrower, a set of corporate financial statements. The lender will consider the borrower's ability to pay should income from the property be insufficient to pay debt services. However, in many cases borrowers and lenders may agree that a **nonrecourse clause** will be included in the note. This clause releases the borrower from personal liability and makes the property the sole source of security for the loan. To obtain a nonrecourse provision, lenders will usually require an additional fee and/or a higher interest rate as compensation for this lesser amount of loan security. From the standpoint of the borrower this nonrecourse provision can be viewed as a **"put option."** If default occurs and the value of the property is lower than the outstanding loan balance, the investor may "put" or give the property security to the lender. The borrower/investor would lose any equity that existed when the loan was closed, plus the fee paid for the nonrecourse loan. These amounts can be thought of as the cost of the investor's option.

In this case after default, assuming that the loan cannot be restructured in a workout agreement, the borrower would give the lender the deed to the property. This is sometimes referred to as deed in lieu of foreclosure, although depending on the state in which the property is located, the lender may have to go through a legal process to assure that title has been transferred to the lender and that the lender will be able to sell and transfer title to another investor.

The Loan-to-Value Ratio

Most lenders usually require that the loan amount being applied will not exceed more than 75 to 80 percent of the value of the property. Therefore, should a borrower default on such a loan, the property serving as security for the loan would have to *decline* in value by 20 to 25 percent from the date of closing before the outstanding loan balance owed to the lender would be jeopardized. As a result, lenders tend to consider this range in the loan-to-value ratio to be important in underwriting.

The Debt Coverage Ratio

An additional underwriting benchmark widely used by lenders to limit default risk is the debt coverage ratio. This ratio measures the extent that the *NOI* from the property is expected to exceed the mortgage payments. The lender would like a sufficient cushion so that if the *NOI* becomes less than anticipated (e.g., from unexpected vacancy or a decline in rents) the borrower will still be able to make the mortgage payments without using personal funds.

The **debt coverage ratio** (*DCR*) is the ratio of *NOI* to the mortgage payment. For example, in Exhibit 11–1 the *NOI* projected in year 1 is $12,000 and the interest-only mortgage payment (debt service) is $8,000; these figures result in a debt coverage ratio of 1.50. Lenders typically want the debt coverage ratio to be at least 1.20. In this way, the operating income could decline by as much as 20 percent before the mortgage payment is in jeopardy. This 20 percent cushion is likely to be sufficient for most lenders. In the case shown in Exhibit 11–1, the cushion is 50 percent which is far greater than 20 percent. Therefore this property should easily meet the *DCR* target desired by the lender. However, one additional question of interest to the inventor would be "How high could the loan-to-value ratio be in order to reduce the loan-to-value ratio to 1.20?" The answer can be found as follows:

$$\frac{NOI}{\text{Desired } DCR \text{ target}} = \text{Max debt service}$$

$$\frac{\$12{,}000}{1.20} = \$10{,}000$$

This calculation indicates that a total of $10,000 *could* be expended on debt service while maintaining the desired debt coverage ratio of 1.20. The maximum loan amount will depend on the interest rate that the lender charges for loans greater than 80 percent. For example, if the lender required 11 percent for loans greater than 80 percent, then the maximum loan amount would be based on the debt service required at 11 percent interest while maintaining a debt coverage ratio of 1.20. This can be calculated as:

$$\frac{\text{Maximum debt service}}{\text{Mortgage loan constant}^{4}} = \text{Max loan amount}$$

$$\frac{\$10{,}000}{.11} = \$90{,}909$$

[4]We are using an interest-only loan in our example so the mortgage loan constant is simply the loan interest rate. In cases where the loan is amortizing, the denominator should be the mortgage loan constant that corresponds to the appropriate interest rate and amortization period, expressed on an annual basis, i.e., 12 × the monthly loan constant discussed in Chapter 4.

However this would amount to a loan of over 90 percent of the property value, which is far in excess of the more typical 75 to 80 percent loan-to-value benchmark. In this example, even though a $90,909 loan at 11 percent interest would meet the 1.20 debt coverage ratio requirement, it is unlikely that a lender would agree to a loan because it is far in excess of 80 percent. Furthermore, the marginal cost of funds to the borrower to obtain such a high leverage loan would also be very high. This cost can be approximated as follows:

$$\frac{(\$90{,}909 \times .11) - (\$80{,}000 \times .10)}{(\$90{,}909 - \$80{,}000)} = 18.3\% \text{ incremental cost}$$

Obviously, the cost of obtaining incremental financing of $10,909 is very expensive. Furthermore, it would increase the $BITRR_E$ only very slightly to 21 percent while significantly increasing risk to the investor. Recall our leverage formula:

$$BTIRR_p + (BTIRR_p - BTIRR_d)\, D/E = BTIRR_E$$
$$12\% + (12\% - 11\%) \times .90 = BTIRR_E$$
$$21\% = BTIRR_E$$

This compares to a 20 percent $BTIRR_E$ at a loan-to-value ratio of 80 percent. Therefore, if the greater amount of leverage were used, the investor would only achieve a 1 percent higher return while risking 10 percent more equity, if the 90 percent loan were made.

In short, when lenders underwrite loans, they assess risk by using benchmark, or target debt coverage ratios and loan-to-value ratios. They attempt to maintain a balance in the risk of default due to (1) an unanticipated decline in property value relative to the amount loaned or (2) significant deterioration in the debt coverage ratio. While these targets may vary depending on market conditions at the time of application, the above example should illustrate the trade-offs faced by lenders and borrowers when different amounts of leverage are considered.

Other Loan Terms and Mortgage Covenants

In addition to underwriting considerations relative to loan-to-value and debt coverage ratios, there are many other requirements that lenders may insist upon as a condition for making a loan. Many of these general requirements were discussed previously in Chapter 2. Recall that the lender will require the borrower to maintain and insure the property and pay property taxes and will not allow a sale of the property on an assumption of the loan by a third party without lender approval.

In commercial lending situations, the lender will also require notification of any material changes that may affect the value of the property. Illustrations of some **covenants** that may be included in the mortgage document are listed as follows:

1. Lender must approve all new major leases made for space exceeding a specified amount of square footage (e.g., 5,000 square feet).
2. Lender must approve any modification to existing leases.
3. Lender must approve any additional construction or modifications to the structure and/or site.
4. Borrower must supply periodic updates of property operating and/or cash flow statements.
5. Borrower must supply an annual property appraisal.
6. Borrower must notify the lender of any lawsuits brought by tenants or outside entities, any regulatory violations (e.g., environmental, building code), eminent domain actions, insurance claims filed by the borrower, and so on.

7. Borrower must notify lender of any major capital expenditures to correct structural or other property defects.
8. Lender will have the right to visit and inspect the property, and so on.

This list is meant to be illustrative and not exhaustive of the notifications, approvals, and so on, that a lender may require. The lender's goal is to be assured that *after the loan is closed,* no material deterioration in (1) the value of the property (the mortgage security) and/or (2) the income-producing ability of the property has occurred. (In the case of loans made *with recourse,* the lender will also require that personal financial statements be provided periodically to the lender.) In the event that any of these covenants/requirements are not met by the borrower, the lender will usually notify the borrower that he is in default, and unless the violation of the covenant is corrected, the lender will accelerate on the note and institute foreclosure proceedings. In addition to the above requirements, the lender will also require that much of the material that was produced as a part of the *due diligence process* detailed in Exhibit 10–10, must accompany the loan application.

Lockout Period and Prepayment Penalties. Finally, one additional area that should be discussed here are the topics of the "lockout clause" and prepayment penalties. The **lockout clause** *prohibits* the borrower from prepaying the loan within a specified period of time (usually 7–10 years). It is used because if the borrower were to sell the property or want to refinance within the lockout period, the lender would receive funds earlier than anticipated and face the prospect of having to reloan such funds at an interest rate that may be lower than the rate at which the loan was made. Similarly, if the loan has a 15-year maturity, the lender may also want protection against prepayment *after* the lockout period but before the loan matures, while still providing the borrower with an option to prepay. To accomplish this, the lender will charge a penalty usually referred to as a **yield maintenance fee** (*YMF*). One of many possible examples of how a *YMF* may be calculated can be explained as follows. Assume that a loan in the amount of \$10,000,000 is made at 8 percent "interest only" with a 15-year maturity and a lockout period of 10 years. At the time the loan is closed, the risk free rate of interest (l0-year Treasury bond) is 6 percent. Therefore, the loan *spread* over Treasuries is 2 percent (8 percent − 6 percent).

We now assume that at the end of year 11 the borrower wants to consider prepaying this loan. However, the risk free interest rate for a 4-year Treasury obligation has fallen to 5 percent at the time of prepayment. Therefore, assuming that the lender and borrower had originally agreed that in the event of prepayment, the lender must continue to earn a minimum of 8 percent for the remaining four years, (hence the term *yield maintenance*), the borrower must pay the *difference* between the lender's lowest potential reinvestment rate (which is the prevailing risk free rate of 5 percent plus the 2 percent spread, or 7 percent) and the 8 percent original yield. Therefore, the yield maintenance fee (*YMF*) to be calculated and paid when the loan is repaid at the end of year 11 (month 132) would be:

$$\begin{aligned} YMF_{132} &= \left(\frac{8\% - 7\%}{12}\right) (\$10{,}000{,}000)\ (MIFPV_a,\ 8\%,\ 48 \text{ mos.}) \\ &= \$8{,}333\ (MIFPV_a,\ 8\%,\ 48 \text{ mos.}) \\ &= \$341{,}336 \end{aligned}$$

This means that in order for the borrower to prepay this loan after the lockout period(sale of property, refinancing, and so on) the borrower must pay the lender a fee of $341,336 upon prepayment. In this case, if the lender collects the fee of $341,336 plus the $10,000,000 loan balance and makes a new loan for $10,000,000 at 7 percent interest (a 2 percent spread over the prevailing risk free rate of 5 percent) for four years, the lender will earn a yield of 8 percent over 15 years. This result would be the same to the lender as though the original loan had remained outstanding for 15 years.[5]

Alternatives to Fixed Rate Loan Structures

Loans on real estate income property can be structured in a variety of ways to meet the needs of the borrower and the lender. Lenders generally want the loan to be structured in such a way that the income generated by the property is expected to be sufficient to cover the mortgage payments each year. This relationship is often achieved by setting a minimum debt coverage ratio such as 1.20. At the same time, borrowers generally want to have a relatively high loan-to-value ratio.[6]

The income from real estate income property may be expected to increase substantially over the investment holding period for several reasons. First, in an inflationary environment income may be expected to rise—especially when the lease is structured to allow the lease payments to increase each year.[7] Second, the income for a building that was just developed may be expected to increase for several years because of the time required to lease the new space. Third, the income may be expected to increase because the property has below-market leases at the time it is purchased. If these leases will expire during the investment holding period, the investor may project that income will rise as the leases are renewed at the higher projected market rate.

When the income from the property is expected to increase over time, it becomes difficult to structure a conventional (fixed rate, level payment) mortgage loan such that the loan-to-value ratio is high and the debt coverage ratio exceeds the minimum during the initial years of the loan term. This is because the present value of property includes the higher expected *future increases* in income, whereas the debt coverage ratio is based on the *current* income. The difference between future income and current income has an especially strong impact in an inflationary environment because fixed-rate mortgages include a premium for expected inflation as discussed in Chapter 4. Because the payments on a conventional mortgage are level, the expected inflation results in higher payments during the first year of the loan term. These higher initial payments result in a mismatch between the level payments on the mortgage and the income from the property, which is expected to increase each year to offset the effect of inflation. This mismatch is greatest during the first year of the investment holding period and results in a low and often unacceptable debt coverage ratio.

---

[5]Obviously, there is some risk that the lender may not be able to maintain the 2 percent spread when making a new loan after prepayment. Therefore, when determining the calculation for *YMF* the lender and borrower may also have to negotiate the spread that will be added to the risk free rate for the remainder of the loan period.

[6]Although financial risk increases with the loan-to-value ratio, investors are often willing to incur this additional risk either because they have limited funds to invest and want to minimize their equity investment or because they desire the higher expected rate of return as part of their investment strategy.

[7]For example, an office building lease could include a CPI adjustment and/or expense stops as discussed in Chapter 10.

Because of the problems discussed, the mortgage may have to be structured so that the initial payments are lower but the lender receives additional compensation in the future to insure a competitive rate of return. This compensation can come in a variety of ways. For example, the mortgage payments could increase over time (like a graduated payment mortgage). Or the lender could receive a portion of the proceeds from sale of the property (like a shared appreciation mortgage). Sometimes the lender receives an option to purchase the property at a specified exercise price, which allows the lender to earn a greater return if the value of the property exceeds the exercise price when acquired by the lender.[8]

The remaining part of this chapter will focus on the analysis of alternative loan structures such as the ones mentioned above. We will examine how these structures affect the payment pattern, and the way that the loan structure affects the risk and expected rates of return to both the borrower and lender.

Participation Loans

We begin our discussion of financing alternatives by introducing **equity participation loans,** also referred to as *participations* or *equity kickers.* Actually the term *equity participation* is somewhat a misnomer because the lender does not actually acquire an ownership interest in the property. Rather, in return for a lower stated interest rate on the loan, the lender *participates* in some way in the income or cash flow from the property. Thus, the lender's rate of return depends, in part, on the performance of the property.

Determining the amount of participation can be done in many ways. For example, the lender might receive a percentage of one or more of the following: (1) potential gross income, (2) net operating income (*NOI*), and (3) cash flow after regular debt service (but before the participation). In addition, there might be a participation at the time the property is sold based on total sale proceeds or the appreciation in property value since it was purchased.

A participation in cash flows often begins for newly developed properties after some preagreed amount of leasing and rental achievement is reached. For example, the participation might be based on a percentage of all *NOI in excess* of \$100,000. In the case of existing properties, the break-even point is typically set so that the participation begins after the first operating year. For example, *NOI* might be expected to be \$100,000 during the first year. Thus, the lender would receive a participation only when *NOI* increases to more than \$100,000, which might occur in the second year.

In return for receiving a participation, the lender charges a lower stated interest rate on the loan—how much lower depends on the amount of participation. Participations are highly negotiable, and there is no standard way of structuring them.

Lender Motivations

Why would a lender be willing to make a participation loan? As we will discuss, the lender will want to structure the participation in such a way that the lender's rate of return (including the expected participation) is at least comparable to what the return would have been with a fixed interest rate loan (no participation). Whether the

[8]The exercise price of the option is the price that the lender must pay for the property. It is normally greater than the value of the property when the loan is made but could be less than the value of the property when the option can be exercised.

lender will accept a lower expected return with the participation or demand a premium depends on how risky the participation loan is perceived to be relative to a fixed interest rate loan. Clearly, some uncertainty is associated with a participation because receipts depend on the performance of the property. At the same time, however, the lender does not participate in any losses. The lender still receives some minimum interest rate (unless the borrower defaults). Furthermore, the participation provides the lender with a hedge of sorts against unanticipated inflation because the *NOI* and resale prices for an income property often increase as a result of inflation. Thus, to some extent a participation protects the lender's "real" rate of return.

Investor Motivations

Why would an investor-borrower want a participation loan? As indicated above, participation loans are often structured so that the lender's participation is based on income or cash flow above some specified break-even point. Hence, the participation may be very little or zero for one or more years. During this time period the borrower will be paying less than he would have with a straight loan. Lower initial payments may be quite desirable for the investor since *NOI* may be lower during the first couple of years of ownership, especially on a new project that is not fully rented. Thus, the investor may have more cash flow during the early years of a participation loan than with a straight loan. Increased early cash flow also increases the debt coverage ratio. That is, the investor may be better able to meet debt service during the initial years of the loan with a participation.

You may wonder why the investor wouldn't accept a participation loan with a lower rate and a participation that doesn't kick in for a couple of years, and sell the property before the participation kicks in! This problem is handled by having a **lockout period** during which the property cannot be sold or refinanced without a prepayment penalty to compensate the lender.

Participation Example

To illustrate a participation loan, we assume that an apartment project that an investor is considering for purchase is projected to have *NOI* of $100,000 during the first year. After that the *NOI* is projected to increase 3 percent per year. The property can be purchased for $1 million. This price includes a building value of $900,000, which will be depreciated over 27.5 years. The property value is projected to increase 3 percent per year over a five-year holding period.

The lender has offered the following alternatives:

- A conventional, fixed-rate, constant-payment loan for $700,000 at a 10 percent interest rate (with monthly payments) over a 15-year term.
- A loan for $700,000 at 8 percent interest with monthly payments over 15 years and a participation in 50 percent of any *NOI* in excess of $100,000, plus a participation in 45 percent of any gain (Sale price − Original cost) when the property is sold.

Note that the *amount* of the loan for the two alternatives is the same. This is important because otherwise financial leverage would cause differences in risk. At this point we want to focus on analyzing different ways of *structuring* the debt independent of the decision about the *amount* of debt, which we have already discussed.

Exhibit 11–10 shows the cash flows for the conventional loan. Note that the debt coverage ratio (*DCR*) during the first year of the conventional loan is only 1.11. This is lower than many lenders would find acceptable. Recall that lenders typically require a minimum *DCR* of 1.2. Thus the borrower may have difficulty borrowing $700,000 with a conventional loan. Of course, the amount of the loan could be

EXHIBIT 11–10 Conventional Loan

Estimates of Cash Flow from Operations

	Year 1	2	3	4	5
A. Before-tax cash flow:					
Net operating income (*NOI*)	$100,000	$103,000	$106,090	$109,273	$112,551
Less debt service (*DS*)	90,267	90,267	90,267	90,267	90,267
Cash flow before participation	9,733	12,733	15,823	19,006	22,284
Participation	0	0	0	0	0
Before-tax cash flow	$ 9,733	$ 12,733	$ 15,823	$ 19,006	$ 22,284
B. Taxable income or loss:					
Net operating income (*NOI*)	$100,000	$103,000	$106,090	$109,273	$112,551
Less interest	69,045	66,823	64,368	61,656	58,660
Participation	0	0	0	0	0
Depreciation	32,727	32,727	32,727	32,727	32,727
Taxable income (loss)	−1,772	3,450	8,995	14,890	21,164
Tax	$ −496	$ 966	$ 2,519	$ 4,169	$ 5,926
C. After-tax cash flow:					
Before-tax cash flow (*BTCF*)	$ 9,733	$ 12,733	$ 15,823	$ 19,006	$ 22,284
Less tax*	−496	966	2,519	4,169	5,926
After-tax cash flow (*ATCF*)	$ 10,229	$ 11,767	$ 13,305	$ 14,837	$ 16,358

Estimates of Cash Flows from Sale in Year 5

Sale price			$1,159,274
Less mortgage balance			569,216
Before-tax cash flow (*BTCF*s)			$ 590,058
Taxes in year of sale			
Sale price		$1,159,274	
Original cost basis	$1,000,000		
Accumulated depreciation	163,636		
Adjusted basis		836,364	
Capital gain		$ 322,910	
Tax from sale			90,415
After-tax cash flow from sale (*ATCF*s)			$ 499,643

Cash Flow Summary
End of Year

	0	1	2	3	4	5
BTCF	$−300,000	$ 9,733	$12,733	$15,823	$19,006	$612,342
ATCF	−300,000	10,229	11,767	13,305	14,837	516,001

Before-tax *IRR* = 18.37%
After-tax *IRR* = 14.30%

*It is assumed that the investor is not subject to passive activity loss limitations.

reduced to increase the debt coverage ratio. As we will see, however, a participation loan may be structured to alleviate the *DCR* problem.

Exhibit 11–11 shows the cash flows for the participation loan. The cash flow patterns differ significantly due to the different nature of the participation. Note that the participation loan offers lower payments (debt service plus participation payments) during the early years. This is because of the lower interest rate on the participation loan plus the fact that the participation does not start until the second year. Also, part of the payments to the lender from the participation loan do not come until the property is sold.

Despite the difference in payment patterns, the before-tax *IRR* ($BTIRR_E$) is virtually the same for both the conventional loan and the participation loan as a result of the terms for this particular participation loan.

For a participation loan to be attractive to the lender, the expected rate of return to the lender, which is also the effective cost of the loan, must be attractive relative to the interest rate available on conventional loans. In this case, the lender's *IRR*, considering both debt service and participation payments, is about 10 percent.[9] This *IRR* is the same as the *IRR* for the conventional loan, which is also 10 percent (the same as the interest rate on the loan because there are no points).

Although the lender's *IRR* is also about the same for each alternative, note that the *DCR* for the first year is 1.25 for the participation loan, whereas it is only 1.11 for the conventional loan. Recall that lenders typically require a *DCR* of at least 1.2. Thus, the participation loan might be much more acceptable to the lender. The investor may also prefer this payment pattern because the pattern of debt service (regular mortgage payment plus the participation) is a better match with the pattern of *NOI*. In an inflationary environment, the nominal increase in *NOI* will be greater than the real increase in *NOI*. Recall our discussion in Chapter 4 of problems associated with a constant payment mortgage in an inflationary environment. A participating mortgage helps alleviate the tilt effect by allowing the nominal debt service to start at a lower amount than necessary for a conventional loan, and then increase in nominal terms as a function of the nominal increase in the *NOI*.

Note that because part of the lender's return depends on the likelihood of income being produced by the property, the participation payments are referred to as *contingent* interest. Because the contingent interest is contingent on the performance of the property and its ability to produce income, this interest is also tax-deductible, as shown in Exhibit 11–11. Thus, one feature of a participation loan is that the entire participation payment is tax-deductible, whereas only the interest portion of a conventional loan is deductible. However, because the amount of participation is lower during the early years in this case, the present value of the interest deductions on the conventional loan is greater than the present value of the deductions for interest and participation payments on the participation loan. This results in an after-tax *IRR* ($ATIRR_E$) that is lower for the participation loan even though the before-tax *IRR* ($BTIRR_E$) is virtually the same for each loan alternative. Exhibit 11–12 summarizes the *IRR*s for each financing alternative and shows the *DCR* for each case (based on first-year cash flows).

[9]This *IRR* is found by calculating the interest rate that equates the amount of loan ($700,000) with the present value of *both* the debt service paid each year ($80,275) *plus* the participation paid each year *plus* the loan balance and participation paid at the end of the holding period. The cash flows differ each year due to the participation. The answer we calculated (10.17 percent) was based on the assumption that the debt service and participation were paid monthly.

EXHIBIT 11–11 Participation Example

	Estimates of Cash Flow from Operations Year				
	1	*2*	*3*	*4*	*5*
A. Before-tax cash flow:					
Net operating income (*NOI*)	$100,000	$103,000	$106,090	$109,273	$112,551
Less debt service (*DS*)	80,275	80,275	80,275	80,275	80,275
Cash flow before participation	19,725	22,725	25,815	28,998	32,276
Participation	0	1,500	3,045	4,636	6,275
Before-tax cash flow	$ 19,725	$ 21,225	$ 22,770	$ 24,362	$ 26,001
B. Taxable income or loss:					
Net operating income (*NOI*)	$100,000	$103,000	$106,090	$109,273	$112,551
Less interest	55,090	53,000	50,736	48,284	45,629
Participation	0	1,500	3,045	4,636	6,275
Depreciation	32,727	32,727	32,727	32,727	32,727
Taxable income (loss)	12,183	15,773	19,582	23,625	27,919
Tax	$3,411	$ 4,417	$ 5,483	$ 6,615	$ 7,817
C. After-tax cash flow:					
Before-tax cash flow (*BTCF*)	$ 19,725	$ 21,225	$ 22,770	$ 24,362	$ 26,001
Less tax	3,411	4,417	5,483	6,615	7,817
After-tax cash flow(*ATCF*)	$ 16,314	$ 16,809	$ 17,287	$ 17,747	$ 18,183

Estimates of Cash Flows from Sale in Year 5

Sale price			$1,159,274
Less mortgage balance			551,364
Cash flow before participation			607,910
Less participation in gain from sale			71,673
Before tax cash flow (*BTCF*s)			$ 536,237
Taxes in year of sale			
Sale price		$1,159,274	
Participation		71,673	
Original cost basis	$1,000,000		
Accumulated depreciation	163,636		
Adjusted basis		836,364	
Capital gain		$ 251,237	
Tax from sale			70,346
After-tax cash flow from sale (*ATCF*s)			$ 465,891

Cash Flow Summary: Investor
End of Year

	0	*1*	*2*	*3*	*4*	*5*
Before-tax cash flow	$−300,000	$19,725	$21,225	$22,770	$24,362	$562,238
After-tax cash flow	−300,000	16,314	16,809	17,287	17,747	484,074

Before-tax *IRR* = 18.36%
After-tax *IRR* = 14.07%

EXHIBIT 11–11 Participation Example (continued)

	Cash Flow Summary: Lender						
	0	*1–12*	*13–24*	*25–36*	*37–48*	*49–60*	*60*
Loan amount	$−700,000						
Debt service		$6,690	$6,690	$6,690	$6,690	$6,690	
Participation		0	125	254	386	523	$ 71,673
Loan balance							551,364
Total $	−700,000	$6,690	$6,815	$6,944	$7,076	$7,213	$623,037
Lender's *IRR* 10%							

EXHIBIT 11–12 Summary of Returns to the Lender and Investor

	Before-Tax IRR	*After-Tax IRR*	*DCR*	*Lender's IRR*
Conventional loan	18.37%	14.30%	1.11	10.00%
Participation loan	18.36	14.07	1.25	10.17

From the foregoing analysis, it appears that the participation loan is a viable alternative to the conventional loan. The lender receives virtually the same *IRR*, and the *DCR* is higher. The expected *BTIRR* for the investor is also virtually the same for each, and the expected *ATIRR* is only slightly less. Furthermore, the borrower might have difficulty obtaining the conventional loan due to the low *DCR*.

Sale-Leaseback of the Land

Up to this point in this chapter we have considered alternative ways of financing acquisition of a property (land and building). We have assumed that the investor finances both the land and building with the same loan. It is possible, however, to obtain financing on the building only (e.g., with the building as collateral for the loan). The investor may obtain a separate loan on the land or finance it with a land lease. That is, the investor would own the building but lease the land from a different investor. If the investor already owns the land, she can sell it with an agreement to lease the land back from the purchaser. This is referred to as a **sale-leaseback of the land.** Either way, the investor is, in effect, financing the land.

To illustrate the use of a sale-leaseback of the land, we will use the same example used in the previous section. We now assume that the land could be sold for $100,000 and leased back at an annual payment of $7,800 per year for 25 years. The building would be financed for $630,000 (70 percent of the *building* value) at a 10 percent rate and a 15-year term. The amount of equity invested is therefore equal to the purchase price ($1 million) less the price of the land ($100,000) less the amount of loan on the building ($630,000), resulting in equity of $270,000. Exhibit 11–13 shows the cash flows for this alternative. Note that the resale price is now lower because only the building is being sold.[10]

An investor may find a sale-leaseback an attractive financing alternative for several reasons. First, it is, in effect, a way of obtaining 100 percent financing on the land. For example, a loan on the entire property (land and building) for 70 percent of the value also amounts to a 70 percent loan on the land. With the sale-leaseback, the investor receives funds in an amount equal to 100 percent of the value of the land. Instead of a mortgage payment on the land, the investor would make lease payments on the land.

A second benefit of a sale-leaseback is that lease payments are tax-deductible. Recall that only the interest, not the principal portion of the payment, is tax-deductible with a mortgage.

Third, whereas the building can be depreciated for tax purposes, the land cannot be depreciated. Thus, the investor may deduct the same depreciation charges whether or not he owns the land. Because, as discussed above, less equity is required with a sale-leaseback of the land, the sale-leaseback results in the same depreciation for a smaller equity investment.

Finally, the investor may have the option to purchase the land back at the end of the lease. This option provides the investor the opportunity to regain ownership of the land if desired.

Whether or not the sale-leaseback is a desirable financing alternative depends on the "cost" of obtaining funds this way. One of the obvious costs is the lease payments that must be made. Another aspect of the cost is the "opportunity cost" associated with any appreciation in the value of the land over the holding period. That is, by doing a sale-leaseback the investor gives up the opportunity to sell the land at the end of the holding period along with the building.

Effective Cost of the Sale-Leaseback

Calculating the effective cost of the sale-leaseback (before-tax return to the investor who purchases the land) is similar to calculating the cost of other financing alternatives. However, we must consider the opportunity cost of the proceeds from sale of the land.

When the land is sold at the time of the sale-leaseback, the building investor receives $100,000. During the five years of the holding period, the investor makes lease payments of $7,800. At the end of the five-year holding period, the investor receives $115,927 *less* than if he had not done the sale-leaseback (Exhibit 11–13). That is, the entire property could be sold for $1,159,274 without the sale-and-leaseback (see Exhibit 11–11). In other words, if the sale-leaseback is used, the building alone will sell for $1,043,347 at the end of the holding period, for a difference of $115,927. We can now solve for the effective cost as follows:

$$100{,}000 = 7{,}800/12\ (MPVIFA,\ ?\%,\ 5\text{ yrs.}) + 115{,}927\ (MPVIF,\ ?\%,\ 5\text{ yrs.})$$

---

[10]We assumed that the building will still increase in value 3 percent per year, the same rate that we assumed the property value (land and building) would grow. Obviously the building value may grow at a slower rate than the land, with the 3 percent growth rate for the property being a weighted average of the land and building growth rates. Using a rate of 3 percent for the building, the sale price is $(\$900{,}000)(1.03)^5 = \$1{,}043{,}347$.

EXHIBIT 11–13 Sale-Leaseback of the Land

Estimates of Cash Flow from Operations

	Year 1	2	3	4	5
A. Before-tax cash flow:					
Net operating income	$100,000	$103,000	$106,090	$109,273	$112,551
Less debt service	81,240	81,240	81,240	81,240	81,240
Less land lease payment	7,800	7,800	7,800	7,800	7,800
Before-tax cash flow	$ 10,960	$ 13,960	$ 17,050	$ 20,233	$ 23,511
B. Taxable income or loss:					
Net operating income (*NOI*)	$100,000	$103,000	$106,090	$109,273	$112,551
Less interest	62,140	60,140	57,931	55,490	52,794
Land lease payment	7,800	7,800	7,800	7,800	7,800
Depreciation	32,727	32,727	32,727	32,727	32,727
Taxable income (loss)	−2,668	2,332	7,632	13,255	19,230
Tax	$ −747	$ 653	$ 2,137	$ 3,711	$ 5,384
C. After-tax cash flow:					
Before-tax cash flow (*BTCF*)	$ 10,960	$ 13,960	$ 17,050	$ 20,233	$ 23,511
Less tax	−747	653	2,137	3,711	5,384
After-tax cash flow (*ATCF*)	$ 11,707	$ 13,307	$ 14,913	$ 16,521	$ 18,126

Estimates of Cash Flows from Sale in Year 5

Sale price			$1,043,347
Less mortgage balance			512,295
Before-tax cash flow (*BTCFs*)			$ 531,052
Taxes in year of sale			
Sale price		$1,043,347	
Original cost basis	$900,000		
Accumulated depreciation	163,636		
Adjusted basis		736,364	
Capital gain		$ 306,983	
Tax from sale			85,955
After-tax cash flow from sale (*ATCFs*)			$ 445,097

Cash Flow Summary
End of Year

	0	1	2	3	4	5
Before-tax cash flow	$−270,000	$10,960	$13,960	$17,050	$20,233	$554,563
After-tax cash flow	−270,000	11,707	13,307	14,913	16,521	463,223

Before-tax *IRR* = 19.16%
After-tax *IRR* = 14.98%

The resulting yield is 10.25 percent. Thus, the cost of the sale-and-leaseback of the land (return to the purchaser-lessor of the land) is 10.25 percent, which is about 25 percentage points more than the return from the conventional loan. At the same

EXHIBIT 11–14 Interest-Only Loan

	Estimates of Cash Flow from Operations				
	Year				
	1	*2*	*3*	*4*	*5*
A. Before-tax cash flow:					
Net operating income	$100,000	$103,000	$106,090	$109,273	$112,551
Less debt service	70,000	70,000	70,000	70,000	70,000
Before-tax cash flow	$ 30,000	$ 33,000	$ 36,090	$ 39,273	$ 42,551
B. Taxable income or loss:					
Net operating income (*NOI*)	$100,000	$103,000	$106,090	$109,273	$112,551
Less interest	70,000	70,000	70,000	70,000	70,000
Depreciation	32,727	32,727	32,727	32,727	32,727
Taxable income (loss)	−2,727	273	3,363	6,546	9,824
Tax	$ −764	$ 76	$ 942	$ 1,833	$ 2,751
C. After-tax cash flow:					
Before-tax cash flow (*BTCF*)	$ 30,000	$ 33,000	$ 36,090	$ 39,273	$ 42,551
Less tax	−764	76	942	1,833	2,751
After-tax cash flow (*ATCF*)	$ 30,764	$ 32,924	$ 35,148	$ 37,440	$ 39,800

Estimates of Cash Flows from Sale in Year 5

Sale price			$1,159,274
Less mortgage balance			700,000
Before-tax cash flow (*BTCFs*)			$ 459,274
Sale price		$1,159,274	
Original cost basis	$1,000,000		
Accumulated depreciation	163,636		
Adjusted basis		836,364	
Capital gain			322,910
Tax from sale			90,415
After-tax cash flow from sale (*ATCFs*)			$ 368,859

Cash Flow Summary
End of Year

	0	*1*	*2*	*3*	*4*	*5*
Before-tax cash flow	$−300,000	$30,000	$33,000	$36,090	$39,273	$501,825
After-tax cash flow	−300,000	30,764	32,924	35,148	37,440	408,659

Before-tax *IRR* = 18.98%
After-tax *IRR* = 14.94%

time, the building investor's return on equity invested is greater than that for a straight loan. Furthermore, the lender for the building loan is still receiving the 10 percent return that would have been available on a straight loan on the land and building, and the building lender's risk is slightly less if the land lease is subordinated to the building loan.

Interest-Only Loans

Loans on real estate income properties are sometimes structured such that no amortization is required for a specified period of time, for example, three to five years. This is referred to as an **interest-only loan** because the monthly payment is just sufficient to cover the interest charges. Because the loan is not amortized, the balance of the loan does not change over time. At the end of the interest-only period, the loan is either amortized over the remaining loan term or the balance of the loan is due as a **balloon payment.** Lenders for income-producing properties refer to these loans as **bullet loans** because they are short term and require little or no amortization. Since the loan does not fully amortize, the term *balloon payment* refers to payment of the loan balance at maturity. Most of these loans are refinanced at maturity based on appraised values at that time.

To illustrate an interest-only loan, we use the same basic assumptions as in the previous two examples (a $700,000 loan at 10 percent interest), but assume that the investor makes interest-only payments for the first five years of the loan with a balloon payment due in year 5 when the property is sold. Exhibit 11–14 illustrates the after-tax cash flows. In contrast to the conventional loan, the after-tax *IRR* increases slightly from 14.30 percent to 14.94 percent. This increase is due to the higher cash flows during the operating years, which, in present value terms, more than offset the lower cash flow from sale due to the larger loan balance. Another benefit of the interest-only loan is that the debt coverage ratio increases to 1.43 versus 1.11 for the conventional loan. The rate of return to the lender would still be 10 percent because the lender earns interest on the outstanding balance of the loan at this rate. Of course, the lender might require a slightly higher interest rate if the loan is viewed as riskier because it is not amortized for five years.

Accrual Loans

In the previous example we analyzed a loan with interest-only payments. In that case the monthly payment just covered the interest payment and the amortization was zero. Sometimes loans are structured so the payments for a specified number of years are lower than the amount that would be required to cover the monthly interest charge. These loans, when made on income properties, are referred to as **accrual loans,** and they have negative amortization. The structure of these loans is similar to the graduated payment mortgage as illustrated in Chapter 4 for residential loans.

Loan payments are sometimes calculated by using a rate to calculate the loan payment (referred to as the **pay rate**) that is different from the rate used to calculate the interest charged (referred to as the **accrual rate**). The pay rate is used in place of the interest rate when calculating monthly payments. The pay rate is not the same as the loan constant. The accrual rate is the interest rate that the borrower is legally required to pay on the loan. If the payment rate is less than the accrual rate, the loan will have negative amortization. To illustrate, we now assume that a loan is obtained with a payment rate of 8 percent and an accrual rate of 10 percent. To further lower the payments, the payments are based on a 30-year amortization term although the loan will be due in 15 years with a balloon payment. All other assumptions remain the same as in the previous examples. Exhibit 11–15 illustrates the cash flows for this loan. The annual debt service (12 times the monthly loan payment) is now $61,636 versus $90,267 for the conventional loan. (The annual loan constant is 8.81 percent.) The

EXHIBIT 11–15 Negative Amortization Loan

Estimates of Cash Flow from Operations

	Year 1	2	3	4	5
A. Before-tax cash flow:					
Net operating income	$100,000	$103,000	$106,090	$109,273	$112,551
Less debt service	61,636	61,636	61,636	61,636	61,636
Before-tax cash flow	$ 38,364	$ 41,364	$ 44,454	$ 47,637	$ 50,915
B. Taxable income or loss:					
Net operating income	$100,000	$103,000	$106,090	$109,273	$112,551
Less interest*	70,394	71,311	72,324	73,444	74,680
Depreciation	32,727	32,727	32,727	32,727	32,727
Taxable income (loss)	−3,121	−1,038	1,039	3,102	5,144
Tax	$ −874	$ −291	$ 291	$ 869	$ 1,440
C. After-tax cash flow:					
Before-tax cash flow (*BTCF*)	$ 38,364	$ 41,364	$ 44,454	$ 47,637	$ 50,915
Less tax	−874	−291	291	869	1,440
After-tax cash flow (*ATCF*)	$ 39,238	$ 41,655	$ 44,163	$ 46,768	$ 49,475

Estimates of Cash Flow from Sale in Year 5

Sale price			$1,159,274
Less mortgage balance			753,972
Before-tax cash flow (*BTCFs*)			$ 405,302
Sale price		$1,159,274	
Original cost basis	$1,000,000		
Accumulated depreciation	163,636		
Adjusted basis		836,364	
Capital gain		$ 322,910	
Tax from sale			90,415
After-tax cash flow from sale (*ATCFs*)			$ 314,887

Cash Flow Summary
End of Year

	0	1	2	3	4	5
Before-tax cash flow	$300,000	$38,364	$41,364	$44,454	$47,637	$456,217
After-tax cash flow	−300,000	39,238	41,655	44,163	46,768	364,362

Before-tax *IRR* = 19.27%
After-tax *IRR* = 15.25%

*The table assumes that interest can be deducted on an accrual basis for tax purposes.

lender's yield is still 10 percent because the lender earns interest on the outstanding balance at the accrual rate. The lender may view a negative amortization loan as riskier and might charge a higher accrual rate relative to a conventional loan. The debt coverage ratio has increased from 1.11 for the conventional loan to 1.62 for the negative amortization loan because of the lower annual debt service. Note that the loan balance reaches $753,972 in year 5 as a result of negative amortization. (Recall that the monthly interest differential between the 8 percent pay rate and the 10 percent accrual rate must be compounded at 10 percent and added to the loan balance.)

In many cases, loan payments may be structured based on the pay rate with no amortization. Regardless of whether amortization is required or not, when loans are structured with a pay rate that is lower than the accrual rate, a loan payment that is less than the amount of interest due on the outstanding loan balance usually results. This shortfall (**negative amortization**) causes the loan balance to increase. However, the lender will still require that the loan either be repaid at the end of a specified time period or that the loan begin to amortize at some point. These requirements can be met in a variety of ways. Frequently, negative amortization loans have a term of about 7 to 10 years; hence the loan balance, which includes accrued interest, will be repaid at that time. Alternatively, when loans have longer terms, say 10 to 15 years, the pay rate increases after a specified number of years. At that point, the pay rate may be increased so that the loan will be amortized over the remaining loan term. Sometimes loan agreements are structured so that the pay rate increases each year for a certain number of years. For example, the loan may require that the pay rate begin at 8 percent the first year, then increase by 0.5 percent each year until the 10th year when the pay rate remains at 12.5 percent until the loan is fully amortized.

Structuring the Payment for a Target Debt Coverage Ratio

One of the primary motivations for structuring loans with negative amortization is to increase the debt coverage ratio without reducing the loan amount. As previously discussed, lenders typically require a loan to have a minimum debt coverage ratio (*DCR*). In the above example, the conventional loan had a *DCR* of 1.11. Suppose the lender required a minimum debt coverage ratio of 1.25. The negative amortization loan discussed above resulted in a *DCR* that exceeded this minimum. Another way of determining the mortgage payment is to calculate the mortgage payment necessary to have a specified debt coverage ratio during the first year. To do so, we can simply divide the *NOI* by the specified debt coverage ratio. For example, the mortgage payment that results in a *DCR* of 1.25 during the first year is $\$100{,}000 \div 1.25 = \$80{,}000$. This amount is greater than the payment for the negative amortization loan discussed above, but less than the payment on the conventional loan. In this case the payment would not result in negative amortization because it is sufficient to cover the required interest payment. However, the loan amortization period is not sufficient to fully amortize the loan. For full amortization to occur, the loan has to be extended beyond 30 years. Hence, it is likely that the lender would require a balloon payment on or before the 30th year. Alternatively, the lender could shorten the amortization period by increasing payments each year or after a specified number of years. One possibility is to recalculate the payment each year to maintain a constant debt coverage ratio over time. For example, the above loan may have a payment during year 2 of $\$103{,}000 \div 1.25 = \$82{,}400$, and so on, until the loan begins to amortize sufficiently to be repaid at the end of the term. At that point, loan payments would remain fixed.

Convertible Mortgages

A **convertible mortgage** gives the lender an option to purchase a full or a partial interest in the property at the end of some specified period of time. This purchase option allows the lender to convert its mortgage to equity ownership, hence the term *convertible mortgage.* The lender may view a convertible mortgage as a combination of a mortgage loan and purchase of a call option, or as a right to acquire a full or partial equity interest for a predetermined price on the option's expiration date.

To illustrate, we assume that the property evaluated in the previous examples will be financed with a $700,000 (70 percent of value) convertible mortgage that allows the lender to acquire 65 percent of the equity ownership in the property at the end of the fifth year.[11] The loan will be amortized over 30 years with monthly payments. We assume the interest rate on the loan to be 8.5 percent versus 10 percent for the conventional loan. The lender is willing to accept the lower interest rate in exchange for the conversion option. The 150 basis point difference in interest rates between the conventional mortgage and the convertible mortgage represents the "price" that the lender must pay for the option associated with the convertible loan.[12]

Exhibit 11–16 illustrates the after-tax cash flows for the investor under the assumption that the property is financed with the convertible mortgage described above and that the lender exercises the option to purchase a 65 percent interest in the property at the end of the fifth year. We would expect the lender to exercise this option because 65 percent of the estimated sale price ($753,528) is greater than the mortgage balance at the end of the fifth year ($668,432). That is, the option is "in the money" at the time it can be exercised. For comparison with the previous examples, we also assume that the investor will sell the remaining 35 percent interest in the property.

Lender's Yield on Convertible Mortgage

The lender's yield on a convertible mortgage depends on the interest rate charged on the mortgage as well as any gain on conversion of the mortgage into an equity position. If the mortgage is not converted, the lender's yield will equal the interest rate on the loan.[13] The interest rate is the lower limit of the yield, assuming that the borrower does not default on the mortgage. In the above example, the lender's yield on the convertible mortgage is greater than the 8.5 percent interest rate on the loan because of the gain on conversion of the mortgage balance into an equity position. This gain occurred because the conversion option included with the mortgage was assumed to be "in the money" on its exercise date. Thus, the mortgage lender receives mortgage payments of $5,382.39 per month, plus a 65 percent interest in the property worth $753,528 at the end of the fifth year. The lender's effective yield is calculated as follows:

$$700{,}000 = 64{,}589 \div 12\ (MPVIFA,\ ?\%,\ 5\text{ yrs.}) + \$753{,}528\ (MPVIF,\ ?\%,\ 5\text{ years})$$

Using a financial calculator we obtain a yield of 10.40 percent. This is the lender's before-tax rate of return on the convertible mortgage.[14] The yield can also be interpreted as the borrower's effective borrowing cost for the convertible mortgage (before tax).

---

[11]Generally, the Internal Revenue Service requires that the loan-to-value ratio on the date of financing must be greater than the conversion ratio. This is because if the conversion ratio is greater, the IRS considers the option to be "in the money." Although the lender may have to wait to exercise the conversion option, the lender may have the right to sell or assign the convertible mortgage before the exercise date.

[12]That is, rather than pay an amount up front for the call option, the lender accepts a lower interest rate on the mortgage loan.

[13]Of course, the yield would be higher if points were also charged on the loan.

[14]It should be noted that the borrower has a taxable gain when the mortgage balance is converted into an equity interest in the property. This would have to be considered if the lender's after-tax yield is calculated.

EXHIBIT 11–16 Convertible Mortgage

Estimate of Cash Flow from Operations

	Year 1	2	3	4	5
A. Before-tax cash flow:					
Net operating income	$100,000	$103,000	$106,090	$109,273	$112,551
Less debt service	64,589	64,589	64,589	64,589	64,589
Before-tax cash flow	$ 35,411	$ 38,411	$ 41,501	$ 44,684	$ 47,962
B. Taxable income or loss:					
Net operating income	$100,000	$103,000	$106,090	$109,273	$112,551
Less interest	59,297	58,829	58,320	57,766	57,163
Depreciation	32,727	32,727	32,727	32,727	32,727
Taxable income (loss)	7,976	11,443	15,043	18,779	22,661
Tax	$ 2,233	$ 3,204	$ 4,212	$ 5,258	$ 6,345
C. After-tax cash flow:					
Before-tax cash flow (*BTCF*)	$ 35,411	$ 38,411	$ 41,501	$ 44,684	$ 47,962
Less tax	2,233	3,204	4,212	5,258	6,345
After-tax cash flow (*ATCF*)	$ 33,178	$ 35,207	$ 37,289	$ 39,426	$ 41,617

Estimate of Cash Flow from Sale in Year 5

Exchange of 65% interest in property for loan balance*			$000,000
Sale of remaining 35% interest in the property			405,746
Before-tax cash flow (*BTCF*s)			$405,746
Sale price		$1,159,274	
Original cost basis	$1,000,000		
Accumulated depreciation	163,636		
Adjusted basis		836,364	
Capital gain		$ 322,910	
Tax from sale			90,415
After-tax cash flow from sale (*ATCF*s)			$315,331

Cash Flow Summary
End of Year

	0	1	2	3	4	5
Before-tax cash flow	$300,000	$35,411	$38,411	$41,501	$44,684	$453,708
After-tax cash flow	−300,000	33,178	35,207	37,289	39,426	356,948

Before-tax *IRR* = 18.40%
After-tax *IRR* = 13.06%

*The lender receives 65 percent of the property in exchange for the loan balance. The net cash flow to the investor is zero.

Comparison of Financing Alternatives

Exhibit 11–17 shows a summary of performance measures for each of the financing alternatives evaluated in the previous examples. In this case, the accrual loan results

EXHIBIT 11–17 Comparison of Financing Alternatives

	$BTIRR_E$	$ATIRR_E$	DCR	IRR_{D^*}
Conventional mortgage	18.37%	14.30%	1.11	10.00%
Participating mortgage	18.36	14.07	1.25	10.17
Sale-and-leaseback of land	19.16	14.98	1.12†	10.25‡
Interest-only mortgage	18.98	14.94	1.43	10.00
Accrual mortgage	19.27	15.25	1.62	10.00
Convertible mortgage	18.40	13.06	1.55	10.40

*Based on monthly cash flows for debt service and participation payments.

†Includes land lease payment with debt service. The *DCR* is 1.23 when land lease payments are not included.

‡This is the yield to the purchaser of the land who provides the sale-leaseback financing. The yield (IRR_D) on the building loan is 10 percent.

in the highest return to the investor on both a before- and after-tax basis. This loan also has the highest debt coverage ratio. Thus, it would appear to be the most attractive from the borrower's point of view. This result, however, is based on the assumption that the lender is willing to charge the same interest rate (10 percent) as a conventional loan. Although the debt coverage ratio is lower for the negative amortization loan, the loan balance *increases* over time, thereby *decreasing* equity in the property and *increasing* the default risk. Thus, we might expect the lender to charge a higher interest rate on the negative amortization loan.

Based on the above discussion, it is not surprising that the interest-only loan results in a lower return to the investor than the negative amortization loan but a higher return than the conventional loan. It requires lower payments than the conventional loan but higher payments than the negative amortization loan. Considering the differences in default risk, we would expect lenders to charge a slightly higher rate on the interest-only loan than the conventional loan, but not as high as for the negative amortization loan.

The before- and after-tax returns to the investor for the sale-leaseback of the land are the second highest of the financing alternatives even though the effective borrowing cost for the sale-leaseback is slightly higher than for the conventional loan (10.25 percent versus 10.00 percent). Note, however, that less equity ($30,000) is required when the land is leased rather than owned because the land lease is, in effect, equivalent to a 100 percent loan on the land. Thus, the amount of financing for the land has increased from 70 percent (in the case of a conventional mortgage) to 100 percent of the land value. This increases the amount of financial leverage and financial risk. Thus, the investor should expect to earn a slightly higher rate of return with a sale-leaseback than a conventional mortgage loan.

Another reason that the investor's return is higher with the sale-leaseback of the land is that the payments on the land lease are less than the debt service would be if a loan were made on the land. Furthermore, a significant portion of the cost of the sale-leaseback to the borrower is because of the opportunity rate, or increase in land value, which is given up. This opportunity cost is not incurred, however, until the property is sold.

The debt coverage ratio for the sale-leaseback is 1.2, which is about the same as a conventional loan. To be consistent with the other examples, we calculate this ratio with the land lease payments added to the mortgage payments. We use the combination of mortgage and land lease payments because the land lease payment is a substitute for mortgage debt service.

The participating loan allows the lender to share in any increase in the net operating income from the property as well as any increase in the value of the property. This type of loan, then, is similar to the convertible mortgage in the sense that the lender receives an additional return if the property performs well; that is, its income and value increase. Although the participation loan does not allow the lender to obtain an equity position, part of the lender's interest is contingent on the performance of the property. In both cases the lender accepts a lower contract interest rate in exchange for a "piece of the action" on the upside. In the above examples, the convertible mortgage results in a higher return to the lender than the participating loan and a lower after-tax return to the investor. At the same time, the lender would view the convertible mortgage as having greater risk than the participation loan. This is because the participation payments are expected sooner as *NOI* increases in the second year whereas the gain from conversion does not occur until the fifth year.

If we assume all the mortgages discussed above are nonrecourse to the borrower,[15] as is often the case, the lender bears the downside risk of receiving the property through default. In effect, the borrower has an option to "put" the property to the mortgage lender if the value decreases below the mortgage balance. Thus, with a convertible loan, and to some extent with a participation loan, the lender bears both the upside and downside risk of property ownership. Consequently, the expected return on each loan structure should be commensurate with this risk.

We approached the analysis of different financing alternatives by considering each one independently. However, features of the different financing alternatives are often combined. For example, a convertible mortgage could also include a participation in *NOI* during the operating years as well as interest-only or negative amortization feature.

The above discussion provides a structure for thinking about the risk and return trade-offs for different financing alternatives. These alternatives allow the investor and lender to structure the financing so that the risk and return for the property are shared acceptably. The expected rate of return to each party must be commensurate with the risk. To a large extent, structuring the loan in different ways simply determines how that risk is shared between the borrower and the lender. Different tax status for the borrower and lender, however, may provide gains to both with some loan structures. For example, the lender may have a lower marginal tax rate than the investor, which would make the tax depreciation allowance associated with ownership of the property more valuable to the investor than to the lender. Thus, a participation loan that allows the investor to retain all of the ownership and tax depreciation may be more desirable than a convertible mortgage with the same before-tax cash flows to each party. Alternatively, the lender may desire to eventually own the property. By using a convertible mortgage the investor would receive all the tax benefits of depreciation until the mortgage is converted into equity. In return for allowing the investor to capture these tax benefits and for taking the risk of buying the ownership option under a convertible mortgage, the lender would expect to earn a return higher than the interest rate on a more conventional loan structure. Thus, both parties may gain by attempting to structure the transaction in an optimal manner.

[15]Recall that this means that the borrower incurs no personal liability in the event of loan default.

Conclusion

This chapter illustrated the concept of financial leverage and discussed the conditions for favorable leverage on both before-tax and after-tax bases. We also showed that the use of financial leverage in the hopes of increasing the rate of return on equity is *not riskless*. That is, increasing the level of debt increases the riskiness of the investment, as we illustrated by showing that debt increases the variance of the rate of returns. Thus, when investors use leverage, they must consider whether the additional risk is commensurate with the higher expected return (assuming positive leverage).

Financial leverage deals with the *amount* of financing. The chapter also discussed several financing alternatives, including different types of participation loans and a sale-leaseback of the land. We also considered the effect of each of these alternatives on the investor's cash flows, rates of return, and the debt coverage ratio, and we calculated the effective cost of each alternative. These calculations are used to make decisions regarding the type of financing alternative to choose (the *structure* of the debt).

It is impossible to discuss all the possible types of financing alternatives. However, the concepts discussed in this chapter should help you analyze any alternative encountered in practice.

Key Terms

Questions

1. What is financial leverage? Why is a one-year measure of return on investment inadequate in determining whether positive or negative financial leverage exists?
2. What is the break-even mortgage interest rate *(BEIR)* in the context of financial leverage? Would you ever expect an investor to pay a break-even interest rate when financing a property? Why or why not?
3. What are *positive* and *negative* financial leverage? How are returns or losses magnified as the degree of leverage increases? How does leverage on a before-tax basis differ from leverage on an after-tax basis?
4. In what way does leverage increase the riskiness of a loan?
5. What is meant by a participation loan? What does the lender participate in? Why would a lender want to make a participation loan? Why would an investor want to obtain a participation loan?
6. What is meant by a sale-leaseback? Why would a building investor want to do a sale-leaseback of the land? What is the benefit to the party that purchases the land under a sale-leaseback?
7. Why might an investor prefer a loan with a lower interest rate and a participation?
8. Why might a lender prefer a loan with a lower interest rate and a participation?
9. How do you think participations affect the riskiness of a loan?
10. What is the motivation for a sale-leaseback of the land?
11. What criteria should be used to choose between two financing alternatives?
12. What is the traditional cash equivalency approach to determine how below-market rate loans affect value?
13. How can the effect of below-market rate loans on value be determined using investor criteria?

Problems

1. An investor would like to purchase a new apartment property for $2 million. However, she faces the decision of whether to use 70 percent or 80 percent financing. The 70 percent loan can be obtained at 10 percent interest for 25 years. The 80 percent loan can be obtained at 11 percent interest for 25 years.

   NOI is expected to be $190,000 per year and increase at 3 percent annually, the same rate at which the property is expected to increase in value. The building and improvements represent 80 percent of value and will be depreciated over 27.5 years (1 ÷ 27.5 per year). The project is expected to be sold after five years. Assume a 36% tax bracket for all income and capital gain.

   a. What would the *BTIRR* and *ATIRR* be at each level of financing (assume monthly mortgage amortization)?

   b. What is the break-even interest rate *(BEIR)* for this project?

   c. What is the marginal cost of the 80 percent loan? What does this mean?

   d. Does each loan offer favorable financial leverage? Which would you recommend?

2. You are advising a group of investors that is considering the purchase of a shopping center complex. They would like to finance 75 percent of the purchase price. A loan has been offered to them on the following terms: The contract interest rate is 10 percent and will be amortized with monthly payments over 25 years. The loan also will have an equity participation of 40 percent of the cash flow after debt service. The loan has a "lockout" provision that prevents it from being prepaid before year 5.

   The property is expected to cost $5 million. *NOI* is estimated to be $475,000, including overages during the first year, and to increase at the rate of 3 percent per year for the next five years. The property is expected to be worth $6 million at the end of five years. The improvement represents 80 percent of cost, and depreciation will be over 39 years. Assume a 28% tax bracket for all income and capital gains and a holding period of five years.

   a. Compute the *BTIRR* and *ATIRR* after five years, taking into account the equity participation.

   b. What would the *BEIR* be on such a project? What is the projected cost of the equity participation financing?

   c. Is there favorable leverage with the proposed loan?

3. Use the same information as in problem 5 in Chapter 10. Now assume a loan for $1.5 million is obtained at a 10 percent interest rate and a 15-year term.

   a. Calculate the expected *IRR* on equity and the standard deviation of the return on equity.

   b. Contrast the results from (*a*) with those from problem 5 in Chapter 10. Has the loan increased the risk? Explain.

4. A developer wants to finance a project costing $1.5 million with a 70 percent, 25-year loan at an interest rate of 8 percent. The project's *NOI* is expected to be $120,000 during year 1 and the *NOI*, as well as its value, is expected to increase at an annual rate of 3 percent thereafter. The lender will require an initial debt coverage ratio of at least 1.20.

   a. Would the lender be likely to make the loan to the developer? Support your answer with a cash flow statement for a five-year period. What would be the developer's before-tax yield on equity (*BTIRR*)?

   b. Based on the projection in (*a*), what would be the maximum loan amount that the lender would make if the debt coverage ratio was 1.15 for year 1? What would be the loan-to-value ratio?

   c. Assuming conditions in part (*a*), suppose that mortgage interest rates suddenly increase from 8 percent to 10 percent. *NOI* and value will now increase at a rate of 5 percent. If the desired *DCR* is 1.20, will the lender be as willing to make a conventional loan now? Support your answer with a cash flow statement.

5. Ace Development Company is trying to structure a loan with the First National Bank. Ace would like to purchase a property for $2.5 million. The property is projected to produce a first year *NOI* of $200,000. The lender will only allow up to an 80 percent loan on the property and requires a *DCR* in the first year of at least 1.25. All loan payments are to be made monthly, but will increase by 10 percent at the beginning of each year for five years. The contract rate of interest on the loan is 12 percent. The lender is willing to allow the loan to negatively amortize; however, the loan will mature at the end of the five-year period.

   a. What will the balloon payment be at the end of the fifth year?

   b. If the property value does not change, what will the loan-to-value ratio be at the end of the five-year period?

6. An institutional lender is willing to make a loan for $1 million on an office building at a 10 percent interest (accrual) rate with payments calculated using an 8 percent pay rate and a 30-year loan term. (That is, payments are calculated as if the interest rate were 8 percent with monthly payments over 30 years.) After the first five years the payments are to be adjusted so that the loan can be amortized over the remaining 25-year term.
   a. What is the initial payment?
   b. How much interest will accrue during the first year?
   c. What will the balance be after five years?
   d. What will the monthly payments be starting in year 6?
7. A property is expected to have *NOI* of $100,000 the first year. The *NOI* is expected to increase by 3 percent per year thereafter. The appraised value of the property is currently $1 million and the lender is willing to make a $900,000 participation loan with a contract interest rate of 8 percent. The loan will be amortized with monthly payments over a 20-year term. In addition to the regular mortgage payments, the lender will receive 50 percent of the *NOI* in excess of $100,000 each year until the loan is repaid. The lender also will receive 50 percent of any increase in the value of the property. The loan includes a substantial prepayment penalty for repayment before year 5, and the balance of the loan is due in year 10. (If the property has not been sold the participation will be based on the appraised value of the property.) Assume that the appraiser would estimate the value in year 10 by dividing the *NOI* for year 11 by a 10 percent capitalization rate.

   Calculate the effective cost (to the borrower) of the participation loan assuming the loan is held for 10 years. (Note that this is also the expected return to the lender.)
8. Refer to problem 7. Assume that another alternative is a convertible mortgage (instead of a participation loan) that gives the lender the option to convert the mortgage balance into a 60 percent equity position at the end of year 10. That is, instead of receiving the payoff on the mortgage, the lender would own 60 percent of the property. The loan would be for $900,000 with a contract rate of 9 percent, and it would be amortized over 20 years. Assume that the borrower will default if the property value is less than the loan balance in year 10.
   a. What is the lender's *IRR* if the property sells for the same price in year 10 as the previous example?
   b. What is the lender's *IRR* if the property only sells for $1 million after 10 years?
   c. What is the lender's *IRR* if the property only sells for $500,000 after 10 years?
9. A borrower and lender negotiate a $20,000,000 interest only loan at a 9 percent interest rate for a term of 15 years. There is a lockout period of 10 years. Should the borrower choose to prepay this loan at anytime after the end of the 10th year, a yield maintenance fee (*YMF*) will be charged. The *YMF* will be calculated as follows: A treasury security with a maturity equal to the number of months remaining on the loan will be selected, to which a spread of 150 basis points (1.50 percent) will be added to determine the lender's reinvestment rate. The penalty will be determined as the present value of the difference between the original loan rate and the lender's reinvestment rate.
   a. How much will the *YMF* be if the loan is repaid at the end of year 13 if 2-year treasury rates are 6 percent? What if 2-year treasury rates are 8 percent?

CHAPTER

12

Partnerships, Joint Ventures, and Syndications

Introduction: What Is a Syndicate?

The concept of real estate **syndication** extends generally to any group of investors who have combined their financial resources with the expertise of a real estate professional for the common purpose of carrying out a real estate project. A syndication is not an organization form per se. It may take any of the legal business forms such as a corporation, limited partnership, or general partnership.

A syndicate can be formed to acquire, develop, manage, operate, or market real estate. Syndication can be viewed as a type of financing that offers smaller investors the opportunity to invest in ventures that would otherwise be beyond their financial and management capabilities. Syndicators benefit from the fees they receive for their services and the interest they may retain in the syndicated property. Many syndication firms are in the business of acquiring, managing, and then selling real estate projects. In order to acquire property, they bring in other investors with capital that forms the equity base with which the property is acquired. Syndicators do not usually invest much of their own capital. Rather, they act more as agent-managers earning fees for acquiring, managing, and selling properties owned by the investors who have contributed capital to the syndication.

Developers who need additional equity capital to undertake a project often raise funds through syndications, either directly or by using a firm that specializes in raising capital by selling interests in the syndication. The syndication may become involved during the development and construction of the project or after the building is completed and leased. In the latter case, the syndication provides a means for the developer to remove equity from the project, especially if the value of the project upon completion and lease-up is greater than the construction cost. The developer also typically receives a development fee. This strategy allows the developer to focus on developing projects, earning a development fee, retaining some ownership in the project, and going on to the next development project.

In cases where one or a small number of projects are to be syndicated, investors often choose a **limited partnership.** For a smaller project that requires a limited number of investors, the capital for the partnership will usually be raised by what is referred to as a **private offering.** Syndicators must adhere to certain regulations when offering ownership interests in partnerships to investors.

In other cases a syndicator may desire to raise a large amount of funds to acquire many properties. The particular properties to be acquired may or may not be identified when the funds are raised. If not, the offering is referred to as a **blind pool.** A blind pool offering allows the syndicator discretion over what properties are purchased, subject to broad guidelines in an offering prospectus to investors. In cases where ownership interests will be sold to investors in many states, the syndication is usually undertaken through a **public syndicate.** This type of syndication is subject to numerous state and federal regulations that are discussed later in this chapter.

The purpose of this chapter is to familiarize students with basic approaches to understanding and evaluating investment in an ownership interest in a real estate syndication. This information is important for both potential investors and developers. The investor must evaluate how the rate of return and risk for investment in a share of a syndicate compares with other investment opportunities. The developer must evaluate how the *cost* of obtaining equity funds through syndication (in terms of what the developer must give up) compares with other financing alternatives.

The focus of our discussion in this chapter will be on the analysis of a *private* offering in which a *single* property is to be acquired by a limited partnership. The emphasis is on understanding how ownership of shares in a partnership that owns the property differs from direct ownership of the property, as we have assumed in previous chapters.

Use of the Limited Partnership in Private and Public Syndicates

Limited partnerships have often been used as vehicles for raising equity capital for real estate ventures. They combine the limited liability feature of an investment in a corporation with the advantages of a general partnership, such as the ability to make special allocations of income and cash flow to the partners. An investor's liability (**limited partner**) is limited to his initial contribution plus any unpaid contributions he has agreed to make in the future. Furthermore, the responsibility for the management of the partnership rests with the **general partners** who are frequently knowledgeable in real estate matters, thus providing the partnership with professional management.

The Tax Reform Act of 1986 removed many of the tax advantages associated with the use of limited partnerships relative to other forms of real estate ownership. For example, any tax losses resulting from investments in limited partnerships are subject to the passive activity limitation rules (see Chapter 10). These tax changes led to a significant decline in real estate syndicates' use of the limited partnership form of ownership. It remains important to understand this ownership vehicle, however, since a large number of real estate limited partnerships still exist. Furthermore, a large number of the Real Estate Investment Trusts (REITs) formed during the early 1990s were structured so that the REIT was a general partner in a limited partnership. This structure allowed limited partners in existing syndications (including ones that were formed prior to the Tax Reform Act of 1986) to exchange their limited partnership interests for interests in the new partnership formed by the REIT as a "tax free exchange." We discuss Real Estate Investment Trusts further in Chapter 19. The point here is simply that limited partnerships continue to play an important role in real estate finance.

Private Syndication Problem Illustrated

When embarking on a syndication with other investors, it is essential for all parties, whether investors or lenders, to understand the framework in which the venture will operate. What follows is an analysis of a *private* real estate syndication formed to acquire and operate the Plaza Office Building. In this syndication, 35 individuals have been approached by Dallac Investment Corporation, which has agreed to act as the sole general partner in a *limited partnership.*[1] Dallac is trying to raise sufficient equity capital to undertake the purchase and has decided to use the *limited partnership* form of organization, which will limit the liability of all partners to their agreed upon capital contribution to the venture.

The venture to be undertaken and relevant cost and financial data are summarized in Exhibit 12–1. Dallac has obtained an option to purchase the property and has a commitment for a nonrecourse loan from Prudent Life Insurance Company. The loan requires prior approval of any change in the general partner at any time in the future.

Financial Considerations—Partnership Agreement

Exhibit 12–2 summarizes the financial aspects of the partnership agreement and the equity requirements of the general and limited partners for this example. The partnership agreement governs the business relationship among the general and limited partners and is often long and rather involved. At a minimum, partnership agreements should specify how and in what proportions the equity will be initially contributed and whether assessments will be made should a cash shortfall occur or should the improvement need substantial repair in the future. In this example, Dallac has agreed as general partner to contribute 5 percent of the required equity, with the 35 limited partners investing 95 percent.[2] There is no provision for future assessments of the limited partners. Since limited partners are not liable for future capital contributions, Dallac will have to address the issue of what happens in the event the property generates negative before-tax cash flow. Dallac could guarantee to cover negative before-tax cash flow (and will likely charge a fee for doing so), raise sufficient equity capital initially to cover future negative cash flows, arrange for additional borrowing, or reserve the right to raise new capital by admitting additional partners.

The partnership agreement should also specify how income or loss from operating the property and capital gain or loss from sale of the property should be distributed. In our example, profits, losses, and cash flow from operations will be distributed 5 percent to the general partner (Dallac) and 95 percent to the limited partners. However, gain (or loss) from sale of the property is to be allocated 10 percent to the general partner and 90 percent to the limited partners. As mentioned earlier, an important characteristic of a partnership is that all items of income and loss (including gain or loss from resale) and cash do not have to be distributed in the same proportion. This **special allocation** allows flexibility in the ability to allocate the benefits of the real estate investment between the general and limited partners. We will see that these allocations affect the rate of return to each of the partners and are, therefore, important considerations in the analysis of partnerships.

---

[1]For clarity, we will consider all 35 limited partners as a single entity. As we will discuss later in this chapter, when more than 35 investors become partners, it is generally considered a public offering.

[2]In this case we assume each limited partner invests an equal percentage of the cash required from each partner. In practice, however, partners could purchase different proportional interests. Also, in many syndications, the general partner may invest as little as 1 percent of the equity or no equity at all.

EXHIBIT 12–1 Plaza Office Building Acquisition Cost and Financing Summary

Cost breakdown		
Land	$ 525,000	
Improvements	3,475,000	(capitalized)
Points	60,000	(amortized over loan term)
Subtotal	$4,060,000	
Organization fee	20,000	(amortized over 5 years)
Syndication expenses	100,000	(capitalized but not depreciated)
Total funding required	$4,180,000	
Loan amount	$3,000,000	(71.77% of total funding)
Interest rate	12%	
Term	25 years	(monthly payments)
Points	$ 60,000	
Annual debt service	$ 379,161	

EXHIBIT 12–2 Partnership Facts and Equity Requirements for Plaza Office Building Syndication

a. Organization: December, year 1
b. Number of partners: 1 general partner and 35 limited partners
c. Equity capital contribution: general partner, 5%; limited partners, 95%
d. Cash assessments: none
e. Cash distributions from operations: general partner, 5%; limited partners, 95%
f. Taxable income and losses from operations: general partner, 5%; limited partners, 95%
g. Allocation of gain or loss from sale: general partner, 10%; limited partners, 90%
h. Cash distributions at sale: Based on capital account balances (capital accounts will be explained in the following discussion)

Initial equity requirements	
Land and improvements	$4,000,000
Points on mortgage loan	60,000
Organization fee	20,000
Syndication fees	100,000
Total cash requirements	$4,180,000
Less mortgage financing	3,000,000
Equals equity requirements	$1,180,000
General partners (5%)	59,000
Limited partners (95%)*	$1,121,000

*As indicated earlier, it is common to allow limited partners to pay in their equity contribution over time. The general partner arranges for additional financing during this pay-in period, using the limited partners' notes as collateral. To keep this example manageable, we have not assumed such a pay-in.

When special allocations are used to allocate items of income and cash flow in different proportions to different partners, it becomes important to know how to determine the amount of cash that should be distributed to each partner upon sale of the property. This final cash distribution must take into consideration the initial equity contribution, allocations of cash flow during the operating years of the property, and allocations of income (or loss) from operation and sale of the property. These

EXHIBIT 12–3 Plaza Operating and Tax Projections

Potential gross income (year 2)	$750,000
Vacancy and collection loss	5% of potential gross income
Operating expenses (year 2)	35% of effective gross income
Depreciation method	Straight line, 31.5 years*
Amortization of loan points	$60,000 over 25 years or $2,400 annually
Amortization of organization fees	$20,000 over 5 years or $4,000 annually
Projected growth in income	3% per year
Projected resale price after 5 years	$5,000,000
Limited partners' tax rate	28%
General partner's tax rate	28%

*Depreciable life allowed at the time this syndication is assumed to be formed. As indicated in Chapter 10, depreciation rules change frequently. Partnerships formed after 1993 would be required to use a depreciable life of 27.5 years for residential property and 39 years for nonresidential property.

items are accounted for in the partner's **capital account.** The nature and importance of the capital account will be discussed in more detail later in the chapter. For now we point out that the partnership agreement specifies that the cash flow from sale of the property will be allocated according to the capital account balances at that time.

Operating Projections

Exhibit 12–3 summarizes Dallac's projections about operations. All projections in a syndication offering must be made carefully and prudently since any misrepresentation or failure to disclose all material risks of the investment may result in a lawsuit for rescission of the partnership or damages by investors, or an action by regulatory authorities.[3] Because of this scrutiny by public agencies and the potential for legal action by limited partners, many general partner–syndicators make very general projections regarding future results or provide only a description of the projects that will be invested in, along with some information on the business background of the general partner or partners.

In addition to projections for rental income, operating expenses, management fees, and the like, Dallac has also disclosed the method of depreciation to be used, the period over which loan fees and organization fees will be amortized, and when syndication fees will be deducted for federal income tax purposes. Syndication fees cannot be deducted in the year in which payment occurs; they must be capitalized and amortized over a prescribed time period established by tax regulations. These expenses are important from the investor's perspective because the cash flow requirement occurs when the expenses are paid; however, their tax influence occurs over the period of years during which amortization occurs or when the item is appropriately deductible.

[3]In the case of public offerings most states require that a prospectus be filed with the state securities and exchange commission, and such projections are carefully scrutinized before approval to offer the securities is granted. Interstate offerings must be filed with the U.S. Securities and Exchange Commission and undergo a similar examination. Review and examination of securities offerings by state or federal agencies in no way indicate approval or disapproval of the economic merits of the investment, but only that the offering substantially complies with the disclosure and other requirements for registration or exemption.

EXHIBIT 12–4 Pro Forma Statement of Before-Tax Cash Flow for Plaza Office Building

	Year				
	(2)	(3)	(4)	(5)	(6)
Potential gross income	$750,000	$772,500	$795,675	$819,545	$844,132
Less vacancy and collection	37,500	38,625	39,784	40,977	42,207
Effective gross income	712,500	733,875	755,891	778,568	801,925
Less operating expenses	249,375	256,856	264,562	272,499	$280,674
Net operating income	463,125	477,019	491,329	506,069	521,251
Less debt service	379,161	379,161	379,161	379,161	379,161
Before-tax cash flow (*BTCF*)	$ 83,964	$ 97,858	$112,169	$126,909	$142,091
Allocation					
General partners	5%				
Limited partners	95%				
Distribution of *BTCF*					
General partners	$ 4,198	$ 4,893	$ 5,608	$ 6,345	$ 7,105
Limited partners	$ 79,766	$ 92,965	$106,560	$120,563	$134,986

Statement of Before-Tax Cash Flow (BTCF)

An important projection to be considered when analyzing a partnership is the statement of cash flow. In addition to the $1,121,000 investment made by limited partners in December, or the end of year 1, the statement shown in Exhibit 12–4 summarizes the before-tax cash inflow (*BTCF*) or cash shortfalls expected from the operation of the Plaza Office Building.

Another important aspect of the statement of cash flow deals with the distribution of cash to partners. In year 2 the project is expected to generate $83,964 in cash for distribution. Of this amount $79,766 will be distributed to limited partners. This represents an equity dividend rate of about 7 percent.

Calculation of Net Income or Loss

To illustrate the tax effect of the projections made in Exhibit 12–3, we have constructed a statement of taxable income or loss in Exhibit 12–5 for the syndication-partnership investment in the Plaza Office Building. The exhibit shows that limited partners making a $1,121,000 (total for all partners) investment at the end of December would have a $12,502 taxable loss to report during year 2. The syndication loss is a passive loss, as discussed in Chapter 10, and subject to the passive activity loss limitation rules. In this example we assume that each of the 35 partners has sufficient passive activity income from other investments (e.g., other real estate partnership investments that now have taxable income) to use the share of the loss (11,877 ÷ 35) in year 2. Beginning in year 3, investors would have to report taxable income, which would be subject to ordinary rates of taxation at that time.

Calculation of Capital Gain from Sale

The calculation of capital gains and the resulting tax due from sale of the property is the same for a syndicated investment property sale as it is for the sale of property held by an individual. Exhibit 12–6 shows the calculation of the capital gain and its allocation to the general and limited partners pursuant to the partnership agreement, which provides that 10 percent of the gain be allocated to the general partner and 90 percent of the gain to the limited partner.

EXHIBIT 12–5 Pro Forma Statement of Income (loss), Plaza Office Building Syndication

	Year (2)	(3)	(4)	(5)	(6)
Net operating income	$ 463,125	$477,019	$491,329	$506,069	$521,251
Less					
Interest	358,910	356,342	353,448	350,187	346,512
Depreciation	110,317	110,317	110,317	110,317	110,317
Amortization					
Organization fee	4,000	4,000	4,000	4,000	4,000
Loan fee	2,400	2,400	2,400	2,400	50,400
Taxable income	$−12,502	$ 3,960	$ 21,164	$ 39,165	$ 10,022
Distribution					
General partners	5%				
Limited partners	95%				
Distribution					
General partners	$ −625	$ 198	$ 1,058	$ 1,958	$ 501
Limited partners	−11,877	$ 3,761	$ 20,106	$ 37,207	$ 9,521

EXHIBIT 12–6 Calculation of Capital Gain and Allocation to Partners

Calculation of Capital Gain from Reversion in Year 6		
Sale price		$5,000,000
Selling costs		250,000
Original cost basis	$4,100,000	
Less accumulated depreciation	551,587	
Adjusted basis		3,548,413
Total taxable gain		$1,201,587
Allocation of Gain		
General partners (10% of gain)		$ 120,159
Limited partners (90% of gain)		$1,081,428

Capital Accounts

Capital accounts represent the partners' ownership equity in partnership assets. Capital accounts are maintained by *crediting* the account for all *cash contributed* to the partnership and all *income* and *gain* allocated to each partner. The account is then *debited* for *cash distributed* to the partner plus any loss allocated to the partner. Exhibit 12–7 shows the capital account balances for the partners after accounting for the initial equity contribution, all income allocated from operating the property, all cash distributed while operating the property, and the allocation of gain from sale of the property. Thus, capital account balances include everything but cash proceeds from sale of the property because, according to the partnership agreement, the distribution of cash proceeds from sale of the property is to be based on the capital account balance.

The capital account balance at the end of year 1 is $1,121,000 for the limited partners and $59,000 for the general partner. This represents the initial equity contributions. In year 2 those balances are reduced by both the losses allocated and the cash distributed. Of course, the reason that cash is available for distribution at the same time losses are allocated is because losses are due to noncash deductions (depreciation and amortization), as discussed in Chapter 10. Note that beginning in year 3, income allocations increase capital accounts, but cash distributions reduce them. Finally, in year 6, capital accounts are increased by the gain from sale allocated to each partner. In an accounting sense, the balances in year 6 show what each partner has in the way of equity capital invested in the partnership at that time. This is important to know because cash proceeds from sale of the property will be distributed in accordance with these capital account balances. We will further discuss the importance of these capital accounts later.

Distribution of Cash from Sale of Asset

Exhibit 12–8 shows a breakdown of the cash distribution from the sale of the property. As indicated in the agreement, after paying selling expenses and the outstanding mortgage, both the limited partners and the general partner will receive cash distributions from the sale that are equal to their capital account balances. Capital account balances for all of the partners will be exactly zero after this distribution of cash because all prior allocations of income, cash flows, and losses have been accounted for in the partners' capital accounts (see Exhibit 12–7).

Calculation of After-Tax Cash Flow and ATIRR on Equity

Based on all of the preceding exhibits and an assumed marginal tax bracket of 28 percent, after-tax cash flows from operations and reversion can be calculated and the *ATIRR* on the investment can be determined. This is done in Exhibit 12–9, where the initial equity investment is a cash outflow in year 1 and before-tax cash flows plus tax savings (or less taxes due) are cash inflows. After-tax cash flows from operations and reversion result in an *ATIRR* of 13.15 percent for limited partners and 22.24 percent for the general partner. The higher return to the general partner is due to the additional allocation of gain and, consequently, additional cash flow when the property is sold. That is, the general partner was allocated 10 percent of the gain from the sale, whereas the general partner contributed 5 percent of the equity and received 5 percent of the income and cash flow during the operating years. If the allocation of gain was also 5 percent for the general partner, then the *ATIRR* would have been exactly the same for both general and limited partners. (This return would be 13.68 percent. Of course, the general and limited partners must also be in the same tax bracket for their after-tax returns to be the same.)

Based on our analysis of Dallac, you should have a general framework in mind to consider potential investments involving limited partnerships. We should stress that the Dallac case example is meant to illustrate one possible way in which an investment can be structured. Indeed, many consider the field of real estate syndication financing and partnerships one of the most complex areas of federal tax law, subject to great variations in structuring terms among partners. Hence, much study of the law and federal taxation beyond the information presented here is required to gain expertise in the area.

However, you can keep in mind a few underlying generalizations when evaluating such investments. One generalization is that syndication arrangements are subject to the same economic influences that all investments are, that is, risk and return. Any real estate investment is capable of producing only so much income, regardless of whether or not it is syndicated. When syndicated under a limited

EXHIBIT 12–7 Capital Accounts Prior to Distribution of Cash Flow from Sale

	End of Year					
	(1)	*(2)*	*(3)*	*(4)*	*(5)*	*(6)*
Limited Partners						
Equity	$1,121,000					
Plus income	0	$ 0	$ 3,761	$ 20,106	$ 37,207	$ 9,521
Less loss	0	−1,877	0	0	0	0
Plus gain from sale	0					1,081,428
Less cash distributed	0	−79,766	−92,965	−106,560	−120,563	−134,986
Total for year	1,121,000	−91,643	−89,204	−86,455	−83,357	955,963
Balance	$1,121,000	$1,029,357	$ 940,153	$ 853,698	$ 770,341	$1,726,304
General Partner						
Equity	$59,000					
Plus income	0	$ 0	$ 198	$ 1,058	$ 1,958	$ 501
Less loss	0	−625	0	0	0	0
Plus gain from sale						120,159
Less cash distributed	0	−4,198	4,893	−5,608	−6,345	−7,105
Total for year	59,000	−4,823	−4,695	−4,550	−4,387	113,555
Balance	$59,000	$54,177	$49,482	$44,932	$40,545	$154,100

EXHIBIT 12–8 Cash Distribution from Sale—Year 6

Sale price	$5,000,000
Less selling costs	250,000
Less mortgage balance	2,869,596
Before-tax cash flow	1,880,404
Distribution (based on capital account balances):	
General partners	154,100
Limited partners	1,726,304
Balance (should be zero)	$ 0

partnership, cash flows and tax items from operating and the eventual sale of assets are simply split among different parties. The promoter of the syndicate, who in many cases becomes the general partner, will offer limited partners only what is necessary under current competitive conditions to induce them to invest in the project. Such a return must be commensurate with the risk and return available to investors from comparable syndication offerings or other investment opportunities. Hence the *ratios* used to establish contribution of equity assessments, splitting of cash flows, and so on, should be structured in such a way that given reasonable projections of income and property value, investors will earn a competitive return as measured by the procedure described in this section of the chapter.

Investors should be in a position to compare terms offered by competing syndicators given the risk and required equity investment, and to judge whether expected

EXHIBIT 12–9 Calculation of After-Tax Cash Flow and *ATIRR*

	End of Year					
	(1)	(2)	(3)	(4)	(5)	(6)
	General Partner					
Operation						
*BTCF**	$ −59,000	$ 4,198	$ 4,893	$ 5,608	$ 6,345	$ 7,105
Taxable income†	0	−625	198	1,058	1,958	501
Taxes (28%)	0	−175	55	296	548	140
ATCF	$ −59,000	$ 4,373	$ 4,838	$ 5,312	$ 5,797	$6,965
Reversion						
BTCF‡						$ 154,100
Capital gain§						120,159
Taxes (28%)						33,644
ATCF						120,456
Total *ATCF*	$ −59,000	$ 4,373	$ 4,838	$ 5,312	$ 5,797	$ 127,421
ATIRR = 22.24%						
	Limited Partners					
Operation						
*BTCF**	$−1,121,000	$ 79,766	$92,965	$106,560	$120,563	$ 134,986
Taxable income†		−11,877	3,761	20,106	37,207	9,521
Taxes (28%)	0	−3,326	1,053	5,630	10,418	2,666
ATCF	$−1,121,000	$ 83,092	$91,912	$100,930	$110,145	$ 132,320
Reversion						
BTCF‡						$1,726,304
Capital gain§						1,081,428
Taxes (28%)						302,800
ATCF						1,423,504
Total *ATCF*	$−1,121,000	$ 83,092	$91,912	$100,931	$110,145	$1,555,824
ATIRR = 13.15%						

*From Exhibits 12–2 and 12–4.
†From Exhibit 12–5.
‡From Exhibit 12–7.
§From Exhibit 12–6.

returns are adequate. However, keep in mind that the general partner must also earn a competitive return in order to profitably perform the economic function of syndicating. Essentially, syndicators view their role in the investment process more like that of an agent who seeks and finds properties for acquisition or development, finds equity investors, operates and manages properties during ownership by the syndication, and eventually disposes of them. Because syndicators perform these services, they must also be reasonably assured of being compensated. Hence, they attempt to charge *fees* for all services such as finding properties for purchase, renting facilities, promoting the sale of partnership interests, and managing and accounting for the partnership investment. Investors pay these fees in addition to legal and accounting costs of organizing the partnership.

Limited partners must consider the reasonableness of syndicators' fees and partnership fees, plus the general partner's share in cash flows and appreciation in property value, when comparing syndication alternatives. The primary concern of the limited partner is whether the general partner is "carving out" too much in fees and participation in future cash flows that would make the return on investment unattractive to limited partners. On the other hand, the general partner must be assured of earning a reasonable return for the risk and time involved in promoting the investment. Further, if the syndicator is attempting to earn all compensation from fees and is not taking some equity risk in the project, it may appear to a limited partner that the syndicator–general partner really has no stake in the project and has little concern over the long-run performance of the investment. If *expertise* in the operation and management of the investment is the part of the syndication that appeals to the limited partner, then the limited partner may be more satisfied if the general partner has a stake in the profits instead of receiving fees. Clearly, many facets of reimbursement must be considered, and the partners must reach some balance. Although fees to the general partner may ultimately reduce the limited partner's rate of return, these fees represent the cost of transferring certain risks and responsibilities to the general partner. Thus, the limited partner should not expect as high a return as in a situation where he must incur these risks and costs himself.

Partnership Allocations and Substantial Economic Effect

One of the advantages of a partnership, whether a limited partnership or a general partnership between a few individuals, is the ability to allocate profit and loss to different partners in different proportions than their equity contribution. However, certain guidelines must be followed to ensure that the benefits of these allocations won't be disallowed. Syndicates typically attempt to allocate the greatest amount of tax loss from the venture as quickly as possible to the individuals (usually limited partners) who have contributed capital to the partnership. In effect, it is these tax losses that the investors have purchased. Various means, such as disproportionate allocations of specific items (such as depreciation deductions), have been used to accelerate the allocation of losses to limited partners.[4] A partner's distributive share of each item of income, gain, loss, deduction, or credit is generally determined by the partnership agreement. However, for the IRS to accept the allocations as valid, the allocations must result in what is referred to as a **substantial economic effect.** Where the allocation in the partnership agreement lacks substantial economic effect, the item that is subject to the allocation will be reallocated by the IRS according to the partner's "interest in the partnership."[5]

In determining whether an allocation had a substantial economic effect on the partners, the courts have long inquired whether the allocation was reflected by an appropriate adjustment in the partners' capital accounts. The new proposed regulations governing special allocations adopt this view and provide rules for the proper maintenance of the partners' capital accounts.[6] As we have seen, capital accounts are used for

---

[4]For a more complete discussion see Richard B. Peiser, "Partnership Allocations in Real Estate Joint Ventures," *Real Estate Review* 13, no. 3.

[5]A partner's "interest in the partnership" is determined by taking into account all of the facts and circumstances, including the partner's initial investment, interest in profits, losses, and cash flow, and distributions of capital upon liquidation.

[6]Treasury Regulation Section 1.704–1.

accounting purposes and reflect the economic contribution of partners to the partnership. In general, the proposed regulations provide that if (1) an allocation to a partner is reflected in her capital account and the liquidation proceeds (cash flows from sale of the property) are distributed in accordance with the capital accounts, and (2) following the distribution of the proceeds the partners are liable to the partnership (either pursuant to the partnership agreement or under state law) to restore any deficit in their capital accounts (by contributing cash to partners with positive capital account balances), the allocation has substantial economic effect and will be recognized by the IRS.

Capital Accounts and Gain Charge-Backs

Assume A and B form a partnership where A, the limited partner, contributes $100,000 and B, the general partner, contributes no cash. The partnership secures a $400,000 (10 percent interest only) nonrecourse loan and acquires AB Apartments for $500,000. Assume that the results from the first year of operations of AB Apartments are as follows:

Gross income	$ 70,000
Less vacancy and collection loss	−4,000
Effective gross income	$ 66,000
Less operating expenses	−21,000
Net operating income	$ 45,000
Less debt service (interest only)	−40,000
Before-tax cash flow	$ 5,000

Assume that tax depreciation the first year is $50,000. This results in taxable income as follows:

Net operating income	$ 45,000
Less depreciation	50,000
Less interest cost	40,000
Taxable income	$ −45,000

Now assume that the partnership agreement provides that 90 percent of all taxable income, loss, and cash flow from operations is to be allocated to A and 10 percent to B. At the end of year 1 the capital accounts of A and B would appear as follows:

Capital Accounts after First Year of Operations

	A's Capital Account	*B's Capital Account*
Initial equity contribution	$100,000	0
Less loss allocation	−40,500	$−4,500
Less cash flow distribution	−4,500	−500
Ending balance	$ 55,000	$−5,000

Assume that AB Apartments are sold after year 1 for $550,000 with no expenses of sale. This results in a taxable gain as follows:

Sales price		$550,000
Purchase price	$500,000	
Depreciation taken	50,000	
Adjusted basis		450,000
Gain		$100,000

Cash proceeds from the sale would be as follows:

Sale price	$550,000
Less mortgage balance	400,000
Cash flow	$150,000

Now suppose that upon resale, taxable gains or losses are split 50–50 between A and B. Cash proceeds are distributed first to A in an amount equal to his original investment less any cash distributions previously received. Any remaining cash proceeds are split 50–50 between A and B. Exhibit 12–10 shows the impact this arrangement would have on the capital accounts of A and B. Notice that the *net* balance of the two capital accounts is zero (this will always be true if all items of income, cash, and so on, are properly accounted for), but A's capital account is negative and B's is positive. As mentioned above, for an allocation to have a substantial economic effect, liquidation proceeds to be distributed must reflect the disparities in the partners' capital accounts. Where A's capital account is negative and B's is positive, A has in effect recovered his investment at the expense of B. If A is not obligated to restore the deficit in his capital account (by a $17,500 cash payment to B), he may not have borne the entire economic burden equivalent to his share of the depreciation deductions, and the allocations lack substantial economic effect. Therefore, in order for the allocations to be recognized, the capital accounts of the partners must be equalized before the partners in this example can split the remaining cash 50–50. Two acceptable methods of equalizing the capital accounts are discussed below.

The first method of equalizing capital accounts is to adjust the cash distribution to the partners. This adjustment would be done by allocating $17,750 less cash from sale to A and $17,750 more to B. The accounts would now be equal. The second method would be to credit A's capital account for an additional $17,750 in *gain from*

EXHIBIT 12–10 Capital Accounts after Sale of Building

	A's Capital Account	*B's Capital Account*
Balance prior to sale	$ 55,000	$ −5,000
Return of original equity		
Less previous cash distribution	$−95,500	NA
50% of gain	50,000	50,000
50% remaining cash proceeds	−27,250	−27,250
Ending balance	$−17,750	$ 17,750

EXHIBIT 12–11 Capital Accounts after Sale of Building Using Gain Charge-Back

	A's Capital Account	*B's Capital Account*
Balance prior to sale	$ 55,000	$−5,000
Return of original equity		
Less previous cash distribution	$−95,500	
Gain charge-back	35,500	
50% of remaining gain*	32,250	32,250
50% remaining cash proceeds	−27,250	27,250
Ending balance	$ 0	$ 0

*Total gain from sale is $100,000. After the gain charge-back, $65,000 remains to be distributed.

sale, thereby reducing B's share of the gain proportionally. By allocating more gain to A, capital account balances will be zero after cash is distributed.

Exhibit 12–11 illustrates a valid partnership allocation using the second approach or **gain charge-back** method, and shows its impact on the capital accounts of A and B.

Careful examination of the above example should make it clear that the requirement that capital account balances for both partners be zero after sale of the building is one way for the IRS to ensure that a partner who is allocated proportionately more losses for tax purposes is also either allocated more taxable gain at sale of the property or receives less cash. Otherwise, partnerships could be structured in such a way that the partners in higher tax brackets would receive most of the losses, whereas the partners in lower tax brackets would receive most of the gains! Furthermore, the partners in higher tax brackets would be willing to give up some of the cash flow in exchange for receiving the losses and not receiving the gains. The ending capital account balances would then most likely be negative for the partners in higher tax brackets and positive for partners in the lower tax bracket. While the partners may be perfectly happy with this arrangement, the government loses tax revenue. Thus, as we have emphasized, partnership agreements must provide for ending capital account balances to be zero to avoid challenge from the IRS.

Recall that in the case of the Plaza Office Building, the gain was first allocated to the capital accounts, and then the final cash flow was based on the capital account balances. This approach ensured that the capital account balances would be zero for both partners after all allocations and distributions to partners. The partnership agreement could have been structured in other ways for Plaza Office Building and still result in zero capital account balances. For example, a specified percentage of the *cash* available from sale could first be distributed to each partner—the general partners in the Plaza Office Building might receive 10 percent and the limited partners 90 percent. Then to ensure zero capital account balances, the allocation of gain could be based on the capital account balances. (In this case the capital account balances would be negative after the distribution of cash. Allocation of gain to the partners would then eliminate the negative balance.) The point is that allocations of all items of income and cash flow cannot be made without some provision for ensuring that the capital account balances are zero after all allocations and distributions are made.

Use of the Limited Partnership in Private and Public Syndicates

Limited partnerships are widely used as vehicles for raising equity capital for real estate ventures. They combine the limited liability feature of an investment in a corporation with the advantages of a general partnership, such as the ability to make special allocations of income and cash flow to the partners. An investor's liability (limited partner) is limited to the initial contribution plus any unpaid contributions agreed to in the future. Furthermore, the responsibility for the management of the partnership rests with the general partners who are frequently knowledgeable in real estate matters, thus providing the partnership with professional management.

In establishing the limited partnership, great care must be taken that the contractual terms identify it in effect as a partnership and not as an "association" as understood by the Internal Revenue Service. An association is taxed like a corporation. The six criteria for treatment like a corporation are:

1. Business association.
2. An objective to carry on the business and divide the gains therefrom.
3. Continuity of life.
4. Centralization of management.
5. Limited liability.
6. Free transferability of interest.

A corporation must have more corporate than noncorporate characteristics to be classified as a corporation for tax purposes. Criteria 1 and 2 are common to corporations and partnerships. Therefore a business firm generally will be treated as a partnership if two of criteria 3 through 6 are absent.

Most limited partnerships have centralized management similar to that of corporations, so differentiation normally takes place in criteria 3, 5, and 6. Under the Uniform Partnership Act, after which most state statutes are patterned, the general partner has the power to dissolve the partnership at any time, thus denying it continuity of life. Otherwise, a terminal date may be provided in the partnership articles. The criterion of limited liability is negated by the very fact that one partner is a general partner with unlimited liability. Finally, free transferability of interests can be limited by requiring permission of the general or other limited partners to effect a change of ownership. This restriction has been deemed by the Treasury regulations as a legal curtailment of transferability of interests. By proper combination of these provisions, tax treatment as a partnership can be achieved.

Use of Corporate General Partners

The sole general partner of a limited partnership is often a corporation. The advantage of this arrangement lies in the limits on personal liability for the builder-sponsor of a project whose interest in the limited partnership is through a corporation. An incorporated general partner can also provide better continuity of management. To avoid "dummy" corporations as the sole corporate general partner, the Internal Revenue Service follows internal guidelines (called **safe harbor rules**) that impose certain ownership and minimum capital requirements. Limited partners may not own, individually or in the aggregate, more than 20 percent of the corporate stock. The net worth requirement of the corporate general partner depends on the total contributed capital of the partnership. If the contributed capital is less than $2.5 million, the corporate general partner must have a net worth at least equal to 15 percent of the total partnership capital, but not to exceed $250,000. Where the contributed partnership capital is $2.5 million or more, the corporate general partner must maintain at all times a net worth of at least 10 percent of the partnership capital.

Private versus Public Syndicates

An important way to classify syndicates is as **private** and **public.** Most private offerings are issued under Regulation D of the Securities Act of 1933 so as to be exempt from the registration requirements of that act. The Securities and Exchange Commission proposed Regulation D in 1982 to simplify and expand the exemptions from federal securities registration. It exempts syndicates from the registration requirement of the Securities Act, not from the full disclosure and antifraud provisions of securities laws. But that exemption can be significant—the costs of registration essentially eliminate all but the largest syndicated offerings, so exemption from registration under certain conditions facilitates small and medium-sized offerings. Compliance with the regulation does not by itself exempt syndications under *state* securities laws; many states, however, do have similar exemption statutes. Although Regulation D codifies and expands prior exemption statutes, it also defines important concepts, including that of the **accredited investor,** which is discussed in the following section. Anyone involved in making an offering pursuant to the regulation should read and understand it thoroughly to ensure careful compliance with its provisions.

Accredited Investors—Regulation D

If the securities are sold only to accredited investors, it is not necessary to provide investors with the information otherwise required to obtain an exemption under Regulation D. Accredited investors purchasing securities also are not counted in determining the maximum number of potential purchasers that may be solicited to retain exemption from Regulation D. Also, accredited investors do not need to meet the "sophistication and experience" requirements in financial and business matters that are applicable to other investors under the private placement exemption rule in Regulation D. General examples of criteria used to describe accredited investors include the following:

- Any director, executive officer, or general partner of the issuer of the securities being offered or sold, or a director, executive officer, or general partner of a general partner of that issuer.
- Any person who purchases at least $150,000 of the securities being offered, where the purchaser's total purchase price does not exceed 20 percent of the purchaser's net worth at the time of sale.
- Any natural person whose individual net worth, or joint net worth with that person's spouse, at the time of purchase exceeds $1 million.
- Any natural person who had an individual income in excess of $200,000 in each of the two most recent years and who reasonably expects an income in excess of $200,000 in the current year.

Private offerings are usually limited to 35 or fewer investors. A public offering, on the other hand, is characterized by rigorous compliance requirements of the federal and state securities divisions governing the sale of securities to the public. Numerous reports, brochures, prospectuses, and the like are required to qualify an issue for sale to the public. The minimum cost for a registration with the Securities and Exchange Commission is about $50,000 and can run as high as $300,000 to $500,000 for large syndications that register and sell shares in many states. Given the high cost of registering a public syndication under federal and state laws, it makes sense to have a public syndication for large transactions that raise a large amount of capital.

Certificates of participation in public syndicates have been sold in units as low as $500, $1,000, or $5,000. Minimum investments in private syndicates are usually 10 times this amount. Recently, public syndicates have reduced their investment minimums in an attempt to attract Individual Retirement Account and Keogh (self-employed retirement plan) money. The result has been that instead of a few participants of substantial means and risk-taking ability, the syndicate membership may be composed of thousands of small investors. Individuals now have a chance to invest in prime real estate that would normally be beyond the reach of all but wealthy or institutional investors.

Caveats. In a large public syndication, the syndication general partners usually share very few of the risks. They may have originally bought property through another business entity and sold it to the syndicate at a profit. Through other companies that they may also own, they may receive substantial remuneration for the sale of securities to the public, management services, and so on. As the general partners, all earnings and capital gains not contracted to the limited partners accrue to their benefit. These activities may or may not be fully disclosed to potential investors. The role of general partners has been a matter of increasingly grave concern to state and federal securities sales regulators.

Regulation of Syndicates

The great flexibility of the limited partnership has led to abuses. In 1980 a statement of policy or guidelines that established standards for limited partnership offerings of real estate was adopted by the North American Securities Administrators Association (NASAA). State registration agencies, in those states where the guidelines are applicable, generally look with disfavor upon applications that do not conform to the standards contained in the guidelines. All states except California (which in some respects has even more stringent guidelines) belong to NASAA, but not all states have adopted the NASAA guidelines. However, a substantial number of states follow the guidelines, and although the guidelines are intended to *apply only to public syndicates,* many securities administrators look to them for guidance when considering requests for exemptions from registration. The guidelines address syndicates' investment policies, promoters' and managers' compensation, and investor suitability standards. It is in these areas that federal and state regulatory authorities have expressed their greatest concern.

Investment Objectives and Policies

Syndicates differ widely in the investment objectives they seek to accomplish and policies they follow to achieve them. If targeted syndicate investors are in a low tax bracket and seek current income (e.g., IRA and pension fund investors), the syndicate will acquire properties that produce the greatest cash flow. Some of these properties may be purchased for all cash. Other investors may not need current income and seek properties (such as raw land in the path of urban growth) that offer the greatest potential for future capital gain. Still other investors may emphasize investments that generate tax shelters through high depreciation and mortgage interest deductions. The targeted investors for the syndicate will dictate the investment objectives and policies of the syndicator.

In early experience with limited partnerships until the late 1960s, syndicates normally raised capital to finance identifiable parcels, which were described in the prospectus or offering circular in detail so the investor could evaluate them before investing money. Such syndicates are referred to as "specified property" syndicates. Other syndicates raise capital before identifying any or all of the properties it will eventually own. They are known as **blind pool** syndicates and should be recognized as pure venture capital funds since no property descriptions or relevant economic or financial data are available to guide the investor. Specific investment criteria (e.g., type of property and geographic location) should be disclosed in the prospectus for such a blind pool syndicate, as well as the sponsor's background, experience, and previous results, because an investment in a blind pool is essentially an investment in the syndicator's track record and reputation. Investors in such offerings should carefully scrutinize the statement of investment objectives contained in the prospectus, as well as the background and track record of the syndicator. Syndicates' investment objectives generally vary around the following partial list of attributes:

- Fully identified properties.
- Blind pool investment.
- Use of leverage.
- Period of ownership expected before assets are sold.
- Land development investments to be allowed.
- Joint ventures with developers and other investors.
- Acquisition of foreclosed properties for resale.

Promoters' and Managers' Compensation

A major area of concern for syndicate investors is promotional and management fees. Keeping these fees to reasonable levels becomes especially difficult because of the many ways in which competition can be paid. Syndicators often charge fees for providing services such as acquiring properties for the portfolio, managing them, guaranteeing investors a minimum cash flow, selling properties, or arranging refinancing. Obviously up-front fees reduce the amount of funds available for investment in the actual real estate. Additional fees may also be charged on the "back end" out of proceeds from sale of the property.

Management fees have been based on gross assets, net assets, gross rentals, net income, and cash flow. Each method yields its own unique results depending on the fortunes of the syndicate operation. Unfortunately, projections of results are often based on hypotheticals without valid underlying assumptions. Bad projections distort judgments of appropriate compensation and the proper method for determining it. In all instances, full disclosure of conflicts of interest of principals, as well as all direct and indirect compensation payable by the partners to promoters, general partners, underwriters, and affiliates, should be made. This disclosure should describe the time of payment and amount of compensation, and it should detail the service rendered to earn it.

As we just pointed out, fees charged by syndicators and others promoting the syndicate vary widely. Because up-front fees reduce amounts available for investment, investors should look closely at deals where more than 20 percent of the equity raised is paid out in fees. Typical up-front fees include 7 to 10 percent for sales commissions to brokers selling syndicate interests, 1 to 3 percent for legal and accounting expenses, and 5 to 15 percent for organizational and financing fees.

Investor Suitability Standards

An outstanding weakness of a limited partnership interest as an investment is its lack of liquidity or marketability. Because of the restrictions on the assignability of the capital interest, a new partner must have the consent of the existing partners to acquire and enjoy the full interest of a selling partner. Furthermore, state-imposed requirements of financial responsibility of potential investors have made it more difficult to develop a secondary market for such interests. Even an issue of certificates of beneficial interest in a limited partnership is complicated because the limited partner selling an interest becomes a securities issuer and is subject to separate registration requirements. This lack of liquidity and marketability increases the riskiness of a limited partnership investment.

Another weakness of the syndicate is that many syndications have limited appeal to any but the investor in the high tax bracket. Yields other than from a tax shelter may be negligible. The low-income investor may acquire such a syndicate interest with too little appreciation of the weak economic viability of the venture. Minimum suitability standards for investors as recommended by the NASAA guidelines include either an annual gross income of $30,000 and net worth (exclusive of home, furnishings, and automobiles) of at least $30,000 or net worth of at least $75,000. Tax-oriented offerings may require higher standards, such as being in the highest federal income tax bracket, and high-risk offerings may impose higher income and net worth standards. In any case, the prospectus should clearly present the nature of the investor's expected return in the traditional sense, as well as the potential tax savings.

Federal and State Securities Authorities

The federal and state securities laws and regulations are relevant to any real estate syndication. Disclosure requirements under the Securities Act of 1933 and the Securities Exchange Act of 1934 make up the federal basis for civil liability and criminal fraud liability for principals and their professional counsels who fail to disclose full information about a public issue. Most state laws require securities salespersons to be registered in the local jurisdiction. These laws often go beyond the federal requirements in permitting the state commissioner to disqualify a securities offering on its merits, in addition to determining the required degree of disclosure of specific facts about the issue. Neglect by the issuer to qualify the issue may permit investors to rescind the whole transaction and demand their money back. Beyond these laws are the antifraud statutes that deal with fraudulent practices in connection with securities registration. Although the degree of applicability of federal or state laws and regulations differs with the characteristics of each issue, full and active compliance yields the best results for both the syndicator and investors.

Joint Ventures

The term **joint venture** refers to the joining of two or more parties to undertake a business venture such as developing a real estate property. In contrast to syndications which typically include a number of small investors who contribute capital, a joint venture typically includes only a few individuals or institutional investors. For example an insurance company that wants to invest in real estate may form a joint venture with a developer with real estate expertise. A joint venture can be structured as a partnership and provide allocations of cash flows and taxable income as discussed in this chapter. When one of the joint venture partners contributes a substantial portion of the capital they often receive a **preferential return.** For example, they would be allocated a specified amount of cash flow that must be paid before the other partner is paid.

Conclusion

Excessive amounts of capital flowed into real estate during the late 1970s and early 1980s, especially after the Economic Recovery Tax Act of 1981 gave significant impetus to the syndication industry. Prior to the Tax Reform Act of 1986, real estate syndications were aimed at individual investors who were seeking a tax shelter. Partnership interests were often marketed by sponsors and purchased by investors based on unrealistic assumptions regarding the expected performance of the property. This was at least one of the factors that led to overbuilding during this period.

Real estate syndication has undergone dramatic changes subsequent to the TRA of 1986. Syndications are now aimed at individuals and corporations with very high net worth, institutions, pension funds, and overseas investors. Tax losses are no longer the focus. Rather, sponsors of the syndication must make realistic assumptions about the performance of the underlying real estate and offer a competitive before-tax rate of return. Syndications also have been formed to purchase troubled properties at distressed prices. These are sometimes referred to as **vulture funds.** Although public syndications may never reach the level of activity that they did during the early 1980s, the use of partnerships remains a viable alternative to corporations as an ownership vehicle.

Although the focus of this chapter was on limited partnerships, the same concepts apply to simpler partnerships such as a general partnership that does not have limited partners. Finally, as noted at the beginning of this chapter, most REITs formed in the past 10 years were structured such that the REIT is the general partner in a limited partnership that owns the properties. The limited partners are investors who exchanged their partnership interest in a syndication for a partnership interest in the limited partnership owned by the REIT. This is discussed further in Chapter 19.

Key Terms

accredited investor 382
blind pool 368, 384
capital account 371
gain charge-back 380
general partner 368
joint venture 385
limited partner 368
limited partnership 367
preferential return 385
private offering 367
private syndicate 382
public syndicate 368, 382
safe harbor rules 381
special allocation 369
substantial economic effect 377
syndication 367
vulture fund 386

Questions

1. What is the advantage of the limited partnership ownership form for real estate syndications?
2. How can the general partner–syndicator structure the partnership to offer incentives to limited partners?
3. Why is the Internal Revenue Service concerned with how partnership agreements in real estate are structured?
4. What is the main difference between the way a partnership is taxed versus the way a corporation is taxed?
5. What are special allocations?
6. What causes the after-tax *IRR* ($ATIRR_e$) for the general partner to differ from that of the limited partner?
7. What is the significance of capital accounts? What causes the balance in a capital account to change each year?
8. How does the risk associated with investment in a partnership differ for the general partner versus a limited partner?
9. What are the different ways that the general partner is compensated?
10. Why do you think the Tax Reform Act of 1986 affected the desirability of investing in real estate syndications?
11. What concerns should an investor in a real estate syndication have regarding general partners?
12. Differentiate between public and private syndications. What is an accredited investor? Why is this distinction used?
13. How are general partners usually compensated in a syndication? What major concerns should investors consider when making an investment with a syndication?

Problems

1. Venture Capital Limited has formed a *private* real estate syndication to acquire and operate the Tower Office Building, with Venture acting as the general partner and 35 individual limited partners. The venture to be undertaken and relevant cost and financial data are summarized as follows:

Cost breakdown		
Land	$ 1,000,000	
Improvements	9,000,000	(capitalized)
Points	100,000	(amortized over loan term)
Subtotal	$10,100,000	
Organization fee	100,000	(amortized over 5 years)
Syndication expenses	100,000	(capitalized)
Total funding required	$10,300,000	
Financing		
Loan amount	$ 8,000,000	
Interest rate	11%	
Term	25 years	(monthly payments)
Points	$ 100,000	

Partnership facts and equity requirements

Organization: December, year 1
Number of partners: 1 general partner and 35 limited partners
Equity capital contribution: general partner, 10%; limited partners, 90%
Cash assessments: none
Cash distributions from operations: general partner, 10%; limited partners, 90%
Taxable income and losses from operations: general partner, 10%; limited partners, 90%
Allocation of gain or loss from sale: general partner, 15%; limited partners, 85%
Cash distribution at sale: based on capital account balances

Operating and tax projections	
Potential gross income (year 2)	$1,750,000
Vacancy and collection loss	10% of potential gross income
Operating expenses (year 2)	35% of effective gross income
Depreciation method	Straight line, 31.5 years
Projected growth in income	3% per year
Projected resale price after 5 years	$13,500,000
Limited partners' tax rate	28%
General partner's tax rate	28%
Selling expenses	5%

a. Determine an estimated return ($ATIRR_e$) for a limited partner. (Hint: Consider all 35 limited partners as a single investor.)

b. Determine an estimated return ($ATIRR_e$) for the general partner.

c. Why do the returns differ for the general and limited partners?

2. A and B form a partnership where A, the limited partner, contributes $500,000 and B, the general partner, contributes no cash. The partnership secures a $2 million (10 percent interest only) nonrecourse loan and acquires AB Apartments for $2.5 million. Assume that the results from the first year of operations of AB Apartments are as follows:

Net operating income	$ 250,000
Less debt service (interest only)	−200,000
Before-tax cash flow	$ 50,000

Assume that tax depreciation the first year is $250,000.

The partnership agreement provides that 90 percent of all taxable income, loss, and cash flow from operations is to be allocated to A and 10 percent to B. At resale, taxable gains or losses are to be split 50–50 between A and B, and cash proceeds are distributed first to A in an amount equal to his original investment less any cash distributions previously received, and then split 50–50 between A and B.

a. What are the capital account balances for A and B after one year?

b. Assume that AB Apartments are sold after year 1 for $3 million with no expenses of sale. How much cash is available (before tax) from sale?

c. How much cash would be distributed to A and B upon sale of the property?

d. How much capital gain would be allocated to A and B upon sale of the property?

e. Calculate the capital account balances for A and B after sale.

CHAPTER

13

Disposition And Renovation of Income Properties

In the preceding chapters dealing with income properties, we have given much attention to measuring returns on investment in real estate and the extent to which financial leverage, federal income taxes, and other factors affect that return. Returns were always calculated based on a projected holding period for the property. In this chapter we take a closer look at the factors that would affect an investor's decision to choose a particular holding period. We also consider alternatives to disposition, such as renovating and refinancing the property.

Disposition Decisions

An investor purchases a real estate investment based on the benefits expected to be received over an *anticipated* holding period. That is, the investor computes the various measures of investment performance based on expectations at the time the property is purchased. After the property is purchased, however, many things can change that affect the actual performance of the property. These same factors may affect the investor's decision as to whether the property continues to meet investment objectives. For example, market rents may not be increasing as fast as expected, thus reducing the investor's cash flow. Tax laws also may have changed. As we saw in Chapter 10, tax laws are frequently revised, which can affect potential new investors in a property differently than existing investors. Hence investors should periodically evaluate whether it is time for **disposition,** that is, sale of the property.

Even if the investor's projections for a property are accurate, other factors may influence the investor to sell after a specified number of years. One important factor is the potential benefits associated with leverage that we have discussed in several previous chapters. Assuming that the mortgage on the property has positive amortization, the outstanding mortgage balance decreases each year and the investor's equity position increases. Although this **equity buildup** may appear desirable in the sense that the investor will get more cash from the property when it is sold, it also means that each year the investor has more funds tied up in the property. Any increase in the value of the property over time, whether anticipated or not, also contributes to an increase in the investor's equity buildup.

EXHIBIT 13–1 Past Operating Results, Apex Center

	Year				
	1	*2*	*3*	*4*	*5*
A. Before-tax cash flow:					
Rents	$ 39,000	$ 40,560	$ 42,182	$ 43,870	$ 45,624
Less operating expenses	19,500	20,280	21,091	21,935	22,812
Net operating income (*NOI*)	19,500	20,280	21,091	21,935	22,812
Less debt service (*DS*)	17,642	17,642	17,642	17,642	17,642
Before-tax cash flow	$ 1,858	$ 2,638	$ 3,449	$ 4,293	$ 5,170
B. Taxable income or loss:					
Net operating income (*NOI*)	$ 19,500	$ 20,280	$ 21,091	$ 21,935	$ 22,812
Less interest	16,441	16,302	16,146	15,973	15,780
Depreciation	8,421	8,421	8,421	8,421	8,421
Taxable income (loss)	−5,362	−4,443	−3,476	−2,460	−1,389
Tax	$ −2,681	$ −2,221	$ −1,738	$−1,230	$ −695
C. After-tax cash flow:					
Before-tax cash flow (*BTCF*)	$ 1,858	$ 2,638	$ 3,449	$ 4,293	$ 5,170
Less tax	−2,681	−2,221	−1,738	−1,230	−695
After-tax cash flow (*ATCF*)	$ 4,539	$ 4,859	$ 5,187	$ 5,523	$ 5,865

Equity buildup represents funds that the investor could place in another investment if the current property were sold. This is the *opportunity cost* of *not* selling the property. The proceeds that the investor could have received if the property were sold can be thought of as the amount of equity investment made to *keep* the property for an additional period of time. But unless the property is refinanced, a greater portion of equity capital remains invested in relation to the cash flow being received from continuing to operate the property. Further, while the total mortgage payment (debt service) remains the same, the interest portion of the payment decreases each year, resulting in lower tax deductions. Hence, the investor is also losing the benefits of financial leverage each year.

A Decision Rule for Property Disposition

Next we discuss the factors that investors should consider to determine whether to sell a property or retain ownership. This discussion is based on incremental, or marginal, return criteria that investors should utilize when faced with such decisions.

To illustrate the criteria that should be applied when making a decision to keep a property or to sell it, we assume that an investor acquired a very small retail property five years ago at a cost of $200,000. The Apex Center was 15 years old at the time of purchase and was financed with a 75 percent mortgage made at 11 percent interest for 25 years. The investor uses straight-line depreciation with 80 percent of the original cost ($160,000) allocated to the building and 20 percent allocated to land. We assume that when originally purchased the property could be depreciated on a straight-line basis over depreciable life of 19 years and that the investor has had

EXHIBIT 13–2 Estimates of Cash Flows from Sale Today

Sale price			$250,000
Less sale costs (at 6%)			15,000
Less mortgage balance			142,432
Before-tax cash flow (*BTCF*)			$ 92,568
Taxes in year of sale:			
Sale price		$250,000	
Less selling expenses		15,000	
Original cost basis	$200,000		
Less accumulated depreciation	42,105		
Adjusted basis		157,895	
Capital gains tax at 28%		77,105	
Tax from sale			21,589
After-tax cash flow from sale (*ATCFs*)			$ 70,979

EXHIBIT 13–3 Cash Flow Summary Assuming Sale Today

	End of Year					
	0	*1*	*2*	*3*	*4*	*5*
Before-tax cash flow	$−50,000	$1,858	$2,638	$3,449	$4,293	$97,738
After-tax cash flow	−50,000	4,539	4,859	5,187	5,523	76,843

Before-tax *IRR* = 18.26%
After-tax *IRR* = 14.83%

a marginal tax rate of 50 percent over the past five years.[1] Exhibit 13–1 shows operating results during the *past* five years of operation.

If Apex were sold *today,* it is estimated that the property could be sold for $250,000. Selling costs equal to 6 percent of the sale price would have to be paid. Exhibit 13–2 shows the cash flows from sale of the property (if sold today). We assume that the capital gain from sale of the property is taxed at a maximum rate of 28 percent, the rate that the investor would have to pay if the property were sold today (a function of the tax law in effect at the time of sale). This rate could be different than what the investor expected when the property was originally purchased due to changes in the tax law.

Using the information in Exhibit 13–2, we can calculate the rate of return that the investor would have realized for the past five years if the property were sold. Exhibit 13–3 shows the cash flow summary.

[1]Tax laws change frequently. The purpose of this example is to illustrate how changes in the tax law and other factors affect disposition decisions. The intent is not to replicate a particular tax regime. See Chapter 10 for a summary of the tax law at the time of this revision.

We see that if the property were sold today, the investor would earn an ex post (historical) before-tax return (*BTIRR*) of 18.26 percent and an after-tax return (*ATIRR*) of 14.83 percent. But do these figures really help us decide whether to sell the property? For example, suppose that the investor had expected an after-tax return of 16 percent and now finds that sale of the property produces a return of only 14.83 percent. Does that mean the property should be sold? We really cannot say. All we can say is that the property did not perform as well as originally expected. It may be a good investment in the future.

If the historic return calculated above is also an indication of *future* performance, then it will likely be reflected in the price that the property can be sold for today. The current sale price of the property depends on expected *future* performance for a typical buyer. However, future performance does not necessarily have any relationship to historic returns.

IRR for Holding versus Sale of the Property

If we are to determine whether the investor should keep the property, we must evaluate the *expected future performance* of the property. The essential question facing the investor at this time is whether Apex should be sold and funds from the sale invested in another property. Assuming that the investor believes that a reliable forecast for Apex can be made for the *next* five years, Exhibit 13–4 presents estimates of *ATCF* for years 6 to 10. The investor believes that rents and expenses will *not* continue to grow at the same 4 percent per year rate as for the past five years and projects them to increase at a 3 percent rate for the next five years. Note in the

EXHIBIT 13–4 Estimated Future Operating Results: Apex Center (if not sold)

	Year (since purchase)				
	6	*7*	*8*	*9*	*10*
A. Before-tax cash flow:					
Rent	$47,450	$48,872	$50,340	$51,850	$53,404
Less expenses	23,725	24,436	25,170	25,925	26,702
Net operating income (*NOI*)	23,725	24,436	25,170	25,925	26,702
Less debt service	17,642	17,642	17,642	17,642	17,642
Before-tax cash flow (*BTCF*)	$ 6,083	$ 6,794	$ 7,528	$ 8,283	$ 9,060
B. Taxable income or loss:					
Net operating income (*NOI*)	$23,725	$24,436	$25,170	$25,925	$26,702
Less interest	15,565	15,325	15,056	14,757	14,423
Depreciation	8,421	8,421	8,421	8,421	8,421
Taxable income (loss)	−261	691	1,692	2,746	3,858
Tax	$ −73	$ 193	$ 474	$ 769	$ 1,080
C. After-tax cash flow:					
Before-tax cash flow (*BTCF*)	6,083	6,794	7,528	8,283	9,060
Less tax	−73	193	474	769	1,080
After-tax cash flow (*ATCF*)	$ 6,156	$ 6,601	$ 7,054	$ 7,514	$ 7,980

exhibit that depreciation charges remain at $8,421 per year based on *original cost* and the *original depreciation method.* Although our example will assume that a new buyer will be subject to a different depreciation rule, investors who already own a property prior to a tax law change are not usually required to change their method of depreciation. However, the investor's tax rate is now assumed to be 28 percent under the assumption that the investor's tax rate over the next five years is based on the current tax law. Also note that mortgage payments and interest charges are still based on original financing.

If the forecast period is considered to be 5 years (10 years from the date of purchase), the investor must also compute $ATCF_s$. Using a 3 percent per year rate of price appreciation, the owner estimates that Apex should increase in value to $289,819 by then. Exhibit 13–5 computes an estimate of what $ATCF_s$ will be. Note that the mortgage balance and adjusted basis are based on a total period of 10 years, the time from the date of acquisition.

To fully analyze whether a property should be sold also requires investigation into (1) the alternative investments available in which cash realized from a sale may be reinvested and (2) the tax consequences of selling one property and acquiring another. Clearly, if the investor sells Apex and makes an alternative investment, that investment will have to provide a high enough return to make up for the return given up. The question is how much of an *ATIRR* must the alternative investment provide if Apex is sold?

If Apex is sold to acquire another property, the investor must pay capital gains taxes and selling expenses (if any) before funds are available for reinvestment. Hence, when considering the sale of one property and the acquisition of another, the first task is to ascertain how much cash would be available for reinvestment. The estimated sale price for the Apex Center at this time is $250,000. However, the investor must consider how much cash will be available for reinvestment after payment of the mortgage balance, taxes, and selling expenses. We find that figure by computing *ATCF* as if the property were being sold *immediately,* as we did before. We saw in Exhibit 13–2 that if the property were sold today the investor would net $70,978 after repayment of the mortgage and payment of capital gains taxes.

EXHIBIT 13–5 Calculation of After-Tax Cash Flow from Sale after Five Additional Years

Sales price			$289,819
Mortgage balance			129,348
Selling expenses at 6 percent			17,389
Before-tax cash flow			$143,081
Taxes in year of sale:			
Sales price		$289,819	
Selling expenses		17,389	
Original cost basis	$200,000		
Less: Accumulated depreciation	84,211		
Adjusted basis		115,789	
Total taxable gain		$156,640	
Capital gains tax at 28%			43,859
After-tax cash flow from sale ($ATCF_s$)			$ 99,222

Thus $70,978 would be available for reinvestment should the investor decide to *sell* Apex at this time. Note that capital gains tax rates are expected to remain at 28 percent for the next five years. Sale calculations should always be based on the tax laws that are expected to be in effect when the property is sold. In our case, for example, even though the property was *purchased* at a time when a 60 percent capital gains exclusion was available, because the property is being sold under the new tax law, the capital gains exclusion is no longer available. However, the maximum marginal tax has declined from 50 percent to 28 percent.

The owner must now consider whether or not the $70,978 can be reinvested at a greater rate of return (*ATIRR*) than the return that would be earned *if Apex were not sold.* In other words, we want to know what the *minimum ATIRR* would have to be on an alternative investment (equivalent in risk to Apex) to make the investor indifferent between continuing to own Apex and purchasing the alternative property.

The answer is relatively straightforward. We know that the cash available to reinvest is $70,978 if Apex is sold. Also, we know that if Apex is sold, the investor gives up *ATCF* for the next five years (Exhibit 13–2) and the $ATCF_s$ of $99,222 at the end of the five years. Hence the $70,978 must generate a high enough *ATIRR* to offset the cash flows that would be lost by selling Apex. The cash flow summary and return calculation is as follows:

	Cash Flow Summary Year					
	5	*6*	*7*	*8*	*9*	*10*
After-tax cash flow	$−70,978	$6,156	$6,601	$7,054	$7,514	$107,202
Internal rate of return =	15.60%					

Therefore, the investor would have to earn an *ATIRR* greater than 15.60 percent on the funds obtained from the sale of the Apex Center. These funds must be used to purchase some alternative investment, *equal in risk,* to justify selling Apex. In this case, if an alternative investment is equal in risk to Apex and the investor estimates that the $ATIRR_e$ from that alternative would *exceed* 15.60 percent, then the sale of Apex and the acquisition of the alternative would be justified. If the $ATIRR_e$ on the alternative is expected to be less than 15.6 percent, then Apex should be retained.

Return to a New Investor

To examine how incentives for the current investor to hold the property can differ from the incentives for a new investor to invest in the same property, even if both have the same expectations for future rents and expenses, we will assume a new investor purchases the property at the current value. Recall that Apex is currently worth $250,000 and was financed 5 years ago with a $150,000 loan that is being amortized over 25 years with monthly payments at an 11 percent interest rate. To eliminate the effect of financing (leverage) on our comparison with the present owner, we assume that the new investor takes over the existing loan and does not obtain any additional financing. Thus, the only difference for a new investor will be the effect of tax law. First, the new investor will have a new adjusted basis in the property. Assuming that the building is still 80 percent of the total value in year 5, the new investor will be able to depreciate 80 percent of \$250,000 or \$200,000, compared to depreciation for the present owner based on the original basis of \$160,000. Second, a new investor must depreciate the property based on the tax law in effect at the time of purchase. We assume that the new investor would have to depreciate the property over a 31.5-year depreciable life, a much longer period than the 19-year schedule that would still apply to the present owner. In summary, the new investor gets an increased depreciable basis but must use a longer depreciable life. Note, however, that although this example assumes the buyer would have a longer depreciable life than the existing investor, the reverse could also be true. Again, as noted in Chapter 10, depreciable lives for real estate have been shortened and lengthened frequently over time depending on the whims of Congress.

Exhibit 13–6 shows the projected cash flows and $ATIRR_e$. We see that a new investor would earn an $ATIRR_e$ of 9.1 percent. Although this may be a competitive return for a new investor, given opportunity cost, it is less than the current investor can earn (15.6 percent) by keeping the property, primarily because the existing investor can continue to use a depreciation schedule based on the old tax law. Thus, we see that tax law changes affect the relative benefits of existing versus new investors in the same property. If the tax law becomes *less* favorable as it did in 1986, it tends to favor existing investors. If the tax law becomes *more* favorable, as it did in 1981 when *ACRS* was passed and depreciable lives were shortened considerably, then new investors tend to be favored. Thus, tax law changes tend to affect the turnover, or sale, of real estate. It is important that you understand these concepts since tax laws are always subject to change, and these changes affect the relative risk and return opportunities for new and existing investors.

Marginal Rate of Return

The return for selling versus holding the property calculated earlier (15.6 percent, using cash flows from Exhibits 13–4 and 13–5) is an $ATIRR_e$ based on holding the property for *five additional years.* We chose this period of time based on the assumption that if the property were sold the funds would be placed in a similar investment, which would also be evaluated on the basis of a holding period of five additional years. A slightly different approach is to consider the return that would result from holding the property only *one* additional year. This return would be calculated the same way as above, but would project only one additional year of operating cash flow, and the $ATCF_s$ from sale after one year. We refer to this one-year $ATIRR_e$ as the **marginal rate of return.** For example, in the year that we are considering the sale of the property, we can ask, "What will the marginal return be if the property is held one more year?" Then (assuming the property has not been sold) at the end of that additional year we ask, "What is the marginal return for holding one more year?" This process can be continued until the property is actually sold (or renovated).

To illustrate calculation of the marginal return, we assume that *NOI* will actually increase 3 percent per year (the same rate used for our projections) over the next 10 years. We assume that the resale price will also actually increase 3 percent per year. Exhibit 13–7 shows the projected after-tax cash flows from operating the property over the next 10 years ($ATCF_o$). For each of the 10 years (years 6 through 15), the exhibit also shows the projected after-tax cash flow ($ATCF_s$) that would result *if* the property were sold at the end of that year.

We can use the information in Exhibit 13–7 to calculate the marginal rate of return for each of the next 10 years. Each year the marginal rate of return is based on

EXHIBIT 13–6 Projections for a New Investor

Calculation of After-Tax Cash Flow from Operations

	Year 6	7	8	9	10
Rent	$47,449	$48,873	$50,339	$51,849	$53,405
Less expenses	23,725	24,436	25,170	25,925	26,702
Net operating income	23,725	24,436	25,170	25,925	26,702
Less debt service	17,642	17,642	17,642	17,642	17,642
Before-tax cash flow	$ 6,083	$ 6,794	$ 7,528	$ 8,283	$ 9,060
Net operating income	$23,725	$24,436	$25,170	$25,925	$26,702
Less interest	15,565	15,325	15,065	14,757	14,423
Depreciation	6,349	6,349	6,349	6,349	6,349
Taxable income	1,811	2,763	3,764	4,818	5,930
Tax	$ 507	$ 774	$ 1,054	$ 1,349	$ 1,660
Before-tax cash flow	$ 6,083	$ 6,794	$ 7,528	$ 8,283	$ 9,060
Tax	507	774	1,054	1,349	1,660
After-tax cash flow	$ 5,576	$ 6,021	$ 6,474	$ 6,934	$ 7,400

Calculation of After-Tax Cash Flow from Sale after 5 Years

Sale price			$289,819
Less mortgage balance			129,348
Less selling expenses at 6%			17,389
Before-tax cash flow ($BTCF_s$)			$143,081
Taxes in year of sale			
Sale price		$289,819	
Less selling expenses		17,389	
Original cost basis	$250,000		
Less accumulated depreciation	31,746		
Adjusted basis		218,254	
Total taxable gain		$ 54,176	
Capital gains tax at 28%			15,169
After-tax cash flow from sale ($ATCF_s$)			$127,912

Cash Flow Year Summary

	5	6	7	8	9	10
ATCF	$−107,568	$5,576	$6,021	$6,474	$6,934	$135,312

Internal rate of return ($ATIRR_e$) = 9.10%

the benefit of receiving $ATCF_o$ for one additional year and $ATCF_s$ at the end of the additional year. The cost of receiving this cash flow is $ATCF_s$ for the current year. Since only one year is involved, the return calculation is simply as follows:

$$MRR = \frac{ATCF_s\text{ (year } t+1) + ATCF_o\text{ (year } t+1) - ATCF_s\text{ (year } t)}{ATCF_s\text{ (year } t)}$$

EXHIBIT 13–7 Projections of $ATCF_o$ and $ATCF_s$ for 10 Additional Years

	Calculation of After-Tax Cash Flow from Operations Year (after purchase)									
	6	*7*	*8*	*9*	*10*	*11*	*12*	*13*	*14*	*15*
Rent	$ 47,450	$ 48,872	$ 50,340	$ 51,850	$ 53,404	$ 55,006	$ 56,658	$ 58,356	$ 60,108	$ 61,910
Less expenses	23,725	24,436	25,170	25,925	26,702	27,503	28,329	29,178	30,054	30,955
NOI	23,725	24,436	25,170	25,925	26,702	27,503	28,329	29,178	30,054	30,955
Debt service	17,642	17,642	17,642	17,642	17,642	17,642	17,642	17,642	17,642	17,642
BTCF	$ 6,083	$ 6,794	$ 7,528	$ 8,283	$ 9,060	$ 9,861	$ 10,687	$ 11,536	$ 12,412	$ 13,313
NOI	$ 23,725	$ 24,436	$ 25,170	$ 25,925	$ 26,702	$ 27,503	$ 28,329	$ 29,178	$ 30,054	$ 30,955
Less interest	15,565	15,325	15,056	14,757	14,423	14,051	13,635	13,172	12,654	12,077
Depreciation	8,421	8,421	8,421	8,421	8,421	8,421	8,421	8,421	8,421	8,421
Taxable income	−261	691	1,692	2,746	3,858	5,032	6,272	7,586	8,978	10,457
Tax	$ −73	$ 193	$ 474	$ 769	$ 1,080	$ 1,409	$ 1,756	$ 2,124	$ 2,514	$ 2,928
BTCF	$ 6,083	$ 6,794	$ 7,528	$ 8,283	$ 9,060	$ 9,861	$ 10,687	$ 11,536	$ 12,412	$ 13,313
Tax	−73	193	474	769	1,080	1,409	1,756	2,124	2,514	2,928
ATCF	$ 6,156	$ 6,601	$ 7,054	$ 7,514	$ 7,980	$ 8,453	$ 8,930	$ 9,412	$ 9,898	$ 10,385
	Calculation of After-Tax Cash Flow from Sale									
Sale price	$257,500	$265,225	$273,182	$281,377	$289,819	$298,513	$307,468	$316,693	$326,193	$335,979
Mortgage balance	140,355	138,037	135,452	132,567	129,348	125,757	121,750	117,280	112,292	106,727
Selling expenses	15,450	15,914	16,391	16,883	17,389	17,911	18,448	19,002	19,572	20,159
BTCF	$101,695	$111,274	$121,339	$131,928	$143,081	$154,845	$167,270	$180,411	$194,330	$209,093
Original cost basis	$200,000	$200,000	$200,000	$200,000	$200,000	$200,000	$200,000	$200,000	$200,000	$200,000
Accumulated depreciation	50,526	58,947	67,368	75,789	84,211	092,632	101,053	109,474	117,895	126,316
Adjusted basis	$149,474	$141,053	$132,632	$124,211	$115,789	$107,368	$ 98,947	$ 90,526	$ 82,105	$ 73,684
Sale price	$257,500	$265,225	$273,182	$281,377	$289,819	$298,513	$307,468	$316,693	$326,193	$335,979
Selling expenses	15,450	15,914	16,391	16,883	17,389	17,911	18,448	19,002	19,572	20,159
Adjusted basis	149,474	141,053	132,632	124,211	115,789	107,368	98,947	90,526	82,105	73,684
Total taxable gain	$ 92,576	$108,259	$124,159	$140,284	$156,640	$173,234	$190,073	$207,165	$224,516	$242,136
BTCF	$101,695	$111,274	$121,339	$131,928	$143,081	$154,845	$167,270	$180,411	$194,330	$209,093
Capital gains tax	25,921	30,312	34,765	39,280	43,859	48,505	53,220	58,006	62,865	67,798
ATCF	$ 75,774	$ 80,962	$ 86,575	$ 92,648	$ 99,222	$106,340	$114,050	$122,405	$131,465	$141,295

Exhibit 13–8 shows what the *MRR* (marginal rate of return) is for years 6 through 15, and Exhibit 13–9 plots those *MRR*s. We see that the *MRR* rises until year 10 and then begins to fall. Increasing rents and increases in the value of the property tend to increase the *MRR*. Equity buildup from the price appreciation and loan repayment, however, tends to lower the *MRR*. Also, because the depreciation deduction is fixed but rents are rising, the relative amount of tax benefits from depreciation decreases each year. After year 10 the effect of equity buildup dominates. How long should the property be held? The answer is that *the property should be sold when the marginal rate of return falls below the rate at which funds can be reinvested.* For example, suppose the investor believes that funds can be reinvested in a different property (with the same risk) at a rate of 15.5 percent. This means that the property should be sold in the 14th year, because the *MRR* falls below 15.5 percent after year 14.

EXHIBIT 13–8 Marginal Rate of Return for the Next 10 Years

Year	*Marginal Rate of Return (percent)*
6	15.43
7	15.56
8	15.65
9	15.69
10	15.71
11	15.69
12	15.65
13	15.58
14	15.49
15	15.38

EXHIBIT 13–9 Holding Period Analysis

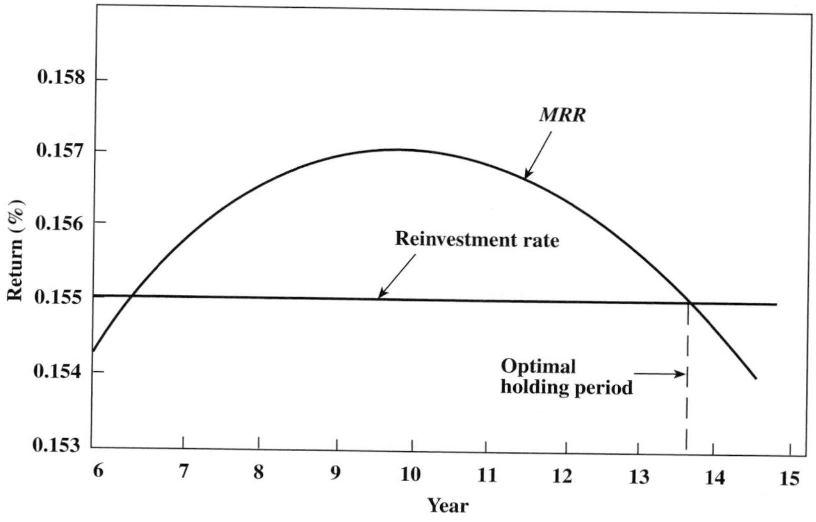

EXHIBIT 13–10 Holding Period Analysis

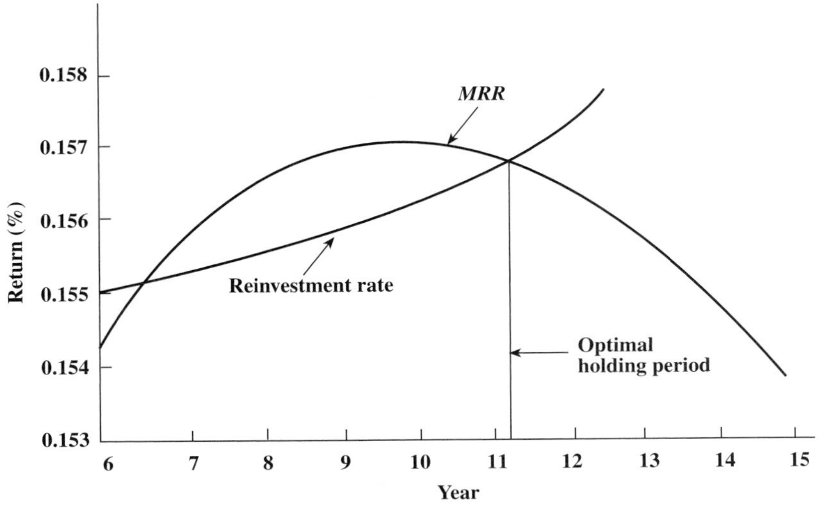

The above analysis assumes that the **reinvestment rate** would be constant throughout the next 10 years. It is not necessary to make this assumption. For example, the reinvestment rate may be expected to rise through time due to an increase in the general level of interest rates and yields on alternative investments. This increase could obviously change the optimal holding period, as illustrated in Exhibit 13–10. Because of the rising reinvestment rate, the **optimal holding period** would be about 11 years.

Refinancing as an Alternative to Disposition

As we have discussed, after an investor has owned a property for a number of years, equity may build up as a result of an increase in the property value and amortization of the loan. Thus, the loan balance relative to the *current* value of the property will be lower than when the property was originally purchased. In this situation the investor has less financial leverage than when the property was originally financed and may consider *refinancing* the property. Refinancing would allow the investor to increase financial leverage. Because refinancing at a higher loan-to-current-value ratio may provide additional funds to invest, it is, to some extent, an alternative to sale of the property.

If the investor's equity has increased due to an increase in the value of the property and amortization of the existing loan, then the investor should be able to obtain a new loan based on some percentage of the *current* property value. The current property value would normally be based on an appraisal of the property. Of course, points, appraisal fees, and other expenses may be incurred to obtain the new loan. However, no taxes have to be paid on funds received by additional borrowing, whereas taxes would have to be paid if the property is sold.

How should an investor decide whether it is profitable to refinance? To answer this question, we must first determine the cost of the additional funds obtained from refinancing. This is the topic of the next section.

Incremental Cost of Refinancing

In Chapter 7 we discussed the importance of considering the incremental borrowing cost when the borrower is faced with a choice between two different amounts of debt. Recall that when the interest rate is higher on the larger loan amount, the incremental cost of the additional funds borrowed is even higher than the rate on the larger loan because the higher rate had to be paid on all the funds borrowed, not just the additional funds.

The same concept applies to the analysis of refinancing. By refinancing we obtain additional funds. If the interest rate on the new loan is higher than that on the existing loan, the incremental cost of the additional funds will be even higher than the rate on the new loan. To illustrate, we return to the Apex Center example introduced at the beginning of this chapter. Now assume that Apex Center could be refinanced with a loan that is 75 percent of the current value of the property. Thus, the loan would be for 75 percent of $250,000 or $187,500. Suppose the rate on this loan would be 12 percent with a 25-year term. We can calculate the incremental cost of refinancing as follows:

	Current Balance	*Monthly Payment*	*Balance after Five Years*
New loan	$187,500	$1,975	$179,350
Existing loan	142,432	1,470	129,348
Difference	$ 45,068	$ 505	$ 50,002

$45,068 = $505 × (*MPVIFA*, ?%, 5 years) + $50,002 × (*MPVIF*, ?%, 5 years)

The difference between the new loan amount of $187,500 and the existing loan balance of $142,432 represents the additional funds obtained by refinancing, $45,068. The incremental cost of these funds depends on the additional payment made after refinancing ($505) and the additional loan balance after five years ($50,002). Solving for the interest rate we obtain 14.93 percent. We refer to this as the *incremental cost of financing.* To justify refinancing, the investor must be able to reinvest the proceeds from refinancing Apex Center in another project earning more than 14.93 percent. Otherwise, favorable financing leverage would not result from use of the funds obtained by refinancing Apex Center.

Refinancing at a Lower Interest Rate

The previous example assumed that the investor had to pay a higher interest rate when refinancing. The methodology would be the same if a lower rate could be obtained on the new loan. In this case the savings associated with the lower interest rate would be reflected in a lower incremental cost of the additional funds obtained from refinancing. To illustrate, suppose the rate on the loan used for refinancing Apex Center was at a 10.5 percent rate for 25 years. The incremental cost of refinancing would be as follows:

	Current Balance	*Monthly Payment*	*Balance after Five Years*
New loan	$187,500	$1,770	$177,321
Existing loan	142,432	1,470	129,348
Difference	$ 45,068	$ 300	$ 47,973

$45,068 = $300 × (*MPVIFA*, ?%, 5 years) + $47,973 × (*MPVIF*, ?%, 5 years)

The incremental cost of refinancing in this case is 9.01 percent. Thus, the investor would achieve favorable financial leverage by investing the funds obtained from refinancing Apex Center in a project earning more than 9.01 percent.

Diversification Benefits. As we have pointed out, additional funds can often be obtained by refinancing a property because the property has increased in value since it was initially purchased and the loan balance has been reduced through amortization. The additional funds that are obtained from refinancing the property represent equity capital that can be reinvested in a second property. So refinancing enables the investor to increase the amount of property owned. Furthermore, the investor may be able to diversify investments further by owning more than two properties, especially if different property types could be acquired in different locations. For example, suppose an investor currently owns a property that has a value of $1 million and has an existing loan balance of $500,000. Equity in the project is therefore $500,000. By refinancing with a 75 percent loan, the investor has $250,000 to reinvest in a second project. Assuming the investor could also obtain a 75 percent loan on the second project, she could purchase a second project that has a property value of $1 million. Note that the investor has the same total amount of equity capital invested ($500,000), but it is now being used to acquire *two* projects with a total value of $2 million. The investor has also incurred additional total debt of $1 million. Again, as stressed above, for refinancing to be a profitable strategy, the effective cost of this debt must be less than the unlevered return on the projects being financed. We discuss diversification much more extensively in Chapter 20.

Renovation as an Alternative to Disposition

Rather than selling one property to acquire another, an additional option would be to consider **renovation** of the property. For example, depending on economic trends in the local market and in the area where the property is located, the investor may consider improving a property by enlarging it or by making major capital improvements to upgrade quality and reduce operating costs. Alternatively, the investor may consider converting the improvement to accommodate a different economic use, such as converting a small multifamily residence to a small professional office building in an urban neighborhood (assuming zoning allows such a conversion).

The issue we address here is how to properly analyze such an option. To illustrate, we reconsider renovating the same property we analyzed in the first part of the chapter. Apex Center, which you recall is presently 20-years old, is owned by an investor who purchased it five years ago at a cost of $200,000. It was financed 5 years ago with a $150,000 loan at 11 percent interest for 25 years. We know that the property could be sold today for $250,000 if it is not renovated (Exhibit 13–2). We also know what the return would be if the property was held for five *additional* years and not renovated (Exhibits 13–4 and 13–5). We will now see how to evaluate the return associated with making an additional investment to renovate the property.

The owner is considering renovation that would cost $200,000. We initially assume that, because of the risk involved in the project, the bank will only agree to refinancing the present loan balance ($142,432) plus 75 percent of the $200,000 renovation cost, for a total loan of $292,432.[2] The new mortgage would carry an interest rate of 11 percent for 15 years.[3]

If the owner, who is in a 28 percent tax bracket, undertakes the modernization project and wants to conduct an after-tax analysis of the investment proposal, the *additional* equity that the owner will have to invest in the property must be determined. This will equal the renovation cost less the additional financing (including both the financing for the renovation plus any existing financing on the remainder of the property). In this case, the lender would only provide additional financing to cover 75 percent of the renovation cost. However, it is also common on renovation projects to get an appraisal of what the entire property will be worth after the renovation and to borrow a percent of that value. This approach may allow the investor to get some equity out of the property.

In this case, the renovation cost is $200,000, and the additional financing amounts to 75 percent of the renovation cost or $150,000. Thus, the *additional* equity investment is $200,000 − $150,000 = $50,000. What does the investor get in return for investing an additional $50,000 in the property? In general, renovation can have many benefits, including increasing rents, lowering vacancy, lowering operating expenses, and increasing the future property value.

Given the estimated cost of modernization and refinancing, the critical elements facing the investor are the estimates of rents, expenses, property values, and expected period of ownership. Obviously the results of a planned renovation depend on such estimates, which require a careful market analysis and planning, as we have previously discussed. Assuming such a plan is carried out, the owner-investor's five-year projection for the modernized Apex Center is shown in Exhibit 13–11.

Looking at Exhibit 13–11, we should note that, based on the modernization plan, *NOI* in year 1 is estimated to increase from $23,725 without renovation (see Exhibit 13–4) to $45,000 with modernization. After the renovation, *NOI* is expected to increase at 4 percent per year instead of 3 percent. Debt service is based on the new $292,432 mortgage loan made at 11 percent for 15 years. The depreciation charge of $14,770 is computed by first calculating depreciation for the renovation expenditure, which increases the depreciable basis by $200,000. We assume the renovation depreciates over 31.5 years based on the tax law in effect at the time. Thus, the renovation results in depreciation of $200,000 ÷ 31.5 = $6,349 per year. The depreciation for the existing building (the original depreciable basis) is not affected by the renovation. This depreciation is still $8,421 per year. Adding the original depreciation to the $6,349 depreciation resulting from the renovation results in the total depreciation of $14,770.

---

[2]The lender will often make a loan based on the present market value rather than on the existing loan balance, which was based on the market value at the time the loan was originally made, plus the cost of improvement. This is considered in the following section.

[3]Another alternative could be a second mortgage for $50,000. The procedure provided here would still be applicable to the problem.

EXHIBIT 13–11 Projections for Apex Center after Renovation

Calculation of After-Tax Cash Flow from Operations

	Year					
	6	*7*	*8*	*9*	*10*	*11*
Net operating income (*NOI*)	$45,000	$46,800	$48,672	$50,619	$52,644	$54,749*
Less debt service	39,885	39,885	39,885	39,885	39,885	
Before-tax cash flow	$ 5,115	$ 6,915	$ 8,787	$10,734	$12,758	
Net operating income	$45,000	$46,800	$48,672	$50,619	$52,644	
Less interest	31,766	30,827	29,779	28,609	27,304	
Depreciation	14,770	14,770	14,770	14,770	14,770	
Taxable income	−1,537	1,203	4,123	7,240	10,569	
Tax	$ −430	$ 337	$ 1,155	$ 2,027	$ 2,959	
Before-tax cash flow	$ 5,115	$ 6,915	$ 8,787	$10,734	$12,758	
Tax	−430	337	1,155	2,027	2,959	
After-tax cash flow	$ 5,545	$ 6,578	$ 7,632	$ 8,707	$ 9,749	

Calculation of After-Tax Cash Flow from Reversion

Sale price			$547,494
Less selling costs at 6%			32,850
Less mortgage balance			241,290
Before-tax cash flow ($BTCF_s$)			$273,354
Taxes in year of sale			
Sale price		$547,494	
Less selling expenses		32,850	
Original cost basis	$400,000		
Accumulated depreciation	115,957		
Adjusted basis		284,043	
Capital gain		$230,601	
Capital gains tax at 28%			64,568
After-tax cash flow from sale ($ATCF_s$)			$208,786

*Projected *NOI* for year 11 is used to estimate the sale price at the end of year 10.

A five-year expected investment period has been selected for analysis. To estimate the resale price, the investor uses a 10 percent terminal capitalization rate applied to an estimate of *NOI* six years from now. This method is based on the assumption that the benefit of the renovation will be reflected in the future *NOI,* and a new investor purchasing the property after five years will purchase on the basis of *NOI* starting in year 11.

Now we are interested in determining how much the after-tax cash flow increases as a result of the renovation. That is, how much greater, if any, is the after-tax cash flow *after* renovation compared with the after-tax cash flow *before* renovation? The after-tax cash flow assuming no renovation is the same as determined in Exhibits 13–4 and 13–5 when we analyzed Apex Center assuming no sale. Exhibit 13–12 summarizes the after-tax cash flows for renovation versus no renovation.

Exhibit 13–12 Incremental Analysis—Renovation versus No Renovation

	Year					
	5	6	7	8	9	10
ATCF assuming renovation		$5,545	$6,578	$7,632	$8,707	$218,585
ATCF assuming no renovation		6,156	6,601	7,054	7,514	107,202
Incremental cash flow	$−50,000	−611	−23	578	1,193	111,382
IRR on incremental cash flows =	17.58%					

From Exhibit 13–12 we see that after-tax cash flows are actually slightly less for the first two years if the property is renovated. After that, however, the after-tax cash flows are increasingly higher. And the after-tax cash flow from sale is higher if the property is renovated. Using the incremental cash flows, we can compute an *IRR* on the additional equity investment of 17.58 percent. This *IRR* means that the investor would earn 17.58 percent on the additional $50,000 spent to renovate the property. Whether this is a good investment depends on what rate the $50,000 could earn in a different investment of comparable risk.

It is important to realize that the 17.58 percent return we have calculated is not a return for the entire investment in Apex. It does not tell us anything about whether Apex is a good investment before renovation. That was the purpose of the analysis in the first part of the chapter. We are now assuming the investor already owns Apex and wants to know whether an additional investment to renovate the property is a viable investment.

Renovation and Refinancing

The previous example assumed that if the property were renovated, the additional financing would equal the existing loan balance of the property (before renovation) plus 75 percent of the renovation costs. When properties are renovated, the investor often uses that opportunity to refinance the entire property. For example, the existing loan balance on the Apex building is only 57 percent of the current value of the property ($142,432 ÷ $250,000). Thus, the investor may be able to borrow more than the renovation requires, especially if the investor plans to obtain a new loan on the entire property rather than a second mortgage to cover the renovation costs.

The total amount of funds that the investor will be able to borrow is usually based on a percentage of estimated value of the property after renovation is completed. This value would be based on an appraisal. If we assume that the *value* added by the renovation is equal to the *cost* of the renovation, then this value would be equal to the existing value of $250,000 plus the renovation cost of $200,000, or $450,000. If the investor can borrow 75 percent of this value, a loan for $337,500 could be obtained. Because the existing loan balance is $142,432, the net additional loan proceeds would be $195,068. Thus the investor would only have to invest $4,932 of his own equity capital to renovate the property. Obviously this is a highly leveraged situation, and the incremental rate of return should be significantly higher. Exhibit 13–13 shows the cash flows for Apex under the assumption that a loan is obtained for $337,500 at an 11 percent interest rate and a 15-year loan term.

EXHIBIT 13–13 After-Tax Cash Flow from Renovation with Refinancing

Calculation of After-Tax Cash Flow from Operations

	Year					
	6	7	8	9	10	11
Net operating income	$ 45,000	$ 46,800	$ 48,672	$50,619	$52,644	$54,749*
Less debt service	46,032	46,032	46,032	46,032	46,032	
Before-tax cash flow	$−1,032	$ 768	$ 2,640	$ 4,587	$ 6,612	
Net operating income	$ 45,000	$ 46,800	$ 48,672	$50,619	$52,644	
Interest	36,662	35,578	34,368	33,018	31,512	
Depreciation	14,770	14,770	14,770	14,770	14,770	
Taxable income	−6,432	3,548	−466	2,831	6,361	
Tax	−1,801	$ −993	$ −131	$ 793	$ 1,781	
Before-tax cash flow	−1,032	$ 768	$ 2,640	$ 4,587	$ 6,612	
Tax	−1,801	−993	−131	793	1,781	
After-tax cash flow	$ 769	$ 1,761	$ 2,770	$ 3,794	$ 4,831	

Calculation of After-Tax Cash Flow from Reversion, Year 10

Sale price			$547,494
Less selling costs (at 6%)			32,850
Less mortgage balance			278,477
Before-tax cash flow ($BTCF_s$)			$236,168
Taxes in year of sale			
Sale price		$547,494	
Selling costs		32,850	
Original cost basis	$400,000		
Accumulated depreciation	115,957		
Adjusted basis		284,043	
Capital gain		$230,601	
Capital gains tax at 28%			64,568
After-tax cash flow from sale ($ATCF_s$)			$171,599

*Projected *NOI* for year 11 is used to estimate the sale price at the end of year 10.

Exhibit 13–14 shows the results of the incremental analysis. As indicated, only $4,932 must be invested to complete the renovation. However, because the new loan is much higher than the existing loan, the additional payments result in negative incremental cash flows for each of the years until the property is sold. Because of the higher value resulting from the renovation, a significant amount of additional cash flow occurs when the property is sold, resulting in an incremental *ATIRR* for the investor of 37.47 percent. Thus, the additional financing (leverage) significantly increases the incremental return from renovating the property. As we know, however, there is also more risk due to the additional debt. The investor must decide whether the additional return is commensurate with the additional risk. Some of the additional debt resulted from, in effect, bringing the original loan balance up to a 75 percent loan-to-value ratio. Thus, although the renovation cost is highly levered, total leverage on the property is at a typical level. The investor must consider all of these factors to make an informed investment decision.

EXHIBIT 13–14 Incremental Analysis Assuming Refinancing

	Year					
	5	6	7	8	9	10
ATCF after renovation		$ 769	$ 1,761	$ 2,770	$ 3,794	$176,430
ATCF before renovation		6,156	6,601	7,054	7,514	107,202
Incremental cash flow	$−4,932	$−5,387	$−4,840	$−4,283	$−3,720	$ 69,227

IRR on incremental cash flow = 37.47%

Rehabilitation Investment Tax Credits

Investment tax credits are available for certain rehabilitation expenditures during the year (or when expenditures occur). Investment tax credits reduce the investor's *tax liability* (e.g., a dollar of tax credit generally reduces a dollar of taxes otherwise payable). Thus, a dollar of tax credit is usually more valuable to an investor than a dollar of additional deductions (e.g., depreciation) because an additional deduction reduces taxable income that would be taxed at the investor's marginal tax rate. For an investor in the 28 percent tax bracket a dollar of deduction reduces taxes by 28 cents. However, a $1 tax credit reduces taxes by $1.

In general, the credits available for rehabilitation are as follows:

Category	*Credit*
Placed in service before 1936	10%
Certified historic structures	20%

The credit is available to the investor in the year the property is placed in service—when the property is open for tenants to occupy. The depreciable basis for the property is reduced by the *full* amount of the credit in the year it is deducted. For example, suppose an investor spends $50,000 to rehabilitate a property that is a certified historic structure and meets the necessary requirements for a rehabilitation tax credit. The amount of tax credit will be $10,000 (20 percent of $50,000). The depreciable basis for the rehabilitation expenditures must be reduced by the amount of credit or by $10,000. The depreciable basis will therefore be $40,000 ($50,000 − $10,000).

Certified historic structures have no age requirement. However, the building must be located in a registered historic district and approval must be obtained from the secretary of the interior. The rehabilitation must also be "substantial," which means that the amount of rehabilitation exceeds the *greater* of (1) the adjusted basis of the property prior to rehabilitation, or (2) $5,000. (Note that this requirement favors investors who have owned the property for a long time and have a low adjusted basis.) Furthermore, at least 75 percent of the existing external walls of the building must have been retained (at least 50 percent still used as external walls) after the rehabilitation. Also, at least 75 percent of the building's internal structural framework must be retained.

If an investor takes a rehabilitation investment tax credit, and disposes of the property during the first five years after the rehabilitated building was placed in service, some of the credit will be recaptured. The amount of recapture as a percent of the original tax credit is as follows:

Year of Disposition	*Recapture Percent*
One full year after placed in service	100%
Second year	80
Third year	60
Fourth year	40
Fifth year	20

Low-Income Housing

A new **low-income housing tax credit** that was introduced with the Tax Reform Act of 1986 allows a tax credit to be claimed by owners of residential rental property providing low-income housing. The credits are claimed annually for a period of 10 years. The *annual* credit has a maximum rate of 9 percent for new construction and rehabilitation, and a maximum rate of 4 percent for the acquisition cost of existing housing. To qualify, the expenditure for construction or rehabilitation must exceed $2,000 per low-income unit. For the property to qualify for the credit, either (1) at least 20 percent of the housing units in the project must be occupied by individuals with incomes 50 percent or less of the area median income, or (2) at least 40 percent of the housing units in the project must be occupied by individuals with incomes of 60 percent or less of area median income. The basis for project depreciation is *not* reduced by the amount of low-income credits claimed.

Conclusion

The primary purpose of this chapter was to answer the following two questions: (1) When should a property be sold? (2) Should a property be renovated? We saw that once a property has been purchased, the return associated with keeping the property might be quite different than the return originally estimated. The concept of a marginal rate of return helps evaluate whether a property should be sold or held for an additional period. The marginal rate of return considers what the investor could get in the future by keeping the property versus what he could get today by selling the property.

To determine whether a property should be renovated, we considered the incremental benefit associated with renovating the property versus not renovating the property. This approach is appropriate when the investor already owns the property and the question is whether an *additional* investment made to renovate the property is justified. If the investor did *not* already own the property, we would take a different approach. In this case the investor would want to know the total rate of return associated with both purchasing and renovating the property. The investor would also want to know the return for purchasing the property but not renovating it, since it still might make sense to purchase the property but not renovate it.

From the above discussion, it should be obvious that the approach we take when analyzing an investment depends on the particular question that we are trying to answer. Poor investment decisions are often made because the analyst did not answer the right question.

Key Terms

disposition 388
equity buildup 388
low-income housing tax credits 406
marginal rate of return 394
optimal holding period 398
rehabilitation tax credits 405
reinvestment rate 398
renovation 400

Questions

1. What factors should an investor consider when trying to decide whether to dispose of a property that he has owned for several years?
2. Why might the actual holding period for a property be different from the holding period that was anticipated when the property was purchased?
3. What is the marginal rate of return? How is it calculated?
4. What causes the marginal rate of return to change over time? How can the marginal rate of return be used to decide when to sell a property?
5. Why might the after-tax internal rate of return on equity ($ATIRR_e$) differ for a new investor versus an existing investor who keeps the property?
6. What factors should be considered when deciding whether to renovate a property?
7. Why is refinancing often done in conjunction with renovation?
8. Why would refinancing be an alternative to sale of the property?
9. How can tax law changes create incentives for investors to sell their properties to other investors?
10. How important are taxes in the decision to sell a property?
11. Are tax considerations important in renovation decisions?
12. What are the benefits and costs of renovation?
13. Do you think renovation is more or less risky than a new investment?
14. What is meant by the *incremental cost of refinancing?*
15. In general, what kinds of tax incentives are available for rehabilitation of real estate income property?

Problems

1. A property could be sold today for $2 million. It has a loan balance of $1 million and if sold the investor would incur a capital gains tax of $250,000. The investor has determined that if sold today, she would earn an *IRR* of 15 percent on equity for the past five years. If not sold, the property is expected to produce after-tax cash flow of $50,000 over the next year. At the end of the year, the property value is expected to increase to $2.1 million, the loan balance would decrease to $900,000 and the amount of capital gains tax due is expected to increase to $255,000.
   a. What is the marginal rate of return for keeping the property one additional year?
   b. What advice would you give the investor?
2. Refer to problem 1. The owner determines that if the property were renovated instead of sold, after-tax cash flow over the next year would increase to $60,000 and the property could be sold after one year for $2.4 million. Renovation would cost $250,000. The investor would not borrow any additional funds to renovate the property.
   a. What is the rate of return that the investor would earn on the additional funds invested in renovating the property?
   b. Would you recommend that the property be renovated?
3. Lonnie Carson purchased Royal Oaks Apartments two years ago. An opportunity has arisen for Carson to purchase a larger apartment project called Royal Palms, but Carson believes that he would have to sell Royal Oaks to have sufficient equity capital to purchase Royal Palms. Carson paid $2 million for Royal Oaks two years ago, with the land representing approximately $200,000 of that value. A recent appraisal indicated that the property is worth about $2.2 million today. When purchased two years ago, Carson financed the property with a 70 percent mortgage at 10 percent interest for 25 years (monthly payments). The property is being depreciated over 27.5 years (1/27.5 per year for simplicity). Effective gross income during the next year is expected to be $350,000, and operating expenses are projected to be

40 percent of effective gross income. Carson expects the effective gross income to increase 3 percent per year. The property value is expected to increase at the same 3 percent annual rate. Carson is currently in the 36 percent tax bracket and expects to remain in that bracket in the future. Because Carson has other real estate investments that are now generating taxable income, he does not expect any tax losses from Royal Oaks to be subject to the passive activity loss limitations. If he sells Royal Oaks, selling expenses would be 6 percent of the sale price.

a. How much after-tax cash flow ($ATCF_s$) would Carson receive if Royal Oaks was sold today (exactly two years after he purchased it)?

b. What is the projected after-tax cash flow ($ATCF_o$) for the *next* five years if Carson does *not* sell Royal Oaks?

c. How much after-tax cash flow ($ATCF_s$) would Carson receive if he sold Royal Oaks five years from now?

d. Using the results from (*a*) through (*c*), find the after-tax rate of return ($ATIRR_e$) that Carson can expect to earn if he holds Royal Oaks for five additional years versus selling it today.

e. What is the marginal rate of return (*MRR*) if Carson holds the property for *one additional year* (if he sells *next* year versus this year)?

f. Why do you think the *MRR* in (*e*) is higher than the return calculated in (*d*)?

g. Can you think of any other ways that Carson could use to purchase Royal Palms and still retain ownership of Royal Oaks?

h. What is your recommendation to Carson?

i. *Optional for computer users.* What is the *MRR* for each of the next 10 years? How can this calculation be used to determine when Royal Oaks should be sold?

4. Richard Rambo presently owns the Marine Tower office building, which is 20 years old, and is considering renovating it. He purchased the property two years ago for $800,000 and financed it with a 20-year, 75 percent loan at 10 percent interest (monthly payments). Of the $800,000, the appraiser indicated that the land was worth $200,000 and the building $600,000. Rambo has been using straight-line depreciation over 39 years (1/39 per year for simplicity). At the present time Marine Tower is producing $90,000 in *NOI,* and the *NOI* and property value are expected to increase 2 percent per year. The current market value of the property is $820,000. Rambo estimates that if the Marine Tower office building is renovated at a cost of $200,000, *NOI* would be about 20 percent higher next year ($108,000 versus $90,000) due to higher rents and lower expenses. He also expects that with the renovation the *NOI* would increase 3 percent per year instead of 2 percent. Furthermore, Rambo believes that after five years, a new investor would purchase the Marine Tower office building at a price based on capitalizing the projected *NOI* six years from now at a 10 percent capitalization rate. Selling costs would be 6 percent of the sale price. Rambo is in the 28 percent tax bracket and expects to continue to be in that bracket. He also would not be subject to any passive activity loss limitations. If Rambo does the renovation, he believes he could obtain a new loan at an 11 percent interest rate and a 20-year loan term (monthly payments).

a. Assume that if Rambo does the renovation, he will be able to obtain a new loan that is equal to the balance of the existing loan plus 75 percent of the renovation costs. What is the *incremental* return ($ATIRR_e$) for doing the renovation versus not doing the renovation? Assume a five-year holding period.

b. Repeat (*a*) but assume that Rambo is able to obtain a new loan that is equal to 75 percent of the *sum* of the existing value of the property ($820,000) plus the renovation costs ($200,000). (This assumes that after renovation the value of the property will at least increase by the cost of the renovation.)

c. Explain the difference between the returns calculated in (*b*) and (*c*). Is there a difference in the risk associated with each financing alternative?

d. What advice would you give Rambo?

CHAPTER

14

FINANCING CORPORATE REAL ESTATE

The focus of the previous chapters dealing with income properties has been that of an owner/investor who leases space to tenants. These tenants would generally be firms that use space as part of business operations. For example, a typical user could be a corporation that leases some, or all, of the space in an office building for use by its employees. Thus, the corporation uses the office space but does not own the building as an operating asset. This chapter analyzes real estate from the point of view of firms that are not real estate investors, but use real estate as part of business operations. Because so many of these "user firms" are corporations, their real estate activities are commonly referred to as **corporate real estate**.[1] However, this chapter is intended for any *user* of real estate assets and is not limited to corporations. Even though the primary business of these corporations is not real estate investment, they have to make many decisions regarding the use of real estate because real estate is typically an integral part of the firm's operations. For example, real estate is used for office space, warehouse space, manufacturing, and so on. In addition to using real estate, firms may choose to own real estate for a variety of other reasons, including these:[2]

- Owning rather than leasing space used in the operation of the business.
- Investing in real estate as one means of diversification from the core business.
- Retaining, rather than selling, real estate that may have been used previously in business operations.
- Acquiring real estate for future business expansion or relocation.

For these reasons, corporations are by far the largest owners of commercial real estate in the United States. Corporate users control as much as 75 percent of all commercial real estate according to some estimates. On a book-value basis, moreover, roughly one-third of the total assets of Fortune 500 companies is estimated to be real estate. With such a large concentration of corporate wealth in commercial

---

[1]Portions of this chapter are based on an article by William B. Brueggeman, Jeffrey D. Fisher, and David M. Porter, "Rethinking Corporate Real Estate," *Journal of Applied Corporate Finance*, 1991 (published by Continental Bank, Chicago).

[2]By "owning" real estate we are referring to fee simple ownership in the property. A corporation may also have a leasehold interest in real estate that has value because the property is leased at a below market rate.

property, it is worth taking a closer look at the way that businesses or users of real estate should make real estate investment and financing decisions.

Benefits associated with ownership of real estate for a corporate user include many of the same benefits realized by a pure investor. For example, a corporate owner that would otherwise lease space saves lease payments, which is analogous to an investor earning lease income. By owning real estate, the corporation also receives the tax benefits from depreciation allowances. Furthermore, by owning real estate the corporation retains the right to sell the property in the future. At that time, the property can be leased back from the purchaser if the firm still needs to use the space. Firms whose core business is not real estate investment, however, must consider additional factors. In particular, the user must consider the opportunity cost of capital invested in real estate, the impact that ownership of the real estate will have on corporate financial statements, and the corporation's ability to use space efficiently. These are some of the issues that this chapter will consider. We begin by considering how a corporate user should analyze whether or not to lease or own space necessary in its business operations.

Lease-versus-Own Analysis

Corporations can either lease or own space needed in business operations. If a corporation owns space, it is essentially "investing" in real estate. When purchasing these assets, a corporation may decide to finance the purchase by taking out a mortgage secured by the property in addition to equity capital, or it may decide to use only equity capital. Alternatively, depending on the extent of debt already used to finance business operations, capital could consist of a combination of unsecured corporate debt and equity obtained from sale of stock or retained earnings.

If the firm leases space, on the other hand, it can use the space without investing corporate equity, freeing the equity capital for other investment opportunities available to the firm. Whether these investment opportunities are better than investing in the real estate depends on the after-tax rate of return and risk of these opportunities relative to that of the real estate.

Leasing versus Owning—An Example

To illustrate the decision to own rather than lease real estate that the corporation plans to use in its operations, consider the following example. Assume the XYZ Corporation is considering opening an office in a new market area that would allow it to increase its annual sales by $1.5 million. Cost of goods sold is estimated to be 50 percent of sales, and corporate overhead would increase by $200,000 not including the cost of either acquiring or leasing office space. XYZ will also have to invest $1.3 million in office furniture, office equipment, and other up-front costs associated with opening the new office before considering the costs of owning or leasing the office space.[3]

XYZ could purchase a small office building for its sole use at a total price of $1.8 million, of which $225,000 (12.5 percent) of the purchase price would represent land value, and $1,575,000 (87.5 percent) would represent building value. The cost of the building would be depreciated over 31.5 years.[4] XYZ is in a 30 percent tax bracket. As an alternative to owning, an investor has approached XYZ and indicated

[3]Other costs might include sales training, relocating employees, and the like.

[4]For illustration only. The depreciable life would depend on the tax law in effect at the time of purchase.

EXHIBIT 14–1 After-Tax Cash Flow: Leasing Office Building

Cash Flow from Operations

	Lease
Sales	$1,500,000
Cost of goods sold	750,000
Gross income	750,000
Less operating expenses:	
Business	200,000
Real estate*	90,000
Less: Lease payments	180,000
Taxable income	$ 280,000
Tax	84,000
Income after tax	$ 196,000
After-tax cash flow	$ 196,000

Summary of After-Tax Cash Flows

	Outlay	*Cash Flow*
Year	0	1–15
	$−1,300,000	$196,000
IRR	12.50%	

*Operating expenses on the real estate such as property taxes and insurance that the tenant is responsible for paying under the net lease.

a willingness to purchase the same building and lease it to XYZ for $180,000 per year for a term of 15 years. XYZ would pay all real estate operating expenses (absolute net lease), which are estimated to be 50 percent of the lease payments. XYZ has estimated that the property value should increase over the 15-year lease term, and the building could be sold for $3 million at the end of the 15 years.[5] XYZ has also determined that if it purchases the property, it could arrange financing with an interest-only mortgage on the property for $1,369,000 (76 percent of the purchase price) at an interest rate of 10 percent with a balloon payment due after 10 years.[6]

Cash Flow from Leasing

Exhibit 14–1 shows the calculation of after-tax cash flow associated with opening the office building and obtaining use of the space by leasing. Recall that the initial cash outlay of $1.3 million is the up-front cost of setting up the office. After-tax cash flow of $196,000 is received each year for 15 years. We also assume that XYZ will close the office at the end of the lease, and that the furniture and equipment will have no residual value. An after-tax rate of return of 12.5 percent is assumed to be the opportunity cost, or after-tax reinvestment rate savings of $1.3 million, if XYZ chooses to lease rather than own the office building. This is the rate of return after

[5]Even if the corporation still needs to use the space, it could sell the property and lease it back at the end of the lease term. Sale-leaseback is considered later in this chapter. The corporation could also decide to sell the building and relocate its sales office to another property that is leased or owned.

[6]For purposes of illustration, we assume the loan amount to be equal to the present value of the lease payments of $180,000 per year, discounted at the mortgage loan interest rate of 10 percent. This makes the financing comparable with leasing as we will discuss later in the chapter.

EXHIBIT 14–2 After-Tax Cash Flow: Owning Office Building

Operating Years

Sales	$1,500,000
Cost of goods sold	750,000
Gross income	750,000
Less operating expenses:	
Business	200,000
Building or property	90,000
Less: Interest	136,900
Depreciation	50,000
Taxable Income	273,100
Less: Tax	81,930
Income after tax	191,170
Plus: Depreciation	50,000
Cash flow	$ 241,170

Sale at End of Lease

Reversion		$ 3,000,000
Mortgage balance		−1,369,000
Reversion	$ 3,000,000	
Basis	−1,050,000	
Gain	$ 1,950,000	
Tax		−585,000
Cash flow		$ 1,046,000

Calculation of *IRR* Summary

	Outlay	*Cash flow*	*Reversion*
Year	0	1–15	15
Cash flow	$−1,731,000	$241,170	$1,046,000
IRR	12.95%		

tax that XYZ can compare with other investment alternatives of equal risk when considering whether it should invest the $1.3 million necessary to open the new office building.

Assuming that XYZ believes that it should open a new regional office, the next question is whether the firm should lease or own the property that will house the new operation. One way to answer this question is to calculate the after-tax cash flows and after-tax rate of return assuming that the space is owned rather than leased.

Cash Flow from Owning

Exhibit 14–2 shows the after-tax cash flow from opening the office building under the assumption that it is owned. The initial cash outlay of $1,731,000 includes the equity invested in the office building of $431,000 as well as the other up-front costs of $1.3 million. During the first 15 years the after-tax cash flow is $241,170. After-tax cash flow from sale of the real estate is $1,046,000. The after-tax *IRR* under this scenario is 12.95 percent. This return is slightly higher than the after-tax rate of return of 12.50 percent if XYZ chooses to lease the space as shown in Exhibit 14–1.

This return suggests that owning is better than leasing. Note, however, that the 12.95 percent rate of return is the after-tax rate of return on *both* the funds invested in opening the office building ($1.3 million) and the additional equity invested in owning the building ($431,000). That is, this rate of return is for two combined investment decisions: (1) to open the office building, and (2) to own the office building. Although the rate of return associated with owning the office building is greater than leasing it, the risk may also be greater, depending on the risk of holding the real estate as an investment.[7] To evaluate risk further, we have to isolate the after-tax rate of return associated with making the investment in the real estate only.

Cash Flow from Owning versus Leasing

Thus far we have been dealing with two interrelated decisions. The first decision is whether the corporation should expand its operations by investing funds to *use* the additional office space. The second decision is how to pay for the use of the space. In the preceding analysis, we calculated the rate of return under two different assumptions about how the firm would pay for the use of the space. Assuming that the rate of return under one or both of these alternatives meets the firm's investment criteria, the firm should decide to use the space. It is not clear, however, that the risk and rate of return should be the same for both alternative ways of obtaining use of the space. In this example, both scenarios involve use of the same building with the same sales potential and non–real estate costs.[8]

As we have seen, however, the decision to own the space involves an additional equity investment in the property that is not required when leasing. To look more closely at the equity investment in the property that is included with the decision to own versus lease, we must consider the *difference* in the cash flow to the corporation if it leases the space rather than owns the space. Exhibit 14–3 replicates the after-tax cash flow under both the lease and own scenarios and computes the difference in these cash flows.

The first two columns of Exhibit 14–3 repeat calculations of the after-tax cash flows for owning and leasing respectively. As we have discussed, these cash flows to the firm would result from using the office building based on each alternative. The $431,000 initial outlay now represents only the equity for investment in the property. During the first 15 years, after-tax cash flow would be $241,000 per year if the property were owned, as compared to $196,000 per year if the property were leased—a difference of $45,170 per year. The firm would realize the $1,046,000 cash flow from sale if it chooses to own the project. When making the lease versus own decision, remember that the volume of sales and the operating costs associated with generating those sales will be the same whether the space is leased or owned. Therefore, the decision to lease or own should depend only on the *difference* in cash flows under the two alternatives. In other words, owning or leasing a building should in no way affect XYZ's business operations. The difference in cash flows is shown in column 3 of Exhibit 14–3. By owning rather than leasing, XYZ should

---

[7]The decision whether or not to use the space for an office building should normally be made by considering the after-tax cash flow from leasing the space. This ensures that the decision to use the space is based on the market-determined cost of using the space. It also separates the benefits of owning the space from the benefits of using the space for a new sales office.

[8]In practice, space that is available for leasing may not be available for purchase, so that the space that would be leased would not be the same as the space that would be owned. This could result in slightly different assumptions about the sales potential of each alternative. For simplicity we have ignored this potential difference.

EXHIBIT 14–3 Lease-versus-Own Analysis

Cash Flow from Operations

	Own	*Lease*	*Difference (Own − Lease)*
Sales	$1,500,000	$1,500,000	0
Cost of goods sold	750,000	750,000	0
Gross income	750,000	750,000	0
Operating expenses:			
Business	200,000	200,000	0
Real estate	90,000	90,000	0
Lease payments	0	180,000	−180,000
Interest	136,900	0	136,900
Depreciation	50,000	0	50,000
Taxable income	273,100	280,000	6,900
Tax	81,930	84,000	2,070
Income after tax	191,170	196,000	4,830
Plus: Depreciation	50,000	0	50,000
After-tax cash flow	$ 241,170	$ 196,000	$ 45,170

Cash Flow from Sale

Reversion/owning		$ 3,000,000
Mortgage balance		−1,369,000
Reversion	$ 3,000,000	
Basis	−1,050,000	
Gain	$ 1,950,000	
Tax		−585,000
After-tax cash flow		$ 1,046,000

Summary After-Tax Cash Flows

	Outlay	*Savings*	*Reversion*
Year	0	1–15	15
Own–Lease	$−431,000	$45,170	$1,046,000
IRR	13.79%		

save $45,170 per year after taxes.[9] Furthermore, if XYZ owns the space, it will receive $1,046,000 at the end of the 15th year from sale of the office building.

Return from Owning versus Leasing

Recall that the equity investment required to own the property was $431,000. Based on this investment and the incremental cash flows of $45,170 per year and $1,046,000 in year 15 (owning versus leasing), the after-tax *IRR* is 13.79 percent. Whether this is sufficient to justify the additional investment in ownership versus leasing the space depends on the opportunity cost and risk associated with the investment of equity capital in the property. If XYZ believes that an after-tax rate of return of 13.79 percent is not sufficient to warrant the risk associated with owning

[9]Alternatively, by leasing rather than owning, the corporation must pay an additional $45,170 per year.

the space, it should decide to lease rather than own the space. On the other hand, if XYZ thinks that 13.79 percent is an adequate return given the risk of owning and eventually selling the property after 15 years, then it should own.

Importance of the Residual Value of Real Estate

Leasing and owning are often viewed as two financing alternatives because lease payments substitute for debt payments as discussed above. As we saw in the above example, however, the debt liability that is comparable to a lease liability does not cover the portion of the purchase price that represents an investment in the right to the residual value. Hence leasing property differs from equipment leasing, where the residual value can usually be assumed to be zero.

Generally, leasing or owning real estate differs from leasing or owning equipment because real estate may have a substantial residual value. The owner of the real estate has the right to the residual value and incurs the risk that the residual value will be different from the cost of the property at the time it was purchased. Thus, in addition to having use of the real estate during the term of the lease, *a corporation that chooses to own real estate has also made an investment in its residual value*. This means that deciding to own versus lease real estate is not simply a choice between two financing alternatives. Although they are both ways of financing the use of the real estate over the lease term, ownership includes the right to the residual value of the property at the end of the lease term.[10] Leasing does not give the company any interest in the residual value of the property.[11] This residual value can be quite substantial if the property has retained its value or appreciated in value over the lease term, whereas with corporate equipment the expected residual value is so small in most cases that it can usually be ignored.

The residual value of the property is affected by changes in the supply and demand for real estate over the term of the lease and is usually more uncertain than the contract lease payments. Thus, the required rate of return from owning (discount rate) used to evaluate the incremental cash flows from owning versus leasing should probably be higher than the after-tax cost of corporate debt, although the rate of return may not have to be as high as the cost of capital used for the typical corporate investment.[12]

Estimating the Residual Value. **Residual value**—that is, the reversion value of land and improvements at the end of the lease term—is an important part of the decision to lease or own that causes confusion for corporate managers. Some analysts assume that the residual value of the real estate will be equal to the book value of the

---

[10]Assume that the property in our lease-versus-own example is financed with a nonrecourse mortgage loan. The difference between owning and leasing (aside from the tax benefits) would be an option to keep the property if its value at the end of the lease exceeds the loan balance. If the value of the property is less than the loan balance, the corporation could default on the mortgage, and the property would revert to the lender just as it would to the lessor at the end of the lease. In this case, owning differs from leasing by including the investment made to purchase a call option on the residual value property. The exercise price of the option is the mortgage balance at the end of the lease term. Because we assumed the loan amount to be equal to the present value of the lease payments, the price paid for the call option is essentially the amount of equity that must be invested.

[11]Leases can also be structured to include a claim on the residual value of the property. For example, an "equity lease" gives the lessee an ownership interest in the building. The lessee might also have an option to buy the property at the end of the lease.

[12]The cost of capital typically used by corporations is a weighted average of the cost of corporate debt and equity capital. Because equity is more expensive than debt, the weighted average cost of capital is greater than the cost of debt. (See chapter appendix.)

property or the original acquisition cost less accounting depreciation at the expiration of the lease term. Others go to the extreme of assuming that there will be no residual value. Why? Because there will always be a need for a facility and the residual sale price received must be reinvested in a lease or on a new facility at that time.

Because real estate does not typically decline in value as fast as accounting depreciation and rarely has zero value at the end of a typical lease term, assuming no residual value biases the lease-versus-own decision toward leasing. However, it is just as incorrect to assume unrealistically high rates of appreciation that bias the analysis toward ownership. The correct approach is to make a realistic estimate of the residual value of the real estate and the uncertainty of the value estimate. This estimate should consider the *market value* of the real estate (as discussed in Chapter 8), not the investment value to the corporation.

By deciding to own, a corporation chooses, in effect, to bear a residual real estate risk that may be completely unrelated to its operating success. Real estate is different from other corporate assets in that, at the end of the lease term, the range of possible residual values runs from well below to well above the initial cost of the property. Over the life of a medium- to long-term lease, local, regional, and even international economic factors can cause the market values of corporate real estate to change significantly. By deciding to own rather than lease space, the company must bear the risk of any unexpected changes in the residual value of the real estate.

Some analysts argue that the residual value of the real estate is irrelevant because the corporation needs to use space on an ongoing basis. That is, there will always be a need for a facility, and proceeds from the residual sale must be reinvested in a new facility at that time. But this approach ignores the fact that by owning, the corporation retains ownership of an asset with value at the end of the typical lease term. At that time (when the lease ends) management may or may not decide to continue to *use* the same space. The corporation has the option to relocate if a change in the highest and best use of the site makes the space inefficient for continued use.[13] If the corporation decides to continue to use the space, it can then decide whether to continue to own the space or sell the space and lease it back.[14]

Regardless of what the firm decides to do in the future, the initial decision to own versus lease means that the firm has an asset with an expected market value when the initial lease term would have ended. If property values have risen, the corporation has an asset that is more valuable than when it was purchased. If property values have fallen, the asset is less valuable than when purchased. In either case, the corporation has an asset on the balance sheet that it would not have had if it had decided to lease. If the market capitalization rate for the property has remained fairly constant, any change in the market value of the property and market rental rates should be highly correlated. Thus, by owning, the corporation has in effect invested in an asset that has a rate of return that is correlated with changes in the corporation's cost of leasing the space. As suggested above, this may or may not be correlated with the return on the corporation's core business. If market values and rental rates rise, the opportunity cost of using the space will be greater in the future whether the space is leased or owned. The difference is that by having decided to own, the company has an asset that has appreciated in value and a gain on the value

[13]Options available to the corporation when the highest and best use of the space has changed are considered in a later section.

[14]Sale-leaseback is examined in more detail later in the chapter.

of the real estate. As noted, it can realize this historical gain by a sale and leaseback or by relocating.[15]

Alternatively, if the company had leased, it would still face higher lease costs but may or may not have invested funds in an asset that has increased in value. Of course, if rental rates fall, the company can now lease the space at a lower rate. But by owning instead of leasing, the company has also incurred a loss on the real estate.

The point is that by owning rather than leasing, the corporation has made an investment with a rate of return that depends on what happens to local real estate values. Own-versus-lease decisions must consider how the risk and expected return from this investment fit in the overall corporate investment and financing strategy.

The Investor's Perspective

In the above analysis, we considered the incremental cash flow associated with owning versus leasing. The return from owning (and cost of leasing) from the corporation's point of view was calculated to be 13.79 percent. If the corporation decides to lease the space, our analysis assumes that there is an investor willing to own the space and lease it to the corporation. What rate of return would the investor expect? This depends, of course, on how the investor finances the property, and the investor's tax situation. For sake of comparison, assume that the investor is in the same tax bracket as the corporation and that the property would be financed the same way. Exhibit 14–4 shows the projected after-tax cash flows from operating the property during the term of the lease and resale at the end of the lease.

The rate of return for the investor is exactly the same as it was for the corporation. This should be no surprise because we have emphasized that the difference between owning and leasing is a real estate equity investment.

A Note on Project Financing

In the lease-versus-own analysis considered earlier, we assumed the corporation took out a mortgage on the property. Rather than a mortgage, the corporation could have used unsecured corporate debt. Using a mortgage loan utilizing real estate as security substitutes for the use of unsecured corporate debt under the assumption that the corporation wants to maintain a constant proportion of total debt (e.g., mortgages on real estate, corporate bonds). However, corporations may find that the rate on a mortgage secured by the real estate is less than the rate it has to pay on a new issue of unsecured corporate debt. This is because the rate on a mortgage tends to reflect the risk of the real estate, whereas the risk for unsecured corporate debt reflects the risk of the corporation.

A corporation with a high credit rating may pay less for unsecured debt than for a mortgage because the rate on mortgage loans, particularly those made without recourse to the borrower, reflects the risk of default—the inability of the cash flows produced by the property to service the debt rather than the default risk associated with the borrower. That is, in the case of nonrecourse financing, the rate on the mortgage includes a risk premium to the lender because the borrower has the "option to default" in the event that the property value is less than the loan or cash flow cannot service the debt. In such cases, the financial community may consider debt based on the assets of the corporation less risky than the real estate, and, therefore,

[15]If lease payments have risen as well as property values, the company may still be better off by continuing to own rather than selling and leasing back the space. This does not negate the fact that the return from owning the real estate may or may not have been greater than the return that the corporation could have earned leasing instead of owning and investing the funds elsewhere.

EXHIBIT 14–4 Investment Analysis

Lease income		$180,000
Operating expenses (net lease)		0
Net operating income		180,000
Less: Depreciation		50,000
Less: Interest		136,900
Taxable income		−6,900
Tax		−2,070
Net operating income		180,000
Less: Debt service		136,900
Less: Taxes		−2,070
After-tax cash flow		45,170

Sale at End of Lease

Reversion		$3,000,000
Mortgage balance		−1,369,000
Reversion	$3,000,000	
Basis	−1,050,000	
Gain	$1,950,000	
Tax		−585,000
Cash flow		$1,046,000

Summary

	Outlay	*ATCF*	*Reversion*
Year	0	1–15	15
Cash flow	$−431,000	$45,170	$1,046,000
IRR	13.79%		

the unsecured corporate borrowing rate may be lower than that of a mortgage loan based solely on the real estate as security.

On the other hand, a corporation that has assets that are riskier than the real estate may have to pay more for unsecured corporate debt than the mortgage rate used to finance the acquisition of real estate when real estate is the only collateral for the debt.

If the corporation can obtain unsecured corporate debt at a lower rate than a mortgage on the property, we can assume the lower rate in the analysis in Exhibits 14–2 and 14–3. Alternatively, analysts sometimes calculate the incremental cash flows from owning versus leasing (as in Exhibit 14–3) *without explicitly considering the debt financing*. This type of analysis is analogous to calculating the return from owning the real estate (as in Exhibit 14–4) by using the cash flows before considering financing, that is, as if the property were unlevered. In this case the rate of return from owning (versus leasing) must be compared to the firm's weighted average cost of capital, which is an average of the firm's cost of debt and equity capital. This approach allows the cost of debt financing to be reflected in the required rate of return from owning the real estate rather than considering financing in the calculation of the cash flows.[16] As shown in the appendix to this chapter, this approach

[16]This approach is typically taken in corporate finance texts. The appendix to this chapter discusses the use of the weighted average cost of capital approach.

does not change the conclusion about the rate of return earned by investing in real estate. Analysts often argue that for lease-versus-own decisions, the rate of return on the incremental cash flows from owning versus leasing (when financing is not explicitly considered) should be compared with the corporation's cost-of-debt capital rather than a weighted average cost of debt and equity. This argument is based on the assumption that the lease liability (based on the present value of the lease payments) is equivalent to the amount of debt financing and that no additional equity would be invested in owning. This assumption is realistic for equipment leasing because equipment has no substantial residual value. However, as our example illustrated, even if we can borrow an amount equal to the present value of the lease payments, real estate requires an additional equity investment due to the expected present value of the residual.

Factors Affecting Own-versus-Lease Decisions

The above example provides insight into key financial factors that affect the decision to own or lease space. Additional considerations, however, must be considered. Some of these are difficult to incorporate explicitly in a lease-versus-own analysis, but they may affect the final decision.

Space Requirements. Leasing would be preferable when the company's space requirements are far less than the optimal development on a given site. In cases where the amount of space a corporate user desires is less than the optimal building scale that should be developed on a site, we expect (and typically find) corporate users leasing and developers (and their investment partners) assuming real estate risks. Even in cases where a corporate lessee will be the dominant tenant, it may be preferable for the corporate user to lease. For example, companies like IBM may be able to negotiate lease concessions (or a share of the developer's profits) that reflect the developer's use of the corporate credit when obtaining development financing.

Amount of Time Space Is Needed. In cases where the expected life of an asset far exceeds the company's projected period of use, companies will also generally choose to lease rather than bear the costs associated with selling an illiquid asset. This tendency can be explained, in part, by the comparative advantage of lessors in creating or locating alternative uses for such assets.

Risk Bearing. We have discussed the importance of the residual value of the real estate, which is affected by changes in local property values. Lease-versus-own analysis should carefully consider any relationship between the factors that influence the company's operating value and those driving local property markets. The aim of such consideration should be to determine whether other real estate investors have a comparative advantage in bearing the risk associated with local real estate markets. Pension funds, for example, generally hold unlevered portfolios of real estate diversified both by property type (offices, warehouses, etc.) and by geographic region. These funds, as well as REITs, are likely to be able to diversify risks in property markets much more efficiently than all but the largest corporations. When a given real estate investment represents a large proportion of the company's total capital, the comparative advantage of other investors in bearing such risks may create a strong preference for leasing. For these reasons of relative risk-bearing capacity, larger companies with broadly dispersed operations are more likely to own than are smaller companies with geographically concentrated operations.

Management Expertise. Owning and managing real estate is not typically a primary part of a corporation's business activity. Thus the corporation can be at a disadvantage when it comes to owning real estate. The corporation may not have the expertise to manage real estate assets. When property is owned rather than leased, managers may not be as aware of the true cost of using the space, leading to inefficient use of real estate. Leasing is favored when the company does not have a comparative advantage relative to developers and other investors in managing property and eventually selling it.

Maintenance. Companies are more likely to own assets whose values are highly sensitive to the level of maintenance. Lessors that own maintenance sensitive buildings, unless protected by enforceable maintenance provisions,[17] are likely to charge higher lease rates to compensate for lower expected levels of maintenance undertaken by (particularly short-term) tenants. Therefore, unless corporate users find some means of reassuring lessors that maintenance is in the user's as well as the owner's best interest (perhaps through a very long-term lease), corporate users are likely to find it more economical to own.

Special Purpose Buildings. Companies are more likely to own buildings that have been "customized" for their operations, especially when those operations are unusual and the company has few competitors. To illustrate the case of "customized" corporate real estate, we typically observe corporations owning rather than leasing buildings outfitted for hi-tech, R&D operations.[18] (Bulk distribution warehouses, by contrast, are far more likely to be leased than owned.) The high costs of relocating specialized corporate fixtures and machinery are an obvious incentive to own rather than lease. In the case of many single-tenant, special-purpose buildings, the value of the real estate may well be far higher in its current corporate use than in any conceivable alternative use. To the extent this is the case, a lessor would be effectively holding a corporate security whose value depended almost entirely on the company's operating success. In such cases, corporate users would likely have a considerable advantage over real estate investors in bearing such firm-specific risk.

Tax Considerations. Tax considerations have historically played a major role in the standard lease-versus-buy analysis. It is less clear today than it was prior to 1986 whether corporations or individuals (either through the medium of partnerships or institutions) are the tax-favored owners of real estate.

The simple rule of thumb on taxes in lease-versus-buy decisions is as follows: If the lessor is in a higher tax bracket than the lessee, then leasing puts "ownership" of the asset in the hands of the party that can most benefit from the tax shelter provided by depreciation. From 1981 to 1986, two elements of the tax code together encouraged the ownership of real estate by individuals in high tax brackets: (1) Depreciation

---

[17]Effective contracting may be very difficult to achieve even if a net lease is negotiated with the lessor because of time losses in monitoring, assessing blame, and resolving disputes over excessive equipment failures or other problems caused by poor building design or other flaws believed to be the responsibility of the lessor.

[18]The maintenance and specialization issues may in fact be closely related. For example, in an R&D facility requiring specific hardware in its design, technicians employed by the corporate entity may be better able to diagnose and respond to maintenance problems. In such cases, ownership would be preferable to constructing intricate provisions in lease contracts for the lessor to maintain such assets.

lives were considerably shorter for real estate assets, thus increasing the depreciation tax shield; and (2) The marginal tax rate for wealthy individuals (50 percent) was higher than the highest marginal tax rate for corporations (46 percent), and many companies had other tax shields that effectively lowered their marginal rate well below the statutory 46 percent rate. These two conditions, combined with the ability of partnerships to pass through operating losses directly to investors and avoid the double taxation of corporate dividends, created strong incentives for partnerships of high-tax individuals to own real estate and lease it to corporations. These tax incentives for corporations to sell real estate to individuals coupled with the market's perceived reluctance to reflect corporate real estate values in stock prices explain much of the real estate sales and sale-leaseback that occurred during this time period.

The Tax Reform Act of 1986 substantially reduced the incentive for individuals to lease to corporations in several ways. First, it lengthened tax depreciation lives, thus lowering the tax shield. Second, the highest marginal tax rate for corporations (34 percent) is now slightly higher than that of wealthy individuals (31 percent). Third, individuals are subject to limitations on "passive" losses that restrict their ability to use accounting losses from real estate to offset other income. These tax law changes have leveled the playing field among partnerships, corporations, and tax-exempt entities such as pension funds as owners of real estate.[19] For this reason, taxes are far less likely today to be the deciding factor in corporate lease-versus-own decisions.

Access to Capital Markets. Real estate is very capital intensive. The cost of owning real estate is a function of the cost of obtaining debt and equity capital. As mentioned previously, corporations with a high credit rating may be able to obtain unsecured corporate debt and equity at a cost less than the cost of capital for the individual or institutional investor that would be willing to own and lease the real estate to the corporation. This would tend to make owning preferable because the lease rate must cover the owner's cost of capital. On the other hand, a corporation that has a high cost of capital relative to a potential lessor might find leasing more attractive than owning.

If a property is mortgaged, we might expect the rate to be the same for the corporation or the investor, assuming the rate is based on the risk of the real estate rather than the risk of the borrower. If the loan is made with recourse to the borrower, however, the mortgage rate for corporations and investors could differ.

Control. The corporation may want to control the real estate by owning the property for financial reasons not considered in the above example. For example, as the corporation does business at a particular site it may build up goodwill that is difficult to transfer to another location. If the space is leased, the lessor may attempt to extract some of this firm-specific value from the corporation by charging a lease rate that is higher than the prevailing market rate. Owning the real estate ensures that the corporation retains goodwill at a reasonable cost.

---

[19]In fact, some researchers now claim that, for tax purposes under certain conditions, corporations rather than partnerships may be the optimal organizational form for holding real estate. See Jeffrey D. Fisher and George Lentz, "Tax Reform and Organizational Forms for Holding Investment Real Estate: Corporations vs. Partnerships," *The American Real Estate and Urban Economics Association Journal* 17, no. 3, 1989.

Effect on Financial Statements. The decision to own versus lease space has an impact on the financial statements of the corporation, which, in turn, may affect the value placed on the corporation by investors and lenders and, consequently, the cost of capital for the corporation. These financial considerations can have a substantial impact on the decision to own versus lease. In fact, because of the nature of real estate versus other corporate assets, corporations are often at a disadvantage owning real estate versus other investors.

Looking again at Exhibit 14–3, note that by owning versus leasing, income after tax is only $4,830 higher during the first 15 years, even though the after-tax cash flow is higher by $45,170. Income based on accounting statements versus cash flows presents potential problems because investors may be aware only of the "earnings per share" reported by the corporation, not the cash flow. Furthermore, much of the benefit of owning in this example comes from the residual value of the real estate at the end of the lease term. This unrealized source of potential gain would not be reflected in the annual income statements. Another potential problem is that real estate is carried at book value on corporate balance sheets. Because book values are based on cost, they are equal to the original acquisition cost less accumulated depreciation. The investment community may not be aware of the market value of real estate held by corporations, or at least real estate value is difficult to determine. Thus, many analysts argue that a corporation's stock price may not reflect the benefit of any above-average appreciation in any real estate assets that it owns.[20]

Indeed, unless real estate assets are valued periodically, corporate managers may not realize that the corporation's real estate is worth more than book value. Thus they may use real estate inefficiently because they do not consider the true cost of the space. Corporations' inefficient use of real estate can lead to takeover attempts by investors who recognize the value of the real estate and the fact that it is not being put to its highest and best use. After such takeovers, the new owners sell real estate assets, and shift operations to cost facilities elsewhere.

Another distortion in corporate balance sheets occurs when real estate is carried at book value but is financed with a mortgage based on its current market value. If this occurs, the proportion of financing (loan-to-market-value ratio) is lower than the loan-to-book value. Thus, a mortgage can increase a corporation's overall debt ratio, which is based on assets carried at book value. The debt ratio can make the corporation appear riskier to shareholders and result in a lower stock price because the assets of the firm may appear to be more highly levered than they actually are. Many have argued that this distortion partially accounts for premiums paid over the prevailing stock prices by investors, who are aware of this difference when they seek to take over a firm.

Off-Balance-Sheet Financing. Because ownership of real estate often has an unfavorable impact on the company's financial statements, corporations often attempt to avoid showing real estate on the financial statements. Leasing may allow the corporation to get the real estate off the balance sheet if the lease meets certain criteria. If the lease is accounted for as an **operating lease**, the lease contract does not affect the corporation's balance sheet. If the lease is accounted for as a **capital lease**, however, the lease is recorded on the balance sheet as both a long-term asset and a long-

[20]Investors may know that real estate has a higher value on average than its book value. But without details as to the market value of the real estate for a specific company, the best they can do is assume the market value is higher than the book value by some arbitrary amount.

term liability. Both are recorded on the balance sheet at an amount equal to the present value of the lease payments.[21] This obviously increases the corporation's debt-to-assets ratio. Thus, many corporations prefer to account for the lease as an operating lease. Under Financial Accounting Standards Board (FASB) guidelines, however, the lease must be accounted for as a capital lease if it meets any one of four conditions.[22] A lease is a capital lease if it extends for at least 75 percent of the asset's life, if it transfers ownership to the lessee at the end of the lease term, or if it seems likely that ownership will be transferred to the lessee because of a "bargain purchase" option.[23] Finally, if the present value of the contractual lease payments equals or exceeds 90 percent of the fair market value of the asset at the time the lease is signed, then the lease is a capital lease.

In the past, many corporations used unconsolidated subsidiaries to provide a way to own real estate assets but report only the equity ownership interest (not the purchase price and the debt liability) and still report the earnings on consolidated financial statements. Corporations could use subsidiaries in this way when the subsidiary was considered to engage in "nonhomogeneous," or unrelated activities. Thus, if real estate was unrelated to the firm's core business, the corporation could use an unconsolidated subsidiary to own the real estate without affecting the consolidated balance sheet. FASB guidelines have since been revised, however, to severely restrict the use of unconsolidated subsidiaries for this purpose. Companies wanting to use unconsolidated subsidiaries to keep the real estate off the balance sheet must own less than 50 percent of the subsidiary, which means that they must give up control of the subsidiary.

The Problem of "Hidden Value." The appreciation in value of some corporate real estate poses a critical problem for management. Many observers claim that, because accounting conventions require companies to carry real estate assets on a "lower of cost or market" basis and many properties contribute little to reported earnings, the value of corporate real estate is "hidden" from investors and, therefore, not fully reflected in stock prices. To the extent that real estate values are not reflected in share prices, corporate management is vulnerable to the predations of raiders who are able to buy companies at bargain prices and then sell off the undervalued assets.

The perceived undervaluation of corporate real estate is leading corporate managers to take careful inventory of real assets and to evaluate their alternative uses. In some cases, this process has led to outright property sales accompanied by major relocations, in others to sale-leaseback, and in still others to a variety of asset-backed refinancing designed to capture "hidden" values. At the same time, some companies are attempting to reduce occupancy costs as well as the potential for future hidden value problems through the use of equity leases and joint ventures. Such methods allow corporations to participate in the appreciation of real estate projects

---

[21]This was one of the reasons that we assumed in the lease-versus-own example that the loan would equal the present value of the lease payments. FASB guidelines require that the discount rate be appropriate given the creditworthiness of the lessee. Recall that we assumed that the loan amount was equal to the present value of the lease payments discounted at the mortgage interest rate. A lease and a mortgage to the same corporation would be of comparable risk.

[22]FASB, *Statement of Financial Accounting Standards No. 13*, par. 7.

[23]A bargain purchase option gives the lessee the right to purchase the asset for a price less than the fair market value of the asset expected when the option is exercised.

in which they are major tenants, while avoiding the costs associated with a major capital commitment to real estate.

The case of real estate presents several special problems that may result in a discount in the share price. For one thing, the costs for outside investors to ascertain the values of such real estate may be large enough to warrant a large discount, especially if management (1) does not know the value of its own real estate or (2) does know it but fails to communicate it to investors.

Second, investors may discount too heavily (if they consider at all) the expected future value of real estate that produces no current operating cash flow—especially if they believe that management has no intention of selling or developing the real estate. For example, if prices of undeveloped land have risen dramatically but management does not inspire confidence that it has a plan to harvest such value, then investors may be justified in assigning low value to such growth options. Investors, after all, do not have the control necessary to realize hidden values.

Third, in the case of operating real estate, the fact that management persists in using assets with much higher valued alternative uses in marginally profitable operations would also warrant a large discount in the stock—again, provided management does not signal to the market its intent to sell or convert the asset.

Still another potential problem in valuing real estate arises even in the case of income-producing properties. Because accounting depreciation charges generally exceed true economic depreciation, the reported earnings of real estate companies typically understate the level of operating cash flow. And if the market responds mechanically to reported earnings, then it could systematically undervalue real estate assets, thus leaving companies prey to raiders concerned only about cash flow. But if markets do look through earnings to cash flow, as much academic research suggests, then accounting conventions should not lead to the undervaluation of real estate.

On the other hand, as mentioned earlier, the ability of acquirers to take over asset-rich companies, write up the value of acquired real estate assets to market, and then depreciate their values over shorter lives (provided by the Economic Recovery Tax Act of 1981) clearly provided an artificial stimulus to takeover activity in the early 1980s. Such a stimulus was removed, however, with the Tax Reform Act of 1986.

To summarize, then, besides the possibility of market inefficiency, information and control problems could be responsible for large disparities between stock prices and perceived real estate values. First, in the case of large industrial companies with dispersed real estate assets, the costs to investors of ascertaining such values may be very large. Second, even if the market knows the value of such assets, the remaining uncertainty about whether management will take steps to realize the value of such real estate options, and about when such steps will be taken, could lead investors to heavily discount real assets in setting stock prices.

The Role of Real Estate in Corporate Restructuring

The business environment of the 1980s, which featured widespread deregulation, heightened international competition, and increased shareholder activism, forced American corporations to reexamine many aspects of their operations in the attempt to increase shareholder value (and, in some cases, to defend against raiders). By stepping up the urgency of management's search for efficiencies, these competitive forces produced an unprecedented number of mergers and acquisitions, divestitures, spinoffs, leveraged buyouts, and other major recapitalizations. Real estate assets were often a focal point in these restructurings.

As a consequence of this restructuring activity, corporate managements today are far more likely to question the traditional notion that corporations have a comparative advantage in owning real estate. It is important to remember that corporate real assets, while functioning as facilities in corporate operations, are part of local and regional property markets. And unless the company is a dominant force in a small local economy, the market value of those assets is typically governed by factors very different from those that drive the value of the firm's operating business. Developers and real estate investors are likely to be more alert to changes in property values, and to opportunities to take advantage of such changes, than a corporate management focused on operations.

Sale-Leaseback

An additional analysis that is relevant for a corporation that has owned real estate for some time is whether it should sell the real estate and lease it back from the new owner. This procedure would be attractive in cases where the company wants to sell the real estate but needs to continue to use the space because relocation is not practicable. In 1988, for example, Time, Inc., sold its 45 percent interest in its Rockefeller Center headquarters to the building's former co-owner, the Rockefeller Group, and then arranged a long-term lease.

Why might the corporation benefit from a sale-leaseback? In such cases, the corporation receives cash from sale of the property, and assuming that it still needs to use the real estate, leases the facilities back and makes lease payments. It also loses any remaining depreciation allowance on the book value on the building. However, it also removes the risk associated with the residual value of the property.

As discussed in the analysis of leasing versus owning, whether a corporation benefits from continuing to be an investor in the real estate will dictate whether to do a sale-leaseback. In fact, the analysis is very similar to that of leasing versus owning. There is one main difference: Because the corporation already owns the real estate, it has to consider the after-tax cash flow it receives from sale of the property (rather than the purchase price), as the amount of funds invested if it decides to continue to own the property.

The after-tax cash flow from sale will be less than the cost of purchasing the property if capital gains tax must be paid. Thus, the rate of return received on funds left in the property (if the company does not do a sale-leaseback) may be greater than if the company were deciding to own or lease the same property that it did not already own.

To see how we might analyze whether a corporation should sell and lease back space, we will extend the example we considered earlier in the lease-versus-own analysis. Suppose that five years ago, the corporation had decided to own rather than lease the real estate. Assume that it is now five years later and management is considering a sale-leaseback of the property. The property can be sold today for $2 million and leased back at a rate of $200,000 per year on a 15-year lease starting today. Exhibit 14–5 shows the after-tax cash flow if the property is sold today, taking into consideration that the company purchased the property five years ago for

EXHIBIT 14–5 Sale-Leaseback

Original price: (5 years ago)		
Land	$ 225,000	12.50%
Building	1,575,000	87.50%
Total	1,800,000	100.00%
Depreciation	31.5 years	
Tax rate	30.00%	
ATCF if sold today:		
Reversion		$ 2,000,000
Mortgage balance		−1,369,000
Reversion	$ 2,000,000	
Basis	−1,550,000	
Gain	$ 450,000	
Tax		−135,000
Cash flow		$ 496,000
Lease payment		$200,000 (15-year net lease)
Operating expense		50.00% of lease payment

	Own	*Lease*	*Difference (Own − Lease)*
Sales	$1,500,000	$1,500,000	0
Cost of goods sold	750,000	750,000	0
Gross income	750,000	750,000	0
Operating expenses:			
Business	200,000	200,000	0
Real estate	100,000	100,000	0
Lease payments	0	200,000	−200,000
Interest	−136,900	0	−136,900
Depreciation	−50,000	0	−50,000
Taxable income	263,100	250,000	13,100
Tax	78,930	75,000	3,930
Income after tax	184,170	175,000	9,170
Plus: Depreciation	50,000	0	50,000
Less: Principal	0	0	0
Cash flow	234,170	175,000	59,170
Reversion			$3,000,000
Mortgage balance			−1,369,000
Reversion		$3,000,000	
Basis (after 20 yrs.)		−800,000	
Gain		$2,200,000	
Tax			−660,000
Cash flow			$ 971,000
Year	0	1–15	15
Own − Lease	$−496,000	$ 59,170	$ 971,000
IRR 14.10%			

$1.8 million. Because it has depreciated the property over the past five years, the firm must pay capital gains tax of $135,000, making the after-tax cash flow from the sale today $1,865,000. By leasing instead of owning for the next 15 years, management must pay an additional $155,000 in after-tax cash flow each year.[24] Further, if the property is sold today, the firm will not receive the cash flow from sale of the property at the end of the lease. We assume that the property will be worth $3 million at the end of the 15-year lease.

As shown in Exhibit 14–5, the *IRR* from owning versus leasing is 14.10 percent. This is the *return from continuing to own* instead of leasing. Alternatively, the *IRR* can be viewed as the *cost of the sale-leaseback financing*, that is, the cost of obtaining $496,000 today by selling the property, then leasing it back. The return from continuing to own is slightly greater than in the original lease-versus-own example. Why? One reason is that taxes must be paid if the property is sold, which increases the benefit of continuing to own. Lease payments are also higher because market rents increased during the past five years. In this situation there are more benefits from owning because the higher lease payments are now saved. Should the firm choose to lease, higher lease payments offset the higher price of the property that would be realized if the property were sold and reduces the benefit of owning relative to leasing.

A sale-leaseback also has implications for the corporation's financial statements. As we discussed, sale of the property results in capital gains tax. At the same time, however, it allows the corporation to report additional income because of the gain on the sale. Additional income results in an increase in reported earnings per share. Managers may have the incentive to do a real estate sale-leaseback to recognize a capital gain when they want to show an increase in earnings per share. Sale-leaseback for that reason is not necessarily in the best interest of the corporation, however.

A sale-leaseback, like any asset sale, removes an option for potential raiders to use real estate as a means of financing. Provided management can profitably reinvest the sale proceeds in its basic business or returns the cash to shareholders, then the opportunity for outside investors to profit from takeover by selling or refinancing the real estate is foreclosed. Furthermore, if the company leases with a short-term lease, it retains its option to relocate. But, if a company simply sells and then commits itself to a long-term lease, the ownership transfer may offer no economic gain. The capital inflow from the sale may simply be offset over time by the higher rent charged by the new owner. Moreover, if the sale triggers a large tax liability payment, then the transaction could actually reduce shareholder value.

Assuming, however, that companies can shelter capital gains,[25] corporate shareholders could benefit from sale-leaseback to the extent that U.S. institutional or foreign investors are willing to accept lower yields than the returns required by corporate investors (again, adjusted for risk and leverage). In such cases, the sale proceeds to the company could exceed the present value of the new lease stream as well as any foregone tax savings from ownership.

Another potential benefit of sale-leaseback is its role as a "signaling" device. To the extent investors have been unable or unwilling to recognize real estate values, a sale-leaseback clearly demonstrates those values to the marketplace. Perhaps equally important, a sale-leaseback, especially when combined with stock repurchases, may also persuade investors that management has become more serious about its commitment to increasing shareholder value. For companies in mature industries with

---

[24]Alternatively, by continuing to own, the corporation saves $155,000 in after-tax cash flow.

[25]Of course, there will always be cases where sale-leaseback may be used to recognize gains from the sale of assets to offset any loss carry-forwards that a corporation may want to utilize.

limited investment opportunities, a sale-leaseback together with a large distribution to shareholders may add value by returning excess capital to investors.[26]

Still another possible benefit from sale-leaseback is to provide a source of capital that can be used to fund growth opportunities or to refinance existing high-priced debt. Fred Meyer, Inc., for example, recently sold and leased back 35 stores and a distribution center, thereby raising $400 million. Each store was leased for 20 years with a fixed-payment, net-lease rate and an operating lease structure that allowed off-balance-sheet treatment. This transaction effectively enabled the company to capture the full market value of real estate assets, use the sale proceeds to retire some of its higher-yielding debt, and retain control of the assets by means of long-term leases.

Refinancing

One reason that the corporation might be considering a sale-leaseback as discussed in the previous section is to raise capital. An alternative might be to refinance the real estate with a mortgage, especially if unsecured corporate financing sources were initially used. As discussed earlier, mortgage financing may be a substitute for corporate debt if it is shown on the balance sheet and increases the corporation's debt ratio. Thus, the corporation must consider whether a mortgage on the real estate can be obtained at a lower cost than unsecured corporate debt. An additional option available to the corporation is refinancing with a hybrid mortgage as discussed in Chapter 11.

Investing in Real Estate for Diversification

Corporations may view ownership of real estate as a way of diversifying their business activities, leading to purchase of more real estate than it needs for its operations. For example, the corporation may decide to develop or purchase an office building that is larger than it needs for its own use. The rest of the office building is held as an investment.[27]

A corporation may also own space that was formerly used for the core business but is no longer needed. This excess space might be kept as an investment. In both of these cases, the question is whether the corporation has the expertise to own and manage investment real estate and whether the value of the company's stock will fully reflect the value of the real estate investments. That is, would the real estate be considered more valuable if held by a different entity such as a real estate investment trust or a real estate limited partnership? These investment vehicles will be discussed further in later chapters. The point here is that corporations need to determine whether holding real estate as an investment is in the best interests of their shareholders. Shareholders may prefer to have the corporation own only assets related to its core business.

---

[26] This is the substance of Michael Jensen's argument known as the "agency costs of free cash flow." For a nontechnical explanation of this concept and its reflection in corporate restructuring activity, see Michael Jensen, "The Takeover Controversy: Analysis and Evidence," *Midland Corporate Finance Journal* 4, no. 2 (Summer 1986).

[27] If the corporation needs to expand, building ownership can be an advantage because, in effect, the corporation has the first option on space in the building it owns when another tenant's lease expires.

Conclusion

This chapter focused on the decision to own or lease real estate that is used by a corporation as part of its core business. We showed the decision to own versus lease real estate to be similar to the pure real estate investment decision we analyzed extensively in earlier chapters. A key difference, however, is the impact that ownership or sale-leaseback of real estate can have on the corporation's financial statements. Whether a particular corporation should own or lease depends on whether it has a comparative advantage owning real estate relative to other investors or investment vehicles.

CFOs are increasingly giving corporate real estate more attention, realizing the importance of property to their bottom line and share price. Facilities managers today must justify ownership of real estate against a variety of alternatives that combine the operating control provided by ownership with reduced investment and greater flexibility. Corporations are more likely to accept such alternatives, which include a variety of leasing forms as well as joint-venture ownership, as ownership becomes unnecessary to maintaining operating control of real estate.

Key Terms

capital lease 422
corporate real estate 409
hidden value 423
lease-versus-own analysis 410
off-balance-sheet financing 422
operating lease 422
residual value 415
sale-leaseback 425
special purpose buildings 420

Questions

1. What are the main reasons that corporations may choose to own real estate?
2. What factors would tend to make leasing more desirable than owning?
3. Why might the cost of a mortgage loan be greater than the cost of using unsecured corporate debt to finance corporate real estate?
4. Why might the riskiness of cash flow from the residual value of the real estate differ from the riskiness of cash flow from the corporation's core business? What would cause these cash flows to be correlated?
5. What would cause the rate of return for an investor that purchases real estate and leases it to the corporation to differ from the rate of return earned by the corporation on the incremental investment in owning versus leasing the same property?
6. Why might the decision to own rather than lease real estate have an unfavorable effect on the corporation's financial statements?
7. Why is the value of corporate real estate often considered "hidden" from shareholders?
8. How does the analysis of a sale-leaseback differ from the analysis of owning versus leasing?
9. Why is the cost of financing with a sale-leaseback essentially the same as the return from continuing to own?
10. Why might it be argued that corporations do not have a comparative advantage when investing in real estate as a means of diversification from the core business?
11. Why has real estate often been a key factor in corporate restructuring?
12. Why might refinancing be considered an alternative to a sale-leaseback?
13. What factors might cause the highest and best use of real estate to change during the course of typical lease term?
14. Why should corporations have their real estate appraised on a regular basis?
15. What factors would tend to affect the value of a lease?

Problems

1. The ABC Corporation is considering opening an office in a new market area that would allow it to increase its annual sales by $2.5 million. Cost of goods sold is estimated to be 40 percent of sales, and corporate overhead would increase by $300,000, not including the cost of either acquiring or leasing office space. The corporation will have to invest $2.5 million in office furniture, office equipment, and other up-front costs associated with opening the new office before considering the costs of owning or leasing the office space.

   A small office building could be purchased for sole use by the corporation at a total price of $3.9 million, of which $600,000 of the purchase price would represent land value, and $3.3 million would represent building value. The cost of the building would be depreciated over 39 years. The corporation is in a 30 percent tax bracket. An investor is willing to purchase the same building and lease it to the corporation for $450,000 per year for a term of 15 years, with the corporation paying all real estate operating expenses (absolute net lease). Real estate operating expenses are estimated to be 50 percent of the lease payments. Estimates are that the property value will increase over the 15-year lease term for a sale price of $4.9 million at the end of the 15 years. If the property is purchased, it would be financed with an interest-only mortgage for $2,730,000 at an interest rate of 10 percent with a balloon payment due after 15 years.

   a. What is the return from opening the office building under the assumption that it is leased?

   b. What is the return from opening the office building under the assumption that it is owned?

   c. What is the return on the incremental cash flow from owning versus leasing?

   d. In general, what other factors might the firm consider before deciding whether to lease or own?

2. Refer to problem 1. Suppose that five years ago the corporation had decided to own rather than lease the real estate. Assume that it is now five years later and management is considering a sale-leaseback of the property. The property can be sold today for $4,240,000 and leased back at a rate of $450,000 per year on a 15-year lease starting today. It was purchased five years ago for $3.9 million. Assume that the property will be worth $5.7 million at the end of the 15-year lease.

   a. How much would the corporation receive from a sale-leaseback of the property?

   b. What is the cost of obtaining financing with a sale-leaseback?

   c. What is the return from continuing to own the property?

   d. In general, what other factors and alternatives might the firm consider in order to decide whether to do a sale-leaseback?

3. Refer to problem 1. ABC realizes that the benefits of leasing versus owning may be sensitive to many of the assumptions being made. Management wants to know how the return on the incremental cash flow from owning versus leasing is affected by different assumptions. (This problem is best done using a spreadsheet.)

   a. How would the return be affected by the corporation being in a zero tax bracket?

   b. How would the return be affected if the property value does not increase over time, if it remains constant?

   c. How would the return be affected if the mortgage were at an 8 percent (rather than 10 percent) interest rate?

Appendix: Real Estate Asset Pricing and Capital Budgeting Analysis: A Synthesis

Introduction

As we have discussed beginning with Chapter 10, real estate income property is usually valued from the point of view of the equity investor. That is, we discount the cash flows (before or after tax) available to the equity investor based on explicit assumptions about the cost and terms of the mortgage used to finance the property. We use an after-tax discount rate to discount the after-tax cash flows. When analyzing the after-tax basis, the calculation of the after-tax cash flow to the equity investor reflects the tax deductibility of interest. The amount of equity an investor is willing to invest represents the value of the equity position. The amount of loan that a mortgage lender will lend on the property represents the value of the mortgage position. The total property value is the sum of the value of the mortgage and equity positions.

In contrast, the traditional capital budgeting procedures shown in corporate finance text books suggests that after-tax cash flows produced by the project *before deducting any financing costs* should be discounted by a weighted average cost of capital that considers after-tax cost of debt and equity. Tax deductibility of interest on debt is treated in one of two ways: (1) the after-tax cost of debt is used when calculating the weighted average cost of capital, or (2) the tax shield created by the interest deduction on debt is added back to the after-tax cash flow produced by the project. In this latter case, the before-tax cost of debt is used to calculate the weighted average cost of capital. In both of these approaches, the after-tax cost of equity is included in the weighted average cost of capital.

This appendix demonstrates that all three approaches mentioned above are consistent and result in the same property value when applied correctly.

Mortgage-Equity Approach

As we saw in Chapter 9, the term *mortgage-equity analysis* is often used in real estate to refer to the valuation of real estate income property by explicitly considering how the property will be financed. For simplicity, in this appendix we assume that all cash flows are a level perpetuity, the loan is interest-only (no amortization), and there is no depreciation allowance.[1] In general, the value of the property can be found with the mortgage-equity approach as follows:

$$V = \frac{(NOI - r_d D)(1 - t)}{R_e} + D$$

where:

V = Estimated property value
D = Amount of debt
NOI = Net operating income
I = Tax rate
r_d = Cost of debt (before tax)
R_e = Cost of equity (after tax)

Example

Assume that NOI is \$115,000 per year. A loan (D) is available for \$800,000 with an interest rate (r_d) of 10 percent. The investor's tax rate (t) is 20 percent and the investor's required after-tax rate of return (R_e) is 14 percent.

[1]Assuming that cash flows are not level and that the project is sold after a finite holding period or assuming that there is a depreciation allowance does not change any of the conclusions of this appendix.

Using the preceding formula, we have:

$$V = \frac{(115{,}000 - .10 \times 80{,}000)(1 - .20)}{.14} + 800{,}000$$

$$V = 200{,}000 + 800{,}000$$
$$V = 1{,}000{,}000$$

Weighted-Average Cost of Capital—Alternative 1

Use of a weighted-average cost of capital assumes that the project will have the same proportion of debt as in other projects. In the above example, debt represented 80 percent of property value. Assuming another project is undertaken with the same proportion of debt, the weighted-average cost of capital is as follows:

$$R_a = [D/V \times r_d \times (1 - t)]\ 1\ [E/V \times R_e]$$

where

R_a is the Weighted average cost of capital
E is the Amount of equity
D/V is the Proportion of debt
E/V is the Proportion of equity

The value of the property is found as follows:

$$V = \frac{NOI(1 - t)}{R_a}$$

For the example considered earlier, we have:

$$V = \frac{115{,}000(1 - .20)}{[.80 \times .10 \times (1 - .2)] + (.20 \times .14)}$$

$$V = \frac{92{,}000}{.092}$$

$$V = 1{,}000{,}000$$

This is obviously the same answer as before.

Weighted-Average Cost of Capital—Alternative 2

An alternative way of valuing the property is to adjust the after-tax cash flows available on the project for the tax shield associated with the deductibility of the debt. This tax shield is equal to the annual interest payment ($r_d \times D$) multiplied by the tax rate (t). In terms of the above symbols, the tax shield is equal to $r_d \times D \times t$. When the cash flows are adjusted by the tax shield, the cost of capital is calculated by using the *before-tax* cost of debt (r_d) rather than the after-tax cost. The after-tax cost of equity (r_e) is still used. In this case the value can be expressed as follows:

$$V = \frac{(NOI)(1 - t) + (r_d \times D \times t)}{(D/V \times r_d) + (E/V \times R_e)}$$

Note that the numerator in the above formula is not the cash flow to the equity investor. It represents the cash flow on the entire property plus an adjustment for the additional tax benefit associated with the debt.[2]

For the same example considered above, we have:

$$V = \frac{115{,}000\,(1 - .20) + (.10 \times 800{,}000 \times .20)}{(.80 \times .10) + (.20 \times .14)}$$

$$V = \frac{108{,}000}{.1080}$$

$$V = 1{,}000{,}000$$

Again, the answer is the same as before.

Conclusion

Use of the mortgage-equity approach is consistent with traditional capital budgeting procedures when valuing real estate. When using the mortgage-equity approach the after-tax cost of equity is used in place of the weighted average cost of capital when discounting the cash flows produced after payment of interest. When using the traditional weighted average cost of capital calculation, an after-tax cost of debt and equity is used to discount before-tax cash flows. An alternative to the latter approach is to adjust the after-tax cash flow from the property by adding back an amount that represents the tax savings associated with the debt. When using this approach, a before-tax cost of debt must be used when calculating the weighted average cost of capital. In either case, the estimated value is the same as the mortgage-equity approach, which is typically used to value real estate.

We simplified the above analysis by assuming cash flows were perpetuities and that the debt was not amortized. This approach implies that the proportion of debt and equity remains constant over time. Analysts argue that corporations can maintain a target proportion of debt in their capital structure by alternating between issuing debt and equity. Thus, it may not be appropriate to value a *particular* project based on the amount of debt or equity used to finance that project. However, mortgage loans are typically amortized and are usually secured by a specific property. Refinancing is expensive and, therefore, it is not feasible to maintain a constant proportion of debt from year to year. As this appendix points out, the value produced by the mortgage-equity approach is the same as that found with traditional capital budgeting techniques if consistent assumptions are made about the use of financing. However, because real estate is used as security for debt and refinancing to maintain a constant ratio of debt to assets is costly, using the mortgage-equity approach may be more appropriate because it allows financing to be considered explicitly.

---

[2]This adjustment does not necessarily assume that the use of debt adds to the value of the property relative to an unlevered property. It simply recognizes the fact that interest is tax deductible.

CHAPTER

15

Financing Project Development

Introduction

This chapter deals with financing the development of income-producing real estate projects such as apartment complexes, office buildings, warehouses, and shopping centers. Developers of such projects face changing conditions in the national and local economies, competitive pressures from other developments, and changes in locational preferences of tenants, all of which influence the long-run profitability of developing and operating an income-producing property. Together they affect the ability of the developer to acquire land, build improvements, lease space to tenants, and earn sufficient revenues to cover operating expenses.

The Development of Income-Producing Property—An Overview

As the introduction points out, many types of income property may be developed, and each has its own special set of characteristics. Differences in market demand affect the economic feasibility of each of them. However, a few general concepts are common to all project developments.

The simplified diagram in Exhibit 15–1 shows the typical development process. With the possible exception of the management phase, this process is generally applicable to most categories of project development. Essentially, a developer (1) acquires a site, (2) develops the site and constructs building improvements, (3) provides the finish-out and readies the space for occupancy by tenants, (4) manages the property after completion, and (5) may eventually sell the project. How long after development the developer sells the project depends on the business strategy employed. The project has been an economic success if its market value exceeds the sum total of the land and development costs extended to complete it. It is in this sense that developers are said to "create value." That is, by combining land and building improvements, in any way that is highly valued by rent-paying tenants, the developer creates value in excess of the sum of the cost of individual components.

Developers' business strategies can be categorized in three general ways. First, many development firms undertake projects with the intention of owning and managing them for many years after completion. These developers view leasing and

EXHIBIT 15–1 Phases of Real Estate Project Development and Risk

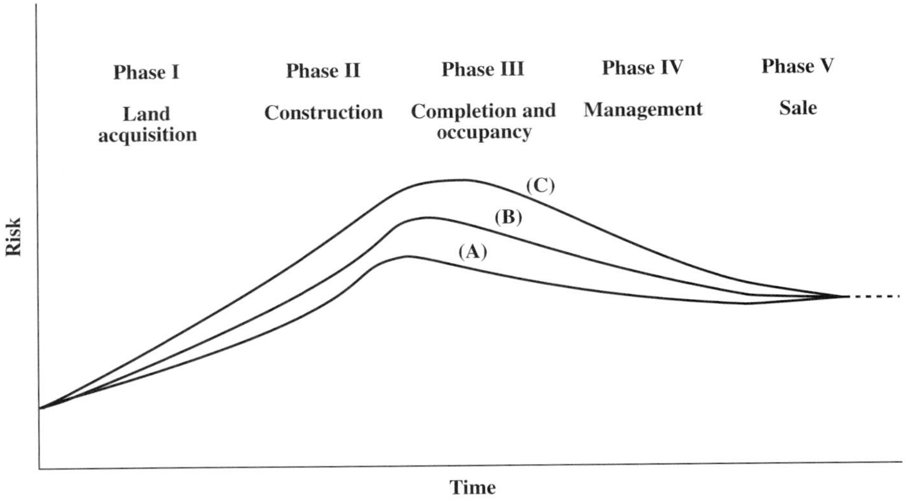

(A) Greater than normal predevelopment leasing, completion ahead of schedule.
(B) Normal predevelopment leasing, completion on schedule.
(C) Lower than normal predevelopment leasing, completion behind schedule.

management as integral parts of their business in addition to the development function. Second, some developers expect to sell their developments after the lease-up phase, or when normal occupancy has been achieved. These developers usually sell projects to institutional investors such as insurance companies or other investment entities, or they may sell completely or in part to syndication firms that form limited partnerships. In these cases, even though they sell the project, development companies may continue to manage them. Third, some developers, particularly those involved in a combination of land development and the development of commercial property such as business parks and industrial parks, normally develop land and buildings for lease in a master-planned development. However, they may also **"build to suit"** for single tenants.

The point is that many developers intentionally *specialize* their business activities in one or more phases of the generalized diagram shown in Exhibit 15–1. Those developers intending to sell soon after lease-up rely heavily on external contractors, architects, real estate brokers, leasing agents, and property managers to accomplish much of phases II through V. Alternatively, very large, integrated development firms with activities in many regional markets find it profitable to provide most of the functions shown in the exhibit themselves, using external firms only when it is cost-effective to do so. For firms on both ends of the spectrum, however, it is possible that an unanticipated sale of a project may occur in any phase of development. Most developers are never averse to considering a serious offer to purchase a project at anytime.

Market Risks

Exhibit 15–1 also depicts a typical risk scenario in a "normal" market, as represented by case (B), or one in which market rents are believed to be sufficient to justify development (a subject that we will elaborate upon later in the chapter). Risk begins with land acquisition and increases steadily as construction commences until expected cash flows from the leasing phase materialize. After lease-up is completed, occupancy takes place and the property management phase begins. At that point, project risk declines because tenants are committed to leases with terms of varying lengths. Assuming that the property is performing well, it is during phase IV that it may be described as a **"seasoned" property**. An example of a market scenario with less risk is shown as case (A), where market demand for space is increasing and predevelopment leasing, or leasing *prior* to project completion, is occurring at an "above normal" rate, thereby increasing expected cash inflows. The expected increase in cash inflows usually reflects a greater than anticipated demand for the type of space being developed and, therefore, a reduction in project risk. Obviously, if market demand and expected revenues were to decline or if the time required for the leasing phase lengthened considerably, as in case (C), project risk would increase dramatically. Factors such as construction delays, price increases in materials, and interest rate increases cause changes in project risk.

Although regional and urban economics and employment are not the focus of this book, it should be clear that factors determining the demand for the type of space (e.g., office, retail, warehouse) being developed are critical to project risk. These factors may manifest themselves in current market indicators, such as vacancy rate levels, rent levels, or the extent of predevelopment leasing commitments from tenants. A very good understanding of the underlying economic base of an urban area or region is critical when assessing the viability of real estate development because not only is the demand for rental space important during development, but it is important long *after* development is completed. Demand may decline and rents may fall in markets at any time, and tenants may find more attractive space at lower rents. Simply because a project has been developed and leased up does *not* mean that it is no longer vulnerable to competition. As space in new developments is supplied to the market, owners of existing projects become subject to the possibility of a loss in tenants. Indeed, many developers are not willing to undertake this longer-term market risk and the intensive amount of property management necessary to retain tenants. As mentioned earlier, they may prefer to sell to institutional or other investors who are willing to specialize in real estate managing and leasing and bear that risk.

Contrasted with developers who generally sell projects shortly after lease-up, larger, more geographically diversified developers may be willing to manage projects in various regions. They view this risk in the context of a portfolio in which risks emanating from longer-term economic growth and declines in individual regions can be sufficiently diversified to provide an adequate risk-adjusted return on their total property holdings. These firms may derive other benefits from continuing to perform the leasing and property management functions after development is completed. One benefit is that leads for future development opportunities may be obtained from the existing tenant base under management. These leads can take the form of (1) expansion of existing tenant facilities, (2) expansion opportunities in other cities as the businesses in which existing tenants are engaged need facilities to pursue growth opportunities elsewhere, and (3) development of different product types (e.g., the development of an office building for a satisfied tenant who currently leases warehouse space elsewhere).

Project Risks

The general market demand and leasing activity are not the only sources of risk that developers must consider in project development. Obviously, the location of the site to be acquired for the project development is an important consideration because its spatial proximity to other sites in an urban area will affect the cost of doing business for tenants or the demand for the product or service that tenants are selling. It follows that the better the spatial proximity, or location, as perceived by the tenant, the greater the value of site. When developers acquire sites in a given market, the cost of acquisition is an important determinant of the quality and cost of building improvements. Generally, as the cost of a given site increases, the building improvements will be of higher quality and will cost more to develop. Further, as the price of the land increases, the site is likely to be more densely developed. These basic economic relationships partially explain why certain areas of cities, such as downtowns, are more densely developed with high-rise office buildings while suburban areas are less densely developed (e.g., warehouses on relatively low-cost suburban or agricultural land).

A few of the major components for which cost and quality can be differentiated include physical design, functionality in interior layout, quality of interior finish, density on the site and its adequacy of access and egress from transportation, amenities (dining, athletic, retail, etc.), landscaping, parking and circulation on the site, common areas, elevators, quality of heat, ventilation, and air-conditioning (HVAC), and exterior finish (granite, aggregate, wood, etc.). Because of uncertainty about how the quantity and quality of services provided as a part of the development should be combined or "packaged" to meet demand, each of these elements presents a potential source of project risk.

Not all new projects are initially constructed as luxury "class A" space, which is usually complemented with higher-quality interior, exterior, and mechanical components. Indeed, many large national corporations seeking to expand facilities will have set policies regarding the quality of space necessary for various categories of employees. They may provide some employees involved with primary customer contacts (such as marketing) with relatively high-quality space; on the other hand, they may not see the need for such costly space for support services (accounting, computer, etc.). Indeed, if the majority of the expansion space will be required for support service, not only will the corporate tenant be looking for a facility with average finish and construction quality, but also the tenant may prefer a suburban location. Proximity to a residential location for its employees may be an extremely important corporate consideration, since a support facility does not usually involve customer contact. On the other hand, a building to be occupied by tenants who have frequent face-to-face contact with customers (law firms, high-fashion retail shops) generally require facilities with significantly higher finish costs.

The point is that investors must examine the demand for space in terms of the characteristics of the demand by *end users* (tenants) in a given market. This demand, in turn, depends on the type of employment in the local market and the nature of the functions that tenants will perform. Only by understanding the local economy and the nature of employment can the developer anticipate demand accurately and produce or supply the quantity and quality of space in the proper combination to satisfy market demand.

Project Development Financing—An Overview

In phase I of Exhibit 15–1, the developer may use equity or combine equity with debt financing to acquire the land, perhaps after taking an option to purchase the land (to be discussed in Chapter 16). The developer may provide the equity capital, or it may come from a partnership between the developer and the landowner or other investors. Should the developer expect to move forward on the project immediately after land acquisition, he may negotiate a loan for the cost of constructing improvements, providing his equity requirements from one or a combination of the sources just described. Generally, the loan used for funds to construct the building and other site improvements is referred to as a **construction**, or **interim loan**. This loan usually comes from a commercial bank, a mortgage banking company, or in some cases, a savings and loan association. It generally is used to fund all the **hard costs** of construction such as materials and labor for site improvements. However, it may also cover some **soft costs**, such as leasing costs, planning costs, and management. It may also include some of the costs of finishing the interior space for tenants through the lease-up stage. If the developer owns the land free and clear of debt, it may also be possible to obtain additional financing using the value of the land as security. Lenders prefer to make loans only for the cost of site improvements. However, in a rapidly expanding market, competition among lenders may result in more flexible lending policies. Also, in most cases when interim financing is sought, the developer is personally liable for the note. When construction is complete and the project is leased, the lender may fully or partially release the developer from personal liability. At this point the note becomes nonrecourse against the borrower/developer.

There are three general loan structures that are used to finance development.[1] Generally, the structure chosen will depend on what the developer expects to do with the property after construction and leasing are completed. In most cases developers expect to do one of three things:

1. The property may be sold upon completion and lease-up to investors who want to own real estate but who do not want to bear the risk of development and initial leasing. In this case, the difference between the developer's cost and the price received for the completed property represents profit to the developer. In this case, the developer will usually consider short-term financing structures.
2. The developer may retain ownership with the expectation that she will continue to manage, operate, and lease the property as an integral part of her business. Many developers maintain relationships with tenants and may have opportunities to develop and lease to them if future expansion becomes necessary. In this event, a developer will seek a longer-term financing structure. This may consist of two loans, a permanent loan and a construction loan.
3. A developer may consider the sale or refinancing of a property upon completion. This is an option that combines elements of (1) and (2) above. In this case, the developer may seek short-term construction financing, coupled with either an option, or a commitment, to extend financing for one or two years beyond the construction period. This allows additional time beyond construction to (1) prepare the property for sale, or (2) provide actual financial data from operations to lenders. The latter may provide the opportunity for refinancing at more attractive interest rates as the project should be less risky to lenders. Many of these loans may have maturities ranging from five to seven years and are commonly referred to

[1]There are many possible loan structures. We focus on three commonly used forms in this chapter.

as **mini-perm loans**. However, the downside of this strategy is that interest rates may be higher than was the case when construction began and the developer may be forced to pay a higher interest rate than may have otherwise been available had a precommitment for a permanent loan been made at the beginning of the development process. If this strategy was chosen, a developer should also investigate the possibility of an interest rate swap or hedge against higher interest rates. After the lease-up stage is completed and normal occupancy levels are achieved, the interim loan will usually be repaid by using either proceeds from the sale of the property or funds obtained from a permanent mortgage loan. Permanent loans usually come from life insurance companies, pension funds, or in some cases, large commercial banks.

In cases where a developer expects to have long-term ownership of a property, a commitment for permanent debt financing may be acquired *before* a commitment for the construction loan is obtained. Even in cases where developers expect to sell or refinance property when a project is completed, if leasing market conditions warrant it, the interim lender may require the developer to obtain a permanent loan commitment or to provide contractual evidence that he will sell the project to an identified buyer before the maturity date of the interim loan. Justification for such loan requirements may occur if the demand for space in a local market is expected to weaken, but the likelihood of sale of a project upon lease-up is high. Too much **speculative** and **open-ended** construction lending in a local market may result in significant overbuilding or an excess supply of space, which in turn may result in more vacancies and a reduction in rents. Property values may then decline, resulting in foreclosures.[2] In this case, a construction lender may want more assurance that the loan will be repaid from a sale or from a permanent loan committed to by another lender.

Lender Requirements in Financing Project Development

When developing income properties, the process of obtaining financing may be more complicated because in many cases *two* lenders, construction and permanent, are involved. Hence the developer must satisfy *two* sets of lending criteria. *While many components of these two criteria may be the same, some will be specific to each of the lenders.* A further complication is that the nature of the agreement reached with the permanent lender may affect the nature of the agreement that must be reached with the construction lender. When a permanent lender considers making a take-out commitment, that lender is literally "taking out" the construction lender and releasing that lender from any further lending responsibility to the developer. The take-out agreement may create a problem for a developer in that if the requirements of the commitment (lease-up requirements, lease approvals, etc.) are too stringent, it may be difficult to find a construction lender who is willing to comply. In this situation the developer's financing options are narrower and considerable delay may result. Exhibit 15–2 will help you understand the process of

[2]Many observers believe that the availability of funds is the primary determinant of development activity. Indeed, these observers believe that if funds are available, developers will build regardless of general market indications because they are so optimistic that they believe that their individual projects will always succeed in spite of the nature of competition and local market conditions.

obtaining project financing and the nature of the documentation that is generally required by both lenders.[3]

Loan Submission Information for Loan Requests—An Overview

While many of the items in Section A of Exhibit 15–2 are self-explanatory, the initial submission to the *permanent lender* will focus on what can be developed on the site; that is, it will provide a fairly detailed description of the size, design, and cost of the project. The submission will also provide a detailed market and competitive analysis, identify the team that will develop the project, and document all public approvals obtained or needed relative to zoning and permitting. Detailed pro forma operating statements and a set of financial statements from the borrower or borrowing entity will also be included. As just indicated, if the permanent lender gives the developer an indication of interest in financing the project, the permanent lender will request more detailed information, and the developer will be required to support the assumptions used in the pro forma operating statements from the market analysis and provide other data requested. Assuming that the developer provides data to the satisfaction of the lender, the lender usually issues an *intent* to provide financing, and the developer may proceed to work on much more detailed cost breakdowns, drawings, plans, and so on. This intent to finance is usually necessary before the developer invests additional funds in more detailed planning. However, this detailed planning must be completed before the permanent lender issues a *commitment*. The interim lender, who will be monitoring construction progress and compliance with plans and specifications, will certainly require detailed plans. The methods used to underwrite and analyze market and financial data will be covered in a case example later in the chapter.

The information in Part A of Exhibit 15–2 will generally not be complete when the developer first approaches a permanent lender for funding, because in most cases the development concept and strategy will not be finalized. Keep in mind that the submission should contain as much information as possible; however, both lenders will have specific questions and requests for supporting data that the developer must provide. Hence, obtaining both permanent and construction financing should be viewed as a continuing process between all of the parties that may take several rounds of review by all concerned before any written commitments are made.

The Permanent or Take-Out Commitment. Assuming that an interim and a permanent loan are to be used, the permanent lender makes a commitment in writing and specifies *contingencies* (to be discussed in more detail below) that the developer-borrower must meet before the permanent lender's commitment becomes legally binding. When these contingencies are met, the permanent lender will provide funds for the developer to repay the construction loan. If any of the contingencies in the take-out commitment are not met, the permanent lender is not obligated to fund the permanent loan. In this event, the developer must seek another permanent loan, or the construction lender may have to continue to carry financing on the completed project, or the developer may face a foreclosure proceeding initiated by the interim lender when the interim loan expires. The

[3]The information contained in Exhibit 15–2 is not meant to be an exhaustive list of required documentation and requirements for obtaining loans. For a good treatment of legal considerations in construction lending, see Richard Harris, *Construction and Development Financing* (New York: Warren, Gorham, and Lamont, 1982).

EXHIBIT 15–2 General Submission and Closing Requirements for Project Development Loans

A. General requirements for a loan submission package.

1. Project information.

    a. Project description—legal description of site, survey, photographs of site, renderings of building and any parking facilities, development strategy and timing.

    b. Site and circulation plan, identification of any easements, availability of utilities, description of adjacent land uses, soil tests.

    c. Plans for building improvements. Detailed list of amenities.

    d. Identification of architect, general contractor, principal subcontractors. Supporting financial data and past performance of parties. Copies of any agreements executed among parties. Description of construction and development procedures.

2. Market and financial data.

    a. Full set of financial statements on the borrower and any other principal project sponsors, past development experience, list of previous project lenders.

    b. Pro forma operating statement. Detail on proposed leasing terms to tenants including base rent, escalations, expense stops, renewal options, common area expense allocation, overage (retail leases), finish-out allowances, other commitments.

    c. Detailed cost breakdowns including:

    - Any land acquisition costs.
    - Any necessary land development costs.
    - Any required demolition costs.
    - Direct or hard costs with breakdowns for excavation, grading, foundation, masonry, steel work, drywall or plastering, HVAC, plumbing, electrical, elevator, and other mechanical items, any special finish-out or fixtures.
    - Indirect or soft costs, including architects, engineering fees, legal fees, property taxes, interest-construction period, development fees, insurance and bonding fees, estimated contingency reserve, anticipated permanent loan fees.

    d. Any executed lease commitments or letters of intent from tenants detailing all terms of leases.

    e. Market study and appraisal including all comparables and detached schedule of rents charged by competitors.

    f. Loan request, terms, anticipated interest rate, amortization period, anticipated participation options.

    g. Equity to be provided by developer and/or other sponsors (cash and/or land); anticipated financing of draws/repayment.

3. Government and regulatory information.

    a. Statement as to zoning status.

    b. Ad valorem taxes, method of payment, reappraisal dates.

    c. All necessary permits, evidence of approved zoning variances, etc. (see list in Exhibit 16–2).

4. Legal documentation.

    a. Legal entity applying for loan (evidence of incorporation, partnership agreement).

    b. Statement of land cost or contract evidencing purchase.

    c. Detail regarding deed restrictions, etc. (see Exhibit 18–2).

    d. Subordination agreements (see Exhibit 18–2).

    e. Force majeure provisions (events beyond the control of the developer such as an "act of God").

B. Additional information needed for interim loan package (if two loans are used).

1. A copy of the permanent or standby commitment from the permanent lender. Details on the amount, rate, term, fees, options relative to prepayment, calls, and participation. Details on contingencies that the developer must meet before the commitment is binding (the chapter explains these contingencies).
2. *Detailed* architectural plans and specifications.
3. *Detailed* cost breakdown.
4. All data relative to requirements listed in Part A and *updated* as appropriate.

Assuming that (1) upon review of all relevant materials in A and B, the interim lender makes a commitment and (2) the developer goes forward with the project, the next step will be to close the interim loan.

C. Interim lender closing requirements.

1. Project information: *final* drawings, cost estimates, site plan, etc.

2. Market and financial information: statement that no adverse change in borrower's financial position has occurred since application date.
3. Government and regulatory information: all necessary permits, notification of any approved zoning variances, etc. (also see list in Exhibit 16–2).
4. Legal documentation.
   a. Documentation indicating that the permanent lender has reviewed and approved all information in Part A and all updates in Part B.
   b. All documentation relative to contracts for general contractors, architects, planners, subcontractors. Evidence of bonding, conditional assignment of all contracts to interim lender. Agreements of all contractors to perform for interim lender. Verification of property tax insurance contracts, etc. (see list B in Exhibit 18–2 dealing with closing requirements in land development financing).
   c. Inventory of all personal property that will serve as security for the interim loan (particularly important for shopping centers and hotels).
   d. Any executed leases and approvals by permanent lender.
   e. Copies of ground leases and verification of current payment status by the lessor/owner.
   f. The interim lender will also insist on an assignment of all leases, rents, and other income in the event of default *and* a guarantee of loan payments by the borrower (personal liability). After review of all items indicated above, the interim lender will provide the borrower with a loan commitment detailing the terms of the loan including amount, rate, term, fees, prepayment and call options, and any participations. However, the *permanent* lender may require certain agreements with the interim lender, including a buy-sell agreement or triparty agreement (discussed in chapter).

D. Permanent lender closing requirements.

These requirements are necessary *if* the developer (1) completes construction and (2) satisfies all contingencies (including lease-up requirements) contained in the permanent loan commitment before the expiration date of the permanent commitment.

1. Market and financial data.
   a. Statement of no material changes in financial status of borrower, or,
   b. A certified list of tenants, executed leases, and estoppel certificates indicating verification of rents currently being collected, any amounts owed, and any dispute relative to payments on finish-out costs agreements with the developer.
2. Project information.
   a. Final appraisal of project value.
   b. Final survey of building on site.
3. Government and regulatory information.
   a. Updates on currency of property taxes.
   b. Certificate of occupancy issued by building inspector.
   c. Other permit requirements (fire, safety, health, etc.)
4. Legal documentation.
   a. Delivery of the construction loan mortgage (if assigned to the permanent lender).
   b. Architect's certificate of completion with detailed survey and final plans, etc.
   c. Endorsements of all casualty and hazard insurance policies indicating permanent lender as new loss payee.
   d. Updated title insurance policy.
   e. Updated verification on status of ground rents (if relevant).
   f. An exculpation agreement, relieving the borrower of personal liability (if applicable).
   g. Lien releases from general subcontractors verification of any payments outstanding and proposed disposition.

---

intent of the take-out commitment, then, is to create a legally binding agreement between the developer and permanent lender, whereby the permanent lender fully intends to make a long-term loan on the property after the building is completed, satisfactory levels of leasing have been accomplished, and other contingencies have been satisfied.

Standby Commitments

Standby commitments may be obtained occasionally from a "standby" lender when (1) the developer cannot or does not want to pay fees to obtain a permanent loan commitment, or because (2) the borrower expects to find a permanent loan commitment elsewhere after construction is underway and preleasing occurs, on better borrowing terms, or (3) the developer is planning to sell the project upon completion and lease-up and does not believe a permanent loan will be needed. Like the permanent loan, standby commitment funds are used to repay the construction loan. While standby commitments are similar to a permanent take-out loan in terms of the contingencies and other contents of the agreement, they differ from permanent take-outs in that neither the borrower nor the standby lender really *expects* the standby commitment to be used. However, because the developer-borrower wants to begin development, and the interim lender wants assurance of a take-out, the developer may have to find a standby commitment *at the insistence* of the interim lender. If the developer does not sell the project, or a permanent take-out cannot be found upon completion of the project, then the standby commitment will be used and the permanent loan will be closed with the lender who made the standby commitment.

Even though permanent lenders who offer standby commitments charge a commitment fee and are legally bound to deliver mortgage funds on the completion date, many banks are unwilling to make construction loans when a borrower has only a standby commitment because the commitment is made with a low expectation of being used. In many cases, should the borrower decide to use the commitment, the standby lender may be very inflexible concerning contingencies in it. For example, lenders who have issued standbys may look for "technical violations" of contingencies in the commitment (for example, minor changes in construction plans and substitution of building materials that were not approved by the standby lender, and so on). One problem interim lenders face is determining when the developer and provider of permanent funding *intend* a commitment to be permanent and when they *intend* it as a standby. The agreement may not have explicit wording as to whether it is a take-out or standby commitment. Careful analysis of the permanent funding agreement the developer provides is important because if market conditions change, the developer and interim lender may consider the standby lender legally bound to provide funds, while the standby lender may balk because of the expectation that the project would be sold or long-term financing would be found on more attractive terms and the standby lender would not have to deliver.

Contingencies in Lending Commitments

When a developer obtains a permanent loan commitment prior to actual development and prior to obtaining a construction loan, the permanent lender usually includes **contingencies** in the commitment. In cases where an interim loan or mini-perm loan is to be used, many of these same contingencies must be satisfied before a lender is willing to release the developer from personal liability, thereby making the note *nonrecourse* against the borrower. As pointed out, if the developer does not fulfill the requirements under these contingencies, the permanent lender does not have to fund the loan. Common contingencies found in take-out commitments obtained from permanent lenders include these:

- The maximum period of time allowed for the developer to acquire a construction loan commitment.
- Completion date for the construction phase of the project.
- Minimum rent-up (leasing) requirements and approval of all major leases in order for permanent financing to become effective.

- Provisions for gap financing should the rent-up requirement not be met.
- Expiration date of the permanent loan commitment and any provisions for extensions.
- Approval of design changes and substitution of any building materials by the permanent lender.

Essentially, these items represent common contingencies that must be negotiated before a lender issues a permanent loan commitment. When financing is being sought on proposed projects, these contingencies are especially important because they establish that the permanent loan will be made when the developer has performed as promised.

These contingencies are indispensable to permanent lenders because they require that developers carry out certain responsibilities during development or prior to the expiration date of the permanent commitment. For example, the first two provisions in the preceding list require that the borrower have a specified time to find an interim lender willing to make a loan to cover construction and development costs, and that the project be completed by a specific date. The permanent lender must rely on a local lender such as a bank to provide construction, or interim, funds and to monitor construction quality. Because large permanent lenders are usually life insurance companies, pension funds, and the like, they are not likely to be located in the city where the project is to be developed. The completion date contingency provides an incentive for developers to work as efficiently as possible toward completion of construction and leasing the building space or face the possibility of losing the loan commitment.

As for leasing requirements, this contingency is used to help assure permanent lenders that local economic conditions, that are being used to justify the appraised value and feasibility of the project are favorable. The permanent lender requires a provision such as this to shift some project risk to the interim lender who should be very familiar with the local market and who specializes in construction lending in that market. The interim lender must carefully consider conditions in the local market because should the project not rent up to a specified percentage of occupancy by the expiration date, the rent-up contingency will not be met. This means that the permanent lender will not have to fund the commitment. Unless the permanent lender is willing to modify the terms of the permanent commitment, expiration would force the construction lender to extend its interim loan beyond the term originally intended and, perhaps, to become the permanent lender.

In many cases, the permanent lender may agree that if the occupancy requirement is not met, funds will be advanced on a pro rata basis or in proportion to occupancy achieved by the expiration date. Advances would then be made toward full funding as occupancy increases.

When a construction lender is unwilling to accept a pro rata funding takeout, however, the developer may have to find a third-party lender to stand by and provide a **gap financing** commitment. This commitment provides that the "gap" between any partial funding advanced by the permanent lender (because a rental achievement has not been met by the developer as of the date the permanent loan is scheduled to close) and the funds needed to repay the construction lender will be provided by a gap lender. The gap lender usually takes a second lien position and earns interest at a higher rate than both the interim and permanent lenders plus a nonrefundable gap commitment fee. Funds provided by the gap lender and permanent lender repay the interim lender. As the project leases up and the permanent lender releases more funds, the developer uses them to repay the gap lender.[4] The developer also uses gap lending when cost overruns in excess of both the construction and permanent commitments occur, or if a permanent loan commitment is less than the construction loan. In either instance, the gap lender will analyze the project and, if convinced that it is acceptable risk, may take a second lien position.

The last item in the preceding list of contingencies, that is, approval of construction and design changes, assures permanent lenders that developers will complete projects substantially as agreed—they will not substitute substandard materials and use shortcuts to save costs that may jeopardize project quality. Poor project quality could obviously affect the leasing success of a project and, therefore, the collateral security for the permanent loan. Consequently, interim lenders usually insist that they retain the right to approve all substitutions of material and design changes.

The Construction or Interim Loan

As indicated previously, before developers and lenders negotiate construction loans on income-producing properties, the developer may have already obtained a commitment for a permanent loan or a standby loan. The developer presents much of the same information about the proposed project used to obtain the permanent loan (shown in Part A of Exhibit 15–2) as support for obtaining interim financing. The permanent lender is generally not interested in making the interim loan because construction lenders are knowledgeable about local market conditions and are able to monitor construction progress and disburse funds as phases of the project are completed. This activity in development lending requires knowledge of construction methods and materials, and the construction lender can usually perform it more cost-effectively. However, because of the contingencies the permanent lender requires of the developer, the construction lender must also evaluate the information in the permanent loan submission very carefully. In the event that the construction lender makes a commitment to fund the project's development and the developer does not meet the take-out contingencies, the permanent loan will not be funded and the construction lender will be forced to provide permanent funding for the project or call the construction loan due on the completion date, which could force the developer into bankruptcy.

In some cases, rather than negotiating a construction loan and a permanent loan, a developer may obtain a *single* loan from an interim lender and use it to finance construction and operations for a year or two beyond the lease-up stage. This variation, used in place of obtaining both a construction loan and a permanent loan, is the so-called **mini-perm loan**.[5] It was used extensively during the 1980 development boom throughout the United States as lenders aggressively competed against one another for a larger share of the construction loan market. Developers using this approach expected either to sell or refinance the project on very attractive terms at or before maturity. Lenders, primarily savings and loans and commercial banks, offered these loans as "one-stop shopping" that enabled developers to proceed without obtaining a permanent loan.

---

[4]In some cases, as the expiration date for closing the permanent loan nears, the construction lender may agree to become a "gap lender" if the rental achievement is not met. The construction lender may do so to keep the permanent commitment alive, particularly if the borrower cannot find a third-party gap lender.

[5]In cases where a mini-perm loan is negotiated, most of the material presented in the chapter is relevant, although some redundancy in documentation and other requirements is eliminated when one loan is used to finance a project.

Methods of Disbursement—Construction Lending

Generally, the construction loan is secured by a mortgage for future advances or by an open-end mortgage. The construction lender usually requires a first lien on the land and all improvements as they are constructed on the site. Construction lenders follow the cardinal rule of never advancing loan funds in excess of the economic value of the property that serves as security for the loan. In other words, the construction lender never wants the developer "to get ahead" on a draw schedule by drawing down funds in excess of the cost of construction improvements made to date.

The most commonly used method to disburse funds for commercial development is the **monthly draw method**. This method is used extensively in the construction of larger-scale projects requiring sizable loans. The developer requests a draw each month based on the work completed during the preceding month. If an architect or engineer verifies to the lender that such work is in place, the lender disburses the funds. Again, the collateral value for the loan increases simultaneously with the disbursement of funds.

In some cases, the developer submits invoices to a title insurance company, if the lender is using one, which updates the title abstract between each draw and then approves payment on the invoices. As payments are made, contractors and subcontractors sign an agreement that they have been paid for work done to date.[6] This usually precludes them from filing mechanics' liens.[7]

Interest Rates and Fees

As with many business loans, interest rates on construction loans are generally based on short-term interest rates that may vary considerably from period to period in response to current lending conditions. Most lenders, particularly commercial banks, usually rely on a system of floating interest rates on construction loans. Floating rates may be based on the bank's prime lending rate or the short-term interest rate charged on commercial loans to the bank's most creditworthy customers. However, some short-term loans may be based on either Treasury bill rates or the London Interbank Offering Rate (LIBOR). The lender normally evaluates a construction loan as to risk during the underwriting process, and the interest rate quoted on the loan reflects the short-term rate to which the loan will be tied *plus* a premium that is added to that rate. For example, an interest rate on a construction loan may be quoted as "two points over prime." This means that if the loan is tied to a 10 percent prime rate at closing, the interest rate charged on the construction loan will be 12 percent. Because the interest rate on construction loans is a "floating rate," the actual interest expense that the developer must pay can differ substantially from the amount budgeted or included in the loan request. In other words, the developer may bear the interest rate risk during the development period. The construction lender may also charge loan commitment fees.

Additional Information for Interim Loan Submission

Section B of Exhibit 15–2 summarizes some additional requirements for an interim loan submission that generally supplements and updates the material provided to the permanent lender. The developer provides this additional information, *assuming* that the preliminary data supplied to the permanent lender are satisfactory and the developer has obtained a permanent take-out commitment. Much of the documentation

---

[6]On a very large scale (projects that will take an extensive period of time to finish and involve many vendors and contractors), title companies frequently make disbursements and verify that no liens have been filed since the previous draw.

[7]Liens created during construction can cause problems for a developer in closing the permanent loan or selling the property when it is completed.

required by the *construction lender* depends on the terms and conditions contained in the permanent loan commitment. Hence, the interim lender must be in a position to review the permanent, or take-out, commitment as well as the final set of development plans and updated information for each component of the loan submission listed in Part A. Further, the interim lender will usually want assurance that the permanent lender reviews all of these updates prior to closing the construction loan.

Requirements to Close the Interim Loan

Although this chapter focuses on financing, Part C in Exhibit 15–2 lists general requirements the developer supplies to close the interim loan. Generally speaking, if the interim lender has expressed an interest to fund construction, the lender will issue a commitment letter containing all necessary requirements and documentation to close the loan.

Assignment of Commitment Letter. When a developer obtains commitments for two loans to finance a project, a legal obligation exists between the developer and each of the two lenders, but no legal obligation exists between the two lenders. To create such an obligation, the construction lender may require that the borrower obtain the right to assign the take-out commitment from the permanent lender to the interim lender. In this way, if the project is finished by the completion date and all contingencies are met, the construction lender can collect mortgage funds directly from the permanent lender, bypassing the developer. Also, should any disagreement occur between the developer and permanent lender, the construction lender, by obtaining assignment of the commitment, may pursue enforcement of the commitment directly with the permanent lender. Assignment of the commitment also limits the developer's ability to terminate the permanent loan commitment and seek another during construction.

Triparty Buy-Sell Agreement. In lieu of assignment of the take-out commitment, the developer, construction lender, and long-term lender may enter into a more formal agreement in which (1) the permanent lender agrees to buy the construction mortgage loan directly from the construction lender on the completion date, assuming all contingencies are met, and (2) the two lenders agree about their duties and responsibilities. This formal agreement goes beyond the assignment of the take-out commitment and provides that the permanent lender will notify the interim lender that the take-out commitment is in full effect, that the permanent lender will indicate whether all necessary plans and documents have been reviewed and approved prior to closing the construction loan, and that the permanent lender will provide the construction lender with notice of any violations in the terms of the loan commitment by the developer and the time available to cure such a violation.

The goal of this agreement is to create legal responsibilities between the borrower, the permanent lender, and the construction lender. In this way, both lenders are more likely to be better informed as to the progress that the developer is making and whether any problems are likely to occur when it is time to close the permanent loan. With this approach, the permanent lender also has more assurance that the permanent loan will be made at the agreed-upon rate of interest and other terms. Otherwise, when the permanent lender makes the take-out commitment, some question may remain about whether the developer has a mandatory commitment to close the permanent loan. Indeed, if the developer finds another commitment on more favorable terms, he may choose to forfeit any commitment fees and close with the new lender. In that case, since funding will be available to repay the construction loan, the original lender may not object. But, by using a triparty agreement, the construction lender agrees not to accept funding from any source other than the initial permanent lender.

The Permanent Loan Closing

After completion of the construction and lease-up period, assuming that all contingencies enumerated in the take-out commitment are met, the permanent loan will be closed and the construction lender is "taken out," or repaid, with funds advanced from the permanent lender. From this point, the borrower will begin to make monthly mortgage payments from rental revenues. Part D of Exhibit 15–2 lists some of the general requirements for the permanent loan closing. Keep in mind that even though the permanent lender may have made a take-out or permanent commitment, that commitment will not be funded until the loan is ready to be closed, or after the project has been completed. Hence, the permanent lender will be in a position to evaluate whether all building and material specifications, leasing, and so on, have been carried out in conformance with what the developer promised when the permanent funding commitment was issued. Further, the permanent lender will also be in a position to ascertain whether all contingencies have been met before the permanent loan is closed.

A recent trend in the field of real estate finance has been to limit the liability of borrowers after all contingencies have been met, the permanent loan has been closed, and the project is operating normally. Liability can be limited by including an **exculpation,** or **nonrecourse, clause** in the permanent mortgage. Essentially, this clause limits the liability of borrowers by restricting the claim of lenders to proceeds from the sale of the real estate in the event of default. Because this relieves the developer of part of, or all, personal liability, it potentially reduces the lender's ability to recover losses in the event of default and foreclosure. This is a point that lenders and borrowers negotiate seriously. Liability limitations also place more underwriting emphasis on the quality of the property from the lender's perspective, since income produced from the property must repay the loan, and the property value must always be sufficiently high to repay the loan balance should a property become financially troubled.

If an exculpation clause is not a part of the permanent loan, the permanent lender will want to be very careful to ascertain that no material change in the financial status of the borrower has occurred since the commitment date. No lender wants to be in a position of funding a developer heading toward bankruptcy. But "material change" can present a problem because the criteria used to ascertain what constitutes a material change may differ between the interim and permanent lenders, and the permanent lender may refuse to close the loan. In some cases, enhancements, such as letters of credit or third-party guarantees, may be required of the developer by either the interim lender or the permanent lender at the outset, in anticipation of potential problems.

Project Development Illustrated

Project Description and Project Costs

What follows is a case example of Rolling Meadows Center, a high-quality shopping center development located in an upper-income neighborhood proposed by Southfork Development Co. Southfork plans to develop, then own and operate Rolling Meadows for a long period of time. It plans to use both interim and permanent

Exhibit 15–3 Project Description for Rolling Meadows

A. Site and proposed improvements	
Site area (in acres)	9.5
Gross buildable area (*GBA*)	120,000 sq. ft.
Gross leasable area (*GLA*)	110,000 sq. ft.
Percent leasable area	91.67%
Floor area ratio (site area)	29.00%
Parking index	5 spaces/1,000 sq.ft. (*GLA*)
Parking spaces	550
B. Development period	12 months
C. Site plan	
Building coverage	29%
Street parking	45%
Open space/landscaping	26%
Total	100%
D. Loan information	
Construction loan	
Loan term	12 months
% of construction loan drawn in the first 4 months	75%
% of construction loan drawn in the last months	25%
Interest rate	12%
Construction loan fee	2%
Permanent loan	
Debt amortization	25 years
Term of loan	10 years
Interest rate	12%
Permanent loan fee	3%
E. Anticipated hold after completion	5 years

financing and has approached the Citadel Life Insurance Company to provide permanent financing. If Southfork planned to sell the shopping center after completion and lease-up, it might have elected to pursue a mini-perm loan. In either case, much of the underwriting analysis and contingencies that follow would be applicable. Exhibit 15–3 contains a breakdown of site size, floor-to-area ratio, parking, and anticipated construction and permanent financing. It also provides percentage breakdowns for building coverage, parking, and open space. The lender will review the percentage breakdowns to ascertain whether the density of the project development on the site is too high and whether parking is adequate. The lender will pay particular attention to the site plan and ease of traffic circulation on the site. Citadel will have access to comparative data for this project from previous project financing files and from industry statistics.[8]

Exhibit 15–4 breaks down development costs into land acquisition costs, off-site costs, hard costs, and soft costs. These costs are also broken down as a percentage of total cost and cost per square foot of gross building area (*GBA*).

Depending on the type of shopping center (e.g., strip, neighborhood, specialty, regional mall), lenders will want to know whether the relative breakdown of costs conforms to average breakdowns for recently developed neighborhood centers in comparable locations. Land costs that are too high or hard costs that are too low relative to land costs may mean that the total cost of developing an adequate mix of

[8]One important source of data is the Urban Land Institute's *Dollars and Cents of Shopping Centers*.

EXHIBIT 15–4 Summary of Cost Information for Rolling Meadows

		Cost	Percent of Total Cost	Cost per Sq. Ft. GBA
A. Land and site improvements:				
Site acquisition and closing costs		$ 2,500,000	20.9%	$20.83
On/off-site improvement costs:				
Off-site improvements	$ 250,000			
On-site improvements:				
Excavation and grading	50,000			
Sewer/water	150,000			
Paving	200,000			
Curbs/sidewalks	100,000			
Landscaping	100,000			
Total on/off-site costs		$ 850,000	7.1%	$ 7.08
B. Construction costs:				
Hard costs:				
Shell structure	$3,925,000			
HVAC	528,500			
Electrical	613,000			
Plumbing	221,580			
Project management fees	300,250			
Finish-out	1,400,600			
Graphics/signage	66,570			
Total hard costs		$ 7,055,500	58.9%	$58.80
Soft costs:				
Architect engineering	$ 147,000			
Fees and permits	24,300			
Legal fees	26,900			
Construction interest	692,416			
Construction loan fees	180,028			
Permanent loan fees	270,042			
Leasing commissions	45,300			
Direct overhead	160,000			
Indirect overhead	30,800			
Total soft costs		$ 1,576,787	13.2%	$13.14
Total project costs		$11,982,287	100.0%	$99.85

Construction Loan Request:	
Total on/off-site improvements	$ 850,000
Total hard construction costs	7,055,500
Soft costs	403,500
Total costs to be financed	8,309,000
Estimated interest carry	692,416
Total loan amount	9,001,416
Equity requirements	2,980,871
Total project cost	$11,982,287

retail space of adequate quality may not be achievable at prevailing market rents. Similarly, common areas (difference between gross building area and gross leasable area) that are too large or too small may affect the ability to lease space and can be detrimental to profitability. The "correct" mix of location improvements, density, parking, circulation, and design is crucial to success.

In many cases, lenders will not fund any land acquisition costs or base loans as a percentage of appraised value. In other words, lenders prefer to make loans to cover improvement costs only, and the developer may be expected to contribute the land as equity. Further, lenders usually require a first lien on the land and all improvements made with the proceeds of the construction loan. They do so because loans based on appraised value alone may result in the lender advancing funds in excess of the market value of the property if the appraisal is in error. For example, if the lender agrees to lend 80 percent of the total project value and the appraisal (which you must realize is being done for a project that is still in the planning and design stages) results in an overestimate of value in the range of 130 percent of actual value upon completion, then the loan advances would equal 104 percent of actual value (80 percent of 130 percent). Further, if an overoptimistic assessment of future rental achievement caused the overestimate of project value, the developer may have difficulty servicing the mortgage debt. This difficulty obviously creates problems for the developer and for the interim lender who may be looking to a permanent lender to take out the construction loan. Recall that the take-out commitment may contain contingencies relative to leasing and rental achievement and may also contain a requirement that the final project appraised value exceed the permanent loan commitment by a specified percentage. If these provisions are not achieved, the interim lender and developer may have difficulty enforcing the take-out commitment.

We do not mean to say that lenders never consider appraised values in loan requests. Most lenders realize that the loan being requested must represent a reasonable percentage of appraised value. Reasonable percentage generally means that if the loan-to-value ratio for the proposed project is 80 percent, the lender anticipates that the improvement costs plus any other development costs that the lender is willing to fund should also be in the range of 80 percent. The funding percentage, in turn, implies that land values and other costs not funded in the loan should be in the range of 20 percent. In other words, the lender is looking for an equity contribution of 20 percent by the developer. If improvement costs were estimated to be 90 percent of value, for example, the lender may still be willing to fund only 80 percent of value. In this case, all improvement costs would not be funded. An alternative way of looking at the loan-to-appraised-value relationship is that a lender may, in our example, prefer to provide funds equal to the lower of either all improvement costs or 80 percent of project value.

Many lenders will not fund off-site improvements that are part of a loan request because other parties may have title to the land on which improvements will be made. Even if the developer has title to the off-site land, the construction lender may have difficulty acquiring satisfactory lien security on the land where the off-site improvements will be made. The ability to acquire funding of off-site costs depends on the lender's judgment as to how far in excess of the total loan amount the value of the project will be when completed.

Most lenders will fund all hard costs if they can be documented and are commensurate with the overall quality of the development. Lenders, however, vary in their willingness to fund many soft-cost items. They may not be willing to fund closing fees associated with the land acquisition, financing fees, planning and design fees, permitting fees, and/or any overhead charges the developer requests as a part of the project cost. This is because these changes represent fees for services, or intangibles which may be regarded as difficult to recover in the event of default or bankruptcy should a property have to be auctioned or sold to repay the construction loan. Hard costs represent outlays for tangible improvements (e.g., bricks and mortar) and are thought to be better security than outlays for intangibles, even though the latter are necessary. In most cases, however, an estimate of construction interest carry is *included* in the loan request.

Construction Loan Request. Exhibit 15–4 also contains a breakdown of the *loan request*. Note that this particular loan request does not include land cost. Also note that it does not ask for financing for all soft costs. However, Southfork is requesting funding for some off-site improvements. The total loan request is $9,001,416, which represents about 75 percent of the $11,982,287 estimate of total project cost (land plus all other outlays). Also, note in Exhibit 15–4 that the request includes construction period interest as part of the loan. This is very common in construction lending because the project will not provide any rent or cash inflow during development. Therefore, the developer will usually be allowed to borrow the interest as one additional cost of construction. An estimate of *construction period interest* is made by computing the *monthly draw rate* for construction costs to be funded by the lender over the 12-month period. This is illustrated in Exhibit 15–5.

Note in the exhibit that the draw rates shown in column (*a*) are calculated by determining expected monthly draws for direct costs ($8,309,000). Also note that the estimated interest is $692,416. This consists of interest calculated at 12% ÷ 12 months, or 1 percent per month on the cumulative loan balance shown in column (*c*). Interest draws are computed on the outstanding monthly loan balance and are borrowed as a part of the construction cost draws at the end of each month. The developer makes cash interest payments (column *d*) to the bank each month. However, because all of the interest carry is borrowed it becomes part of the loan balance and because all monthly payments made by the developer are interest only, no reduction of principal occurs. In short, this pattern is analogous to an interest-only loan discussed in previous chapters. The reader may recall that these loans require no reduction in loan principal because payments are computed to include interest payments only. Also note that the interest payments in column (*d*) are exactly offset by the interest draw in column (*b*). Thus the net effect is as if there were no payment to the lender until the entire loan balance is repaid at the end of the construction period. This is analogous to a negative amortization loan with the loan balance increasing by the amount of interest accrued each month.

In summary, Exhibit 15–5 shows that the loan balance will increase each month by the amount of the project cost draws plus interest borrowed. The total ending balance, $9,001,416, will be equal to the total construction loan amount at the end of the 12-month period. This amount will be funded by the permanent lender, thereby taking out the construction lender at that time. In most cases, the permanent loan and the interim loan commitments are made for the same amount.

Even though developers may estimate costs very carefully, the *actual* costs of development and interest carry will differ from such estimates because of uncertainties in the rate at which work will progress and because interest rates may change. Hence, it is likely that the *actual* interest draw pattern will deviate from the *estimated* pattern. Once the $9,001,416 commitment amount is reached however, the construction lender *is not required to fund any more draws, and the permanent lender is not required to fund any more than the committed amount.* If the developer does not want to bear the risk of unanticipated interest rate changes and the possibility of interest cost overruns, she can eliminate, or at least reduce, that risk for a fee by purchasing an interest rate swap.

EXHIBIT 15–5 Projected Loan Repayment Schedule for Rolling Meadows Center

	Loan Draws			Payments		
End of Month	(a) Project Costs	(b) Construction Interest	(c) Loan Balance	(d) Interest	(e) Principal Reduction	(f) Ending Loan Balance
0	$ 0	$ 0	$ 0	$ 0	$ 0	$ 0
1	1,557,938	0	1,557,938	0	0	1,557,938
2	1,557,938	15,579	3,131,454	15,579	0	3,131,454
3	1,557,938	31,315	4,720,706	31,315	0	4,720,706
4	1,557,938	47,207	6,325,851	47,207	0	6,325,851
5	259,656	63,259	6,648,766	63,259	0	6,648,766
6	259,656	66,488	6,974,910	66,488	0	6,974,910
7	259,656	69,749	7,304,315	69,749	0	7,304,315
8	259,656	73,043	7,637,014	73,043	0	7,637,014
9	259,656	76,370	7,973,041	76,370	0	7,973,041
10	259,656	79,730	8,312,427	79,730	0	8,312,427
11	259,656	83,124	8,655,208	83,124	0	8,655,208
12	259,656	86,552	9,001,416	86,552	$9,001,416	0
Total	$8,309,000	$692,416				

If the developer does not want to bear the cost of eliminating interest rate risk, she will have to provide additional funds (perhaps by attracting more partners to the venture) or find a gap lender or equity partners. If actual costs exceed estimated costs because of material and labor cost overruns, unanticipated changes in interest rates,[9] a longer than anticipated lease-up period because of a declining market, and so on, and if the developer cannot find other sources of equity (through a partnership or similar arrangement) or a gap loan, and if the interim lender refuses to extend additional funds, the developer may face foreclosure.

Lenders and developers also use a draw, interest, and repayment schedule similar to that shown in Exhibit 15–5 as a tool for financial control. They may use this schedule in conjunction with field surveys completed by staff engineers to verify that the total percentage of *work in place* at the end of each month corresponds to the outstanding loan balance at the end of each month. If the lender feels that total funds drawn down are in excess of construction in place, the lender will not allow further draws until offsetting improvements are made. Note that because the construction lender charges a 2 percent loan origination fee, the loan yield will be about 15.5 percent, as compared with the 12 percent rate of interest used to compute interest on the loan. This yield is calculated by finding the rate of discount that makes the present value of monthly outflows in months 1 through 12 plus the lump sum inflow also in month 12 equal to the loan fees charged at closing by the interim lender, or $180,028.

[9]Some developers use the interest rate futures to hedge against interest rate risk when using floating interest rate loans.

A final note regarding the draw schedule has to do with lenders' use of **holdbacks**. Generally, when project developers contract with various building contractors to perform work, developers hold back a percentage (10 percent) of each progress payment made to such contractors until all work is satisfactorily completed. Holding back payments assures the developer that all work has been completed in accordance with plans and specifications. When work is completed to the developer's satisfaction, the final payment is made to the contractors. Most lenders are aware of holdback practices and will in turn hold back a percentage (10 percent) of all loan draw requests from developers. Lender holdbacks prevent developers from drawing down funds at a faster rate than they must pay to contractors. Exhibit 15–5 does not take holdbacks into account. However, you should be aware of this practice and take holdbacks into account in the draw schedule if applicable.

Permanent Loan Request. Upon completion of the project, Citadel Life Insurance Company will replace the construction loan with permanent financing, assuming that all conditions in the construction loan and all contingencies outlined in the permanent financing commitment have been met. Remember, the permanent loan terms outlined in Exhibit 15–6 were predetermined before construction began. Any additional development costs over $9,001,416 are Southfork's responsibility. For a 3 percent loan fee, Citadel Life Insurance Company will provide Southfork with a 10-year mortgage. Monthly payments will be $94,805 based on a 25-year amortization schedule at an interest rate of 12 percent.

Market Data and Tenant Mix

Exhibit 15–7 contains a breakdown of the expected tenant mix for Rolling Meadows and the space tenants are expected to occupy. For a neighborhood center, most lenders would expect at least one predevelopment lease commitment from a food chain and/or general merchandiser. Obviously, if favorable predevelopment lease commitments accompany the loan request, it is more likely that a commitment will be made. The other data in the exhibit are based on experience from U.S. data averages and with averages obtained from local market surveys. It should be stressed that exact comparability in tenant mix is not expected in each and every project submitted for review. However, past experience usually indicates that certain types of tenants are not compatible (e.g., auto parts and jewelry stores) in the same center, whereas other tenants are compatible (e.g., jewelry stores and furriers). A submission that indicates a lack of understanding regarding tenant mix may reveal developer inexperience. Further, the tenant breakdown should be realistic—if the developer projects too many "high-end" retail stores (which usually pay high rents), it may indicate overoptimism.

EXHIBIT 15–6 Summary of Permanent Loan Terms

Total loan	$9,001,416
Debt amortization	25
Term of loan	10
Interest rate	12.00%
Debt service/month	$ 94,805
Debt service/year	$1,137,661
3% permanent loan fee	$ 270,042
Yield to permanent lender	12.55%

EXHIBIT 15–7 Market Survey Data—Shopping Centers (tenant information)

Classification	*Number of Stores*	*% of Tenants**	*Sq. Ft. of GLA*	*% GLA*	*U.S. Avg.%*	*Local Avg.%*
General merchandise	1	3.57%	4,950	4.50%	5.60%	5.20%
Food	2	7.14	37,400	34.00	30.80	36.00
Food service	1	3.57	8,800	8.00	8.80	7.00
Clothing	3	10.71	7,700	7.00	5.00	6.00
Shoes	1	3.57	1,155	1.05	1.30	0.70
Home furnishings	1	3.57	1,100	1.00	2.60	2.30
Home appliances	1	3.57	990	0.90	2.40	1.00
Building materials	1	3.57	1,320	1.20	3.40	2.00
Automotive supplies	0	0.00	0	0.00	1.70	1.50
Hobby	1	3.57	2,035	1.85	2.70	2.50
Gifts and specialty	2	7.14	2,860	2.60	2.50	2.30
Jewelry and cosmetics	1	3.57	1,650	1.50	0.70	2.00
Liquor	1	3.57	1,430	1.30	1.50	1.50
Drugs	1	3.57	9,900	9.00	8.50	8.00
Other retail	6	21.46	12,100	11.00	4.40	6.00
Personal services	2	7.14	8,910	8.10	6.50	7.00
Recreational	1	3.57	2,200	2.00	3.50	3.00
Financial	1	3.57	3,300	3.00	4.10	3.00
Offices	1	3.57	2,200	2.00	4.00	3.00
Total	28	100.00%	110,000	100.00%	100.00%	100.00%

*Rounded.

In addition to the data shown in Exhibit 15–7, the developer will have to provide more detail regarding the trade area expected to be served by the center, a competitive analysis of other centers, and proof that the addition of another center will not oversupply that market with retail space. Additional information relative to population growth, age, households, income, retail spending patterns, and so forth (not shown), in the trade area must also support the loan request. The importance of these data cannot be stressed enough.

Pro Forma Construction Costs and Cash Flow Projections

Another necessary ingredient in the submission of data to the permanent lender is a pro forma (estimate) of construction costs and net operating income. Exhibit 15–8 contains annual estimates for expenditures during the construction period for land acquisition, site improvements, hard costs, and soft costs. Total loan draws are based on the $9,001,416 loan request (including interest), for which financing is being sought, over the two-year development period. Note that the developer will require $2,950,071 from internal sources at closing to cover land acquisition and loan fees, plus an additional $30,800 to cover indirect overhead, or total equity of $2,980,871. Citadel Life Insurance Co. will review Southfork's financial statements (not shown) to determine whether it has the ability to provide such funding from internal sources.

Exhibit 15–9 details the pro forma operating statement for Rolling Meadows. The lease-up or marketing effort should result in 70 percent occupancy during the second year and 95 percent thereafter. Southfork is estimating a base rent of $15 per square foot of gross leasable area, with average increases based on leases indexed to the CPI of 6 percent per year after the first year of operation (leases are expected to have terms ranging from one to five years). An overage provision requires tenants to also pay 5

EXHIBIT 15–8 Pro Forma Statement of Cash Flows—Construction Period

	Draws per Year		
	(0)	*(1)*	*Total*
Site acquisition and closing costs	$2,500,000		$ 2,500,000
Site improvements (on/off)		$ 850,000	850,000
Hard costs		7,055,500	7,055,500
Soft costs		$ 434,300	$ 434,300
Permanent loan fee	270,042		270,042
Construction loan fee	180,028		180,028
Construction interest		692,416	692,416
Total construction cash outflow	2,950,071	9,032,216	11,982,287
Less: Total draws	0	9,001,416	9,001,416
Total equity needed	$2,950,071	$ 30,800	$ 2,980,871

percent of gross sales in excess of a base sales level each month.[10] In a retail operation, rent is usually divided into two components. The first is a minimum rent per square foot. The other component is called **percentage rent**. Developers frequently charge percentage rent, calculated as a percentage of the sales of a tenant in excess of a predetermined *breakpoint* or sales volume. As long as the tenant's sales are below the breakpoint, the owner receives only the minimum rent. When a tenant's sales increase above the breakpoint, the percentage rent rate is applied to the sales volume in excess of the breakpoint and is added to the minimum rent, thus increasing the total rent. In this way, should the shopping center become very successful, the owner shares in the increased revenue produced by the tenants. The percentage rent shown in Exhibit 15–9 is estimated for all tenants in Rolling Meadows.

Tenant reimbursements are also shown in Exhibit 15–9. These amounts are based on negotiations between the owner and tenants and represent the amount of operating expenses over expense stops for which the tenant is responsible (recall the discussion of such stops in Chapter 10 for office buildings). Hence base rents, percentage rents, and expenses for which tenants are responsible over some preagreed amount (stop) all represent gross income to the owner of Rolling Meadows.

Operating expenses are also detailed in Exhibit 15–9. These amounts represent the actual expenses that must be paid to operate Rolling Meadows. They are deducted from rents, overage, and tenant reimbursements. All leases are to be *net to the tenant*, with a direct pass-through for insurance and property taxes. Tenants will also be billed for their share of common area maintenance (parking lot, circulation space in center, etc.) and utilities. An additional premium will be added to the utility charge to provide for a replacement reserve on HVAC equipment.[11] Tenants will pay these expenses to Southfork as reimbursement. Southfork management will, in

[10]Overages are common in retail leasing. The breakpoint is commonly determined by dividing the tenant's base rental amount (rate per square foot times rentable area) by the percentage rent negotiated between the owner and tenant. For further discussion see *Shopping Center Development Handbook Series* (Washington, DC) published by the Urban Land Institute.

[11]Note the difference in utility income to be collected from tenants and actual costs to be paid by Southfork management. This difference is a depreciation charge for utility equipment. Depending on competition for space in the retail market, the developer may or may not be able to negotiate this change.

EXHIBIT 15–9 Pro Forma Statement of Cash Flows—Operating Period

Cash Flows (EOP)	*(2)*	*(3)*	*(4)*	*(5)*	*(6)*
Income:					
Minimum rent	$1,650,000	$1,749,000	$1,853,940	$1,965,176	$2,083,087
Overage (5% of gross sales)	30,000	124,800	129,792	134,984	140,383
Tenant reimbursements					
Real estate taxes	137,500	143,000	148,720	154,669	160,856
Common area maintenance	385,000	400,400	416,416	433,073	450,396
Utilities	367,500	382,200	397,488	413,388	429,923
Insurance	33,000	34,320	35,693	37,121	38,605
Gross potential income	$2,603,000	$2,833,720	$2,982,049	$3,138,410	$3,303,249
Less: Vacancy allowance	780,900	141,686	149,102	156,920	165,162
Expected gross income	$1,822,100	$2,692,034	$2,832,947	$2,981,490	$3,138,087
Expenses:					
Management and leasing fees	$ 104,500	$93,690	$99,187	$ 105,008	$ 111,174
General and administrative	77,000	80,080	83,283	86,615	90,079
Real estate taxes	137,500	143,000	148,720	154,669	160,856
Common area maintenance	385,000	400,400	416,416	433,073	450,396
Utilities	300,300	312,312	324,804	337,797	351,309
Insurance	33,000	34,320	35,693	37,121	38,605
Other	27,500	28,600	29,744	30,934	32,171
Total expenses	$1,064,800	$1,092,402	$1,137,847	$1,185,215	$1,234,589
Net operating income	$ 757,300	$1,599,632	$1,695,099	$1,796,275	$1,903,498
Less: Debt service	1,137,661	1,137,661	1,137,661	1,137,661	1,137,661
Before-tax cash flow	$−380,361	$ 461,971	$ 557,438	$ 658,614	$ 765,837
Ratios:					
Operating expense		40.58%	40.16%	39.75%	39.34%
Debt coverage ratio		1.41	1.49	1.58	1.67
Free and clear return		13.35%	14.15%	14.99%	15.89%
Return on equity		15.50%	18.70%	22.09%	25.69%
Vacancy-collection loss		5.00%	5.00%	5.00%	5.00%
Break-even occupancy rate		78.70%	76.31%	74.01%	71.82%

turn, pay any expenses to third parties as they become due. Southfork will also incur expenses of its own for property management, leasing commissions, and general and administrative expenses that will not be recoverable from tenants. These amounts are deducted from rents, overage, and tenant reimbursements. The projections assume that a sufficient number of leases will be signed at the end of the second year to warrant closing the permanent loan.

Pay particular attention to the ratios that appear at the bottom of Exhibit 15–9. These ratios, calculated beginning with data for year 3 when "normal" operation is anticipated, are used to evaluate the performance of the property. The permanent lender will review these and other ratios to ascertain whether they fall into acceptable underwriting ranges. We must stress again that market data supporting rents and overages, proof of estimates of operating costs from the management of comparable centers, realistic estimates of the lease-up rate, and lease terms that tenants are willing to accept in the retail market are all critical to the underwriting process.

The operating expense ratio, which is calculated by dividing total annual operating expenses by the effective gross income (*EGI*), indicates that at most 40.5 percent of *EGI* from Rolling Meadows goes into servicing operating expenses. In contrast, Rolling Meadows' debt coverage ratio, or net operating income divided by debt service, exceeds 1.41. This ratio demonstrates the property's ability to meet its debt payments. The cash returns earned on the total investment will be positive and exceed the mortgage interest rate.[12] This free and clear return is calculated by dividing net operating income by the total project costs. Return on equity, a second cash return measurement, is calculated by dividing net operating income by the total equity contributions. These returns do not include any appreciation in project value. Finally, the break-even occupancy rate approximates the level of occupancy required to service both the debt service and the operating expenses of a project. This ratio is calculated by dividing the annual debt service and operating expenses by the gross potential income. Clearly, with occupancy projected to be 95 percent, Rolling Meadows easily meets its debt service and operating expense obligations.

Assuming that the permanent lender makes the take-out commitment, the developer will incorporate the actual amount of the loan commitment into the pro forma statements and seek out a construction lender.[13] During this time, the developer will refine and update cost and market estimates and provide more detailed construction plans in order to acquire interim financing. After the permanent financing commitment is acquired, however, all changes in design, cost, predevelopment lease agreements, and so on, must be submitted to both the permanent and interim lenders for review.

Feasibility, Profitability, and Risk—Additional Issues

Most of the analysis that the interim and permanent lenders conduct focuses on the pro forma statements and market data supplied with the loan requests. This is because lenders are concerned about market conditions, rents, and the ability of the project to cover expenses and debt service. Southfork is equally concerned with these issues; however, it is also interested in knowing how well this project will perform as an investment, both before and after taxes. Also, from the standpoint of assessing risk, it needs to know how sensitive the estimates provided in the pro forma statements are to various assumptions made in the analysis. Much of what follows are analytic tools for assessing project performance. These tools may be used at any time during development as market data, building costs, interest rates, and so on, change. They also may be used to ascertain the maximum price that should be paid for the land *prior to its acquisition*. To illustrate these ideas, we will use the pro forma estimates presented thus far and change them by introducing sensitivity analysis.

Profitability before and after Taxes

For Southfork to assess the profitability of the Rolling Meadows Center before and after taxes, additional assumptions regarding the number of operating periods and the appreciation rate on the property value must be made. We have assumed that a sale will occur five years after construction.

[12]Total project cost is estimated at $11,982,287. When divided into *NOI* a 13.35 percent return on total investment results.

[13]The actual take-out commitment will contain contingencies that may affect the pro forma statements presented here. Recall that all of the statements produced thus far are part of a *proposal* to the permanent lender. Should the lender decide to fund less than the total amount requested or insist on a higher lease-up requirement, among other things, those changes would have to be incorporated in the data submitted to potential interim lenders.

Exhibit 15–10 summarizes estimates of before-tax cash flow (*BTCF*) during the development and operating periods, based on information contained in Exhibits 15–8 and 15–9. The before-tax estimate for *NPV* comprises all negative cash flows consisting of equity requirements at closing (land acquisition and loan fees), cash equity needed during development for costs not financed (indirect overhead), and cash requirements needed during year 2, or the lease-up phase. Positive cash flows are based on operations from years 3 through 6 plus cash flow from the sale of the project in year 6 (all figures are rounded).

Exhibit 15–11 contains estimates of before-tax cash flows when Rolling Meadows Center reevaluates its investment plans and instead of owning and operating, it decides to sell to Mony Mutual Realty Advisors, which acquires projects and manages them on behalf of pension fund sponsors. We see that after paying selling expenses and repaying the mortgage loan balance to Citadel, Southfork will have $7,104,160 in cash before taxes (*BTCF*s). The sale price for the project,

EXHIBIT 15–10 Profitability Analysis for Rolling Meadows Center

	Before-Tax Cash Flows						
	Year						
	0	*1*	*2*	*3*	*4*	*5*	*6*
Equity	($2,950,071)	($ 30,800)					
BTCF—operations			($ 380,361)	$ 461,971	$ 557,438	$ 658,614	$ 765,837
BTCF—sale							7,104,160
Total *BTCF*	($2,950,071)	($ 30,800)	($ 380,361)	$ 461,971	$ 557,438	$ 658,614	$7,869,997
BTIRR = 21.33%							
BTNPV @21% = $47,050							
	Taxable Income						
Net operating income			($ 757,300)	$1,599,632	$1,695,099	$1,796,275	$1,903,498
Less:							
Interest			1,076,900	1,069,194	1,060,511	1,050,726	1,039,701
Depreciation:							
Capital improvements			256,769	256,769	256,769	256,769	256,769
Tenant improvements			256,769	183,406	131,005	93,575	77,979
Amortization:							
Construction loan fees		180,028					
Permanent loan fees			27,004	27,004	27,004	27,004	27,004
Taxable income	$ 0	$(180,028)	$ (860,142)	$ 63,258	$ 219,811	$ 368,200	$ 502,045
Tax @ 28%	0	(50,408)	(240,840)	17,712	61,547	103,096	140,573
	After-Tax Cash Flows						
Total *BTCF*	($2,950,071)	($ 30,800)	($ 380,361)	$ 461,971	$ 557,438	$ 658,614	$7,869,997
Less: Ord. Tax	0	(50,408)	(240,840)	17,712	61,547	103,096	140,573
Cap. Gain Tax	—	—	—	—	—	—	1,713,304*
ATCF	($2,950,071)	$ 19,608	($ 139,521)	$ 444,259	$ 495,891	$ 555,518	$6,016,120
ATIRR = 17.74%							

*Includes $1,713,304 in taxes from the sale of Rolling Meadows at the end of year 6 (see Exhibit 15–11).

EXHIBIT 15–11 Sale of Rolling Meadows Center

	Before-Tax Cash Flow
Sale price	$16,035,003
Less:	
Selling expenses	320,700
Mortgage balance	8,610,143
Before-tax cash flow on the sale	$ 7,104,160
	Gain in Year of Sale
Sale price	$16,035,003
Less:	
Selling expenses	320,700
Adjusted basis	9,595,358
Total gain on the sale	$ 6,118,945
	After-Tax Cash Flow
Before-tax cash flow on the sale	$ 7,104,160
Less: Tax on gain @ 28%	1,713,304
After-tax cash flow on the sale	$ 5,390,856

$16,035,003, is based on the initial total project cost, $11,982,287 (Exhibit 15–8), compounded at an appreciation rate of 6 percent per year for five years.

From Exhibit 15–10, we can calculate an estimate for *NPV* before taxes based on all before-tax cash flows expected to occur from years 1 to 6, discounted at a required before-tax rate of 21 percent. This results in a positive *NPV* of $47,050. This 21 percent required rate of return represents a 9 percent risk premium over the mortgage interest rate that Southfork management believes would be a satisfactory return on its equity after recovery of all project costs, given the risk of the Rolling Meadows project.

The *after-tax internal rate of return* for Southfork is also presented in Exhibit 15–10. To arrive at net cash flow after tax during development and in each operating year, we need additional information to take income taxes into account.

Exhibit 15–12 provides the information about depreciation and amortization of various project costs that we need to estimate taxable income. Part A in Exhibit 15–12 contains a list of costs that must be capitalized as part of the improvement and depreciated. Of total depreciable costs, we see in Part B that 90 percent are capital improvements and, therefore, subject to depreciation on a straight-line basis over 31.5 years.[14] Southfork estimates 10 percent of these costs to be tenant improvements, which are categorized as personal rather than real property. This category of improvement may be depreciated on a double-declining basis over seven years.[15] Part C contains a description of project soft costs that may be amortized.

[14]See Chapter 10 for an explanation of depreciation methods. The depreciable life of 31.5 years used in this example is not necessarily representative of the current tax law. It is for illustration only.

[15]An explanation of double-declining-balance depreciation may be found in introductory accounting texts. Switching to straight-line is also allowed and carried out in the analysis here.

EXHIBIT 15–12 Depreciation and Amortization Schedule for Rolling Meadows Center

A. Depreciable costs:			
Site improvements (on/off)		$ 850,000	
Hard costs		7,055,500	
Soft costs:			
Architect engineering	$147,000		
Fees and permits	24,300		
Legal fees	26,900		
Construction interest	692,416		
Direct overhead	160,000		
Indirect overhead	30,800		
Total soft costs		$ 1,081,416	
Total depreciable costs		$ 8,986,916	
			Depreciation Period
B. Depreciation schedule:			
Capital improvements (90% of total)		$ 8,088,225	31.5 years
Tenant improvements (10% of total)		898,692	7 years
			Amortization Period
C. Amortization schedule:			
Construction loan fees		$ 180,028	1 year
Permanent loan fees		270,042	10 years
Leasing commissions		45,300	5 years
Total depreciable/amortized costs		9,482,287	
Add: Land		2,500,000	
Total project costs		$11,982,287	

Adjusted Basis at the End of Year 6

Item	*Total Cost*	*Less: Accumulated Depreciation/Amortization*	*Adjusted Basis*
Land	$ 2,500,000	$ 0	$2,500,000
Capital improvements	8,088,225	1,283,845	6,804,379
Tenant improvements	898,692	742,734	155,958
Permanent loan fees	270,042	135,021	135,021
Leasing commissions	45,300	45,300	0
Construction loan fees	180,028	180,028	0
Total	$11,982,287	$2,386,928	$9,595,358

Because we assume two loans used to fund the project, we amortize loan fees over the respective terms of each loan.[16] Finally, we capitalize leasing commissions and write them off over the average of lease terms for the project.

[16]The permanent loan fees are assumed to be paid when the commitment is obtained. However, amortization is assumed not to begin until the loan is closed at the beginning of the third year.

We also need after-tax cash flow in the year of *sale* (*ATCF*s) to complete the computation of the after-tax *IRR*. From Exhibit 15–11, tax in the year of sale ($1,713,304) is the difference between the estimated net selling price less the adjusted basis times the 28 percent tax rate. As noted in Chapter 10, capital gains might be taxed at a lower rate than ordinary income. In this example we assume the same tax rate is used for ordinary income and capital gains. The adjusted basis is computed as the cost of land plus all improvements, or $11,982,287, less the sum of all depreciation and amortization taken over the seven-year period.[17] The adjusted basis, or cost to be recovered from the sale of the asset prior to computing the tax on the gain, is $9,595,358. We can then estimate after-tax cash flow to be $5,390,856.

We can solve for the *ATIRR* shown in Exhibit 15–10 by setting the equity requirements at closing equal to *ATCF* in each year and in the year of sale and solving for the rate of interest that makes the after-tax *NPV* equal zero. Note that although *BTCF* is negative in year 1, after-tax cash flow is positive during that year because of the tax deductibility of loan fees. Those deductions result in a net loss, or an offset against any other active income earned by Southfork during that year. Hence, they *reduce* taxes, *save* cash, and offset negative *BTCF*. Taxes are calculated by assuming a tax rate of 28 percent,[18] and after-tax cash flows are determined and used to determine the *ATIRR*, which is 17.74 percent for Rolling Meadows. Note that this return is *not* equal to the *BTIRR* (shown in Exhibit 15–10) times 1 minus tax rate, or 21.33 percent (1 − .28 = 15.36%) because of the higher rates allowable for amortization of tenant improvements and fees (Exhibit 15–12) relative to the 31.5 year straight-line depreciation allowed for real property.

Sensitivity Analysis, Risk, and Feasibility Analysis

Based on the preceding analysis, we have concluded that if Southfork is satisfied that a 21 percent before-tax rate return on equity is adequate to undertake the Rolling Meadows Center development, it will earn a positive *NPV*. This implies that the $2.5 million land acquisition price would be warranted, given estimates of construction costs, market rents, expenses, and the appreciation rate in property value. An interesting question that could be raised at this point is, "Suppose market rents were estimated to be $12 per square foot instead of $15 and all other assumptions remained constant (quantity of space, construction costs, interest rates, appreciation rates, and operating expenses). Would the project still be feasible—would it cover all costs and provide the developer with a competitive return on equity?"

To consider this question, refer to Exhibit 15–13. This diagram represents the relationship between *BTNPV* (vertical axis) and market rents per square foot of leasable area (horizontal axis). Note that at the average rent of $15 per square foot assumed in our analysis, the *BTNPV* is slightly above zero (the discount rate is held constant at 21 percent). If, however, the market rent averaged $12 per square foot and all other assumptions remained the same, it is clear that the *NPV* would be negative. In that case, Southfork would not be interested in pursuing the development.

---

[17]In years prior to the 1986 Tax Reform Act, tax rates on capital gains and on ordinary income were different. Further, the tax treatment of construction period interest and property taxes and certain other fees also differed. Because of these differences, interest, taxes, and fees were capitalized from the improvement, and the unamortized balance in the year of sale was either deducted as an ordinary expense or added to the undepreciated basis. Stay informed about real estate taxation, particularly when analyzing project development, because the tax treatment of various cost categories changes frequently.

[18]We assume that Southfork is a sole proprietorship or a partnership whose owners are taxed at ordinary rates. We also assume that Southfork's owners have other passive income that they can use to offset the passive losses produced by this project (see Chapter 10 for a discussion of passive income).

EXHIBIT 15–13 ***BTNPV* of Rolling Meadows Center and Rents**

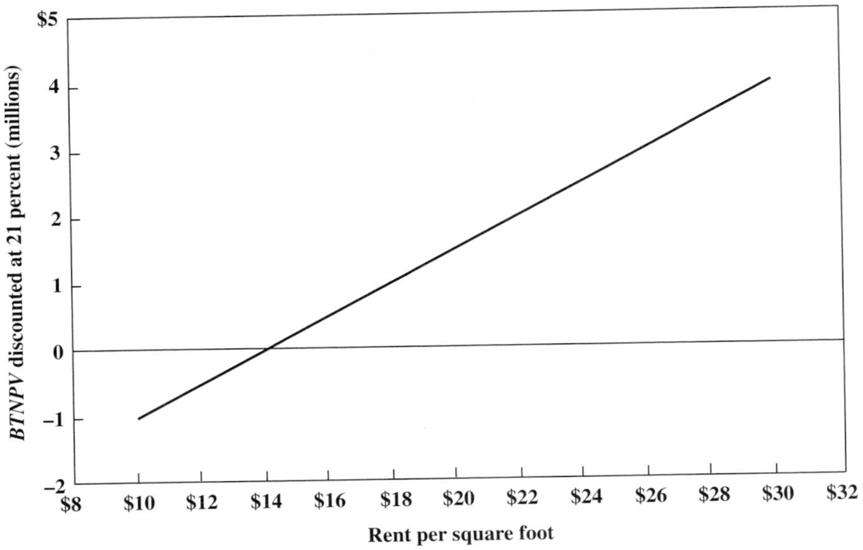

An even more critical aspect of this analysis becomes clear if, after both loan commitments were made, construction went forward on the project and market rents then fell from $15 to $12 per square foot as the lease-up phase was underway. In this event, Southfork would be facing a negative *NPV* and would be committed to the development. If it was not able to produce more equity or to find additional investors to provide equity at that point, it would not be able to meet project expenses and debt service. At that point, the interim lender would be faced with the prospect that the permanent lender may not be compelled to honor its take-out commitment because the developer would not meet rental requirements. The interim lender would have to negotiate the interim loan terms with the developer (sometimes referred to as a *workout*), or possibly foreclose. You can now begin to see how changing market conditions can affect project risk.

Another important consideration is apparent in Exhibit 15–14, where *BTNPV* is related to land cost (horizontal axis). Recall that we estimated a slightly positive *NPV*, assuming that the land was acquired at $2.5 million. If Southfork was too optimistic and paid $3 million for the land, we can see from the diagram that the *NPV* would be negative (again, discounting at 21 percent and holding all other variables constant). On the other hand, if the land could be acquired for less than $2.5 million, the *NPV* would become more favorable. The value of this *sensitivity analysis* should be obvious at this point.[19] This analysis is also referred to as **feasibility analysis**, or a determination of whether a project is commercially feasible at prevailing market rents, land prices, and construction and financing costs.

[19]The same analysis may be carried out by changing other variables, such as construction costs, interest rates, or operating expenses one at a time to assess the impact on before-tax *NPV*.

EXHIBIT 15–14 ***BTNPV* of Rolling Meadows Center and Land Cost**

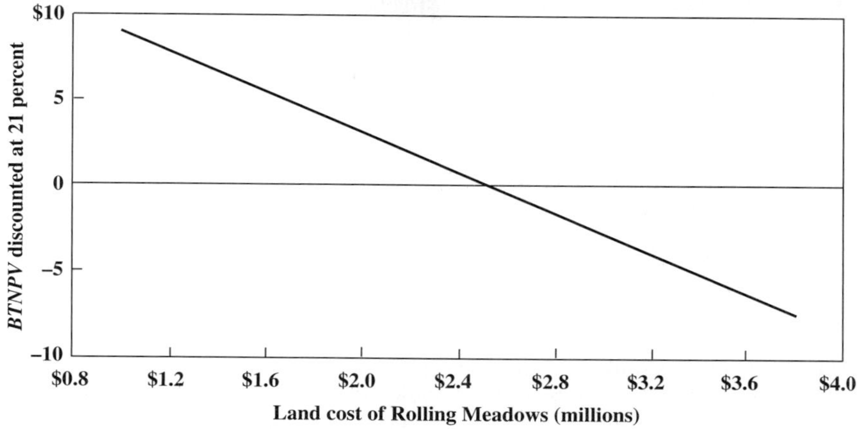

Conclusion

This chapter dealt with financing the development of income-producing real estate such as apartment complexes, office buildings, warehouses, and shopping centers. Development projects include many risks in addition to those we have discussed in previous chapters for existing projects. We have seen that developers of such projects face changing conditions in the national and local economies, competitive pressures from other developments, and changes in locational preferences of tenants, all of which influence the profitability of developing and operating an income-producing property. All these forces combined affect the developer's ability to acquire land, build improvements, lease space to tenants, and earn sufficient revenues to cover operating expenses and repay both a construction and a permanent mortgage loan. This chapter illustrated the mechanics of construction loans, which differ from the permanent loans we have already discussed extensively because they involve draws over the construction period. The next chapter explores land development projects, which extends the concepts of this chapter to development and financing land for subdivision.

Key Terms

build to suit 434
construction (interim) loan 437
contingencies 442
exculpation (nonrecourse) clause 447
feasibility analysis 462
gap financing 443
hard costs 437
holdbacks 453
mini-perm loan 438, 444
monthly draw method 445
percentage rent 455
permanent financing 447
seasoned property 435
soft costs 437
speculative/open-ended construction lending 438
standby commitment 442
triparty buy-sell agreement 446

Questions

1. What are the sources of risk associated with project development?
2. What are some development strategies that many developers follow? Why do they follow such strategies?

3. How can development projects be differentiated from one another in the marketplace?
4. Describe the process of financing the construction and operation of a typical real estate development. Indicate the order in which lenders who fund project development financing are sought and why this pattern is followed.
5. What contingencies are commonly found in permanent or take-out loan commitments? Why are they used? What happens if they are not met by the developer?
6. What is a *standby commitment*? When and why is it used?
7. What is a *mini-perm* or *bullet loan*? When and why is this loan used?
8. Third-party lenders sometimes provide gap financing for project developments. Why is this lending used? How does it work?
9. A presale agreement is said to be equivalent to a take-out commitment. What will the construction lender be concerned about if the developer plans to use such an agreement in lieu of a take-out?
10. Why don't permanent lenders usually provide construction loans to developers? Do construction lenders ever provide permanent loans to developers?
11. What is the difference between the assignment of a take-out commitment to the construction lender and a triparty agreement? If neither device is used in project financing, what is the relationship between lenders in such a case?
12. What is the major concern construction lenders express about the income approach to estimating value? Why do they prefer to use the cost approach when possible? In the latter case, if the developer has owned the land for five years prior to development would the cost approach be more effective? Why or why not?
13. What do we mean by *overage* in a retail lease agreement? How might it be calculated?
14. What is *sensitivity analysis*? How might it be used in real estate development?
15. It is sometimes said that land represents "residual" value. This statement reflects the fact that improvement costs do not vary materially from one location to another whereas rents vary considerably. Hence, land values reflect changes in rents (both up and down) from location to location. Do you agree or disagree?
16. Why is the practice of "holdbacks" used? Who is involved in this practice? How does it affect construction lending?

Problems

1. The CEO of Kuehner Development Co. has just come from a meeting with his marketing staff where he was given the latest market study of a proposed new shopping center, Parker Road Plaza. The study calls for a construction phase of one year and an operation phase of five years. The property is to be sold at the end of the fifth year of operation.

   Part I. *Construction Phase*:

   The marketing staff has chosen a 12-acre site for the project that they believe they can acquire for $2.25 million. The initial studies indicate that this shopping center will support a floor-to-area ratio of 36.35 percent and a 92.11 percent leasable area ratio. (This means that the gross building area [*GBA*] will be 190,000 square feet, and the gross leasable area [*GLA*] will be 175,000 square feet.)

   The head of Kuehner's construction division assures the CEO that construction can keep hard costs to $54 per square foot (*GBA*) and soft costs (excluding interest carry and all loan fees) to $4.50 per square foot (*GBA*). The division has decided to subcontract all of the site improvements at a total cost of $750,000.

   The Shawmut Bank has agreed to provide interim financing for the project. The bank will finance all of the construction costs and site improvements at an annual rate of 13 percent plus a loan commitment fee of two points. The construction division estimates that 60 percent of the total direct cost will be taken down evenly during the first six months of the construction phase. Kuehner expects to obtain permanent financing from the Acme Insurance Co. at an interest rate of 12 percent for 20 years with a 2.5 percent prepaid loan fee and a 10-year call. Kuehner is expected to make monthly loan payments.

   a. What will be the total project cost for Parker Road Plaza (excluding loan commitment fees and interest carry)? What will be the total direct costs?

   b. What will be the interest carry for the Parker Road Plaza project? What will be the total loan amount that Kuehner must borrow (including interest carry)? What will be the yield to the lender on this construction loan?

   c. What is the total project cost and how much equity must be put into the project each year during the construction phase? (Kuehner will fund both loan commitment fees from project equity.)

Part II. *Operations and Final Sale Phase*:

Kuehner estimates that it can lease Parker Road Plaza for $18.50 per square foot (*GLA*) base rent with a 3 percent overage on gross sales in excess of $200 per square foot (*GLA*). The company expects rents to increase by 5 percent per year during the lease period and tenant reimbursements to run $8 per square foot (*GLA*) and to increase at the same rate as rents. Kuehner expects to have the shopping center 70 percent leased during the first year of operation. After that, vacancies should average about 5 percent per year. The vacancy losses should be calculated on the entire gross potential income, which includes minimum rents, percentage rents, and tenant reimbursements. Sales, which are expected to average $210 per square foot (*GLA*) for the first year of operation, should grow at 6 percent per year. The operating expenses are expected to average $14 per square foot of *GLA* for the first year and will increase at the same rate as the rents. Kuehner will collect an additional 5 percent of *EGI* as an annual management fee. The final sales price is expected to be $18.4 million and Kuehner will incur sales expenses of 2 percent. Two schedules provide necessary information about this phase of the project: (1) the gross potential income of Parker Road Plaza for the five-year operation period; (2) the schedule of amortization and depreciation expenses for the project.

d. What cash flows would Kuehner Development Co. earn before and after taxes for Parker Road Plaza if it were operated for five years (assuming the marginal tax rate to be 28 percent for ordinary income and capital gains)? What cash flows will Kuehner realize before and after taxes from the sale of the project after five years?

e. Assuming that Kuehner's before-tax required rate of return is 16 percent, should the company develop Parker Road Plaza? Justify your answer based on *BTNPV* and *BTIRR*.

2. As a financial advisor for the Spain Development Co., you have been given the construction and marketing studies for the proposed Timbercreek office project. Several potential sites have been selected, but a final decision has not been made. Your manager needs to know how much she can afford to pay for the land and still manage to return 16 percent on the entire project over its lifetime.

The strategic plan calls for a construction phase of one year and an operation phase of five years, after which time the property will be sold. The marketing staff says that a 1.3-acre site will be adequate because the initial studies indicate that this site will support an office building with a gross leasable area (*GLA*) of 26,520 square feet. The gross building area (*GBA*) will be 31,200 square feet, giving a leasable ratio of 85 percent. The marketing staff further assures you that

Pro Forma Operating Statement—Parker Road Plaza

Cash Flows (EOP)	*2*	*3*	*4*	*5*	*6*
Income					
Minimum rent	$3,237,500	$3,399,375	$3,569,344	$3,747,811	$3,935,201
Overage (% of gross sales)	52,500	118,650	188,769	263,095	341,881
Tenant reimbursements (per *GLA*)	1,400,000	1,470,000	1,543,500	1,620,675	1,701,709
Potential gross income	$4,690,000	$4,988,025	$5,301,613	$5,631,581	$5,978,791

Item	*Amortization Period*
Construction loan fees	1 year
Permanent loan fees	10 years

	Depreciation Period
Capital improvements (90% of total)	31.5 years S/L
Tenant improvements (10% of total)	7 years DDB

the space can be rented for $19 per square foot. The head of the construction division maintains that all direct costs (excluding interest carry and all loan fees) will be $2.4 million.

The First Street Bank will provide the construction loan for the project. The bank will finance all of the construction costs, site improvements, and interest carry at an annual rate of 13 percent plus a loan origination fee of 1.5 points. The construction division estimates that the direct cost draws will be taken down in six equal amounts commencing with the first month after close. The permanent financing for the project will come at the end of the first year from the Reliable Co. at an interest rate of 11.5 percent with a 4 percent prepaid loan fee. The loan has an eight-year term and is to be paid back monthly over a 25-year amortization schedule. No financing fees will be included in either loan amount. Spain will fund acquisition of the land with its own equity.

Spain expects tenant reimbursements for the project to be $3.25 per square foot and the office building to be 75 percent leased during the first year of operation. After that, vacancies should average about 5 percent of GPI per year. Rents, tenant reimbursement, and operating expenses are expected to increase by 3 percent per year during the lease period. The operating expenses are expected to be $9.50 per square foot. The final sales price is based on the *NOI* in the sixth year of the project (the fifth year of operation) capitalized at 9.5 percent. The project will incur sales expenses of 4 percent. Spain is concerned that it may not be able to afford to pay for the land and still earn 16 percent (before taxes) on its equity (remember that the land acquisition cost must be paid from Spain's equity).

To consider project feasibility,

a. Estimate construction draw schedule, interest carry, and total loan amount for improvements. Determine total project cost (including fees) less financing and the equity needed to fund improvements.

b. Estimate cash flows from operations and eventual sale.

c. Establish whether a positive or negative *NPV* exists by discounting equity cash inflows and outflows in (*b*).

d. What does the *NPV* mean in this case? If the asking price of the land were $195,000, would this project be feasible?

CHAPTER

16

Financing Land Development Projects

As the last chapter indicated, real estate development is a very complex process to analyze, from the standpoint of both lenders and investors. This chapter deals with **land development**, which involves the acquisition of land with the intention of constructing utilities and surface improvements, then reselling some or all of the developed sites to project developers or, in the case of housing, home builders. As described in the previous chapter, *project development* deals with the acquisition of a specific site, then construction of an office building, shopping center, or other property type. This chapter contains a basic description of land development and financing. However, many attributes of real estate development are common to both types of development, so to avoid redundancy we do not repeat them here. After completing both chapters, you should have a general understanding of investment financing in the development process.

In this chapter, we provide insight into the land development process and how to determine the feasibility of land development projects. We discuss how to structure development loans, how to determine terms for disbursement and repayment, and how to make profitability projections. Structuring loan agreements and repayment schedules and estimating interest carry for land development projects are detailed and complex processes. You may want to refer to the appendix in the previous chapter for a more in-depth treatment of these subjects if you have problems mastering the material in this chapter.

Characterization of the Land Development Business

When generalizing about the land development process, it is useful to think of the land developer as an individual with a general development concept. Before proceeding with the development, however, there must be evidence that the project is feasible or that market acceptance of the end product (single family houses, offices, warehouses, etc.) is highly likely. This step is important even though the land developer may, or may not, be the developer of the final product. In other words, in the land development phase, the developer must anticipate and understand the demand for the final product (or products in the case of a mixed use land development, which may contain sites for sale to single family builders, apartment developers, and/or shopping center developers, for example). Demand for the end product obviously affects the demand for individual sites, lots, or pads within the land development. Every land acquisition decision must also be based on whether the tract of unimproved land on which the plan is to be executed is of sufficient size and contains adequate amounts of usable area to accommodate the development plan. While development plans will differ based on the general development concept, all plans include the subdivision, or platting, of sites within a tract of land to be acquired. Decisions as to how to subdivide the larger development into lot sizes and how to price individual sites are based on expected end uses envisioned as a part of the general development concept.

In residential land development, it is common to find firms specializing in the acquisition of raw land in suburban fringe areas and developing sites for single family detached units or for multiple uses, such as combinations of single family units, multifamily apartments, and cluster housing. Based on the market segment in which the end use will likely sell, the land developer acquires land, develops a land use and traffic circulation plan, then constructs streets, lighting, and subsurface improvements (utilities, drainage, sewer). The developer then subdivides individual sites, and sells smaller sites to builders and project developers. The developer may also retain some retail sites for later sale if the site has suitable highway frontage.

One point that must be stressed here is that land developers and builders or project developers may, or may not, be the same entities. Land developers may or may not have the expertise to undertake building construction and/or project development. These functions differ in their respective production technologies and market risks. However, a few large firms may engage in both activities. For example, where residential sites are being developed for housing in lower price ranges, the land developer may also engage in some home building. On the other hand, when land is more expensive, the land developer usually sells lots to custom home builders and engages in little, if any, home building.

In business parks and industrial development, land developers (discussed in the previous chapter) may prepare sites for sale to project developers, but they usually retain some sites for project development of their own. For example, a major single tenant may want to have a building constructed in a business park. In this case, the park developer may design and **build to suit** a structure for the tenant and enter a long-term lease arrangement. Alternatively, the developer may construct a building on a site and sell it to the tenant on a **turnkey basis**. In business and industrial park development, the land developer may also construct some building improvements on a speculative basis to attract other tenants to the park. However, these developers usually stand ready to sell sites in the park to other project developers as long as those project developers abide by required development controls. These controls usually include construction of buildings of adequate quality, maintenance, landscaping, and so on. These controls are usually specified deed restrictions and/or provisions in an agreement governing the operation of a business park owners association.

Another observation about land development is that the industry is highly fragmented, localized, and competitive. Many land development firms usually exist in a given urban market. They enter the market for raw land by contacting landowners or land brokers and obtaining information on tracts of land available for sale. These developers then engage consultants to conduct market studies to assess the demand for end uses that would ultimately be developed and price ranges for each use. The developer then completes a preliminary land plan, estimates the land development cost, and analyzes whether the tract can be purchased and developed profitably. This process is referred to as a **feasibility study.** It should be stressed that in many cases the developer is more of a facilitator of the development process than a firm that undertakes all necessary functions in the land development process. Thus many functions required to complete a land development project may be done by consulting firms (land planners, civil engineers, landscape architects) and contractors (roads and utility construction companies). In these instances, the developer owns the land, obtains the necessary financing, and implements the overall development plan, but may not employ a staff that is directly involved in construction or design. The developer must also interact with public sector officials in obtaining various project approvals and changes in zoning when necessary, and then market sites to project developers and/or builders.

The Land Development Process—An Overview

Exhibit 16–1 contains a general description of activities performed at various stages in the process. Generally, the process begins when a land broker who represents the owner of a tract of land available for sale contacts a developer. At this point (Stage I), the developer conducts a very preliminary investigation of the site, the condition of the market, how a tract might be developed, and at what cost. Should sufficient interest exist to pursue negotiation, the developer usually negotiates an **option agreement** with the landowner. An option usually provides that the developer has the right, but no obligation, to purchase the land for a specific price at a future date. The developer pays an option price to the landowner, which is usually applied to the purchase price of the land if the developer purchases it (exercises the option). In the event that the developer decides not to purchase the land on the expiration date, the landowner may keep the money paid for the option.

Acquisition of Land—Use of the Option Contract

The developer usually negotiates an option contract because it takes time to accomplish various tasks and activities prior to the decision to actually purchase the land. Some of these activities are shown in Stage II in the exhibit. Inasmuch as the developer's final decision to purchase depends on the information obtained from the activities indicated, the decision to purchase land obviously cannot be made quickly. Consequently, the developer would prefer to negotiate an option at the lowest price possible for the longest period of time possible in order to accomplish these tasks. Further, the developer will incur costs while carrying out the research about whether land should be purchased. The developer wants assurance that the land will not be sold while these costs are being incurred. On the other hand, if the landowner wants to sell as quickly as possible, an option with a short exercise period at the highest possible price would be preferred. While the option agreement provides the developer time to conduct research, it also ties up the land or precludes the landowner from selling it until the expiration date.[1] Consequently, the landowner may give up opportunities to sell the land during the option period with no assurance that the developer may actually close the transaction. Option periods

[1]Because all terms of sale should be included in the option contract, in many cases a contract to purchase the land may be used instead of an option agreement. The contract would be executed with a closing date that would make it equivalent to the option period. All terms, conditions, contingencies, and so on, would be negotiated and included in the sale contract at the time that the contract is executed. This approach usually eliminates contractual ambiguities between the buyer and seller that could arise if they used an option.

EXHIBIT 16–1 Land Development Process

Stage I Initial Contact by Land Broker	*Stage II Option Period*	*Stage III Development Period*	*Stage IV Sales Period*
Site inspection	Soil studies, engineering	Purchase land	Implement marketing program
Preliminary market study	Feasibility, appraisal, and design strategy	Close on land development loan Begin construction of improvements	Additional coordination with builders
Preliminary cost estimates	Bidding and/or negotiating with contractors subject to closing	Implement financial controls	Implement design controls with builders
	Submit plan for public approvals, submit package for financing	Coordinate with contractors, consultants, public sector	Implement facility management and/or begin homeowner association

can be very short (e.g., one month for small residential land developments) or as long as three years or more (e.g., regional shopping centers).[2]

Assuming that the developer obtains an option for an acceptable period of time and cost, some important activities must be undertaken before the expiration date, when the decision to acquire the land must be made. The site must be studied to establish how much of the surface area needs excavating and grading, and at what cost. These decisions are a function of the topography, drainage characteristics, soil condition, and subsurface characteristics. The market must be studied to estimate what the demand will be for a mix of lot sizes. The supply of sites coming into the market in competing areas must also be considered. An estimate of the project's value upon completion of development must be made to determine whether it will be profitable or whether the market value will exceed the cost of the land plus all improvements, interest carry, and marketing costs. Improvement costs must be estimated by obtaining bids from contractors, consulting engineers, and land planners. These estimates must be based on an anticipated land development plan, which usually has to undergo several iterations before it (1) complies with the overall development concept that is intended to meet market demand and (2) meets the approval

[2]Options with assignment clauses have also been used in land speculation. In these cases, the prospective land buyer obtains an option from the landowner with little or no expectation of purchasing the land (although he may not indicate this). The owner of the option hopes to find another buyer to purchase the land at a price higher than the exercise price prior to the expiration of the option. If he can do so, he realizes a gain. If he cannot find a buyer, the speculator loses the option price. This practice has been referred to as *flipping* a contract. In some cases, developers with options that have lengthy expiration dates inadvertently realize gains. These gains occur when, after developers undertake feasibility studies, they realize that land values have risen. In this case, they may engage a land broker or try to find a buyer prior to the option expiration date, or they may negotiate an extension period on the option with the landowner. In some instances, landowners face situations in which a subsequent offer of a higher price is received after an option has been given to a developer. In this case, if the new bidder wants to close the transaction prior to the expiration date of the option, the landowner may try to repurchase the option from the developer and hope that the new buyer and the developer do not meet and negotiate directly.

of various public agencies (city departments, planning commissions, city council, etc.). Results from all of these activities must then be interpreted and used to develop a loan submission request. Without approval from a lender, who may be asked to provide a large portion of the funds necessary to acquire the land and construct improvements, the project is not likely to go forward.

One aspect of the process depicted in Stage II of Exhibit 16–1 should become clear at this point. The response time of the developer to accomplish these functions is critical and usually requires the commitment of other firms to the developer's timetable. If the developer cannot obtain the necessary approvals from public officials or find a lender, he may lose the cost of the option plus all fees and costs incurred while trying to accomplish the activities in Stage II. If approvals and the loan commitment are not secured by the expiration date, the developer may try to negotiate an extension of the option period with the landowner. Failing that, the developer may have to raise equity from partners to acquire the land with the expectation that approvals and/or a loan will be obtained shortly after the option period expires and the land is acquired. Clearly, this approach can be risky because if the land is acquired, long delays may occur before financing and necessary approvals are obtained. Market conditions and costs can also change during this time, thereby increasing the risk of development.

Financing and Development

Assuming that the land developer successfully accomplishes all activities in Stage II, the purchase and financing of the land, the construction of utilities, and surface improvements must occur next in Stage III. As discussed earlier, the developer generally acts as a facilitator in coordinating, controlling, and paying for the construction of land improvements as funds are acquired from a lender. When financing the land acquisition and development process, a number of structures may be available to the developer; however, we will discuss three of the more common alternatives here.

1. The developer may purchase the land for cash. The developer may then obtain a loan for the cost of improvements and interest carry.
2. The developer may purchase the land by making a down payment only. The seller finances all or a portion of the land sale by taking back a purchase-money mortgage from the developer. The developer then acquires a loan for improvements only. The seller of land (mortgagee) agrees to subordinate the lien represented by the purchase-money mortgage to the development loan, and the developer repays the seller's mortgage from funds as parcels are sold and after payments on the development loan are made.
3. The developer purchases the land by making a down payment and obtaining one loan based on a percentage of the appraised value of land plus improvements. The funds pay off the seller and construction improvements.

The extent to which developers use each of these techniques depends on conditions in the market for land and the price paid for the land. If the demand for developable land is strong, sellers may demand cash and may not be willing to sell "on terms" or take back purchase-money mortgages. However, during such times, lenders are generally more willing to provide funds for improvements and a part of the land acquisition price. During periods when demand is not as strong, sellers of land are more willing to finance a portion of the sale price; however, lenders are usually more cautious as uncertainty becomes more prevalent in the marketplace.[3]

Regardless of the financing technique used to acquire the land, lenders usually make loans for land improvements that allow developers to "draw down" funds in stages, usually monthly, based on the percentage of development work completed and verified by the lender. The developer uses an open-end mortgage as security for the loan. Such loans are usually made on a floating rate basis. That is, the lender usually makes the loan at 2 or 3 percent above the prime lending rate. Hence, the developer bears the risk of an interest rate change during the development period. As previously indicated, the lender providing the funds for improvements will insist on obtaining first lien on the land being developed and first lien on all improvements as they are completed and as funds are disbursed.

Repayment of land development loans ultimately depends on the sale of the subdivided sites to builders or other developers. Because repayments depend on lot sales and lenders view such loans as very risky, they must accurately assess the risk of projects and the rate at which parcels will be sold in order to determine whether such loans can be repaid. Lenders closely analyze financial statements, appraisal reports, and market studies. In addition, as a development progresses, monthly inspections must be made to verify all work done before a draw can be made against a loan commitment.

As previously indicated, as the developer eventually obtains funds from the sale of individual parcels, a portion of the proceeds from each parcel sale must be used to repay loans used to make improvements and/or acquire the land. Developers and lenders usually negotiate amounts to be paid for each type of developed site in a project, which is referred to as a **release schedule**. When a developer sells a parcel and repays a lender or lenders, the developer obtains a release statement in which lenders waive all liens on the parcel to be sold. Clear title may then pass from the developer to the buyer of the parcel. Lenders use these release provisions as a control on development loans to ensure that repayment will occur as parcels are sold. Developers must also deal with risks of cost overruns, changes in market demand, and supply conditions that cause delays and increases in carrying costs (interest on loans, taxes, etc.) during this phase.

In Stage IV, the final stage, promotion, marketing, and sales to builders or project developers occur. Generally, the developer will have designed a marketing program utilizing various media (newspapers, trade publications, etc.) to advertise the development to the builders and developers that are constructing improvements based on the nature of the land being developed (homesites, office parks, etc.).

Lender Requirements in Financing Land Development

While the focus of this chapter is on financial analysis and the feasibility of land development projects, some understanding of the financing process and interaction between lender and borrower is essential. A general understanding of the documentation requirements associated with the development process will also help the

[3]It is difficult to generalize how much a lender is willing to provide to a land developer. If the developer does not own the land and is in the process of acquiring it for development, and if the lender is satisfied that the value of the land will not decline, the lender may be willing to make a land acquisition and development loan. Further, if the developer has considerable personal net worth and is personally liable on the loan, the lender may be more willing to advance a portion of the funds to acquire the land in view of the additional security behind the loan.

reader understand the nature of the liability and performance requirements created when projects are financed and developed. Exhibit 16–2 contains a general list consisting of (A) typical requirements for a land development loan submission to the lender, (B) requirements for closing the loan if the submission is approved, and (C) the final commitment and attendant terms of financing after closing. Be aware that this is a very general list of requirements and that each land development will have unique requirements of its own. Also, during the process of trying to finance a project and close a loan, the lender will raise other questions and require additional documentation and verification that the developer will have to supply during the application period. (Some of the material in Exhibit 16–2 is relevant to the land component of project development covered in Chapter 15. It was not included in Exhibit 15–2 to avoid redundancy.)

Much of the required information listed in Exhibit 16–2 deals with (1) the capacity of third parties (such as contractors and architects) to perform, (2) verification by public sector officials that the use and density of the proposed development conforms with both appropriate zoning ordinances and the capacity of utilities on the site (the lender cannot rely on the developer to provide such information; the municipality or county must give an unambiguous statement on these issues because officials will have to provide permits to allow development to commence), and (3) verification that third parties are committed to bear unforeseen risks such as indicated by the items listed in part 4 in category B. If the developer was unable to obtain any of these verifications, it would obviously be a signal to the lender that more factual information is necessary to support the loan application.

Detailed Cost Breakdowns

The developer usually must submit detailed cost estimates and plans for constructing the improvements. The lender generally verifies the cost breakdown for accuracy in accordance with construction plans and specifications. The lender will usually require verification of all costs on a monthly basis as development work progresses and as the lender disburses funds.

General Contracts and Subcontracts

Normally, lenders prefer that developers obtain fixed-price contracts from subcontractors. The lender may require these contracts as a means of protecting against cost overruns that may occur if material or labor prices rise during development.

Labor and Material Payment Bonds and Completion Bonds. Many lenders require that contractors purchase labor and material payment bonds and **completion bonds.** The first type of bond assures the lender that any unpaid bills for labor and material will be paid by the bonding company should a contractor default. The completion bond assures the lender that the bonding company will provide funds needed to complete in the event that a contractor defaults during construction.

Title Insurance. As a condition for obtaining a land development loan, the developer generally must purchase title insurance. Such insurance assures the lender that no liens superior to its lien exist on the property when construction commences.

Holdbacks. As we discussed in the previous chapter dealing with project development, land development loans may also provide for a **holdback** of a proportion of each disbursement payable to a developer. This occurs when the developer and/or a general contractor engage a number of subcontractors and hold back a portion of the funds due under subcontracts. The developer holds back these funds to be sure

Exhibit 16–2 General Loan Submission and Closing Requirements—Land Development and Closing

A. General requirements for *loan submission* package—land development

1. Project information
   - *a.* Project description: all details for land use plan, aerials, soil reports, platting, circulation, amenities, renderings, environmental impact statement
   - *b.* Survey and legal description of site showing property lines, easements, utility lines
   - *c.* Preliminary plan for improvements and specifications
   - *d.* Project cost breakdown
   - *e.* Identification of architect, land planner, and general contractor with bank references and/or supporting data indicating their ability to complete the project if approved
2. Market financial data
   - *a.* Requested loan terms: amount, rate, maturity period, proposed release schedule (to be dealt with later in chapter)
   - *b.* Financial statements of borrowers (including bank references) and development background
   - *c.* Feasibility study, including market comparables, appraisals, pro forma operating statement (which will be dealt with later in chapter), schedule of estimated selling prices
   - *d.* Projected loan closing date
3. Government and regulatory information
   - *a.* Statement of zoning status: current zoning status and disclosure of any zoning changes required before undertaking development
   - *b.* Ad valorem taxes: any impending change in the method of levy, any pending reappraisal, and the current status of payment
4. Legal documentation
   - *a.* Legal documents including corporate charters, partnership agreements (there should be no ambiguity as to the entity requesting the loan and where liability will rest)
   - *b.* Statement of land cost and proof of ownership (deed) or impending ownership, as evidenced by an option or purchase agreement
   - *c.* Detailed description of any deed restrictions or restrictive covenants regarding land use
   - *d.* Subordination agreements: in the event of seller financing or debt financing used or to be used to acquire the land, evidence that such parties are willing to subordinate their liens to that of the development lender; if the land mortgages are to be repaid from advances from the development loan being requested, the exact amount should be stipulated, and the nature of any releases being obtained should be disclosed

B. General requirements for *loan closing*—land development

1. Project information: land site plan containing platting, renderings, circulation, utility lines, landscaping, etc.
2. Market and financial data: statement that borrowers have had no adverse impact in financial condition since the initial loan submission
3. Government and regulatory information
   - *a.* Copies of all permits from all relevant agencies and jurisdictions; includes building permits, approved zoning variances needed, health, water, sewer, environmental impact statement, etc.
   - *b.* Availability of utilities: letters from appropriate municipal or county departments indicating extent of utilities available to the site. Any off-site utility extensions must be detailed and the extension cost disclosed
4. Legal documentation
   - *a.* Detail on contracts to be let with general contractor and all subcontractors, including size of contracts
   - *b.* Evidence of contractor performance and payment bond
   - *c.* Agreement from general contractor, architect, and land planner to perform for the lender in the event of developer default

continued

Exhibit 16–2 General Loan Submission and Closing Requirements—Land Development and Closing (concluded)

d. Evidence of all casualty, hazard, and other insurance policies naming the lender as loss payee
e. Evidence of all liability and workman's compensation coverage needed by the developer
f. Title insurance binder

C. Final commitment and agreements

a. Loan commitment and terms: requirements for lender approval of draws, methods of calculating holdback requirements, prepayment options and any extension agreement
b. Note and mortgage or deed of trust evidencing debt and lien status of lender
c. Borrower's personal guarantee for repayment of loan
d. Conditional assignment agreement covering all contracts made with architects, planners, and the general contractor to be assigned to the interim lender in the event of borrower default

that subcontractors perform all work completely before receiving final payment. Consequently, the lender holds back from the developer so that no excess funds are made available to the developer during the period the developer is holding back from subcontractors.

Extension Agreements. Because it is possible that the loan will not be paid on time due to development problems or the slow sale of parcels, the lender usually requires an **extension agreement** clause in the initial loan contract. This clause specifies that an additional charge will be made for any extra time needed to repay the loan. This arrangement amounts to gap financing or additional interim financing, and the lender usually charges an extension fee in addition to interest on the outstanding loan balance if an extension is needed. In fact, these amounts may never be collectible. Indeed, if the project encounters extreme difficulty, the lender may have to foreclose and assume ownership of the development.

Residential Land Development Illustrated

To illustrate one of the many land development scenarios that are possible, we have chosen a medium-size residential land development project. However, many of the same *general* concepts and the framework for analysis apply to business/office parks and industrial/warehouse/distribution centers. Our illustration is based on the 50-acre Grayson tract, the availability of which has been brought to the attention of Landco Development Company by a land broker. Based on the combination of the description of the tract provided by the broker, Landco's knowledge of the area, and information obtained from the owner of the tract, a summary of important facts is provided in Exhibit 16–3.

Information in Exhibit 16–3 indicates that the tract is farmland at the fringe of suburban development 15 miles north of the central business district (CBD) with good proximity to highways. The present owner has recently had the property rezoned to allow for the development of single family detached units. Most of the surface area may be developed; however, five acres consist of creek and floodplain. Current zoning provides for an *average* maximum development density of one

EXHIBIT 16–3 Data on Grayson Tract

Size of tract	50 acres
Asking price	$40,000 per acre, for a total of $2,000,000
Option	30-day "free look," $20,000 for next five months
Current zoning	Single family detached, with a maximum average development density of 1 unit per 7,500 sq. ft. of developable area
Legal status	No deed restrictions or easements are currently indicated; no encumbrances exist
Site characteristics	Creek and floodplain comprise five acres of surface area. Terrain is gently rolling and moderately treed. A creek flows through the northeast quadrant, and the floodplain is contained within a channel to the edge of a steep embankment. The soil is stable with normal percolation.
Utilities	Water, sewer, electricity, and gas, all with adequate capacity, are extended to the site
Proximity	1,500 feet of highway frontage (state highway 66), 1 mile west of U.S. Interstate 166, 15 miles north of CBD
Current use	Farmland in suburban fringe area

single family detached unit per 7,500 square feet of developable surface space (gross land area, less floodplain area, less circulation such as roads, alleys, etc). The terrain appears to present little, if any, problem to constructing land improvements. The broker has indicated that the owner is willing to entertain an offer to sell the property for $2 million, and will give the developer an option to purchase it for 30 days at no cost. At the end of such time, the developer may acquire another option for an additional five months at 1 percent of the price of the land, or $20,000. Should the purchaser exercise the option to purchase the land, credit for the option price would be applied toward the purchase of the land.[4]

Inasmuch as the owner is allowing a 30-day "free look" at the property, Landco has decided to expend effort to determine if the project is feasible and whether the $2 million asking price is justified. To accomplish this, Landco must complete a preliminary development plan and conduct a market study to assess the demand for residential sites and the competitive supply conditions, both currently and in the near future. If results from the land plan and market study appear positive, information will be compiled to apply for a loan commitment and public approvals.

Market Conditions and Site Plan

As previously indicated, this illustration is intended to focus on approaches that can be used to evaluate the economic feasibility of residential land development. Estimates used to make projections for such developments are heavily based on market and cost information. While we do not provide the reader with an in-depth discussion of how to conduct market studies and how to make cost estimates, we do not mean to imply that these are minor considerations when one is deciding whether to enter into a land development project. Indeed, these studies are extremely important, and you should consult other sources of information for additional insights into this process.[5]

[4]In many cases, the buyer may be able to use a letter of credit in lieu of a cash option payment to the seller. This approach, if acceptable to the seller, is usually a lower-cost alternative to the buyer, who may have a more profitable use for the funds during the option period.

[5]For an illustration see John M. Clapp, *Handbook for Real Estate Market Analysis* (Englewood Cliffs, NJ: Prentice Hall, 1987).

Exhibit 16–4 provides a brief summary of important facts that should be the objective of market and engineering studies. These studies should be carried out during the option period, before acquiring the land and applying for financing. In addition to gauging how strong builder demand for lots is before committing to purchase the land, the developer must have a clear vision of the proposed development and how it will be viewed by buyers who have the choice of acquiring homes in competing developments.

Essentially, Landco's plan is to develop cluster-type housing sites and standard and oversized creek lots. The project will also include community facilities (pool, tennis courts). Five acres of the tract are not developable because they lie in a floodplain, and to the extent that competing land development projects do not have this loss in developable land, Landco may be at a competitive disadvantage unless (1) The loss of acreage is reflected in a lower acquisition price for the tract (holding all else equal), or (2) Landco can develop the creek area into a positive, complementary feature. If lots can be developed contiguous to the creek they may command a premium price. This may fully or partially offset the loss of developable space in the floodplain. In any event, the developer must carefully consider how much of the land is developable relative to comparable sites and their respective prices when deciding whether the development is economically feasible. In Landco's case, the issue is whether the asking price for the Grayson land ($2 million) plus development costs will be too high relative to the market value of competing homesites.

One aspect of the site plan that must be considered when investing in and financing land development is the percent of land available for lot development. For example, gross acreage in our case is 50 acres. However, the amount of land actually available for development is equal to gross land area, less floodplain area, less circulation requirements. In our example, this would be $[(50 - 5) \times (1 - .20)] \div 50 = 72$ percent, or 36 net acres of the total 50-acre tract. The lot yield in this case could be 180 lots $\div$ 50 or 3.6 lots to the acre. This also means that an average of 8,712 square feet of developable land would be available per developed lot (36 acres $\times$ 43,560 square feet per acre $\div$ 180 lots).

The value in knowing these relationships lies in conducting comparative analysis with competing developments. Large differences in developable land and lot yields may indicate that a development would contain a relatively low-density housing pattern or that the site has soil, terrain, or other characteristics that make a significant part of it unusable. These ratios also give us a basis to compare the *density* of housing that will be built with competing projects. For example, if Landco's estimated gross and net lot yield are greater or less than lot yields in competing developments, Landco may be over- or underdeveloping the tract relative to competing developments. A more careful analysis of market data and a competitive analysis should reveal why this is the case.

For example, if a developer overpays for a site relative to the competition, she must attempt to recapture the higher land cost with more density (higher net lot yield). However, this strategy may not be successful because it depends on the price that builders (and eventually home buyers) are willing to pay for higher-density housing or smaller sites. Do not assume that developers always try to maximize net lot yield per acre. This approach may appear to be a more "efficient" utilization of land and provide the developer with more lots to sell, but market demand may prove that home buyers prefer larger lot sizes, wider streets and alleys (circulation), and a lower development density. Although this lower density may only be provided at higher prices, if household incomes and preferences will support the pattern, it

EXHIBIT 16–4 Summary of Market Data and Development Strategy

A. Market conditions	Based on a survey of three land developments underway in the area, absorption of building sites appears to be excellent. Builder surveys indicate a strong desire to purchase sites for future development. Average lot sizes in competing developments are approximately 8,700 sq. ft.
B. Lot mix and development plan	Landco plans to utilize the creek area to enhance the development by configuring the circulation pattern to accommodate larger lot sizes on both sides of the creek. The lots for cluster-type housing units would be placed adjacent to the highway frontage as a buffer. These would be complemented with heavy landscaping. Cul-de-sacs would be utilized where possible in the interior of the development. Lot sizes would be ranging from 5,000 to 20,000 sq. ft. within the development with the average lot size being 8,712 sq. ft.
C. Deed restrictions	Private deed restrictions would be used to insure that detached housing units with a minimum of 2,000 sq. ft. would be constructed on each lot. Restriction regarding setbacks, external finish materials (percent of brick and wood, roof composition), landscaping, fencing, and future additions to structures would continue to apply after completion of the development to ensure neighborhood quality.
D. Developable area	50 acres less 5 acres of creek and floodplain, less an additional 20% for circulation (alleys, streets, amenities, etc.) or 36 net acres. Lot yield should be 3.6 units per gross surface acre. Setbacks, lot lines, street and alley widths, and utility easements easily meet all city regulatory requirements.
E. Amenities	Clubhouse, two swimming pools, eight lighted tennis courts. A homeowners association will assume management upon completion and sell-out of development.
F. Construction of land improvements	Paving streets, curbing, water mains, hydrants, sewer, and all connections to be constructed in accordance with current city and county standards.
G. Development restrictions	Zoning allows an average of 1 unit per 7,500 sq. ft. of net developable area as the maximum density of development.

would be a mistake to proceed with higher densities. On the other hand, if this tract were closer to the central business district, higher density may be acceptable to households that may have preferences for smaller lot sizes with closer proximity to the city center. Hence, lot yield calculations should only be used as a tool to investigate why *deviations* from yields in comparable developments exist. Using them should provide a better understanding of the market segment that developers are appealing to. No absolute maximum or minimum rules apply.

Public agencies also use lot yield per acre to determine if the development adheres to zoning restrictions. As shown in Exhibit 16–4, we see that zoning provides that an *average* of one lot per 7,500 square feet of developable area is the maximum density allowed in this project. Landco projects that an *average* of 8,712 square feet per unit will be the maximum *average* density, which easily meets zoning restrictions. Notice that developers do not always design to the maximum density allowed by zoning regulations. In all cases, *market demand* and household preferences dictate what densities should be developed. As previously indicated, home buyers may prefer to pay higher prices for lower densities and corresponding increases in privacy (larger lots) and reductions in traffic and congestion. In this event, developers may take excessive risks if they attempt to increase densities, even if current zoning allows them to do so and lower average lot prices for buyers could result.

To consider some of the market conditions Landco faces, refer to the competitive market analysis summary provided in Exhibit 16–5. For example, note that relative to Grayson, project A has about the same net development density, but it has no amenities or creek sites and it has a slightly lower average asking price per standard lot. Project B is larger in scale than Grayson, has much lower net density, larger average lot sizes, slightly greater circulation requirement (because of hilly terrain), a slightly better amenity package, and bluff sites as a special feature. Its sites are priced higher in each category. Development C is largest in scale and has no special topographic features. It has a higher development density and more amenities than the Grayson project. Landco believes, based on this competitive analysis, its price structure is justified (all other important characteristics, such as access to schools, shopping, churches, and so on, are thought to be equal).

From the above considerations, it should be apparent that estimating market demand and pricing the end product are very important. In cases where competing projects are very similar, pricing must be similar because the package of attributes being provided by each is the same. On the other hand, the more dissimilar projects are, the more variation in pricing is likely. In these cases, pricing must be based on the desirability of the relative attributes of each development. In these instances, pricing risk will be greater. Based on the estimated market prices for these lots, a preliminary estimate of the market value for the Grayson tract, *assuming all lots were completely developed and sold immediately*, would be $6,840,000.

Estimating Development Cost and Interest Carry

Landco has retained Robert Whole and Associates, an engineering firm, to estimate direct development costs based on the anticipated land plan Landco has presented to them. Exhibit 16–6 provides cost estimates. These costs are broken down into (A) land acquisition and development costs (hard and soft), and (B) operating expenses.

Land Acquisition and Development Costs. Many direct costs must be evaluated when acquiring a site for land development. Site acquisition is only one part of these costs. A developer must also evaluate the hard costs, which include site preparation and utilities installation, and the soft costs, which include site engineering, public approval fees, construction interest, and loan fees. Not all soft costs will be financed by the lender; however, to the extent that Landco is able to borrow the land acquisition and development costs, interest carry will become a significant cost of the Grayson project, as it will take several years to complete.

Operating Expenses. Other items included in Exhibit 16–6 are expenses that the developer will incur for marketing, taxes, legal, and other outlays when the project is developed and parcels are ready for sale.

Landco Development Company has approached Mid City Savings Association regarding its 50-acre Grayson tract. Mid City has reviewed the project and believes it to be viable. It has agreed to finance $1 million of the land acquisition cost, all

Exhibit 16–5 Competitive Market Analysis Survey: Grayson Project

	Grayson	*A*	*B*	*C*
Gross acres	50	40	70	100
Number of lots	180	160	210	420
Density:				
Percent developable	72%	80%	75%	80%
Lot yield	3.6	4.0	3.0	4.2
Range in sq. ft./lot	5–20,000	5–10,000	5–25,000	5–22,000
Average sq. ft./lot	8,712	8,712	10,890	8,300
Circulation requirements	20%	20%	25%	20%
Amenities:				
Pools/cabanas	2	N/A	2	2
Tennis courts	8	N/A	10	12
Exercise rooms	N/A	N/A	1	2
Clubhouse	N/A	N/A	N/A	1
Other features	Creek sites	—	Bluff sites	—
Prices:				
Cluster	$19,000	N/A	$36,000	$19,000
Standard	45,600	40,000	48,000	40,000
Creek/bluff	47,500	N/A	60,000	N/A

	Number of Parcels	*Price*	*Total*	*% Total*
Cluster	54	$19,000	$1,026,000	15.0
Standard	90	45,600	4,104,000	60.0
Creek	36	47,500	1,710,000	25.0
Gross project value/Grayson tract			$6,840,000	%100.0

Construction period:	6 months
Approval period:	6 months
Likely financing terms:	$1,000,000 of the land acquisition cost, 100 percent of the improvement cost (subject to appraisal and feasibility analysis). Loan draws are to be made as improvements are completed, interest is to be paid monthly.
Interest rate:	12 percent, or prime rate of 10 percent plus 2 percent with 3 points to be paid at loan closing.

hard costs, $700,000 of soft costs, plus the interest carry on the project. The interest rate will be tied to the prime rate plus 2 percent. For the Grayson project, the interest rate will be 12 percent on the outstanding monthly loan balance. Landco also believes that the interest rate should remain the same during the development period.[6] As in the project development we discussed in the preceding chapter, financing interest carry as a part of a land development loan is very common, even though the developer will earn no income until much of the development is complete and lots are sold to builders. As long as the lender is convinced that the value added to the site from development exceeds the cost of the site plus the cost of improvements by more than the interest cost that will be incurred on the development loan, then making a loan that includes interest carry is feasible.

[6]The interest rate risk may be reduced by using interest rate swaps.

EXHIBIT 16–6 Grayson Project Cost Estimates

A. Land and development costs:		
Site acquisition and closing costs:		
50 acres @$48,000 each		$2,400,000
Development costs:		
Hard costs		
Grading/clearing	$390,000	
Paving	540,000	
Storm sewers	70,000	
Sanitary sewers	125,000	
Water	125,000	
Electricity	120,000	
Landscaping	90,000	
Other (signage, etc.)	90,000	
Amenities (pool, cabana, tennis)	390,000	
Subtotal—Hard costs		$1,940,000
Soft costs		
Engineering	$110,000	
Direct overhead—Landco	80,000	
Public approvals, tap fees, etc.	90,000	
Miscellaneous direct costs	80,000	
Legal and accounting fees	100,000	
Contingencies	240,000	
Construction interest	451,052	
Construction loan fees (3%)	122,732	
Subtotal—Soft costs		$1,273,783
Total land, hard, and soft costs		$5,613,783
B. Operating expenses:		
Selling commissions (5%)	$342,000	
Property taxes	87,500	
General and administrative	210,000	
Marketing costs	100,000	
Total operating expenses		$ 739,500
Total project cost		$6,353,283

Draws and Revenue Estimates. Estimating the amount of interest carry is somewhat complicated because (1) The loan will be taken down in "draws" or stages, and interest will be calculated only as funds are drawn down, (2) The revenue from the sale of each type of site varies, (3) The rate of repayment of the loan depends on when parcels are actually sold, and (4) As indicated earlier, the interest rate is usually tied to a floating rate and, hence, is subject to change. Exhibits 16–7, 16–8, and 16–9 show the procedures used to estimate interest carry. Exhibit 16–7A contains a breakdown of the *loan request*, and Exhibit 16–7B contains a schedule of dollar draws and draw rates for direct development costs envisioned by Landco. Recall that Exhibit 16–5 shows that although the cluster lots represent 30 percent of the sites to be developed, they will produce only 15 percent of total revenue. Cluster lots produce less revenue because the individual sites are smaller; hence, the average cost of improving those sites is lower (not shown). Standard-size sites, which make up the majority of total sites, represent 60 percent of sites and will produce 50 percent of total revenue, whereas the creek sites represent only 20 percent of the

EXHIBIT 16–7A Estimate of Costs to be Funded by Loan Proceeds

Land costs financed		$1,000,000
Total hard development costs		1,940,000
Soft construction costs financed		
Engineering	$110,000	
Direct overhead—Landco	80,000	
Public approvals, tap fees, etc.	90,000	
Miscellaneous direct costs	80,000	
Legal and accounting fees	100,000	
Contingencies	240,000	
Total soft construction costs		700,000
Total direct costs that will be financed		$3,640,000
Estimated interest carry (calculated in Exhibit 16–12)		448,109
Total loan amount		$4,088,109
Equity required:		
Total project cost		$6,353,283
– Total loan amount		4,088,109
Equity		$2,265,174

EXHIBIT 16–7B Schedule of Estimated Monthly Cash Draws for Development Costs

Month	*Amount*	*Rate (percent)*
Closing*	$1,019,200	28.00%
1	655,200	18.00
2	655,200	18.00
3	655,200	18.00
4	218,400	6.00
5	218,400	6.00
6	218,400	6.00
Total	$3,640,000	100.00%

*$1,000,000 of land costs, plus an additional draw of $19,200 for direct costs incurred by Landco to be funded at closing (28% of $3,640,000 = $1,019,200).

sites but will produce 25 percent of total revenue. The latter sites are larger and require more than the average cost to develop.

It might be inferred from this allocation that the project may be more profitable if more standard and creek sites were developed, which would also lower the total density of the development. However, market demand may not be high enough to sell more of these sites. The point is that the *relative demand* for each type of homesite is important in determining the configuration of sites and prices that will maximize project value. For example, creek sites also will be most expensive to develop and consequently are priced highest. Cluster sites may be the only type of site amenable to the terrain on which the development of improvements must be constructed. In other words, the mix of all sites may be necessary to maintain an

EXHIBIT 16–7C Estimated Monthly Absorption Rate after Loan Closing

Month	*Cluster**	*Standard*†	*Creek*‡	*Cumulative Unit Sales*	*Cumulative Sales Volume*	*Monthly Sales Revenue*	*Monthly Revenue Rate (percent of total)*
Close	0	0	0	0	$ 0	$ 0	0.000000%
1–3	0	0	0	0	0	0	0.000000
4–6	2	2	0	12	387,600	129,200	1.888889
7–12	4	3	1	60	1,949,400	260,300	3.805556
13–18	3	6	3	132	4,788,000	473,100	6.916667
19–24	1	5	2	180	6,840,000	342,000	5.000000
Total	54	90	36	180	$6,840,000	–	100.000000%

*Price per lot = $19,000.
†Price per lot = $45,600.
‡Price per lot = $47,500.

acceptable level of total development density, to utilize the sites along the creek, and to maximize total project value.

Sales and Repayment Rates. Exhibit 16–7C provides an estimated schedule of how sales of the three categories of lots will occur and how funds will be drawn down for direct development costs for the Grayson project. Landco makes its sales estimates based on information obtained from market studies of competing projects and its own recent experience with similar projects. This sales estimate is necessary because the lender is to be repaid from revenue as lot sales occur. Exhibit 16–7C shows the revenue produced from the sale of each type of lot and the number of lots to be sold per month. These monthly revenue rates are important because as a parcel is sold the lender will receive a partial repayment of the loan that corresponds to the revenue produced from each sale.

Exhibit 16–8 shows a summary of the monthly construction draws and monthly sales revenue including the total and present value of the monthly amounts for each. We can use this information to calculate the percentage of each lot sale that needs to be paid to the lender so that the loan is repaid when the last lot is sold. (Later we will discuss accelerating the payment schedule so that the loan is repaid before the last lot is sold.) In essence, what lenders will generally do is *match* the loan repayment with the revenue produced from each parcel sale. Then, as parcels are sold, the lender *releases* the lien held on that parcel as a part of the loan security, thus clearing the way for the developer to sell to a builder. The amount that the borrower pays the lender to obtain this release is referred to as the **release price**.

You might recall from early chapters of this book that the amount that the borrower receives on a loan (initial loan amount) is equal to the present value of the future payments, discounted at the interest rate on the loan. We can generalize this to say that the present value of the amounts the borrower receives over time (e.g., loan draws) must be equal to the present value of the future payments. In Exhibit 16–8 the two present values in the exhibit are not equal because the sales revenue includes both the amount necessary to repay the loan plus the amount that the developer will get to keep to cover his expenses and provide a return on equity

EXHIBIT 16–8 Summary of Monthly Construction Draws and Sales Revenue

(a) Month	(b) Construction Draw	(c) Sales Revenue (lot sales)
Close	$1,019,200	0
1	655,200	0
2	655,200	0
3	655,200	0
4	218,400	$129,200
5	218,400	129,200
6	218,400	129,200
7		260,300
8		260,300
9		260,300
10		260,300
11		260,300
12		260,300
13		473,100
14		473,100
15		473,100
16		473,100
17		473,100
18		473,100
19		342,000
20		342,000
21		342,000
22		342,000
23		342,000
24		342,000
Total	$3,640,000	$6,840,000
Present value @ 12%	$3,569,554	$5,880,209

invested. Therefore, if we take the ratio of the present value of the loan draws to the present value of the sales revenue we get the percent of each dollar of lot sales revenue that needs to be used to repay the loan. Using the present values in the exhibit,

$$\% \text{ of revenue to lender} = \$3{,}569{,}554/\$5{,}880{,}209 = 60.7045\%.$$

This means that whenever a lot is sold, the lender must receive 60.7045 percent of the sales revenue if the loan is to be repaid *exactly when the last lot is sold.* This can be used to determine the amount that must be repaid for each type of lot as follows:

Lot Type	*Sale Price*	*% to Lender*	*Release Price*
Cluster	$19,000	.607045	$11,534
Standard	45,600	.607045	27,681
Creek	47,500	.607045	28,835

The lender would normally contract for a fixed dollar amount rather than a percent of revenue to be repaid from each lot sale. This is because the lender doesn't want to be concerned about whether the developer will decide to cut the price on a lot at a later point in time in order to make a sale. More important, the lender will not want to wait until the last lot is sold to have the loan completely repaid. The lender does not want to incur the risk that a slowdown in lot sales or difficulty selling some of the lots will significantly delay loan repayment. Thus, the actual release price negotiated with the lender will normally be higher than the release prices shown above. Before we consider this, however, we will demonstrate that the release price above does repay the loan by the time the last lot is sold.

Exhibit 16–9 shows a loan repayment schedule based on the release prices calculated above. Note that, during months 1 through 3, the interest draw pattern in column (*b*) is based on the interest rate (12 percent) divided by 12 months, or 1 percent of the previous month's ending loan balance. Also, note that because the interest carry is *borrowed,* it is accumulated in the loan balance.[7] The ending monthly loan balance continues to increase until enough parcels are sold each month to provide a paydown of principal in excess of interest draws (month 7). However, monthly interest payments continue to be based on the preceding month's loan balance.[8]

Principal payments in Exhibit 16–9 are based on the projected lot sales and release prices calculated above. For example, in month 4 two cluster lots sold for $11,534 and two standard lots sold for $27,681 for a total of $78,430. Note that the ending balance is exactly zero in month 24. This proves that the loan is repaid when the last lot is sold.

Release Schedule. Regarding the expected period that the loan will be outstanding, most lenders insist that the loan be repaid *prior* to the time expected for the borrower to sell all the parcels in the development. The lender usually does not want to take the risk associated with a possible slowdown in sales in the later stages of the project. In many land developments, choice parcels are sold early and less desirable ones may remain unsold as time passes. Because some parcels may be more difficult to sell, the lender wants assurance that the developer will take this added risk. Consequently, the lender will bargain for a faster rate of loan payments, thereby making sure that the loan will be repaid before all 180 parcels are sold.

Another reason for negotiating faster repayment rates is, since Mid City will put most of the "front-end" money into the development during the first six months, it wants assurance that the loan repayment is given preference as sales proceeds are realized. Further, because the developer will realize some markup on each sale, the lender has some room to negotiate a satisfactory release schedule and still leave the developer with a reasonable amount of cash inflow.

---

[7]This is analogous to a negative amortization loan.

[8]We show in Exhibit 16–9 that the developer actually receives interest draws in cash (column *b*). Then the developer simultaneously makes a cash interest payment in the same amount (column *c*). Notice that the same loan balance would result if the lender provided a draw for the direct cost only (column *a*), *computed* interest on those draws as in column (*b*), added it to the loan balance (instead of actually paying out cash), reduced the loan balance as principal repayments occur (column *d*), and did not require cash interest payments from the developer (column *e*). If this pattern were followed, the ending balance would be the same and no cash disbursement for interest would have to be made by the lender or repaid by the developer. In the pattern just described, interest carry is simply being accrued in the loan balance.

EXHIBIT 16–9 Loan Repayment Schedule Assuming Loan Payments Proportional with Lot Sales

	Draws			Payments			
Month	*(a) Construction Draw*	*(b) Interest*	*(c) Total Draw*	*(d) Payments Principal*	*(e) Interest*	*(f) Total Payments*	*(g) Ending Balance*
Close 0	$1,019,200	$ 0	$1,019,200	$ 0	$ 0	$ 0	$1,019,200
1	655,200	10,192	665,392	0	10,192	10,192	1,684,592
2	655,200	16,846	672,046	0	16,846	16,846	2,356,638
3	655,200	23,566	678,766	0	23,566	23,566	3,035,404
4	218,400	30,354	248,754	78,430	30,354	108,784	3,205,728
5	218,400	32,057	250,457	78,430	32,057	110,488	3,377,755
6	218,400	33,778	252,178	78,430	33,778	112,208	3,551,502
7	0	35,515	35,515	158,014	35,515	193,529	3,429,003
8	0	34,290	34,290	158,014	34,290	192,304	3,305,279
9	0	33,053	33,053	158,014	33,053	191,067	3,180,318
10	0	31,803	31,803	158,014	31,803	189,817	3,054,108
11	0	30,541	30,541	158,014	30,541	188,555	2,926,635
12	0	29,266	29,266	158,014	29,266	187,280	2,797,887
13	0	27,979	27,979	287,193	27,979	315,172	2,538,673
14	0	25,387	25,387	287,193	25,387	312,580	2,276,866
15	0	22,769	22,769	287,193	22,769	309,962	2,012,442
16	0	20,124	20,124	287,193	20,124	307,318	1,745,373
17	0	17,454	17,454	287,193	17,454	304,647	1,475,633
18	0	14,756	14,756	287,193	14,756	301,950	1,203,196
19	0	12,032	12,032	207,610	12,032	219,642	1,007,619
20	0	10,076	10,076	207,610	10,076	217,686	810,085
21	0	8,101	8,101	207,610	8,101	215,710	610,577
22	0	6,106	6,106	207,610	6,106	213,715	409,073
23	0	4,091	4,091	207,610	4,091	211,700	205,554
24	0	2,056	2,056	207,610	2,056	209,665	0
Totals	$3,640,000	$512,191	$4,152,191	$4,152,191	$512,191	$4,664,383	

Many land development loans set the repayment rate so that the loan is repaid when about 80 to 90 percent of total project revenue is realized. The exact schedule is negotiated based on how fast the lender wants the loan repaid, how much cash the developer must retain from each parcel sale to cover expenses not funded in the loan, and conditions in the loan market.

In Exhibit 16–10, the duration of the construction loan is estimated assuming the lender wants to be repaid when approximately 83.33 percent of project revenues, or $5.7 million, is realized. This means that the lender wants to be repaid at a rate equal to 120 percent of the rate at which monthly revenue is received (100%/83.33% = 120%). If the borrower and lender had agreed that the loan would be repaid over the entire life of the project (24 months), then 100 percent of the loan would be repaid when 100 percent of project revenues were received, as was illustrated in Exhibit 16–9. Accelerating the repayment rate by 16.67 percent means that for every $1 of sales revenue realized, the developer repays the loan by an amount 120 percent greater than would be the case if the loan were repaid over the entire life of the project. In our illustration, based on the cumulative sales revenue shown in Exhibit 16–7C, a total of 80 percent of project revenues will be received during the month 21. Hence, the lender would like the loan to be repaid at that time.

EXHIBIT 16–10 Determining the Duration of the Construction Loan

				Monthly		
Month	*Cluster*	*Standard*	*Creek*	*Cumulative Sales ($)*	*Sales Revenue*	
4–6	6	6	0	$ 387,600	$129,200	
7–12	24	18	6	1,949,400	260,300	
13–18	18	36	18	4,788,000	473,100	
19	1	5	2	5,130,000	342,000	
20	1	5	2	5,472,000	342,000	
21	1	5	2	5,814,000	342,000	←Repaid during this month

EXHIBIT 16–11 Calculation of the Release Price per Parcel

Lot Type	*Release Price before Acceleration*	*Acceleration Factor*	*Accelerated Release Price*
Cluster	$11,534	1.2	$13,840
Standard	27,681	1.2	33,217
Creek	28,835	1.2	34,602

Estimating Release Prices per Parcel Sold

We have already indicated that the lender will generally insist on a loan repayment rate in excess of the rate estimated for revenue to be earned. Indeed, in our example, we have indicated that the lender would like the loan to be repaid at 120 percent of the rate at which revenue will be received. However, as we have seen, when lenders and developers negotiate land development loans, they also usually assign a release price *to each parcel* in the development. When each parcel is sold, that release amount is paid to the lender, who then releases the lien, thereby assuring the buyer of an unencumbered title. In Exhibit 16–11, the release prices for the three types of lots in our example are calculated.[9]

Loan Request and Repayment Schedule

Exhibit 16–12 shows the revised loan schedule with the new release price. Note that the loan is now repaid in month 21 as we projected in Exhibit 16–10.[10] The exhibit indicates that total interest carry will be $448,109. This is the amount that the developer must include in his loan request. If sales were to slow down, the loan balance would increase rapidly because *actual* interest draws would increase at a faster rate than *estimated* draws. If this slowdown occurred, the interest reserve of

[9]There are alternative ways of calculating the accelerated release price. Previous editions of this text used a slightly different approach. In this edition we have simplified the approach while obtaining virtually the same answer. The point of any approach taken is simply to arrive at proposed release prices that are acceptable to both the lender and developer.

[10]The reader should keep in mind that the approach in Exhibit 16–10 was an estimate to determine when the loan would be repaid to determine what release price to use. The actual month it is repaid may differ slightly when calculated using the more detailed projections in Exhibit 16–12 that actually calculates the interest, loan balance, and so on, every month.

EXHIBIT 16–12 Accelerated Loan Repayment Schedule—Landco Development Company

	Draws			Payments			
Month	(a) Construction Draw	(b) Interest	(c) Total Draw	(d) Principal	(e) Interest	(f) Total Payments	(g) Ending Balance
Close 0	$1,019,200	$ 0	$1,019,200	$ 0	$ 0	$ 0	$1,019,200
1	655,200	10,192	665,392	0	10,192	10,192	1,684,592
2	655,200	16,846	672,046	0	16,846	16,846	2,356,638
3	655,200	23,566	678,766	0	23,566	23,566	3,035,404
4	218,400	30,354	248,754	94,116	30,354	124,470	3,190,042
5	218,400	31,900	250,300	94,116	31,900	126,017	3,346,226
6	218,400	33,462	251,862	94,116	33,462	127,579	3,503,972
7	0	35,040	35,040	189,617	35,040	224,656	3,349,395
8	0	33,494	33,494	189,617	33,494	223,111	3,193,272
9	0	31,933	31,933	189,617	31,933	221,549	3,035,588
10	0	30,356	30,356	189,617	30,356	219,973	2,876,327
11	0	28,763	28,763	189,617	28,763	218,380	2,715,474
12	0	27,155	27,155	189,617	27,155	216,771	2,553,012
13	0	25,530	25,530	344,632	25,530	370,162	2,233,910
14	0	22,339	22,339	344,632	22,339	366,971	1,911,617
15	0	19,116	19,116	344,632	19,116	363,748	1,586,102
16	0	15,861	15,861	344,632	15,861	360,493	1,257,331
17	0	12,573	12,573	344,632	12,573	357,205	925,272
18	0	9,253	9,253	344,632	9,253	353,885	589,893
19	0	5,899	5,899	249,131	5,899	255,030	346,660
20	0	3,467	3,467	249,131	3,467	252,598	100,996
21	0	1,010	1,010	102,005	1,010	103,015	0
22	0	0	0	0	0	0	0
23	0	0	0	0	0	0	0
24	0	0	0	0	0	0	0
Totals	$3,640,000	$448,109	$4,088,109	$4,982,630	$448,109	$5,430,739	

$448,109 might be depleted. Further, if the loan balance ever reached $4,088,109, the lender would not allow further draws. The developer would have to make interest payments from other sources. This is one reason why the loan request is a low percentage of gross project value ($4,088,109/$6,840,000) = 60 percent (rounded). Indeed, most lenders prefer to keep the loan-to-value ratio for land development projects in the range of 70 percent, so they have a better chance of recovering the loan balance should the project go into default.

Project Feasibility and Profitability

From the developer's viewpoint, the economic feasibility of the project is based on whether the market value of the sites after development will exceed the acquisition cost of the land, plus direct improvement costs, plus the interest carry and any other costs not included in the loan provided by Mid City. Exhibit 16–6 discussed previously summarizes total costs, including closing costs and other costs that Landco must pay but that will not be funded in the loan for the Grayson project. The loan fees and interest carry *is included* in the total loan amount of $4,088,109. We can now do a more detailed projection of how the project costs will be incurred over time and how income will be generated over time from lot sales.

To investigate the developer's ability to carry this project until the loan is repaid and to establish whether the project is feasible for the developer to pursue and meet the expected return on investment, the lender must analyze a schedule of cash flows that the developer prepares. This statement should contain not only direct costs but also additional day-to-day operating expenses that the Grayson project may require. In this way, the lender can project the developer's cash position, better analyze the risk of loan default, and establish the profitability of the project. Exhibit 16–13 contains a quarterly summary of all cash inflows and outflows for Landco over the entire life of the project. The inflows are estimated based on the sales prices for each type of parcel, plus loan draws and equity required from the developer for the land purchase price and closing costs. The outflows include expenditures for direct development costs taken from the schedule of monthly draws (Exhibit 16–12). Loan repayments are taken from the schedule of loan repayments (Exhibit 16–12). Other operating expenses, including general and administrative expenses, sales commissions, and property taxes, have been estimated on a quarterly basis and included in the exhibit.

The developer will have negative cash flow during the first two quarters. Adding up these two negative cash flows results in a total of $1,648,893, which is the total equity that the developer is likely to need for the project. Based on the loan repayment schedule detailed above, the developer will retain all cash flow from sale proceeds beginning in month 21 through month 24. Although some cash flow will be retained from earlier sales, clearly the developer will receive the greatest cash flow during the later quarters.

From the beginning of the development period until the 21st month, a question arises concerning the developer's ability to meet operating expenses and other cash outflow requirements not funded in the loan request from Mid City. The amount loaned to the developer covers only part of the land cost, direct costs, and interest carry. Other obligations, such as overhead and loan fees, must be paid during development. Sales commissions, property taxes, and general and administrative expenses were not funded as a part of the development loan and must also be covered from the cash retained by the developer from each parcel sale.

Exhibit 16–13 provides insight into Landco's ability to carry the cash needs of the entire project. At closing and in the first quarter Landco will have negative cash flow. However, from the second through eighth quarters, cash flow will be positive. It is during such periods that estimates concerning costs, sales, rates, and repayment conditions become crucial to both Landco and Mid City. If the time needed for development exceeds initial estimates, if actual development costs exceed estimates, or if sales do not materialize as projected, Landco's cash flow position during these months will change dramatically. Similarly, if Mid City demands a release schedule calling for loan repayments that are too high, cash flow to Landco from sales revenue would be reduced, which may jeopardize Landco's ability to carry out the project and to repay the loan. For this reason, Mid City must consider Landco's own financial resources in the event that any of these adverse factors materialize. Clearly, if Landco's cash position in this project becomes questionable, Landco will be expected to share in some of the risk by contributing working capital from its own resources to complete sale of the project successfully. To analyze Landco's ability to provide working capital, should it be necessary, Mid City will thoroughly review the company's income statement and balance sheet as well as possibly requiring additional loan security or guarantees from Landco beyond the land that serves as security for the loan.

Finally, based on Exhibit 16–13, Landco's cash flow does not materialize significantly until the later quarters of the project. This timing is in keeping with the way risk is taken during the project. Because the lender puts in front-end capital, they want assurance of a high priority in the sales proceeds as the development matures. Consequently, Landco must wait until the lender's prior claim is satisfied before it realizes a return. However, from Landco's viewpoint, its equity in the project increases as value is added to the project as actual development occurs. Hence, most of its returns are appropriately deferred to the later stages of the project.

Project IRR *and Net Present Value*

Up to this point in the analysis, we have made some rough estimates as to the economic viability of the project. Recall that we estimated that the market value of the project if it were developed and all parcels were sold today was $6,840,000, and costs were estimated to be $6,353,283, indicating that a margin between total revenues and total costs existed. Although such a margin exists, the cash inflows and outflows related to the development and subsequent sales *do not occur immediately*. Consequently, the *time value of money* must be taken into account. To do this for the Grayson project, we *estimate* that a risk premium of at least 3 percent over the borrowing rate of 12 percent, or 15 percent, would be the *minimum* before-tax return that Landco is willing to accept on its equity investment at this time.[11] Applying this rate to the quarterly net cash flows shown in Exhibit 16–13 results in a net present value of $41,558. This figure indicates that the project is economically feasible and meets Landco's required return.[12] Stated another way, based on the assumptions used in our analysis, Landco can pay $2.4 million for the land and still earn a positive net present value. Finally, again using the cash flows in Exhibit 16–13 we see that the *IRR* for the project is 16.64 percent. As expected, since the *NPV* was positive, this exceeds Landco's required *IRR* of 15 percent.

Entrepreneurial Profits

In the preceding section, we noted that revenues produced by the Grayson project as projected by Landco would cover all costs, and the resultant cash flows, when discounted by the required rate of return (assumed to be 15 percent before taxes in the example), would provide a positive *NPV* of about $42,000. When such estimates are made, *all costs* associated with development, *particularly general overhead costs* relating to time spent by all Landco staff, executives, and other personnel should be included (see Exhibit 16–6). The goal of the analysis is to produce an estimate of net cash flow that can be used to evaluate whether a required before-tax return of 15 percent (net of *all* relevant costs) will be earned on the $2,262,231 of

[11]An annual rate of 15 percent, compounded quarterly, is the rate of return used for discounting. This discount rate represents the required return that Landco must earn as a development company or a going concern, *net of all direct and indirect costs* associated with this project. It represents a rate of return to the owners or shareholders of the Landco company.

[12]Because the project shows a positive net present value, Landco could pay slightly more that $2.4 million and still earn its required return. If the seller of the land, however, is satisfied with $2.4 million, Landco may be in a position to earn a higher return (assuming all projections materialize). Such a difference between what buyers and sellers are willing to pay and receive occurs because of differences in expectations concerning future development revenues, or because of differences in information (e.g., market knowledge) possessed by each party. You should now see that the exhibits presented in this chapter can be linked in a spreadsheet format and with a computer, various "what if" scenarios or simulation analyses can be carried out.

EXHIBIT 16–13 Developer's Cash Flow

Quarter	*Close*	*(1)*	*(2)*	*(3)*	*(4)*	*(5)*	*(6)*	*(7)*	*(8)*
Inflow									
Sales		$ 0	$ 387,600	$780,900	$ 780,900	$1,419,300	$1,419,300	$1,026,000	$1,026,000
Construction draw	$ 1,019,200	$1,965,600	655,200	0	0	0	0	0	0
Interest draw		50,604	95,717	100,466	86,274	66,985	37,687	10,375	0
Total inflow	$ 1,019,200	$2,016,204	$1,138,517	$881,366	$ 867,174	$1,486,285	$1,456,987	$1,036,375	$1,026,000
Outflow									
Land purchase	$ 2,400,000								
Closing costs	100,000								
Loan fees	122,643								
Principal		$ 0	$ 282,349	$568,850	$568,850	$1,033,896	$1,033,896	$ 600,268	$ 0
Direct costs	19,200	1,965,600	655,200	0	0	0	0	0	0
Interest costs		50,604	95,717	100,466	86,274	66,985	37,687	10,375	0
General and admin.		26,250	26,250	26,250	26,250	26,250	26,250	26,250	26,250
Property tax					43,750				43,750
Sales expense		0	19,380	39,045	39,045	70,965	70,965	51,300	51,300
Total outflow	2,641,843	2,042,454	1,078,896	734,612	764,169	1,198,096	1,168,798	688,194	121,300
Net cash flow	$(1,622,643)	$ (26,250)	$ 59,621	$146,755	$ 103,005	$ 288,189	$ 288,189	$ 348,182	$ 904,700

Developer's *IRR* = 16.64% (*IRR* of quarterly cash flows multiplied by 4)
NPV @15.00% = $41,558

equity Landco invests in the Grayson project. This required return should be viewed as a minimum rate of return that Landco must earn to justify allocating the equity to the project.

Some professionals in the real estate field may also include in their projections an estimate for developer profit, say 10 or 15 percent, as an additional cost of development when projecting net cash flow. Net cash flow is then discounted by a required return on equity. When doing this, one must be careful to avoid "double counting" profit by including a developer profit and discounting by a required return that includes a premium for taking development risk. We have included all costs relative to land, labor, and capital explicitly in our projections and have not included an estimate of markup or developer profit as an *additional* cost of development. Thus the 16.64 percent projected return for this project includes compensation for Landco's entrepreneurial ability to develop the project.

Sensitivity Analysis

Based on the analysis just concluded, because Landco estimated a positive *NPV*, the \$2.4 million land price is justified. Indeed, the analysis shows that based on the assumptions used to make projections for the project, Landco could actually pay slightly more and still earn its desired return of 15 percent. However, Landco should also use sensitivity analysis to determine how sensitive this return is to lower market prices, larger development periods, cost overruns, higher interest rates, and the like, before acquiring the land. We discussed this analysis at the conclusion of the previous chapter. It applies to land development as well as to project development.

Conclusion

This chapter dealt with *land development*, which involves the acquisition of land with the intention of constructing utilities and surface improvements, then reselling some or all of the developed sites to project developers or, in the case of housing, home builders. Our discussion of land development extends many of the concepts introduced in the previous chapter that dealt with financing development projects. After completing both chapters, you should have a good understanding of the development process including the mechanics of construction and land development loans.

Key Terms

acquisition and development costs 479
build to suit 468
completion bonds 473
draws 481
entrepreneurial profits 490
extension agreements 475
feasibility study 469
holdbacks 473
land development 467
option agreement 469
release price 483
release schedule 472
turnkey basis 468

Questions

1. How might land development activities be specialized? Why is this activity different from project development discussed in the preceding chapter?
2. What is an option contract? How is it used in land acquisition? What should developers be concerned

with when using such options? What contingencies may be included in a land option?

3. What are some of the physical considerations that a developer should be concerned with when purchasing land? How should such considerations be taken into account when determining the price that should be paid?

4. In land development projects, why do lenders insist on loan repayment rates in excess of sales revenue? What is a *release price*?

5. What are the unique risks of land development projects from the developer's and lender's points of view?

Problems

1. Treetop Associated Group (TAG) is seeking financing for acquisition and development of 147 homesites. The land will cost \$1.5 million, and TAG estimates direct development costs to be an additional \$2.7 million. City Federal Bank will make a loan covering 40 percent of the land acquisition cost, 100 percent of direct improvement cost, and interest carry at 11 percent interest with a 3 percent loan origination fee.

   TAG has decided to split the development into *two* parcel types, standard and deluxe, with the standard parcels comprising 87 of the total. Also, TAG thinks that the deluxe sites will be priced at a \$2,000 premium over the standard parcel price of \$36,000. Total project revenue will be \$5,412,000. After making a 60 percent down payment for the land and incurring closing costs of \$50,000, TAG believes that the remaining development costs will be drawn down at \$600,000 a month for the first three months and \$300,000 a month for the next three months. Parcel sales are expected to begin during the fourth month after closing. TAG estimates that they will sell three standard parcels and four deluxe parcels a month for the remainder of the first year, and five standards and two deluxes per month for the second year.

   The company and the bank have agreed to a repayment schedule calling for the loan to be repaid at a rate 20 percent faster than the receipt of sales revenues; that is, the loan plus interest carry per parcel will be repaid when approximately 83.33 percent of all revenues are realized. Other costs to consider include sales expense (paid quarterly at a rate of *S* percent on parcels sold during the quarter), administrative costs of \$7,500 per quarter, and property taxes of \$19,000 at the end of each year.

   a. Estimate the total loan amount including interest carry for TAG.

   b. Based on your answer in (*a*), what will be the release price for each type of lot?

   c. Based on (*b*) and the pattern of loan draws, prepare a schedule showing when TAG will have the loan fully repaid. What will be the total cash payments on the project loan?

   d. What will total project costs be? What percentage of total project costs are being financed?

   e. What will be the *NPV* and *IRR* of this project if TAG's before-tax required rate of return is 15 percent? (Hint: Prepare a cash flow analysis on a quarterly basis over the life of the project.)

2. Lee Development Co. has found a site that it believes will support 75 homesites. The company also believes that the land can be purchased for \$225,000 while direct development costs will run an additional \$775,000. The Last National Bank of Texas will underwrite 100 percent of the improvements plus the interest carry. The loan would be made at 13 percent interest with a *3 percent loan origination fee*. Lee believes that the development will sell faster with two types of parcels, standard and deluxe, with the standard parcel comprising 57 percent of the total parcels.

   Lee's marketing staff believes that the deluxe sites can be sold for \$24,000 while the standard sites should bring \$13,500. Lee estimates that the direct cost draws will be taken down in four equal amounts, with the first draw commencing with the close of the loan. Other up-front fees include closing costs of \$10,000 and a 3 percent loan fee (not covered by the loan). Lee's sales staff supervisor assures him that she can generate sales activity starting in the fourth month that will result in the sale of five standard parcels per month and four deluxe parcels per month for three months. For the next six months, activity should be seven standard parcels per month and only one deluxe parcel per month. The Last National Bank wants its money out of the project early and wants Lee to agree to a release price per parcel that will result in the loan being repaid at a rate 25 percent faster than sales revenue is expected to be earned. Other costs to consider include sales expense (paid quarterly on 5 percent of the sales price of parcels sold during the quarter), administrative costs of \$11,000 per quarter, and property taxes of \$7,000. None of these latter items are to be funded in the loan.

   a. Develop a total monthly sales schedule for Lee. What will be Lee's total revenue? How many months will it take Lee to fully repay the loan?

b. What will be the total interest carry funded in the loan amount? What will be the release price for each type of lot? Compute the loan repayment schedule. What will be Lee's total cash payments to the Last National Bank?

c. What will Lee's total equity requirement be? Should Lee undertake this project if its required return on equity is 18 percent? (Hint: Do a cash flow analysis on a quarterly basis for the life of the project.) What will be the *IRR* on the project?

3. Refer to problem 1. (Optional for spreadsheet users.)

a. Determine the release price based on a repayment schedule calling for the loan to be repaid at the following rates: 0 percent, 10 percent, and 30 percent faster than the receipt of sales revenues. (Note: the original problem assumes a rate 20 percent faster.)

b. Develop a loan schedule to demonstrate that with 0 percent acceleration the loan is paid off exactly when the last lot is sold.

c. Calculate the lender's *IRR* (effective cost of the loan) for each of the rates in part (*a*).

CHAPTER

17

The Secondary Mortgage Market

Pass-Through Securities

Introduction

We begin this chapter with a brief description of the evolution of the secondary market. Particular attention is paid to the need for this kind of market and identifying the major organizations that participate in it. We then describe the various types of mortgage-backed securities that have evolved in recent years and provide a framework for analyzing their investment characteristics. Although mortgage-related securities may be offered on many types of mortgage pools, we generally limit our discussion to residential mortgage-backed pools. The chapter concludes with a section on "pricing" two types of mortgage-related securities, and provides an evaluation of characteristics that differentiate these more important security types. The next chapter is a continuation of this one. It provides a detailed analysis of collateralized mortgage obligations (CMOs) and "derivative" securities. It also contains an introduction to commercial mortgage-backed securities.

Evolution of the Secondary Mortgage Market

The **secondary mortgage market**, as we know it today, evolved as a result of a combination of the following influences:

(1) A need existed for a market in which specialized mortgage originators, such as mortgage banking companies, could sell mortgages and thereby replenish funds with which new loans could be originated.

(2) A need also existed for a market mechanism to facilitate a geographic flow of funds. Such a market would allow lenders located in regions where the demand for housing and mortgage financing far exceeded the availability of deposits to sell mortgages to other intermediaries in regions with a surplus of savings.

(3) Beginning in the late 1960s, many innovations in securitization occurred in response to the trend toward deregulation of depository-type financial institutions. Because of this trend, savers were no longer limited to traditional methods of saving, such as savings accounts and certificates of deposit. Further, with the passage of legislation giving individual retirement accounts (IRAs) favorable tax treatment, and the aging of the U.S. population increasing the flow of funds to pension

accounts, the market for investible funds became much broader. Hence, mortgage lenders, with the aid of organizations specializing in underwriting and selling securities to the public and institutional investors, were faced with the challenge of attracting savings from the public in different ways so as to replenish funds for new mortgage loans. There has been a long-standing commitment on the part of the federal government to encourage home ownership and to provide support for a strong system of housing finance.

Early Buyers of Mortgage Loans

There has always been a secondary mortgage market of some type. Prior to the mid-1950s, primary mortgage originators involved in the secondary market included mortgage companies and, to a lesser extent, thrift institutions. Investors who purchased these mortgages included large life insurance companies and eastern thrifts. The former generally purchased mortgages from mortgage companies, and the latter generally purchased them from thrifts in other regions. By purchasing mortgages, these institutional investors helped to provide funds necessary for the housing boom during the postwar era.

One major factor enhancing the early development of the secondary market was that the federal government, through programs initiated with the Federal Housing Administration (FHA) and later the Veterans Administration (VA), protected mortgage investors from losses by providing either default insurance (FHA) or loan guarantees (VA). One outcome of these programs was a system of minimum underwriting standards for borrower qualifications, appraisals, and building specifications. Uniform administrative procedures required by the FHA and VA were followed by mortgage companies and helped to accommodate significant volumes of FHA and VA originations and facilitated servicing activities. Given (1) the availability of default insurance and loan guarantees, (2) the development of standardized loan underwriting, processing, and servicing, and (3) the availability of hazard and title insurance, investors in mortgages could acquire a large quantity of loans and expect to receive interest and principal payments with little or no risk. Administrative problems regarding defaults, late payments, and so forth were usually handled for a fee by the servicer, making mortgage investments resemble those of a bond or fixed-income security. With funds acquired from sales of mortgages to institutional investors, originators (primarily mortgage companies) replenished funds with which they could originate new loans.

The Government's Role in Market Development

Government involvement in the secondary mortgage market was formally established in 1916 when the first farmer's credit program was created at the Federal Land Bank as a result of federal concerns with rural housing finance. However, the two most important factors in the early development of the secondary mortgage market were the creation of the Federal Housing Administration (FHA) in 1934 and the chartering of the Federal National Mortgage Association (FNMA) in 1938. As previously indicated, FHA programs helped found a national mortgage market with the creation of mortgage underwriting standards and mortgage default insurance. This program and the Veterans Administration loan guarantee program created in 1944 were very important events in the evolution of the secondary market.

In 1935, Congress authorized the Reconstruction Finance Corporation (RFC)[1] to form a subsidiary to be known as the RFC Mortgage Company, to initiate a

[1]This agency was charged with the responsibility of raising capital to provide loans for construction of new physical facilities after the Depression.

secondary mortgage market. This venture was not successful, and in 1938 a subsidiary was formed to focus only on a secondary market for government-insured residential mortgages. This institution, the **Federal National Mortgage Association**, often designated by its initials FNMA, is now commonly known as "Fannie Mae."

FNMA was a subsidiary of the RFC until 1950, when it was transferred to the Housing and Home Finance Agency,[2] which had been created in 1942. By becoming a part of the federal agency primarily concerned with housing and home finance, FNMA's activities in the secondary market for home mortgages could be more closely coordinated with activities of the Federal Home Loan Bank Board and its affiliated agencies as well as with those of the FHA. It should be stressed that FNMA's role at this time was limited to very specialized activities, such as direct lending on FHA-insured housing located in remote areas not reached by the existing mortgage market and selling these mortgages to private investors. During this time, it had no real comparative advantage in borrowing or purchasing relative to private entities and hence was not a major force in the secondary market.

The Secondary Market after 1954

In 1954, Congress rechartered FNMA, assigning it three separate and distinct activities: (1) enhancement of secondary market operations in federally insured and guaranteed mortgages, (2) management of direct loans previously made and, where necessary, liquidation of properties and mortgages acquired by default, and (3) management of special assistance programs, including support for subsidized mortgage loan programs. Each function was carried out as though it was operated as a separate corporation.

Throughout this and earlier periods, interest rates on FHA and VA mortgages were *regulated* by those agencies. Instead of deregulating interest rates on FHA and VA mortgages, Congress, in its attempt to keep mortgage interest rates as low as possible to would-be home buyers, preferred to maintain a system under which FHA-VA interest rates would remain regulated. FNMA's role would be to raise capital by issuing debt when necessary to purchase mortgages, thereby replenishing capital to originators during periods of rising interest rates. It was thought that those mortgages would be sold at a gain when interest rates declined, thereby providing FNMA with funds to retire debt that was previously issued to acquire mortgages. FNMA was thus viewed as a vehicle that would provide liquidity to the home finance system when needed, and would assume the interest rate risk associated with its role as an intermediary between mortgage originators (primary originators of FHA and VA loans) and investors in its bonds. Ostensibly, over many periodic cycles of interest rate movements, it was hoped that FNMA would, on the average, earn a "spread" between interest earned on mortgages and interest paid on its bonds, while providing liquidity to the home finance system.[3]

---

[2]This agency, along with FHA, would ultimately become part of the U.S. Department of Housing and Urban Development (HUD).

[3]Obviously, the risk of such a strategy is that the *net* cost of bonds and notes used to raise funds over periods of rising and falling interest rates would exceed the *net* interest income from mortgages held in a portfolio. This could occur if, over several cycles, net purchases of mortgages exceeded net sales.

FNMA's Changing Role

As market interest rates gradually increased and FHA-VA mortgage interest rates lagged, life insurance companies began to adopt a policy of shifting funds from mortgages to other investments. At the same time, life insurance companies developed considerable interest in the acquisition of common stock, which was previously thought to be too risky. Hence, investment by life insurance companies in common stocks and corporate bonds grew at the expense of mortgages. The traditional channel between mortgage companies and life insurance companies was seriously disrupted. Mortgage companies and other originators became concerned because their traditional source of funds from secondary mortgage sales diminished. Recognizing these changes in investment policy, organizations such as the National Association of Home Builders, the Mortgage Bankers Association of America, the National Association of Real Estate Boards, and the United States Savings and Loan League advocated that FNMA's secondary market operations be expanded.

These influences prompted Congress to review the operations of FNMA and culminated in the Charter Act of 1954. Among the provisions in the act, however, was an additional provision that governmental participation in the operation of the principal secondary market facility should be gradually replaced by a private enterprise. The act included a procedure whereby FNMA would, over a period of time, be transformed into a privately owned and managed organization. By converting FNMA to a private operation rather than setting up a new one, FNMA's years of experience in the secondary market could be utilized during the transition period and eventually would concentrate the whole operation in private hands.

To provide a financial base to operate FNMA, the Charter Act also authorized issuance of nonvoting preferred and common stock for the financing of secondary market operations. The preferred stock was issued to the secretary of the treasury. Sellers of mortgages to FNMA were required to purchase FNMA stock as a condition of sale, which provided additional capital for operations and resulted in widespread ownership of FNMA. Additional funding for FNMA came from its issuance of notes and debt instruments. The act provided that, if necessary, the U.S. Treasury would be permitted to acquire up to $2.25 billion of these notes. This "backstop" was intended to provide assurance of liquidity to FNMA bond and note purchasers and a price support for such securities, should FNMA's profitability or inability to issue more of these obligations ever come into question. It also provided FNMA with a distinct advantage when borrowing in capital markets to finance its activities. FNMA could now borrow at lower rates of interest than it otherwise could have in the absence of the Treasury backstop.

The Housing and Urban Development Act of 1968

Under the Housing and Urban Development Act of 1968, the assets, liabilities, and management of the secondary market operations were transferred to a completely private corporation. This corporation became the Federal National Mortgage Association as we know it today: a government-sponsored corporation owned solely by private investors. All Treasury-held preferred shares provided for in the 1954 Act were retired, thereby eliminating government ownership.

The special assistance and management and liquidating functions, largely dealing with subsidized mortgage purchases for special federal housing programs, remained in the Department of Housing and Urban Development. To perform these functions, the 1968 Act created another corporation, the Government National Mortgage Association (GNMA), now commonly known as "Ginnie Mae."

The Government National Mortgage Association

The **Government National Mortgage Association** (GNMA) was organized to perform three principal functions: (1) management and liquidation of mortgages previously acquired by FNMA—the liquidation of the portfolio acquired from FNMA at the time of its partition comes through regular principal repayments and sales; (2) special assistance lending in support of certain federal subsidized housing programs; GNMA, also known as "Ginnie Mae," is authorized to purchase mortgages that are originated under various housing programs designed by FHA, to provide housing in areas where it cannot be provided by conventional market lending; and (3) provision of a guarantee for FHA-VA mortgage pools, which would provide a guarantee for mortgage-backed securities. Its operations are financed through funds from the U.S. Treasury and from public borrowing.

Mortgage-Backed Securities and the GNMA Payment Guarantee

The guarantee program provided for in 1968 was one of the most significant provisions in the development of the secondary mortgage market as we know it today. Essentially, GNMA was empowered to guarantee the timely payment of principal and interest on securities backed or secured by pools of mortgages insured by the FHA and the Farmers Home Administration (FmHA), or guaranteed by the VA. One of the problems in the secondary mortgage market prior to this time was that even though FHA-insured mortgages could be purchased by investors who received monthly payments of principal and interest (less servicing fees), investors often experienced delays in payments when borrower defaults occurred. In these cases, servicers would have to make a claim for any payments in arrears plus remittance of the loan balance from FHA or the guarantee from VA. Settlement of these claims could be time-consuming and required additional administrative effort on the part of investors.

Many investors in mortgage packages disliked this waiting period, which resulted in unpredictable cash flows and a reduction in investment yields. By providing the buyer with a guarantee of timely payment of interest and principal, GNMA was, in essence, guaranteeing monthly payments of interest and principal from amortization. The guarantee also included repayment of outstanding loan balances should mortgages be prepaid before maturity or should borrowers default. GNMA would make timely payments to the security purchaser, then take responsibility for settling accounts with the servicer. This would relieve investors from administrative problems and delays in receiving mortgage payments. For this guarantee, the buyer was charged a guarantee fee, which provided GNMA with operating funds to perform this function.

As a result of this GNMA guarantee program, a virtual explosion in the secondary market occured. This guarantee enabled originators of FHA and VA mortgages to pool or package mortgages and to *issue securities*, called *pass-through securities*, which were collateralized by the mortgages, and were based on the notion of investors buying an undivided security interest in a pool of mortgages with interest and principal passed through to investors as received from borrowers. These securities would be underwritten by investment banking firms and sold to investors in markets that were not reached prior to this innovation. Funds received by originators from the sales of pass-through securities would be used to originate new mortgages.

Investors were attracted to these securities because default risk on them was minimized as a result of either FHA insurance or a VA guarantee. Securities issued against such pools were viewed by investors as virtually riskless or very similar to an investment in a government security. With the added guarantee of timely payment of interest and principal by GNMA, these securities also took on the repayment characteristics of a bond, although repayment of the outstanding principal could occur at any time. Repayment could occur when a borrower defaulted, refinanced, or repaid the outstanding loan balance.[4]

The Federal Home Loan Mortgage Corporation

By the early 1970s, the mortgage-backed securities market based on pools of FHA-insured and VA home mortgages was well established under the operation of FNMA and GNMA. However, no such secondary market existed for the resale of *conventional* loans originated by thrifts. These mortgages have historically accounted for the vast majority of residential loan originations. For example, conventional mortgage originations accounted for approximately 79 percent of total residential loans, while FHA and VA mortgages accounted for only 21 percent of the total. Thrifts originated the majority of conventional loans (58 percent), and mortgage companies originated the majority of FHA-VA mortgages (80 percent). Hence, finding a way to securitize conventional loans was very important if funds were to continue to flow to originators.

Periods of intermittent interest rate volatility, particularly during the mid- and late-1960s, was also causing liquidity problems that plagued thrifts.[5] This resulted in a reduction in the flow of funds to the conventional mortgage market and prompted Congress, under Title III of the Emergency Home Finance Act of 1970, to charter the **Federal Home Loan Mortgage Corporation (FHLMC)**, more commonly known as "Freddie Mac." Its primary purpose was to provide a secondary market and, hence, liquidity for conventional mortgage originators just as Fannie Mae and Ginnie Mae did for originators of FHA-VA mortgages.

Initially, Freddie Mac was authorized to purchase and make commitments to purchase first lien, fixed-rate conventional residential mortgage loans and participations. This bill also allowed Fannie Mae to purchase conventional mortgages, and Freddie Mac was given the authority to purchase FHA-VA loans as well. This provision would, in essence, allow both organizations to *compete* for all mortgage loans. However, the vast majority of Freddie Mac's business was, and continues to be, conventional mortgages, and FNMA continues to be the dominant purchaser of FHA-VA mortgages, although its acquisition of conventional loans now exceeds its FHA-VA acquisition volume.

Operation of the Secondary Mortgage Market

To understand how the secondary mortgage market functions, remember that the primary function of this market is to provide a mechanism for replenishing funds

[4]Repayment could also occur if a property was sold and the loan was not assumed by the buyer, or, in the event of a hazard (fire, etc.), if proceeds from hazard insurance were used to repay the mortgage rather than to reconstruct the improvement.

[5]Prior to the era of interest rate deregulation (on savings deposits), the small investor would deposit funds in a thrift or bank, which would in turn originate and retain the mortgage as an investment. During this period of regulated interest rates, savers withdrew deposits and began investing directly in financial securities. This change, as well as legislation allowing individuals to open individual retirement accounts (outside of savings institutions), forced thrifts to find a way to compete for funds that they once had been able to acquire by offering savings accounts.

used by mortgage originators. This, in turn, enables them to maintain a flow of new mortgage originations during periods of rising and falling interest rates. They may accomplish this by selling mortgages directly to Fannie Mae, Freddie Mac, or other private entities. Or they may form mortgage pools and issue various securities, thereby attracting funds from investors who may not otherwise make investments directly in mortgage loans. Hence, much like any corporation raising funds for doing business, the primary goal of mortgage originators in today's market is to replenish funds by reaching broader investor markets.

Direct Sale Programs

Exhibit 17–1 illustrates the direct sale approach used by mortgage originators to replenish funds. As previously indicated, prior to the mid-1950s, the secondary market was utilized by mortgage companies and some thrifts who originated FHA and VA mortgages, which were in turn sold to life insurance companies and some large eastern thrifts. These institutions utilized funds obtained from policyholder reserves and savings deposits, respectively, to acquire mortgage packages. This market changed during the mid-1950s as FNMA became the predominant purchaser of FHA-VA mortgages from mortgage bankers. The FHLMC entered the market by 1970, offering savings and loan associations the opportunity to sell conventional and FHA-VA mortgages.

At the present time, originators may now sell to both Fannie Mae and Freddie Mac, which now purchase a myriad of mortgages through their direct "standard purchase" programs. These standard programs include the purchase of 30-year fixed-rate loans, various adjustable rate loans, participations in individual or package loans, and second mortgage loans. In addition to the standard purchase programs, both agencies offer their version of a negotiated purchase program in which they will purchase a loan that does not fit into any of the standard categories.

A by-product of the standard purchase programs instituted by FNMA and FHLMC was the development of standardized procedures in areas such as qualifying borrowers, property appraisals, and obtaining insurance when originating loans. This came about because neither FNMA or FHLMC would purchase loans unless underwriting and documentation procedures conformed to their requirements. Originators had to follow these requirements or the mortgage could not be sold. With the institution of standardized procedures came the recognition that a more standardized

EXHIBIT 17–1 Funds Flow Analysis (Direct Purchase Programs)

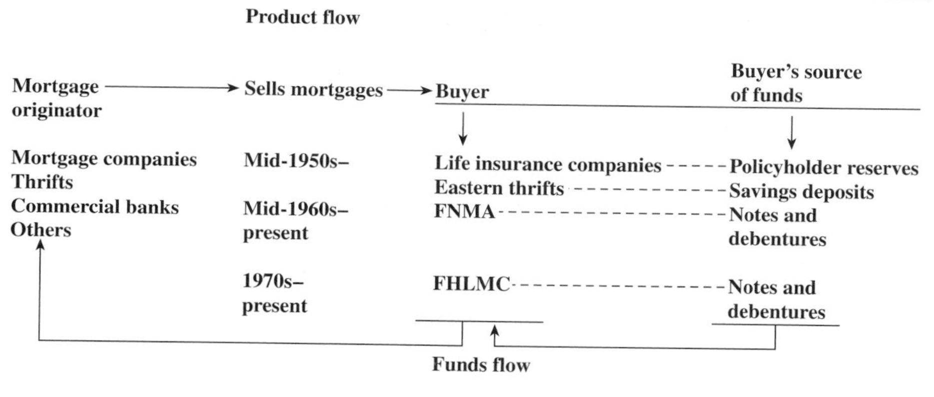

product was beginning to emerge that could be sold and resold in substantial market volumes.

FNMA's current commitment program is divided into two parts: mandatory and optional. Under the mandatory commitment option, Fannie Mae is obligated to purchase a certain amount of mortgages at a certain price at a certain time, and mortgage originators are *obligated* to deliver the mortgages. Originators pay a commitment fee to Fannie Mae for the privilege of selling mortgages under the commitment program. Under the optional delivery program, originators pay Fannie Mae a fee (the amount is higher than the corresponding commitment fee under the mandatory commitment program) for the *option* to deliver their mortgages to Fannie Mae. Under the mandatory commitment program, mortgage originators will benefit if market interest rates rise, but they could lose if market interest rates fall because they could have received a higher price elsewhere. On the other hand, the optional delivery commitment program gives the mortgage originator the "right but not the obligation" to sell the mortgages to Fannie Mae. Hence, if interest rates increase, originators can sell mortgages to Fannie Mae, but if rates fall, they retain the option to sell mortgages to another party for a better price (or even to renegotiate a price with Fannie Mae). With the advent of these commitment programs, mortgage originators were able to continue to shift most interest rate risk to Fannie Mae; however, this can now only be done for a fee. The program became so successful for Fannie Mae that Freddie Mac instituted a similar program in 1970.

The Development of Mortgage-Related Security Pools

As discussed previously, in addition to direct sales of mortgages from originators to investors, many large mortgage originators found that they could place mortgages in pools and sell securities of various types, using the mortgages in these pools as collateral. With the aid of investment bankers, large originators could issue securities in small denominations which would be purchased by many more investors. Firms with smaller mortgage origination volumes could continue to sell mortgages directly to FNMA and FHLMC, who in turn would create large pools of their own and issue securities. Creation of mortgage pools for securitization has clearly changed the previous pattern of thrifts *originating and holding* mortgages in their own portfolios and mortgage companies originating and selling mortgages directly to life insurance companies or large thrifts in regions where a surplus of savings existed. As we will see, many originators are no longer willing to take the interest rate risk associated with originating loans with funds obtained from deposits and have found a way, through securitization, to raise funds and shift interest rate risk to various classes of investors who are willing to take that risk.

There are many types of mortgage-related securities that have been developed in recent years. The number and types of securities is continuing to increase as mortgage originators, investment bankers, and the three federally related institutions discussed thus far (FNMA, FHLMC, and GNMA) continue to innovate and reach investor markets that provide the ultimate sources for many of the funds used in new mortgage originations. In this chapter and the next, we will deal in depth with the major types of mortgage-backed securities currently in use:

1. Mortgage-backed bonds (MBBs).
2. Mortgage pass-through securities (MPTs).
3. Mortgage pay-through bonds (MPTBs).
4. Collateralized mortgage obligations (CMOs).

Mortgage-Backed Bonds

One approach to mortgage securitization that has been used by private mortgage originators such as mortgage companies, commercial banks, and savings and loans to replenish funds for new originators has been to issue **mortgage-backed bonds (MBBs)**. When issuing MBBs, the issuer establishes a pool of mortgages—this pool usually includes residential mortgages, but commercial mortgages and other mortgage-related securities may also be used—and issues bonds to investors. The issuer retains ownership of the mortgages, but they are pledged as security and are usually placed in trust with a third-party trustee. This trustee makes certain that the provisions of the bond issue are adhered to on behalf of the security owners. Like corporate bonds, MBBs are usually issued with fixed-coupon rates and specific maturities.

To assure investors that the income from mortgages will be sufficient to pay interest on the bonds and to repay principal on the maturity date, the issuer usually "overcollateralizes" the bond issue. This is done by placing mortgages in the pool with outstanding loan balances in excess of the dollar amount of the securities issued. Historically, issuers have pledged from 125 percent to 240 percent in mortgage collateral in excess of the par value of securities issued. This practice is followed because some borrowers may default or fall behind in payments on mortgage loans in the pool. In this case, the overcollateralization ensures that interest payments promised to security holders will continue even though some mortgages may be in default. Further, some loans may be prepaid either before the maturity date of the mortgage or before the bond maturity date. Because mortgage-backed bonds are issued for a specified number of years, overcollateralization ensures that, as mortgages are prepaid, others will still be in the pool to replace them. Another reason for overcollateralization is that bond issues usually provide that the trustee "mark all mortgage collateral to the market." This is done periodically to make sure that the market values of mortgages used for overcollateralization are maintained at the level agreed upon at the time of issue (e.g., 125 percent or 240 percent) or at other levels agreed upon throughout the life of the bond issue. Should the market value of the mortgages in trust fall below the agreed-upon level of overcollateralization or be reduced because of an excessive number of defaults or prepayment on mortgages in the pool, the issuer must *replenish* the pool with additional mortgages of the same quality. If the issuer doesn't replenish or doesn't abide by the provisions of the security issue, the trustee may sell all collateral in the trust to protect the security owners.

Mortgage-backed bonds, like all mortgage-related securities, are usually underwritten by investment banking companies, given an investment rating by an independent bond-rating agency,[6] and sold through an underwriting syndicate.[7] The investment rating depends on (1) the quality of the mortgages in the underlying pool, which is a reflection of the types of mortgages and their loan-to-value ratios, and whether they are insured or guaranted against default, either fully or partially; (2) the extent of geographic diversification in the mortgage security; (3) the interest rates on mortgages in the pool; (4) the likelihood that mortgages will be prepaid before maturity; (5) the extent of overcollateralization; and (6) in the case of commercial mortgages, the appraised value and debt coverage ratio.

Obviously for mortgage pools containing FHA-VA mortgages or conventional mortgages with private mortgage insurance, the risk of default losses would be

[6]Such agencies might be Moody's or Standard & Poor's Corporation.

[7]Prominent underwriters of mortgage-related securities have included First Boston Company, Salomon Brothers, and Goldman Sachs & Co.

lower than if such mortgages were not insured or guaranteed. In some cases, however, the issuer may include some additional types of credit enhancement from a third party as additional security against default losses to bondholders. This enhancement could be a letter of credit from a bank, based on the issuer's credit standing and deposit requirements maintained at the bank issuing the letter, or some types of surety in the form of an insurance or other agreement negotiated with a creditworthy third party for a fee. When credit enhancements are used, the investor must also evaluate the ability of the third party to perform on the guarantee or to evaluate the terms and conditions of letters of credit when provided by the issuer or third parties. The quality of the enhancement will generally affect the amount of overcollateralization required or the coupon rate offered on the bonds.

In summary, the quality and types of mortgages in the pool are the primary determinants of whether the cash flows used to pay interest on the bonds and to eventually retire them will be adequate. These characteristics will affect the ability of the issuer to meet the requirements of the bond issue and, hence, affect the risk to investors. This risk will determine the yields required by investors on such bonds and, hence, the price that the issuer will receive for them. This pricing issue is considered next.

Pricing Mortgage-Backed Bonds

To illustrate how mortgage-backed bonds are priced by issuers when negotiating with underwriters, we assume that $200 million of MBBs will be issued against a $300 million pool of mortgages, in denominations of $10,000 for a period of 10 years. The bonds will carry a coupon, or interest rate, of 8 percent, payable annually,[8] based on the quality of the mortgage security in trust, the overcollateralization, and the creditworthiness of the issuer (and/or credit enhancement provided by the issuer). We assume that the securities receive a rating of Aaa or AAA.[9] To determine the *price* at which the security will be offered on the *date of issue*, we must discount the present value of the future interest payments and return of principal at the market rate of return demanded by investors (who will purchase them from underwriters). This rate is obviously a reflection of the riskiness of the bond relative to other securities and the yields on comparable securities in the marketplace.

In our example, the price of the security is determined by finding the present value of a stream of $800 interest payments (made annually for 10 years, plus the return of $10,000 in principal at the end of the 10th year). Assuming that the issuer, in concert with the underwriters, agrees that the rate of return that will be required to sell the bonds is 9 percent, then the price will be established as follows:

$$\begin{aligned} PV &= \$800(PVIFA, 9\%, 10 \text{ yrs.}) + \$10{,}000(PVIF, 9\%, 10 \text{ yrs.}) \\ &= \$9{,}358 \end{aligned}$$

Hence, the bond would be priced at a discount of $642, or at 93.58 percent of par value ($10,000), resulting in a yield to maturity of 9 percent.[10] The issuer would receive $187,160,000 from the underwriter,[11] less an underwriting fee, in exchange

[8]Most bonds pay interest semiannually. We are simplifying the analysis here.

[9]This is the highest rating obtainable. An explanation of the meaning and determination of ratings can be obtained from Moody's or Standard & Poor's.

[10]*Yield to maturity* is a term used by bond investors that is identical to the internal rate of return. It is calculated upon whether the coupon (interest) payments are made semiannually, quarterly, and so on.

[11]We assume that the underwriter makes a firm commitment to purchase the entire offering from the originator for an agreed price. The underwriter then forms a syndicate with other underwriters, who then take the risk of reselling securities to the public and institutional investors through a network of securities dealers.

EXHIBIT 17–2 Prices for an 8 Percent Coupon versus a Zero Coupon MBB at Varying Interest Rates

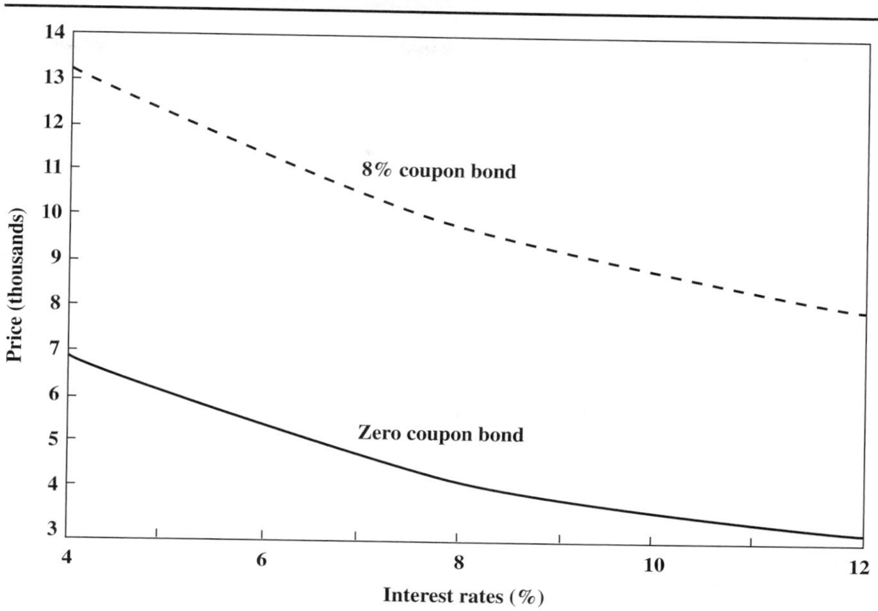

for the securities. On the other hand, if the yield was deemed to be 7 percent, then the present value of the bonds would be \$10,702 or they would sell at a premium of \$702 and the issuer would receive \$214,400,000. Hence, the price of the issue will depend on the relationship between the coupon rate on the bond and prevailing required rates of return. When market rates exceed the coupon rate, the price of the bond will be lower, and vice versa. Exhibit 17–2 shows the relationship between price and the market yield or rate of return at the time that the 8 percent MBB is issued. Note the inverse relationship between prices and demanded rates of return.

Subsequent Prices

The bonds referred to will be traded after they are issued and, although the prices at which they trade will no longer affect funds received by the issuer, these prices are important to investors as well as issuers who plan to make additional security offerings. For example, if we assume that two years after issue the required rate of return is again 9 percent, then the bond price would be:

$$\begin{aligned} PV &= \$800(PVIFA, 9\%, 8 \text{ yrs.}) + \$10{,}000(PVIF, 9\%, 8 \text{ yrs.}) \\ &= \$9{,}447 \end{aligned}$$

Hence, we can see that the price of security would now be 94.47 percent of par value. The discount is now lower than at the time of issue because the remaining number of years to maturity is now 8 instead of 10. Alternatively, if the demanded return was 7 percent after two years, then the premium would be \$10,597, or a price 105.97 percent of par. Hence, the extent of premium and discount when the maturity period is 10 years is different from the pattern illustrated when the remaining maturity is eight years. However, regardless of the remaining maturity period, when the market rate of return is 8 percent or equal to the coupon rate, the security will always sell at par value. The student should verify this.

Zero Coupon Mortgage-Backed Bonds. In some cases, bonds issued against mortgages will carry zero coupons or will not pay any interest. These MBBs accrue interest until the principal amount is returned at maturity. To illustrate, we assume the bond in our previous example is to be issued with a zero coupon, but interest is to be accrued at 8 percent until maturity. At maturity, the *par value* of the security will be redeemed for $10,000. If, however, at the time of issue, the rate of return demanded by investors in these securities is 8 percent, then the security will be *priced* as follows:

$$\begin{aligned} PV &= \$10{,}000(PVIF, 8\%, 10 \text{ yrs.}) \\ &= \$4{,}632 \end{aligned}$$

Based on this result, the security would be priced to sell at $4,632, or 46.32 percent of par value at maturity ($10,000). Should market rates of interest be 7.5 percent at the time of issue, the security would be priced at $4,852, or 48.52 percent of par. Exhibit 17–2 also shows the relationship between prices and various market rates of return for a zero coupon MBB with a 10-year maturity period at the time of issue. When compared with the 8 percent coupon bond, the price sensitivity of a zero coupon bond, as a percentage of par value, is far greater than that of the more standard bonds that pay interest currently. For example, when the required return is 4 percent, the 8 percent interest-bearing coupon bond would sell at 130 percent of par, while the zero coupon would sell at about 68 percent of par. The greater price sensitivity for zero coupon bonds relative to interest-bearing bonds occurs because all income is deferred until maturity with the zero coupon bond. Therefore, its present value will always be more sensitive to changes in interest rates than that of investments returning some cash flows during the investment period.

Marketing the Mortgage Portfolio to Market. As mentioned previously, the trustee selected to oversee that the provisions of the bond issue are carried out must ascertain periodically whether the market value of the mortgages placed in trust is equal to the agreed-upon level of overcolleralization. The pricing techniques used by the trustee to establish the market value of the pledged mortgages are very complex because (1) there are generally many different interest rates on mortgages placed in trust, (2) those mortgages will be amortizing principal, (3) many of the mortgages in the pool may be prepaid because many of them may allow the borrower to repay the outstanding loan balance at any time, and (4) some borrowers may default on loans. These latter two factors would obviously reduce the amount and number of mortgages in the pool.

To make an estimate of the value of mortgages in the pool (referred to as *marking the mortgages to market*), the trustee must value each of the mortgages in the pool by first establishing the number and outstanding balance of each mortgage in trust. Estimates must then be made of the current market yield demanded by investors for each type of mortgage based on assumptions about the period that each mortgage is expected to be outstanding (not the contract maturity period, because most mortgages on single family residential properties are prepaid as properties are sold, loans refinanced, borrowers default, etc.).[12] Hence, the valuation of the underlying security is a more complex undertaking, particularly when the prepayment patterns are considered. Many of the techniques that must be considered in evaluating such securities are also important when valuing mortgage pass-through securities.

[12]Other methods of principal repayment may also be used, such as sinking fund retirements and call provisions. For a discussion see any basic text dealing with investments.

Mortgage Pass-Through Securities

In 1968, Ginnie Mae initiated the mortgage-backed guarantee program. This program represented an attempt to create a mortgage-backed investment capable of competing with corporate and government securities for investment funds. As previously pointed out, one of the most serious objections that had to be overcome with this type of security was the issue of safety. Because mortgage-related securities would represent loans made by many individual borrowers with different income and household characteristics, an investment vehicle had to be created whereby the collateral underlying the mortgage security could be easily understood and yet be comparable to other securities.

We know that mortgages are subject to default risk and interest rate risk. Although fixed interest rate mortgage securities, like corporate and government bonds, would also be subject to interest rate risk, default risk could be eliminated by FHA insurance or dramatically reduced with a VA guarantee. Another characteristic of concern to potential investors in mortgage-related securities was the predictability of the income stream. Substitute investments, such as noncallable bonds, have very predictable interest payment schedules. As pointed out previously, mortgage payments can be delayed because of a household's inability to keep payments current or because of default. To overcome this lack of timeliness in payments, Ginnie Mae guaranteed the full and timely payment of principal and interest. GNMA's position as guarantor was that of a surety, with securities carrying the GNMA guarantee having full faith and credit of the U.S. government behind them. This full faith and credit guarantee meant that GNMA could borrow without limit from the Treasury. This unique guarantee had made the GNMA security the most liquid of all secondary mortgage market securities.

Before the advent of the first mortgage-backed security, the pass-through, the only way an originator could sell a package of mortgage investments was to sell whole loans, which involved the transfer of ownership in addition to all of the investor concerns mentioned above. The mortgage pass-through overcame many of these problems. **Mortgage pass-through securities (MPTs)** are issued by a mortgage originator (e.g., mortgage company, thrift) and represent an undivided ownership interest in a pool of mortgages. The pool may consist of one or many mortgages. However, the usual minimum size of such a pool is $100 million, which could represent 1,000 or more residential mortgages. Each mortgage placed in the pool continues to be serviced by its originator or an approved servicer. A trustee is designated as the owner of the mortgages in the pool and ensures that all payments are made to individual security owners. Cash flows from the pool, which consists of principal and interest, less servicing and guarantee fees, are distributed to security holders. That is why the securities are called "pass-throughs," because cash flows are "passed-through" to the investors by the mortgage servicer.

Exhibit 17–3 presents a flowchart showing how mortgage pass-through securities are originated and sold. Essentially, mortgages are originated by lenders and are pooled by them or sold to FNMA or FHLMC. If pooled by the originator, the originator will work with a securities underwriter to issue securities. These securities are then sold through security dealers to mutual funds, individuals with individual retirement accounts (IRAs), trust and pension fund administrators, life insurance companies, or even thrifts and commercial banks in geographic areas with a surplus of savings. This pattern of securitization enabled originators of mortgages to ultimately reach the relatively small investor, who could now purchase an interest in a

EXHIBIT 17–3 Mortgage Pass-Through Securities: Issuance and Funds Flow

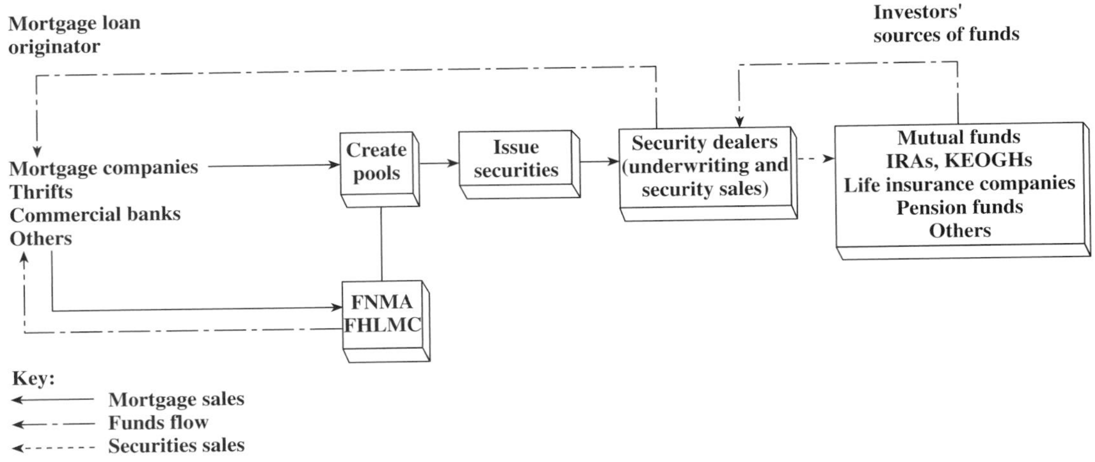

Ginnie Mae pass-through or another pass-through security by investing in a mutual fund or buying it directly.

The pattern shown in the upper portion of Exhibit 17–3 represents the approach generally used for issuing mortgage-backed securities until 1970. After that time, both FHLMC and FNMA instituted their own mortgage pass-through programs—their securities were referred to as **participation certificates (PCs)** and mortgage-backed securities (MBS), respectively. These securities were backed by mortgage pools from direct purchases made under both the optional and mandatory commitment direct purchase programs. Guarantees for timely payment of interest and principal were also provided by FNMA and FHLMC. Rather than securitizing themselves, originators of small mortgage volumes would sell directly to FNMA and FHLMC, who would in turn create mortgage pools and issue securities. These securities could then be placed directly with large institutional buyers or sold through security dealers to generally the same investors that would purchase GNMA pass-throughs.

The process of mortgage securitization changed again in 1981 when Freddie Mac instituted its "swap program." A similar program was later implemented by Fannie Mae. The major information brought about with **mortgage pass-through security swaps** is shown in Exhibit 17–4. Essentially, in the swap program one originator pools mortgages, then swaps them for pass-through mortgage securities issued simultaneously by Fannie Mae or Freddie Mac. Contrary to the direct sale programs discussed earlier in which mortgage packages are sold to either Fannie Mae or Freddy Mac for cash, the swap program allows mortgages with the same interest rate to be swapped for securities guaranteed by Fannie Mae or Freddie Mac (for a fee), bearing the same coupon rate. Depending on market interest rates, the originator may then choose to sell part or all of the mortgage securities at a premium or discount. These securities could be sold directly by the originator to institutional investors, to security dealers, or through the trading department operated by FHLMC. By swapping securities for mortgages, the originator has more flexibility when deciding whether to own securities or how and when such securities will be

EXHIBIT 17–4 Mortgage Pass-Through Security Swaps

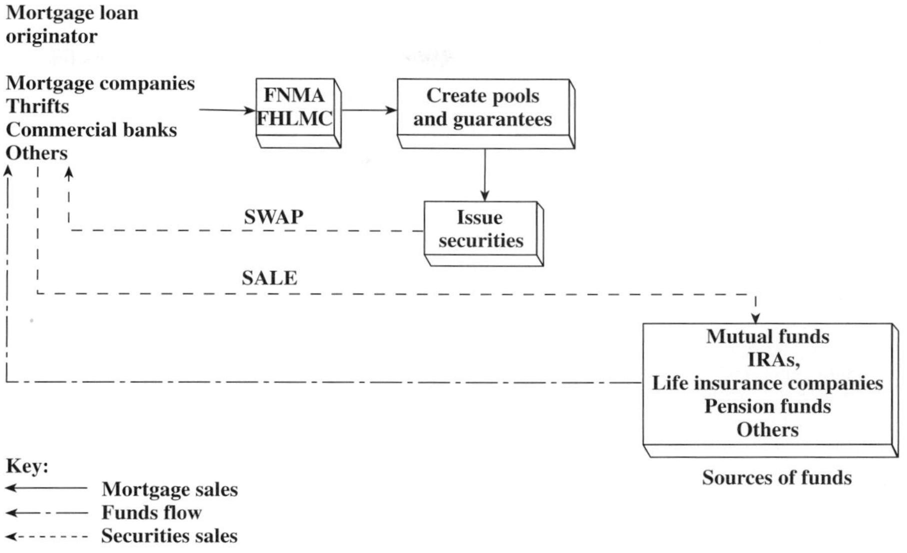

sold to raise cash. Further, in an attempt to provide a market outlet for such securities, Freddie Mac maintains a trading department that makes a market in mortgage-backed securities.

Important Characteristics of Mortgage Pools

Exhibit 17–5 provides information on the most important types of pass-through securities that have been used. Although all pass-through securities have the same underlying structure, some major differences between them should be pointed out. These differences are extremely important to issuers when creating mortgage pools and are equally important to investors when evaluating the possibility of investing in a mortgage pass-through security as opposed to a government bond, corporate bond, or another interest-bearing security.

Not all mortgage-backed securities are alike. When reviewing the characteristics listed in Exhibit 17–5, pay particular attention to how the market value of a pass-through security, which is backed by an underlying pool of mortgage loans made to borrowers, will respond to general changes in market interest rates. The change in market value of a particular security depends on the characteristics of the mortgages in the underlying pool, the response of borrowers to changes in interest rates, and the changes in borrower behavior in response to changes affecting their demand for housing, employment opportunities, and other influences. Borrowers may choose to refinance or repay their loans in response to changes in interest rates. As economic conditions change, they may sell their present house to buy another or to take a job transfer to another region. In these cases, they would very likely prepay their outstanding mortgages. These factors are extremely important to investors who must evaluate the timing of the receipt of cash flows when estimating value.

Security Issuers and Guarantors. The first security type listed in Exhibit 17–5 is referred to as a GNMA pass-through, which is usually issued by mortgage

Exhibit 17–5 Selected Characteristics of Mortgage Pass-Through Securities

Security	GNMA pass-through	Participation certificate	Mortgage-backed security
Issuer	Mortgage companies, thrifts, others	FHLMC	FNMA
Guarantor against default on mortgages	FHA, VA, FmHA	Private mortgage insurance, FHA/VA	FHA/VA, private mortgage insurance
Types of mortgages in pool*	*FRM*, *GPM*, *MH*, *ARM*	*FRM*, *GPM*, *ARM*, *MF*, seconds	*FRM*, *GPM*, *ARM*, *MF*, seconds
Interest rate on mortgages in underlying pools allowed to vary?	Yes	Yes	Yes
Seasoned mortgages allowed in pools?	Yes	Yes	Yes
Nature of payment guarantee	Timely payment of P & I and prepayments	Timely payment of P & I and eventual prepayments	Timely payment of P & I and prepayments
Guarantor	GNMA and credit of U.S. government	FHLMC only	FNMA only

*Key
FRM = 1–4 single family, 30-year fixed-rate mortgages.
GPM = Graduated payment mortgage.
ARM = Adjustable-rate mortgages.
CL = Construction loan mortgages.
MH = Manufactured housing mortgages.
PL = Federally financed housing project loans.
MF = Multifamily housing mortgages.
Seconds = Mortgage pools secured by second mortgages.

companies, thrifts, commercial banks, and other organizations that originate FHA and VA mortgages. The remaining two security types, participation certificates and mortgage-backed securities, are securities issued by FHLMC and FNMA, respectively. As previously mentioned, the latter two securities are backed by pools of mortgages that are purchased from originators by FHLMC and FNMA, which, in turn, provide a timely payment guarantee. In these cases, FNMA and FHLMC act as intermediaries, purchasing smaller quantities of mortgages from many originators, then accumulating larger pools against which they issue securities.

Default Insurance. GNMA pass-through securities are backed with FHA-VA mortgages that carry either insurance or a guarantee against default losses. When it first began, this program was limited to FHA-VA pools because private mortgage default insurance on conventional mortgages was not generally available. Even today, with the availability of private mortgage insurance, major issuers of pass-through securities usually do not mix *both* FHA-VA and conventional mortgages in the same pool because of the greater depth of FHA default insurance coverage and the VA guarantee compared with conventional default coverage. As shown in Exhibit 17–5, GNMAs still contain mortgages with FHA-VA backing, whereas FNMA and FHLMC pass-throughs may be based on separate pools of either FHA-VA backing or conventional mortgages. In their conventional mortgage-backed programs, both FNMA and FHLMC require conventional mortgages with loan-to-value ratios greater than 80 percent to carry private mortgage insurance.

Payment Patterns and Security for Mortgages in Pools. As Exhibit 17–5 indicates, most mortgage varieties may be individually pooled for a pass-through security issue. This is true for mortgages with adjustable payment patterns such as adjustable rate mortgages (ARMs); graduated payment mortgages (GPMs); mortgages secured by single family, multifamily, and mobile homes; and even second-lien mortgages. However, the vast majority of mortgages used in the pass-through security market are fixed interest rate loans secured by mortgages on single family houses.

The rule about not mixing FHA-VA and conventional mortgages in the same pool generally applies to payment patterns and the nature of loan security and loan maturity. In other words, mortgage pools are usually grouped according to (1) payment patterns (e.g., ARMs), (2) maturity (e.g., second mortgages with 10-year terms), or (3) security (e.g., single family homes, mobile homes). The reason this is done is that investors must be able to predict the cash flow pattern that they can expect to receive in a pass-through security with some confidence. If pools contained mortgages with many different payment patterns, investors would have a more difficult time assessing the likely cash flow pattern that they could expect to receive. The payment pattern of individuals making fixed interest rate loans may vary considerably from those making ARMs, second liens, and so on. As we will see in the material on pricing securities, expected prepayment patterns dramatically affect expected yields on mortgage securities. Hence, a general rule followed thus far has been to keep mortgage pools as homogeneous as possible so that their prepayment patterns are somewhat easier for investors to assess.

Coupon Rates, Interest Rates, and Number of Seasoned Mortgages in Pools. Pass-through securities issues guaranteed by Fannie Mae and Freddie Mac have allowed for a mixture of *interest rates* on mortgages included in a pool to enable a faster accumulation of larger pools for securitization. This pattern has been followed by security issuers, who believe that the variation in cash flows caused by mixing such mortgages is not large enough to offset the lower issuance costs on very large mortgage pools (i.e., economies of scale).

When Freddie Mac began its PC pass-through program, it allowed a variation of 200 basis points (from highest to lowest) in interest rates on mortgages packaged in the same pool, Fannie Mae allowed a 200-basis-point range with its first mortgage-backed security offering in 1981. The GNMA pass-through programs provide that some pools contain mortgages with the same interest rate, while others allow a variation of 100 basis points on mortgages in the underlying pool. These ranges are subject to revision by the guarantors from time to time.[13]

The variation in interest rates on a mortgage pool may be very important for investors to consider, because in each case the *coupon rate* promised to investors purchasing securities is generally based on the *lowest* interest rate on *any* mortgage in the pool, less servicing and guarantee fees. This means that for two security issues bearing the same coupon rate, expected cash flows to investors in the pool containing mortgages with different rates will be less variable than cash flows to investors in the pool with the same interest rates. This occurs because each mortgage included in a pool with different interest rates will have a lower likelihood of prepayment than pooled mortgages with the same interest rate. This likelihood exists because mortgages with one interest rate are *all* more likely to be prepaid, should interest rates decline. This would obviously make the pattern of expected cash flows more variable.

[13]The GNMA I pass-through program requires all mortgages in a pool to have the same interest rate.

Another important factor relating to the amount and timing of cash flows received by investors is the maturity distribution of mortgages and the extent to which "seasoned" mortgages are included in a pool. *Seasoning* is a term used to describe the age or number of years that a loan has been outstanding before it is placed in a pool. The scheduled maturity date for a pass-through security issue is generally the date on which the mortgage with the longest remaining maturity in the pool is scheduled to be repaid, assuming no prepayment. Each guarantor listed in Exhibit 17–5 places limitations on the number of seasoned mortgages allowed in a pool. Most GNMA insured mortgage pools generally contain mortgages made within one year of pool formation. Fannie Mae and Freddie Mac generally allow for more variation in seasoning in pools that they guarantee. The concern over seasoning is important because the more seasoned a mortgage is, the greater the likelihood of prepayment. The likelihood that borrowers will sell houses, change job locations, and so on increases with the length of time the mortgage has been outstanding.

On the other hand, the risk of default is usually greatest in the early years of the life of a mortgage. Hence, seasoned mortgages tend to reduce the possibility of prepayment because of default. However, to the extent seasoning reduces or increases the likelihood of prepayment, more variation in cash flows results, which makes evaluation of the security more difficult for investors. This will, in turn, affect the price investors are willing to pay for the security.

Number of Mortgages and Geographic Distribution. Other factors relating to mortgages in the underlying pool that may affect the predictability and, hence, the variability of the monthly cash flows on pass-through securities are the *number* and *geographic* distribution of mortgages in the pool.

Both of these factors may be critical when estimating the yield on a pass-through security because they influence the expected repayment of principal. Generally, the larger the dollar amount of the pool issue, the more individual mortgages will be contained in the pool and the larger the number of mortgages in the pool, all else being equal, the more predictable the monthly cash flow. This means that the likelihood of a major change in cash flows owing to default or prepayment of one or a few individual mortgages will not significantly affect future cash flows paid to investors. Most mortgage pools underlying pass-throughs are in minimum denominations of $100 million. If the average mortgage size is about $100,000, most pools of residential mortgages will contain at least 1,000 mortgages. This may be enough to assure investors that changes in cash flows caused by a small number of mortgages are minimal.

Geographic factors are important because they may affect the likelihood of prepayment and default. Certain regions of the country may be affected more by economic downturns and resulting unemployment than others and, hence, may have higher default rates. Prepayment rates, because of mobility by borrowers due to their age and family status, may be higher in some areas than others. A mortgage pool with more geographic diversity tends to insulate investors from cash flow irregularities.

Borrower Characteristics and Loan Prepayment. Perhaps more important than any of the other explicit pool characteristics discussed in conjunction with Exhibit 17–5 are borrower characteristics, or the socioeconomic makeup of individuals who have made the mortgage loans and are the ultimate source of cash flows for the mortgage pool. These characteristics are important because (1) households prepay existing mortgage loans as they adjust their consumption of housing over time in response to changes in income, family size, and tastes; (2) like other economic entities, households respond to changes in interest rates by refinancing their loans when interest rates fall and postponing adjustments in housing consumption when interest rates rise; and (3) households may default on loan obligations because of loss of employment, divorce, and so on, and although most pools have default insurance, the mortgage balance is prepaid upon default. Therefore, changes in borrower behavior with respect to these characteristics will affect the expected cash flows on loans and expected maturities. Indeed, depending on borrower behavior, the expected maturity of a loan may vary significantly, therefore affecting the expected yield on the mortgage. Unfortunately, not much information about borrower characteristics for individual loans in an underlying mortgage pool is made available to investors in pass-through securities. Hence, even though it is an important variable affecting cash flows on mortgage securities, no reliable source of information is generally available to investors.

Nuisance Calls. Where the prepayment rate reaches the point where a diminishing number and amount of mortgages remain in the pool, say about 10 percent of the initial pool amount, the servicer may call the remainder of the securities. This call is referred to as a *nuisance* or *cleanup call* and is used when the cost of servicing begins to become large relative to servicing income.

Mortgage Pass-Through Securities: A General Approach to Pricing

As we have seen, many things influence the pricing of a mortgage pass-through security (or any mortgage-backed security). We can summarize these influences as follows:

1. *Interest rate risk*—Reductions in market value due to an unanticipated rise in interest rates. This risk is generally greatest for pools containing fixed interest rate loans.
2. *Default risk*—Losses due to borrower default. For single family loans, the likelihood of default losses is lowest for FHA-insured mortgages, slightly greater for VA-guaranteed mortgages, and generally greater for privately insured mortgages. This source of risk is also generally higher for ARMs and variable payment mortgages.
3. *Risk of delayed payment of principal and interest*—This source of risk can be evaluated in relation to the financial strength of the guarantor because the guarantee of *timely payment* is only as good as the ability of the guarantor to perform on the guarantee. GNMA is backed by the full faith and credit of the U.S. government. FNMA has a $2.25 billion commitment from the U.S. Treasury to purchase its notes and bonds, which provides some assurance that a market will be available for Fannie Mae's ability to raise funds, maintain liquidity, and make good on its timely payment guarantee. However, neither FNMA nor FHLMC has the direct backing of the U.S. government.
4. *Prepayment risk*—Loss in yield because of greater than anticipated loan repayments. In general, most mortgage loans are prepaid before the stated maturity date. Hence, when investing in a pass-through, an investor must estimate expected cash flows by including an assessment of the prepayment rate on loans in the underlying pools. In the case of fixed interest rate mortgage pools, the impact of prepayment on cash flows passed through to investors will vary according to the:

   a. Number of mortgages in the pool.
   b. Distribution of interest rates on such mortgages.
   c. Number of seasoned mortgages included in the pool.
   d. Geographic location of borrowers.

e. Household (borrower) characteristics.
f. Unanticipated events (e.g., flood, earthquake).

Although the above sources of risk are important to issuers and investors, information available on mortgage pools is usually limited to very general borrower and mortgage characteristics. Information usually available on mortgage pools is discussed in the following sections.

Pass-Through Rates, Yields, and Servicing Fee. The pass-through rate is the coupon rate of interest promised by the issuer of a pass-through security to the investor. The yield to maturity, or internal rate of return, on such a security is equal to this rate only when it is issued at par value.

The coupon rate on pass-throughs is lower than the lowest rate of interest on any mortgage in the pool. The difference between the two rates is known as the *servicing fee*. The GNMA I, which allows no variance in interest rates in the underlying pool, has a total servicing fee of .5 percent, or 50 basis points below the interest rates on all mortgages in the pool. The servicing fee is divided between the guarantor fee and the loan services fee and is calculated as a percentage of the outstanding principal balance of the pool. As an example, GNMA takes .06 percent or 6 basis points of the outstanding principal balance of the pool as its fee for guarantee of timely payment of principal and interest, while the remaining 44 basis points of the servicing fee are retained by the servicer. For mortgage pass-through securities that allow a range of interest rates on mortgages in the pool (e.g., GNMA II), the coupon rate will be set lower than the lowest mortgage rate in the pool.

Weighted Average Coupon. The **weighted average coupon** (WAC) is a measure of the homogeneity of the coupon rates on mortgages in a pool. It is calculated as the average of the underlying mortgage interest rates weighted by the dollar balance of each mortgage as of the security issue date. WACs are meaningful only for pools that allow a variance in interest rates on mortgages. In most instances, the servicing and guarantee fee can be approximated as the difference between the WAC and the pass-through coupon rate.

Stated Maturity Date of Pool. The stated maturity date of the pass-through pool is the longest maturity date for any mortgage in the pool, assuming that no prepayments occur. For example, if 75 percent of the pool contained 15-year mortgages and the remaining 25 percent contained 20-year mortgages, the stated pool maturity would be 20 years. GNMA generally imposes more restrictions on the variance in mortgage maturities allowed in pools. FNMA and FHLMC pools may contain more seasoned loans with a wider range in stated maturity dates.

Weighted Average Maturity. Because the remaining term to stated maturity of mortgages in a pool may affect the prepayment rate of mortgages and, consequently, the yield of securities issued against the pool, the concept of a **weighted average maturity** was developed. The weighted average maturity is calculated as the average remaining term of the underlying mortgages as of the pass-through issue date, with the principal balance of the mortgage as the weighting factor.

Payment Delays by Servicer. Payment delay is the time lag between the time that the homeowners make their mortgage payments and the date that the servicing agent actually pays the investors holding the pass-through securities. This delay may range from 14 to 55 days. As with other securities, the timing of cash flows is important. Delays in payments received by investors obviously reduce yields.

Pool Factor. The **pool factor** is the outstanding principal balance divided by the original pool balance. This balance changes every month as mortgages are amortized and balances prepaid. The pool factor starts out as 1 and usually declines. (However, it may increase above 1 if the pool includes mortgages that allow negative amortization.) The pool factor is used to determine the current principal balance of the pool based on the outstanding balance of all mortgages remaining in the pool at any point in time. For example, if the pool factor is .9050 and the pool initially contained mortgages with $50,000 in balances outstanding, the current principal balance of the pool would be $50,000 × .9050 = $45,250. This factor is particularly important when securities are traded *after* the issue date, when subsequent buyers are considering how much to pay for a security. For example, as the pool factor becomes smaller, the remaining balances on mortgages in the pool are also becoming smaller; hence, the likelihood of prepayment becomes greater (holding all else constant).

Mortgage Pass-Through Payment Mechanics Illustrated

Exhibit 17–6 illustrates cash flow patterns that are important when evaluating mortgage pass-through securities. In this exhibit, it is assumed that $1,000,000 of 10 percent fixed interest rate mortgages have been pooled as security for an issue of pass-through securities. The pass-through will carry a coupon, or pass-through, rate of 9.5 percent. The difference between the pooled mortgage rates and coupon rate, or .5 percent, is the servicing fee, which is assessed on the outstanding loan balances. To simplify the discussion, we have assumed that all mortgages in the pool have a maturity of 10 years and that mortgage payments, or cash flows and outflows in and out of the pool, occur annually.[14]

The cash flows passed through to individual security holders (column *g*) are based on annual mortgage payments for a 10 percent, 10-year mortgage on the initial pool balance of $1,000,000, resulting in total principal and interest payments generated by the pool (column *c*).[15] The servicing fee of .5 percent (column *e*) is then assessed on the outstanding loan balance at the end of each previous period and subtracted from total principal and interest payments. This results in actual payments to be made to all investors (column *f*). Because of the way servicing fees are calculated, payments passed through to investors (column *f*) are not the same from year to year, even though payments into the pool (column *d*) are level.[16] If no mortgages in the pool are prepaid (column *c*)—that is, all mortgages remain outstanding for their stated maturities—the principal balance in the pool will not reach zero until the end of the 10th year.

The amount of cash that will be received by an issuer when this type of pool is formed and securitized depends on the prevailing market rate of return that investors demand on the investment. If it is assumed that, based on the pool characteristics discussed above, the market or desired rate of return is *equal* to the coupon rate (9.5 percent), then the amount to be received (paid) by the issuers (investors)

[14]For most pass-through issues, payments are made to investors monthly.

[15]Because all mortgages in the pool are 10 percent, 10-year loans, the constant payment in column *c* is computed as one annual payment on a $1,000,000 loan.

[16]If there are any prepayments (column *c*), this will also cause payments passed through to investors to vary from year to year.

EXHIBIT 17–6 Cash Flows from Mortgage Pass-Through Security (constant payment, fixed rate, 10-year mortgage pool, interest rate = 10 percent, prepayment assumed to be 0 percent, coupon rate = 9.5 percent rounded)

End of Period	*(a)* Pool Balance	*(b)* P&I Payment	*(c)* Principal Prepayment	*(d)* Total Payments* (b) + (c)	*(e)* Guarantee and Service Fees (0.5%)†	*(f)* Total PMTs to Investors (d) − (e)	*(g)* Payment to Individual Investor (f) ÷ 40
0	$1,000,000						($25,000)
1	937,255	$162,745	$0	$162,745	$5,000	$157,745	3,944
2	868,235	162,745	0	$162,745	4,686	158,059	3,951
3	792,313	162,745	0	$162,745	4,341	158,404	3,960
4	708,799	162,745	0	$162,745	3,962	158,784	3,970
5	616,933	162,745	0	$162,745	3,544	159,201	3,980
6	515,881	162,745	0	$162,745	3,085	159,661	3,992
7	404,724	162,745	0	$162,745	2,579	160,166	4,004
8	282,451	162,745	0	$162,745	2,024	160,722	4,018
9	147,950	162,745	0	$162,745	1,412	161,333	4,033
10	0	162,745	0	$162,745	740	162,006	4,050

A.
Value of cash flows to issuer if required rate is 9.50 percent = $1,000,000
Value of cash flows to individual investors at 9.50 = 25,000

B.
Value of cash flows to issuer if required rate is 8.50 percent = $1,045,219
Value of cash flows to individual investors at 8.50 = 26,130

C.
Value of cash flows to issuer if required rate is 10.50 percent = $ 957,754
Value of cash flows to individual investors at 10.50 = 23,944

*Payments calculated on an annual basis.
†Based on pool balance at the end of the previous year.

will be $1,000,000 (or 40 securities with a face value of $25,000 will be sold). This is based on the stream of annual cash flow payments in the exhibit, discounted at 9.5 percent. In this instance, the securities would be sold at par value or $25,000 each.

It is rarely ever true, however, that the rate of return demanded by investors is *exactly* equal to the coupon rate on a security. As we know, market interest rates change continually; hence, it would only be coincidental that interest rates on mortgages originated at some previous time and placed in a pool would bear interest rates exactly equal to the market rate demanded by investors at the time the securities were issued. Inasmuch as the annual cash flows into the pool based on payments received by borrowers are known at the time of issue and passed through to investors, the price received by the issuer will depend on the present value of all payments received by investors, discounted at the prevailing market rate of return. As discussed earlier, the latter rate is determined by the real rate of interest, inflationary expectations, and a premium for the various sources of risk. It is also based on yields available on alternative investments. We shall see that the periods that mortgages are expected to remain outstanding is also very important in the determination of the prices that investors are willing to pay for pass-through securities.

To illustrate the effect that market interest rates have on the price of pass-through securities, note that if the stream of cash flows paid to investors (column *g*) in Exhibit 17–6 is discounted at a market rate of 8.5 percent, the securities will sell at a premium or $26,130 (part B), the result of discounting payments in column *g* by 8.5 percent. If market rates were to rise to 10.50 percent at the time of issue, the security prices would reflect a *discount* of $23,944 (see part C). Both of these calculations assume, however, that the expected maturity of the pass-through security is equal to the stated maturity of mortgages in the pool (10 years). Hence, the amortization of principal is assumed to occur over the full 10-year period; that is, no prepayment is assumed.

To provide some idea of the effect of the sensitivity of security prices to changes in market interest rates, Exhibit 17–7 shows the effect of rising and falling interest rates on the issue *price* of the mortgage pass-through securities in our example. (Keep in mind that the assumption regarding repayment of principal over the 10-year period remains the same.) Results show that for all rates of return desired by investors in excess of 9.5 percent, the pass-through will be issued at a discount; when required rates decrease, the security would be sold at a premium. Note that only when the required rate of return is *equal* to the promised coupon rate (9.5 percent) does the security sell at par value (an amount equal to the initial pool balance of $1,000,000, or $25,000 per security).

Prepayment Patterns and Security Prices

One problem that affects how securities are priced and is unique to the mortgage-backed securities market is the option that most borrowers have to prepay or repay the outstanding mortgage balance at any time.[17] This topic is important because when investors make comparisons between pass-throughs, corporate bonds, U.S. government bonds, and various state and local bond issues, the *expected* maturity period for pass-throughs is usually more difficult to estimate relative to the other investments. For example, when corporate bonds are issued, an *option to call* the outstanding principal is usually made explicit in the indenture agreement by specifying the price at which the bond may be called by the corporation each year that the bond issue is outstanding. Such options to call are usually included in the event that interest rates decline and the company wants to refinance the debt at a lower interest rate.[18]

As an alternative to call provisions, bond indentures issued by both corporations and state and local issuers may specify that a *scheduled* number of bonds will be called and retired in specific years after issue, regardless of what the current level of interest rates is at that time. This is not an option but a requirement of the

---

[17]There are some exceptions and additional facts that should be mentioned that affect mortgage prepayment. FHA and VA mortgages are assembled by buyers of properties. Hence, they are not always repaid when a property is sold. Conventional mortgages may contain a due-on-sale clause, which prohibits assumptions; hence, they would be more likely to be repaid if a property is sold. Some older conventional fixed interest rate mortgages may also contain prepayment penalties, which tend to discourage early repayment. Conventional mortgages made more recently and ARMs generally do not include such penalties.

[18]To include this option in the agreement with investors, however, the issuer usually includes a schedule of premiums in excess of par value that will be paid to bondholders if the option to call is exercised by the corporation. This premium is paid because (1) the market value of the bonds will have increased if market rates have fallen and calling in the bond would deprive bondholders of an increase in market value, and (2) if investors expect to own the bonds for the entire maturity period, refinancing by the company may represent an unanticipated interruption in cash flows, and bondholders would have to reinvest at lower interest rates.

EXHIBIT 17–7 Relationship between Security Price and Required Rates of Return (prepayment rate assumed to be 0 percent)

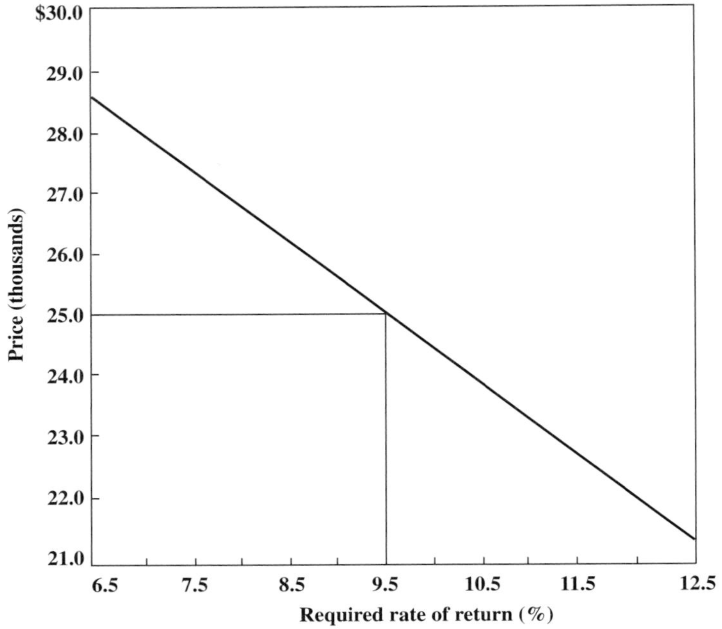

indenture agreement.[19] The vast majority of U.S. government securities are issued for a stated maturity and are generally not callable. In other words, they are generally issued to run until maturity.[20]

The point is that other fixed-interest securities are generally more predictable with respect to when repayment of principal can be expected. This is not true for mortgage pass-through securities. Hence, when comparing yields on pass-throughs with other securities, there is definitely some additional uncertainty regarding the rate of repayment of principal that investors must take into account.

Prepayment Assumptions

Because some prepayments by borrowers are likely to occur over time, as outstanding balances on mortgages contained in pools are repaid, proceeds are passed through to investors in pass-through securities. Pass-throughs of mortgage balances can be zero in months when interest rates increase and accelerate rapidly when market interest rates decline. During the latter periods, many households choose to refinance. Mortgages are then paid off and removed from the pool as principal is passed through to investors.

[19]These retirements amount to an implicit method of amortization (e.g., a mortgage) and are usually accomplished with a sinking fund that is used to (1) call bonds as scheduled, by serial number at either a premium or at par value, (2) call a percentage of the original issue at random by serial number at either par value or at a premium, or (3) use sinking funds to enter the market and repurchase bonds at market value.

[20]A limited number of U.S. government bond issues are callable for a specified number of years prior to maturity.

When issuing pass-through securities, the issuer generally specifies both a coupon rate of interest (9.5 percent in our preceding example) *and* an offering price on the securities being issued. This offering price may be above or below par value. This specification is made because investors may demand a rate of return that is different from the coupon rate of 9.5 percent as market conditions vary at the time of issue. Even when no prepayments are assumed, the range in security prices may vary considerably, depending on the market rate of return demanded by investors (see Exhibit 17–7). However, because investors realize that there is also a strong likelihood that some prepayments will occur while they own these securities, issuers usually take into account some *assumed prepayment pattern* when pricing these securities. This is necessary to provide a more accurate estimate of cash flows (hence, yield to investors) rather than to assume that all borrowers will repay loans in accordance with a stated amortization schedule.

Methods that issuers use to include prepayment assumptions when pricing securities fall into four broad classes:

1. *Average maturity.* This method assumes, for example, that a pool of 10-year mortgages is scheduled to amortize principal based on a 10-year maturity, but the pool is totally paid off after some average period of time, such as the 5th year. Hence, when calculating yields or pricing securities, it is assumed that regular mortgage payments would be made for 5 years, and the principal due at that time would amount to a balloon payment. This method has the advantage of simplicity because an average prepayment rate is chosen to represent all mortgages in the pool. Further, choosing an average maturity has the effect of facilitating comparison with traditional bonds.

The disadvantages of this technique far outweigh its advantages. There is considerable evidence that the so-called 5-year average life convention is not an adequate method of handling the prepayment problem and will usually result in under- or overestimation of yield. As previously explained, prepayments are the product of numerous factors, including interest rate changes and household characteristics. Hence, using an average maturity may not reflect changes underlying these characteristics.

2. *Constant rates of prepayment.* This method of handling prepayment assumes that a constant percentage of the total mortgages in the pool will be paid off every year. The advantages of the **constant prepayment assumption** are that it is simple to understand and prepayments are easy to compute. However, empirical evidence suggests that prepayments due to defaults occur more frequently early in the life of most mortgages. Hence, most constant prepayment rates tend to understate prepayment in earlier years and overstate it in later years. While this method may be preferable to an average maturity, it also is not likely to reflect underlying pool characteristics.

3. *FHA prepayment experience.* Prepayment assumptions based on empirical evidence from actual prepayment experience collected by the FHA over several decades have been suggested as a guide for making more accurate prepayment assumptions. The FHA has developed an extensive data base on mortgage terminations as a part of its insurance program. This data base contains the total number of mortgage terminations during a single policy year, including information on the number resulting from defaults and repayments. Many argue that prepayment assumptions could be based on this FHA "experience." For example, if slower or faster prepayment on pools of mortgages is expected because of differences in investor expectations, those rates could be adjusted to be less than 100 percent or greater than 100 percent of FHA experience, and yields could be disclosed to investors.

However, the FHA data on prepayment experience are not without shortcomings. Major problems are encountered when applying historic FHA experience to current mortgage pools because the precise causes of prepayment (e.g., changes in interest rates, borrowers' employment) over time are difficult to determine. There is no assurance that this pattern will repeat in the future; the FHA does not keep enough detailed data on each mortgage and borrower to enable a systematic investigation into the causes of prepayment behavior.

4. *The PSA prepayment model.* The **PSA prepayment model** was developed by the Public Securities Association to simplify the FHA experience prepayment model. Even though it suffers from the same shortcomings as the FHA prepayment experience, it has become an industry standard for prepayment assumptions used by most issuers of mortgage-backed securities. Simply put, the model is based on monthly prepayment rates, which vary during the life of a mortgage pool underlying the security. At present, the standard PSA prepayment rate curve (referred to as *100 percent PSA*) begins at 0.2 percent per month for the first year, then increases by 0.2 percent each month until month 30. It then remains at 0.5 percent per month, or 6 percent per year for the remaining stated maturity period of the pool. The model combines both FHA experience and the constant rate of repayment approach.

Because investors and issuers are aware that yields are likely to be affected by the rate of loan repayment, the PSA assumption is widely used to convey both price and yield information to investors at the time of issue. To provide prospective security buyers with additional information about the sensitivity of yields to different prepayment rates at the time of issue, a series of yield quotes based on various PSA repayment rates (e.g., 75 percent PSA, 150 percent PSA) are placed on the prospectus.

The Effects of Prepayment Illustrated

To illustrate the effects of prepayment on cash flows to investors in mortgage pass-through securities, a schedule of payments is shown in Exhibit 17–8. The rate of prepayment is assumed to be 10 percent each year based on the pool balance at the end of the preceding period. Payments in column *g* should be compared to those in Exhibit 17–7, which are based on a zero prepayment rate. However, in spite of these differences, when cash flows in column *g* of both exhibits are discounted at 9.5 percent, the present value in both cases equals \$1,000,000, or \$25,000 per investor. This result occurs because even though the 10 percent prepayment assumption results in more cash flows early in the life of the pool, interest is still calculated at 9.5 percent on the outstanding balance at all times. Therefore, even though the investor is receiving *principal* on the pass-through faster, interest continues on the outstanding balance at 9.5 percent. Hence, the present value of both columns *g* in Exhibits 17–7 and 17–8, when discounted at 9.5 percent, equal \$25,000.

Exhibit 17–9 depicts cash flows from a pool assuming 0 percent, 10 percent, and 50 percent prepayment. Obviously, the cash flow to investors will vary dramatically, depending on the repayment rate. Also, as previously discussed, in the unlikely event that the market rate of return demanded by investors is equal to the coupon rate on the pass-through security, the security will always sell at par value, or \$25,000, regardless of the prepayment rate. (Think about why this result is true.)

EXHIBIT 17–8 Cash Flows from Mortgage Pass-Through Security (constant payment, fixed rate, 10-year mortgage pool, interest rate = 10 percent, prepayment assumed to be 10 percent, coupon rate = 9.5 percent rounded)

End of Period	*(a) Pool Balance*	*(b) P&I Payment*	*(c) Principal Prepayment*	*(d) Total Payments* (b) + (c)*	*(e) Guarantee and Service Fees (0,5%)†*	*(f) Total PMTs to Investors (d) − (e)*	*(g) Payment to Individual Investor (f) ÷ 40*
0	$1,000,000						($25,000)
1	837,255	$162,745	$100,000	$262,745	$5,000	$257,745	6,444
2	691,873	145,381	83,725	229,107	4,186	224,921	5,623
3	562,186	129,688	69,187	198,875	3,459	195,415	4,885
4	446,710	115,476	56,219	171,695	2,811	168,884	4,222
5	344,142	102,568	44,671	147,239	2,234	145,005	3,625
6	253,358	90,784	34,414	125,198	1,721	123,477	3,087
7	173,431	79,927	25,336	105,263	1,267	103,996	2,600
8	103,692	69,739	17,343	87,082	867	86,215	2,155
9	43,946	59,746	10,369	70,115	518	69,597	1,740
10	0	48,340	0	48,340	220	48,120	1,203

A.
Value of cash flows to issuer if required rate is 9.50 percent = $1,000,000
Value of cash flows to individual investors at 9.50 = 25,000

B.
Value of cash flows to issuer if required rate is 8.50 percent = $1,033,908
Value of cash flows to individual investors at 8.50 = 25,848

C.
Value of cash flows to issuer if required rate is 10.50 percent = $967,970
Value of cash flows to individual investors at 10.50 = 24,199

*Payments calculated on an annual basis.
†Based on pool balance at the end of the previous year.

Security Prices and Expected Yields

As previously pointed out, when mortgage pass-through securities are priced by the issuer (with the advice of security underwriters), some assessment of yields expected by investors *at the time of issue* must be made. Further, this yield is likely to be different from the coupon rate on securities at the time of issue. This assessment is usually made by (1) establishing the extent of the premium that investors expect in excess of current yields on government securities with maturities in the same expected maturity range, or (2) considering the current yields on other pass-throughs currently trading in the market. Establishing the premium may be difficult in the former case because of the uncertainty in repayment rates on pass-throughs. It may be difficult in the latter case because pricing of other pass-throughs assumes that the characteristics underlying both pools are the same. Nonetheless, the securities must be priced to sell to investors at the time of issue.

Turning back to our example, if we *assume* after considering all current market conditions and future expectations regarding repayment that the issuer decides that an expected yield of 8.5 percent will be required to successfully sell all securities to investors *and* that the prepayment rate will be 10 percent, then the security price will be equal to the present value of cash flows in column *g* of Exhibit 17–8 discounted at 8.5 percent. This yields a price of $25,848, or a premium of $848 over

EXHIBIT 17–9 Mortgage Pass-Through Security Cash Flow Payments to Individual Investors at Various Prepayment Rates

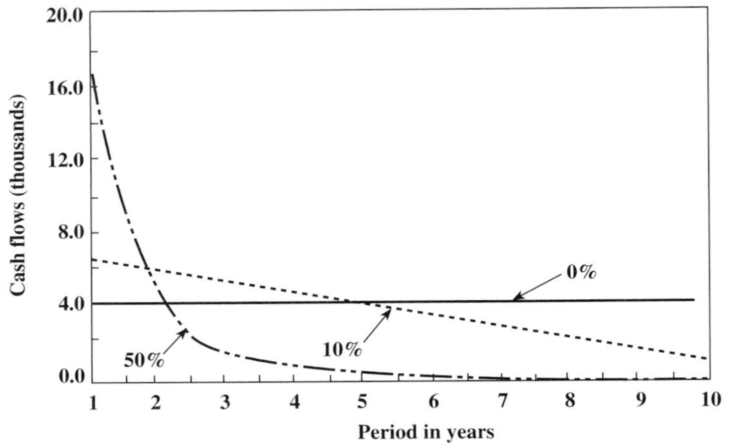

the $25,000 par value (see part B of Exhibit 17–8). The security is now said to be "priced at 103.39 percent of par ($25,848 ÷ $25,000) to yield 8.5 percent." However, the issuer will usually provide yield information to the investor by assuming *faster* and *slower prepayment rates*. This is accomplished by taking the offering price for the security ($25,848) and setting it equal to the expected cash flows that would occur above and below 10 percent prepayment, then solving for the internal rate of return. Faster (or slower) rates of prepayment will cause the yield to be lower (or higher) in this example. The investor is willing to pay a premium of $848 in this example because the coupon rate is higher than the investor's required yield. But because the mortgages in the pool are likely to be prepaid sooner than expected, the investor will not benefit from the higher coupon rate for very long because of the increase in prepayments. Hence, the premium must reflect not only the relationship between the coupon rate on the security and the market yield on similar investments demanded by investors, but also the expected rate of repayment by home owners. On the other hand, if market yields indicated that at the time of issue the security should be priced to yield 10.5 percent at 10 percent prepayment, it would be issued at a discount, or at a price of $24,199 (see part C of Exhibit 17–8). In this case, mortgages are not likely to be prepaid so quickly by homeowners; hence, the expected rate of repayment decreases and the discount paid on the security must reflect this as well as coupon rates and market yields.

Market Interest Rates and Price Behavior on Mortgage Pass-Throughs

To illustrate the very important relationships between changes in interest rates and varying rates of prepayment, Exhibit 17–10 shows that if the market rate of interest were to fall to 7.5 percent, investors having a 9.5 percent coupon rate pass-through security would expect an *increase* in its *price* because of the decline in interest rates. Further, if there were no prepayment assumed (i.e., 0 percent), the price of the pass-through would increase from $25,000 to approximately $27,500. However, if interest rates decline and the prepayment rate accelerates because more borrowers chose to refinance or pay off loans, the price will not rise to the extent that it would have if no

EXHIBIT 17–10 Mortgage Pass-Through Security Prices at Various Required Rates of Return and Prepayment Rates

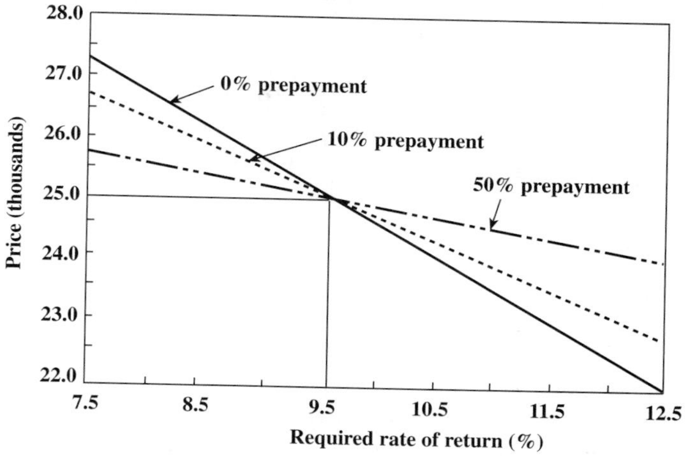

increase in prepayments occurred. This can be seen by comparing prices at extreme rates of repayment, such as prices at 0 percent PSA (no prepayment), with prices at 50 percent for interest rates less than 9.5 percent. Note that even if interest rates *decline*, if the prepayment rate accelerates to 50 percent, the price at a 7.5 percent demanded yield would now be only slightly in excess of $25,000 compared with about $27,500 assuming no prepayment. On the other hand, when market interest rates are *greater* than the coupon rate, prices of mortgage pass-throughs (MPTs) will fall, and by a greater amount as repayments slow. This can also be seen by comparing prices for interest rates greater than 9.5 percent at 0 percent and 50 percent. Hence, prices of mortgage pass-throughs (MPTs) are *inversely* related to interest rates; however, they are less sensitive to declines in interest rates and more sensitive to increases in interest rates because rates of repayment are likely to accelerate as interest rates fall and slow as interest rates rise. This asymmetry affects the duration of the investment and its convexity. **Convexity** is a measure of the sensitivity of duration to changes in interest rates. For example, because prepayments may decelerate with rising interest rates, MPTs usually exhibit negative convexity resulting from an increase in duration. This limit on premiums is referred to as **price compression**. Further, as interest rates decline and prepayments accelerate, all cash flows received by investors must be reinvested at lower interest rates. This prospect is perhaps the most serious problem that investors perceive when investing in mortgage pass-through securities. It is this problem, coupled with other factors, that has given rise to collateralized mortgage obligations (CMOs), one of the mortgage-related securities that we will cover in the next chapter.

A Note on MBBs and MPTs

We have previously indicated that the trustee was required to periodically "mark the mortgage collateral to the market" to determine whether the overcollateralization requirements of bond issues were being maintained. The methodology just outlined for pricing MPTs is the methodology that a trustee would generally follow to establish the market value of the mortgage pool for an issue of mortgage-backed bonds (MBBs). Further, with MBBs, *issuers bear prepayment risk* by virtue of the overcollateralization requirement. In other words, as prepayments accelerate and mortgages are prepaid, more mortgages must be replaced in the pool. With MPTs, *security holders bear prepayment risk* because all prepayments are passed through to investors. This means that (1) MBBs should be priced to provide lower yields than MPTs because the MBB issuer bears prepayment risk, and (2) as market interest rates change, the price of MBBs will not reflect accelerated prepayment rates. As shown in Exhibit 17–10, this is not the case for MPTs. If all other terms of the MPT offering described in our examples were exactly the same for an MBB offering, the price behavior for the MBB would be represented by the 0 percent curve.

Key Terms

constant prepayment assumption 519
convexity 523
Federal Home Loan Mortgage Corp. (FHLMC) 500
Federal National Mortgage Association (FNMA) 497
Government National Mortgage Association (GNMA) 499
mortgage-backed bonds (MBBs) 503
mortgage pass-through securities (MPTs) 507
mortgage pass-through security swaps 508
participation certificates (PCs) 508
pool factor 515
price compression 523
PSA prepayment model 520
secondary mortgage market 495
weighted average coupon 514
weighted average maturity 514

Questions

1. What is the secondary mortgage market? List three reasons why it is important.
2. What were the three principal activities of FNMA under its 1954 charter? What is its principal function now?
3. Name two ways that FNMA currently finances its secondary mortgage operations.
4. When did GNMA come into existence? What was its original function? What is its main function now?
5. Why was the formation of FHLMC so important?
6. What is a mortgage-related security? What are the similarities and differences between mortgage securities and corporate bonds?
7. Name the principal types of mortgage-related securities. What are the differences between them?
8. There are several ways that mortgages can be sold in the secondary market. Choose two and compare and contrast their length of distribution channel, relative ease of transaction, and efficiency as they relate to maximizing funds flow from sale.
9. What is the function of the optional delivery commitment?
10. What is a mortgage swap certificate?
11. Name five important characteristics of mortgage pools. Tell why each is important.
12. In general, would a falling rate of market interest cause the price of an MPT security to increase or decrease? Would the increase or decrease be greater if the security was issued at a discount? Would an increase in prepayment be likely or unlikely? Describe with an example.

Problems

1. Two 25-year maturity mortgage-backed bonds are issued. The first bond has a par value of $10,000 and promises to pay a 10.5 percent annual coupon, while the second is a zero coupon bond that promises to pay $10,000 (par) after 25 years including accrued interest at 10 percent. At issue, bond market investors require a 12 percent interest rate on both bonds.

   a. What is the initial price on each bond?

b. Assume both bonds promise interest at 10.5 percent, compounded semiannually. What will be the initial price for each bond?

c. If market interest rates fall to 9.5 percent at the end of five years, what will be the value of each bond, assuming annual payments as in (*a*) (state both as a percentage of par value and actual dollar value)?

2. The Green S & L originated a pool containing 75 ten-year fixed interest rate mortgages with an average balance of $100,000 each. All mortgages in the pool carry a coupon of 12 percent. (For simplicity, assume all mortgage payments are made *annually* at 12 percent interest.) Green would now like to sell the pool to FNMA.

   a. Assuming a constant annual prepayment rate of 10 percent (for simplicity assume that prepayments are based on the pool balance at the end of the preceding year and begin at the *end* of year 1), what is the price that Green could obtain if market interest rates were 11 percent, 12 percent, 9 percent?

   b. Assume that five years have passed since the date in (*a*). What will the pool factor be? If market interest rates were 12 percent, what price could Green obtain now?

   c. Instead of selling the pool of mortgages in (*a*), Green decides to securitize the mortgages by issuing 100 pass-through securities. The coupon rate will be 11.5 percent and the servicing and guarantee fee will be .5 percent. However, the current market rate of return is 10.5 percent. How much will Green obtain for this offering of MPTs? What will each purchaser pay for an MPT security, assuming the same prepayment rate as in (*a*)?

   d. Assume now that immediately after purchase in (*c*), interest rates fall to 9 percent and that the prepayment rates are expected to accelerate to 20 percent per year, beginning at the end of the first year. What will the MPT security be worth now?

CHAPTER

18

The Secondary Mortgage Market

CMOs and Derivative Securities

Introduction

Two additional securities have been introduced to securitize mortgage pools. The first is referred to as a mortgage pay-through bond (MPTB). It contains elements of mortgage-backed bonds and mortgage pass-through securities. The second security, referred to as a collateralized mortgage obligation (CMO), was developed in conjunction with investment underwriters by Freddie Mac in 1983 and adopted by Fannie Mae in 1987. These securities should be viewed as a natural outgrowth of the initial success of the mortgage-backed bond and pass-through security programs. Recall that many risks and investor concerns with purchasing whole mortgages discussed in the previous chapter were alleviated to some extent by mortgage pass-throughs. However, several key concerns with prepayment risk and reinvestment risk remained for some investors. Innovators of mortgage-backed securities believed that in addition to CMOs, new product types called **derivative securities,** or simply "derivatives," had to be developed to address these concerns.

Mortgage Pay-Through Bonds (MPTBs)

These bonds can be best described as hybrid securities or ones containing elements of both mortgage pass-throughs and mortgage-backed bonds. Mortgage pay-through bonds (MPTBs) are issued against mortgage pools and, like MPTs, cash flows from the pool (i.e., principal and interest) are passed through to security holders. However, unlike an MPT, this security is a *bond* and not an undivided *equity* ownership interest in a mortgage pool. Like the MBB, the MPTB is a debt obligation of the issuer, who retains ownership of the mortgage pool. However, like the MPT, cash flows paid to bondholders are based on a coupon rate of interest while principal is passed through as it is received from normal amortization and prepayment of loans in the pool. Hence, an MPTB can be viewed as an MBB with the pass-through of principal and prepayment features of an MPT.

Most pay-through issues are based on residential pools and, like MBBs, will generally be overcollateralized by including (1) more mortgages in the pool than the sum of the securities issued against it or (2) additional collateral in the form of U.S.

government bonds or other agency obligations. The income from this additional collateral is used as added assurance that sufficient cash flows will be available to service the bonds. Again, like MBBs, MPTBs may be issued either with a coupon rate or on a zero coupon basis.

An MPTB credit rating depends on (1) the riskiness of mortgages in the pool, (2) the extent of overcollateralization, and (3) the nature of any government-related securities constituting the excess collateral. Emphasis is placed on the extent of cash flow that will be produced by the pool, the reinvestment period that the issuer faces between receipt of principal and interest from the mortgage pool and periodic (usually semiannual) payments to bondholders, the securities making up the overcollateralization, and its relationship to promised coupon payments. All of these features are evaluated relative to prepayment risk. Because of the pass-through of amortization and prepayments, the market value of the collateral is not as important as it is with MBBs. Hence, there is usually no need to mark the collateral to the market or to provide for replenishment of collateral as long as the amount of overcollateralization is adequate. Because of the pass-through of principal, overcollateral requirements are not as great as for MBBs. Credit enhancements in the form of letters of credit and third-party guarantees or insurance are used by MPTB issuers to acquire higher credit ratings. In the absence of these enhancements, the creditworthiness of the issuer is very important because, should the mortgage pool experience a high rate of default losses and prepayments, the issuer must be looked to for satisfaction by the debt security holders.[1]

Although we do not provide a detailed analysis of MPTBs, the cash flow patterns are similar to those shown in the illustrations used for MBBs and MPTs in Chapter 17. However, contrary to the MBB, the issuer of MPTBs does not bear prepayment risk. It is borne by the investor. Hence, when pricing MPTBs, the risks that are so important when evaluating MPT prepayment patterns and reinvestment rates are equally important to MPTBs. This uncertainty regarding cash flows from prepayments has resulted in yet another security type, one that provides more protection against prepayment risk than MPTs and MPTBs, but less than that of an MBB. This security, referred to as the collateralized mortgage obligation (CMO), is the subject of the next section.

Collateralized Mortgage Obligations

To understand how **collateralized mortgage obligations (CMOs)** help to alleviate some of the reinvestment and prepayment risk for investors, we must understand the concept of a CMO and how it differs from MPTs and MPTBs. CMOs are debt instruments (like MBBs) that are issued using a pool of mortgages for collateral. In the pass-through, investors own an individual interest in the entire pool. In contrast, the issuer of a CMO offering *retains the ownership* of the mortgage pool and issues the bonds as debt against the mortgage pool. However, like the MPT and MPTB, the CMO is a pay-through security in that all amortization and prepayments flow through to investors. This means that the *security holder* continues to assume prepayment risk. However, the CMO modifies how the risk is allocated. Like both the

[1]Like other mortgage-related securities, default risk can be reduced by using FHA-VA mortgages or conventional loans with private mortgage insurance.

MBB and MPTB, the difference between assets pledged as security and the amount of the debt issued against the pool constitutes the equity position of the issuer.

The major difference between CMOs and the other mortgage-backed securities is that CMOs are securities issued in multiple classes against the same pool of mortgages. These securities may have a number of maturity classes, such as three, five, or seven years. Such maturities are chosen by the issuer to meet the investment needs of various classes of investors. By issuing multiple classes of securities, each with a different maturity, the issuer is effectively creating different securities with maturity and payment streams that are vastly different from the underlying mortgage pool.

There are several fundamental differences between CMOs and MPTs. To reduce prepayment risk (and the coincident reinvestment risk), a mechanism had to be developed for an entity other than the investor to assume this risk while retaining the basic procedure of issuing securities against a mortgage pool. This was accomplished by the *issuer* retaining the ownership of the mortgage pool and prioritizing the payment of interest and principal among the various classes of debt securities issued against the pool. This prioritization is accomplished by issuing CMOs in classes referred to as **tranches** with different stated maturity dates. To achieve the desired number and maturity of these tranches, a prioritization of interest, principal, and prepayment proceeds from the mortgage pool to bondholders is made. Based on this prioritization, some classes of CMO investors receive cash flows like investors in conventional debt securities, while other investors agree to defer cash flows to later periods. This allocation was designed to appeal to more investor groups than would be willing to invest in MPTs, but who also were willing to bear some prepayment risk at yields that would be higher than those earned on MBBs. A CMO can also be referred to as a *multiple security class, mortgage pay-through security.*

Since its inception in 1983, the CMO has evolved into an extremely complex investment alternative. Although the sequential pay structure (see Exhibit 18–1) was used extensively during the initial years of CMO offerings and did much to stimulate investor interest, high demand and rather specific investor needs have led to the creation of a wide array of tranche alternatives. By slightly modifying either the method of principal repayment or coupon calculation, investment bankers have created a multitude of unique derivative investment vehicles that dominate the current CMO market.[2]

CMOs Illustrated

Exhibit 18–1 shows provisions that a very simplified offering of a CMO security might contain. On the "asset" side of the exhibit, the pool used for the bond collateral is assumed to be either FHA, VA, or conventional mortgages with interest rates fixed at 11 percent interest over a 10-year maturity. As with pass-throughs, mortgages placed in CMO pools are generally secured by very similar kinds of real estate and have equally similar payment patterns. It is also possible to pool GNMAs or other pass-through securities for a CMO offering.[3] The latter securities can be used in a pool because they ultimately represent securities based on a pool of mortgages.

---

[2]The term *derivative* refers to any investment with an underlying value that is dependent in another security, index, or pool of securities. For example, if an investor purchased a call option in the S&P 500 index, that option would be classified as a derivative because its price would be dependent on changes in the value of the S&P 500 index. Many derivative-type investments have been created with prices that are dependent on the changes in the cash flows from mortgages in an underlying pool. These derivatives are discussed later in this chapter.

[3]CMOs can be created based on many different mortgage pools (e.g., ARMs, GPMs), such as those discussed in the previous chapter.

EXHIBIT 18–1 Contents of a CMO Security Offering with Sequential Pay Tranches

			Estimated Maturity (years)	Coupon Rate (percent)	Amount Issued	Weight	Weighted Average Coupon (percent)
Assets:		**Liabilities:**					
Mortgages (11% interest) 10-yr. maturity	$75,000,000	Class A Bonds	2–5	9.25%	$27,000,000	0.375	3.47%
		Class B Bonds	4–7	10.00	15,000,000	0.208	2.08
		Class Z Bonds	6–10	11.00	30,000,000	0.417	4.58
		Total bonds			72,000,000	1.000	10.14%
		Equity:			3,000,000		
Total assets	$75,000,000	Total debt and net worth			$75,000,000		

Major investors:
Class A—Thrifts, commercial banks, money market funds, corporations
Class B—Insurance companies, pension funds, trusts, international investors
Class Z—Pension funds, trusts, international investors and hedge bonds

On the "liability" side of the exhibit, four classes of bonds are created with different maturities and coupon rates. The amount of CMOs issued against the $75 million pool is $72 million. The difference ($3 million) is overcollateral, which is the equity contribution made by the issuer. The need for the overcollateralization will be apparent as the structure of the CMO issue is explained. Another observation that can be made in our example is that the 11 percent rate to be earned on the asset pool exceeds the coupon rates promised to each class of bondholders except the Z class. The difference between the 11 percent earned on the $75 million pool, or $8,250,000, and the *weighted average rate of interest* promised to security holders or 10.14 percent on $72,000,000, which is an interest cost of $7,297,500, represents the source of profit at about $956,400 to be earned by the issuer. This residual cash flow will represent a return on the $3 million in overcollateral, or equity, invested in the venture. The issuer earns a profit on the equity that is used for creating the security issue. Fees may also be earned for providing any credit enhancements, managing, and administering the mortgage pool.

To achieve the desired maturity pattern for the CMOs shown in Exhibit 18–1, the conditions of the issue are such that the coupon rate of interest is not paid currently on all tranches. This structure, which is one of many possible payout possibilities, is referred to as a *sequential payout tranche* structure and is used to achieve the desired maturity pattern. For example, interest is paid currently on tranches A and B, but it is not paid on tranche Z until principal on the other tranches is repaid. For securities in tranche Z, interest will be accrued and accumulated into the investment balance. To ensure that the maturity of tranche A securities is kept relatively short, all interest accrued on the portion of the security offering contributed by the tranche Z is also allocated first to the tranche A security holders as additional principal. Further, all current amortization of principal and prepayments from the *entire* mortgage pool will also be allocated *first* to tranche A. Hence, tranche A investors, representing $27 million of the CMO issue, will receive principal on all mortgages in the pool (including prepayments), plus interest that would have been paid to tranche Z until the $27 million tranche is repaid, in addition to a coupon rate of 9.25 percent on their outstanding investment balance. Their investment balance is reduced by all principal payments from the pool plus the interest not currently paid but accrued on the Z class investment balance. As to the spread in stated maturities for tranche A securities (five to nine years), it represents (*a*) the maximum number of years that it would take for class A investors to recover their principal, *assuming that no prepayments* occurred on the underlying mortgage pool, and (*b*) an *estimate* of the minimum number of years (five) that it would take them to recover their investment. Of course, this latter estimate could be longer or shorter, depending on the *actual* rate of prepayment.

Until tranche A is repaid, tranche B receives "interest only" payments. After class A is repaid, all principal allocations are made to B, and so on. As pointed out, the Z class of security holders receives no interest payments or principal payments while the A and B tranches are being repaid. Instead, interest is accrued on the $15 million invested by this class of investors and is compounded at the 10 percent coupon rate. The accrued interest is then added to the amount owed. After classes A and B are repaid, cash interest payments are made to the Z class, and all principal payments from the pool are then directed toward this class.

The $3,000,000 in extra mortgages placed in the pool, which represents overcollateralization or equity invested in the issue, is required for several reasons. First, in addition to the cash flow patterns described, most CMO issues promise payments to investors quarterly or semiannually; we know however, that payments into the mortgage pool occur monthly. Because monthly mortgage payments may be reinvested by the issuer until semiannual payments are due to investors, the issuer promises a minimum rate of interest on these investable funds *in addition to* promised coupon payments and priority repayment of principal. Hence, in addition to the risk of prepayment, a reinvestment risk exists in the event that market interest rates fall dramatically. In this event, prepayments into the pool would accelerate, thereby repaying all tranches *much faster* than expected. Further, the issuer may not be able to earn the promised rate of return on interim cash flows as interest rates fall (reinvestment risk). In this event, any cash shortfall to CMO investors will be paid from the $3 million of additional mortgage collateral. Hence, as with MBBs and MPTBs, the extent of overcollateralization is an important consideration that investors must make when evaluating a CMO investment. Obviously, the greater the amount of overcollateralization, the more likely that promised coupon rates and rates on interim cash flows will be paid. However, lower risk also implies that the coupon rate and rate on reinvested funds promised to the shorter-term tranches may also be lower.

Another important consideration with these securities is whether the CMO issuer is liable beyond the $3 million of equity. Usually issued by a corporation, CMOs are debt instruments that can be made with or without recourse to the issuer. Hence, like an issue of corporate bonds, CMO security owners may have recourse against the assets of the issuing corporation should the issuer become bankrupt and not perform as promised and liability exceeds $3 million.

CMO Mechanics

Some idea of cash flow patterns from a CMO offering is given in Exhibit 18–2, in which the data from Exhibit 18–1 are used to produce cash flows. To simplify this analysis, we have assumed that payments into the pool from mortgage borrowers occur annually. Consequently, we do not consider any reinvestment of interim cash flows between receipt of mortgage payments into the pool and payment to the

EXHIBIT 18–2 Annual Cash Flows into CMO Mortgage Pool (prepayment rate = 0 percent)

Period	(1) Mortgage Pool: 10-Year Term 11% Fixed Rate	(2) Principal and Interest Payments into Pool	(4) Total Amortization Excluding Prepayments	(5) Interest	(6) Amount Owed to Security Holders
0	$75,000,000				$72,000,000
1	70,514,893	$12,735,107	$ 4,485,107	$8,250,000	67,514,893
2	65,536,424	12,735,107	4,978,469	7,756,638	62,536,424
3	60,010,324	12,735,107	5,526,100	7,209,007	57,010,324
4	53,876,352	12,735,107	6,133,971	6,601,136	50,876,352
5	47,067,644	12,735,107	6,808,708	5,926,399	44,067,644
6	39,509,978	12,735,107	7,557,666	5,177,441	36,509,978
7	31,120,968	12,735,107	8,389,009	4,346,098	28,120,968
8	21,809,168	12,735,107	9,311,801	3,423,307	18,809,168
9	11,473,069	12,735,107	10,336,099	2,399,008	8,473,069
10	0	12,735,107	11,473,069	1,262,038	0

various tranches of securities. We begin by assuming a rate of prepayment equal to 0 percent. Essentially, the exhibit details the source and composition of cash flows into the mortgage pool backing the CMO offering. Exhibit 18–3 provides a breakdown of cash flows for the various tranches of securities. Based on the assumption that no prepayments occur, tranche A security holders would be paid (*a*) interest at 9.25 percent of $27,000,000, or $2,497,500 (*b*) all principal repayments of $4,485,107 flowing into the pool (see column 4 in Exhibit 18–2), plus (*c*) the $3,300,00 in interest that would have been paid to the Z class of securities, or a total of $10,282,607 at end of the first year (see Exhibit 18–3). The cash flow pattern just described continues each year until the class A securities are repaid, which occurs at the end of the fourth year. Note again that class Z investors receive no current cash payments because interest is being accrued in that class.

Exhibit 18–3 provides a similar breakdown for class B and Z security holders. Note that class B securities receive current interest payments from years 1 to 3, but they do not receive any repayment of principal until class A is repaid. They then receive current interest plus all amortization flowing into the pool and interest from the tranche Z accrual. Note that when no prepayment is assumed, the B class would have a maturity period of five years based on normal amortization of the underlying mortgage pool. Note that the Z tranche accumulates interest until year 5 when investors in this tranche begin to receive cash flow.

Exhibit 18–4 provides detail on what is referred to as the cash flow to the **residual,** or equity, position in the CMO offering. Recall in our example that the firm that issues the CMO securities had collateralized the issue by $3 million, which represents the equivalent of an equity investment in the CMO offering. Hence, the issuer is entitled to retain any excess cash flow after payments are made to all security owners, and servicing fees and so on are paid. These cash flows represent the source of any return to the residual or equity position. Note that the cash flows are simply the sum of all cash flows into the pool, less all cash flows paid out to all tranches according to the CMO agreement. The cash flow available to the residual equity

EXHIBIT 18–3 Cash Flows to Class A, B, and Z Investors (prepayment rate = 0 percent)

Tranche A (coupon rate = 9.25%; amount invested = $27,000,000)

Period	Amount Owed to Security Holder at End of Period	All Principal from Pool and Interest from Z Class	Coupon Interest	Total Payments
0	$27,000,000			
1	19,214,893	$7,785,107	$2,497,500	$10,282,607
2	10,573,424	8,641,469	1,777,378	10,418,846
3	981,394	9,592,030	978,042	10,570,072
4	0	981,394	90,779	1,072,173
5	0	0	0	0
6	0	0	0	0
7	0	0	0	0
8	0	0	0	0
9	0	0	0	0
10	0	0	0	0

Tranche B (coupon rate = 10.00%; amount invested = $15,000,000)

Period	Amount Owed to Security Holder at End of Period	All Principal from Pool and Interest from Z Class	Coupon Interest	Total Payments
0	$15,000,000			
1	15,000,000	0	$1,500,000	$ 1,500,000
2	15,000,000	0	1,500,000	1,500,000
3	15,000,000	0	1,500,000	1,500,000
4	5,334,240	$9,665,760	1,500,000	11,165,760
5	0	5,334,240	533,424	5,867,664
6	0	0	0	0
7	0	0	0	0
8	0	0	0	0
9	0	0	0	0
10	0	0	0	0

Tranche Z (coupon rate = 11.00%; amount invested = $30,000,000)

Period	Amount Owed to Security Holder at End of Period	Interest	Accrued Interest	Principal Allocation	Total Payments
0	$30,000,000				
1	33,300,000	$3,300,000	$3,300,000		
2	36,963,000	3,663,000	3,663,000		
3	41,028,930	4,065,930	4,065,930		
4	45,542,112	4,513,182	4,513,182		
5	44,067,644	5,009,632		$ 1,474,468	$ 6,484,101
6	36,509,978	4,847,441		7,557,666	12,405,107
7	28,120,968	4,016,098		8,389,009	12,405,107
8	18,809,168	3,093,307		9,311,801	12,405,107
9	8,473,069	2,069,008		10,336,099	12,405,107
10	0	932,038		8,473,069	9,405,107i

depends on how much interest is earned on the mortgage pool relative to the amount of interest paid to the A, B, and Z security holders. In our example, cash flow residuals

Exhibit 18–4 Residual Cash Flows (prepayment rate = 0 percent)

Residual Equity Class ($3,000,000 invested)			
Period	*Total Cash Flows into Pool*	*Total Payments to A, B, and Z classes*	*Residual Cash Flows to Equity Class*
0			($3,000,000)
1	$12,735,107	$11,782,607	952,500
2	12,735,107	11,918,846	816,261
3	12,735,107	12,070,072	665,035
4	12,735,107	12,237,933	497,174
5	12,735,107	12,351,765	383,342
6	12,735,107	12,405,107	330,000
7	12,735,107	12,405,107	330,000
8	12,735,107	12,405,107	330,000
9	12,735,107	12,405,107	330,000
10	12,735,107	9,405,107	3,330,000

Residual *IRR* 20.19%

are received by the equity investor each year, even when the Z class of securities does not receive any cash flows.[4] Also, the $952,500 initial cash flow to the residual interest represents a very small margin (less than 1 percent) relative to the $75 million security issue. This residual cash flow includes any servicing fees that are earned by the issuer, who we assume also retains the servicing responsibility for the mortgage pool. This margin is important because, for example, if $10 million of the mortgage pool was to unexpectedly prepay immediately after the securities were issued, this large amount of prepayments would significantly reduce the interest flow into the pool. Further, these unanticipated prepayments must be reinvested to compensate for the loss in interest and to pay the class A tranche at the end of the year. Consequently, the $952,500 cash flow to the residual would have to be used to offset the difference between interest lost because of prepayment and any interest earned on interim reinvestment.

The possibility of unanticipated prepayment and the potential problem with reinvesting in a period of declining interest rates (which is also likely to cause even more prepayments) should clarify why the $3 million overcollateralization is required. Further, we have assumed that the mortgages used to form the pool for the CMO issue are FHA, VA, or conventional fixed-rate mortgages. In any case, we have assumed that there is adequate insurance protection against default losses. Where there are no limited or no full guarantees against default losses (e.g., where CMOs are issued against commercial mortgages or second mortgages), the investor would have to consider the possibility of greater losses because of the impact of default on cash flows. Hence, in the latter instances we would expect to see (1) larger amounts of overcollateralization, and/or (2) pool insurance purchased by the issuer from a third party who is willing to insure investors against part or all default loss, or (3) a provision referred to as a

[4]Some CMO provisions may require that this payment be placed in reserve until termination of the issue. In this event, the internal rate of return shown at the bottom of the exhibit would be lower because residual cash flows would not be realized by the issuer until mortgages in the pool are completely amortized.

calamity call, which allows the issuer to recall all securities for a specified time after issue in the event interest rates declined sharply, prepayments accelerated, and reinvestment rates were below rates promised to investors. However, if cash flows were to occur as shown in Exhibit 18–4, the issuer would earn a *BTIRR* of 20.19 percent on the $3 million in equity (servicing and other fees not removed from residual cash flows). This rate obviously exceeds the rates earned by each security class, which has a prior claim on all cash flows paid into the pool.

CMO Cash Flows and Prepayment Assumptions. Because there will always be some prepayment of principal from mortgages in an underlying pool, the expected maturity for each security class will affect profitability to the issuer. To illustrate this effect, we now assume that prepayment will occur at approximately 10 percent instead of zero as illustrated in the preceding exhibits.

Cash payments from the pool to each of the classes of security holders are shown in Exhibit 18–5. Note that in addition to normal amortization payments into the pool, prepayments are assumed to occur at 10 percent per year. As shown in Exhibit 18–6, investors in tranche A receive their promised coupon payments, $2,497,500, plus the tranche Z portion of interest in $3,300,000, plus all amortization $4,485,107 and prepayments of $7,500,000 flowing into the pool during the first year, or a total of $17,782,607. Based on this accelerated pattern of cash flows, class A investors would now be repaid after two years. This compares with four years when no prepayment was assumed. For this reason, class A securities are sometimes referred to as the "fast pay tranche." After two years, class B investors, who receive current interest only payments, would begin receiving the interest accrued on tranche Z plus all principal from mortgages paid into the pool during the third year. Based on this pattern of cash receipts, tranche B would now be repaid after one additional year, or a total of three years from the date of issue. This compares to five years with no prepayment.

As indicated earlier, tranche Z security holders do not receive interest or principal payments until the A and B tranches are repaid. Exhibit 18–6 shows that during

EXHIBIT 18–5 Annual Cash Flows into CMO Mortgage Pool (prepayment rate = 10 percent)

Period	(1) Mortgage Pool: 10-Year Term 11% Fixed Rate	(2) Principal and Interest Payment into Pool	(3) Assumed Prepayments* (10%)	(4) Total Amortization Excluding Prepayments	(5) Interest	(6) Amount Owed to Security Holders	(7) Total Available for Distribution (2) + (3)
0	$75,000,000					$72,000,000	
1	63,014,893	$12,735,107	$7,500,000	$4,485,107	$8,250,000	60,014,893	$20,235,107
2	52,264,447	11,380,595	6,301,489	4,448,956	6,931,638	49,264,447	17,682,084
3	42,631,009	10,156,083	5,226,445	4,406,993	5,749,089	39,631,009	15,382,527
4	34,010,368	9,046,951	4,263,101	4,357,540	4,689,411	31,010,368	13,310,052
5	26,311,218	8,039,254	3,401,037	4,298,113	3,741,141	23,311,218	11,440,291
6	19,455,296	7,119,034	2,631,122	4,224,800	2,894,234	16,455,296	9,750,156
7	13,378,894	6,270,955	1,945,530	4,130,872	2,140,083	10,378,894	8,216,484
8	8,037,865	5,474,818	1,337,889	4,003,140	1,471,678	5,037,865	6,812,708
9	3,424,664	4,693,580	803,786	3,809,415	884,165	424,664	5,497,366
10	0	3,801,377	0	3,424,664	376,713	0	3,801,377

*Based on pool balance at the end of the preceding year.

EXHIBIT 18–6 Cash Flows to Class A, B, and Z Investors (prepayment rate = 10 percent)

Tranche A (coupon rate = 9.25%; amount invested = $27,000,000)

Period	*Amount Owed to Security Holder at End of Period*	*All Principal from Pool and Interest from Z Class*	*Coupon Interest*	*Total Payments*
0	$27,000,000			
1	11,714,893	$15,285,107	$2,497,500	$17,782,607
2	0	11,714,893	1,083,628	12,798,521
3	0	0	0	0
4	0	0	0	0
5	0	0	0	0
6	0	0	0	0
7	0	0	0	0
8	0	0	0	0
9	0	0	0	0
10	0	0	0	0

Tranche B (coupon rate = 10.00%; amount invested = $15,000,000)

Period	*Amount Owed to Security Holder at End of Period*	*All Principal from Pool and Interest from Z Class*	*Coupon Interest*	*Total Payments*
0	$15,000,000			
1	15,000,000	0	$1,500,000	$ 1,500,000
2	12,301,447	$ 2,698,553	1,500,000	4,198,553
3	0	12,301,447	1,230,145	13,531,592
4	0	0	0	0
5	0	0	0	0
6	0	0	0	0
7	0	0	0	0
8	0	0	0	0
9	0	0	0	0
10	0	0	0	0

Tranche Z (coupon rate = 11.00%; amount invested = $30,000,000)

Period	*Amount Owed to Security Holder at End of Period*	*Interest*	*Accrued Interest*	*Principal Allocation*	*Total Payments*
0	$30,000,000				
1	33,300,000	$3,300,000	$3,300,000		
2	36,963,000	3,663,000	3,663,000		
3	39,631,009	4,065,930	2,668,009		$ 1,397,921
4	31,010,368	4,359,411		$8,620,641	12,980,052
5	23,311,218	3,411,141		7,699,150	11,110,291
6	16,455,296	2,564,234		6,855,922	9,420,156
7	10,378,894	1,810,083		6,076,402	7,886,484
8	5,037,865	1,141,678		5,341,029	6,482,708
9	424,664	554,165		4,613,201	5,167,366
10	0	46,713		424,664	471,377

the first three years, interest would be accrued on the Z class by compounding the $30 million invested at 11 percent. Interest is calculated at the coupon rate (11 percent) on the accumulated investment balance, which contains $30 million plus all

EXHIBIT 18–7 Residual Class Flows (prepayment rate = 10 percent)

Residual Equity Class ($3,000,000 invested)			
Period	*Total Cash Flows into Pool*	*Total Payments to A, B, and Z classes*	*Residual Cash Flows to Equity Class*
0			($3,000,000)
1	$20,235,107	$19,282,607	952,500
2	17,682,084	16,997,073	685,011
3	15,382,527	14,929,513	453,014
4	13,310,052	12,980,052	330,000
5	11,440,291	11,110,291	330,000
6	9,750,156	9,420,156	330,000
7	8,216,484	7,886,484	330,000
8	6,812,708	6,482,708	330,000
9	5,497,366	5,167,366	330,000
10	3,801,377	471,377	3,330,000
Residual *IRR* 17.25%			

accrued interest. In year 3 the Z class begins to receive some payments but it is not enough to cover the interest until year 4 when all other securities have been paid off. All principal payments flowing into the pool at this point are also allocated to the Z class. The Z class, based on our prepayment assumptions, will now be repaid in the 10th year.

Finally, the issuer retains residual cash flows remaining after all cash payments are made to each tranche of securities. This residual amounts to, in essence, the spread earned by the issuer for investing equity (overcollateralization) and for managing the provisions of the CMO issue. Exhibit 18–7 shows the residual cash flows, or the difference between total payments into the pool and cash payments made to all of the investor classes (based on all preceding exhibits). Recall that these residuals are based on the assumption that the repayment rate remains at 10 percent. Obviously, these residuals would vary considerably at different rates of repayment. When the residual cash flows received over 10 years by the issuer are set equal to the $3 million in equity invested at the time of issue, a yield, or internal rate of return, of 17.25 percent results. As expected, this yield still represents a higher return than is earned on the A, B, or Z tranches. Further, this yield would obviously increase if the amount of equity used to finance the CMO issue is reduced (because of the use of financial leverage).[5]

Also note that in the case of faster prepayment, the *BTIRR* (Exhibit 18–7) will fall to 17.25 percent from the slower prepayment example (Exhibit 18–4), where the *IRR* was 20.19 percent. This occurs because the total interest collected from the pool will be lower if prepayment accelerates; therefore, the dollar spread between interest inflow and outflow becomes smaller.

[5]The reader may think of leverage in the financial structure of a CMO issue much like that of leveraging any income-producing asset with debt. Similarly, the risk assumed by the various classes of bondholders and the issuer will vary based on the amount of overcollateralization.

CMOs: Pricing and Expected Maturities

Exhibit 18–8 provides additional insights to aid in understanding how the patterns of cash flow payments to each tranche of securities vary with prepayment rates. The graph in panel A shows the expected cash flows to each class of CMO investors based on a zero percent prepayment rate. In panel B, four very distinct cash flow patterns emerge. This is exactly the goal of the CMO issuer; that is, to reach different *market segments* of investors who have more specific maturity requirements than a mortgage pass-through security provides, but who may not need the exact maturity requirements that an MBB provides. As indicated, however, the CMO does not completely eliminate prepayment risk. Indeed, if mortgage interest rates declined substantially, these securities may provide investors with only slightly more prepayment protection than a pass-through security. To illustrate what cash flows and the maturity of security classes may look like, assuming a significant increase in prepayment, Exhibit 18–9 shows results assuming a 10 percent prepayment rate.

EXHIBIT 18–8 Annual Cash Flows to CMO Tranches and Residual Equity (prepayment rate = 0 percent)

Panel A

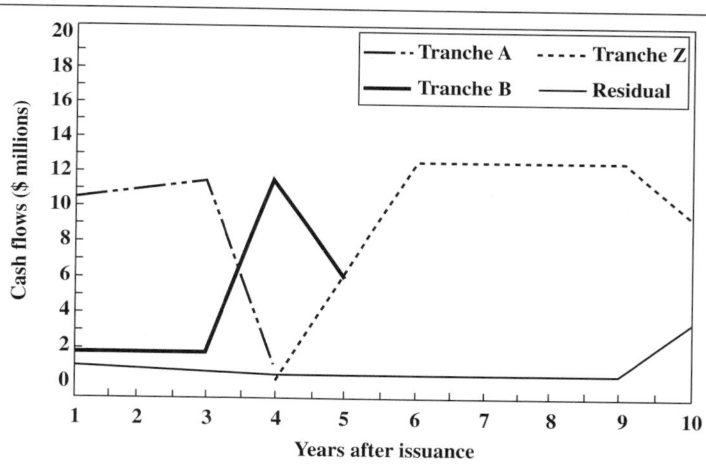

Panel B

Period	*Cash Flows Tranche A*	*Cash Flows Tranche B*	*Cash Flows Tranche Z*	*Cash Flows Residual*
1	$10,282,607	$ 1,500,000	0	$ 952,500
2	10,418,846	1,500,000	0	816,261
3	10,570,072	1,500,000	0	665,035
4	1,072,173	11,165,760	0	497,174
5	0	5,867,664	$ 6,484,101	383,342
6	0	0	12,405,107	330,000
7	0	0	12,405,107	330,000
8	0	0	12,405,107	330,000
9	0	0	12,405,107	330,000
10	0	0	9,405,107	3,330,000

EXHIBIT 18–9 Annual Cash Flows to CMO Tranches and Residual Equity (prepayment rate = 10 percent)

Panel A

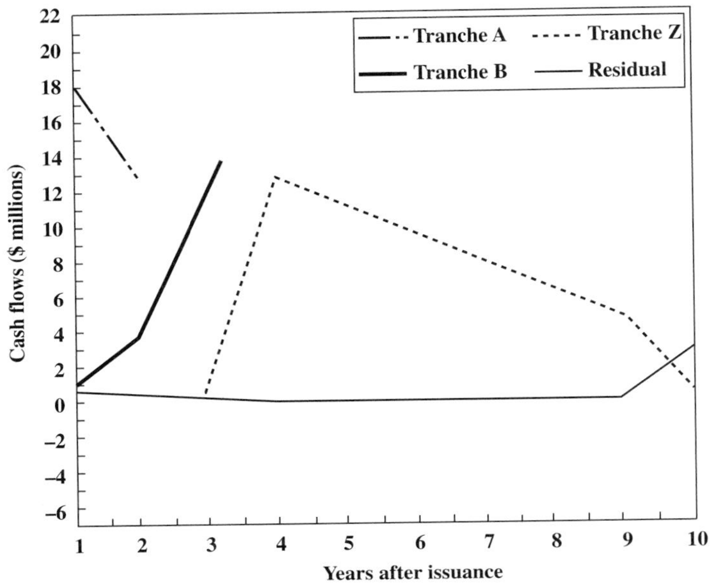

Panel B

Period	*Cash Flows Tranche A*	*Cash Flows Tranche B*	*Cash Flows Tranche Z*	*Cash Flows Residual*
1	$17,782,607	$ 1,500,000	0	$ 952,500
2	12,798,521	4,198,553	0	685,011
3	0	13,531,592	$ 1,397,921	453,014
4	0	0	12,980,052	330,000
5	0	0	11,110,291	330,000
6	0	0	9,420,156	330,000
7	0	0	7,886,484	330,000
8	0	0	6,482,708	330,000
9	0	0	5,167,366	330,000
10	0	0	471,377	3,330,000

By placing a priority on the distribution of cash flows to various classes of security owners, the CMO generally provides more predictability with respect to expected maturity periods and cash flows than a mortgage pass-through. Recall that in our simplified example in Chapter 17, MPT investors could be committed for a period of up to 10 years, with substantial variation in cash flows received from period to period, depending on the repayment rate.

CMO securities, when based on a pool of FHA, VA, or conventionally insured mortgages, should provide a yield in excess of U.S. Treasury securities with equivalent maturity classes[6] because of added cash flow uncertainty. In any case, if no significant decline in interest rates is expected by security holders, the pattern of cash flows shown in Exhibit 18–9 may be appealing to some investors who would otherwise be interested in a pass-through security. This may be particularly true for class A, or fast-pay tranche, which would compete with short-term Treasury bills and notes and may be attractive to managers of money market funds. Tranche B may be more appealing to insurance companies and pension funds, while tranche Z may be preferred by either long-term or hedge-type mutual funds. Hence, prioritization of cash flows does create the possibility of reaching a broader class of investors with more specific maturity requirements than would be the case with MPTs.[7]

To establish some idea of the sensitivity of expected *maturity* to expected rates of prepayment, Exhibit 18–10 shows the outstanding amount owed for each tranche under the repayment assumption of 0 percent PSA (panel A) and 10 percent. As expected, the balances shown for tranche A in panel A begin to amortize immediately, and tranche B amortizes in accordance with the priority allocation of cash flows. However, the amount owed to the Z class increases sharply as interest accrues (like that on a GPM mortgage). In the event that the repayment rate increases sharply (as in panel B), the amounts owed to each security class decrease significantly and all investors in the CMO offering would be repaid within 10 years.

CMO Price Behavior and Prepayment Rates

As with MPTs, CMO prices will vary with both changes in interest rates and prepayment rates. The relationship for 0 percent PSA is shown in panel A of Exhibit 18–11. An important characteristic of the prices is their relatively narrow range (vertical axis) that results from changes in demanded market rates of return (interest rates, horizontal axis) for the A and B tranches. The reason is the prioritization of cash flows, which has a "smoothing effect" on prices. However, with respect to prices for tranche Z and present value of the residual interest, these two classes exhibit more volatility in price behavior than tranches A and B. This volatility is a byproduct of the market segmentation chosen for this CMO security issue.

Even when an extremely significant increase in the prepayment rate occurs, as shown in panel B of Exhibit 18–11, the range in prices tends to narrow for all tranches in the CMO issue. This can be seen by comparing the ranges in panels A and B. However, also keep in mind that the *expected maturity period* also declines significantly as rate of prepayment increases (see Exhibit 18–10). Hence, this CMO structure makes a trade-off in price stability from the Z and residual classes to the A and B tranches as the maturity period contracts for all classes. However, relative to mortgage pass-through securities, the A and B tranches of CMOs receive some additional prepayment and price protection not given to MPT security holders. Investors in MPTs would receive an increase in cash flows as the rate of prepayment increases, but not necessarily as dramatic a reduction in maturity (although the cash

---

[6]Because the investor in a CMO is dealing with an *expected* range in maturity, that expected maturity must be used as a basis of comparison for maturities of alternative investments.

[7]The reader may have reached the conclusion that a CMO issue with its various classes of expected maturities resembles tax-exempt serial bonds, which are frequently issued by state and local municipalities. Recall that bond issues with serial and sinking fund provisions call for the retirement of specific amounts of bonds at specific time intervals. This pattern of different maturities appeals to many investor groups that have a specific need to match liabilities coming due on specific dates with an interest-bearing asset with the same maturity. The different pattern of CMO maturities does emulate such bond issues offerings in this respect. However, the use of a Z class of security and residual or equity interest is the truly innovative aspect of this type of offering.

Exhibit 18–10 Maturity of CMO Tranches at Various Prepayment Rates

Panel A. Annual Balance Owed on CMO Tranches at 0 Percent Prepayment

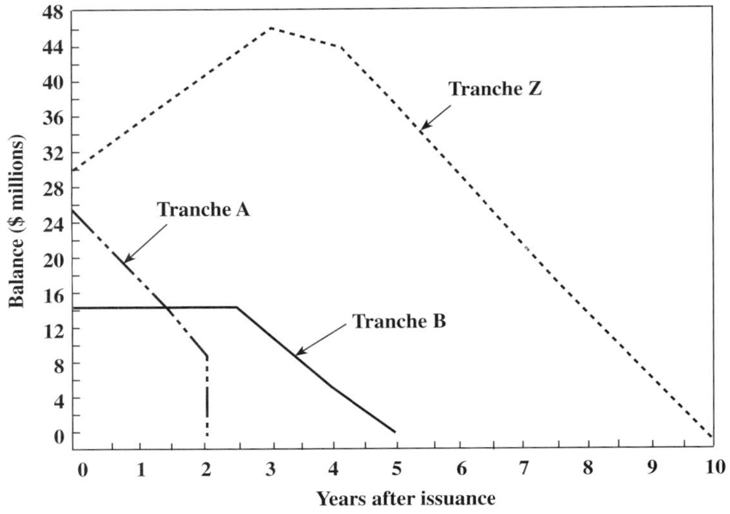

Panel B. Annual Balance Owed on CMO Tranches at 10 Percent Prepayment

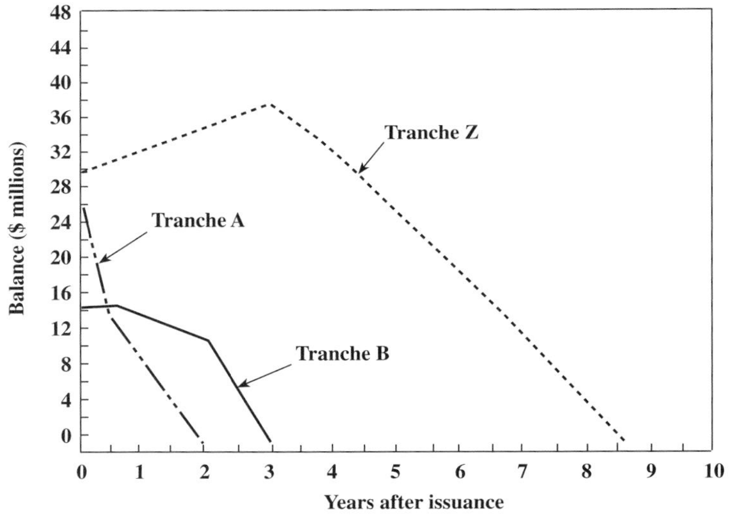

flows in the later years may be relatively small). Consequently, structuring a CMO offering with a maturity and cash flow pattern for one Z tranche, while retaining shorter maturities for the A and B tranches, may make it possible to appeal to investors who have a preference for shorter maturities and a strong dislike for the MPT. One measure that is often used to measure the relationship between price,

EXHIBIT 18–11 **CMO Price Behavior in Response to Changes in Interest Rates and Prepayment Rates**

Panel A. Prices at 0 Percent Prepayment

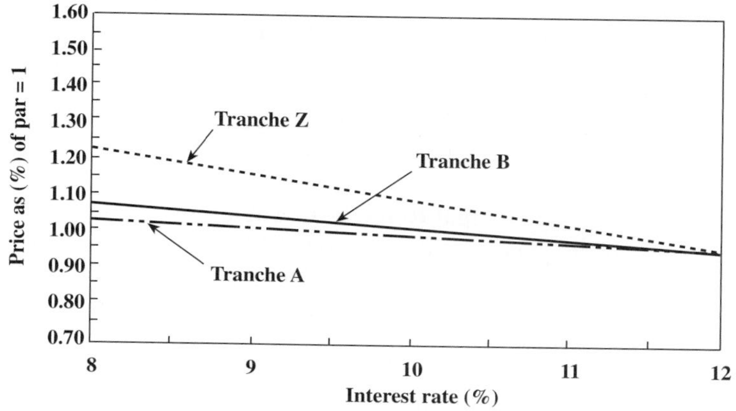

Tranche A		*Tranche B*		*Tranche Z*	
8.25%	$27,503,902	9.0%	$15,520,627	10.0%	$32,068,383
9.25	27,000,000	10.0	15,000,000	11.0	30,000,000
10.25	26,511,478	11.0	14,502,977	12.0	28,087,320

Panel B. Prices at 10 Percent Prepayment

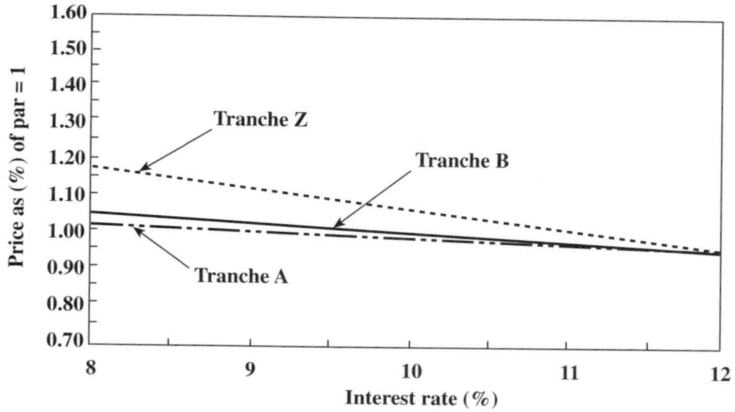

Tranche A		*Tranche B*		*Tranche Z*	
8.25%	$27,349,396	9.0%	$15,358,856	10.0%	$31,576,326
9.25	27,000,000	10.0	15,000,000	11.0	30,000,000
10.25	26,658,723	11.0	14,653,174	12.0	28,521,768

yield, and maturity for tranches with sequential payment and other structures is called *duration*. This measure is discussed in considerable detail in the Appendix to this chapter.

CMO Tranche Variations

Although the preceding illustration is useful in gaining a basic understanding of the mechanics of a CMO, the elementary structure used in this example reflects only a small portion of today's CMO market. In today's market up to 20 CMO different tranches may be used to create many derivative security types from a single mortgage pool. What follows is a discussion of a select number of other classes that, because of their importance in the multiclass mortgage-backed security market, deserve further discussion.

Principal Repayment Variations. Instead of the *sequential pay tranches* used to construct the previous CMO example, issuers may use a sinking fund structure to redeem the securities' principal balance. This method of principal repayment allows issuers to create tranches with more cash flow certainty. In a sinking fund structure, two or more tranches are eligible to receive paydowns of principal on a payment date. The actual amount of payment to each is dependent upon the sinking fund schedule for the structure and the amount of prepayments received.

Under a sinking fund structure, a **planned amortization class (PAC) tranche** offers the greatest degree of cash flow certainty. Instead of being allocated all principal repayments from the underlying pool, the PAC receives *fixed payments* over a predetermined period of time under a range of prepayment scenarios. This range, or *PAC band*, is delineated by a minimum and maximum constant payment speed under which the PAC scheduled repayment will remain unchanged. A **targeted amortization class (TAC)** schedule, on the other hand, corresponds to a single "targeted" prepayment speed (e.g., 150 percent PSA). This targeted prepayment speed is often referred to as the TAC's *pricing speed*. For either of these classes, prepayments in excess of the amounts specified in the sinking fund schedule will be applied to one or more of the non-PAC and non-TAC tranches in the structure, which are often called *companion* or *support tranches* because they are issued in tandem with PACs and TACs and absorb any significant variation in prepayments. As a consequence, when PACs and TACs are present an attempt to insulate the security holder from the prepayment risk of the underlying pool is desired. However, the prepayment risk must be transferred to the other non-PACs or non-TACs in the structure.

Coupon Variations. As shown in the earlier example, class Z tranches, also known as *accrual* or *accretion bonds*, provide for the unpaid coupon to be added to the outstanding principal balance, resulting in automatic reinvestment at the coupon rate. Since the interest that accrues on Z tranches is used to pay down principal on other tranches, the issuer can offer shorter average life securities as companions.

Derivatives Illustrated

Floating rate tranches are generally attractive to institutional investors seeking assets to match floating rate liabilities. The **floater tranche**, as it is often called, has coupon rates that adjust periodically to a fixed spread over an index. For example, if a floater's corresponding index fell from 7 percent to 6.75 percent and the tranche offered a spread of 75 basis points, the coupon rate of the floating rate tranche would adjust from 7.75 percent to 7.5 percent on its reset date. The indexes currently used in the CMO market include the **LIBOR**,[8] the 11th district cost of funds (COF), the one-year Treasury rate and the certificate of deposit (CD) rate. Reset intervals for these tranches typically range from one to six months.

To offset the variable payout for the floating rate tranche, an *inverted floating rate tranche* is often used in the same CMO issue. The **inverse floater tranche** has a coupon interest rate that adjusts in the *opposite* direction to its index. By setting the ratio of the floating rate tranche to inverted floating rate tranche equal to one, the CMO issuer can ensure that the weighted average rate of interest for the two classes will be stabilized with respect to changes in the index.

An illustration of the floater–inverse floater structure is as follows: Assume that in our example, a portion of one tranche is subdivided into equal amounts of $10 million. Each subdivided amount is now referred to as a floater (F) and inverse floater (IF) tranche. If we assume that the F tranche is tied to LIBOR, with coupon interest on the floater portion *increasing* with increases in LIBOR and the inverse floater portion *decreasing* with declines in LIBOR, and on the day of issue LIBOR is 6 percent, then the interest allocation to each tranche within this portion of the mortgage pool on the date of issue is as follows:

Interest due to the (F) and (IF) tranches on *date of issue*, LIBOR = 6 percent.

Case 1

(F) floater inverse $10,000,000	= .50 × .06 =	$ 600,000
(IF) inverse floater $10,000,000	= .50 × .06 =	600,000
	Interest payable =	$1,200,000

If, after the issue date, LIBOR were to *increase* by 1 percent, the interest payable to *both* classes of investors would be:

Interest due if LIBOR increases by 1 percent to 7 percent:

Case 2

(F) floater inverse $10,000,000	= .50 × .07 =	$ 700,000
(IF) inverse floater $10,000,000	= .50 × .05 =	500,000
	Interest payable =	$1,200,000

Note that total interest payable remains at $1,200,000 and that the relative share received by (F) and (IF) investors changes in case 2. Investors in the floaters would now receive $700,000, or $100,000 more than they received in case 1. IF investors would receive $100,000 *less* than they received in case 1. Also, if LIBOR were ever to increase by 6 percent to 12 percent, the F tranche would receive *all* interest available for distribution, or $1,200,000, and IF investors would receive zero. Since IF investors cannot receive negative interest payments, this implies that a cap for F tranche investors must always be specified at the time of issue. The *maximum* cap would be equal to $1,200,000 divided by $20,000,000, or LIBOR = 12 percent. However, depending on investor demand for F and IF securities at the time of issue, caps may be

[8] LIBOR, or the London Interbank Offer Rate is a very important deposit rate that is quoted daily among banks that do business in the Eurocurrency market. This interest rate is widely used throughout the world as an index upon which interest rates on many financial instruments are based.

set at various levels below 12 percent. Conversely, if LIBOR *declines* by 2 percent when payments are due, then IF tranche investors would receive base LIBOR of 6 percent plus 2 percent, or a total of 8 percent, and F tranche investors would receive 6 percent less 2 percent, or 4 percent. Again, interest payments must sum to $1,200,000, the total available to both investor classes. A minimum, or *floor* must also be set for IF investors. In this case, it happens to be a 6 percent decline from base LIBOR. However, floors may also be set at other levels between base LIBOR and zero. This is essentially the purpose of the floater/inverse floater structure. If LIBOR increases, the share of interest that F tranche investors receive increases by the amount of the increase in LIBOR and the share of total interest received by IF investors declines by a like amount. When LIBOR declines, the opposite pattern applies.

Based on these basic relationships, it is now possible to show how underwriters may change the above investment structure to meet whatever investor preferences are relative to prevailing market conditions. This can be done by **scaling** the ratio of the relative composition of interest to be received by the F and IF tranche investors. For example, if the F investors in the example accounted for 60 percent of the tranche and the IF investors 40 percent, then the scale of F to IF is 60 percent divided by 40 percent or 1.5. In this case, we would have the following relationship at the time of issue:

Total interest allocation at time of issue:

(F) tranche	60%	=	12,000,000 × .06	=	$ 720,000
(IF) tranche	40%	=	8,000,000 × .06	=	480,000
	100%	=	20,000,000		$1,200,000

Note that even though the scale of F to IF has changed, total interest payable is $1,200,000. However, because the relative share that results from scaling the F and IF tranches is 1.5, if LIBOR increases by 1 percent to a level of 7 percent, we would have:

(F) tranche	60%	=	12,000,000 × .070	=	$ 840,000
(IF) tranche	40%	=	8,000,000 × .045	=	360,000
	100%	=	20,000,000		$1,200,000

Note that interest due to F tranche investors is tied directly to increases in LIBOR, which is now 6 percent plus 1 percent equals 7 percent. Therefore, F investors must now receive $840,000. However, because the total interest payment on both tranches must sum to $1,200,000, or the total available for distribution, the inverse floater tranche will earn only 4.5 percent or the original LIBOR rate of 6 percent less the 1 percent increase in LIBOR times 1.5. The 1.5 multiple, times the inverse of the *change* from the base LIBOR, is also specified at the time of issue. Therefore, IF investors will always receive interest based on the scale of 1.5 times the inverse of the change from base LIBOR. As pointed out above, a *cap* for the maximum increase in LIBOR must also be included. The maximum cap would be an increase of 4 percent, at which point LIBOR equals 10 percent. At that level, the F tranche would receive $1,200,000 and the IF tranche would receive zero. The theoretical floor for IF investors would be the point where IF investors receive all interest available to both investor classes, or $1,200,000 divided by $8,000,000 equals 15 percent. However, since base LIBOR is 6 percent, the maximum decline that can occur is 6 percent, at which point LIBOR would equal zero and IF tranche investors would receive 6 percent times 1.5, or 9 percent. Therefore, 6 percent represents the minimum, or floor. F investors would continue to receive \$480,000 divided by \$12,000,000, or 4 percent.

Returning to our example, if base LIBOR *decreased* by 4 percent from 6 percent to a level of 2 percent, we would have:

(F) tranche	60%	= 12,000,000 × .02	=	\$ 240,000
(IF) tranche	40%	= 8,000,000 × .12	=	960,000
	100%			\$1,200,000

In this case, the 4 percent *decline* in LIBOR from its initial 6 percent level to 2 percent would result in interest to IF tranche equal to 4 percent times 1.5, or 6 percent. When added to the base LIBOR of 6 percent, a total of 12 percent results. The total interest payment of \$960,000 would now be distributed to IF tranche investors. Clearly, with a 4 percent decline from base LIBOR, the total interest payable to IF investors would increase by 100 percent from the allocation determined on the date of issue.

From this simple example, it should be clear that the ratio of F to IF can be scaled and both floors and caps can be set for specified maximum increases or decreases in LIBOR. Also, the greater the scaler used to differentiate interest payable to F and IF investors, the greater the "leverage" applied to the IF investors. Our examples show that when such leverage is applied, it increases the potential volatility (hence, risk) in cash flows to F and IF investors. In practice, the scaler that will be used depends on how much potential volatility versus return F and IF investors want to buy at the time the securities are offered for sale. Underwriters and issuers also must decide then what structure will be most marketable to investors.

Why would investors ever purchase an F or IF derivative investment in the first place? They would do so if they believe that interest rates are likely to rise or fall and if they have *liabilities* that must be paid at some future date based on interest rates that prevail on the date that these liabilities are payable. Derivatives may be purchased to protect the yield on another portfolio of mortgage or bonds. For example, assume that an investor holds a portfolio of fixed interest rate bonds with a current market value of \$1,000,000, which are being used as *collateral* for a business loan that matures in *six months* and the value of the collateral *must* remain \$1,000,000 at all times. If interest rates rise, the value of the collateral will fall. In this event, the investor is required to *add* more collateral to the portfolio. Instead of buying more bonds to add to the collateral, an investor might consider purchasing a floating rate (F) tranche CMO with an expected maturity corresponding to either the maturity of the business loan or six months. This approach may be less costly than purchasing more bonds that have to be sold after six months at a gain or loss.[9]

Based on the changing amounts of interest payments that are to be received, the *range in prices* for F or IF tranche securities are likely to be extremely volatile. Indeed, derivative securities generally exhibit greater price volatility, or a much greater high or low trading range, than is the case when the underlying security

[9]Obviously, there are many other ways to hedge this kind of risk. An investor desiring to hedge could produce a financial futures contract on T-bills, which could also be sold short as a hedge against collateral loss. Similarly, a put option could be purchased on an interest rate futures contract against interest increases. This alternative may also be suitable if the investor is not concerned about receiving interest income in the interim. When an F or IF CMO is purchased, interest income is also received in addition to a price hedge against increases or decreases in collateral value. This may also be important to the investor.

(e.g., mortgage) is purchased directly. Consequently, the potential for greater gains (and losses) exists for investors seeking riskier investments.

Yield Enhancement

It also should be apparent that instead of hedging, investors may want to purchase F and IF securities to enhance yields on a portfolio. For example, if an investor holds a portfolio of lower-risk investments (e.g., short-term U.S. Treasury bills), declines in interest rates will not materially affect the *value* of the portfolio because of its very short-term nature. As these securities rapidly mature, proceeds are also being reinvested at *current, lower interest rates*. By purchasing an IF tranche CMO investment with a relatively short-term expected maturity, loss in income in the base portfolio from falling interest rates may be offset by increasing interest payment from the IF investment. Of course, the opposite effect occurs if interest rates suddenly rise.

A *super floating rate tranche* incorporates the characteristics of the standard floating rate tranche along with the scaling factor found in inverted floating rate tranches. The result is that the coupon rate on this type of security floats in the same direction as, but has much more volatility than, its associated index.

IO and PO Strips

Principal only (PO) tranches are created with a coupon set at zero, producing a "principal only" security that resembles a zero coupon bond. Payment patterns are generally slow in early years and increase over time as amortization and prepayment increase. If a CMO structure contains both a PAC (or a TAC) and a PO class, the PO is often referred to as a super PO because the prepayment risk that is directed from the PAC causes the *companion* super PO to become far more volatile than its generic counterpart.

Interest only (IO) tranches are created to allocate interest to investors that is generally high in the beginning years, then declines over time as amortization and prepayments of underlying principal increase. These are usually issued with PO tranches and are referred to as "stripped" mortgage-backed security issues. These derivative securities have increased in importance in recent years. To illustrate IO and PO strip tranches consider the following greatly simplified example.

Exhibit 18–12 shows that the two security types are created by "stripping" interest and principal from one segment, or tranche, of the mortgage pool; hence, the terms **IO strips** and **PO strips.** Note that if no prepayment occurs on any of the mortgages in the pool and if investors demand an 11 percent return on each strip, which is equal to the interest rate on all mortgages in the pool, the present value (PV) of the IO strip is $461,248 while that of the PO strip is $538,752. Obviously, the sum of the two present values must equal $1,000,000 when the discount rate that investors demand equals 11 percent. In practice, this will rarely occur.

However, there are very specific risks regarding prepayment that must be taken into account when making IO and PO strip investments. As discussed many times before, in the event that interest rates decline significantly after issuance, there is a high probability that a number of mortgages in the pool will be *prepaid*. When this occurs, holders of the PO strip will receive flows from repayments sooner than expected. This unexpected increase in the rate of cash flow coupled with the decline in interest rates, will tend to drive the price of the PO strips higher. Conversely, when prepayments increase, IO strip holders receive less cash flow as the pool gets smaller because they receive "interest only" from the pool; when mortgages are paid off, interest ceases altogether. In the limit, if *all* mortgages are paid off, the *value of the IO strip becomes zero*. Therefore, the investment return to IO strip investors is comprised of interest *only*. If we assume that prepayment *accelerates*

EXHIBIT 18–12 Pool Segment Used to Create IO/PO Strips

Pool characteristics: $1,000,000 mortgages
11% interest annually
10-year maturity

Panel A. Cash Flow to the IO and PO Strip Investors at 0% Prepayment Rate

Period	Beginning Balance	Interest IO/Strip	Principal PO/Strip	PO Prepayment	Ending Balance
1	$1,000,000	$110,000	$ 59,801	0	$940,199
2	940,199	103,422	66,380	0	873,819
3	873,819	96,120	73,681	0	800,138
4	800,138	88,015	81,786	0	718,351
5	718,351	79,019	90,783	0	627,569
6	627,569	69,033	100,769	0	526,800
7	526,800	57,948	111,853	0	414,946
8	414,946	45,644	124,157	0	290,789
9	290,789	31,987	137,815	0	152,974
10	152,974	16,827	152,974	0	0
			$1,000,000	0	
	PV at 11% =	$461,248	$ 538,752		

Panel B. Cash Flow to the IO and PO Strip Investors at 20% Prepayment Rate

Period	Beginning Balance	Interest IO/Strip	Principal PO/Strip	PO Prepayment	Ending Balance
1	$1,000,000	$110,000	$ 59,801	$200,000	$740,199
2	740,199	81,422	52,259	148,040	539,900
3	539,900	59,389	45,525	107,980	386,395
4	386,395	42,503	39,495	77,279	269,620
5	269,620	29,658	34,074	53,924	181,623
6	181,623	19,978	29,163	36,325	116,135
7	116,135	12,775	24,658	23,227	68,249
8	68,249	7,507	20,421	13,650	34,178
9	34,178	3,760	16,198	6,836	11,144
10	11,144	1,226	11,144	0	0
			$332,738	$667,261	
	PV at 11% =	$276,200	$222,403	$501,397	

from zero to 20 percent per year, the cash flow pattern of panel B in Exhibit 18–12 results. IO strip investors will receive far less cash flow; when discounted by 11 percent, the present value of those floors falls from $461,248 in panel A to $276,200 in panel B, a decline of $184,048 or about 40 percent in value. The PO strip, on the other hand, with receipt of accelerated prepayments (see PO prepayment in panel B), receives *more* cash flow much sooner. When the PO strip is discounted to present value at 11 percent, it shows an increase of 34 percent from panel A (normal amortization of $222,403 + prepayments of $501,397 = $723,806). Note that the PO strip receives the same *total* cash flow ($1,000,000) regardless of prepayment.

In Exhibit 18–13, we see the combined effects of prepayment and changing interest rates on IO and PO prices. Note that the present value of the IO strip *declines* dramatically from a 10-year normal amortization to a 20 percent prepayment throughout the range of discount rates. The PO strip, on the other hand, *increases* in value because more cash flow is recovered *sooner* than if interest rates had remained stable.

This comparison points out the *potentially volatile price behavior* of IO and PO strips. It also implies that, in practice, when investors consider IOs and POs, they must take into account or form expectations about likely future movements in mortgage interest rates (either up or down) *and* the rate of repayment from the mortgage pool (faster or slower). In addition to investment considerations, these derivative-type investments, like the F and IF investments discussed earlier, may also be purchased when investors expect interest rate volatility to occur and choose to hedge against it.

Convexity

Another useful way to describe the present value patterns shown in panels A and B of Exhibit 18–13 is to say that the curve representing the PO strip exhibits greater

EXHIBIT 18–13 IO and PO Prices at Various Discount Rates: Prepayment Rate (PPR) at 0% and 20%

Panel A

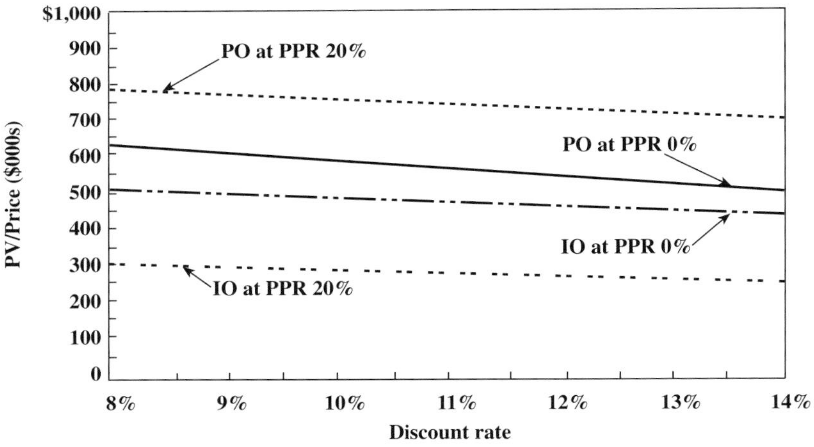

Panel B

Discount Rate	*PPR = 0% PV of IO*	*PPR = 20% PV of IO*	*PPR = 0% PV of PO*	*PPR = 20% PV of PO*
8%	511	297	628	784
9	494	290	596	763
10	477	283	566	743
11	461	276	539	724
12	446	270	513	706
13	432	264	489	688
14	419	258	467	671

convexity than the IO curve. This can be seen by examining the range in *PVs* when the $PPR = 0$. Note that at $PPR = 0$, the PO curve has a greater slope than the IO curve over the range of discount rates. This means that the price of the PO in our example is *more sensitive* than the IO to changes in market rates of interest (discount rates). In other words, the PO has greater price convexity. However, note that when the prepayment rate increases to 20 percent, the price of the PO *rises* because mortgages are repaid sooner. However, note that the price of the IO *declines*. The IO declines in price because interest payments *cease* on 20 percent of the mortgage portfolio. In the latter case, the prepayment rate must be taken into account when estimating prices of IOs at various discount rates. The resulting prices for IOs will show much greater sensitivity to prepayment and interest rate changes.

Residential Mortgage-Related Securities: A Summary

We now briefly summarize some of the major characteristics of the four major types of securities covered thus far. Exhibit 18–14 contains a summary of some important terms and definitions used in the mortgage-backed securities (MBS) business. Exhibit 18–15 is a classification of some of the more important aspects of these securities that should aid you in understanding cash flow and risk-bearing patterns associated with each type.

With the exception of MPTs, which represent an undivided ownership equity interest in a pool of mortgages, all other securities discussed in the chapter are actually debt. An MPT should be viewed as a stand-alone investment that is placed in trust after it is sold to investors in a securitized form. Because the mortgage pools backing the issue are usually FHA/VA or conventionally insured mortgages and a timely payment guarantee is usually provided by the issuer or GNMA, MPTs can be a stand-alone investment; that is, there is no need for overcollateralization or credit enhancements. The success of the investment is based solely on the income produced by mortgages in the pool, and the recovery of investment by investors depends on how amortization and prepayments from the mortgage pool occur. However, because of the pass-through of principal, investors bear all prepayment and reinvestment risk since they do not know exactly what cash flows will be from period to period, nor do they know when the security that they own will mature.

The debt securities listed in Exhibit 18–15 may be differentiated on the basis of (1) who bears prepayment risk and (2) the extent and type of overcollateralization or the use of credit enhancements. Issuers of MBBs bear all of this prepayment risk; hence, the extent of overcollateralization or credit enhancements for these securities must be greatest. Conversely, to the extent that the investor bears prepayment risk—or to the extent that the pass-through of principal flows directly to investors—the need for overcollateralization or credit enhancements is reduced somewhat (holding all else constant). This is true because, for example, as prepayments accelerate on MPTBs and CMOs, maturities are reduced, whereas the maturity for MBBs remains constant regardless of the prepayment rate on the underlying pool. Therefore, in anticipation of the possibility of prepayment in the latter case, the issuer will have to provide more collateral than with the other two debt securities. This means that in each case, the use of overcollateralization and credit enhancements and the extent to which the investor bears prepayment risk must all be taken into account when assessing the relative attractiveness of each security type.

EXHIBIT 18–14 Summary of Important Terms Used in the Market for CMOs and Derivative Securities*

CMO
A collateralized mortgage obligation, or CMO, is a bond or debt obligation that is backed by mortgages or mortgage-backed securities. Its cash distributions from the mortgage pool are designed to provide mortgage pass-through (MPT) and CMO investors with a broader selection of cash flows, and maturities risk.

Contraction risk
When mortgage market rates fall, homeowners tend to accelerate refinancing. Contraction risk affects the price of an MBS in two ways: (1) Because of the prepayment risk on an MBS, price will not increase as much as a noncallable alternative with an equivalent maturity such as a Treasury bond. (2) As MBS investors receive prepayments of principal, they must reinvest at prevailing lower market interest rates. The combination of these two effects is referred to as contraction.

Convexity
The rate of change in the price of an investment with respect to a change in market interest rates (investor discount rates).

Derivative security
A derivative security derives its value from another security, index, or financial claim. Because the value of mortgage-backed securities (MBSs), such as MPTs and CMOs, are based on pools of mortgages, both are referred to as "derivatives." There are many other derivatives such as options, swaps, and so forth.

Duration
When prepayment rates increase (decrease) in response to declining (increasing) interest rates, the expected maturity of an MBS becomes shorter (longer) as cash flows from amortization change. The present value of such investments obviously changes, but so does the maturity. Duration is a measure of the time-weighted pattern of the receipt of cash flow and is a companion tool that helps investors rank present values on the weight and timing of the receipt of cash flows.

Extension risk
Extension risk is the opposite of contraction risk. It is the risk investors face when interest rates increase. Rising rates affect MBS investors in two ways: (1) The price of the MBS security declines like other fixed-income securities; however, because the rate of prepayment slows with rising interest rates, cash flows to the investor decline and the expected maturity increases. This causes the price of the MBS to fall more than equivalent noncallable alternative, such as a Treasury bond. (2) As prepayment rates decline, opportunities to reinvest greater cash flows at higher interest rates are lost. The combination of these two effects, MBS price declines and lower reinvestment returns, is referred to as extension risk.

IO/PO strips
IO and PO strips occur when mortgages are split ("stripped") into two securities. IO (interest only) strip investors receive only the interest payments from the mortgage pool. PO (principal only) strip investors receive the principal payments. Declining interest rates cause the price of PO strip securities to increase because lower rates induce borrowers to refinance, thereby providing PO investors with an acceleration in cash flows. Rising interest rates are providing PO investors with an acceleration in cash flows. Rising interest rates are beneficial to IO investors because refinancing slows as homeowners prefer to keep their original mortgages. IO holders then receive interest payments for a longer time than expected, thereby increasing the cash flows over that time.

LIBOR
The London Interbank Offer Rate, LIBOR, is a widely quoted interest rate on deposit-based transactions between banks in the Eurocurrency market.

Prepayment risk
Because home owners can choose to prepay or keep their original mortgages, MBS investors must forecast mortgage repayment rates when analyzing their investments. This is important because the timing of cash flows (i.e., investor returns) are affected by the rate of prepayment.

Tranche
Tranches are bond classes in a CMO, which differ from one another either by priority of the receipt of cash flows or in some other way. The word comes from the French *trancher*, which means "to cut."

*For a review of terminology and a basic understanding of mortgage pass-throughs and derivatives, see R. S. Guttery and E. McCarthy, "Real Estate Derivative Assets: CMOs, IOs, POs and Inverse Floaters," *Real Estate Finance*, Winter 1995, pp. 18–29.

EXHIBIT 18–15 Summary of Important Investment Characteristics of Mortgage-Related Securities

	MBB	*MPT**	*MPTB*	*CMO*
(*a*) Type of security interest acquired	Debt	Equity	Debt	Debt
(*b*) Number of security classes	One	One	One	Multiple
(*c*) Pass-through of principal	None	Direct	Direct	Prioritized
(*d*) Party bearing prepayment risk	Issuer	Investor	Investor	Investor
(*e*) Overcollateralization	Yes	No	Yes	Yes
(*f*) Overcollateral marked to market?	Yes	NA	No	No
(*g*) Credit enhancements used?	Yes	No	Yes	No
(*h*) Maturity period known?	Yes	No	No	No
(*i*) Call provisions?	Possibly	Cleanup	Possibly	Calamity and nuisance
(*j*) Off-balance-sheet financing possible?	No	Yes	No	Yes

*Assumed to be a GNMA/MPT, FNMA/MBS, or FHLMC/PC.

Finally, with respect to the issuer, the use of MBBs and MPTBs should be viewed as a method of debt financing. Although the securitized mortgages are placed with a trustee, they are still carried as an asset on the issuer's balance sheet while the MBBs are categorized as debt. This would also apply to CMOs unless the issuer sells the residual interest to a third party, in which case the issuer would no longer retain an ownership interest and would not have to carry the mortgage pool as an asset or the CMO securities as liabilities. As an alternative to a CMO issue the issuer could create a real estate mortgage investment conduit (REMIC) to achieve off-balance-sheet financing. With this vehicle, the issuer is selling the mortgage pool to investors and the transaction is completely off-balance-sheet financing. The issuer must only recognize a gain or loss on the sale of mortgages when they are securitized and sold.

Residential Mortgage-Related Securities: Some Closing Observations

Much of what has been discussed strongly suggests that there may exist some market segmentation among investors based on a strong preference for investments with specific maturities. This preference results from the demand by investment managers for interest-bearing assets with the same maturities as liabilities that come due at specified times (e.g., pension plan assets may be acquired with maturities that match liabilities coming due as a number of beneficiaries retire each year).

Finally, because of the different cash flow patterns that are likely to be encountered when choosing among an MBB, MPT, MPTB, or CMO, additional questions are related to receipt of cash flows and the measurement of yields that must be addressed. With an MBB, for example, a level stream of interest payments for a fixed maturity plus a lump-sum return of principal will be received, whereas an

MPT may have more variable cash flows due to prepayments and the Z tranche on a CMO issue may pay cash flows to the investor toward the end of a maturity period. If we assume that each security type was offered at the same yield,[10] should an investor consider each as equivalent? Or, if all three investments existed in a portfolio and payments were to be used to pay liabilities coming due at specific time periods, how can we assess the relationship between the maturity periods over which cash inflows will be received and the rate at which liabilities mature? The appendix to this chapter develops a measure that combines both cash flows constituting the yields *and* maturity into a measure called *duration*, which may be useful in assessing these questions.

Commercial Mortgage-Backed Securities (CMBSs)

In this and the preceding chapters, we have dealt primarily with mortgage-related securities backed by *residential* mortgage pools. Essentially, the methods and structures used to issue *commercial* mortgage-backed securities are very similar. However, the nature of the mortgage collateral, its ability to produce income, and the risk associated with commercial mortgage pools differ from a residential pool in very important ways. These differences are elaborated and contrasted in this section.

Like residential-backed securities, most commercial mortgage-backed offerings take the form of a mortgage-backed bond, pass-through security, or a collateralized mortgage obligation. The primary distinction between residential-backed and commercial-backed pools centers around the likelihood of losses due to **default risk.** Recall that in most residential offerings, mortgages in the pool are usually FHA insured, VA guaranteed, or conventional mortgages with private mortgage insurance. In most cases, timely payment of principal and interest is usually guaranteed by a branch of the U.S. government (GNMA) or an agency (FNMA, FHLMC). While private entities have issued many mortgage-backed bonds and mortgage pay-through bonds with no government guarantees, the dollar volume of government-backed securities has been far greater in amount.

In contrast to residential-backed issues, commercial-backed securities are secured by mortgages on income-producing properties. Tenants in these properties sign lease agreements that provide the source of income from which mortgage payments are made. Hence, the quality of properties, geographic regions in which they are located, and the creditworthiness of the tenant must play some part in assessing the risk of a commercial-backed security offering. Clearly, *if tenants default on lease payments or if the geographic market in which the property is located becomes overbuilt and rents generally decline, the income stream used to make mortgage payments will become jeopardized*. Further, because such permanent mortgage loans are made on a nonrecourse basis, the lender may look only to proceeds from the sale of the property to satisfy the loan in the event of default. A CMBS offering has certain distinctive elements (see Exhibit 18–16). First, commercial mortgage assets in the pool are likely to have short maturities (5–15 years) and they are likely to

[10]Generally, the yield on the three security types would not be the same even if backed by the same pool of securities because the issuer of an MBB bears repayment risk and the investor would earn a lower yield than with an MPT, where the investor bears that risk. A Z tranche security, such as the one demonstrated in the chapter, would yield more than an MPT because not only does that investor bear prepayment risk but interest is also accrued and paid later in the life of the security.

EXHIBIT 18–16 Simplified Example of a Commercial Mortgage-Backed Security (CMO) Offering

Pool Characteristics
$10,000,000 mortgages
10% interest rate
5-year maturity

Assets		Liabilities	Coupon	
Commercial mortgages	$10,000,000	Senior securities: Class A bonds	8%	$ 6,000,000
		Subordinated securities: Class B bonds	10%	3,000,000
		Total		9,000,000
		Net worth (residual)		1,000,000
Total	$10,000,000	Total		$10,000,000

be "interest only." This means that—like a corporate or U.S. government bond—flows into the pool will consist of monthly interest only with the *full amount* of principal repaid by the borrowers at maturity. A second difference lies in the structure of the CMO securities. Two major classes of debt securities are usually offered as a part of a CMBS offering; *senior* and *subordinated* tranches. Sometimes these are referred to as the "A piece" and "B piece," respectively. In practice there will be several subclasses within each of these major classes. The distinction between the two classes is largely based on the *priority of claims* on all payments flowing into the pool, with the **senior tranche** receiving highest priority and the **subordinated tranche** coming second. As before, any cash flow remaining after paying the senior and subordinated tranche is received by residual- or equity-class shareholders.

Another important aspect of these securities concerns repayment of principal. Repayments of residential loans are *expected* to occur long before most mortgages reach maturity, as home owners sell properties to pay off existing loans and buy new homes as they change employment, refinance, and so on. This is not likely to be true of commercial mortgages. Little or no principal payments or prepayments are likely to flow into the CMBS pool because of **"lockouts"** that prevent prepayment for a specified number of years. As a result, a *major* focus of CMBS–CMO investors centers on the likelihood of borrowers making full repayment of principal when mortgages mature.

Commercial mortgages often have a "balloon payment" that is due before the loan is fully amortized. When the balloon payment is due, there must be a source to refund or refinance the properties serving as security for the mortgages. This source may be the original lender who agrees to refinance, or "roll over," the mortgage at maturity. In this case, funds from refinancing are used to repay existing loans in the pool, and recovery of principal will flow through to commercial investors in the CMBS pool. The risk that borrowers can refinance their properties when the balloon payment is due may be significant for commercial real estate loans because *at the time of refunding, property markets may be poor, interest rates high*, and so on. As a result, original lenders may choose not to refinance loans at all or to refinance them only at a reduced loan amount. As a result, borrowers may not be able to fully repay loans or they may be able to refinance only a portion of the loan balance. This will pose problems for commercial mortgage-backed security holders who are expecting to be repaid when the underlying mortgages mature. If this happens, CMO investors may have to wait for the trustee administering the pool to foreclose, negotiate loan extensions, and so forth, as most commercial mortgages in the pool will be nonrecourse mortgages against both the borrower and lender-issuer. The risk that borrowers won't be able to refinance their properties when the loan matures is called **extension risk.** If the borrower defaults and foreclosure results, the property may eventually be sold and the proceeds used to repay the loan balance. A deficiency results if the value of the property is *less* than the loan balance. In this event, some CMO investors are not likely to recover all principal due at maturity, resulting in a loss. Therefore, considerable investor focus is centered on the *likelihood of borrower default* resulting in a full, or partial loss in cash flows when the commercial mortgage matures.

Exhibit 18–17 illustrates the distribution of cash flows and potential risk associated with the CMBS offering shown in Exhibit 18–16. In panel A, cash inflows consisting of interest only is distributed first to the senior tranche, which is due 8 percent interest and accounts for 60 percent of the offering. The subordinated tranche than receives interest at a rate of 10 percent on its segment, or 30 percent of the offering. The remainder goes to the residual class, which contributed $1,000,000, or 10 percent of the offering. If no default occurs, investors in each security class receive cash flows as promised, plus recovery of the initial investment in year 5 when underlying mortgages mature and borrowers repay outstanding balances.

Panel B of Exhibit 18–17 illustrates what happens to the cash flow patterns if default and foreclosure occur when mortgages mature and the sale of properties brings only 80 percent of the total loan balances due at the end of year 5. Note that cash flows into the pool in year 5 total $9,000,000, or $1,000,000 in interest only plus $8,000,000, or 80 percent of the principal amount due at that time. From this cash flow, the senior tranche receives its full amount of interest, or $480,000 plus $6,000,000 on the total initial investment. However, the subordinated tranche investors receive interest due of $300,000 plus only $2,000,000 in loan repayments. This represents a $1,000,000 loss to subordinated investors because of default. Residual investors lose all their initial investment of $1,000,000. Based on these distributions, the internal rate of return earned by senior tranche investors remains at 8 percent; however, the *IRR* declines from 10 percent to 7.23 percent for the subordinated tranche investors. The residual class does not recover its investment; its return falls from a projected 22 percent (see panel A) to −4.92 percent.

Exhibit 18–17 illustrates the basic mechanics of a CMBS offering. Because of the potential for default loss, residual investors obviously take the greatest risk while the subordinated tranche investors stand to lose their investment next. For this reason, the subordinated tranche is usually referred to as the **first loss position** among the bond investors. It should be obvious that the size of investment made by each security class and its priority in cash distributions relative to the likelihood of default are the critical variables that must be assessed by investors when evaluating a CMBS offering.

Because of the importance of default risk, the source for many mortgages used in forming mortgage pools comes from insurance companies and commercial banks that have previously originated loans on commercial (and multifamily) properties. These loans are usually seasoned and have a payment record spanning a number of

EXHIBIT 18–17 Cash Flows to CMBS Security Holders

Panel A. No Default or Mortgage Prepayment

End of Period	*Cash Inflow to Pool*	*Senior*	*Subordinated*	*Residual*
1	$ 1,000,000	$ 480,000	$ 300,000	$ 220,000
2	1,000,000	480,000	300,000	220,000
3	1,000,000	480,000	300,000	220,000
4	1,000,000	480,000	300,000	220,000
5	11,000,000	6,480,000	3,300,000	1,220,000
	IRR =	8%	10%	22%

Panel B. Default Occurs at Maturity and Sale of Property is 80% of Outstanding Loan Balance

End of Period	*Cash Inflow to Pool*	*Senior*	*Subordinated*	*Residual*
1	$1,000,000	$ 480,000	$ 300,000	$220,000
2	1,000,000	480,000	300,000	220,000
3	1,000,000	480,000	300,000	220,000
4	1,000,000	480,000	300,000	220,000
5	9,000,000	6,480,000	2,300,000	−0−
	IRR =	8%	7.23%	−4.92%

years. This is useful information for potential investors. As the market value of these loans increases during periods of declining interest rates, many lenders want to sell them. However, the very thin secondary market for such individual loans, which tend to be relatively large in amount and are not standardized in terms of loan provisions, makes finding buyers difficult. Hence, by placing these mortgages in a pool and issuing securities against them, the lender may issue securities in smaller denominations which are ultimately sold to many investors, thereby converting the mortgages to cash and realizing gains because of lower interest rates. Other motivations for lenders to securitize may be simply to obtain more funds for operating requirements by converting previously originated loans.

The security for a commercial-backed mortgage pool, therefore, can range from one mortgage on a very large mixed use, multitenant property to a group of smaller income-producing properties on which mortgages have been made by a lender. In general, however, securities are issued based on mortgage pools owned by one lender. Further, properties serving as collateral for the mortgages are generally the same type (i.e., either office buildings or retail) and are geographically diverse.

Rating Commercial Mortgage-Backed Securities

Most security offerings backed by commercial mortgages are rated by independent credit rating firms. However, because of the nature of mortgage collateral in the pool, the criteria used for rating differ dramatically from those used in rating residential pools. Where the securities being rated are based on the credit standing of the issuer and do not contain guarantees or insurance from third parties, the cash flows expected to be earned on each mortgaged property in the pool are usually subjected to a worst-case scenario regarding rents, vacancy allowances, operating expenses, and so on, and a judgment about the property's ability to cover debt service is made. This is particularly important when only one or a few mortgages will make up the pool. Where several mortgages are in a pool, more emphasis is placed on the past underwriting record of the lender. In other words, losses due to defaults from previous loan originations (unrelated to the mortgage pool) are given serious consideration. To provide the worst-case scenario, data specific to the local market area are used as input to the cash flow projections. Generally, rating agencies will only give the senior tranche, or A piece, an investment-grade rating (e.g., AAA, AA, or A). The subordinated tranches will have a lower rating (BBB to B) or remain "unrated," which means that they are not investment-grade quality and therefore cannot be purchased by many pension and trust funds. Exhibit 18–18 illustrates the likely ratings for classes (bonds) with different levels of subordination. The exhibit also shows the LTV and DSCR for each security.

For a commercial-backed offering to be successful, the issuer may have to provide enough credit enhancement to the investor to reduce default risk to an acceptable level. These enhancements may include one or more of the following types of support.

1. *Issuer of third-party guarantees.* These may include (*a*) a guarantee of timely payment and/or (*b*) a guarantee of payments to the security holder in the event of a cash flow shortfall from the mortgage pool jeopardizing promised coupon payments, and/or (*c*) a guarantee of repayment of principal to the security holder. Such guarantees may be limited, and they may be provided in part by the issuer with a third-party guarantee for any losses in excess of some specified limit. In any case, the ability of the issuer or third party to perform on the guarantee must be considered by the investor.

2. *Surety bonds and letters of credit.* These are provided by banks and insurance companies for a fee and may be used to guarantee interest and principal payments. In this case, the third-party guarantor is assuming default risk. These guarantees may be made in addition to the guarantee provided in (1). The amount of the guarantee may also vary.

3. *Advance payment agreements.* These are timely payment guarantees made by the issuer and may be limited to a specified number of payments after default.

4. *Loan substitutions and repurchase agreements.* Some commercial-backed issues may provide that the issuer will substitute a defective mortgage with one of better quality, or that issuers stand ready to repurchase any nonperforming mortgages.

5. *Lease assignments.* This provision simply provides that the property owner will assign lease payments directly to the mortgage lender who, in turn, makes payments to the security holder (instead of loan payments being made first to a property manager, or owner, and then to the lender). In this way, the probability that cash flow would not be received by security holders is reduced should the property owner or manager ever become threatened with the possibility of bankruptcy.

6. *Overcollateralization.* As discussed previously, overcollateralization amounts to a lender providing a mortgage pool with a dollar value in excess of the value of securities being used against the pool. By doing this, more income flows into the pool from the larger amount of mortgages relative to required coupon payments to investors. Defaults would have to be approximately equal to the amount of overcollateralization before investors would suffer losses. The extent of overcollateralization necessary in commercial-backed issues is usually based on a desired debt coverage ratio (i.e., the number of mortgages needed to provide an adequate amount of income relative to the interest payment) to investors in the pool.

7. *Cross-collateralization and cross-default provision.* When a pool of mortgages is used for a security issue, the lender may be able to provide a blanket

EXHIBIT 18–18 CMBS General Bond Risk Considerations

Rating	Subordination	DSCR	LTV	Price
AAA	30%	2.00	52.50%	102
AA	24%	1.84	57.00%	101
A	18%	1.71	61.50%	100
BBB	11%	1.57	66.75%	98
BB	6%	1.49	70.50%	75
B	3%	1.44	72.75%	65
NR	0%	1.40	75.00%	35

Premium → *Discount*

Source: Diagram created by Mr. Josh Marston, Mass Financial Services, and provided by Charter Research.

mortgage or cross-collateralization agreement for all mortgages in the pool. This can occur if the lender has made loans to one developer or investor. A cross-collateralization agreement provides that all properties serving as collateral for individual loans will serve to collateralize the entire debt as represented by the blanket mortgage. Hence, in the event that one mortgage defaults, the lender may accelerate prepayments on all mortgages that are a part of the agreement. This means that any loss on one mortgage in a pool because of default may be made up by the security provided by the properties, which may have appreciated in value and are now a part of the blanket mortgage security. By also accelerating on the notes secured by the appreciated properties, the owner-borrower will generally find a way (e.g., second lien, syndication) to raise additional equity and make up any payments on a defaulted loan rather than lose all of the properties.[11] Thus, a blanket mortgage or cross-collateralization agreement is usually beneficial to mortgage-backed security holders.

[11]Cross-collateralization is used by lenders when dealing with developers who pledge previously developed properties as security to obtain financing for new developments. They do this to reduce cash equity in new developments. Lenders may also insist on this additional security because most permanent mortgages are made on a nonrecourse basis; hence, lenders must look to the real estate pledged as security for loans in the event of default.

Perhaps the most important impediment to growth in this market is the refinancing risk associated with mortgages when the maturity date is reached. Contrary to the residential market where there are frequent sales and refinancing is available (1) as households sell and purchase new homes (2) default risk is minimized by the FHA or private insurance, this is not true in the commercial mortgage market. As a result, when a commercial mortgage matures and refinancing is not readily available, investors in the mortgage pool may have to extend financing beyond the original maturity date.

In the event that a third party provides a letter of credit or other guarantee of principal and interest on the mortgage pool, the ability of the third party to perform is more important than the mortgages in the underlying pool because default risk shifts from the issuer to the third party. Hence, the security holder will be more concerned with the creditworthiness of the insurer or guarantor.

Mortgage-Related Securities and REMICs

Prior to the creation of CMOs, most mortgage-related securities would have been issued as mortgage-backed bonds or mortgage pass-through securities. The federal tax treatment of these securities is relatively straightforward. For MBBs and MPTs, a grantor trust is generally utilized on which mortgages are usually placed under the administration of a trustee who oversees the provision of the trust agreement on behalf of security owners. While such provisions may have varied, if federal income tax regulations defining a qualified trust are met, the trust avoids taxation, and interest that flows through to investors is taxed only at the investor level. The primary conditions that such a trust has to meet are that (1) it have a limited life, (2) it be self-liquidating, and (3) it needs no substantive amount of management after the assets are placed in trust. In essence, to avoid classification as an association doing business as a corporation and thus becoming subject to taxation, investment income from the trust has to be passive in nature. Hence, for MBBs and MPTs, the payment of principal and interest from a pool of mortgages under the maintenance of a trustee would generally be sufficient to avoid tax at the entity level. This means that only interest received by investors (or beneficiaries of the trust) would be taxed.

When CMOs were first offered, the IRS ruled mortgage-backed securities with multiple tranches and an equity or residential ownership interest retained by an issuer were too similar to a corporation retaining control of the vehicle used to raise funds. In effect, the issuing entity could use a CMO offering as financing for a business purpose, as opposed to creating a passive investment entity. Further, it required more active management than a pass-through offering. This would be particularly true with respect to selecting securities when reinvesting interim cash flows between the date of receipt from the mortgage pool and disbursement to CMO security holders. Hence, the IRS took the position that if a mortgage-related security offering had more than one class of securities issued against a pool, it ran the risk of being classified as a corporation for tax purposes, resulting in double taxation of income, at both the entity and investor levels. If this tax treatment were applied, CMOs could obviously not compete effectively with MPTs and MBBs, the income from which was generally taxable only at the individual level.

As part of the Tax Reform Act of 1986, Congress passed legislation creating real estate mortgage investment conduits (REMICs, pronounced "remicks"). This legislation provided regulations that, if adhered to, allowed mortgage-backed offerings with multiple security classes to be issued without the risk of taxation at the entity level. The intent of the legislation was to provide the issuer some flexibility in managing a mortgage pool and its income while retaining the basic passive character of the trust and the flow of income to security holders.

Regulatory Provisions. Generally, a REMIC is considered to be a tax entity (not necessarily a legal form of organization such as a corporation or partnership) that can be created by simply selecting a REMIC tax status and maintaining separate records relative to the mortgage pool and the management of funds related to the pool. A corporation, partnership, trust, or association may also elect REMIC status. To retain REMIC status, very stringent rules must be followed by the issuer. For example, substantially all assets must consist of "qualified mortgages," foreclosure property, cash flow investments, and a qualified reserve fund.

1. Qualified mortgages generally include any mortgages secured directly or indirectly by an interest (full or partial) in real estate (residential, commercial, and all other real estate). This definition is very broad and encompasses virtually all first mortgages, participations, seconds, other pass-through securities, and so on. Mortgages must be placed in the pool prior to its creation or within three months thereafter. New mortgages may not be acquired or sold by the REMIC after its creation; however, the REMIC is allowed to substitute new mortgages for defective mortgages up to two years after its creation.
2. Foreclosure property may include real estate, the title to which is retained only by virtue of defaults of a mortgage in the pool.
3. Additional investments are limited to short-term, passive, interest-bearing assets that may be used to reinvest interim cash flows received from mortgages but not yet paid out to investors (e.g., T-bills or guaranteed investment contracts, or GICs).
4. A qualified reserve fund may contain longer-term investments, the income from which may be used to pay expenses for managing the REMIC pool because it may be used as added assurance to investors against losses from defaults on mortgages in the pool. These reserves may take the form of passive investments, letters of credit, mortgage pool insurance, and other forms of credit enhancement. This fund is generally more important for commercial mortgage-backed securities or other mortgages that are not backed by the FHA, VA, or private mortgage default insurance.

REMICs: Other Considerations

Because of the pass-through nature of a REMIC, owners of residual interests (usually the issuers) may avoid including REMIC assets, liabilities, and residual interests in REMICs and may avoid taxes at the entity level. Also, if regulations pertaining to REMICs are followed, the owner of the residual interests does not have to participate in balance-sheet reporting to the public because REMICs are intended to be more like a passive, stand-alone entity. In theory, creation of a REMIC is akin to a sale of assets from an origination to the REMIC with a gain or loss on sale realized by the seller and subject to taxation either immediately or over the life of the REMIC.

As such, the seller no longer carries the assets or liabilities created by the REMIC on its balance sheet. However, if the seller chooses not to recognize gain or loss when the sale of assets to the REMIC occurs, the value of the residual interest owned in the REMIC as an asset will be reported. Generally, this off-balance-sheet accounting treatment has been allowed on issues of mortgage-related securities only if the residual interest was sold or transferred by the issuer to a third party.

In summary, by providing for REMICs, Congress has created a tax-exempt conduit through which CMOs may be issued. This allows for the creation of mortgage-backed securities with multiple maturity classes and other investment choices that would not be available with mortgage pass-through securities. This should provide more choices to more investors and broaden the participation in mortgage-related securities.

Conclusion

The explosion in the market for mortgage-backed securities (MBSs) has led to some of the most significant capital market innovations in recent history. This market began with relatively simple mortgage pass-through securities in which mortgages were pooled, securities were issued, and investors received a pro rata share of principal and interest less servicing fees. Investor concerns over unanticipated cash flow due to borrower prepayment prompted investment bankers and underwriters to innovate and develop the collateralized mortgage obligation (CMO). Rather than simply "passing through" cash flow, the new CMO structure provided for debt securities secured by a mortgage pool. Cash flows were prioritized according to different security classes. Investors in CMOs usually receive a coupon rate of interest and select a priority for the receipt of cash flow from amortization and prepayments on mortgages in the pool. The latter allocation effectively allows investment bankers to pool longer-term mortgages with higher interest rates as security for debt securities that range from short-term, lower interest rate securities to longer-term, higher interest rate securities. More investors can be reached in this structure, with its greater variety of securities, than in a simple pass-through structure. More recent innovations in this market include stripped securities and inverse floaters. These "derivatives" are intended to broaden the market even further as well as to offer investors the opportunity to hedge and manage interest rate risk.

Key Terms

collateralized mortgage obligation (CMO) 527
convexity 549
default risk 552
derivative securities 526
extension risk 554
first loss position 554
floater tranche 542
inverse floater tranche 543
IO strips 546
LIBOR 543
"lockouts" 543
planned amortization class (PAC) tranche 542
PO strips 546
residual 531
scaling 544
senior tranche 553
subordinated tranche 553
targeted amortization class (TAC) 542
tranches 528

Questions

1. What is a mortgage pay-through bond (MPTB)? How does it resemble a mortgage-backed bond (MBB)? How does it differ?
2. Are the overcollateralization requirements the same for mortgage pay-through bonds as for the mortgage-backed bonds?
3. Name two different ways that MPTBs can be overcollateralized.
4. What is a CMO? Explain why a CMO has been called as much of a marketing innovation as a financial innovation.
5. What is meant by a derivative investment?
6. Name the four major classes of mortgage-related securities. As an issuer, explain the reasons for choosing one type over another.
7. What is the major difference between a CMO and the other types of mortgage-related securities?
8. Why are CMOs overcollateralized?
9. What is the purpose of the accrual tranche? Could a CMO exist without a Z class? What would be the difference between the CMO with and without the accrual class?
10. Which tranches in a CMO issue are least subject to price variances related to changes in market interest rates? Why?
11. What is the primary distinction between mortgage-related securities backed by residential mortgages and those backed by commercial mortgages?
12. Name the major types of credit enhancement used for commercial-backed mortgage securities.
13. What is a "floater"/"inverse-floater" tranche in a CMO offering?
14. What is the role of the "scaler" in structuring an (F) and (IF) structure?

15. Why would anyone want to purchase an (F) or (IF) derivative type of investment?
16. What are (IO) and (PO) strips? Which tends to be more volatile in price? Why?
17. In what ways is a CMBS structure different from a CMO backed by residential mortgages? Why is default F risk in a CMBS offering given more attention?

Problems

1. The MZ Mortgage Company is issuing a CMO with three tranches. The A tranche will consist of $40.5 million with a coupon of 8.25 percent. The B tranche will be issued with a coupon of 9.0 percent and a principal of $22.5 million. The Z tranche will carry a coupon of 10.0 percent with a principal of $45 million. The mortgages backing the security issue were originated at a fixed rate of 10 percent with a maturity of 10 years (annual payments). The issue will be overcollateralized by $4.5 million, and issuer will receive all net cash flows after priority payments are made to each class of securities. Priority payments will be made to the class A tranche and will include the promised coupon, all amortization from the mortgage pool, and interest that will be accrued to the Z class until the principal of $40.5 million due to the A tranche is repaid. The B class securities receive interest only payments until the A class is repaid, then receive priority payments of amortization and accrued interest. The Z class will accrue interest at 10 percent until both A and B classes are repaid. It will receive current interest and principal payments at that time.
   a. What will be the weighted average coupon (WAC) on the CMO when issued?
   b. What will be the maturity of each tranche assuming no prepayment of mortgages in the pool?
   c. What will be the WAC at the end of the year 3? year 4? year 8?
   d. If class A, B, and Z investors demand an 8.5 percent, 9.5 percent, and 9.75 percent yield to maturity, respectively, at the time of issue, what price should MZ Mortgage Company ask for each security? How much will the company receive as proceeds from the CMO issue?
   e. What are the residual cash flows to MZ? What rate of return will be earned on the equity overcollateralization?
   f. Optional. Assume that the mortgages in the underlying pool prepay at the rate of 10 percent per year. How will your answers in (*b*)–(*e*) change?
   g. Optional. Assume that immediately after the securities are issued in case (*f*), the price of all securities suddenly trades up by 10 percent over the issue price. What will the yield to maturity be for each security?
2. An investor is considering the purchase of either an IO or PO strip from a CMO offering. The portion of the mortgage pool backing this tranche consists of $1,000,000 in mortgages with a remaining maturity of 10 years and an 8 percent interest rate.
   a. Assuming annual payments and a zero prepayment rate, prepare a schedule showing the IO and PO cash flows that would be payable to investors in this tranche. If the interest rate demanded by investors on this investment is also 8 percent, what would be the prices of the IO and PO strips?
   b. If interest rates *increased* to 10 percent and prepayments remained at a zero rate, how would the price of the IO and PO strips change? Which security, the IO or PO, exhibits the greatest price change from (*a*)? Why?
   c. Investor interest rates now *decline* to 6 percent. What is the price of the IO? PO? Prepayments now increase to a rate of 20 percent per year because mortgage borrowers in the pool begin to refinance at lower interest rates. What would prices for the IO and PO be now? (Assume that the 20 percent prepayment received at the end of each year is based on the outstanding loan balances at the end of the preceding year). Which security, the IO or PO, exhibits the greatest change in price when compared to (*a*) and (*b*) above? Why? What does this pattern suggest about the relative risk of each security?
3. An issuer is trying to structure a floating rate tranche in a CMO offering. The tranche will be backed by mortgages with an 8 percent interest rate and a current balance of $2,000,000. Interest payable to investors in the floating rate securities (F) and inverse floater securities (IF) will be based on an initial, or base market rate of 8 percent. Investors in the F portion of the tranche will benefit to the extent of any *increases* from the base rate of interest and IF investors will benefit to the extent of any *decreases* from the base rate.
   a. Assuming that the F and IF portions of the tranche are equal (50 percent each), what will the share of interest be for each class of investors on the day of issue? A maximum cap must be set on increases in the base rate of interest for the F investors. What would such a cap be? What would be the floor for the IF portion of the offering?

b. Assume that the IF buyers prefer a leveraged offering. If the terms in (*a*) were altered to a ratio of 60 percent to F investors and 40 percent to IF investors, what would the interest allocation be on the day of issue? What would the cap and floor be?

c. Compare the terms in (*a*) and (*b*). Assume now that a 2 percent *increase* from the base rate of 8 percent occurs immediately after the CMO offering. What happens to the cash distributions to the F and IF investors? Assume that a 2 percent *decrease* from the base rate occurs. What happens to cash distributions? Which class of investors experiences more volatility in cash flow and, therefore, price volatility? Why?

APPENDIX: DURATION—AN ADDITIONAL CONSIDERATION IN YIELD MEASUREMENT

We have presented many examples of mortgage-related or derivative securities. Recall that most mortgage-backed bonds (MBBs) are very much like corporate bonds in that they promise a coupon rate of interest and repayment of principal at maturity. Mortgage-pass-throughs (MPTs) also promise an interest payment; however, principal is also passed through to the investor from the mortgage pool as it is received from borrowers. Hence, repayment of principal is received over the life of the MPT security. Collateralized mortgage obligations (CMOs) differ from both of the above securities. They promise a coupon rate of interest but also promise priority to some tranches of securities concerning receipt of interest and principal payments as they are made into the pool. Interest on some tranches may be deferred and distributed after repayment of principal on other tranches with a higher priority.

The very different patterns of cash flows on the securities just described raise significant problems when investors are comparing yields. These problems come about because if the yield to maturity (*IRR*) is the tool used to measure return on investment, it is possible for the investments to have the same yield but drastically different cash flow patterns. How should two securities with the same yield but different cash flows be compared? Should the magnitude and timing of each cash flow be taken into account as an additional consideration when comparing the investments?

One measure that has been developed to aid in the analysis is *duration*. Recall that it is a measure that takes into account *both* size of cash flows and timing of receipt. Specifically, it is a measure of the *weighted-average* time required before all principal and interest is received on an investment.

Duration (D) is defined mathematically as:

$$D = \sum_{t=1}^{n} w_t(t)$$

where t is the time period in which a payment is received, n is the total number of periods during which payments will be received, and w is a weight representing the annual proportion of the investment's present value received each year. If we assume that security A has a current price of \$10,000 and a coupon of 10 percent, that its maturity is five years and interest only is to be paid to investors annually, the yield to maturity, or *IRR*, would be calculated for the investment as follows:

$$\begin{aligned}\$10{,}000 &= \$1{,}000(PVIFA, ?\%, 5 \text{ yrs}) + \\ &= \$10{,}000(PVIF, ?\%, 5 \text{ yrs})\end{aligned}$$

Substituting an estimated interest rate of 10 percent, we have:

$$\begin{aligned}&= \$1{,}000(3.790787) + \$10{,}000(.620921) \\ &= \$10{,}000\end{aligned}$$

Hence, we know that the yield to maturity on the bond is 10 percent.

Alternatively, if we assume that investment B is also priced at \$10,000, and that five payments of principal and interest equal to \$2,637.97 are to be received annually at the end of each year for five years, the yield to maturity would also be 10 percent. This can be seen as follows:

$$\begin{aligned}\$10{,}000 &= \$2{,}637.97(PVIFA, ?\%, 5 \text{ yrs}) \\ &= \$2{,}637.97(3.790787) \\ &= \$10{,}000\end{aligned}$$

Hence, by construction, both yields are 10 percent. However, when cash flows are compared, they differ dramatically. Duration provides us with a measure that can be used to determine the weighted-average time to full recovery of principal and interest payments. More specifically, for a required rate of return (i), the weight (w) for each period (t) is computed as:

$$w_t = t \left[\frac{\frac{R_t}{(1+i)^t}}{PV} \right] \text{ where } PV = \sum_{t=1}^{n} \frac{R_t}{(1+i)^t}$$

Given the above defined terms, we calculate duration for any asset (j) as :

$$D_j = (1) \left[\frac{\frac{R_t}{(1+i)^1}}{PV} \right] + (2) \left[\frac{\frac{R_2}{(1+i)^2}}{PV} \right]$$

$$+ \ldots (n) \left[\frac{\frac{R_n}{(1+i)^n}}{PV} \right]$$

Note in this equation that the proportion that each cash flow received is each period (R_t) bears to the present value (or price) of the investment is calculated and multiplied by the year in the sequence during which each cash flow is received.

In our example, we would have for investment A:

$$D_A = (1) \left[\frac{\frac{1{,}000}{(1+.10)^1}}{10{,}000} \right] + (2) \left[\frac{\frac{1{,}000}{(1+.10)^2}}{10{,}000} \right]$$

$$+(3) \left[\frac{\frac{1{,}000}{(1+.10)^3}}{10{,}000} \right] + (4) \left[\frac{\frac{1{,}000}{(1+.10)^4}}{10{,}000} \right]$$

$$+(5) \left[\frac{\frac{\$11{,}000}{(1+.10)^5}}{10{,}000} \right]$$

$$= .0909 + .1653 + .2254 + .2732 + 3.4151$$

$$= 4.170 \text{ years}$$

For investment B we have:

$$D_B = (1) \left[\frac{\frac{2{,}367.97}{(1+.10)^1}}{10{,}000} \right] + (2) \left[\frac{\frac{2{,}367.97}{(1+.10)^2}}{10{,}000} \right]$$

$$+(3) \left[\frac{\frac{2{,}367.97}{(1+.10)^3}}{10{,}000} \right] + (4) \left[\frac{\frac{2{,}367.97}{(1+.10)^4}}{10{,}000} \right]$$

$$+(5) \left[\frac{\frac{2{,}367.97}{(1+.10)^5}}{10{,}000} \right]$$

$$= .2398 + .4360 + .5946 + .7207 + .8190$$

$$= 2.810 \text{ years}$$

From the preceding calculations, we can see that the duration (D) for investment B is lower than the duration for investment A. This implies that although the yields and maturities on the two investments are identical, the weighted-average number of years required to realize total cash flows from investment B is far less than that for A. Hence, depending on the likelihood of better reinvestment opportunities as cash flows are received each year, the investor may choose investment B over A. For example, if the yield curve is expected to take on a more steep, positive slope, the larger cash flows from investment B may be viewed as more favorable, as it may be possible to reinvest them at higher rates of interest.

Duration is also a measure of the extent to which different investments expose investors to interest rate risk. For example, if interest rates were to increase suddenly, it is clear that the price of investment A, with its longer duration, is likely to decline by a greater amount than that of B. For example, if interest rates suddenly increased to 15 percent, the likely percentage change in the prices of the two securities can be approximated as follows:

$$\%\text{ decline in price of investment} = -D\left(\frac{\Delta i}{1+i_t}\right) \text{ when } \Delta i > 0 \text{ and}$$

$$D\left(\frac{\Delta i}{1+i_t}\right) \text{ when } \Delta i < 0.$$

In our example for A we have:

$$\%\text{ decline} = -4.170\left(\frac{.05}{1.10}\right)$$

$$= -.1895, \text{ or a } 18.95\% \text{ decline in price to } \$8{,}105$$

For B we have:

$$\%\text{ decline} = -2.180\left(\frac{.05}{1.10}\right)$$

$$= -.0991, \text{ or a } 9.91\% \text{ decline in price to } \$9{,}009$$

Other applications of duration may involve a portfolio or pool, of assets and liabilities where each component of the portfolio may have different cash flow patterns and the same, or different, maturities. When assessing exposure to interest rate risk, duration provides a better measure of risk exposure than reliance on a simple weighted-average maturity for assets and liabilities because it takes into account the magnitude and timing of cash flows. To illustrate, if investment A represented an asset and B represented a liability even though the maturities for both investments are equal (five years) and there was an interest rate change to 15 percent, the market value of our asset A (\$8,105) would be less than that of liability B (\$9,009). Depending on the circumstances, this imbalance could cause serious problems for a portfolio manager of an investment fund or an asset-liability manager of a financial institution. Hence, in addition to making yield comparisons, duration may provide an alternative approach to matching assets and liabilities that fluctuate in value when interest rates change.

Effective Duration

When dealing in the world of mortgage pools and derivative investments, the notion of *effective duration* is used. Because prepayment rates are estimated when analyzing these investments, the above or standard, measure of duration is modified to take into account various rates of prepayments on cash flows. The standard duration formula detailed above is modified to take account of changes in cash flow (faster or slower repayment at various interest rates). An estimate of duration is made for a range of various assumptions regarding prepayment and is referred to as "effective" duration.

Problem

A–1. The Provincial Insurance Company has the choice of investing $100,000 in either a mortgage bond with annual payments based on a 10-year amortization schedule with a maturity of five years at 10 percent or a 5-year corporate bond with annual interest payments and a final principal payment also yielding 10 percent.

a. Find the duration of each instrument if they are issued at par.

b. If the market rate of interest on each bond fell from 10 percent to 7 percent and the durations found in part (*a*) remained constant, what would be the new price for each bond?

CHAPTER

19

Real Estate Investment Trusts (REITs)

Introduction

The concept of the real estate investment trust goes back to the 1880s. In the early years, trusts were not taxed if trust income was distributed to beneficiaries. In the 1930s, however, a Supreme Court decision required all passive investment vehicles that were centrally organized and managed like corporations to be taxed as corporations. This included real estate investment trusts.

Stock and bond investment companies, also affected by the same Supreme Court decision, promptly secured legislation (in 1936) that exempted regulated investment companies, including mutual funds, from federal taxation. At this time, real estate trusts were not organized to press for equal consideration, and the trust did not develop into importance as a legal form for investing in real estate.

After World War II, however, the need for large sums of real estate equity and mortgage funds renewed interest in more extensive use of the **real estate investment trust,** which also became known as the **REIT** (pronounced "reet"), and a campaign was begun to achieve for the REIT special tax considerations comparable to those accorded mutual funds. In 1960, Congress passed the necessary legislation.

Legal Requirements

A real estate investment trust is basically a creation of the Internal Revenue Code. It is a real estate company or trust that has elected to qualify under certain tax provisions to become a pass-through entity that distributes to its shareholders substantially all of its earnings in addition to any capital gains generated from the sale of disposition of its properties. In accordance with the tax provisions under which it was established, the real estate investment trust does not pay taxes on its earnings, but the distributed earnings do represent dividend income to its shareholders and are taxed accordingly. Similarly, any distributed capital gains are taxed at the shareholder's applicable tax rate.

Effective January 1, 1961, special income tax benefits were accorded a new type of investment institution by an amendment to the Internal Revenue Code (Sections 856–858). Under this amendment, a real estate investment trust meeting prescribed requirements during the taxable year may be treated simply as a conduit with respect to the income distributed to beneficiaries of the trust. Thus, the unincorporated trust or association ordinarily taxed as a corporation is not taxed on distributed taxable income when it qualifies for the special tax benefits. Only the beneficiaries pay the tax on the distributed income. To qualify as a real estate investment trust for tax purposes, the trust must satisfy the following requirements:

Asset Requirements.

- At least 75 percent of the value of a REIT's assets must consist of real estate assets, cash, and government securities.
- Not more than 5 percent of the value of the assets may consist of the securities of any one issuer if the securities are not includable under the 75 percent test.
- A REIT may not hold more than 10 percent of the outstanding voting securities of any one issuer if those securities are not includable under the 75 percent test.

Income Requirements.

- At least 95 percent of the entity's gross income must be derived from dividends, interest, rents, or gains from the sale of certain assets.
- At least 75 percent of gross income must be derived from rents, interest on obligations secured by mortgages, gains from the sale of certain assets, or income attributable to investments in other REITs.
- Not more than 30 percent of the entity's gross income can be derived from sale or disposition of stock or securities held for less than six months or real property held for less than four years other than property involuntarily converted or foreclosed on.

Distribution Requirements.

- Distributions to shareholders must equal or exceed the sum of 95 percent of REIT taxable income.

Stock and Ownership Requirements.

- Shares in a REIT must be transferable and must be held by a minimum of 100 persons.
- No more than 50 percent of REIT shares may be held by five or fewer individuals during the last half of a taxable year.

Prior to 1986, a management activity restriction existed to ensure the passive nature of REITs. Trustees, directors, or employees of a REIT were not permitted to actively engage in managing or operating REIT property, rendering services to tenants of REIT property, or collecting rents from tenants. These functions are generally performed by an independent contractor. In 1986, The Tax Reform Act relaxed the management limitations, allowing REITs to render normal and customary maintenance and other services for tenants, eliminating the need for an outside independent contractor for property-related functions like property management. The result of this change is that REIT managers now have the ability to internalize these functions, creating vertically-integrated operating companies and fundamentally altering the REIT vehicle.

In the pre-1986 era, many REITs were organized or sponsored by a financial institution, such as an insurance company, a commercial bank, or a mortgage banker. The sponsoring institution also served as an advisor to the REIT, either directly or through an affiliate. Responsibility was delegated to the advisor for managing the operations of the REIT, including management of the REIT's assets and liabilities. Following the 1986 Tax Act, the REIT became a more attractive vehicle for real estate developers who had not been interested in a passive investment vehicle. Real estate developers and operators have become the dominant sponsors of REITs, particularly for larger companies.

There were two landmark initial public offerings that helped to shape the modern REIT industry. The first was the 1991 Kimco Realty offering, which was the first offering of a modern vertically integrated REIT, providing its own property and asset management. Although some existing REITs adapted following the 1986 Act, Kimco Realty was the first significant REIT initial public offering designed to be internally managed and advised. The second significant offering was the Taubman Realty offering, which launched the public **Umbrella Partnership REIT** or UPREIT.

An **UPREIT** is a REIT that owns a controlling interest in a limited partnership that owns the real estate, as opposed to a traditional structure in which the REIT directly owns the real estate. This structure was created in 1992 as a tax-deferred mechanism through which real estate developers and other real estate owners could transfer their properties to the REIT form of ownership. Since the transfer is an exchange of one partnership interest for another, it is not a taxable event. These partnership interests, known as operating partnership units or OP units, are generally convertible into shares of the REIT, offering voting rights and dividend payments matching those of the REIT shares.

In 1992, traditional real estate capital sources were largely absent from the market, creating a credit crunch. In these conditions, the "modern" REIT structure featuring active management and tax deferred exchanges of assets was attractive to owners and investors alike. The result was massive growth in REIT equity market capitalization, as shown in Exhibit 19–1.

The vast majority of today's equity REITs are self-advised, vertically integrated operating companies. They actively manage their portfolios in an effort to grow their cash flow and their portfolios, a fundamentally different entity from the earlier "passive" REIT. The industry continues to change in response to real estate market dynamics and investor preferences.

EXHIBIT 19–1 Market Capitalization of Publicly Traded REITs

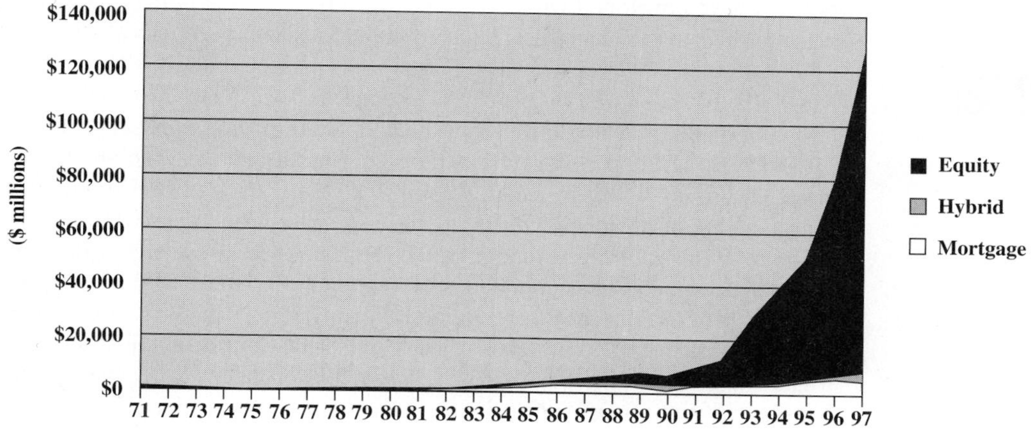

Tax Treatment

One area of importance in accounting for REITs is the treatment of depreciation for financial reporting and the determination of taxable income. For example, a REIT may use an accelerated method of depreciation in its determination of taxable income, but when determining income available for dividends it is required to use a 40-year asset life. The use of inconsistent methods of income calculation sometimes results in shareholders receiving dividends in excess of the REIT's calculated taxable income. However, to the extent that the distribution represents a return on investment, these dividends will be taxed as normal income. Any additional amounts distributed, such as those representing depreciation, will be considered a return of original capital and thus will simply reduce the shareholder's tax basis. REITS report the breakdown of their distribution annually on Form 1099 and investors may choose to hold specific REITs in taxable or nontaxable accounts based on the breakdown of their distribution.

Violation Penalties and Status Termination

In the event that an entity fails to qualify as a REIT or voluntarily revokes its REIT status, the entity's election to be taxed as a REIT terminates for that and subsequent years. Once this termination has occurred, the entity cannot make a new election to be taxed as a REIT until five years after the termination date. However, if the entity's REIT status was terminated as a result of a failure to satisfy the qualifying requirements, the entity may reelect REIT status within the five-year time period if it can prove to the IRS that its failure to qualify was due to reasonable cause and not willful neglect.

Types of Trusts

The three principal types of real estate trusts are *equity trusts, mortgage trusts,* and *hybrid trusts.* The equity trust was prevalent in an early period, but during the mid-1970s, the mortgage trust became more important. More recently, the equity trust has again grown in importance and is now the dominant REIT type by both number and market capitalization figures.

The difference between assets held by the equity trust and those held by the mortgage trust is fairly obvious. The equity trust acquires property interests, while the mortgage trust purchases mortgage obligations and thus becomes a creditor with mortgage liens given priority to equity holders. Over time, more heterogeneous investment policies have developed which combine the advantages of both types of trusts to suit specific investment objectives. Such combinations are called *hybrid trusts.*

Equity Trusts

Most REITs specialize by property type; some specialize by geographic location. Others specialize by both property type and location. Not all REITs specialize; some diversify by both property type and geographic location. Specialization implies a concentration of effort to create a comparative advantage. REITs and analysts generally use the term specialization to cover a fairly broad range of concentration. In reality, specialization is a matter of degree. The extent to which a REIT is specialized impacts the risks associated with ownership of the REIT. Therefore, it is important to determine how specialized an individual REIT is in comparison with other REITs, in order to assess relative risks. For purposes of description, equity trusts have generally been broken down by property type specialization. The National Association of Real Estate Investment Trusts (NAREIT) divides Equity REITS into the following property types:

1. **Industrial/Office.** These REITs are further subdivided into those that own industrial, office, or a mix of office and industrial properties. Some analysts further segregate these REITs by property location (i.e., whether they are in central business district (CBD) or suburban locations).
2. **Retail.** These REITs are further subdivided into those that own strip centers, regional malls, outlet centers, and free-standing retail properties.
3. **Residential.** These REITs are further subdivided into those that own multifamily apartments and manufactured home communities.
4. **Diversified.** REITs that own a variety of property types.
5. **Lodging/Resorts.** REITS that primarily own hotels, motels, and resorts.
6. **Health Care.** These REITs specialize in owning hospitals and related health care facilities that are leased back to private health care providers who operate such facilities. This is a highly specialized form of REIT and one which many do not consider to be a "true, real estate-backed" security.
7. **Self Storage.** These REITs specialize in ownership of self-storage facilities.
8. **Specialty.** These REITs specialize in numerous types of properties, including prisons, theaters, golf courses, automobile dealerships, and timberland. Specialty REITs have been a rapidly evolving segment of the industry.

The distribution of REIT ownership by property type changes over time. In September 1991, residential properties accounted for more than half of all total publicly traded REIT real estate investments, followed by office, retail, health care, industrial, hotels, and other properties. By year-end 1998, industrial/office REITs represented the largest sector at just over one-quarter of the total, followed by retail, residential, diversified, lodging/resorts, health care, self-storage and specialty properties.

REITs may also be categorized by other variables, including duration of the trust, i.e., finite-life versus nonfinite-life REITs. A finite-life (or self-liquidating) REIT is undertaken with the goal of disposing of its assets and distributing all proceeds to shareholders by a specified date. These REITs were instituted in response to the criticism of many investors that the prices of REIT shares tended to behave more like shares of common stock; that is, they were based on current and expected future earnings instead of the underlying real estate value of the REIT. Hence, by the establishment of a terminal distribution date, it is argued that REIT share prices would more closely match asset values because investors could make better estimates of the terminal value of the underlying properties. This, it is argued, is not the case with nonfinite-life REITs, which reinvest any sale and financing proceeds in new or existing properties and tend to operate more like a going concern, as opposed to an investment conduit. One potential problem with finite-life REITs has to do with general market conditions at the time the REIT plans to dispose of assets. If interest rates are high and occupancies and rents are low, the timing of such disposition activity may not be good and distribution dates may have to be extended. Most new REITs are nonfinite life REITs, and several existing finite-life REITs amended their articles of incorporation to become nonfinite life REITs.

The Investment Appeal of Equity Trusts

The equity-oriented real estate investment trust has provided investors with opportunities (1) to invest funds in a diversified portfolio of real estate under professional management and (2) to own equity shares that trade on organized exchanges, thus providing more liquidity than if a property were acquired outright. Because the individual investor has the opportunity to pool his or her resources with those of persons of like interests, funds are assembled to permit purchase of buildings, shopping centers, and land in whatever proportion seems to offer the most attractive returns. Investments must be approved and management activities reviewed by a board of trustees who are accountable to shareholders and are ordinarily well qualified to make such decisions. The trust certificate is usually readily salable in the over-the-counter market or on major stock exchanges. The tax exemption feature of REITs places the small shareholder in a tax position similar to that of an individual real estate operator making the same investment.

Caveats. As described above, when an equity REIT is created, existing properties or projects to be developed will be acquired as investments. In addition, during the life of the REIT, management fees, advisory fees, and commissions will be paid to affiliates and other parties doing business with the trust. Typically, a real estate owner working with an investment banker can form a REIT that is capitalized through a public securities offering. The REIT may then use the funds it has raised to acquire the owner's properties. The prices that prevail in these transactions are generally not based on "arms-length" negotiations and there is generally no appraisal or other independent indication of value.

Obviously, the formation transactions and the close association of REITs with other real estate organizations or individuals who sponsor them can create potential conflicts of interest or conflicts. These conflicts can come in several forms including preferential treatment given to properties owned by management but not owned by REIT investors, and so on. Investors have reacted harshly to REITs perceived as "holding out" properties of exceptional value and have forced management to make provision for the REIT to acquire all noncontributed properties. Other conflicts include managers negotiating an excessive price for their contributed real estate operating companies, including third-party management contracts. The UPREIT form adds more potential conflicts, including the fact that OP units holders, often the managers, have a different tax position relative to contributed properties, and a sale or refinancing of properties they contributed may be taxable. A number of safeguards attempt to protect investors against the problems of such conflicts, including the provision in the articles of incorporation of most REITs that a *majority* of the trustees or directors may not be affiliated with the sponsors of a REIT. Some REITs also engage independent appraisers to determine whether the purchase prices of properties acquired from the sponsors are at fair market value and that "fees paid to the REIT's management and advisory companies are reasonable." Many REITs are "self-advised" and avoid many of these conflicts by not using external advisors. Self-advised REITs will disclose and identify specific managers, their responsibilities, compensation, and so on, thereby providing information that investors can use when evaluating the shares.

Importance of FFO (Funds from Operations)

FFO stands for **funds from operations,** which most analysts consider the REIT equivalent of earnings in industrial stocks. FFO is used by analysts and investors as a measure of the cash flow available to the REIT for distributions (dividends) to shareholders. Most investors are familiar with the use of earnings per share in this capacity. However, for REITs, earnings are not the best measure of cash flow, largely due to the element of depreciation. Because REITs own real estate assets that are subject to large depreciation allowances, the reader should be aware of the difference between REIT earnings per share (EPS) and funds from operations (FFO) per share. The distinction between the two can be best made with a simple example:

	REIT Income Statement	*REIT Cash Flow*
Rent	$100	$100
−Operating expenses	40	40
Net operating income	60	60
−Depreciation	40	—
Net income	20	—
Cash flow	—	60
EPS	$ 2	—
FFO per share	—	$ 6

Assuming that the REIT above has 10 shares of stock outstanding, its earnings per share (EPS) would be reported as $2.00 per share. However, its funds from operations (FFO) per share would be $6.00. *Generally Accepted Accounting Practices* (GAAP) provide for depreciation of assets over time as their useful life is expended. Depreciation is assumed to occur in a predictable fashion and the time periods and rates of depreciation for different types of assets are well established. Most people are familiar with the concept and logic of depreciation based on their experiences with automobiles and other durable goods. As these goods get older, their mechanical parts break down and function less efficiently, decreasing their value. Real estate values tend to rise and fall over time based more on market conditions than physical conditions, although physical conditions can and do play a role in value. The result is that GAAP earnings calculations that use historical cost depreciation do not provide an accurate or meaningful picture of REIT financial performance.

The National Association of Real Estate Investment Trusts (NAREIT) recognized this problem and has worked to develop and promulgate FFO as a more representative measure of REIT performance. In 1991, NAREIT adopted a definition of FFO that follows:

> *Fund from operations* means net income (computed in accordance with generally accepted accounting principles), excluding gains (or losses) from debt restructuring and sales of property, plus depreciation and amortization, and after adjustments for unconsolidated partnerships and joint ventures. Adjustments for unconsolidated partnerships and joint ventures will be calculated to reflect funds from operations on the same basis.

The definition was well accepted in the industry and FFO became a standard measure of REIT performance. FFO provided analysts and investors with an "apples to apples" measure for comparing performance among REITs. NAREIT suggests that the adoption of the FFO measure made it easier for investors to understand REIT operations. They claim that increased understanding facilitated the growth in REITs as an ownership form, a claim that has some merit.

As REITs grew, FFO and its reporting emerged as an important issue. The definition adopted by NAREIT was, of necessity, rather broad. It left considerable room for interpretation. During the IPO boom in 1992 and 1993, REIT initial pricing was generally couched in terms of a **dividend yield** supported (at least in theory) by a projected FFO. The value of management's ownership position was a function of the initial price, so there was a strong incentive to project FFO at maximum levels. By mid-1993, the page of the prospectus dealing with the projected FFO had become known as the "magic page." The implication was that FFO was being created to support overly aggressive initial pricing.

Many analysts and investors have gone beyond the FFO to look at adjusted funds from operations (AFFO), funds available for distribution (FAD), or cash available for distribution (CAD). AFFO, FAD, and CAD are largely interchangeable, with different analysts using the term they prefer. The major difference between FFO and these supplementals relates to the issue of capital improvements, particularly ongoing capital improvements. To understand the difference, consider a multifamily apartment building. There are several major expenditures, such as painting and replacement of carpets that have to be made on a recurring basis. For example, carpeting may be replaced every five years, and painting redone every three years. Accounting policies vary from REIT to REIT on how to handle these expenses. The most conservative treatment is to classify these as expenses, counting against the current year's income. Others choose to classify them as capital improvements, capitalizing them on the balance sheet and amortizing them over time. In the latter case, the amount spent for capital expenditures will not affect FFO because amortization is added back to EPS when calculating FFO. Thus although either treatment is valid, the variation causes difficulty in comparing income and expense figures across REITs.

REIT Expansion and Growth

Because of the requirement that 95 percent of earnings be paid out as dividends, REITs have limited opportunities to retain earnings or cash flow to acquire additional real estate assets. Stated another way, REITs have very little free cash flow. Consequently, most REITs must plan for expansion by reserving the right to issue additional stock at some future time. This is referred to as a secondary, or follow-on stock offering to raise more equity capital, which may in turn be used to acquire additional real estate assets. Analysts may view eventual issuance of these shares as a potential source of *dilution* of future earnings. The general tendency in the industry is to evaluate the use of funds from follow-on offerings to determine if they will generate an increase in cash flow that more than offsets the dilution. In the industry, this is referred to as an *accretive* transaction. This is particularly important when looking at the period just after additional shares are issued and before additional cash flow is realized from the newly acquired assets. Furthermore, any interim problems with developing, leasing, managing, and renovating of the new real estate assets could require time to correct and thus serve as a potential drag on earnings. The dilution of earnings from issuing additional shares also might have a depressing effect on the stock price of the REIT, through the impact on the dividend.

REITs also make use of significant amounts of debt financing, including individual property mortgages, mortgage pools, secured debt, unsecured debt, and corporate lines of credit. Many REITs have been assigned investment ratings by the various ratings agencies, and use multiple sources of debt capital for growth. Proceeds from debt financing may be used to finance additional asset acquisitions. In some cases, lines of credit or unsecured debt financing can be used as an interim source of funds until long-term mortgage financing or a supplemental stock offering can be accomplished. In any event, because REITs are "asset-intensive" entities with a considerable restriction on earnings retention, their ability to finance any future expansion must be planned with great care. The advent of the UPREIT structure has provided another mechanism for incremental growth. Unlike many manufacturing and service corporations that add to capacity incrementally, REIT expansions are likely to involve large asset acquisitions. How these acquisitions are financed can affect earnings for considerable periods of time.

There are four ways in which a REIT can grow income and increase funds from operations, thus securing its dividend and making dividend increases possible. These four methods are (1) growing income from existing properties, (2) growing income through acquisitions, (3) growing income through development, and (4) financial engineering. The relative balance among these areas is a strategic decision, as are the mechanisms for operations within the areas.

Growing Income from Existing Properties. The most obvious method for growing income in an existing portfolio is increasing occupancy by renting more space. The second is by raising rents. Obviously, the two are intrinsically related and both are dependent on the supply and demand conditions in the market. Redevelopment offers a third alternative. Redevelopment primarily refers to remodeling of space to meet changing tenant needs. This can result in income growth because it results in either more aesthetically appealing space or space that is more suitable for prospective tenants, both of which can result in higher rents. Redevelopment may address other physical problems, such as the lack of an elevator in a three-story office building. Expansion can increase income by providing more physical space for rental purposes and is fairly common in retail facilities, where an anchor tenant may expand, or outlying parcels may be developed to generate additional rental income. Office and industrial REITs, particularly those that specialize in industrial/office parks often hold substantial amounts of land in close proximity to their existing parks. This land, which is usually permitted and approved, is simply held in anticipation of growing demand for space. Where the demand does not emerge, the property can be sold and the assets reallocated to more productive areas. Another means of growing income is in altering the market segments addressed. A mall might shift to a fashion focus, essentially developing a retenanting focus. Marketing and policies may also change, as is the case in eliminating a no-pets policy at an apartment community.

Growing Income through Acquisitions. There are two methods of growing the portfolio through acquisitions. These two methods are: (1) purchasing properties with cash at positive spreads, utilizing the arbitrage between cost of capital and the yield of the property, and (2) swapping shares in the REIT or operating partnership units for interests in properties, taking advantage of the tax and form benefits. Positive spread acquisitions are fairly common in periods when REITs are trading at low cap rates relative to the underlying real estate, but more difficult to achieve as REIT yields come closer to or exceed the cap rates on the underlying properties. Another way of looking at this is in terms of **net asset value (NAV).** Net asset value is the net "market value" of all a company's assets, including but not limited to its properties, after subtracting all its liabilities and obligations. When a REIT is trading above NAV, it is more likely to find attractive spreads than when it is trading below NAV. When yields (prices) are very close, it may not be wise to acquire properties in this fashion because of the costs associated with securing capital.

Swapping shares in the REIT or operating partnership units for interests in properties has the advantage of a minimal cash requirement. As a general rule, operating partnership swaps are the more attractive of the two options because of the potential for tax timing. Existing shareholders can benefit because the swaps are generally done at favorable cap rates, with the owners of the acquired property willing to accept a discount for their properties in exchange for liquidity. In some cases, these swaps also include other business enterprises or personnel that are beneficial to the acquiring REIT. For example, an existing REIT with limited development capacity might work out a swap with a private company in the REIT IPO pipeline that has development capacity. The acquiring REIT gets the benefits associated with a larger portfolio and a set of skills that it did not have previous to the transaction. The owners of the acquired properties satisfy some of their goals that led to the consideration of going public, without incurring the substantial costs associated with the legal process of becoming a REIT.

Growing Income through Development. REITs may also choose to grow their income through development of properties. Risk is generally higher than in redevelopment or acquisition, but can be mitigated. For example, the risks associated with build-to-suit development of properties subject to long-term net leases with quality credit tenants are considerably lower than those associated with speculative development. In either case, thorough market analysis is an absolute necessity. Development offers an opportunity to secure entrepreneurial profits and increase funds from operations significantly. However, the returns are offset by a series of risks. There are always risks of construction delays, cost overruns, and lease-up problems. In the market, many investors are extremely concerned with quarterly performance, a focus where it probably does not make a great deal of sense to invest in a long-term asset like real estate, but which can influence pricing. As acquisition opportunities decline, REITs may shift to a development orientation. In some cases, the REITs have a long and distinguished development history and are capitalizing on in-house expertise. In other cases, the REIT does not have the expertise in-house and is forced to acquire it through acquisition of operating companies or through hiring. A third alternative is to develop a relationship with an existing developer and act as the take-out on their construction projects.

Financial Engineering. A fourth alternative is to grow the funds from operation through financial engineering. Financial engineering includes a variety of accounting treatments and uses of leverage that tend to magnify the funds from operations, which many view as the best short-term measure of the REIT's income-producing ability. Financial engineering also includes the ability to secure favorable rates, financing terms, and sources of capital. These factors can influence the long-term cost of capital for the REIT. Essentially, the idea is that REIT management can manipulate the capital structure in order to maximize distributions. The following outline some of the risks and rewards of various financial engineering alternatives.

Accounting treatments can be used to magnify funds from operation (FFO). Since REITs have tended to trade at some multiple of funds from operations, magnifying funds from operations often results in higher stock prices. The risk is that the REIT will be unable to meet the expectations of its shareholders based on magnified FFO numbers. These shareholders may view these magnified numbers as indicative of future growth and expect corresponding increases in dividends. REITs that fail to meet FFO projections or sustain high growth levels have been treated harshly by investors.

As an example of the influence of accounting treatments, some recurring expense items can be either expensed or capitalized. In some property types, particularly multifamily residential properties, recurring expenses are cyclical, impacting the REITs ability to distribute funds on a regular basis. REITs vary as to their treatment of these expenses, making comparisons among REITs difficult. As a result, many analysts have moved to **cash available for distribution (CAD)** as discussed earlier. Cash available for distribution treats recurring expenses as expenses rather than capital items, providing a more conservative estimate of the potential stream of income available for dividend purposes. The problem is that CAD calculation is not standardized, and the information necessary for standardization is often not available.

REITs can also use leverage to magnify FFO in the short term. One way is for the REIT to use short-term variable-rate loans to acquire properties. The rates on this type of loan are lower than those that can be obtained for long-term fixed-rate debt, so the rate of return on the investment is higher, at least in the short run. Higher return on the investment leads to higher FFO and dividends, which in an ideal situation, will lead to an increased multiple, making it feasible to replace the debt with attractively priced equity. Unfortunately, the higher rates of return are accompanied by greater risks and the leverage can reverse, magnifying losses and moving prices in the other direction. The result can be an inability to replace debt with equity and a need to refinance at a less than opportune time. This refinancing risk needs to be evaluated and priced.

REITs can also alter payout ratios. The payout ratio is the percentage of FFO, or alternatively CAD, that is used to pay out the dividend. The payout ratio is an important indicator of the financial flexibility of an organization and its ability to maintain its dividend. As an example, consider two REITs. REIT 1 has FFO of $1.00 per share and pays a dividend of $0.85, resulting in a payout ratio of 85 percent. REIT 2 has FFO of $0.93 and a dividend of $0.85, resulting in a payout ratio of 91.4 percent. If both REITs were subject to a $0.10 per share drop in income, then the resulting payout ratios at the same dividend rate would be 94.4 percent and 102.4 percent, respectively. While REIT 1 can maintain its dividend without dipping into cash reserves, REIT 2 is required to dip into cash reserves, essentially giving the shareholders their money back. While this type of distribution can be maintained for short periods under unusual circumstances, it cannot be maintained indefinitely without hampering growth prospects.

Important Issues in Accounting and Financial Disclosure: Equity REITs[1]

When analyzing financial statements, one must understand that REITs, like other economic entities, have considerable latitude when accounting for their operations. This section covers some issues and interpretations that REIT investors should bear in mind when performing a financial analysis based on financial statements and other documents. These issues are widely covered in various industry reports provided by investment bankers and other REIT market analysts. The following presents some of the basic issues and explains their significance in evaluating REITs and their financial statements.

---

[1]The authors thank Eric Hemel and Neil Barsky for providing them with the report, "Do You Believe in Magic? Understanding a REIT IPO's Pro Forma Funds from Operation." (Morgan Stanley: *U.S. Investment Research,* January 24, 1994.)

Tenant Improvements and Free Rents: Effects on FFO

When markets are soft and vacancies are above normal, tenants may be induced by owners to sign leases with free rent or improvements provided by REIT management. This possibility is important to understanding REIT revenue, particularly where leases are long term. Occupancy and revenues are obviously important items when reporting income for industrial, office, and retail properties. Occupancy rates can be raised and rental revenues increased by providing important concessions to tenants, often in the form of tenant improvements. Generally, new commercial tenants must always incur some costs to reconfigure the space and make it suitable for their operations. Landlord allowances for some tenant improvements are a common practice in much of the real estate industry, but concessions could be a concern if they are very large relative to what other owners are offering. Tenant improvements paid by the landlord are often capitalized and then depreciated. Thus, the cash flows for tenant improvements are not included in FFO calculations because FFO represents earnings before depreciation. Therefore, the investor should be aware that this cash outflow may be occurring currently but accounted for in depreciation expense *over time*. Investors should also pay particularly close attention to any notes to FFO estimates that include "signed leases scheduled to commence." This may indicate that the REIT is currently including the effect of leases not taking effect until a future date.

One way investors can evaluate the implications of new leases is to determine the "cost" per square foot and the extent that tenant improvements and free rent are included in the leases. This determination may be particularly important when the REIT is about to go public with an initial public offering (IPO). For example, suppose that tenant improvement costs averaged $7 per square foot of newly leased space during the three years before the IPO. However, the company spent $20 per square foot *in the year* prior to the IPO. The additional amounts spent on tenant improvements could suggest that the company was preparing for the impending IPO by attempting to boost its occupancy rates and nominal rent levels to make itself more attractive to investors. Many companies do not explicitly disclose the cost per square foot of tenant improvements, but they may disclose enough information about historical leasing activity and aggregate tenant improvement levels so that investors can make their own estimates.

Leasing Commissions and Related Costs

A number of REITs pay outside leasing brokers a commission to solicit tenants. These commissions are usually paid in cash, and the cost is capitalized over the life of the lease. These costs are included in depreciation and amortization expense. Because investors traditionally measure REIT profitability according to funds from operations (earnings before depreciation and amortization), any deferred leasing costs may be overlooked. There is no single, accepted standard for disclosing deferred leasing costs. Many REITs do their own leasing and pay their employee-brokers salaries or commissions, or both. These REITs may then either expense or capitalize and defer the costs. The deferral of leasing costs raises two issues: (1) Leasing costs are an ongoing source of operating expense; omitting them as an operating expense reduces expenses and increases FFO. (2) In rare instances, brokers are paid commissions over the life of the leases instead of up front. In that case, investors in a REIT that is about to embark on an IPO will be paying commissions incurred on leases signed *prior* to the IPO; this means that the REIT may have to pay out cash in the future for leases signed in previous periods.

Use of Straight-Line Rents

Another accounting issue arises when a REIT relies on long-term leases with rent increases contractually stipulated over the life of the lease. This is rarely a factor in apartment companies, which usually have year-to-year or month-to-month leases, but it can be important for REITs with long-term leases, and this includes virtually every category of commercial and industrial property.

To understand the potential problem, consider a simple solution in which a tenant signs a 10-year lease with step-ups: The lease is \$8 per square foot in years 1 through 3, \$10 per square foot in years 4 through 7, and \$12 per square foot in years 8 through 10. If revenue recognition is based on "straight-line" reporting, the rent will be averaged over the full lease term, which in this case is \$10 per square foot. Thus, rental revenues in year 1 are counted as \$10 even though the actual cash flow is \$8. Since FFO is calculated as earnings before depreciation, a pro forma FFO may use \$10 instead of the actual \$8, unless the assumptions underlying the pro forma calculation clearly specify otherwise. Obviously, the FFO estimate will be lower than the actual revenue in the later years of the lease, when \$12 of cash flow exceeds the \$10 average. However, in an IPO, considerable attention is given to the initial, or near-term estimates of FFO. In this case, investors may want to bend the straight line of the rental stream. Management should provide clear guidance to investors about the cash flow without the straight-line rent adjustment in year 1. In this way, investors can better assess the dividend-paying ability of the REIT and accurately evaluate the company on the basis of potential cash flow growth resulting from contractual rent adjustments well into the future. This is one of the primary reasons that many analysts have moved to estimating adjusted FFO, CAD, and other supplemental measures of cash flow as previously discussed.

FFO and Income from Managing Other Properties

A number of REITs receive third-party management income, or income in exchange for managing other properties not owned by the REIT. While third-party management income may provide additional earnings, its associated revenue stream is likely to vary more than the underlying rental income from REIT-owned properties because many management contracts may be cancelable by third-party owners on short notice. Moreover, other events might affect this source of income: Other properties managed by the REIT may be sold, or the management of REIT-owned properties could suffer if the REIT gives too much attention to managing third-party properties. As a result, many REIT security analysts assign a lower multiple to the portion of FFO produced by management income. Investors should always be aware of any fee based on other sources of income that the REIT reports because a large portion of these fees may be short term. The character of the third-party relationship is also important, in that the REIT's managers may have a partnership interest that effectively locks in the contracts. It is important to understand the nature of third-party management contracts and other sources of income. Additionally, some sources of income may not constitute income from real properties and may jeopardize the REIT's tax status if in excess of allowable levels.

Types of Mortgage Debt and Other Obligations

When examining a REIT investment, it is important to consider the terms of the company's mortgage debt. Mortgages may be either short or long term, floating rate or fixed, and nonamortizing or amortizing. As a practical matter, most REITS do not amortize much of their debt. The result is a continual return to the debt market to replace maturing debt. By using short-term, floating rate debt, the REIT borrower may enjoy a lower mortgage rate in exchange for assuming some portion of the risk of inflation and increasing interest rates. The use of a short-term floating rate may be favorable in the near term because of low-interest charges, but it exposes the REIT to significantly greater risk. The REIT can hedge this risk through the use of interest rate "caps" or "swaps," the extent and cost of which should be disclosed to shareholders.

Existence of Ground Leases

As the name suggests, ground leases encumber the land underneath buildings. They are typically made for long periods of time, sometimes up to 99 years. Ground leases tend to be "net" leases, which means the tenant pays for all costs associated with operating the building, including utilities, taxes, renovations, and so on. The landowner, or "fee" owner, pays no operating role other than to collect land rents from the building owner or operator. At the time the lease expires, the landowner owns residual rights to all buildings and improvements situated on the land.

Two basic arrangements of ground leases are likely to apply to REITs. First, the REIT *owns buildings subject to* a ground lease owned by another party. The REIT may have a potential advantage if the ground-lease payments are *fixed.* In this event, the REIT is using the equivalence of leverage because, if the cash flow from the building rental income continues to grow relative to the fixed ground lease payments, a higher return on equity will be achieved. The universal disadvantage of the ground lease is that the REIT will give up ownership of the buildings at the time of lease expiration or it must renegotiate the lease prior to its expiration. In their valuation process, investors should discount heavily the cash flow from any buildings on a ground lease with an approaching expiration date. In addition, some ground leases may call for the lessor to participate in revenue growth. This is similar to a participating debt and may be negative from a REIT investor's perspective. Obviously, the terms and conditions of all ground leases should probably be renegotiated *long before* the lease term expires.

The second case applies to a REIT that *owns a ground lease* that it has acquired from the landowner. Ground leases are allowable investments for REITs, which simply put the REIT between the landowner, who retains all rights of reversion, and the building owner. This arrangement is known as "spread investing," where the REIT takes the risk of collecting a stream of rents from the building owner and pays a lower and perhaps fixed payment to the landowner. Ground leasing to third parties, depending on their credit, can be a safe and reliable way to assure an income stream.

Some ground leases are important and complex enough to warrant detailed financial analysis. Many *retail* REITs, for example, own shopping malls subject to ground leases. In this case, lessors and landowners usually enjoy a substantial share of the cash flow once certain retail revenue thresholds are exceeded, but payments to the ground lease may reduce the ultimate growth prospects of the REIT.

Lease Renewal Options and REIT Rent Growth

Investors should review the lease rollover schedules of REITs. This is particularly important for REITs that concentrate in sectors with long-term leases: regional malls, industrial properties, and offices. Most initial public offerings for these REITs should disclose the average rent of recently expired leases as well as the new rents. Following the initial public offerings, most REITS disclose a schedule of aggregate annual lease expirations in the supplemental materials to their financial statements. This, combined with notes and management discussion, should enable investors to determine how many new leases are being made at or below previous rents and how much or how little growth is occurring from lease rollovers.

Expected lease rollovers should be examined to determine the amount of space subject to *renewal options* and the range of rent levels at which those options are set. Rents could be far below the prevailing rents at the time of lease expiration. Investors should also question the likelihood that some tenants will elect not to renew their leases. This may occur because tenants find that the existing space is inadequate for their expanding operations, or for any one of a number of reasons. Therefore, investors must consider the probability that the space will be leased to new tenants, and how long it will take and how much it will cost a REIT (lease commissions and finish-out) to attract new tenants.

Occupancy Numbers: Leased Space or Occupied Space?

When discussing occupancy numbers, nearly all REITs use the term *occupied space* in notes to financial statements and operating results. Like other disclosure issues, this at first appears innocuous, but on closer examination it opens the way for potential distortion. Occupied space quantifies the space for which tenants are now paying rent. *Leased space* includes all space for which leases are signed, even if the lease does not go into effect for another 6 to 12 months. The amount of leased space is often several percentage points higher than occupied space. Investors who compare occupied space in one REIT against leased space in another, may be using two different—and non-comparable—methods of counting occupancy. For example, one REIT may report as occupied, space that is currently leased but which has been, or is about to be, vacated by tenants, while another may report that space as vacant. There is also variation by property sector, largely due to difference in structure and length of leases. To be conservative, REITs should either not claim credit for occupied space that it has reason to believe will be vacant in the immediate future or disclose the impending vacancy.

Retail REITs and Sales per Square Foot

There is no standard way to measure retail sales per square foot of a small store. Several methods of calculation have evolved, but investors should beware of the implications of each. For example, one method excludes sales per square foot from "in-line stores in regional malls." Another method uses "mall store sales" but excludes sales of "large space users" where space is used less intensively or where a portion of the total space is owned by the tenant or governed by a highly restricted operating agreement. The problem with both definitions is that total retail sales and sales per square foot in a mall are affected by excluding large space users. Even though many large space users may own their space in a mall or have a very strict operating agreement that gives them considerable control over their space, investors are in a sense paying for the lease portfolio or tenant roster and "sales power" of all tenants. A better approach may be to report total sales per square foot rather than to exclude large space users. Some REITs separate anchor tenant sales from in-line tenant sales.

One legitimate defense of excluding large space users from financial statements is that many older malls have large variety-type stores that bring down average sales per square foot. Lease rollovers may provide the mall with significant opportunities for sales and revenue growth, particularly if the leases of variety-type stores is about to expire. Consequently, the more inclusive definition of sales per square foot may tend to understate the long-term sales potential of a mall.

A third definition of sales per square foot is based on "mall store tenants that reported 12 months of sales for the operating period." This definition may exclude tenants that reported less than 12 months of sales, possibly because of bankruptcy or deliberate lease terminations. This measure may suffer from "tenant survivorship bias," or the counting of only those tenants that survived and the exclusion of those that did not. The excluded tenants probably experienced lower sales per square foot than their healthier counterparts; if included, they would have pulled down the average. Alternatively, the measure leaves off sales of seasonal "kiosk" or "cart" operators that sell goods in common areas during holidays and other periods of heavy demand.

Additional Costs of Being a Public Company

REITs typically have to purchase insurance for directors and officers, pay directors' fees, pay for listings on the stock exchanges, and file annual and quarterly reports with the Securities and Exchange Commission. While these costs are usually included in general and administrative costs, the actual amounts may be considerably more than a REIT initially estimated.

The Investment Appeal of Mortgage REITs

The mortgage real estate investment trust is unlike the equity trust in that it does not own the real property. Rather, it owns mortgage paper secured by the underlying real property. Income generated by the mortgage paper is affected by the interest rate on the mortgage note, the discount (or premium) at which the obligation is acquired, and the amount of funds outstanding on loan. Trust expenses applicable against this income are the interest paid for the funds to make payments on loans, management company costs, and other lesser expenses incident to the operations of this kind of investment company.

During the late 1960s and early 1970s, the mortgage trust was used as a source of loans, particularly for construction and development, that were beyond the legal or policy limits of the highly regulated banks, savings and loans, insurance companies, or other real estate-oriented financing institutions. Because their lending policies were relatively unregulated and because they had access to public securities markets, mortgage trusts were in a position to fill a void in the real estate financing market. Even though their cost for short-term borrowed funds was relatively high, there was always the reasonable expectation that the trust could make construction or development loans at rates 3.5 to 4 percent higher than rates available from other lending sources. The spread between borrowing costs and loan income thus held the promise of increasing earnings on the shareholders' equity as the loan portfolio grew. This earnings growth would support further sales of shares in the trust at higher prices, and so on. Following this pattern, the expansion of mortgage trusts during the early 1970s was spectacular.

However, during 1974 a general economic recession set in, and the prime bank lending rate rose to unprecedented heights. Because of the unanticipated rise in their cost of funds, many mortgage trusts were forced into an operating loss position because they were not able to pass on a sufficient amount of these higher costs to borrowers. Further, many advance mortgage commitments had already been made at lower rates with inadequate flexibility for upward rate adjustments. During this period of rising interest rates, many developers were unable to sell completed units or could not complete projects because of rapidly inflating construction costs. Consequently, they were thrown into default on their construction loans. The share values of mortgage trusts fell dramatically, thus reducing the possibilities for further stock offerings as a source of funds.

Because of loan default expectations, the commercial paper market also dried up for trusts and forced them to rely almost exclusively on bank credit lines. As the defaults continued to increase during 1975, many large commercial banks were forced to extend the maturities on notes taken pursuant to these credit lines, which had usually been extended by banks as a group under a revolving credit agreement. The extensions were granted to avoid the cumulative impact on the total financial system if the trusts were forced to undertake mass foreclosures during a serious business recession. When credit became so tight that commercial bank lines could no longer be reasonably renewed, a number of bank sponsors took large blocks of mortgages out of the trust portfolios and put them into their own loan and liquidation accounts to reduce trust debts. These actions had an impact on overall commercial bank liquidity and removed the mortgage trusts generally from the construction and development loan markets as a supplier of funds for the foreseeable future. As a practical matter, most mortgage REITs invest in Commercial Mortgage-Backed Securities (CMBS) of pools of residential mortgages rather than whole loans.

Caveats. As was the case with equity REITs, the potential for a conflict of interest exists when sponsors and affiliates of mortgage REITs (e.g., mortgage companies, thrifts, commercial banks) are also originators of mortgage loans. In these instances, there may be incentives to sell the submarginal loans of REITs while charging fees for servicing them. As indicated earlier, the rules governing the appointment of nonaffiliated trustees and the use of outside appraisers must also be followed in the creation and operation of mortgage REITs. Additionally, CMBS portfolios often contain fairly high risk tranches, known as "B" pieces, that offer significantly higher risks and returns than other tranches. Mortgage REITs, under pressure to grow income, have been prime buyers of "B" pieces. Investors should review a mortgage REIT's investment policy and the quality of its loans as carefully as an equity REIT's properties.

Financial Analysis of an Equity REIT Illustrated

What follows is an analysis of an equity REIT that a prospective investor or shareholder might make. The financial statement for Midwestern America Property Trust is provided in Exhibit 19–2. Midwestern America owns and manages approximately five million square feet of suburban office, office-warehouse, and specialty office/distribution space, which it has assembled over the years in three Midwestern

EXHIBIT 19–2 Financial Statement Midwestern America Property Trust

Panel A. Operating Statement Summary

Net revenue	$70,000,000
Less:	
Operating expenses	30,000,000
Depreciation and amortization	15,000,000
General and administrative expenses	4,000,000
Management expense	1,000,000
Income from operations	$20,000,000
Less:	
Interest expense	6,400,000
Net income (loss)	$13,600,000
Net income (loss) per share	$ 2.72

Panel B. Balance Sheet Summary

Assets			Liabilities	
Cash		$ 500,000	Short term	$ 2,000,000
Rents receivable		1,500,000	Mortgage debt	80,000,000
Properties @ cost	$300,000,000		Total	$ 82,000,000
Less: Acc. depr.	130,000,000		Shareholders' equity	90,000,000
Properties—net		170,000,000		
Net assets		$172,000,000	Total liabilities and equity	$172,000,000

states. The cost basis for these assets is $300 million; the REIT has made or assumed mortgages totaling $80 million as part of financing its asset acquisitions. Midwestern America's stock is currently trading at $75 per share, making its current market value worth $375 million.

When analyzing an equity REIT, two key financial relationships must be understood: (1) the judgment of investment performance and risk and (2) the comparison of Midwestern America (MA) with other equity REITs. Referring to Exhibit 19–2, we see that MA earned $13,600,000 in net income, or $2.72 per share, during the past year. However, additional data (see Exhibit 19–3) indicate that other interesting and important relationships must be understood. As is always the case with real estate investment, considerable emphasis is given to *cash flow.* For example, section II of Exhibit 19–3 includes additional performance measures. **Net income from operations** is analogous to net operating income (*NOI*), which has been discussed at length in earlier chapters. It represents the operating cash flow exclusive of interest, and was $7.00 per share for the past year. The second measure, funds from operations (FFO), is analogous to net cash flow per share. As you may recall, it is derived by adding all noncash expense items to net income (loss). Noncash accounting charges generally include depreciation and amortization. Most industry analysts rely heavily on FFO when making judgments and comparisons among REITs. We can see that the FFO per share for MA was $5.72 during the past year versus **earnings per share (EPS)** of $2.72. The difference in this simplified example is due to the $15 million depreciation allowance.

One REIT regulation previously detailed indicates that 95 percent of net income must be paid out as dividends. Therefore, another very important relationship shown in section III is the dividend payment per share. In our example, the payment of $4.00 per share meets the 95 percent requirement, but this amount is also greater than the earnings per share; thus, MA paid dividends of $4.00 per share even though EPS was only $2.72. This can occur because FFO, or *cash flow* per share, was $5.72, which exceeded earnings per share. Indeed, MA could have paid dividends of $5.72 per share even though it was required to pay only 95 percent of $2.72, or only $2.58 per share. By paying a $4.00 dividend, Midwestern America met the 95 percent of earnings requirement and retained cash of $1.72 per share for operations and acquisitions of new assets.

The difference between REIT earnings and dividends has a very important effect on the taxes that shareholders pay. Tax regulations provide that even though investors in Midwestern America receive $4.00 per share, only $2.72 of earnings are reported as a taxable dividend. The remaining $1.28 is treated as **recovery of capital (ROC)** and serves to reduce the cost basis of the stock acquired by the investor. For example, if a share of MA stock was purchased for $75 prior to the dividend declaration date, the investor would reduce the investment basis of the stock by $1.28, from $75.00 to $73.72. When the stock is eventually sold, the investor would then calculate any gain or loss based on the sale price, less $73.72, or the reduced basis of the stock. If the stock has been owned for one year or more and results in a gain, it would be taxed at the prevailing capital gains tax rate. This also means that if there is a difference between ordinary and capital gains tax rates, the investor saves taxes in the amount of $1.28 times the difference in the two tax rates. Consequently, this treatment allows investors to receive a portion of the dividend ($1.28) "tax free" until the stock is sold or the REIT is liquidated. At that point, if the investor has owned the stock long enough to qualify for capital gains treatment and capital gains tax rates are lower than tax on ordinary income, the investor will also save taxes.

EXHIBIT 19–3 Summary Indicators of Financial Performance: Midwestern America Property Trust

I. General Summary:

Properties: 5 million sq. ft.	Mortgage debt: $80,000,000
Original cost: $300 million	Avg. interest 8%, 10-yr. maturity
Depreciated cost: $170 million	Number of common shares: 5 million

II. Profit Summary:

	$ Amount	Per Share
Earnings per share (*EPS*)[1]	13,600,000	$ 2.72
Income from operations plus depreciation and amortization (*NOI per share*)[2]	35,000,000	$ 7.00
Funds from operations (*FFO per share*)[3]	28,600,000	$ 5.72

III. Other Important Financial Data:

Market price per share of common stock	$75.00
Dividend per share	$ 4.00
Shareholder recovery of capital (*ROC per share*)[4]	$ 1.28
Cash retention per share (*CRPS*)[5]	$ 1.72
Earnings yield[6]	3.62%
FFO yield[7]	7.62%
Dividend yield[8]	5.33%
Current earnings multiple[9]	27.6x
Current *FFO* multiple[10]	13.1x
Net assets per share (*NAPS*)[11]	$34.00
Equity or book value per share (*BVPS*)[12]	$18.00

IV. Explanation and calculations:

[1]*EPS:* Net income $13,600,000/5,000,000 shares outstanding
[2]*NOI:* Income from operations plus depreciation and amortization ($20,000,000 + $15,000,000)/5,000,000 shares outstanding
[3]*FFO:* Net Income + Depreciation & Amortization ($13,600,000 + $15,000,000)/5,000,000 shares outstanding
[4]*ROC:* Dividend per share − *EPS* = $4.00 − $2.72 = $1.28
[5]*CRPS: FFO* − Dividend per share $5.72 − $4.00 = $1.72
[6]*EPS*/Market Price per share = $2.72/$75 = 3.62%
[7]*FFO*/Market Price per share = $5.72/$75 = 7.62%
[8]Dividend per share/Market price per share = $4.00/$75 = 5.33%
[9]Current price per share/*EPS* = $75/$2.72 = 27.6x
[10]Current price per share/*FFO* = $75/$5.72 = 13.1x
[11]*NAPS*: Net assets $172,000,000/5,000,000
[12]*BVPS:* (Assets − Liabilities)/shares = $90,000,000/5,000,000

When REITs report operating losses, none of the losses can be passed through to investors. Instead, losses must be carried forward to offset income in future periods. The passive loss limitation provision does not materially affect REITs because their losses cannot be passed through to investors. REIT dividends are considered to be *portfolio income* and thus do not qualify as passive income to offset passive losses.

With respect to capital gains from the sale of property, REITs may either (1) retain the gain and defer its distribution to shareholders, in which case the gain is taxed at the appropriate corporate capital gains rate, or (2) distribute the gain as a dividend to shareholders. In the latter case, the REIT is not taxed on the distributed gain; however, the REIT is required to designate such dividends as a capital gain distribution to shareholders, who must recognize it as a capital gain in their individual taxes. Capital losses cannot be passed through to individual investors, but must be carried forward by the REIT and offset against any future capital gains.

Also important in section III of Exhibit 19–3 is cash flow retention, or the difference between FFO per share and dividends per share, which amounts to $1.72. Midwestern America may have retained this amount as a cash reserve or to acquire properties during the past year. As pointed out, MA could have paid this amount as a dividend and been taxed at ordinary income rates. However, because it was not paid currently, the cash flow retention converted eventually into a capital gain if the *price* of MA stock responds favorably to management's decision to retain and invest these funds instead of paying dividends. Unlike corporations that may choose not to pay any dividends and retain all earnings for future expansion, MA must pay at least 95 percent of $2.72, or $2.58 per share. In other words, MA has far less discretion than corporations with respect to paying a minimum dividend—a major difference between REITs and corporate entities, which affects REIT dividend reinvestment and expansion policy in very important ways.

Conclusion

The resurgence of real estate investment trusts (REITs) in the early 1990s is another indication of the extent that real estate has become "securitized." Compared with traditional methods of investing, real estate-backed securities appear to be gaining in importance because of their marketability, the public accountability of management, and numerous other reasons. REITs, which provide a structure similar to that of mutual funds for common stock investors, allow investors to participate in a portfolio of properties that may be geographically diversified and professionally managed. Further, REITs are usually tax-exempt and must pass through as dividends to investors most of the cash flow produced from managing the portfolio. Accounting practices for depreciation and amortization and the resultant effects on net income may allow a portion of the tax on REIT dividends to be deferred. Today the market value of REITs exceeds $140 billion, and many of the premier real estate operators in the United States are operating within the REIT format, so market research and analysis for individual REITs and the industry are widely available from investment banks and other investment firms.

Key Terms

book value per share 583
cash available for distribution (CAD) 575
dividend yield 571
earnings multiple 583
earnings per share (EPS) 582
earnings yield 583
FFO multiple 583
FFO yield 583
funds from operations (FFO) 570
net asset value (NAV) 573
net income from operations 582
real estate investment trust (REIT) 565
recovery of capital (ROC) 582
umbrella partnership REIT (UPREIT) 567

Questions

1. What are the general requirements regarding income, investments, and dividends with which a REIT must comply to maintain its tax-exempt status?
2. What are the three principal types of REITs?
3. List and characterize equity REITs based on their property types.
4. What is the difference between earnings per share (*EPS*), funds from operations (*FFO*), adjusted funds from operations (AFFO) and dividends per share?
5. Explain how an investor in an equity REIT may receive a current dividend, part of which may be tax-deferred.

6. What are some important lease provisions which investors should be aware of when analyzing the financial statements of REITs?

7. What is a mortgage REIT?

Problems

1. You have been presented with the following set of financial statements for National Property Trust, a REIT that is about to make an initial stock offering to the public. This REIT specializes in the acquisition and management of warehouses. Your firm, Blue Street Advisors, is an investment management company that is considering the purchase of National Property Trust shares. You have been asked to prepare a financial analysis of the REIT. National believes that it should pay a dividend of at least $3.00 per share to be comparable with other REITs at this time. However, it is not sure whether this amount will be sufficient.

National Property Trust

Panel A. Operating Statement Summary

Net revenue	$100,000,000
Less:	
Operating expenses	40,000,000
Depreciation and amortization	22,000,000
General and administrative expenses	6,000,000
Management expense	3,000,000
Income from operations	29,000,000
Less:	
Interest expense*	6,400,000
Net income (loss)	$ 22,600,000

*At 8% interest only.

Panel B. Balance Sheet Summary

Assets

Cash	$ 1,500,000
Rents receivable	2,500,000
Properties @ cost	750,000,000
Less: Accumulated depreciation	450,000,000
Properties—net	300,000,000
Total net assets	$304,000,000

Liabilities

Short term	$ 12,000,000
Mortgage debt*	80,000,000
Total	92,000,000
Shareholder equity†	212,000,000
Total liabilities and equity	$304,000,000

*At 8% interest only.
†10,000,000 shares outstanding.

a. Develop a set of financial ratios that will provide Blue Street Advisors with useful information in the evaluation and comparison of National Property Trust with other REITs.

b. Your research also indicates that the shares of comparable REITs specializing in warehouse acquisitions in the same regions are selling at dividend yields in the range of 8 percent. Price multiples for these REITs are about 12 × current FFO. What price range does this suggest for National shares? What would you expect National's dividend and cash retention policy to be in order to recommend its purchase?

2. Robust Properties is planning to go public by creating a REIT that will offer 1 million shares of stock. It is currently trying to develop a pro forma set of financial statements. Robust is faced with a number of questions about its handling of some accounting and financial disclosure issues.

Robust Properties

I. Major Financial Information:	
a. Assets—properties (actual cost)	$100,000,000
b. Depreciable basis—buildings only	$80,000,000
c. Useful life	40 years
d. Operating expenses	38% of rents
e. Management expenses—3rd parties	5% of rents
f. General and administrative expenses	3% of rents
g. Mortgage @ 8% interest only, 10 yrs.	$30,000,000
h. Financing fees	$900,000
II. Lease Information:	
a. Average lease term	5 years
b. Leasable space	1,000,000sf.
c. Base rents (year 1)	$15 psf.
d. Escalation factor—rents per year	5%
e. Lease commissions	4% of yr 1 rent
f. Tenant improvements	$10 psf.

The management of Robust Properties has asked you to prepare preliminary pro forma financials for the next *three years.* Specifically, you should have (1) a *beginning* balance sheet, (2) operating statements for each of the next three years, and (3) all relevant financial ratios for year 1 results only. Robust will pay all financing fees, tenant improvements, and lease commissions upon commencing operations. It would like to pay a minimum dividend of $4.00 per share.

In preparing your pro forma operating statements, Robust wants you to consider the effects of reporting in the following two ways:

Approach	(1)	(2)
Lease commissions	Amortize, 5 years	Expense in year 1
Finance fees	Amortize, 10 years	Expense in year 1
Tenant improvments	Depreciate, 40 years	Depr. over 5-year lease term
Buildings	Depreciate, 40 years	Depr., 40 years

a. What would EPS, FFO, and ROC be under both approaches? How should Robust think about its accounting policy?

CHAPTER

20 Real Estate Investment Performance and Portfolio Considerations

Introduction

Thus far, our discussion of risk and required rates of return has stressed a methodology or an approach that should be used when evaluating a specific project or mortgage financing alternative. In this chapter, we provide some insight into the measurement of return and risk for various real estate investment vehicles and investment portfolios.

We will apply concepts and methodologies based on financial theory and demonstrate possible applications to real estate investments. The use of many of these applications is gaining in importance to institutional investors, such as life insurance companies, investment advisors, consultants to pension funds, bank trust departments, and other entities that manage portfolios with real estate assets. Portfolio managers must be able to measure the performance of real estate assets and be able to compare it to the performance of stocks, bonds, and other investments. Also, many portfolio managers are interested in knowing how well investment portfolios perform when real estate investments are *combined* with other securities.

The Nature of Real Estate Investment Data

When measuring the investment performance of something as broadly defined as real estate, one must keep many things in mind. Ideally, to measure real estate investment performance, we would like to have data on prices for all investment property transactions—ranging from hotels to warehouses to apartment units—taking place in the economy, a detailed description of the land, improvements, and cash flows produced by these properties. We would also like to have data on repeated sales of the same properties over time. We could then calculate various measures of return on investment over time. Unfortunately, such a data series, or even an adequate sample of transactions in the many areas of real estate, is not available because the market is one in which the price for a relatively nonhomogeneous asset is negotiated between two parties. Generally, this price does not have to be disclosed to any public or private agency. Hence, unlike securities markets, there is no centralized collection of real estate transactions and operating income data.[1]

Because of these limitations, current attempts to measure real estate investment performance are based on limited data that are made available from a few select sources. The available data may not be representative of (1) the many types of properties, (2) the many geographic areas in which commercial real estate is located, or (3) the frequency of transactions indicative of real estate investment activity in the economy as a whole. Consequently, you must be careful when making generalizations about real estate performance.

Sources of Data Used for Real Estate Performance Measurement

In this section, we provide information on two sources of real estate data that are used to a limited extent when measuring real estate investment performance. We also consider investment returns from data that are available on common stocks, corporate bonds, and government securities. Exhibit 20–1 summarizes the data available for these investments. We rely on two sources for real estate returns in this chapter. The first is security prices as represented by REIT shares. The second data source is based on estimates of value of individual properties owned by pension plan sponsors. Note that the primary differences in these data is that one source is based on real estate-backed securities and the other is based on estimates of individual properties.

REIT Data: Security Prices

One of the two sources of data used to produce investment returns on real estate in this chapter are based on REITs. The **NAREIT** (National Association of Real Estate Investment Trusts) REIT Share Price Index is a monthly index based on ending market prices for shares owned by REIT investors. Data for this series are available beginning with January 1972 and include all REITs actively traded on the New York and American Stock Exchanges as well as the Nasdaq National Market System.[2]

The data used in this chapter are based on only those REITs that *own* real estate, or equity REITs. NAREIT compiles a monthly index for equity REITs based on month-end prices and dividends on securities owned by investors in each equity REIT contained in the index. Hence, the prices of REIT shares are determined by how successful investors believe the trustees of an individual REIT will be in finding properties at favorable prices, managing them, and then selling them. While equity REIT share prices certainly reflect investors' perceptions of the quality, diversity, and risk of real estate assets owned, investors are also evaluating the effectiveness of trustees in their valuation of equity REIT securities. Further, when purchasing shares, investors do not give up as much liquidity as they would if they acquired and managed real estate assets directly, because a continuous auction market (e.g., NYSE) exists in which shares are traded. Thus, investing in an equity REIT may be less risky than investing directly in real estate.

Hybrid and Mortgage REITs

A mortgage REIT investment return series and a hybrid REIT return series are also shown in Exhibit 20–1. The mortgage REIT index is based on security prices of

[1]In some states, actual transaction prices must be disclosed to property tax assessors. However, other data relating to property characteristics and operating cash flows are generally not available.

[2]Obtained from various publications of the National Association of Real Estate Investment Trusts, Washington, DC

EXHIBIT 20–1 Common Sources of Data Used for Measuring Investment Performance

Real Estate–Equity Returns	*Description of Data*
NAREIT—Equity REIT Share Price Index and Dividend Yield Series	Monthly index computed based on share prices of REITs that own and manage real estate assets. Security prices used in the index are obtained from the New York Stock Exchange (NYSE), American Stock Exchange (AMEX), and National Association of Security Dealers Automated Quotation (Nasdaq) system. Divided data are collected by NAREIT. Properties owned may be levered or unlevered. Index values are available from 1972 to the present.
NAREIT—Mortgage REIT Share Price Index and Dividend Yield Series	Monthly index computed on share price data of REITs that make primarily commercial real estate loans (construction, development, and permanent) although some make or purchase residential loans (both multifamily and single family). Prices obtained from NYSE, AMEX, and Nasdaq market system. Dividend data are collected by NAREIT. Monthly index data available from 1972 to the present.
NAREIT—Hybrid REIT Index	Monthly index compiled by NAREIT from share prices and dividends for REITs that (1) own properties and (2) make mortgage loans. Sources of data are the same as for equity and mortgage REITs. Index values are available from 1972 to the present
NCREIF Property Index—National Council of Real Estate Investment Fiduciaries	Data are contributed by members of NCREIF, based on about 3,000 properties with an aggregate market value of about $100 billion that are owned by pension fund plan sponsors through investment managers. An index is calculated quarterly and data consist of: (1) net operating income and (2) beginning- and end-of-quarter appraised values for all properties. Actual sale prices are used, as available. Quarterly index values are available from 1978 to the present.
Common stocks—Standard & Poor's (S&P) 500	Daily index based on common stock prices for the 500 corporations with the highest market value of common stock outstanding. Data available from the financial press. Dividend data compiled by Wilshire and Associates and included in a monthly and annual total return index by Ibbotson Associates, Chicago. Daily index data available from 1926 to the present.
Corporate bonds—Salomon Brothers High-Grade Corporate Bond Index	Monthly index based on high-grade, long-term (20-year) bond prices. Interest based on bond coupons and total returns (interest, beginning, and ending index values) compiled by Ibbotson Associates, Chicago. Daily index available from 1926 to the present.
Government securities	U.S. Treasury bills and bonds. Price data obtained from *The Wall Street Journal*. A monthly total return series compiled by Ibbotson Associates, Chicago. Daily index data available from 1926 to the present.

shares outstanding in REITs that specialize in acquiring various types of mortgage loans on many types of properties. Hence, when investing in a mortgage REIT, an investor is buying equity shares in an entity whose assets are primarily mortgage loans. Hybrid REITs operate by buying real estate *and* by acquiring mortgages on both commercial and residential real estate.

NCREIF Property Index: Property Values

The NCREIF Property Index measures the historic performance of income-producing properties either (1) acquired by open-end or commingled investment funds that sell investment units owned by qualified pension and profit-sharing trusts, or (2) acquired by investment advisors and managed on separate account bases. The data incorporated in the **NCREIF Index** are voluntarily contributed and based on the performance of properties managed by members of the National Council of Real Estate Investment Fiduciaries (NCREIF).[3] Quarterly rates of return are calculated for all properties included in the index and are based on two distinct components of return: (1) net operating income and (2) the quarterly change in property market value (appreciation or depreciation). The NCREIF Index contains data on five major property categories: apartment complexes, office buildings, warehouses, office/showrooms/research and development facilities, and retail properties (including regional, community, and neighborhood shopping centers as well as freestanding store buildings). Property values are based on either appraised values or, for properties that are sold, net sales proceeds, which are entered as the final market value in the quarter in which the property is sold. The index returns represent an aggregate of individual property returns calculated quarterly before deduction of investment advisory fees. The quarterly series is calculated by summing the increase or decrease in the value of each property plus its net operating income for the quarter. To obtain changes in value, *quarterly appraisals* are made, and when sales occur, actual transaction prices negotiated by the buyer and seller are a part of the index.

Data Sources for Other Investments

In contrast to the scarcity of real estate return data, data on financial assets are plentiful and easily obtainable. In this chapter, we will also develop measures of investment performance for common stocks from the Standard & Poor's 500 Index of Common Stocks (S&P 500), U.S. Treasury bills (T-bills), longer-term U.S. Treasury bonds, and long-term corporate bonds contained in the Salomon Brothers Index of Corporate Bonds. These indexes (see Exhibit 20–1) are generally computed daily, weekly, monthly, quarterly, and annually and are published regularly in the financial press.

Cumulative Investment Return Patterns

A series of historic total return indexes (see Exhibit 20–2) have been developed to begin the discussion of real estate equity investment performance. We have included three equity indexes: the S&P 500, EREIT (equity REITs), and NCREIF Property Index. Debt securities are represented by indexes for T-bills and corporate bonds (for sources see Exhibit 20–1). These indexes are cumulative total returns based on quarterly data for each security: Each series is indexed at 100 beginning in 1985 (1Q) and is compiled through 2000 (4Q) and includes reinvestment of dividends, income, or interest as appropriate.[4]

The patterns indicate that $100 invested from the end of 1985 through 2000 would have produced the greatest total return (based on quarterly price changes and

[3]See the *NCREIF Real Estate Performance Report,* various issues, published by National Council of Real Estate Fiduciaries (Chicago), www.NCREIF.org.

[4]Dividends are included for the S&P 500 and EREITs. Net operating income is included in the NCREIF Index. Interest is included in the corporate bond index. T-bills include price changes only as no interest is paid on these instruments. They are bought and sold at discounts to maturity.

EXHIBIT 20–2 Cumulative Total Returns REITs, S&P 500, NCREIF, Bonds, and T-Bill Indices, 1985–2000

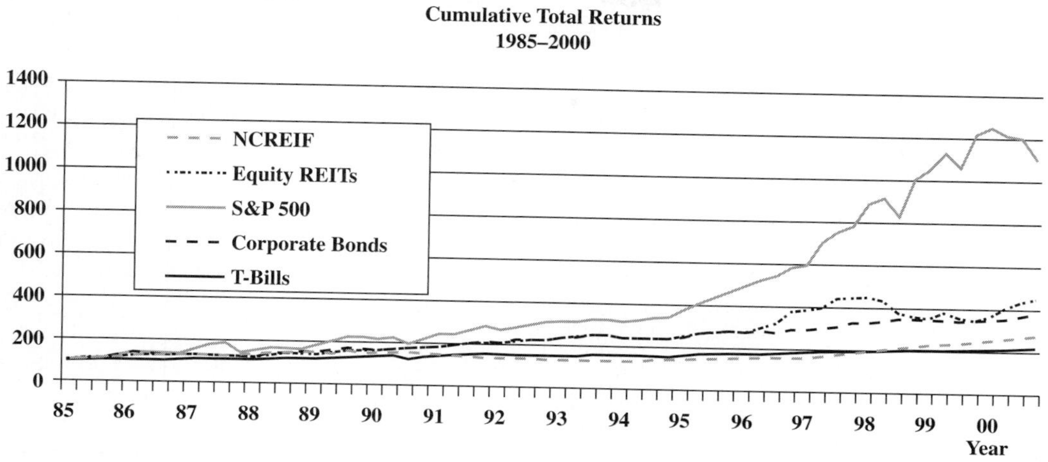

reinvestment of all dividends, interest, or income) if it had been invested in securities comprising the S&P 500 index. Total return rankings of the other indexes were as follows: Equity REITs, Corporate Bond Index, NCREIF Index, and T-bills. We stress, however, that although these return patterns are informative, it should not be implied that each investment is equivalent in *risk*. When attempting to make comparisons among different securities, cumulative return data must be broken down into an appropriate time series so that various measures of volatility can be calculated to provide some idea about the relative risk of each security. It should be stressed that when analyzing investments, returns provide us with only one-half of the information that we need. Information on the risk characteristics of investment are equally important.

Computing Holding Period Returns

While the cumulative total returns shown in Exhibit 20–2 are useful information, additional insight into the risk-return characteristics of each security can be obtained by examining returns over shorter time periods. The most fundamental unit of measure used by portfolio managers to measure investment returns for individual securities, or a class of securities in a portfolio, is the **holding period return *(HPR)***. This is generally defined as follows:

$$HPR = \frac{P_t - P_{t-1} + D_t}{P_{t-1}}$$

where P_t is the end-of-period price for the asset, or value of an index for an investment, or index representing a class of investments, whose performance is being assessed, $P_{t-1}$is the beginning of period value, and D represents any dividends or other cash payouts that may have occurred during the period over which the *HPR* is being measured.

EXHIBIT 20–3 Sample Computation of Holding Period Returns (*HPR*s) and Related Statistics: Hypothetical Security

Period Ending	*Index*	*HPR*	$HPR - \overline{HPR}$	$(HPR - \overline{HPR})^2$
Quarter				
1	673.7	—	—	—
2	764.6	0.1349	0.1240	0.0154
3	787.6	0.0301	0.0192	0.0004
4	803.6	0.0203	0.0094	0.0001
5	802.5	−0.0014	−0.0123	0.0002
6	886.3	0.1044	0.0935	0.0087
7	890.6	0.0049	−0.0061	0.0000
8	855.3	−0.0396	−0.0505	0.0026
9	773.1	−0.0961	−0.1070	0.0115
10	844.3	0.0921	0.0812	0.0066
11	867.8	0.0278	0.0169	0.0003
12	878.5	0.0123	0.0014	0.0000
13	874.4	−0.0047	−0.0156	0.0002
14	895.6	0.0242	0.0133	0.0002
15	948.5	0.0591	0.0482	0.0023
16	982.6	0.0360	0.0250	0.0006
17	952.5	−0.0306	−0.0415	0.0017
18	914.5	−0.0399	−0.0508	0.0026
19	911.8	−0.0030	−0.0139	0.0002
20	780.7	−0.1438	−0.1547	0.0239
21	804.9	0.0310	0.0201	0.0004
		Σ0.2181		Σ0.0779

1st quarter $HPR = (764.6 - 673.7) \div 673.7 = 0.1349$

Mean $HPR = \overline{HPR} = \Sigma HPR \div n = 0.2181/20 = 0.0109$

Variance $= \sigma^2 = \Sigma\,(HPR - \overline{HPR})^2 \div n = 0.0779/20 = 0.0039$

Standard deviation $= \sigma = \sqrt{\sigma^2} = \sqrt{.0039} = 0.0624$

Coefficient of variation $= 0.0624 \div 0.0109 = 5.7219$

Geometric mean return $= \sqrt[n]{(1 + HPR_1)(1 + HPR_2)\cdots(1 + HPR_n)} - 1 = 0.0013$

An example of how holding period returns are calculated for a hypothetical security index is demonstrated in Exhibit 20–3. The first quarter's return was calculated by subtracting the end-of-period value and dividing by the beginning-of-period value. The arithmetic mean, variance, standard deviation, and coefficient of variation have also been calculated. These measures will be used in our discussion of risk later in the chapter. The *HPR* for the first quarter in the series was 13.49 percent. The mean *HPR*, or $\overline{HPR}$, all quarterly returns in the series were 1.09 percent.

An alternative way of considering these return data is to calculate the **geometric mean return.** This return is calculated by finding the *n*th root of the product of each quarterly *HPR* in series multiplied together, minus 1 (see bottom of exhibit). The geometric mean return was equal to .13 percent, a measure of the quarterly *compounded* rate of return that an investor would have earned on $1 invested in the index during the period.

Although the values of the arithmetic mean and geometric mean are sometimes very close, this will not always be the case, particularly if values in the series rise and fall sharply or the series is longer than the sample shown in the exhibit. There

EXHIBIT 20–4 Summary Statistics of Performance Measures for Selected Investment Alternatives

	CPI	*Corp. Bonds*	*S&P 500*	*T-Bills*	*NCREIF*	*EREIT*
Arithmetic mean	1.13%	2.31%	4.06%	1.76%	2.32%	3.94%
Standard deviation	0.90%	3.80%	7.41%	0.70%	1.76%	10.26%
Coefficient of variation	0.80	1.64	1.83	0.40	0.76	2.60
Geometric mean	0.79%	2.24%	3.98%	1.40%	1.73%	2.58%

is a distinct conceptual difference between the arithmetic and geometric mean returns. The geometric mean is used by portfolio managers when considering the performance of an investment and is expressed as a compound rate of interest from the beginning to the end of a specific period of time. **Arithmetic mean returns** are simple averages (not compounded) and are widely used in statistical studies spanning very long periods of time.[5]

Exhibit 20–4 contains summary statistics for various investments that we have chosen to include in the chapter. Note that for each of the return series, we have calculated quarterly arithmetic mean and geometric mean returns and related statistics. The exhibit also includes data for the Consumer Price Index (CPI).

Comparing Investment Returns

We can now begin to compare total returns for the various investment categories contained in Exhibit 20–4. A number of patterns should be apparent from the data. The geometric mean returns (also called time weighted returns by many portfolio managers), show that from 1985 to 2000, stocks constituting the Standard and Poor's 500 Index (S&P 500) produced quarterly returns of 3.98 percent, which exceeded all other returns shown in the exhibit. Equity REIT (NAREIT) returns were 2.58 percent, followed by corporate bonds which were 2.24 percent, then by returns on the NCREIF Index, which were 1.73 percent, and T-bills (1.40 percent).

***HPR*s and Inflation.** All returns shown in Exhibit 20–4 may also be compared with the quarterly rate of inflation, as represented by the CPI, which was .79 percent. The comparison with the CPI provides some insight into whether returns from each investment category exceeded the rate of inflation (thereby earning *real* returns).

Comparing Risk Premiums. In addition to returns, risk premiums may be calculated for each investment class relative to T-bills. Risk premiums may also be

[5]The geometric mean is considered to superior to the arithmetic mean when the past performance of an investment is being considered for a specified period of time, say from the date of purchase until the present time, or for an investment portfolio where funds are flowing in and out and the investment base is changing. For example, suppose the price of a security is 100, 110, 100 at the end of each of three consecutive years. The *HPR*s are 10 percent and − 9.09 percent. The arithmetic mean is .45 percent; however, the geometric mean is zero. The latter result occurs because the beginning and ending security prices are equal. This return better represents the performance of a security from the time of purchase until the present. Arithmetic mean returns are used in statistical studies where some inference about the future is based on averages of past performance. In these cases, an entire series of returns may be used to justify a long-term future decision and no specific time interval is considered any more important than another.

calculated for each investment relative to all other investments. For example, during the 1985–2000 period, EREITs earned an average *risk premium* of 1.18 percent per quarter, in excess of T-bills (2.58% − 1.40%). T-bills are generally used to represent a riskless investment; hence, T-bill returns provide a measure of a risk-free return. Investors in EREITs would also have earned a premium of .34 percent relative to returns on corporate bonds (2.58% − 2.24%). When compared to the NCREIF Index, which provided returns of 1.73 percent compounded quarterly, EREIT returns were higher by .85 percent. We should recall, however, that the NCREIF Index is compiled on an *unleveraged* basis; that is, the properties in the index were purchased on an all-cash basis or "free and clear" of debt. Hence, a more appropriate comparison for the NCREIF Property Index would be relative to equity REITs that purchase properties on an all-cash basis, or unleveraged basis, because EREIT returns include the effects of leverage, while the NCREIF Index does not. Hence, EREITs are more risky. Therefore, holding all else constant, a premium should be earned on EREIT shares relative to returns based on the NCREIF Index.

Risk, Return, and Performance Measurement

While comparing investment returns is an important starting point in evaluating investment performance, it represents only one part of the analysis. We know from material presented earlier that investments that produce higher returns usually exhibit greater price volatility and are generally *riskier* than investments that produce lower returns. In cases involving *individual real estate* investments, such risks may be a function of the type of property, its location, design, lease structure, and so on. Those attributes, and the attendant risks associated with those attributes, can be thought of as a type of *business risk.*

Another source of risk occurs when real estate investments are leveraged. In these cases, default risk is present. Finally, because of the relative difficulty and time required to sell property, liquidity risk is certainly present. As we know, when these three major sources of risk are compared among properties or among alternative investments, when more risk is taken by investors, a risk premium, or higher investment return should be earned by investors who bear that additional risk. One way of considering this risk-return relationship is to compute risk premiums, as we did above. A subjective assessment can then be made about whether risk premiums earned on riskier assets are adequate relative to the additional risk taken. An investor may then judge whether the premium earned on EREITs is sufficient to compensate for their added risk taken if EREITs are purchased instead of corporate bonds.

Another way of looking at the risk-return relationship is to think about the way in which business, default, and liquidity risks affect the pattern of returns that investors expect to earn. Over time, returns (dividends and price changes) on investments with more of these risks present are likely to exhibit more *variation* than investments with fewer of these risks. Recalling our earlier discussions on investment risk, we would expect a property with more risk to provide higher, but more variable investment returns than a property with less risk. The point is that greater variability in market prices and cash flows can be thought of as commensurate with increased risk because an investor owning a risky asset with a highly variable price pattern (up and down) faces having to sell it for a more unpredictable price than a less risky asset. *The assumption that variability in asset returns represents risk and that premiums over what could be earned on a riskless investment represent the price of risk is the foundation for modern finance theory.* It is also a premise that must be understood if the techniques for risk-adjusting returns that are described below are to be used.

Risk-Adjusted Returns: Basic Elements

Given that the combined effects of the sources of risk described above will be reflected in the variability in investment returns, one way of taking into account investment risk when evaluating performance is to consider the variability of returns. The variability of holding period returns for specific assets or classes of assets enables one to make a better comparison among investments exhibiting different risk.

One approach that may be used to consider risk and returns is to compute the **coefficient of variation** of the returns. This is defined as the standard deviation of returns divided by the mean return (this can be based on either the arithmetic or geometric mean returns for a given investment or investment index). This concept is sometimes referred to as a *risk-to-reward ratio* and is intended to relate total risk, as represented by the standard deviation, to the mean return with the idea of determining how much return an investor could expect to earn relative to the total risk taken if the investment was made. For example, if an investor holds a portfolio containing securities with a mean return of 2 percent and a standard deviation of 3 percent the coefficient of variation is 1.5. This may be interpreted as taking 1.5 units of risk for every unit of return that is earned.[6]

An interesting comparison may now be made between the investment performance of EREITs and the NCREIF Index. Recall from Exhibit 20–4 that the NCREIF Index produced a lower mean return compared with EREITs. However, when mean returns for both investment categories are risk-adjusted, the NCREIF Index appears to have outperformed the EREIT index on a risk-adjusted basis. When the coefficient of variation for EREITs and the NCREIF Index are compared, the NCREIF had better *risk-adjusted return* than the EREITs.

It has already been pointed out that the NCREIF Index (1) does not include the effect of leverage in investment returns, and (2) property values used to compute the NCREIF Index are based largely on quarterly appraisals plus a relatively small number of actual sale transactions. Using appraisals may have a smoothing effect on returns and reduce variability. If property appraisals are (1) significantly different from actual market values and (2) affect the variation in the index, then the NCREIF Index may not be representative of true real estate returns or volatility in those returns. For example, results in Exhibit 20–4 for EREITs indicate that the mean return was 3.94 percent and the standard deviation of returns was 10.26 percent, resulting in a coefficient of variation of 2.60. This compares to a mean return of 2.32 percent for the NCREIF Index and a coefficient of variation of .76. These results indicate a material difference in both return and risk for the two indexes. This difference also may be due to considerable differences in the types of properties (e.g., office, retail; apartment), in the geographic distribution of their locations (e.g., north, south, east, or west and suburban or urban sites); and in the investment strategies employed by investment managers (e.g., investing in raw land in predevelopment stages or in fully leased properties only). Such differences may affect the relative risk of investments

[6]This calculation also assumes that the risk premium, or return, is proportional to the risk taken on all investments by all investors. This assumption clearly *does not hold* for all investors, some of whom are more risk-averse than others. Even for the same investor, risk aversion cannot be considered for individual assets independently of one another. Rather, risk must be assessed in terms of the additional risk assumed relative to the total portfolio of assets owned. More will be said about this later.

in each index. Further, equity REIT shares are bought and sold in an *auction* market with continuous trading, whereas the individual properties that make up the NCREIF Index are bought and sold in a much more limited, *negotiated* market between parties. Premiums for liquidity and transaction costs when making such comparisons are really not well understood, nor have such premiums been isolated in research studies. Finally, the definition of income used in calculating the holding period returns for both indexes may not be exactly comparable because of advisory and other management fees that are deducted from REIT income, but not for properties in the NCREIF Index. More research must be done before the nature of risk and return for investments made in REIT shares versus direct investment in real estate, as represented by the NCREIF Index, is well understood.

Elements of Portfolio Theory

The preceding section dealt with one approach that may be used to compare investments by considering the investment's mean return (we used the geometric) and the standard deviation of those returns. The standard deviation was used as a measure of risk when making comparisons among investments. In addition, investors must consider the extent to which the acquisition of an investment affects the risk and return of a *portfolio* of assets. This question is very important because of the interaction between returns when investments are *combined* in a portfolio. This interaction may cause the variance of return on a portfolio to be less than the average of the individual investments. When investors add to an existing portfolio it is important to understand how the acquisition of new assets may *impact* the return and risk of the entire portfolio.

Building a portfolio by considering the return and standard deviation of returns for *individual* investments will not always ensure that an optimum portfolio will be obtained. Indeed, any new asset that is being considered as an addition to a portfolio should be judged on the grounds of "efficiency", that is, whether its addition to an existing portfolio will increase expected portfolio returns while maintaining, or lowering, portfolio risk. Alternatively, an investor may also judge whether the portfolio efficiency of an asset will lower portfolio risk while maintaining or increasing, the expected portfolio return.[7]

To illustrate how the interaction between investment returns occurs, we consider the data in Exhibit 20–5. Returns in column 1 are calculated on quarterly *HPR*s for another stock *i*, abbreviated as HPR_i. Returns in column 2 are the quarterly returns computed for stock over the same time period. The statistics presented at the bottom of the exhibit indicate that the quarterly mean return for stock *j* was 3.59 percent and the standard deviation was 9.33 percent. The mean return for stock *i* was 1.09 percent, and the standard deviation of the return was 6.24 percent (calculations not shown). Obviously, risk and returns for these two investments are very different. Stock *j* produced both a higher mean return and higher standard deviation (risk) when compared with the returns from stock *i*. Assuming that an investor was holding a portfolio *composed only* of stock *j* at the beginning of the investment period, the question to answer is, how would the addition of another investment (as represented by real estate stock *i*)

[7]The basis for modern portfolio theory was developed by Harry Markowitz, "Portfolio Selection," *Journal of Finance* 7, no. 1 (March 1952), pp. 77–91.

EXHIBIT 20–5 Computation of the Mean *HPR* and Standard Deviation for a Hypothetical Portfolio Containing Stocks *i* and *j* in Equal Proportions

	Stock i HPR	Stock j HPR	$HPR_p = .5(HPR_i) + .5(HPR_j)$	$(HPR_p - \overline{HPR_p})$	$(HPR_p - \overline{HPR})^2$
Quarter					
1	0.1350	0.1407	0.1379	0.1145	0.0131
2	0.0301	0.0591	0.0446	0.0212	0.0004
3	0.0202	−0.0697	−0.0247	−0.0481	0.0023
4	−0.0013	0.0540	0.0264	0.0030	0.0000
5	0.1044	0.2133	0.1588	0.1354	0.0183
6	0.0048	0.0514	0.0281	0.0047	0.0000
7	−0.0396	0.0662	0.0133	−0.0101	0.0001
8	−0.0961	−0.2263	−0.1612	−0.1846	0.0341
9	0.0921	0.0587	0.0754	0.0520	0.0027
10	0.0279	0.0660	0.0469	0.0235	0.0006
11	0.0123	0.0039	0.0081	−0.0153	0.0002
12	−0.0047	0.0310	0.0132	−0.0102	0.0001
13	0.0242	0.0703	0.0472	0.0238	0.0006
14	0.0591	0.0880	0.0735	0.0501	0.0025
15	0.0360	0.1065	0.0713	0.0478	0.0023
16	−0.0307	0.0205	−0.0051	−0.0285	0.0008
17	−0.0399	−0.0302	−0.0351	−0.0585	0.0034
18	−0.0029	0.0629	0.0300	0.0066	0.0000
19	−0.1438	−0.1378	−0.1408	−0.1642	0.0270
20	0.0310	0.0895	0.0603	0.0369	0.0014
$n = 20$	0.2181	0.7180	0.4681		0.1100

Portfolio$_p$ holding period return $\overline{HPR_p} = 0.4681 \div 20 = 0.0234$

Portfolio variance $= \sigma^2_p = (HPR_p - \overline{HPR_p})^2 \div n = 01100/20 = 0.0055$

Portfolio standard deviation $= \sigma_p = \sqrt{\sigma^2_p} = 0.0742$

affect the quarterly mean *portfolio* return and its standard deviation? Would the investor have been better off adding real estate securities to this portfolio?

Calculating Portfolio Returns

To demonstrate an approach that may be used to answer these questions, we will assume that both stocks *i* and *j* were *weighted equally* in one portfolio at the beginning of the period. We will then compute the mean return and standard deviation for the *combined portfolio* (see Exhibit 20–5). The mean return for the portfolio, $\overline{HPR_p}$, is calculated as:

$$\begin{aligned}\overline{HPR_p} &= W_i(\overline{HPR_i}) + W_j(\overline{HPR_j})\\ &= .5(.0109) + .5(.0359)\\ &= .0055 + .0179\\ &= .0234\end{aligned}$$

where W represents the weights that securities i and j represent as a proportion of the total value of the portfolio (i.e., $W_i + W_j = 1.0$). Based on this calculation, we see that the *portfolio* return would have been 2.34 percent quarterly, which is less than what would have been earned on stock *j* alone. However, we cannot really conclude much from this result until we consider how portfolio *risk* may have been affected when the two investments were combined.

Portfolio Risk

To consider how total portfolio risk would have been affected by the *addition* of stock *i* to an existing portfolio of continuing stock *i* and *j* only, the standard deviation of the *new portfolio* returns is calculated (see Exhibit 20–5). Based on those results, we can see that the portfolio standard deviation is 7.42 percent, which is far less than the standard deviation of stock *j* which was 9.33 percent.

However, it is important to note that unlike the mean *HPR* for the portfolio, the *standard deviation of portfolio returns* for the two indexes is not equal to the simple weighted average of the individual standard deviations of the two indexes; that is, [(.5)(6.24%)] + [(.5)(9.33%)] does *not* equal the standard deviation of the portfolio returns. This is because when the returns of the two assets are combined, a greater than proportionate reduction in the variance in portfolio returns is achieved. In other words, there is *interaction* between the two returns in the sense that the pattern, or direction of movement, in each of the individual *HPR*s is not the same in each period.[8] Indeed, in some quarters, the *HPR*s for EREITs are positive and the *HPR*s for the stocks are negative. Hence, when combined in one portfolio, the returns on the portfolio are less volatile than the individual assets. The nature of this interaction is important to understand when measuring the risk of an investment portfolio because it demonstrates whether a portfolio investor will benefit from diversification.

Covariance and Correlation of Returns; Key Statistical Relationships. One important aspect of individual investment returns to consider is how the return on a prospective new asset will vary with returns on an existing portfolio. Clearly, if the asset is producing returns that move up and down in a pattern that is very *similar* to movements in portfolio returns, the inclusion of that asset in the portfolio will not reduce total variation (*risk*) by very much. This pattern, when considered with the mean of portfolio returns and mean return of the prospective asset, will give us an indication of how efficient the acquisition of an asset will be when combined with another asset or with an existing portfolio. Two statistics provide a numerical measure of the extent to which returns tend to either move together, in opposite directions, or have no relationship to one another. These statistics are the *covariance* and *correlation* between the two return series.

The **covariance** between returns on two assets is an *absolute* measure of the extent to which two data series (*HPR*s) move together over time. It is calculated for our example in Exhibit 20–6. Essentially, the covariance is computed for two investments by first finding the deviation of each investment's *HPR* from its mean ($\overline{HPR}$). These deviations for each security in each period are then multiplied and summed. The summed deviations are divided by the number of observations in each series. The result is the *covariance* or statistic that provides an *absolute* measure of the extent to which returns between two securities move together. In our example, the covariance between *i* and *j* is .47 percent.

Because the covariance was positive, the returns on the two securities tended to move *together*, or in the same direction, during the period over which we made the calculation. Hence, we have *positive covariance* between the two stocks. It is also

---

[8]As shown in Exhibit 20–5, the portfolio standard deviation can be calculated each time weights for stocks change. Another method of computation for the two-security case can be made by simply changing the weights W_E and W_S for stocks *E* and *S* in the following equation: $[(W_E)^2(S_E)^2 + (W_S)^2(S_S)^2 + 2(W_S)(W_E)(S_S)(S_E)_{pSE}]1^{1/2}$ = portfolio standard deviation, where W = weight of security types *E*, *S* (all W_S must total 1), S = standard deviation of security, and p_{SE} is the coefficient of correlation between *S* and *E*. Exhibit 20–6 shows the calculations for the standard deviation for each security as well as the correlation between the securities.

EXHIBIT 20–6 Computation of Covariance for Stocks *i* and *j*

Period Ending	*HPR Stock i*	*HPR Stock j*	$HPR_i - \overline{HPR}_i$	$HPR_j - \overline{HPR}_j$	$(HPR_i - \overline{HPR}_i) \times (HPR_j - \overline{HPR}_j)$	*Stock i* $(HPR_i - \overline{HPR}_i)^2$	*Stock j* $(HPR_j - \overline{HPR}_j)^2$
Quarter							
1	0.1350	0.1407	0.1241	0.1048	0.0130	0.0154	0.0110
2	0.0301	0.0591	0.0192	0.0232	0.0004	0.0004	0.0005
3	0.0202	−0.0697	0.0093	−0.1056	−0.0010	0.0001	0.0111
4	−0.0013	0.0540	−0.0122	0.0181	−0.0002	0.0001	0.0003
5	0.1044	0.2133	0.0935	0.1774	0.0166	0.0087	0.0315
6	0.0048	0.0514	−0.0061	0.0155	−0.0001	0.0000	0.0002
7	−0.0396	0.0662	−0.0505	0.0303	−0.0015	0.0026	0.0009
8	−0.0961	−0.2263	−0.1070	−0.2622	0.0281	0.0115	0.0687
9	0.0921	0.0587	0.0812	0.0228	0.0019	0.0066	0.0005
10	0.0279	0.0660	0.0170	0.0300	0.0005	0.0003	0.0009
11	0.0123	0.0039	0.0014	−0.0320	−0.0000	0.0000	0.0010
12	−0.0047	0.0310	−0.0156	−0.0049	0.0001	0.0002	0.0000
13	0.0242	0.0703	0.0133	0.0344	0.0005	0.0002	0.0012
14	0.0591	0.0880	0.0482	0.0521	0.0025	0.0023	0.0027
15	0.0360	0.1065	0.0251	0.0706	0.0018	0.0006	0.0050
16	−0.0307	0.0205	−0.0416	−0.0154	0.0006	0.0017	0.0002
17	−0.0399	−0.0302	−0.0508	−0.0661	0.0034	0.0026	0.0044
18	−0.0029	0.0629	−0.0138	0.0270	−0.0004	0.0002	0.0007
19	−0.1438	−0.1378	−0.1547	−0.1737	0.0269	0.0239	0.0302
20	0.0310	0.0895	0.0201	0.0536	0.0011	0.0004	0.0029
$n = 20$	0.2181	0.7180			0.0940	0.0779	0.1741

Stock *i* holding period return $\overline{HPRi} = 0.2181 \div 20 = 0.0109$

Stock *i* variance $= \sigma_i^2 = 0.0779 \div 20 = 0.0039$

Stock *i* standard deviation $= \sigma_i = \sqrt{\sigma_i^2} = 0.0624$

Stock *j* holding period return $\overline{HPR}_j = 0.7180 \div 20 = 0.0359$

Stock *j* variance $= \sigma_j^2 = 0.1741 \div 20 = 0.0087$

Stock *j* standard deviation $= \sigma_j = \sqrt{\sigma_j^2} = 0.0933$

$$COV_{ij} = \Sigma[HPR_i - \overline{HPR}_i][HPR_j - \overline{HPR}_j] \div n$$
$$= 0.0940 \div 20$$
$$= 0.0047$$

Correlation between stocks *i* and *j*

$$= [COV_{ij}] \div [\sigma_i\,\sigma_j] = 0.8070$$

possible to have *negative covariance,* indicating that returns tend to move in opposite directions. While the covariance measure is useful, it is somewhat difficult to interpret because it is an *absolute* measure of the relationship between returns. We would expect that very large covariance values may indicate a very strong relationship (either positive or negative) between investment returns. However, the covariance statistic can take on values ranging from $+\infty$ to $-\infty$, and, as a result, it is difficult to know when a covariance value is "large" or "small." Because of this problem, we need a method to gauge the importance of the statistic on a *relative* scale of importance. The coefficient of **correlation** (ρ) is used to obtain this *relative* measure or the extent to which one set of numbers moves in the same or opposite direction with another series. The formula for the correlation statistic ρ is:

$$\rho_{ij} = COV_{ij} \div (\sigma_i \sigma_j)$$

In our example we have:

$$\rho_{ij} = .0047 \div (.0624)(.0933)$$
$$= .8070$$

The correlation statistic may only range between +1 and −1; therefore, it is a much easier way to interpret the extent to which returns are related. For example, as the coefficient of correlation approaches +1, two series are said to move very closely together, or be highly correlated. Hence, given a change in one of the series, there is a high likelihood of a change in the other series in the same direction.[9] Conversely, as the coefficient approaches −1, the series are negatively correlated because they move in exactly opposite directions. Hence, given a change in one series, the other would be expected to move in the opposite direction. If the correlation coefficient is close to zero, the implication is that no relationship exists between the two series. In our example, a correlation coefficient of .8070 indicates a strong positive correlation between stocks i and j over the period considered because the coefficient is equal to .8070, has a positive sign, and is much closer to +1.0 than it is to zero.[10]

What are some other important relationships at this point? It should be clear that if two investments are *highly positively correlated,* the reduction in the variance in portfolio returns (hence, risk) is likely to be smaller than if there were no correlation or negative correlation because, in the latter case, the distribution of two returns would be either unrelated or negatively related, and the interaction between returns would not be reinforced. If returns were negatively correlated, they would be offsetting and the sum of the deviations from the portfolio mean would be smaller after the security is added; hence, the standard deviation of portfolio returns would be lower (i.e., lower risk). Consequently, it should be stressed that anytime the correlation between returns on two assets is less than +1, *some* reduction in risk (standard deviation) may be obtained by combining investments, as opposed to holding one investment (or one portfolio) with higher standard deviation than the prospective investment. However, the potential for risk reduction is much greater as the correlation approaches −1.

Based on the foregoing analysis, it should be clear why the standard deviation of portfolio returns in our example is not equal to a simple, weighted average of the standard deviation of the two individual investment returns. Further, if variation in security returns is a reasonable representation of risk to investors, then it should become apparent that there may be some benefit, in the form of risk reduction, by *diversifying* an investment portfolio to include assets with returns that are negatively correlated, or assets with returns showing little or no correlation. Of course, the other critical dimension that has to be considered is how the *mean return* of the portfolio will be affected when the individual securities are combined. For example, if two securities have the *same* positive mean returns and these returns were perfectly, negatively correlated (e.g., −1), then it may be inferred that an investor could

---

[9]Obviously there would have to be an underlying cause-and-effect relationship between the two series to make an assertion that any past relationship can be used to predict a future relationship.

[10]When the coefficient of correlation has a value greater than .5, the association between two series is considered high. There are also statistical tests of significance that enable us to say with more confidence whether two series are correlated or whether the correlation statistic calculated between the series resulted from an unrepresentative sample taken from the underlying distribution of returns. For a discussion of correlation, normal distribution assumptions, and related statistics, see a standard college textbook on elementary statistics.

earn a positive portfolio return with zero risk if both investments were purchased (the standard deviation of the combined returns would be zero). The possibility that this will ever occur is slight, however, because the likelihood of finding perfectly negatively correlated (−1) securities is small. However, many investments with returns that are negatively correlated, uncorrelated, or less than perfectly positively correlated may be candidates for addition to a portfolio on the grounds of efficiency outlined above. These basic elements of portfolio analysis should make the reader aware of a framework that may be used to consider many questions regarding risk and returns.

Portfolio Weighting: Trading Off Risk and Return

In our hypothetical example, we have seen that adding stock *i* to a portfolio containing stock *j* would have reduced portfolio risk (standard deviation) by a lesser amount (percent) than the reduction in portfolio mean return. This implies that a portfolio containing both stocks (indexes) would not have been more efficient than a portfolio containing only one stock. However, in our computations, we assumed that *both assets were equally weighted.* Could a more optimal portfolio, that is, one containing some other combination of stocks that would have either increased returns relative to an increase in risk or maintained returns while decreasing risk, been attained by *varying the weight (proportion) of the two securities in the portfolio?* To answer this question, we first consider the *sample* of NCREIF and S&P 500 returns from Exhibit 20–4, or those returns that comprised the *period* 1985–2000. The arithmetic quarterly means *HPR* for the S&P 500 index was 4.06 percent with a standard deviation of 7.41 percent, and the *HPR* for NCREIF was 2.32 percent with a standard deviation of 1.76 percent. The correlation between both return series was −.0521 (see Exhibit 20–7).[11] Because the correlation coefficient was less than 1, some reduction in risk would have been possible by combining the two assets.

Second, we want to understand the importance of weighting securities in a portfolio. To determine the optimal *weighting, all combinations* of both assets must be considered. In our example, the weight of each security was changed in increments of 10 percent, and the mean portfolio return and standard deviation were calculated for each weighting. The result is shown in Exhibit 20–8. The diagram shows all values lying between the two extreme cases, that is, the case where the portfolio would be composed entirely of S&P 500 stocks and no NCREIF properties (100 percent in the exhibit) and the case where the portfolio would be composed of 100 percent NCREIF properties and no S&P shares (0 percent in the exhibit). Hence, the curve in the exhibit shows the *trade-off* between return and risk for the portfolio as the two asset classes are combined in varying proportions.

Note that even though the NCREIF Index had a lower mean *HPR* during this period, when compared with the S&P index (see Exhibit 20–4), diversification benefits may be realized by *combining* assets as opposed to holding only S&P 500 or NCREIF properties. This is illustrated in Exhibit 20–8.

In Exhibit 20–8, note that having a portfolio of 100 percent NCREIF has a lower return but greater risk than holding some S&P with NCREIF. This results from the diversification benefits of including both stocks (S&P) and properties (NCREIF) in a portfolio. The portion of the curve with a positive slope (returns increase as risk increases) is known as the *efficient frontier*. It represents the most

[11]The correlations are calculated over a longer time period to capture the long-run correlation between the different assets.

EXHIBIT 20–7 Correlation Matrix for Selected Assets: Quarterly Returns, 1978–2000

	1978–2000					
	CPI	*Bonds*	*S&P 500*	*T-Bills*	*NCREIF*	*REITs*
CPI	1					
Bonds	−0.2440	1				
S&P 500	−0.1349	0.2766	1			
T-Bills	0.5868	0.1284	−0.0737	1		
NCREIF	0.3317	−0.1469	−0.0521	0.4700	1	
REITs	−0.0199	0.4862	0.5986	0.0044	−0.0642	1

EXHIBIT 20–8 Portfolio Returns of NCREIF and S&P 500 Stocks, 1978–2000

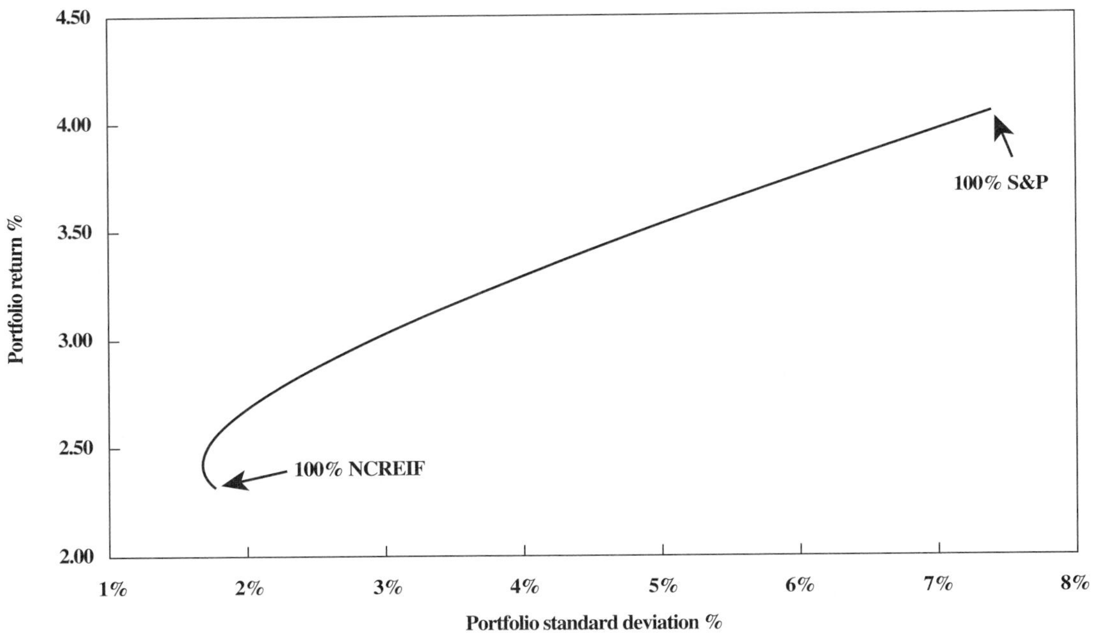

efficient combination of securities that provides investors with maximum portfolio returns as portfolio risk increases. Returns below the efficient frontier (or in the interior of the ellipse) are *inferior* because there is always a better combination of securities that will increase returns for a given level of risk. Investors will choose the combination of securities along the efficient frontier in accordance with their willingness to take risk. Investors who are risk-averse would tend to hold a mix with more properties (NCREIF) in this example. Less risk-averse investors would tend to weigh stocks (S&P) more heavily in their portfolio. Holding all stocks (100 percent S&P) has the greatest expected return but also the greatest risk.

Real Estate Returns, Other Investments, and the Potential for Portfolio Diversification

From the preceding analysis, it should be clear that there are many different assets that have the potential to be combined efficiently in a portfolio that will provide an optimal risk-return relationship for investors. Clearly, our example consisting of only NCREIFs and S&P 500 assets shows this potential. However, many other assets can be considered by investors when selecting assets. One of the key relationships that indicates the potential for combining assets in a portfolio is the correlation between asset returns. Exhibit 20–7 is a *correlation matrix,* or table, that contains the coefficient of correlation for returns on all securities listed in Exhibit 20–4. The purpose of calculating these coefficients is to consider how various *investment vehicles* might be combined efficiently with various other assets when building a portfolio.

We can gain some insight into the question of whether portfolios containing certain securities would be more efficient if *real estate investment vehicles* were added. We will focus on this more narrow question, because to consider the question of what *the* optimum portfolio *should* contain would have to include an examination of the risk and returns for the global, or worldwide set of securities and assets that are available to investors. Such a portfolio might contain bonds, stock, real estate, gold, jewelry, coins, stamps, and virtually any asset that can be owned by investors. Based on mean standard deviation of returns and covariance between returns, investors would hold portfolios containing the optimum combination of available investments. An efficient frontier, such as the one shown in our two-investment case in Exhibit 20–8, would also exist for this larger, diversified "market portfolio." If all investors made decisions based on whether or not the ratio of risk to return for the total portfolio would be improved, all investor portfolios would tend to be diversified and efficient. Returns on any additional investments would be evaluated on the basis of any incremental increases or decreases in total portfolio risk, and the risk premium paid by investors for these securities would reflect that incremental risk. In short, risk premiums for investments would be determined on the basis of the expected addition or reduction in portfolio risk and all investments would be priced in accordance with that relationship.[12]

In this section, we consider the question of portfolio performance, diversification, and real estate. Portfolio managers have seriously considered real estate as an investment class for only about 20 years. Only in recent years has equity ownership in real estate become widely available in a "securitized" form such as a REIT share or in ownership "units" in open- and closed-ended commingled investment funds. Also regulatory restrictions governing pension funds have been relaxed to include real estate as an acceptable investment. However, many institutions, which heretofore considered only government securities, corporate bonds, and common stocks have shown increasing interest in real estate.

We now consider the question of whether real estate investments are likely to provide **diversification benefits** to investors with portfolios consisting of some government securities, stocks, and bonds. In other words, we begin with some assumptions about the nature of existing investment portfolios. We then consider whether these portfolios could have benefited from diversifying by acquiring real estate investments over the period 1985–2000.

---

[12]For additional information regarding capital market theory and efficient markets, see Z. Bodie, A. Kane, and A. Marcus, *Investments,* 2nd ed. (Homewood, IL., Richard D. Irwin, 1994).

Portfolio Diversification: EREITs and Other Investments

Looking again at Exhibit 20–7, we can see what the historical (or ex-post) correlation in quarterly returns was for each investment relative to all others for the period 1978–2000. Focusing our attention on equity investments in real estate, note, for example, that returns on EREITs tended to be positively correlated with common stocks (.5986) and corporate bonds (.4862) and a correlation of almost zero (.0044) with T-bills. This relationship suggests that because EREITs have less than perfect correlation with the S&P 500 and corporate bonds and the correlation coefficient between both EREITs and T-bills is very low, there is a good chance that if this real estate investment was combined in a portfolio containing common stock, bonds, and T-bills, diversification benefits could be achieved. Furthermore, NCREIF has a negative coefficient with the S&P 500 (−.0521) and bonds (−.1469) although it has a positive correlation with T-bills (.47). This suggests that adding direct investment in properties may provide more diversification benefits than just adding REITs.

To illustrate the diversification benefits of adding equity real estate to a portfolio of stocks and bonds, we will use the mean (arithmetic) returns from Exhibit 20–4 and the correlations from Exhibit 20–7.[13] Exhibit 20–9 shows two efficient frontiers. The lower frontier consists of only stocks (S&P 500) and bonds. The upper frontier includes stocks, bonds and private real estate investments (NCREIF Index). Note that the frontier that includes real estate has higher returns at each level of risk (standard deviation). The only exception is the highest risk/highest return portfolio which in both cases consists entirely of stocks. Including private real estate with stocks and bonds also provides a wider spectrum of risk-return combinations at the lower end of the frontier (i.e., where there is less return but lower levels of risk).

It should be noted that these results are based on historical returns over a specific time period and may not be indicative of future performance. Investors make investment decisions based on future or expected risks and returns. This example has used ex-post, or past returns to illustrate concepts. There is no assurance that these results will be repeated in the future. In practice, investors often use historic correlations as was done in this example unless there is evidence that there has been a significant change in the correlation between different assets. Similarly, historic standard deviations for securities are used unless there is a reason to believe that the underlying risk of the asset has changed. But expected future rather than historic returns are used for each asset. Historic returns are only used as one indication of what might be realistic to expect in the future.

We also used the NCREIF Index as an indication of the return and risk (standard deviation) for private real estate. The NCREIF index has a very low mean return and standard deviation of returns. As noted in the beginning of this chapter, this index may not fully capture the true variability in returns for private real estate because it is based on appraised values rather than transaction prices. Some have argued that the use of appraised values may reduce or "smooth" the variation in returns. This does not mean that the estimates of value are erroneous. Rather, the appraisal process is such that sudden shifts in the market as reflected in a few transactions are not fully captured in appraised values until the change in market conditions can be sufficiently confirmed by additional market evidence. Thus indices based on appraised values may not fully capture quarterly changes in property values in an index like the NCREIF Index.

[13]In practice we might use expected future returns rather than historical return for this type of analysis. We use historic returns to illustrate the diversification benefits based on what was actually achieved for each asset.

EXHIBIT 20–9 Efficient Frontiers

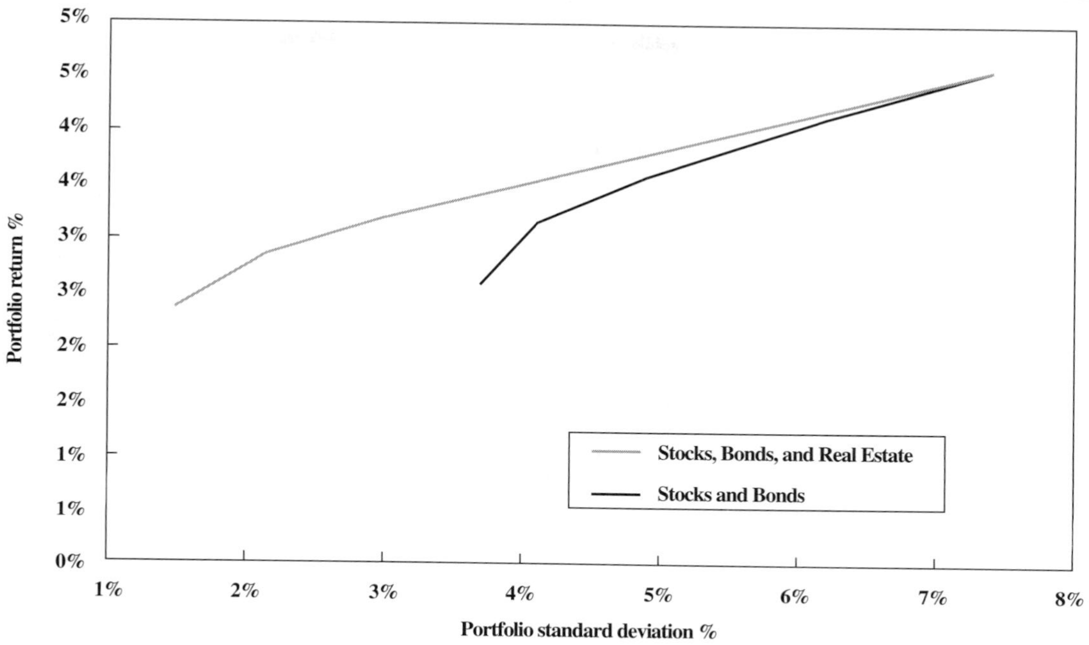

Public versus Private Real Estate Investments

We saw previously that the performance of private real estate as reflected in the NCREIF Index and the performance of REITs as reflected in the NAREIT Index were quite different in terms of historic returns, standard deviations, and correlations with other assets. For example, the standard deviation of the NAREIT Index is higher than that of the NCREIF Index. One explanation for this might be that the NCREIF Index does not capture all of the variability of returns because it is based on appraised values, as discussed earlier. An alternative explanation, however, is that when real estate is owned by publicly traded REITs, it takes on more of the risk of public markets in general. As we saw in Exhibit 20–7, REITs have a much higher correlation with the S&P 500 than NCREIF. Also, we saw that the NCREIF Index has a relatively high correlation with the CPI indicating that it may be an inflation hedge whereas the NAREIT Index has a slightly negative correlation with the CPI.

There is likely to be truth in both arguments—that appraisals reduce the variance of the true returns in the NCREIF Index but publicly traded REITs take on additional variance because they trade in more active markets that are influenced more by short-term flows of capital into and out of the stock market. To see what the difference in variability is between NCREIF and NAREIT, we have plotted the historic returns for each in Exhibit 20–10. Note that in order to better compare the returns over time, we have used a different scale for the NCREIF returns (−6% to +6%) than for NAREIT returns (−20% to +25%). The NAREIT Index clearly has more volatility in its returns than the NCREIF Index and the two indices perform quite differently during many time periods.

Although some people argue about which index is a better indication of the performance of equity real estate, it is quite possible that the conclusion should be that

Exhibit 20–10 NCREIF versus NAREIT (REITs) Quarterly Returns, 1985–2000

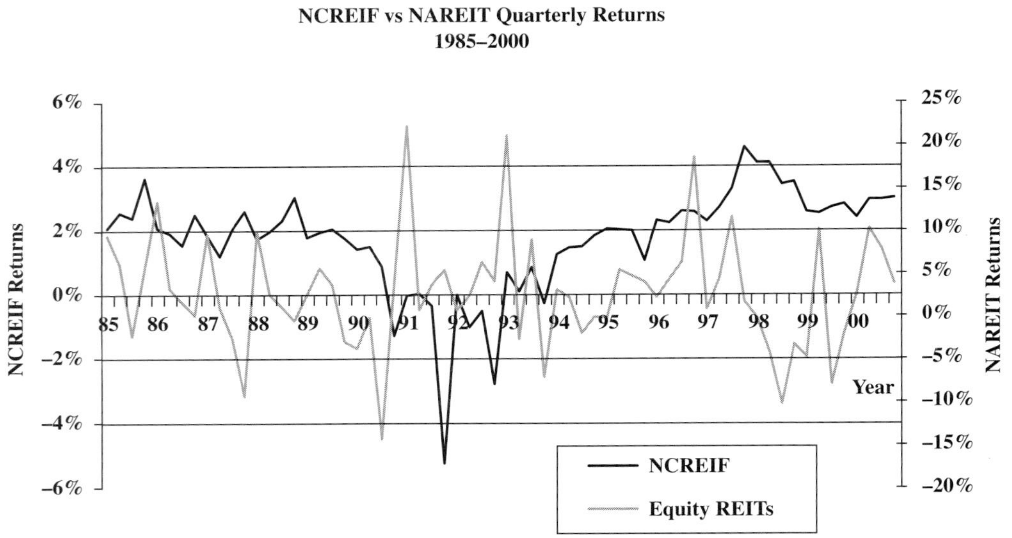

both private real estate investments (represented by the NCREIF Index) and public real estate investments (represented by the NAREIT Index) could play a role in a portfolio. Both provide diversification benefits to a pure stock and bond portfolio, and there are advantages and disadvantages of each as an investment alternative. For example, REITs are more liquid than private real estate but the investor does not have control over decisions as to when to sell individual properties as he or she would by owning properties instead of shares of stock. The purpose of this chapter is not to suggest which type of investment is better for a particular investor, but rather to illustrate what tools an investor can use to evaluate the role of either one or both ways of including equity real estate in a portfolio.

Real Estate Performance and Inflation

One final comparison of interest to portfolio managers is the relationship between real estate performance and *inflation*. More specifically, did real estate returns exceed the rate of inflation? To provide some insight into this question, we recall our earlier comparisons between the EREIT and NCREIF indexes and the CPI. In all cases, the real estate indexes exceeded the rate of growth in the CPI. This implies that at least for the period 1985–2000, real estate investments, as represented by the data used in Exhibit 20–4, exceeded the rate of inflation and produced real investment returns. Another question of importance is whether real estate returns are *correlated* with inflation. Using the correlation matrix in Exhibit 20–7, it would appear that based on the NCREIF Index and the CPI, it is. However, the same comparison with EREITs indicates that it is not. In this context it is important to realize that a *positive* correlation with inflation is desirable because it indicates that the asset is an inflation hedge. That is, if inflation increases then returns also increase which preserves the real rate of return.

Conclusion

This chapter has introduced the measurement of investment performance and the basic elements of portfolio theory. We have also dealt with the question of whether real estate investments tend to provide diversification benefits to portfolios that have traditionally consisted of government securities, common stocks, and corporate bonds.

We have stressed that the nature of real estate investment return data is very limited and may not be representative of a broad measure of real estate returns. Further, some of the data are based on a group of properties owned by investment advisors. In this case, an index is calculated on reported net operating income and appraised property values with very few actual transaction prices.

Results from the portfolio simulations conducted and reported in the last part of the chapter indicate that there appeared to be significant gains available from portfolio diversification into real estate during the period 1985–2000 based on these limited data sets. In all simulations, real estate increased portfolio efficiency. Of course, these results are based on historical data from a limited sample of real estate investments and may not be indicative of future results or apply generally to all real estate investments.

Key Terms

arithmetic mean returns 593
coefficient of variation 595
correlation 599
covariance 598
diversification benefits 603
geometric mean return 592
holding period return (*HPR*) 591
NAREIT Index 588
NCREIF Index 590

Questions

1. What are some of the difficulties in obtaining data to measure real estate investment performance?
2. What are the distinguishing characteristics between REIT data and the NCREIF Property Index?
3. What is the difference between arithmetic and geometric mean returns?
4. What statistical concept do many portfolio managers use to represent risk when considering investment performance?
5. When NCREIF returns and REIT returns are compared, NCREIF returns exhibit a much lower pattern of variation. Why might this be the case?
6. Mean returns for portfolios are calculated by taking the weighted average of the mean returns for each investment in the portfolio. Why won't this approach work to calculate the standard deviation of portfolio returns?
7. What is the difference between covariance and correlation? Why are these concepts so important in portfolio analysis?
8. Results reported in the chapter showed that by including either REITs or the NCREIF Index in a portfolio containing S&P 500 securities, corporate bonds, and T-bills, diversification benefits resulted. Why was this true? Did those benefits come about for the same reason for each category of real estate investment?
9. Results presented in the chapter are based on historical data. Of what use are these results to a portfolio manager who may be making an investment decision today? Elaborate.

Problem

1. As an investment advisor for MREAF (Momentum Real Estate Advisory Fund), you are about to make a presentation to the portfolio manager of the ET&T pension fund. You would like to show what would have happened had ET&T made an investment in MREAF during the last 13 quarters. The ET&T manager has provided you with historical data on the performance of its portfolio, which is made up entirely of common stock. Historical data for the ET&T portfolio and the MREAF fund are as follows:

	ET&T Common Stock Fund		MREAF Real Estate Fund	
Period Ending	*Unit Value*	*Quarterly Dividend*	*Unit Value*	*Quarterly Dividend*
Quarter				
1	$ 701.00	$ 8.28	$ 70.00	$2.17
2	752.50	8.11	80.05	2.14
3	850.52	10.30	90.80	2.01
4	953.75	9.81	100.50	2.01
5	1,047.57	12.05	99.14	1.87
6	1,221.70	14.17	95.50	1.81
7	1,443.90	17.18	93.77	1.79
8	1,263.31	14.91	80.31	1.54
9	1,258.56	13.84	77.34	1.49
10	1,526.72	18.32	76.53	1.44
11	1,616.81	19.73	78.42	1.51
12	1,624.08	19.98	79.01	1.53
13	1,560.25	18.88	81.75	1.55

a. Calculate the quarterly *HPR* for each investment.

b. Calculate the arithmetic mean *HPR*, the standard deviation of the *HPR*s, and the geometric mean for each fund. Which fund contained more risk per unit of return?

c. Was there any correlation between returns on the ET&T fund and MREAF?

d. Would a portfolio that contained equal amounts of ET&T securities and MREAF have provided any investment diversification? Why?

e. (Optional) Assume each investment could have been combined in a portfolio with weights ranging from 0 percent to 100 percent. What pattern of risk and return would result if each investment was added (deleted) in increments of 10 percent (remember that the sum of the two proportions must always sum to 100 percent)? What combination of securities would have comprised the "efficient frontier" (if any)?

f. If the manager of ET&T is considering making an investment in MREAF, of what use is this analysis?

APPENDIX

A

ANNUAL COMPOUND INTEREST TABLES

ANNUAL COMPOUND INTEREST TABLES

6.00% ANNUAL INTEREST RATE

YEARS	1 AMOUNT OF $1 AT COMPOUND INTEREST	2 ACCUMULATION OF $1 PER PERIOD	3 SINKING FUND FACTOR	4 PRESENT VALUE REVERSION OF $1	5 PRESENT VALUE ORD. ANNUITY $1 PER PERIOD	6 INSTALLMENT TO AMORTIZE $1	YEARS
1	1.060000	1.000000	1.000000	0.943396	0.943396	1.060000	1
2	1.123600	2.060000	0.485437	0.889996	1.833393	0.545437	2
3	1.191016	3.183600	0.314110	0.839619	2.673012	0.374110	3
4	1.262477	4.374616	0.228591	0.792094	3.465106	0.288591	4
5	1.338226	5.637093	0.177396	0.747258	4.212364	0.237396	5
6	1.418519	6.975319	0.143363	0.704961	4.917324	0.203363	6
7	1.503630	8.393838	0.119135	0.665057	5.582381	0.179135	7
8	1.593848	9.897468	0.101036	0.627412	6.209794	0.161036	8
9	1.689479	11.491316	0.087022	0.591898	6.801692	0.147022	9
10	1.790848	13.180795	0.075868	0.558395	7.360087	0.135868	10
11	1.898299	14.971643	0.066793	0.526788	7.886875	0.126793	11
12	2.012196	16.869941	0.059277	0.496969	8.383844	0.119277	12
13	2.132928	18.882138	0.052960	0.468839	8.852683	0.112960	13
14	2.260904	21.015066	0.047585	0.442301	9.294984	0.107585	14
15	2.396558	23.275970	0.042963	0.417265	9.712249	0.102963	15
16	2.540352	25.672528	0.038952	0.393646	10.105895	0.098952	16
17	2.692773	28.212880	0.035445	0.371364	10.477260	0.095445	17
18	2.854339	30.905653	0.032357	0.350344	10.827603	0.092357	18
19	3.025600	33.759992	0.029621	0.330513	11.158116	0.089621	19
20	3.207135	36.785591	0.027185	0.311805	11.469921	0.087185	20
21	3.399564	39.992727	0.025005	0.294155	11.764077	0.085005	21
22	3.603537	43.392290	0.023046	0.277505	12.041582	0.083046	22
23	3.819750	46.995828	0.021278	0.261797	12.303379	0.081278	23
24	4.048935	50.815577	0.019679	0.246979	12.550358	0.079679	24
25	4.291871	54.864512	0.018227	0.232999	12.783356	0.078227	25
26	4.549383	59.156383	0.016904	0.219810	13.003166	0.076904	26
27	4.822346	63.705766	0.015697	0.207368	13.210534	0.075697	27
28	5.111687	68.528112	0.014593	0.195630	13.406164	0.074593	28
29	5.418388	73.639798	0.013580	0.184557	13.590721	0.073580	29
30	5.743491	79.058186	0.012649	0.174110	13.764831	0.072649	30
31	6.088101	84.801677	0.011792	0.164255	13.929086	0.071792	31
32	6.453387	90.889778	0.011002	0.154957	14.084043	0.071002	32
33	6.840590	97.343165	0.010273	0.146186	14.230230	0.070273	33
34	7.251025	104.183755	0.009598	0.137912	14.368141	0.069598	34
35	7.686087	111.434780	0.008974	0.130105	14.498246	0.068974	35
36	8.147252	119.120867	0.008395	0.122741	14.620987	0.068395	36
37	8.636087	127.268119	0.007857	0.115793	14.736780	0.067857	37
38	9.154252	135.904206	0.007358	0.109239	14.846019	0.067358	38
39	9.703507	145.058458	0.006894	0.103056	14.949075	0.066894	39
40	10.285718	154.761966	0.006462	0.097222	15.046297	0.066462	40
41	10.902861	165.047684	0.006059	0.091719	15.138016	0.066059	41
42	11.557033	175.950545	0.005683	0.086527	15.224543	0.065683	42
43	12.250455	187.507577	0.005333	0.081630	15.306173	0.065333	43
44	12.985482	199.758032	0.005006	0.077009	15.383182	0.065006	44
45	13.764611	212.743514	0.004700	0.072650	15.455832	0.064700	45
46	14.590487	226.508125	0.004415	0.068538	15.524370	0.064415	46
47	15.465917	241.098612	0.004148	0.064658	15.589028	0.064148	47
48	16.393872	256.564529	0.003898	0.060998	15.650027	0.063898	48
49	17.377504	272.958401	0.003664	0.057546	15.707572	0.063664	49
50	18.420154	290.335905	0.003444	0.054288	15.761861	0.063444	50

ANNUAL COMPOUND INTEREST TABLES

7.00% ANNUAL INTEREST RATE

YEARS	1 AMOUNT OF $1 AT COMPOUND INTEREST	2 ACCUMULATION OF $1 PER PERIOD	3 SINKING FUND FACTOR	4 PRESENT VALUE REVERSION OF $1	5 PRESENT VALUE ORD. ANNUITY $1 PER PERIOD	6 INSTALLMENT TO AMORTIZE $1	YEARS
1	1.070000	1.000000	1.000000	0.934579	0.934579	1.070000	1
2	1.144900	2.070000	0.483092	0.873439	1.808018	0.553092	2
3	1.225043	3.214900	0.311052	0.816298	2.624316	0.381052	3
4	1.310796	4.439943	0.225228	0.762895	3.387211	0.295228	4
5	1.402552	5.750739	0.173891	0.712986	4.100197	0.243891	5
6	1.500730	7.153291	0.139796	0.666342	4.766540	0.209796	6
7	1.605781	8.654021	0.115553	0.622750	5.389289	0.185553	7
8	1.718186	10.259803	0.097468	0.582009	5.971299	0.167468	8
9	1.838459	11.977989	0.083486	0.543934	6.515232	0.153486	9
10	1.967151	13.816448	0.072378	0.508349	7.023582	0.142378	10
11	2.104852	15.783599	0.063357	0.475093	7.498674	0.133357	11
12	2.252192	17.888451	0.055902	0.444012	7.942686	0.125902	12
13	2.409845	20.140643	0.049651	0.414964	8.357651	0.119651	13
14	2.578534	22.550488	0.044345	0.387817	8.745468	0.114345	14
15	2.759032	25.129022	0.039795	0.362446	9.107914	0.109795	15
16	2.952164	27.888054	0.035858	0.338735	9.446649	0.105858	16
17	3.158815	30.840217	0.032425	0.316574	9.763223	0.102425	17
18	3.379932	33.999033	0.029413	0.295864	10.059087	0.099413	18
19	3.616528	37.378965	0.026753	0.276508	10.335595	0.096753	19
20	3.869684	40.995492	0.024393	0.258419	10.594014	0.094393	20
21	4.140562	44.865177	0.022289	0.241513	10.835527	0.092289	21
22	4.430402	49.005739	0.020406	0.225713	11.061240	0.090406	22
23	4.740530	53.436141	0.018714	0.210947	11.272187	0.088714	23
24	5.072367	58.176671	0.017189	0.197147	11.469334	0.087189	24
25	5.427433	63.249038	0.015811	0.184249	11.653583	0.085811	25
26	5.807353	68.676470	0.014561	0.172195	11.825779	0.084561	26
27	6.213868	74.483823	0.013426	0.160930	11.986709	0.083426	27
28	6.648838	80.697691	0.012392	0.150402	12.137111	0.082392	28
29	7.114257	87.346529	0.011449	0.140563	12.277674	0.081449	29
30	7.612255	94.460786	0.010586	0.131367	12.409041	0.080586	30
31	8.145113	102.073041	0.009797	0.122773	12.531814	0.079797	31
32	8.715271	110.218154	0.009073	0.114741	12.646555	0.079073	32
33	9.325340	118.933425	0.008408	0.107235	12.753790	0.078408	33
34	9.978114	128.258765	0.007797	0.100219	12.854009	0.077797	34
35	10.676581	138.236878	0.007234	0.093663	12.947672	0.077234	35
36	11.423942	148.913460	0.006715	0.087535	13.035208	0.076715	36
37	12.223618	160.337402	0.006237	0.081809	13.117017	0.076237	37
38	13.079271	172.561020	0.005795	0.076457	13.193473	0.075795	38
39	13.994820	185.640292	0.005387	0.071455	13.264928	0.075387	39
40	14.974458	199.635112	0.005009	0.066780	13.331709	0.075009	40
41	16.022670	214.609570	0.004660	0.062412	13.394120	0.074660	41
42	17.144257	230.632240	0.004336	0.058329	13.452449	0.074336	42
43	18.344355	247.776496	0.004036	0.054513	13.506962	0.074036	43
44	19.628460	266.120851	0.003758	0.050946	13.557908	0.073758	44
45	21.002452	285.749311	0.003500	0.047613	13.605522	0.073500	45
46	22.472623	306.751763	0.003260	0.044499	13.650020	0.073260	46
47	24.045707	329.224386	0.003037	0.041587	13.691608	0.073037	47
48	25.728907	353.270093	0.002831	0.038867	13.730474	0.072831	48
49	27.529930	378.999000	0.002639	0.036324	13.766799	0.072639	49
50	29.457025	406.528929	0.002460	0.033948	13.800746	0.072460	50

ANNUAL COMPOUND INTEREST TABLES

8.00% ANNUAL INTEREST RATE

YEARS	1 AMOUNT OF $1 AT COMPOUND INTEREST	2 ACCUMULATION OF $1 PER PERIOD	3 SINKING FUND FACTOR	4 PRESENT VALUE REVERSION OF $1	5 PRESENT VALUE ORD. ANNUITY $1 PER PERIOD	6 INSTALLMENT TO AMORTIZE $1	YEARS
1	1.080000	1.000000	1.000000	0.925926	0.925926	1.080000	1
2	1.166400	2.080000	0.480769	0.857339	1.783265	0.560769	2
3	1.259712	3.246400	0.308034	0.793832	2.577097	0.388034	3
4	1.360489	4.506112	0.221921	0.735030	3.312127	0.301921	4
5	1.469328	5.866601	0.170456	0.680583	3.992710	0.250456	5
6	1.586874	7.335929	0.136315	0.630170	4.622880	0.216315	6
7	1.713824	8.922803	0.112072	0.583490	5.206370	0.192072	7
8	1.850930	10.636628	0.094015	0.540269	5.746639	0.174015	8
9	1.999005	12.487558	0.080080	0.500249	6.246888	0.160080	9
10	2.158925	14.486562	0.069029	0.463193	6.710081	0.149029	10
11	2.331639	16.645487	0.060076	0.428883	7.138964	0.140076	11
12	2.518170	18.977126	0.052695	0.397114	7.536078	0.132695	12
13	2.719624	21.495297	0.046522	0.367698	7.903776	0.126522	13
14	2.937194	24.214920	0.041297	0.340461	8.244237	0.121297	14
15	3.172169	27.152114	0.036830	0.315242	8.559479	0.116830	15
16	3.425943	30.324283	0.032977	0.291890	8.851369	0.112977	16
17	3.700018	33.750226	0.029629	0.270269	9.121638	0.109629	17
18	3.996019	37.450244	0.026702	0.250249	9.371887	0.106702	18
19	4.315701	41.446263	0.024128	0.231712	9.603599	0.104128	19
20	4.660957	45.761964	0.021852	0.214548	9.818147	0.101852	20
21	5.033834	50.422921	0.019832	0.198656	10.016803	0.099832	21
22	5.436540	55.456755	0.018032	0.183941	10.200744	0.098032	22
23	5.871464	60.893296	0.016422	0.170315	10.371059	0.096422	23
24	6.341181	66.764759	0.014978	0.157699	10.528758	0.094978	24
25	6.848475	73.105940	0.013679	0.146018	10.674776	0.093679	25
26	7.396353	79.954415	0.012507	0.135202	10.809978	0.092507	26
27	7.988061	87.350768	0.011448	0.125187	10.935165	0.091448	27
28	8.627106	95.338830	0.010489	0.115914	11.051078	0.090489	28
29	9.317275	103.965936	0.009619	0.107328	11.158406	0.089619	29
30	10.062657	113.283211	0.008827	0.099377	11.257783	0.088827	30
31	10.867669	123.345868	0.008107	0.092016	11.349799	0.088107	31
32	11.737083	134.213537	0.007451	0.085200	11.434999	0.087451	32
33	12.676050	145.950620	0.006852	0.078889	11.513888	0.086852	33
34	13.690134	158.626670	0.006304	0.073045	11.586934	0.086304	34
35	14.785344	172.316804	0.005803	0.067635	11.654568	0.085803	35
36	15.968172	187.102148	0.005345	0.062625	11.717193	0.085345	36
37	17.245626	203.070320	0.004924	0.057986	11.775179	0.084924	37
38	18.625276	220.315945	0.004539	0.053690	11.828869	0.084539	38
39	20.115298	238.941221	0.004185	0.049713	11.878582	0.084185	39
40	21.724521	259.056519	0.003860	0.046031	11.924613	0.083860	40
41	23.462483	280.781040	0.003561	0.042621	11.967235	0.083561	41
42	25.339482	304.243523	0.003287	0.039464	12.006699	0.083287	42
43	27.366640	329.583005	0.003034	0.036541	12.043240	0.083034	43
44	29.555972	356.949646	0.002802	0.033834	12.077074	0.082802	44
45	31.920449	386.505617	0.002587	0.031328	12.108402	0.082587	45
46	34.474085	418.426067	0.002390	0.029007	12.137409	0.082390	46
47	37.232012	452.900152	0.002208	0.026859	12.164267	0.082208	47
48	40.210573	490.132164	0.002040	0.024869	12.189136	0.082040	48
49	43.427419	530.342737	0.001886	0.023027	12.212163	0.081886	49
50	46.901613	573.770156	0.001743	0.021321	12.233485	0.081743	50

ANNUAL COMPOUND INTEREST TABLES

9.00% ANNUAL INTEREST RATE

YEARS	1 AMOUNT OF $1 AT COMPOUND INTEREST	2 ACCUMULATION OF $1 PER PERIOD	3 SINKING FUND FACTOR	4 PRESENT VALUE REVERSION OF $1	5 PRESENT VALUE ORD. ANNUITY $1 PER PERIOD	6 INSTALLMENT TO AMORTIZE $1	YEARS
1	1.090000	1.000000	1.000000	0.917431	0.917431	1.090000	1
2	1.188100	2.090000	0.478469	0.841680	1.759111	0.568469	2
3	1.295029	3.278100	0.305055	0.772183	2.531295	0.395055	3
4	1.411582	4.573129	0.218669	0.708425	3.239720	0.308669	4
5	1.538624	5.984711	0.167092	0.649931	3.889651	0.257092	5
6	1.677100	7.523335	0.132920	0.596267	4.485919	0.222920	6
7	1.828039	9.200435	0.108691	0.547034	5.032953	0.198691	7
8	1.992563	11.028474	0.090674	0.501866	5.534819	0.180674	8
9	2.171893	13.021036	0.076799	0.460428	5.995247	0.166799	9
10	2.367364	15.192930	0.065820	0.422411	6.417658	0.155820	10
11	2.580426	17.560293	0.056947	0.387533	6.805191	0.146947	11
12	2.812665	20.140720	0.049651	0.355535	7.160725	0.139651	12
13	3.065805	22.953385	0.043567	0.326179	7.486904	0.133567	13
14	3.341727	26.019189	0.038433	0.299246	7.786150	0.128433	14
15	3.642482	29.360916	0.034059	0.274538	8.060688	0.124059	15
16	3.970306	33.003399	0.030300	0.251870	8.312558	0.120300	16
17	4.327633	36.973705	0.027046	0.231073	8.543631	0.117046	17
18	4.717120	41.301338	0.024212	0.211994	8.755625	0.114212	18
19	5.141661	46.018458	0.021730	0.194490	8.950115	0.111730	19
20	5.604411	51.160120	0.019546	0.178431	9.128546	0.109546	20
21	6.108808	56.764530	0.017617	0.163698	9.292244	0.107617	21
22	6.658600	62.873338	0.015905	0.150182	9.442425	0.105905	22
23	7.257874	69.531939	0.014382	0.137781	9.580207	0.104382	23
24	7.911083	76.789813	0.013023	0.126405	9.706612	0.103023	24
25	8.623081	84.700896	0.011806	0.115968	9.822580	0.101806	25
26	9.399158	93.323977	0.010715	0.106393	9.928972	0.100715	26
27	10.245082	102.723135	0.009735	0.097608	10.026580	0.099735	27
28	11.167140	112.968217	0.008852	0.089548	10.116128	0.098852	28
29	12.172182	124.135356	0.008056	0.082155	10.198283	0.098056	29
30	13.267678	136.307539	0.007336	0.075371	10.273654	0.097336	30
31	14.461770	149.575217	0.006686	0.069148	10.342802	0.096686	31
32	15.763329	164.036987	0.006096	0.063438	10.406240	0.096096	32
33	17.182028	179.800315	0.005562	0.058200	10.464441	0.095562	33
34	18.728411	196.982344	0.005077	0.053395	10.517835	0.095077	34
35	20.413968	215.710755	0.004636	0.048986	10.566821	0.094636	35
36	22.251225	236.124723	0.004235	0.044941	10.611763	0.094235	36
37	24.253835	258.375948	0.003870	0.041231	10.652993	0.093870	37
38	26.436680	282.629783	0.003538	0.037826	10.690820	0.093538	38
39	28.815982	309.066463	0.003236	0.034703	10.725523	0.093236	39
40	31.409420	337.882445	0.002960	0.031838	10.757360	0.092960	40
41	34.236268	369.291865	0.002708	0.029209	10.786569	0.092708	41
42	37.317532	403.528133	0.002478	0.026797	10.813366	0.092478	42
43	40.676110	440.845665	0.002268	0.024584	10.837950	0.092268	43
44	44.336960	481.521775	0.002077	0.022555	10.860505	0.092077	44
45	48.327286	525.858734	0.001902	0.020692	10.881197	0.091902	45
46	52.676742	574.186021	0.001742	0.018984	10.900181	0.091742	46
47	57.417649	626.862762	0.001595	0.017416	10.917597	0.091595	47
48	62.585237	684.280411	0.001461	0.015978	10.933575	0.091461	48
49	68.217908	746.865648	0.001339	0.014659	10.948234	0.091339	49
50	74.357520	815.083556	0.001227	0.013449	10.961683	0.091227	50

ANNUAL COMPOUND INTEREST TABLES

10.00% ANNUAL INTEREST RATE

YEARS	1 AMOUNT OF $1 AT COMPOUND INTEREST	2 ACCUMULATION OF $1 PER PERIOD	3 SINKING FUND FACTOR	4 PRESENT VALUE REVERSION OF $1	5 PRESENT VALUE ORD. ANNUITY $1 PER PERIOD	6 INSTALLMENT TO AMORTIZE $1	YEARS
1	1.100000	1.000000	1.000000	0.909091	0.909091	1.100000	1
2	1.210000	2.100000	0.476190	0.826446	1.735537	0.576190	2
3	1.331000	3.310000	0.302115	0.751315	2.486852	0.402115	3
4	1.464100	4.641000	0.215471	0.683013	3.169865	0.315471	4
5	1.610510	6.105100	0.163797	0.620921	3.790787	0.263797	5
6	1.771561	7.715610	0.129607	0.564474	4.355261	0.229607	6
7	1.948717	9.487171	0.105405	0.513158	4.868419	0.205405	7
8	2.143589	11.435888	0.087444	0.466507	5.334926	0.187444	8
9	2.357948	13.579477	0.073641	0.424098	5.759024	0.173641	9
10	2.593742	15.937425	0.062745	0.385543	6.144567	0.162745	10
11	2.853117	18.531167	0.053963	0.350494	6.495061	0.153963	11
12	3.138428	21.384284	0.046763	0.318631	6.813692	0.146763	12
13	3.452271	24.522712	0.040779	0.289664	7.103356	0.140779	13
14	3.797498	27.974983	0.035746	0.263331	7.366687	0.135746	14
15	4.177248	31.772482	0.031474	0.239392	7.606080	0.131474	15
16	4.594973	35.949730	0.027817	0.217629	7.823709	0.127817	16
17	5.054470	40.544703	0.024664	0.197845	8.021553	0.124664	17
18	5.559917	45.599173	0.021930	0.179859	8.201412	0.121930	18
19	6.115909	51.159090	0.019547	0.163508	8.364920	0.119547	19
20	6.727500	57.274999	0.017460	0.148644	8.513564	0.117460	20
21	7.400250	64.002499	0.015624	0.135131	8.648694	0.115624	21
22	8.140275	71.402749	0.014005	0.122846	8.771540	0.114005	22
23	8.954302	79.543024	0.012572	0.111678	8.883218	0.112572	23
24	9.849733	88.497327	0.011300	0.101526	8.984744	0.111300	24
25	10.834706	98.347059	0.010168	0.092296	9.077040	0.110168	25
26	11.918177	109.181765	0.009159	0.083905	9.160945	0.109159	26
27	13.109994	121.099942	0.008258	0.076278	9.237223	0.108258	27
28	14.420994	134.209936	0.007451	0.069343	9.306567	0.107451	28
29	15.863093	148.630930	0.006728	0.063039	9.369606	0.106728	29
30	17.449402	164.494023	0.006079	0.057309	9.426914	0.106079	30
31	19.194342	181.943425	0.005496	0.052099	9.479013	0.105496	31
32	21.113777	201.137767	0.004972	0.047362	9.526376	0.104972	32
33	23.225154	222.251544	0.004499	0.043057	9.569432	0.104499	33
34	25.547670	245.476699	0.004074	0.039143	9.608575	0.104074	34
35	28.102437	271.024368	0.003690	0.035584	9.644159	0.103690	35
36	30.912681	299.126805	0.003343	0.032349	9.676508	0.103343	36
37	34.003949	330.039486	0.003030	0.029408	9.705917	0.103030	37
38	37.404343	364.043434	0.002747	0.026735	9.732651	0.102747	38
39	41.144778	401.447778	0.002491	0.024304	9.756956	0.102491	39
40	45.259256	442.592556	0.002259	0.022095	9.779051	0.102259	40
41	49.785181	487.851811	0.002050	0.020086	9.799137	0.102050	41
42	54.763699	537.636992	0.001860	0.018260	9.817397	0.101860	42
43	60.240069	592.400692	0.001688	0.016600	9.833998	0.101688	43
44	66.264076	652.640761	0.001532	0.015091	9.849089	0.101532	44
45	72.890484	718.904837	0.001391	0.013719	9.862808	0.101391	45
46	80.179532	791.795321	0.001263	0.012472	9.875280	0.101263	46
47	88.197485	871.974853	0.001147	0.011338	9.886618	0.101147	47
48	97.017234	960.172338	0.001041	0.010307	9.896926	0.101041	48
49	106.718957	1057.189572	0.000946	0.009370	9.906296	0.100946	49
50	117.390853	1163.908529	0.000859	0.008519	9.914814	0.100859	50

ANNUAL COMPOUND INTEREST TABLES

11.00% ANNUAL INTEREST RATE

YEARS	1 AMOUNT OF $1 AT COMPOUND INTEREST	2 ACCUMULATION OF $1 PER PERIOD	3 SINKING FUND FACTOR	4 PRESENT VALUE REVERSION OF $1	5 PRESENT VALUE ORD. ANNUITY $1 PER PERIOD	6 INSTALLMENT TO AMORTIZE $1	YEARS
1	1.110000	1.000000	1.000000	0.900901	0.900901	1.110000	1
2	1.232100	2.110000	0.473934	0.811622	1.712523	0.583934	2
3	1.367631	3.342100	0.299213	0.731191	2.443715	0.409213	3
4	1.518070	4.709731	0.212326	0.658731	3.102446	0.322326	4
5	1.685058	6.227801	0.160570	0.593451	3.695897	0.270570	5
6	1.870415	7.912860	0.126377	0.534641	4.230538	0.236377	6
7	2.076160	9.783274	0.102215	0.481658	4.712196	0.212215	7
8	2.304538	11.859434	0.084321	0.433926	5.146123	0.194321	8
9	2.558037	14.163972	0.070602	0.390925	5.537048	0.180602	9
10	2.839421	16.722009	0.059801	0.352184	5.889232	0.169801	10
11	3.151757	19.561430	0.051121	0.317283	6.206515	0.161121	11
12	3.498451	22.713187	0.044027	0.285841	6.492356	0.154027	12
13	3.883280	26.211638	0.038151	0.257514	6.749870	0.148151	13
14	4.310441	30.094918	0.033228	0.231995	6.981865	0.143228	14
15	4.784589	34.405359	0.029065	0.209004	7.190870	0.139065	15
16	5.310894	39.189948	0.025517	0.188292	7.379162	0.135517	16
17	5.895093	44.500843	0.022471	0.169633	7.548794	0.132471	17
18	6.543553	50.395936	0.019843	0.152822	7.701617	0.129843	18
19	7.263344	56.939488	0.017563	0.137678	7.839294	0.127563	19
20	8.062312	64.202832	0.015576	0.124034	7.963328	0.125576	20
21	8.949166	72.265144	0.013838	0.111742	8.075070	0.123838	21
22	9.933574	81.214309	0.012313	0.100669	8.175739	0.122313	22
23	11.026267	91.147884	0.010971	0.090693	8.266432	0.120971	23
24	12.239157	102.174151	0.009787	0.081705	8.348137	0.119787	24
25	13.585464	114.413307	0.008740	0.073608	8.421745	0.118740	25
26	15.079865	127.998771	0.007813	0.066314	8.488058	0.117813	26
27	16.738650	143.078636	0.006989	0.059742	8.547800	0.116989	27
28	18.579901	159.817286	0.006257	0.053822	8.601622	0.116257	28
29	20.623691	178.397187	0.005605	0.048488	8.650110	0.115605	29
30	22.892297	199.020878	0.005025	0.043683	8.693793	0.115025	30
31	25.410449	221.913174	0.004506	0.039354	8.733146	0.114506	31
32	28.205599	247.323624	0.004043	0.035454	8.768600	0.114043	32
33	31.308214	275.529222	0.003629	0.031940	8.800541	0.113629	33
34	34.752118	306.837437	0.003259	0.028775	8.829316	0.113259	34
35	38.574851	341.589555	0.002927	0.025924	8.855240	0.112927	35
36	42.818085	380.164406	0.002630	0.023355	8.878594	0.112630	36
37	47.528074	422.982490	0.002364	0.021040	8.899635	0.112364	37
38	52.756162	470.510564	0.002125	0.018955	8.918590	0.112125	38
39	58.559340	523.266726	0.001911	0.017077	8.935666	0.111911	39
40	65.000867	581.826066	0.001719	0.015384	8.951051	0.111719	40
41	72.150963	646.826934	0.001546	0.013860	8.964911	0.111546	41
42	80.087569	718.977896	0.001391	0.012486	8.977397	0.111391	42
43	88.897201	799.065465	0.001251	0.011249	8.988646	0.111251	43
44	98.675893	887.962666	0.001126	0.010134	8.998780	0.111126	44
45	109.530242	986.638559	0.001014	0.009130	9.007910	0.111014	45
46	121.578568	1096.168801	0.000912	0.008225	9.016135	0.110912	46
47	134.952211	1217.747369	0.000821	0.007410	9.023545	0.110821	47
48	149.796954	1352.699580	0.000739	0.006676	9.030221	0.110739	48
49	166.274619	1502.496533	0.000666	0.006014	9.036235	0.110666	49
50	184.564827	1668.771152	0.000599	0.005418	9.041653	0.110599	50

ANNUAL COMPOUND INTEREST TABLES

12.00% ANNUAL INTEREST RATE

	1	2	3	4	5	6	
	AMOUNT OF $1 AT COMPOUND INTEREST	ACCUMULATION OF $1 PER PERIOD	SINKING FUND FACTOR	PRESENT VALUE REVERSION OF $1	PRESENT VALUE ORD. ANNUITY $1 PER PERIOD	INSTALLMENT TO AMORTIZE $1	
YEARS							YEARS
1	1.120000	1.000000	1.000000	0.892857	0.892857	1.120000	1
2	1.254400	2.120000	0.471698	0.797194	1.690051	0.591698	2
3	1.404928	3.374400	0.296349	0.711780	2.401831	0.416349	3
4	1.573519	4.779328	0.209234	0.635518	3.037349	0.329234	4
5	1.762342	6.352847	0.157410	0.567427	3.604776	0.277410	5
6	1.973823	8.115189	0.123226	0.506631	4.111407	0.243226	6
7	2.210681	10.089012	0.099118	0.452349	4.563757	0.219118	7
8	2.475963	12.299693	0.081303	0.403883	4.967640	0.201303	8
9	2.773079	14.775656	0.067679	0.360610	5.328250	0.187679	9
10	3.105848	17.548735	0.056984	0.321973	5.650223	0.176984	10
11	3.478550	20.654583	0.048415	0.287476	5.937699	0.168415	11
12	3.895976	24.133133	0.041437	0.256675	6.194374	0.161437	12
13	4.363493	28.029109	0.035677	0.229174	6.423548	0.155677	13
14	4.887112	32.392602	0.030871	0.204620	6.628168	0.150871	14
15	5.473566	37.279715	0.026824	0.182696	6.810864	0.146824	15
16	6.130394	42.753280	0.023390	0.163122	6.973986	0.143390	16
17	6.866041	48.883674	0.020457	0.145644	7.119630	0.140457	17
18	7.689966	55.749715	0.017937	0.130040	7.249670	0.137937	18
19	8.612762	63.439681	0.015763	0.116107	7.365777	0.135763	19
20	9.646293	72.052442	0.013879	0.103667	7.469444	0.133879	20
21	10.803848	81.698736	0.012240	0.092560	7.562003	0.132240	21
22	12.100310	92.502584	0.010811	0.082643	7.644646	0.130811	22
23	13.552347	104.602894	0.009560	0.073788	7.718434	0.129560	23
24	15.178629	118.155241	0.008463	0.065882	7.784316	0.128463	24
25	17.000064	133.333870	0.007500	0.058823	7.843139	0.127500	25
26	19.040072	150.333934	0.006652	0.052521	7.895660	0.126652	26
27	21.324881	169.374007	0.005904	0.046894	7.942554	0.125904	27
28	23.883866	190.698887	0.005244	0.041869	7.984423	0.125244	28
29	26.749930	214.582754	0.004660	0.037383	8.021806	0.124660	29
30	29.959922	241.332684	0.004144	0.033378	8.055184	0.124144	30
31	33.555113	271.292606	0.003686	0.029802	8.084986	0.123686	31
32	37.581726	304.847719	0.003280	0.026609	8.111594	0.123280	32
33	42.091533	342.429446	0.002920	0.023758	8.135352	0.122920	33
34	47.142517	384.520979	0.002601	0.021212	8.156564	0.122601	34
35	52.799620	431.663496	0.002317	0.018940	8.175504	0.122317	35
36	59.135574	484.463116	0.002064	0.016910	8.192414	0.122064	36
37	66.231843	543.598690	0.001840	0.015098	8.207513	0.121840	37
38	74.179664	609.830533	0.001640	0.013481	8.220993	0.121640	38
39	83.081224	684.010197	0.001462	0.012036	8.233030	0.121462	39
40	93.050970	767.091420	0.001304	0.010747	8.243777	0.121304	40
41	104.217087	860.142391	0.001163	0.009595	8.253372	0.121163	41
42	116.723137	964.359478	0.001037	0.008567	8.261939	0.121037	42
43	130.729914	1081.082615	0.000925	0.007649	8.269589	0.120925	43
44	146.417503	1211.812529	0.000825	0.006830	8.276418	0.120825	44
45	163.987604	1358.230032	0.000736	0.006098	8.282516	0.120736	45
46	183.666116	1522.217636	0.000657	0.005445	8.287961	0.120657	46
47	205.706050	1705.883752	0.000586	0.004861	8.292822	0.120586	47
48	230.390776	1911.589803	0.000523	0.004340	8.297163	0.120523	48
49	258.037669	2141.980579	0.000467	0.003875	8.301038	0.120467	49
50	289.002190	2400.018249	0.000417	0.003460	8.304498	0.120417	50

ANNUAL COMPOUND INTEREST TABLES

13.00% ANNUAL INTEREST RATE

YEARS	1 AMOUNT OF $1 AT COMPOUND INTEREST	2 ACCUMULATION OF $1 PER PERIOD	3 SINKING FUND FACTOR	4 PRESENT VALUE REVERSION OF $1	5 PRESENT VALUE ORD. ANNUITY $1 PER PERIOD	6 INSTALLMENT TO AMORTIZE $1	YEARS
1	1.130000	1.000000	1.000000	0.884956	0.884956	1.130000	1
2	1.276900	2.130000	0.469484	0.783147	1.668102	0.599484	2
3	1.442897	3.406900	0.293522	0.693050	2.361153	0.423522	3
4	1.630474	4.849797	0.206194	0.613319	2.974471	0.336194	4
5	1.842435	6.480271	0.154315	0.542760	3.517231	0.284315	5
6	2.081952	8.322706	0.120153	0.480319	3.997550	0.250153	6
7	2.352605	10.404658	0.096111	0.425061	4.422610	0.226111	7
8	2.658444	12.757263	0.078387	0.376160	4.798770	0.208387	8
9	3.004042	15.415707	0.064869	0.332885	5.131655	0.194869	9
10	3.394567	18.419749	0.054290	0.294588	5.426243	0.184290	10
11	3.835861	21.814317	0.045841	0.260698	5.686941	0.175841	11
12	4.334523	25.650178	0.038986	0.230706	5.917647	0.168986	12
13	4.898011	29.984701	0.033350	0.204165	6.121812	0.163350	13
14	5.534753	34.882712	0.028667	0.180677	6.302488	0.158667	14
15	6.254270	40.417464	0.024742	0.159891	6.462379	0.154742	15
16	7.067326	46.671735	0.021426	0.141496	6.603875	0.151426	16
17	7.986078	53.739060	0.018608	0.125218	6.729093	0.148608	17
18	9.024268	61.725138	0.016201	0.110812	6.839905	0.146201	18
19	10.197423	70.749406	0.014134	0.098064	6.937969	0.144134	19
20	11.523088	80.946829	0.012354	0.086782	7.024752	0.142354	20
21	13.021089	92.469917	0.010814	0.076798	7.101550	0.140814	21
22	14.713831	105.491006	0.009479	0.067963	7.169513	0.139479	22
23	16.626629	120.204837	0.008319	0.060144	7.229658	0.138319	23
24	18.788091	136.831465	0.007308	0.053225	7.282883	0.137308	24
25	21.230542	155.619556	0.006426	0.047102	7.329985	0.136426	25
26	23.990513	176.850098	0.005655	0.041683	7.371668	0.135655	26
27	27.109279	200.840611	0.004979	0.036888	7.408556	0.134979	27
28	30.633486	227.949890	0.004387	0.032644	7.441200	0.134387	28
29	34.615839	258.583376	0.003867	0.028889	7.470088	0.133867	29
30	39.115898	293.199215	0.003411	0.025565	7.495653	0.133411	30
31	44.200965	332.315113	0.003009	0.022624	7.518277	0.133009	31
32	49.947090	376.516078	0.002656	0.020021	7.538299	0.132656	32
33	56.440212	426.463168	0.002345	0.017718	7.556016	0.132345	33
34	63.777439	482.903380	0.002071	0.015680	7.571696	0.132071	34
35	72.068506	546.680819	0.001829	0.013876	7.585572	0.131829	35
36	81.437412	618.749325	0.001616	0.012279	7.597851	0.131616	36
37	92.024276	700.186738	0.001428	0.010867	7.608718	0.131428	37
38	103.987432	792.211014	0.001262	0.009617	7.618334	0.131262	38
39	117.505798	896.198445	0.001116	0.008510	7.626844	0.131116	39
40	132.781552	1013.704243	0.000986	0.007531	7.634376	0.130986	40
41	150.043153	1146.485795	0.000872	0.006665	7.641040	0.130872	41
42	169.548763	1296.528948	0.000771	0.005898	7.646938	0.130771	42
43	191.590103	1466.077712	0.000682	0.005219	7.652158	0.130682	43
44	216.496816	1657.667814	0.000603	0.004619	7.656777	0.130603	44
45	244.641402	1874.164630	0.000534	0.004088	7.660864	0.130534	45
46	276.444784	2118.806032	0.000472	0.003617	7.664482	0.130472	46
47	312.382606	2395.250816	0.000417	0.003201	7.667683	0.130417	47
48	352.992345	2707.633422	0.000369	0.002833	7.670516	0.130369	48
49	398.881350	3060.625767	0.000327	0.002507	7.673023	0.130327	49
50	450.735925	3459.507117	0.000289	0.002219	7.675242	0.130289	50

ANNUAL COMPOUND INTEREST TABLES

14.00% ANNUAL INTEREST RATE

YEARS	1 AMOUNT OF $1 AT COMPOUND INTEREST	2 ACCUMULATION OF $1 PER PERIOD	3 SINKING FUND FACTOR	4 PRESENT VALUE REVERSION OF $1	5 PRESENT VALUE ORD. ANNUITY $1 PER PERIOD	6 INSTALLMENT TO AMORTIZE $1	YEARS
1	1.140000	1.000000	1.000000	0.877193	0.877193	1.140000	1
2	1.299600	2.140000	0.467290	0.769468	1.646661	0.607290	2
3	1.481544	3.439600	0.290731	0.674972	2.321632	0.430731	3
4	1.688960	4.921144	0.203205	0.592080	2.913712	0.343205	4
5	1.925415	6.610104	0.151284	0.519369	3.433081	0.291284	5
6	2.194973	8.535519	0.117157	0.455587	3.888668	0.257157	6
7	2.502269	10.730491	0.093192	0.399637	4.288305	0.233192	7
8	2.852586	13.232760	0.075570	0.350559	4.638864	0.215570	8
9	3.251949	16.085347	0.062168	0.307508	4.946372	0.202168	9
10	3.707221	19.337295	0.051714	0.269744	5.216116	0.191714	10
11	4.226232	23.044516	0.043394	0.236617	5.452733	0.183394	11
12	4.817905	27.270749	0.036669	0.207559	5.660292	0.176669	12
13	5.492411	32.088654	0.031164	0.182069	5.842362	0.171164	13
14	6.261349	37.581065	0.026609	0.159710	6.002072	0.166609	14
15	7.137938	43.842414	0.022809	0.140096	6.142168	0.162809	15
16	8.137249	50.980352	0.019615	0.122892	6.265060	0.159615	16
17	9.276464	59.117601	0.016915	0.107800	6.372859	0.156915	17
18	10.575169	68.394066	0.014621	0.094561	6.467420	0.154621	18
19	12.055693	78.969235	0.012663	0.082948	6.550369	0.152663	19
20	13.743490	91.024928	0.010986	0.072762	6.623131	0.150986	20
21	15.667578	104.768418	0.009545	0.063826	6.686957	0.149545	21
22	17.861039	120.435996	0.008303	0.055988	6.742944	0.148303	22
23	20.361585	138.297035	0.007231	0.049112	6.792056	0.147231	23
24	23.212207	158.658620	0.006303	0.043081	6.835137	0.146303	24
25	26.461916	181.870827	0.005498	0.037790	6.872927	0.145498	25
26	30.166584	208.332743	0.004800	0.033149	6.906077	0.144800	26
27	34.389906	238.499327	0.004193	0.029078	6.935155	0.144193	27
28	39.204493	272.889233	0.003664	0.025507	6.960662	0.143664	28
29	44.693122	312.093725	0.003204	0.022375	6.983037	0.143204	29
30	50.950159	356.786847	0.002803	0.019627	7.002664	0.142803	30
31	58.083181	407.737006	0.002453	0.017217	7.019881	0.142453	31
32	66.214826	465.820186	0.002147	0.015102	7.034983	0.142147	32
33	75.484902	532.035012	0.001880	0.013248	7.048231	0.141880	33
34	86.052788	607.519914	0.001646	0.011621	7.059852	0.141646	34
35	98.100178	693.572702	0.001442	0.010194	7.070045	0.141442	35
36	111.834203	791.672881	0.001263	0.008942	7.078987	0.141263	36
37	127.490992	903.507084	0.001107	0.007844	7.086831	0.141107	37
38	145.339731	1030.998076	0.000970	0.006880	7.093711	0.140970	38
39	165.687293	1176.337806	0.000850	0.006035	7.099747	0.140850	39
40	188.883514	1342.025099	0.000745	0.005294	7.105041	0.140745	40
41	215.327206	1530.908613	0.000653	0.004644	7.109685	0.140653	41
42	245.473015	1746.235819	0.000573	0.004074	7.113759	0.140573	42
43	279.839237	1991.708833	0.000502	0.003573	7.117332	0.140502	43
44	319.016730	2271.548070	0.000440	0.003135	7.120467	0.140440	44
45	363.679072	2590.564800	0.000386	0.002750	7.123217	0.140386	45
46	414.594142	2954.243872	0.000338	0.002412	7.125629	0.140338	46
47	472.637322	3368.838014	0.000297	0.002116	7.127744	0.140297	47
48	538.806547	3841.475336	0.000260	0.001856	7.129600	0.140260	48
49	614.239464	4380.281883	0.000228	0.001628	7.131228	0.140228	49
50	700.232988	4994.521346	0.000200	0.001428	7.132656	0.140200	50

ANNUAL COMPOUND INTEREST TABLES

15.00% ANNUAL INTEREST RATE

YEARS	1 AMOUNT OF $1 AT COMPOUND INTEREST	2 ACCUMULATION OF $1 PER PERIOD	3 SINKING FUND FACTOR	4 PRESENT VALUE REVERSION OF $1	5 PRESENT VALUE ORD. ANNUITY $1 PER PERIOD	6 INSTALLMENT TO AMORTIZE $1	YEARS
1	1.150000	1.000000	1.000000	0.869565	0.869565	1.150000	1
2	1.322500	2.150000	0.465116	0.756144	1.625709	0.615116	2
3	1.520875	3.472500	0.287977	0.657516	2.283225	0.437977	3
4	1.749006	4.993375	0.200265	0.571753	2.854978	0.350265	4
5	2.011357	6.742381	0.148316	0.497177	3.352155	0.298316	5
6	2.313061	8.753738	0.114237	0.432328	3.784483	0.264237	6
7	2.660020	11.066799	0.090360	0.375937	4.160420	0.240360	7
8	3.059023	13.726819	0.072850	0.326902	4.487322	0.222850	8
9	3.517876	16.785842	0.059574	0.284262	4.771584	0.209574	9
10	4.045558	20.303718	0.049252	0.247185	5.018769	0.199252	10
11	4.652391	24.349276	0.041069	0.214943	5.233712	0.191069	11
12	5.350250	29.001667	0.034481	0.186907	5.420619	0.184481	12
13	6.152788	34.351917	0.029110	0.162528	5.583147	0.179110	13
14	7.075706	40.504705	0.024688	0.141329	5.724476	0.174688	14
15	8.137062	47.580411	0.021017	0.122894	5.847370	0.171017	15
16	9.357621	55.717472	0.017948	0.106865	5.954235	0.167948	16
17	10.761264	65.075093	0.015367	0.092926	6.047161	0.165367	17
18	12.375454	75.836357	0.013186	0.080805	6.127966	0.163186	18
19	14.231772	88.211811	0.011336	0.070265	6.198231	0.161336	19
20	16.366537	102.443583	0.009761	0.061100	6.259331	0.159761	20
21	18.821518	118.810120	0.008417	0.053131	6.312462	0.158417	21
22	21.644746	137.631638	0.007266	0.046201	6.358663	0.157266	22
23	24.891458	159.276384	0.006278	0.040174	6.398837	0.156278	23
24	28.625176	184.167841	0.005430	0.034934	6.433771	0.155430	24
25	32.918953	212.793017	0.004699	0.030378	6.464149	0.154699	25
26	37.856796	245.711970	0.004070	0.026415	6.490564	0.154070	26
27	43.535315	283.568766	0.003526	0.022970	6.513534	0.153526	27
28	50.065612	327.104080	0.003057	0.019974	6.533508	0.153057	28
29	57.575454	377.169693	0.002651	0.017369	6.550877	0.152651	29
30	66.211772	434.745146	0.002300	0.015103	6.565980	0.152300	30
31	76.143538	500.956918	0.001996	0.013133	6.579113	0.151996	31
32	87.565068	577.100456	0.001733	0.011420	6.590533	0.151733	32
33	100.699829	664.665524	0.001505	0.009931	6.600463	0.151505	33
34	115.804803	765.365353	0.001307	0.008635	6.609099	0.151307	34
35	133.175523	881.170156	0.001135	0.007509	6.616607	0.151135	35
36	153.151852	1014.345680	0.000986	0.006529	6.623137	0.150986	36
37	176.124630	1167.497532	0.000857	0.005678	6.628815	0.150857	37
38	202.543324	1343.622161	0.000744	0.004937	6.633752	0.150744	38
39	232.924823	1546.165485	0.000647	0.004293	6.638045	0.150647	39
40	267.863546	1779.090308	0.000562	0.003733	6.641778	0.150562	40
41	308.043078	2046.953854	0.000489	0.003246	6.645025	0.150489	41
42	354.249540	2354.996933	0.000425	0.002823	6.647848	0.150425	42
43	407.386971	2709.246473	0.000369	0.002455	6.650302	0.150369	43
44	468.495017	3116.633443	0.000321	0.002134	6.652437	0.150321	44
45	538.769269	3585.128460	0.000279	0.001856	6.654293	0.150279	45
46	619.584659	4123.897729	0.000242	0.001614	6.655907	0.150242	46
47	712.522358	4743.482388	0.000211	0.001403	6.657310	0.150211	47
48	819.400712	5456.004746	0.000183	0.001220	6.658531	0.150183	48
49	942.310819	6275.405458	0.000159	0.001061	6.659592	0.150159	49
50	1083.657442	7217.716277	0.000139	0.000923	6.660515	0.150139	50

ANNUAL COMPOUND INTEREST TABLES

16.00% ANNUAL INTEREST RATE

YEARS	1 AMOUNT OF $1 AT COMPOUND INTEREST	2 ACCUMULATION OF $1 PER PERIOD	3 SINKING FUND FACTOR	4 PRESENT VALUE REVERSION OF $1	5 PRESENT VALUE ORD. ANNUITY $1 PER PERIOD	6 INSTALLMENT TO AMORTIZE $1	YEARS
1	1.160000	1.000000	1.000000	0.862069	0.862069	1.160000	1
2	1.345600	2.160000	0.462963	0.743163	1.605232	0.622963	2
3	1.560896	3.505600	0.285258	0.640658	2.245890	0.445258	3
4	1.810639	5.066496	0.197375	0.552291	2.798181	0.357375	4
5	2.100342	6.877135	0.145409	0.476113	3.274294	0.305409	5
6	2.436396	8.977477	0.111390	0.410442	3.684736	0.271390	6
7	2.826220	11.413873	0.087613	0.353830	4.038565	0.247613	7
8	3.278415	14.240093	0.070224	0.305025	4.343591	0.230224	8
9	3.802961	17.518508	0.057082	0.262953	4.606544	0.217082	9
10	4.411435	21.321469	0.046901	0.226684	4.833227	0.206901	10
11	5.117265	25.732904	0.038861	0.195417	5.028644	0.198861	11
12	5.936027	30.850169	0.032415	0.168463	5.197107	0.192415	12
13	6.885791	36.786196	0.027184	0.145227	5.342334	0.187184	13
14	7.987518	43.671987	0.022898	0.125195	5.467529	0.182898	14
15	9.265521	51.659505	0.019358	0.107927	5.575456	0.179358	15
16	10.748004	60.925026	0.016414	0.093041	5.668497	0.176414	16
17	12.467685	71.673030	0.013952	0.080207	5.748704	0.173952	17
18	14.462514	84.140715	0.011885	0.069144	5.817848	0.171885	18
19	16.776517	98.603230	0.010142	0.059607	5.877455	0.170142	19
20	19.460759	115.379747	0.008667	0.051385	5.928841	0.168667	20
21	22.574481	134.840506	0.007416	0.044298	5.973139	0.167416	21
22	26.186398	157.414987	0.006353	0.038188	6.011326	0.166353	22
23	30.376222	183.601385	0.005447	0.032920	6.044247	0.165447	23
24	35.236417	213.977607	0.004673	0.028380	6.072627	0.164673	24
25	40.874244	249.214024	0.004013	0.024465	6.097092	0.164013	25
26	47.414123	290.088267	0.003447	0.021091	6.118183	0.163447	26
27	55.000382	337.502390	0.002963	0.018182	6.136364	0.162963	27
28	63.800444	392.502773	0.002548	0.015674	6.152038	0.162548	28
29	74.008515	456.303216	0.002192	0.013512	6.165550	0.162192	29
30	85.849877	530.311731	0.001886	0.011648	6.177198	0.161886	30
31	99.585857	616.161608	0.001623	0.010042	6.187240	0.161623	31
32	115.519594	715.747465	0.001397	0.008657	6.195897	0.161397	32
33	134.002729	831.267059	0.001203	0.007463	6.203359	0.161203	33
34	155.443166	965.269789	0.001036	0.006433	6.209792	0.161036	34
35	180.314073	1120.712955	0.000892	0.005546	6.215338	0.160892	35
36	209.164324	1301.027028	0.000769	0.004781	6.220119	0.160769	36
37	242.630616	1510.191352	0.000662	0.004121	6.224241	0.160662	37
38	281.451515	1752.821968	0.000571	0.003553	6.227794	0.160571	38
39	326.483757	2034.273483	0.000492	0.003063	6.230857	0.160492	39
40	378.721158	2360.757241	0.000424	0.002640	6.233497	0.160424	40
41	439.316544	2739.478399	0.000365	0.002276	6.235773	0.160365	41
42	509.607191	3178.794943	0.000315	0.001962	6.237736	0.160315	42
43	591.144341	3688.402134	0.000271	0.001692	6.239427	0.160271	43
44	685.727436	4279.546475	0.000234	0.001458	6.240886	0.160234	44
45	795.443826	4965.273911	0.000201	0.001257	6.242143	0.160201	45
46	922.714838	5760.717737	0.000174	0.001084	6.243227	0.160174	46
47	1070.349212	6683.432575	0.000150	0.000934	6.244161	0.160150	47
48	1241.605086	7753.781787	0.000129	0.000805	6.244966	0.160129	48
49	1440.261900	8995.386873	0.000111	0.000694	6.245661	0.160111	49
50	1670.703804	10435.648773	0.000096	0.000599	6.246259	0.160096	50

ANNUAL COMPOUND INTEREST TABLES

17.00% ANNUAL INTEREST RATE

YEARS	1 AMOUNT OF $1 AT COMPOUND INTEREST	2 ACCUMULATION OF $1 PER PERIOD	3 SINKING FUND FACTOR	4 PRESENT VALUE REVERSION OF $1	5 PRESENT VALUE ORD. ANNUITY $1 PER PERIOD	6 INSTALLMENT TO AMORTIZE $1	YEARS
1	1.170000	1.000000	1.000000	0.854701	0.854701	1.170000	1
2	1.368900	2.170000	0.460829	0.730514	1.585214	0.630829	2
3	1.601613	3.538900	0.282574	0.624371	2.209585	0.452574	3
4	1.873887	5.140513	0.194533	0.533650	2.743235	0.364533	4
5	2.192448	7.014400	0.142564	0.456111	3.199346	0.312564	5
6	2.565164	9.206848	0.108615	0.389839	3.589185	0.278615	6
7	3.001242	11.772012	0.084947	0.333195	3.922380	0.254947	7
8	3.511453	14.773255	0.067690	0.284782	4.207163	0.237690	8
9	4.108400	18.284708	0.054691	0.243404	4.450566	0.224691	9
10	4.806828	22.393108	0.044657	0.208037	4.658604	0.214657	10
11	5.623989	27.199937	0.036765	0.177810	4.836413	0.206765	11
12	6.580067	32.823926	0.030466	0.151974	4.988387	0.200466	12
13	7.698679	39.403993	0.025378	0.129892	5.118280	0.195378	13
14	9.007454	47.102672	0.021230	0.111019	5.229299	0.191230	14
15	10.538721	56.110126	0.017822	0.094888	5.324187	0.187822	15
16	12.330304	66.648848	0.015004	0.081101	5.405288	0.185004	16
17	14.426456	78.979152	0.012662	0.069317	5.474605	0.182662	17
18	16.878953	93.405608	0.010706	0.059245	5.533851	0.180706	18
19	19.748375	110.284561	0.009067	0.050637	5.584488	0.179067	19
20	23.105599	130.032936	0.007690	0.043280	5.627767	0.177690	20
21	27.033551	153.138535	0.006530	0.036991	5.664758	0.176530	21
22	31.629255	180.172086	0.005550	0.031616	5.696375	0.175550	22
23	37.006228	211.801341	0.004721	0.027022	5.723397	0.174721	23
24	43.297287	248.807569	0.004019	0.023096	5.746493	0.174019	24
25	50.657826	292.104856	0.003423	0.019740	5.766234	0.173423	25
26	59.269656	342.762681	0.002917	0.016872	5.783106	0.172917	26
27	69.345497	402.032337	0.002487	0.014421	5.797526	0.172487	27
28	81.134232	471.377835	0.002121	0.012325	5.809851	0.172121	28
29	94.927051	552.512066	0.001810	0.010534	5.820386	0.171810	29
30	111.064650	647.439118	0.001545	0.009004	5.829390	0.171545	30
31	129.945641	758.503768	0.001318	0.007696	5.837085	0.171318	31
32	152.036399	888.449408	0.001126	0.006577	5.843663	0.171126	32
33	177.882587	1040.485808	0.000961	0.005622	5.849284	0.170961	33
34	208.122627	1218.368395	0.000821	0.004805	5.854089	0.170821	34
35	243.503474	1426.491022	0.000701	0.004107	5.858196	0.170701	35
36	284.899064	1669.994496	0.000599	0.003510	5.861706	0.170599	36
37	333.331905	1954.893560	0.000512	0.003000	5.864706	0.170512	37
38	389.998329	2288.225465	0.000437	0.002564	5.867270	0.170437	38
39	456.298045	2678.223794	0.000373	0.002192	5.869461	0.170373	39
40	533.868713	3134.521839	0.000319	0.001873	5.871335	0.170319	40
41	624.626394	3668.390552	0.000273	0.001601	5.872936	0.170273	41
42	730.812881	4293.016946	0.000233	0.001368	5.874304	0.170233	42
43	855.051071	5023.829827	0.000199	0.001170	5.875473	0.170199	43
44	1000.409753	5878.880897	0.000170	0.001000	5.876473	0.170170	44
45	1170.479411	6879.290650	0.000145	0.000854	5.877327	0.170145	45
46	1369.460910	8049.770061	0.000124	0.000730	5.878058	0.170124	46
47	1602.269265	9419.230971	0.000106	0.000624	5.878682	0.170106	47
48	1874.655040	11021.500236	0.000091	0.000533	5.879215	0.170091	48
49	2193.346397	12896.155276	0.000078	0.000456	5.879671	0.170078	49
50	2566.215284	15089.501673	0.000066	0.000390	5.880061	0.170066	50

ANNUAL COMPOUND INTEREST TABLES

18.00% ANNUAL INTEREST RATE

YEARS	1 AMOUNT OF $1 AT COMPOUND INTEREST	2 ACCUMULATION OF $1 PER PERIOD	3 SINKING FUND FACTOR	4 PRESENT VALUE REVERSION OF $1	5 PRESENT VALUE ORD. ANNUITY $1 PER PERIOD	6 INSTALLMENT TO AMORTIZE $1	YEARS
1	1.180000	1.000000	1.000000	0.847458	0.847458	1.180000	1
2	1.392400	2.180000	0.458716	0.718184	1.565642	0.638716	2
3	1.643032	3.572400	0.279924	0.608631	2.174273	0.459924	3
4	1.938778	5.215432	0.191739	0.515789	2.690062	0.371739	4
5	2.287758	7.154210	0.139778	0.437109	3.127171	0.319778	5
6	2.699554	9.441968	0.105910	0.370432	3.497603	0.285910	6
7	3.185474	12.141522	0.082362	0.313925	3.811528	0.262362	7
8	3.758859	15.326996	0.065244	0.266038	4.077566	0.245244	8
9	4.435454	19.085855	0.052395	0.225456	4.303022	0.232395	9
10	5.233836	23.521309	0.042515	0.191064	4.494086	0.222515	10
11	6.175926	28.755144	0.034776	0.161919	4.656005	0.214776	11
12	7.287593	34.931070	0.028628	0.137220	4.793225	0.208628	12
13	8.599359	42.218663	0.023686	0.116288	4.909513	0.203686	13
14	10.147244	50.818022	0.019678	0.098549	5.008062	0.199678	14
15	11.973748	60.965266	0.016403	0.083516	5.091578	0.196403	15
16	14.129023	72.939014	0.013710	0.070776	5.162354	0.193710	16
17	16.672247	87.068036	0.011485	0.059980	5.222334	0.191485	17
18	19.673251	103.740283	0.009639	0.050830	5.273164	0.189639	18
19	23.214436	123.413534	0.008103	0.043077	5.316241	0.188103	19
20	27.393035	146.627970	0.006820	0.036506	5.352746	0.186820	20
21	32.323781	174.021005	0.005746	0.030937	5.383683	0.185746	21
22	38.142061	206.344785	0.004846	0.026218	5.409901	0.184846	22
23	45.007632	244.486847	0.004090	0.022218	5.432120	0.184090	23
24	53.109006	289.494479	0.003454	0.018829	5.450949	0.183454	24
25	62.668627	342.603486	0.002919	0.015957	5.466906	0.182919	25
26	73.948980	405.272113	0.002467	0.013523	5.480429	0.182467	26
27	87.259797	479.221093	0.002087	0.011460	5.491889	0.182087	27
28	102.966560	566.480890	0.001765	0.009712	5.501601	0.181765	28
29	121.500541	669.447450	0.001494	0.008230	5.509831	0.181494	29
30	143.370638	790.947991	0.001264	0.006975	5.516806	0.181264	30
31	169.177353	934.318630	0.001070	0.005911	5.522717	0.181070	31
32	199.629277	1103.495983	0.000906	0.005009	5.527726	0.180906	32
33	235.562547	1303.125260	0.000767	0.004245	5.531971	0.180767	33
34	277.963805	1538.687807	0.000650	0.003598	5.535569	0.180650	34
35	327.997290	1816.651612	0.000550	0.003049	5.538618	0.180550	35
36	387.036802	2144.648902	0.000466	0.002584	5.541201	0.180466	36
37	456.703427	2531.685705	0.000395	0.002190	5.543391	0.180395	37
38	538.910044	2988.389132	0.000335	0.001856	5.545247	0.180335	38
39	635.913852	3527.299175	0.000284	0.001573	5.546819	0.180284	39
40	750.378345	4163.213027	0.000240	0.001333	5.548152	0.180240	40
41	885.446447	4913.591372	0.000204	0.001129	5.549281	0.180204	41
42	1044.826807	5799.037819	0.000172	0.000957	5.550238	0.180172	42
43	1232.895633	6843.864626	0.000146	0.000811	5.551049	0.180146	43
44	1454.816847	8076.760259	0.000124	0.000687	5.551737	0.180124	44
45	1716.683879	9531.577105	0.000105	0.000583	5.552319	0.180105	45
46	2025.686977	11248.260984	0.000089	0.000494	5.552813	0.180089	46
47	2390.310633	13273.947961	0.000075	0.000418	5.553231	0.180075	47
48	2820.566547	15664.258594	0.000064	0.000355	5.553586	0.180064	48
49	3328.268525	18484.825141	0.000054	0.000300	5.553886	0.180054	49
50	3927.356860	21813.093666	0.000046	0.000255	5.554141	0.180046	50

ANNUAL COMPOUND INTEREST TABLES

19.00% ANNUAL INTEREST RATE

YEARS	1 AMOUNT OF $1 AT COMPOUND INTEREST	2 ACCUMULATION OF $1 PER PERIOD	3 SINKING FUND FACTOR	4 PRESENT VALUE REVERSION OF $1	5 PRESENT VALUE ORD. ANNUITY $1 PER PERIOD	6 INSTALLMENT TO AMORTIZE $1	YEARS
1	1.190000	1.000000	1.000000	0.840336	0.840336	1.190000	1
2	1.416100	2.190000	0.456621	0.706165	1.546501	0.646621	2
3	1.685159	3.606100	0.277308	0.593416	2.139917	0.467308	3
4	2.005339	5.291259	0.188991	0.498669	2.638586	0.378991	4
5	2.386354	7.296598	0.137050	0.419049	3.057635	0.327050	5
6	2.839761	9.682952	0.103274	0.352142	3.409777	0.293274	6
7	3.379315	12.522713	0.079855	0.295918	3.705695	0.269855	7
8	4.021385	15.902028	0.062885	0.248671	3.954366	0.252885	8
9	4.785449	19.923413	0.050192	0.208967	4.163332	0.240192	9
10	5.694684	24.708862	0.040471	0.175602	4.338935	0.230471	10
11	6.776674	30.403546	0.032891	0.147565	4.486500	0.222891	11
12	8.064242	37.180220	0.026896	0.124004	4.610504	0.216896	12
13	9.596448	45.244461	0.022102	0.104205	4.714709	0.212102	13
14	11.419773	54.840909	0.018235	0.087567	4.802277	0.208235	14
15	13.589530	66.260682	0.015092	0.073586	4.875863	0.205092	15
16	16.171540	79.850211	0.012523	0.061837	4.937700	0.202523	16
17	19.244133	96.021751	0.010414	0.051964	4.989664	0.200414	17
18	22.900518	115.265884	0.008676	0.043667	5.033331	0.198676	18
19	27.251616	138.166402	0.007238	0.036695	5.070026	0.197238	19
20	32.429423	165.418018	0.006045	0.030836	5.100862	0.196045	20
21	38.591014	197.847442	0.005054	0.025913	5.126775	0.195054	21
22	45.923307	236.438456	0.004229	0.021775	5.148550	0.194229	22
23	54.648735	282.361762	0.003542	0.018299	5.166849	0.193542	23
24	65.031994	337.010497	0.002967	0.015377	5.182226	0.192967	24
25	77.388073	402.042491	0.002487	0.012922	5.195148	0.192487	25
26	92.091807	479.430565	0.002086	0.010859	5.206007	0.192086	26
27	109.589251	571.522372	0.001750	0.009125	5.215132	0.191750	27
28	130.411208	681.111623	0.001468	0.007668	5.222800	0.191468	28
29	155.189338	811.522831	0.001232	0.006444	5.229243	0.191232	29
30	184.675312	966.712169	0.001034	0.005415	5.234658	0.191034	30
31	219.763621	1151.387481	0.000869	0.004550	5.239209	0.190869	31
32	261.518710	1371.151103	0.000729	0.003824	5.243033	0.190729	32
33	311.207264	1632.669812	0.000612	0.003213	5.246246	0.190612	33
34	370.336645	1943.877077	0.000514	0.002700	5.248946	0.190514	34
35	440.700607	2314.213721	0.000432	0.002269	5.251215	0.190432	35
36	524.433722	2754.914328	0.000363	0.001907	5.253122	0.190363	36
37	624.076130	3279.348051	0.000305	0.001602	5.254724	0.190305	37
38	742.650594	3903.424180	0.000256	0.001347	5.256071	0.190256	38
39	883.754207	4646.074775	0.000215	0.001132	5.257202	0.190215	39
40	1051.667507	5529.828982	0.000181	0.000951	5.258153	0.190181	40
41	1251.484333	6581.496488	0.000152	0.000799	5.258952	0.190152	41
42	1489.266356	7832.980821	0.000128	0.000671	5.259624	0.190128	42
43	1772.226964	9322.247177	0.000107	0.000564	5.260188	0.190107	43
44	2108.950087	11094.474141	0.000090	0.000474	5.260662	0.190090	44
45	2509.650603	13203.424228	0.000076	0.000398	5.261061	0.190076	45
46	2986.484218	15713.074831	0.000064	0.000335	5.261396	0.190064	46
47	3553.916219	18699.559049	0.000053	0.000281	5.261677	0.190053	47
48	4229.160301	22253.475268	0.000045	0.000236	5.261913	0.190045	48
49	5032.700758	26482.635569	0.000038	0.000199	5.262112	0.190038	49
50	5988.913902	31515.336327	0.000032	0.000167	5.262279	0.190032	50

ANNUAL COMPOUND INTEREST TABLES

20.00% ANNUAL INTEREST RATE

YEARS	1 AMOUNT OF $1 AT COMPOUND INTEREST	2 ACCUMULATION OF $1 PER PERIOD	3 SINKING FUND FACTOR	4 PRESENT VALUE REVERSION OF $1	5 PRESENT VALUE ORD. ANNUITY $1 PER PERIOD	6 INSTALLMENT TO AMORTIZE $1	YEARS
1	1.200000	1.000000	1.000000	0.833333	0.833333	1.200000	1
2	1.440000	2.200000	0.454545	0.694444	1.527778	0.654545	2
3	1.728000	3.640000	0.274725	0.578704	2.106481	0.474725	3
4	2.073600	5.368000	0.186289	0.482253	2.588735	0.386289	4
5	2.488320	7.441600	0.134380	0.401878	2.990612	0.334380	5
6	2.985984	9.929920	0.100706	0.334898	3.325510	0.300706	6
7	3.583181	12.915904	0.077424	0.279082	3.604592	0.277424	7
8	4.299817	16.499085	0.060609	0.232568	3.837160	0.260609	8
9	5.159780	20.798902	0.048079	0.193807	4.030967	0.248079	9
10	6.191736	25.958682	0.038523	0.161506	4.192472	0.238523	10
11	7.430084	32.150419	0.031104	0.134588	4.327060	0.231104	11
12	8.916100	39.580502	0.025265	0.112157	4.439217	0.225265	12
13	10.699321	48.496603	0.020620	0.093464	4.532681	0.220620	13
14	12.839185	59.195923	0.016893	0.077887	4.610567	0.216893	14
15	15.407022	72.035108	0.013882	0.064905	4.675473	0.213882	15
16	18.488426	87.442129	0.011436	0.054088	4.729561	0.211436	16
17	22.186111	105.930555	0.009440	0.045073	4.774634	0.209440	17
18	26.623333	128.116666	0.007805	0.037561	4.812195	0.207805	18
19	31.948000	154.740000	0.006462	0.031301	4.843496	0.206462	19
20	38.337600	186.688000	0.005357	0.026084	4.869580	0.205357	20
21	46.005120	225.025600	0.004444	0.021737	4.891316	0.204444	21
22	55.206144	271.030719	0.003690	0.018114	4.909430	0.203690	22
23	66.247373	326.236863	0.003065	0.015095	4.924525	0.203065	23
24	79.496847	392.484236	0.002548	0.012579	4.937104	0.202548	24
25	95.396217	471.981083	0.002119	0.010483	4.947587	0.202119	25
26	114.475460	567.377300	0.001762	0.008735	4.956323	0.201762	26
27	137.370552	681.852760	0.001467	0.007280	4.963602	0.201467	27
28	164.844662	819.223312	0.001221	0.006066	4.969668	0.201221	28
29	197.813595	984.067974	0.001016	0.005055	4.974724	0.201016	29
30	237.376314	1181.881569	0.000846	0.004213	4.978936	0.200846	30
31	284.851577	1419.257883	0.000705	0.003511	4.982447	0.200705	31
32	341.821892	1704.109459	0.000587	0.002926	4.985372	0.200587	32
33	410.186270	2045.931351	0.000489	0.002438	4.987810	0.200489	33
34	492.223524	2456.117621	0.000407	0.002032	4.989842	0.200407	34
35	590.668229	2948.341146	0.000339	0.001693	4.991535	0.200339	35
36	708.801875	3539.009375	0.000283	0.001411	4.992946	0.200283	36
37	850.562250	4247.811250	0.000235	0.001176	4.994122	0.200235	37
38	1020.674700	5098.373500	0.000196	0.000980	4.995101	0.200196	38
39	1224.809640	6119.048200	0.000163	0.000816	4.995918	0.200163	39
40	1469.771568	7343.857840	0.000136	0.000680	4.996598	0.200136	40
41	1763.725882	8813.629408	0.000113	0.000567	4.997165	0.200113	41
42	2116.471058	10577.355289	0.000095	0.000472	4.997638	0.200095	42
43	2539.765269	12693.826347	0.000079	0.000394	4.998031	0.200079	43
44	3047.718323	15233.591617	0.000066	0.000328	4.998359	0.200066	44
45	3657.261988	18281.309940	0.000055	0.000273	4.998633	0.200055	45
46	4388.714386	21938.571928	0.000046	0.000228	4.998861	0.200046	46
47	5266.457263	26327.286314	0.000038	0.000190	4.999051	0.200038	47
48	6319.748715	31593.743576	0.000032	0.000158	4.999209	0.200032	48
49	7583.698458	37913.492292	0.000026	0.000132	4.999341	0.200026	49
50	9100.438150	45497.190750	0.000022	0.000110	4.999451	0.200022	50

APPENDIX

B

Monthly Compound Interest Tables

MONTHLY COMPOUND INTEREST TABLES

6.00% ANNUAL INTEREST RATE

0.5000% MONTHLY EFFECTIVE INTEREST RATE

	1 AMOUNT OF $1 AT COMPOUND INTEREST	2 ACCUMULATION OF $1 PER PERIOD	3 SINKING FUND FACTOR	4 PRESENT VALUE REVERSION OF $1	5 PRESENT VALUE ORD. ANNUITY $1 PER PERIOD	6 INSTALLMENT TO AMORTIZE $1	
MONTHS							MONTHS
1	1.005000	1.000000	1.000000	0.995025	0.995025	1.005000	1
2	1.010025	2.005000	0.498753	0.990075	1.985099	0.503753	2
3	1.015075	3.015025	0.331672	0.985149	2.970248	0.336672	3
4	1.020151	4.030100	0.248133	0.980248	3.950496	0.253133	4
5	1.025251	5.050251	0.198010	0.975371	4.925866	0.203010	5
6	1.030378	6.075502	0.164595	0.970518	5.896384	0.169595	6
7	1.035529	7.105879	0.140729	0.965690	6.862074	0.145729	7
8	1.040707	8.141409	0.122829	0.960885	7.822959	0.127829	8
9	1.045911	9.182116	0.108907	0.956105	8.779064	0.113907	9
10	1.051140	10.228026	0.097771	0.951348	9.730412	0.102771	10
11	1.056396	11.279167	0.088659	0.946615	10.677027	0.093659	11
12	1.061678	12.335562	0.081066	0.941905	11.618932	0.086066	12
YEARS							MONTHS
1	1.061678	12.335562	0.081066	0.941905	11.618932	0.086066	12
2	1.127160	25.431955	0.039321	0.887186	22.562866	0.044321	24
3	1.196681	39.336105	0.025422	0.835645	32.871016	0.030422	36
4	1.270489	54.097832	0.018485	0.787098	42.580318	0.023485	48
5	1.348850	69.770031	0.014333	0.741372	51.725561	0.019333	60
6	1.432044	86.408856	0.011573	0.698302	60.339514	0.016573	72
7	1.520370	104.073927	0.009609	0.657735	68.453042	0.014609	84
8	1.614143	122.828542	0.008141	0.619524	76.095218	0.013141	96
9	1.713699	142.739900	0.007006	0.583533	83.293424	0.012006	108
10	1.819397	163.879347	0.006102	0.549633	90.073453	0.011102	120
11	1.931613	186.322629	0.005367	0.517702	96.459599	0.010367	132
12	2.050751	210.150163	0.004759	0.487626	102.474743	0.009759	144
13	2.177237	235.447328	0.004247	0.459298	108.140440	0.009247	156
14	2.311524	262.304766	0.003812	0.432615	113.476990	0.008812	168
15	2.454094	290.818712	0.003439	0.407482	118.503515	0.008439	180
16	2.605457	321.091337	0.003114	0.383810	123.238025	0.008114	192
17	2.766156	353.231110	0.002831	0.361513	127.697486	0.007831	204
18	2.936766	387.353194	0.002582	0.340511	131.897876	0.007582	216
19	3.117899	423.579854	0.002361	0.320729	135.854246	0.007361	228
20	3.310204	462.040895	0.002164	0.302096	139.580772	0.007164	240
21	3.514371	502.874129	0.001989	0.284546	143.090806	0.006989	252
22	3.731129	546.225867	0.001831	0.268015	146.396927	0.006831	264
23	3.961257	592.251446	0.001688	0.252445	149.510979	0.006688	276
24	4.205579	641.115782	0.001560	0.237779	152.444121	0.006560	288
25	4.464970	692.993962	0.001443	0.223966	155.206864	0.006443	300
26	4.740359	748.071876	0.001337	0.210954	157.809106	0.006337	312
27	5.032734	806.546875	0.001240	0.198699	160.260172	0.006240	324
28	5.343142	868.628484	0.001151	0.187156	162.568844	0.006151	336
29	5.672696	934.539150	0.001070	0.176283	164.743394	0.006070	348
30	6.022575	1004.515042	0.000996	0.166042	166.791614	0.005996	360
31	6.394034	1078.806895	0.000927	0.156396	168.720844	0.005927	372
32	6.788405	1157.680906	0.000864	0.147310	170.537996	0.005864	384
33	7.207098	1241.419693	0.000806	0.138752	172.249581	0.005806	396
34	7.651617	1330.323306	0.000752	0.130691	173.861732	0.005752	408
35	8.123551	1424.710299	0.000702	0.123099	175.380226	0.005702	420
36	8.624594	1524.918875	0.000656	0.115947	176.810504	0.005656	432
37	9.156540	1631.308097	0.000613	0.109212	178.157690	0.005613	444
38	9.721296	1744.259173	0.000573	0.102867	179.426611	0.005573	456
39	10.320884	1864.176824	0.000536	0.096891	180.621815	0.005536	468
40	10.957454	1991.490734	0.000502	0.091262	181.747584	0.005502	480

MONTHLY COMPOUND INTEREST TABLES

7.00% ANNUAL INTEREST RATE

0.5833% MONTHLY EFFECTIVE INTEREST RATE

	1 AMOUNT OF $1 AT COMPOUND INTEREST	2 ACCUMULATION OF $1 PER PERIOD	3 SINKING FUND FACTOR	4 PRESENT VALUE REVERSION OF $1	5 PRESENT VALUE ORD. ANNUITY $1 PER PERIOD	6 INSTALLMENT TO AMORTIZE $1	
MONTHS							MONTHS
1	1.005833	1.000000	1.000000	0.994200	0.994200	1.005833	1
2	1.011701	2.005833	0.498546	0.988435	1.982635	0.504379	2
3	1.017602	3.017534	0.331396	0.982702	2.965337	0.337230	3
4	1.023538	4.035136	0.247823	0.977003	3.942340	0.253656	4
5	1.029509	5.058675	0.197680	0.971337	4.913677	0.203514	5
6	1.035514	6.088184	0.164253	0.965704	5.879381	0.170086	6
7	1.041555	7.123698	0.140377	0.960103	6.839484	0.146210	7
8	1.047631	8.165253	0.122470	0.954535	7.794019	0.128304	8
9	1.053742	9.212883	0.108544	0.948999	8.743018	0.114377	9
10	1.059889	10.266625	0.097403	0.943495	9.686513	0.103236	10
11	1.066071	11.326514	0.088288	0.938024	10.624537	0.094122	11
12	1.072290	12.392585	0.080693	0.932583	11.557120	0.086527	12
YEARS							MONTHS
1	1.072290	12.392585	0.080693	0.932583	11.557120	0.086527	12
2	1.149806	25.681032	0.038939	0.869712	22.335099	0.044773	24
3	1.232926	39.930101	0.025044	0.811079	32.386464	0.030877	36
4	1.322054	55.209236	0.018113	0.756399	41.760201	0.023946	48
5	1.417625	71.592902	0.013968	0.705405	50.501994	0.019801	60
6	1.520106	89.160944	0.011216	0.657849	58.654444	0.017049	72
7	1.629994	107.998981	0.009259	0.613499	66.257285	0.015093	84
8	1.747826	128.198821	0.007800	0.572139	73.347569	0.013634	96
9	1.874177	149.858909	0.006673	0.533568	79.959850	0.012506	108
10	2.009661	173.084807	0.005778	0.497596	86.126354	0.011611	120
11	2.154940	197.989707	0.005051	0.464050	91.877134	0.010884	132
12	2.310721	224.694985	0.004450	0.432765	97.240216	0.010284	144
13	2.477763	253.330789	0.003947	0.403590	102.241738	0.009781	156
14	2.656881	284.036677	0.003521	0.376381	106.906074	0.009354	168
15	2.848947	316.962297	0.003155	0.351007	111.255958	0.008988	180
16	3.054897	352.268112	0.002839	0.327343	115.312587	0.008672	192
17	3.275736	390.126188	0.002563	0.305275	119.095732	0.008397	204
18	3.512539	430.721027	0.002322	0.284694	122.623831	0.008155	216
19	3.766461	474.250470	0.002109	0.265501	125.914077	0.007942	228
20	4.038739	520.926660	0.001920	0.247602	128.982506	0.007753	240
21	4.330700	570.977075	0.001751	0.230910	131.844073	0.007585	252
22	4.643766	624.645640	0.001601	0.215342	134.512723	0.007434	264
23	4.979464	682.193909	0.001466	0.200825	137.001461	0.007299	276
24	5.339430	743.902347	0.001344	0.187286	139.322418	0.007178	288
25	5.725418	810.071693	0.001234	0.174660	141.486903	0.007068	300
26	6.139309	881.024427	0.001135	0.162885	143.505467	0.006968	312
27	6.583120	957.106339	0.001045	0.151904	145.387946	0.006878	324
28	7.059015	1038.688219	0.000963	0.141663	147.143515	0.006796	336
29	7.569311	1126.167659	0.000888	0.132112	148.780729	0.006721	348
30	8.116497	1219.970996	0.000820	0.123206	150.307568	0.006653	360
31	8.703240	1320.555383	0.000757	0.114900	151.731473	0.006591	372
32	9.332398	1428.411024	0.000700	0.107154	153.059383	0.006533	384
33	10.007037	1544.063557	0.000648	0.099930	154.297770	0.006481	396
34	10.730447	1668.076622	0.000599	0.093193	155.452669	0.006433	408
35	11.506152	1801.054601	0.000555	0.086910	156.529709	0.006389	420
36	12.337932	1943.645569	0.000514	0.081051	157.534139	0.006348	432
37	13.229843	2096.544450	0.000477	0.075587	158.470853	0.006310	444
38	14.186229	2260.496403	0.000442	0.070491	159.344418	0.006276	456
39	15.211753	2436.300456	0.000410	0.065739	160.159090	0.006244	468
40	16.311411	2624.813398	0.000381	0.061307	160.918839	0.006214	480

MONTHLY COMPOUND INTEREST TABLES

8.00% ANNUAL INTEREST RATE

0.6667% MONTHLY EFFECTIVE INTEREST RATE

	1 AMOUNT OF $1 AT COMPOUND INTEREST	2 ACCUMULATION OF $1 PER PERIOD	3 SINKING FUND FACTOR	4 PRESENT VALUE REVERSION OF $1	5 PRESENT VALUE ORD. ANNUITY $1 PER PERIOD	6 INSTALLMENT TO AMORTIZE $1	
MONTHS							MONTHS
1	1.006667	1.000000	1.000000	0.993377	0.993377	1.006667	1
2	1.013378	2.006667	0.498339	0.986799	1.980176	0.505006	2
3	1.020134	3.020044	0.331121	0.980264	2.960440	0.337788	3
4	1.026935	4.040178	0.247514	0.973772	3.934212	0.254181	4
5	1.033781	5.067113	0.197351	0.967323	4.901535	0.204018	5
6	1.040673	6.100893	0.163910	0.960917	5.862452	0.170577	6
7	1.047610	7.141566	0.140025	0.954553	6.817005	0.146692	7
8	1.054595	8.189176	0.122112	0.948232	7.765237	0.128779	8
9	1.061625	9.243771	0.108181	0.941952	8.707189	0.114848	9
10	1.068703	10.305396	0.097037	0.935714	9.642903	0.103703	10
11	1.075827	11.374099	0.087919	0.929517	10.572420	0.094586	11
12	1.083000	12.449926	0.080322	0.923361	11.495782	0.086988	12
YEARS							MONTHS
1	1.083000	12.449926	0.080322	0.923361	11.495782	0.086988	12
2	1.172888	25.933190	0.038561	0.852596	22.110544	0.045227	24
3	1.270237	40.535558	0.024670	0.787255	31.911806	0.031336	36
4	1.375666	56.349915	0.017746	0.726921	40.961913	0.024413	48
5	1.489846	73.476856	0.013610	0.671210	49.318433	0.020276	60
6	1.613502	92.025325	0.010867	0.619770	57.034522	0.017533	72
7	1.747422	112.113308	0.008920	0.572272	64.159261	0.015586	84
8	1.892457	133.868583	0.007470	0.528414	70.737970	0.014137	96
9	2.049530	157.429535	0.006352	0.487917	76.812497	0.013019	108
10	2.219640	182.946035	0.005466	0.450523	82.421481	0.012133	120
11	2.403869	210.580392	0.004749	0.415996	87.600600	0.011415	132
12	2.603389	240.508387	0.004158	0.384115	92.382800	0.010825	144
13	2.819469	272.920390	0.003664	0.354677	96.798498	0.010331	156
14	3.053484	308.022574	0.003247	0.327495	100.875784	0.009913	168
15	3.306921	346.038222	0.002890	0.302396	104.640592	0.009557	180
16	3.581394	387.209149	0.002583	0.279221	108.116871	0.009249	192
17	3.878648	431.797244	0.002316	0.257822	111.326733	0.008983	204
18	4.200574	480.086128	0.002083	0.238063	114.290596	0.008750	216
19	4.549220	532.382966	0.001878	0.219818	117.027313	0.008545	228
20	4.926803	589.020416	0.001698	0.202971	119.554292	0.008364	240
21	5.335725	650.358746	0.001538	0.187416	121.887606	0.008204	252
22	5.778588	716.788127	0.001395	0.173053	124.042099	0.008062	264
23	6.258207	788.731114	0.001268	0.159790	126.031475	0.007935	276
24	6.777636	866.645333	0.001154	0.147544	127.868388	0.007821	288
25	7.340176	951.026395	0.001051	0.136237	129.564523	0.007718	300
26	7.949407	1042.411042	0.000959	0.125796	131.130668	0.007626	312
27	8.609204	1141.380571	0.000876	0.116155	132.576786	0.007543	324
28	9.323763	1248.564521	0.000801	0.107253	133.912076	0.007468	336
29	10.097631	1364.644687	0.000733	0.099033	135.145031	0.007399	348
30	10.935730	1490.359449	0.000671	0.091443	136.283494	0.007338	360
31	11.843390	1626.508474	0.000615	0.084435	137.334707	0.007281	372
32	12.826385	1773.957801	0.000564	0.077964	138.305357	0.007230	384
33	13.890969	1933.645350	0.000517	0.071989	139.201617	0.007184	396
34	15.043913	2106.586886	0.000475	0.066472	140.029190	0.007141	408
35	16.292550	2293.882485	0.000436	0.061378	140.793338	0.007103	420
36	17.644824	2496.723526	0.000401	0.056674	141.498923	0.007067	432
37	19.109335	2716.400273	0.000368	0.052330	142.150433	0.007035	444
38	20.695401	2954.310082	0.000338	0.048320	142.752013	0.007005	456
39	22.413109	3211.966288	0.000311	0.044617	143.307488	0.006978	468
40	24.273386	3491.007831	0.000286	0.041197	143.820392	0.006953	480

MONTHLY COMPOUND INTEREST TABLES

9.00% ANNUAL INTEREST RATE — 0.7500% MONTHLY EFFECTIVE INTEREST RATE

	1 AMOUNT OF $1 AT COMPOUND INTEREST	2 ACCUMULATION OF $1 PER PERIOD	3 SINKING FUND FACTOR	4 PRESENT VALUE REVERSION OF $1	5 PRESENT VALUE ORD. ANNUITY $1 PER PERIOD	6 INSTALLMENT TO AMORTIZE $1	
MONTHS							MONTHS
1	1.007500	1.000000	1.000000	0.992556	0.992556	1.007500	1
2	1.015056	2.007500	0.498132	0.985167	1.977723	0.505632	2
3	1.022669	3.022556	0.330846	0.977833	2.955556	0.338346	3
4	1.030339	4.045225	0.247205	0.970554	3.926110	0.254705	4
5	1.038067	5.075565	0.197022	0.963329	4.889440	0.204522	5
6	1.045852	6.113631	0.163569	0.956158	5.845598	0.171069	6
7	1.053696	7.159484	0.139675	0.949040	6.794638	0.147175	7
8	1.061599	8.213180	0.121756	0.941975	7.736613	0.129256	8
9	1.069561	9.274779	0.107819	0.934963	8.671576	0.115319	9
10	1.077583	10.344339	0.096671	0.928003	9.599580	0.104171	10
11	1.085664	11.421922	0.087551	0.921095	10.520675	0.095051	11
12	1.093807	12.507586	0.079951	0.914238	11.434913	0.087451	12
YEARS							MONTHS
1	1.093807	12.507586	0.079951	0.914238	11.434913	0.087451	12
2	1.196414	26.188471	0.038185	0.835831	21.889146	0.045685	24
3	1.308645	41.152716	0.024300	0.764149	31.446805	0.031800	36
4	1.431405	57.520711	0.017385	0.698614	40.184782	0.024885	48
5	1.565681	75.424137	0.013258	0.638700	48.173374	0.020758	60
6	1.712553	95.007028	0.010526	0.583924	55.476849	0.018026	72
7	1.873202	116.426928	0.008589	0.533845	62.153965	0.016089	84
8	2.048921	139.856164	0.007150	0.488062	68.258439	0.014650	96
9	2.241124	165.483223	0.006043	0.446205	73.839382	0.013543	108
10	2.451357	193.514277	0.005168	0.407937	78.941693	0.012668	120
11	2.681311	224.174837	0.004461	0.372952	83.606420	0.011961	132
12	2.932837	257.711570	0.003880	0.340967	87.871092	0.011380	144
13	3.207957	294.394279	0.003397	0.311725	91.770018	0.010897	156
14	3.508886	334.518079	0.002989	0.284991	95.334564	0.010489	168
15	3.838043	378.405769	0.002643	0.260549	98.593409	0.010143	180
16	4.198078	426.410427	0.002345	0.238204	101.572769	0.009845	192
17	4.591887	478.918252	0.002088	0.217775	104.296613	0.009588	204
18	5.022638	536.351674	0.001864	0.199099	106.786856	0.009364	216
19	5.493796	599.172747	0.001669	0.182024	109.063531	0.009169	228
20	6.009152	667.886870	0.001497	0.166413	111.144954	0.008997	240
21	6.572851	743.046852	0.001346	0.152141	113.047870	0.008846	252
22	7.189430	825.257358	0.001212	0.139093	114.787589	0.008712	264
23	7.863848	915.179777	0.001093	0.127164	116.378106	0.008593	276
24	8.601532	1013.537539	0.000987	0.116258	117.832218	0.008487	288
25	9.408415	1121.121937	0.000892	0.106288	119.161622	0.008392	300
26	10.290989	1238.798495	0.000807	0.097172	120.377014	0.008307	312
27	11.256354	1367.513924	0.000731	0.088839	121.488172	0.008231	324
28	12.312278	1508.303750	0.000663	0.081220	122.504035	0.008163	336
29	13.467255	1662.300631	0.000602	0.074254	123.432776	0.008102	348
30	14.730576	1830.743483	0.000546	0.067886	124.281866	0.008046	360
31	16.112406	2014.987436	0.000496	0.062064	125.058136	0.007996	372
32	17.623861	2216.514743	0.000451	0.056741	125.767832	0.007951	384
33	19.277100	2436.946701	0.000410	0.051875	126.416664	0.007910	396
34	21.085425	2678.056697	0.000373	0.047426	127.009850	0.007873	408
35	23.063384	2941.784474	0.000340	0.043359	127.552164	0.007840	420
36	25.226888	3230.251735	0.000310	0.039640	128.047967	0.007810	432
37	27.593344	3545.779215	0.000282	0.036241	128.501250	0.007782	444
38	30.181790	3890.905350	0.000257	0.033133	128.915659	0.007757	456
39	33.013050	4268.406696	0.000234	0.030291	129.294526	0.007734	468
40	36.109902	4681.320273	0.000214	0.027693	129.640902	0.007714	480

MONTHLY COMPOUND INTEREST TABLES

10.00% ANNUAL INTEREST RATE 0.8333% MONTHLY EFFECTIVE INTEREST RATE

	1 AMOUNT OF $1 AT COMPOUND INTEREST	2 ACCUMULATION OF $1 PER PERIOD	3 SINKING FUND FACTOR	4 PRESENT VALUE REVERSION OF $1	5 PRESENT VALUE ORD. ANNUITY $1 PER PERIOD	6 INSTALLMENT TO AMORTIZE $1	
MONTHS							MONTHS
1	1.008333	1.000000	1.000000	0.991736	0.991736	1.008333	1
2	1.016736	2.008333	0.497925	0.983539	1.975275	0.506259	2
3	1.025209	3.025069	0.330571	0.975411	2.950686	0.338904	3
4	1.033752	4.050278	0.246897	0.967350	3.918036	0.255230	4
5	1.042367	5.084031	0.196694	0.959355	4.877391	0.205028	5
6	1.051053	6.126398	0.163228	0.951427	5.828817	0.171561	6
7	1.059812	7.177451	0.139325	0.943563	6.772381	0.147659	7
8	1.068644	8.237263	0.121400	0.935765	7.708146	0.129733	8
9	1.077549	9.305907	0.107459	0.928032	8.636178	0.115792	9
10	1.086529	10.383456	0.096307	0.920362	9.556540	0.104640	10
11	1.095583	11.469985	0.087184	0.912756	10.469296	0.095517	11
12	1.104713	12.565568	0.079583	0.905212	11.374508	0.087916	12

YEARS	1	2	3	4	5	6	MONTHS
1	1.104713	12.565568	0.079583	0.905212	11.374508	0.087916	12
2	1.220391	26.446915	0.037812	0.819410	21.670855	0.046145	24
3	1.348182	41.781821	0.023934	0.741740	30.991236	0.032267	36
4	1.489354	58.722492	0.017029	0.671432	39.428160	0.025363	48
5	1.645309	77.437072	0.012914	0.607789	47.065369	0.021247	60
6	1.817594	98.111314	0.010193	0.550178	53.978665	0.018526	72
7	2.007920	120.950418	0.008268	0.498028	60.236667	0.016601	84
8	2.218176	146.181076	0.006841	0.450821	65.901488	0.015174	96
9	2.450448	174.053713	0.005745	0.408089	71.029355	0.014079	108
10	2.707041	204.844979	0.004882	0.369407	75.671163	0.013215	120
11	2.990504	238.860493	0.004187	0.334392	79.872986	0.012520	132
12	3.303649	276.437876	0.003617	0.302696	83.676528	0.011951	144
13	3.649584	317.950102	0.003145	0.274004	87.119542	0.011478	156
14	4.031743	363.809201	0.002749	0.248032	90.236201	0.011082	168
15	4.453920	414.470346	0.002413	0.224521	93.057439	0.010746	180
16	4.920303	470.436376	0.002126	0.203240	95.611259	0.010459	192
17	5.435523	532.262780	0.001879	0.183975	97.923008	0.010212	204
18	6.004693	600.563216	0.001665	0.166536	100.015633	0.009998	216
19	6.633463	676.015601	0.001479	0.150751	101.909902	0.009813	228
20	7.328074	759.368836	0.001317	0.136462	103.624619	0.009650	240
21	8.095419	851.450244	0.001174	0.123527	105.176801	0.009508	252
22	8.943115	953.173779	0.001049	0.111818	106.581856	0.009382	264
23	9.879576	1065.549097	0.000938	0.101219	107.853730	0.009272	276
24	10.914097	1189.691580	0.000841	0.091625	109.005045	0.009174	288
25	12.056945	1326.833403	0.000754	0.082940	110.047230	0.009087	300
26	13.319465	1478.335767	0.000676	0.075078	110.990629	0.009010	312
27	14.714187	1645.702407	0.000608	0.067962	111.844605	0.008941	324
28	16.254954	1830.594523	0.000546	0.061520	112.617635	0.008880	336
29	17.957060	2034.847258	0.000491	0.055688	113.317392	0.008825	348
30	19.837399	2260.487925	0.000442	0.050410	113.950820	0.008776	360
31	21.914634	2509.756117	0.000398	0.045632	114.524207	0.008732	372
32	24.209383	2785.125947	0.000359	0.041306	115.043244	0.008692	384
33	26.744422	3089.330596	0.000324	0.037391	115.513083	0.008657	396
34	29.544912	3425.389447	0.000292	0.033847	115.938387	0.008625	408
35	32.638650	3796.638052	0.000263	0.030639	116.323377	0.008597	420
36	36.056344	4206.761236	0.000238	0.027734	116.671876	0.008571	432
37	39.831914	4659.829677	0.000215	0.025105	116.987340	0.008548	444
38	44.002836	5160.340305	0.000194	0.022726	117.272903	0.008527	456
39	48.610508	5713.260935	0.000175	0.020572	117.531398	0.008508	468
40	53.700663	6324.079581	0.000158	0.018622	117.765391	0.008491	480

MONTHLY COMPOUND INTEREST TABLES

11.00% ANNUAL INTEREST RATE — 0.9167% MONTHLY EFFECTIVE INTEREST RATE

	1 AMOUNT OF $1 AT COMPOUND INTEREST	2 ACCUMULATION OF $1 PER PERIOD	3 SINKING FUND FACTOR	4 PRESENT VALUE REVERSION OF $1	5 PRESENT VALUE ORD. ANNUITY $1 PER PERIOD	6 INSTALLMENT TO AMORTIZE $1	
MONTHS							MONTHS
1	1.009167	1.000000	1.000000	0.990917	0.990917	1.009167	1
2	1.018417	2.009167	0.497719	0.981916	1.972832	0.506885	2
3	1.027753	3.027584	0.330296	0.972997	2.945829	0.339463	3
4	1.037174	4.055337	0.246589	0.964158	3.909987	0.255755	4
5	1.046681	5.092511	0.196367	0.955401	4.865388	0.205533	5
6	1.056276	6.139192	0.162888	0.946722	5.812110	0.172055	6
7	1.065958	7.195468	0.138976	0.938123	6.750233	0.148143	7
8	1.075730	8.261427	0.121044	0.929602	7.679835	0.130211	8
9	1.085591	9.337156	0.107099	0.921158	8.600992	0.116266	9
10	1.095542	10.422747	0.095944	0.912790	9.513783	0.105111	10
11	1.105584	11.518289	0.086818	0.904499	10.418282	0.095985	11
12	1.115719	12.623873	0.079215	0.896283	11.314565	0.088382	12
YEARS							MONTHS
1	1.115719	12.623873	0.079215	0.896283	11.314565	0.088382	12
2	1.244829	26.708566	0.037441	0.803323	21.455619	0.046608	24
3	1.388879	42.423123	0.023572	0.720005	30.544874	0.032739	36
4	1.549598	59.956151	0.016679	0.645329	38.691421	0.025846	48
5	1.728916	79.518080	0.012576	0.578397	45.993034	0.021742	60
6	1.928984	101.343692	0.009867	0.518408	52.537346	0.019034	72
7	2.152204	125.694940	0.007956	0.464640	58.402903	0.017122	84
8	2.401254	152.864085	0.006542	0.416449	63.660103	0.015708	96
9	2.679124	183.177212	0.005459	0.373256	68.372043	0.014626	108
10	2.989150	216.998139	0.004608	0.334543	72.595275	0.013775	120
11	3.335051	254.732784	0.003926	0.299846	76.380487	0.013092	132
12	3.720979	296.834038	0.003369	0.268747	79.773109	0.012536	144
13	4.151566	343.807200	0.002909	0.240873	82.813859	0.012075	156
14	4.631980	396.216042	0.002524	0.215890	85.539231	0.011691	168
15	5.167988	454.689575	0.002199	0.193499	87.981937	0.011366	180
16	5.766021	519.929596	0.001923	0.173430	90.171293	0.011090	192
17	6.433259	592.719117	0.001687	0.155442	92.133576	0.010854	204
18	7.177708	673.931757	0.001484	0.139320	93.892337	0.010650	216
19	8.008304	764.542228	0.001308	0.124870	95.468685	0.010475	228
20	8.935015	865.638038	0.001155	0.111919	96.881539	0.010322	240
21	9.968965	978.432537	0.001022	0.100311	98.147856	0.010189	252
22	11.122562	1104.279485	0.000906	0.089907	99.282835	0.010072	264
23	12.409652	1244.689295	0.000803	0.080582	100.300098	0.009970	276
24	13.845682	1401.347165	0.000714	0.072225	101.211853	0.009880	288
25	15.447889	1576.133301	0.000634	0.064734	102.029044	0.009801	300
26	17.235500	1771.145485	0.000565	0.058020	102.761478	0.009731	312
27	19.229972	1988.724252	0.000503	0.052002	103.417947	0.009670	324
28	21.455242	2231.480981	0.000448	0.046609	104.006328	0.009615	336
29	23.938018	2502.329236	0.000400	0.041775	104.533685	0.009566	348
30	26.708098	2804.519736	0.000357	0.037442	105.006346	0.009523	360
31	29.798728	3141.679369	0.000318	0.033558	105.429984	0.009485	372
32	33.247002	3517.854723	0.000284	0.030078	105.809684	0.009451	384
33	37.094306	3937.560650	0.000254	0.026958	106.150002	0.009421	396
34	41.386816	4405.834459	0.000227	0.024162	106.455024	0.009394	408
35	46.176050	4928.296368	0.000203	0.021656	106.728409	0.009370	420
36	51.519489	5511.216962	0.000181	0.019410	106.973440	0.009348	432
37	57.481264	6161.592447	0.000162	0.017397	107.193057	0.009329	444
38	64.132929	6887.228628	0.000145	0.015593	107.389897	0.009312	456
39	71.554317	7696.834582	0.000130	0.013975	107.566320	0.009297	468
40	79.834499	8600.127195	0.000116	0.012526	107.724446	0.009283	480

MONTHLY COMPOUND INTEREST TABLES

12.00% ANNUAL INTEREST RATE

1.0000% MONTHLY EFFECTIVE INTEREST RATE

	1 AMOUNT OF $1 AT COMPOUND INTEREST	2 ACCUMULATION OF $1 PER PERIOD	3 SINKING FUND FACTOR	4 PRESENT VALUE REVERSION OF $1	5 PRESENT VALUE ORD. ANNUITY $1 PER PERIOD	6 INSTALLMENT TO AMORTIZE $1	
MONTHS							MONTHS
1	1.010000	1.000000	1.000000	0.990099	0.990099	1.010000	1
2	1.020100	2.010000	0.497512	0.980296	1.970395	0.507512	2
3	1.030301	3.030100	0.330022	0.970590	2.940985	0.340022	3
4	1.040604	4.060401	0.246281	0.960980	3.901966	0.256281	4
5	1.051010	5.101005	0.196040	0.951466	4.853431	0.206040	5
6	1.061520	6.152015	0.162548	0.942045	5.795476	0.172548	6
7	1.072135	7.213535	0.138628	0.932718	6.728195	0.148628	7
8	1.082857	8.285671	0.120690	0.923483	7.651678	0.130690	8
9	1.093685	9.368527	0.106740	0.914340	8.566018	0.116740	9
10	1.104622	10.462213	0.095582	0.905287	9.471305	0.105582	10
11	1.115668	11.566835	0.086454	0.896324	10.367628	0.096454	11
12	1.126825	12.682503	0.078849	0.887449	11.255077	0.088849	12
YEARS							MONTHS
1	1.126825	12.682503	0.078849	0.887449	11.255077	0.088849	12
2	1.269735	26.973465	0.037073	0.787566	21.243387	0.047073	24
3	1.430769	43.076878	0.023214	0.698925	30.107505	0.033214	36
4	1.612226	61.222608	0.016334	0.620260	37.973959	0.026334	48
5	1.816697	81.669670	0.012244	0.550450	44.955038	0.022244	60
6	2.047099	104.709931	0.009550	0.488496	51.150391	0.019550	72
7	2.306723	130.672274	0.007653	0.433515	56.648453	0.017653	84
8	2.599273	159.927293	0.006253	0.384723	61.527703	0.016253	96
9	2.928926	192.892579	0.005184	0.341422	65.857790	0.015184	108
10	3.300387	230.038689	0.004347	0.302995	69.700522	0.014347	120
11	3.718959	271.895856	0.003678	0.268892	73.110752	0.013678	132
12	4.190616	319.061559	0.003134	0.238628	76.137157	0.013134	144
13	4.722091	372.209054	0.002687	0.211771	78.822939	0.012687	156
14	5.320970	432.096982	0.002314	0.187936	81.206434	0.012314	168
15	5.995802	499.580198	0.002002	0.166783	83.321664	0.012002	180
16	6.756220	575.621974	0.001737	0.148012	85.198824	0.011737	192
17	7.613078	661.307751	0.001512	0.131353	86.864707	0.011512	204
18	8.578606	757.860630	0.001320	0.116569	88.343095	0.011320	216
19	9.666588	866.658830	0.001154	0.103449	89.655089	0.011154	228
20	10.892554	989.255365	0.001011	0.091806	90.819416	0.011011	240
21	12.274002	1127.400210	0.000887	0.081473	91.852698	0.010887	252
22	13.830653	1283.065279	0.000779	0.072303	92.769683	0.010779	264
23	15.584726	1458.472574	0.000686	0.064165	93.583461	0.010686	276
24	17.561259	1656.125905	0.000604	0.056944	94.305647	0.010604	288
25	19.788466	1878.846626	0.000532	0.050534	94.946551	0.010532	300
26	22.298139	2129.813909	0.000470	0.044847	95.515321	0.010470	312
27	25.126101	2412.610125	0.000414	0.039799	96.020075	0.010414	324
28	28.312720	2731.271980	0.000366	0.035320	96.468019	0.010366	336
29	31.903481	3090.348134	0.000324	0.031345	96.865546	0.010324	348
30	35.949641	3494.964133	0.000286	0.027817	97.218331	0.010286	360
31	40.508956	3950.895567	0.000253	0.024686	97.531410	0.010253	372
32	45.646505	4464.650520	0.000224	0.021907	97.809252	0.010224	384
33	51.435625	5043.562459	0.000198	0.019442	98.055822	0.010198	396
34	57.958949	5695.894923	0.000176	0.017254	98.274641	0.010176	408
35	65.309595	6430.959471	0.000155	0.015312	98.468831	0.010155	420
36	73.592486	7259.248603	0.000138	0.013588	98.641166	0.010138	432
37	82.925855	8192.585529	0.000122	0.012059	98.794103	0.010122	444
38	93.442929	9244.292939	0.000108	0.010702	98.929828	0.010108	456
39	105.293832	10429.383172	0.000096	0.009497	99.050277	0.010096	468
40	118.647725	11764.772510	0.000085	0.008428	99.157169	0.010085	480

MONTHLY COMPOUND INTEREST TABLES

13.00% ANNUAL INTEREST RATE

1.0833% MONTHLY EFFECTIVE INTEREST RATE

	1 AMOUNT OF $1 AT COMPOUND INTEREST	2 ACCUMULATION OF $1 PER PERIOD	3 SINKING FUND FACTOR	4 PRESENT VALUE REVERSION OF $1	5 PRESENT VALUE ORD. ANNUITY $1 PER PERIOD	6 INSTALLMENT TO AMORTIZE $1	
MONTHS							MONTHS
1	1.010833	1.000000	1.000000	0.989283	0.989283	1.010833	1
2	1.021784	2.010833	0.497306	0.978680	1.967963	0.508140	2
3	1.032853	3.032617	0.329748	0.968192	2.936155	0.340581	3
4	1.044043	4.065471	0.245974	0.957815	3.893970	0.256807	4
5	1.055353	5.109513	0.195713	0.947550	4.841520	0.206547	5
6	1.066786	6.164866	0.162210	0.937395	5.778915	0.173043	6
7	1.078343	7.231652	0.138281	0.927349	6.706264	0.149114	7
8	1.090025	8.309995	0.120337	0.917410	7.623674	0.131170	8
9	1.101834	9.400020	0.106383	0.907578	8.531253	0.117216	9
10	1.113770	10.501854	0.095221	0.897851	9.429104	0.106055	10
11	1.125836	11.615624	0.086091	0.888229	10.317333	0.096924	11
12	1.138032	12.741460	0.078484	0.878710	11.196042	0.089317	12
YEARS							MONTHS
1	1.138032	12.741460	0.078484	0.878710	11.196042	0.089317	12
2	1.295118	27.241655	0.036708	0.772130	21.034112	0.047542	24
3	1.473886	43.743348	0.022861	0.678478	29.678917	0.033694	36
4	1.677330	62.522811	0.015994	0.596185	37.275190	0.026827	48
5	1.908857	83.894449	0.011920	0.523874	43.950107	0.022753	60
6	2.172341	108.216068	0.009241	0.460333	49.815421	0.020074	72
7	2.472194	135.894861	0.007359	0.404499	54.969328	0.018192	84
8	2.813437	167.394225	0.005974	0.355437	59.498115	0.016807	96
9	3.201783	203.241525	0.004920	0.312326	63.477604	0.015754	108
10	3.643733	244.036917	0.004098	0.274444	66.974419	0.014931	120
11	4.146687	290.463399	0.003443	0.241156	70.047103	0.014276	132
12	4.719064	343.298242	0.002913	0.211906	72.747100	0.013746	144
13	5.370448	403.426010	0.002479	0.186204	75.119613	0.013312	156
14	6.111745	471.853363	0.002119	0.163619	77.204363	0.012953	168
15	6.955364	549.725914	0.001819	0.143774	79.036253	0.012652	180
16	7.915430	638.347406	0.001567	0.126336	80.645952	0.012400	192
17	9.008017	739.201542	0.001353	0.111012	82.060410	0.012186	204
18	10.251416	853.976825	0.001171	0.097548	83.303307	0.012004	216
19	11.666444	984.594826	0.001016	0.085716	84.395453	0.011849	228
20	13.276792	1133.242353	0.000882	0.075319	85.355132	0.011716	240
21	15.109421	1302.408067	0.000768	0.066184	86.198412	0.011601	252
22	17.195012	1494.924144	0.000669	0.058156	86.939409	0.011502	264
23	19.568482	1714.013694	0.000583	0.051103	87.590531	0.011417	276
24	22.269568	1963.344717	0.000509	0.044904	88.162677	0.011343	288
25	25.343491	2247.091520	0.000445	0.039458	88.665428	0.011278	300
26	28.841716	2570.004599	0.000389	0.034672	89.107200	0.011222	312
27	32.822810	2937.490172	0.000340	0.030467	89.495389	0.011174	324
28	37.353424	3355.700690	0.000298	0.026771	89.836495	0.011131	336
29	42.509410	3831.637843	0.000261	0.023524	90.136227	0.011094	348
30	48.377089	4373.269783	0.000229	0.020671	90.399605	0.011062	360
31	55.054699	4989.664524	0.000200	0.018164	90.631038	0.011034	372
32	62.654036	5691.141761	0.000176	0.015961	90.834400	0.011009	384
33	71.302328	6489.445641	0.000154	0.014025	91.013097	0.010987	396
34	81.144365	7397.941387	0.000135	0.012324	91.170119	0.010969	408
35	92.344923	8431.839055	0.000119	0.010829	91.308095	0.010952	420
36	105.091522	9608.448184	0.000104	0.009516	91.429337	0.010937	432
37	119.597566	10947.467591	0.000091	0.008361	91.535873	0.010925	444
38	136.105914	12471.315170	0.000080	0.007347	91.629487	0.010914	456
39	154.892951	14205.503212	0.000070	0.006456	91.711747	0.010904	468
40	176.273210	16179.065533	0.000062	0.005673	91.784030	0.010895	480

MONTHLY COMPOUND INTEREST TABLES

14.00% ANNUAL INTEREST RATE 1.1667% MONTHLY EFFECTIVE INTEREST RATE

	1 AMOUNT OF $1 AT COMPOUND INTEREST	2 ACCUMULATION OF $1 PER PERIOD	3 SINKING FUND FACTOR	4 PRESENT VALUE REVERSION OF $1	5 PRESENT VALUE ORD. ANNUITY $1 PER PERIOD	6 INSTALLMENT TO AMORTIZE $1	
MONTHS							MONTHS
1	1.011667	1.000000	1.000000	0.988468	0.988468	1.011667	1
2	1.023469	2.011667	0.497100	0.977069	1.965537	0.508767	2
3	1.035410	3.035136	0.329475	0.965801	2.931338	0.341141	3
4	1.047490	4.070546	0.245667	0.954663	3.886001	0.257334	4
5	1.059710	5.118036	0.195387	0.943654	4.829655	0.207054	5
6	1.072074	6.177746	0.161871	0.932772	5.762427	0.173538	6
7	1.084581	7.249820	0.137934	0.922015	6.684442	0.149601	7
8	1.097235	8.334401	0.119985	0.911382	7.595824	0.131651	8
9	1.110036	9.431636	0.106026	0.900872	8.496696	0.117693	9
10	1.122986	10.541672	0.094862	0.890483	9.387178	0.106528	10
11	1.136088	11.664658	0.085729	0.880214	10.267392	0.097396	11
12	1.149342	12.800745	0.078120	0.870063	11.137455	0.089787	12
YEARS							MONTHS
1	1.149342	12.800745	0.078120	0.870063	11.137455	0.089787	12
2	1.320987	27.513180	0.036346	0.757010	20.827743	0.048013	24
3	1.518266	44.422800	0.022511	0.658646	29.258904	0.034178	36
4	1.745007	63.857736	0.015660	0.573064	36.594546	0.027326	48
5	2.005610	86.195125	0.011602	0.498601	42.977016	0.023268	60
6	2.305132	111.868425	0.008939	0.433815	48.530168	0.020606	72
7	2.649385	141.375828	0.007073	0.377446	53.361760	0.018740	84
8	3.045049	175.289927	0.005705	0.328402	57.565549	0.017372	96
9	3.499803	214.268826	0.004667	0.285730	61.223111	0.016334	108
10	4.022471	259.068912	0.003860	0.248603	64.405420	0.015527	120
11	4.623195	310.559534	0.003220	0.216301	67.174230	0.014887	132
12	5.313632	369.739871	0.002705	0.188195	69.583269	0.014371	144
13	6.107180	437.758319	0.002284	0.163742	71.679284	0.013951	156
14	7.019239	515.934780	0.001938	0.142466	73.502950	0.013605	168
15	8.067507	605.786272	0.001651	0.123954	75.089654	0.013317	180
16	9.272324	709.056369	0.001410	0.107848	76.470187	0.013077	192
17	10.657072	827.749031	0.001208	0.093834	77.671337	0.012875	204
18	12.248621	964.167496	0.001037	0.081642	78.716413	0.012704	216
19	14.077855	1120.958972	0.000892	0.071034	79.625696	0.012559	228
20	16.180270	1301.166005	0.000769	0.061804	80.416829	0.012435	240
21	18.596664	1508.285522	0.000663	0.053773	81.105164	0.012330	252
22	21.373928	1746.336688	0.000573	0.046786	81.704060	0.012239	264
23	24.565954	2019.938898	0.000495	0.040707	82.225136	0.012162	276
24	28.234683	2334.401417	0.000428	0.035417	82.678506	0.012095	288
25	32.451308	2695.826407	0.000371	0.030815	83.072966	0.012038	300
26	37.297652	3111.227338	0.000321	0.026811	83.416171	0.011988	312
27	42.867759	3588.665088	0.000279	0.023328	83.714781	0.011945	324
28	49.269718	4137.404359	0.000242	0.020296	83.974591	0.011908	336
29	56.627757	4768.093467	0.000210	0.017659	84.200641	0.011876	348
30	65.084661	5492.970967	0.000182	0.015365	84.397320	0.011849	360
31	74.804537	6326.103143	0.000158	0.013368	84.568442	0.011825	372
32	85.975998	7283.656968	0.000137	0.011631	84.717330	0.011804	384
33	98.815828	8384.213825	0.000119	0.010120	84.846871	0.011786	396
34	113.573184	9649.130077	0.000104	0.008805	84.959580	0.011770	408
35	130.534434	11102.951488	0.000090	0.007661	85.057645	0.011757	420
36	150.028711	12773.889538	0.000078	0.006665	85.142966	0.011745	432
37	172.434303	14694.368868	0.000068	0.005799	85.217202	0.011735	444
38	198.185992	16901.656478	0.000059	0.005046	85.281792	0.011726	456
39	227.783490	19438.584899	0.000051	0.004390	85.337989	0.011718	468
40	261.801139	22354.383358	0.000045	0.003820	85.386883	0.011711	480

MONTHLY COMPOUND INTEREST TABLES

15.00% ANNUAL INTEREST RATE

1.2500% MONTHLY EFFECTIVE INTEREST RATE

	1 AMOUNT OF $1 AT COMPOUND INTEREST	2 ACCUMULATION OF $1 PER PERIOD	3 SINKING FUND FACTOR	4 PRESENT VALUE REVERSION OF $1	5 PRESENT VALUE ORD. ANNUITY $1 PER PERIOD	6 INSTALLMENT TO AMORTIZE $1	
MONTHS							MONTHS
1	1.012500	1.000000	1.000000	0.987654	0.987654	1.012500	1
2	1.025156	2.012500	0.496894	0.975461	1.963115	0.509394	2
3	1.037971	3.037656	0.329201	0.963418	2.926534	0.341701	3
4	1.050945	4.075627	0.245361	0.951524	3.878058	0.257861	4
5	1.064082	5.126572	0.195062	0.939777	4.817835	0.207562	5
6	1.077383	6.190654	0.161534	0.928175	5.746010	0.174034	6
7	1.090850	7.268038	0.137589	0.916716	6.662726	0.150089	7
8	1.104486	8.358888	0.119633	0.905398	7.568124	0.132133	8
9	1.118292	9.463374	0.105671	0.894221	8.462345	0.118171	9
10	1.132271	10.581666	0.094503	0.883181	9.345526	0.107003	10
11	1.146424	11.713937	0.085368	0.872277	10.217803	0.097868	11
12	1.160755	12.860361	0.077758	0.861509	11.079312	0.090258	12
YEARS							MONTHS
1	1.160755	12.860361	0.077758	0.861509	11.079312	0.090258	12
2	1.347351	27.788084	0.035987	0.742197	20.624235	0.048487	24
3	1.563944	45.115505	0.022165	0.639409	28.847267	0.034665	36
4	1.815355	65.228388	0.015331	0.550856	35.931481	0.027831	48
5	2.107181	88.574508	0.011290	0.474568	42.034592	0.023790	60
6	2.445920	115.673621	0.008645	0.408844	47.292474	0.021145	72
7	2.839113	147.129040	0.006797	0.352223	51.822185	0.019297	84
8	3.295513	183.641059	0.005445	0.303443	55.724570	0.017945	96
9	3.825282	226.022551	0.004424	0.261419	59.086509	0.016924	108
10	4.440213	275.217058	0.003633	0.225214	61.982847	0.016133	120
11	5.153998	332.319805	0.003009	0.194024	64.478068	0.015509	132
12	5.982526	398.602077	0.002509	0.167153	66.627722	0.015009	144
13	6.944244	475.539523	0.002103	0.144004	68.479668	0.014603	156
14	8.060563	564.845011	0.001770	0.124061	70.075134	0.014270	168
15	9.356334	668.506759	0.001496	0.106879	71.449643	0.013996	180
16	10.860408	788.832603	0.001268	0.092078	72.633794	0.013768	192
17	12.606267	928.501369	0.001077	0.079326	73.653950	0.013577	204
18	14.632781	1090.622520	0.000917	0.068340	74.532823	0.013417	216
19	16.985067	1278.805378	0.000782	0.058875	75.289980	0.013282	228
20	19.715494	1497.239481	0.000668	0.050722	75.942278	0.013168	240
21	22.884848	1750.787854	0.000571	0.043697	76.504237	0.013071	252
22	26.563691	2045.095272	0.000489	0.037645	76.988370	0.012989	264
23	30.833924	2386.713938	0.000419	0.032432	77.405455	0.012919	276
24	35.790617	2783.249347	0.000359	0.027940	77.764777	0.012859	288
25	41.544120	3243.529615	0.000308	0.024071	78.074336	0.012808	300
26	48.222525	3777.802015	0.000265	0.020737	78.341024	0.012765	312
27	55.974514	4397.961118	0.000227	0.017865	78.570778	0.012727	324
28	64.972670	5117.813598	0.000195	0.015391	78.768713	0.012695	336
29	75.417320	5953.385616	0.000168	0.013260	78.939236	0.012668	348
30	87.540995	6923.279611	0.000144	0.011423	79.086142	0.012644	360
31	101.613606	8049.088447	0.000124	0.009841	79.212704	0.012624	372
32	117.948452	9355.876140	0.000107	0.008478	79.321738	0.012607	384
33	136.909198	10872.735858	0.000092	0.007304	79.415671	0.012592	396
34	158.917970	12633.437629	0.000079	0.006293	79.496596	0.012579	408
35	184.464752	14677.180163	0.000068	0.005421	79.566313	0.012568	420
36	214.118294	17049.463544	0.000059	0.004670	79.626375	0.012559	432
37	248.538777	19803.102194	0.000050	0.004024	79.678119	0.012550	444
38	288.492509	22999.400699	0.000043	0.003466	79.722696	0.012543	456
39	334.868983	26709.518627	0.000037	0.002986	79.761101	0.012537	468
40	388.700685	31016.054774	0.000032	0.002573	79.794186	0.012532	480

MONTHLY COMPOUND INTEREST TABLES

16.00% ANNUAL INTEREST RATE 1.3333% MONTHLY EFFECTIVE INTEREST RATE

	1 AMOUNT OF $1 AT COMPOUND INTEREST	2 ACCUMULATION OF $1 PER PERIOD	3 SINKING FUND FACTOR	4 PRESENT VALUE REVERSION OF $1	5 PRESENT VALUE ORD. ANNUITY $1 PER PERIOD	6 INSTALLMENT TO AMORTIZE $1	
MONTHS							MONTHS
1	1.013333	1.000000	1.000000	0.986842	0.986842	1.013333	1
2	1.026844	2.013333	0.496689	0.973857	1.960699	0.510022	2
3	1.040536	3.040178	0.328928	0.961043	2.921743	0.342261	3
4	1.054410	4.080713	0.245055	0.948398	3.870141	0.258389	4
5	1.068468	5.135123	0.194737	0.935919	4.806060	0.208071	5
6	1.082715	6.203591	0.161197	0.923604	5.729665	0.174530	6
7	1.097151	7.286306	0.137244	0.911452	6.641116	0.150577	7
8	1.111779	8.383457	0.119283	0.899459	7.540575	0.132616	8
9	1.126603	9.495236	0.105316	0.887624	8.428199	0.118649	9
10	1.141625	10.621839	0.094146	0.875945	9.304144	0.107479	10
11	1.156846	11.763464	0.085009	0.864419	10.168563	0.098342	11
12	1.172271	12.920310	0.077398	0.853045	11.021609	0.090731	12
YEARS							MONTHS
1	1.172271	12.920310	0.077398	0.853045	11.021609	0.090731	12
2	1.374219	28.066412	0.035630	0.727686	20.423539	0.048963	24
3	1.610957	45.821745	0.021824	0.620749	28.443811	0.035157	36
4	1.888477	66.635803	0.015007	0.529527	35.285465	0.028340	48
5	2.213807	91.035516	0.010985	0.451711	41.121706	0.024318	60
6	2.595181	119.638587	0.008359	0.385330	46.100283	0.021692	72
7	3.042255	153.169132	0.006529	0.328704	50.347235	0.019862	84
8	3.566347	192.476010	0.005195	0.280399	53.970077	0.018529	96
9	4.180724	238.554316	0.004192	0.239193	57.060524	0.017525	108
10	4.900941	292.570569	0.003418	0.204042	59.696816	0.016751	120
11	5.745230	355.892244	0.002810	0.174057	61.945692	0.016143	132
12	6.734965	430.122395	0.002325	0.148479	63.864085	0.015658	144
13	7.895203	517.140233	0.001934	0.126659	65.500561	0.015267	156
14	9.255316	619.148703	0.001615	0.108046	66.896549	0.014948	168
15	10.849737	738.730255	0.001354	0.092168	68.087390	0.014687	180
16	12.718830	878.912215	0.001138	0.078624	69.103231	0.014471	192
17	14.909912	1043.243434	0.000959	0.067069	69.969789	0.014292	204
18	17.478455	1235.884123	0.000809	0.057213	70.709003	0.014142	216
19	20.489482	1461.711177	0.000684	0.048806	71.339585	0.014017	228
20	24.019222	1726.441638	0.000579	0.041633	71.877501	0.013913	240
21	28.157032	2036.777427	0.000491	0.035515	72.336367	0.013824	252
22	33.007667	2400.575011	0.000417	0.030296	72.727801	0.013750	264
23	38.693924	2827.044294	0.000354	0.025844	73.061711	0.013687	276
24	45.359757	3326.981781	0.000301	0.022046	73.346552	0.013634	288
25	53.173919	3913.043898	0.000256	0.018806	73.589534	0.013589	300
26	62.334232	4600.067404	0.000217	0.016043	73.796809	0.013551	312
27	73.072600	5405.444997	0.000185	0.013685	73.973623	0.013518	324
28	85.660875	6349.565632	0.000157	0.011674	74.124454	0.013491	336
29	100.417742	7456.330682	0.000134	0.009958	74.253120	0.013467	348
30	117.716787	8753.759030	0.000114	0.008495	74.362878	0.013448	360
31	137.995952	10274.696396	0.000097	0.007247	74.456506	0.013431	372
32	161.768625	12057.646856	0.000083	0.006182	74.536375	0.013416	384
33	189.636635	14147.747615	0.000071	0.005273	74.604507	0.013404	396
34	222.305489	16597.911700	0.000060	0.004498	74.662626	0.013394	408
35	260.602233	19470.167508	0.000051	0.003837	74.712205	0.013385	420
36	305.496388	22837.229116	0.000044	0.003273	74.754498	0.013377	432
37	358.124495	26784.337116	0.000037	0.002792	74.790576	0.013371	444
38	419.818887	31411.416562	0.000032	0.002382	74.821352	0.013365	456
39	492.141422	36835.606677	0.000027	0.002032	74.847605	0.013360	468
40	576.923018	43194.226353	0.000023	0.001733	74.870000	0.013356	480

MONTHLY COMPOUND INTEREST TABLES

17.00% ANNUAL INTEREST RATE 1.4167% MONTHLY EFFECTIVE INTEREST RATE

	1 AMOUNT OF $1 AT COMPOUND INTEREST	2 ACCUMULATION OF $1 PER PERIOD	3 SINKING FUND FACTOR	4 PRESENT VALUE REVERSION OF $1	5 PRESENT VALUE ORD. ANNUITY $1 PER PERIOD	6 INSTALLMENT TO AMORTIZE $1	
MONTHS							MONTHS
1	1.014167	1.000000	1.000000	0.986031	0.986031	1.014167	1
2	1.028534	2.014167	0.496483	0.972258	1.958289	0.510650	2
3	1.043105	3.042701	0.328655	0.958676	2.916965	0.342822	3
4	1.057882	4.085806	0.244750	0.945285	3.862250	0.258916	4
5	1.072869	5.143688	0.194413	0.932080	4.794330	0.208580	5
6	1.088068	6.216557	0.160861	0.919060	5.713391	0.175027	6
7	1.103482	7.304625	0.136900	0.906222	6.619613	0.151066	7
8	1.119115	8.408107	0.118933	0.893563	7.513176	0.133100	8
9	1.134969	9.527222	0.104962	0.881081	8.394257	0.119129	9
10	1.151048	10.662191	0.093789	0.868774	9.263031	0.107956	10
11	1.167354	11.813238	0.084651	0.856638	10.119669	0.098817	11
12	1.183892	12.980593	0.077038	0.844672	10.964341	0.091205	12
YEARS							MONTHS
1	1.183892	12.980593	0.077038	0.844672	10.964341	0.091205	12
2	1.401600	28.348209	0.035276	0.713471	20.225611	0.049442	24
3	1.659342	46.541802	0.021486	0.602648	28.048345	0.035653	36
4	1.964482	68.081048	0.014688	0.509040	34.655988	0.028855	48
5	2.325733	93.581182	0.010686	0.429972	40.237278	0.024853	60
6	2.753417	123.770579	0.008079	0.363185	44.951636	0.022246	72
7	3.259747	159.511558	0.006269	0.306772	48.933722	0.020436	84
8	3.859188	201.825006	0.004955	0.259122	52.297278	0.019121	96
9	4.568860	251.919548	0.003970	0.218873	55.138379	0.018136	108
10	5.409036	311.226062	0.003213	0.184876	57.538177	0.017380	120
11	6.403713	381.438553	0.002622	0.156159	59.565218	0.016788	132
12	7.581303	464.562540	0.002153	0.131903	61.277403	0.016319	144
13	8.975441	562.972341	0.001776	0.111415	62.723638	0.015943	156
14	10.625951	679.478890	0.001472	0.094109	63.945231	0.015638	168
15	12.579975	817.410030	0.001223	0.079491	64.977077	0.015390	180
16	14.893329	980.705566	0.001020	0.067144	65.848648	0.015186	192
17	17.632089	1174.029800	0.000852	0.056715	66.584839	0.015018	204
18	20.874484	1402.904761	0.000713	0.047905	67.206679	0.014879	216
19	24.713129	1673.867935	0.000597	0.040464	67.731930	0.014764	228
20	29.257669	1994.658995	0.000501	0.034179	68.175595	0.014668	240
21	34.637912	2374.440878	0.000421	0.028870	68.550346	0.014588	252
22	41.007538	2824.061507	0.000354	0.024386	68.866887	0.014521	264
23	48.548485	3356.363651	0.000298	0.020598	69.134261	0.014465	276
24	57.476150	3986.551756	0.000251	0.017399	69.360104	0.014418	288
25	68.045538	4732.626240	0.000211	0.014696	69.550868	0.014378	300
26	80.558550	5615.897651	0.000178	0.012413	69.712000	0.014345	312
27	95.372601	6661.595368	0.000150	0.010485	69.848104	0.014317	324
28	112.910833	7899.588246	0.000127	0.008857	69.963067	0.014293	336
29	133.674202	9365.237774	0.000107	0.007481	70.060174	0.014273	348
30	158.255782	11100.408126	0.000090	0.006319	70.142196	0.014257	360
31	187.357711	13154.661953	0.000076	0.005337	70.211479	0.014243	372
32	221.811244	15586.676066	0.000064	0.004508	70.270000	0.014231	384
33	262.600497	18465.917458	0.000054	0.003808	70.319431	0.014221	396
34	310.890557	21874.627526	0.000046	0.003217	70.361184	0.014212	408
35	368.060758	25910.171179	0.000039	0.002717	70.396451	0.014205	420
36	435.744087	30687.817929	0.000033	0.002295	70.426241	0.014199	432
37	515.873821	36344.034396	0.000028	0.001938	70.451403	0.014194	444
38	610.738749	43040.382285	0.000023	0.001637	70.472657	0.014190	456
39	723.048553	50968.133160	0.000020	0.001383	70.490609	0.014186	468
40	856.011201	60353.731845	0.000017	0.001168	70.505773	0.014183	480

MONTHLY COMPOUND INTEREST TABLES

18.00% ANNUAL INTEREST RATE

1.5000% MONTHLY EFFECTIVE INTEREST RATE

	1 AMOUNT OF $1 AT COMPOUND INTEREST	2 ACCUMULATION OF $1 PER PERIOD	3 SINKING FUND FACTOR	4 PRESENT VALUE REVERSION OF $1	5 PRESENT VALUE ORD. ANNUITY $1 PER PERIOD	6 INSTALLMENT TO AMORTIZE $.	
MONTHS							MONTHS
1	1.015000	1.000000	1.000000	0.985222	0.985222	1.015000	1
2	1.030225	2.015000	0.496278	0.970662	1.955883	0.511278	2
3	1.045678	3.045225	0.328383	0.956317	2.912200	0.343383	3
4	1.061364	4.090903	0.244445	0.942184	3.854385	0.259445	4
5	1.077284	5.152267	0.194089	0.928260	4.782645	0.209089	5
6	1.093443	6.229551	0.160525	0.914542	5.697187	0.175525	6
7	1.109845	7.322994	0.136556	0.901027	6.598214	0.151556	7
8	1.126493	8.432839	0.118584	0.887711	7.485925	0.133584	8
9	1.143390	9.559332	0.104610	0.874592	8.360517	0.119610	9
10	1.160541	10.702722	0.093434	0.861667	9.222185	0.108434	10
11	1.177949	11.863262	0.084294	0.848933	10.071118	0.099294	11
12	1.195618	13.041211	0.076680	0.836387	10.907505	0.091680	12
YEARS							MONTHS
1	1.195618	13.041211	0.076680	0.836387	10.907505	0.091680	12
2	1.429503	28.633521	0.034924	0.699544	20.030405	0.049924	24
3	1.709140	47.275969	0.021152	0.585090	27.660684	0.036152	36
4	2.043478	69.565219	0.014375	0.489362	34.042554	0.029375	48
5	2.443220	96.214652	0.010393	0.409296	39.380269	0.025393	60
6	2.921158	128.077197	0.007808	0.342330	43.844667	0.022808	72
7	3.492590	166.172636	0.006018	0.286321	47.578633	0.021018	84
8	4.175804	211.720235	0.004723	0.239475	50.701675	0.019723	96
9	4.992667	266.177771	0.003757	0.200294	53.313749	0.018757	108
10	5.969323	331.288191	0.003019	0.167523	55.498454	0.018019	120
11	7.137031	409.135393	0.002444	0.140114	57.325714	0.017444	132
12	8.533164	502.210922	0.001991	0.117190	58.854011	0.016991	144
13	10.202406	613.493716	0.001630	0.098016	60.132260	0.016630	156
14	12.198182	746.545446	0.001340	0.081979	61.201371	0.016340	168
15	14.584368	905.624513	0.001104	0.068567	62.095562	0.016104	180
16	17.437335	1095.822335	0.000913	0.057348	62.843452	0.015913	192
17	20.848395	1323.226308	0.000756	0.047965	63.468978	0.015756	204
18	24.926719	1595.114630	0.000627	0.040118	63.992160	0.015627	216
19	29.802839	1920.189249	0.000521	0.033554	64.429743	0.015521	228
20	35.632816	2308.854370	0.000433	0.028064	64.795732	0.015433	240
21	42.603242	2773.549452	0.000361	0.023472	65.101841	0.015361	252
22	50.937210	3329.147335	0.000300	0.019632	65.357866	0.015300	264
23	60.901454	3993.430261	0.000250	0.016420	65.572002	0.015250	276
24	72.814885	4787.658998	0.000209	0.013733	65.751103	0.015209	288
25	87.058800	5737.253308	0.000174	0.011486	65.900901	0.015174	300
26	104.089083	6872.605521	0.000146	0.009607	66.026190	0.015146	312
27	124.450799	8230.053258	0.000122	0.008035	66.130980	0.015122	324
28	148.795637	9853.042439	0.000101	0.006721	66.218625	0.015101	336
29	177.902767	11793.517795	0.000085	0.005621	66.291930	0.015085	348
30	212.703781	14113.585393	0.000071	0.004701	66.353242	0.015071	360
31	254.312506	16887.500372	0.000059	0.003932	66.404522	0.015059	372
32	304.060653	20204.043526	0.000049	0.003289	66.447412	0.015049	384
33	363.540442	24169.362788	0.000041	0.002751	66.483285	0.015041	396
34	434.655558	28910.370554	0.000035	0.002301	66.513289	0.015035	408
35	519.682084	34578.805589	0.000029	0.001924	66.538383	0.015029	420
36	621.341343	41356.089521	0.000024	0.001609	66.559372	0.015024	432
37	742.887000	49459.133344	0.000020	0.001346	66.576927	0.015020	444
38	888.209197	59147.279782	0.000017	0.001126	66.591609	0.015017	456
39	1061.959056	70730.603711	0.000014	0.000942	66.603890	0.015014	468
40	1269.697544	84579.836287	0.000012	0.000788	66.614161	0.015012	480

MONTHLY COMPOUND INTEREST TABLES

19.00% ANNUAL INTEREST RATE 1.5833% MONTHLY EFFECTIVE INTEREST RATE

	1 AMOUNT OF $1 AT COMPOUND INTEREST	2 ACCUMULATION OF $1 PER PERIOD	3 SINKING FUND FACTOR	4 PRESENT VALUE REVERSION OF $1	5 PRESENT VALUE ORD. ANNUITY $1 PER PERIOD	6 INSTALLMENT TO AMORTIZE $1	
MONTHS							MONTHS
1	1.015833	1.000000	1.000000	0.984413	0.984413	1.015833	1
2	1.031917	2.015833	0.496073	0.969070	1.953483	0.511906	2
3	1.048256	3.047751	0.328111	0.953965	2.907449	0.343944	3
4	1.064853	4.096007	0.244140	0.939096	3.846545	0.259974	4
5	1.081714	5.160860	0.193766	0.924459	4.771004	0.209599	5
6	1.098841	6.242574	0.160190	0.910050	5.681054	0.176024	6
7	1.116239	7.341415	0.136214	0.895865	6.576920	0.152047	7
8	1.133913	8.457654	0.118236	0.881902	7.458822	0.134069	8
9	1.151866	9.591566	0.104258	0.868156	8.326978	0.120092	9
10	1.170104	10.743433	0.093080	0.854625	9.181602	0.108913	10
11	1.188631	11.913537	0.083938	0.841304	10.022906	0.099771	11
12	1.207451	13.102168	0.076323	0.828191	10.851097	0.092157	12
YEARS							MONTHS
1	1.207451	13.102168	0.076323	0.828191	10.851097	0.092157	12
2	1.457938	28.922394	0.034575	0.685900	19.837878	0.050409	24
3	1.760389	48.024542	0.020823	0.568056	27.280649	0.036656	36
4	2.125583	71.089450	0.014067	0.470459	33.444684	0.029900	48
5	2.566537	98.939196	0.010107	0.389630	38.549682	0.025941	60
6	3.098968	132.566399	0.007543	0.322688	42.777596	0.023377	72
7	3.741852	173.169599	0.005775	0.267247	46.279115	0.021608	84
8	4.518103	222.195973	0.004501	0.221332	49.179042	0.020334	96
9	5.455388	281.392918	0.003554	0.183305	51.580735	0.019387	108
10	6.587114	352.870328	0.002834	0.151812	53.569796	0.018667	120
11	7.953617	439.175798	0.002277	0.125729	55.217118	0.018110	132
12	9.603603	543.385424	0.001840	0.104128	56.581415	0.017674	144
13	11.595879	669.213441	0.001494	0.086238	57.711314	0.017328	156
14	14.001456	821.144606	0.001218	0.071421	58.647086	0.017051	168
15	16.906072	1004.594042	0.000995	0.059150	59.422084	0.016829	180
16	20.413254	1226.100247	0.000816	0.048988	60.063930	0.016649	192
17	24.648004	1493.558135	0.000670	0.040571	60.595501	0.016503	204
18	29.761257	1816.500430	0.000551	0.033601	61.035743	0.016384	216
19	35.935259	2206.437425	0.000453	0.027828	61.400348	0.016287	228
20	43.390065	2677.267240	0.000374	0.023047	61.702310	0.016207	240
21	52.391377	3245.771169	0.000308	0.019087	61.952393	0.016141	252
22	63.260020	3932.211806	0.000254	0.015808	62.159509	0.016088	264
23	76.383375	4761.055238	0.000210	0.013092	62.331041	0.016043	276
24	92.229182	5761.843068	0.000174	0.010843	62.473102	0.016007	288
25	111.362218	6970.245332	0.000143	0.008980	62.590755	0.015977	300
26	134.464421	8429.331851	0.000119	0.007437	62.688195	0.015952	312
27	162.359199	10191.107326	0.000098	0.006159	62.768894	0.015931	324
28	196.040777	12318.364881	0.000081	0.005101	62.835728	0.015915	336
29	236.709632	14886.924139	0.000067	0.004225	62.891079	0.015901	348
30	285.815282	17988.333579	0.000056	0.003499	62.936920	0.015889	360
31	345.107947	21733.133503	0.000046	0.002898	62.974886	0.015879	372
32	416.700935	26254.795909	0.000038	0.002400	63.006328	0.015871	384
33	503.145960	31714.481694	0.000032	0.001987	63.032369	0.015865	396
34	607.524092	38306.784745	0.000026	0.001646	63.053935	0.015859	408
35	733.555571	46266.667644	0.000022	0.001363	63.071796	0.015855	420
36	885.732406	55877.836195	0.000018	0.001129	63.086589	0.015851	432
37	1069.478478	67482.851256	0.000015	0.000935	63.098840	0.015848	444
38	1291.342856	81495.338274	0.000012	0.000774	63.108986	0.015846	456
39	1559.233220	98414.729710	0.000010	0.000641	63.117389	0.015843	468
40	1882.697708	118844.065787	0.000008	0.000531	63.124348	0.015842	480

MONTHLY COMPOUND INTEREST TABLES

20.00% ANNUAL INTEREST RATE 1.6667% MONTHLY EFFECTIVE INTEREST RATE

MONTHS	1 AMOUNT OF $1 AT COMPOUND INTEREST	2 ACCUMULATION OF $1 PER PERIOD	3 SINKING FUND FACTOR	4 PRESENT VALUE REVERSION OF $1	5 PRESENT VALUE ORD. ANNUITY $1 PER PERIOD	6 INSTALLMENT TO AMORTIZE $1	MONTHS
1	1.016667	1.000000	1.000000	0.983607	0.983607	1.016667	1
2	1.033611	2.016667	0.495868	0.967482	1.951088	0.512534	2
3	1.050838	3.050278	0.327839	0.951622	2.902710	0.344506	3
4	1.068352	4.101116	0.243836	0.936021	3.838731	0.260503	4
5	1.086158	5.169468	0.193444	0.920677	4.759408	0.210110	5
6	1.104260	6.255625	0.159856	0.905583	5.664991	0.176523	6
7	1.122665	7.359886	0.135872	0.890738	6.555729	0.152538	7
8	1.141376	8.482551	0.117889	0.876136	7.431865	0.134556	8
9	1.160399	9.623926	0.103908	0.861773	8.293637	0.120574	9
10	1.179739	10.784325	0.092727	0.847645	9.141283	0.109394	10
11	1.199401	11.964064	0.083584	0.833749	9.975032	0.100250	11
12	1.219391	13.163465	0.075968	0.820081	10.795113	0.092635	12

YEARS	1	2	3	4	5	6	MONTHS
1	1.219391	13.163465	0.075968	0.820081	10.795113	0.092635	12
2	1.486915	29.214877	0.034229	0.672534	19.647986	0.050896	24
3	1.813130	48.787826	0.020497	0.551532	26.908062	0.037164	36
4	2.210915	72.654905	0.013764	0.452301	32.861916	0.030430	48
5	2.695970	101.758208	0.009827	0.370924	37.744561	0.026494	60
6	3.287442	137.246517	0.007286	0.304188	41.748727	0.023953	72
7	4.008677	180.520645	0.005540	0.249459	45.032470	0.022206	84
8	4.888145	233.288730	0.004287	0.204577	47.725406	0.020953	96
9	5.960561	297.633662	0.003360	0.167769	49.933833	0.020027	108
10	7.268255	376.095300	0.002659	0.137585	51.744924	0.019326	120
11	8.862845	471.770720	0.002120	0.112831	53.230165	0.018786	132
12	10.807275	588.436476	0.001699	0.092530	54.448184	0.018366	144
13	13.178294	730.697658	0.001369	0.075882	55.447059	0.018035	156
14	16.069495	904.169675	0.001106	0.062230	56.266217	0.017773	168
15	19.594998	1115.699905	0.000896	0.051033	56.937994	0.017563	180
16	23.893966	1373.637983	0.000728	0.041852	57.488906	0.017395	192
17	29.136090	1688.165376	0.000592	0.034322	57.940698	0.017259	204
18	35.528288	2071.697274	0.000483	0.028147	58.311205	0.017149	216
19	43.322878	2539.372652	0.000394	0.023082	58.615050	0.017060	228
20	52.827531	3109.651838	0.000322	0.018930	58.864229	0.016988	240
21	64.417420	3805.045193	0.000263	0.015524	59.068575	0.016929	252
22	78.550028	4653.001652	0.000215	0.012731	59.236156	0.016882	264
23	95.783203	5686.992197	0.000176	0.010440	59.373585	0.016843	276
24	116.797184	6947.831050	0.000144	0.008562	59.486289	0.016811	288
25	142.421445	8485.286707	0.000118	0.007021	59.578715	0.016785	300
26	173.667440	10360.046428	0.000097	0.005758	59.654512	0.016763	312
27	211.768529	12646.111719	0.000079	0.004722	59.716672	0.016746	324
28	258.228656	15433.719354	0.000065	0.003873	59.767648	0.016731	336
29	314.881721	18832.903252	0.000053	0.003176	59.809452	0.016720	348
30	383.963963	22977.837794	0.000044	0.002604	59.843735	0.016710	360
31	468.202234	28032.134021	0.000036	0.002136	59.871850	0.016702	372
32	570.921630	34195.297782	0.000029	0.001752	59.894907	0.016696	384
33	696.176745	41710.604726	0.000024	0.001436	59.913815	0.016691	396
34	848.911717	50874.703014	0.000020	0.001178	59.929321	0.016686	408
35	1035.155379	62049.322767	0.000016	0.000966	59.942038	0.016683	420
36	1262.259241	75675.554472	0.000013	0.000792	59.952466	0.016680	432
37	1539.187666	92291.259933	0.000011	0.000650	59.961018	0.016678	444
38	1876.871717	112552.303043	0.000009	0.000533	59.968032	0.016676	456
39	2288.640640	137258.438381	0.000007	0.000437	59.973784	0.016674	468
40	2790.747993	167384.879555	0.000006	0.000358	59.978500	0.016673	480

INDEX

Words in **bold** indicate key words